The Search for Personal Freedom

Volume 2

The Search for Personal Freedom
seventh edition

Robert C. Lamm
Arizona State University

Neal M. Cross

Rudy H. Turk
Arizona State University

wcb

Wm. C. Brown Publishers
Dubuque, Iowa

Book Team

Karen Speerstra
Senior Developmental Editor

Lynne Niznik
Assistant Developmental Editor

Karen Slaght
Production Editor

Catherine Dinsmore
Designer

Mavis M. Oeth
Permissions Editor

Carol M. Schiessl
Visual Research Editor

wcb
group

Wm. C. Brown
Chairman of the Board

Mark C. Falb
President and Chief Executive Officer

wcb
Wm. C. Brown Publishers, College Division

Lawrence E. Cremer
President

James L. Romig
Vice-President, Product Development

David Wm. Smith
Vice-President, Marketing

David A. Corona
Vice-President, Production and Design

E. F. Jogerst
Vice-President, Cost Analyst

Marcia H. Stout
Marketing Manager

Linda M. Galarowicz
Director of Marketing Research

William A. Moss
Production Editorial Manager

Marilyn A. Phelps
Manager of Design

Mary M. Heller
Visual Research Manager

Contents

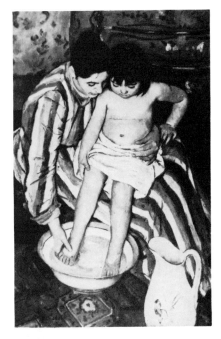

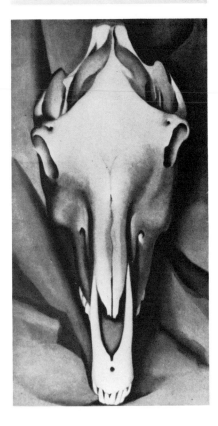

Illustrations

Colorplates

Volume 1

Volume 2

Figures

Preface

This is a text for the integrated humanities: the arts of literature, painting, music, sculpture, film, and architecture, and the discipline of philosophy. Though not an "art" in the strictest sense, philosophical ideas so consistently permeate each of the arts that theories of major philosophers are, of necessity, interwoven throughout the book. The components of the humanities—philosophy and the arts—are presented not as separate technical disciplines but as interrelated manifestations of human creativity. This is, therefore, a book about people and about "art's eternal victory over the human situation" (André Malraux).

In order to better understand why we are the way we are, our studies have been centered on our cultural heritage, from ancient Greece to the present day. For a better comprehension of the great sweep of Western civilization, the text has been divided into nine units:

Throughout the book the accomplishments of the past are considered not as museum pieces but as living evidence of enduring responses to the perplexities of life. These achievements have become, in our day, a basic part of our attempts to make sense of the universe.

Because artists naturally respond to the issues of their own time, each unit is prefaced by an overview of the social, scientific, religious, and philosophical climate of the period. Forming the core of these volumes are the primary sources, the artworks themselves, many complete works rather than bits and pieces: plays, poetry, short stories, entire sections of large works, hundreds of art illustrations (many in color), and numerous musical examples. Introduced with appropriate commentary, many of the selections are followed by practical exercises and questions. Additionally, there are maps, graphs, time charts, record lists, and, at the end of each volume, there is a glossary of important terms in philosophy and the arts. An Instructor's Manual is available highlighting key points and including many suggestions for supplementary materials: slides, sound filmstrips, sound slidesets, and films. There is more than enough material for a two-semester course based entirely on the book, or the book can be used as a central text embellished by additional primary sources.

Since the publication of the first edition in 1948, our text has gone through many changes and a whole generation of students and teachers. The framework remains intact, but some of the parts have changed. In the Renaissance unit we have added Mirandola's *Oration on the Dignity of Man,* selections from Castiglione's *Book of the Courtier* and *The Praise of Folly* by Erasmus plus a delightful essay by Montaigne. The unit now concludes with the complete text of Shakespeare's powerful *King Lear.*

Added to Unit 7 on The Early Modern World (1600–1789) are poems by John Donne, Andrew Marvell, John Milton, and Thomas Gray. Jonathan Swift is represented with his pungent satire entitled *A Modest Proposal*.

Unit 8 on The Middle Modern World (1789–1914) now includes works by major English Romantic and Victorian poets. Also added are selections by notable American writers like Poe, Whitman, Emerson, Thoreau, Melville, Twain, Dickinson, Dunbar, and Crane.

In the last unit on The Twentieth Century we have kept most of the literary selections and added works by Countee Cullen, Richard Wright, Langston Hughes, Flannery O'Connor, Denise Levertov, Nadine Gordimer, Don L. Lee, and Nikki Giovanni. We now have a very broad range of important twentieth-century literature: seven short stories, eighteen poems, and selections from five essays and four novels.

In the music chapters technicalities have been pared to a bare minimum. An Appendix on Music Listening and Notation has been added to help students acquire a basic literacy in music notation.

The art chapters have been completely rewritten and now include many more important artists: Cranach the Younger, Fra Angelico, Bellini, van Eyck, van der Weyden, Memling, Bosch, Veronese, Leyster, Ruisdael, Gainsborough, Gilbert Stuart, Constable, Corot, Cassatt, H. Rousseau, Toulouse-Lautrec, and numerous additional twentieth-century artists. In reorganizing these chapters, our primary concern has been the overall evolution of artistic styles. No longer are sculpture, painting, and architecture treated as separate categories; rather, artworks are considered chronologically as reflections of an overall cultural evolution. Like literature and music, art is presented as an interrelated component of the integrated humanities.

No longer confined to the art chapters, illustrations are used throughout the book to point up the text and help clarify some issues. All in all, this is a broader and richer version of *The Search for Personal Freedom*.

Acknowledgments

This book could not have been written without the patience, forebearance, and expert editorial assistance of Katy Lamm.

We also wish to thank the following professors whose careful reading of the manuscript proved invaluable for this seventh edition.

M. Barbara Akin
Grove City College

Lee Ball, Jr.
Southeastern Oklahoma State
    University

Robert H. Canary
University of Wisconsin–Parkside

Ralph D. Cole
Northeastern Oklahoma A&M
    College

Charles G. Davis
Boise State University

Dale W. Davis
Texas Tech University

Cynthia Donahue
Brevard Community College

Henry Hall
Diablo Valley College

Michael A. Jacobsen
University of Georgia, Athens

Carla M. Krantz
Pasco-Hernando Community
    College

Richard W. Leach
Lakeland College

James V. Mehl
Missouri Western State College

Phil Mullins
Missouri Western State College

Clifton L. Warren
Central State University, Edmond

Frederick W. Westphal
California State University,
    Sacramento

6

Unit

The Renaissance, 1350–1600

17
New Ideas and Discoveries Result from a New Way of Looking at the World

The Renaissance (ca. 1350–1600) was a remarkable period of intellectual energy and artistic creativity that ushered out the Middle Ages and set the stage for the emergence of the modern world. *Renaissance,* the French word for *rebirth,* refers not only to the rediscovery of classical Greece and Rome but also, in a larger sense, to fresh ideas about the nature of human beings and their place in the universe. The medieval conception of God as the ultimate reality was superseded by the idea that men and women were unique beings, the noblest creations of God. Everyone had worth and dignity and a free will that made it possible to be and to do, to utilize their God-given capacities to transform the world. They could develop their minds by study and reflection, activities advocated by Cicero as worthy of the "dignity of the human race" (Offices I.30).

The rediscovery of the ancient world originated in Italy, but there were Renaissance stirrings in northern countries that had no classical heritage. Vigorous trade, the beginnings of capitalism, the expansion of trade guilds, growing cities, burgeoning industries, and a spirit of creative enterprise fueled the rebirth of Europe both in the South and in the North.

The Rise of Humanism

On April 8, 1341, Petrarch (Francesco Petrarca; 1304–1374) was crowned with a laurel wreath as the first poet laureate of modern times. Symbolizing an intellectual movement called *humanism* that had begun in Verona and Padua a century earlier, the ceremony honoring the leading humanist took place, fittingly enough, in Rome. Humanism was the rediscovery of the total culture of classical antiquity: literature, history, rhetoric, ethics, and politics. Describing his abandoned law studies at Bologna as "the art of selling justice," Petrarch devoted his life to acquiring what he called the "golden wisdom" of the ancients: the proper conduct of one's private life; the rational governance of the state; the enjoyment of beauty; and the quest for truth. Humanism was a union of love and reason that stressed earthly fulfillment rather than medieval preparations for paradise. The humanists had rediscovered their ancestors, seeing them as real people lending assistance in the restatement of human values. Petrarch wrote letters to Cicero, whom he called his father, and to Virgil, who was, he said, his brother.

There had been earlier stirrings of classical revivals in the ninth-century Carolingian Renaissance and in the twelfth century at the Cathedral School of Chartres and at the Court of Eleanor of Aquitaine, but not until the middle of the fourteenth century did the rediscovery of antiquity become a true cultural movement. Petrarch's friend, the writer Giovanni Boccaccio (bo-KOTCH-yo; 1313-1375), was one of the first Westerners to study Greek, but by 1400 nearly all the Greek authors had been recovered and translated into Latin and Italian: Homer, Herodotos, Thucydides, Aeschylus, Sophokles, Euripides, and all the dialogues of Plato. For the humanists there were three ages of humankind: ancient, middle, and modern. The middle period, the Middle Ages, was seen as a benighted period between the fall of Rome and the rebirth of classical cultures. The men and women of the Renaissance were, in effect, discovering themselves as they recovered the past. They were aware that their age was significantly different from the Middle Ages, that they were the spiritual heirs of a distant past that was being reborn through their own efforts. There was no Latin word for rebirth, but Giorgio Vasari (1511-1574; see chap. 18) invented the word *Renaissance (Rinascita)* in his *Lives of the Most Excellent Italian Architects, Painters, and Sculptors from Cimabue to our own Times* (Florence, 1550). Vasari's term was applied to the fine arts that had developed out of early humanism, but the label now describes an era that consciously freed itself from the bondage of medievalism.

The most influential center of humanistic studies was the Platonic Academy founded at Florence in 1462 by the banker Cosimo de' Medici (1389-1464), the sire of a family that was to control Florence throughout most of the Renaissance. The guiding force of the academy, Marsilio Ficino (fi-CHEE-no; 1433-1499), promoted the study of Platonism through his translations into Latin of Plato, Plotinus, and other philosophers. In his major work, the *Theologia Platonica* (1482), Ficino described a universe presided over by a gracious and loving God who sought to bring humankind to Him through Beauty, one of His attributes. The contemplation of the beauty of nature, of beautiful things, of glorious art became a sort of worship of this God. When beauty was arranged in words or paintings (see colorplate 22), these works of art, too, became a part of the circle of love by which people reached beyond themselves to a loving God. Ficino's theory of "Platonic love," a spiritual bond between lovers of beauty, had strong repercussions in later English, French, and Italian literature.

Pico della Mirandola (PEA-ko della mere-AN-do-luh; 1463-1494) was a friend of Ficino's and a major influence on the humanists of the Forentine academy. His broadly based classical education in Greek and Latin was enriched by studies in Hebrew and Arabic that brought him into contact with Jewish and Arabic philosophy. Pico's attack on astrology impressed even the astronomer Johannes Kepler. More importantly, his conception of the dignity of the human race and the ideal of the unity of truth were significant contributions to Renaissance thought. His *Oration on the Dignity of Man* has been called "The Manifesto of Humanism." The following excerpts from Pico's ringing affirmation of the nobility of humankind epitomize the optimistic Renaissance point of view.

Literary Selection

ORATION ON THE DIGNITY OF MAN
Pico della Mirandola (1463-1494)

I have read in the records of the Arabians, reverend Fathers, that Abdala the Saracen, when questioned as to what on this stage of the world, as it were, could be seen most worthy of wonder, replied: "There is nothing to be seen more wonderful than man." In agreement with this opinion is the saying of Hermes Trismegistus: "A great miracle, Asclepius, is man." But when I weighed the reason for these maxims, the many grounds for the excellence of human nature reported by many men failed to satisfy me—that man is the intermediary between creatures, the intimate of the gods, the king of the lower beings, by the acuteness of his senses, by the discernment of his reason, and by the light of his intelligence the interpreter of nature, the interval between fixed eternity and fleeting time, and (as the Persians say) the bond, nay, rather, the marriage song of the world, on David's testimony but little lower than the angels. Admittedly great though these reasons be, they are not the principal grounds, that is, those which may rightfully claim for themselves the privilege of the highest admiration. For why should we not admire more the angels themselves and the blessed choirs of heaven? At last it seems to me I have come to understand why man is the most fortunate of creatures and consequently worthy of all admiration and what precisely is that rank which is his lot in the universal chain of Being—a rank to be envied not only by brutes but even by the stars and by minds beyond this world. It is a matter past faith and a wondrous one. Why should it not be? For it is on this very account that man is rightly called and judged a great miracle and a wonderful creature indeed.

2. But hear, Fathers, exactly what this rank is and, as friendly auditors, conformably to your kindness, do me this favor. God the Father, the supreme Architect, had already built this cosmic home we behold, the most sacred temple of His godhead, by the laws of His mysterious wisdom. The region above the heavens He had adorned with Intelligences, the heavenly spheres He had quickened with eternal souls, and the excrementary and filthy parts of the lower world He had filled with a multitude of animals of every kind. But, when the work

was finished, the Craftsman kept wishing that there were someone to ponder the plan of so great a work, to love its beauty, and to wonder at its vastness. Therefore, when everything was done (as Moses and Timaeus bear witness), He finally took thought concerning the creation of man. But there was not among His archetypes that from which He could fashion a new offspring, nor was there in His treasurehouses anything which He might bestow on His new son as an inheritance, nor was there in the seats of all the world a place where the latter might sit to contemplate the universe. All was now complete; all things had been assigned to the highest, the middle, and the lowest orders. But in its final creation it was not the part of the Father's power to fail as though exhausted. It was not the part of His wisdom to waver in a needful matter through poverty of counsel. It was not the part of His kindly love that he who was to praise God's divine generosity in regard to others should be compelled to condemn it in regard to himself.

3. At last the best of artisans ordained that that creature to whom He had been able to give nothing proper to himself should have joint possession of whatever had been peculiar to each of the different kinds of being. He therefore took man as a creature of indeterminate nature and, assigning him a place in the middle of the world, addressed him thus: "Neither a fixed abode nor a form that is thine alone nor any function peculiar to thyself have we given thee, Adam, to the end that according to thy longing and according to thy judgment thou mayest have and possess what abode, what form, and what functions thou thyself shalt desire. The nature of all other beings is limited and constrained within the bounds of laws prescribed by Us. Thou, constrained by no limits, in accordance with thine own free will, in whose hand We have placed thee, shalt ordain for thyself the limits of thy nature. We have set thee at the world's center that thou mayest from thence more easily observe whatever is in the world. We have made thee neither of heaven nor of earth, neither mortal nor immortal, so that with freedom of choice and with honor, as though the maker and molder of thyself, thou mayest fashion thyself in whatever shape thou shalt prefer. Thou shalt have the power to degenerate into the lower forms of life, which are brutish. Thou shalt have the power, out of thy soul's judgment, to be reborn into the higher forms, which are divine."

4. O supreme generosity of God the Father, O highest and most marvelous felicity of man! To him it is granted to have whatever he chooses, to be whatever he wills. Beasts as soon as they are born (so says Lucilius) bring with them from their mother's womb all they will ever possess. Spiritual beings, either from the beginning or soon thereafter, become what they are to be for ever and ever. On man when he came into life the Father conferred the seeds of all kinds and the germs of every way of life. Whatever seeds each man cultivates will grow to maturity and bear in him their own fruit. If they be vegetative, he will be like a plant. If sensitive, he will become brutish. If rational, he will grow into a heavenly being. If intellectual, he will be an angel and the son of God. And if, happy in the lot of no created thing, he withdraws into the center of his own unity, his spirit, made one with God, in the solitary darkness of God, who is set above all things, shall surpass them all. Who would not admire this our chameleon? Or who could more

greatly admire aught else whatever? It is man who Asclepius of Athens, arguing from his mutability of character and from his self-transforming nature, on just grounds says was symbolized by Proteus in the mysteries. Hence those metamorphoses renowned among the Hebrews and the Pythagoreans.

5. For the occult theology of the Hebrews sometimes transforms the holy Enoch into an angel of divinity whom they call "Mal'akh Adonay Shebaoth," and sometimes transforms others into other divinities. The Pythagoreans degrade impious men into brutes and, if one is to believe Empedocles, even into plants. Mohammed, in imitation, often had this saying on his tongue: "They who have deviated from divine law become beasts," and surely he spoke justly. For it is not the bark that makes the plant but its senseless and insentient nature; neither is it the hide that makes the beast of burden but its irrational, sensitive soul; neither is it the orbed form that makes the heavens but its undeviating order; nor is it the sundering from body but his spiritual intelligence that makes the angel. For if you see one abandoned to his appetites crawling on the ground, it is a plant and not a man you see; if you see one blinded by the vain illusions of imagery, as it were of Calypso, and softened by their gnawing allurement, delivered over to his senses, it is a beast and not a man you see. If you see a philosopher determining all things by means of right reason, him you shall reverence: he is a heavenly being and not of this earth. If you see a pure contemplator, one unaware of the body and confined to the inner reaches of the mind, he is neither an earthly nor a heavenly being; he is a more reverend divinity vested with human flesh. . . .

7. Let us disdain earthly things, despise heavenly things, and, finally, esteeming less whatever is of the world, hasten to that court which is beyond the world and nearest to the Godhead. There, as the sacred mysteries relate, Seraphim, Cherubim, and Thrones hold the first places; let us, incapable of yielding to them, and intolerant of a lower place, emulate their dignity and their glory. If we have willed it, we shall be second to them in nothing.

Perhaps the greatest teaching of these inspired scholars was that *virtu* was the highest goal of human existence. *Virtu* is not our word *virtue;* it can be defined as "excellence as a person." *Virtu* includes physical courage and daring, a high degree of intelligence, skill in many fields, and, above all, *action* that reveals all these characteristics. The aspiration toward *virtu* led to the "Renaissance man" and "Renaissance woman" of the period, as exemplified by Leonardo da Vinci and Isabella d'Este (see chap. 18).

Renaissance Science: The Secular View of the Universe

The Copernican Revolution

The idea of the universe on which medieval life had been based was that of Ptolemy. The Ptolemaic concept supposed the earth was the center of the universe, with the moon, the planets, and the fixed stars

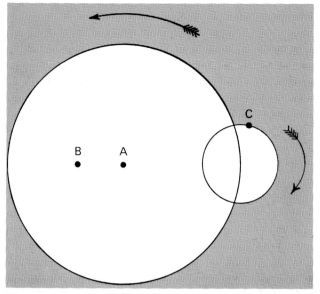

Figure 17.1 The earth in the center of the universe (A), the sun (B), and a heavenly body rotating around the earth (C). Also indicated is its orbit or epicycle (the clockwise arrow orbit). Try to imagine this whole system revolving at once. What figure would it make? If you cannot imagine, see figure 17.2.

revolving around the earth in more or less fixed spheres (see fig. 17.1). Around the whole lay the crystalline sphere, outside of which lay the realm of God. Throughout the Middle Ages, however, many scientists, particularly the Arabic astronomers, had made observations about the movement of stars and planets that did not readily fit into this scheme and required the addition of more and more spheres. These scientists, working within the limits of Ptolemaic astronomy, also had to postulate certain backward loops of the heavenly bodies to account for variations in their periods of rotation. By the time of the Renaissance, the astronomers had built up an enormously complicated system of more than seventy spheres surrounding the earth, with each of the heavenly bodies performing an epicycle, or little backward rotation of its own around a central point on its orbit.

The Ptolemaic system was first questioned by the Polish astronomer and mathematician Nicholas Copernicus, who lived from 1473 to 1543. Copernicus never advanced the theory that the earth was not the center of the universe; he only discovered that mathematical calculations would be simpler if one accepted the sun as a stationary point and based one's calculations upon that. His conclusions were based upon the diagram shown in figure 17.2, which reveals the path a heavenly body performing its grand cycle about the earth (and also its little epicycle) would make.

Copernicus calculated that if we shifted the center of our system of sun and planets from the earth to the sun, we could eliminate the idea of the epicycles, for, as the heavenly body makes its circle around the

earth and also makes its little epicyclical journey, it actually describes a new orbit in which the sun is the center. The dotted line in figure 17.2 is the circumference of this circle. Copernicus, as we have said, only suggested this as a method of simplifying the mathematical calculations. Actually he gave an entirely new description of the world, which yielded a new concept of humanity's relation to the universe.

Once one gets the idea of this change in point of view, it seems simple. One wonders how people who had the intelligence to make the complicated calculations concerned with the epicycles could not have gotten this simple idea of changing their perspective. Copernicus could do this because he had the courage to look at the thing *as it was,* uncolored by all the ideas that had been handed down to him. He was willing to junk all of his traditional learning and tell what he really saw. Here, better than any place else, one can see the difference between the Renaissance and the medieval point of view.

The Copernican system, with many modifications, is essentially the concept of our solar system we accept as true today. Some of the modifications of the principle occurred during the Renaissance itself. Tycho Brahe (TIE-ko BRA-hee; 1546–1601) made careful observations of stars and planets that were to serve as factual material for later astronomers' interpretation. Kepler (1571–1630), a German astronomer, refined the calculations of Copernicus, pointing out that the orbits of the planets were ellipses rather than circles and accounting for the fact that the motion of planets was more rapid at some points in their orbits than at others. Galileo (gal–i–LAY–oh; 1564–1642) did more with his telescope than any other person to establish the Copernican system as an astronomical fact, remembering that Copernicus only advanced the idea as a method of simplifying mathematical calculations. Indeed, this phase of Galileo's work was probably as important as any other that he did. While he is best known for his discovery of the laws of motion (one immediately remembers the stories of his experiments in dropping objects from the leaning tower of Pisa), these experiments took place after the Church had banned his further observations with the telescope. (Galileo's work is discussed in greater detail in chap. 21.)

All of these advances in our knowledge about the vast universe of which we are a part were summed up in what is known as the Cartesian revolution, after René Descartes (day–KART; 1596–1650), a French philosopher who formulated the more or less fragmentary evidence into a unified system of scientific philosophy. (Descartes is also discussed in chap. 21.) He reaffirmed the ideas first expressed by the Greek atomist Demokritos that the whole of matter was composed of items of identical substance. All reality for Descartes, then, lay in the motion of this absolute substance through space and time. For him, and the many who followed him, God was reduced to an engineer who had built a very complicated machine and

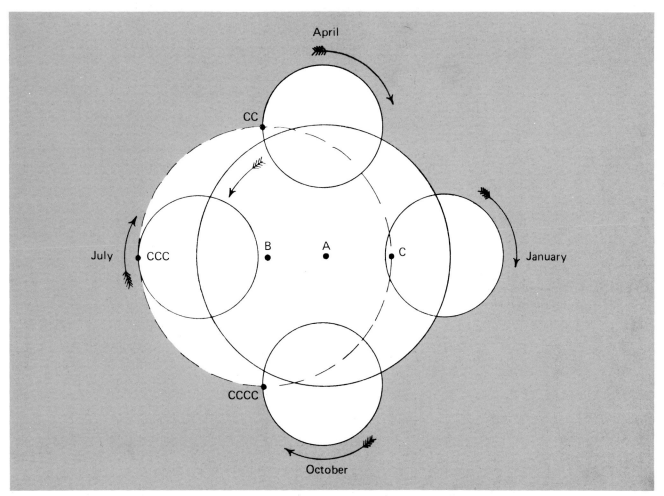

Figure 17.2 The earth (A), the sun (B), and a heavenly body (C) making its epicycle in the same time it makes its orbit around the earth: a full year. Suppose that in January the heavenly body is at point C. Then by April it will have gone a quarter of the way around its orbit with the earth as the center, and it will also have gone a quarter of the way around its epicycle. It will be at point CC. By July it will have gone around another quarter of its circles and will be at point CCC. By October it will be at point CCCC. By January it will be back at its starting point. If we join these points with the line that the planet traveled, we will find its path to be a circle (dotted line), which has the sun at its center.

set it in motion. From that time forth, God had no function in the world. By Descartes's division of primary (measurable) qualities and secondary (nonmeasurable) qualities, he brought about a new kind of dualism. Henceforth, the body was the only part of the human that was of real importance; the soul, if it existed at all, belonged to the secondary, the less important group of qualities. From Descartes onward, scientists were only to concern themselves with the question "How does something work?" not "Why does it work?" As Randall has summed up the thought of the Cartesian revolution:

> To Descartes thenceforth space or extension became the fundamental reality in the world, motion the source of all change, and mathematics the only relation between its parts. . . . He made of nature a machine and nothing but a machine; purposes and spiritual significance had alike vanished.[1]

We have said many times that one of humankind's great questions was that of our relation to the universe and to God. Henceforth, we must separate the two and ask about our relationship to the universe and our relationship to God. Of the two questions, the world since the scientific revolution has considered the former question the more important. Human institutions, from that day forth, have been built upon the idea of a mathematically ordered universe rather than one actively ruled by God.

1. J. H. Randall Jr., *The Making of the Modern Mind* (New York: Columbia University Press, 1976), pp. 241–42.

Inventions and Discoveries

In China printing was invented in 756, gunpowder in about 1100, and the magnetic compass a decade or two later. All were strictly controlled by the existing social order, enabling the imperial government to maintain control, most of the time, in all of China. There was no central authority in Europe, and so the changes caused by just these three inventions were dramatic. During the 1440s movable type was invented in the Mainz river valley in Germany, possibly by Johannes Gutenberg (1398?–1468). Up to this time learning had been the privilege of the few who could afford to have books copied by hand. The invention of printing made possible the most rapid expansion of knowledge that we have known prior to the proliferation of computers that has occurred in our own time. By 1500 there were over a thousand print shops and millions of volumes in print. Without printing Erasmus of Rotterdam (see chap. 20) would not have achieved his eminence as Europe's foremost man of letters. Printing was a vital factor in the success of the Protestant Reformation; Martin Luther's tracts attacking the Roman church were rushed into print and spread like wildfire throughout Europe.

The technique of making gunpowder was imported from China and first used during the latter years of the Hundred Years' War (1337–1453) between England and France. Subsequent improvements in firearms and artillery made gunpowder, in effect, a great leveler. One man with a gun was more than a match for a knight on horseback, and even early cannons could bombard medieval castles into submission. The feudal age ended abruptly and, one might say, explosively.

Exploration and Discovery

As mentioned earlier, trade between European cities and those of the Near and Middle East was an important factor in the evolution of the Renaissance, but limited navigational aids forced sailing vessels to generally remain within sight of land. A few intrepid travelers, the most famous of which was the Venetian Marco Polo (1254?–1324?), made their way along the great land routes to India and China. Marco Polo returned to Venice after spending seventeen years in China (1271–1295), but no one at the time believed any of the wonders that he related. Not until the fifteenth century would European sailors have the capability to circumnavigate Africa to reach China, and the driving force behind this exploration was Prince Henry the Navigator (1394–1460), son of King John I of Portugal. Apparently without referring to the Chinese work, a crude magnetic compass had been invented in the twelfth century. Henry improved this crucial device, had accurate maps and tables drawn, improved the design of ships, and reintroduced the use of the astrolabe that had been invented by the Arabs. A ship's latitude (north-south) could be calculated to within about thirty miles by using the astrolabe to determine the angle of the sun above the horizon at noon. This figure was then compared with Henry's tables of the sun's declination at known latitudes for each day of the year.

Navigation could not be made more precise until the marine chronometer was invented in 1760 to determine longitude (east-west). Nevertheless, navigational aids were adequate for voyages of exploration. In 1497, for example, Vasco da Gama (ca. 1469–1524) sailed southwest and then south from Portugal for ninety-seven days before turning east and sailing directly to the known latitude of his African destination, the Cape of Good Hope. He continued around Africa and on to India, returning to Lisbon in 1799 (see fig. 17.3). Prior to da Gama's successful voyage, India had been the destination of Christopher Columbus (ca. 1451–1506), who sailed west rather than south and discovered instead a New World—new to Europeans, that is, with the exception of much earlier Viking voyages. Columbus claimed the land for Spain, which was confirmed when Spain and Portugal drew a vertical line in the Atlantic, with the Americas awarded to Spain and Africa to Portugal. No one knew at the time that the line ran through Brazil, until it was accidentally discovered by the Portuguese captain Pedro Cabral (1460–ca. 1526), who was blown off course as he sailed down the African coast. A treaty later confirmed Portugal's ownership of Brazil. It apparently occurred to no one that the Americas and Africa were already inhabited by people who were never consulted by their new owners. European colonialism had begun.

Vasco de Balboa (1475–1517) marched across the Isthmus of Panama in 1513 to discover a Pacific Ocean that residents of the Pacific Basin had always known was there. Ferdinand Magellan (1480–1521), a Portuguese in the service of Spain, sailed west in 1519 with five ships to find a passage, now called the Straits of Magellan, around South America and across the Pacific to Asia. He was killed in the Philippines, but his explorations proved empirically that the world was round.

Spain and Portugal intended to divide between them the entire overseas world, but England and France had other ideas. An Italian mariner who the English called John Cabot (1450–1498) was dispatched in 1497 to find a "northwest passage" to the Indies. The passage did not exist, of course, but Cabot's landings somewhere around Labrador and Newfoundland provided England with an opportunity to claim all of North America. The explorations of Jacques Cartier (1494–1553) plus later discoveries by Samuel de Champlain (1567?–1635) gave France competing claims, while the Dutch joined the competition with the explorations of Henry Hudson (?–1611), an Englishman who entered Dutch service in 1609.

Maritime explorers were followed by adventurers like Hernando Cortés (1485–1547) and Francisco Pizarro (1471–1541), who conquered the only two high civilizations of the New World. Cortés took the Aztec empire of Mexico in 1519 with 600 soldiers, and Pizarro conquered the Inca empire of Peru in 1531–1533 with only 180 soldiers.

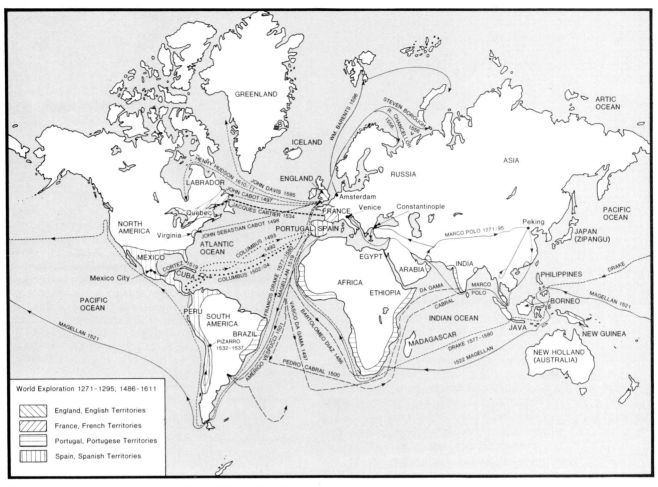

Figure 17.3 World Exploration 1271–1295; 1486–1611.

There was treasure aplenty in the New World, but Europeans found another in their own minds. Accounts of the voyages of explorers seized the Renaissance mind much as the exploration of space engages the minds of our time. Renaissance Europe had opened up new frontiers in art, literature, philosophy, and science, and now there was the lure and challenge of new lands as well. America became, for many Europeans, the literal utopia that Sir Thomas More used as the setting for his fictional *Utopia* (see chap. 20).

The Reformation: New Ideas about God and Humankind

Not only did concepts about the universe and the world change rapidly during the Renaissance, but the Reformation changed the face of Europe. It not only created a major schism in a once monolithic church but also constituted a major social, political, economic, and intellectual revolution. There had been earlier challenges to the authority of the Church of Rome, but the Reformation started by Martin Luther was the first to succeed on a large scale.

In 1170, for instance, a French merchant named Peter Waldo (d. 1217) founded a puritan sect known as the Waldenses. Preaching apostolic poverty, they rejected Rome and its papal claims. Though excommunicated in 1184 and persecuted for centuries, the sect survives today as the *Vaudois* in the Alps of Italy and France.

In England John Wiclif (or Wycliffe; ca. 1320–1384), an Oxford scholar, revived interest in St. Augustine and openly questioned the need for a priestly hierarchy. Contending that God and the Scriptures were the sole sources of spiritual authority, he translated the Vulgate into English and urged everyone to read it for themselves. He was silenced by the Church, but the Wiclif Bible became important after 1534 when Henry VIII, with his Act of Supremacy, broke away from the Roman Catholic church and confiscated church property.

Jan Hus (or Huss; 1369–1415) was a follower of Wiclif and a priest/professor at Charles University in Prague. His opposition to the sale of indulgences led to charges of the Wiclif heresy, and he was burned at the stake on July 6, 1415. His martyrdom caused bloody riots in Bohemia followed by an evangelical movement of the Unitas Fratrum (Unity of Brethren).

By 1500 the Brethren (later called the Moravian Church), had over 200,000 members in 400 parishes. In 1501 the church published the first hymnal in the vernacular and placed it, along with the Bible, in the hands of the people.

The term *reformation* was used in the late Middle Ages by individuals and groups who protested the secularization of Christianity and the abuses of power and privilege by the church hierarchy from the popes down to parish priests. An unbroken succession of corrupt Renaissance popes from Sixtus IV (1471–1484) to Leo X(1513–1521) fueled the flames of a revolt that was touched off when Martin Luther (1483–1546) posted his ninety-five Theses on the door of the castle church at Wittenberg on October 31, 1517. Luther was incensed at what he called the "sale" of indulgences, particularly the fund-raising activities of a Dominican monk named Tetzel. Operating under papal authority, Tetzel was dealing in indulgences, soliciting contributions to swell the papal treasury (that Leo X had depleted) and to pay for the construction of the new St. Peter's in Rome. Indulgences were the issue and will be discussed later; initially, Luther intended only a clarification of the teachings of the Church. The *origins* of the Reformation are found primarily in Luther's religion.

An Augustinian friar and professor of theology at the University of Wittenberg, Luther had experienced a spiritual crisis. Convinced that he was a lost soul and destined for Hell, Luther took the advice of a confessor and plunged with characteristic fervor into intensive study of the Bible. In the epistles of Paul he rediscovered a faith in salvation by grace. The central doctrines of the early church fathers, especially Augustine, confirmed his belief in the authority of the Word of God: faith alone was sufficient for salvation. Church doctrine stipulated that faith *and* good works were necessary, but Luther stood firm in the conviction that he articulated the true faith of the Church. Faith and the Bible were enough for Luther; the break with Rome was inevitable.

Indulgences were remissions by the Church of temporal punishment either on earth or in purgatory. The Sacrament of Penance of the Roman Catholic church consists of contrition, confession, absolution, and satisfaction on the part of the penitent. The penitent must feel contrition for his or her sins, confess to the priest, and be absolved of guilt. The sinner must satisfy God's justice by working out the penalties assigned by the priest, penalties that could be commuted by the granting of an indulgence. According to the doctrine of *Thesaurus Meritorum*, the Church had a treasury of spiritual merits accumulated from the satisfaction of Christ for the sins of the world and the martyrdom of the Saints. Indulgences transferred spiritual merit from this treasury to the penitent. Too complex for laypersons to understand, many people believed that even sins could be absolved if they could buy enough indulgences, which as Luther observed, "put a grievous instrument in the hands of avarice."

Figure 17.4 Lucas Cranach the Younger (1515–1586), *Martin Luther and the Wittenberg Reformers,* ca. 1543. Oil on panel, 27⅝ × 15⅝". Luther is at the far left and Ulrich Zwingli at the far right. Looming large in the center is John Frederick the Magnanimous, Elector of Saxony and patron of the reformers and the Lutheran Church. The Toledo Museum of Art. Gift of Edward Drummond Libbey.

"Therefore those preachers of indulgences err who say that a papal pardon frees a man from all penalty and assures his salvation" was one of Luther's theses, actually statements that he would publicly debate. Arguing some of these points with the theologian John Eck, Luther publicly admitted that his statements really did challenge the authority of the Church. When shown that his position was similar to that of Jan Hus, Luther asserted that the Church was in error in burning Hus. Jan Hus was a condemned heretic, and Luther, basing his defense on the Scriptures, openly challenged the authority of the pope and the councils of the Church.

In 1521 Emperor Charles V convened the estates of the German empire in the town of Worms to force Luther, who had already been excommunicated by the pope, to retract his writings. "I neither can nor will make any retraction, since it is neither safe nor honorable to act against conscience" was his response. Insisting that "the Church universal is the number of the elect," Luther concluded his defense, according to tradition, with the words, "Here I stand. I cannot do otherwise. God help me. Amen." The Diet adopted an edict declaring Luther an outlaw, but the verdict was academic because Luther had many supporters among the German princes (see fig. 17.4). Corruption in the Church and the formation of a new faith helped promote Luther's church, but a rising tide of nationalism and an opportunity to send no more money to Rome were perhaps even more significant in the triumph of the Reformation.

The principles of Lutheranism were later formulated by a Lutheran scholar, Melancthon (1497–1560), who stated them as follows:

1. The only final authority either for conduct or belief is in the Scriptures *(Sola Scriptura)*.
2. The one condition of salvation is faith or trust in Divine Love *(Sola Fide)*.
3. Faith itself is a gift of God, not an achievement of man *(Sola Gratia)*.
4. The community of the faithful is the true church whose only head is Christ. The growth of this church is fostered by preaching the gospel and the observance of two sacraments, Baptism and the Lord's Supper.

The Lutheran belief stresses individuality; salvation and a knowledge of God is a direct process, needing no church or priestly intercessor.

The Reformation in Germany was closely followed by a notable movement in Switzerland, first led by Ulrich Zwingli (1484–1531; see fig. 17.4), who even more than Luther believed in the individuality of worship and the authority of the Scriptures. Later this group was led by John Calvin (1509–1564), a French Protestant who was originally educated for the law as well as theology. When the Protestants were persecuted in France he fled to Geneva, where he lived for the rest of his life. There he established a theocratic republic, that is, a government that was ruled by the elders of the church.

Calvin was a strong believer in predestination, for since God is all-knowing and all-powerful, Calvin reasoned that he must know the fate of every person. In this faith, only a few of the elect were to be saved. The outward sign of salvation was right moral conduct. In 1536 Calvin published *The Institutes of the Christian Religion* (revised into its final form in 1559) in which he stated the philosophy upon which his faith was founded. This includes the unconditional sovereignty of God, which means that whatever happens, happens because God wills it so. He believed in humanity's total depravity and abject helplessness, which makes the help of a Saviour necessary. He stated his belief in a rigorous predestination of all people; some few of the elect will be saved through faith in God, and many will be forever damned. Finally, he stated that the group of the elect constitutes the Church. It is the duty of civil authorities as well as religious authorities to preserve the Church. Therefore an infraction of divine law required civil punishment, and the civil authorities should be under the direction of church authorities. This, as one can see, was a very strict sort of belief, and Calvin forbade many of the ordinary pleasures of life in Geneva and persecuted all those who did not follow his own faith.

Various forms of Calvinism spread throughout Europe. John Knox (1505–1572) founded the Presbyterian church in Scotland and England following the principles laid down by the Swiss leader. The English Puritans who came to America, and whose first colony was a theocracy like that of Geneva, were Calvinists.

The emphasis upon the individual's right to interpret the Scriptures in a personal way, almost the cornerstone of the churches that grew out of the Reformation, quite naturally led to the separation into many sects. Both Lutheranism and Calvinism attracted their members from the rising middle class. Many of the newer sects drew their following from the poorer classes. Among these latter were the Anabaptists, who believed in baptism only when the individual had reached adulthood, and was able to make a free choice. Very strongly present here was the concept of rebirth through baptism. From the Anabaptists came such modern denominations as the Friends (Quakers) and Baptists. The Socinians, who took their name from Faustus Socinus (1539–1604), were anti-trinitarians who refused to hold serfs or take part in any war. Persecuted in Poland by the Catholic church led by the Jesuits, they were banished in 1658 on pain of death. The Socinians were the single most important source for the Unitarian church. The Arminian church was led by the Dutch theologian Jacobus Arminius (1560–1609). They were an offshoot of Calvinism, but asserted that each person was free to choose his or her own way of living, thus denying the doctrine of predestination. Their theology was, in essence, accepted in England by the Wesley brothers, who founded the Methodist church.

The English church, known in America as the Episcopal church, came into being during the reign of Henry VIII in England. Although the immediate cause of the break with Rome came when the pope refused to sanction the annulment of Henry's marriage to Catherine of Aragon, the real causes of the break went much deeper than that. In the main, the English monarchs were tired of sending money to Rome, and of seeing much of their land in the possession of the Church. In 1534 the break between England and Rome was completed, and the Act of Supremacy stated that the king of England was the official head of the organization of the English church. At the time, there was little difference in the theology of the English and the Roman churches, and most of the forms of worship, though translated into English, remained the same as they had been in the Roman Catholic church.

The Catholic Reformation, also called the Counter-Reformation, was the papal response to Luther's revolt against Rome. Convened by Pope Paul III (1534–1549), the Council of Trent met from 1545 to 1563 to redefine every phase of Catholic doctrine attacked by the reformers: original sin, grace, redemption, the Sacraments, the Sacrifice of the Mass, and Purgatory. Every violation of discipline was denounced, reforms were enacted, and observance was demanded under pain of censure. The music of the Church was reformed, and there was a strong thrust of Counter-Reformation art and architecture (see chap. 22). The Counter-Reformation was given a mighty assist by the Jesuits (Society of Jesus) founded by Ignatius Loyola in 1534 and formally approved by Pope Paul III in 1540. The Jesuits represented the disciplined drive of the movement, but the popes also revived the Inquisition, an old instrument for the stamping out of heresy. Sitting as medieval courts and using medieval methods of torture, the papal and Spanish Inquisitions were relatively ineffective, however, in stemming the Protestant tide, especially in northern Europe.

How can we sum up the influence of the Reformation upon the lives of people? First, it was a strong prop to nationalism, which was perhaps the greatest single force moving through this whole period of the Renaissance. Second, it had a marked influence on education, in many cases divorcing it from ecclesiastical domination. On the other hand, under the strict influence of the Calvinists in particular, the scope of education was limited largely to the subjects of immediate utilitarian value. As far as the rise of individuality is concerned, the Reformation is almost a declaration of religious independence, for when one admits that the Bible alone is the basis for religious beliefs, one is immediately confronted with the great variety of possible interpretations of that book. As a result, under Protestantism there has risen such a host of sects that the individual can find almost any type of religious belief that appeals to him or her. Finally, Protestantism was a strong influence in the rise of capitalism, for the ideal Calvinist, Methodist or Lutheran took the first psalm strongly to heart:

> Blessed is the man that walketh not in the counsel of the ungodly, nor standeth in the way of sinners, nor sitteth in the seat of the scornful. But his delight is in the law of the Lord; and in his law doth he meditate day and night. And he shall be like a tree planted by the rivers of water, that bringeth forth his fruit in his season; his leaf also shall not wither; and whatsoever he doeth shall prosper.

Clearly this psalm tells us that the good man and good woman shall prosper. In a time when making, saving, and spending money was becoming more and more the sign of success, we come to the conclusion that we can recognize good people because they have prospered in this way. Furthermore, the sober, steady, hard-working way of life advocated by most of the new sects was exactly the sort of life that would promote industrious work and careful spending. And so began the Protestant work ethic, which produces the ideal person for a capitalist system.

The Relation of the Individual to the Group

Capitalism

We have already hinted in the previous paragraph at another of the forces that came into being during the Renaissance: capitalism. This is true. We who live in a capitalist society are prone to take our institutions and arrangements for granted, and assume that they have existed forever. However, until the late Middle Ages, at least, the thing we call capitalism had not existed, and it only came into full flower in the Renaissance. This is another example of the trend toward individualism that moved through this time, for up until now the economic arrangements of life had always been under political and religious domination. Now, exactly as the knowledge of the universe divorced itself from religion, so, too, did economic arrangements become an entirely separate field of human thought and human relationships. Indeed, it appears that much of the strife of our time occurs because of our conscious or unconscious attempts to bring politics and economics together again.

In order to make the distinction clear between the guild system and the capitalist system, it would probably be wise to point out some of the characteristics of the guild system. Under this type of economic organization there was production for human need alone. Furthermore, manufacturing and selling were a part of the same process. For example, a shoemaker made shoes only when someone ordered them. When there were no orders, he made no shoes. His sole purpose in his economic life was to make shoes for people when they wanted them. Furthermore, when the shoemaker died, unless his son inherited the business, the business died with the man. The quality of materials and work and the price of the finished article were rigidly controlled, so that there was no competition in business.

Now, to make the difference clear, let us watch the development of a capitalistic business. Anton Fugger settled in the city of Augsburg in 1380 where he became a weaver, that is, a member of the leading industry of that town. Soon, however, he began to collect and sell the products of other weavers. Before very long he employed weavers, paying them for their labor, and taking their product for his own. His son, Jacob Fugger I, continued this business, which was expanded under Jacob Fugger II, the leading capitalist of the Renaissance. This member of the family expanded his interests outside of weaving, dealing in metals as well as textiles. He confined his workings largely within the Hapsburg empire, dealing in silver and copper in Austria, and in silver and quicksilver in Spain. He also lent large sums of money to the Hapsburg emperors (they were engaged in at least a half-dozen wars during the Renaissance and were constantly in need of money), in return for which Fugger obtained monopoly rights on the ores of the metals in which he traded. Finally he bought the mines themselves so that he, like many great capitalists in our own time, employed thousands of workmen to whom he paid a wage; he controlled all of his products from raw material to market; there was no supervision over the quality of his products or the price he charged except the amount that the traffic would bear. Finally, he formed a company that existed outside of himself. Fugger had mined silver, copper, and mer-

Figure 17.5 Quentin Matsys (1465?–1530), *The Money Lender and His Wife,* 1514. Oil on wood, 28 × 26¾". Distracted from reading her Bible, the wife is as fascinated as her husband as he lovingly examines his money. The Louvre, Paris.

cury in quantity, with little relation to life-needs. His company piled up "profits," almost a new term, quite aside from the needs of the Fugger family; and these profits were measured in money rather than in lands or goods. From this example, we can, perhaps, discover some of the essential qualities of capitalism.

Perhaps the first characteristic of capitalism is that it creates "companies" that exist quite separately from the people who make them up. That is, the company can be sued, it can contract debts, and it may even do things of which the people who make up the company disapprove.

A second characteristic lies in the fact that the sole purpose of the company is the acquisition of money, and the demand for more money is never satisfied. Again, let us take a modern example: A single capitalist family acquires more money than it can ever spend. They can buy all sorts of luxury items but ride in only one chauffeur-driven limousine (or Lear jet), live in one house at a time, and consume just so much food in a lifetime. There is a physical limit to what can be bought and actually used. However, there is no limit to the amount of money that can be amassed, and the capitalist system assumes that the acquisition of money is the goal of economic activity (see fig. 17.5).

A third characteristic of capitalism is its rational organization within the "company." The company must plan ahead to assure itself of raw materials in the proper quantity and at the proper time. It must plan ahead to assure itself that it can get rid of the products of its effort. It must utilize the time of its workers and machines to the utmost, which means that there must be an even flow of work throughout the whole concern. The company must know exactly how much of its raw materials, how much of its finished product, and how much money is on hand at any given moment. All this means that it must have a rigid accounting system, both of materials and money, and of human energies as well. Capitalism shapes means to ends, and the end is the making of money profit. It is entirely rational and has no room for emotion in its organization. Any part of the organization that does not make a direct and efficient contribution to the purpose of the company must be cut away.

If the internal organization of the company is marked by this rationality, a fourth characteristic is that the system itself is completely irrational insofar as it is not controlled by government or by agreements within the member-companies of a particular industry. Since each company must grow, the resultant competition is completely ruthless, opportunistic, and irrational. Finally, as one writer points out:

> Profits, no matter how large, can never reach a level sufficiently high to satisfy the economic agent— acquisition therefore becomes unconditional, absolute. Not only does it seize upon all phenomena within the economic realm, but it reaches over into other cultural fields and develops a tendency to proclaim the supremacy of business interest over all other values.[2]

What were some of the immediate effects of the introduction of this new system of economic endeavor? In the first place, it increased the possibilities for individualism. If people could get to the top of the economic heap, all religious or guild restraints were removed, and they could do exactly what they had the power to do. The only limits on individuals lay in their own imagination, their own ability to plan ahead, their own ability to seize opportunity. A second effect of capitalism was in the increase of goods that were available. Under the handicraft-guild system, goods were available only when people wanted them. Now, capitalists created them and went out to find markets for the products. They made more of everything than was ordered and went out to "sell" these goods to people. In terms of the ownership of material things, capitalism has increased our standard of living manyfold. Not the least of the changes wrought by capitalism was the change in the appearance of cities. Up to this time, stores had not existed except as the booths at fairs could be called stores. Up to this time, the factory—a workshop and living quarters for the craftsman, his apprentices, and his family—had also been the store. The show-windows of today, with their enticing display of goods, the practice of shopping for everything from soup to hats and automobiles: these

2. Edwin R. Seligman, ed., "Capitalism," in *Encyclopedia of the Social Sciences,* vol. 3 (New York: Macmillan, 1937), p. 197.

are the result of the capitalistic system, and the planning of our cities today is a direct result of the new type of merchandising.

One caution must be added. Capitalism did not spring full-fledged into the world. In its first stages during the Renaissance it is called *mercantile capitalism,* in a later stage it is called *industrial capitalism,* recently it has been termed *finance capitalism,* and presently *state capitalism.* In each of these stages its characteristics were somewhat different from those of other stages; each stage had its particular qualities; each stage had its peculiar problems.

The Development of the Sovereign Power

Perhaps the most striking development of the Renaissance was the increase of royal power. We saw the beginning of this movement during the latter part of the Middle Ages, when the inadequacies of feudalism—the lack of a common currency, the blocking of trade by feudal tariff barriers, the inconsistencies in the administration of justice, and the lack of civil servants who were trained for their work—revealed themselves, and the kings drove to new power. Still another force that lent importance to the sovereign was the rich pouring of treasure from the newly discovered lands across the sea. For example, the Spanish monarch claimed a fifth of all treasure brought to Spain by the *conquistadores.* With these funds the kings were able to set up brilliant courts that attracted the nobles from their muddy country estates and made these nobles dependent upon the king for their livelihood and for their amusement. Most of the nobility were more than willing to sell out their rural independence for the ritual of seeing the king rise in the morning, or participating, vicariously, at least, in the brilliant art and the sparkling drama with which the kings surrounded themselves, and of taking their part in the great balls and festivals the king provided.

Not only did the nobles give their allegiance to the sovereign, but the common people looked to the throne as the single source of order in a world changing so rapidly that the people could scarcely keep up. "Future shock" was present in the Renaissance as it is today. Order had been the rule of the Middle Ages. Suddenly the authority of the Church was broken in much of northern Europe, the unity of the universe was shattered by the new science, and the economic order that had been controlled by the guilds was shattered by capitalism. People needed some sort of order-giving source to take the place of the shattered systems. The king was the single stabilizing influence in all this chaos. Wherever we turn, we find references to this central position the sovereign held. In Shakespeare's play *Hamlet,* Rosencrantz speaks of the monarch's importance thus:

> The cease of majesty
> Dies not alone, but, like a gulf doth draw
> What's near it with it; it is a massy wheel,
> Fix'd on the summit of the highest mount,
> To whose huge spokes ten thousand lesser things

> Are mortis'd and adjoin'd; which, when it falls,
> Each small annexment, petty consequence.
> Attends the boisterous ruin. Never alone
> Did the king sigh, but with a general groan.

Historically the Renaissance saw the brilliant reigns of the Tudor rulers in England, especially Henry VIII (ruled 1509–1547) and Elizabeth I (ruled 1558–1603). These were two monarchs who understood the rising importance of trade and commerce and the vital role that the middle class played in England's growing prosperity. It was under Elizabeth, too, that the English navy defeated the great Spanish Armada in 1588, making England mistress of the seas until well into the twentieth century.

In France, Francis I (ruled 1515–1547) set a pattern for later kings, such as Louis XIV (ruled 1643–1715), by bringing the best artists to a sumptuously furnished court that became a model for all of Europe. He, too, cemented national feeling by a series of wars fought largely by mercenary soldiers in helpless and divided Italy. France was later bitterly embroiled in a struggle between the Protestant Huguenots, led by the house of Bourbon, and the Catholics, led by the house of Guise. This struggle reached its conclusion in 1598 when Henry of Navarre took the throne as Henry IV, the first Bourbon king (ruled 1598–1610). Henry professed himself a Catholic, but guaranteed certain rights to the Huguenots in selected cities, rights that Louis XIV later cancelled, at which time thousands of Huguenots left the country.

Spain reached its single high point of brilliance at this time, at first under the rule of Ferdinand and Isabella (1474–1504). They and later rulers enjoyed tremendous profits from their conquests in Central and South America. As a matter of fact, the decline of Spain can be attributed to their disinterest in permanent colonies, preferring instead to plunder their holdings. Later, Spain became one of the countries ruled over by the Hapsburgs, for Charles I of Spain (ruled 1519–1556) also held the title of Archduke of Austria. He was, moreover, Charles V, Emperor of the Holy Roman Empire. His holdings included the kingdom of Naples and Sicily plus the Netherlands. The Spanish Hapsburgs became the leading Catholic monarchs in Europe and had the force of the Catholic church as a part of their spiritual and secular power.

In 1566 the Netherlands revolted against the Hapsburg kings, a revolt provoked in large part by the importation of the Inquisition. After a series of bloody wars, Holland became an independent nation, but the area known today as Belgium did not free itself until 1713. Portugal also achieved full independence during the Renaissance, and like Spain, achieved a short-lived glory as a result of the wealth and plunder from its explorers and merchants.

Germany became the battleground of the Thirty Years' War (1618–1648), which began as a conflict between Catholics and Protestants and ended as a political struggle against the Hapsburgs by Holland, France, Sweden, and other nations. Germany was devastated as the largest armies since Roman days surged over the countryside. Sweden alone had over 200,000 men in the field. The ferocity of the struggle prompted the writing of the *Law of War and Peace* (1625) by the Dutch jurist Hugo Grotius. Though he recognized war as "legitimate," he did distinguish between just and unjust conflicts and laid down principles for "humane" warfare. Drawing on actual events of the war, he condemned such acts as poisoning wells, mutilating prisoners, massacring hostages, rape, and pillage. In time the work of Grotius became the basis of the Geneva Conventions. It was this bitter and disastrous war that spurred emigration to America, where there would be a clear separation of church and state and no more religious disagreements fought out on a battlefield.

Italy's fate deserves a special note, for it was in Italy that humanism first appeared, not to mention the inspired creations of artists like Leonardo da Vinci, Michelangelo, and Raphael (see chap. 18). One of the most important stresses in this period was the development of the individual. The Italian cities early fostered ambitious individuals who plied their trade with the cities of the eastern Mediterranean during the late Middle Ages, and had already begun to develop a mercantile capitalism. As a result, a few powerful families rose in Italy, each controlling one of the important cities. The Visconti family ruled in Milan, a council of rich merchants took over the Venetian republic, and the Sforza family was a power in Lombardy and later in Milan. The most notable of the ruling families was the Medici clan in Florence, whose leading member was the famous Lorenzo the Magnificent (1449–1492), a banker, ruler, artist, and patron of the arts. Like the Greek city states of old, however, the rich and powerful cities of Italy could never unite, and they went into decline after 1500, when Italy became a battleground for internal squabbles and rampaging foreign armies that were more efficiently organized under central sovereign powers.

In Summary: A Restatement of the Enduring Questions

There has scarcely been a time, except perhaps our own, when people busied themselves so industriously exploring the dark room of their universe. Wherever they went they turned up new facts that upset any and all old balances and old institutions. Humanism, as one of the instruments of the whole secular spirit, stripped the allegory from all manifestations of nature and aided people in looking at the world as it really was. Humanism also stressed the importance of the individual and the harmonious and complete functioning of the natural person, guided, the humanists hoped, by moderation and good sense, in a rich world. To a certain extent humanism was a revolt against Christian ethics, not only in its turning back to classical sources but also in its insistence on the reasons for leading the good life; it was not in the hope of eternal bliss in heaven, but because the good life was its own reward. At its height humanism was the bridge between medievalism and modernity.

The new science, of which the high points were the heliocentric view of the solar system and the mechanistic theory of the universe, completely shifted the base of all human institutions. Before that time God had been the whole purpose and goal of human life, and it was upon these teleological assumptions that people had based their lives. That basis for human aspirations was swept aside, and men and women saw themselves as inhabitants of a brave new world.

Not only was the theoretical foundation for human values invalidated by scientific discoveries, but the institution that had formerly controlled life's most important functions was questioned and rejected. The keystone of the revolt against the Catholic church was the dazzling realization that people could live in a direct relation to God with no need for an intermediary hierarchy. People who needed religious authority to direct their lives could turn to the Scriptures and read and interpret for themselves. And those who did not need or want religious authority could live their lives without fear.

Vast areas for human endeavor opened at the same time. The idea, as much as the reality, of the New World swept aside musty medieval walls and liberated the European intellect. One tangible reality did come from the New World and that was money. Wealth poured into the countries who sent their buccaneers forth, and the new money bought ease and luxury. Capitalism offered another marvelously stimulating outlet for individual enterprise. If one were resourceful enough and unscrupulous enough, the sky was the limit.

Each of these freedoms brought with it an undercurrent of doubt and pessimism. If the earth and its inhabitants were no longer the center of God's attention, and God no longer the goal and purpose of men and women, then what were we and what was our purpose, if any, here on earth? If the Bible was to be read and interpreted by each person, where was there any certainty? In a world that ran like a machine, where could people find answers about their relationship to each other and to the Creator of that world? Was the new relationship between people only dog eat dog as the new capitalism suggested? The sole answer the Renaissance could suggest to the necessity for order and stability was that of the absolute monarch. In the seventeenth century these monarchs would claim that they were ordained by God to care for his people. They would, therefore, rule by divine right. As the people observed the actions of their rulers, they had good reason to be uneasy about this new basis for an orderly existence.

Another trend, too small and remote as yet to cause pessimism, but present nevertheless in the intellectual currents of the time deserves mention. Science had discovered a rational world that appeared to operate like a machine, and capitalism, while it guaranteed near freedom for the captains of commerce and industry, operated "rationally," as we have said, within the companies that composed it. This meant that the men and women who worked in capitalistic units were not free. They had cast off their heavenly bondage and guild regulations, but they had gained a new bondage: that of the clock, production quotas, and the account book. The coming Industrial Revolution would exacerbate that bondage.

Renaissance Men and Women: Real and Ideal

> What a piece of work is man! How noble in reason! how infinite in faculty! In form, in moving, how express and admirable! In action how like an Angel! In apprehension, how like a God! The beauty of the world! the paragon of animals! And yet to me what is this quintessence of dust? Man delights not me. . . .
>
> *Hamlet*

When one thinks of the Renaissance, the first thought is usually of the glories of discovery throughout the world or the reforms of Luther, or perhaps one thinks of the prodigious output in the arts. Michelangelo, Shakespeare, Palestrina, Cervantes, Leonardo—the names of the remarkable creators tumble through the mind (see the Time Chart for the Renaissance at the end of this chapter). All of these add up to a picture of the Renaissance as a time of glorious optimism and expansion of the human spirit. It would seem that the possible zones of human action were widened in every respect: geographically, with the new discoveries; spiritually, with the Reformation; economically, with the rise of capitalism. This, of course, is true. But it is only a part of the total picture. Hamlet ends his soliloquy: "What is this quintessence of dust? Man delights not me."

This hints at another aspect of the Renaissance that is as important as the first exuberant picture. Throughout the whole period ran a deep-seated pessimism concerning the nature of human beings. In much of the thought of the time one finds this melancholy strain. What is Hamlet saying? Primarily, that in all appearances, in actions, and in potentialities, men (and women) are great. Yet somehow in reality they fall short of greatness. Such pessimism usually indicates a failure to reach some ideal.

The Renaissance Problem

With the information we now have at hand, we can state the problem that confronted the thinkers of the time. On the one hand they had opportunity unlimited. Wide horizons stretched in all directions. At last it seemed that human beings, with their mighty achievements, could become Godlike creatures.

Yet at the same moment, the very forces that opened these new possibilities undermined the very concept of humans as the special and most loved of all of God's creations. The matters of the soul, of divinity, and even of human emotions were relegated to a secondary position in relation to the physical and quantifiable equalities. Even further, the more purposes and hopes that were held out for humankind, the more did it seem that people's animal nature won ascendancy over their nobler qualities. When the opportunities for advancement opened before them, people seized them savagely and selfishly. Not only did those of low station who had been released by the changing events show themselves unworthy, but even the best and the wisest, the noblest among men and women, saw deeply into their own personalities and found the same base instincts there.

Here, then, is the problem. How can this animal nature of human beings, which now seemed dominant over all other aspects of their character, be dealt with so they could become the noble creatures that, on the surface, they seemed to be? How could the rough, crude, and selfish person be disciplined so that all men and women could proceed in some sort of order to the fulfillment of the total promise of their character and the expanding world in which they lived? Philosophers, theologians, artists, psychologists, and men and women in all walks of life have wrestled with the problem, but the question remains.

Bibliography

Alexander, Sidney. *Lions and Foxes: Men and Ideas of the Italian Renaissance.* New York: Macmillan, 1974. Fascinating reading and up-to-date material.

Breisach, Ernest. *Renaissance Europe 1300–1517.* New York: Macmillan, 1973. A good history of all important aspects of the period.

Burkhardt, Jacob C. *The Civilization of the Renaissance in Italy.* New York: Harper & Row, n. d. A translation of the classic work that almost "invented" the Renaissance and gave us our first glowing picture of that golden age. Originally published over a century ago, this was a pioneering work that inevitably contained mistakes, not the least of which was ignoring the Renaissance in northern Europe.

Chamberlin, E. R. *Everyday Life in Renaissance Times.* New York: G. P. Putnam's Sons, 1967. Includes 124 illustrations.

Clark, Kenneth. *Civilization: A Personal View.* New York: Harper & Row, 1970. As in volume 1 of this text, we like to recommend this transcription of Clark's brilliant television series (itself an act of civilization) as a companion to this volume. The series is particularly good for the dimensions it gives to the Renaissance.

Clements, Robert J. and Lorna Levant, eds. *Renaissance Letters: Revelations of a World Reborn.* New York: New York University Press, 1976. A carefully edited collection of letters of many of the important individuals in all fields. Fascinating primary sources.

De Santillana, George, ed. *The Age of Adventure: The Renaissance Philosophers*. New York: New American Library, 1956. Like the other volumes of the series, a compendium of the thought of the age.

Elton, Geoffrey R. *Renaissance and Reformation, Thirteen Hundred to Sixteen Forty Eight*. 3d ed. Ideas and Institutions in Western Civilization, vol. 3. New York: Macmillan, 1976. A collection of many of the important documents of the period plus good editorial comments.

Hale, John R. *Renaissance*. Great Ages of Man Series. Alexandria, Va.: Time-Life Books, 1965. Superb coverage in the Time-Life series.

———. *Renaissance Exploration*. New York: W. W. Norton, 1972. Informative little book.

Kinsman, Robert S. *Darker Vision of the Renaissance: Beyond the Fields of Reason*. Berkeley: University of California Press, 1975. Essays on political, literary, social, religious, medical, and artistic phenomena— irrational, nonrational, suprarational. Some of the reasons for the pessimism of the age.

Mates, Julian, and Eugene Cantelupe. *Renaissance Culture*. New York: George Braziller, n. d. Excellent collection of readings, arranged by problem areas, which reveal wide disparities of thought on each topic.

Nauert, Charles G., Jr. *The Age of Renaissance and Reformation*. Boston: University Press of America, 1982. Paperback. Includes up-to-date research.

Rachum, Ilan. *The Renaissance: An Illustrated Encyclopedia*. New York: W. W. Smith Publishers, 1980. Exceptionally useful. Names, places, people and movements, events, photographs, maps, tables, and many illustrations of artworks, some in color.

Simon, Edith. *The Reformation*. Great Ages of Man Series. Alexandria, Va.: Time-Life Books, 1966. More excellent coverage by the Time-Life series.

Symonds, J. A. *The Renaissance in Italy,* 3 vols. Gloucester, Mass.: Peter Smith, n. d. One of the standard, almost classic, treatments of the panorama of the Italian Renaissance.

Tawny, H. O. *Religion and the Rise of Capitalism*. Gloucester, Mass.: Peter Smith, n. d. Calvinism and the Protestant work ethic.

Wilcox, Donald J. *In Search of God and Self; Renaissance and Reformation Thought*. Boston: Houghton Mifflin, 1975. A clear presentation of the intellectual issues and problems.

Williams, Neville, ed. *The Expanding World of Man, 1215–1588*. Milestones of History, vol. III. New York: Newsweek Books, 1970. Panoramic view.

Time Chart for the Renaissance

	1350	1400	1450	1500	1550	1600
Art and Music		Brunelleschi 1377–1446	Limbourg Bros. fl. 1416	Bramante 1444–1510	Bruegel the Elder 1525–1569	
		Donatello 1386–1466		Botticelli 1445–1510	Palestrina 1526–1594	
		van Eyck 1390–1441		Josquin des Pres 1450–1521	El Greco 1548–1625	
		Dufay 1400–1474		Bosch 1450–1516	G. Gabrieli 1557–1612	
		van der Weyden 1400–1464		Grunewald 1470–1528		
		Masaccio 1401–1429		Dürer 1471–1528		
				Michelangelo 1475–1564		
				Raphael 1483–1520		
				Titian 1488–1576		
				Holbein 1497–1543		
Literary Figures	Petrarch 1304–1374		Erasmus 1466–1536	Montaigne 1533–1592		
	Boccaccio 1313–1375		Machiavelli 1469–1527	Cervantes 1546–1616		
			Sir Thomas More 1478–1535	Spenser 1552–1599		
			Castiglione 1478–1529	Shakespeare 1564–1616		
			Rabelais 1494–1553			
Some Important Religious Events		Wycliffe's English Bible, 1382	Dedication of Florence Cathedral, 1436	Martin Luther 1483–1546 Started the Reformation	King James Bible 1611	
		Jan Hus burned at stake, 1415		Posting of 95 Theses, 1517	Geneva Bible 1560	
				Diet of Worms, formal break with church 1521	Calvin's Bible ca. 1547	
				Martin Luther's Bible, 1532	Society of Jesus received official sanction, 1540	
				Henry VIII, Act of Supremacy 1534 Church of England	Loyola 1491–1556 Founder of Society of Jesus	
					John Calvin 1509–1564	

Science and Exploration

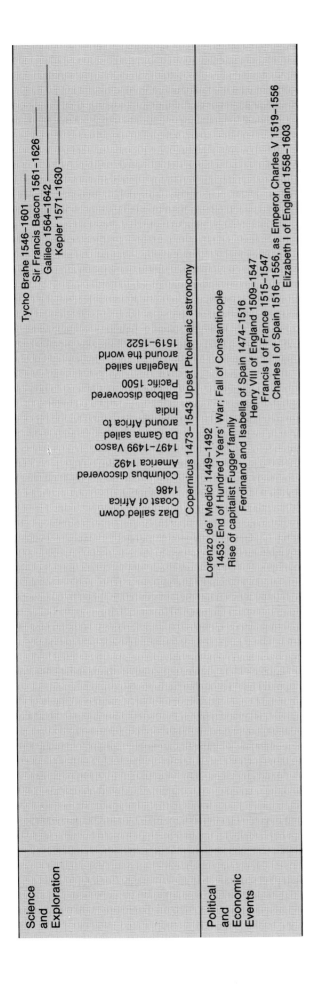

Tycho Brahe 1546–1601 ———
Sir Francis Bacon 1561–1626 ———
Galileo 1564–1642 ———
Kepler 1571–1630 ———

Magellan sailed around the world 1519–1522
Balboa discovered Pacific 1500
Vasco Da Gama sailed around Africa to India 1497–1499
Columbus discovered America 1492
Diaz sailed down Coast of Africa 1486
Copernicus 1473–1543 Upset Ptolemaic astronomy

Political and Economic Events

Lorenzo de' Medici 1449–1492
1453: End of Hundred Years' War; Fall of Constantinople
Rise of capitalist Fugger family
Ferdinand and Isabella of Spain 1474–1516
Henry VIII of England 1509–1547
Francis I of France 1515–1547
Charles I of Spain 1516–1556, as Emperor Charles V 1519–1556
Elizabeth I of England 1558–1603

18

Renaissance Art: A New Golden Age

The Early Renaissance in Fifteenth-Century Italy

Founded by the Romans in the rolling and verdant hills of the Arno River valley, Florence (from *Flora*), the city of flowers, was as early as 1199 a city of bankers and craft guilds. It was destined to become one of the leading financial centers of Europe and the city most closely identified with the Renaissance (fig. 18.1). Intended to symbolize Florentine wealth and influence, the great cathedral Santa Maria del Fiore (St. Mary of the Flower) was begun by Arnolfo di Cambio in 1296. Work slowed down after Arnolfo's death in 1302 and stopped altogether during the terrible days of the Black Death in 1348 and several subsequent years. Like many cities

Figure 18.1 View of Florence from the Boboli Gardens of the Pitti Palace. Reading from left to right: Giotto's Campanile (see fig. 18.3), the dome of the Florence Cathedral, and the Gothic tower of the Palazzo Vecchio.

in Europe, Florence was devastated by the plague, its population falling in just a few summer months from about 130,000 to around 65,000. Recovery was relatively swift, however, and in 1368 the cathedral design was finalized and building resumed, though no one had the faintest idea of how the dome was to be constructed.

In 1417 a special commission announced a competition for the design of the dome, optimistically trusting in Italian genius to solve the problem. The expected genius materialized in the person of Filippo Brunelleschi (broo-nuh-LES-key; ca. 1377–1446), the greatest architect of the Renaissance. His design was selected in 1420 and triumphantly completed about sixteen years later.

On 25 March 1436 all of Florence was bursting with anticipation. Pope Eugene IV, then residing in the Florentine monastery of Sta. Maria Novella, was to preside over the long-awaited consecration of the cathedral. On the day of the Feast of the Annunciation, the pope, accompanied by thirty-seven bishops, seven cardinals, the ruling Signoria, and envoys of foreign powers, began the solemn procession from the doors of the monastery. Moving along the specially constructed passageway (sumptuously carpeted and decorated with tapestries, damask, silk, and fresh flowers), the notables turned into the Via de' Banchi—most fittingly—where the major banking houses were located. Passing through the eleventh-century Baptistery, the dignitaries entered the spacious nave of the cathedral, where a five-hour service celebrated the completion of what was then the largest church in Christendom.

The most famous composer of the time, Guillaume Dufay (doo-FYE; see chap. 19), was present to hear the choir sing his motet *Nuper Rosarum Flores (Flower of Rose),* commissioned for the occasion by the Florentine Republic. A member of the papal choir, Dufay also represented the Flemish musical tradition of the court of the Dukes of Burgundy, the most elegant and powerful court in nothern Europe.

Brunelleschi began his artistic career as a sculptor, but after losing the 1401 competition for the north doors of the Baptistery to Ghiberti he turned his attention to architecture. According to later sources, he made several trips to Rome in the company of the young sculptor Donatello to study and measure the existing buildings of ancient Rome. His design for the largest dome since the Pantheon consisted of eight massive ribs arching upward from an octagonal drum and held in place by a classically inspired lantern (fig. 18.2).

Within the dome a complex web of smaller ribs and horizontal buttresses tied the main ribs firmly together. The design was not only exceptionally stable but was also economical, as it eliminated the need for expensive scaffolding. In addition to designing ribs that could be erected without centering, Brunelleschi invented a hoisting device so practical and simple that city authorities had to issue injunctions

Figure 18.2 Florentine Cathedral Group (aerial view). The Romanesque Baptistery (1060–1150) is at the upper right, partly obscured by Giotto's Campanile (1334–1350s). Cathedral 1296–1436.

Figure 18.3 Giotto, Campanile, 1334–1350s, Florence.

forbidding children from riding it to the dome. Averaging 140′ in diameter, the dome was 367′ high, the dominant feature of the Florentine skyline from that day to this.

The 269′ campanile situated at the southwest corner of the 508′-long cathedral was designed by Giotto (see chap. 15, vol. 1) in 1334 and completed by Talenti in the 1350s (fig. 18.3). Though many of the design elements are Gothic, the multicolored marble facing and the lucid proportions of the basically horizontal design reflect Italy's classical heritage. When compared with the dynamic thrust of the South Tower of Chartres Cathedral (fig. 18.4), Giotto's Campanile is cooly restrained, poised, and serene.

Figure 18.4 South Tower, Chartres Cathedral, ca. 1280. Height 344′.

Figure 18.5 Brunelleschi, Pazzi Chapel, Cloister of Church of Santa Croce, Florence, ca. 1441–1460.

Figure 18.6 Interior, Pazzi Chapel

It was in the Pazzi Chapel (fig. 18.5) in the cloister of the Church of Santa Croce that Brunelleschi applied his knowledge of classical designs. A diminutive building measuring only 59′9″ X 35′8″, its Renaissance design is clearly apparent, perhaps because the architect was not preoccupied with complex structural problems. In this beautifully proportioned building the break with the Gothic tradition is total. Gothic pointed arches are replaced with Corinthian columns and pilasters in even, harmonious spacing. The walls are treated as solid, flat surfaces and, overall, there is a subtle and graceful balance of horizontal and vertical elements. The portico was perhaps designed by Giuliano da Maiano and added after Brunelleschi's death.

Rather than dominating the building, the central dome rests effortlessly on its supporting rim. From within (fig. 18.6), it seems to float on the light of the twelve *occuli,* somewhat in the manner of Hagia Sophia (see fig. 12.20). The white stucco is articulated by the *pietra serena* (It., clear stone) pilasters and moldings of clear gray Tuscan limestone and highlighted by the deep blue backgrounds of the terracotta reliefs and the Pazzi coats of arms on the pendentives. The harmonious proportions of the facade are confirmed by an interior space that is also shaped into clear geometric units. The Pazzi Chapel is a prototype of the new Renaissance style, which revived the concept of harmonious proportions on a human scale, a point of view even more germane to the work of Renaissance sculptors.

When Donatello (don-a-TEL-o; 1386?–1466), the greatest of Early Renaissance sculptors, completed his statue of a Biblical prophet (fig. 18.7), he is said to have commanded it to "Speak, speak or the plague take you." The story may be apocryphal, but Renaissance artists did view themselves as creators, not as mere makers of things. With an assurance that the ancient Greeks would have admired, these artists hacked, hewed, painted, and composed as though

Figure 18.7 Donatello, Prophet ("Zuccone"), ca. 1423–1425. Marble, height 6′5″. Originally on the campanile, Florence; now in the Museo dell'Opera del Duomo, Florence.

Figure 18.8 Donatello, *David,* ca. 1430–1432 but maybe later. Bronze, height 62″. Museo Nazionale del Bargello, Florence.

they partook of the Divine Spirit. Though still regarded by society as craftsmen engaged in manual labor, they repeatedly proclaimed their preeminence as *artists,* an elevated status finally accorded men like Leonardo, Raphael, and Michelangelo in the sixteenth century. Created for a niche in Giotto's campanile, Donatello's Biblical prophet displays the rude power of a zealot, a man of God fiercely denouncing wickedness and vice. Known in Donatello's time as Zuccone ("pumpkin head," i.e., baldy), the figure is classical not in Greek terms but in human terms as an individual. Wearing a cloak thrown hurriedly over his body, the prophet is intent upon his mission: calling down the wrath of God on the faithless.

After a prolonged stay in Rome studying Roman art, Donatello returned in the early 1430s to Florence, where he created the *David* (fig. 18.8), a favorite image of Republican Florence, which saw itself as a latter-day David, champion of liberty. Representing a second stage in the development of Renaissance art, *David* is more classical than the Biblical prophet (see fig. 18.7), standing in a pose reminiscent of the *Hermes* by Praxiteles (see fig. 7.61). While the sinuous grace of the flowing lines and the balance of tension and relaxation is classical, this is the body of an

adolescent boy and not that of a Greek athlete or warrior. The Tuscan shepherd's cap and warrior boots emphasize what is possibly the first life-size free-standing nude since antiquity. The agony evident in the face of the slain Goliath offers a strong contrast to the curiously impassive facial expression of the shepherd boy. The Middle Ages interpreted David's triumph as symbolic of Christ's victory over death, but Donatello's intentions remain a tantalizing mystery.

The intentions of Early Renaissance painters are quite clear, however; they were concerned with creating the illusion of the natural world without regard to metaphysical symbols. Artists studied anatomy to determine how the human body was constructed and how it functioned. By using scientific procedures, they developed linear and aerial perspectives to create the illusion of actual space. They studied optics, light, and color to add the final touches to the illusion of light and personality. Through keen observation they confidently developed new forms for the new age.

Renaissance painting appeared in the 1420s in fully developed form in the work of a single artist. Though only in his mid-twenties, Masaccio (ma-SOT-cho; 1401–1428?) created a fresh repertory of illusionist techniques that were avidly studied by later Renaissance painters, especially Leonardo and Michelangelo. Working with his colleague Masolino, Masaccio painted a series of frescoes in the Brancacci

Figure 18.9 Masaccio, *Tribute Money,* ca. 1425. Fresco, 8'4" × 19'8". Brancacci, Chapel, Church of Santa Maria del Carmine, Florence.

Chapel, of which his *Tribute Money* (fig. 18.9) is the acknowledged masterpiece. The subject is based on Matthew 17:24–27 in which the Roman tax collector, wearing the short tunic, demands his tribute of Peter. Christ instructs Peter to cast a hook and take the first fish caught. In the fish's mouth Peter will find a shekel that he will give to the tax collector "for me and for yourself." Told in continuous narration in the Roman manner (see Trajan's Column, fig. 10.19), Peter appears first in the center, fishing at the left, and finally handing the coin to the tax man at the right. At the time of the painting, Florence was debating a new tax, the *catasto,* based in the modern manner on the ability to pay. Given the outdoor setting of the Arno Valley, rather than the Sea of Galilee, it is possible that the fresco appealed to people to pay their proper earthly taxes, or so the painting was interpreted by a fifteenth-century Florentine archbishop.

Masaccio used three Renaissance illusionist devices in this painting: linear perspective, atmospheric perspective, and chiaroscuro. Apparently developed by Brunelleschi, *linear perspective* is based on the principle of all lines converging on a single vanishing point, located at the head of Christ in this case. Perhaps invented in Italy by Masaccio, *atmospheric perspective* is based on the optical fact that colors become dimmer and outlines hazier as they recede into the distance. Flooding the painting from outside the pictorial space, light strikes the figures at an angle, outlining the bodies in a tangible space, a technique also utilized by the contemporaneous Northern Renaissance painters Robert Campin and Jan van Eyck (see colorplate 3). With light sculpting the bodies in gradations of light and dark, called *chiaroscuro* (key-AR-o-SCOOR-o), the illusion communicates weight, substance, and bulk. In the North, the Boucicaut Master

Figure 18.10 Fra Angelico and Fra Filippi Lippi, *The Adoration of the Magi,* ca. 1445. Tempera on wood, ca. 54" in diameter. Samuel H. Kress Collection. National Gallery of Art, Washington, D.C.

in Paris and van Eyck in Bruges also used atmospheric perspective, indicating that naturalistic painting had become, virtually simultaneously, the goal of a number of widely separated artists.

Fra Angelico (ca. 1400–1455) began his career as a painter in the Late Gothic tradition. Entering the Dominican Order in about 1423, Angelico devoted himself to the religious life and to reverential paintings of sacred subjects. He was hailed in his day as one of the two notable Florentine masters after Masaccio (the other was Fra Filippo Lippi), and was a superb painter of landscape and light. His *Adoration of the Magi* (fig. 18.10), completed by his collaborator, Fra Filippo Lippi, was listed in the 1492 Medici inventory as the most valuable piece of a fabulous

Figure 18.11 Paolo Uccello, "The Unhorsing of Bernardino della Carda," *Battle of San Romano,* ca. 1455. Tempera on wood, 6' × 10'5". Uffizi Gallery, Florence.

collection. Apparently designed by Angelico, who probably painted the Holy Family, the work is filled with a multitude of people who have followed the shepherds and magi to celebrate the Advent of the Messiah. There is a sense of deep space but no chiaroscuro or atmospheric perspective, even though Lippo supposedly decided to become a painter after viewing Masaccio's frescoes in the Brancacci Chapel. Instead, light is suffused throughout the painting with figures in sharp outlines and with colors remaining vibrant deep into the painting. Symbolism abounds. The dog stands for faithfulness, while the peacock represents resurrection and immortality. The looming mountain probably represents Golgotha, and the ruins could symbolize the classical past. Strikingly representative of the new age was the collaboration of two such disparate personalities. Fra Angelico became prior of the Monastery of San Marco in Florence; Fra Filippo Lippi was eventually defrocked by his order, but not before he sired two children by a nun and otherwise scandalized the church. That Renaissance artists usually portrayed religious subject matter was no sure guide to their spiritual orientation; it was their patrons, rather, who determined the subject matter of works of art.

For an age already using crossbows, gunpowder, and cannons, Renaissance warfare was paradoxical, a cultivated legacy from the Age of Chivalry. Based on soldiering for pay, the so-called *condottiere* (kondot-TYAY-ray; It., one hired as leader) system followed the tradition of medieval lists: armored knights in formal combat complete with code of honor and the pageantry of wheeling and charging with trumpets blowing and banners flying. For the Florentines, the relatively minor fray at San Romano epitomized fifteenth-century concepts of honor and, most especially, *virtu* (It., excellence, manliness). Immortalized by Paolo Uccello (oot-TSCHELL-o; 1397–1475) in three magnificent panels, the *Battle of San Romano* originally hung in the bedchamber of Lorenzo the Magnificent. Now divided among three museums, the left panel (National Gallery, London) depicts the Florentine condottiere Niccolò da Tolentino directing the attack. The right panel (Louvre, Paris) shows a counterattack, while the central panel (Uffizi Gallery, Florence; fig. 18.11) portrays the climax of the battle. One more incident in the wars between Siena and Florence, the Sienese, under Bernardino della Carda, were ravaging the Tuscan countryside until challenged on 1 June 1432 by Florence's military hero Niccolò da Tolentino. After an eight-hour battle capped by the unhorsing of their leader, the Sienese were routed. Uccello was obsessed with the problems of scientific linear perspective and thus more concerned with the patterns of lances, armor, trumpets, and crossbows than with the ferocity of warfare. The result is a stylized composition of a bloodless battle, with horses looking like transplants from a merry-go-round. The work is both a study in perspective and a memorial to military honor, Renaissance style.

Figure 18.12 Donatello, *Equestrian Monument of Gattamelata*, 1443–1453. Bronze, height 12'2". Piazza del Santo, Padua.

Figure 18.13 Leonbattista Alberti (design) and Bernardo Rossellino (architect), Facade, Palazzo Rucellai. Begun 1461, Florence.

Also commemorating a military hero, Donatello's colossal equestrian statue of the Venetian condottiere Gattamelata (fig. 18.12) was commissioned by the general's family, undoubtedly as authorized by the Venetian Senate. Donatello's ten-year sojourn in Padua in effect exported the Florentine Renaissance to northern Italy, spawning a whole school of painting and sculpture influenced by his powerful personality. The statue itself was possibly influenced by the Roman vigor of the equestrian statue of Marcus Aurelius in Rome (see fig. 10.22), then thought to portray Constantine. Donatello's work, however, exceeded the representation of the Roman emperor in the concentrated power of his figure's commanding presence. Apparently guiding his charger by sheer willpower (note the slack reins and spurs), the general is an idealized image of majestic power. Outfitted with a combination of Roman and Venetian armor, the composition of horse and rider is unified by the vigorous diagonals of the general's baton and long sword. Donatello not only solved the technical problems of large-scale bronze casting but created a masterpiece in the process.

During the first half of the fifteenth century, the Roman past was examined by Brunelleschi, Donatello, and others in terms of such classical elements as columns, capitals, and arches. By mid century the whole of antiquity was scrutinized, led by the remarkable humanist Leonbattista Alberti (1404–1472), who adopted the glorious past as a way of life. The first to study in detail the works of the Roman architect Vitruvius (first century B.C.), Alberti wrote enormously influential scientific treatises on painting, architecture, and sculpture. His design for the facade

of a wealthy merchant's townhouse was inspired by Roman architecture but, there being no precedents in an ancient society in which rich men lived in country villas, Alberti invented for the Palazzo Rucellai (fig. 18.13) a new architecture based upon his classically derived system of ideal proportions. Divided into three even and clearly articulated stories separated by friezes and architraves, the structure is faced with rusticated blocks of identical patterns in each bay, changing to related patterns in the upper two stories. Alberti adapted the articulation of superimposed pilasters from the Colosseum (see fig. 10.14), but without the deep spaces of that impressive exterior. He used the Tuscan order for the ground floor and the Corinthian for the top floor. In between he invented his own composite order, a layer of acanthus leaves around a palmette, maintaining that a thorough knowledge of classical designs enabled architects to extend the vocabulary, and then proving his point.

Alberti was responsible for two buildings in Florence, the Palazzo Rucellai and the facade of the Church of Santa Maria Novella, neither of which had any noticeable effect on Florentine artists of the time. Outside of Florence, however, and continuing into the sixteenth century, Alberti's classical designs influenced all Renaissance architects, especially Bramante, Michelangelo, and Palladio. His design for the

Figure 18.14 Leonbattista Alberti, Facade, Santa Maria Novella. Completed 1470, Florence.

Figure 18.15 Andrea del Verrocchio, *David*. Bronze, height 49⅝". Museo Nazionale del Bargello, Florence.

facade of Santa Maria Novella (fig. 18.14) had to cope with the existing Gothic arches on the ground level, which he accomplished brilliantly by topping them with blind arches and matching their green and white marbles with the corner pilasters and the four pilasters on the second story. His masterstroke was the addition of the volutes on both sides of the narrow upper temple, which solved two problems: (1) it supplied needed buttressing for the nave walls and (2) it beautifully filled the space above the side aisles of a basilica-plan church. The harmonious whole of the facade was the result of a rigorous set of proportions. Width and height are identical with a ratio of 1:1. The upper structure can be encased in a square one-fourth the size of the basic square, or a ratio of 1:4. The lower portion is a rectangle of double squares forming a ratio of 1:2. Throughout the facade the proportions can be expressed in whole-number relationships: 1:1, 1:2, 1:3, and so on. Along with Brunelleschi, Alberti was convinced that beauty was inherent in these ratios.

An overriding characteristic of Renaissance artists was their individuality, their need to be uniquely and unmistakably themselves. In three works by Andrea del Verrocchio (veh-ROE-key-o; 1435–1488) we see clear manifestations of this drive for individuality when treating the same subject. Verrocchio's *David* (fig. 18.15) is totally different from Donatello's conception. Donatello's figure is essentially a composition of sinuous and graceful lines; in his young warrior Verrocchio emphasizes texture, a delicate rendering in gleaming bronze of skin, underlying veins, muscle, and bone. These are qualities that, unfortunately, can be best appreciated only when walking around the actual work. The tactile qualities are enhanced by clothing the figure in a skintight short skirt designed to look like leather. That Verrocchio used his pupil Leonardo da Vinci as a model may or may not be true, but Leonardo would have been about the right age.

Donatello's *Equestrian Monument of Gattamelata* (see fig. 18.12) is idealized, but Verrocchio's portrayal of Bartolommea Colleoni (fig. 18.16) is strikingly realistic, with the fiercely scowling general readying his mace as he rides boldly into battle. Twisting in his saddle, the powerful figure seems almost too massive for the sprightly horse to carry. The tensions of horse and rider are portrayed in a dynamic moment in time. The battle is clearly at hand.

Also naturalistic is Verrocchio's portrait bust of Lorenzo the Magnificent (fig. 18.17), banker, poet, patron of the arts, and autocrat of Florence. Any accomplished craftsman can reproduce the crooked ski-slide nose, tight lips, and knitted brow. These are details that assist in the communication of a tangible presence: the overpowering personality of a unique human being. Classical portraiture had been revived and, without question, this is a masterful portrait of one of the dominant figures of the Italian Renaissance.

Three of the leading painters of the last quarter of the century—Botticelli, Ghirlandaio, and Perugino—were all vastly different in temperament and style. Sandro Botticelli (bot-tee-CHEL-lee; 1445–1510), in fact, stands alone as one of the great masters in the use of line. In his *The Adoration of the Magi* (fig. 18.18), Botticelli has painted a circular composition that is opened in the center foreground to admit the spectator. The architectural perspective

Figure 18.16 Andrea del Verrocchio (completed by Leopardi), *Equestrian Monument of Bartolommeo Colleoni,* ca. 1481–1496. Bronze, height ca. 13′. Campo SS Giovanni a Paolo, Venice.

Figure 18.17 Andrea del Verrocchio, *Lorenzo de' Medici,* ca. 1480. Terra-cotta, life size. Samuel H. Kress Collection. National Gallery of Art, Washington, D.C.

Figure 18.18 Sandro Botticelli, *The Adoration of the Magi,* after 1482. Panel, 27⅝ X 41″. Andrew W. Mellon Collection. National Gallery of Art, Washington, D.C.

is tilted upward, inviting the viewer into the work, to complete, as it were, the broken circle of adoration. The shed housing the Nativity group recalls Roman ruins, while the truss roof resembles that of old St. Peter's in Rome. Verrocchio's other famous pupil, Leonardo, claimed that Botticelli's paintings were not "correct" in terms of detail and atmosphere. Botticelli, in fact, deliberately violated the "rules" in this and other paintings; the vanishing point behind the Holy Family differs from the landscape perspective on either side of the Roman-style shed. Conforming to Alberti's doctrine of visual unity in terms of single-point perspective was an option. Renaissance perspective was, after all, only one of several systems for depicting the illusion of depth, an artificial method of representing space and therefore not *the* "correct" method of portraying reality. Botticelli's landscape is not incorrect; it is, in fact, brilliantly conceived for what the artist intends the viewer to experience.

In his celebrated *Birth of Venus* (colorplate 22) Botticelli subordinates perspective and "correct" anatomical proportions and details to the elegant and sensual lines that make his style so delightfully unique. Like many of his generation, especially the elite circle of Lorenzo de' Medici and the "Platonic Academy," Botticelli was fascinated with themes from classical mythology. According to an ancient myth, Venus was born from the sea, a legend interpreted by Ficino as an allegory of the birth of beauty. What the Florentine Neoplatonists actually did believe is still debated. Much of Plato's work had become available but there was also a large body of Neoplatonist writings with Christian elements superimposed on Platonic theories. Whether Botticelli's Venus symbolizes non-Christian or Christian ideas, or both, she is certainly lovely. Possibly inspired by a poem by Poliziano, Botticelli has painted her poised lightly on a conch shell as she is blown gently to shore by two Zephyrs, while one of the Hours hastens to drape her body with a flowered mantle. This is poetry in motion. The sea is flat, marked by upward thrusting V-shaped lines and bound by a stylized shoreline to form a serene setting for the sinuous lines of the moving figures. Probably inspired by classical statues in the Medici collection, the body of the goddess of spiritual and intellectual beauty is elongated and exquisitely curved, proportionately larger than the scale of the landscape. The gold-line shading on the trees is a further indication that Botticelli intended no realistic representation of the landscape. It was, in fact, this sort of stylized treatment of the background that led to Leonardo's comment that Botticelli created landscapes by throwing a sponge at the canvas.

Botticelli was favored by the intellectual elite of Florence, while the style of Domenico del Ghirlandaio (gear-lan-DAH-yo; 1449–1494) was preferred by the merchants and bankers of the city. Not interested in mythological fantasies, Ghirlandaio was a conservative painter for a conservative clientele and, as might be expected, a very successful artist. His *Old Man with*

Figure 18.19 Domenico del Ghirlandaio, *Old Man with a Child*, ca. 1480. Panel, 24⅜″ × 18′12″. The Louvre, Paris.

a Child (fig. 18.19), one of his most endearing works, is a compassionate portrayal of an elderly man holding an adoring child who could be his grandson, though the subjects have never been identified. Perhaps influenced by the naturalism of Flemish painting, which was well-known in Italy by this time, the objective treatment of thinning hair and a deformed nose actually adds to the tender scene of familial love. As was customary in Renaissance portraiture, the human subjects totally dominate the composition, reinforced by the lovely and distant landscape.

Until about the middle of the fifteenth century, the Early Renaissance was essentially Florentine; the second half of the century saw the dissemination of Renaissance techniques throughout Italy, notably by artists like Perugino and Bellini. Though his early training is a mystery, Pietro Vanucci was in Florence by 1472, where he acquired his knowledge of drawing and perspective, possibly from Verrocchio. It was in the Umbrian city of Perugia that he established his reputation and acquired the name by which he is known today: Perugino (pay-roo-GEE-no; ca. 1445–1523), the "Perugian." In his *Crucifixion with Saints* (colorplate 23), Perugino created a masterful pictorial space that is much more open than Florentine landscapes, with a sky stretching to infinity. As polished and cool as the work of the Flemish painter

Colorplate 22 Sandro Botticelli, *Birth of Venus,* after 1482. Tempera on canvas, 5'9″ × 9'½″. Uffizi Gallery, Florence.

Colorplate 23 Perugino, *Crucifixion with Saints,* before 1481. Panel, transferred to canvas: center, 40 × 22¼″; wings, 37¼ × 12″ each. Andrew W. Mellon Collection. National Gallery of Art, Washington, D.C.

Colorplate 24 Jan van Eyck, *Annunciation,* ca. 1430.
Oil on panel, 36½ × 14⅜″. Andrew W. Mellon
Collection. National Gallery of Art, Washington, D.C.

Colorplate 25 Leonardo da Vinci, *Ginevra de'Benci,* ca. 1480/81. Oil and tempera on panel, 15⅛ × 14½". Ailsa Mellon Bruce Fund. National Gallery of Art, Washington, D.C.

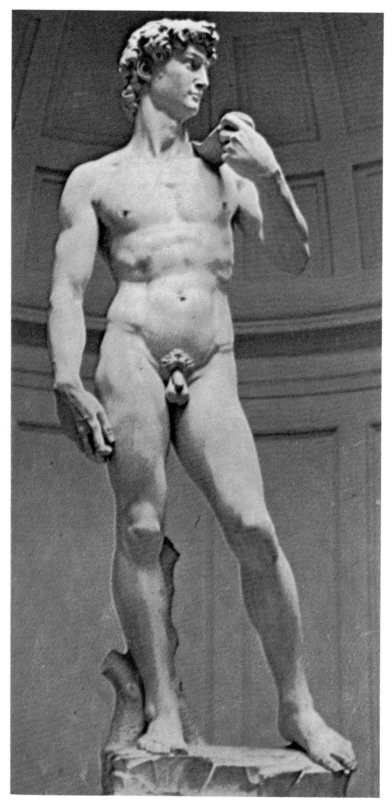

Colorplate 26 Michelangelo, *David,* 1501–1504. Marble, height of figure 14′3″. Academy, Florence.

Colorplate 27 Raphael, *The Alba Madonna,* ca. 1510. Transferred from wood to canvas, diameter of 37¼″. Andrew W. Mellon Collection. National Gallery of Art, Washington, D.C.

Colorplate 28 Giorgione, *Adoration of the Shepherds,* ca. 1505. Oil on panel, 35¾ × 43¼″. Samuel H. Kress Collection. National Gallery of Art, Washington, D.C.

Colorplate 29 Titian, *Venus with a Mirror,* ca. 1555. Oil on canvas, 49 × 41½″. Andrew W. Mellon Collection. National Gallery of Art, Washington, D.C.

Colorplate 30 Tintoretto, *Christ at the Sea of Galilee,* ca. 1555/1575. Oil on canvas, 66¼ × 46″. Samuel H. Kress Collection. National Gallery of Art, Washington, D.C.

Colorplate 31 El Greco, *Laokoön,* ca. 1610–1614. Oil on canvas, 54⅛ × 67⅞". Samuel H. Kress Collection. National Gallery of Art, Washington, D.C.

Colorplate 32 Matthias Grunewald, *The Small Crucifixion,* ca. 1510. Oil on canvas, 70 × 60″. Samuel H. Kress Collection. National Gallery of Art, Washington, D.C.

Figure 18.20 Giovanni Bellini and Titian, *The Feast of the Gods,* ca. 1514. Oil on canvas, 67 × 74". Widener Collection. National Gallery of Art, Washington, D.C.

Hans Memling (see fig. 18.26), and probably influenced by his work, the altarpiece shows none of the usual emotions of Florentine crucifixions. Christ is not racked by pain nor do Mary at the left or John at the right display any grief. In the wings St. Jerome and Mary Magdalene stand serenely in counterbalancing poses. In the vast expanse of the natural setting all is quietude. Whether the absence of emotion reflects Vasari's statement (in his *Lives of the Most Eminent Painters, Sculptors, and Architects,* 1550) that Perugino was an atheist may be a moot point. Though religious convictions were important for many people at that time, Renaissance artists were valued chiefly for their skills not their spirits.

Religious beliefs apparently interfered with some of the work of Giovanni Bellini (ca. 1430–1516), the foremost Venetian painter of the Early Renaissance. *The Feast of the Gods* (fig. 18.20), painted late in his long and productive career, was commissioned by the Duke of Ferrara and intended for the collection of Isabella d'Este, one of the most discerning and demanding patrons of the arts in Renaissance Italy (see chap. 20). Based on a story told by Ovid, the jackass at the left has just brayed, arousing the gods from satiated slumber and saving the wood nymph at the right from the amorous advances of Priapus, Roman god of procreation. Although placed in a glorious Arcadian setting, the nymphs, satyrs, and gods are portrayed more as peasants than as immortals. Bellini may have included portraits of some of his contemporaries; the dreamy goddess in the center (holding a bowl) may be Lucrezia Borgia, daughter of Pope Alexander VI. The lush landscape and pastoral but sensual mood are typical of the Venetian school, of which Bellini was the first master and the probable teacher of Giorgione

and Titian. He was among the first to adopt the Flemish invention of oil painting as developed by van Eyck (see fig. 18.22). Because Bellini was too devout for the secular tastes of the Duke and Isabella d'Este, Titian was commissioned to complete the work while converting it into more appropriate pagan terms, which was accomplished by partially disrobing the nymphs and changing some of the gestures to better fit Ovid's story. For the remainder of the Italian Renaissance the Venetian school followed the poetic tradition of vibrant colors depicting the pleasures of men and women, while the Roman and Florentine schools were mainly preoccupied with formal designs and noble themes.

The Early Renaissance in the North

The focus of significant new developments in art and music (see chap. 19) was the sumptuous court of the Dukes of Burgundy, from which the dukes governed the most prosperous lands in all of Europe (see the map of Burgundy on page 56). Philip the Bold and his brother, the Duke of Berry, sponsored leading artists like the Limbourg Brothers: Paul, Herman, and Jean (ca. 1385–1416). Their work in manuscript illumination marked the high point of the International Style (Late Gothic), while also moving beyond to a new naturalism. Commissioned by the Duke of Berry, they created for him a personal prayer book, a Book of Hours containing passages of Scripture, prayers, and Office Hours, all lavishly decorated and illustrated with paintings. Of particular interest are the twelve illuminated calendar pages; ten include peasants and aristocrats and two are devoted solely to peasant genre scenes. The month of *February* (fig. 18.21) has, at the top, a zodiac representing the route of the chariot of the sun and including, in this case, the zodiacal signs of Aquarius and Pisces. The scene is an intensely cold, snowy landscape, the first convincing snow scene in Western art. On the upper level a peasant cuts firewood, while another herds a donkey laden with faggots toward a distant village. In the tiny farmyard snow caps the beehives and covers the roof of the sheep pen except for the unrepaired hole in the roof. At the right a woman blows on her icy hands and stamps her feet to try to restore circulation. With the front wall removed for our benefit, we see a man and a woman seated before the fire with skirts raised high to gather in the welcome warmth. At the doorway, the lady of the house rather more decorously lifts her skirt, while the cat is, of course, cozily warm and comfortable. The perspective that gives the illusion of depth is empirical rather than mathematically precise, the way the artists actually perceived the scene. Marking the beginning of the Northern tradition of naturalistic art, the overriding concern is with the visible world, with loving care devoted to minute details in all their complexity.

The decisive victory of the English king Henry V at Agincourt in 1415 effectively ended, for some forty years, the dominance of the French court and thus

Figure 18.21 The Limbourg Brothers, *February* from the *Tres Riches Heures du Duc de Berry,* 1413–1416. Illumination. Musée Condé, Chantilly, France.

Figure 18.22 Jan van Eyck, *Ghent Altarpiece* (closed), ca. 1425–1432. St. Bavon, Ghent, Belgium. Copyright A. C. L. Bruxelles.

royal sponsorship of the courtly International Style. The center for art shifted to the Low Countries, where Philip the Good (ruled 1419–1467) maintained his Burgundian court and negotiated hardheaded trade alliances with England. Artists found in the flourishing cities of Flanders—Bruges, Ghent, Louvain, Brussels—new patrons in the bankers and merchants who were the true rulers of the wealthiest society in Europe. The society was bourgeois, but cosmopolitan rather than provincial with powerful banking and trade connections throughout Europe. This solid middle class wanted art that pictured the real world and, by a strange coincidence, there were several artists of genius available to help fulfill the passion for naturalism.

The leading painter of the early Flemish school, indeed of any age, Jan van Eyck (Yahn van Ike; ca. 1390–1441) first served the court of John of Bavaria and later at the Burgundian court of Philip the Good. Credited by Vasari with inventing oil painting, it is likely that van Eyck perfected an existing technique. Until the fifteenth century, panel painters worked in tempera, an emulsion of pigment and egg yolk capable of detail and bright color but limited to a narrow range between light and dark. Too dark colors became dead and very light ones became chalklike.

Using a technique still not fully understood, van Eyck probably used a *gesso* coating on his panel, a mixture of plaster and water, followed by successive coats of pigments suspended in linseed oil. Applying alternate layers of opaque and translucent color, van Eyck enhanced the brilliance of his colors from the darkest to the lightest with no loss of intensity. With slow-drying oil paints he made infinitely subtle and smooth gradations between color tones, obtaining a jewellike radiance comparable to medieval stained glass. He undoubtedly learned some of his techniques from manuscript painters like the Limbourg Brothers, but it also seems likely that van Eyck was influenced, or possibly inspired, by the stained glass of Gothic churches.

The greatest work of early Flemish painting and a monumental accomplishment in any age, the *Ghent Altarpiece* (fig. 18.22) is a polyptych, a central painting with two hinged wings measuring 11'3" X 7'2" when closed and 11'3" X 14'5" in the open position. The twenty different panels of the work range from the Annunciation on the outer panels to the Adoration of the Mystic Lamb within. In the lunettes of figure 18.22, the prophet Zechariah (left) with the Erythraean Sibyl, Cumean Sibyl, and prophet Micah symbolize the coming of Christ. The annunciation

Figure 18.23 Jan van Eyck, *Ghent Altarpiece* (open).

figures are placed in a contemporary room containing Romanesque and Gothic elements that probably symbolize the Old and New Testaments. In the center panels below, the simulated sculptural figures of St. John the Baptist and St. John the Evangelist are flanked by the donors Jodoc Vyt and his wife.

In the open altarpiece (fig. 18.23) the lower central panel shows the community of saints, come from the four corners of the world to worship at the altar of the Mystic Lamb, from whose heart blood cascades into a chalice. In the foreground the Fountain of Life pours from spigots into an octagonal basin, running toward the observer as the "river of life" (Rev. 22:1). In the left-hand panel, judges and knights ride to the altar, while on the right hermits, pilgrims, and the giant St. Christopher walk to an altar scene backed by the heavenly Jerusalem in the distance. Forming a continuous view of Paradise, the five lower panels are designed with a rising perspective, another of the innovations of the artist. On the upper level, the Lord has Mary as the Queen of Heaven on his right hand and St. John the Baptist on his left. To either side are choirs of angels with St. Cecelia seated at the portative (portable) organ, flanked by Adam and Eve on the outer panels. The first large nudes in Northern panel painting, the figures of Adam and Eve reveal a keen appreciation of the human body and innovative painting techniques in perspective and lighting. Once bowed by shame, the figures stand erect as the First Man and First Woman. The placement of the altarpiece puts the feet of the two nudes at about eye level, which accounts for the view of the sole of Adam's foot. This bit of naturalism is typical of a visual reality so precise that botanists can identify dozens of flowers and plants in this awesome work.

Probably completed while he was working on the *Ghent Altarpiece,* the *Annunciation* (colorplate 24) is a relatively small work that, with its strong control of space, has a monumental quality. Set in an imaginary church whose mixed Romanesque and Gothic details probably symbolize the Old and New Testaments, the scene is dominated by an oversized Virgin, portrayed here as the Queen of Heaven. Heavenly light streams in through an upper window, bearing the Dove of the Holy Spirit, its diagonal thrust balanced at the lower right by the lilies of purity. No detail is extraneous; even the designs of the stained glass window and floor tiles foretell the Advent of Christ.

Figure 18.24 Jan van Eyck, *Giovanni Arnolfini and His Bride,* 1434. Oil on canvas, 32¼ × 23½". National Gallery, London.

Figure 18.25 Rogier van der Weyden, *Portrait of a Lady,* ca. 1455–1460. Oil on wood, 14½ × 10¾". Andrew W. Mellon Collection. National Gallery of Art, Washington, D.C.

The meticulous details in a van Eyck painting are fascinating, but the whole of a picture—its unity—is greater than the sum of its parts. In a work commissioned by Giovanni Arnolfini, an Italian merchant, he and his bride, Jeanne Cenami, apparently pose for a wedding portrait as a form of wedding certificate, duly witnessed by the artist (seen in the mirror) and notarized on the back wall: "Jan van Eyck was here" (fig. 18.24). In terms of light, space, volume, and the two distinct personalities, all is unified, both visually and psychologically. Patron and artist must have been more than acquaintances; two individuals make up this wedding couple, joined together in a tender moment without the slightest hint of sentimentality. The texture of cloth, glass, metal, wood, and even the furry little dog are exquisitely detailed. Though unobtrusive, symbols abound. The single lighted candle is, according to custom, the last to be extinguished on the wedding night, but it may also symbolize Christ as the Light of the World. Carved on the post of a bedside chair is the image of St. Margaret, the patron saint of childbirth. The dog represents fidelity (*fides,* "Fido") and the abandoned slippers are a reminder that the couple is standing on holy ground. Craftsmanship at this level verges on the superhuman; indeed, nothing like this had ever been done before.

Because his paintings were perfect in their own marvelously unique way, van Eyck had many admirers in Northern Europe, Spain, and Italy but no emulators. There were imitators, of course, but no disciples who could even approach his rare gifts. Adopting a more expressive and emotional style than that of van Eyck, Rogier van der Weyden (van dur VYE-den; ca. 1400–1464) was the leading Flemish painter of the next generation, becoming City Painter for Brussels in 1435. When he traveled to Italy for the Holy Year of 1450, he influenced Italian art and was, in turn, impressed by what he saw there, probably including the work of Fra Angelico in Florence and Rome. As technically accomplished as van Eyck, his portraits had a psychological depth then unknown in Flemish painting. *Portrait of a Lady* (fig. 18.25) is a study of a young woman tentatively identified as Marie de Valengin, the daughter of Philip the Good, Duke of Burgundy. Her forehead and eyebrows are shaved, a fashionable indication of intellectual acumen. Also high fashions, the high-waisted dress and triangular coif focus attention on the exquisite modeling of the face. The portrait is both beautiful and baffling. The impression of an almost ascetic contemplation is contradicted by the sensuality of the full mouth with its ripe underlip. The overall impression is that of an assertive personality, an intelligent, self-confident, and strong-willed young woman. She certainly looks like a princess of the most

Figure 18.26 Hans Memling, *The Presentation in the Temple,* ca. 1463. Oil on panel, 23½ × 19″. Samuel H. Kress Collection. National Gallery of Art, Washington, D.C.

Figure 18.27 Hieronymus Bosch, *Death and the Miser,* ca. 1510. Oil on panel, 36⅝ × 12⅛″. Samuel H. Kress Collection. National Gallery of Art, Washington, D.C.

powerful court in Northern Europe. Contrasting curiously with the broad facial planes, the thin fingers are almost Gothic in style. Bewitching and beguiling, this is a masterful psychological study by one of the first of a long line of Low Country painters leading directly to Hals and Rembrandt.

Hans Memling (ca. 1440–1494) served his apprenticeship in his native Germany but then moved to Flanders where he apparently studied with van der Weyden. A contemporary of Ghirlandaio in Italy, his style is similarly genial and rather naive; it appealed to a large clientele of merchants and led ultimately to a considerable fortune. Utilizing extensive studies of earlier Flemish masters, particularly van Eyck, he developed a somewhat melancholy art of extreme refinement. In *The Presentation in the Temple* (fig. 18.26) the figures are immobile, frozen in time, or even outside of time. The light falls on people grouped in harmony with their imaginary setting, which appears to be neither inside nor outside a church. The overall feeling is unworldly and slightly sad.

Memling's work was in tune with a general feeling of pessimism, an erosion of confidence in the moral authority of the church, an almost prophetic feeling of the impending Reformation. In Italy the pessimism was fully warranted, for it was in 1494—the year of Memling's death—that the Medicis were expelled from Florence, coinciding with the invasion of the French armies of Charles VIII, which launched a tumultuous era of warfare in Italy.

This pessimistic age found its supreme artist in the person of Hieronymus Bosch (BOS; ca. 1450–1516), one of history's most enthralling and enigmatic painters. He lived and worked in present-day southern Holland, but little else is known about either his life or his artistic intentions. Art historians have wondered about his bizarre iconography but so have psychiatrists. This was an age obsessed with death and with an almost pathological fear of the devil and his demons. Based on his work, it is plain that Bosch had a pessimistic view of human nature—though some would call his vision realistic—and he certainly raged against sinfulness. In the small panel *Death and the Miser* (fig. 18.27), death waits at the door but the miser cannot decide between the crucifix pointed out by the angel or the bag of gold offered by the demon. At the foot of the bed the miser appears as greed personified, clutching a rosary with one hand and storing, with the other hand, money in a strongbox held by another demon. The weapons and armor in the foreground probably indicate warfare as an earlier source of wealth. Other figures and objects are also symbolic, probably literal depictions of folk sayings and tales. Within the carefully defined setting we witness life, death, and human nature.

Enormously popular in the sixteenth century, Bosch's paintings typify an age that had a sickening undercurrent of fear of the devil, leading to fierce, misdirected religious zeal. In 1484 Pope Innocent VIII declared witchcraft (possession by the Devil) a prime heresy. During the next two centuries a wave of sadism and misogyny led to the torture, hanging, and burning of more than 100,000 women plus a few children and men who were enveloped in the madness. Two unscrupulous Dominican monks wrote a handbook for witch-hunters, *The Witches Hammer* (1498), a best-seller that went to thirty editions, an ironic testimony to the spread of books following the invention of movable type in the Rhine River valley during the 1430s.

The career of Hieronymus Bosch marked the end of the Early Northern Renaissance and the beginning of a tormented period of warfare in Italy, of corrupt and dissolute Renaissance popes, and of spiritually bankrupt religious orders. One year after Bosch's death Martin Luther published his *Ninety-five Theses* to set in motion the irrepressible Reformation.

The High Renaissance in Italy, ca. 1495–1520

The relatively peaceful and prosperous existence of Florence ended in two rough jolts in the fateful years of 1492 and 1494. Lorenzo the Magnificent, a strong, moderating force in the fortunes of Florence, died in 1492, the same year in which Ferdinand and Isabella captured Cordoba, the last Moorish stronghold in Spain. Columbus, using a map drawn in Florence, discovered the New World and in Rome, Rodrigo Borgia was crowned as Pope Alexander VI, the epitome of a decadent and corrupt Renaissance pontiff and an enemy of the Florentine Republic.

In 1494, concerned about the military support of Lorenzo's dim and feckless son Piero, Ludovico Sforza of Milan encouraged Charles VIII of France to invade Italy. Charles, who was spoiling for a fight, willingly did so. For the next thirty-five years French and Spanish armies, the latter freed by the removal of the Moors, fought the Italian city-states and, for good measure, each other. Always thinking that each invasion was the last, the Italian cities never banded together to expel their foreign tormenters. Paradoxically, it was against this backdrop of almost constant warfare that High Renaissance art flourished. Exploiting and refining Early Renaissance discoveries in Italy and the North, Leonardo da Vinci, Michelangelo, Raphael, and Bramante created masterworks that crowned the Italian Renaissance.

Leonardo da Vinci

The illegitimate son of a peasant girl known only as Caterina and Piero da Vinci, a notary, Leonardo da Vinci (lay-o-NAR-do da VIN-chee; 1452–1519) was the acknowledged universal man of the Renaissance, the most astounding genius in an age of giants. Inventor, civil and military engineer, architect, musician, geologist, botanist, physicist, anatomist, sculptor, and painter, Leonardo left untouched only classical scholarship, poetry, and philosophy. Theology was of no interest to him; he was a lifelong skeptic who recognized no authority higher than the eye, which he called the "window of the soul."

As was customary with bastardy during the Renaissance, Leonardo was acknowledged by his father and, at about age fifteen, was apprenticed to Verrocchio in Florence. Though little else is known about the first thirty years of his life, records indicate that Leonardo, like Masaccio and Botticelli before him, was admitted to the guild as a craftsman in painting. Unlike Early Renaissance masters, however, Leonardo along with Michelangelo launched a successful campaign to raise the status of artists to the highest level of society.

In 1481 Pope Sixtus IV summoned the "best" Tuscan artists to work in the Vatican, including Botticelli, Ghirlandaio, and Perugino, but not Leonardo. Furious at the slight, Leonardo decided to leave Florence, but not before he had completed a commission for the de'Benci family of wealthy bankers. His portrait of Ginevra de'Benci (colorplate 25), the only Leonardo painting in the United States, is an enchanting study of a lovely but strangely tense and wary young woman. She was known to be a very devout person, ill at ease in the fun-loving exuberance of Florence, and sternly disapproving of Lorenzo de' Medici's long-term affair with her aunt. Framing her golden curls in juniper branches (Ginevra means "juniper"), Leonardo has created a melancholy work, the pallid face set against a thinly misted background, with details deliberately softened and blurred. Though not invented by Leonardo, this *sfumato* (sfoo-MAH-toh) technique (literally "smoky") was one of that artist's significant contributions to the art of painting. The twilight atmosphere is another innovation, contrasting sharply with the sunlit paintings of other masters. The painting is minus some six inches at the bottom, which may explain why the lady's hands are not shown, as they are in the *Mona Lisa* and two of Leonardo's other portraits.

Seeking a more appreciative patron than the Medicis or the pope, Leonardo wrote to Ludovico Sforza, Duke of Milan, touting his expertise as a military engineer but mentioning, in just two sentences, that he was also a sculptor and a painter. During his stay in Milan (1482–1499) Leonardo produced *The Last Supper* (fig. 18.28), a treatment of the familiar theme unlike anything done before or since. The High Renaissance begins with this magnificent composition. After suffering the indignities of damp walls, Napoleon's troops, and World War II bombing, the painting has been restored, but only to an approximation of its original condition. The moment of the painting is not the traditional one of the Eucharist but

Figure 18.28 Leonardo da Vinci, *The Last Supper,* ca. 1495–1498. Mural, oil and tempera on plaster, 14'5" × 28'. Refectory of Sta. Maria della Grazie, Milan.

Christ's electrifying statement, "One of you shall betray me." Except for Christ, Leonardo used life models for the disciples, and had difficulty only in finding a suitable Judas. According to Vasari, when the prior of Sta. Maria complained to Sforza that Leonardo was "lazy" in his execution of the painting, Leonardo remarked that locating a Judas was difficult but that the prior would serve nicely. Leonardo's contemporaries would have looked for Judas where other artists had placed him—across the table from Jesus. Instead, we see Judas as part of the first group of three Apostles to the left of Christ, composed in a tight, dark triangle with no light shining on his face. Clutching a bag of money, Judas is in the group but not a part of it. His dark bulk is in sharp contrast to the lighted profile of Peter and the luminous radiance of John. In fact, each Apostle is an individual psychological study, reacting to Christ's startling statement in a manner consistent with his personality.

The design of *The Last Supper* has a mathematical unity, with divisions of groups of threes and fours that add up to seven (3 + 4) and multiply into twelve (3 × 4). The three windows place Christ's head in the center window as the second person of the Trinity. The shocked Apostles are grouped into four units of three each, divided in the middle by the isolated triangular (three-sided) design of Christ. Echoing the four groups are the wall panels on either side, and on the ceiling there are seven beams running from both front to back and side to side. Leonardo may have had Christian number symbolism in mind (Holy Trinity, Four Gospels, Seven Cardinal Virtues, Twelve Gates

of the New Jerusalem, and so on) but three, four and seven also stand for the Trivium and Quadrivium of the Seven Liberal Arts. Moreover, Pythagorean number symbolism includes the concept of one as unity, three as the most logical number (beginning, middle, end), and four as symbolizing Justice (see chap. 4). Given Leonardo's skepticism and explicit anticlerical feelings, something other than Christian symbolism may be a more appropriate interpretation. There is no question, however, about the picture as a whole. Despite the mathematical precision of the perspective, there is no place from which a spectator can view the perspective "correctly"; it exists as a work apart, on an ideal level beyond everyday experience. As mentioned previously, this is the elevated style of formal design and noble theme that characterizes the High Renaissance.

Leonardo insisted that painters were noble creatures and that painting should be a part of the seven liberal arts. For him, sculptors were craftsmen standing in dust and debris while hammering away at stubborn marble. Michelangelo, on the other hand, claimed that sculpture was as superior to painting as the sun was to the moon.

Michelangelo

Perhaps the greatest artistic genius who ever lived, Michelangelo Buonarroti (me-kell-AHN-djay-lo boo-on-na-ROE-tea; 1475–1564) excelled in four arts: sculpture, painting, architecture, and poetry. A towering figure even in his own time, he was the "Divine

Figure 18.29 Michelangelo, *Pietà*, 1498–1499/1500. Marble, height 68½″. St. Peter's, Rome.

Michelangelo." Words and more words have been written trying to account for such a man, but there is no accounting for him. Born of a vain and mean-spirited father and a dimly pathetic mother to whom he never referred, he appeared with prodigious gifts at a time and place seemingly destined to make him divine. He learned painting techniques in Ghirlandaio's studio and sculpting from a pupil of Donatello and from ancient works in the Medici collection. His first masterpiece, the *Pietà* (fig. 18.29), is more fifteenth than sixteenth century in style, with elegant lines reminiscent of Botticelli. The triangular composition is made up of contradictions. Though Christ is dead, the blood pumps through his veins as if he were asleep. The Virgin is portrayed as younger than her son, her lovely face composed rather than distorted by grief; only her left hand indicates her sorrow. The figure of Christ is life size but that of the Virgin is elongated; her head is the same size as Christ's but in proportion she would be about seven feet tall if she were standing. The overall visual effect of these distortions is a super reality beyond earthbound reality.

The *Pietà* was a youthful work but the *David* (colorplate 26), started only a year or so later, was the first monumental statue of the High Renaissance, a product of Michelangelo's already mature genius. Though the Palazzo della Signoria already possessed three Davids, two by Donatello (see fig. 18.8) and one by Verrocchio (see fig. 18.15), one more was not too

many for a city battling to maintain its power and independence. After the Medicis were expelled in 1494, the crusading monk Savonarola ruled Florence, having had Christ declared King of Florence. Savonarola then legally banned all acts he considered sinful. By 1498 the corrupt but powerful Borgia pope Alexander VI had excommunicated Savonarola. Incredibly, Savonarola excommunicated the pope; following this he was arrested by the Florentine Signory and, with two associates, hanged and then burned. While Michelangelo was working on his David, the dangerous Alexander VI died, in 1503, and shortly thereafter the incompetent Piero de' Medici, known as Piero the Unfortunate, drowned while fighting with the French in an attempt to gain reentry to the city. By 1504 Florence was finally at peace and the prime civic concern was where to place Michelangelo's mighty *David*. The commission to select the site included Leonardo, Botticelli, Perugino, and others, attesting to the status the nearly completed work had already acquired. Originally scheduled to be placed high on Florence Cathedral, *David* was triumphantly set in front of the center of government, the Palazzo Vecchio, where it became the symbol of a republic ready to battle all enemies. (During the nineteenth century the statue was moved indoors to protect it from the weather.)

The Davids of Donatello and Verrocchio were adolescent boys; this is a strapping young man who is standing alert, every muscle vibrant with power. The head might be that of Apollo and the body of Herakles yet this is the portrait of an ideal, a Platonic ideal as well as David the King. His father was both Hebrew and, collectively, Lorenzo, Ficino, and the "Platonic Academy" of Florence.

The fame of the *David* was instant, and Michelangelo had more commissions than he could handle, including one to construct a vast tomb for Pope Julius II. The tomb project was never finished as originally planned, instead, somehow, Michelangelo found himself in 1508 lying on his back atop the scaffolding in the Sistine Chapel. How all this came about has never been satisfactorily explained, but one plausible theory concerns the possible machinations of Bramante, the recently appointed architect of the new St. Peter's. He was known to be concerned about funds for his project and was also intensely jealous of Michelangelo. Julius had lavished enormous sums on his tomb project, money that Bramante needed for his mighty basilica. If the pope could be encouraged to put Michelangelo to work painting the Sistine Chapel ceiling, a monumental undertaking Bramante felt not even Michelangelo could bring off, then he would have no further financial or artistic competition. Whatever transpired behind the scenes, Michelangelo was, in fact, the only artist who was capable of tackling the project.

With a 68′ high ceiling that is proportionately too high for its 44 × 132′ dimensions, the private chapel of the popes was neither intimate nor monumental; Michelangelo's frescoes *made* it monumental. In only

Figure 18.30 Michelangelo, *Creation of Adam,* detail of Sistine Chapel Ceiling, 1511. Fresco. Vatican, Rome.

four years, 1508–1512, he filled the entire 700 square yards of barrel-vaulted ceiling with over 300 powerful figures. Relating the Genesis story from the Creation through the Flood, Michelangelo fused Judeo-Christian theology with ancient mythology and Neoplatonic philosophy to create one of the truly awesome works of Western art. In just one detail, the *Creation of Adam* (fig. 18.30), one can perceive some of the majesty of the total work. Embracing an awestruck Eve and with his left hand resting on the shoulder of the Christ Child, God the Father extends his finger and the spark of life to an inert Adam. Against a background of generations waiting to be born, the twisting, dynamic figure is lovingly paternal, imparting to Adam the soul that will actuate his potential nobility. After protesting for four years that he was a sculptor, not a painter, Michelangelo proved that he was both; all of the figures are sculptural forms, conceived in the mind's eye of a sculptor and executed in paint on wet plaster. Totally overwhelming the work of many notable artists on the walls, the ceiling frescoes express the optimism of a supreme artist at the peak of his powers.

The following sonnet[1] illustrates Michelangelo's personal and agonizingly physical reaction to the task the pope set for him:

SONNET V
To Giovanni da Pistoia
"On the Painting of the Sistine Chapel"
(I' ho già fatto un gozzo)

I've grown a goitre by dwelling in this den—
    As cats from stagnant streams in Lombardy,
    Or in what other land they hap to be—
    Which drives the belly close beneath the chin:

My beard turns up to heaven; my nape falls in,
    Fixed on my spine: my breast-bone visibly
    Grows like a harp: a rich embroidery
    Bedews my face from brush-drops thick and thin.
My loins into my paunch like levers grind:
    My buttock like a crupper bears my weight;
    My feet unguided wander to and fro;
In front my skin grows loose and long; behind,
    By bending it becomes more taut and strait;
    Crosswise I strain me like a Syrian bow:
      Whence false and quaint, I know,
    Must be the fruit of squinting brain and eye;
    For ill can aim the gun that bends awry.
      Come then, Giovanni, try
    To succour my dead pictures and my fame;
    Since foul I fare and painting is my shame.

Bramante

The dominant political figure and artistic patron of the High Renaissance was Pope Julius II (1503–1513), known as the Warrior Pope. Determined to obliterate the awful memories of Alexander VI and the Borgia crimes, he refused to even live in the apartment of his decadent predecessor. Julius II restored order to the city of Rome, reconquered papal provinces with the sword, and proceeded energetically to rebuild his beloved Rome. A fortuitous quirk of history put a dynamic pope in power at precisely the time when he

1. John Addington Symonds, trans., *The Sonnets of Michelangelo Buonarotti and Tommaso Campanella* (London: Smith, Elder & Co., 1878), p. 35.

Figure 18.31 Donato Bramante, *Tempietto,* 1502. Height 46' with external diameter of 29'. S. Pietro in Montorio, Rome.

could utilize the mature talents of Michelangelo, Raphael, and Bramante. Donato Bramante of Urbino (1444–1514), the foremost architect of the High Renaissance and a close personal friend of the pope, was entrusted with many building projects, the greatest of which was the construction of a new St. Peter's. Julius II decided, in 1505, that the 1100-year-old Basilica of St. Peter's was to be replaced by a Renaissance structure worthy of the imperial splendor of the new Rome, a project that was not completely finished until 1626 (see fig. 18.40), some 14 architects, 20 popes, and one Reformation later.

Though much of Bramante's design can still be seen in St. Peter's, his architectural genius is better illustrated by a circular structure of only modest size but of immense influence in architectural history. Constructed on the spot where St. Peter was supposedly crucified, the Tempietto (little temple; fig. 18.31) became the prototype of classical domed architecture in Europe and the United States. Placed on a three-step base like a Greek temple, the exquisitely proportioned building was conceived as an articulated work of sculpture in the manner of classical Greek architecture (see chap. 7). Influenced by Leonardo's radial designs, the building is distinguished by the severely Doric colonnade, above which are classical triglyphs and metopes topped by a lightly rhythmical balustrade. The overall effect of majestic serenity in a small building may have been the decisive factor in Bramante's selection as the architect of the pope.

Raphael

The third artist working in the Vatican, in addition to Bramante and Michelangelo, was Raphael (RAHF-ee-el; 1483–1520), one of the greatest painters in Western art, of whom the English painter Reynolds said, "Of the just hyperbole the perpetual instance is the divine Raphael." Born in Urbino like Bramante, Raphael studied first with Perugino and then, as so many artists had done before him, moved to Florence. Over the four-year period of 1504–1508, he studied the works of Leonardo and Michelangelo and painted many of his famous Madonnas.

The most reproduced painter of the Renaissance, the work of Raphael, especially the Madonnas, is perhaps too familiar. Raphael was an intellectual painter whose works should be studied for both form and content, but viewers tend to see his Madonnas as pretty and sweet, partly because they were intended as sympathetic portrayals of Mother and Child and partly because of countless sentimental imitations of Raphael's style. *The Alba Madonna* (colorplate 27) is a tightly controlled triangular composition derived from Leonardo's style but designed as a *tondo* (circular painting). Unlike Leonardo and other Madonna painters, Raphael used life models, usually in the nude, sketching the basic figure until he had all elements just right. In this work he was concerned with subtly contrasting the humanity of John the Baptist with the divinity of the Christ Child, who is the actual focal point of the painting. The counterbalancing diagonals of the left arm of the Madonna and the back of the kneeling John form the top of the pyramid, while the left leg of Christ echoes the reverse diagonal that extends from the Madonna's left forearm and down her leg. Enclosed within the space between the blue-draped leg and the fur-covered back of John, the figure of the Christ Child is essentially vertical. The one horizontal element in the composition is the right arm of Christ, leading our eye to the slender cross so lightly held. Like so many of Raphael's paintings, this masterpiece suffers perhaps from too much loving care; it has been so vigorously cleaned that the colors are not as vibrant as they undoubtedly once were.

Characterized as Aristotelian in his approach to art, Raphael was a keen observer of nature and of people. His mastery of his craft combined with his perceptive examination of the world about him enabled Raphael to be one of the foremost portrait painters of his age. A member of the circle of Baldassare Castiglione, author of the *Courtier,* a book about courtesy

Figure 18.32 Raphael, *Baldassare Castiglione*, ca. 1515. Oil on canvas, 32¼ × 26½". The Louvre, Paris.

Giorgione ("big George"; giorge-o-NAY; ca. 1475/77–1510). Very little is known about the man or even his work. He perhaps studied with Bellini and was the teacher of Titian and was, according to Vassari, a humanist, musician, and lover of conversation, parties, nature, and women, probably in reverse order.

Though another hand has added some distant figures in the left landscape, Giorgione's *Adoration of the Shepherds* (colorplate 28) is a superb example of the new pastoral poetic style that Giorgione introduced to painting in general and to the Venetian school in particular. One of the most innovative and influential painters of the Renaissance, Giorgione used his mastery of light and color to paint magical landscapes in which human figures become part of the Arcadian mood. In fact, in colorplate 28 the landscape is so predominant that the work can be viewed as a landscape with Nativity Scene. The landscape itself is depicted not in naturalistic terms, as in the works of van Eyck or Leonardo, but as nature in the raw as viewed by the eye of the poet. The figures are not drawn but rather formed of contrasting light and shadow, with the body of the child and the heads of the parents radiating a heavenly light against the gloomy recesses of the cave. The high moral tone and noble values of the Florentine/Roman High Renaissance are utterly foreign to this romantic evocation of mood and feeling.

Giorgione died at an early age of the plague, leaving a number of unfinished works. Though it is known that Titian completed some of the paintings, what may never be known is which paintings were involved and what "completed by Titian" really means. In the *Fête Champêtre* (fig. 18.33) we see two opulent nudes painted in the lush Venetian manner; the one on the left is gracefully emptying a crystal pitcher and the other holds a recorder while gazing dreamily into the distance. The fully clothed men are deep in conversation, but only the man casually playing the lute is fashionably dressed. Having been labeled at various times "Pastoral Symphony," "Fountain of Love," or, as here, "Country Festival," the work has even been called an allegory of poetry. In other words, the subject matter may never be known or even be important. The painting exists as an enchanting combination of forms and shapes in a poetic setting, all created by an artist who may have had in mind nothing more than that.

and conduct (see chap. 20), Raphael was described by the writer Aretino as having "every virtue and every grace that is appropriate to a gentleman." It was, in fact, Raphael's social graces and material success that lay at the heart of his cold war with the socially inept Michelangelo. In his portrait of Castiglione (fig. 18.32) Raphael depicts his friend in the cooly composed pose of a Renaissance gentleman. The poise and quiet confidence are emphasized by the restrained elegance of his dress, which exemplifies a cultured society reacting against the flamboyant dress of the preceding century. With the premature death of the frail Raphael, the High Renaissance in Rome came to an end. By this time the innovations of Leonardo, Michelangelo, Bramante, and Raphael were being studied and applied throughout Italy, especially in Venice, and northward into Germany, France, and the Netherlands (today's Holland and Belgium).

High and Late Renaissance and Mannerism in Sixteenth-Century Italy

The High Renaissance style appeared only in elements of the later work of the long-lived Bellini (see fig. 18.20) but very clearly in the work of a shadowy figure first known as Giorgio and, later, as the famous

Michelangelo and Mannerism

The art of the remainder of the century can be considered as two basic streams of styles: Mannerism and Late Renaissance. The beauty, harmony, and proportions of the High Renaissance were seen at this time as a golden age, an era in which Leonardo, Michelangelo, and Raphael had convincingly demonstrated that there was nothing an artist could not do.

Figure 18.33 Giorgione (and Titian?), *Fête Champêtre,* ca. 1505. Oil on canvas, 43¼ × 54¼". The Louvre, Paris.

What was left for later artists? Vasari used the term *maniera,* meaning style, of working "in the manner of" supreme artists like Raphael and Michelangelo. Later artists could either adopt the techniques of the masters or use these techniques as a point of departure, to replace the serenity of the High Renaissance with a Mannerist virtuosity that delighted in twisting, confusing, and distorting human figures. Raphael and Michelangelo studied nature; the Mannerists studied Raphael and Michelangelo, especially Michelangelo.

The so-called Mannerist Crisis may also have been a reaction to the momentous events of the 1520s, some local and others international, that affected the viewpoints and lives of just about everyone.

1. The power of Florence came to an end, as the proud city became a pawn in the hands of the Medici popes Leo X (1513–1521) and Clement VII (1523–1534).
2. During the 1520s Luther's defiance of Pope Leo X led to the dissolution of unified Christianity, followed by over a century of sectarian warfare.
3. In 1526 Suleiman the Turk defeated the Hungarians at Monac and, for decades, continued to menace Christian Europe.

4. In 1527 the political machinations of Clement VII led to the Sack of Rome by the rampaging armies of the Holy Roman Emperor Charles V of Germany.
5. In 1529 Clement VII refused to recognize the marriage of Henry VIII of England and Anne Boleyn, leading to England's break with Rome.

Artistically, the Mannerists were greatly influenced by Michelangelo's sculptures in the Medici Chapel and his *Last Judgment* fresco in the Sistine Chapel. Michelangelo's designs for the New Sacristy of the Medici Chapel were the most nearly complete of his architectural-sculptural conceptions. Signing the contract in 1519, he labored for fifteen years on a mortuary chapel for the tombs of Lorenzo and Giuliano de' Medici (son and grandson of Lorenzo the Magnificent; d. 1516), Lorenzo the Magnificent (d. 1492), and his brother Giuliano de' Medici (murdered in 1478). For most of its construction the project was threatened by exterior forces as outlined above, particularly the humiliation of the papacy during the 1527 Sack of Rome. By the time the poverty-stricken Clement VII had returned to his burned-out city in 1528, Florence had successfully revolted against the Medici for the third time. However, the

Figure 18.34 Michelangelo, *Tomb of Giuliano de' Medici,* 1519–1534. Marble, 20'9" × 13'10". New Sacristy.

Figure 18.35 Michelangelo, *Tomb of Lorenzo de' Medici,* 1519–1534. Marble, 20'9" × 13'10". New Sacristy, Medici Chapel, S. Lorenzo, Florence.

1530 reconquest of the Republic put a Medici governor in charge again, leading to an order for Michelangelo's assassination because he had helped the city fortify itself. Protected by the canon of the Church of San Lorenzo, Michelangelo was pardoned by the Medici pope Clement VII so he could complete the family tomb. With the installation of the pope's illegitimate son, the vicious Alessandro, Duke of Florence, Michelangelo's position was so precarious that when Clement VII died in 1534, he fled to Rome, never again to return to Florence. It is difficult to conceive of a project that was more plagued by violent events or more successful in artistic terms.

The *Tomb of Giuliano de' Medici* (fig. 18.34) is a triangular composition with the contemplative figure of Lorenzo's son, Giuliano, at the top and the figures of Night and Day reclining on either side. According to the sculptor's own explanation, Night and Day caused the Duke's death but, in death, he has conquered time. Beneath Night's shoulder a grinning mask seems to symbolize earthly vanities, while the

owl beneath her leg is the common symbol of night. Her heavily muscled and twisted body is complemented by the extraordinary musculature of Day, whose contorted extremities imprison the figure in an anguished tension, a characteristic of Michelangelo's second style that strongly influenced the Mannerists.

On the opposite side of the *Madonna and Child* (see fig. 18.37) at which both men are looking, is the figure of Lorenzo (fig. 18.35), grandson of the great Lorenzo. Like Giuliano, he wears Roman armor as a Prince of the Church of Rome, but is flanked by a masculine Twilight and feminine Dawn. Night was portrayed as a mother but Dawn is depicted as a virgin, just starting to sleepily stir in the faint light of the new day (fig. 18.36).

The *Madonna and Child* (fig. 18.37), who are the focus of the design, were intended originally for the tomb of Lorenzo the Magnificent. The twisting, serpentine design draws the two figures together in a unity of love and affection, a design that also influenced the Mannerists.

Figure 18.36 Dawn (detail), *Tomb of Lorenzo de' Medici.*

Figure 18.37 Michelangelo, *Madonna and Child,* 1519–1534. Marble. New Sacristy, Medici Chapel, S. Lorenzo, Florence.

During Michelangelo's visit to Rome to obtain Clement VII's pardon, the discussion concerned the Sistine Chapel perhaps even more than the New Sacristy that was destined to remain incomplete. The end wall of the Sistine Chapel contained the *Assumption of the Virgin* by Perugino but Clement proposed to Michelangelo that this be replaced with a Resurrection. By the time the new pope Paul III (1534–1549) had commissioned the artist to paint the entire wall, the subject had become the Last Judgment, though how this came about is unclear. Paul III was a Counter-Reformation pope whose most significant act was the convening of the Council of Trent (1545–1564) to systematically reform the church to counter the challenge of Protestantism. However, nepotism was rampant during Paul's reign and he, along with his sons and daughters, lived the lavish life of a Renaissance pope. Michelangelo, on the other hand, was deeply religious and was, moreover, sixty-one years old when he accepted the commission.

Preoccupied with the fate of humanity and that of his own soul, Michelangelo apparently began *The Last Judgment* (fig. 18.38) with the conviction that the world had gone mad. The ideal beauty and optimism of the chapel ceiling had been superseded by a mood of terror and doom, with the gigantic figure of Christ come to judge the quick and the dead. Based on Matthew 24:30–31, everyone "will see the Son of Man coming on clouds of Heaven with power and great glory," his body twisted and his arm raised in a gesture of damnation. In an energetic clockwise motion, the figures at the bottom rise toward Christ and are either gathered in by waiting angels or pulled by demons down into Hell. The resurrected women (always clothed) and men (generally nude) float into the helping arms of angels, who are unencumbered by wings or halos. The scale of the figures is from small in the region of the Damned, close to eye level, to monumental at the distant top section in the region of the Blessed. The nervous energy and the twisting, writhing, elongated figures are techniques adopted by the Mannerists. In this powerful fresco, however, they

are manifestations of the unique artistic vision of a master, a natural evolution, given the subject matter, of his style for the Medici tombs in Florence.

Only a few days before his death, Michelangelo was reworking his *Rondanini Pieta* (fig. 18.39), cutting the head back into the Virgin's shoulder and making the composition a slender, unified work of infinite pathos. Far removed from the High Renaissance style, the elongated figures are reminiscent of the jamb statues of the Royal Portal of Chartres Cathedral (see fig. 15.39), seeming to symbolize the artist's direct appeal to God. His death in his eighty-eighth year, probably of pneumonia, left this sculpture unfinished and his major project, the dome of St. Peter's, still under construction.

Michelangelo's apse and dome of St. Peter's (fig. 18.40) was not a commission but, in his words, done "solely for the love of God." Whether or not Michelangelo's late style can be described as Mannerist, still a moot point, his late architectural style is powerful and confident. The great dome is a huge sculptured shape rising above an apse distinguished by enormous pilasters, Michelangelo's "colossal order," pilasters that are both decorative and structural. The upward thrust of the pilasters is repeated and reinforced by the double columns of the drum, and carried ever upward by the arching ribs to a climax in the lantern. The vertical stress of classic forms, a new Renaissance procedure, is visible proof that classicism can be as emotional and as transcendal as the High Gothic style of Chartres Cathedral (see fig. 15.38).

Figure 18.38 Michelangelo, *The Last Judgment,* 1536–1540. Fresco, 48 × 44'. Altar wall of the Sistine Chapel, Vatican, Rome.

Figure 18.39 Michelangelo, *Rondanini Pieta,* ca. 1554–1564. Marble, height 64". Castello Sforza, Milan.

Figure 18.40 Michelangelo, Dome of St. Peter's (view from the west), 1546–1564. Height of dome 452'. Completed by della Porta in 1590. Vatican, Rome.

Renaissance Art: A New Golden Age   **45**

Figure 18.41 Parmigianino, *Madonna with the Long Neck,* 1534–1540. Oil on panel, 7'1" × 4'4". Uffizi Gallery, Florence.

Though the nave was extended far beyond Michelangelo's Greek-cross plan, the dome is still the major landmark of Rome, a fitting symbol for the art and life of Michelangelo.

Unquestionably a Mannerist, Parmigianino (par-me-dja-ah-NEE-no; 1503–1540) painted in an elaborate, tense, elegant, and artificial style in sharp and deliberate contrast to the harmonious naturalism of the High Renaissance. His *Madonna with the Long Neck* (fig. 18.41) is a marvel of decorative beauty. With a swanlike neck, exceptionally long fingers, and cold, ivory-smooth flesh, the Madonna smiles tenderly on a seemingly lifeless Christ Child. The background figure of the biblical prophet is dramatically small, and the rising, uncompleted columns add to the artificiality and strange mood of unreality. Parmigianino planned a complete temple in the background but left it incomplete, further illustrating, perhaps, the perverseness of an artist known to deliberately flaunt social and artistic conventions.

Late Renaissance and Mannerism in Italy and Spain

With an artistic career spanning sixty-eight years, Titian (TISH-n; ca. 1488–1576) was a giant of the High and Late Renaissance, excelling in every aspect of the painter's craft. After Raphael he was the finest portrait artist of the century, courted by the nobles and kings of Europe. Titian achieved the social status advocated by Leonardo, acquiring a towering reputation that led to many honors, the title of count, and a princely life. Repeatedly celebrating the goddess of love, his late painting, *Venus with a Mirror* (colorplate 29) is permeated with a tangible sensuality that is, however, not erotic, expressing instead the natural loveliness of woman. The famous color tones are exceptionally rich rather than just brilliant, mellowed by layer-upon-layer of glazes. Titian produced several variations upon the Venus-and-mirror theme, but this painting he kept for himself and willed to his son. Perhaps more than any other Renaissance artist, Titian understood the spirit of classical art. Drawing upon the Greeks, he incorporated High Renaissance techniques and some Mannerist devices in what is best described, in this work, as Late Renaissance style.

Titian's Venetian contemporary, Tintoretto (tin-toe-RET-toe; 1518–1594), developed a more fervent style blending Mannerist devices with the drawing technique of Michelangelo. In *Christ at the Sea of Galilee* (colorplate 30) we view a turbulent sea with wave edges as sharp as the blade of a knife, spottily applied white highlights, and deliberately atonal combinations that heighten the emotional content. The curved and elongated figure of Christ dominates an intensely dramatic scene in which the frightened fishermen look to the Savior for deliverance.

A comparison of Tintoretto's *The Last Supper* (fig. 18.42) with that by Leonardo (see fig. 18.28) dramatically illustrates the differences between the High Renaissance and the Mannerist style of the Late Renaissance. In Tintoretto's version the table is sharply angled and placed at the left. The size of the disciples diminishes from foreground to background, with Christ highlighted only by the brilliant glow of his halo. Almost lost in the agitation, Judas, dressed like a servant, sits on the opposite side of the table, a pathetic, isolated figure. This is the moment of the Eucharist, the transubstantiation of consecrated bread and wine into the flesh and blood of Christ. The agitated clutter of servants, hovering angels, flaming lamp, and radiant halo combine to express the emotional spirit of the Counter-Reformation.

The intense dramatic style of Tintoretto heralds the coming age of the Baroque, but the architectural designs of Palladio (pah-LAH-djo; 1518–1580) are clearly, lucidly classical. The only North Italian architect comparable to Brunelleschi, Alberti, Bramante, and Michelangelo, Palladio was born Andrea di Pietro but is known to posterity by a name derived from Pallas Athena, goddess of wisdom. An avid student of classical and Renaissance architecture, Palladio designed churches, public buildings, and private homes. His Villa Rotunda (fig. 18.43), one of nineteen Palladian villas still in existence, was built in the countryside near Venice, much in the manner and style of Roman villas. From a central square identical porticoes thrust out from each side, each with a different view and a slightly variable climate at different

Figure 18.42 Tintoretto, *The Last Supper,* 1592–1594. Oil on canvas, 12′ × 18′8″. S. Giorgio Maggiore, Venice.

Figure 18.43 Palladio, Villa Rotunda, Vicenza. Begun 1550 and finished by Vencenzo Scamozzi.

hours of the day. Palladian designs became popular for English stately homes, and this particular design became a model for southern plantation homes in the American South, where outdoor living was common for much of the year. In the Villa Rotunda the proportions of length and breadth, height and width, of and between the rooms were based on the Pythagorean ratios of the Greek musical scale (see chap. 4), as in Alberti's proportions for his Church of Santa Maria Novella (see fig. 18.14) but even more rigorously applied.

Paradoxically, only the country villas of Palladio were placed in the natural settings that the Venetian painters Giorgione, Titian, Tintoretto, and Veronese celebrated in their richly colored paintings. Venice itself, except for private gardens, was a congested city of marble, brick, stone, and waterways with few plants, flowers, or trees. The fourth of the great Venetian masters, Paolo Veronese (vair-oh-NAY-se; 1528–1588), like his contemporaries, glorified nature in his work, but unlike other artists he concentrated on the sumptuous material world. Pleasure-loving Venetians preferred luxurious paintings that dazzled the eye and soothed the conscience. In *The Finding of Moses* (fig. 18.44) Veronese created a cheerful biblical scene redolent with the elegance and luxury that the Venetians themselves enjoyed. The Egyptian princess is richly clothed in Venetian dress, presiding benignly over the rescue of the abandoned child. The composition unwinds from the black page at the lower left up through the lady-in-waiting, who is handing Moses to the Pharaoh's daughter. On the right there is a similar unwinding upward but with a tighter rhythm. The tableau is set in a lush countryside in front of a sturdy Italian bridge and a suitably exotic and fanciful Egyptian city.

Figure 18.44 Paolo Veronese, *The Finding of Moses,* ca. 1570. Oil on canvas, 22¾ × 17½". Andrew W. Mellon Collection. National Gallery of Art, Washington, D.C.

Figure 18.45 El Greco, *The Pentitent St. Peter,* ca. 1598–1600. The San Diego Museum of Art, San Diego, California.

Veronese's style is lavishly and opulently Late Renaissance and basically secular, but that of El Greco is mystical, a fervent expression of the Counter-Reformation spirit. The last and possibly the most gifted of the Mannerists, Domenikos Theotokopoulos, known as El Greco (the Greek; 1541–1614), was born in Crete, then a Venetian possession, and trained in Late Byzantine art and Venetian Mannerism before moving to Spain in 1576. Even before the defeat of the Spanish Armada in 1588 Spain was a fading power, artistically provincial and obsessed with the Counter-Reformation, yet it was the proper environment for an artist of El Greco's religious convictions. Combining the Byzantine tradition with his thorough knowledge of the Venetian masters, El Greco created a passionately religious art that was the embodiment of Spanish mysticism. In his *The Penitent St. Peter* (fig. 18.45) the elongated figure with hands clasped in prayer and anguished eyes turned heavenward in repentance for having denied Christ is set against a dark and mysterious background in which a distant angel is softly illuminated. Although physically tranquil, the scene is turbulent with the emotion of spiritual forces in a triangular composition that directs our eyes to the agonized face. The oft-debated topic of El Greco's astigmatism being responsible for his elongated figures has no basis in fact; the distortions are deliberate and reflect the artist's exposure to Byzantine art and Venetian Mannerism.

Though the subject is secular, El Greco's *Laokoön* (colorplate 31) is equally tormented. Unlike the Hellenistic sculptural version (see fig. 7.74), the Trojan priest and no less than five sons are depicted as attenuated silvery figures, fighting off slender snakes that may be venomous but certainly are not capable of crushing anyone, unlike the powerful sea serpents of the sculptural group. In the background, dramatic clouds hover over the brooding city of Toledo, El Greco's version of Troy before its fall to Agamemnon and his Argive army.

A nation supercharged with religious zeal, Spain formed the spearhead of the Counter-Reformation and was the birthplace of the Society of Jesus (Jesuits) and the stronghold of the Inquisition. El Greco was its peerless master of religious subjects, an artist who, more than any other, made visible the spiritual content of the Catholic faith. Widely admired in his time, El Greco's reputation declined rapidly as Western Europe, but not Spain, plunged enthusiastically into the scientific and intellectual discoveries of the Age of Reason. It was not until the twentieth century that El Greco's unique and intensely personal art received proper recognition.

High and Late Renaissance in the North, ca. 1500–1600

For most of the fifteenth century, Northern artists and some Italians were influenced by the dazzling naturalism of the Flemish masters. Not until the end of the century did Italian influences begin to beguile Northern patrons with their scientific rules and, especially, a literary tradition that included a vocabulary of art criticism. Noble patrons were delighted with classical examples of "good" and "bad" art. Increasingly, this came to mean that art based on models from antiquity was good while the rest, including the entire Flemish tradition was "wrong" or at best "primitive." With remarkable suddenness, Italian artists were busily engaged with important projects for patrons like Henry VII of England and the French royal family, while Northern artists were traveling to Italy to study the masters of the Early and High Renaissance.

During the sixteenth century it became fashionable to view Northern culture as backwards and its artists as inferior, especially those who had not been blessed with Italian instruction in the rules of perspective and proportion. Speaking, in essence, for the Italian Renaissance, Michelangelo remarked to the Portuguese painter Francesco da Hollanda that Flemish landscape paintings were fit only for "young women, nuns, and certain noble persons with no sense of true harmony." "Furthermore," he observed, "their painting is of stuffs, bricks, mortar, the grass of the fields, the shadows of trees and little figures here and there. And all this," said he, "though it may appear good in some eyes, is in truth done without symmetry or proportion." Consigned to the attic of Northern art, the matchless paintings of the Flemish masters were, for over three centuries, derided as primitive or naive. It was not until 1902 that the first international show of fifteenth-century Flemish art was opened in Bruges and only considerably later in this century that the derogatory labels were finally dropped.

For reasons still unknown, Italian art caught on first in Germany, where Albrecht Dürer (DOO-er; 1471–1528) became the founder of the brief but brilliant German High Renaissance. His two trips to Italy (1494–1495 and 1505–1507) exposed him to all of the Italian techniques, but he was never attuned to Italian form, preferring instead the strong lines of the Northern tradition. Though he became a master painter, Dürer's greatest achievements were in the graphic arts of engraving and woodcuts, which were printed in quantity and sold throughout Germany, making the artist a wealthy man.

Dürer's *Virgin with a Monkey* (fig. 18.46), one of his many Madonnas, reveals Dürer's own combination of German and Italian styles. Holding a finch, symbol of his passion, the chubby Christ Child looks properly Italian, but the blond Madonna, wearing what appears to be a heavy woolen dress, is clearly Germanic, as is the medieval building in the background.

Figure 18.46 Albrecht Dürer, *The Virgin with the Monkey,* ca. 1498–1499. Engraving, 7¼ × 4¹³⁄₁₆". University Art Collections, Arizona State University, Tempe. Gift of Mr. and Mrs. Read Mullen.

The monkey may have a symbolic meaning or may be included simply to add a touch of exoticism. The fleecy, billowing clouds and meticulous perspective are comparable to Italian art, but the strong details of the dress and the naturalism of the grass and foliage indicate the work of a Northern master.

Dürer was deeply involved in the religious and political movements in Germany and in the Italian humanism that flourished briefly on German soil until the winds of the Reformation blew away what was essentially a Catholic point of view. The leading humanist of sixteenth-century Europe, Erasmus of Rotterdam (1466–1536), influenced many intellectuals of the period including artists like Dürer and Hans Holbein the Younger. In the Erasmus portrait by Dürer (see fig. 20.1) the scholar sits in his study surrounded by books, some presumably his own publications, while he writes a new work. Behind him in Latin is the elaborate title of the print and the name of the artist. At the bottom is Dürer's monogram, above which is the date and above that a Greek inscription that translates as, "His writings portray him even better," meaning that his books were a more accurate measure of the man than Dürer's reverential portrait. The Northern passion for detail is, to say the least, clearly evident in this print.

Figure 18.47 Chateau of Azay-le-Rideau, 1518–1529.

Figure 18.48 Chateau of Chambord, north front, begun 1519.

Dürer was internationally famous but his worthy contemporary Matthias Grunewald (1483?–1528), though widely known in his own time, was neglected until this century. A highly original artist, Grunewald, whose name was actually Mathis Gothardt Neithardt, was familiar with the work of Dürer and possibly that of Bosch, but there is no evidence of Italian classical influence, as one glance at his *Small Crucifixion* (colorplate 32) will immediately reveal. This is the brutal reality of nailing a man to a cross and leaving him there to die. His body a mass of cuts and suppurating sores, his limbs twisted, his skin grey and speckled with dried blood, Christ is depicted in relentless detail as having died for the sins of all people. The grief of John, Mary, and Mary Magdalene is vibrant with intense pain and sorrow. Grunewald has elevated the horror of the passion to the level of universal tragedy, producing a composition as convincing as anything in Western art.

Fully conversant with all that the Italians had to teach, Hans Holbein the Younger (hol-bine; 1497–1543) was the last of the great painters of the German High Renaissance and one of the finest portrait painters in the history of art. He traveled widely in France, Switzerland, and Italy, then finally settled down in London, where he became the favorite painter of Henry VIII, who furnished a special suite in St.

James's Palace for "master Hans." Holbein gained access to the English court through Erasmus of Rotterdam, who provided him with a letter of recommendation to Sir Thomas More. His portrait of More (see fig. 20.2) is a noble portrayal of the humanist-statesman. Depicted realistically, including a stubble of beard, More wears the luxurious clothes of his rank and the heavy chain of his office as Lord Chancellor of England. With meticulous attention to detail in the manner of van Eyck, Holbein depicts the dignity and determination of a man who will one day be executed for opposing Henry's establishment of the Church of England.

The Italian influence in France is epitomized in the chain of elegant chateaux built throughout the scenic Loire River valley. Combining the French Gothic heritage with Italian details, the Chateau of Azay-le-Rideau (fig. 18.47) has a Gothic silhouette, but the walls and windows are proportioned and decorated in the manner of an Italian palazzo (see fig. 18.13). Entirely surrounded by a wide moat, this tiny jewel of a chateau is harmonious, elegant, and wholly French.

Imposing and elaborate as befits the king of a prosperous nation, the Chateau of Chambord (fig. 18.48) was originally a hunting lodge that was later redesigned for Francis I by an Italian architect who may have been influenced by a nearby resident named Leonardo da Vinci. The huge central block is connected by corridors leading outwards to sets of apartments designed in the modern manner as self-contained units. Anchored at the four corners by large round towers, the entire complex is surrounded by a moat (not visible here). The matching of horizontal and vertical features in windows and moldings is taken directly from the Italian palazzos, but the forest of dormers, chimneys, and lanterns is right out of the Gothic tradition and flamboyantly French.

Figure 18.49 Pieter Bruegel the Elder, *Landscape with the Fall of Ikarus,* ca. 1558. Oil on canvas, 44⅛ × 29″. Musee Royaux des Beaux Arts, Brussels.

Most of the Renaissance art of France was courtly but, as mentioned previously, there was a growing middle class of art patrons in the Netherlands, which in the sixteenth century had become a battleground of religious and political strife. Militantly Protestant, particularly in the north (today's Holland), the Netherlands fought a rigid Spanish rule that became even more brutal under the fanatical Philip II and the imported Spanish Inquisition. Nevertheless, the Netherlandish school of painting flourished and produced Pieter Bruegel the Elder (BRU-gul; 1525?–1569), the only Northern genius to appear between Dürer and Rubens. A highly educated humanist and philosopher, Bruegel studied in Italy in 1551–1555, returning home with a love of Italian landscapes and a profound knowledge of Italian control of form and space. In *Landscape with the Fall of Ikarus* (fig. 18.49) Bruegel depicts the myth of the reckless one who ignored the advice of his father, Daidalos, and flew so near the sun that the wings fashioned by his father melted, and he plunged to his death in the sea. In the painting Bruegel emphasizes everything but Ikarus, who is just a pair of kicking legs and a splash in the sea in front of the sailing galleon. The plowman and the singing shepherd are oblivious of the fate of a foolish boy who has caused his own destruction. He dies in the sea, but the plowing, the shepherding, the world go serenely on. Bruegel viewed humankind as basically noble, but depicted men and women as faulty individuals who were easily degraded or destroyed by materialism, avarice, or, like Ikarus, just plain folly.

In *The Blind Leading the Blind* (fig. 18.50) Bruegel has drawn upon Matthew 15:12–19 in which Christ warns, "If a blind man leads a blind man, both will fall into a pit." A common moralizing issue of the time, Bosch painted the subject with the two men stipulated by the Bible, but Bruegel increased the number to set up a horizontal composition. With each man suffering from an identifiable eye disease, the design can be followed from the upright man at the left, and then in a descending line dropping to the man who has fallen "into a pit," in this case, a brook. Though this is a strong didactic statement the meaning is not clear. It could be a warning against following false prophets, thus referring to the raging religious controversies of the time. Or the artist may be cautioning against the folly of worldly ambitions that can blind one to the teachings of Christ. The latter interpretation may or may not explain the solid little church in the background, a dignified structure played against six ugly and pathetic individuals reduced to helpless cripples by their own folly. Bruegel seems to be saying that people are free to choose their own fate.

Figure 18.50 Pieter Bruegel the Elder, *The Blind Leading the Blind,* 1568. Tempera on canvas, 60 × 34". National Museum, Naples.

Summary

Symbolized by Brunelleschi's dome and the dedication of Florence Cathedral in 1436, a new age came into being in fifteenth-century Florence, a city of bankers and craftsmen whose self-image was personified by the Davids of Donatello, Verrocchio, and Michelangelo. To create the new style, a fresh repertory of illusionist devices was developed by Masaccio and later utilized by Fra Angelico, Fra Filippo Lippi, and Uccello.

By the second half of the century classical designs had been fully assimilated, leading to the classically based architecture of Alberti and the mythological painting of Botticelli. Florentine innovations spread throughout Italy, promoted by Perugino and by Bellini, the founder of the Venetian school.

The Renaissance in the North took another course. Influenced by the International Style and a long tradition of craftsmanship in manuscript illuminations and stained glass, van Eyck perfected the new technique of oil painting and created matchless works of meticulous naturalism. Rogier van der Weyden and Hans Memling continued in the naturalistic style but, coinciding with the rising pessimism and fear of death and the devil, the bizarre art of Hieronymus Bosch epitomized the religious torment of a society on the brink of the Lutheran Reformation.

The High Renaissance in Italy was a time of constant warfare highlighted by the incredible achievements of Leonardo in scientific investigation, invention, and painting. Excelling in the arts of sculpture, architecture, painting, and poetry, the "divine Michelangelo" created, among other works, the *Pieta, David,* and the frescoes of the Sistine Chapel ceiling. Raphael achieved a classic balance of form and content that became the hallmark of the High Renaissance, and Bramante, in his Tempietto, designed the prototype of classical domed structures.

In sixteenth-century Venice Giorgione was the first of the Venetian colorists, followed by the assured painting of Titian and the luxuriant style of Veronese. Michelangelo designed the Medici tombs and influenced Mannerist painters like Parmigianino, Tintoretto, and the Spanish painter from Crete called El Greco. During the latter stages of his career Michelangelo painted the awesome *Last Judgment* and designed the apse and dome of St. Peter's. Marking the end of the Renaissance in Italy, Palladio's villas became models for eighteenth- and nineteenth-century domestic architecture in England and the United States.

In sixteenth-century Germany Albrecht Dürer, Matthias Grunewald, and Hans Holbein the Younger were the leading painters of the High Renaissance, while in France, Italian styles influenced French courtly art and contributed to the designs of elegant chateaux in the Loire River valley. Renaissance art in the strife-torn Netherlands culminated in the work of Pieter Bruegel the Elder.

By the end of the sixteenth century the ideals and aspirations of the Renaissance had perished in the wreckage of cultures beset by religious wars with the worst yet to come. Marking the end of an era, the Renaissance set the stage for the emergence of the modern world.

Bibliography

Ackerman, James S. *Palladio*. rev. ed. New York: Penguin, 1977. Paperback. Fine study of a very influential architect.

Berenson, Bernard. *Italian Painters of the Renaissance*. Ithaca, N.Y.: Cornell University Press, 1980. Paperback. A classic study and still the most influential.

Cellini, Benvenuto. *Autobiography*. New York: Penguin, 1956. Paperback. A unique and inimitable personal view of Renaissance life and customs.

Clark, Sir Kenneth. *Leonardo da Vinci*. New York: Penguin, 1976. An urbane analysis of a fascinating genius.

De Tolnay, Charles. *Michelangelo: Sculptor, Painter, Architect*. Princeton, N.J.: Princeton University Press, 1982. A fine study of a towering figure in art, regardless of the period.

Janson, H. W. *The Sculpture of Donatello*. 2 vols. Princeton, N.J.: Princeton University Press, 1979. Paperback. A magnificent edition.

MacCurdy, Edward, trans. *The Notebooks of Leonardo da Vinci*. 2 vols. London: Chatto Bodley Jonathan, 1978. Only in the notebooks can one even begin to appreciate the range of one of the greatest minds in human history.

Panofsky, Erwin. *Life & Art of Albrecht Dürer*. Princeton, N.J.: Princeton University Press, 1955. Paperback. This is probably the finest single work in English on the German genius.

19 *Renaissance Music: Court and Church*

The conviction that music was inherently sacred or secular was a medieval idea that ended with the Renaissance. Subject matter was a primary concern, and in the Renaissance, the subject was human life. There were still many threads from the Middle Ages, but the Renaissance flowered and flourished when men and women turned to the physical world of the here and now. Enriched by music, art, and literature, the good life was its own reward and it was attainable on this earth.

Renaissance music dates from about 1420 to 1600. It can be characterized, in large part, as optimistic, lively, and worldly. The once-rigid distinctions between sacred and secular music no longer applied. Sacred music was not always synonymous with devotional, noble, and edifying sounds any more than secular music was necessarily shallow, common, or folksy.

The subject matter rather than the style now determined whether the work was sacred or secular. Renaissance painters used local models for their madonnas, the same models who posed as Aphrodites or nymphs. Composers used melodies where they worked best. The music for Latin poetry, for example, could also be used to accompany a portion of the Mass. Popular songs of the time were sometimes used as a basis for liturgical motets and even for entire masses.

As stated in chapter 17, the Renaissance began around 1350 in Italy and in the North. By the fifteenth century, humanism had spread from Italy to the North, and the work of Flemish painters Jan van Eyck and Rogier van der Weyden (see chap. 18) strongly influenced a number of Italian painters, especially their technique of oil painting. For reasons still not clearly understood, the *musical* Renaissance began in the North—in England, the Low Countries, and in northern France. The most notable of the English composers, John Dunstable (d. 1453) was a contemporary of the early Renaissance composers on the continent and probably influenced them with what his admirers called his "sweet style." On the continent some court and church composers of northern France and the Low Countries (Flanders) formed a group known today as the Franco-Flemish school. True Renaissance artists, they were individualistic, materialistic, and boldly experimental. They had mastered the craft and art of a new style of music, and they delighted in demonstrating their compositional skills with intricate canons and musical puzzles for educated amateurs.

In their quest for new materials and fresh ideas they traveled to Italy, where the simple folk melodies and dance tunes provided further opportunities for polyphonic devices and techniques. Considering the travel hardships then, the mobility of Franco-Flemish composers in the fifteenth century was astounding. The composer Dufay, for example, was discovered at the age of nine in Cambrai in France by talent scouts seeking out precocious young musicians. Before he was twenty-six Dufay had traveled to Italy and then studied in Paris, held a post in northern France, served the court in Bologna, and sung in the papal choir in Rome.

Franco-Flemish composers like Dufay and others dominated Italian musical life in the courts and in the churches for over a century. St. Mark's in Venice, one of the most important musical centers in Europe, employed only Flemish composers until the latter part of the sixteenth century. When Florence decided to dedicate its magnificent cathedral (1436), Dufay was commissioned to write special music for the occasion (see chap. 18).

Music was an integral part of the complex fabric of Renaissance society. A retinue of musicians became a fixture of court life, with the dukes of Burgundy, Philip the Good and Charles the Bold, setting the style. Castiglione (see chap. 20), the chief social arbiter of the Renaissance, thought that his ideal Courtier should be proficient in both vocal and instrumental music:

> I regard as beautiful music, to sing well by note, with ease and beautiful style; but as even far more beautiful, to sing to the accompaniment of the viol, because nearly all the sweetness lies in the solo part, and we note and observe the fine manner and the melody with much greater attention when our ears are not occupied with more than a single voice, and moreover every little fault is more clearly discerned,—which is not the case when several sing together, because each singer helps his neighbor. But above all, singing to the viol by way of recitative seems to me most delightful, which adds to the words a charm and grace that are very admirable.
>
> All keyed instruments also are pleasing to the ear, because they produce very perfect consonances, and upon them one can play many things that fill the mind with musical delight. And not less charming is the music of the stringed quartet, which is most sweet and exquisite. The human voice lends much ornament and grace to all these instruments, with which I would have our Courtier at least to some degree acquainted, albeit the more he excels with them, the better.[1]

At different times a kingdom, a county, and a duchy, Burgundy became the most powerful and influential political entity in Europe during the fifteenth century. From Philip the Bold in 1336 through

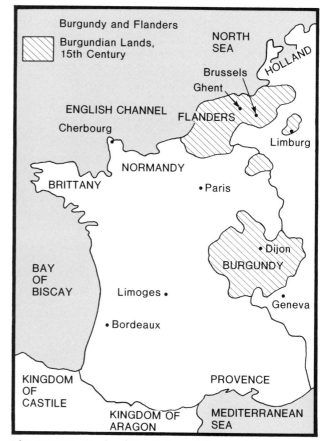

Figure 19.1 Lands of the Dukes of Burgundy

John the Fearless and Philip the Good to Charles the Bold (ruled 1467–1477), the rulers of Burgundy made the court in the capital city of Dijon one of the most magnificent in Europe (see fig. 19.1).

The Flemish sculptor Claus Sluter and the painter Jan van Eyck served the "court of plume and panoply" of Philip the Good at the time of its greatest splendor. The court was ostentatious and even flamboyant, but nevertheless according to contemporary accounts, it resembled a sort of fairyland. Women wore hennins, cone-shaped headdresses with long sheer veils hanging from the pointed tops. Their gowns were opulent, frequently decorated with fur and set off by gold throat bands and necklaces. Elaborate furniture and interior designs furnished the proper setting for the elegance of the court.

The court of the dukes of Burgundy set the styles in dress, manners, dancing, music, and the other arts. The principal court dance was the *basse dance,* which was performed with gliding steps, possibly accounting for the designation *basse* (low). The basse dance belonged to a family of related dances: the basse dance proper and the *pas de Brabant* (Italian *saltarello*). It

---

1. Baldassare Castiglione, *The Book of the Courtier,* trans. Leonard Eckstein Opdycke (New York: Horace Liveright, 1929).

was the custom to follow the dignified basse dance, referred to as the "imperial measure," by the quicker pas de Brabant, thus producing a contrasting pair of slow and fast dance movements, a typical procedure for Renaissance dances. Both used the same basic music; only the rhythms were changed.

Tapestries and miniatures of the period show instrumental ensembles playing for the dancers. The standard group of instruments consisted of two shawms (early oboes) and a slide-trumpet, while the harp, lute, and flute made up the other group. The former group consisted of *hauts* (high, loud) instruments, the latter of *bas* (low, soft) instruments. The hauts instruments were used for festive occasions and were usually played from a balcony or loggia. The bas instruments were used for more intimate dancing and were placed near the dancers.

Court life at Dijon was lively and elegant. In many respects, it was an updated version of the medieval Court of Love with music, both lively and sedate, for dancing and for songs, true French *chansons* extolling love, joy, and beauty. Secular music was in great demand for everything from the intimate rites of courtship to elaborate ceremonial music for the court. There was a remarkable development of sophisticated secular music, but not at the expense of sacred music, which incorporated the techniques and some of the melodies of secular music into a highly refined style.

The Burgundian School

Guillaume Dufay (doo–FYE; ca. 1400–1474) was the most famous composer of the Burgundian school of the Franco-Flemish tradition and one of the greatest of French composers. Following is the beginning of a Dufay mass movement that illustrates the smoother, fuller sounds of Renaissance music. Dufay has broken down the *Kyrie Eleison* into three separate movements: *Kyrie eleison, Christe eleison,* and *Kyrie eleison.* The texture is characteristic of early Renaissance music with mixed vocal and instrumental sounds and with instruments playing the wordless portions of the Mass.

First Kyrie from the Mass
"Se la face ay pale"[2]

Time: 1:40
(Complete)
Guillaume Dufay (ca. 1400–1474)

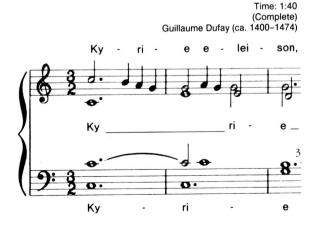

Dufay also composed a wealth of secular music, some of which is indicated in the Record List at the end of this chapter. *Note*: The Record List always follows the exact sequence in which examples are presented.

Gilles Binchois (bann–SWAH; ca. 1400–1460) did not have the versatility of Dufay but was a superb composer of French chansons. Some, like the famous "De plus en plus," are as fresh, witty, and bright today as when they were written. Although composed for aristocrats of the court, Binchois's music has a comfortable middle-class air of easy informality. Bourgeois influences had now become significant. Wealthy Flemish merchants were beginning to make their presence felt in the world of art, music, and manners, once the exclusive preserve of aristocracy and clergy.

The Franco-Flemish Tradition

During the latter part of the fifteenth century the center of musical activity gradually shifted from Burgundy to northern France and the Low Countries of Flanders and the Netherlands. The fusion of French elegance, Flemish polyphonic techniques, and Italian vigor led to the highly sophisticated style of the Late Renaissance. Whatever followed from this—even the music of such giants as Palestrina and Lassus—was actually a continuation of northern genius suffused with Italian taste and supported by Italian patronage.

No one person was responsible for the development of the new music. It simply happened that a large group of gifted composers in one geographic area was active at about the same time and that all, at varying times, were involved in Italian musical life. The most important composers were Obrecht and Agricola of the Netherlands; Brumel and de la Rue of northern France; and Isaac, Compère, and Josquin of Flanders. Each was brilliant in his own right, but Josquin outshone them all.

Martin Luther is reported to have said that "Others follow the notes, Josquin makes them do as he wishes." Josquin des Prés (ca. 1450–1521), usually referred to as Josquin (JOSS–can), did indeed know what to do with the notes; in his own time he was referred to as the "prince of music." He and his Franco-Flemish contemporaries developed all of the basic

2. Smijers, *Algemeene Muziek Geschiedenis,* Utrecht, 1938, p. 101.

3. Musical notation is used on a modest scale throughout this book in order to give brief quotes from works to be studied. These are guides to listening just as literary quotations are guides to reading. Using musical quotes is a necessary, basic procedure that is in no way "technical." Performing music is technical; *reading* music is a simple procedure easily learned by anyone. Please consult the Appendix, Music Listening and Notation. This has been abstracted from volume 1 and included here so that everyone can acquire, perhaps for the first time, a basic music literacy.

features of the Late Renaissance and, in so doing, established music as an international style in western European culture. Josquin was to music what Leonardo, Michelangelo, and Raphael were to the visual arts. A master of compositional techniques, he sometimes invented and consistently refined the methods and materials of Renaissance polyphonic music.

Musical development moved to the north of France and to the Low Countries after the beginning of the slow decline of the Duchy of Burgundy. Both Josquin and the great Orlandus di Lassus were born in Flanders, the latter in 1532. In between these two towering figures there were literally hundreds of excellent composers and performers in the Franco-Flemish school.

While Italy was exporting artists and works of art, it was also importing music and musicians. Western Europeans flowed into Italy to study her literary and visual arts, while musicians from the north moved in to take over most of the major musical positions. Northern dominance was so prevalent that Franco-Flemish music flourished on foreign soil for over a century before Italy was able to produce a Palestrina.

The motet "Ave Maria" by Josquin is an example of the serene lucidity and beauty of music of the High Renaissance. The smoothly flowing lines are woven into an elegant tapestry of luminous sound, a sound somehow comparable to the undulating arches of a Renaissance arcade. Motets are still sacred music, similar to polyphonic masses, but the text is nonscriptural. Instruments are no longer combined or alternated with the voices as in Early Renaissance music; the singing is now consistently unaccompanied (*a cappella*). The vocal texture is continuous with new phrases overlapping preceding phrases to produce an unbroken stream of simultaneous melodies. This ceaseless flow of intricately intertwined melodies is a hallmark of High and Late Renaissance vocal music.

The voices enter one at a time in *imitation;* that is, each of the four voices has essentially the same melodic line when it makes its entrance. Josquin used the text of the "Ave Maria" ("Hail Mary, full of grace . . .") and selected his basic theme from a portion of an "Ave Maria" chant:

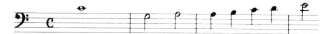

Motet: "Ave Maria"[4]

Time: 3:50
Josquin des Près (ca. 1450–1521)

= Listening Cue

The Flemish composer Orlandus Lassus (1532–1594) was one of the finest composers of a celebrated era, the Golden Age of Polyphony of the sixteenth century. His 1250 compositions were literally international: Latin masses and motets; secular vocal music in French, German, and Italian; and instrumental music in different national styles. Representative of his sacred music, the "Tristis est anima mea" is quoted below in a simplified musical score illustrating the rich and sonorous sound of his music. (See "motet" in the Glossary.)

Motet: "Tristis est anima mea"[5]

Time: 4:00
Orlandus Lassus (1532–1594)

The Italian Style

During the latter part of the sixteenth century, Italian genius manifested itself in the music of native Italians. Italian music had been invigorated by the presence of resident Flemish composers and by the dynamic Counter-Reformation response to Luther's revolt. Flemish composers had fled Spanish tyranny in the Low Countries to pursue their profession in a less hostile setting. There was, moreover, a real need to develop a new style of sacred music because things had gotten out of hand, as Erasmus of Rotterdam cogently pointed out.

> We have introduced an artificial and theatrical music into the church, a bawling and agitation of various voices, such as I believe had never been heard in the theatres of the Greeks and Romans. Horns, trumpets, pipes vie and sound along constantly with the voices. Amorous and lascivious melodies are heard such as elsewhere accompany only the dances of courtesans and clowns.[6]

The Council of Trent (1545–1564) was convened to deal with the abuses pointed out by Luther and other reformers. The problem of music was only incidental to overall concerns, but musical difficulties occupied most of the attention of the Council for over a year. Final recommendations were negative rather than positive. Certain practices were forbidden and

4. Josquin des Près, *Werke*, Motets, vol. I, Amsterdam, 1935, p. 1.
5. Orlando di Lasso, *Sämtliche Werke*, vol. V, Leipzig, 1895, p. 48.
6. Desiderius Erasmus, *Opera Omnia*, VI, 1705, col. 731.

certain results were prescribed without, however, specifying the means. The canon finally adopted by the Council in 1562 banned all seductive or impure melodies, whether vocal or instrumental, all vain and worldly texts, all outcries and uproars, that "the House of God may in truth be called a House of prayer."

Shortly after passing the canon against decadent musical practices, the Council took under consideration the possible banning of all polyphonic music, especially polyphonic masses. This ultraconservative movement was countered by Lassus and Palestrina, who, among others, submitted polyphonic music to a special Commission in order to promote a favorable decision. Polyphonic music was preserved when the Council approved, after considerable deliberation, the reformed style of polyphonic music advocated by the composers of the Church.

Giovanni Pierluigi da Palestrina (1524–1594) was one of the supreme exponents of Catholic polyphonic music of the Renaissance, but his secular music is equally outstanding. Romanticized in the nineteenth century as a lonely and poverty-stricken artist who was wedded to the church, Palestrina was actually a successful professional musician. He briefly considered the priesthood after the death of his first wife, but chose instead to marry a wealthy widow. He was paid well for the music that he wrote for the church and even refused several more lucrative positions rather than leave Rome.

Present-day music students study Palestrina's music for classes in "strict counterpoint," that is, writing polyphonic music in the manner of the sixteenth century with Palestrina as the model composer. Though his compositions serve as a guide to correct contrapuntal writing, Palestrina's music is anything but dogmatic. A model it is but one of clarity, conciseness, and consistency. Using existing plainsong melodies as a point of departure, he wrote in a beautifully balanced style of simultaneous plainsong.

The following plainsong, "Veni sponsa Christi," forms the basis for a Palestrina mass:

Palestrina began with this simple melody, transforming it into a serenely flowing melodic theme:

A-gnus De-i, A _____ gnus De-i.

"Veni sponsa Christi" (named after the plainsong) is a short composition based on this characteristic Palestrina melody. Notice how the smoothly flowing text is fitted to graceful melodic lines.

First Agnus Dei from the Mass: "Veni sponsa Christi"[7]

Time: 2:15
G.P. da Palestrina (1524–1594)

Italian Vocal-Instrumental Music

Instrumental music came to the fore during the late Renaissance assisted particularly by the musical directors of the Cathedral of St. Mark's in Venice. St. Mark's Byzantine splendor was typical of the grandiose palaces, churches, ceremonies, and even paintings of that ornate city (see fig. 19.2). As a trading center and crossroads of the world, much of the pomp and pageantry was a deliberate (and successful) attempt to impress visitors with the magnificence of Venice. Grand productions inside the cathedral were also necessary for the desired effect, but the arrangement of the church did not lend itself to large musical groups.

St. Mark's floor plan was that of a Greek cross (fig. 19.3). Following the conventions of the Eastern church, the main floor was reserved for men and the smaller balcony level for women. This design was exploited by creating a new *polychoral* style of *antiphonal* singing, or a procedure whereby the ensemble (chorus with or without orchestra) was divided into several different groups singing and/or playing in *alternation*. Musical productions would include the use of the two organs in their fixed positions plus choirs and brass choirs stationed on several balconies throughout the church. The listener would be overwhelmed with vocal and instrumental music alternating between left and right, front and rear, etc. Arrangements of choirs and brass choirs could be selected from some of the possibilities indicated in figure 19.3 (also see fig. 19.4).

---

7. Ioannis Petraloysii Praenestini, *Opera omnia*, Leipzig, 1886, vol. 18, p. 35.

Figure 19.2 St. Mark's Cathedral, begun 1063, Venice. With its five portals and five glittering domes, St. Mark's functioned as a sumptuous backdrop for the elaborate civic ceremonies staged in the great piazza stretched before it. Also see figure 12.22 in volume 1.

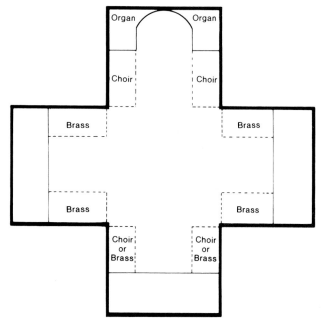

Figure 19.3 Simplified floor plan of St. Mark's, Venice

Figure 19.4 Interior, St. Mark's, Venice. This view is from the west balcony where one organ is located, looking east to the small chancel with the other organ and space for a small choir. Brass choirs were placed at one or more of the four upper corners under massive arches. The conductor stood on the high podium in front of the main-floor choir.

Following is the motet "In ecclesiis" by G. Gabrieli (1557–1612) for:

Chorus I
Chorus II
Solo voices
Orchestra
    Three cornettos (usually played by trumpets)
    Viola (bowed string instrument in alto register)
    Two trombones
    Pipe organ

The motet consists of five verses and five alleluias and has the following overall structure of text and performing groups (which sing or play from four different locations in the church):

Verse 1.	*In ecclesiis benedicite Domino,* (Praise the Lord in the congregation)	Sopranos (Chorus I) Organ
	Alleluia	Sopranos (Chorus I) Chorus II Organ
Verse 2.	*In omnia loco . . . ,* (In every place of worship praise him)	Tenors (Chorus I) Organ
	Alleluia	Tenors (Chorus I) Chorus II Organ

Sinfonia (orchestral interlude)

Verse 3.	*In Deo, salutari meo . . . ,* (In God, who is my salvation and glory, is my help, and my hope is in God)	Altos (Chorus I) Tenors (Chorus I) Orchestra
	Alleluia	Altos (Chorus I) Tenors (Chorus I) Chorus II Orchestra
Verse 4.	*Deus meus, te invocamus . . . ,* (My God, we invoke thee, we worship thee; deliver us, quicken us)	Sopranos (Chorus I) Tenors (Chorus I) Organ
	Alleluia	Chorus I Chorus II Organ
Verse 5.	*Deus, adjutor noster aeternam,* (My God, judge us eternally)	Chorus I Chorus II Orchestra
	Alleluia	Chorus I Chorus II Orchestra Organ

Music Printing

Venice was also the setting for the development of printed music. Over nine million books had been printed by the year 1500, but no one had thought of printing music on that scale. A 1457 *Psalterium* that included music had been printed at Mainz and a Roman *Missale* was printed in 1476 in Milan using, for the first time, movable type.

Ottaviano de' Petrucci (peh–TROO–tchee; 1466–1539) used movable type in his printing shop, but he was also an enterprising businessman. On May 25, 1498, he petitioned the Signoria of Venice for a twenty-year license (amounting to a monopoly) to print music to meet a growing demand for domestic music. In 1501 he produced the *Harmonice Musices Odhecaton A (One Hundred Songs of Harmonic Music)*, the earliest printed collection of part-music. Rich in Franco-Flemish chansons, this anthology was followed by fifty-eight more volumes of secular and sacred music produced for music-hungry amateurs and an increasing number of professional musicians. An expanding market led, of course, to lower prices and even wider dissemination of music. By the end of the sixteenth century, music publishers were in business throughout Europe.

Instrumental Music

Renaissance instrumental music continued to be primarily functional; that is, it was associated with dances, plays, masquerades, and extravaganzas of noble courts rather than as a performance art with its own special audience.

Dance and music have always been associated and rarely more effectively than in the sixteenth century, which has been called "the century of the dance." The church had long suppressed dancing as both heathenish and lascivious. However, the frantic, compulsive dances of the flagellants of the fourteenth century symbolized a violent reaction against this stifling authority. Simultaneously in the Italian and French courts, men and women joined hands for the first time for folklike round dances and courtly pair dances such as the *danse royale*.

A large variety of dances appeared in the lute, keyboard, and other instrumental music of the sixteenth century. The pair of dances "Der Prinzen-Tanz" and "Proportz" is for the lute, a plucked string instrument with a mellow and resonant tone. This "Prince's Dance" is in slow duple meter (two beats per measure) followed by the same melody "proportionately altered"—designated as "Proportz"—in a

Figure 19.5 *Lady Playing a Dulcimer* from the early sixteenth-century manuscript of the fourteenth-century poem "Les Echecs Amoreux." A few of the many Renaissance instruments are depicted here. The elegantly gowned lady is playing her dulcimer (an instrument still in use) with small hammers. A harp leans against the wall at the left, and a portable organ rests on the floor at the right. In the background are singers and players. Reading from left to right, the instruments are: recorder (still used today and also ancestor of the flute), shawm (ancestor of the oboe), and bagpipes (probably of Asian origin; introduced to Europe by the Romans during the first century A.D.). Biblioteque Nazional fv. 143, Paris.

fast triple meter (three beats per measure). The dance is organized into four short sections, each repeated, which can be labeled *a–b–c–d.* The graph of "Lute Dances" given below is drawn to scale and uses a letter for each section of the music. The numerals indicate the number of measures in each section.[8] Any number of Renaissance dances can be designed and danced to the basic musical structure.

Lute Dances: "Der Prinzen-Tanz; Proportz" (ca.1550)

Scale: 1/8" = 1 measure
Arabic numerals indicate number of measures
in each section.

Time: 1:35

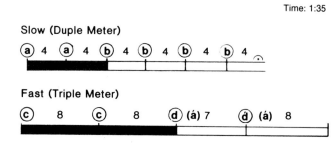

Slow (Duple Meter)

Fast (Triple Meter)

The chief instrumental rival of the lute was the *harpsichord*—also called cembalo, clavecin, virginal, spinet—the principal keyboard instrument of the sixteenth through the eighteenth centuries. Harpsichords have various shapes, which are generally similar in external appearance to grand, upright, and spinet pianos. The tone is produced by quills plucking the strings and is bright and sharp. Unlike the piano, harpsichords cannot vary their *dynamics* (degrees of loudness or softness) except by using two keyboards, muted strings, or different types of quills. Whole sections are played at one dynamic level; variation is achieved by changing to a louder or softer tone quality in the next section.

In England, the harpsichord was called a *virginal,* supposedly in honor of the "maiden Queen Elizabeth." English music had flourished under Henry VIII, Edward VI, and Mary, and reached, under Elizabeth, a level rarely approached thereafter. English power and wealth, the importation of foreign talent, and increased travel, all combined to make the English assimilation of the Italian Renaissance one of the outstanding periods in Western history. Tudor sacred music was superb, but the secular forms of English music—the madrigals, lute music, virginal music, and fancies for viols—had special importance in the richness of the Elizabethan Age.

The composition "Loth to Depart" for a "pair of virginals"—harpsichord with two keyboards—is by the English composer Giles Farnaby. The piece is written in what had become a common and preferred instrumental form of *theme and variations.* In this case, the theme is in triple meter and is sixteen measures long. After the theme, there is a set of five variations, each patterned after the original theme in structure, melody, and harmony. The formal structure of the piece does not change; the composer achieves variety by making alterations in rhythm, melody, and texture.

Variations for Virginals: "Loth to Depart"[9]

Time: 4:25
Giles Farnaby (ca. 1560–1600)
Theme (beginning)

8. If there are four measures they can be counted audibly as 1–2, 2–2, 3–2, 4–2. Four measures of triple meter would count as: 1–2–3, 2–2–3, 3–2–3, 4–2–3.

9. *Fitzwilliam Virginal Book,* vol. II, London, 1899, p. 317.

English Secular Vocal Music

The English madrigal school was inspired by Italian models, but its growth and development has made the English madrigal virtually synonymous with Elizabethan England. A *madrigal,* whether English or Italian, is a secular, unaccompanied part-song, usually in four voices. English madrigals tend toward a balanced texture of polyphonic and homophonic writing and are frequently either merry or melancholy. The outstanding characteristic, however, is the sheer delight in the sounds, rhythms, and meanings of the English language.

The madrigalists are fond of natural word rhythms. They also like to play with onomatopoeia, alliteration, metaphor, and simile and take exceptional pleasure in exploiting double meanings. Word play with triple meanings is even better. Word painting is another notable characteristic whereby composers manipulate the sounds of the music so that they can imitate, imply, or describe the sounds of nature and/or the meaning and sounds of words.

In the following *pastoral madrigal,* the composer quietly poses the question, "Thyrsis? Sleepest thou?" and then continues to press the question until Thyrsis is awakened with some vigorous "hollas." The cuckoo song is imitated, the music "sighs" as the shepherd "sighed as one all undone" and requests to be "let alone alas." The repetitious text of "drive him back to London" pushes the madrigal to an animated conclusion.

Madrigal: "Thyrsis, Sleepest Thou?"[10]

Time: 1:40
John Bennet (ca. 1575–1625)

The *catch* is one of the most interesting and ingenious types of English secular music. Written as a three-part round for male voices, it was designed for double and triple entendre as the texts of the second and third voice parts blended into the gaps in the text of the top voice part. This blending process may be illustrated as follows:

Part 1. Show me now the ____ way ____ .
Part 2.　　Lead me to the best man.
Part 3.　　　Now is the time to ride home.
　　　(Show me now the best way home.)

The following catches illustrate two characteristic types of humorous songs, which were sung by "gentlemen of quality." These gentlemen had to be good singers so that they could "catch" the melody at the right time.

Tom the Taylor[11]
Henry Purcell (1659–1695)

Tom making a Mantua[12] for a Lass of pleasure,
Pull'd out, pull'd out, pull'd out his long, his long and
　　lawful measure,
But quickly found, tho' woundily streight lac'd Sir
Nine Inches, nine Inches, nine Inches, nine Inches
　　would not half surround her wast, Sir.
Three Inches more at length brisk Tom advances,
Yet all, yet all too short, yet all too short, all too short, all
　　too short, yet all too short, all too short to reach her
　　swinging hances.

A Catch in the Play of the Knight of Malta[13]
Henry Purcell

At the close of the Evening the Watches were set,
The Guards went the Round, and the Ta-ta-ta-too, Ta-ta-ta-
　　too, ta-ta-ta-too, ta-ta-ta-too, ta-ta-ta-too, ta-ta-ta-ta-ta-
　　ta-too was beat, the ta-ta-ta-ta-ta-ta-too was beat,
But now yonder stars appear in the Sky,
And Ta-ra-ra-ra, Ra-ra-ra-ra, Ra-ra-ra-ra, Ra-ra-ra-ra, Ra-ra-ra-
　　ra, Ra-ra-ra-ra, Ra-ra-ra-ra is sounded on high.
We shall soon be reliev'd, then drink, drink away, then
　　drink away, then drink, drink, drink away,
Here's to you, and to you, and to you, let us drink, let us
　　drink, till 'tis day, let, let us drink till 'tis day.

Summary

The environment of music underwent notable changes during the Renaissance with the inevitable result that the forms of music changed accordingly. The forces of secularization, which were set in motion during the Gothic period, began to equalize the power of the church. The expansion of the universities, the development of city centers of trade and commerce, and the rise of a mercantile middle class helped bring about a concurrent development of secular music.

Outdoor concerts using orchestras composed of violins, shawms, trombones, and drums and indoor concerts of recorders, viols, and harpsichord became common. Some of the outdoor performances provided music for dancing, which had changed from improvised music for one or two instruments to composed music for groups of instruments (*consorts*).

The demand for musical instruments for domestic use spurred the development and production of lutes, viols, and especially the instrument that could play both homophonic and polyphonic music, the harpsichord. An even more common household instrument was the *clavichord.*[14]

---

10. John Bennet, *Madrigals to Four Voices,* London, 1599, no. 8.

11. *The Catch Club or Merry Companions,* I, Walsh, London, 1762, p. 2.

12. Mantle.

13. *The Catch Club,* p. 38.

14. The tone of the clavichord is produced by depressing the keys so that a metal tangent on the other end of the key would strike the string. The instrument is portable and the tone light and flexible. The principle of striking a string was later, in the eighteenth century, developed into the hammer action of the piano.

The newly awakened interest in classical culture, in humanism, and in the creative individual was reflected in the active participation in the arts by educated amateurs. Large and small social gatherings featured performances of solo songs accompanied by lute or harpsichord (or clavichord), a variety of chamber music, and, particularly in England, the singing of part-songs such as madrigals and catches.

The proliferation of secular music did not provoke a decline in sacred music; rather there was a merging of techniques, instruments, and styles. Burgundian composers such as Dufay combined vocal with instrumental music in the Church. Binchois specialized in secular music with particular emphasis upon the special qualities of the French chanson.

Josquin des Près wrote masses and motets, Italian secular music, and French chansons. Lassus wrote 1250 compositions in Latin, French, German, and Italian. Palestrina, serving the church in Rome, wrote mostly sacred music, but did compose a number of Italian madrigals. In Venice, Gabrieli wrote antiphonal, vocal-instrumental music and considerable instrumental music.

The growth of music during the Renaissance was astounding. Within a single century, music changed from an esoteric, church-dominated art form to an international language heard in every court, noble residence, and many middle-class homes throughout Europe.

Listening Outline (Third Stage)

Note: As a guide to listening, this outline represents a *maximum* of elements to listen for. Perhaps no one can hear everything the first or even the tenth time through. Hearing everything is not crucial, but having an objective listening procedure is important. That is the purpose of this guide.

I. Listening outline
   A. Medium
      1. Vocal (text: English, Latin, German, French, other)
      2. Instrumental
      3. Vocal and instrumental (text)
   B. Tempo—very slow, slow, moderate, fast, very fast
   C. Loudness—soft, medium loud, loud, combination
   D. Number of performers
      1. Solo
      2. Ensemble
         a) Small (2 to 5)
         b) Medium (6 to 20)
         c) Medium large (21 to 59)
         d) Large (60 to 100 or more)
   E. Rhythm
      1. Regular beat (or pulsation)
      2. Pulsation irregular or indistinct
   F. Meter
      1. Duple (2 beats per measure)
      2. Triple (3 beats per measure)
      3. Quadruple (4 beats per measure)
   G. Texture
      1. One melody, unaccompanied (monophonic)
      2. Melody with accompaniment (homophonic)
      3. Simultaneous melodies (polyphonic)
   H. Form
      1. AB (two-part) or variant
      2. ABA (three-part) or variant
      3. Other
II. Conclusions
   A. Period: 600–1420 (medieval), 1420–1600 (Renaissance)
   B. General musical form—mass, madrigal, motet, catch, folk song, instrumental dance music, other
   C. National origin—England, France, Germany, Italy, Flanders, other

Note: See the Glossary for terms that may not be familiar.

Record List

Except for special records and standard anthologies, specific records are not listed. The market is unstable at best and digital recordings have added to the confusion.

1. Dufay, G. 1st Kyrie from the Mass: "Se la face ay pale." In *Masterpieces of Music before 1750* (referred to as *Masterpieces*). 3 vols. Haydn Society 9038/9040.
2. Binchois. "De plus en plus." In *The Art of Courtly Love.* EMI SLS 863.
3. Josquin des Près. "Ave Maria." In *Masterpieces.*
4. Lassus. Motet, "Tristis est anima mea." In *Masterpieces.*
5. Palestrina, G. P. da. 1st Agnus Dei from the Mass: "Veni sponsa Christi." In *Masterpieces.*
6. Gabrieli, G. "In ecclesiis." RCA Victor LM 6029—2.
7. Lute Dances: "Der Prinzen-Tanz; Proportz." In *Masterpieces.*
8. Farnaby, G. Variations for Virginals: "Loth to Depart." In *Masterpieces.*
9. Bennet, J. "Thyrsis, Sleepest Thou?" In *Masterpieces.*
10. Purcell, H. "Tom the Taylor" and "A Catch in the Play of the Knight of Malta." In *Catch That Catch Can* (Music of the Sixteenth and Seventeenth Centuries, vol. 8). Musical Heritage Society MHS 690.

Also Recommended

1. Dufay. Mass, *Se le face ay pale.*
2. ———. *Missa, L'Homme armé.*
3. ———. *Secular and Sacred Music for Voices and Instruments.* Dover HCR—5261.
4. ———. *Secular Works.* EMS 206.
5. ———. Chansons und Motetten: *Adieu M'Amour.* EMI C 063—30 124.
6. *Dances of the Renaissance.* L'Oiseau-lyre SOL—R330.
7. *French Chansons and Dances of the 16th Century.* Dover HCR 5221.
8. *French Dances of the Renaissance and other Celebrated Pieces of the Renaissance and Baroque.* Nonesuch H 1036.
9. Josquin. *Ave, Christe, immolate.*
10. ———. *Chansons.*
11. ———. *Deploration sur la mort d'Ockeghem.*
12. ———. *Chansons, Frottole and Instrumental Pieces.* Nonesuch LL 71261.
13. ———. *Missa, Pange lingua, 8 Secular Works.* Archive ARC 3159.
14. Lassus. *Missa Bell' Amfitrit' altera.*
15. ———. *St. Matthew Passion.*
16. Palestrina. *Missa Assumpta est Maria.*
17. ———. *Missa brevis.*
18. ———. *Missa Hodie Christus natus est.*
19. ———. *Missa Papae Marcelli, 8 Motets.* Archive ARC 3182.
20. ———. *Madrigali e ricercari.* Archive ARC 198 434.
21. Gabrieli. *Sacrae symphoniae and Canzoni.* Bach Guild BG 611.
22. ———. *Madrigals and Dialogues.* Dover HCR—ST 97271.
23. ———. *The Antiphonal Music of Gabrieli.* Columbia MS 7209.
24. ———. *Music for Brass.* Vox STPL 514,240.
25. ———. *The Glory of Gabrieli.* Columbia MS 7071.
26. ———. *The Glory of Venice.* Columbia M 30937.
27. *The English Madrigal School.* Bach Guild BG—553–554, 577–578.
28. *English Madrigals and Folk Songs.* Odyssey 32 16 0017.
29. *An Evening of Elizabethan Verse and Its Music.* Columbia ML 5051.
30. *Shakespearean Songs and Consort Music.* RCA Victor VIC 1266.
31. *Music of the High Renaissance in England.* Turnabout TV 34017S.
32. *The Triumphs of Oriana, Music to Entertain Elizabeth I.* Argo ZRG 643.
33. *Lute Music by Dowland and Byrd.* RCA Victor LM 2819.
34. Byrd, William. *Madrigals, Motets, Anthems and Keyboard Music.* Musical Heritage Society MHS 877S.
35. ———. *Works, Virginal.* EMI Electrola 1C 063—30120.

Bibliography

Brown, Howard M. *Music in the Renaissance.* Englewood Cliffs, N.J.: Prentice-Hall, 1976. Good overview and not too technical.

Reese, Gustav. *Music in the Renaissance.* New York: W. W. Norton, 1959. Thorough but technical.

Robertson, Alec, and Denis Stevens, eds. *Renaissance and Baroque.* The Pelican History of Music, vol. 2. New York: Penguin Books, 1963. Relatively nontechnical survey.

20

Shadow and Substance: Literary Insights into the Renaissance

The linguistic dualism of the Renaissance had a very positive effect on the development of literature, philosophy, and science. The Latin that the Church had preserved was the common language of all intellectuals and, moreover, a direct link to the classical past. No wonder Petrarch and other humanists viewed Cicero and Virgil as contemporaries; all wrote in the same language. Developing during the Middle Ages as the spoken languages of the people, the vernaculars became the accepted languages of popular culture. Latin was still viewed as the proper language for scholarly work, but the vernaculars developed during the Renaissance into recognized national languages that became acceptable vehicles for literary expression. Latin provided a kind of intellectual unity; English, French, and Spanish each reinforced a sense of national unity and purpose. Each nation developed its own modern literary tradition, but languages were not isolated by the rise of nationalism. Translations of every language, including Latin, flowed back and forth over national borders, making Renaissance literature as international, in its own way, as art and music.

From the treasure-house of Renaissance literature we can select only a few writers and a variety of literary forms that are realistic, romantic, optimistic, or pessimistic, each mirroring one (or more) of these Renaissance attitudes.

Literary Selections

Though Petrarch (see chap. 17) intended his epic poem *Africa* to be his major work, his Italian sonnets have been far more influential. His love poetry was inspired by Laura, whom he first saw in the Church of St. Clara of Avignon on April 6, 1327. The following sonnet commemorates that momentous meeting, while also alluding to the day on which Christ supposedly died: April 6.

SONNET III

(Era il giorno ch'al sol si scolarara)
Petrarch (Francesco Petrarca; 1304–1374)

'Twas on the morn when heaven its blessed ray
    In pity to its suffering master veil'd,
    First did I, lady, to your beauty yield,
    Of your victorious eyes th' unguarded prey.
Ah, little reck'd I that, on such a day,
    Needed against Love's arrows any shield;
    And trod, securely trod, the fatal field:
    Whence, with the world's, began my heart's dismay.
On every side Love found his victim bare,
    And through mine eyes transfix'd my throbbing
        heart;
    Those eyes which now with constant sorrows flow:
But poor the triumph of his boasted art,
    Who thus could pierce a naked youth, nor dare
    To you in armor mail'd even to display his bow!

Like Dante's Beatrice, Laura was an ideal, the object throughout Petrarch's life of an unrequited poetic passion. Unlike Beatrice, whom Dante idealized from afar, Laura accepted the poet as a friend—but no more than that. She was married and destined to be the mother of ten children. A sonnet is, by definition, a fourteen-line lyric poem that expresses a single idea or thought, in this case the poet's reaction to Laura's physical beauty.

SONNET LXIX

(Erano i capei d'oro all' aura sparsi)
Petrarch (Francesco Petrarca; 1304–1374)

Her golden tresses were spread loose to air,
    And by the wind in thousand tangles blown,
    And a sweet light beyond all brightness shone
    From those grand eyes, though now of brilliance
        bare;
And did that face a flush of feeling wear?
    I now thought yes, then no, the truth unknown.
    My heart was then for love like tinder grown,
    What wonder if it flamed with sudden flare?
Not like the walk of mortals was her walk,
    But as when angels glide; and seemed her talk
    With other than mere human voice, to flow.
A spirit heavenly, a living sun
    I saw, and if she be no longer so,
    A wound heals not, because the bow's undone.

Petrarch was tormented by his passion, but he was also inspired as a poet because the one-way love affair appealed to his vanity. He was a Renaissance artist, a self-conscious man of letters seeking earthly fame, as the following sonnet clearly reveals.

SONNET XLVII

(Benedetto sia l' giorno e l' mese e l' anno)
Petrarch (Francesco Petrarca; 1304–1374)

Blest be the day, and blest the month, the year,
    The spring, the hour, the very moment blest,
    The lovely scene, the spot, where first oppress'd
    I sunk, of two bright eyes the prisoner:

And blest the first soft pang, to me most dear,
    Which thrill'd my heart, when Love became its guest;
    And blest the bow, the shafts which pierced my
        breast.
    And even the wounds, which bosom'd thence I bear.
Blest too the strains which, pour'd through glade and
        grove,
    Have made the woodlands echo with her name;
    The sighs, the tears, the languishment, the love:
And blest those sonnets, sources of my fame;
    And blest that thought—Oh! never to remove!—
    Which turns to her alone, from her alone which
        came.

Laura died on April 6, 1348, of the Black Death, as did millions of Europeans during that ghastly summer. Petrarch was devastated, as well as transfixed by the date.

SONNET CCXCII

(Gli occhi di ch' io parlai sì caldamente)
Petrarch (Francesco Petrarca; 1304–1374)

Those eyes, 'neath which my passionate rapture rose,
    The arms, hands, feet, the beauty that erewhile
    Could my own soul from its own self beguile,
    And in a separate world of dreams enclose,
The hair's bright tresses, full of golden glows,
    And the soft lightning of the angelic smile
    That changed this earth to some celestial isle,—
    Are now but dust, poor dust, that nothing knows.
And yet *I* live! Myself *I* grieve and scorn,
    Left dark without the light I loved in vain,
    Adrift in tempest on a bark forlorn;
Dead is the source of all my amorous strain,
    Dry is the channel of my thoughts outworn,
    And my sad harp can sound but notes of pain.

Throughout the rest of the poet's long life, Laura remained the ideal object, becoming in death the mediator between the penitent and the Divine.

SONNET CCCXIII

(I'vo piangendo i miei passati tempi)
Petrarch (Francesco Petrarca; 1304–1374)

I now am weeping, for the years passed by,
    Wasted in loving but a mortal thing,
    Though I could fly, not rising on the wing,
    To leave some work, perhaps not far from high.
My deeds unworthy, impious, from the sky,
    Thy realm, thou see'st, unseen, immortal King;
    To me, astray and feeble, succour bring,
    And with Thy grace, my soul's defect supply:
So that if tempest-tost, and oft in strife,
    I lived, I yet may die in port, at peace,
    And nobly quit, though spent in vain, my life.
Through my remaining years, so soon to cease,
    Let Thy right hand, my guide, in dying, be
    My stay; Thou know'st I have no hope but Thee.

Exercises

1. In line 11 of Sonnet III, the image of the eyes as a gateway to the heart was a poetic commonplace. Is that image still used today in poetry and songs? Give a few examples.
2. What is the meaning of the image of the "bow" in the last line of sonnets III and LXIX?
3. In the sonnets given here, what are some of the clues that mark these as Renaissance rather than medieval poetry?

Desiderius Erasmus (1466–1536)

Italian humanism had a distinctly pagan flavor, but across the Alps the movement was entirely Christian, with Erasmus (fig. 20.1), the "prince of humanists," in the forefront. He was a true cosmopolitan, making all Europe his home from England to Italy. Although at first well-disposed toward Luther's reforms, he could not accept Luther's denial of free will. "I laid a hen's egg," wrote Erasmus; "Luther hatched a bird of quite another species." With equal clarity he saw the corruption within the Church and the intransigence of Luther and chose to stay aloof. His advice to Pope Adrian VI, a personal friend, was characteristically levelheaded:

> As to writing against Luther, I have not learned enough. . . . One party says I agree with Luther because I do not oppose him. . . . The other finds fault with me because I do oppose him. . . . I did what I could. I advised him to be moderate, and I only made his friends my enemies. . . . They quote this and that to show we are alike. I could find a hundred passages where St. Paul seems to teach the doctrines which they condemn in Luther. I did not anticipate what a time was coming. I did, I admit, help to bring it on; but I was always willing to submit what I wrote to the Church. . . . Those counsel you best who advise gentle measures. . . . For myself, I should say, discover the roots of the disease. Clean out those to begin with. Punish no one. Let what has taken place be regarded as a chastisement sent by Providence, and grant a universal amnesty. If God forgives so many sins, God's vicar may forgive.

Erasmus was a strong supporter of overdue reforms. In his *Colloquies* he wrote that "Luther was guilty of two great crimes—he struck the Pope in his crown, and the monks in their belly." In another vein he sternly admonished his church: "By identifying the new learning with heresy you make orthodoxy synonymous with ignorance." Erasmus preferred a purified church to a divided one.

Erasmus conceived the idea of a satire on just about every aspect of contemporary society during a journey from Italy to England. Written partly during his stay with the English humanist Sir Thomas More

Figure 20.1 Albrecht Dürer (1471–1528), *Erasmus of Rotterdam,* 1526. Engraving, 9¾ × 7½". The Latin inscription states that this was a drawing from life (also see p. 49). Metropolitan Museum of Art, New York. Fletcher Fund, 1919.

and dedicated to More, he called the book *Moria* (the Greek word for Folly) in a punning reference to his English friend's name. Appearing in 36 editions in his own lifetime, the *Praise of Folly* was the most widely read book of the century after the Bible. Erasmus had brilliantly reinvented the classical paradoxical encomium in which everyone and everything unworthy of praise are ironically celebrated.

Literary Selection

THE PRAISE OF FOLLY
Desiderius Erasmus

Erasmus uses a dramatic setting and a woman, Folly Herself, who speaks wisely and foolishly, learnedly and jokingly. The underlying issue seems to be knowledge versus ignorance, with Erasmus holding to the middle ground. Don't put too much faith in knowledge and scholars, Folly implies, and try to be tolerant and gentle with fools and with ignorance.

Folly Herself Speaks
Whatever the world says of me (for I am not ignorant of Folly's poor reputation, even among the most foolish), yet I and I alone provide joy for gods and men. I no sooner step up to speak to this full assembly than all your faces put on a kind of new and unwonted pleasantness. So suddenly have you cleared your brows, and with so pleasant and hearty a laughter given me your applause, that in truth, as many of you as I behold on every side of me, seem to me no less than Homer's gods drunk with nectar and the drug nepenthe; whereas before, you sat as lumpish and pensive as if you had come from consulting an oracle. And as it usually happens when the sun begins to show his beams, or when after a sharp winter the spring breathes afresh on the earth, all things

immediately get a new face, new color, and recover as it were a certain kind of youth again: in like manner, but by beholding me, you have in an instant gotten another kind of countenance; and so what the otherwise great orators with their tedious and long-studied speeches can hardly effect, to wit, to remove the trouble of the mind, I have done it at once, with my single look.

But if you ask me why I appear before you in this strange dress, be pleased to lend me your ears, and I will tell you; not those ears, I mean, you carry to church, but abroad with you, such as you are wont to prick up to jugglers, fools, and buffoons, and such as our friend Midas once gave to Pan. For I am disposed awhile to play the sophist with you; not of their sort who nowadays cram boys' heads with certain empty notions and curious trifles, yet teach them nothing but a more than womanish obstinacy of scolding: but I'll imitate those ancients, who, that they might the better avoid that infamous appellation of *Sophi* or *Wise,* chose rather to be called "sophists." Their business was to celebrate the praises of the gods and valiant men. And the like encomium shall you hear from me, but neither of Herakles nor Solon, but mine own dear self, that is to say, Folly.

I think it high time to look down a little on the earth; wherein you'll find nothing frolicky or fortunate, that it owes not to me. So provident has that great parent of mankind, nature, been, that there should not be anything without its mixture, as it were seasoning, of Folly. For since according to the definition of the Stoics, wisdom is nothing else than to be governed by reason; and on the contrary Folly, to be given up to the will of our passions; that the life of man might not be altogether disconsolate and hard to put up with, of how much more passion than reason has Jupiter composed us? putting in, as one would say, "scarce half an ounce to the pound." Besides, he has confined reason to a narrow corner of the brain, and left all the rest of the body to our passions; as also set up, against this one, two as it were, masterless tyrants—anger that possesses the region of the heart, and consequently the very fountain of life, the heart itself; and lust, that stretches its empire everywhere. Against which double force how powerful reason is, let common experience declare, inasmuch as she, which yet is all she can do, may call out to us until she's hoarse, and tell us the rules of honesty and virtue; while they give up the reins to their governor, and make a hideous clamor, till at last being wearied, he suffer himself to be carried wherever they please to hurry him.

Is not war the very root and matter of all famed enterprise? And yet what more foolish than to undertake it for I know not what trifles, especially when both parties are sure to lose more than they get in the bargain? For of those that are slain, not a word of them; and for the rest, when both sides are close engaged "and the trumpets make an ugly noise," what use of these wise men, I pray, that are so exhausted with study that their thin cold blood has scarcely any spirits left? No, it must be those blunt fat fellows, that by how much more they excel in courage, fall short in understanding. Unless perhaps one had rather choose Demosthenes for a soldier, who, following the example of Archilochius, threw away his arms and took to his heels e'er he had scarcely seen his enemy; as ill a soldier, as happy an orator.

But good judgment, you'll say, is not of the least concern in matters of war. In a general way I grant it; but this thing of warring is no part of philosophy, but managed by parasites, pimps, thieves, assassins, peasants, sots, spendthrifts and such other dregs of mankind, not philosophers; who how inept they are in everyday conversation, let Sokrates, whom the oracle of Apollo, though not so wisely, judged "the wisest of all men living," be witness; who stepping up to speak about something, I know not what, in public, was forced to come down again well laughed at for his pains. Though yet in this he was not altogether a fool, that he refused the appellation of wise, and returning it back to the oracle, delivered his opinion that a wise man should abstain from meddling with public business; unless perhaps he should have admonished us to beware of wisdom if we intended to be reckoned among the living, there being nothing but his wisdom that first accused and afterwards sentenced him to the drinking of his poisoned cup. For while, as you find him in Aristophanes, philosophying about clouds and ideas, measuring how far a flea could leap, and admiring that so small a creature as a fly should make so great a buzz, he meddled not with anything that concerned common life.

What should I speak of Theophrastus, who being about to make a speech, became as dumb as if he had met a wolf in his way, which yet would have put courage in a man of war? Or Isokrates, who was so fainthearted that he never tried a speech? Or Tully, that great founder of the Roman eloquence, who could never begin to speak without an odd kind of trembling, like a boy that had the hiccups; which Fabius interprets as an argument of a wise orator and one that was sensible of what he was doing; and while he says it, does he not plainly confess that wisdom is a great obstacle to the true management of business? What would become of them were they to fight it out at blows, that are so dead through fear, when the contest is only with empty words?

Even among the professions those only are in high esteem that come nearest to common sense, that is to say, Folly. Theologians are half-starved, physicists out of heart, astronomers laughed at, and logicians slighted; only the physician is worth all the rest. And among them too, the more unlearned, impudent, or unadvised he is, the more he is esteemed, even among princes. For medicine, especially as it is now practiced by most men, is nothing but a branch of flattery, no less so than rhetoric. Next to them, the second place is given to our lawyers, if not the first; whose profession, though I say it myself, most men laugh at as the ass of philosophy; yet there's scarcely any business, either great or small, but is managed by these asses. These purchase their great titles, while in the meantime the theologian, having run through the whole body of religious thought, sits gnawing a radish as he wars with lice and fleas.

Why should I bother discussing our professors of arts? Self-love is so natural to them all that they had rather part with their father's land than their foolish opinions; but especially actors, fiddlers, orators, and poets, of which the more ignorant each of them is, the more insolently he pleases himself, that is to say struts and spreads out his plumes. And like will to like; nay, the more foolish anything is, the more it is admired; the greater number being ever tickled at the worst things, because, as I said before, most men are so subject to Folly. And therefore if the more foolish a man is, the more he pleases himself and is admired by others, to what purpose should he beat his brains about true knowledge, which first will cost him dear, and next render him the more troublesome and less confident, and, lastly, please only a few?

And now that I consider it, nature has planted, not only in particular men but even in every nation, and scarcely any city is without it, a kind of common self-love. And thus it is that the English, besides other things, lay claim to beauty, music, and feasting. The Scots are proud of their nobility, blood-ties to the crown, and dialectical subtleties. The French think themselves the only well-bred men. The Parisians, excluding all others, arrogate to themselves the only knowledge of theological learning. The Italians affirm they are the only masters of good letters and eloquence, and flatter themselves on this account, that of all others they only are not barbarous. In which kind of happiness those of Rome claim the first place, still dreaming to themselves of somewhat, I know not what, of old Rome. The Venetians fancy themselves happy in the reputation of their nobility. The Greeks, as if they were the only authors of all learning, swell themselves with titles of ancient heroes. The Turks, and all that scum of the truly barbarous, claim for themselves the only true religion and laugh at Christians as superstitious. To this day the Jews confidently expect the coming of the Messiah and obstinately quarrel over their law of Moses. The Spaniards give place to none in the reputation of soldiery. The Germans pride themselves in their tallness of stature and skill in magic.

And not to list every instance, you see, I think, how much satisfaction this Self-love gives to mankind and, in this, her sister Flattery is nearly her equal.

Now if I seem to anyone to have spoken more boldly than truthfully, let us, if you please, look a little into the lives of men, and it will easily appear not only how much they owe to me, but how much they esteem me even from the highest to the lowest. And yet we will not run over the lives of everyone, for that would be too long; but only some few of the great ones, from whence we shall easily conjecture the rest.

For to what purpose is it to say anything of the common people, who without dispute are wholly mine? For they abound everywhere with so many several sorts of Folly, and are every day so busy in inventing new, that a thousand Democritus's are too few for so general a laughter, though we need one more Democritus to laugh at the thousand. It is almost incredible what sport and delight they daily provide for the Gods; for though the Gods set aside their sober morning hours to dispatch business and receive prayers, yet when they begin to be well soused with nectar, and cannot think of anything that's serious, they get themselves up into some part of heaven that's better for viewing, and then look down upon the actions of men. Nor is there anything that pleases them better. Good, good! what an excellent sight it is! How many varieties of fools! for I myself sometimes sit among the poetical Gods.

Here's one desperately in love with a young wench, and the more she slights him the more outrageously he loves her. Another marries a woman's money, not her self. Another's jealousy keeps more eyes on her than Argos. Another becomes a fulltime mourner, and how foolishly he carries it! nay, hires others to bear him company, to make it more ridiculous. Another weeps over his mother-in-law's grave. Another spends all he can on his belly, to be the more hungry after it. Another thinks there is no happiness but in sleep and idleness. Another frets about other men's business, and neglects his own. Another thinks himself rich in refinancing and buying on credit, as we say borrowing from Peter to pay Paul, and in a short

time becomes bankrupt. Another starves himself to enrich his heir. Another for a small and uncertain gain exposes his life to the dangers of seas and storms, which yet no money can restore. Another had rather get riches by war than live peaceably at home.

And some there are that think money easiest attained by courting childless old men with presents; and others again by making love to rich old women; both which afford the Gods most excellent pastime, to see them cheated by those persons they thought to have outwitted. But the most foolish and basest of all others are our merchants, to wit such as venture on everything be it never so dishonest, and manage it no better; who though they lie unceasingly, swear and perjure themselves, steal, deceive, and cheat, yet shuffle themselves into the first rank, and all because they have gold rings on their fingers. Nor are they without their flattering friars that admire them and give them openly the title of honorable, in hopes, no doubt, to get some small snip of it themselves.

There are also a kind of Pythagoreans, with whom all things are held in common, that if they get anything under their cloaks, they make no more scruple of carrying it away than if it were their own by inheritance. There are others too that are only rich in wishful thinking, and while they fancy to themselves pleasant dreams, conceive that enough to make them happy. Some desire to be accounted wealthy abroad, and are yet ready to starve at home. One makes what haste he can to fritter his money away, and another rakes it together by right or wrong. This man is ever laboring for public honors; and another lies sleeping in a chimney corner. A great many undertake endless lawsuits and outvie one another who shall most enrich the crooked judge or corrupt lawyer. One is all for innovations; and another for some great-he-knows-not-what. Another leaves his wife and children at home, and goes to Jerusalem, Rome, or on a pilgrimage to St. James's, where he has no business.

In short, if a man like Menippus of old could look down from the moon, and behold those innumerable rufflings of mankind, he would think he saw a swarm of flies and gnats quarreling among themselves, fighting, laying traps for one another, snatching, playing, wantoning, growing up, growing old, and dying. Nor is it to be believed what stir, what commotions this little creature raises, and yet in how short a time it comes to nothing at all; while sometimes war, other times pestilence, sweeps many thousands away.

But let me be most foolish myself, and one whom Democritus may not only laugh at but deride, if I go one foot further in the discovery of the follies and madnesses of the common people. I'll betake me to them that carry the reputation of wise men, and hunt after that "golden bough," as says the proverb. Among whom the school teachers hold the first place, a generation of men than whom nothing would be more miserable, nothing more wretched, nothing more hated of the Gods, did not I allay the troubles of that pitiful profession with a certain kind of pleasant madness. For they are not only subject to those five afflictions with which Homer begins his Iliad, but six hundred; as being ever hungry and slovenly in their schools—schools, did I say? Nay, rather prisons, sweat shops, or torture chambers—, grown old among a company of boys, deaf with their noise, and wasted away in the stench and nastiness. And yet by my courtesy it is that they think themselves the most excellent of all men; so greatly do they please themselves in frightening a company of fearful boys with a thundering voice and fierce scowls; tormenting them with switches, rods, and whips; and, laying about them without fear or wit, imitate the ass in the lion's skin. In the meantime all that nastiness seems absolute spruceness, that stench a perfume, and that miserable slavery of theirs a kingdom, and such too as they would not exchange their tyranny for the empires of Phalaris or Dionysius.

Nor are they less happy in that new opinion they have taken up of being learned; for whereas most of them beat into boys' heads nothing but nonsense, yet, ye good Gods! what Palemon, what Donatus, do they not scorn in comparison with themselves? And so, I know not by what tricks, they bring it about to their boys' foolish mothers and dolt-headed fathers they pass for such as they fancy themselves.

Perhaps I had better pass over our theologians in silence and not stir this pool, or touch this fair but unsavory stinkweed; as a kind of men that are supercilious beyond comparison, and to that too, implacable; lest setting them about my ears, they attack me with proofs and force me to recant, which if I refuse, they straight away pronounce me a heretic. For this is the thunderbolt with which they frighten those whom they are resolved not to favor. And truly, though there are few others that less willingly acknowledge the kindnesses I have done for them, yet even these too are bound to me for no ordinary benefits; meanwhile being happy in their own opinion, and as if they dwelt in the third heaven, they look with haughtiness on all others as poor creeping things, and could almost find in their hearts to pity them.

And next come those that commonly call themselves "religious" and "monks"; most false in both titles, when a large part of them are farthest from religion, and no men swarm thicker in all places than themselves. Nor can I think of anything that could be more miserable, did I not support them in so many ways. For whereas all men detest them so much, that they take it for ill luck to meet one of them by chance, yet such is their happiness that they flatter themselves. For first, they reckon it one of the main points of piety if they are so illiterate that they can't so much as read. And then when they run over their Offices, which they carry about them, rather by rote than understanding, they believe the Gods more than ordinarily pleased with their braying. And some there are among them that make a great show about their pious poverty, yet roam up and down for the bread they eat; nay, there is scarcely an inn, coach, or ship into which they intrude not, to the no small damage of the commonwealth of beggars. And yet, like pleasant fellows, with all this vileness, ignorance, rudeness, and impudence, they represent to us, for so they call it, the lives of the apostles.

And as to the popes, what should I mention about them? than most of whom though there be nothing more indebted, more servile, more witless, more contemptible, yet they would seem as they were the most excellent of all others. And yet in this only thing no men more' modest, in that they are contented to wear about them gold, jewels, purple, and those other marks of virtue and wisdom, but for the study of the things themselves, they remit it to others; thinking it happiness enough for them that they can call the King Master, having learned the cringe *a la mode,* know when and where to use those titles of Your Grace, My Lord, Your Magnificence; in a word that they are past all shame and can flatter pleasantly. For these are the arts that bespeak a man truly noble and a model courtier.

But if you look into their manner of life you'll find them mere sots, as debauched as Penelope's wooers. They sleep till noon, and have their mercenary Levite come to their bedside, where he chops over his Matins before they are half up. Then to breakfast, which is scarcely done when dinner is ready for them. From thence they go to dice, tables, cards, or entertain themselves with jesters, fools, and gamblers. In the meantime they have one or two snacks and then supper, and after that a banquet, and it would be well, by Jupiter, that there be no more than one.

And in this manner do their hours, days, months, years, age slide away without the least irksomeness. Nay, I have sometimes gone away many inches fatter, to see them speak big words; while each of the ladies believes herself so much nearer the Gods, by how much the longer train she trails after her; while one cardinal edges out another, that he may get the nearer to Jupiter himself; and every one of them pleases himself the more by how much heavier is the gold chain he drapes on his shoulders, as if he meant to show his strength as well as his wealth.

But I forget myself and run beyond my bounds. Though yet, if I shall seem to have spoken anything more boldly or impertinently than I ought, be pleased to consider that not only Folly but a woman said it; remembering in the meantime that Greek proverb, "Sometimes a fool may speak a word in season," unless perhaps you'll say this concerns not women. I see you expect an Epilogue, but give me leave to tell you that you are mistaken if you think I remember anything of what I have said, having foolishly bolted out such a hodgepodge of words. It is an old proverb, "I hate one that remembers what's done over the cup." This is a new one of my own making: "I hate a man that remembers what he hears." Wherefore farewell, clap your hands, live, and drink lustily, my most excellent Disciples of Folly.

Exercises

1. Try to imagine that you are a sixteenth-century college professor. What would be your reaction to Folly's description of "professors of arts." Does her account fit any of your professors?
2. Folly makes some general statements about countries and cities, e.g., the "English lay claim to beauty, music, and feasting." Are any of these observations still valid today? Which ones?
3. Does Folly's description of "school teachers" (elementary and secondary) still have any truth today? To what extent?
4. What does the great popularity of this satire indicate about the literate public of that time? Would a twentieth-century Praise of Folly be equally popular? Why or why not?

Niccolo Machiavelli (1469–1527)

The thorough humanistic education of Niccolo Machiavelli (MAHK-iya-VEL-lee) and his own political experience helped him to reevaluate the role of the state. For medieval thinkers, the Church looked after the spiritual salvation of its flock, the State attended to their physical well-being, and all operated under Divine Law. Machiavelli observed that the Romans had encouraged civic duties and civic pride, but Christians were supposed to detach themselves from public affairs. The obvious solution was to secularize politics. Make the state preeminent and its own justification, and have it function in accordance with the observable facts of human nature. Machiavelli wrote *The Prince* as a guide for the man he and many Italians fervently longed to see: a ruler who would unite Italy under one jurisdiction. This was a manual for action, the first objective analysis of how political power was obtained and kept. Machiavelli's brilliant analysis is detached, objective, and nonjudgmental. It gave the Renaissance its first candid picture of human nature with all of the idealism, both of medievalism and humanism, stripped away.

> For of men it may generally be affirmed that they are thankless, fickle, false, studious to avoid danger, greedy of gain, devoted to you while you are able to confer benefits upon them, and ready, as I have said before, while danger is distant, to shed their blood, and sacrifice their property, their lives and their children for you; but in the hour of need they turn against you. . . . Love is held by the tie of obligation, which, because men are a sorry breed, is broken on every whisper of private interest.

Machiavelli's verdict was not simply the opinion of a misanthrope, soured on the world. The author was a social scientist who investigated human affairs with the same cold detachment that Copernicus used to chart the courses of the planets. After considering the fate of governments from that of Athens to all those of his own time, he came to the conclusion that human beings were beasts, at best, and that the successful ruler is the one who treats people accordingly. Though Italy did not achieve unification until the nineteenth century, Machiavelli's theory of absolutism became a model for the rest of Europe.

Literary Selection

THE PRINCE
Niccolo Machiavelli

Men Who Gain a Princedom through Wicked Deeds

In our times, when Alexander VI was reigning, Liverotto of Fermo—who many years before had been left when little without a father—was brought up by his maternal uncle, named Giovanni Fogliani, and in the early years of his youth was placed to serve as a soldier under Paulo Vitelli, in order that, well versed in that profession, he might attain some excellent position in an army. Paulo afterward dying, he served under Vitellozzo his brother; in a very short time, being quickwitted and vigorous in body and mind, he became the first man in his army. But since he thought it servile to be a subordinate, he determined, with the aid of some citizens of Fermo who preferred slavery rather than freedom for their native city, and with the help of the Vitelleschi, to capture Fermo. So he wrote to Giovanni Fogliani that, having been many years away from home, he wished to come to visit him and his native city and also to inspect his inheritance; and—because he had not striven for anything except to gain honor—in order that his fellow citizens might see that he had not spent his time without results, he wished to come with honor escorted by a hundred horsemen from among his friends and servants; and he begged his uncle to be so kind as to arrange that the people of Fermo would receive him honorably. This would bring honor not merely to him but to Giovanni, whose foster child he was. In no way, thereupon, did Giovanni fall short in any duty he owed his nephew, and he had the people of Fermo receive him honorably. Liverotto then took up his lodging in his own mansion. There, having spent some days and carefully made the secret arrangements that his future wickedness required, he gave a splendid banquet, to which he invited Giovanni Fogliani and all the leading men of Fermo. When the meal was finished and all the other matters customary at such banquets, Liverotto, according to plan, started certain serious discourses, talking of Pope Alexander's greatness and of Cesare his son and of their enterprises. After Giovanni and the others had replied to these discourses, he at once rose up, saying these were things to speak of in a place more secret; and he withdrew to a chamber to which Giovanni and all the other citizens followed. No sooner were they seated than, from secret places in the room, out came soldiers who killed Giovanni and all the others. After this slaughter, Liverotto mounted his horse and overran the city and besieged in the Palace the chief magistrates, so that for fear they were compelled to obey him and to confirm a government of which he made himself prince.

[Liverotto's Success]

When all those were dead who, if they had been discontented, could have injured him, he strengthened himself with new dispositions both civil and military in such a way that for a year, during which he held the princedom, not merely was he safe in the city of Fermo, but he had become an object of fear to all his neighbors. His overthrow, indeed, would have been as difficult as that of Agathocles if he had not let Cesare Borgia deceive him at Sinigaglia when, as I said above, the Duke captured the Orsini and Vitelli. There Liverotto too was taken, a year after the parricide he committed, and along with Vitellozzo, who had been his instructor in good and evil, he was strangled.

[Cruelty Prudently Used]

Some may wonder how it came about that Agathocles and others like him, after countless betrayals and cruelties, could for a long time live safely in their native places and defend themselves from foreign enemies, and the citizens never plotted against them; yet many others, even in peaceful times, could not by means of cruelty carry on their governments—and so much the less in the uncertain times of war. I believe this comes from cruelties badly used or well used. *Well used* we call those (if of what is bad we can use the word *well*) that a conqueror carries out at a single stroke, as a result of his need to secure himself, and then does not persist in, but transmutes into the greatest possible benefits to his subjects. *Badly used* are those which, though few in the beginning, rather increase with time than disappear. Princes who follow the first method can, before God and before men, make some improvement in their position, as Agathocles could; the others cannot possibly sustain themselves.

On Taking a State

It is to be noted, that in taking a state the conqueror must arrange to commit all his cruelties at once, so as not to have to recur to them every day, and so as to be able, by not making fresh changes, to reassure people and win them over by benefiting them. Whoever acts otherwise, either through timidity or bad counsels, is always obliged to stand with knife in hand, and can never depend on his subjects, because they, owing to continually fresh injuries, are unable to depend upon him. For injuries should be done all together, so that being less tasted, they will give less offence. Benefits should be granted little by little, so that they may be better enjoyed. And above all, a prince must live with his subjects in such a way that no accident of good or evil fortune can deflect him from his course; for necessity arising in adverse times, severe measures are too late, and the good that you do does not profit, as it is judged to be forced upon you, and you will derive no benefit whatever from it.

Of the Things for Which Men, and Especially Princes, Are Praised or Blamed

It now remains to be seen what are the methods and rules for a prince as regards his subjects and friends. And as I know that many have written of this, I fear that my writing about it may be deemed presumptuous, differing as I do, especially in this matter, from the opinions of others. But my intention being to write something of use to those who understand, it appears to me more proper to go to the real truth of the matter than to its imagination; and many have imagined republics and principalities which have never been seen or known to exist in reality; for how we live is so far removed from how we ought to live, that he who abandons what is done for what ought to be done, will rather learn to bring about his own ruin than his preservation. A man who wishes to make a profession of goodness in everything must necessarily come to grief among so many who are not good. Therefore it is necessary for a prince, who wishes to maintain himself, to learn how not to be good, and to use this knowledge and not use it, according to the necessity of the case.

Leaving on one side, then, those things which concern only an imaginary prince, and speaking of those that are real, I state that all men, and especially princes, who are placed at a greater height, are reputed for certain qualities which bring them either praise or blame. Thus one is considered liberal, another miserly; one a free giver, another rapacious: one cruel, another merciful; one a breaker of his word, another trust-worthy; one effeminate and pusillanimous, another fierce and high-spirited; one humane, another haughty; one lascivious, another chaste; one frank, another astute; one hard, another easy; one serious, another frivolous; one religious, another an unbeliever, and so on. I know that every one will admit that it would be highly praiseworthy in a prince to possess all the above-named qualities that are reputed good, but as they cannot all be possessed or observed, human conditions not permitting of it, it is necessary that he should be prudent enough to avoid the scandal of those vices which would lose him the state, and guard himself if possible against those which will not lose it to him, but if not able to, he can indulge them with less scruple. And yet he must not mind incurring the scandal of those vices, without which it would be difficult to save the state, for if one considers well, it will be found that some things which seem virtues would, if followed, lead to one's ruin, and some others which appear vices result in one's greater security and well-being.

Beginning now with the first qualities above named, I say that it would be well to be considered liberal; nevertheless liberality such as the world understands it will injure you, because if used virtuously and in the proper way, it will not be known, and you will incur the disgrace of the contrary vice. But one who wishes to obtain the reputation of liberality among men, must not omit every kind of sumptuous display, and to such an extent that a prince of this character will consume by such means all his resources, and will be at last compelled, if he wishes to maintain his name for liberality, to impose heavy taxes on his people, become extortionate, and do everything possible to obtain money. This will make his subjects begin to hate him, and he will be little esteemed being poor, so that having by this liberality injured many and benefited but few, he will feel the first little disturbance and be endangered by every peril. If he recognizes this and wishes to change his system, he incurs at once the charge of niggardliness.

A prince, therefore, not being able to exercise this virtue of liberality without risk if it be known, must not, if he be prudent, object to be called miserly. In course of time he will be thought more liberal, when it is seen that by his parsimony his revenue is sufficient, that he can defend himself against those who make war on him, and undertake enterprises without burdening his people, so that he is really liberal to all those from whom he does not take, who are infinite in number, and niggardly to all to whom he does not give, who are few. In our times we have seen nothing great done except by those who have been esteemed niggardly; the others have all been ruined.

Of Cruelty and Clemency, and Whether It Is Better To Be Loved or Feared

Proceeding to the other qualities before named, I say that every prince must desire to be considered merciful and not cruel. He must, however, take care not to misuse this mercifulness. Cesare Borgia was considered cruel, but his cruelty had brought order to the Romagna, united it, and reduced it to peace and fealty. If this is considered well, it will be seen that he was really much more merciful than the Florentine people, who, to avoid the name of cruelty, allowed Pistoia to be destroyed. A prince, therefore, must not mind incurring the charge of cruelty for the purpose of keeping his subjects united and faithful; for, with a very few examples, he will be more merciful than those, who, from excess of tenderness, allow disorders to arise, from whence spring bloodshed and rapine; for these as a rule injure the whole community, while the executions carried out by the prince injure only individuals. And of all princes, it is impossible for a new prince to escape the reputation of cruelty, new states being always full of dangers.

Nevertheless, he must be cautious in believing and acting, and must not be afraid of his own shadow, and must proceed in a temperate manner with prudence and humanity, so that too much confidence does not render him incautious, and too much diffidence does not render him intolerant.

From this arises the question whether it is better to be loved more than feared, or feared more than loved. The reply is, that one ought to be both feared and loved, but as it is difficult for the two to go together, it is much safer to be feared than loved, if one of the two has to be wanting. For it may be said of men in general that they are ungrateful, voluble, dissemblers, anxious to avoid danger, and covetous of gain; as long as you benefit them, they are entirely yours; they offer you their blood, their goods, their life, and their children, as I have before said, when the necessity is remote; but when it approaches, they revolt. And the prince who has relied solely on their words, without making other preparations, is ruined; for the friendship which is gained by purchase and not through grandeur and nobility of spirit is bought but not secured, and at a pinch is not to be expended in your service. And men have less scruple in offending one who makes himself loved than one who makes himself feared; for love is held by a chain of obligation which, men being selfish, is broken whenever it serves their purpose; but fear is maintained by a dread of punishment which never fails.

In What Way Princes Must Keep Faith

How laudable it is for a prince to keep good faith and live with integrity, and not with astuteness, every one knows. Still the experience of our times shows those princes to have done great things who have had little regard for good faith, and who have been able by astuteness to confuse men's brains, and who have ultimately overcome those who have made loyalty their foundation.

You must know, then, that there are two methods of fighting, the one by law, the other by force: the first method is that of men, the second of beasts; but as the first method is often insufficient, one must have recourse to the second. It is therefore necessary for a prince to know well how to use both the beast and the man.

A prince being thus obligated to know well how to act as a beast must imitate the fox and the lion, for the lion cannot protect himself from traps, and the fox cannot defend himself from wolves. One must therefore be a fox to recognize traps, and a lion to frighten wolves. Those that wish to be only lions do not understand this. Therefore, a prudent ruler ought not to keep faith when by so doing it would be against his interest, and when the reasons which made him bind himself no longer exist. If men were all good, this precept would not be a good one; but as they are bad, and would not observe their faith with you, so you are not bound to keep faith with them. Nor have legitimate grounds ever failed a prince who wished to show tolerable excuse for the non-fulfillment of his promise. Of this one could furnish an infinite number of modern examples, and show how many times peace has been broken, and how many promises rendered worthless, by the faithlessness of princes, and those that have been able to imitate the fox have succeeded best. But it is necessary to be able to disguise this character well, and to be a great feigner and dissembler; and men are so simple and so ready to obey present necessities, that one who deceives will always find those who allow themselves to be deceived.

I will only mention one modern instance. Alexander VI did nothing else but deceive men, he thought of nothing else, and found the occasion for it; no man was ever more able to give assurances, or affirmed things with stronger oaths, and no man observed them less; however, he always succeeded in his deceptions, as he well knew this aspect of things.

It is not, therefore, necessary for a prince to have all the above-named qualities, but it is very necessary to seem to have them. I would even be bold to say that to possess them and always to observe them is dangerous, but to appear to possess them is useful. Thus it is well to seem merciful, faithful, humane, sincere, religious, and also to be so; but you must have the mind so disposed that when it is needful to be otherwise you may be able to change to the opposite qualities. And it must be understood that a prince, and especially a new prince, cannot observe all those things which are considered good in men, being often obliged, in order to maintain the state, to act against faith, against charity, against humanity, and against religion. And, therefore, he must have a mind disposed to adapt itself according to the wind, and as the variations of fortune dictate, and, as I said before, not deviate from what is good, if possible, but be able to do evil if constrained.

A prince must take great care that nothing goes out of his mouth which is not full of the above-named five qualities, and, to see and hear him, he should seem to be all mercy, faith, integrity, humanity, and religion. And nothing is more necessary than to seem to have this last quality, for men in general judge more by the eyes than by the hands, for every one can see, but very few have to feel. Everybody sees what you appear to be, few feel what you are, and those few will not dare to oppose themselves to the many, who have the majesty of the state to defend them; and in the actions of men, and especially of princes, from which there is no appeal, the end justifies the means. Let a prince therefore aim at conquering and maintaining the state, and the means will always be judged honourable and praised by everyone, for the vulgar is always taken by appearances and the issue of the event; and the world consists only of the vulgar, and the few who are not vulgar are isolated when the many have a rallying point in the prince. A certain prince of the present time, whom it is well not to name, never does anything but preach peace and good faith, but he is really a great enemy to both, and either of them, had he observed them, would have lost him state or reputation on many occasions.

Exercises

1. What does Machiavelli mean by cruelty "well used"? Give some contemporary examples of cruelty both "well used" and "badly used." Is Machiavelli correct? Have there been any twentieth-century rulers who were overthrown because of their badly used cruelties? Which ones? Regimes that are headed for destruction?
2. Is it better, according to Machiavelli, for a ruler to be loved or feared? How would the leaders of the U.S.S.R. and the People's Republic of China respond?

3. Machiavelli contends that a ruler does not have to keep good faith. Why not? Under what circumstances? Have any American presidents acted like "a fox and a lion"? Name one or two.

Michelangelo Buonarotti (1475–1564)

The musicality of sonnets by Petrarch and his followers was the accepted style of the Italian Renaissance, but Michelangelo followed his own course in his poetry just as he did in sculpting and painting. His sonnets were, as he himself said, "unprofessional, rude, and rough." Michelangelo did not consider himself a poet in Petrarchian terms but he was praised at the time as a poet in his own right. His sonnets, like the personality of their creator, are powerful and unique and constitute, at their best, the finest lyric Italian poetry of the Renaissance. No knowledge of Michelangelo the sculptor and painter can be complete without knowing the artist as poet. The following two poems were written for Michelangelo's close friend Tommaso de' Cavalieri.

Literary Selections

SONNET XXX

(Veggio co' bei vostri occhi)
Michelangelo Buonarotti

With your fair eyes a charming light I see,
　　For which my own blind eyes would peer in vain;
　　Stayed by your feet the burden I sustain
　　Which my lame feet find all too strong for me;
Wingless upon your pinions forth I fly;
　　Heavenward your spirit stirreth me to strain;
　　E'en as you will, I blush and blanch again,
　　Freeze in the sun, burn 'neath a frosty sky.
Your will includes and is the lord of mine;
　　Life to my thoughts within your heart is given;
　　My words begin to breathe upon your breath:
Like to the moon am I, that cannot shine
　　Alone; for lo! our eyes see nought in heaven
　　Save what the living sun illumineth.

SONNET XXXII

(S'un casto amor)
Michelangelo Buonarotti

If love be chaste, if virtue conquer ill,
　　If fortune bind both lovers in one bond,
　　If either at the other's grief despond,
　　If both be governed by one life, one will;
If in two bodies one soul triumph still,
　　Raising the twain from earth to heaven beyond,
　　If Love with one blow and one golden wand
　　Have power both smitten breasts to pierce and thrill;
If each the other love, himself forgoing,
　　With such delight, such savour, and so well,
　　That both to one sole end their wills combine;
If thousands of these thoughts, all thought outgoing,
　　Fail the least part of their firm love to tell:
　　Say, can mere angry spite this knot untwine?

Michelangelo met Vittoria Colonna, the marquise of Pescara, while he was working on the Last Judgment (1536–1541; see fig. 18.38) in the Sistine Chapel. Probably the only woman he ever loved, Vittoria was an astute judge of his work, but valued the man even above his creations. Michelangelo viewed her as "God inside a woman." Her death in 1547 was a painful loss for a seventy-two-year-old artist who was already obsessed with the fear of death and hell. Like much of the poetry written for Vittoria, Michelangelo used sculpture as a theme; God had created Adam and that made him a sculptor.

SONNET LXI

(Se'l mie rozzo martello)
After the Death of Vittoria Colonna
Michelangelo Buonarotti

When my rude hammer to the stubborn stone
　　Gives human shape, now that, now this, at will,
　　Following his hand who wields and guides it still,
　　It moves upon another's feet alone:
But that which dwells in heaven, the world doth fill
　　With beauty by pure motions of its own;
　　And since tools fashion tools which else were none,
　　Its life makes all that lives with living skill.
Now, for that every stroke excels the more
　　The higher at the forge it doth ascend,
　　Her soul that fashioned mine hath sought the skies:
Wherefore unfinished I must meet my end,
　　If God, the great artificer, denies
　　That aid which was unique on earth before.

Exercise

1. Compare the style of these sonnets with that of Petrarch's poems, granting that all are in English translation. Compare and contrast the vocabulary of the two poets. Petrarch, for example, uses verbs like *shone, flamed, flow, beguile, smile,* and *rising;* Michelangelo's verbs include *fly, stirreth, strain, bind, conquer, pierce, thrill,* and *spite.* Are there similar parallels in the adjectives and adverbs?

Baldassare Castiglione (1478–1529)

As discussed previously, Renaissance civilization reasserted "the dignity of the human race" (Cicero) and the worth of the individual. Life and human institutions could be shaped to be more efficient and more pleasant, leading to a good life that became, at its best, an art form—the art of gracious living. True ladies and gentlemen had disciplined intellects, good manners, and impeccable taste. Those who aspired to this ideal studied the countless manuals that became available, most especially *The Book of the Courtier* by Count Baldassare Castiglione (kas-teel-YO-nay; see fig. 18.32). Using personalities from his own circle at the court of the Duke of Urbino, Castiglione designed a kind of Platonic dialogue to set up his utopian social society, a model for civilized people of every age, including today.

As was the custom, the evening gathering of the court circle proposed various games, actually civil discourses about subjects agreeable to all. This selection begins in Book I, Chapter 12, when Federico Fregoso proposes the game that will be played for four evenings.

Literary Selection

THE BOOK OF THE COURTIER
Baldassare Castiglione

"My Lady, I would it were permitted me, as it sometimes is, to assent to another's proposal; since for my part I would readily approve any of the games proposed by these gentlemen, for I really think that all of them would be amusing. But not to break our rule, I say that anyone who wished to praise our court,—laying aside the merit of our lady Duchess, which with her divine virtue would suffice to lift from earth to heaven the meanest souls that are in the world,—might well say without suspicion of flattery, that in all Italy it would perhaps be hard to find so many cavaliers so singularly admirable and so excellent in divers other matters besides the chief concerns of chivalry, as are now to be found here: wherefore if anywhere there be men who deserve to be called good Courtiers and who are able to judge of what pertains to the perfection of Courtiership, it is reasonable to believe that they are here. So, to repress the many fools who by impudence and folly think to win the name of good Courtier, I would that this evening's game might be, that we select some one of the company and give him the task of portraying a perfect Courtier, explaining all the conditions and special qualities requisite in one who deserves this title; and as to those things that shall not appear sound, let everyone be allowed to contradict, as in the schools of the philosophers it is allowed to contradict anyone who proposes a thesis."

Messer Federico was continuing his discourse still further, when my lady Emilia interrupted him and said:

"This, if it pleases my lady Duchess, shall for the present be our game."

My lady Duchess answered:

"It does please me."

Then nearly all those present began to say, both to my lady Duchess and among themselves, that this was the finest game that could possibly be; and without waiting for each other's answer, they entreated my lady Emilia to decide who should begin. She turned to my lady Duchess and said:

"Command, my Lady, him who it best pleases you should have this task; for I do not wish, by selecting one rather than another, to seem to decide whom I think more competent in this matter than the rest, and so do wrong to anyone."

My lady Duchess replied:

"Nay, make this choice yourself, and take heed lest by not obeying you give an example to the others, so that they too prove disobedient in their turn."

13.—At this my lady Emilia laughed and said to Count Ludovico da Canossa:

"Then not to lose more time, you, Count, shall be the one to take this enterprise after the manner that messer Federico has described; not indeed because we account you so good a Courtier that you know what befits one, but because, if you say everything wrong as we hope you will, the game will be more lively, for everyone will then have something to answer you; while if someone else had this task who knew more than you, it would be impossible to contradict him in anything, because he would tell the truth, and so the game would be tedious."

The Count answered quickly:

"Whoever told the truth, my Lady, would run no risk of lacking contradiction, so long as you were present;" and after some laughter at this retort, he continued: "But truly I would fain escape this burden, it seeming to me too heavy, and I being conscious that what you said in jest is very true; that is, that I do not know what befits a good Courtier: and I do not seek to prove this with further argument, because, as I do not practise the rules of Courtiership, one may judge that I do not know them; and I think my blame may be the less, for sure it is worse not to wish to do well than not to know how. Yet, since it so happens that you are pleased to have me bear this burden, I neither can nor will refuse it, in order not to contravene our rule and your judgment, which I rate far higher than my own."

14.—"I wish, then, that this Courtier of ours should be nobly born and of gentle race; because it is far less unseemly for one of ignoble birth to fail in worthy deeds, than for one of noble birth, who, if he strays from the path of his predecessors, stains his family name, and not only fails to achieve but loses what has been achieved already; for noble birth is like a bright lamp that manifests and makes visible good and evil deeds, and kindles and stimulates to virtue both by fear of shame and by hope of praise. And since this splendour of nobility does not illumine the deeds of the humbly born, they lack that stimulus and fear of shame, nor do they feel any obligation to advance beyond what their predecessors have done; while to the nobly born it seems a reproach not to reach at least the goal set them by their ancestors. And thus it nearly always happens that both in the profession of arms and in other worthy pursuits the most famous men have been of noble birth, because nature has implanted in everything that hidden seed which gives a certain force and quality of its own essence to all things that are derived from it, and makes them like itself: as we see not only in the breeds of horses and of other animals, but also in trees, the shoots of which nearly always resemble the trunk; and if they sometimes degenerate, it arises from poor cultivation. And so it is with men, who if rightly trained are nearly always like those from whom they spring, and often better; but if there be no one to give them proper care, they become like savages and never reach perfection.

"It is true that, by favour of the stars or of nature, some men are endowed at birth with such graces that they seem not to have been born, but rather as if some god had formed them with his very hands and adorned them with every excellence of mind and body. So too there are many men so foolish and rude that one cannot but think that nature brought them into the world out of contempt or mockery. Just as these can usually accomplish little even with constant diligence and good training, so with slight pains those others reach the highest summit of excellence. And to give you an instance: you see my lord Don Ippolito d'Este, Cardinal of

Ferrara, who has enjoyed such fortune from his birth, that his person, his aspect, his words and all his movements are so disposed and imbued with this grace, that—although he is young—he exhibits among the most aged prelates such weight of character that he seems fitter to teach than to be taught; likewise in conversation with men and women of every rank, in games, in pleasantry and in banter, he has a certain sweetness and manners so gracious, that whoso speaks with him or even sees him, must needs remain attached to him forever.

"But to return to our subject: I say that there is a middle state between perfect grace on the one hand and senseless folly on the other; and those who are not thus perfectly endowed by nature, with study and toil can in great part polish and amend their natural defects. Besides his noble birth, then, I would have the Courtier favored in this regard also, and endowed by nature not only with talent and beauty of person and feature, but with a certain grace and (as we say) air that shall make him at first sight pleasing and agreeable to all who see him; and I would have this an ornament that should dispose and unite all his actions, and in his outward aspect give promise of whatever is worthy the society and favour of every great lord."

15.—Here, without waiting longer, my lord Gaspar Pallavicino said:

"In order that our game may have the form prescribed, and that we may not seem to slight the privilege given us to contradict, I say that this nobility of birth does not appear to me so essential in the Courtier; and if I thought I were saying what was new to any of us, I should cite instances of many men born of the noblest blood who have been full of vices; and on the other hand, of many men among the humbly born who by their virtue have made their posterity illustrious. And if what you just said be true, namely that there is in everything this occult influence of the original seed, then we should all be in the same case, because we had the same origin, nor would any man be more noble than another. But as to our differences and grades of eminence and obscurity, I believe there are many other causes: among which I rate fortune to be chief; for we see her holding sway in all mundane affairs, often amusing herself by lifting to heaven whom she pleases (although wholly without merit), and burying in the depths those most worthy to be exalted.

"I quite agree with what you say as to the good fortune of those endowed from birth with advantages of mind and body: but this is seen as well among the humbly born as among the nobly born, since nature has no such subtle distinctions as these; and often, as I said, the highest gifts of nature are found among the most obscure. Therefore, since this nobility of birth is won neither by talent nor by strength nor by craft, and is rather the merit of our predecessors than our own, it seems to me too extravagant to maintain that if our Courtier's parents be humbly born, all his good qualities are spoiled, and that all those other qualifications that you mentioned do not avail to raise him to the summit of perfection; I mean talent, beauty of feature, comeliness of person, and that grace which makes him always charming to everyone at first sight."

16.—Then Count Ludovico replied:

"I do not deny that the same virtues may rule the low-born and the noble: but (not to repeat what we have said already or the many other arguments that could be adduced in praise of noble birth, which is honoured always and by everyone, it being reasonable that good should beget good), since we have to form a Courtier without flaw and endowed with every praiseworthy quality, it seems to me necessary to make him nobly born, as well for many other reasons as for universal opinion, which is at once disposed in favour of noble birth. For if there be two Courtiers who have as yet given no impression of themselves by good or evil acts, as soon as the one is known to have been born a gentleman and the other not, he who is low-born will be far less esteemed by everyone than he who is high-born, and will need much effort and time to make upon men's minds that good impression which the other will have achieved in a moment and merely by being a gentleman. And how important these impressions are, everyone can easily understand: for in our own case we have seen men present themselves in this house, who, being silly and awkward in the extreme, yet had throughout Italy the reputation of very great Courtiers; and although they were detected and recognized at last, still they imposed upon us for many days, and maintained in our minds that opinion of them which they first found impressed there, although they conducted themselves after the slightness of their worth. We have seen others, held at first in small esteem, then admirably successful at the last.

"And of these mistakes there are various causes: and among others, the regard of princes, who in their wish to perform miracles sometimes undertake to bestow favour on a man who seems to them to merit disfavour. And often too they are themselves deceived; but since they always have a host of imitators, their favour begets very great fame, which chiefly guides our judgments: and if we find anything that seems contrary to common opinion, we suspect that it is we ourselves who are wrong, and always seek for something hidden: because it seems that these universal opinions must after all be founded on fact and spring from rational causes; and because our minds are very prone to love and hate, as is seen in battle-shows and games and every other sort of contest, wherein the spectators without apparent cause become partisans of one side, with eager wish that it may win and the other lose. In our opinion of men's character also, good or evil fame sways our minds to one of these two passions from the start; and thus it happens that we usually judge with love or hate. You see then how important this first impression is, and how he ought to strive to make a good one at the outset, who thinks to hold the rank and name of good Courtier.

17.—"But to come to some details, I am of opinion that the principal and true profession of the Courtier ought to be that of arms; which I would have him follow actively above all else, and be known among others as bold and strong, and loyal to whomsoever he serves. And he will win a reputation for these good qualities by exercising them at all times and in all places, since one may never fail in this without severest censure. And just as among women, their fair fame once sullied never recovers its first lustre, so the reputation of a gentleman who bears arms, if once it be in the least tarnished with cowardice or other disgrace, remains forever infamous before the world and full of ignominy. Therefore the more our Courtier excels in this art, the more he will be worthy of praise; and yet I do not deem essential in him that perfect knowledge of things and those other qualities that befit a commander; since this would be too wide a sea, let us be content, as we have said, with perfect loyalty and unconquered courage, and that he be always seen to possess them. For the courageous are often recognized even more in small things than in great; and frequently in perils of importance and where there are many spectators, some men are to be found, who, although their hearts be dead within them, yet, moved by shame or by the presence of others, press forward almost with their eyes shut, and do their duty God knows how. While on occasions of little moment, when they think they can avoid putting themselves in danger without being detected, they are glad to keep safe. But those who, even when they do not expect to be observed or seen or recognized by anyone, show their ardour and neglect nothing, however paltry, that may be laid to their charge,—they have that strength of mind which we seek in our Courtier.

"Not that we would have him look so fierce, or go about blustering, or say that he has taken his cuirass to wife, or threaten with those grim scowls that we have often seen in Berto; because to such men as this, one might justly say that which a brave lady jestingly said in gentle company to one whom I will not name at present; who, being invited by her out of compliment to dance, refused not only that, but to listen to the music, and many other entertainments proposed to him,—saying always that such silly trifles were not his business; so that at last the lady said, 'What is your business, then?' He replied with a sour look, 'To fight.' Then the lady at once said, 'Now that you are in no war and out of fighting trim, I should think it were a good thing to have yourself well oiled, and to stow yourself with all your battle harness in a closet until you be needed, lest you grow more rusty than you are;' and so, amid much laughter from the bystanders, she left the discomfited fellow to his silly presumption.

"Therefore let the man we are seeking, be very bold, stern, and always among the first, where the enemy are to be seen; and in every other place, gentle, modest, reserved, above all things avoiding ostentation and that impudent self-praise by which men ever excite hatred and disgust in all who hear them."

18.—Then my lord Gaspar replied:

"As for me, I have known few men excellent in anything whatever, who do not praise themselves; and it seems to me that this may well be permitted them; for when anyone who feels himself to be of worth, sees that he is not known to the ignorant by his works, he is offended that his worth should lie buried, and needs must in some way hold it up to view, in order that he may not be cheated of the fame that is the true reward of worthy effort. Thus among the ancient authors, whoever carries weight seldom fails to praise himself. They indeed are insufferable who do this without desert, but such we do not presume our Courtier to be."

The Count then said:

"If you heard what I said, it was impudent and indiscriminate self-praise that I censured: and as you say, we surely ought not to form a bad opinion of a brave man who praises himself modestly, nay we ought rather to regard such praise as better evidence than if it came from the mouth of others. I say, however, that he, who in praising himself runs into no error and incurs no annoyance or envy at the hands of those that hear him, is a very discreet man indeed and merits praise from others in addition to that which he bestows upon himself; because it is a very difficult matter."

Then my lord Gaspar said:

"You must teach us that."

The Count replied:

"Among the ancient authors there is no lack of those who have taught it; but to my thinking, the whole art consists in saying things in such a way that they shall not seem to be said to that end, but let fall so naturally that it was impossible not to say them, and while seeming always to avoid self-praise, yet to achieve it; but not after the manner of those boasters, who open their mouths and let the words come forth haphazard. Like one of our friends a few days ago, who, being quite run through the thigh with a spear at Pisa, said he thought it was a fly that had stung him; and another man said he kept no mirror in his room because, when angry, he became so terrible to look at, that the sight of himself would have frightened him too much."

Everyone laughed at this, but messer Cesare Gonzaga added:

"Why do you laugh? Do you not know that Alexander the Great, on hearing the opinion of a philosopher to be that there was an infinite number of worlds, began to weep, and being asked why he wept, replied, 'Because I have not yet conquered one of them;' as if he would fain have vanquished all? Does not this seem to you a greater boast than that about the fly-sting?"

Then the Count said:

"Yes, and Alexander was a greater man than he who made the other speech. But extraordinary men are surely to be pardoned when they assume much; for he who has great things to do must needs have daring to do them, and confidence in himself, and must not be abject or mean in spirit, yet very modest in speech, showing less confidence in himself that he has, lest his self-confidence lead to rashness."

19.—The Count now paused a little, and messer Bernardo Bibbiena said, laughing:

"I remember what you said earlier, that this Courtier of ours must be endowed by nature with beauty of countenance and person, and with a grace that shall make him so agreeable. Grace and beauty of countenance I think I certainly possess, and this is the reason why so many ladies are ardently in love with me, as you know; but I am rather doubtful as to the beauty of my person, especially as regards these legs of mine, which seem to me decidedly less well proportioned than I should wish: as to my bust and other members however, I am quite content. Pray, now, describe a little more in particular the sort of body that the Courtier is to have, so that I may dismiss this doubt and set my mind at rest."

After some laughter at this, the Count continued:

"Of a certainty that grace of countenance can be truly said to be yours, nor need I cite further example than this to show what manner of thing it is, for we unquestionably perceive your aspect to be most agreeable and pleasing to everyone, albeit the lineaments of it are not very delicate. Still it is of a manly cast and at the same time full of grace; and this characteristic is to be found in many different types of countenance. And of such sort I would have our Courtier's aspect; not so soft and effeminate as is sought by many, who not only curl their hair and pluck their brows, but gloss their faces with all those arts employed by the most wanton and unchaste women in the world; and in their walk, posture and every act, they seem so limp and languid that their limbs are like to fall apart; and they pronounce their words so mournfully that they appear about to expire upon the spot: and the more they find themselves with men of rank, the more they affect such tricks. Since nature has not made them women, as they seem to wish to appear and be, they should be treated not as good women but as public harlots, and driven not merely from the courts of great lords but from the society of honest men.

20.—"Then coming to the bodily frame, I say it is enough if this be neither extremely short nor tall, for both of these conditions excite a certain contemptuous surprise, and men of either sort are gazed upon in much the same way that we gaze on monsters. Yet if we must offend in one of the two extremes, it is preferable to fall a little short of the just measure of height than to exceed it, for besides often being dull of intellect, men thus huge of body are also unfit for every exercise of agility, which thing I should much wish in the Courtier. And so I would have him well built and shapely of limb, and would have him show strength and lightness and suppleness, and know all bodily exercises that befit a man of war; whereof I think the first should be to handle every sort of weapon well on foot and on horse, to understand the advantages of each, and especially to be familiar with those weapons that are ordinarily used among gentlemen; for besides the use of them in war, where such subtlety in contrivance is perhaps not needful, there frequently arise differences between one gentleman and another, which afterwards result in duels often fought with such weapons as happen at the moment to be within reach: thus knowledge of this kind is a very safe thing. Nor am I one of those who say that skill is forgotten in the hour of need; for he whose skill forsakes him at such a time, indeed gives token that he has already lost heart and head through fear.

21.—"Moreover I deem it very important to know how to wrestle, for it is a great help in the use of all kinds of weapons on foot. Then, both for his own sake and for that of his friends, he must understand the quarrels and differences that may arise, and must be quick to seize an advantage, always showing courage and prudence in all things. Nor should he be too ready to fight except when honour demands it; for besides the great danger that the uncertainty of fate entails, he who rushes into such affairs recklessly and without urgent cause, merits the severest censure even though he be successful. But when he finds himself so far engaged that he cannot withdraw without reproach, he ought to be most deliberate, both in the preliminaries to the duel and in the duel itself, and always show readiness and daring. Nor must he act like some, who fritter the affair away in disputes and controversies, and who, having the choice of weapons, select those that neither cut nor pierce, and arm themselves as if they were expecting a cannonade; and thinking it enough not to be defeated, stand ever on the defensive and retreat,—showing therein their utter cowardice. And thus they make themselves a laughing-stock for boys, like those two men of Ancona who fought at Perugia not long since, and made everyone laugh who saw them."

"And who were they?" asked my lord Gaspar Pallavicino.

"Two cousins," replied messer Cesare.

Then the Count said:

"In their fighting they were as like as two brothers;" and soon continued: "Even in time of peace weapons are often used in various exercises, and gentlemen appear in public shows before the people and ladies and great lords. For this reason I would have our Courtier a perfect horseman in every kind of seat; and besides understanding horses and what pertains to riding, I would have him use all possible care and diligence to lift himself a little beyond the rest in everything, so that he may be ever recognized as eminent above all others. And as we read of Alcibiades that he surpassed all the nations with whom he lived, each in their particular province, so I would have this Courtier of ours excel all others, and each in that which is most their profession. And as it is the especial pride of the Italians to ride well with the rein, to govern wild horses with consummate skill, and to play at tilting and jousting,—in these things let him be among the best of the Italians. In tourneys and in the arts of defence and attack, let him shine among the best in France. In stick-throwing, bull-fighting, and in casting spears and darts, let him excel among the Spaniards. But above everything he should temper all his movements with a certain good judgment and grace, if he wishes to merit that universal favour which is too greatly prized.

22.—"There are also many other exercises, which although not immediately dependent upon arms, yet are closely connected therewith, and greatly foster manly sturdiness; and one of the chief among these seems to me to be the chase, because it bears a certain likeness to war: and truly it is an amusement for great lords and befitting a man at court, and furthermore it is seen to have been much cultivated among the ancients. It is fitting also to know how to swim, to leap, to run, to throw stones, for besides the use that may be made of this in war, a man often has occasion to show what he can do in such matters; whence good esteem is to be won, especially with the multitude, who must be taken into account withal. Another admirable exercise, and one very befitting a man at court, is the game of tennis, in which are well shown the disposition of the body, the quickness and suppleness of every member, and all those qualities that are seen in nearly every other exercise. Nor less highly do I esteem vaulting on horse, which although it be fatiguing and difficult, makes a man very light and dexterous more than any other thing; and besides its utility, if this lightness is accompanied by grace, it is to my thinking a finer show than any of the others.

"Our Courtier having once become more than fairly expert in these exercises, I think he should leave the others on one side: such as turning summersaults, rope-walking, and the like, which savour of the mountebank and little befit a gentleman.

"But since one cannot devote himself to such fatiguing exercises continually, and since repetition becomes very tiresome and abates the admiration felt for what is rare, we must always diversify our life with various occupations. For this reason I would have our Courtier sometimes descend to quieter and more tranquil exercises, and in order to escape envy and to entertain himself agreeably with everyone, let him do whatever others do, yet never departing from praiseworthy deeds, and governing himself with that good judgment which will keep him from all folly; but let him laugh, jest, banter, frolic and dance, yet in such fashion that he shall always appear genial and discreet, and that everything he may do or say shall be stamped with grace."

Book III is devoted to the qualities of the Court Lady, who should be affable, modest, decorous, virtuous, courageous, educated, and intelligent. The following excerpt summarizes the qualities of the ideal Court Lady.

9.—"And since my lord Gaspar further asks what these many things are whereof she ought to have knowledge, and in what manner she ought to converse, and whether her virtues ought to contribute to her conversation,—I say I would have her acquainted with that which these gentlemen wished the Courtier to know. And of the exercises that we have said do not befit her, I would have her at least possess such understanding as we may have of things that we do not practise; and this in order that she may know how to praise and value cavaliers more or less, according to their deserts.

"And to repeat in a few words part of what has been already said, I wish this Lady to have knowledge of letters, music, painting, and to know how to dance and make merry; accompanying the other precepts that have been taught the Courtier with discreet modesty and with the giving of a good impression of herself. And thus, in her talk, her laughter, her play, her jesting, in short, in everything, she will be very graceful, and will entertain appropriately, and with witticisms and pleasantries befitting her, everyone who shall come before her. And although continence, magnanimity, temperance, strength of mind, prudence, and the other virtues, seem to have little to do with entertainment, I would have her adorned with all of them, not so much for the sake of entertainment (albeit even there they can be of service), as in order that she may be full of virtue, and to the end that these virtues may render her worthy of being honoured, and that her every act may be governed by them."

10.—My lord Gaspar then said, laughing:

"Since you have given women letters and continence and magnanimity and temperance, I only marvel that you would not also have them govern cities, make laws, and lead armies, and let the men stay at home to cook or spin."

The Magnifico replied, also laughing:

"Perhaps even this would not be amiss." Then he added: "Do you not know that Plato, who certainly was no great friend to women, gave them charge over the city, and gave all other martial duties to the men? Do you not believe that there are many to be found who would know how to govern cities and armies as well as men do? But I have not laid these duties on them, because I am fashioning a Court Lady and not a Queen.

Castiglione wrote his book as a tribute to Giubaldo di Montefeltro, Duke of Urbino (1472–1509), who was a real-life courtier. Isabella d'Este, Marchioness of Mantua (1474–1539), epitomized the court lady. Praised by Castiglione and many others for her intellect and moral qualities, she used her fine literary and artistic training to create a court at Mantua that became one of the brightest centers of Italian culture.

Exercises

1. According to Castiglione "the principal and true profession of the Courtier ought to be that of arms." What is your reaction to this statement? Why?
2. Itemize the virtues of a Courtier. Which of these still apply in contemporary society? Which do not? How do you account for the changes in attitude?
3. Compare the virtues of a Court Lady with those of a Courtier. How might modern feminists react to these statements? Would they, for example, prefer a Queen to a Court Lady?

François Rabelais (1494?–1553)

An ebullient humanist and an outspoken rebel who detested all regimentation, Rabelais (rab-LAY) insisted that the good life was a natural consequence of freedom combined with a solid classical education. His masterwork, *Gargantua and Pantagruel,* is a long, boisterous fable about two giant-kings, father and son. In the following excerpt Gargantua writes to his son in Paris, where he was receiving, as had his father before him, the best possible education. The style of the letter is eloquent in the manner of Cicero, but the instructions are explicit, for example: "I intend, and will have it so, that thou learn the languages perfectly." This fictional letter summarizes Rabelais's view of an ideal education, an attitude in accord with what was generally expected of the intellectual elite.

Literary Selections

GARGANTUA AND PANTAGRUEL
François Rabelais

Chapter VIII.

How Pantagruel, being at Paris, received letters from his father Gargantua, and the copy of them.

Pantagruel studied very hard, as you may well conceive, and profited accordingly; for he had an excellent understanding and notable wit, together with a capacity in memory equal to the measure of twelve oil budgets or butts of olives. And, as he was there abiding one day, he received a letter from his father in manner as followeth.

Most dear Son,—Amongst the gifts, graces, and prerogatives, with which the sovereign psalmator God Almighty hath endowed and adorned human nature at the beginning, that seems to me most singular and excellent, by which we may in a moral state attain to a kind of immortality, and in the course of this transitory life perpetuate our name and seed, which is done by a progeny issued from us in the lawful bonds of matrimony.

Whereby that in some measure is restored unto us which was taken from us by the sin of our first parents, to whom it was said that, because they had not obeyed the commandment of God their Creator, they should die, and by death should be brought to nought that so stately frame and psalmature wherein the man at first had been created.

But by this means of seminal propagation there continueth in the children what was lost in the parents, and in the grandchildren that which perished in their fathers, and so successively until the day of the last judgment, when Jesus Christ shall have rendered up to God the Father his kingdom in a peaceable condition, out of all danger and contamination of sin; for then shall cease all generations and corruptions, and the elements leave off their continual transmutations, seeing the so much desired peace shall be attained unto and enjoyed, and that all things shall be brought to their end and period. And, therefore, not without just and reasonable cause do I give thanks to God my Saviour and Preserver, for that he hath enabled me to see my bald old age reflourish in thy youth; for when, at his good pleasure, who rules and governs all things, my soul shall leave this mortal habitation, I shall not account myself wholly to die, but to pass from one place unto another, considering that, in and by that, I continue in my visible image living in world, visiting and conversing with people of honour, and other my good friends, as I was wont to do. Which conversation of mine, although it was not without sin, because we are all of us trespassers, and therefore ought continually to beseech his divine majesty to blot our transgressions out of his memory, yet was it, by the help and grace of God, without all manner of reproach before men.

Wherefore, if those qualities of the mind but shine in thee wherewith I am endowed, as in thee remaineth the perfect image of my body, thou wilt be esteemed by all men to be the perfect guardian and treasure of the immortality of our name. But, if otherwise, I shall truly take but small pleasure to see it, considering that the lesser part of me, which is the body, would abide in thee, and the best, to wit, that which is the soul, and by which our name continues blessed amongst men, would be degenerate and abastardized. This I do not speak out of any distrust that I have of thy virtue, which I have heretofore already tried, but to encourage thee yet more earnestly to proceed from good to better. And that which I now write unto thee is not so much that thou shouldst live in this virtuous course, as that thou shouldst rejoice in so living and having lived, and cheer up thyself with the like resolution in time to come; to the prosecution and accomplishment of which enterprise and generous undertaking thou mayst easily remember how that I have spared nothing, but have so helped thee, as if I had had no other treasure in this world, but to see thee once in my life completely well-bred and accomplished as well in virtue, honesty, and valour, as in all liberal knowledge and civility, and so to leave thee after my death, as a mirror representing the person of me thy father, and if not so excellent, and such in deed as I do wish thee, yet such is my desire.

But although my deceased father of happy memory, Grangousier, had bent his endeavors to make me profit in all perfection and political knowledge, and that my labour and study was fully correspondent to, yea, went beyond his desire, nevertheless, as thou mayst well understand, the time then was not so proper and fit for learning as it is at present, neither had I plenty of such good masters as thou hast had. For that time was darksome, obscured with clouds of ignorance, and savouring a little of the infelicity and calamity of the Goths, who had, wherever they set footing, destroyed all good literature, which in my age hath by the divine goodness been restored unto its former light and dignity, and that with such amendment and increase of the knowledge, that now hardly should I be admitted unto the first form of the little grammar-schoolboys—I say, I, who in my youthful days was, and that justly, reputed the most learned of that age. Which I do not speak in vain boasting, although I might lawfully do it in writing unto thee—in verification whereof thou hast the authority of Marcus Tullius in his book of old age, and the sentence of Plutarch in the book entitled How a man may praise himself without envy—but to give thee an emulous encouragement to strive yet further.

Now is it that the minds of men are qualified with all manner of discipline, and the old sciences revived which for many ages were extinct. Now is it that the learned languages are to their pristine purity restored, viz., Greek, without which a man may be ashamed to account himself a scholar, Hebrew, Arabic, Chaldean, and Latin. Printing likewise is now in use, so elegant and so correct that better cannot be imagined, although it was found out but in my time by divine inspiration, as by a diabolical suggestion on the other side was the invention of ordnance. All the world is full of knowing men, of most learned schoolmasters, and vast libraries; and it appears to me as a truth, that neither in Plato's time, nor Cicero's, nor Papinian's, there was ever such conveniency for studying as we see at this day there is. Nor must any adventure henceforward to come in public, or present himself in company, that hath not been pretty well polished in the shop of Minerva. I see robbers, hangmen, freebooters, tapsters, ostlers, and such like, of the very rubbish of the people, more learned now than the doctors and preachers were in my time.

What shall I say? The very women and children have aspired to this praise and celestial manner of good learning. Yet so it is that, in the age I am now of, I have been constrained to learn the Greek tongue—which I contemned not like Cato, but had not the leisure in my younger years to attend the study of it—and take much delight in the reading of Plutarch's Morals, the pleasant Dialogues of Plato, the Monuments of Pausanias, and the Antiquities of Athenæus, in waiting on the hour wherein God my Creator shall call me and command me to depart from this earth and transitory pilgrimage. Wherefore, my son, I admonish thee to employ thy youth to profit as well as thou canst, both in thy studies and in virtue. Thou art at Paris, where the laudable examples of many brave men may stir up thy mind to gallant actions, and hast likewise for thy tutor and pedagogue the learned Epistemon, who by his lively and vocal documents may instruct thee in the arts and sciences.

I intend, and will have it so, that thou learn the languages perfectly; first of all, the Greek, as Quintilian will have it; secondly, the Latin; and then the Hebrew, for the Holy Scripture sake; and then the Chaldee and Arabic likewise, and that thou frame thy style in Greek in imitation of Plato, and for the Latin after Cicero. Let there be no history which thou shalt not have ready in thy memory; unto the prosecuting of which design, books of cosmography will be very conducible and help thee much. Of the liberal arts of geometry, arithmetic, and music, I gave thee some taste when thou wert yet little, and not above five or six years old. Proceed further in them, and learn the remainder if thou canst. As for astronomy, study all the rules thereof. Let pass, nevertheless, the divining and judicial astrology, and the art of Lullius, as being nothing else but plain abuses and vanities. As for the civil law, of that I would have thee to know the texts by heart, and then to confer them with philosophy.

Now, in matter of the knowledge of the works of nature, I would have thee to study that exactly, and that so there be no sea, river, nor fountain, of which thou dost not know the fishes; all the fowls of the air; all the several kinds of shrubs and trees, whether in forests or orchards; all sorts of herbs and flowers that grow upon the ground; all the various metals that are hid within the bowels of the earth; together with all the diversity of precious stones that are to be seen in the orient and south parts of the world. Let nothing of all these be hidden from thee. Then fail not most carefully to peruse the books of the Greek, Arabian, and Latin physicians, not despising the Talmudists and Cabalists; and by frequent anatomies get thee the perfect knowledge of the other world, called microcosm, which is man. And at some hours of the day apply thy mind to the study of the Holy Scriptures; first in Greek, the New Testament, with the Epistles of the Apostles; and then the old Testament in Hebrew. In brief, let me see thee an abyss and bottomless pit of knowledge; for from hence forward as thou growest great and becomest a man, thou must part from this tranquillity and rest of study, thou must learn chivalry, warfare, and the exercises of the field, the better thereby to defend my house and our friends, and to succour and protect them at all their needs against the invasion and assaults of evildoers.

Furthermore, I will that very shortly thou try how much thou has profited, which thou canst not better do than by maintaining publicly theses and conclusions in all arts against all persons whatsoever, and by haunting the company of learned men, both at Paris and otherwhere. But because, as the wise man Solomon saith, Wisdom entereth not into a malicious mind, and that knowledge without conscience is but the ruin of the soul, it behooveth thee to serve, to love, to fear God, and on him to cast all thy thoughts and all thy hope, and by faith formed in charity to cleave unto him, so that thou mayst never be separated from him by thy sins. Suspect the abuses of the world. Set not thy heart upon vanity, for this life is transitory, but the Word of the Lord endureth for ever. Be serviceable to all thy neighbors, and love them as thyself. Reverence thy preceptors: shun the conversation of those whom thou desirest not to resemble, and receive not in vain the graces which God hath bestowed upon thee. And, when thou shalt see that thou hast attained to all the knowledge that is to be acquired in that part, return unto me, that I may see thee and give thee my blessing before I die. My son, the peace and grace of our Lord be with thee. Amen.

Thy Father Gargantua.
From Utopia the 17th day of the month of March.

These letters being received and read, Pantagruel plucked up his heart, took a fresh courage to him, and was inflamed with a desire to profit in his studies more than ever, so that if you had seen him, how he took pains, and how he advanced in learning, you would have said that the vivacity of his spirit amidst the books, was like a great fire amongst dry wood, so active it was, vigorous and indefatigable.

Exercises

1. Gargantua writes about his son's education but not his vocation. Why not? What does this imply? Is education more important than what one does for a living? *Should* education be more important than a particular job?
2. Compare the education of Pantagruel with today's typical B.A. in a liberal arts discipline. What happened!? Why? Would *you* aspire to Pantagruel's college education? Why or why not?

Gargantua wrote his letter from "Utopia," a commonly-used term after the appearance of Sir Thomas More's *Utopia* (Gk., no place), a novel about an ideal state. Utopianism was in the air. Machiavelli's Prince was an ideal autocrat and Castiglione's Courtier functioned gracefully in an ideal society. In the "Abbey of Theleme" from *Gargantua and Pantagruel,* Rabelais describes the good life as the opposite extreme from monasticism, which he had experienced firsthand and thoroughly detested. He was, in fact, expelled from several monasteries. The motto over the gate of the sardonically titled "Abbey" is "Do What Thou Wilt," an inversion of the monastic vows of poverty, chastity, and obedience.

Abbey of Theleme
François Rabelais

There was left only the monk to provide for, whom Gargantua would have made abbot of Seuilly, but he refused it. He would have given him the abbey of Bourgueil or of Saint-Florent, which was better, or both if it pleased him. But the monk gave him a very peremptory answer, that he would never take upon him the charge nor government of monks. "For how shall I be able," said he, "to rule over others, that have not full power and command of myself? If you think I have done you, or may hereafter do you any acceptable service, give me leave to found an abbey after my own mind and fancy."

The notion pleased Gargantua very well, who thereupon offered him all the country of Theleme by the river of Loire. The monk then requested Gargantua to institute his religious order contrary to all others.

"First then," said Gargantua, "you must not build a wall about your convent, for all other abbeys are strongly walled and mured[1] about."

---

1. Mured—walled in with bricks and mortar.

Moreover, seeing there are certain convents in the world whereof the custom is, if any women come in they immediately sweep the ground which they have trod upon; therefore was it ordained that if any man or woman, entered into religious orders, should by chance come within this new abbey, all the rooms should be thoroughly washed and cleansed through which they had passed. And because in all other monasteries and nunneries all is compassed, limited, and regulated by hours, it was decreed that in this new structure there should be neither clock nor dial, but that according to the opportunities and incident occasions all their hours should be disposed of. "For," said Gargantua, "the greatest loss of time that I know is to count the hours. What good comes of it? Nor can there be any greater dotage in the world than for one to guide and direct his courses by the sound of a bell, and not by his own judgment and discretion."

Then was it ordained that into this religious order should be admitted no women that were not fair, well-featured, and of a sweet disposition; nor men that were not comely, personable, and well-conditioned.

Item, because in the convents of women men come not but underhand, privily, and by stealth, it was therefore enacted that in this house there shall be no women in case there be not men, nor men in case there be not women.

Item, because both men and women that are received into religious orders, after the expiring of their novitiate, or probation year, were constrained and forced perpetually to stay there all the days of their life, it was therefore ordered that all whatever, men or women, admitted within this abbey, should have full leave to depart with peace and contentment, whensoever it should seem good to them so to do.

Item, for that religious men and women did ordinarily make vows, to wit, those of chastity, poverty, and obedience, it was therefore constituted and appointed that in this convent they might be honorably married, that they might be rich, and live at liberty. In regard of the legitimate time of the persons to be initiated, and years under and above which they were not capable of reception, the women were to be admitted from ten till fifteen, and the men from twelve to eighteen.

The architecture was in a figure hexagonal, and in such a fashion that in every one of the six corners there was built a great round tower of threescore feet in diameter, and were all of a like form and bigness. Upon the north side ran along the River Loire, on the bank whereof was situated the tower called Arctic. Going towards the east, there was another called Calaer; the next following, Anatole; the next, Mesembrine; the next, Hesperia; and the last, Crière. Every tower was distant from the other the space of three hundred and twelve paces. The whole edifice was everywhere six stories high, reckoning the cellars underground for one.

This same building was a hundred times more sumptuous and magnificent than ever was Bonnivet, Chambord, or Chantilly.[2] For there were in it nine thousand, three hundred and two-and-thirty chambers; every one whereof had a withdrawing room, a handsome closet, a wardrobe, an oratory, and neat passage leading into a great and spacious hall. Between every tower, in the midst of the said body of building, there was a pair of winding stairs, whereof the steps were part of porphyry, part of Numidian stone, and part of serpentine marble; each of those steps being two-and-twenty feet in length

and three fingers thick and the just number of twelve betwixt every rest or landing place. In every resting place were two fair antique arches, where the light came in, and by those they went into a cabinet made even with, and of the breadth of the said winding; and the reascending above the roofs of the house ended conically in a pavilion. By that vize, or winding, they entered on every side into a great hall and from the halls into the chambers.

From the Arctic tower unto the Crière were the fair great libraries in Greek, Latin, Hebrew, French, Italian, and Spanish, respectively distributed in their several cantons,[3] according to the diversity of these languages. In the midst there was a wonderful winding stair, the entry whereof was without the house, in a vault or arch six fathoms broad. It was made in such symmetry and largeness that six men-at-arms, with their lances in their rests, might together in a breast ride all up to the very top of all the palace.

From the tower Anatole to the Mesembrine were spacious galleries, all colored over and painted with the ancient prowesses, histories, and descriptions of the world. In the midst thereof there was likewise such another ascent and gate, as we said there was on the river side. Upon that gate was written, in great antique letters, that which followeth:

Here enter not, religious boobies, sots.
Impostors, sniveling hypocrites, bigots,
Dark brain-distorted owls, worse than the Huns
Or Ostrogoths, forerunners of baboons,
Cursed snakes, dissembling varlets,[4] seeming saints,
Slipshod cafards,[5] beggars pretending wants,
Fomenters of divisions and debates;
Elsewhere, not here, make sale of your deceits.
 Your filthy trumperies,
 Stuffed with pernicious lies,
  (Not worth a bubble)
  Would only trouble
 Our earthly Paradise,
 Your filthy trumperies!
Here enter not attorneys, barristers,
Nor bridle-champing law practitioners;
Clerks, commissaries, scribes, nor Pharisees,
Willful disturbers of the people's ease,
Judges, destroyers, with an unjust breath,
That, like dogs, worry honest men to death.
We want not your demurrers,[6] nor your pleas;
So at the gibbet[7] go and seek your fees,
We are not for attendance or delays,
But would with ease and quiet pass our days.
 Lawsuits, debates, and wrangling
 Hence are exiled, and jangling.
  Here we are very
  Frolic and merry,
 And free from all entangling
 Lawsuits, debates, and wrangling.

---

2. Bonnivet, Chambord, Chantilly—regarded as fine, sumptuous castles.

3. Cantons—sections; division.

4. Varlets—scoundrels.

5. Cafards—hypocrites.

6. Demurrers—motions for delay or dismissal on a point of law.

7. Gibbet—gallows.

Here enter not base pinching usurers,
Pelf-lickers, everlasting gatherers;
    Gold-graspers, coin-gripers, gulpers of mists,
With harpy-griping claws, who, though your chests
Vast sums of money should to you afford,
Would nevertheless be adding to the hoard,
And yet not be content; ye clunch-fist dastards,
Insatiable fiends, and Pluto's bastards,
Greedy devourers, chichy, sneakbill[8] rogues;
Hell-mastiffs gnaw your bones, you ravenous dogs
        You beastly-looking fellows.
        Reason doth plainly tell us,
            That we should not
            To you allot
        Room here, but at the gallows;
        You beastly-looking fellows.

        Here enter not, unsociable wight,
Humorsome[9] churl, by day, nor yet by night;
No grumbling oaf, none of the sharping trade,
No huff-cap[10] squire, or brother of the blade,
A Tartar bred, or in Alsatian wars,
The ruffian comes not hither with his bears.
Elsewhere for shelter scour, ye bully-rooks
And rogues, that rot with infamy and pox.
        Grace, honor, praise, delight,
        Here sojourn day and night,
            Sound bodies, lined
            With a good mind,
        Do here pursue with might
        Grace, honor, praise, delight.

        Here enter you, and welcome from our hearts,
All noble sparks, endowed with gallant parts!
This is the glorious place which nobly shall
Afford sufficient to content you all;
Were you a thousand, here you shall not want
For anything; for what you ask, we grant.
The brave, the witty, here we entertain,
And, in a word, all worthy gentlemen.
        Men of heroic breasts
        Shall taste here of the feasts,
            Both privily
                And civilly;
        All you are welcome guests,
        Men of heroic breasts.

        Here enter you, pure, honest, faithful, true,
Expounders of the Scriptures, old and new;
Whose glosses do not the plain truth disguise,
And with false light distract or blind our eyes.
Here shall we find a safe and warm retreat,
When Error beats about and spreads her net.
Strange doctrines here must neither reap nor sow
But Faith and Charity together grow.
In short, confounded be their first device,
Who are the holy Scriptures' enemies.
Here in the holy Word
Trust all, with one accord,
        It will some help afford;
        Though you be knight or lord,
    You may find shield and sword,
    Here in the holy Word.

        Here enter ladies all of high degree,
Of goodly shape; of humor gay and free,
Of lovely looks, of sprightly flesh and blood,
Here take, here choose, here settle your abode;
The gentle, the brisk, the fair, whoever comes,
With eyes that sparkle, or whose beauty blooms.

This bower is fashioned by a gentle knight,
Ladies, for you, and innocent delight.
        This is designed a place
        For every charming grace;
            The witty and the fair
            Hither may all repair;
        For every lovely face
        This is designed a place.

How the Thelemites Were Governed and of Their Manner of Living

All their life was spent not in laws, statutes, or rules, but according to their own free will and pleasure. They rose out of their beds when they thought good; they did eat, drink, labor, sleep, when they had a mind to it and were disposed for it. None did awake them, none did offer to constrain them to eat, drink, nor do any other things; for so had Gargantua established it. In all their rule and strictest tie of their order, there was but this one clause to be observed: DO WHAT THOU WILT. Because men that are free, well-born, well-bred, and conversant in honest companies have naturally an instinct and spur that prompteth them unto virtuous actions and withdraws them from vice, which is called honor. Those same men, when by base subjection and constraint they are brought under and kept down, turn aside from that noble disposition by which they formerly were inclined to virtue, to shake off that bond of servitude where in they are so tyrannously enslaved; for it is agreeable to the nature of man to long after things forbidden, and to desire what is denied us.

By this liberty they entered into a very laudable emulation to do, all of them, what they saw did please one. If any of the gallants or ladies should say, "Let us drink," they would all drink. If any one of them said, "Let us play," they all played. If one said, "Let us go a-walking into the fields," they went all. If it were to go a-hawking or a-hunting, the ladies, mounted upon dainty well-paced nags, seated in a stately palfrey saddle, carried on their lovely fists, miniardly begloved every one of them, either a sparhawk, or a lanneret, or a merlin, and the young gallants carried the other kinds of hawks.

So nobly were they taught that there was neither he nor she amongst them but could read, write, sing, play upon several instruments, speak five or six several languages, and compose in them all very quaintly both in verse and prose. Never were seen so valiant knights, so noble and worthy, so dextrous and skillful both on foot and horseback, more brisk and lively, more nimble and quick, or better handling all manner of weapons, than were there. Never were seen ladies so proper and handsome, so miniard and dainty, less forward, or more ready with their hand and with their needle, in every honest and free action belonging to that sex, than were there.

For this reason, when the time came that any man of the said abbey, either at the request of his parents or for some other cause, had a mind to go out of it, he carried along with him one of the ladies, namely her whom he

---

8. Sneakbill—stingy; paltry.
9. Humorsome—quarrelsome; ill-natured.
10. Huff-cap—quarrelsome.

had before that chosen for his mistress, and they were married together. And if they had formerly in Theleme lived in good devotion and amity, they did continue therein and increase it to a greater height in their state of matrimony; and did entertain that mutual love till the very last day of their life, in no less vigor and fervency than at the very day of their wedding.

Exercise

1. "Do what thou wilt" was the motto of the Abbey of Theleme. Suppose that you seriously and studiously followed that precept for one day in your life. What would your day be like? What difficulties might you encounter?

Sir Thomas More (1478–1535)

As discussed previously, Europeans were entranced with the hope and promise of the New World. It was in these newly discovered lands that More (fig. 20.2) placed his *Utopia* (1516). To give his philosophical romance a framework, he relates his conversation with a sailor, Raphael Hythloday, who had sailed with Amerigo Vespucci. Hythloday tells More of a fabulous country that they had discovered named Utopia.

Literary Selection
UTOPIA
Sir Thomas More

More, like Machiavelli, was a realist, but an optimistic realist. He was careful, however, to retain certain checks on human conduct. Like Rabelais, More insists on equality under a representative form of government, much like the system in Switzerland, which he knew. Like Plato, who was his inspiration, he has to resort to a class of slaves to do the dirty work. Warfare, which was incessant during the Renaissance, would be waged outside *Utopia* by mercenaries. (More was also acquainted with Swiss mercenaries.) The limitation of More's thinking is interesting here, for he can extend his ideal state of culture only to the borders of the nation. He was able to place his exploitable savages just beyond the boundaries; yet, in everyday life, they are here and now and with us always.

One characteristic of Renaissance life was particularly revolting to More. This was the religious dissension that split the nations and which was to cost More his life. So in *Utopia,* we find complete religious freedom. Most Utopians adhere to a single faith, but the options are open and protected. Those who seek to impose their beliefs on anyone else will be severely punished.

Figure 20.2 Hans Holbein the Younger (1497/8–1543). *Sir Thomas More,* ca. 1530. Holbein's superb portrait reveals a visionary and a man of conscience ("a man for all seasons"), who died at the hands of Henry VIII rather than compromise his religious convictions. Copyright the Frick Collection, New York.

More did not write a manual for a perfect civilization, and he knew this as well as any modern reader. All of his ideas do, however, merit serious consideration. The world may never be perfect, but we must always aspire to something better.

The island of Utopia containeth in breadth in the middle part of it (for there it is broadest) two hundred miles. Which breadth continueth through the most part of the land, saving that by little and little it cometh in, and waxeth narrower towards both the ends. Which fetching about a circuit or compass of five hundred miles, do fashion the whole island like to the new moon. Between these two corners the sea runneth in, dividing them asunder by the distance of eleven miles or thereabouts, and there surmounteth into a large and wide sea, which by reason that the land on every side compasseth it about, and sheltereth it from the winds, is not rough, nor mounteth not with great waves, but almost floweth quietly, not much unlike a great standing pool: and maketh almost all the space within the belly of the land in manner of a haven: and to the great commodity of the inhabitants receiveth in ships towards every part of the land. The forefronts or frontiers of the two corners, what with fords and shelves, and what with rocks be very jeopardous and dangerous. In the middle distance between them both standeth up above the water a great rock, which therefore is nothing perilous because it is in sight. Upon the top of this rock is a fair and a strong tower builded, which they hold with a garrison of men. Other rocks there be that lie hid under the water, and therefore be dangerous. The channels be known only to themselves. And therefore it seldom chanceth that any stranger unless he be guided by a Utopian can come into this haven. Insomuch that they themselves could scarcely enter without jeopardy, but that their way is directed and ruled by certain landmarks standing on the shore. By turning, translating, and removing these marks into other places they may destroy their enemies' navies, be they never so many. The outside of the land is also full of havens, but the landing is so surely defenced, what by nature, and what by workmanship of man's hand, that a few defenders may drive back many armies.

There be in the island fifty-four large and fair cities, or shire towns, agreeing all together in one tongue, in like manners, institutions and laws. They be all set and situate alike, and in all points fashioned alike, as far forth as the place or plot suffereth.

Of these cities they that be nighest together be twenty-four miles asunder. Again there is none of them distant from the next above one day's journey afoot. There come yearly to Amaurote out of every city three old men wise and well experienced, there to entreat and debate, of the common matters of the land. For this city (because it standeth just in the midst of the island, and is therefore most meet for the ambassadors of all parts of the realm) is taken for the chief and head city. The precincts and bounds of the shires be so commodiously appointed out, and set forth for the cities, that never a one of them all hath of any side less than twenty miles of ground, and of some side also much more, as of that part where the cities be of farther distance asunder. None of the cities desire to enlarge the bounds and limits of their shires. For they count themselves rather the good husbands[11] than the owners of their lands. They have in the country in all parts of the shire houses or farms builded, well appointed and furnished with all sorts of instruments and tools belonging to husbandry. These houses be inhabited of the citizens, which come thither to dwell by course. No household or farm in the country hath fewer than forty persons, men and women, besides two bondmen, which be all under the rule and order of the good man, and the good wife of the house, being both very sage and discreet persons. And every thirty farms or families have one head ruler, which is called a philarch, being as it were a head bailiff. Out of every one of these families or farms cometh every year into the city twenty persons which have continued two years before in the country. In their place so many fresh be sent thither out of the city, which of them that have been there a year already, and be therefore expert and cunning in husbandry, shall be instructed and taught. And they the next year shall teach others. This order is used for fear that either scarceness of victuals, or some other like incommodity should chance, through lack of knowledge, if they should be altogether new, and fresh, and unexpert in husbandry. This manner and fashion of yearly changing and renewing the occupiers of husbandry, though it be solemn and customably used, to the intent that no man shall be constrained against his will to continue long in that hard and sharp kind of life, yet many of them have such a pleasure and delight in husbandry, that they obtain a longer space of years. These husbandmen plough and till the ground, and breed up cattle, and make ready wood, which they carry to the city either by land, or by water, as

they may most conveniently. They bring up a great multitude of poultry, and that by a marvellous policy. For the hens do not sit upon the eggs; but by keeping them in a certain equal heat they bring life into them, and hatch them. The chickens, as soon as they come out of the shell, follow men and women instead of the hens. They bring up very few horses: nor none, but very fierce ones: and for none other use or purpose, but only to exercise their youth in riding and feats of arms. For oxen be put to all the labour of ploughing and drawing. Which they grant to be not so good as horses at a sudden brunt, and (as we say) at a dead lift, but yet they hold opinion that they will abide and suffer much more labour and pain than horses will. And they think that they be not in danger and subject unto so many diseases, and that they be kept and maintained with much less cost and charge: and finally that they be good for meat, when they be past labour. They sow corn only for bread. For their drink is either wine made of grapes, or else of apples, or pears, or else it is clean water. And many times mead made of honey or liquorice sodden in water, for thereof they have great store. And though they know certainly (for they know it perfectly indeed) how much victuals the city with the whole country or shire round about it doth spend: yet they sow much more corn, and breed up much more cattle, than serveth for their own use, and the over-plus they part among their borderers.[12] Whatsoever necessary things be lacking in the country, all such stuff they fetch out of the city: where without any exchange they easily obtain it of the magistrates of the city. For every month many of them go into the city on the holy day. When their harvest day draweth near and is at hand, then the philarchs, which be the head officers and bailiffs of husbandry, send word to the magistrates of the city what number of harvest men is needful to be sent to them out of the city. The which company of harvest men being there ready at the day appointed, almost in one fair day despatcheth all the harvest work.

Of the Cities, and Namely of Amaurote

As for their cities, he that knoweth one of them, knoweth them all: they be all like one to another, as farforth as the nature of the place permitteth. I will describe therefore to you one or other of them, for it skilleth[13] not greatly which: but which rather than Amaurote? Of them all this is the worthiest and of most dignity. For the residue acknowledge it for the head city, because there is the council house. Nor to me any of them all is better beloved, as wherein I lived five whole years together. The city of Amaurote standeth upon the side of a low hill in fashion almost four square. For the breadth of it beginneth a little beneath the top of the hill, and still continueth by the space of two miles, until it come to the river of Anyder. The length of it, which lieth by the river's side, is somewhat more. The river of Anyder riseth twenty-four miles above Amaurote out of a little spring. But being increased by other small floods and brooks that run into it, and among other two somewhat big ones, before the city it is half a mile broad, and farther broader. And sixty miles beyond the city it falleth into the Ocean sea.

---

11. Husbands—caretakers or farmers.
12. Borderers—the surrounding countries.
13. Skilleth—matters.

By all that space that lieth between the sea and the city, and a good sort of miles also above the city, the water ebbeth and floweth six hours together with a swift tide. When the sea floweth in, for the length of thirty miles it filleth all the Anyder with salt water, and driveth back the fresh water of the river. And somewhat further it changeth the sweetness of the fresh water with saltness. But a little beyond that the river waxeth sweet, and runneth forby the city fresh and pleasant. And when the sea ebbeth, and goeth back again, the fresh water followeth it almost even to the very fall into the sea. There goeth a bridge over the river made not of piles of timber, but of stonework with gorgeous and substantial arches at that part of the city that is farthest from the sea: to the intent that ships may go along forby all the side of the city without let.[14] They have also another river which indeed is not very great. But it runneth gently and pleasantly. For it riseth even out of the same hill that the city standeth upon, and runneth down a slope through the midst of the city into Anyder. And because it riseth a little without the city, the Amaurotians have inclosed the head spring of it with strong fences and bulwarks, and so have joined it to the city. This is done to the intent that the water should not be stopped nor turned away, or poisoned, if their enemies should chance to come upon them. From thence the water is derived and brought down in canals of brick divers ways into the lower parts of the city. Where that cannot be done, by reason that the place will not suffer it, there they gather the rain water in great cisterns, which doth them as good service. The city is compassed about with a high and thick wall full of turrets and bulwarks. A dry ditch, but deep, and broad, and overgrown with bushes, briers and thorns, goeth about three sides or quarters of the city. To the fourth side the river itself serveth for a ditch. The streets be appointed and set forth very commodious and handsome, both for carriage, and also against the winds. The houses be of fair and gorgeous building, and in the street side they stand joined together in a long row through the whole street without any partition or separation. The streets be twenty feet broad. On the back side of the houses through the whole length of the street, lie large gardens which be closed in round about with the back part of the streets. Every house hath two doors, one into the street, and a postern door on the back side into the garden. These doors be made with two leaves, never locked nor bolted, so easy to be opened, that they will follow the least drawing of a finger, and shut again by themselves. Every man that will, may go in, for there is nothing within the houses that is private, or any man's own. And every tenth year they change their houses by lot. They set great store by their gardens. In them they have vineyards, all manner of fruit, herbs, and flowers, so pleasant, so well furnished and so finely kept, that I never saw thing more fruitful, nor better trimmed in any place. Their study and diligence herein cometh not only of pleasure, but also of a certain strife and contention that is between street and street, concerning the trimming, husbanding, and furnishing of their gardens: every man for his own part. And verily you shall not lightly find in all the city anything that is more commodious, either for the profit of the citizens, or for pleasure.

Of the Magistrates

Every thirty families or farms, choose them yearly an officer, which is called the philarch. Every ten philarchs with all their 300 families be under an officer which is called the chief philarch. Moreover, as concerning the election of the prince, all the philarchs which be in number 200, first be sworn to choose him whom they think most meet and expedient. Then by a secret election, they name prince, one of those four whom the people before named unto them. For out of the four quarters of the city there be four chosen, out of every quarter one, to stand for the election: which be put up to the council. The prince's office continueth all his lifetime, unless he be deposed or put down for suspicion of tyranny. They choose the chief philarchs yearly, but lightly they change them not. All the other offices be but for one year. The chief philarchs every third day, and sometimes, if need be, oftener, come into the council house with the prince. Their council is concerning the commonwealth. If there be any controversies among the commoners, which be very few, they despatch and end them by-and-by. They take ever two philarchs to them in counsel, and every day a new couple. And it is provided that nothing touching the commonwealth shall be confirmed and ratified unless it have been reasoned of and debated three days in the council, before it be decreed. It is death to have any consultation for the commonwealth out of the council, or the place of the common election. This statute, they say, was made to the intent that the prince and chief philarchs might not easily conspire together to oppress the people by tyranny, and to change the state of the weal public. Therefore matters of great weight and importance be brought to the election house of the philarchs, which open the matter to their families. And afterward, when they have consulted among themselves, they show their device to the council. Sometimes the matter is brought before the council of the whole island. Furthermore this custom also the council useth, to dispute or reason of no matter the same day that it is first proposed or put forth, but to defer it to the next sitting of the council. Because that no man when he hath rashly there spoken what cometh first to his tongue's end, shall then afterwards rather study for reasons wherewith to defend and confirm his first foolish sentence, than for the commodity of the commonwealth: as one rather willing the harm or hindrance of the weal public than any loss or diminution of his own existimation. And as one that would not for shame (which is a very foolish shame) be counted anything overseen in the matter at the first. Who at the first ought to have spoken rather wisely, then hastily, or rashly.

Of Sciences, Crafts, and Occupations

Husbandry is a science common to them all in general, both men and women, wherein they be all expert and cunning. In this they be all instruct even from their youth: partly in schools with traditions and precepts, and partly in the country nigh the city, brought up as it were in playing, not only beholding the use of it, but by occasion of exercising their bodies practising it also. Besides husbandry, which (as I said) is common to them all, every one of them learneth one or other several and particular science, as his own proper craft. That is most commonly either clothworking in wool or flax, or masonry, or the smith's craft, or the carpenter's science. For there is none other occupation that any number to

---

14. Let—hindrance.

speak of doth use there. For their garments, which throughout all the island be of one fashion (saving that there is a difference between the man's garment and the woman's, between the married and the unmarried) and this one continueth for evermore unchanged, seemly and comely to the eye, no let to the moving and wielding of the body, also fit both for winter and summer: as for these garments (I say) every family maketh their own. But of the other foresaid crafts every man learneth one. And not only the men, but also the women. But the women, as the weaker sort, be put to the easier crafts: they work wool and flax. The other more laboursome sciences be committed to the men. For the most part every man is brought up in his father's craft. For most commonly they be naturally thereto bent and inclined. But if a man's mind stand to any other, he is by adoption put into a family of that occupation, which he doth most fantasy.[15] Whom not only his father, but also the magistrates do diligently look to, that he be put to a discreet and an honest householder. Yea, and if any person, when he hath learned one craft, be desirous to learn also another, he is likewise suffered and permitted.

When he hath learned both, he occupieth whether he will: unless the city have more need of the one, than of the other. The chief and almost the only office of the philarchs is, to see and take heed that no man sit idle: but that every one apply his own craft with earnest diligence. And yet for all that, not be wearied from early in the morning, to late in the evening, with continual work, like labouring and toiling beasts.

For this is worse than the miserable and wretched condition of bondmen. Which nevertheless is almost everywhere the life of workmen and artificers, saving in Utopia. For they dividing the day and the night into twenty-four just hours, appoint and assign only six of those hours to work; three before noon, upon the which they go straight to dinner: and after dinner, when they have rested two hours, then they work three and upon that they go to supper. About eight of the clock in the evening (counting one of clock as the first hour after noon) they go to bed: eight hours they give to sleep. All the void time, that is between the hours of work, sleep, and meat, that they be suffered to bestow, every man as he liketh best himself. Not to the intent that they should misspend this time in riot or slothfulness: but being then licensed from the labour of their own occupations, to bestow the time well and thriftly upon some other good science, as shall please them. For it is a solemn custom there, to have lectures daily early in the morning, where to be present they only be constrained that be chosen and appointed to learning. Howbeit a great multitude of every sort of people, both men and women, go to hear lectures, some one and some another, as every man's nature is inclined. Yet, this notwithstanding, if any man had rather bestow this time upon his own occupation (as it chanceth in many, whose minds rise not in the contemplation of any science liberal) he is not letted, nor prohibited, but is also praised and commended, as profitable to the commonwealth. After supper they bestow one hour in play: in summer in their gardens: in winter in their common halls: where they dine and sup. There they exercise themselves in music, or else in honest and wholesome communication. But lest you be deceived, one thing you must look more narrowly upon. For seeing they bestow but six hours in work perchance you may think that the lack of some necessary things hereof may ensue. But this is nothing so. For that small time is not only enough but also too much for the store and abundance of all things that be requisite, either for the necessity, or commodity of life. The which thing you also shall perceive, if you weigh and consider with yourselves how great a part of the people in other countries liveth idle. First almost all women, which be the half of the whole number: or else if the women be anywhere occupied, there most commonly in their stead the men be idle. Beside this how great, and how idle a company is there of priests, and religious men, as they call them? Put thereto all rich men, especially all landed men, which commonly be called gentlemen, and noblemen. Take into this number also their servants: I mean all that flock of stout bragging rush-bucklers. Join to them also sturdy and valiant beggars, cloaking their idle life under the colour of some disease or sickness. And truly you shall find them much fewer than you thought, by whose labour all these things be gotten that men use and live by. Now consider with yourself, of these few that do work, how few be occupied, in necessary works. For where money beareth all the swing, there many vain and superfluous occupations must needs be used, to serve only for riotous superfluity and unhonest pleasure. For the same multitude that now is occupied in work, if they were divided into so few occupations as the necessary use of nature requireth; in so great plenty of things as then of necessity would ensue, doubtless the prices would be too little for the artificers to maintain their livings. But if all these, that be now busied about unprofitable occupations, with all the whole flock of them that live idly and slothfully, which consume and waste every one of them more of these things that come by other men's labour, then two of the workmen themselves do: if all these (I say) were set to profitable occupations, you easily perceive how little time would be enough, yea and too much to store us with all things that may be requisite either for necessity, or for commodity, yea or for pleasure, so that the same pleasure be true and natural. And this in Utopia the thing itself maketh manifest and plain. For there in all the city, with the whole country, or shire adjoining to it scarcely 500 persons of all the whole number of men and women, that be neither too old, nor too weak to work, be licensed from labour. Among them be the philarchs which (though they be by the laws exempt and privileged from labour) yet they exempt not themselves: to the intent they may the rather by their example provoke others to work. The same vacation from labour do they also enjoy, to whom the people persuaded by the commendation of the priests, and secret election of the philarchs, have given a perpetual license from labour to learning. But if any one of them prove not according to the expectation and hope of him conceived, he is forthwith plucked back to the company of artificers. And contrariwise, often it chanceth that a handicraftsman doth so earnestly bestow his vacant and spare hours in learning, and through diligence to profit therein, that he is taken from his handy occupation, and promoted to the company of the learned. Out of this order of the learned be chosen ambassadors, priests, chief philarchs, and finally the prince himself.

---

15. Fantasy—desire or choose.

Of Warfare

Immediately after that war is once solemnly announced, they procure many proclamations signed with their own common seal to be set up privily at one time in their enemies' land, in places most frequented. In these proclamations they promise great rewards to him that will kill their enemies' prince, and somewhat less gifts, but them very great also, for every head of them, whose names be in the said proclamations contained. They be those whom they count their chief adversaries, next unto the prince. Whatsoever is prescribed unto him that killeth any of the proclaimed persons, that is doubled to him that bringeth any of the same to them alive; yea, and to the proclaimed persons themselves, if they will change their minds and come into them, taking their parts, they proffer the same great rewards with pardon and surety of their lives. Therefore it quickly cometh to pass that they have all other men in suspicion, and be unfaithful and mistrusting among themselves one to another, living in great fear, and in no less jeopardy. For it is well known, that divers times the most part of them (and specially the prince himself) hath been betrayed of them, in whom they put their most hope and trust. So that there is no manner of act nor deed that gifts and rewards do not enforce men unto. And in rewards they keep no measure. But remembering and considering into how great hazard and jeopardy they call them, endeavor themselves to recompense the greatness of the danger with like great benefits. And therefore they promise not only wonderful great abundance of gold, but also lands of great revenues lying in most places among their friends. And their promises they perform faithfully without any fraud or deceit. This custom of buying and selling adversaries among other people is disallowed, as a cruel act of a base and a cowardish mind. But they in this behalf think themselves much praiseworthy, as who like wise men by this means despatch great wars without any battle or skirmish. Yea they count it also a deed of pity and mercy, because that by the death of a few offenders the lives of a great number of innocents, as well of their own men as also of their enemies, be ransomed and saved, which in fighting should have been slain. For they do no less pity the base and common sort of their enemies' people, than they do their own; knowing that they be driven to war against their wills by the furious madness of their princes and heads. If by none of these means the matter go forward as they would have it, then they procure occasions of debate and dissension to be spread among their enemies. As by causing the prince's brother, or some of the noblemen, to hope to obtain the kingdom. If this way prevail not, then they raise up the people that be next neighbors and borderers to their enemies, and them they set in their necks under the colour of some old title of right, such as kings do never lack. To them they promise their help and aid in their war. And as for money they give them abundance. But of their own citizens they send to them few or none. Whom they make so much of and love so entirely, that they would not be willing to change any of them for their adversary's prince. But their gold and silver, because they keep it all for this only purpose, they lay it out frankly and freely; as who[16] should live even as wealthily, if they had bestowed it every penny. Yea, and besides their riches, which they keep at home, that have also an infinite treasure abroad, by reason that (as I said before) many nations be in their debt. Therefore they hire soldiers out of all countries and send them to battle, but chiefly of the Zapoletes. This people is

five hundred miles from Utopia eastward. They be hideous, savage and fierce, dwelling in wild woods and high mountains, where they were bred and brought up. They be of an hard nature, able to abide and sustain heat, cold and labour, abhorring from all delicate dainties, occupying no husbandry nor tillage of the ground, homely and rude both in the building of their houses and in their apparel, given unto no goodness, but only to the breeding and bringing up of cattle. The most part of their living is by hunting and stealing. They be born only to war, which they diligently and earnestly seek for. And when they have gotten it, they be wonders glad thereof. They go forth of their country in great companies together, and whosoever lacketh soldiers, there they proffer their service for small wages. This is only the craft that they have to get their living by. They maintain their life by seeking their death. For them with whom they be in wages they fight hardily, fiercely, and faithfully. But they bind themselves for no certain time. But upon this condition they enter into bonds, that the next day they will take part with the other side for greater wages, and the next day after that, they will be ready to come back again for a little more money. There be few wars thereaway, wherein is not a great number of them in both parties. Therefore it daily chanceth that nigh kinsfolk, which were hired together on one part, and there very friendly and familiarly used themselves one with another, shortly after being separate into contrary parts, run one against another enviously and fiercely, and forgetting both kindred and friendship, thrust their swords one in another. And that for none other cause, but that they be hired of contrary princes for a little money. Which they do so highly regard and esteem, that they will easily be provoked to change parts for a halfpenny more wages by the day. So quickly they have taken a smack in covetousness. Which for all that is to them no profit. For that they get by fighting, immediately they spend unthriftily and wretchedly in riot. This people fight for the Utopians against all nations, because they give them greater wages than any other nation will. For the Utopians like as they seek good men to use well, so they seek these evil and vicious men to abuse. Whom, when need requireth, with promises of great rewards, they put forth into great jeopardies. From whence the most part of them never cometh again to ask their rewards. But to them that remain alive they pay that which they promised faithfully, that they may be more willing to put themselves in like dangers another time. Nor the Utopians pass not how many of them they bring to destruction. For they believe that they should do a very good deed for all mankind, if they could rid out of the world all that foul stinking den of that most wicked and cursed people.

Of the Religions in Utopia

There be divers kinds of religion not only in sundry parts of the island, but also in divers places of every city. Some worship for God, the sun; some, the moon; some other of the planets. There be that give worship to a man that was once of excellent virtue or of famous glory, not only as God, but also as the chiefest and highest God. But the most and the wisest part (rejecting all these) believe that

---

16. "As who should live," etc.: read this "as people who would live just as richly. . ."

there is a certain godly power unknown, everlasting, incomprehensible, inexplicable, far above the capacity and reach of man's wit, dispersed throughout all the world, not in bigness, but in virtue and power. Him they call the father of all. To him alone they attribute the beginnings, the increasings, the proceedings, the changes and the ends of all things. Neither they give divine honours to any other than to him. Yea all the other also, though they be in divers opinions, yet in this point they agree all together with the wisest sort, in believing that there is one chief and principal God, the maker and ruler of the whole world: whom they all commonly in their country language call Mithra. But after they heard us speak of the name of Christ, of his doctrine, laws, miracles, and of the no less wonderful constancy of so many martyrs, whose blood willingly shed brought a great number of nations throughout all parts of the world into their sect; you will not believe with how glad minds, they agreed unto the same: whether it were by the secret inspiration of God, or else for that they thought it next unto that opinion, which among them is counted the chiefest. Howbeit I think this was no small help and furtherance in the matter, that they heard us say, that Christ instituted among his, all things common; and that the same community doth yet remain amongst the rightest Christian companies. Verily howsoever it come to pass, many of them consented together in our religion, and were washed in the holy water of baptism. They also which do not agree to Christ's religion, fear no man from it, nor speak against any man that hath received it. Saving that one of our company in my presence was sharply punished. He as soon as he was baptised began against our wills, with more earnest affection than wisdom, to reason of Christ's religion; and began to wax so hot in his matter, that he did not only prefer our religion before all other, but also did utterly despise and condemn all other, calling them profane, and the followers of them wicked and devilish and the children of everlasting damnation. When he had thus long reasoned the matter, they laid hold on him, accused him and condemned him into exile, not as a despiser of religion, but as a seditious person and a raiser up of dissension among the people. For this is one of the ancientest laws among them; that no man shall be blamed for reasoning in the maintenance of his own religion. For King Utopus, even at the first beginning, hearing that the inhabitants of the land were, before his coming thither, at continual dissention and strife among themselves for their religions; as soon as he had gotten the victory, first of all he made a decree, that it should be lawful for every man to favour and follow what religion he would, and that he might do the best he could to bring other to this opinion, so that he did it peaceably, gently, quietly, and soberly, without haste and contentious rebuking and inveighing against other. If he could not by fair and gentle speech induce them unto his opinion yet he should use no kind of violence, and refrain from displeasant and seditious words. To him that would vehemently and fervently in this cause strive and contend was decreed banishment or bondage. This law did King Utopus make not only for the maintenance of peace, which he saw through continual contention and mortal hatred utterly extinguished; but also because he thought this decree should make for the furtherance of religion. Whereof he durst define and determine nothing unadvisedly, as doubting whether God desiring manifold and divers sorts of honour, would inspire sundry men with sundry kinds of religion. And this surely he thought a very unmeet and foolish thing, and a point of arrogant presumption, to compel all other by violence and threatenings to agree to the same that thou believest to be true. Furthermore though there be one religion which alone is true, and all other vain and superstitious, yet did he well foresee (so that the matter were handled with reason, and sober modesty) that the truth of its own power would at the last issue out and come to light. But if contention and debate in that behalf should continually be used, as the worst men be most obstinate and stubborn, and in their evil opinion most constant; he perceived that then the best and holiest religion would be trodden underfoot and destroyed by most vain superstitions, even as good corn is by thorns and weeds overgrown and choked. Therefore all this matter he left undiscussed, and gave to every man free liberty and choice to believe what he would.

Exercises

1. Try making a sketch-map or diagram of Amaurote, the Utopian capital. What considerations or specifications does More give that are unnecessary in a modern American city? Are there any specifications that might improve American cities? Such as?
2. The Zapoletes, Utopia's mercenary soldiers, must have presented some problems to their employers. What might these be? Would *you* be willing to serve as a mercenary soldier? Why or why not?

Michel de Montaigne (1533–1592)

Michel de Montaigne (mon-TAN), like Erasmus, remained within the Catholic church, but he was far more interested in the secular world, in the classics, and, most notably, in himself. Montaigne was a rationalist and he was a skeptic. He was convinced that all knowledge was necessarily incomplete and would always be less than total. Like More, he saw that absolutist beliefs of church or state led to religious strife and warfare. He deliberately withdrew from his troubled world to study Latin and Greek authors and to write, essentially for his own gratification, personal essays on a wide range of subjects that interested him. No other Renaissance writer speaks as openly, clearly, and unpretentiously as does Montaigne. In the foreword to his *Essays* he writes:

> This, reader, is a book without guile. Had I proposed to court the favor of the world, I had set myself out in borrowed beauties; but it was my wish to be seen in my simple, natural and ordinary garb without study or artifice, for it was myself I had to paint.

Elsewhere he wrote, "If the world finds fault with me for speaking too much of myself, I find fault with the world for not even thinking of itself."

The cannibals described by Montaigne also live in the New World, in Brazil, but these are real people. More used his Utopians to criticize his own society, but Montaigne is more direct. His cannibals are compared with Europeans and, cannibalism notwithstanding, judged superior:

> We may, then, well call these people barbarians in respect to the rules of reason, but not in respect to ourselves, who, in all sorts of barbarity, exceed them.

Literary Selection

On Cannibals from ESSAYS
Michel de Montaigne

When Pyrrhus, king of Epirus, invaded Italy, having viewed and considered the order of the army the Romans sent out to meet him,—"I know not," said he, "what kind of barbarians (for so the Greeks called all other nations) these may be; but the disposition of this army that I see has nothing of the barbarian in it." As much said the Greeks of that which Flaminius brought into their country; and Philip, beholding, from an eminence, the order and disposition of the Roman camp, led into his kingdom by Publius Sulpitus Galba, spoke to the same effect. By which it appears how cautious men ought to be of taking things upon trust from vulgar opinion, and that we are to judge by the eye of reason, and not from common report. I have long had a man in my house that lived ten or twelve years in the new world discovered in these latter days, and in that part of it where Villegaignon landed, which he called Antartic France.[17] This discovery of so vast a country seems to be of very great consideration; and we are not sure that hereafter there may not be another found, so many wiser men than we having been deceived in this. I am afraid our eyes are bigger than our bellies, and that we have more curiosity than capacity; for we grasp at all, but catch nothing but air.

Plato brings in Solon, relating that he had heard from the Priests of Sais, in Egypt, that of old, and before the deluge, there was a great island, called Atlantis, situated directly at the mouth of the Strait of Gibraltar, which contained more ground than both Africa and Asia put together; that the kings of that country, who not only possessed that isle, but extended their dominion so far into the continent that they had a country as large as Africa to Egypt, and as long as Europe to Tuscany, had attempted to encroach even upon Asia, and to subjugate all the nations that border upon the Mediterranean Sea, as far as the Great Gulph,[18] and to that effect had overrun all Spain, the Gauls, and Italy, as far as Greece, where the Athenians stopped the torrent of their arms: but some time after both the Athenians, they, and their island, were swallowed by the flood. It is very likely that this violent eruption and inundation of water made strange alterations in the habitable parts of the earth; as 'tis said, for instance, that the sea then cut off Sicily from Italy; Cyprus from Syria; the isle of Negropont from the continent of Baeotia; and elsewhere, united lands that were separate before, by filling up the channel betwixt them with sand and mud. But there is no great appearance that this isle was this new world so lately discovered; for that almost touched upon Spain,[19] and it were an incredible effect of an inundation to have carried so prodigious a mass above

twelve hundred leagues: besides that our modern navigators have already almost discovered it to be no island, but firm land and continent, with the East Indies on the one side, and the land under the two poles on the other; or, if it be separated from them, 'tis by so narrow a strait that it never more deserves the name of an island for that. It should seem that, in this great body, there are two sorts of motions, the one natural, and the other feverish, as there are in ours. When I consider the impression that my own river, Dordogne, has made, in my time, on the right bank of its descent, and that, in twenty years, it has gained so much, and undermined the foundation of so many houses, I perceive it to be an extraordinary agitation; for, had it always gone on at this rate, or were hereafter to do it, the aspect of the world would be totally changed. But rivers alter in this respect, sometimes spreading out against the one side, and sometimes against the other, and sometimes quietly keeping the channel. I do not speak of sudden inundations, the causes of which every body understands.

The other testimony from antiquity, to which some would apply this discovery of the new world, is in Aristotle; at least, if that little book of unheard-of miracles be his. He there tells us that certain Carthaginians, having crossed the Atlantic sea, without the Straits of Gibraltar, and sailed a very long time, discovered, at last, a great and fruitful island, all covered over with wood, and watered with several broad and deep rivers, far remote from any continent, and that they, and others after them, allured by the pleasantness and fertility of the soil, went thither, with their wives and children, and began to plant a colony. But the senate of Carthage, perceiving their people, by little and little, to grow thin, issued out an express prohibition, that no one, upon pain of death, should transport themselves thither; and also drove out the new inhabitants, fearing, 'tis said, lest, in process of time, they should so multiply as to supplant themselves and ruin their state. But this relation of Aristotle's does no more agree with our new found lands than the other.

This man that I have[20] is a plain ignorant fellow, and therefore, the more likely to tell truth: for though your better-bred sort of men are much more curious in their observation, and discover a great deal more, they gloss upon it, and, to give the greater weight to what they deliver, and allure your belief, they cannot forbear a little to alter the story. They never represent things to you simply as they are, but rather as they appear to them, or as they would have them appear to you, and, to gain the reputation of men of judgment, and the better to induce your faith, are willing to help out the business with something more than is really true, of their own invention. Now, in this case, we should either have a man of irreproachable veracity, or so simple that he has not wherewithal to contrive and to give a color of truth to false relations, and that can have no ends in forging an

---

17. Brazil, where he arrived in 1557.

18. The Black Sea

19. Plato does not say any thing of the sort. The reader will observe in the following passages several geographical blunders, which were, doubtless, spread abroad by the first travellers in America.

20. Montaigne is referring to the man in his house who lived for ten or twelve years in the new world.

untruth. Such a one is mine; and, besides the little suspicion the man lies under, he has divers time brought me several seamen and merchants that, at the same time, went the same voyage. I shall, therefore, content myself with his information, without inquiring what the cosmographers say to the business. We need topographers to trace out to us the particular places where they have been; but for having had this advantage over us, to have seen the Holy Land, they would have the privilege to tell us stories of all the other parts of the world besides. I would have every one write what he knows, but no more; and that not in this only, but in all other subjects: for such a person may have some particular knowledge and experience of the nature of such a river, or such a fountain, that as to other things knows no more than what every body does, and yet, to keep a clutter with this little pittance of his, will undertake to write the whole body of physics: a vice whence many great inconveniences derive their original.

Now, to return to my subject, I find that there is nothing barbarous and savage in this nation, by any things that I can gather, excepting that every one gives the title of barbarism to every thing that is not in use in his own country: as, indeed, we have no other level of truth and reason than the example and idea of the opinions and customs of the place wherein we live. There is always the perfect religion, there the perfect government, there the perfect everything. This nation are savages, in the same way that we say fruits are wild, which nature produces of herself, and by her own ordinary progress; whereas, in truth, we ought rather to call those wild whose natures we have changed by our artifice, and diverted from the common order. In those, the genuine, most useful, and natural virtues and properties, are vigorous and active, which we have degenerated in these, by accommodating them to the pleasure of our own corrupted palate. And yet, for all this, our taste confesses a flavor and delicacy, excellent even to emulation of the best of ours, in several fruits those countries abound with, without art or culture; nor is it reasonable that art should gain the point over our great and powerful mother, Nature. We have so oppressed her beauty and the richness of her works, by our inventions, that we have almost smothered her; but, where she shines in her own purity and proper luster, she marvellously baffles and disgraces all our vain and frivolous attempts.

Our utmost endeavours cannot arrive at so much as to imitate the nest of the least of birds, its contexture, its elegance, its convenience; not so much as the web of a contemptible spider. "All things," says Plato, "are produced either by nature, or by fortune, or by art; the greatest and most beautiful by the one, or the other of the former, the least and most imperfect by the last."

These nations then seem to me to be so far barbarous, as having received but very little form and fashion from art and human invention, and being consequently not much remote from their original simplicity. The laws of nature govern them still, not as yet much vitiated with any mixture of ours; nay, in such purity that I am sometimes troubled we were no sooner acquainted with these people, and that they were not discovered in those better times, when there were men much more able to judge of them than we are. I am sorry that Lycurgus and Plato had no knowledge of them: for, to my apprehension, what we now see in those natives does not only surpass all the images with which the poets have adorned the golden age, and all their inventions in feigning a happy state of man, but moreover the fancy, and even the wish and desire of philosophy itself. So native and so pure a simplicity as we by experience see to be in them, could never enter into their imagination, nor could they ever believe that human society could have been maintained with so little artifice. Should I tell Plato that it is a nation wherein there is no manner of traffic, no knowledge of letters, no science of numbers, no name of magistrate, nor political superiority; no use of service, riches or poverty; no contracts, no successions, no dividends, no properties, no employments, but those of leisure; no respect of kindred, but in common; no clothing, no agriculture, no metal, no use of corn or wine; and where so much as the very words that signify lying, treachery, dissimulation, avarice, envy, detraction, and pardon were never heard of—how much would he find his imaginary republic short of this perfection?

As to the rest, they live in a country beautiful and pleasant, and so temperate, as my intelligence informs me, that 'tis very rare to hear of a sick person there; and they moreover assure me that they never saw any of the natives either paralytic, blear-eyed, toothless, or crooked with age. The situation of their country is along the seashore, and enclosed on the side towards the land with great and high mountains, having about an hundred leagues in breadth between. They have great store of fish and flesh meat that have no resemblance to ours, which they eat without any other cookery than plain boiling, roasting, or broiling. The first that carried a horse thither, though in several other voyages he had contracted an acquaintance and familiarity with them, put them into so terrible a fright at his appearance so mounted, that they killed him with their arrows before they could come to discover who he was. Their buildings, which are very long, and of capacity to hold two or three hundred people, are made of the barks of tall trees, reared with one end upon the ground, and leaning against and supporting one another at the top, like some of our barns, of which the covering hangs down to the very ground, and serves for the side walls. They have wood so hard that they cleave it into swords, and make grills of it to broil their meat. Their beds are of cotton, hung swinging from the roof, like our seamen's hammocks: for every one, the wives lying apart from their husbands. They rise with the sun, and so soon as they are up eat for all day: for they have no more meals but that. They do not drink then (as Suidas reports of some other people of the east, that never drink at their meals), but drink very often in the day, and sometimes a great deal. Their liquor is made of a certain root, and is as red as our claret; and this they never drink but lukewarm. It will keep only two or three days, has a sharp taste, is nothing heady, but very wholesome to the stomach, laxative for strangers, and a very pleasant beverage to such as are used to it. Instead of bread they make use of a certain white matter, like preserved coriander; I have tasted of it, the taste is sweet, but somewhat insipid. The whole day is spent in dancing. The young men go hunting after wild beasts with bows and arrows, and one part of their women are employed in preparing their drink the while, which is their chief employment. Some of their old men in the morning, before they fall to eating, preach to the whole family, walking to and fro from the one end of the house to the other, several times repeating the same sentence, till they have finished their round (for their houses are at least a hundred yards long); enjoining valor towards their enemies and love towards their wives are the two heads of his discourse, never failing, as a burden, to put them in mind that 'tis to their wives they are obliged for providing them their drink warm and relishing. The fashion of their beds, ropes, swords, and the wooden bracelets, which they tie about their wrists when they go to fight, and of their great canes, bored hollow at one end, by the sound of which they keep the cadence of their dances, it to be seen in several places, and among others at my house. They shave all over, and much more closely than we, without any other razor than one of wood or of stone.

They believe the immortality of the soul, and that those who have merited well of the gods are lodged in that part of heaven where the sun rises, and the accursed in the west. They have a kind of priests and prophets that rarely present themselves to the people, having their abode in the mountains. At their arrival there is a great feast and solemn assembly of many villages made, that is, all the neighboring families, for every house, as I have described it, makes a village, and are about a French league distant from one another. This prophet declaims to them in public, exhorting them to virtue and their duty; but all their ethics consist in these two articles—resolution in war and affection to their wives. He also prophesies to them events to come, and the issues they are to expect from their enterprises, prompts them to, or diverts them from, war. But let him look to it; for if he fail in his divination, and anything happen otherwise than he has foretold, he is cut into a thousand pieces, if he be caught and condemned for a false prophet; and for that reason, if any of them finds himself mistaken, he is no more to be heard of. Divination is a gift of God, and therefore to abuse it ought to be a punishable offense. Among the Scythians, when their diviners failed in the promised effect, they were laid, bound hand and foot, upon carts laden with firewood, and drawn with oxen, on which they were burned to death. Such as only meddle with things subject to the conduct of human capacity are excusable in doing the best they can; but those other sort of people that come to delude us with assurances of an extraordinary faculty beyond our understanding, ought they not to be punished for the temerity of their imposture?

They have wars with the nations that live farther within the main land, beyond their mountains, to which they go naked, and without other arms than their bows and wooden swords, pointed at one end like the head of a javelin. The obstinacy of their battles is wonderful: they never end without great effusion of blood; for as to running away, or fear, they know not what it is. Every one for a trophy brings home the head of an enemy he has killed, which he fixes over the door of his house. After having a long time treated their prisoners very well, and given them all the luxuries they can think of, he to whom the prisoner belongs invites a great assembly of his kindred and friends, who being come, he ties a rope to one of the arms of the prisoner, of which at a distance, out of his reach, he holds the one end himself, and gives to the friend he loves best the other arm, to hold after the same manner; which being done, they two, in the presence of all the assembly, dispatch him with their swords. After that they roast him, eat him amongst them, and send some chops to their absent friends; which nevertheless they do not do, as some think, for nourishment, as the Scythians anciently did, but as a representation of an extreme revenge, as will immediately appear. Having observed the Portuguese, who were in league with their enemies, to inflict another sort of death

upon any of them they took as prisoners, which was to bury them up to the waist, to shoot at the remaining part till it was stuck full of arrows, and then to hang them; they who thought those people of the other world (as men who had sown the knowledge of a great many vices amongst their neighbors, and were much greater masters in all kind of malignity than they,) did not exercise this sort of revenge without reason, and that it must needs be more painful than theirs, began to leave their old way and to follow this. I am not sorry that we should here take notice of the barbarous horror of so cruel an act, but that, seeing so clearly into their faults, we should be so blind to our own. I conceive there is more barbarity in eating a man alive than when he is dead; in tearing a body that is still full of feeling limb from limb, by racks and torments, in roasting it by degrees, causing it to be bit and worried by dogs and swine (as we have not only read, but lately seen, not among inveterate and mortal enemies, but among neighbors and fellow-citizens, and, what is worse, under color of piety and religion), than to roast and eat him after he is dead.

Chrysippus and Zeno, chiefs of the Stoic sect, were of opinion that there was no harm in making use of our dead carcasses, in any way, for our necessity, and in feeding upon them too; as our ancestors, who, being besieged by Caesar in the City of Alésia, resolved to sustain the famine of the siege with the bodies of their old men, women, and other persons, who were incapable of bearing arms. And the physicians made no scruple of employing it to all sorts of use, either to apply it outwardly, or to give it inwardly for the health of the patient. But there never was any opinion so irregular as to excuse treachery, disloyalty, tyranny and cruelty, which are our familiar vices. We may, then, well call these people barbarous, in respect to the rules of reason; but not in respect to ourselves, who, in all sorts of barbarity, exceed them. Their wars are throughout noble and generous, and carry as much excuse and fair pretence as this human malady is capable of; having with them no other foundation than the sole jealousy of valor. Their disputes are not for the conquests of new lands, those they already possess being so fruitful by nature as to supply them, without labor or concern, with all things necessary, in such abundance that they have no need to enlarge their borders. And they are moreover happy in this, that they only covet so much as their natural necessities require; all beyond that is superfluous to them. Men of the same age generally call one another brothers, those who are younger, sons and daughters, and the old men are fathers to all. These leave to their heirs in common this full possession of goods, without any manner of division, or other title than what nature bestows upon her creatures in bringing them into the world. If their neighbors pass the mountains, and come to attack them, and obtain a victory, all the victors gain by it is glory only, and the advantage of having proved themselves the better in valor and virtue: for they never meddle with the goods of the conquered, but presently return into their own country, where they have no want of any necessity; nor of this greatest of all goods, to know how to enjoy their condition happily, and to be content. And these in turn do the same. They demand of their prisoners no other ransom than acknowledgment that they are overcome. But there is not one found in an age that will not rather choose to die than make such a concession; or either by word or look recede from the grandeur of an invincible courage. There is not a man among them who had not rather be killed and eaten, than so much as to open his mouth to entreat he may not. They use them with all liberality and freedom, to the end their lives may be so much the dearer to them; but frequently entertain them with menaces of their approaching death, of the torments they are to suffer, of the preparations that are making in order to it, of the mangling their limbs, and of the feast that is to be made, where their carcass is to be the only dish. All which they do to no other end but only to extort some gently or submissive word from them, or to frighten them so as to make them run away; so that they may obtain this advantage, that they had terrified them, and that their constancy was shaken. And indeed, if rightly taken, it is in this point only that a true victory consists.

These prisoners are so far from discovering the least weakness for all the terrors can be represented to them, that on the contrary, during the two or three months that they are kept, they always appear with a cheerful countenance; importune their masters to make haste to bring them to the test; defy, rail at them and reproach them with cowardice, and the number of battles they have lost against those of their country. I have a song made by one of these prisoners, wherein he bids them come all and dine upon him, and welcome, for they shall at the same time eat their own fathers and grandfathers, whose flesh has served to feed and nourish him. "These muscles" says he, "this flesh, and these veins, are your own. Poor fools that you are, you little think that the substance of your ancestors' limbs is here yet: taste it well, and you will find in it the relish of your own flesh." In which song there is to be observed an invention that smacks nothing of the barbarian. Those that paint these people dying after this manner, represent the prisoner spitting in the face of his executioners, and making at them a wry mouth. And 'tis most certain that, to the very last gasp, they never cease to brave and defy them both in word and gesture. In plain truth, these men are very savage in comparison with us, for, of necessity, they must either be absolutely so, or else we are savages; for there is a vast difference between their manners and ours.

The men there have several wives, and so much the greater number by how much they have the greater reputation for valor, and it is one very remarkable virtue their women have, that the same endeavors our wives jealously use to hinder and divert us from the friendship and familiarity of other women, these employ to acquire it for their husbands; being, above all things, solicitous of their husband's honor, 'tis their chiefest care to procure for him the most companions in his affections they can, forasmuch as it is a testimony of their husbands' valor. Ours will cry out that 'tis monstrous: it is not so; 'tis a truly matrimonial virtue, though of the highest form.

And, that it may not be supposed that all this is done by a simple and servile observance of their common practice, or by any authoritative impression of their ancient custom, without judgment or reason, or, from having a soul so stupid that it cannot contrive what else to do, I must here give you some touches of their sufficiency in point of understanding. Besides what I repeated to you before, which was one of their songs of war, I have another, a love song, that begins thus: "Stay, adder, stay, that, by thy pattern, my sister may draw the fashion and work of a rich belt I would present to my beloved; so may thy beauty and the excellent order of thy scales be forever preferred before all other serpents." Now I have conversed enough with poetry to judge thus much: that not only there is nothing barbarous in this composition,

but, moreover, that it is perfectly Anacreontic. Indeed, their language is soft, of a pleasing accent, and something bordering upon the Greek terminations. Three of these people, not foreseeing how dear their knowledge of the corruptions of this part of the world will, one day, cost their happiness and repose, and that the effect of this commerce will be their ruin; which, I suppose, is in a very fair way (miserable men, to suffer themselves to be deluded with desire of novelty, and to have left the serenity of their own heaven to come so far to gaze at ours!), went to Rouen, at the time that the late King Charles the Ninth was there. The king himself talked to them a good while, and there were made to see our fashions, our pomp, and the form of a great city; after which some one asked their opinion, and would know of them, what of all the things they had seen they found most to be admired? To which they made answer, three things, of which I have forgot the third, and am vexed at it, but two I yet remember. They said that, in the first place, they thought it very strange that so many tall men wearing beards, strong and well armed, who were about the king ('tis like, they meant the Swiss of the guard), should submit to obey a child, and that they did not rather choose out one among themselves to command: secondly, (they have a way of speaking in their language, to call men the half of one another,) that they had observed that there were, among us, men full and crammed with all manner of luxuries, while, in the meantime, their halves were begging at their doors, lean and half-starved with hunger and poverty; and thought it strange that these needy halves were able to suffer so great an inequality and injustice, and that they did not take the others by the throats, or set fire to their houses. I talked to one of them a long while, but I had an interpreter, who followed me so ill, and whose stupidity kept him from understanding my questions so almost entirely that I could get nothing out of him of any moment. Asking him what advantage he reaped from the superiority he had among his own people—for he was a captain, and our mariners called him king,—he told me, to march at the head of them to war; and demanding of him, farther, how many men he had to follow him, he showed me a space of ground, to signify as many as could march in such a compass; which might be four or five thousand men; and, putting the question to him, whether or not his authority expired with the war, he told me this remained; that when he went to visit the villages in his dependency, they cleared him paths through the thick of their woods, through which he might pass at his ease. All this does not sound very ill, but then, hold on, they wear no breeches!

Exercises

1. Montaigne contends that the cannibals are less barbaric than his European contemporaries. Is this sardonic irony or is he serious? How serious?
2. Compare Montaigne's cannibals with today's society. Of course there are differences, but are all of the ethics of the cannibals clearly inferior? Are they, in all respects, more barbaric than we? As in Montaigne's essay, try to view our society through the eyes of the cannibals.

William Shakespeare (1564–1616)

Will Shakespeare was not a classical scholar, having, as he said, "little Latin and less Greek." His formal schooling was limited. His plots were mostly borrowed and his plays intended as box-office hits, which they were. Yet he is the supreme figure of Renaissance literature and the most quoted writer in the English language. How can this be? Critics have said that no human being could have written Mozart's music and the same can be said for the plays of Shakespeare. There is no accounting for genius; we have the music and the plays, and the world is infinitely richer because of them. Shakespeare understood human nature in all its complexity and perversity and was able to translate his perceptions into dramatic speech and action. Whether borrowed, created, or actual historical figures, his characters are unforgettable: Hamlet, King Lear, Falstaff, Macbeth, Romeo, Juliet, Othello, Iago, Portia, Richard III, Cleopatra, and Julius Caesar, to name a few.

The themes in the 37 plays—chronicle-plays, comedies, and tragedies—are timeless, but the flavor of the Renaissance is unmistakable. Like other Renaissance writers, Shakespeare was concerned with the active role of men and women in the lusty and prosperous Elizabethan age: their passions, problems, and aspirations. Like Machiavelli, he saw people as they really were and the vision was, for Shakespeare if not for Machiavelli, profoundly disturbing. Nevertheless, his pessimistic view of the baser instincts of people was tempered by his belief in their ability to achieve, usually through suffering, some measure of dignity and even nobility, as exemplified in *King Lear*.

Literary Selection

KING LEAR
William Shakespeare

Set somewhere in pre-Roman Britain, the play is a dark and powerful tragedy centered around a legendary king. The scope is vast, as described by A. C. Bradley in his *Shakespearean Tragedy:*

> . . . the feeling not of a scene or of a particular place, but of a world; or, so to speak more accurately, of a particular place which is also a world. This world is dim to us, partly from its immensity, and partly because it is filled with gloom; and in the gloom shapes approach and recede, whose half-seen faces and motions touch us with dread, horror, or the most painful pity,—sympathies and antipathies which we seem to be feeling not only for them but for the whole race. This world, we are told, is called Britain: but we should no more look for it in an atlas than for the place called Caucasus, where Prometheus was chained by Strength and Force and comforted by the daughters of Ocean. . . .

The plot, in brief, is the story of a haughty King Lear, who decides to hand over his power and wealth to his three daughters and their husbands. He will keep his title and base his bequests on how much love they have for him. Regan and Goneril lie about their deep affection and are richly rewarded, but the favorite daughter, Cordelia, says truthfully that "I love your Majesty according to my bond, no more nor less." Cordelia is summarily disinherited, but nevertheless taken in marriage by the King of France. For the remainder of the play Lear deteriorates physically and mentally as he is betrayed by Regan and Goneril, and finally goes mad during a mighty storm. The subplot parallels and reinforces the main plot. One of Lear's last faithful followers, Gloucester, has disinherited Edgar, his favorite son, and put in his place Edmund, his evil bastard son. Finally, a pitiful party of unfortunates—Lear, Gloucester, Edgar, and Lear's fool—band together, too late, to try to right the accumulation of wrongs. The invading King of France crushes the forces of evil, specifically Regan, Goneril, and Edmund, who have assisted in their own downfall. Cordelia, however, has been killed and Lear, now totally mad, dies of grief.

In simple terms, a tragedy ends with the hero dead. In Greek tragedy a noble man, because of a fatal flaw, is brought low. In the Elizabethan theatre the essentially good person is destroyed, one way or another, in the process of casting out evil. All of the above apply to Lear, but there is more. Lear's pride in keeping his title and demanding overt responses of love assist in his downfall. More importantly, he has no right to abdicate his kingly oath of office and turn the kingdom over to anyone. He is, moreover, blind to the hypocrisy of two of his daughters and to the faithfulness of his favorite child. For his part, Gloucester is unrepentant over his broken marriage vows and blind to the true nature of a son he barely knows. His blindness will become literal. Both Lear and Gloucester suddenly believe evil of a beloved and faithful daughter and son; the horrors that follow are unnatural and inevitable.

Throughout the play there are constant references to lower animals and how like them people are, a consistent dark theme throughout the Renaissance. Swinburne and other critics claim that the pessimism in Lear is total, that all succumbs to utter despair. Terror and pity are indeed carried to extreme limits, but Lear, who suffered mightily because of his own folly, is regenerated. There are flashes of his royal hauteur and vengefulness, but these emphasize the greatness and nobility of spirit that he recovers despite—or because of—his humiliation. In Act III, Lear and the other victims grow in spirit through suffering, but the villains become victims of their own material success. Adversity is constructive but evil is destructive and, in the end, self-destructive. Lear is reborn in the process of resisting evil, and he lives to see it destroyed.

CHARACTERS

Lear, King of Britain
King of France
Duke of Burgundy
Duke of Cornwall, husband to Regan
Duke of Albany, husband to Goneril
Earl of Kent
Earl of Gloucester
Edgar, son of Gloucester
Edmund, bastard son of Gloucester
Curan, a courtier
Old man, tenant of Gloucester
Doctor
Lear's Fool
Oswald, steward to Goneril
Captain, employed by Edmund
Gentleman, attending Cordelia
Herald
Servants to Cornwall
Goneril ⎫
Regan   ⎬ daughters of Lear
Cordelia ⎭
Knights attending Lear, Officers,
  Messengers, Soldiers, Attendants
          Scene: Britain

Act I.

Scene I.—KING LEAR'S palace.

Enter KENT, GLOUCESTER, *and* EDMUND.

Kent: I thought the king had more affected the Duke of Albany than Cornwall.

Gloucester: It did always seem so to us: but now, in the division of the kingdom, it appears not which of the dukes he values most; for equalities are so weighed that curiosity in neither can make choice of either's moiety.

Kent: Is not this your son, my lord?

Gloucester: His breeding, sir, hath been at my charge: I have so often blushed to acknowledge him that now I am brazed to it.

Kent: I cannot conceive you.

Gloucester: Sir, this young fellow's mother could: whereupon she grew round-wombed, and had indeed, sir, a son for her cradle ere she had a husband for her bed. Do you smell a fault?

Kent: I cannot wish the fault undone, the issue of it being so proper.

Gloucester: But I have, sir, a son by order of law, some year elder than this, who yet is no dearer in my account: though this knave came something saucily into the world before he was sent for, yet was his mother fair; there was good sport at his making, and the whoreson must be acknowledged. Do you know this noble gentleman, Edmund?

Edmund: No, my lord.

Gloucester: My lord of Kent: remember him hereafter as my honorable friend.

Edmund: My services to your lordship.

Kent: I must love you, and sue to know you better.

Edmund: Sir, I shall study deserving.

Gloucester: He hath been out nine years, and away he shall again. The king is coming.

Sennet. Enter one bearing a coronet, KING LEAR,
   CORNWALL, ALBANY, GONERIL, REGAN,
   CORDELIA, *and* ATTENDANTS.

Lear: Attend the lords of France and Burgundy, Gloucester.

Gloucester: I shall, my liege.
                        [*Exeunt* GLOUCESTER *and* EDMUND]

Lear: Meantime we shall express our darker purpose.
Give me the map there. Know we have divided
In three our kingdom: and 'tis our fast intent
To shake all cares and business from our age,
Conferring them on younger strengths, while we
Unburthen'd crawl toward death. Our son of Cornwall,
And you, our no less loving son of Albany,
We have this hour a constant will to publish
Our daughters' several dowers, that future strife
May be prevented now. The princes, France and
          Burgundy,
Great rivals in our youngest daughter's love,
Long in our court have made their amorous sojourn,
And here are to be answer'd. Tell me, my daughters,
Since now we will divest us both of rule,
Interest of territory, cares of state,
Which of you shall we say doth love us most?
That we our largest bounty may extend
Where nature doth with merit challenge.
          Goneril,
Our eldest-born, speak first.

Goneril: Sir, I love you more than words can wield the
          matter,
Dearer than eye-sight, space and liberty,
Beyond what can be valued, rich or rare,
No less than life, with grace, health, beauty, honor,
As much as child e'er loved or father found;
A love that makes breath poor and speech unable;
Beyond all manner of so much I love you.

Cordelia: [*Aside*] What shall Cordelia do? Love, and be silent.

Lear: Of all these bounds, even from this line to this,
With shadowy forests and with champains rich'd,
With plenteous rivers and wide-skirted meads,
We make thee lady. To thine and Albany's issue
Be this perpetual. What says our second daughter,
Our dearest Regan, wife to Cornwall? Speak.

Regan: I am made of that self metal as my sister,
And prize me at her worth. In my true heart
I find she names my very deed of love;
Only she comes too short: that I profess
Myself an enemy to all other joys
Which the most precious square of sense possesses,
And find I am alone felicitate
In your dear highness' love.

Cordelia: [*Aside*] Then poor Cordelia!
And yet not so, since I am sure my love's
More ponderous than my tongue.

Lear: To thee and thine hereditary ever
Remain this ample third of our fair kingdom,
No less in space, validity and pleasure,
Than that conferr'd on Goneril. Now, our joy,
Although the last, not least, to whose young love
The vines of France and milk of Burgundy
Strive to be interess'd, what can you say to draw
A third more opulent than your sisters? Speak.

Cordelia: Nothing, my lord.

Lear: Nothing!

Cordelia: Nothing.

Lear: Nothing will come of nothing: speak again.

Cordelia: Unhappy that I am, I cannot heave
My heart into my mouth: I love your majesty
According to my bond; nor more nor less.

Lear: How, how, Cordelia! mend your speech a little,
Lest it may mar your fortunes.
Cordelia: Good my lord,
You have begot me, bred me, loved me: I
Return those duties back as are right fit,
Obey you, love you, and most honor you.
Why have my sisters husbands, if they say
They love you all? Haply, when I shall wed,
That lord whose hand must take my plight shall carry
Half my love with him, half my care and duty:
Sure, I shall never marry like my sisters,
To love my father all.
Lear: But goes thy heart with this?
Cordelia: Aye, good my lord.
Lear: So young, and so untender?
Cordelia: So young, my lord, and true.
Lear: Let it be so; thy truth then be thy dower:
For, by the sacred radiance of the sun,
The mysteries of Hecate, and the night;
By all the operation of the orbs
From whom we do exist and cease to be;
Here I disclaim all my paternal care,
Propinquity and property of blood,
And as a stranger to my heart and me
Hold thee from this for ever. The barbarous Scythian,
Or he that makes his generation messes
To gorge his appetite, shall to my bosom
Be as well neighbor'd, pitied and relieved,
As thou my sometime daughter.
Kent: Good my liege,—
Lear: Peace, Kent!
Come not between the dragon and his wrath.
I loved her most, and thought to set my rest
On her kind nursery. Hence, and avoid my sight!
So be my grave my peace, as here I give
Her father's heart from her! Call France. Who stirs?
Call Burgundy. Cornwall and Albany,
With my two daughters' dowers digest this third:
Let pride, which she calls plainness, marry her.
I do invest you jointly with my power,
Pre-eminence and all the large effects
That troop with majesty. Ourself, by monthly course,
With reservation of an hundred knights
By you to be sustain'd, shall our abode
Make with you by due turns. Only we still retain
The name and all the additions to a king;
The sway, revenue, execution of the rest,
Beloved sons, be yours: which to confirm
This coronet part betwixt you.
Kent: Royal Lear,
Whom I have ever honor'd as my king,
Loved as my father, as my master follow'd,
As my great patron thought on in my prayers,—
Lear: The bow is bent and drawn, make from the shaft.
Kent: Let it fall rather, though the fork invade
The region of my heart: be Kent unmannerly,
When Lear is mad. What wouldst thou do, old man?
Think'st thou that duty shall have dread to speak,
When power to flattery bows? To plainness honor's
         bound,
When majesty stoops to folly. Reverse thy doom,
And in thy best consideration check
This hideous rashness: answer my life my judgment,
Thy youngest daughter does not love thee least;
Nor are those empty-hearted whose low sound
Reverbs no hollowness.

Lear: Kent, on thy life, no more.
Kent: My life I never held but as a pawn
To wage against thy enemies, nor fear to lose it,
Thy safety being the motive.
Lear: Out of my sight!
Kent: See better, Lear, and let me still remain
The true blank of thine eye.
Lear: Now, by Apollo,—
Kent: Now, by Apollo, king,
Thou swear'st thy gods in vain.
Lear: O, vassal! miscreant!
                              [*Laying his hand on his sword*]
Albany: }
Cornwall: }   Dear sir, forbear.
Kent: Do;
Kill thy physician, and the fee bestow
Upon the foul disease. Revoke thy doom;
Or, whilst I can vent clamor from my throat,
I'll tell thee thou dost evil.
Lear: Hear me, recreant!
On thy allegiance, hear me!
Since thou hast sought to make us break our vow,
Which we durst never yet, and with strain'd pride
To come between our sentence and our power,
Which nor our nature nor our place can bear,
Our potency made good, take thy reward.
Five days we do allot thee, for provision
To shield thee from diseases of the world,
And on the sixth to turn thy hated back
Upon our kingdom: if on the tenth day following
Thy banish'd trunk be found in our dominions,
The moment is thy death. Away! By Jupiter,
This shall not be revoked.
Kent: Fare thee well, king: sith thus thou wilt appear,
Freedom lives hence, and banishment is here.
[*To* CORDELIA] The gods to their dear shelter take thee,
         maid,
That justly think'st and hath most rightly said!
[*To* REGAN *and* GONERIL] And your large speeches may
         your deeds approve,
That good effects may spring from words of love.
Thus Kent, O princes, bids you all adieu;
He'll shape his old course in a country new.   [*Exit*]

Flourish. Re-enter GLOUCESTER, *with* FRANCE,
      BURGUNDY, *and* ATTENDANTS.

Gloucester: Here's France and Burgundy, my noble
lord.
Lear: My lord of Burgundy.
We first address towards you, who with this king
Hath rival'd for our daughter: what, in the least,
Will you require in present dower with her,
Or cease your quest of love?
Burgundy: Most royal majesty,
I crave no more than what your highness offer'd,
Nor will you tender less.
Lear: Right noble Burgundy,
When she was dear to us, we did hold her so;
But now her price is fall'n. Sir, there she stands:
If aught within that little seeming substance,
Or all of it, with our displeasure pierced,
And nothing more, may fitly like your grace,
She's there, and she is yours.
Burgundy: I know no answer.
Lear: Will you, with those infirmities she owes,
Unfriended, new adopted to our hate,
Dower'd with our curse and stranger'd with our oath,
Take her, or leave her?

Burgundy: Pardon me, royal sir;
Election makes not up on such conditions.
Lear: Then leave her, sir; for, by the power that made me,
I tell you all her wealth. [*To* FRANCE] For you, great king,
I would not from your love make such a stray,
To match you where I hate; therefore beseech you
To avert your liking a more worthier way
Than on a wretch whom nature is ashamed
Almost to acknowledge hers.
France: This is most strange,
That she, that even but now was your best object,
The argument of your praise, balm of your age,
Most best, most dearest, should in this trice of time
Commit a thing so monstrous, to dismantle
So many folds of favor. Sure, her offense
Must be of such unnatural degree
That monsters it, or your fore-vouch'd affection
Fall'n into taint: which to believe of her,
Must be a faith that reason without miracle
Could never plant in me.
Cordelia: I yet beseech your majesty,—
If for I want that glib and oily art,
To speak and purpose not, since what I well intend,
I'll do't before I speak,—that you make known
It is no vicious blot, murder, or foulness,
No unchaste action, or dishonor'd step,
That hath deprived me of your grace and favor;
But even for want of that for which I am richer,
A still-soliciting eye, and such a tongue
As I am glad I have not, though not to have it
Hath lost me in your liking.
Lear: Better thou
Hadst not been born than not to have pleased me better.
France: Is it but this? a tardiness in nature
Which often leaves the history unspoke
That it intends to do? My lord of Burgundy,
What say you to the lady? Love's not love
When it is mingled with regards that stand
Aloof from the entire point. Will you have her?
She is herself a dowry.
Burgundy: Royal Lear,
Give but that portion which yourself proposed,
And here I take Cordelia by the hand,
Duchess of Burgundy.
Lear: Nothing: I have sworn, I am firm.
Burgundy: I am sorry then you have so lost a father
That you must lose a husband.
Cordelia: Peace be with Burgundy!
Since that respects of fortune are his love,
I shall not be his wife.
France: Fairest Cordelia, that are most rich being poor,
Most choice forsaken, and most loved despised,
Thee and thy virtues here I seize upon:
Be it lawful I take up what's cast away.
Gods, gods! 'tis strange that from their cold'st neglect
My love should kindle to inflamed respect.
Thy dowerless daughter, king, thrown to my chance,
Is queen of us, of ours, and our fair France:
Not all the dukes of waterish Burgundy
Can buy this unprized precious maid of me.
Bid them farewell, Cordelia, though unkind:
Thou losest here, a better where to find.
Lear: Thou hast her, France: let her be thine, for we
Have no such daughter, nor shall ever see
That face of hers again. Therefore be gone

Without our grace, our love, our benison.
Come, noble Burgundy. [*Flourish. Exeunt all but*
FRANCE, GONERIL, REGAN, *and* CORDELIA.]
France: Bid farewell to your sisters.
Cordelia: The jewels of our father, with wash'd eyes
Cordelia leaves you: I know you what you are;
And, like a sister, am most loath to call
Your faults as they are named. Use well our father:
To your professed bosoms I commit him:
But yet, alas, stood I within his grace,
I would prefer him to a better place,
So farewell to you both.
Regan: Prescribe not us our duties.
Goneril: Let your study
Be to content your lord, who hath received you
At fortune's alms. You have obedience scanted,
And well are worth the want that you have wanted.
Cordelia: Time shall unfold what plaited cunning hides:
Who covers faults, at last shame them derides.
Well may you prosper!
France: Come, my fair Cordelia.
[*Exeunt* FRANCE *and* CORDELIA]
Goneril: Sister, it is not a little I have to say of what most nearly appertains to us both. I think our father will hence to-night.
Regan: That's most certain, and with you; next month with us.
Goneril: You see how full of changes his age is; the observation we have made of it hath not been little: he always loved our sister most; and with what poor judgment he hath now cast her off appears too grossly.
Regan: 'Tis the infirmity of his age: yet he hath ever but slenderly known himself.
Goneril: The best and soundest of his time hath been but rash; then must we look to receive from his age, not alone the imperfections of long ingrafted condition, but therewithal the unruly waywardness that infirm and choleric years bring with them.
Regan: Such unconstant starts are we like to have from him as this of Kent's banishment.
Goneril: There is further compliment of leave-taking between France and him. Pray you, let's hit together: if our father carry authority with such dispositions as he bears, this last surrender of his will but offend us.
Regan: We shall further think on't.
Goneril: We must do something, and i' the heat.
[*Exeunt*]

Scene II.—The EARL OF GLOUCESTER'S castle.
Enter EDMUND, *with a letter.*

Edmund: Thou, nature, art my goddess; to thy law
My services are bound. Wherefore should I
Stand in the plague of custom, and permit
The curiosity of nations to deprive me,
For that I am some twelve or fourteen moonshines
Lag of a brother? Why bastard? wherefore base?
When my dimensions are as well compact,
My mind as generous and my shape as true,
As honest madam's issue? Why brand they us
With base? with baseness? bastardy? base, base?
Who in the lusty stealth of nature take
More composition and fierce quality
Than doth, within a dull, stale, tired bed,
Go to the creating a whole tribe of fops,
Got 'tween asleep and wake? Well then,
Legitimate Edgar, I must have your land:

Our father's love is to the bastard Edmund
As to the legitimate: fine word, 'legitimate'!
Well, my legitimate, if this letter speed
And my invention thrive, Edmund the base
Shall top the legitimate. I grow; I prosper:
Now, gods, stand up for bastards!

Enter GLOUCESTER.

Gloucester: Kent banish'd thus! and France in choler parted!
And the king gone to-night! subscribed his power!
Confined to exhibition! All this done
Upon the gad! Edmund, how now! what news?

Edmund: So please your lordship, none.

[Putting up the letter]

Gloucester: Why so earnestly seek you to put up that letter?

Edmund: I know no news, my lord.

Gloucester: What paper were you reading?

Edmund: Nothing, my lord.

Gloucester: No? What needed then that terrible dispatch of it into your pocket? the quality of nothing hath not such need to hide itself. Let's see: come, if it be nothing, I shall not need spectacles.

Edmund: I beseech you, sir, pardon me: it is a letter from my brother, that I have not all o'er-read, and for so much as I have perused, I find it not fit for your o'er-looking.

Gloucester: Give me the letter, sir.

Edmund: I shall offend, either to detain or give it. The contents, as in part I understand them, are to blame.

Gloucester: Let's see, let's see.

Edmund: I hope, for my brother's justification, he wrote this but as an essay or taste of my virtue.

Gloucester: *[Reads]* 'This policy and reverence of age makes the world bitter to the best of our times; keeps our fortunes from us till our oldness cannot relish them. I begin to find an idle and fond bondage in the oppression of aged tyranny; who sways, not as it hath power, but as it is suffered. Come to me, that of this I may speak more. If our father would sleep till I waked him, you should enjoy half his revenue for ever, and live the beloved of your brother, EDGAR.' Hum! Conspiracy!—'Sleep till I waked him, you should enjoy half his revenue!'—My son Edgar! Had he a hand to write this? a heart and brain to breed it in? When came this to you? who brought it?

Edmund: It was not brought me, my lord; there's the cunning of it; I found it thrown in at the casement of my closet.

Goucester: You know the character to be your brother's?

Edmund: If the matter were good, my lord, I durst swear it were his; but, in respect of that, I would fain think it were not.

Gloucester: It is his.

Edmund: It is his hand, my lord; but I hope his heart is not in the contents.

Gloucester: Hath he never heretofore sounded you in this business?

Edmund: Never, my lord: but I have heard him oft maintain it to be fit, that, sons at perfect age, and fathers declining, the father should be as ward to the son, and the son manage his revenue.

Gloucester: O villain, villain! His very opinion in the letter! Abhorred villain! Unnatural, detested, brutish villain! worse than brutish! Go, sirrah, seek him; aye, apprehend him: abominable villain! Where is he?

Edmund: I do not well know, my lord. If it shall please you to suspend your indignation against my brother till you can derive from him better testimony of his intent, you should run a certain course; where, if you violently proceed against him, mistaking his purpose, it would make a great gap in your own honor and shake in pieces the heart of his obedience. I dare pawn down my life for him that he hath wrote this to feel my affection to your honor and to no further pretense of danger.

Gloucester: Think you so?

Edmund: If your honor judge it meet, I will place you where you shall hear us confer of this, and by an auricular assurance have your satisfaction, and that without any further delay than this very evening.

Gloucester: He cannot be such a monster—

Edmund: Nor is not, sure.

Gloucester: To his father, that so tenderly and entirely loves him. Heaven and earth! Edmund, seek him out; wind me into him, I pray you: frame the business after your own wisdom. I would unstate myself, to be in a due resolution.

Edmund: I will seek him, sir, presently, convey the business as I shall find means, and acquaint you withal.

Gloucester: These late eclipses in the sun and moon portend no good to us: though the wisdom of nature can reason it thus and thus, yet nature finds itself scourged by the sequent effects: love cools, friendship falls off, brothers divide: in cities, mutinies; in countries, discord; in palaces, treason; and the bond cracked 'twixt son and father. This villain of mine comes under the prediction; there's son against father: the king falls from bias of nature; there's father against child. We have seen the best of our time: machinations, hollowness, treachery and all ruinous disorders follow us disquietly to our graves. Find out this villain, Edmund; it shall lose thee nothing; do it carefully. And the noble and truehearted Kent banished! his offense, honesty! 'Tis strange.

[Exit]

Edmund: This is the excellent foppery of the world, that when we are sick in fortune—often the surfeit of our own behavior—we make guilty of our disasters the sun, the moon and the stars: as if we were villains by necessity, fools by heavenly compulsion; knaves, thieves and treachers, by spherical predominance; drunkards, liars and adulterers, by an enforced obedience of planetary influence; and all that we are evil in, by a divine thrusting on: an admirable evasion of whore-master man, to lay his goatish disposition to the charge of a star! My father compounded with my mother under the dragon's tail, and my nativity was under Ursa major; so that it follows I am rough and lecherous. Tut, I should have been that I am, had the maidenliest star in the firmament twinkled on my bastardizing, Edgar—

Enter EDGAR.

And pat he comes like the catastrophe of the old comedy: my cue is villainous melancholy, with a sigh like Tom o' Bedlam. O, these eclipses do portend these divisions! fa, sol, la, mi.

Edgar: How now, brother Edmund! what serious contemplation are you in?

Edmund: I am thinking, brother, of a prediction I read this other day, what should follow these eclipses.

Edgar: Do you busy yourself about that?

Edmund: I promise you, the effects he writ of succeed unhappily; as of unnaturalness between the child and the parent; death, dearth, dissolutions of ancient amities; divisions in state, menaces and maledictions against king and nobles; needless diffidences, banishment of friends, dissipation of cohorts, nuptial breeches, and I know not what.

Edgar: How long have you been a sectary astronomical?

Edmund: Come, come; when saw you my father last?

Edgar: Why, the night gone by.

Edmund: Spake you with him?

Edgar: Aye, two hours together.

Edmund: Parted you in good terms? Found you no displeasure in him by word or countenance?

Edgar: None at all.

Edmund: Bethink yourself wherein you may have offended him: and at my entreaty forbear his presence till some little time hath qualified the heat of his displeasure, which at this instant so rageth in him that with the mischief of your person it would scarcely allay.

Edgar: Some villain hath done me wrong.

Edmund: That's my fear. I pray you, have a continent forbearance till the speed of his rage goes slower, and, as I say, retire with me to my lodging, from whence I will fitly bring you to hear my lord speak: pray ye, go; there's my key: if you do stir abroad, go armed.

Edgar: Armed, brother!

Edmund: Brother, I advise you to the best; go armed: I am no honest man if there be any good meaning towards you: I have told you what I have seen and heard; but faintly, nothing like the image and horror of it: pray you, away.

Edgar: Shall I hear from you anon?

Edmund: I do serve you in this business. [*Exit* EDGAR]
A credulous father, and a brother noble,
Whose nature is so far from doing harms
That he suspects none; on whose foolish honesty
My practices ride easy. I see the business.
Let me, if not by birth, have lands by wit:
All with me's meet that I can fashion it.   [*Exit*]

Scene III.—The DUKE OF ALBANY'S *palace.*

Enter GONERIL *and* OSWALD, *her steward.*

Goneril: Did my father strike my gentleman for chiding of his fool?

Oswald: Yes, madam.

Goneril: By day and night he wrongs me; every hour
He flashes into one gross crime or other,
That sets us all at odds: I'll not endure it:
His knights grow riotous, and himself upbraids us
On every trifle. When he returns from hunting,
I will not speak with him; say I am sick:
If you come slack of former services,
You shall do well; the fault of it I'll answer.

Oswald: He's coming, madam; I hear him. [*Horns within*]

Goneril: Put on what weary negligence you please,
You and your fellows; I 'ld have it come to question:
If he distaste it, let him to our sister,
Whose mind and mine, I know, in that are one,
Not to be over-ruled. Idle old man,
That still would manage those authorities
That he hath given away! Now, by my life
Old fools are babes again, and must be used
With checks as flatteries, when they are seen abused.
Remember what I tell you.

Oswald: Very well, madam.

Goneril: And let his knights have colder looks among you;
What grows of it, no matter; advise your fellows so:
I would breed from hence occasions, and I shall,

That I may speak: I'll write straight to my sister,
To hold my very course. Prepare for dinner.   [*Exeunt*]

Scene IV.—A hall in the same.

Enter KENT, *disguised.*

Kent: If but as well I other accents borrow,
That can my speech defuse, my good intent
May carry through itself to that full issue
For which I razed my likeness. Now, banish'd Kent,
If thou canst serve where thou dost stand condemn'd,
So may it come, thy master whom thou lovest
Shall find thee full of labors.

Horns within. Enter LEAR, KNIGHTS, *and* ATTENDANTS.

Lear: Let me not stay a jot for dinner; go get it ready.
[*Exit an* ATTENDANT] How now! what art thou?

Kent: A man, sir.

Lear: What dost thou profess? What wouldst thou with us?

Kent: I do profess to be no less than I seem; to serve him truly that will put me in trust; to love him that is honest; to converse with him that is wise and says little; to fear judgment; to fight when I cannot choose, and to eat no fish.

Lear: What art thou?

Kent: A very honest-hearted fellow, and as poor as the king.

Lear: If thou be as poor for a subject as he is for a king, thou art poor enough. What wouldst thou?

Kent: Service.

Lear: Who wouldst thou serve?

Kent: You.

Lear: Dost thou know me, fellow?

Kent: No, sir; but you have that in your countenance which I would fain call master.

Lear: What's that?

Kent: Authority.

Lear: What services canst thou do?

Kent: I can keep honest counsel, ride, run, mar a curious tale in telling it, and deliver a plain message bluntly: that which ordinary men are fit for, I am qualified in, and the best of me is diligence.

Lear: How old art thou?

Kent: Not so young, sir, to love a woman for singing, nor so old to dote on her for any thing: I have years on my back forty eight.

Lear: Follow me; thou shalt serve me: if I like thee no worse after dinner, I will not part from thee yet. Dinner, ho, dinner! Where's my knave? my fool? Go you, and call my fool hither.

Exit an ATTENDANT.

Enter OSWALD.

You, you, sirrah, where's my daughter?

Oswald: So please you,—   [*Exit*]

Lear: What says the fellow there? Call the clotpoll back.
[*Exit a* KNIGHT] Where's my fool, ho? I think the world's asleep.

Re-enter KNIGHT.

How now! where's that mongrel?

Knight: He says, my lord, your daughter is not well.

Lear: Why came not the slave back to me when I called him?

Knight: Sir, he answered me in the roundest manner, he would not.

Lear: He would not!

Knight: My lord, I know not what the matter is; but, to my judgment, your highness is not entertained with that ceremonious affection as you were wont; there's a great abatement of kindness appear as well in the general dependants as in the duke himself also and your daughter.

Lear: Ha! sayest thou so?

Knight: I beseech you, pardon me, my lord, if I be mistaken; for my duty cannot be silent when I think your highness wronged.

Lear: Thou but rememberest me of mine own conception: I have perceived a most faint neglect of late; which I have rather blamed as mine own jealous curiosity than as a very pretense and purpose of unkindness: I will look further into 't. But where's my fool? I have not seen him this two days.

Knight: Since my young lady's going into France, sir, the fool hath much pined away.

Lear: No more of that; I have noted it well. Go you, and tell my daughter I would speak with her. [*Exit an* ATTENDANT] Go you, call hither my fool.

[*Exit an* ATTENDANT]

Re-enter OSWALD.

O, you sir, come you hither, sir: who am I, sir?

Oswald: My lady's father.

Lear: My lady's father! my lord's knave: you whoreson dog! you slave! you cur!

Oswald: I am none of these, my lord; I beseech your pardon.

Lear: Do you bandy looks with me, you rascal?

[*Striking him*]

Oswald: I'll not be struck, my lord.

Kent: Nor tripped neither, you base foot-ball player.

[*Tripping up his heels*]

Lear: I thank thee, fellow; thou servest me, and I'll love thee.

Kent: Come, sir, arise, away! I'll teach you differences: away, away! If you will measure your lubber's length again, tarry: but away! go to; have you wisdom? so.

[*Pushes* OSWALD *out*]

Lear: Now, my friendly knave, I thank thee: there's earnest of thy service.

[*Giving* KENT *money*]

Enter FOOL.

Fool: Let me hire him too: here's my coxcomb.

[*Offering* KENT *his cap*]

Lear: How now, my pretty knave! how dost thou?

Fool: Sirrah, you were best take my coxcomb.

Kent: Why, fool?

Fool: Why, for taking one's part that's out of favor: nay, as thou canst not smile as the wind sits, thou 'lt catch cold shortly: there, take my coxcomb: why, this fellow hath banished two on 's daughters, and done the third a blessing against his will; if thou follow him, thou must needs wear my coxcomb. How now, nuncle! Would I had two coxcombs and two daughters!

Lear: Why, my boy?

Fool: If I gave them all my living, I 'ld keep my coxcombs myself. There's mine; beg another of thy daughters.

Lear: Take heed, sirrah; the whip.

Fool: Truth's a dog must to kennel; he must be whipped out, when Lady the brach may stand by the fire and stink.

Lear: A pestilent gall to me!

Fool: Sirrah, I'll teach thee a speech.

Lear: Do.

Fool: Mark it, nuncle:
Have more than thou showest,
Speak less than thou knowest,
Lend less than thou owest,
Ride more than thou goest,
Learn more than thou trowest,
Set less than thou throwest,
Leave thy drink and thy whore,
And keep in-a-door,
And thou shalt have more
Than two tens to a score.

Kent: This is nothing, fool.

Fool: Then 'tis like the breath of an unfee'd lawyer, you gave me nothing for 't. Can you make no use of nothing, nuncle?

Lear: Why, no, boy; nothing can be made out of nothing.

Fool: [*To* KENT] Prithee, tell him, so much the rent of his land comes to: he will not believe a fool.

Lear: A bitter fool!

Fool: Dost thou know the difference, my boy, Between a bitter fool and a sweet fool?

Lear: No, lad; teach me.

Fool: That lord that counsel'd thee
To give away thy land,
Come place him here by me;
Do thou for him stand:
The sweet and bitter fool
Will presently appear;
The one in motley here,
The other found out there.

Lear: Dost thou call me fool, boy?

Fool: All thy other titles thou has given away; that thou wast born with.

Kent: This is not altogether fool, my lord.

Fool: No, faith, lords and great men will not let me; if I had a monopoly out, they would have part on 't: and ladies too, they will not let me have all the fool to myself; they'll be snatching. Give me an egg, nuncle, and I'll give thee two crowns.

Lear: What two crowns shall they be?

Fool: Why, after I have cut the egg in the middle and eat up the meat, the two crowns of the egg. When thou clovest thy crown i' the middle and gavest away both parts, thou borest thine ass on thy back o'er the dirt: thou hadst little wit in thy bald crown when thou gavest thy golden one away. If I speak like myself in this, let him be whipped that first finds it so.
[*Singing*] Fools had ne'er less wit in a year;
For wise men are grown foppish,
And know not how their wits to wear,
Their manners are so apish.

Lear: When were you wont to be so full of songs, sirrah?

Fool: I have used it, nuncle, ever since thou madest thy daughters thy mother: for when thou gavest them the rod and puttest down thine own breeches,
[*Singing*] Then they for sudden joy did weep,
And I for sorrow sung,
That such a king should play bo-peep,
And go the fools among.
Prithee, nuncle, keep a schoolmaster that can teach thy fool to lie: I would fain learn to lie.

Lear: An you lie, sirrah, we'll have you whipped.

Fool: I marvel what kin thou and thy daughters are: they'll have me whipped for speaking true, thou 'lt have me whipped for lying, and sometimes I am whipped for holding my peace. I had rather be any kind o' thing than a fool: and yet I would not be thee, nuncle; thou hast pared thy wit o' both sides and left nothing i' the middle. Here comes one o' the parings.

Enter GONERIL.

Lear: How now, daughter! what makes that frontlet on? Methinks you are too much of late i' the frown.

Fool: Thou wast a pretty fellow when thou hadst no need to care for her frowning; now thou art an O without a figure: I am better than thou art now; I am a fool, thou art nothing. [*To* GONERIL] Yes, forsooth, I will hold my tongue; so your face bids me, though you say nothing.

> Mum, mum:
> He that keeps nor crust nor crumb,
> Weary of all, shall want some.

[*Pointing to* LEAR] That's a shealed peascod.

Goneril: Not only, sir, this your all-licensed fool,
But other of your insolent retinue
Do hourly carp and quarrel, breaking forth
In rank and not to be endured riots. Sir,
I had thought, by making this well known unto you,
To have found a safe redress; but now grow fearful,
By what yourself too late have spoke and done,
That you protect this course and put it on
By your allowance; which if you should, the fault
Would not 'scape censure, nor the redresses sleep,
Which, in the tender of a wholesome weal,
Might in their working do you that offense
Which else were shame, that then necessity
Will call discreet proceeding.

Fool: For, you know, nuncle,
The hedge-sparrow fed the cuckoo so long,
That it had it head bit off by it young.
So out went the candle, and we were left darkling.

Lear: Are you our daughter?

Goneril: Come, sir,
I would you would make use of that good wisdom
Whereof I know you are fraught, and put away
These dispositions that of late transform you
From what you rightly are.

Fool: May not an ass know when the cart draws the horse? Whoop, Jug! I love thee.

Lear: Doth any here know me? This is not Lear:
Doth Lear walk thus? speak thus? Where are his eyes?
Either his notion weakens, his discernings
Are lethargied—Ha! waking? 'tis not so.
Who is it that can tell me who I am?

Fool: Lear's shadow.

Lear: I would learn that; for, by the marks of sovereignty, knowledge and reason, I should be false persuaded I had daughters.

Fool: Which they will make an obedient father.

Lear: Your name, fair gentlewoman?

Goneril: This admiration, sir, is much o' the savor
Of other your new pranks. I do beseech you
To understand my purposes aright:
As you are old and reverend, you should be wise.
Here do you keep a hundred knights and squires;
Men so disorder'd, so debosh'd and bold,
That this our court, infected with their manners,
Shows like a riotous inn: epicurism and lust
Make it more like a tavern or a brothel
Than a graced palace. The shame itself doth speak
For instant remedy: be then desired

By her that else will take the thing she begs
A little to disquantity your train,
And the remainder that shall still depend,
To be such men as may besort your age,
Which know themselves and you.

Lear: Darkness and devils!
Saddle my horses; call my train together.
Degenerate bastard! I'll not trouble thee:
Yet have I left a daughter.

Goneril: You strike my people, and your disorder'd rabble
Make servants of their betters.

Enter Albany.

Lear: Woe, that too late repents,—[*To* ALBANY] O, sir, are you come?
Is it your will? Speak, sir. Prepare my horses.
Ingratitude, thou marble-hearted fiend,
More hideous when thou show'st thee in a child
Than the sea-monster!

Albany: Pray, sir, be patient.

Lear: [*To* GONERIL] Detested kite! thou liest.
My train are men of choice and rarest parts,
That all particulars of duty know,
And in the most exact regard support
The worships of their name. O most small fault,
How ugly didst thou in Cordelia show!
That, like an engine, wrench'd my frame of nature
From the fix'd place, drew from my heart all love
And added to the gall. O Lear, Lear, Lear!
Beat at this gate, that let thy folly in.

[*Striking his head*]

And thy dear judgment out! Go, go, my people.

Albany: My lord, I am guiltless, as I am ignorant
Of what hath moved you.

Lear: It may be so, my lord.
Hear, nature, hear; dear goddess, hear!
Suspend thy purpose, if thou didst intend
To make this creature fruitful:
Into her womb convey sterility:
Dry up in her the organs of increase,
And from her derogate body never spring
A babe to honor her! If she must teem,
Create her child of spleen, that it may live
And be a thwart disnatured torment to her.
Let it stamp wrinkles in her brow of youth;
With cadent tears fret channels in her cheeks;
Turn all her mother's pains and benefits
To laughter and contempt; that she may feel
How sharper than a serpent's tooth it is
To have a thankless child! Away, away! [*Exit*]

Albany: Now, gods that we adore, whereof comes this?

Goneril: Never afflict yourself to know the cause,
But let his disposition have that scope
That dotage gives it.

Re-enter LEAR.

Lear: What, fifty of my followers at a clap!
Within a fortnight!

Albany: What's the matter, sir?

Lear: I'll tell thee. [*To* GONERIL] Life and death! I am ashamed
That thou hast power to shake my manhood thus;
That these hot tears, which break from me perforce,
Should make thee worth them. Blasts and fogs upon thee!
The untented woundings of a father's curse
Pierce every sense about thee! Old fond eyes,
Beweep this cause again, I'll pluck ye out

And cast you with the waters that you lose
To temper clay. Yea, is it come to this?
Let it be so: yet have I left a daughter,
Who, I am sure, is kind and comfortable:
When she shall hear this of thee, with her nails
She'll flay thy wolfish visage. Thou shalt find
That I'll resume the shape which thou dost think
I have cast off for ever: thou shalt, I warrant thee.

                [*Exeunt* LEAR, KENT, *and* ATTENDANTS]

Goneril: Do you mark that, my lord?
Albany: I cannot be so partial, Goneril,
To the great love I bear you,—
Goneril: Pray you, content. What, Oswald, ho!
[*To the* FOOL] You, sir, more knave than fool, after your
    master.
Fool: Nuncle Lear, Nuncle Lear, tarry; take the fool with
    thee.

       A fox, when one has caught her,
       And such a daughter,
       Should sure to the slaughter,
       If my cap would buy a halter:
       So the fool follows after.   [*Exit*]

Goneril: This man hath had good counsel: a hundred
    knights!
'Tis politic and safe to let him keep
At point a hundred knights: yes, that on every dream,
Each buzz, each fancy, each complaint, dislike,
He may enguard his dotage with their powers
And hold our lives in mercy. Oswald, I say!
Albany: Well, you may fear too far.
Goneril: Safer than trust too far:
Let me still take away the harms I fear,
Not fear still to be taken: I know his heart.
What he hath utter'd I have writ my sister:
If she sustain him and his hundred knights,
When I have show'd the unfitness,—

           Re-enter OSWALD.

               How, now, Oswald!
What, have you writ that letter to my sister?
Oswald: Yes, madam.
Goneril: Take you some company, and away to horse:
Inform her full of my particular fear,
And thereto add such reasons of your own
As may compact it more. Get you gone;
And hasten your return. [*Exit* OSWALD] No, no, my lord,
This milky gentleness and course of yours
Though I condemn not, yet, under pardon,
You are much more attask'd for want of wisdom
Than praised for harmful mildness.
Albany: How far your eyes may pierce I cannot tell:
Striving to better, oft we mar what's well.
Goneril: Nay, then—
Albany: Well, well; the event.   [*Exeunt*]

Scene V.—Court before the same.

       Enter LEAR, KENT, *and* FOOL.

Lear: Go you before to Gloucester with these letters.
Acquaint my daughter no further with any thing you know
than comes from her demand out of the letter. If your
diligence be not speedy, I shall be there afore you.
Kent: I will not sleep, my lord, till I have delivered
your letter.   [*Exit*]
Fool: If a man's brains were in 's heels, were 't not in
danger of kibes?
Lear: Aye, boy.

Fool: Then, I prithee, be merry; thy wit shall ne'er go
slip-shod.
Lear: Ha, ha, ha!
Fool: Shalt see thy other daughter will use thee kindly;
for though she's as like this as a crab 's like an apple, yet I
can tell what I can tell.
Lear: Why, what canst thou tell, my boy?
Fool: She will taste as like this as a crab does to a crab.
Thou canst tell why one's nose stands i' the middle on 's
face?
Lear: No.
Fool: Why, to keep one's eyes of either side's nose, that
what a man cannot smell out he may spy into.
Lear: I did her wrong—
Fool: Canst tell how an oyster makes his shell?
Lear: No.
Fool: Nor I either; but I can tell why a snail has a
house.
Lear: Why?
Fool: Why, to put 's head in; not to give it away to his
daughters, and leave his horns without a case.
Lear: I will forget my nature.—So kind a father!—Be my
horses ready?
Fool: Thy asses are gone about 'em. The reason why the
seven stars are no more than seven is a pretty reason.
Lear: Because they are not eight?
Fool: Yes, indeed: thou wouldst make a good fool.
Lear: To tak 't again perforce! Monster ingratitude!
Fool: If thou wert my fool, nuncle, I 'ld have thee
beaten for being old before thy time.
Lear: How's that?
Fool: Thou shouldst not have been old till thou hadst
been wise.
Lear: O, let me not be mad, not mad, sweet heaven!
Keep me in temper: I would not be mad!

          Enter GENTLEMAN.

How now! are the horses ready?
Gentleman: Ready, my lord.
Lear: Come, boy.
Fool: She that's a maid now and laughts at my departure
Shall not be a maid long, unless things be cut shorter.

                  [*Exeunt*]

Act II.

Scene I.—The EARL OF GLOUCESTER'S castle.

     Enter EDMUND *and* CURAN, *meeting.*

Edmund: Save thee, Curan.
Curan: And you, sir. I have been with your father and
given him notice that the Duke of Cornwall and Regan
his duchess will be here with him this night.
Edmund: How comes that?
Curan: Nay, I know not. You have heard of the news
abroad, I mean the whispered ones, for they are yet but
ear-kissing arguments?
Edmund: Not I: pray you, what are they?
Curan: Have you heard of no likely wars toward, 'twixt
the Dukes of Cornwall and Albany?
Edmund: Not a word.
Curan: You may do then in time. Fare you well, sir.
                    [*Exit*]

Edmund: The duke be here to-night? The better! best!
This weaves itself perforce into my business.
My father hath set guard to take my brother;
And I have one thing, of a queasy question,

Which I must act: briefness and fortune, work!
Brother, a word; descend: brother, I say!

Enter EDGAR.

My father watches: O sir, fly this place;
Intelligence is given where you are hid;
You have now the good advantage of the night:
Have you not spoken 'gainst the Duke of Cornwall?
He's coming hither, now, i' the night, i' the haste,
And Regan with him: have you nothing said
Upon his party 'gainst the Duke of Albany?
Advise yourself.
Edgar: I am sure on 't, not a word.
Edmund: I hear my father coming: pardon me:
In cunning I must draw my sword upon you:
Draw: seem to defend yourself: now quit you well.
Yield: come before my father. Light, ho, here!
Fly, brother. Torches, torches! So farewell. [*Exit* EDGAR]
Some blood drawn on me would beget opinion
                                              [*Wounds his arm*]
Of my more fierce endeavor: I have seen drunkards
Do more than this in sport. Father, father!
Stop, stop! No help?

Enter GLOUCESTER, *and* SERVANTS *with torches.*

Gloucester: Now, Edmund, where 's the villain?
Edmund: Here stood he in the dark, his sharp sword
      out,
Mumbling of wicked charms, conjuring the moon
To stand 's auspicious mistress.
Gloucester: But where is he?
Edmund: Look, sir, I bleed.
Gloucester: Where is the villain, Edmund?
Edmund: Fled this way, sir. When by no means he
      could—
Gloucester: Pursue him, ho!—Go after. [*Exeunt some*
      SERVANTS] 'By no means' what?
Edmund: Persuade me to the murder of your lordship;
But that I told him the revenging gods
'Gainst parricides did all their thunders bend,
Spoke with how manifold and strong a bond
The child was bound to the father; sir, in fine,
Seeing how loathly opposite I stood
To his unnatural purpose, in fell motion
With his prepared sword he charges home
My unprovided body, lanced mine arm:
But when he saw my best alarum'd spirits
Bold in the quarrel's right, roused to the encounter,
Or whether gasted by the noise I made,
Full suddenly he fled.
Gloucester: Let him fly far:
Not in this land shall he remain uncaught:
And found—dispatch. The noble duke my master,
My worthy arch and patron, comes to-night.
By his authority I will proclaim it,
That he which finds him shall deserve our thanks,
Bringing the murderous caitiff to the stake;
He that conceals him, death.
Edmund: When I dissuaded him from his intent
And found him pight to do it, with curst speech
I threaten'd to discover him: he replied,
'Thou unpossessing bastard! dost thou think,
If I would stand against thee, could the reposure
Of any trust, virtue, or worth, in thee
Make thy words faith'd? No: what I should deny—
As this I would; aye, though thou didst produce
My very character—I 'ld turn it all
To thy suggestion, plot, and damned practice:
And thou must make a dullard of the world,

If they not thought the profits of my death
Were very pregnant and potential spurs
To make thee seek it.'
Gloucester: Strong and fasten'd villain!
Would he deny his letter? I never got him.
                                              [*Tucket within*]
Hark, the duke's trumpets! I know not why he comes.
All ports I'll bar; the villain shall not 'scape;
The duke must grant me that: besides, his picture
I will send far and near, that all the kingdom
May have due note of him; and of my land,
Loyal and natural boy, I'll work the means
To make thee capable.

Enter CORNWALL, REGAN, *and* ATTENDANTS.

Cornwall: How now, my noble friend! since I came
      hither,
Which I can call but now, I have heard strange news.
Regan: If it be true, all vengeance comes too short
Which can pursue the offender. How dost, my lord?
Gloucester: O, madam, my old heart is crack'd, is
      crack'd!
Regan: What, did my father's godson seek your life?
He whom my father named? your Edgar?
Gloucester: O, lady, lady, shame would have it hid!
Regan: Was he not companion with the riotous knights
That tend upon my father?
Gloucester: I know not, madam: 'tis too bad, too bad.
Edmund: Yes, madam, he was of that consort.
Regan: No marvel then, though he were ill affected:
'Tis they have put him on the old man's death,
To have the waste and spoil of his revenues.
I have this present evening from my sister
Been well inform'd of them, and with such cautions
That if they come to sojourn at my house,
I'll not be there.
Cornwall: Nor I, assure thee, Regan.
Edmund, I hear that you have shown your father
A child-like office.
Edmund: 'Twas my duty, sir.
Gloucester: He did bewray his practice, and received
This hurt you see, striving to apprehend him.
Cornwall: Is he pursued?
Gloucester: Aye, my good lord.
Cornwall: If he be taken, he shall never more
Be fear'd of doing harm: make your own purpose,
How in my strength you please. For you, Edmund,
Whose virtue and obedience doth this instant
So much commend itself, you shall be ours:
Natures of such deep trust we shall much need:
You we first seize on.
Edmund: I shall serve you, sir,
Truly, however else.
Gloucester: For him I thank your grace.
Cornwall: You know not why we came to visit you,—
Regan: Thus out of season, threading dark-eyed night:
Occasions, noble Gloucester, of some poise,
Wherein we must have use of your advice:
Our father he hath writ, so hath our sister,
Of differences, which I least thought it fit
To answer from our home; the several messengers
From hence attend dispatch. Our good old friend,
Lay comforts to your bosom, and bestow
Your needful counsel to our business,
Which craves the instant use.
Gloucester: I serve you, madam:
Your graces are right welcome.   [*Flourish. Exeunt*]

Scene II.—Before GLOUCESTER'S castle.
Enter KENT and OSWALD, severally.

Oswald: Good dawning to thee, friend: art of this house?

Kent: Aye.

Oswald: Where may we set our horses?

Kent: I' the mire.

Oswald: Prithee, if thou lovest me, tell me.

Kent: I love thee not.

Oswald: Why then I care not for thee.

Kent: If I had thee in Lipsbury pinfold, I would make thee care for me.

Oswald: Why dost thou use me thus? I know thee not.

Kent: Fellow, I know thee.

Oswald: What dost thou know me for?

Kent: A knave; a rascal; an eater of broken meats; a base, proud, shallow, beggarly, three-suited, hundred-pound, filthy, worsted-stocking knave; a lily-livered, action-taking knave; a whoreson, glass-gazing, superserviceable, finical rogue; one-trunk-inheriting slave; one that wouldst be a bawd in way of good service, and art nothing but the composition of a knave, beggar, coward, pandar, and the son and heir of a mongrel bitch: one whom I will beat into a clamorous whining, if thou deniest the least syllable of thy addition.

Oswald: Why, what a monstrous fellow art thou, thus to rail on one that is neither known of thee nor knows thee!

Kent: What a brazen-faced varlet art thou, to deny thou knowest me! Is it two days ago since I tripped up thy heels and beat thee before the king? Draw, you rogue: for, though it be night, yet the moon shines; I'll make a sop o' the moonshine of you: draw, you whoreson cullionly barber-monger, draw.

[Drawing his sword]

Oswald: Away! I have nothing to do with thee.

Kent: Draw, you rascal: you come with letters against the king, and take vanity the puppet's part against the royalty of her father: draw, you rogue, or I'll so carbonado your shanks: draw, you rascal: come your ways.

Oswald: Help, ho! murder! help!

Kent: Strike, you slave; stand, rogue; stand, you neat slave, strike.

[Beating him]

Oswald: Help, ho! murder! help!

Enter EDMUND, with his rapier drawn, CORNWALL,
REGAN, GLOUCESTER, and SERVANTS.

Edmund: How now! What's the matter? *[Parting them]*

Kent: With you, goodman boy, an you please: come, I'll flesh you; come on, young master.

Gloucester: Weapons! arms! What's the matter here?

Cornwall: Keep peace, upon your lives;
He dies that strikes again. What is the matter?

Regan: The messengers from our sister and the king.

Cornwall: What is your difference? speak.

Oswald: I am scarce in breath, my lord.

Kent: No marvel, you have so bestirred your valor. You cowardly rascal, nature disclaims in thee: a tailor made thee.

Cornwall: Thou art a strange fellow: a tailor make a man?

Kent: Aye, a tailor, sir: a stone-cutter or a painter could not have made him so ill, though he had been but two hours at the trade.

Cornwall: Speak yet, how grew your quarrel?

Oswald: This ancient ruffian, sir, whose life I have spared at suit of his gray beard,—

Kent: Thou whoreson zed! thou unnecessary letter! My lord, if you will give me leave, I will tread this unbolted villain into mortar, and daub the walls of a jakes with him. Spare my gray beard, you wagtail?

Cornwall: Peace, sirrah!
You beastly knave, know you no reverence?

Kent: Yes, sir; but anger hath a privilege.

Cornwall: Why art thou angry?

Kent: That such a slave as this should wear a sword,
Who wears no honesty. Such smiling rogues as these,
Like rats, oft bite the holy cords a-twain
Which are too intrinse to unloose; smooth every passion
That in the natures of their lords rebel;
Bring oil to fire, snow to their colder moods;
Renege, affirm, and turn their halcyon beaks
With every gale and vary of their masters,
Knowing nought, like dogs, but following.
A plague upon your epileptic visage!
Smile you my speeches, as I were a fool?
Goose, if I had you upon Sarum plain,
I 'ld drive ye cackling home to Camelot.

Cornwall: What, art thou mad, old fellow?

Gloucester: How fell you out? say that.

Kent: No contraries hold more antipathy
Than I and such a knave.

Cornwall: Why dost thou call him knave? What is his fault?

Kent: His countenance likes me not.

Cornwall: No more perchance does mine, nor his, nor hers.

Kent: Sir, 'tis my occupation to be plain:
I have seen better faces in my time
Than stands on any shoulder that I see
Before me at this instant.

Cornwall: This is some fellow,
Who, having been praised for bluntness, doth affect
A saucy roughness, and constrains the garb
Quite from his nature: he cannot flatter, he,—
An honest mind and plain,—he must speak truth!
An they will take it, so; if not, he's plain.
These kind of knaves I know, which in this plainness
Harbor more craft and more corrupter ends
Than twenty silly ducking observants
That stretch their duties nicely.

Kent: Sir, in good faith, in sincere verity,
Under the allowance of your great aspect,
Whose influence, like the wreath of radiant fire
On flickering Phoebus' front,—

Cornwall: What mean'st by this?

Kent: To go out of my dialect, which you discommend so much. I know, sir, I am no flatterer: he that beguiled you in a plain accent was a plain knave; which, for my part, I will not be, though I should win your displeasure to entreat me to 't.

Cornwall: What was the offense you gave him?

Oswald: I never gave him any:
It pleased the king his master very late
To strike at me, upon his misconstruction;
When he, conjunct, and flattering his displeasure,
Tripp'd me behind; being down, insulted, rail'd,
And put upon him such a deal of man,
That worthied him, got praises of the king
For him attempting who was self-subdued,
And in the fleshment of this dread exploit
Drew on me here again.

Kent: None of these rogues and cowards
But Ajax is their fool.

Cornwall: Fetch forth the stocks!
You stubborn ancient knave, you reverend braggart,
We'll teach you—
Kent: Sir, I am too old to learn:
Call not your stocks for me: I serve the king,
On whose employment I was sent to you:
You shall do small respect, show too bold malice
Against the grace and person of my master,
Stocking his messenger.
Cornwall: Fetch forth the stocks! As I have life and
honor,
There shall he sit till noon.
Regan: Till noon! till night, my lord, and all night too.
Kent: Why, madam, if I were your father's dog,
You should not use me so.
Regan: Sir, being his knave, I will.
Cornwall: This is a fellow of the self-same color
Our sister speaks of. Come, bring away the stocks!
[*Stocks brought out*]
Gloucester: Let me beseech your grace not to do so:
His fault is much, and the good king his master
Will check him for 't: your purposed low correction
Is such as basest and contemned'st wretches
For pilferings and most common trespasses
Are punish'd with: the king must take it ill,
That he, so slightly valued in his messenger,
Should have him thus restrain'd.
Cornwall: I'll answer that.
Regan: My sister may receive it much more worse,
To have her gentleman abused, assaulted,
For following her affairs. Put in his legs.
[*KENT is put in the stocks.*]
Come, my good lord, away.
[*Exeunt all but GLOUCESTER and KENT.*]
Gloucester: I am sorry for thee, friend; 'tis the duke's
pleasure,
Whose disposition, all the world well knows,
Will not be rubb'd nor stopp'd: I'll entreat for thee.
Kent: Pray, do not, sir: I have watch'd and travel'd hard;
Some time I shall sleep out, the rest I'll whistle.
A good man's fortune may grow out at heels:
Give you good morrow!
Gloucester: The duke 's to blame in this; 'twill be ill
taken. [*Exit*]
Kent: Good king, that must approve the common saw,
Thou out of heaven's benediction comest
To the warm sun!
Approach, thou beacon to this under globe,
That by thy comfortable beams I may
Peruse this letter! Nothing almost sees miracles
But misery: I know 'tis from Cordelia,
Who hath most fortunately been inform'd
Of my obscured course; and shall find time
From this enormous state, seeking to give
Losses their remedies. All weary and o'er-watch'd,
Take vantage, heavy eyes, not to behold
This shameful lodging.
Fortune, good night: smile once more; turn thy wheel!
[*Sleeps*]

Scene III.—A wood.

Enter EDGAR.

Edgar: I heard myself proclaim'd;
And by the happy hollow of a tree
Escaped the hunt. No port is free; no place,
That guard and most unusual vigilance

Does not attend my taking. Whiles I may 'scape
I will preserve myself: and am bethought
To take the basest and the most poorest shape
That ever penury in contempt of man
Brought near to beast: my face I'll grime with filth,
Blanket my loins, elf all my hair in knots
And with presented nakedness out-face
The winds and persecutions of the sky.
The country gives me proof and precedent
Of Bedlam beggars, who with roaring voices
Strike in their numb'd and mortified bare arms
Pins, wooden pricks, nails, sprigs of rosemary;
And with this horrible object, from low farms,
Poor pelting villages, sheep-cotes and mills,
Sometime with lunatic bans, sometime with prayers,
Enforce their charity. Poor Turlygod! poor Tom!
That's something yet: Edgar I nothing am. [*Exit*]

Scene IV.—Before GLOUCESTER'S castle.
KENT *in the stocks.*

Enter LEAR, FOOL, and GENTLEMEN.

Lear: 'Tis strange that they should so depart from
home,
And not send back my messenger.
Gentleman: As I learn'd,
The night before there was no purpose in them
Of this remove.
Kent: Hail to thee, noble master!
Lear: Ha!
Makest thou this shame thy pastime?
Kent: No, my lord.
Fool: Ha, ha! he wears cruel garters. Horses are tied by
the heads, dogs and bears by the necks, monkeys by the
loins, and men by the legs: when a man's over-lusty at
legs, then he wears wooden nether-stocks.
Lear: What 's he that hath so much thy place mistook
To set thee here?
Kent: It is both he and she;
Your son and daughter.
Lear: No.
Kent: Yes.
Lear: No, I say.
Kent: I say, yea.
Lear: No, no, they would not.
Kent: Yes, they have.
Lear: By Jupiter, I swear, no.
Kent: By Juno, I swear, aye.
Lear: They durst not do 't;
They could not, would not do 't; 'tis worse than murder,
To do upon respect such violent outrage:
Resolve me with all modest haste which way
Thou mightst deserve, or they impose, this usage,
Coming from us.
Kent: My lord, when at their home
I did commend your highness' letters to them,
Ere I was risen from the place that show'd
My duty kneeling, came there a reeking post,
Stew'd in his haste, half breathless, panting forth
From Goneril his mistress salutations;
Deliver'd letters, spite of intermission,
Which presently they read: on whose contents
They summon'd up their meiny, straight took horse;
Commanded me to follow and attend
The leisure of their answer; gave me cold looks:
And meeting here the other messenger,
Whose welcome, I perceived, had poison'd mine—
Being the very fellow that of late

Display'd so saucily against your highness—
Having more man than wit about me, drew:
He raised the house with loud and coward cries.
Your son and daughter found this trespass worth
The shame which here it suffers.

Fool: Winter's not gone yet, if the wild geese fly that
    way.

> Fathers that wear rags
>   Do make their children blind:
> But fathers that bear bags
>   Shall see their children kind.
> Fortune, that arrant whore,
>   Ne'er turns the key to the poor.

But, for all this, thou shalt have as many dolors for thy
    daughters as thou canst tell in a year.

Lear: O, how this mother swells up toward my heart!
Hysterica passio, down, thou climbing sorrow,
Thy element's below! Where is this daughter?

Kent: With the earl, sir, here within.

Lear: Follow me not; stay here.   [*Exit*]

Gentleman: Made you no more offense but what you
speak of?

Kent: None.
How chance the king comes with so small a train?

Fool: An thou hadst been set i' the stocks for that
question, thou hadst well deserved it.

Kent: Why, fool?

Fool: We'll set thee to school to an aunt, to teach thee
there's no laboring i' the winter. All that follow their
noses are led by their eyes but blind men; and there's not
a nose among twenty but can smell him that's stinking.
Let go thy hold when a great wheel runs down a hill, lest
it break thy neck with following it; but the great one that
goes up the hill, let him draw thee after. When a wise
man gives thee better counsel, give me mine again: I
would have none but knaves follow it, since a fool gives
it.

> That sir which serves and seeks for gain,
>   And follows but for form,
> Will pack when it begins to rain,
>   And leave thee in the storm.
> But I will tarry; the fool will stay,
>   And let the wise man fly:
> The knave turns fool that runs away;
>   The fool no knave, perdy.

Kent: Where learned you this, fool?

Fool: Not i' the stocks, fool.

        Re-enter LEAR, *with* GLOUCESTER.

Lear: Deny to speak with me? They are sick? they are
    weary?
They have travel'd all the night? Mere fetches;
The images of revolt and flying off.
Fetch me a better answer.

Gloucester: My dear lord,
You know the fiery quality of the duke;
How unremovable and fix'd he is
In his own course.

Lear: Vengeance! plague! death! confusion!
Fiery? what quality? Why, Gloucester, Gloucester,
I 'ld speak with the Duke of Cornwall and his wife.

Gloucester: Well, my good lord, I have inform'd them
so.

Lear: Inform'd them! Dost thou understand me, man?

Gloucester: Aye, my good lord.

Lear: The king would speak with Cornwall; the dear
    father

Would with his daughter speak, commands her service:
Are they inform'd of this? My breath and blood!
'Fiery'? 'the fiery duke'? Tell the hot duke that—
No, but not yet: may be he is not well:
Infirmity doth still neglect all office
Whereto our health is bound; we are not ourselves
When nature being oppress'd commands the mind
To suffer with the body; I'll forbear;
And am fall'n out with my more headier will,
To take the indisposed and sickly fit
For the sound man. [*Looking on* KENT] Death on my
    state! wherefore
Should he sit here? This act persuades me
That this remotion of the duke and her
Is practice only. Give me my servant forth.
Go tell the duke and 's wife I 'ld speak with them,
Now, presently: bid them come forth and hear me,
Or at their chamber-door I'll beat the drum
Till it cry sleep to death.

Gloucester: I would have all well betwixt you.   [*Exit*]

Lear: O me, my heart, my rising heart! But down!

Fool: Cry to it, nuncle, as the cockney did to the eels
when she put 'em i' the paste alive; she knapped 'em o'
the coxcombs with a stick, and cried, 'Down, wantons,
down!' 'Twas her brother that, in pure kindness to his
horse, buttered his hay.

Re-enter GLOUCESTER *with* CORNWALL, REGAN, *and*
SERVANTS.

Lear: Good morrow to you both.

Cornwall: Hail to your grace!
                      [KENT *is set at liberty*]

Regan: I am glad to see your highness.

Lear: Regan, I think you are; I know what reason
I have to think so: If thou shouldst not be glad,
I would divorce me from thy mother's tomb,
Sepulchring an adultress. [*To* KENT.] O, are you free?
Some other time for that. Beloved Regan,
Thy sister 's naught: O Regan, she hath tied
Sharp-tooth'd unkindness, like a vulture, here:
                     [*Points to his heart*]
I can scarce speak to thee; thou 'lt not believe
With how depraved a quality—O Regan!

Regan: I pray you, sir, take patience: I have hope
You less know how to value her desert
Than she to scant her duty.

Lear: Say, how is that?

Regan: I cannot think my sister in the least
Would fail her obligation: if, sir, perchance
She have restrain'd the riots of your followers,
'Tis on such ground and to such wholesome end
As clears her from all blame.

Lear: My curses on her!

Regan: O, sir, you are old;
Nature in you stands on the very verge
Of her confine: you should be ruled and led
By some discretion that discerns your state
Better than you yourself. Therefore I pray you
That to our sister you do make return;
Say you have wrong'd her, sir.

Lear: Ask her forgiveness?
Do you but mark how this becomes the house:
[*Kneeling*] 'Dear daughter, I confess that I am old;
Age is unnecessary: on my knees I beg
That you'll vouchsafe me raiment, bed and food.'

Regan: Good sir, no more; these are unsightly tricks:
Return you to my sister.

Lear: [*Rising*] Never Regan:
She hath abated me of half my train;
Look'd black upon me; struck me with her tongue,
Most serpent-like, upon the very heart:
All the stored vengeances of heaven fall
On her ingrateful top! Strike her young bones,
You taking airs, with lameness.
Cornwall: Fie, sir, fie!
Lear: You nimble lightnings, dart your blinding flames
Into her scornful eyes. Infect her beauty,
You fen-suck'd fogs, drawn by the powerful sun
To fall and blast her pride.
Regan: O the blest gods! so will you wish on me,
When the rash mood is on.
Lear: No, Regan, thou shalt never have my curse:
Thy tender-hefted nature shall not give
Thee o'er to harshness: her eyes are fierce, but thine
Do comfort and not burn. 'Tis not in thee
To grudge my pleasures, to cut off my train,
To bandy hasty words, to scant my sizes,
And in conclusion to oppose the bolt
Against my coming in: thou better know'st
The offices of nature, bond of childhood,
Effects of courtesy, dues of gratitude;
Thy half o' the kingdom hast thou not forgot,
Wherein I thee endow'd.
Regan: Good sir, to the purpose.
Lear: Who put my man i' the stocks? [*Tucket within*]
Cornwall: What trumpet's that?
Regan: I know 't; my sister's: this approves her letter,
That she would soon be here.

Enter OSWALD.

Is your lady come?
Lear: This is a slave whose easy-borrow'd pride
Dwells in the fickle grace of her he follows.
Out, varlet, from my sight!
Cornwall: What means your grace?
Lear: Who stock'd my servant? Regan, I have good hope
Thou didst not know on 't. Who comes here?

Enter GONERIL.

O heavens,
If you do love old men, if your sweet sway
Allow obedience, if yourselves are old,
Make it your cause; send down, and take my part!
[*To* GONERIL] Art not ashamed to look upon this beard?
O Regan, wilt thou take her by the hand?
Goneril: Why not by the hand, sir? How have I offended?
All 's not offense that indiscretion finds
And dotage terms so.
Lear: O sides, you are too tough;
Will you yet hold? How came my man i' in the stocks?
Cornwall: I set him there, sir: but his own disorders
Deserved much less advancement.
Lear: You! did you?
Regan: I pray you, father, being weak, seem so.
If, till the expiration of your month,
You will return and sojourn with my sister,
Dismissing half your train, come then to me:
I am now from home and out of that provision
Which shall be needful for your entertainment.
Lear: Return to her, and fifty men dismiss'd?
No, rather I abjure all roofs, and choose
To wage against the enmity o' the air,
To be a comrade with the wolf and owl,—
Necessity's sharp pinch! Return with her?

Why, the hot-blooded France, that dowerless took
Our youngest born, I could as well be brought
To knee his throne, and, squire-like, pension beg
To keep base life afoot. Return with her?
Persuade me rather to be slave and sumpter
To this detested groom. [*Pointing at* OSWALD]
Goneril: At your choice, sir.
Lear: I prithee, daughter, do not make me mad:
I will not trouble thee, my child; farewell:
We'll no more meet, no more see one another:
But yet thou art my flesh, my blood, my daughter;
Or rather a disease that 's in my flesh,
Which I must needs call mine: thou art a boil,
A plague-sore, an embossed carbuncle,
In my corrupted blood. But I'll not chide thee;
Let shame come when it will, I do not call it:
I do not bid the thunder-bearer shoot,
Nor tell tales of thee to high-judging Jove:
Mend when thou canst; be better at thy leisure:
I can be patient; I can stay with Regan,
I and my hundred knights.
Regan: Not altogether so:
I look'd not for you yet, nor am provided
For your fit welcome. Give ear, sir, to my sister;
For those that mingle reason with your passion
Must be content to think you old, and so—
But she knows what she does.
Lear: Is this well spoken?
Regan: I dare avouch it, sir: what, fifty followers?
Is it not well? What should you need of more?
Yea, or so many, sith that both charge and danger
Speak 'gainst so great a number? How in one house
Should many people under two commands
Hold amity? 'Tis hard, almost impossible.
Goneril: Why might not you, my lord, receive attendance
From those that she calls servants or from mine?
Regan: Why not, my lord? If then they chanced to slack you,
We could control them. If you will come to me,
For now I spy a danger, I entreat you
To bring but five and twenty: to no more
Will I give place or notice.
Lear: I gave you all—
Regan: And in good time you gave it.
Lear: Made you my guardians, my depositaries,
But kept a reservation to be follow'd
With such a number. What, must I come to you
With five and twenty, Regan? said you so?
Regan: And speak 't again, my lord; no more with me.
Lear: Those wicked creatures yet do look well-favor'd,
When others are more wicked; not being the worst
Stands in some rank of praise. [*To* GONERIL] I'll go with thee:
Thy fifty yet doth double five and twenty,
And thou art twice her love.
Goneril: Hear me, my lord:
What need you five and twenty, ten, or five,
To follow in a house where twice so many
Have a command to tend you?
Regan: What need one?
Lear: O, reason not the need: our basest beggars
Are in the poorest thing superfluous:
Allow not nature more than nature needs,
Man's life 's as cheap as beast's: thou art a lady;
If only to go warm were gorgeous,
Why, nature needs not what thou gorgeous wear'st,

Which scarcely keeps thee warm. But for true need,—
You heavens, give me that patience, patience I need!
You see me here, you gods, a poor old man,
As full of grief as age; wretched in both:
If it be you that stirs these daughters' hearts
Against their father, fool me not so much
To bear it tamely; touch me with noble anger,
And let not woman's weapons, water-drops,
Stain my man's cheeks! No, you unnatural hags,
I will have such revenges on you both
That all the world shall—I will do such things,—
What they are, yet I know not, but they shall be
The terrors of the earth. You think I'll weep;
No, I'll not weep:
I have full cause of weeping; but this heart
Shall break into a hundred thousand flaws,
Or ere I'll weep. O fool, I shall go mad!
     [*Exeunt* LEAR, GLOUCESTER, KENT, *and* FOOL]
Cornwall: Let us withdraw; 'twill be a storm.
         [*Storm and tempest*]
Regan: This house is little: the old man and his people
Cannot be well bestow'd.
Goneril: 'Tis his own blame; hath put himself from rest,
And must needs taste his folly.
Regan: For his particular, I'll receive him gladly,
But not one follower.
Goneril: So am I purposed.
Where is my lord of Gloucester?
Cornwall: Follow'd the old man forth: he is return'd.

       Re-enter GLOUCESTER.

Gloucester: The king is in high rage.
Cornwall: Whither is he going?
Gloucester: He calls to horse; but will I know not
    whither.
Cornwall: 'Tis best to give him way; he leads himself.
Goneril: My lord, entreat him by no means to stay.
Gloucester: Alack, the night comes on, and the bleak
    winds
Do sorely ruffle; for many miles about
There's scarce a bush.
Regan: O, sir, to willful men
The injuries that they themselves procure
Must be their schoolmasters. Shut up your doors:
He is attended with a desperate train;
And what they may incense him to, being apt
To have his ear abused, wisdom bids fear.
Cornwall: Shut up your doors, my lord; 'tis a wild
    night:
My Regan counsels well: come out o' the storm.
         [*Exeunt*]

Act III.

Scene I.—A heath.

Storm still. Enter KENT *and a* GENTLEMAN, *meeting.*

Kent: Who's there, besides foul weather?
Gentleman: One minded like the weather, most
    unquietly.
Kent: I know you. Where's the king?
Gentleman: Contending with the fretful elements;
Bids the wind blow the earth into the sea,
Or swell the curled waters 'bove the main,
That things might change or cease; tears his white hair,
Which the impetuous blasts, with eyeless rage,
Catch in their fury, and make nothing of;
Strives in his little world of man to out-scorn
The to-and-fro-conflicting wind and rain.

This night, wherein the cub-drawn bear would crouch,
The lion and the belly-pinched wolf
Keep their fur dry, unbonneted he runs,
And bids what will take all.
Kent: But who is with him?
Gentleman: None but the fool; who labors to out-jest
His heart-struck injuries.
Kent: Sir, I do know you;
And dare, upon the warrant of my note,
Commend a dear thing to you. There is division,
Although as yet the face of it be cover'd
With mutual cunning, 'twixt Albany and Cornwall;
Who have—as who have not, that their great stars
Throned and set high?—servants, who seem no less,
Which are to France the spies and speculations
Intelligent of our state; what hath been seen,
Either in snuffs and packings of the dukes,
Or the hard rain which both of them have borne
Against the old kind king, or something deeper,
Whereof perchance these are but furnishings,—
But true it is, from France there comes a power
Into this scatter'd kingdom; who already,
Wise in our negligence, have secret feet
In some of our best ports, and are at point
To show their open banner. Now to you:
If on my credit you dare build so far
To make your speed to Dover, you shall find
Some that will thank you, making just report
Of how unnatural and bemadding sorrow
The king hath cause to plain.
I am a gentleman of blood and breeding,
And from some knowledge and assurance offer
This office to you.
Gentleman: I will talk further with you.
Kent: No, do not.
For confirmation that I am much more
Than my out-wall, open this purse and take
What it contains. If you shall see Cordelia,—
As fear not but you shall,—show her this ring,
And she will tell you who your fellow is
That yet you do not know. Fie on this storm!
I will go seek the king.
Gentleman: Give me your hand:
Have you no more to say?
Kent: Few words, but, to effect, more than all yet;
That when we have found the king,—in which your pain
That way, I'll this,—he that first lights on him
Holla the other.   [*Exeunt severally*]

Scene II.—Another part of the heath. Storm still.
       Enter LEAR *and* FOOL.

Lear: Blow, winds, and crack your cheeks! rage! blow!
You cataracts and hurricanoes, spout
Till you have drench'd our steeples, drown'd the cocks!
You sulphurous and thought-executing fires,
Vaunt-couriers to oak-cleaving thunderbolts,
Singe my white head! And thou, all-shaking thunder,
Smite flat the thick rotundity o' the world!
Crack nature's molds, all germins spill at once
That make ingrateful man!
Fool: O nuncle, court holy-water in a dry house is
better than this rain-water out o' door. Good nuncle, in,
and ask thy daughters' blessing: here 's a night pities
neither wise man nor fool.
Lear: Rumble thy bellyful! Spit, fire! spout, rain.
Nor rain, wind, thunder, fire, are my daughters:
I tax not you, you elements, with unkindness;

I never gave you kingdom, call'd you children,
You owe me no subscription: then let fall
Your horrible pleasure; here I stand, your slave,
A poor, infirm, weak and despised old man:
But yet I call you servile ministers,
That have with two pernicious daughters join'd
Your high-engender'd battles 'gainst a head
So old and white as this. O! O! 'tis foul!
Fool: He that has a house to put 's head in has a good
head-piece.
     The cod-piece that will house
       Before the head has any,
     The head and he shall louse
       So beggars marry many.
     The man that makes his toe
       What he his heart should make
     Shall of a corn cry woe,
       And turn his sleep to wake.
For there was never yet fair woman but she made mouths
in a glass.
Lear: No, I will be the pattern of all patience; I will say
nothing.

Enter KENT.

Kent: Who's there?
Fool: Marry, here's grace and a cod-piece; that's a wise
man and a fool.
Kent: Alas, sir, are you here? things that love night
Love not such nights as these; the wrathful skies
Gallow the very wanderers of the dark,
And make them keep their caves: since I was man,
Such sheets of fire, such bursts of horrid thunder,
Such groans of roaring wind and rain, I never
Remember to have heard: man's nature cannot carry
The affliction nor the fear.
Lear: Let the great gods,
That keep this dreadful pother o'er our heads,
Find out their enemies now. Tremble, thou wretch,
That hast within the undivulged crimes,
Unwhipp'd of justice: hide thee, thou bloody hand;
Thou perjured, and thou similar man of virtue
That art incestuous: caitiff, to pieces shake,
That under covert and convenient seeming
Hast practised on man's life: close pent-up guilts,
Rive your concealing continents and cry
These dreadful summoners grace. I am a man
More sinn'd against than sinning.
Kent: Alack, bare-headed!
Gracious my lord, hard by here is a hovel;
Some friendship will it lend you 'gainst the tempest:
Repose you there; while I to this hard house—
More harder than the stones whereof 'tis raised;
Which even but now, demanding after you,
Denied me to come in—return, and force
Their scanted courtesy.
Lear: My wits begin to turn.
Come on, my boy: how dost, my boy? art cold?
I am cold myself. Where is this straw, my fellow?
The art of our necessities is strange,
That can make vile things precious. Come, your hovel.
Poor fool and knave, I have one part in my heart
That's sorry yet for thee.
Fool: [*Singing*]
He that has and a little tiny wit,—
  With hey, ho, the wind and the rain,—
Must make content with his fortunes fit,
  For the rain it raineth every day.

Lear: True, my good boy. Come, bring us to this hovel.
                           [*Exeunt* LEAR *and* KENT]
Fool: This is a brave night to cool a courtezan.
I'll speak a prophecy ere I go:
When priests are more in word than matter;
When brewers mar their malt with water;
When nobles are their tailors' tutors;
No heretics burn'd, but wenches' suitors;
When every case in law is right;
No squire in debt, nor no poor knight;
When slanders do not live in tongues,
Nor cutpurses come not to throngs;
When usurers tell their gold i' the field,
And bawds and whores do churches build,
Then shall the realm of Albion
Come to great confusion:
Then comes the time, who lives to see 't,
That going shall be used with feet.
This prophecy Merlin shall make; for I live before his
    time.
                                  [*Exit*]

Scene III.—GLOUCESTER'S castle.
Enter GLOUCESTER *and* EDMUND.

Gloucester: Alack, alack, Edmund, I like not this
unnatural dealing. When I desired their leave that I might
pity him, they took from me the use of mine own house;
charged me, on pain of their perpetual displeasure,
neither to speak of him, entreat for him, nor any way
sustain him.
Edmund: Most savage and unnatural!
Gloucester: Go to; say you nothing. There's a division
betwixt the dukes, and a worse matter than that: I have
received a letter this night; 'tis dangerous to be spoken; I
have locked the letter in my closet: these injuries the king
now bears will be revenged home; there is part of a
power already footed; we must incline to the king. I will
seek him and privily relieve him: go you, and maintain
talk with the duke, that my charity be not of him
perceived: if he ask for me, I am ill and gone to bed.
Though I die for it, as no less is threatened me, the king
my old master must be relieved. There is some strange
thing toward, Edmund; pray you, be careful.
                                  [*Exit*]

Edmund: This courtesy, forbid thee, shall the duke
Instantly know, and of that letter too:
This seems a fair deserving, and must draw me
That which my father loses; no less than all:
The younger rises when the old doth fall.
                                  [*Exit*]

Scene IV.—The heath. Before a hovel.
Enter LEAR, KENT, *and* FOOL.

Kent: Here is the place, my lord; good my lord, enter:
The tyranny of the open night's too rough
For nature to endure.   [*Storm still*]
Lear: Let me alone.
Kent: Good my lord, enter here.
Lear: Wilt break my heart?
Kent: I had rather break mine own. Good my lord,
    enter.
Lear: Thou think'st 'tis much that this contentious
    storm
Invades us to the skin: so 'tis to thee;
But where the greater malady is fix'd
The lesser is scarce felt. Thou 'ldst shun a bear,

But if thy flight lay toward the raging sea
Thou 'ldst meet the bear i' the mouth. When the mind's
    free
The body 's delicate: the tempest in my mind
Doth from my senses take all feeling else
Save what beats there. Filial ingratitude!
Is it not as this mouth should tear this hand
For lifting food to 't? But I will punish home
No, I will weep no more. In such a night
To shut me out! Pour on; I will endure.
In such a night as this! O Regan, Goneril!
Your old kind father, whose frank heart gave you all,—
O, that way madness lies; let me shun that;
No more of that.
Kent: Good my lord, enter here.
Lear: Prithee, go in thyself; seek thine own ease:
This tempest will not give me leave to ponder
On things would hurt me more. But I'll go in.
[*To the* FOOL] In, boy; go first. You houseless poverty,—
Nay, get thee in. I'll pray, and then I'll sleep.
                              [FOOL *goes in*]
Poor naked wretches, wheresoe'er you are,
That bide the pelting of this pitiless storm,
How shall your houseless heads and unfed sides,
Your loop'd and window'd raggedness, defend you
From seasons such as these? O, I have ta'en
Too little care of this! Take physic, pomp;
Expose thyself to feel what wretches feel,
That thou mayst shake the superflux to them
And show the heavens more just.
Edgar: [*Within*] Fathom and half, fathom and half!
Poor Tom!   [*The* FOOL *runs out from the hovel.*]
Fool: Come not in here, nuncle, here's a spirit.
Help me, help me!
Kent: Give me thy hand. Who's there?
Fool: A spirit, a spirit: he says his name's poor Tom.
Kent: What are thou that dost grumble there i' the
    straw? Come forth.

          Enter EDGAR *disguised as a madman.*

Edgar: Away! the foul fiend follows me!
'Through the sharp hawthorn blows the cold wind.'
Hum! go to thy cold bed and warm thee.
Lear: Hast thou given all to thy two daughters? and art
thou come to this?
Edgar: Who gives any thing to poor Tom? whom the
foul fiend hath led through fire and through flame,
through ford and whirlpool, o'er bog and quagmire; that
hath laid knives under his pillow and halters in his pew;
set ratsbane by his porridge; made him proud of heart, to
ride on a bay trotting-horse over four-inched bridges, to
course his own shadow for a traitor. Bless thy five wits!
Tom's a-cold. O, do de, do de, do de. Bless thee from
whirlwinds, star-blasting, and taking! Do poor Tom some
charity, whom the foul fiend vexes. There could I have
him now, and there, and there again, and there.
                              [*Storm still*]
Lear: What, have his daughters brought him to this
    pass?
Couldst thou save nothing? Didst thou give them all?
Fool: Nay, he reserved a blanket, else we had been all
shamed.
Lear: Now, all the plagues that in the pendulous air
Hang fated o'er men's faults light on thy daughters!
Kent: He hath no daughters, sir.
Lear: Death, traitor! nothing could have subdued nature
To such a lowness but his unkind daughters.

Is it the fashion that discarded fathers
Should have thus little mercy on their flesh?
Judicious punishment! 'twas this flesh begot
Those pelican daughters.
Edgar: Pillicock say on Pillicock-hill:
               Halloo, halloo, loo, loo!
Fool: This cold night will turn us all to fools and
madmen.
Edgar: Take heed o' the foul fiend: obey thy parents;
keep thy word justly; swear not; commit not with man's
sworn spouse; set not thy sweet heart on proud array.
Tom's a-cold.
Lear: What hast thou been?
Edgar: A serving-man, proud in heart and mind; that
curled my hair; wore gloves in my cap; served the lust of
my mistress' heart and did the act of darkness with her;
swore as many oaths as I spake words and broke them in
the sweet face of heaven: one that slept in the contriving
of lust and waked to do it: wine loved I deeply, dice
dearly, and in woman out-paramoured the Turk: false of
heart, light of ear, bloody of hand; hog in sloth, fox in
stealth, wolf in greediness, dog in madness, lion in prey.
Let not the creaking of shoes nor the rustling of silks
betray thy poor heart to woman: keep thy foot out of
brothels, thy hand out of plackets, thy pen from lenders'
books, and defy the foul fiend.
'Still through the hawthorn blows the cold wind.'
Says suum, mun, ha, no, nonny.
Dolphin my boy, my boy, sessa! let him trot by.
                              [*Storm still*]
Lear: Why, thou wert better in thy grave than to answer
with thy uncovered body this extremity of the skies. Is
man no more than this? Consider him well. Thou owest
the worm no silk, the beast no hide, the sheep no wool,
the cat no perfume. Ha! here's three on 's are
sophisticated. Thou art the thing itself: unaccommodated
man is no more but such a poor, bare, forked animal as
thou art. Off, off, you lendings! come, unbutton here.
                         [*Tearing off his clothes*]
Fool: Prithee, nuncle, be contented; 'tis a naughty night
to swim in. Now a little fire in a wild field were like an
old lecher's heart, a small spark, all the rest on 's body
cold. Look, here comes a walking fire.

         Enter GLOUCESTER, *with a torch.*

Edgar: This is the foul fiend Flibbertigibbet: he begins
at curfew and walks till the first cock; he gives the web
and the pin, squints the eye and makes the hare-lip;
mildews the white wheat and hurts the poor creature of
earth.
        Saint Withold footed thrice the 'old;
        He met the night-mare and her nine-fold;
             Bid her alight,
             And her troth plight,
        And aroint thee, witch, aroint thee!
Kent: How fares your grace?
Lear: What's he?
Kent: Who's there? What is 't you seek?
Gloucester: What are you there? Your names?
Edgar: Poor Tom, that eats the swimming frog, the toad,
the tadpole, the wall-newt and the water; that in the fury
of his heart, when the foul fiend rages, eats cow-dung for
sallets; swallows the old rat and the ditch-dog; drinks the
green mantle of the standing pool; who is whipped from
tithing to tithing, and stock-punished, and imprisoned;
who hath had three suits to his back, six shirts to his
body, horse to ride and weapon to wear;
But mice and rats and such small deer

Have been Tom's food for seven long year.
Beware my follower. Peace, Smulkin; peace, thou fiend!
Gloucester: What, hath your grace no better company?
Edgar: The prince of darkness is a gentleman:
Modo he's call'd, and Mahu.
Gloucester: Our flesh and blood is grown so vile, my lord,
That it doth hate what gets it.
Edgar: Poor Tom's a-cold.
Gloucester: Go in with me: my duty cannot suffer
To obey in all your daughters' hard commands:
Though their injunction be to bar my doors
And let this tyrannous night take hold upon you,
Yet have I ventured to come seek you out
And bring you where both fire and food is ready.
Lear: First let me talk with this philosopher.
What is the cause of thunder?
Kent: Good my lord, take his offer; go into the house.
Lear: I'll talk a word with this same learned Theban.
What is your study?
Edgar: How to prevent the fiend and to kill vermin.
Lear: Let me ask you one word in private.
Kent: Importune him once more to go, my lord;
His wits begin to unsettle.
Gloucester: Canst thou blame him?

[*Storm still*]

His daughters seek his death: ah, that good Kent!
He said it would be thus, poor banish'd man!
Thou say'st the king grows mad; I'll tell thee, friend,
I am almost mad myself: I had a son,
Now outlaw'd from my blood; he sought my life,
But lately, very late: I loved him, friend,
No father his son dearer: truth to tell thee,
The grief hath crazed my wits. What a night's this!
I do beseech your grace,
Lear: O, cry you mercy, sir.
Noble philosopher, your company.
Edgar: Tom's a-cold.
Gloucester: In, fellow, there, into the hovel: keep thee warm.
Lear: Come, let's in all.
Kent: This way, my lord.
Lear: With him;
I will keep still with my philosopher.
Kent: Good my lord, soothe him; let him take the fellow.
Gloucester: Take him you on.
Kent: Sirrah, come on; go along with us.
Lear: Come, good Athenian.
Gloucester: No words, no words: hush.
Edgar: Child Rowland to the dark tower came:
    His word was still 'Fie, foh, and fum,
        I smell the blood of a British man.' [*Exeunt*]

Scene V.—GLOUCESTER'S castle.

Enter CORNWALL *and* EDMUND.

Cornwall: I will have my revenge ere I depart his house.
Edmund: How, my lord, I may be censured, that nature thus gives way to loyalty, something fears me to think of.
Cornwall: I now perceive, it was not altogether your brother's evil disposition made him seek his death, but a provoking merit, set a-work by a reprovable badness in himself.
Edmund: How malicious is my fortune, that I must repent to be just! This is the letter he spoke of, which

approves him an intelligent party to the advantages of France. O heavens! that this treason were not, or not I the detector!
Cornwall: Go with me to the duchess.
Edmund: If the matter of this paper be certain, you have mighty business in hand.
Cornwall: True or false, it hath made thee earl of Gloucester. Seek out where thy father is, that he may be ready for our apprehension.
Edmund: [*Aside*] If I find him comforting the king, it will stuff his suspicion more fully.—I will persever in my course of loyalty, though the conflict be sore between that and my blood.
Cornwall: I will lay trust upon thee, and thou shalt find a dearer father in my love.

[*Exeunt*]

Scene VI.—A chamber in a farmhouse adjoining the castle.

Enter GLOUCESTER, LEAR, KENT, FOOL, *and* EDGAR.

Gloucester: Here is better than the open air; take it thankfully. I will piece out the comfort with what addition I can: I will not be long from you.
Kent: All the power of his wits have given way to his impatience: the gods reward your kindness!

[*Exit* GLOUCESTER]

Edgar: Frateretto calls me, and tells me Nero is an angler in the lake of darkness. Pray, innocent, and beware the foul fiend.
Fool: Prithee, nuncle, tell me whether a madman be a gentleman or a yeoman.
Lear: A king, a king!
Fool: No, he's a yeoman that has a gentleman to his son, for he's a mad yeoman that sees his son a gentleman before him.
Lear: To have a thousand with red burning spits
Come hissing in upon 'em,—
Edgar: The foul fiend bites my back.
Fool: He's mad that trusts in the tameness of a wolf, a horse's health, a boy's love, or a whore's oath.
Lear: It shall be done; I will arraign them straight.
[*To* EDGAR] Come, sit thou here, most learned justicer;
[*To the* FOOL] Thou, sapient sir, sit here. Now, you she foxes!
Edgar: Look, where he stands and glares!
Wantest thou eyes at trial, madam?
        Come o'er the bourn, Bessy, to me.
Fool: Her boat hath a leak,
        And she must not speak
    Why she dares not come over to thee.
Edgar: The foul fiend haunts poor Tom in the voice of a nightingale. Hopdance cries in Tom's belly for two white herring. Croak not, black angel; I have no food for thee.
Kent: How do you, sir? Stand you not so amazed:
Will you lie down and rest upon the cushions?
Lear: I'll see their trial first. Bring in the evidence.
[*To* EDGAR] Thou robed man of justice, take thy place;
[*To the* FOOL] And thou, his yoke-fellow of equity,
Bench by his side. [*To* KENT] You are o' the commission;
Sit you too.
Edgar: Let us deal justly.
        Sleepest or wakest thou, jolly shepherd:
            Thy sheep be in the corn;
        And for one blast of thy minikin mouth,
            Thy sheep shall take no harm.
Pur! the cat is gray.

Lear: Arraign her first; 'tis Goneril. I here take my oath before this honorable assembly, she kicked the poor king her father.
Fool: Come hither, mistress. Is your name Goneril?
Lear: She cannot deny it.
Fool: Cry you mercy, I took you for a joint-stool.
Lear: And here's another, whose warp'd looks proclaim What store her heart is made on. Stop her there! Arms, arms, sword, fire! Corruption in the place! False justicer, why hast thou let her 'scape?
Edgar: Bless thy five wits!
Kent: O pity! Sir, where is the patience now, That you so oft have boasted to retain?
Edgar: [Aside] My tears begin to take his part so much, They'll mar my counterfeiting.
Lear: The little dogs and all, Tray, Blanch, and Sweet-heart, see, they bark at me.
Edgar: Tom will throw his head at them. Avaunt, you curs!
> Be thy mouth or black or white,
> Tooth that poisons if it bite;
> Mastiff, greyhound, mongrel grim,
> Hound or spaniel, brach or lym,
> Or bobtail tike or trundle-tail,
> Tom will make them weep and wail:
> For, with throwing thus my head,
> Dogs leap the hatch, and all are fled.

Do de, de, de. Sessa! Come, march to wakes and fairs and market-towns. Poor Tom, thy horn is dry.
Lear: Then let them anatomize Regan; see what breeds about her heart. Is there any cause in nature that makes these hard hearts? [To EDGAR] You sir, I entertain for one of my hundred; only I do not like the fashion of your garments. You will say they are Persian attire; but let them be changed.
Kent: Now, good my lord, lie here and rest awhile.
Lear: Make no noise, make no noise; draw the curtains: so, so, so. We'll go to supper i' the morning. So, so, so.
Fool: And I'll go to bed at noon.

Re-enter GLOUCESTER.

Gloucester: Come hither, friend: where is the king my master?
Kent: Here, sir; but trouble him not: his wits are gone.
Gloucester: Good friend, I prithee, take him in thy arms;
I have o'erheard a plot of death upon him:
There is a litter ready; lay him in 't,
And drive toward Dover, friend, where thou shalt meet
Both welcome and protection. Take up thy master:
If thou shouldst dally half an hour, his life,
With thine and all that offer to defend him,
Stand in assured loss. Take up, take up,
And follow me, that will to some provision
Give thee quick conduct.
Kent: Oppressed nature sleeps.
This rest might yet have balm'd thy broken sinews,
Which, if convenience will not allow,
Stand in hard cure. [To the FOOL] Come, help to bear thy master;
Thou must not stay behind.
Gloucester: Come, come, away.

[Exeunt all but EDGAR]

Edgar: When we our betters see bearing our woes,
We scarcely think our miseries our foes.
Who alone suffers suffers most i' the mind,

Leaving free things and happy shows behind:
But then the mind much sufferance doth o'erskip,
When grief hath mates, and bearing fellowship.
How light and portable my pain seems now,
When that which makes me bend makes the king bow,
He childed as I father'd! Tom, away!
Mark the high noises, and thyself bewray
When false opinion, whose wrong thought defiles thee,
In thy just proof repeals and reconciles thee.
What will hap more to-night, safe 'scape the king!
Lurk, lurk.   [Exit]

Scene VII.—GLOUCESTER'S castle.

Enter CORNWALL, REGAN, GONERIL, EDMUND, and SERVANTS.

Cornwall: Post speedily to my lord your husband; show him this letter: the army of France is landed. Seek out the traitor Gloucester.

[Exeunt some of the SERVANTS]

Regan: Hang him instantly.
Goneril: Pluck out his eyes.
Cornwall: Leave him to my displeasure. Edmund, keep you our sister company: the revenges we are bound to take upon your traitorous father are not fit for your beholding. Advise the duke, where you are going, to a most festinate preparation: we are bound to the like. Our posts shall be swift and intelligent betwixt us. Farewell, dear sister: farewell, my lord of Gloucester.

Enter OSWALD.

How now! where's the king?
Oswald: My lord of Gloucester hath convey'd him hence:
Some five or six and thirty of his knights,
Hot questrists after him, met him at gate;
Who, with some other of the lord's dependants,
Are gone with him toward Dover; where they boast
To have well-armed friends.
Cornwall: Get horses for your mistress.
Goneril: Farewell, sweet lord, and sister.
Cornwall: Edmund, farewell.

[Exeunt GONERIL, EDMUND, and OSWALD]
                          Go seek the traitor Gloucester.
Pinion him like a thief, bring him before us.

[Exeunt other SERVANTS]
Though well we may not pass upon his life
Without the form of justice, yet our power
Shall do a courtesy to our wrath, which men
May blame but not control. Who's there? the traitor?

Enter GLOUCESTER, brought in by two or three.

Regan: Ingrateful fox! 'tis he.
Cornwall: Bind fast his corky arms.
Gloucester: What mean your graces? Good my friends, consider
You are my guests: do me no foul play, friends.
Cornwall: Bind him, I say.   [SERVANTS bind him]
Regan: Hard, hard. O filthy traitor!
Gloucester: Unmerciful lady as you are, I'm none.
Cornwall: To this chair bind him. Villain, thou shalt find—

[REGAN plucks his beard]

Gloucester: By the kind gods, 'tis most ignobly done
To pluck me by the beard.
Regan: So white, and such a traitor!

Gloucester: Naughty lady,
These hairs which thou dost ravish from my chin
Will quicken and accuse thee: I am your host:
With robbers' hands my hospitable favors
You should not ruffle thus. What will you do?
Cornwall: Come, sir, what letters had you late from
France?
Regan: Be simple answerer, for we know the truth.
Cornwall: And what confederacy have you with the
traitors
Late footed in the kingdom?
Regan: To whose hands have you sent the lunatic king?
Speak.
Gloucester: I have a letter guessingly set down,
Which came from one that's of a neutral heart,
And not from one opposed.
Cornwall: Cunning.
Regan: And false.
Cornwall: Where hast thou sent the king?
Gloucester: To Dover.
Regan: Wherefore to Dover? Wast thou not charged at
peril—
Cornwall: Wherefore to Dover? Let him first answer
that.
Gloucester: I am tied to the stake, and I must stand the
course.
Regan: Wherefore to Dover, sir?
Gloucester: Because I would not see thy cruel nails
Pluck out his poor old eyes, nor thy fierce sister
In his anointed flesh stick boarish fangs.
The sea, with such a storm as his bare head
In hell-black night endured, would have buoy'd up,
And quench'd the stelled fires:
Yet, poor old heart, he holp the heavens to rain.
If wolves had at thy gate howl'd that stern time,
Thou shouldst have said, 'Good porter, turn the key,'
All cruels else subscribed: but I shall see
The winged vengeance overtake such children.
Cornwall: See 't shalt thou never. Fellows, hold the
chair.
Upon these eyes of thine I'll set my foot.
Gloucester: He that will think to live till he be old,
Give me some help! O cruel! O you gods!
Regan: One side will mock another; the other too.
Cornwall: If you see vengeance—
First Servant: Hold your hand, my
lord:
I have served you ever since I was a child;
But better service have I never done you
Than now to bid you hold.
Regan: How now, you dog!
First Servant: If you did wear a beard upon your chin,
I'ld shake it on this quarrel. What do you mean?
Cornwall: My villain! *[They draw and fight.]*
First Servant: Nay, then, come on, and take the chance
of anger.
Regan: Give my thy sword. A peasant stand up thus!
[Takes a sword and runs at him behind]
First Servant: O, I am slain! My lord, you have one eye
left
To see some mischief on him. O! *[Dies]*
Cornwall: Lest it see more, prevent it. Out, vile jelly!
Where is thy luster now?
Gloucester: All dark and comfortless. Where's my son
Edmund?
Edmund, enkindle all the sparks of nature,
To quit this horrid act.

Regan: Out, treacherous villain!
Thou call'st on him that hates thee: it was he
That made the overture of thy treasons to us;
Who is too good to pity thee.
Gloucester: O my follies! Then Edgar was abused.
Kind gods, forgive me that, and prosper him!
Regan: Go thrust him out at gates, and let him smell
His way to Dover. *[Exit one with GLOUCESTER]*
How is 't, my lord, how look you?
Cornwall: I have received a hurt: follow me, lady.
Turn out that eyeless villain: throw his slave
Upon the dunghill. Regan, I bleed apace:
Untimely comes this hurt: give me your arm.
[Exit CORNWALL, led by REGAN]
Second Servant: I'll never care what wickedness I do,
If this man come to good.
Third Servant: If she live long,
And in the end meet the old course of death,
Women will all turn monsters.
Second Servant: Let's follow the old earl, and get the
Bedlam
To lead him where he would: his roguish madness
Allows itself to any thing.
Third Servant: Go thou: I'll fetch some flax and whites
of eggs
To apply to his bleeding face. Now, heaven help him!
[Exeunt severally]

Act IV.

Scene I.—The heath.

Enter EDGAR.

Edgar: Yet better thus, and known to be contemn'd,
Than still contemn'd and flatter'd. To be worst,
The lowest and most dejected thing of fortune,
Stands still in esperance, lives not in fear:
The lamentable change is from the best;
The worst returns to laughter. Welcome then,
Thou unsubstantial air that I embrace!
The wretch that thou hast blown unto the worst
Owes nothing to thy blasts. But who comes here?

Enter GLOUCESTER, led by an OLD MAN.

My father, poorly led? World, world, O world!
But that thy strange mutations make us hate thee,
Life would not yield to age.
Old Man: O, my good lord, I have been your tenant,
and your father's tenant, these four-score years.
Gloucester: Away, get thee away; good friend, be gone:
Thy comforts can do me no good at all;
Thee they may hurt.
Old Man: Alack, sir, you cannot see your way.
Gloucester: I have no way and therefore want no eyes;
I stumbled when I saw: full oft 'tis seen,
Our means secure us, and our mere defects
Prove our commodities. Ah, dear son Edgar,
The food of thy abused father's wrath!
Might I but live to see thee in my touch,
I'ld say I had eyes again.
Old Man: How now! Who's there?
Edgar: *[Aside]* O gods! Who is 't can say 'I am at the
worst'?
I am worse than e'er I was.
Old Man: 'Tis poor mad Tom.

Edgar: [*Aside*] And worse I may be yet, the worst is not
So long as we can say 'This is the worst.'
Old Man: Fellow, where goest?
Gloucester: Is it a beggar-man?
Old Man: Madman and beggar too.
Gloucester: He has some reason, else he could not
     beg.
I' the last night's storm I such a fellow saw,
Which made me think a man a worm: my son
Came then into my mind, and yet my mind
Was then scarce friends with him: I have heard more
     since.
As flies to wanton boys, are we to the gods;
They kill us for their sport.
Edgar: [*Aside*]   How should this be?
Bad is the trade that must play fool to sorrow,
Angering itself and others. Bless thee, master!
Gloucester: Is that the naked fellow?
Old Man: Aye, my lord.
Gloucester: Then, prithee, get thee gone: if for my sake
Thou wilt o'ertake us hence a mile or twain
I' the way toward Dover, do it for ancient love;
And bring some covering for this naked soul,
Who I'll entreat to lead me.
Old Man: Alack, sir, he is mad.
Gloucester: 'Tis the times' plague, when madmen lead
     the blind.
Do as I bid thee, or rather do thy pleasure;
Above the rest, be gone.
Old Man: I'll bring him the best 'parel that I have,
Come on 't what will.   [*Exit*]
Gloucester: Sirrah, naked fellow,—
Edgar: Poor Tom's a-cold. [*Aside*] I cannot daub it
     further.
Gloucester: Come hither, fellow.
Edgar: [*Aside*] And yet I must.—Bless thy sweet eyes,
     they bleed.
Gloucester: Know'st thou the way to Dover?
Edgar: Both stile and gate, horse-way and foot-path.
Poor Tom hath been scared out of his good wits. Bless
thee, good man's son, from the foul fiend! Five fiends
have been in poor Tom at once; of lust, as Obidicut;
Hobbididence, prince of dumbness; Mahu, of stealing;
Modo, of murder; Flibbertigibbet, of mopping and
mowing; who since possesses chambermaids and waiting-
women. So, bless thee, master!
Gloucester: Here, take this purse, thou whom the
     heavens' plagues
Have humble to all strokes: that I am wretched
Makes thee the happier. Heavens, deal so still!
Let the superfluous and lust-dieted man,
That slaves your ordinance, that will not see
Because he doth not feel, feel your power quickly;
So distribution should undo excess
And each man have enough. Dost thou know Dover?
Edgar: Aye, master.
Gloucester: There is a cliff whose high and bending
     head
Looks fearfully in the confined deep:
Bring me but to the very brim of it,
And I'll repair the misery thou dost bear
With something rich about me: from that place
I shall no leading need.
Edgar: Give me thy arm:
Poor Tom shall lead thee.   [*Exeunt*]

Scene II.—Before the DUKE OF ALBANY'S palace.
Enter GONERIL and EDMUND.

Goneril: Welcome, my lord: I marvel our mild husband
Not met us on the way.

Enter OSWALD.
                    Now, where's your master?
Oswald: Madam, within; but never man so changed.
I told him of the army that was landed;
He smiled at it: I told him you were coming;
His answer was, 'The worse:' of Gloucester's treachery
And of the loyal service of his son
When I inform'd him, then he call'd me sot
And told me I had turn'd the wrong side out:
What most he should dislike seems pleasant to him;
What like, offensive.
Goneril: [*To* EDMUND] Then shall you go no further.
It is the cowish terror of his spirit,
That dares not undertake: he'll not feel wrongs,
Which tie him to an answer. Our wishes on the way
May prove effects. Back, Edmund, to my brother;
Hasten his musters and conduct his powers:
I must change arms at home and give the distaff
Into my husband's hands. This trusty servant
Shall pass between us: ere long you are like to hear,
If you dare venture in your own behalf,
A mistress's command. Wear this; spare speech;
                    [*Giving a favor*]
Decline your head: this kiss, if it durst speak,
Would stretch thy spirits up into the air:
Conceive, and fare thee well.
Edmund: Yours in the ranks of death.
Goneril: My most dear Gloucester!
                    [*Exit* EDMUND]
O, the difference of man and man!
To thee a woman's services are due:
My fool usurps my body.
Oswald: Madam, here comes my lord.
                    [*Exit*]

Enter ALBANY.

Goneril: I have been worth the whistle.
Albany: O Goneril!
You are not worth the dust which the rude wind
Blows in your face. I fear your disposition:
That nature which contemns its origin
Cannot be border'd certain in itself;
She that herself will sliver and disbranch
From her material sap, perforce must wither
And come to deadly use.
Goneril: No more; the text is foolish.
Albany: Wisdom and goodness to the vile seem vile:
Filths savor but themselves. What have you done?
Tigers, not daughters, what have you perform'd?
A father, and a gracious aged man,
Whose reverence even the head-lugg'd bear would lick,
Most barbarous, most degenerate! have you madded.
Could my good brother suffer you to do it?
A man, a prince, by him so benefited!
If that the heavens do not their visible spirits
Send quickly down to tame these vile offenses,
It will come,
Humanity must perforce prey on itself,
Like monsters of the deep.
Goneril: Milk-liver'd man!
That bear'st a cheek for blows, a head for wrongs;
Who hast not in thy brows an eye discerning

Thine honor from thy suffering; that not know'st
Fools do those villains pity who are punish'd
Ere they have done their mischief. Where's thy drum?
France spreads his banners in our noiseless land,
With plumed helm thy state begins to threat,
Whiles thou, a moral fool, sit'st still and criest
'Alack, why does he so?'
Albany: See thyself, devil!
Proper deformity seems not in the fiend
So horrid as in woman.
Goneril: O vain fool!
Albany: Thou changed and self-cover'd thing, for
    shame,
Be-monster not thy feature. Were 't my fitness
To let these hands obey my blood,
They are apt enough to dislocate and tear
Thy flesh and bones: howe'er thou art a fiend,
A woman's shape doth shield thee.
Goneril: Marry, your manhood! mew!

Enter a MESSENGER.

Albany: What news?
Messenger: O, my good lord, the Duke of Cornwall's
    dead,
Slain by his servant, going to put out
The other eye of Gloucester.
Albany: Gloucester's eyes!
Messenger: A servant that he bred, thrill'd with
    remorse,
Opposed against the act, bending his sword
To his great master; who thereat enraged
Flew on him and amongst them fell'd him dead,
But not without that harmful stroke which since
Hath pluck'd him after.
Albany: This shows you are above,
You justicers, that these our nether crimes
So speedily can venge. But, O poor Gloucester!
Lost he his other eye?
Messenger: Both, both, my lord.
This letter, madam, craves a speedy answer;
'Tis from your sister.
Goneril: [*Aside*]   One way I like this well;
But being widow, and my Gloucester with her,
May all the building in my fancy pluck
Upon my hateful life: another way,
The news is not so tart.—I'll read, and answer.   [*Exit*]
Albany: Where was his son when they did take his
    eyes?
Messenger: Come with my lady hither.
Albany: He is not here.
Messenger: No, my good lord; I met him back again.
Albany: Knows he the wickedness?
Messenger: Aye, my good lord; 'twas he inform'd
    against him,
And quit the house on purpose, that their punishment
Might have the freer course.
Albany: Gloucester, I live
To thank thee for the love thou show'dst the king,
And to revenge thine eyes. Come hither, friend:
Tell me what more thou know'st.   [*Exeunt*]

Scene III.—The French camp near Dover.
Enter KENT *and a* GENTLEMAN.

Kent: Why the King of France is so suddenly gone back
know you the reason?

Gentleman: Something he left imperfect in the state
which since his coming forth is thought of, which imports
to the kingdom so much fear and danger that his personal
return was most required and necessary.
Kent: Who hath he left behind him general?
Gentleman: The Marshal of France, Monsieur La Far.
Kent: Did your letters pierce the queen to any
demonstration of grief?
Gentleman: Aye, sir; she took them, read them in my
    presence,
And now and then an ample tear trill'd down
Her delicate cheek: it seem'd she was a queen
Over her passion, who most rebel-like
Sought to be king o'er her.
Kent: O, then it moved her.
Gentleman: Not to a rage: patience and sorrow strove
Who should express her goodliest. You have seen
Sunshine and rain at once: her smiles and tears
Were like a better way: those happy smilets
That play'd on her ripe lip seem'd not to know
What guests were in her eyes; which parted thence
As pearls from diamonds dropp'd. In brief,
Sorrow would be a rarity most beloved,
If all could so become it.
Kent: Made she no verbal question?
Gentleman: Faith, once or twice she heaved the name
    of 'father'
Pantingly forth, as if it press'd her heart;
Cried 'Sisters! sisters! Shame of ladies! sisters!
Kent! father! sisters! What, i' the storm! i' the night?
Let pity not be believed!' There she shook
The holy water from her heavenly eyes,
And clamor moisten'd: then away she started
To deal with grief alone.
Kent: It is the stars,
The stars above us, govern our conditions;
Else one self mate and mate could not beget
Such different issues. You spoke not with her since?
Gentleman: No.
Kent: Was this before the king return'd?
Gentleman: No, since.
Kent: Well, sir, the poor distress'd Lear's i' the town:
Who sometime in his better tune remembers
What we are come about, and by no means
Will yield to see his daughter.
Gentleman: Why, good sir?
Kent: A sovereign shame so elbows him: his own
    unkindness
That stripp'd her from his benediction, turn'd her
To foreign casualties, gave her dear rights
To his dog-hearted daughters: these things sting
His mind so venomously that burning shame
Detains him from Cordelia.
Gentleman: Alack, poor
    gentleman!
Kent: Of Albany's and Cornwall's powers you heard
    not?
Gentleman: 'Tis so; they are afoot.
Kent: Well, sir, I'll bring you to our Master Lear,
And leave you to attend him: some dear cause
Will in concealment wrap me up awhile;
When I am known aright, you shall not grieve
Lending me this acquaintance. I pray you, go
Along with me.   [*Exeunt*]

Scene IV.—The same. A tent.

Enter, with drum and colors, CORDELIA, DOCTOR, *and* SOLDIERS.

Cordelia: Alack, 'tis he: why, he was met even now
As mad as the vex'd sea; singing aloud;
Crown'd with rank fumiter and furrow-weeds,
With bur-docks, hemlock, nettles, cuckoo-flowers,
Darnel, and all the idle weeds that grow
In our sustaining corn. A century send forth;
Search every acre in the high-grown field,
And bring him to our eye.   [*Exit an* OFFICER]
        What can man's wisdom
In the restoring his bereaved sense?
He that helps him take all my outward worth.
Doctor: There is means, madam:
Our foster-nurse of nature is repose,
The which he lacks: that to provoke in him,
Are many simples operative, whose power
Will close the eye of anguish.
Cordelia: All blest secrets,
All you unpublish'd virtues of the earth,
Spring with my tears! be aidant and remediate
In the good man's distress! Seek, seek for him;
Lest his ungovern'd rage dissolve the life
That wants the means to lead it.

Enter a MESSENGER.

Messenger: News, madam;
The British powers are marching hitherward.
Cordelia: 'Tis known before; our preparation stands
In expectation of them. O dear father,
It is thy business that I go about;
Therefore great France
My mourning and important tears hath pitied.
No blown ambition doth our arms incite,
But love, dear love, and our aged father's right:
Soon may I hear and see him!   [*Exeunt*]

Scene V.—GLOUCESTER's castle.

Enter REGAN *and* OSWALD.

Regan: But are my brother's powers set forth?
Oswald: Aye, madam.
Regan: Himself in person there?
Oswald: Madam, with much ado:
Your sister is the better soldier.
Regan: Lord Edmund spake not with your lord at home?
Oswald: No, madam.
Regan: What might import my sister's letter to him?
Oswald: I know not, lady.
Regan: Faith, he is posted hence on serious matter.
It was great ignorance, Gloucester's eyes being out,
To let him live: where he arrives he moves
All hearts against us: Edmund, I think is gone,
In pity of his misery, to dispatch
His nighted life; moreover, to descry
The strength o' the enemy.
Oswald: I must needs after him, madam, with my letter.
Regan: Our troops set forth to-morrow: stay with us;
The ways are dangerous.
Oswald: I may not, madam:
My lady charged my duty in this business.
Regan: Why should she write to Edmund? Might not you
Transport her purposes by word? Belike,
Something—I know not what: I'll love thee much,
Let me unseal the letter.

Oswald: Madam, I had rather—
Regan: I know your lady does not love her husband;
I am sure of that: and at her late being here
She gave strange œillades and most speaking looks
To noble Edmund. I know you are of her bosom.
Oswald: I, madam?
Regan: I speak in understanding: you are, I know 't:
Therefore I do advise you, take this note:
My lord is dead; Edmund and I have talk'd;
And more convenient is he for my hand
Than for your lady's: you may gather more.
If you do find him, pray you, give him this;
And when your mistress hears thus much from you,
I pray, desire her call her wisdom to her.
So, fare you well.
If you do chance to hear of that blind traitor,
Preferment falls on him that cuts him off.
Oswald: Would I could meet him, madam! I should show
What party I do follow.
Regan: Fare thee well.   [*Exeunt*]

Scene VI.—Fields near Dover.

Enter GLOUCESTER, *and* EDGAR *dressed like a peasant.*

Gloucester: When shall we come to the top of that same hill?
Edgar: You do climb up it now: look, how we labor.
Gloucester: Methinks the ground is even.
Edgar: Horrible steep.
Hark, do you hear the sea?
Gloucester: No, truly.
Edgar: Why then your other senses grow imperfect
By your eyes' anguish.
Gloucester: So may it be indeed:
Methinks thy voice is alter'd, and thou speak'st
In better phrase and matter than thou didst.
Edgar: You're much deceived: in nothing am I changed
But in my garments.
Gloucester: Methinks you're better spoken.
Edgar: Come on, sir; here's the place: stand still. How fearful
And dizzy 'tis to cast one's eyes so low!
The crows and choughs that wing the midway air
Show scarce so gross as beetles: half way down
Hangs one that gathers samphire, dreadful trade!
Methinks he seems no bigger than his head:
The fishermen that walk upon the beach
Appear like mice; and yond tall anchoring bark
Diminish'd to her cock; her cock, a buoy
Almost too small for sight: the murmuring surge
That on the unnumber'd idle pebbles chafes
Cannot be heard so high. I'll look no more,
Lest my brain turn and the deficient sight
Topple down headlong.
Gloucester: Set me where you stand.
Edgar: Give me your hand: you are now within a foot
Of the extreme verge: for all beneath the moon
Would I not leap upright.
Gloucester: Let go my hand.
Here, friend,'s another purse; in it a jewel
Well worth a poor man's taking: fairies and gods
Prosper it with thee! Go thou further off;
Bid me farewell, and let me hear thee going.
Edgar: Now fare you well, good sir.

Gloucester: With all my heart.
Edgar: Why I do trifle thus with his despair
Is done to cure it.
Gloucester: [*Kneeling*] O you mighty gods!
This world I do renounce, and in your sights
Shake patiently my great affliction off:
If I could bear it longer and not fall
To quarrel with your great opposeless wills,
My snuff and loathed part of nature should
Burn itself out. If Edgar live, O bless him!
Now, fellow, fare thee well.   [*He falls forward*]
Edgar: Gone, sir: farewell.
And yet I know not how conceit may rob
The treasury of life, when life itself
Yields to the theft: had he been where he thought,
By this had thought been past. Alive or dead?
Ho, you sir! friend! Hear you, sir! speak
Thus might he pass indeed: yet he revives.
What are you, sir?
Gloucester: Away, and let me die.
Edgar: Hadst thou been aught but gossamer, feathers,
   air,
So many fathom down precipitating,
Thou'dst shiver'd like an egg: but thou dost breathe;
Hast heavy substance; bleed'st not; speak'st; art sound.
Ten masts at each make not the altitude
Which thou hast perpendicularly fell:
Thy life's a miracle. Speak yet again.
Gloucester: But have I fall'n, or no?
Edgar: From the dread summit of this chalky bourn.
Look up a-height; the shrill-gorged lark so far
Cannot be seen or heard: do but look up.
Gloucester: Alack, I have no eyes.
Is wretchedness deprived that benefit,
To end itself by death? 'Twas yet some comfort,
When misery could beguile the tyrant's rage
And frustrate his proud will.
Edgar: Give me your arm:
Up: so. How is 't? Feel you your legs? You stand.
Gloucester: Too well, too well.
Edgar: This is above all strangeness.
Upon the crown o' the cliff, what thing was that
Which parted from you?
Gloucester: A poor unfortunate beggar.
Edgar: As I stood here below, methought his eyes
Were two full moons; he had a thousand noses,
Horns whelk'd and waved like the enridged sea:
It was some fiend; therefore, thou happy father,
Think that the clearest gods, who make them honors
Of men's impossibilities, have preserved thee.
Gloucester: I do remember now: henceforth I'll bear
Affliction till it do cry out itself
'Enough, enough,' and die. That thing you speak of,
I took it for a man; often 'twould say
'The fiend, the fiend:' he led me to that place.
Edgar: Bear free and patient thoughts. But who comes
   here?
Enter LEAR, *fantastically dressed with wild flowers.*
The safer sense will ne'er accommodate
His master thus.
Lear: No, they cannot touch me for coining; I am the
king himself.
Edgar: O thou side-piercing sight!
Lear: Nature's above art in that respect. There's your
press-money. That fellow handles his bow like a
crowkeeper; draw me a clothier's yard. Look, look, a
mouse! Peace, peace; this piece of toasted cheese will do

't. There's my gauntlet; I'll prove it on a giant. Bring up
the brown bills. O, well flown, bird! i' the clout, i' the
clout: hewgh! Give the word.
Edgar: Sweet marjoram.
Lear: Pass.
Gloucester: I know that voice.
Lear: Ha! Goneril, with a white beard! They flattered me
like a dog, and told me I had white hairs in my beard ere
the black ones were there. To say 'aye' and 'no' to every
thing that I said! 'Aye' and 'no' too was no good divinity.
When the rain came to wet me once and the wind to
make me chatter; when the thunder would not peace at
my bidding; there I found 'em, there I smelt 'em out. Go
to, they are not men o' their words: they told me I was
every thing; 'tis a lie, I am not ague-proof.
Gloucester: The trick of that voice I do well remember:
Is 't not the king?
Lear: Aye, every inch a king:
When I do stare, see how the subject quakes.
I pardon that man's life. What was thy cause?
Adultery?
Thou shalt not die: die for adultery! No:
The wren goes to 't, and the small gilded fly
Does lecher in my sight.
Let copulation thrive; for Gloucester's bastard son
Was kinder to his father than my daughters
Got 'tween the lawful sheets.
To 't, luxury, pell-mell! for I lack soldiers.
Behold yond simpering dame,
Whose face between her forks presages snow,
That minces virtue and does shake the head
To hear of pleasure's name;
The fitchew, nor the soiled horse, goes to 't
With a more riotous appetite.
Down from the waist they are Centaurs,
Though women all above:
But to the girdle do the gods inherit,
Beneath is all the fiends';
There's hell, there's darkness, there's the sulphurous pit,
Burning, scalding, stench, consumption; fie, fie, fie! pah,
pah! Give me an ounce of civit, good apothecary, to
sweeten my imagination: there's money for thee.
Gloucester: O, let me kiss that hand!
Lear: Let me wipe it first; it smells of mortality.
Gloucester: O ruin'd piece of nature! This great world
Shall so wear out to nought. Dost thou know me?
Lear: I remember thine eyes well enough. Dost thou
squiny at me? No, do thy worst, blind Cupid; I'll not love.
Read thou this challenge; mark but the penning on 't.
Gloucester: Were all the letters suns, I could not see
one.
Edgar: I would not take this from report: it is,
And my heart breaks at it.
Lear: Read.
Gloucester: What, with the case of eyes?
Lear: O, ho, are you there with me? No eyes in your
head, nor no money in your purse? Your eyes are in a
heavy case, your purse in a light: yet you see how this
world goes.
Gloucester: I see it feelingly.
Lear: What, art mad? A man may see how this world
goes with no eyes. Look with thine ears: see how yond
justice rails upon yond simple thief. Hark, in thine ear:
change places, and, handy-dandy, which is the justice,
which is the thief? Thou hast seen a farmer's dog bark at a
beggar?

Gloucester: Aye, sir.
Lear: And the creature run from the cur?
There thou mightst behold the great image of authority: a
  dog's obeyed in office.
Thou rascal beadle, hold thy bloody hand!
Why dost thou lash that whore? Strip thine own back;
Thou hotly lust'st to use her in that kind
For which thou whip'st her. The usurer hangs the
  cozener.
Through tatter'd clothes small vices do appear;
Robes and furr'd gowns hide all. Plate sin with gold,
And the strong lance of justice hurtless breaks;
Arm it in rags, a pigmy's straw does pierce it.
None does offend, none, I say, none; I'll able 'em:
Take that of me, my friend, who have the power
To seal the accuser's lips. Get thee glass eyes,
And, like a scurvy politician, seem
To see the things thou dost not.
Now, now, now, now: pull off my boots: harder, harder: so.
Edgar: O, matter and impertinency mix'd!
Reason in madness!
Lear: If thou wilt weep my fortunes, take my eyes.
I know thee well enough; thy name is Gloucester:
Thou must be patient; we came crying hither;
Thou know'st, the first time that we smell the air,
We wawl and cry. I will preach to thee: mark.
Gloucester: Alack, alack the day!
Lear: When we are born, we cry that we are come
To this great stage of fools. This 's a good block.
It were a delicate stratagem, to shoe
A troop of horse with felt: I'll put 't in proof;
And when I have stol'n upon these sons-in-law,
Then, kill, kill, kill, kill, kill, kill!

Enter a GENTLEMAN, *with* ATTENDANTS.

Gentleman: O, here he is: lay hand upon him. Sir,
Your most dear daughter—
Lear: No rescue? What, a prisoner? I am even
The natural fool of fortune. Use me well;
You shall have ransom. Let me have a surgeon;
I am cut to the brains.
Gentleman: You shall have any thing.
Lear: No seconds? all myself?
Why, this would make a man a man of salt,
To use his eyes for garden water-pots,
Aye, and laying autumn's dust.
Gentleman: Good sir,—
Lear: I will die bravely, like a smug bridegroom. What!
I will be jovial: come, come! I am a king,
My masters, know you that.
Gentleman: You are a royal one, and we obey you.
Lear: Then there's life in 't. Nay, an you get it, you shall
get it by running. Sa, sa, sa, sa.
                    [*Exit running;* ATTENDANTS *follow*]
Gentleman: A sight most pitiful in the meanest wretch,
Past speaking of in a king! Thou hast one daughter,
Who redeems nature from the general curse
Which twain have brought her to.
Edgar: Hail, gentle sir.
Gentleman: Sir, speed you: what's your will?
Edgar: Do you hear aught, sir, of a battle toward?
Gentleman: Most sure and vulgar: every one hears that,
Which can distinguish sound.
Edgar: But, by your favor,
How near's the other army?
Gentleman: Near and on speedy foot; the main descry
Stands on the hourly thought.

Edgar: I thank you, sir: that's all.
Gentleman: Though that the queen on special cause is
  here,
Her army is moved on.
Edgar: I thank you, sir.
                    [*Exit* GENTLEMAN]
Gloucester: You ever-gentle gods, take my breath from
  me;
Let not my worser spirit tempt me again
To die before you please!
Edgar: Well pray you, father.
Gloucester: Now, good sir, what are you?
Edgar: A most poor man, made tame to fortune's blows;
Who, by the art of known and feeling sorrows,
Am pregnant to good pity. Give me your hand,
I'll lead you to some biding.
Gloucester: Hearty thanks;
The bounty and the benison of heaven
To boot, and boot!

Enter OSWALD.

Oswald: A proclaim'd prize! Most happy!
That eyeless head of thine was first framed flesh
To raise my fortunes. Thou old unhappy traitor,
Briefly thyself remember: the sword is out
That must destroy thee.
Gloucester: Now let thy friendly hand
Put strength enough to 't.   [EDGAR *interposes*]
Oswald: Wherefore, bold peasant,
Darest thou support a publish'd traitor?
Hence!
Lest that the infection of his fortune take
Like hold on thee. Let go his arm.
Edgar: Chill not let go, zir, without vurther 'casion.
Oswald: Let go, slave, or thou diest!
Edgar: Good gentleman, go your gait, and let poor volk
pass. An chud ha' been zwaggered out of my life, 'twould
not ha' been zo long as 'tis by a vortnight. Nay, come not
near th' old man; keep out, che vor ye, or I 'se try
whether your costard or my ballow be the harder: chill be
plain with you.
Oswald: Out, dunghill!   [*They fight*]
Edgar: Chill pick your teeth, zir: come; no matter vor
  your foins.   [OSWALD *falls*]
Oswald: Slave, thou hast slain me. Villain, take my
  purse:
If ever thou wilt thrive, bury my body;
And give the letters which thou find'st about me
To Edmund earl of Gloucester; seek him out
Upon the British party. O, untimely death!
Death!   [*Dies*]
Edgar: I know thee well: a serviceable villain,
As duteous to the vices of thy mistress
As badness would desire.
Gloucester: What, is he dead?
Edgar: Sit you down, father; rest you.
Let's see these pockets: the letters that he speaks of
May be my friends. He's dead; I am only sorry
He had no other deathsman. Let us see:
Leave, gentle wax; and, manners, blame us not:
To know our enemies' minds, we 'ld rip their hearts;
Their papers, is more lawful.
[*Reads*] 'Let our reciprocal vows be remembered. You
have many opportunities to cut him off: if your will want
not, time and place will be fruitfully offered. There is

nothing done, if he return the conqueror: then am I the
prisoner, and his bed my jail; from the loathed warmth
whereof deliver me, and supply the place for your labor.
                          'Your—wife, so I would say—
                                    'affectionate servant,
                                              'GONERIL.'

O undistinguish'd space of woman's will!
A plot upon her virtuous husband's life;
And the exchange my brother! Here, in the sands,
Thee I'll rake up, the most unsanctified
Of murderous lechers; and in the mature time
With this ungracious paper strike the sight
Of the death-practiced duke: for him 'tis well
That of thy death and business I can tell.
Gloucester: The king is mad: how stiff is my vile sense,
That I stand up, and have ingenious feeling
Of my huge sorrows! Better I were distract:
So should my thoughts be sever'd from my griefs,
And woes by wrong imaginations lose
The knowledge of themselves   [*Drum afar off*]
Edgar: Give me your hand:
Far off, methinks, I hear the beaten drum:
Come, father, I'll bestow you with a friend.   [*Exeunt*]

Scene VII.—A tent in the French camp. LEAR *on a bed
asleep, soft music playing;* GENTLEMEN, *and others
attending.*

              Enter CORDELIA, KENT, *and* DOCTOR

Cordelia: O thou good Kent, how shall I live and work,
To match thy goodness? My life will be too short,
And every measure fail me.
Kent: To be acknowledged, madam, is o'erpaid.
All my reports go with the modest truth,
Nor more nor clipp'd, but so.
Cordelia: Be better suited:
These weeds are memories of those worser hours:
I prithee, put them off.
Kent: Pardon me, dear madam;
Yet to be known shortens my made intent:
My boon I make it, that you know me not
Till time and I think meet.
Cordelia: Then be 't so, my good lord. [*To the*
        DOCTOR]
How does the king?
Doctor: Madam, sleeps still.
Cordelia: O you kind gods,
Cure this great breach in his abused nature!
The untuned and jarring senses, O, wind up
Of this child-changed father!
Doctor: So please your majesty
That we may wake the king: he hath slept long.
Cordelia: Be govern'd by your knowledge, and proceed
I' the sway of your own will. Is he array'd?
Gentleman: Aye, madam; in the heaviness of his sleep
We put fresh garments on him.
Doctor: Be by, good madam, when we do awake him;
I doubt not of his temperance.
Cordelia: Very well.
Doctor: Please you, draw near. Louder the music there!
Cordelia: O my dear father! Restoration hang
Thy medicine on my lips, and let this kiss
Repair those violent harms that my two sisters
Have in thy reverence made!
Kent: Kind and dear
        princess!

Cordelia: Had you not been their father, these white
        flakes
Had challenged pity of them. Was this a face
To be opposed against the warring winds?
To stand against the deep dread-bolted thunder?
In the most terrible and nimble stroke
Of quick, cross lightning? to watch—poor perdu!—
With this thin helm? Mine enemy's dog,
Though he had bit me, should have stood that night
Against my fire; and wast thou fain, poor father,
To hovel thee with swine and rogues forlorn,
In short and musty straw? Alack, alack!
'Tis wonder that thy life and wits at once
Had not concluded all. He wakes; speak to him.
Doctor: Madam, do you; 'tis fittest.
Cordelia: How does my royal lord? How fares your
majesty?
Lear: You do me wrong to take me out o' the grave:
Thou art a soul in bliss; but I am bound
Upon a wheel of fire, that mine own tears
Do scald like molten lead.
Cordelia: Sir, do you know me?
Lear: You are a spirit, I know: when did you die?
Cordelia: Still, still, far wide!
Doctor: He's scarce awake: let him alone awhile.
Lear: Where have I been? Where am I? Fair daylight?
I am mightily abused. I should e'en die with pity,
To see another thus. I know not what to say.
I will not swear these are my hands: let's see;
I feel this pin prick. Would I were assured
Of my condition!
Cordelia: O, look upon me, sir,
And hold your hands in benediction o'er me.
No, sir, you must not kneel.
Lear: Pray, do not mock me:
I am a very foolish fond old man,
Fourscore and upward, not an hour more nor less;
And, to deal plainly,
I fear I am not in my perfect mind.
Methinks I should know you and know this man;
Yet I am doubtful; for I am mainly ignorant
What place this is, and all the skill I have
Remembers not these garments, nor I know not
Where I did lodge last night. Do not laugh at me;
For, as I am a man, I think this lady
To be my child Cordelia.
Cordelia: And so I am, I am.
Lear: Be your tears wet? yes, faith. I pray, weep not:
If you have poison for me, I will drink it.
I know you do not love me; for your sisters
Have, as I do remember, done me wrong:
You have some cause, they have not.
Cordelia: No cause, no cause.
Lear: Am I in France?
Kent: In your own kingdom, sir,
Lear: Do not abuse me.
Doctor: Be comforted, good madam: the great rage,
You see, is kill'd in him: and yet it is danger
To make him even o'er the time he has lost.
Desire him to go in; trouble him no more
Till further settling.
Cordelia: Will 't please your highness walk?
Lear: You must bear with me.
Pray you now, forget and forgive: I am old and foolish.
                          [*Exeunt all but* KENT *and* GENTLEMAN]

Gentleman: Holds it true, sir, that the Duke of Cornwall was so slain?

Kent: Most certain, sir.

Gentleman: Who is conductor of his people?

Kent: As 'tis said, the bastard son of Gloucester.

Gentleman: They say Edgar, his banished son, is with the Earl of Kent in Germany.

Kent: Report is changeable. 'Tis time to look about; the powers of the kingdom approach apace.

Gentleman: The arbitrement is like to be bloody. Fare you well, sir.   [*Exit*]

Kent: My point and period will be thoroughly wrought, Or well or ill, as this day's battle's fought.   [*Exit*]

Act V.

Scene I.—The British camp near Dover.

Enter, with drum and colors, EDMUND, REGAN,
GENTLEMEN, *and* SOLDIERS.

Edmund: Know of the duke if his last purpose hold,
Or whether since he is advised by aught
To change the course; he's full of alteration
And self-reproving: bring his constant pleasure.
                              [*To a* GENTLEMAN, *who goes out*]

Regan: Our sister's man is certainly miscarried.

Edmund: 'Tis to be doubted, madam.

Regan: Now, sweet lord,
You know the goodness I intend upon you:
Tell me, but truly, but then speak the truth,
Do you not love my sister?

Edmund: In honor'd love.

Regan: But have you never found my brother's way
To the forfended place?

Edmund: That thought abuses you.

Regan: I am doubtful that you have been conjunct
And bosom'd with her, as far as we call hers.

Edmund: No, by mine honor, madam.

Regan: I never shall endure her: dear my lord,
Be not familiar with her.

Edmund: Fear me not.—
She and the duke her husband!

Enter, with drum and colors, ALBANY, GONERIL, *and*
SOLDIERS.

Goneril: [*Aside*] I had rather lose the battle than that sister
Should loosen him and me.

Albany: Our very loving sister, well be-met.
Sir, this I hear; the king is come to his daughter,
With others whom the rigor of our state
Forced to cry out. Where I could not be honest,
I never yet was valiant: for this business,
It toucheth us, as France invades our land,
Not bolds the king, with others, whom, I fear,
Most just and heavy causes make oppose.

Edmund: Sir, you speak nobly.

Regan: Why is this reason'd?

Goneril: Combine together 'gainst the enemy;
For these domestic and particular broils
Are not the question here.

Albany: Let's then determine
With the ancient of war on our proceedings.

Edmund: I shall attend you presently at your tent.

Regan: Sister, you'll go with us?

Goneril: No.

Regan: 'Tis most convenient; pray you, go with us.

Goneril: [*Aside*] O, ho, I know the riddle.—I will go.

As they are going out, enter EDGAR *disguised.*

Edgar: If e'er your grace had speech with man so poor,
Hear me one word.

Albany: I'll overtake you. Speak.
                              [*Exeunt all but* ALBANY *and* EDGAR]

Edgar: Before you fight the battle, ope this letter.
If you have victory, let the trumpet sound
For him that brought it: wretched though I seem,
I can produce a champion that will prove
What is avouched there. If you miscarry,
Your business of the world hath so an end,
And machination ceases. Fortune love you!

Albany: Stay till I have read the letter.

Edgar: I was forbid it.
When time shall serve, let but the herald cry,
And I'll appear again.

Albany: Why, fare thee well: I will o'erlook thy paper.
                              [*Exit* EDGAR]

Re-enter EDMUND.

Edmund: The enemy's in view: draw up your powers.
Here is the guess of their true strength and forces
By diligent discovery; but your haste
Is now urged on you.

Albany: We will greet the time. [*Exit*]

Edmund: To both these sisters have I sworn my love;
Each jealous of the other, as the stung
Are of the adder. Which of them shall I take?
Both? one? or neither? Neither can be enjoy'd,
If both remain alive: to take the widow
Exasperates, makes mad her sister Goneril;
And hardly shall I carry out my side,
Her husband being alive. Now then we'll use
His countenance for the battle; which being done,
Let her who would be rid of him devise
His speedy taking off. As for the mercy
Which he intends to Lear and to Cordelia,
The battle done, and they within our power,
Shall never see his pardon; for my state
Stands on me to defend, not to debate.   [*Exit*]

Scene II.—A field between the two camps.

Alarum within. Enter, with drum and colors, LEAR,
CORDELIA, *and* SOLDIERS, *over the stage; and exeunt.*
                              Enter EDGAR *and* GLOUCESTER.

Edgar: Here, father, take the shadow of this tree
For your good host; pray that the right may thrive:
If ever I return to you again,
I'll bring you comfort.

Gloucester: Grace go with you, sir!
                              [*Exit* EDGAR]

Alarum and retreat within. Re-enter EDGAR.

Edgar: Away, old man; give me thy hand; away!
King Lear hath lost, he and his daughter ta'en:
Give me thy hand; come on.

Gloucester: No further, sir; a man may rot even here.

Edgar: What, in ill thoughts again? Men must endure
Their going hence, even as their coming hither:
Ripeness is all: come on.

Gloucester: And that's true too.   [*Exeunt*]

Scene III.—The British camp near Dover.
Enter, in conquest, with drum and colors, EDMUND;
LEAR *and* CORDELIA, *as prisoners;* CAPTAIN,
SOLDIERS, *etc.*

Edmund: Some officers take them away: good guard,
Until their greater pleasures first be known
That are to censure them.

Cordelia: We are not the first
Who with best meaning have incurr'd the worst.
For thee, oppressed king, am I cast down;
Myself could else out-frown false fortune's frown.
Shall we not see these daughters and these sisters?

Lear: No, no, no, no! Come, let's away to prison:
We two alone will sing like birds i' the cage:
When thou dost ask me blessing, I'll kneel down
And ask of thee forgiveness: so we'll live,
And pray, and sing, and tell old tales, and laugh
At gilded butterflies, and hear poor rogues
Talk of court news; and we'll talk with them too,
Who loses and who wins, who's in, who's out;
And take upon's the mystery of things,
As if we were God's spies: and we'll wear out,
In a wall'd prison, packs and sects of great ones
That ebb and flow by the moon.

Edmund: Take them away.

Lear: Upon such sacrifices, my Cordelia,
The gods themselves throw incense. Have I caught thee?
He that parts us shall bring a brand from heaven,
And fire us hence like foxes. Wipe thine eyes;
The good-years shall devour them, flesh and fell,
Ere they shall make us weep: we'll see 'em starve first.
Come.   [*Exeunt* LEAR *and* CORDELIA, *guarded*]

Edmund: Come hither, captain; hark.
Take thou this note: go follow them to prison:
One step I have advanced thee; if thou dost
As this instructs thee, thou dost make thy way
To noble fortunes: know thou this, that men
Are as the time is: to be tender-minded
Does not become a sword: thy great employment
Will not bear question; either say thou'lt do't,
Or thrive by other means.

Captain: I'll do't, my lord.

Edmund: About it; and write happy when thou hast
        done.
Mark; I say, instantly, and carry it so
As I have set it down.

Captain: I cannot draw a cart, nor eat dried oats;
If it be man's work, I'll do't.

                                           [*Exit*]

Flourish. Enter ALBANY, GONERIL, REGAN, *another*
CAPTAIN, *and* SOLDIERS.

Albany: Sir, you have shown to-day your valiant strain,
And fortune led you well: you have the captives
That were the opposites of this day's strife:
We do require them of you, so to use them
As we shall find their merits and our safety
May equally determine.

Edmund: Sir, I thought it fit
To send the old and miserable king
To some retention and appointed guard;
Whose age has charms in it, whose title more,
To pluck the common bosom on his side,
And turn our impress'd lances in our eyes
Which do command them. With him I sent the queen:
My reason all the same; and they are ready
To-morrow or at further space to appear

Where you shall hold your session. At this time
We sweat and bleed: the friend hath lost his friend;
And the best quarrels, in the heat, are cursed
By those that feel their sharpness.
The question of Cordelia and her father
Requires a fitter place.

Albany: Sir, by your patience,
I hold you but a subject of this war,
Not as a brother.

Regan: That's as we list to grace him.
Methinks our pleasure might have been demanded,
Ere you had spoke so far. He led our powers,
Bore the commission of my place and person;
The which immediacy may well stand up
And call itself your brother.

Goneril: Not so hot:
In his own grace he doth exalt himself
More than in your addition.

Regan: In my rights,
By me invested, he compeers the best.

Goneril: That were the most, if he should husband you.

Regan: Jesters do oft prove prophets.

Goneril: Holla, holla!
That eye that told you so look'd but a-squint.

Regan: Lady, I am not well; else I should answer
From a full-flowing stomach. General,
Take thou my soldiers, prisoners, patrimony;
Dispose of them, of me; the walls are thine:
Witness the world, that I create thee here
My lord and master.

Goneril: Mean you to enjoy him?

Albany: The let-alone lies not in your good will.

Edmund: Nor in thine, lord.

Albany: Half-blooded fellow, yes.

Regan: [*To Edmund*] Let the drum strike, and prove my
title thine.

Albany: Stay yet; hear reason. Edmund, I arrest thee
On capital treason; and in thine attaint
This gilded serpent [*pointing to* GONERIL]. For your
        claim, fair sister,
I bar it in the interest of my wife;
'Tis she is sub-contracted to this lord,
And I, her husband, contradict your bans.
If you will marry, make your loves to me;
My lady is bespoke.

Goneril: An interlude!

Albany: Thou art arm'd, Gloucester: let the trumpet
        sound:
If none appear to prove upon thy person
Thy heinous, manifest, and many treasons,
There is my pledge [*throwing down a glove*]:
        I'll prove it on thy heart,
Ere I taste bread, thou art in nothing less
Than I have here proclaim'd thee.

Regan: Sick, O, sick!

Goneril: [*Aside*] If not, I'll ne'er trust medicine.

Edmund: [*Throwing down a glove*] There's my
        exchange: what in the world he is
That names me traitor, villain-like he lies:
Call by thy trumpet: he that dares approach,
On him, on you,—who not?—I will maintain
My truth and honor firmly.

Albany: A herald, ho!

Edmund: A herald, ho, a herald!

Albany: Trust to thy single virtue; for thy soldiers,
All levied in my name, have in my name
Took their discharge.
Regan: My sickness grows upon me.
Albany: She is not well; convey her to my tent.

[*Exit* REGAN, *led*]

Enter a HERALD.

Come hither, herald,—Let the trumpet sound,—
And read out this.
Captain: Sound, trumpet! [*A trumpet sounds*]
Herald: [*Reads*] 'If any man of quality or degree within
the lists of the army will maintain upon Edmund,
supposed Earl of Gloucester that he is a manifold traitor,
let him appear by the third sound of the trumpet: he is
bold in his defense.'
Edmund: Sound! [*First trumpet*]
Herald: Again! [*Second trumpet*]
Herald: Again! [*Third trumpet*]

[*Trumpet answers within*]

Enter EDGAR, *at the third sound, armed, with a trumpet before him.*

Albany: Ask him his purposes, why he appears
Upon this call o' the trumpet.
Herald: What are you?
Your name, your quality? and why you answer
This present summons?
Edgar: Know, my name is lost;
By treason's tooth bare-gnawn and canker-bit:
Yet am I noble as the adversary
I come to cope.
Albany: Which is that adversary?
Edgar: What's he that speaks for Edmund, Earl of
Gloucester?
Edmund: Himself: what say'st thou to him?
Edgar: Draw thy sword,
That if my speech offend a noble heart,
Thy arm may do thee justice: here is mine.
Behold, it is the privilege of mine honors,
My oath, and my profession: I protest,
Maugre thy strength, youth, place and eminence,
Despite thy victor sword and fire-new fortune,
Thy valor and thy heart, thou art a traitor,
False to thy gods, thy brother and thy father,
Conspirant 'gainst this high illustrious prince,
And from the extremest upward of thy head
To the descent and dust below thy foot,
A most toad-spotted traitor. Say thou 'No,'
This sword, this arm and my best spirits are bent
To prove upon thy heart, whereto I speak,
Thou liest.
Edmund: In wisdom I should ask thy name,
But since thy outside looks so fair and warlike
And that thy tongue some say of breeding breathes,
What safe and nicely I might well delay
By rule of knighthood, I disdain and spurn:
Back do I toss these treasons to thy head;
With the hell-hated lie o'erwhelm thy heart;
Which for they yet glance by and scarcely bruise,
This sword of mine shall give them instant way,
Where they shall rest for ever. Trumpets, speak!

[*Alarums. They fight.* EDMUND *falls.*]

Albany: Save him, save him!
Goneril: This is practice, Gloucester:
By the law of arms thou wast not bound to answer
An unknown opposite; thou art not vanquish'd,
But cozen'd and beguiled.

Albany: Shut your mouth,
dame,
Or with this paper shall I stop it. Hold, sir;
Thou worse than any name, read thine own evil.
No tearing, lady; I perceive you know it.
Goneril: Say, if I do, the laws are mine, not thine:
Who can arraign me for't?
Albany: Most monstrous!
Know'st thou this paper?
Goneril: Ask me not what I know.

[*Exit*]

Albany: Go after her: she's desperate; govern her.
Edmund: What you have charged me with, that have I
done;
And more, much more; the time will bring it out;
'Tis past, and so am I. But what art thou
That hast this fortune on me? If thou'rt noble,
I do forgive thee.
Edgar: Let's exchange charity.
I am no less in blood than thou art, Edmund;
If more, the more thou hast wrong'd me.
My name is Edgar, and thy father's son.
The gods are just, and of our pleasant vices
Make instruments to plague us:
The dark and vicious place where thee he got
Cost him his eyes.
Edmund: Thou hast spoken right, 'tis true;
The wheel is come full circle; I am here.
Albany: Methought thy very gait did prophesy
A royal nobleness: I must embrace thee:
Let sorrow split my heart, if ever I
Did hate thee or thy father!
Edgar: Worthy prince, I know't.
Albany: Where have you hid yourself?
How have you known the miseries of your father?
Edgar: By nursing them, my lord. List a brief tale;
And when 'tis told, O, that my heart would burst!
The bloody proclamation to escape
That follow'd me so near,—O, our lives' sweetness:
That we the pain of death would hourly die
Rather than die at once!—taught me to shift
Into a madman's rags, to assume a semblance
That very dogs disdain'd: and in this habit
Met I my father with his bleeding rings,
Their precious stones new lost; became his guide,
Led him, begg'd for him, saved him from despair;
Never—O fault!—reveal'd myself unto him,
Until some half-hour past, when I was arm'd;
Not sure, though hoping, of this good success,
I ask'd his blessing, and from first to last
Told him my pilgrimage: but his flaw'd heart,—
Alack, took weak the conflict to support!—
'Twixt two extremes of passion, joy and grief,
Burst smilingly.
Edmund: This speech of yours hath moved me,
And shall perchance do good: but speak you on;
You look as you had something more to say.
Albany: If there be more, more woeful, hold it in;
For I am almost ready to dissolve,
Hearing of this.
Edgar: This would have seem'd a period
To such as love not sorrow; but another,
To amplify too much, would make much more,
And top extremity.
Whilst I was big in clamor, came there in a man,
Who, having seen me in my worst estate,

Shunn'd my abhorr'd society; but then, finding
Who 'twas that so endured, with his strong arms
He fasten'd on my neck, and bellow'd out
As he'ld burst heaven; threw him on my father;
Told the most piteous tale of Lear and him
That ever ear received; which in recounting
His grief grew puissant, and the strings of life
Began to crack: twice then the trumpet sounded,
And there I left him tranced.
Albany: But who was this?
Edgar: Kent, sir, the banish'd Kent; who in disguise
Follow'd his enemy king, and did him service
Improper for a slave.

Enter a GENTLEMAN, *with a bloody knife.*

Gentleman: Help, help, O, help!
Edgar: What kind of help?
Albany: Speak, man.
Edgar: What means this bloody knife?
Gentleman: 'Tis hot, it smokes;
It came even from the heart of—O, she's dead!
Albany: Who dead? speak, man.
Gentleman: Your lady, sir, your lady: and her sister
By her is poisoned; she hath confess'd it.
Edmund: I was contracted to them both: all three
Now marry in an instant.
Edgar: Here comes Kent.
Albany: Produce the bodies, be they alive or dead.
                              [*Exit* GENTLEMAN]
This judgment of the heavens, that makes us tremble,
Touches us not with pity.

Enter KENT.

                    O, is this he?
The time will not allow the compliment
Which very manners urges.
Kent: I am come
To bid my king and master aye good night:
Is he not here?
Albany: Great thing of us forgot!
Speak, Edmund, where's the king? and where's Cordelia?
See'st thou this object, Kent?

    [*The bodies of* GONERIL *and* REGAN *are brought in.*]

Kent: Alack, why thus?
Edmund: Yet Edmund was beloved:
The one the other poison'd for my sake,
And after slew herself.
Albany: Even so. Cover their faces.
Edmund: I pant for life: some good I mean to do,
Despite of mine own nature. Quickly send,
Be brief in it, to the castle; for my writ
Is on the life of Lear and on Cordelia:
Nay, send in time.
Albany: Run, run, O, run!
Edgar: To who, my lord? Who hath the office? send
Thy token of reprieve.
Edmund: Well thought on: take my sword,
Give it the captain.
Albany: Haste thee, for thy life. [*Exit* EDGAR]
Edmund: He hath commission from thy wife and me
To hang Cordelia in the prison, and
To lay the blame upon her own despair,
That she fordid herself.
Albany: The gods defend her! Bear him hence awhile.
                              [EDMUND *is borne off*]

Re-enter LEAR, *with* CORDELIA *dead in his arms;*
EDGAR, CAPTAIN, *and others following.*

Lear: Howl, howl, howl, howl! O, you are men of
    stones:
Had I your tongues and eyes, I'ld use them so
That heaven's vault should crack. She's gone for ever!
I know when one is dead and when one lives;
She's dead as earth. Lend me a looking-glass;
If that her breath will mist or stain the stone,
Why, then she lives.
Kent: Is this the promised end?
Edgar: Or image of that horror?
Albany: Fall and cease.
Lear: This feather stirs; she lives. If it be so,
It is a chance which does redeem all sorrows
That ever I have felt.
Kent: [*Kneeling*] O my good master!
Lear: Prithee, away.
Edgar: 'Tis noble Kent, your friend.
Lear: A plague upon you, murderers, traitors all!
I might have saved her; now she's gone for ever!
Cordelia, Cordelia! stay a little. Ha!
What is't thou say'st? Her voice was ever soft,
Gentle and low, an excellent thing in woman.
I kill'd the slave that was a-hanging thee.
Captain: 'Tis true, my lords, he did.
Lear: Did I not, fellow?
I have seen the day, with my good biting falchion
I would have made them skip: I am old now,
And these same crosses spoil me. Who are you?
Mine eyes are not o' the best, I'll tell you straight.
Kent: If fortune brag of two she loved and hated,
One of them we behold.
Lear: This is a dull sight. Are you not Kent?
Kent: The same,
Your servant Kent. Where is your servant Caius?
Lear: He's a good fellow, I can tell you that;
He'll strike, and quickly too: he's dead and rotten.
Kent: No, my good lord; I am the very man—
Lear: I'll see that straight.
Kent: That from your first of difference and decay
Have follow'd your sad steps.
Lear: You are welcome hither.
Kent: Nor no man else: all's cheerless, dark and deadly.
Your eldest daughters have fordone themselves,
And desperately are dead.
Lear: Aye, so I think.
Albany: He knows not what he says, and vain is it
That we present us to him.
Edgar: Very bootless.

Enter a CAPTAIN.

Captain: Edmund is dead, my lord.
Albany: That's but a trifle here.
You lords and noble friends, know our intent.
What comfort to this great decay may come
Shall be applied: for us, we will resign,
During the life of this old majesty,
To him our absolute power: [*To* EDGAR *and* KENT] you,
    to your rights;
With boot, and such addition as your honors
Have more than merited. All friends shall taste
The wages of their virtue, and all foes
The cup of their deservings. O, see, see!
Lear: And my poor fool is hang'd! No, no, no life!
Why should a dog, a horse, a rat, have life,
And thou no breath at all? Thou'lt come no more,
Never, never, never, never, never!

Pray you, undo this button: thank you, sir.
Do you see this? Look on her, look, her lips.
Look there, look there!   [*Dies*]
Edgar: He faints. My lord, my lord!
Kent: Break, heart; I prithee, break!
Edgar: Look up, my
    lord.
Kent: Vex not his ghost: O, let him pass! he hates him
That would upon the rack of this tough world
Stretch him out longer.
Edgar: He is gone indeed.
Kent: The wonder is he hath endured so long:
He but usurp'd his life.
Albany: Bear them from hence. Our present business
Is general woe. [*To* KENT *and* EDGAR] Friends of my
    soul, you twain
Rule in this realm and the gored state sustain.
Kent: I have a journey, sir, shortly to go;
My master calls me, I must not say no.
Albany: The weight of this sad time we must obey,
Speak what we feel, not what we ought to say.
The oldest hath borne most: we that are young
Shall never see so much, nor life so long.
                          [*Exeunt, with a dead march*]

Exercises

1. *Lear* is a historical tragedy set in pagan Britain
   but it was written for a Christian Elizabethan
   audience. Identify some of the Christian
   allusions as revealed by the ethics and diction
   of the characters. What are some of the pagan
   elements?
2. Examine the role of the Fool. What do his lines
   mean in relation to the King? Is the Fool more
   or less sane than Lear?
3. Does the Gloucester subplot add or detract
   from the main action? How?
4. One of the great Renaissance themes was the
   difference between appearance and reality;
   things are not always what they seem to be. All
   we can know of the characters in the play is
   what they say, what they do, and what others say
   about them. Consider, in these terms, Goneril,
   Regan, and Lear. Who is truly insane? How
   insane? Who is benign and who is vicious?

5. Cordelia appears less than any other major
   character and yet she is clearly the heroine.
   How did Shakespeare accomplish this?
   Consider what she says, does, and what is said
   about her.
6. Consider Shakespeare's treatment of madness in
   the characters of Lear, the Fool, and Edgar in
   his disguise as Poor Tom. How irrational are
   they? Always irrational? Is Lear rational at the
   end of the play? How rational?
7. Is Edmund depicted as totally evil? Does he
   redeem himself in any way?
8. Lear is far from a regal character. His judgment
   is faulty, he longs for admiration, he loses touch
   with reality. And yet, he arouses our pity and
   even, at the end, our admiration. How does
   Shakespeare accomplish this? What are Lear's
   assets as a person?

Summary

Perhaps more than any other period before our own tumultuous century, the Renaissance was lively, disorderly, and exceedingly violent. In an age of contradictions, masterpieces of art, literature, and music were created in the midst of almost continuous strife and commotion. In terms of the culture-epoch theory of history, the Renaissance was the period of chaos during and following the breakdown of the medieval synthesis. The process was terribly painful. Not until the seventeenth century would a new view of reality slowly begin to take shape.

The Time Chart for the Renaissance at the end of chapter 17 should again be consulted for an overview of this tempestuous but dazzling age. The bibliography for chapter 17 was selected to appeal to a variety of tastes and interests and should also be consulted.

Unit

7

The Early Modern World, 1600–1789

21 *Science, Reason, and Absolutism*

The Seventeenth Century

Europe emerged from medievalism during the tumultuous Renaissance, but not until 1648 did the passions unleashed by the Reformation and Counter-Reformation gradually subside. Beginning as a conflict between Catholics and Protestants, the Thirty Years' War (1618–1648) evolved into an international war between modern nation-states. The Peace of Westphalia of 1648 that finally ended the slaughter was a landmark in European history, finally laying to rest the last vestiges of medievalism. Once viable values and institutions had completely disappeared. The medieval idea of a unified Christian commonwealth was a relic of the now distant past as were the imperial and papal claims to political power. Adopting the strategies of diplomacy and alliances initiated by Italian city-states, sovereign nations staked out boundaries and competed with each other in the struggle for a new balance of power.

Rapid advances in science and technology revealed vast new horizons, and international trade opened up the whole world to European dominance and, inevitably, European exploitation. The English East Indies Company was founded in 1600, its Dutch counterpart chartered only two years later, followed by the French. With growing power and wealth, the prevailing mood in northern Europe was as positive as the joyful optimism voiced by Miranda in Shakespeare's *The Tempest:*

> O Wonder!
> How many goodly creatures are there here!
> How beauteous mankind is! O brave new world,
> That has such people in't!

Science and Philosophy

Francis Bacon (1561–1626), the English lawyer and statesman, ranks with Descartes and Galileo as one of the founders of modern science and philosophy. He formulated no new scientific hypotheses nor did he make any dramatic discoveries, but he did inquire into the function and ethics of science and scientific research in relation to human life. For Bacon, knowledge was not recognition of any given reality but a search for truth, a journey rather than a destination. Bacon saw clearly that the old culture had come to a dead end and that a new epoch was coming into being. Inventions like gunpowder, the printing press, the compound microscope (ca. 1590), and the telescope (ca. 1608) changed the material world and had to change the ways of thinking about the world. Scientific knowledge and invention, Bacon believed, should be public property to be shared democratically and to be used for the benefit of all people. In his *Novum Organum* (1620) Bacon laid out the logic of scientific inquiry and the principles of the inductive method. Through experiment and observation factual information would be gathered, leading to general statements based only on observable data. For Bacon the principle task of scientific investigation was to remedy the poverty of factual information, a search for knowledge taken for granted in this century but by no means in Bacon's time.

During the sixteenth century the Reformation raised the question of the reliability of religious knowledge, of whether Catholic beliefs were more or less true than Protestant convictions. The rise of science extended the question to the reliability of all knowledge. Skeptics maintained that no certain knowledge was possible, that doubt was always present. Bacon argued that the inductive method augmented by mechanical aids like the compound microscope provided certain knowledge about the world. René Descartes (1596–1650) distrusted sensory evidence, claiming that the senses can deceive us. Well acquainted with skeptics like Montaigne and Mersenne, Descartes followed their arguments to their conclusion, rejecting everything as false. With this process of "Cartesian doubt" he could then, in the depths of uncertainty, find truth and a criterion of truth.

In his *Discourse on Method* (1637) Descartes formulated his "natural method" to accept nothing as true except what was "clearly and distinctly" presented to his mind. It was not until his *Meditations* (1641) that Descartes responded to attacks on all knowledge. Admitting that the senses could not be trusted, Descartes went a step further to postulate an evil demon whose business it was to confuse people about the truth or falsity of anything, even whether or not a square had four sides. The solution is to exorcise the demon by believing in the goodness of the all-powerful God. Descartes doubts not that God exists but how does he know whether or not he himself exists? He finds his answer in the realization that he is a thinking person: *cogito ergo sum,* I think, therefore I am.

Whatever is clearly and distinctly perceived by the *cogito* is true. From this point Descartes proceeded to construct a rational philosophy in which he established the reliability of the senses and proved the existence of the physical world. He believed, further, that God had created two substances, spirit and matter. The mind was spirit and its essence was consciousness; the essence of the body, or matter, was extension and movement in space. Cartesian dualism thus established a gulf between mind and body that later philosophers removed by proving that mind, body, and nature were all interconnected.

For Descartes mathematics was the "queen of the sciences" and the universe was mechanistic. Applied mathematics would enable scientists to rationally study and understand an orderly cosmos that operated according to natural laws, a position with which Galileo was in complete agreement. Copernicus had proposed the heliocentric theory; Kepler had confirmed it by observation and, with mathematics, determined the three laws of planetary motion:

1. The planets move around the sun in ellipses with the sun at one focus of the ellipse.
2. We can imagine a line joining the sun and a planet. Though the planet's speed varies in its orbit around the sun, yet this imaginary line "sweeps out" equal areas in equal times.
3. The square of the time for one complete revolution of each planet is proportional to the cube of its average distance from the sun.

Professor of mechanics and astronomy at the University of Padua, Galileo Galilei (1564–1642) proved the heliocentric theory empirically with his improved telescope, discovered sun spots and Jupiter's moons, devised two laws of motion, invented the thermometer, improved the compound microscope, investigated the principles of the lever and the pulley, measured air pressure, and investigated the properties of magnetism and sound vibrations. Perhaps even more importantly, he invented the modern method of forming a theory, testing it experimentally, and adjusting the theory to conform to observable results. His two laws of motion are:

1. When a body is once in motion it will remain in motion in a straight line unless acted upon by other forces. One can state this law in another way by saying that a body moving in a vacuum, with no forces acting on it, will continue in motion in a straight line forever.
2. If force is applied to a moving object, the object will change course in the direction of the force that has been applied.

Later in the century, Newton, who will be discussed later, added the third law of motion: for every action there is an equal and opposite reaction. Every time a rocket rises from Cape Canaveral we can see the third law of motion in action.

Galileo had long believed in the Copernican hypothesis but did not become involved in public controversy until his 1613 letter to a friend in which he discussed his telescopic observations. The contents became public knowledge and, after the publication of his *Dialogues Concerning the Two Chief World Systems* (1632), he was charged by the Inquisition with heresy. The Holy Office (Inquisition) claimed that Galileo had agreed, in a signed statement, not to promulgate his views about the heliocentric theory. The statement was a forgery and Galileo was not allowed to appear before the court in his own defense.[1] Nevertheless, he was judged a heretic, forced to recant, and sentenced to lifetime house arrest. The book was first sentenced to public burning but later merely prohibited.

After leaving Rome, Galileo, with the assistance of trusted friends, sent a copy of his book to Switzerland where it was published in Latin. He followed that up with *The New Sciences* (1638), the first great work on modern physics. Prince Mattia de' Medici smuggled the manuscript out of Italy and the work was ultimately published in Holland. Galileo had thus successfully defied Rome but his life was a shambles and Italian science had been set back for generations.

Absolutism

At the beginning of the century both England and France had absolute monarchs who claimed to rule by Divine Right. The thrones of England and Scotland were united by the accession of James I (1603–1625), the son of Mary Stuart, Queen of Scots. His attempts to govern absolutely brought him into conflict with Parliament, and the absolute rule of Charles I (1625–1649) finally led to Civil War (1642–1646) between the king and Parliament. Charles I was tried and executed for treason and the Interregnum began, the Puritan era of the Commonwealth and the Protectorate (1649–1659) under what amounted to the dictatorship of Oliver Cromwell.

It was during the Civil War and for over a century and a half afterwards that the Social Contract theory of government became prominent. In the seventeenth century the idea of a government by consent of the governed did not imply a liberal democracy, but that power was derived from people of the wealthy and influential class as a curb against kingly excesses. It was rarely suggested that working people had any natural rights. Consent did not imply democracy unless that meant consent of *all* the people, and that was an eighteenth-century development that led to the American Revolution. The idea of a Social Contract was a strong current of political thought but there was an important countercurrent. In 1651 Thomas Hobbes (1588–1679) published his *Leviathan* in which he revived the idea of a contract based on subjection to the sovereign power of the monarch. Hobbes justified absolutism but not rule by Divine Right. Convinced that peace and security were prerequisites of society, Hobbes believed that certain individual freedoms had to be sacrificed for the good of the state. A state of nature was anarchy; there had to be a superior power to restore and maintain the stability of society, and that would be the unlimited power of the king. Given the

Figure 21.1 French school after Gianlorenzo Bernini, *Bust of Louis XIV,* ca. 1665. Bronze, 33½″ high. Versailles was decorated and furnished in the Baroque style represented by this Italian Baroque bust, but the exterior is essentially Neoclassical, the preferred architectural style of Louis XIV. Samuel H. Kress Collection. National Gallery of Art, Washington, D.C.

circumstances of the time, the Civil War and the execution of the king, the position of Hobbes is understandable even if not commendable.

Upon the death of Cromwell in 1659 Charles II (1660–1685), son of Charles I, was invited to restore the Stuart line. Charles did not openly confront Parliament and managed to go his own way. James II (1685–1688) was not as clever and was forced to abdicate, leaving behind the general conviction that a Catholic king was dangerous to English liberties. Mary, the daughter of James II, was Protestant and married to William of Orange, a Dutch Protestant. Providing they accepted the new Bill of Rights, William and Mary were invited to take the English throne. This was the Glorious Revolution, which, without bloodshed, established a constitutional monarchy. Absolutism was virtually finished in England.

Absolutism in France had a far longer and more violent history. Succeeding to the throne after the assassination of Henry IV, Louis XIII reigned from 1610–1643, but royal power was gradually taken over by his chief minister, Cardinal Richelieu, who operated as a virtual dictator from 1624 to 1642. It was Richelieu who established the French absolutism to which Louis XIV succeeded in 1643 at the age of five under the regency of his mother. During the longest reign of any monarch, Louis XIV (1643–1715) promoted the arts, built the magnificent palace at Versailles (see figs. 22.16, 22.17, and 22.18), and made France the most powerful nation in Europe (fig. 21.1).

---

1. For further information on the trial and the judicial forgery, see Giorgio de Santillana, *The Crime of Galileo* (New York: Time Incorporated, 1962).

The nation had, however, an archaic economic system with local customs barriers, tax-farming, and a nobility that paid no taxes at all. Raising revenues simply increased the misery of the people. Further, the king's revocation of the Edict of Nantes that protected the Huguenots from persecution was a disaster. Over 250,000 mostly middle-class craftsmen and their families were forced to flee the country, marking the beginning of the end of Louis's greatness and, ultimately, of the French monarchy itself.

The Enlightenment, ca. 1687–1789

"Enlightenment" and "Age of Reason" are two of several terms that describe the intellectual characteristics of the eighteenth century. The Enlightenment is usually dated from the year in which Newton's epochal *Principia (Mathematical Principles of Natural Philosophy)* appeared (1687) to the beginning of the French Revolution in 1789. An alternate beginning date would be 1688, the year of the Glorious Revolution in England. A difference of a year is insignificant. The *Principia* and the Glorious Revolution were major milestones marking the advance of science, rationalism, and freedom.

The Enlightenment was a self-conscious and extremely articulate movement that was to transform all societies. Europe had experienced some rude shocks, what some writers called the three humiliations. The earth was not at the center of the universe, people were creatures of nature like other animals, and their reason was subject to passions and instincts. For the Enlightenment these new truths represented intellectual advances that enabled people to redefine their responsibilities: discover truth through science; achieve personal happiness in a viable society; explore the full meaning, and limitations, of liberty. The discoveries of Newton provided convincing evidence that the world was orderly and knowable and that, by the same token, human societies could be made orderly and rational through the exercise of enlightened reason.

Science and Philosophy

Sir Isaac Newton (1642–1727) discovered the universal law of gravitation, made important investigations into the nature of light, and invented the branch of mathematics known as the calculus. At this time we are concerned with only the first of these. Newton supposedly remarked, "If I have seen a little farther than others, it is because I have stood on the shoulders of giants." There were many giants, including Copernicus, Brahe, Bruno, Kepler, and Galileo but Newton effected the grand synthesis that explained the operation of the cosmos. First, he refined Galileo's laws of motion:

1. A body remains in a state of rest or of uniform motion in a straight line unless compelled by an external force to change that state. In other

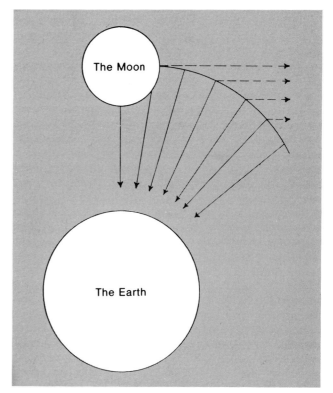

Figure 21.2 Forces acting on the moon to determine its motion.

words, a body's inertia keeps it in a state of rest or its inertia keeps it moving in a straight line. External force has to be applied to move it from either its state of rest or its straight-line motion.
2. A change in momentum is proportional to the force causing the change and takes place in the direction in which the force is acting. In other words, the increase or decrease in velocity is proportional to the force.
3. To every action there is an equal and opposite reaction.

Galileo had demonstrated the principles of movement of bodies on earth but not the motion of heavenly bodies. Why were their orbits curved? Newton hypothesized that all celestial bodies were mutually attracted to each other. He concentrated his studies on the moon, which he treated as having inertial movement in space and then determined that its orbit was curved because it was continuously falling toward the earth (fig. 21.2). Its inertia would cause it to fly out in a straight line, as shown by the dotted arrows but the gravitational pull of the earth balances the straight-line tendency. Action and reaction are equal and the moon remains in orbit at a standard distance from the earth. Newton calculated the mass of the moon and its distance from the earth and determined that the gravitational pull was inversely proportional to the square of its distance from the earth.

Newton also calculated the mass of the sun, the planets and their moons and discovered that each planet would travel according to Kepler's laws only by using the same formula: the gravitational pull of the sun was inversely proportional to the square of a planet's distance from the sun. The mathematical formula was the same whether the object was a terrestrial falling body like an apple or the moon, a law that worked here on earth and far out in space. This was the universal law of gravitation.

Newton (and Edmund Halley) demonstrated that comets obey the same universal principle. He calculated the flattening of the earth at its poles due to its rotation, and proved that the size of a planet determined the length of its day. He showed the effect of latitude on the weight of an object and accounted for the tides as resulting from the combined attraction of the sun and the moon. All of these instances of the operation of gravitation are given here to illustrate some of the different phenomena that can be explained with one law. No wonder Alexander Pope wrote the following couplet:

Nature and nature's laws lay hid in night;
God said, "Let Newton be," and all was light.

The philosophic implications of this unification of scientific principles were astounding. Picture the universe as Newton saw it, a vast and intricate system of whirling bodies in space, a system that was orderly and predictable. Each planet, each moon, each solar system was balanced in the cosmic plan, a balance determined by mechanical forces pulling against each other. Absolute and unvarying, these forces would keep the machine in working order. What, then, was the place of God in this plan? For all practical purposes God was ruled out. Newton was an intensely religious man, however, and he yielded two functions to the Divinity. It was noticed that, over long periods, there were slight irregularities in the motions of the heavenly bodies in terms of Newtonian physics. One function of God was to make certain periodic readjustments. A second function was to maintain an even flow of time and space. In this world picture, then, God became a sort of celestial engineer, turning a wheel here, opening a valve there, keeping an eye on the dials. Even before the close of the eighteenth century, Laplace, a French astronomer, extended the mechanism of gravitation and proved that the irregularities were periodical and subject to a law that kept them within bounds. Many of those who held to the existence of God were deists who looked upon him as the master designer of a perfect world-machine that needed no further tending. In the Declaration of Independence Thomas Jefferson, who was a deist, used the following terminology: laws of nature's God; Creator; Supreme Judge; Divine Providence. Perhaps the most commonly accepted image was that of an "absentee landlord" who had designed the machine and then retired, possibly to a ranch in Mexico.

In these developments we see clearly and distinctly the new reliance upon intellect that characterized the Enlightenment. Human beings using the marvelous mechanisms of their minds could, in time, unlock the most hidden secrets of the universe. And what of human institutions? The cosmos was orderly, rational, and knowable; why couldn't people use their reason to design an orderly and rational society? It was precisely this optimism of the Enlightenment that inspired our Founding Fathers to construct a democracy that would be a model, a beacon of hope for the entire world.

The founders of the Republic had gotten some political ideas from Montesquieu's *Spirit of the Laws* (1748) but they drew mainly from John Locke (1632–1704). Returning from exile after the Glorious Revolution, Locke wrote his *Two Treatises of Government* (1690) to justify constitutional monarchy. In the 15th essay from his *Second Treatise on Civil Government* Locke takes this position:

> Now this power, which every man has in the state of Nature, and which he parts with to the society in all such cases where the society can secure him, is to use such means for the preserving of his own property as he thinks good and Nature allows him; and to punish the breach of the law of Nature in others; so as (according to the best of his reason) may most conduce to the preservation of himself and the rest of mankind. So that the end and measure of this power, when in every other man's hands, in the state of Nature, being the preservation of all his society, that is, all mankind in general; it can have no other end or measure, when in the hands of the magistrate, but to preserve the members of that society in their lives, liberties, and possessions.

Locke assumes a natural law that operated in the affairs of human beings much as Newton's world-machine functioned according to natural law, a position also reflected in the opening paragraph of the Declaration of Independence:

> When, in the course of human events, it becomes necessary for one people to dissolve the political bands which have connected them with another, and to assume, among the powers of the earth, the separate and equal station to which the laws of nature and of nature's God entitle them, a decent respect to the opinions of mankind requires that they should declare the causes which impel them to the separation.

According to this natural law people had, according to Locke, certain rights which were unalienable, and these were life, liberty, and property. Jefferson substituted for "property" a much more striking and challenging phrase:

> We hold these truths to be self-evident, that all men are created equal, that they are endowed by their Creator with certain unalienable Rights, that among these are Life, Liberty, and the pursuit of Happiness. That to secure these rights, Governments are instituted among Men, deriving their just powers from the consent of the governed.

Locke wrote that government existed and had authority only because the people brought it into existence and gave it its authority. If the government violated its trust the people had a right, a natural right, to set up a new government. In short, they had a right to revolt, as Jefferson later stated in the Declaration of Independence.

Economics

Exactly as Locke (and Jefferson) sought natural law as a guide to political affairs and Newton found such a law as the binding force of the universe, so did Adam Smith (1723–1790) seek such a unifying principle for economic affairs. His work, interestingly enough, followed exactly the scientific method which Bacon had established in the previous epoch, for his investigations of the facts of economic life were conducted in a pin factory, and his generalizations were based upon his factual findings.

We are indebted to Smith for the statement of the classical principles of capitalism which were set forth in his volume, *An Inquiry into the Nature and Causes of the Wealth of Nations,* published in 1776. In the time when Smith lived, capitalism had taken the form called *mercantilism,* which was a strictly regulated system of trade, controlled by the government of each nation, and based on the idea that the wealth of a nation depended upon the amount of gold and silver which was held within the nation. In order to achieve a constantly increasing supply of gold and silver, each sought to maintain a favorable balance of trade; that is, each nation tried to keep the value of its yearly exports greater than the value of its yearly imports. With all nations trying to keep such a favorable balance of trade, it is evident that the system is a virtual impossibility, with only one way out. If a nation has colonies, it can make these colonies a source for cheap raw materials and a dumping ground for more expensive manufactured goods. One is reminded of England's policy toward its American colonies. In this way only can the system of mercantilism work, and its faults are obvious: sooner or later the colonies will either develop manufacturing for themselves, or they will be bled white by the mother country. In either case, the system fails.

The first revolt against mercantilism came in France, with a group of economists called the *physiocrats.* They held that the wealth of a nation depended upon the raw materials within the nation rather than the supply of money. They, too, believed that the strict regulation of trade and commerce by a national government was a detriment to economic well-being and progress. Adam Smith studied with this group for a time and mastered their ideas before he worked out his own theories.

Smith's whole effort was to discover a kind of balance in economic affairs that would insure an adequate supply of goods to meet the needs of human beings. He wanted these produced and sold at a fair price so that most people could buy the goods, so that

the laborer would receive a fair wage, and so that the manufacturer could receive a fair profit. In order to solve this intricate problem, he proposed a return to nature in economic affairs. That is, he proposed to remove all restrictions of every sort from the manufacturing and sale of goods and from wages. This is the system we recognize as unfettered competition, or *laissez-faire.* How does it work? Perhaps an example will clarify the process.

Smith's first premise is that people are, by nature, acquisitive. They want to pile up as much wealth as possible. So an enterpriser (a person with capital to invest) looks about and sees that people need shoes. This person sets up a shoe factory and charges as much as the traffic will bear for the product. Let us say that the charge is fifty dollars a pair. Immediately other enterprisers will be attracted to the shoe business, since the profits seem very large. As the number of shoes increases, the price will have to drop, if, according to the doctrine of laissez-faire, all people have equal access to raw materials and to markets with no regulation whatever. If such regulation comes into being, of course, the whole process is thrown out of gear. With such freedom, however, the price drops. Finally there are more shoes than can be sold. The inefficient manufacturer can no longer sell the product, and must drop out of the competition. As this happens, slowly the demand catches up with the supply, and the price regulates itself. Finally, the production is adequate for the needs of people; the price is stabilized at a point at which the most efficient producers can make a fair profit. The only thing omitted from the scheme so far is labor.

Labor, said Smith, is a commodity which is for sale just as shoes are. In a new field, wages will be high. Laborers will flock to this work. As labor becomes more plentiful, wages will decline. Finally the labor market in this field will become glutted, and the wages will fall to a point at which the laborers can no longer live. At that point, the inefficient ones will be eliminated and will seek some other form of employment. Eventually the price of labor, like that of shoes, will stabilize itself at a point at which the most efficient laborers in any field are working in that field at a price for their work which affords them a fair living. Others, squeezed out, will find another kind of work in which they are more efficient, and they will be able to make a good living there.

From these examples, it is possible to derive the principles of Smith's laissez-faire economy. First, he said that labor is the source of all wealth within a nation. Second, all people are acquisitive. Third, we must have completely free and unregulated access to raw materials, labor, and markets. Fourth, each person has a natural endowment of skills that should determine the kind of work to be done. Given a free choice of employment the process should lead the worker into the most congenial type of work. Fifth, if all of the conditions above exist, the law of supply and demand will come into operation and solve the problem of adequate goods, fair price, fair profit, and fair wages. Furthermore, each person will be doing what he or she can do best, and consequently the most enjoyable kind of work. Q.E.D.

Or almost Q.E.D. One problem remained, which Smith recognized, and for which he produced a too facile solution. He recognized that monopolies might grow up that might restrict competition. He proposed that governments must limit and control the growth of monopolies so that free competition could continue. He was not able to point to the exact kind of control that would eliminate monopolies, but that in itself would not be a regulation of industry. This problem has plagued all nations who operate with a capitalistic economy ever since.

In summary, however, it can be pointed out that Smith's economic system was exactly the same sort of plan in its sphere of human activity that John Locke's was in its. The first step is a return to nature. Human limitations and human differences in abilities furnish the natural law that is to operate. If this is done, nature will furnish a mechanism for the economic life of people that will regulate itself. The natural forces of supply and demand, like the gravitational pulls of planets and suns upon each other, like the pulls of executive, legislative, and federative branches of government, will form the whole economic structure into a smoothly operating, functional machine. Again, there is hope here. Smith furnished a principle upon which people could reorganize their economic lives. Then, when the initial adjustments were made, we would have a perfect life in the economic sense, and everyone could enjoy a freedom that had never before been known.

Locke and Educational Theory

In keeping with the complete rationalism of the time, John Locke made one other contribution which had great influence upon education and upon the thinking of the social scientists about the nature of human institutions. Locke proposed that the human mind at the moment of birth was a complete blank. It was, he said, a *tabula rasa,* a blank slate. This position directly countered that of the defenders of political and religious absolutism who contended that an inclination to submit to authority was already present in people's minds when they were born. Not so, said Locke. The mind was a blank slate on which would be written all of the experience the individual had throughout life. If good men and women were desired, then the whole job of creating them lay in the necessity of providing wholesome experience for them. Providing good experiences become the function of education and of human institutions in general, for it is within these institutions that the personality is shaped.

This, one sees immediately, becomes a machine-like process. One starts with the human mind as raw material. One molds it by good experience and the finished product is, at least theoretically, a good person. The process can, of course, work in the opposite direction, for bad experiences could produce a bad person. It is from this basic idea that most of our ideas of universal education, and most of our effort to provide a healthy environment come. Along with Sokrates, men and women of the Enlightenment tended to believe that virtue was knowledge and that ignorance was vice. An educated mind was its own reward. It still is.

David Hume (1711–1776)

Locke's theories of mind and understanding revealed some inconsistencies that were later filled in by the Scottish philosopher David Hume, a sane and urbane man who epitomized the enlightened thinker. Beginning with Locke's empiricist theory of knowledge, Hume went on to prove that there were limits to human reason. Anticipating a great public outcry, he published, in three volumes, *A Treatise of Human Nature being an Attempt to Introduce the Experimental Method of Reasoning into Moral Subjects* (1739–1740). Instead, no one noticed the book at the time; as Hume sadly said: "it fell dead-born from the press." It could not, however, be ignored for long. In volume one Hume granted certain knowledge only to arithmetic and algebra, and to geometry providing the maxims are true. Beyond that, he said, there is only probable knowledge, thus anticipating modern scientific thought.

Hume's principle concern was with cause and effect, or causality. If we observe that a certain event A is always followed by B then we assume that A causes B. If, for example, we hold a match to a piece of paper and see the paper burn, we connect the two events and say that the flaming match caused the paper to burn. Not so, says Hume. That paper always burns when a match is held to it is a *belief* that is developed through *custom,* that is, experience. We have seen this happen so often we assume that it *must* happen every time and therein lies the rub. Since A (the match) does not *cause* B (paper) to burn we cannot assume that paper is *certain* to burn. It is probable but not certain. The paper, for example, could have been soaked in a chemical that no amount of flame would set afire. Further, we cannot bite into an apple with the certainty that it will taste like an apple; it could taste like roast pork. We assume that the sun will rise tomorrow but it is impossible to establish that it must necessarily rise. Newton's law of universal gravitation is therefore probable and not necessarily universal. As American space vehicles have probed ever deeper into the cosmos scientists have watched with extreme curiosity to see if Newton's law remains valid. There have been no inconsistencies to date but no scientist would be willing to predict what the situation might be a thousand light years away. As Hume says, there are limits to human reason. He accepted a world based on probability rather than certainty. Through observation and reasoning we can determine, short of certainty, only *how* nature operates but not *why.*

Hume's skepticism also applied to religion and religious beliefs, and followed a long history of skeptical doubts about the truths of Judeo-Christianity. In the sixteenth century a Portuguese Jewish refugee in Holland, Uriel Da Costa, started out questioning the truth of orthodox Judaism and ended up stating that all religions were made by human beings. The French skeptic Isaac La Peyrère wrote *Man Before Adam* (1656) in which he claimed that there were people all over the world before Adam; the Bible cannot therefore be an accurate account of human history. La Peyrère's work led two Biblical scholars, Baruch de Spinoza (1632–1677) and Father Richard Simon (1638–1712), to reexamine religious knowledge. Spinoza concluded that the Bible was not divine revelation but merely a history of Jewish activities and superstitions. He proposed instead a religious pantheism in which all existence was embraced in one substance (God or Nature), a position of great appeal for the coming Romantic movement. The greatest Biblical scholar of his age, Father Simon set out to prove that scholars could never find an accurate text of the Bible nor discover what it meant. Unlike Spinoza, Simon was convinced that there was a Biblical message and tried, through critical scholarship, to determine what the message was.

The most famous of the French skeptics, Pierre Bayle (1647–1706), wrote his *Historical and Critical Dictionary* (1697–1702), in which he undermined the metaphysical theories of Descartes, Spinoza, Locke, and Leibniz; attacked all existing theologies; ridiculed the heroes of the Old Testament; and challenged all rational knowledge. He advocated abandoning reason in favor of blind faith, but there was little left but doubt about understanding anything at all except by describing everything in historical terms. Voltaire called Bayle's *Dictionary* the "Arsenal of the Enlightenment."

An avid reader of Bayle, Hume saw, as apparently no other Enlightenment thinker did, the plight of human beings if Bayle's doubts could not be answered. Hume never doubted that people could be certain about the evils of murder, stealing, and the like nor should they be uncertain about Newton's laws. Uncertainty belonged in the philosopher's study. People, through a study of human history, had to recognize different kinds of knowledge and live their lives as sane and civilized human beings. There were no absolute truths and one should not believe anything absolutely. He was particularly concerned about religious conflicts. "Errors in religion," he wrote, "are dangerous; those in philosophy only ridiculous." He believed, in the final analysis, that people could lead their lives as he did his, exercising their natural passions and common sense as they cheerfully enjoyed the uncertainties of everyday life.

Immanual Kant (1724–1804)

The leading thinker of the German Enlightenment, Kant responded to Hume's skepticism with the famous remark that he had been "awakened from his dogmatic slumbers." In his three *Critiques (Pure Reason,* 1781; *Practical Reason,* 1788; *Judgement,* 1793) Kant laid out a complete philosophical system. He showed that knowledge *a priori* was possible because people could perceive the world of space, forms, and causality and, because of the intrinsic nature of the human mind, understand phenomena. As he said, we can know only appearances like colors, shapes, and sounds but never the thing-in-itself; true knowledge cannot transcend experience. But, we can have reliable knowledge because all minds function the same way.

In ethics Kant stated that good actions must be done from a sense of duty and that moral law was derived from his categorical imperative: "act only according to the maxim which you at the same time will to be a universal law." People, he said, were independent moral agents with the freedom to choose right actions. As practical necessities Kant postulated the existence of God to insure that virtue was crowned with happiness and immortality so that the pursuit of moral perfection could continue in the afterlife.

Kant was the founder of German idealism. His philosophy appealed to the heart as opposed to the coldness of theoretical reason. This had enormous appeal for the German Romantic movement. In terms of the Enlightenment, his principle that every person was to be considered as an end in herself or himself is a form of the doctrine of the Rights of Man. Kant coined the prevailing motto for the Enlightenment: "Dare to Know!"

The Philosophes

Called *Les Philosophes* (the philosophers) or *Encyclopédistes* because most of them wrote articles for Diderot's monumental *Encyclopedia,* the philosophes were not all philosophers but included writers, poets, artists, mathematicians, dramatists, and scientists. One of the leading philosophes, Denis Diderot (dee-duh-RO; 1713–1784) was editor-in-chief of the *Encyclopedia* (1747–1772). Published in twenty-eight volumes but suppressed in 1759 by the government and thereafter printed clandestinely, the work was a summary of all human knowledge. Its prevailing spirit was scorn for the past and for organized religion, and glorification of reason, the arts, the experimental sciences, and industry. The *Encyclopedia* assumed that religious toleration and freedom of thought would win out and implied throughout that the condition of the common people should be the main concern of the government. A call to arms in twenty-eight volumes, the *Encyclopedia* was perhaps the key influence that led to the French Revolution.

In his *Persian Letters* (published anonymously in 1721) Montesquieu (mon-tes-KYO; 1689–1755) satirized European, especially French, society, leaving no phase of human activity untouched by its devastating wit and irony. His most influential book, *The Spirit of the Laws* (1748), was a scientific study of comparative government whose theories of checks and balances found their way into the United States Constitution.

Diderot, Voltaire, and Rousseau were the most influential of the French philosophes but the latter two will not be considered at this point. Voltaire and his satirical novel *Candide* are considered near the end of this chapter. A kind of reverse image of Voltaire the rationalist, Rousseau was a powerful influence on the Romantic movement and is discussed in chapter 24.

Absolutism and the Enlightenment

Louis XIV was a despot but he could, with some justification, be called an enlightened monarch. The same cannot be said for the next two kings. Louis XV, great grandson of Louis XIV, ruled ineptly but luxuriously from 1715–1774 and his weak and vascillating grandson, Louis XVI (1774–1793) went to the guillotine.

A rival state, the kingdom of Brandenburg-Prussia, rose to power during the decline of French power and influence. Frederick I was crowned the first king of Prussia in 1701, followed by Frederick William I (1713–1740), who began Prussian expansion. Frederick the Great (1740–1786) excelled at waging war and made Prussia the dominant military power in Europe. Known as a "benevolent despot," he promoted social and legal reforms and established a glittering court with musical performances by Johann Sebastian Bach and by Frederick himself. But the king did remark that "my people say what they please and I do as I please." Enlightenment had a way to go.

The founder of the modern Russian state, Peter the Great (1682–1725) mercilessly "Westernized" his country and savagely destroyed his enemies. He was admittedly a genius and he was undoubtedly more than a bit mad. To this day he has been admired as an enlightened leader and viewed with horror as a sadistic monster. Catherine the Great (1762–1791) was of German birth but she became thoroughly Russianized. Influenced by the Enlightenment, she planned vast reforms, but a peasant revolt in 1773–1775 and the French Revolution caused her to reverse course and, among other actions, enslave the serfs.

Only in Britain was there any real political freedom. Under the Hanoverian kings George I (1714–1727) and George II (1727–1760), Robert Walpole became, in fact, if not in name, the prime minister (1721–1742). William Pitt (1757–1761) was a strong prime minister but resigned when the next king, George III (1760–1820), decided he wanted to direct policy. Lord North was an acquiescent prime minister and, between king and prime minister, they inadvertently brought a new democratic republic into being. Absolutism during the Enlightenment was anything but enlightened.

Literature, 1600–1789

John Donne (1573–1631)

Though the seventeenth century is often referred to as the Baroque era, the term is more appropriate for art and music (see chaps. 22 and 23) than it generally is for literature. Donne's poetry does display some of the opulence and splendor associated with the Baroque but Donne has, instead, been characterized as the leader of the Metaphysical school, referring, in general, to the powerful intellectual content of his work, his concentrated images, and his remarkable ability to range between the intensely personal and the cosmic. Poets like Andrew Marvell and others were influenced by Donne, but they formed no organized school nor would they have endorsed the Metaphysical school label that John Dryden and Samuel Johnson affixed to the poetry of Donne and Marvell.

Poet, prose stylist, and preacher, John Donne was an experienced man of the world who spoke with great intellectual vigor in his love poems and in his Holy Sonnets. Neglected for three centuries after his death, he is now recognized as one of the finest poets in the English language, perhaps second only to Shakespeare.

In the following song Donne uses six different vivid images to express the impossibility, as he saw it, of woman's constancy.

Literary Selections
SONG
John Donne

Go and catch a falling star,
    Get with child a mandrake root,
Tell me where all past years are,
    Or who cleft the devil's foot,
Teach me to hear mermaids singing,
Or to keep off envy's stinging,
      And find
      What wind
Serves to advance an honest mind.

If thou be'st born to strange sights,
    Things invisible to see,
Ride ten thousand days and nights,
    Till age snow white hairs on thee;
Thou, when thou return'st, wilt tell me
All strange wonders that befell thee,
      And swear,
      Nowhere
Lives a woman true and fair.

If thou find'st one, let me know;
    Such a pilgrimage were sweet;
Yet do not: I would not go,
    Though at next door we might meet;
Though she were true when you met her,
And last till you write your letter,
      Yet she
      Will be
False, ere I come, to two or three.

The following poem uses unique images that reflect Donne's secret marriage to his patron's niece, a happy union but one that clouded the rest of the poet's life. Only John Donne could effectively express life, love, and loving in terms of a flea.

THE FLEA
John Donne

Mark but this flea, and mark in this,
How little that which thou deniest me is;
It sucked me first, and now sucks thee,
And in this flea our two bloods mingled be;
Thou know'st that this cannot be said
A sin, nor shame, nor loss of maidenhead,
    Yet this enjoys before it woo,
    And pampered swells with one blood made of two,
    And this, alas! is more than we would do.

Oh stay, three lives in one flea spare,
Where we almost, yea, more than married are.
This flea is you and I, and this
Our marriage-bed and marriage-temple is;
Though parents grudge, and you, we 're met
And cloistered in these living walls of jet.
    Though use make you apt to kill me,
    Let not, to that, self-murder added be,
    And sacrilege, three sins in killing three.

"The Good-Morrow" exemplifies Donne's ability to vastly extend personal experience; what lovers discover in their intimacy is raised to the universal and the immortal.

THE GOOD-MORROW
John Donne

I wonder, by my troth, what thou and I
Did till we loved; were we not weaned till then,
But sucked on country pleasures childishly?
Or snorted we in the Seven Sleepers' den?
'T was so; but this, all pleasures fancies be:
If ever any beauty I did see
Which I desired and got, 't was but a dream of thee.

And now good-morrow to our waking souls,
Which watch not one another out of fear;
For love all love of other sights controls,
And makes one little room an everywhere.
Let sea-discoverers to new worlds have gone,
Let maps to other, worlds on worlds have shown,
Let us possess one world; each hath one, and is one.

My face in thine eye, thine in mine appears,
And true plain hearts do in the faces rest;
Where can we find two better hemispheres
Without sharp north, without declining west?
Whatever dies, was not mixed equally;
If our two loves be one, or thou and I
Love so alike that none do slacken, none can die.

Near the end of his career Donne became obsessed with the thought of death. In the following Holy Sonnet he uses intense language and images to try to put death in perspective.

HOLY SONNET X
John Donne

Death, be not proud, though some have callèd thee
Mighty and dreadful, for thou art not so;
For those whom thou think'st thou dost overthrow
Die not, poor Death, nor yet canst thou kill me.
From rest and sleep, which but thy pictures be,
Much pleasure, then from thee much more must flow;
And soonest our best men with thee do go,
Rest of their bones, and soul's delivery.
Thou art slave to Fate, chance, kings, and desperate men,
And dost with poison, war, and sickness dwell,
And poppy or charms can make us sleep as well
And better than thy stroke; why swell'st thou then?
One short sleep past, we wake eternally
And Death shall be no more; Death, thou shalt die.

Exercises

1. Donne's poetry has been aptly called "strong-lined" because of his powerful images and sharp changes in rhythm. Try reading his "Song" aloud, listening for the abrupt change in rhythm of *And find/What wind* plus similar changes in the second and third stanzas. How much do these contribute to "strong-lined" poetry?
2. Identify the three stages in "The Flea": the moral the poet draws from the flea; when the woman proposes to kill it; when she actually does so.
3. Compare, in "The Good-Morrow," personal images with those that are much larger. Consider, for example, *one little room* and *every where, sea-discovers, worlds on worlds*. Look also at verbs like *loved, sucked,* and *snorted*.
4. In the "Holy Sonnet" Donne equates death with extended, restful sleep. Is his point of view convincing? Would it persuade an atheist?

Andrew Marvell (1621–1678)

Late in his career Marvell wrote stinging political satires, but he is best known today for his classically inspired lyric poetry about love and nature. "To his Coy Mistress" is a seduction poem in the tradition of Catullus and other classical writers in which the theme is the fleeting moment and the tone is urgent. We must seize the moment and make love now. Though the theme is serious the style is both graceful and playful and, withal, sophisticated.

TO HIS COY MISTRESS

Andrew Marvell

Had we but World enough, and Time,
This coyness Lady were no crime.
We would sit down, and think which way
To walk, and pass our long Loves Day.
Thou by the *Indian Ganges* side
Should'st Rubies find: I by the Tide
Of *Humber* would complain. I would
Love you ten years before the Flood:
And you should if you please refuse
Till the Conversion of the *Jews.*   10
My vegetable Love should grow
Vaster than Empires, and more slow.
An hundred years should go to praise
Thine Eyes, and on thy Forehead Gaze.
Two hundred to adore each Breast:
But thirty thousand to the rest.
An Age at least to every part,
And the last Age should show your Heart.
For Lady you deserve this State;
Nor would I love at lower rate.   20
    But at my back I alwaies hear
Times winged Charriot hurrying near:
And yonder all before us lye
Desarts of vast Eternity.
Thy Beauty shall no more be found;
Nor, in thy marble Vault, shall sound
My ecchoing Song: then Worms shall try
That long preserv'd Virginity:
And your quaint Honour turn to dust;
And into ashes all my Lust.   30
The Grave's a fine and private place,
But none I think do there embrace.
    Now therefore, while the youthful hew
Sits on thy skin like morning dew,
And while thy willing Soul transpires
At every pore with instant Fires,
Now let us sport us while we may;
And now, like am'rous birds of prey,
Rather at once our Time devour,
Than languish in his slow-chapt pow'r.   40
Let us roll all our Strength, and all
Our sweetness, up into one Ball:
And tear our Pleasures with rough strife,
Thorough the Iron gates of Life.
Thus, though we cannot make our Sun
Stand still, yet we will make him run.

Exercise

1. Did the Coy Mistress acquiesce? Look again at
   the first and last lines, at the progression from
   not having enough time to the illusion of time
   flying by.

John Milton (1608–1674)

An ardent supporter of the Puritan cause, Milton became Latin secretary in Cromwell's government and, in several important tracts, one of its principle defenders. Upon the Restoration of the Stuart line with Charles II (1660) Milton was fined and forcibly retired, after which he dictated his epic poems *Paradise Lost* (1667) and *Paradise Regained* (1671). One of the world's great epic poems, *Paradise Lost* relates the story of Satan's rebellion against God and the Fall of Man. Milton's intention was, as he said, to "justify the ways of God to man."

The epic poems were among the first to use blank verse (unrhymed iambic pentameter), but Milton also wrote some notable sonnets. Considered to be among his finest work in small form, the two sonnets given below are in the standard form of 14 lines in rhymed iambic pentameter.

On Easter Sunday (1655) in the Piedmont region of northwestern Italy, the Duke of Savoy slaughtered about 1,700 members of the Protestant Waldensian sect that dated back to 1170 (see Reformation in chap. 17). Protestant Europe was horrified; Milton's response was a sonnet tense with low-keyed fury. The "martyred blood" refers to Tertullian's statement that "the blood of the martyrs is the seed of the Church." The "Triple tyrant" is the pope, whose tiara has three crowns, and "Babylonian woe" is a reference to Revelation 18 in which the obliteration of the city of luxury and vice is described. Along with many Protestants, especially Puritans, Milton saw the destruction of Babylon as an allegory of the ultimate fate of the Catholic Church.

ON THE LATE MASSACRE IN PIEDMONT (1655)

John Milton

Avenge, O Lord, thy slaughtered Saints, whose bones
    Lie scattered on the Alpine mountains cold;
    Even them who kept thy truth so pure of old,
When all our fathers worshiped stocks and stones,
Forget not: in thy book record their groans
    Who were thy sheep, and in their ancient fold
    Slain by the bloody Piemontese, that rolled
Mother with infant down the rocks. Their moans
The vales redoubled to the hills, and they
    To heaven. Their martyred blood and ashes sow
O'er all the Italian fields, where still doth sway
    The triple Tyrant; that from these may grow
A hundredfold, who, having learnt thy way,
    Early may fly the Babylonian woe.

Because of overwork Milton's eyesight had become impaired as early as 1644, and by 1652 he was totally blind. The first of two sonnets about his blindness, the following poem signals the poet's submission to fate though he had not yet found his way to using, in darkness, "that one talent which is death to hide."

ON HIS BLINDNESS
(1655)
John Milton

When I consider how my light is spent
    Ere half my days in this dark world and wide,
    And that one Talent which is death to hide
    Lodged with me useless, though my soul more bent
To serve therewith my Maker, and present
    My true account, lest He returning chide,
    "Doth God exact day-labour, light denied?"
    I fondly ask. But Patience, to prevent
That murmur, soon replies, "God doth not need
    Either man's work or his own gifts.
        Who best
    Bear his mild yoke, they serve him best.
        His state
Is kingly: thousands at his bidding speed,
    And post o'er land and ocean without rest;
    They also serve who only stand and wait."

Exercise

1. Milton seethes with indignation over the fate of the slaughtered saints in Italy but not over the loss of his sight. What are some of the words that convey this mood of resignation? Consider, for example, words like *spent, bent, mild,* and *murmur.*

Alexander Pope (1688–1744)

Milton's poetry can be reasonably described as Baroque; that of Pope is even more clearly Neoclassic. In *The Essay on Criticism* he formulated an aesthetics of poetry, emphasizing the necessity for precise language, logical order, and clear form. Pope's own poetry was didactic, witty, satiric, technically superb; it epitomized the Neoclassic style of eighteenth-century England. Pope, in fact, expressed his goal in his own verse:

    True wit is nature to advantage dressed,
    What oft was thought, but ne'er so well expressed.

His *Essay on Man* (1733–1734) optimistically summarizes eighteenth-century views on the rational universe, reasonable behavior, and deism. The poem is not profound in philosophic terms but rather admired for its skillful craftsmanship and sparkling wit. Pope's optimism was rejected by Voltaire in *Candide,* as discussed a bit later.

Literary Selection
ESSAY ON MAN
Alexander Pope

Epistle I

Awake, my St. John! leave all meaner things
To low ambition and the pride of kings.
Let us, since life can little more supply
Than just to look about us and to die,
Expatiate free o'er all this scene of man;
A mighty maze! but not without a plan;
A wild, where weeds and flowers promiscuous shoot;
Or garden, tempting with forbidden fruit.
Together let us beat this ample field,
Try what the open, what the covert yield;
The latent tracts, the giddy heights, explore,
Of all who blindly creep, or sightless soar;
Eye Nature's walks, shoot Folly as it flies,
And catch the manners living as they rise;
Laugh where we must, be candid where we can;
But vindicate the ways of God to man.

I

Say first, of God above or man below,
What can we reason but from what we know?
Of man, what see we but his station here,
From which to reason, or to which refer?
Through worlds unnumber'd though the God be known,
'Tis ours to trace him only in our own.
He, who through vast immensity can pierce,
See worlds on worlds compose one universe,
Observe how system into system runs,
What other planets circle other suns,
What varied being peoples every star,
May tell why Heav'n has made us as we are.
But of this frame, the bearings and the ties,
The strong connections, nice dependencies,
Gradations just, has thy pervading soul
Looked through, or can a part contain the whole?
    Is the great chain that draws all to agree,
And drawn supports, upheld by God or thee?

II

Presumptuous man! the reason wouldst thou find,
Why form'd so weak, so little, and so blind?
First, if thou canst, the harder reason guess,
Why form'd no weaker, blinder, and no less?
Ask of thy mother earth, why oaks are made
Taller or stronger than the weeds they shade!
Or ask of yonder argent fields above
Why Jove's satellites are less than Jove!
    Of systems possible, if 't is confest
That wisdom infinite must form the best,
Where all must full or not coherent be,
And all that rises rise in due degree,
Then, in the scale of reas'ning life, 't is plain
There must be somewhere such a rank as Man:
And all the question (wrangle e'er so long)
Is only this, if God has placed him wrong?

Respecting Man, whatever wrong we call,
May, must be right, as relative to all.
In human works, though labor'd on with pain,
A thousand movements scarce one purpose gain;
In God's, one single can its end produce;
Yet serves to second too some other use.
So Man, who here seems principal alone,
Perhaps acts second to some sphere unknown,
Touches some wheel, or verges to some goal;
'Tis but a part we see, and not a whole.
When the proud steed shall know why man restrains
His fiery course, or drives him o'er the plains;
When the dull ox, why now he breaks the clod,
Is now a victim, and now Egypt's god;
Then shall man's pride and dullness comprehend
His actions', passions', being's, use and end;
Why doing, suff'ring, check'd, impell'd; and why
This hour a slave, the next a deity.

    Then say not man's imperfect, Heav'n in fault;
Say rather man's as perfect as he ought:
His knowledge measur'd to his state and place,
His time a moment, and a point his space.
If to be perfect in a certain sphere,
What matter soon or late, or here or there?
The blest today is as completely so,
As who began a thousand years ago.

III

Heav'n from all creatures hides the book of Fate,
All but the page prescrib'd, their present state:
From brutes what men, from men what spirits know:
Or who could suffer Being here below?
The lamb thy riot dooms to bleed today,
Had he thy reason, would he skip and play?
Pleas'd to the last, he crops the flow'ry food,
And licks the hand just rais'd to shed his blood.
Oh blindness to the future! kindly giv'n,
That each may fill the circle mark'd by Heav'n:
Who sees with equal eye, as God of all,
A hero perish, or a sparrow fall,
Atoms or systems into ruin hurl'd,
And now a bubble burst, and now a world.

    Hope humbly then; with trembling pinions soar;
Wait the great teacher Death, and God adore!
What future bliss he gives not thee to know,
But gives that hope to be thy blessing now.
Hope springs eternal in the human breast;
Man never is, but always to be blest.
The soul, uneasy, and confin'd from home,
Rests and expatiates in a life to come.

    Lo! the poor Indian, whose untutor'd mind
Sees God in clouds, or hears him in the wind;
His soul proud Science never taught to stray
Far as the solar walk or milky way;
Yet simple Nature to his hope has giv'n,
Behind the cloud-topt hill, an humbler heav'n;
Some safer world in depth of woods embrac'd,
Some happier island in the watery waste,
Where slaves once more their native land behold,
No fiends torment, no Christians thirst for gold!
To be, contents his natural desire;
He asks no angel's wing, no seraph's fire;
But thinks, admitted to that equal sky,
His faithful dog shall bear him company.

IV

Go, wiser thou! and in thy scale of sense,
Weigh thy opinion against Providence;
Call imperfection what thou fancy'st such,
Say, Here he gives too little, there too much!
Destroy all creatures for thy sport or gust,
Yet cry, If man's unhappy, God's unjust;
If man alone engross not Heav'n's high care,
Alone made perfect here, immortal there:
Snatch from his hand the balance and the rod,
Rejudge his justice, be the God of God!
In pride, in reas'ning pride, our error lies;
All quit their sphere and rush into the skies.
Pride still is aiming at the blest abodes,
Men would be angels, angels would be gods.
Aspiring to be gods if angels fell,
Aspiring to be angels, men rebel:
And who but wishes to invert the laws
Of order, sins against the Eternal Cause.

V

Ask for what end the heav'nly bodies shine,
Earth for whose use? Pride answers, " 'Tis for mine!
For me kind Nature wakes her genial pow'r,
Suckles each herb, and spreads out ev'ry flow'r;
Annual for me, the grape, the rose renew
The juice nectareous and the balmy dew;
For me the mine a thousand treasures brings;
For me health gushes from a thousand springs;
Seas roll to waft me, suns to light me rise;
My footstool earth, my canopy the skies."

    But errs not Nature from this gracious end,
From burning suns when livid deaths descend,
When earthquakes swallow, or when tempests sweep
Towns to one grave, whole nations to the deep?
"No," 't is reply'd, "the first Almighty Cause
Acts not by partial but by gen'ral laws:
Th' exceptions few; some change since all began;
And what created perfect?"—Why then man?
If the great end be human happiness,
Then Nature deviates; and can man do less?
As much that end a constant course requires
Of show'rs and sunshine, as of man's desires:
As much eternal springs and cloudless skies,
As men forever temp'rate, calm, and wise.
If plagues or earthquakes break not Heav'n's design,
Why then a Borgia or a Catiline?
Who knows but he, whose hand the lightning forms,
Why heaves old ocean, and who wings the storms,
Pours fierce ambition in a Caesar's mind,
Or turns young Ammon loose to scourge mankind?
From pride, from pride our very reas'ning springs;
Account for moral, as for natural things:
Why charge we Heav'n in those, in these acquit?
In both, to reason right is to submit.

    Better for us, perhaps, it might appear,
Were there all harmony, all virtue here;
That never air or ocean felt the wind;
That never passion discompos'd the mind.
But all subsists by elemental strife;
And passions are the elements of life.
The gen'ral order, since the whole began,
Is kept in Nature, and is kept in man.

VI

What would this man? Now upward will he soar,
And little less than angel, would be more!
Now looking downwards, just as griev'd appears
To want the strength of bulls, the fur of bears.
Made for his use all creatures if he call,
Say what their use, had he the pow'rs of all?
Nature to these, without profusion, kind,
The proper organs, proper pow'rs assign'd;
Each seeming want compensated of course,
Here with degrees of swiftness, there of force:
All in exact proportion to the state;
Nothing to add, and nothing to abate;
Each beast, each insect happy in its own:
Is Heav'n unkind to man, and man alone?
Shall he alone, whom rational we call,
Be pleas'd with nothing, if not bless'd with all?
The bliss of man (could pride that blessing find),
Is not to act or think beyond mankind;
No powers of body or of soul to share,
But what his nature and his state can bear.
Why has not man a microscopic eye?
For this plain reason, man is not a fly.
Say what the use, were finer optics giv'n,
To inspect a mite, not comprehend the heav'n?
Or touch, if tremblingly alive all o'er,
To smart and agonize at every pore?
Or quick effluvia darting through the brain,
Die of a rose in aromatic pain?
If Nature thunder'd in his opening ears,
And stunn'd him with the music of the spheres,
How would he wish that Heav'n had left him still
The whisp'ring zephyr and the purling rill?
Who finds not Providence all good and wise,
Alike in what it gives, and what denies?

VII

Far as creation's ample range extends,
The scale of sensual, mental powers ascends.
Mark how it mounts to man's imperial race,
From the green myriads in the peopled grass;
What modes of sight betwixt each wide extreme,
The mole's dim curtain, and the lynx's beam:
Of smell, the headlong lioness between,
And hound sagacious on the tainted green:
Of hearing, from the life that fills the flood,
To that which warbles through the vernal wood:
The spider's touch how exquisitely fine!
Feels at each thread, and lives along the line:
In the nice bee, what sense so subtly true
From pois'nous herbs extracts the healing dew?
How instinct varies in the grov'ling swine,
Compar'd, half-reas'ning elephant, with thine!
'Twixt that and reason, what a nice barrier;
Forever sep'rate, yet forever near!
Remembrance and reflection, how ally'd;
What thin partitions sense from thought divide;
And middle natures, how they long to join,
Yet never pass th' insuperable line!
Without this just gradation, could they be
Subjected, these to those, or all to thee?
The pow'rs of all subdu'd by thee alone,
Is not thy reason all these pow'rs in one?
See, through this air, this ocean, and this earth,
All matter quick, and bursting into birth.

Above, how high progressive life may go!
Around, how wide! how deep extend below!
Vast Chain of Being! which from God began,
Natures ethereal, human, angel, man,
Beast, bird, fish, insect, what no eye can see,
No glass can reach; from infinite to thee,
From thee to nothing. On superior pow'rs
Were we to press, inferior might on ours:
Or in the full creation leave a void,
Where, one step broken, the great scale's destroy'd:
From Nature's chain whatever link you strike,
Tenth or ten thousandth, breaks the chain alike.
    And if each system in gradation roll
Alike essential to the amazing Whole,
The least confusion but in one, not all
That system only, but the Whole must fall.
Let earth unbalanc'd from her orbit fly,
Planets and suns run lawless through the sky;
Let ruling angels from their spheres be hurl'd,
Being on being wreck'd, and world on world;
Heav'n's whole foundations to their centre nod,
And Nature tremble to the throne of God!
All this dread Order break—for whom? for thee?
Vile worm!—Oh! madness! pride! impiety!

IX

What if the foot, ordain'd the dust to tread,
Or hand, to toil, aspir'd to be the head?
What if the head, the eye, or ear repin'd
To serve mere engines to the ruling Mind?
Just as absurd for any part to claim
To be another in this gen'ral frame;
Just as absurd to mourn the tasks or pains
The great directing Mind of All ordains.
    All are but parts of one stupendous whole,
Whose body Nature is, and God the soul;
That, chang'd through all, and yet in all the same,
Great in the earth, as in th' ethereal frame,
Warms in the sun, refreshes in the breeze,
Glows in the stars, and blossoms in the trees,
Lives through all life, extends through all extent,
Spreads undivided, operates unspent;
Breathes in our soul, informs our mortal part,
As full, as perfect in a hair as heart;
As full, as perfect in vile man that mourns,
As the rapt seraph that adores and burns:
To him no high, no low, no great, no small;
He fills, he bounds, connects, and equals all.

X

Cease then, nor Order imperfection name:
Our proper bliss depends on what we blame.
Know thy own point: this kind, this due degree
Of blindness, weakness, Heav'n bestows on thee.
Submit: in this or any other sphere,
Secure to be as blest as thou canst bear;
Safe in the hand of one disposing Pow'r
Or in the natal, or the mortal hour.
All Nature is but art unknown to thee;
All chance, direction which thou canst not see;
All discord, harmony not understood;
All partial evil, universal good;
And, spite of pride, in erring reason's spite,
One truth is clear, *whatever is, is right.*

Epistle II

I

Know then thyself, presume not God to scan:
The proper study of mankind is Man.
Plac'd on this isthmus of a middle state,
A being darkly wise and rudely great:
With too much knowledge for the skeptic side,
With too much weakness for the Stoic's pride,
He hangs between; in doubt to act, or rest;
In doubt to deem himself a god or beast;
In doubt his mind or body to prefer;
Born but to die, and reas'ning but to err;
Alike in ignorance, his reason such,
Whether he thinks too little or too much:
Chaos of thought and passion, all confus'd;
Still by himself abus'd, or disabus'd;
Created half to rise, and half to fall;
Great lord of all things, yet a prey to all;
Sole judge of truth, in endless error hurl'd;
The glory, jest, and riddle of the world!

II

Two principles in human nature reign;
Self-love to urge, and reason to restrain;
Nor this a good, nor that a bad we call,
Each works its end to move or govern all:
And to their proper operation still
Ascribe all good; to their improper, ill.
    Self-love, the spring of motion, acts the soul;
Reason's comparing balance rules the whole.
Man, but for that, no action could attend,
And, but for this, were active to no end:
Fix'd like a plant on his peculiar spot,
To draw nutrition, propagate, and rot;
Or, meteor-like, flame lawless thro' the void,
Destroying others, by himself destroyed.
    Most strength the moving principle requires;
Active its task, it prompts, impels, inspires.
Sedate and quiet, the comparing lies,
Form'd but to check, deliberate, and advise.
Self-love still stronger, as its objects nigh;
Reason's at distance and in prospect lie:
That sees immediate good by present sense;
Reason, the future and the consequence.
Thicker than arguments, temptations throng,
At best more watchful this, but that more strong.
The action of the stronger to suspend,
Reason still use, to reason still attend.
Attention, habit and experience gains;
Each strengthens reason, and self-love restrains . . .

V

Vice is a monster of so frightful mien,
As to be hated needs but to be seen;
Yet seen too oft, familiar with her face,
We first endure, then pity, then embrace:
But where the extreme of vice was ne'er agreed:
Ask where's the north? at York, 'tis on the Tweed;
In Scotland, at the Orcades; and there,
At Greenland, Zembla, or the Lord knows where.
No creature owns it in the first degree,
But thinks his neighbor farther gone than he;
Even those who dwell beneath its very zone,
Or never feel the rage, or never own;
What happier natures shrink at with affright
The hard inhabitant contends is right.

Virtuous and vicious every man must be;
Few in the extreme, but all in the degree:
The rogue and fool by fits is fair and wise;
And ev'n the best, by fits, what they despise.
'T is but by parts we follow good or ill;
For, vice or virtue, self directs it still;
Each individual seeks a sev'ral goal;
But Heav'n's great view is one, and that the whole . . .

Epistle III

I

Here then we rest: "The Universal Cause
Acts to one end, but acts by various laws."
In all the madness of superfluous health,
The trim of pride, the impudence of wealth,
Let this great truth be present night and day:
But most be present, if we preach or pray.
    Look round our world, behold the chain of love
Combining all below and all above.
See plastic Nature working to this end:
The single atoms each to other tend;
Attract, attracted to, the next in place
Form'd and impell'd its neighbor to embrace.
See matter next with various life endu'd,
Press to one centre still, the gen'ral good.
See dying vegetables life sustain,
See life dissolving vegetate again:
All forms that perish other forms supply,
(By turns we catch the vital breath, and die,)
Like bubbles on the sea of matter borne,
They rise, they break, and to that sea return.
Nothing is foreign; parts relate to whole;
One all-extending, all-preserving soul
Connects each being, greatest with the least;
Made beast in aid of man, and man of beast;
All serv'd, all serving: nothing stands alone;
The chain holds on, and where it ends, unknown . . .

Exercises

1. In the first section of Epistle I is Pope a "rationalist"—one who believes that the human mind can find answers to all his questions? Why do you answer as you do?
2. In Epistle I:VII Pope refers to the "Vast chain of being." What does he mean by this?
3. Pope speaks of man as the *glory,* the *jest,* and the *riddle* of the world. In what sense does he use each term? Name three men or women, or one person in three different situations that would explain Pope's meaning.
4. In your estimation, what is the point of the brief selection from Epistle III: inescapable Law; constant Change; Continuity and Interdependence; inevitable Death and Decay; the Separateness of all things; or some other idea?
5. Who would have given the more favorable review on the *Essay on Man* (if he could have read it!): Newton or Rousseau? Dante or Machiavelli? Shakespeare or Donne? Why do you think so?

Jonathan Swift (1667–1745)

Born in Ireland of English parents, Jonathan Swift is identified with Ireland and its political troubles and yet, for most of his life, he tried to break away from Ireland. His dream of becoming an English bishop failed; instead he was given the deanship of St. Patrick's Cathedral in Dublin. At first feeling exiled in Ireland he later became closely identified with its poverty and political privation.

A master of language used in a lucid and forceful style, Swift was the greatest English satirist in an age of satire, perhaps because he was more detached, viewing English life and customs from his vantage point in Ireland. His masterpiece, *Gulliver's Travels* (1726), savagely exposed and attacked every human weakness and vice over there in Britain. His brilliant pamphlet, "A Modest Proposal," was written in the white heat of indignation. Ireland's poverty and misery, in his own words, did "tear his heart." His proposal is all the more horrendous in its reasoned logic as he ironically suggests a practical, rational solution to Irish destitution and privation.

Literary Selection

A MODEST PROPOSAL

for Preventing the Children of Poor People in Ireland from Being a Burden to Their Parents or Country, and for Making Them Beneficial to the Public.
1729
Jonathan Swift

It is a melancholy object to those who walk through this great town, or travel in the country, when they see the streets, the roads, and cabin-doors, crowded with beggars of the female sex, followed by three, four, or six children, all in rags, and importuning every passenger for an alms. These mothers, instead of being able to work for their honest livelihood, are forced to employ all their time in strolling to beg sustenance for their helpless infants: who, as they grow up, either turn thieves for want of work, or leave their dear native country to fight for the Pretender in Spain, or sell themselves to the Barbadoes.

I think it is agreed by all parties, that this prodigious number of children in the arms, or on the backs, or at the heels of their mothers, and frequently of their fathers, is, in the present deplorable state of the kingdom, a very great additional grievance; and, therefore, whoever could find out a fair, cheap, and easy method of making these children sound, useful members of the commonwealth, would deserve so well of the public, as to have his statue set up for a preserver of the nation.

But my intention is very far from being confined to provide only for the children of professed beggars; it is of a much greater extent, and shall take in the whole number of infants at a certain age, who are born of parents in effect as little able to support them, as those who demand our charity in the streets.

As to my own part, having turned my thoughts for many years upon this important subject, and maturely weighed the several schemes of our projectors, I have always found them grossly mistaken in their computation. It is true, a child, just born, may be supported by its mother's milk for a solar year, with little other nourishment; at most, not above the value of two shillings, which the mother may certainly get, or the value in scraps, by her lawful occupation of begging; and it is exactly at one year old that I propose to provide for them in such a manner, as, instead of being a charge upon their parents, or the parish, or wanting food and raiment for the rest of their lives, they shall, on the contrary, contribute to the feeding, and partly to the clothing, of many thousands.

There is likewise another great advantage in my scheme, that it will prevent those voluntary abortions, and that horrid practice of women murdering their bastard children, alas, too frequent among us! sacrificing the poor innocent babes, I doubt more to avoid the expense than the shame, which would move tears and pity in the most savage and inhuman breast.

The number of souls in this kingdom being usually reckoned one million and a half, of these I calculate there may be about two hundred thousand couple whose wives are breeders; from which number I subtract thirty thousand couple, who are able to maintain their own children, (although I apprehend there cannot be so many, under the present distresses of the kingdom;) but this being granted, there will remain a hundred and seventy thousand breeders. I again subtract fifty thousand, for those women who miscarry, or whose children die by accident or disease within the year. There only remain a hundred and twenty thousand children of poor parents annually born. The question therefore is, How this number shall be reared and provided for? which, as I have already said, under the present situation of affairs, is utterly impossible by all the methods hitherto proposed. For we can neither employ them in handicraft or agriculture; we neither build houses (I mean in the country,) nor cultivate land: they can very seldom pick up a livelihood by stealing, till they arrive at six years old, except where they are of towardly parts; although I confess they learn the rudiments much earlier; during which time they can, however, be properly looked upon only as probationers; as I have been informed by a principal gentleman in the county of Cavan, who protested to me, that he never knew above one or two instances under the age of six, even in a part of the kingdom so renowned for the quickest proficiency in that art.

I am assured by our merchants, that a boy or a girl before twelve years old is no saleable commodity; and even when they come to this age they will not yield above three pounds or three pounds and half-a-crown at most, on the exchange; which cannot turn to account either to the parents or kingdom, the charge of nutriment and rags having been at least four times that value.

I shall now, therefore, humbly propose my own thoughts, which I hope will not be liable to the least objection.

I have been assured by a very knowing American of my acquaintance in London, that a young healthy child, well nursed, is, at a year old, a most delicious, nourishing, and wholesome food, whether stewed, roasted, baked, or boiled; and I make no doubt that it will equally serve in a fricassee or a ragout.

I do therefore humbly offer it to public consideration, that of the hundred and twenty thousand children already computed, twenty thousand may be reserved for breed, whereof only one-fourth part to be males; which is more than we allow to sheep, black-cattle, or swine; and my reason is, that these children are seldom the fruits of marriage, a circumstance not much regarded by our savages, therefore one male will be sufficient for four females. That the remaining hundred thousand may, at a year old, be offered in sale to the persons of quality and fortune through the kingdom; always advising the mother to let them suck plentifully in the last month, so as to render them plump and fat for a good table. A child will make two dishes at an entertainment for friends; and when the family dines alone, the fore or hind quarter will make a reasonable dish, and, seasoned with a little pepper or salt, will be very good boiled on the fourth day, especially in winter.

I have reckoned, upon a medium, that a child just born will weigh twelve pounds, and in a solar year, if tolerably nursed, will increase to twenty-eight pounds.

I grant this food will be somewhat dear, and therefore very proper for landlords, who, as they have already devoured most of the parents, seem to have the best title to the children.

Infants' flesh will be in season throughout the year, but more plentifully in March, and a little before and after: for we are told by a grave author, an eminent French physician, that fish being a prolific diet, there are more children born in Roman Catholic countries about nine months after Lent, than at any other season; therefore, reckoning a year after Lent, the markets will be more glutted than usual, because the number of Popish infants is at least three to one in this kingdom; and therefore it will have one other collateral advantage, by lessening the number of Papists among us.

I have already computed the charge of nursing a beggar's child (in which list I reckon all cottagers, labourers, and four-fifths of the farmers) to be about two shillings per annum, rags included; and I believe no gentleman would repine to give ten shillings for the carcass of a good fat child, which, as I have said, will make four dishes of excellent nutritive meat, when he has only some particular friend, or his own family, to dine with him. Thus the squire will learn to be a good landlord, and grow popular among his tenants; the mother will have eight shillings net profit, and be fit for work till she produces another child.

Those who are more thrifty (as I must confess the times require) may flay the carcass; the skin of which, artificially dressed, will make admirable gloves for ladies, and summer-boots for fine gentlemen.

As to our city of Dublin, shambles may be appointed for this purpose in the most convenient parts of it, and butchers we may be assured will not be wanting; although I rather recommend buying the children alive, then dressing them hot from the knife, as we do roasting pigs.

A very worthy person, a true lover of his country, and whose virtues I highly esteem, was lately pleased, in discoursing on this matter, to offer a refinement upon my scheme. He said, that many gentlemen of this kingdom, having of late destroyed their deer, he conceived that the want of venison might be well supplied by the bodies of young lads and maidens, not exceeding fourteen years of age, nor under twelve; so great a number of both sexes in every country being now ready to starve for want of work

and service; and these to be disposed of by their parents, if alive, or otherwise by their nearest relations. But, with due deference to so excellent a friend, and so deserving a patriot, I cannot be altogether in his sentiments; for as to the males, my American acquaintance assured me, from frequent experience, that their flesh was generally tough and lean, like that of our schoolboys, by continual exercise, and their taste disagreeable; and to fatten them would not answer the charge. Then as to the females, it would, I think, with humble submission, be a loss to the public, because they soon would become breeders themselves: and besides, it is not improbable that some scrupulous people might be apt to censure such a practice, (although indeed very unjustly,) as a little bordering upon cruelty; which, I confess, has always been with me the strongest objection against any project, how well soever intended.

But in order to justify my friend, he confessed that this expedient was put into his head by the famous Psalmanazar, a native of the island Formosa, who came from thence to London above twenty years ago; and in conversation told my friend, that in his country, when any young person happened to be put to death, the executioner sold the carcass to persons of quality as a prime dainty; and that in his time the body of a plump girl of fifteen, who was crucified for an attempt to poison the emperor, was sold to his imperial majesty's prime minister of state, and other great mandarins of the court, in joints from the gibbet, at four hundred crowns. Neither indeed can I deny, that if the same use were made of several plump young girls in this town, who, without one single groat to their fortunes, cannot stir abroad without a chair, and appear at playhouse and assemblies in foreign fineries which they never will pay for, the kingdom would not be the worse.

Some persons of a desponding spirit are in great concern about that vast number of poor people, who are aged, diseased, or maimed; and I have been desired to employ my thoughts, what course may be taken to ease the nation of so grievous an encumbrance. But I am not in the least pain upon that matter, because it is very well known, that they are every day dying, and rotting, by cold and famine, and filth and vermin, as fast as can be reasonably expected. And as to the young labourers, they are now in almost as hopeful a condition: they cannot get work, and consequently pine away for want of nourishment, to a degree, that if at any time they are accidentally hired to common labour, they have not strength to perform it; and thus the country and themselves are happily delivered from the evils to come.

I have too long digressed, and therefore shall return to my subject. I think the advantages by the proposal which I have made, are obvious and many, as well as of the highest importance.

For first, as I have already observed, it would greatly lessen the number of Papists, with whom we are yearly over-run, being the principal breeders of the nation, as well as our most dangerous enemies; and who stay at home on purpose to deliver the kingdom to the Pretender, hoping to take their advantage by the absence of so many good Protestants, who have chosen rather to leave their country, than stay at home and pay tithes against their conscience to an Episcopal curate.

Secondly, The poorer tenants will have something valuable of their own, which by law may be made liable to distress, and help to pay their landlord's rent; their corn and cattle being already seized, and money a thing unknown.

Thirdly, Whereas the maintenance of a hundred thousand children, from two years old and upward, cannot be computed at less than ten shillings a piece per annum, the nation's stock will be thereby increased fifty thousand pounds per annum, beside the profit of a new dish introduced to the tables of all gentlemen of fortune in the kingdom, who have any refinement in taste. And the money will circulate among ourselves, the goods being entirely of our own growth and manufacture.

Fourthly, The constant breeders, beside the gain of eight shillings sterling per annum by the sale of their children, will be rid of the charge of maintaining them after the first year.

Fifthly, This food would likewise bring great custom to taverns; where the vintners will certainly be so prudent as to procure the best receipts for dressing it to perfection, and, consequently, have their houses frequented by all the fine gentlemen, who justly value themselves upon their knowledge in good eating: and a skilful cook, who understands how to oblige his guests, will contrive to make it as expensive as they please.

Sixthly, This would be a great inducement to marriage, which all wise nations have either encouraged by rewards, or enforced by laws and penalties. It would increase the care and tenderness of mothers toward their children, when they were sure of a settlement for life to the poor babes, provided in some sort by the public, to their annual profit or expense. We should see an honest emulation among the married women, which of them could bring the fattest child to the market. Men would become as fond of their wives during the time of their pregnancy, as they are now of their mares in foal, their cows in calf, their sows when they are ready to farrow; nor offer to beat or kick them (as is too frequent a practice) for fear of a miscarriage.

Many other advantages might be enumerated. For instance, the addition of some thousand carcasses in our exportation of barrelled beef; the propagation of swine's flesh, and improvement in the art of making good bacon, so much wanted among us by the great destruction of pigs, too frequent at our table; which are no way comparable in taste or magnificence to a well-grown, fat, yearling child, which, roasted whole, will make a considerable figure at a lord mayor's feast, or any other public entertainment. But this, and many others, I omit, being studious of brevity.

Supposing that one thousand families in this city would be constant customers for infants' flesh, beside others who might have it at merry-meetings, particularly at weddings and christenings, I compute that Dublin would take off annually about twenty thousand carcasses; and the rest of the kingdom (where probably they will be sold somewhat cheaper) the remaining eighty thousand.

I can think of no one objection, that will possibly be raised against this proposal, unless it should be urged, that the number of people will be thereby much lessened in the kingdom. This I freely own, and it was indeed one principal design in offering it to the world. I desire the reader will observe, that I calculate my remedy for this one individual kingdom of Ireland, and for no other that ever was, is, or I think ever can be, upon earth. Therefore let no man talk to me of other expedients: of taxing our absentees at five shillings a pound: of using neither clothes, nor household-furniture, except what is our own growth and manufacture: of utterly rejecting the materials and instruments that promote foreign luxury: of curing the expensiveness of pride, vanity, idleness, and gaming

in our women; of introducing a vein of parsimony, prudence, and temperance: of learning to love our country, in the want of which we differ even from LAPLANDERS, and the inhabitants of TOPINAMBOO: of quitting our animosities and factions, nor acting any longer like the Jews, who were murdering one another at the very moment their city was taken: of being a little cautious not to sell our country and conscience for nothing: of teaching landlords to have at least one degree of mercy toward their tenants: lastly, of putting a spirit of honesty, industry, and skill into our shopkeepers; who, if a resolution could now be taken to buy only our native goods, would immediately unite to cheat and exact upon us in the price, the measure, and the goodness, nor could ever yet be brought to make one fair proposal of just dealing, though often and earnestly invited to it.

Therefore I repeat, let no man talk to me of these and the like expedients, till he has at least some glimpse of hope, that there will be ever some hearty and sincere attempt to put them in practice.

But, as to myself, having been wearied out for many years with offering vain, idle, visionary thoughts, and at length utterly despairing of success, I fortunately fell upon this proposal; which, as it is wholly new, so it has something solid and real, of no expense and little trouble, full in our own power, and whereby we can incur no danger in disobliging ENGLAND. For this kind of commodity will not bear exportation, the flesh being of too tender a consistence to admit a long continuance in salt, although perhaps I could name a country, which would be glad to eat up our whole nation without it.

After all, I am not so violently bent upon my own opinion as to reject any offer proposed by wise men, which shall be found equally innocent, cheap, easy, and effectual. But before something of that kind shall be advanced in contradiction to my scheme, and offering a better, I desire the author, or authors, will be pleased maturely to consider two points. First, as things now stand, how they will be able to find food and raiment for a hundred thousand useless mouths and backs. And, secondly, there being a round million of creatures in human figure throughout this kingdom, whose whole subsistence put into a common stock would leave them in debt two millions of pounds sterling, adding those who are beggars by profession, to the bulk of farmers, cottagers, and labourers, with the wives and children who are beggars in effect; I desire those politicians who dislike my overture, and may perhaps be so bold as to attempt an answer, that they will first ask the parents of these mortals, whether they would not at this day think it a great happiness to have been sold for food at a year old, in the manner I prescribe, and thereby have avoided such a perpetual scene of misfortunes, as they have since gone through, by the oppression of landlords, the impossibility of paying rent without money or trade, the want of common sustenance, with neither house nor clothes to cover them from the inclemencies of the weather, and the most inevitable prospect of entailing the like, or greater miseries, upon their breed for ever.

I profess, in the sincerity of my heart, that I have not the least personal interest in endeavouring to promote this necessary work, having no other motive than the public good of my country, by advancing our trade, providing for infants, relieving the poor, and giving some pleasure to the rich. I have no children by which I can propose to get a single penny; the youngest being nine years old, and my wife past child-bearing.

Exercise

1. The Irish complained that "the English are devouring the Irish." Swift turned the metaphor into "A Modest Proposal." Forgetting the actual subject matter for the moment, is this proposal rational and practical? Will it help relieve poverty by reducing the population while increasing family incomes? If you answered these questions in the affirmative you are beginning to appreciate the intellectual nature of satire, for satire must be logical and persuasive if it is to accomplish its purpose. The plan is made all the more horrible by Swift's dispassionate tone and flawless logic.

Thomas Gray (1716–1771)

A quiet and solitary professor of modern history at Cambridge, Thomas Gray was a thorough scholar in the classics, old Welsh and Norse literature, and even read Shakespeare, though many classicists at the time regarded the Bard as half barbaric. An expert literary critic, Gray seemed to have criticized his poetry before he wrote it and therefore wrote little. By far his best-known work, his *Elegy* is loved by unsophisticated readers the world over and, paradoxically, is admired by literary critics. It is a classic poem in the classical style: artfully subtle, with a firm control of imagery, cadence, and mood.

Literary Selection

ELEGY WRITTEN IN A COUNTRY CHURCHYARD

Thomas Gray

The curfew tolls the knell of parting day,
    The lowing herd wind slowly o'er the lea,
The plowman homeward plods his weary way,
    And leaves the world to darkness and to me.

Now fades the glimmering landscape on the sight,   5
    And all the air a solemn stillness holds,
Save where the beetle wheels his droning flight,
    And drowsy tinklings lull the distant folds;

Save that from yonder ivy-mantled tow'r,
    The moping owl does to the moon complain   10
Of such as, wand'ring near her secret bow'r,
    Molest her ancient solitary reign.

Beneath those rugged elms, that yew-tree's shade,
    Where heaves the turf in many a mould'ring
    heap,   15
Each in his narrow cell forever laid,
    The rude forefathers of the hamlet sleep.

The breezy call of incense-breathing Morn,
    The swallow twitt'ring from the straw-built shed,
The cock's shrill clarion, or the echoing horn,
    No more shall rouse them from their lowly bed.   20

For them no more the blazing hearth shall burn,
    Or busy housewife ply her evening care;
No children run to lisp their sire's return,
    Or climb his knees the envied kiss to share.

Oft did the harvest to their sickle yield,   25
    Their furrow oft the stubborn glebe has broke;
How jocund did they drive their team afield!
    How bow'd the woods beneath their sturdy stroke!

Let not Ambition mock their useful toil,
    Their homely joys, and destiny obscure;   30
Nor Grandeur hear with a disdainful smile
    The short and simple annals of the poor.

The boast of heraldry, the pomp of pow'r,
    And all that beauty, all that wealth e'er gave,
Await alike th' inevitable hour.   35
    The paths of glory lead but to the grave.

Nor you, ye proud, impute to these the fault,
    If Mem'ry o'er their tomb no trophies raise,
Where thro' the long-drawn aisle and fretted vault
    The pealing anthem swells the note of praise.   40

Can storied urn, or animated bust,
    Back to its mansion call the fleeting breath?
Can Honour's voice provoke the silent dust,
    Or Flatt'ry soothe the dull cold ear of death?

Perhaps in this neglected spot is laid   45
    Some heart once pregnant with celestial fire,
Hands, that the rod of empire might have sway'd,
    Or wak'd to ecstasy the living lyre.

But Knowledge to their eyes her ample page
    Rich with the spoils of time did ne'er unroll;   50
Chill Penury repress'd their noble rage,
    And froze the genial current of the soul.

Full many a gem of purest ray serene
    The dark unfathom'd caves of ocean bear;
Full many a flower is born to blush unseen,   55
    And waste its sweetness on the desert air.

Some village Hampden, that with dauntless breast
    The little Tyrant of his fields withstood,
Some mute inglorious Milton here may rest,
    Some Cromwell guiltless of his country's blood.   60

Th' applause of list'ning senates to command,
    The threats of pain and ruin to despise,
To scatter plenty o'er a smiling land,
    And read their hist'ry in a nation's eyes,

Their lot forbade: nor circumscrib'd alone   65
    Their growing virtues, but their crimes confin'd;
Forbade to wade thro' slaughter to a throne,
    And shut the gates of mercy on mankind;

The struggling pangs of conscious truth to hide,
    To quench the blushes of ingenuous shame,   70
Or heap the shrine of Luxury and Pride
    With incense kindled at the Muse's flame.

Far from the madding crowd's ignoble strife,
    Their sober wishes never learn'd to stray;
Along the cool sequester'd vale of life   75
    They kept the noiseless tenor of their way.

Yet ev'n these bones from insult to protect
    Some frail memorial still erected nigh,
With uncouth rhymes and shapeless sculpture deck'd
    Implores the passing tribute of a sigh.   80

Their name, their years, spelt by th' unletter'd Muse,
    The place of fame and elegy supply;
And many a holy text around she strews,
    That teach the rustic moralist to die.

For who, to dumb Forgetfulness a prey,   85
    This pleasing anxious being e'er resign'd,
Left the warm precincts of the cheerful day,
    Nor cast one longing, ling'ring look behind?

On some fond breast the parting soul relies,
    Some pious drops the closing eye requires;   90
Ev'n from the tomb the voice of Nature cries,
    Ev'n in our ashes live their wonted fires.

For thee, who, mindful of th' unhonour'd dead,
    Dost in these lines their artless tale relate;
If chance, by lonely Contemplation led,   95
    Some kindred spirit shall enquire thy fate,—

Haply some hoary-headed swain may say,
    "Oft have we seen him at the peep of dawn
Brushing with hasty steps the dews away,
    To meet the sun upon the upland lawn: 100

"There at the foot of yonder nodding beech,
    That wreathes its old fantastic roots so high,
His listless length at noontide would he stretch,
    And pore upon the brook that babbles by.

"Hard by yon wood, now smiling as in scorn,   105
    Mutt'ring his wayward fancies he would rove;
Now drooping, woeful-wan, like one forlorn,
    Or craz'd with care, or cross'd in hopeless love.

"One morn I miss'd him on the custom'd hill,
    Along the heath, and near his fav'rite tree;   110
Another came; nor yet beside the rill,
    Nor up the lawn, nor at the wood was he;

"The next, with dirges due in sad array,
    Slow through the church-way path we saw him
      borne:—
Approach and read (for thou canst read) the lay   115
    Grav'd on the stone beneath yon aged thorn."

THE EPITAPH

Here rests his head upon the lap of Earth,
    A youth, to Fortune and to Fame unknown:
Fair Science frown'd not on his humble birth,
    And Melancholy mark'd him for her own.   120

Large was his bounty, and his soul sincere,
    Heav'n did a recompense as largely send;
He gave to Mis'ry all he had, a tear,
    He gain'd from Heav'n ('t was all he wish'd)
      a friend.

No farther seek his merits to disclose,   125
    Or draw his frailties from their dread abode,
(There they alike in trembling hope repose,)
    The bosom of his Father and his God.

Exercises

1. Notice at the beginning of the poem some of
   the words used to establish the melancholy
   mood: *parting, lowing, slowly, weary, darkness.*
   What are some of the other words and images?
2. Does the poem prefer obscurity and ignorance
   to wealth and knowledge? Why?
3. What is the central argument of the poem?
   Consider the type of poem being written and
   where it is composed.

4. The poem is gently melancholy but is it
   pessimistic? Is it, in other words, despairing or
   plaintive?

Voltaire (François Marie de Arouet; 1694–1778)

As philosopher, critic, and writer, Voltaire was the
leading intellectual figure of the Enlightenment. A
tireless opponent of the Church and the *ancien régime* of the Bourbon kings, he was twice imprisoned
in the Bastille (1717, 1726) and exiled in 1726. His
studies in England of Newton and Locke reinforced
his hatred of absolutism and heightened his admiration of English liberalism. Upon his return to France
he published a veritable torrent of works that criticized all of the existing conditions. Whereas Pope had
written, "Whatever is, is right," Voltaire's motto might
well have been, "Whatever is, is wrong." Particularly
did he think that everything was wrong in France.

Voltaire sought his freedom at first in Berlin at
the court of Frederick the Great, where he lived for
three years, but he could not get along with the German king any better than he had with the French king.
So he established himself near Geneva, where he
spent most of the last quarter century of his life. One
may well question Voltaire's sincerity, for he was always concerned with his personal comfort and wealth;
he certainly could not have been too much concerned with the cause of universal freedom when he
went to Berlin and sought to make his permanent
home under the protection of Frederick. But whatever one may say of his personal life, his doubting and
skeptical works found a wide audience. Of all of his
writing, and there is an incredible amount of it, *Candide* is probably the best-known work.

The tone of *Candide* is as important as anything
Voltaire has to say, for he holds up to ridicule everything which the Europe of the time held dear. By his
very tone, Voltaire shows himself to be the debunker
of his time. The trouble with Voltaire is the trouble
with all debunkers: he has little better to offer. As he
looks at his world, everything seems futile and silly:
the glories of war; the church, either Catholic or Protestant; even nature itself. They are all senseless and
unreasonable. When it is all over, the best that he can
suggest is retirement to the farm, where at least one
can cultivate one's garden. One may remark in passing that this is far from a complete answer in the face
of chaotic conditions; but, lacking such a complete
answer, it is much better than none. The development of one's own life and the minding of one's own
business may be better than mistaken activity.

Most of Voltaire's values are negative, and he did
much to contribute to the confusion of his time, for
he brought the faults of his age into sharp focus. That,
however, was of value in itself, for he helped in bringing about the revolutions which upset the old order

of absolutism. Perhaps the painter Jacques Louis David best summed up Voltaire's legacy to his country. During the ceremony of July 10, 1791, when Voltaire's body was transferred to an honored place in the Pantheon, David said, simply: "He taught us to be free."

Literary Selection

CANDIDE
Voltaire

In a castle of Westphalia,[2] belonging to the Baron of Thunder-ten-Tronckh, lived a youth whom nature had endowed with the most gentle manners. His countenance was a true picture of his soul. He combined a true judgment with simplicity of spirit, which was the reason, I apprehend, of his being called Candide. The old servants of the family suspected him to have been the son of the Baron's sister, by a good, honest gentleman of the neighborhood, whom that young lady would never marry because he had been able to prove only seventy-one quarterings, the rest of his genealogical tree having been lost through the injuries of time.

The Baron was one of the most powerful lords in Westphalia, for his castle had not only a gate, but windows. His great hall, even, was hung with tapestry. All the dogs of his farmyards formed a pack of hounds at need; his grooms were his huntsmen; and the curate of the village was his grand almoner.[3] They called him "My Lord," and laughed at all his stories.

The Baron's lady weighed about three hundred and fifty pounds, and was therefore a person of great consideration, and she did the honors of the house with a dignity that commanded still greater respect. Her daughter Cunegonde was seventeen years of age, fresh-colored, comely, plump, and desirable. The Baron's son seemed to be in every respect worthy of his father. The Preceptor Pangloss was the oracle of the family, and little Candide heard his lessons with all the good faith of his age and character.

Pangloss was professor of metaphysicotheologicocosmolo-nigology. He proved admirably that there is no effect without a cause, and that in this best of all possible worlds, the Baron's castle was the most magnificent of castles, and his lady the best of all possible Baronesses.

"It is demonstrable," said he, "that things cannot be otherwise than as they are; for all being created for an end, all is necessarily for the best end. Observe, that the nose has been formed to bear spectacles—thus we have spectacles. Legs are visibly designed for stockings—and we have stockings. Stones were made to be hewn, and to construct castles—therefore my lord has a magnificent castle; for the greatest baron in the province ought to be the best lodged. Pigs were made to be eaten—therefore we eat pork all the year round. Consequently they who assert that all is well have said a foolish thing; they should have said all is for the best."[4]

Candide listened attentively and believed innocently; for he thought Miss Cunegonde extremely beautiful, though he never had the courage to tell her so. He concluded that after the happiness of being born of the Baron of Thunder-ten-Tronckh, the second degree of happiness was to be Miss Cunegonde, the third that of seeing her every day, and the fourth that of hearing Master Pangloss, the greatest philosopher of the whole world.

One day Cunegonde, while walking near the castle, in a little wood which they called a park, . . . became quite pensive, and filled with the desire to be loved, dreamed that she might well be a *sufficient reason* for young Candide, her cousin, and he for her.

She met Candide on reaching the castle and blushed; Candide blushed also; she wished him good morrow in a faltering tone, and Candide spoke to her without knowing what he said. The next day after dinner, as they went from table, Cunegonde and Candide found themselves behind a screen; Cunegonde let fall her handkerchief, Candide picked it up, she took him innocently by the hand, the youth as innocently kissed the young lady's hand with particular vivacity, sensibility, and grace; their lips met, their eyes sparkled, their knees trembled. Baron Thunder-ten-Tronckh passed near the screen and beholding this cause and effect chased Candide from the castle with great kicks; Cunegonde fainted away; she was boxed on the ears by the Baroness, as soon as she came to herself; and all was consternation in this most magnificent and most agreeable of all possible castles.

Candide, driven from this terrestrial paradise, walked a long while without knowing where, weeping, raising his eyes to heaven, turning them often towards the most magnificent of castles which imprisoned the purest of noble young ladies. He lay down to sleep without supper, in the middle of a field between two furrows. The snow fell in large flakes. Next day Candide, all benumbed, dragged himself towards the neighboring town which was called Waldberghofftrarbkdikdorff. Having no money, dying of hunger and fatigue, he stopped sorrowfully at the door of an inn. Two men dressed in blue observed him.

"Comrade," said one, "here is a well-built young fellow, and of proper height."

They went up to Candide and very civilly invited him to dinner.

"Gentlemen," replied Candide, with a most engaging modesty, "you do me great honor, but I have not wherewithal to pay my share."

"Oh, sir," said one of the blues to him, "people of your appearance and of your merit never pay anything: are you not five feet five inches high?"

"Yes, sir, that is my height," answered he, making a low bow.

"Come, sir, seat yourself; not only will we pay your reckoning, but we will never suffer such a man as you to want money; men are only born to assist one another."

"You are right," said Candide; "this is what I was always taught by Mr. Pangloss, and I see plainly that all is for the best."

They begged of him to accept a few crowns. He took them, and wished to give them his note; they refused; they seated themselves at table.

---

2. Westphalia—one of the small Prussian states of Germany.

3. Almoner—official whose duty is to distribute alms.

4. This is not far from Pope's statement, "Whatever is, is right." Actually it comes from the German philosopher, Leibnitz.

"Love you not deeply?"

"Oh, yes," answered he; "I deeply love Miss Cunegonde."

"No," said one of the gentlemen, "we ask you if you do not deeply love the King of the Bulgarians?"

"Not at all," said he; "for I have never seen him."

"What! he is the best of kings, and we must drink his health."

"Oh! very willingly, gentlemen," and he drank.

"That is enough," they told him. "Now you are the help, the support, the defender, the hero of the Bulgarians. Your fortune is made, and your glory is assured."

Instantly they fettered him, and carried him away to the regiment. There he was made to wheel about to the right, and to the left, to draw his rammer,[5] to return his rammer, to present, to fire, to march, and they gave him thirty blows with a cudgel. The next day he did his exercise a little less badly, and he received but twenty blows. The following they gave him only ten, and he was regarded by his comrades as a prodigy.

Candide, all stupefied, could not yet very well realize how he was a hero. He resolved one fine day in spring to go for a walk, marching straight before him, believing that it was a privilege of the human as well as of the animal species to make use of their legs as they pleased. He had advanced two leagues when he was overtaken by four others, heroes of six feet, who bound him and carried him to a dungeon. He was asked which he would like the best, to be whipped six-and-thirty times through all the regiment, or to receive at once twelve balls of lead in his brain. He vainly said that human will is free, and that he chose neither the one nor the other. He was forced to make a choice; he determined, in virtue of that gift of God called liberty, to run the gauntlet six-and-thirty times. He bore this twice. The regiment was composed of two thousand men; that composed for him four thousand strokes, which laid bare all his muscles and nerves, from the nape of his neck quite down to his rump. As they were going to proceed to a third whipping, Candide, able to bear no more, begged as a favor that they would be so good as to shoot him. He obtained this favor; they bandaged his eyes and bade him kneel down. The King of the Bulgarians passed at this moment and ascertained the nature of the crime. As he had great talent, he understood from all that he learned of Candide that he was a young metaphysician, extremely ignorant of the things of this world, and he accorded him his pardon with a clemency which will bring him praise in all the journals, and throughout all ages.

An able surgeon cured Candide in three weeks by means of emollients taught by Dioscorides.[6] He had already a little skin, and was able to march when the King of the Bulgarians gave battle to the King of the Abares.

There was never anything so gallant, so spruce, so brilliant, and so well disposed as the two armies. Trumpets, fifes, hautboys,[7] drums, and cannon made music such as Hell itself had never heard. The cannons first of all laid flat about six thousand men on each side; the muskets swept away from this best of worlds nine or ten thousand ruffians who infested its surface. The bayonet was also a *sufficient reason* for the death of several thousands. The whole might amount to thirty thousand souls. Candide, who trembled like a philosopher, hid himself as well as he could during this heroic butchery.

At length, while the two kings were causing *Te Deum*[8] to be sung each in his own camp, Candide resolved to go and reason elsewhere on effects and causes. He passed over heaps of dead and dying, and first reached a neighboring village; it was in cinders; it was an Abare village which the Bulgarians had burnt according to the laws of war. Here, old men covered with wounds beheld their wives, hugging their children to their bloody breasts, massacred before their faces; there, their daughters, disemboweled and breathing their last after having satisfied the natural wants of Bulgarian heroes, while others, half burnt in the flames, begged to be dispatched. The earth was strewn with brains, arms, and legs.

Candide fled quickly to another village; it belonged to the Bulgarians; and the Abarian heroes had treated it in the same way. Candide, walking always over palpitating limbs or across ruins, arrived at last beyond the seat of war, with a few provisions in his knapsack, and Miss Cunegonde always in his heart. His provisions failed him when he arrived in Holland; but having heard that everyone was rich in that country, and that they were Christians, he did not doubt but he should meet with the same treatment from them as he had met with in the Baron's castle, before Miss Cunegonde's bright eyes were the cause of his expulsion thence.

He asked alms of several grave-looking people, who all answered him that if he continued to follow this trade they would confine him to the house of correction, where he should be taught to get a living.

The next he addressed was a man who had been haranguing a large assembly for a whole hour on the subject of charity. But the orator, looking askew, said:

"What are you doing here? Are you for the good cause?"

"There can be no effect without a cause," modestly answered Candide; "the whole is necessarily concatenated and arranged for the best. It was necessary for me to have been banished from the presence of Miss Cunegonde, to have afterwards run the gauntlet, and now it is necessary I should beg my bread until I learn to earn it; all this cannot be otherwise."

"My friend," said the orator to him, "do you believe the Pope to be Anti-Christ?"

"I have not heard it," answered Candide; "but whether he be, or whether he be not, I want bread."

"Thou dost not deserve to eat," said the other. "Begone, rogue; begone, wretch; do not come near me again."

The orator's wife, putting her head out of the window, and spying a man that doubted whether the Pope was Anti-Christ, poured over him a full bucket of slops. Oh, heavens! to what excess does religious zeal carry the ladies.

A man who had never been christened, a good Anabaptist, named James, beholding the cruel and ignominious treatment shown to one of his brethren, an unfeathered biped with a rational soul, he took him

---

5. Rammer—rod with which to load a muzzle-loading rifle.

6. Dioscorides—ancient Greek medical writer.

7. Hautboys—old form of the modern oboe, a musical instrument.

8. Te Deum—hymn to celebrate victory.

home, cleaned him, gave him bread and beer, presented him with two florins, and even wished to teach him the manufacture of Persian stuffs, which they make in Holland. Candide, almost prostrating himself before him, cried:

"Master Pangloss has well said that all is for the best in this world, for I am infinitely more touched by your extreme generosity than with the inhumanity of that gentleman in the black coat and his lady."

The next day, as he took a walk, he met a beggar all covered with scabs, his eyes diseased, the end of his nose eaten away, his mouth distorted, his teeth black, choking in his throat, tormented with a violent cough, and spitting out a tooth at each effort.

Candide, yet more moved with compassion than with horror, gave to this shocking beggar the two florins which he had received from the honest Anabaptist James. The specter looked at him very earnestly, dropped a few tears, and fell upon his neck. Candide recoiled in disgust.

"Alas!" said one wretch to the other, "do you no longer know your dear Pangloss?"

"What do I hear? You, my dear master! You in this terrible plight! What misfortune has happened to you? Why are you no longer in the most magnificent of castles? What has become of Miss Cunegonde, the pearl of girls, and nature's masterpiece?"

"I am so weak that I cannot stand," said Pangloss.

Upon which Candide carried him to the Anabaptist's stable, and gave him a crust of bread. As soon as Pangloss had refreshed himself a little:

"Well," said Candide, "Cunegonde?"

"She is dead," replied the other.

Candide fainted at this word; his friend recalled his senses with a little bad vinegar which he found by chance in the stable. Candide reopened his eyes.

"Cunegonde is dead! Ah, best of worlds, where art thou? But of what illness did she die? Was it not for grief, upon seeing her father kick me out of his magnificent castle?"

"No," said Pangloss, "she was stabbed by the Bulgarian soldiers, they broke the Baron's head for attempting to defend her; my lady, her mother, was cut in pieces; my poor pupil was served just in the same manner as his sister; and as for the castle, they have not left one stone upon another, not a bar, nor a sheep, nor a duck, nor a tree; but we have had our revenge, for the Abares have done the very same thing to a neighboring barony, which belonged to a Bulgarian lord. . . ."

"Well, this is wonderful!" said Candide, "but you must be cured."

"Alas! how can I?" said Pangloss. "I have not a farthing, my friend, and all over the globe there is no letting of blood or taking a glister[9] without paying, or somebody paying for you."

These last words determined Candide; he went and flung himself at the feet of the charitable Anabaptist James, and gave him so touching a picture of the state to which his friend was reduced that the good man did not scruple to take Dr. Pangloss into his house, and had him cured at his expense. In the cure Pangloss lost only an eye and an ear. He wrote well, and knew arithmetic perfectly. The Anabaptist James made him his bookkeeper. At the end of two months, being obliged to go by sea to Lisbon about some mercantile affairs, he took the two philosophers with him in his ship. Pangloss explained to him how everything was so constituted that it could not be better. James was not of this opinion.

"It is more likely," said he, "mankind have a little corrupted nature, for men were not born wolves, and they have become wolves; God has given them neither cannon or four-and-twenty pounders nor bayonets; and yet they have made cannon and bayonets to destroy one another. Into this account I might throw not only bankrupts, but Justice which seizes on the effects of bankrupts to cheat the creditors."

"All this was indispensable," replied the one-eyed doctor, "for private misfortunes make the general good, so that the more private misfortunes there are the greater is the general good."

While he reasoned, the sky darkened, the winds blew from the four quarters, and the ship was assailed by a most terrible tempest within sight of the port of Lisbon.

Half dead of that inconceivable anguish which the rolling of a ship produces, one half of the passengers were not even sensible of the danger. The other half shrieked and prayed. The sheets were rent, the masts broken, the vessel gaped. Work who would, no one heard, no one commanded. The Anabaptist, being upon deck, bore a hand; then a brutish sailor struck him roughly and laid him sprawling; but with the violence of the blow he himself tumbled head foremost overboard, and struck upon a piece of the broken mast. Honest James ran to his assistance, hauled him up, and from the effort he made was precipitated into the sea in sight of the sailor, who left him to perish, without deigning to look at him. Candide drew near and saw his benefactor, who rose above the water one moment and was then swallowed up forever. He was just going to jump after him, but was prevented by the philosopher Pangloss, who demonstrated to him that the Bay of Lisbon had been made on purpose for the Anabaptist to be drowned. While he was proving this *a priori,* the ship foundered; all perished except Pangloss, Candide, and the brutal sailor who had drowned the good Anabaptist. The villain swam safely to the shore, while Pangloss and Candide were borne thither upon a plank.

As soon as they recovered themselves a little, they walked toward Lisbon. They had some money left, with which they hoped to save themselves from starving, after they had escaped drowning. Scarcely had they reached the city, lamenting the death of their benefactor, when they felt the earth tremble under their feet. The sea swelled and foamed in the harbor and beat to pieces the vessels riding at anchor. Whirlwinds of fire and ashes covered the streets and public places, houses fell, roofs were flung upon the pavements, and the pavements were scattered. Thirty thousand inhabitants of all ages and sexes were crushed under the ruins. The sailor, whistling and swearing, said booty was to be gained here.

"What can be the *sufficient reason* of this phenomenon?" said Pangloss.

"This is the Last Day!" cried Candide.

The sailor ran among the ruins, facing death to find money; finding it, he took it, and got drunk. . . .

Some falling stones had wounded Candide. He lay stretched in the street covered with rubbish.

"Alas!" said he to Pangloss, "get me a little wine and oil; I am dying."

---

9. Glister—a medical treatment.

"This concussion of the earth is no new thing," answered Pangloss. "The city of Lima, in America, experienced the same convulsions last year; the same cause, the same effects; there is certainly a train of sulphur underground from Lima to Lisbon."

"Nothing more probable," said Candide; "but for the love of God get me a little oil and wine."

"How, probable?" replied the philosopher. "I maintain that the point is capable of being demonstrated."

Candide fainted away, and Pangloss fetched him some water from a neighboring fountain. The following day they rummaged among the ruins and found provisions, with which they repaired their exhausted strength. After this they joined with others in relieving those inhabitants who had escaped death. Some, whom they had succored, gave them as good a dinner as they could in such disastrous circumstances; true, the repast was mournful, and the company moistened their bread with tears; but Pangloss consoled them, assuring them that things could not be otherwise.

"For," said he, "all that is is for the best. If there is a volcano at Lisbon it cannot be elsewhere. It is impossible that things should be other than they are; for everything is right."

[In the passage which follows, Candide is whipped and Pangloss is hanged. Candide then meets Cunegonde, who had not been killed in Westphalia. Candide kills two men and flees with Cunegonde and her maid, an old woman, to Cadiz.]

Candide, Cunegonde, and the old woman, having passed through Lucena, Chillas, and Lebrixa, arrived at length at Cadiz. A fleet was there getting ready, and troops assembling to bring to reason the reverend Jesuit Fathers of Paraguay, accused of having made one of the native tribes in the neighborhood of San Sacrament revolt against the kings of Spain and Portugal. Candide, having been in the Bulgarian service, performed the military exercise before the general of this little army with so graceful an address, with so intrepid an air, and with such agility and expedition, that he was given the command of a company of foot. Now, he was a captain! He set sail with Miss Cunegonde, the old woman, two valets, and two Andalusian horses, which had belonged to the Grand Inquisitor of Portugal.

During their voyage they reasoned a good deal on the philosophy of poor Pangloss.

"We are going into another world," said Candide; "and surely it must be there that all is for the best. For I must confess there is reason to complain a little of what passeth in our world in regard to both natural and moral philosophy."

"I love you with all my heart," said Cunegonde; "but my soul is still full of fright at that which I have seen and experienced."

"All will be well," replied Candide; "the sea of this new world is already better than our European sea; it is calmer, the winds more regular. It is certainly the New World which is the best of all possible worlds."

[After landing in Buenos Aires, Candide and his valet, Cacambo, are separated from Cunegonde. Then, Candide, in self-defense, killed an inquisitor, and the two men were forced to flee over much of South America.]

"You see," said Cacambo to Candide, as soon as they had reached the frontiers of the Oreillons, "that this hemisphere is not better than the other, take my word for it; let us go back to Europe by the shortest way."

"How go back?" said Candide, "and where shall we go? to my own country? The Bulgarians and the Abares are slaying all; to Portugal? there I shall be burnt; and if we abide here, we are every moment in danger of being spitted. But how can I resolve to quit a part of the world where my dear Cunegonde resides?"

"Let us turn towards Cayenne," said Cacambo; "there we shall find Frenchmen, who wander all over the world; they may assist us; God will perhaps have pity on us."

It was not easy to get to Cayenne; they knew vaguely in which direction to go, but rivers, precipices, robbers, savages obstructed them all the way. Their horses died of fatigue. Their provisions were consumed; they fed a whole month upon wild fruits, and found themselves at last near a little river bordered with cocoa trees, which sustained their lives and their hopes.

Cacambo, who was a good counselor, said to Candide:

"We are able to hold out no longer; we have walked enough. I see an empty canoe near the riverside; let us fill it with cocoanuts, throw ourselves into it, and go with the current; a river always leads to some inhabited spot. If we do not find pleasant things, we shall at least find new things."

"With all my heart," said Candide; "let us recommend ourselves to Providence."

They rowed a few leagues, between banks, in some places flowery, in others barren; in some parts smooth, in others rugged. The stream widened, and at length lost itself under an arch of frightful rocks which reached to the sky. The two travelers had the courage to commit themselves to the current. The river, suddenly contracting at this place, whirled them along with a dreadful noise and rapidity. At the end of four-and-twenty hours they saw daylight again, but their canoe was dashed to pieces against the rocks. For a league they had to creep from rock to rock, until at length they discovered an extensive plain, bounded by inaccessible mountains. The country was cultivated as much for pleasure as for necessity. On all sides the useful was also the beautiful. The roads were covered, or rather adorned, with carriages of a glittering form and substance, in which were men and women of surprising beauty, drawn by large red sheep which surpassed in fleetness the finest coursers of Andalusia, Tetuan, and Mequinez.

"Here, however, is a country," said Candide, "which is better than Westphalia."

He stepped out with Cacambo toward the first village which he saw. Some children dressed in tattered brocades played at quoits on the outskirts. Our travelers from the other world amused themselves by looking on. The quoits were large round pieces, yellow, red, and green, which cast a singular luster! The travelers picked a few of them off the ground; this was of gold, that of emeralds, the other of rubies—the least of them would have been the greatest ornament on the Mogul's throne.

"Without doubt," said Cacambo, "these children must be the king's sons that are playing at quoits!"

The village schoolmaster appeared at this moment and called them to school.

"There," said Candide, "is the preceptor of the royal family."

The little truants immediately quitted their game, leaving the quoits on the ground with all their other playthings. Candide gathered them up, ran to the master, and presented them to him in a most humble manner, giving him to understand by signs that their royal highnesses had forgotten their gold and jewels. The schoolmaster, smiling, flung them upon the ground; then, looking at Candide with a good deal of surprise, went about his business.

The travelers, however, took care to gather up the gold, the rubies, and the emeralds.

"Where are we?" cried Candide. "The king's children in this country must be well brought up, since they are taught to despise gold and precious stones."

Cacambo was as much surprised as Candide. At length they drew near the first house in the village. It was built like an European palace. A crowd of people pressed about the door, and there were still more in the house. They heard most agreeable music, and were aware of a delicious odor of cooking. Cacambo went up to the door and heard they were talking Peruvian; it was his mother's tongue, for it is well known that Cacambo was born in Tucuman, in a village where no other language was spoken.

"I will be your interpreter here," said he to Candide; "let us go in; it is a public house."

Immediately two waiters and two girls, dressed in cloth of gold, and their hair tied up with ribbons, invited them to sit down to table with the landlord. They served four dishes of soup, each garnished with two young parrots; a boiled condor which weighed two hundred pounds; two roasted monkeys, of excellent flavor; three hundred hummingbirds in one dish, and six hundred fly-birds in another; exquisite ragouts,[10] delicious pastries; the whole served up in dishes of a kind of rock crystal. The waiters and girls poured out several liqueurs drawn from the sugar cane.

Most of the company were chapmen[11] and wagoners, all extremely polite; they asked Cacambo a few questions with the greatest circumspection, and answered his in the most obliging manner.

As soon as dinner was over, Cacambo believed as well as Candide that they might well pay their reckoning by laying down two of those large gold pieces which they had picked up. The landlord and landlady shouted with laughter and held their sides. When the fit was over:

"Gentlemen," said the landlord, "it is plain you are strangers, and such guests we are not accustomed to see; pardon us therefore for laughing when you offered us the pebbles from our highroads in payment of your reckoning. You doubtless have not the money of the country; but it is not necessary to have any money at all to dine in this house. All hostelries established for the convenience of commerce are paid by the government. You have fared but very indifferently because this is a poor village; but everywhere else, you will be received as you deserve."

Cacambo explained this whole discourse with great astonishment to Candide, who was as greatly astonished to hear it.

"What sort of a country then is this," said they to one another; "a country unknown to all the rest of the world, and where nature is of a kind so different from ours? It is probably the country where all is well; for there absolutely must be one such place. And, whatever Master Pangloss might say, I often found that things went very ill in Westphalia."

Cacambo expressed his curiosity to the landlord, who made answer:

"I am very ignorant, but not the worse on that account. However, we have in this neighborhood an old man retired from Court who is the most learned and most communicative person in the kingdom."

At once he took Cacambo to the old man. Candide acted now only a second character, and accompanied his valet. They entered a very plain house, for the door was only of silver, and the ceilings were only of gold, but wrought in so elegant a taste as to vie with the richest. The antechamber, indeed, was only encrusted with rubies and emeralds, but the order in which everything was arranged made amends for this great simplicity.

The old man received the strangers on his sofa, which was stuffed with hummingbirds' feathers, and ordered his servants to present them with liqueurs in diamond goblets; after which he satisfied their curiosity in the following terms:

"I am now one hundred and seventy-two years old, and I learned of my late father, Master of the Horse to the King, the amazing revolutions of Peru, of which he had been an eyewitness. The kingdom we now inhabit is the ancient country of the Incas, who quitted it very imprudently to conquer another part of the world, and were at length destroyed by the Spaniards.

"More wise by far were the princes of their family, who remained in their native country; and they ordained, with the consent of the whole nation, that none of the inhabitants should ever be permitted to quit this little kingdom; and this has preserved our innocence and happiness. The Spaniards have had a confused notion of this country, and have called it *El Dorado;* and an Englishman, whose name was Sir Walter Raleigh, came very near it about a hundred years ago; but being surrounded by inaccessible rocks and precipices, we have hitherto been sheltered from the rapaciousness of European nations, who have an inconceivable passion for the pebbles and dirt of our land, for the sake of which they would murder us to the last man."

The conversation was long: it turned chiefly on their form of government, their manners, their women, their public entertainments, and the arts. At length Candide, having always had a taste for metaphysics, made Cacambo ask whether there was any religion in that country.

The old man reddened a little.

"How then," said he, "can you doubt it? Do you take us for ungrateful wretches?"

Cacambo humbly asked, "What is the religion in El Dorado?"

The old man reddened again, but continued.

"Can there be two religions?" said he. "We have, I believe, the religion of all the world: we worship God night and morning."

"Do you worship but one God?" said Cacambo, who still acted as interpreter in representing Candide's doubts.

"Surely," said the old man, "there are not two, nor three, nor four. I must confess the people from your side of the world ask very extraordinary questions."

Candide was not yet tired of interrogating the good old man; he wanted to know in what manner they prayed to God in El Dorado.

"We do not pray to Him," said the worthy sage; "we have nothing to ask of Him; He has given us all we need, and we return Him thanks without ceasing."

Candide, having a curiosity to see the priests, asked where they were. The good old man smiled.

---

10. Ragouts—highly seasoned stew.
11. Chapmen—peddlers; traders.

"My friend," said he, "we are all priests. The King and all the heads of families sing solemn canticles of thanksgiving every morning, accompanied by five or six thousand musicians. . ."

During this whole discourse Candide was in raptures, and he said to himself:

"This is vastly different from Westphalia and the Baron's castle. Had our friend Pangloss seen El Dorado he would no longer have said that the castle of Thunder-ten-Tronckh was the finest upon earth. It is evident that one must travel."

After this long conversation the old man ordered a coach and six sheep to be got ready, and twelve of his domestics to conduct the travelers to Court.

"Excuse me," said he, "if my age deprives me of the honor of accompanying you. The King will receive you in a manner that cannot displease you; and no doubt you will make there a better entertainment."

Never was more wit shown at a table than that which fell from His Majesty. Cacambo explained the King's bon mots to Candide, and notwithstanding they were translated they still appeared to be bon mots. Of all the things that surprised Candide this was not the least.

They spent a month in this hospitable place. Candide frequently said to Cacambo:

"I own, my friend, once more that the castle where I was born is nothing in comparison with this; but, after all, Miss Cunegonde is not here, and you have, without doubt, some mistress in Europe. If we abide here we shall only be upon a footing with the rest, whereas, if we return to our old world, only with twelve sheep laden with the pebbles of El Dorado, we shall be richer than all the kings in Europe. We shall have no more Inquisitors to fear, and we may easily recover Miss Cunegonde."

This speech was agreeable to Cacambo; mankind are so fond of roving, of making a figure in their own country, and of boasting of what they have seen in their travels that the two happy ones resolved to be no longer so, but to ask His Majesty's leave to quit the country.

"You are foolish," said the King. "I am sensible that my kingdom is but a small place, but when a person is comfortably settled in any part he should abide there. I have not the right to detain strangers. It is a tyranny which neither our manners nor our laws permit. All men are free. Go when you wish, but the going will be very difficult. It is impossible to ascend that rapid river on which you came as by a miracle, and which runs under vaulted rocks. The mountains which surround my kingdom are ten thousand feet high, and as steep as walls; they are each over ten leagues in breadth, and there is no other way to descend them than by precipices. However, since you absolutely wish to depart, I shall give orders to my engineers to construct a machine that will convey you very safely. When we have conducted you over the mountains no one can accompany you further, for my subjects have made a vow never to quit the kingdom, and they are too wise to break it. Ask me besides anything that you please."

"We desire nothing of Your Majesty," said Candide, "but a few sheep laden with provisions, pebbles, and the earth of this country."

The King laughed.

"I cannot conceive," said he, "what pleasure you Europeans find in our yellow clay, but take as much as you like, and great good may it do you!"

At once he gave directions that his engineers should construct a machine to hoist up these two extraordinary men out of the kingdom. Three thousand good mathematicians went to work; it was ready in fifteen days, and did not cost more than twenty million sterling in the specie of that country. They placed Candide and Cacambo on the machine. There were two great red sheep saddled and bridled to ride upon as soon as they were beyond the mountains, twenty pack-sheep laden with provisions, thirty with presents of the curiosities of the country, and fifty with gold, diamonds, and precious stones. The King embraced the two wanderers very tenderly.

Their departure, with the ingenious manner in which they and their sheep were hoisted over the mountains, was a splendid spectacle. The mathematicians took their leave after conveying them to a place of safety, and Candide had no other desire, no other aim, than to present his sheep to Miss Cunegonde.

"Now," said he, "we are able to pay the Governor of Buenos Aires if Miss Cunegonde can be ransomed. Let us journey towards Cayenne. Let us embark, and we will afterwards see what kingdom we shall be able to purchase."

Our travelers spent the first day very agreeably. They were delighted with possessing more treasure than all Asia, Europe, and Africa could scrape together. Candide, in his raptures, cut Cunegonde's name on the trees. The second day two of their sheep plunged into a morass, where they and their burdens were lost; two more died of fatigue a few days after; seven or eight perished with hunger in a desert; and others subsequently fell down precipices. At length, after traveling a hundred days, only two sheep remained. Said Candide to Cacambo:

"My friend, you see how perishable are the riches of this world; there is nothing solid but virtue, and the happiness of seeing Cunegonde once more."

"I grant all you say," said Cacambo, "but we have still two sheep remaining, with more treasure than the King of Spain will ever have; and I see a town which I take to be Surinam, belonging to the Dutch. We are at the end of all our troubles, and at the beginning of happiness."

As they drew near the town, they saw a Negro stretched upon the ground, with only one moiety of his clothes, that is, of his blue linen drawers; the poor man had lost his left leg and his right hand.

"Good God!" said Candide in Dutch, "what art thou doing there, friend, in that shocking condition?"

"I am waiting for my master, Mynheer Vanderdendur, the famous merchant," answered the Negro.

"Was it Mynheer Vanderdendur," said Candide, "that treated thee thus?"

"Yes, sir," said the Negro, "it is the custom. They give us a pair of linen drawers for our whole garment twice a year. When we work at the sugar canes, and the mill snatches hold of a finger, they cut off the hand; and when we attempt to run away, they cut off the leg; both cases have happened to me. This is the price at which you eat sugar in Europe. Yet when my mother sold me for ten patagons on the coast of Guinea, she said to me: 'My child, bless our fetishes adore them forever; they will make thee live happily, thou hast the honor of being the slave of our lord the whites, which is making the fortune of thy father and mother.' Alas! I know not whether I have made their fortunes; this I know, that they have not made mine. Dogs, monkeys, and parrots are a thousand times less wretched than I. The Dutch fetishes, who have converted me, declare every Sunday that we are all of us children of Adam—blacks as well as whites. I am not a genealogist, but if these preachers tell truth, we are all second cousins. Now, you must agree with me it is impossible to treat one's relations in a more barbarous manner."

"Oh, Pangloss!" cried Candide, "thou hadst not guessed at this abomination; it is the end. I must at last renounce thy optimism."

"What is this optimism?" said Cacambo.

"Alas!" said Candide, "it is the madness of maintaining that everything is right when it is wrong."

Looking at the Negro, he shed tears, and weeping, he entered Surinam.

The first thing they inquired after was whether there was a vessel in the harbour which could be sent to Buenos Aires. The person to whom they applied was a Spanish sea-captain, who offered to take them there upon reasonable terms. He appointed to meet them at a public house, whither Candide and the faithful Cacambo went with their two sheep, and awaited his coming.

Candide, who had his heart upon his lips, told the Spaniard all his adventures, and avowed that he intended to elope with Miss Cunegonde.

"Then I will take good care not to carry you to Buenos Aires," said the seaman. "I should be hanged, and so would you. The fair Cunegonde is my lord's favorite mistress!"

This was a thunderclap for Candide: he wept for a long while. At last he drew Cacambo aside.

"Here, my dear friend," said he to him, "this thou must do. We have, each of us in his pocket, five or six millions in diamonds; you are more clever than I; you must go and bring Miss Cunegonde from Buenos Aires. If the Governor makes any difficulty, give him a million; if he will not relinquish her, give him two; as you have not killed an Inquisitor, they will have no suspicion of you; I'll get another ship, and go and wait for you at Venice; that's a free country, where there is no danger either from Bulgarians, Abares, . . . or Inquisitors."

Cacambo applauded this wise resolution. He despaired at parting from so good a master, who had become his intimate friend; but the pleasure of serving him prevailed over the pain of leaving him. They embraced with tears; Candide charged him not to forget the good old woman who had aided them to escape to South America. Cacambo set out that very same day. This Cacambo was a very honest fellow.

Candide stayed some time longer in Surinam, waiting for another captain to carry him and the two remaining sheep to Italy. After he had hired domestics, and purchased everything necessary for a long voyage, Mynheer Vanderdendur, captain of a large vessel, came and offered his services.

"How much will you charge," said he to this man, "to carry me straight to Venice—me, my servants, my baggage, and these two sheep?"

The skipper asked ten thousand piastres. Candide did not hesitate.

"Oh! oh!" said the prudent Vanderdendur to himself, "this stranger gives ten thousand piastres unhesitatingly! He must be very rich."

Returning a little while after, he let him know that, upon second consideration, he could not undertake the voyage for less than twenty thousand piastres.

"Well, you shall have them," said Candide.

"Ay!" said the skipper to himself, "this man agrees to pay twenty thousand piastres with as much ease as ten."

He went back to him again, and declared that he could not carry him to Venice for less than thirty thousand piastres.

"Then you shall have thirty thousand," replied Candide.

"Oh! oh!" said the Dutch skipper once more to himself, "thirty thousand piastres are a trifle to this man; surely these sheep must be laden with an immense treasure; let us say no more about it. First of all, let him pay down the thirty thousand piastres; then we shall see."

Candide sold two small diamonds, the least of which was worth more than what the skipper asked for his freight. He paid him the money in advance.

The two sheep were put on board. Candide followed in a little boat to join the vessel in the roads. The skipper seized his opportunity, set sail, and put out to sea, the wind favoring him. Candide, dismayed and stupefied, soon lost sight of the vessel.

"Alas!" said he, "this is a trick worthy of the old world!"

[Many adventures follow this one in this best of all possible worlds. Finally Candide, Cunegonde, Pangloss (who did not die of hanging), and all the other characters of the story are reunited in Turkey, where they bought a little farm.]

In the neighborhood there lived a very famous Dervish who was esteemed the best philosopher in all Turkey, and so they went to consult him. Pangloss was the speaker.

"Master," said he, "we come to beg you to tell why so strange an animal as man was made."

"With what meddlest thou?" said the Dervish. "Is it thy business?"

"But, reverend father," said Candide, "there is horrible evil in this world."

"What signifies it," said the Dervish, "whether there be evil or good? When His Highness sends a ship to Egypt, does he trouble his head whether the mice on board are at their ease or not?"

"What, then, must we do?" said Pangloss.

"Hold your tongue," answered the Dervish.

"I was in hopes," said Pangloss, "that I should reason with you a little about causes and effects, about the best of possible worlds, the origin of evil, the nature of the soul, and the pre-established harmony."

At these words, the Dervish shut the door in their faces.

During this conversation, the news was spread that two Viziers and the Mufti had been strangled at Constantinople, and that several of their friends had been impaled. This catastrophe made a great noise for some hours. Pangloss, Candide, and Martin, returning to the little farm, saw a good old man taking the fresh air at his door under an orange bower. Pangloss, who was as inquisitive as he was argumentative, asked the old man what was the name of the strangled Mufti.

"I do not know," answered the worthy man, "and I have not known the name of any Mufti, nor of any Vizier. I am entirely ignorant of the event you mention; I presume in general that they who meddle with the administration of public affairs die sometimes miserably, and that they deserve it; but I never trouble my head about what is transacting at Constantinople; I content myself with sending there for sale the fruits of the garden which I cultivate."

Having said these words, he invited the strangers into his house; his two sons and two daughters presented them with several sorts of sherbet, which they made themselves, with Kaimak enriched with the candied peel of citrons, with oranges, lemons, pineapples, pistachio nuts, and Mocha coffee unadulterated with the bad coffee of Batavia or the American islands; after which the two daughters of the honest Mussulman perfumed the strangers' beards.

"You must have a vast and magnificent estate," said Candide to the Turk.

"I have only twenty acres," replied the old man, "I and my children cultivate them; our labor preserves us from three great evils—weariness, vice, and want."

Candide, on his way home, made profound reflections on the old man's conversation.

"This honest Turk," said he to Pangloss and Martin, "seems to be in a situation far preferable to that of the six kings with whom we had the honor of supping."

"Grandeur," said Pangloss, "is extremely dangerous, according to the testimony of philosophers . . ."

"I know also," said Candide, "that we must cultivate our garden."

"You are right," said Pangloss, "for when man was first placed in the Garden of Eden, he was put there *ut operaretur eum,* that he might cultivate it; which shows that man was not born to be idle."

"Let us work," said Martin, "without disputing; it is the only way to render life tolerable."

The whole little society entered into this laudable design, according to their different abilities. Their little plot of land produced plentiful crops. . . . They were all of some service or other. . . .

Pangloss sometimes said to Candide:

"There is a concatenation of events in this best of all possible worlds; for if you had not been kicked out of a magnificent castle for love of Miss Cunegonde; if you had not suffered misfortune in Portugal; if you had not walked over America; if you had not stabbed the Baron; if you had not lost all your sheep from the fine country of El Dorado, you would not be here eating preserved citrons and pistachio nuts."

"All that is very well," answered Candide, "but let us cultivate our garden."

Exercises

1. "El Dorado" sounds suspiciously like "Utopia," at first acquaintance; what different aspects are emphasized from those in More's account?
2. The only "answer" that Voltaire comes up with is "Let us cultivate our garden." What would Perikles have had to say about such an answer? How good an answer is it? What are some of its defects—and virtues?
3. How important a figure is Cunegonde? Why have we not encountered such a figure earlier? In what way is she part of the "New Look" of the eighteenth century?

Thomas Jefferson (1743–1826)

The American Revolution (1775–1783) was hailed throughout the world as the first significant triumph of rationalism. The causes of the uprising were certainly as much economic as ideological yet liberal, rational beliefs were expressed in this war against absolutism and the imposition of authority upon people who had little voice in their own government. One of the clearest voices of the new nation was that of Thomas Jefferson, author of the Declaration of Independence, third president of the United States, and the founder of the University of Virginia, the last being, for Jefferson, his most significant achievement. Jefferson's address upon first assuming the presidency is a masterful speech that effectively summarizes the ideals of the Enlightenment.

Literary Selection

FIRST INAUGURAL ADDRESS
Thomas Jefferson

During the contest of opinion through which we have passed, the animation of discussions and of exertions has sometimes worn an aspect which might impose on strangers unused to think freely and to speak and to write what they think; but this being now decided by the voice of the nation, announced according to the rules of the constitution, all will, of course, arrange themselves under the will of the law, and unite in common efforts for the common good. All, too, will bear in mind this sacred principle, that though the will of the majority is in all cases to prevail, that will, to be rightful, must be reasonable; that the minority possess their equal rights, which equal laws must protect, and to violate which would be oppression. Let us, then, fellow citizens, unite with one heart and one mind. Let us restore to social intercourse that harmony and affection without which liberty and even life itself are but dreary things. And let us reflect that having banished from our land that religious intolerance under which mankind so long bled and suffered, we have yet gained little if we countenance a political intolerance as despotic, as wicked, and capable of as bitter and bloody persecutions. During the throes and convulsions of the ancient world, during the agonizing spasms of infuriated men, seeking through blood and slaughter his long-lost liberty, it was not wonderful that the agitation of the billows should reach even this distant and peaceful shore; that this should be more felt and feared by some and less by others; that this should divide opinions as to measures of safety. But every difference of opinion is not a difference of principle. We have called by different names brethren of the same principle. We are all republicans—we are all federalists. If there be any among us who would wish to dissolve this Union or to change its republican form, let them stand undisturbed as monuments of the safety with which error of opinion may be tolerated where reason is left free to combat it. I know, indeed, that some honest men fear that a republican government cannot be strong; that this government is not strong enough. But would the honest patriot, in the full tide of successful experiment, abandon a government which has so far kept us free and firm, on the theoretic and visionary fear that this government, the world's best hope, may by possibility want energy to preserve itself? I trust not. I believe this, on the contrary, the strongest government on earth. I believe it is the only one where every man, at the call of the law, would fly to the standard of the law, and would meet invasions of the public order as his own personal concern. Sometimes it is said that man cannot be trusted with the government of himself. Can he, then, be trusted with the government of others? Or have we found angels in the form of kings to govern him? Let history answer this question.

Let us, then, with courage and confidence pursue our own federal and republican principles, our attachment to our union and representative government. Kindly separated by nature and a wide ocean from the exterminating havoc of one quarter of the globe; too high-minded to endure the degradations of the others; possessing a chosen country, with room enough for our descendants to the hundredth and thousandth generation; entertaining a due sense of our equal right to the use of our own faculties, to the acquisitions of our own industry, to honor and confidence from our fellow citizens, resulting not from birth but from our actions and their sense of them; enlightened by a benign religion, professed, indeed, and practiced in various forms, yet all of them inculcating honesty, truth, temperance, gratitude, and the love of man; acknowledging and adoring an overruling Providence, which by all its dispensations proves that it delights in the happiness of man here and his greater happiness hereafter; with all these blessings, what more is necessary to make us a happy and a prosperous people? Still one thing more, fellow citizens—a wise and frugal government, which shall restrain men from injuring one another, shall leave them otherwise free to regulate their own pursuits of industry and improvement, and shall not take from the mouth of labor the bread it has earned. This is the sum of good government, and this is necessary to close the circle of our felicities.

About to enter, fellow citizens, on the exercise of duties which comprehend everything dear and valuable to you, it is proper that you should understand what I deem the essential principles of our government, and consequently those which ought to shape its administration. I will compress them within the narrowest compass they will bear, stating the general principle, but not all its limitations. Equal and exact justice to all men, of whatever state or persuasion, religious or political; peace, commerce, and honest friendship, with all nations—entangling alliances with none; the support of the state governments in all their rights, as the most competent administrations for our domestic concerns and the surest bulwarks against anti-republican tendencies; the preservation of the general government in its whole constitutional vigor, as the sheet anchor of our peace at home and safety abroad; a jealous care of the right of election by the people—a mild and safe corrective of abuses which are lopped by the sword of revolution where peaceable remedies are unprovided; absolute acquiescence in the decisions of the majority—the vital principle of republics, from which is no appeal but to force, the vital principles and immediate parent of despotism; a well-disciplined militia—our best reliance in peace and for the first moments of war, till regulars may relieve them; the supremacy of the civil over the military authority; economy in the public expense, that labor may be lightly burdened; the honest payment of our debts and sacred preservation of the public faith; encouragement of agriculture, and of commerce as its handmaid: the

diffusion of information and arraignment of all abuses at the bar of public reason; freedom of religion; freedom of the press; and freedom of person under the protection of the *habeas corpus;* and trial by juries impartially selected—these principles form the bright constellation which has gone before us, and guided our steps through an age of revolution and reformation. The wisdom of our sages and the blood of our heroes have been devoted to their attainment. They should be the creed of our political faith—the text of civil instruction—the touchstone by which to try the services of these we trust; and should we wander from them in moments of error or alarm, let us hasten to retrace our steps and to regain the road which alone leads to peace, liberty, and safety.

I repair, then, fellow citizens, to the post you have assigned me. With experience enough in subordinate offices to have seen the difficulties of this, the greatest of all, I have learned to expect that it will rarely fall to the lot of imperfect man to retire from this station with the reputation and the favor which bring him to it. Without pretentions to that high confidence you reposed in our first and great revolutionary character, whose preeminent services had entitled him to the first place in his country's love, and destined for him the fairest page in the volume of faithful history, I ask so much confidence only as may give firmness and effect to the legal administration of your affairs. I shall often go wrong through defect of judgment. When right, I shall often be thought wrong by those whose positions will not command a view of the whole ground. I ask your indulgence for my own errors, which will never be intentional; and your support against the errors of others, who may condemn what they would not if seen in all its parts. The approbation implied by your suffrage is a consolation to me for the past; and my future solicitude will be to retain the good opinion of those who have bestowed it in advance, to conciliate that of others by doing them all the good in my power and to be instrumental to the happiness and freedom of all.

Relying, then, on the patronage of your good will, I advance with obedience to the work, ready to retire from it whenever you become sensible how much better choice it is in your power to make. And may that Infinite Power which rules the destinies of the universe, lead our councils to what is best, and give them a favorable issue for your peace and prosperity.

Bibliography

Recommended are two books that provide excellent overviews of the period.

1. Blitzer, Charles. *Age of Kings.* Great Ages of Man. New York: Time Incorporated, 1967. Good bibliography.
2. *Twilight of Princes (1601–1789).* Milestones of History, vol. 4. New York: Newsweek, n.d.

Plus a few more-specialized books:

3. Bennett, Jonathan. *Locke, Berkeley, Hume: Central Themes.* New York: Oxford University Press, 1971.
4. Fulton, Robert. *Adam Smith Speaks to Our Time.* North Quincy, Mass.: Christopher Publishing House, 1963.
5. Ronan, Colin. *Newton and Gravitation.* New York: Grossman, 1968.

Time Chart for the Early Modern World, 1600–1789

	1600	1650	1700	1750	1800
Artists and Musicians					

Inigo Jones 1573–1652 —
Caravaggio 1573–1610
Rubens 1577–1640 —
Hals 1580/85–1666 —
Poussin 1594–1665 —
Bernini 1598–1680
Zurburan 1598–1640
Velasquez 1599–1660
Borromini 1599–1644
van Dyck 1599–1641 –
Rembrandt 1606–1669
Leyster 1609–1660
Ruisdael 1628–1682
Vermeer 1632–1675
Wren 1632–1723
Mansart 1646–1708
Corelli 1653–1713
Couperin 1668–1733
Watteau 1684–1721
Bach 1685–1750
Vivaldi 1685–1743
Chardin 1699–1779
Boucher 1703–1770
Gainsborough 1727–1788
Fragonard 1732–1806
Haydn 1732–1809
Houdon 1741–1828
Jefferson 1743–1826
David 1748–1825
Stuart 1755–1828
Mozart 1756–1791
Canova 1757–1822
Beethoven 1770–1827

	1600	1650	1700	1750	1800
Literary Figures					

Donne 1573–1631
Milton 1608–1674
Marvell 1621–1678
Swift 1667–1745
Pope 1688–1744
Montesquieu 1689–1755
Voltaire 1694–1778
Diderot 1713–1784
Gray 1716–1771
Rousseau 1718–1778

Philosophers and Scientists

- Bacon 1561–1626
- Galileo 1564–1642
- Hobbes 1588–1679
- Descartes 1596–1650
- Locke 1632–1704
- Spinoza 1632–1677
- Newton 1641–1727
- Halley 1656–1742
- Hume 1711–1776
- Kant 1724–1804

Rulers

England
- James I 1603–1625
- Charles I 1625–1649
- Cromwell 1649–1659
- Charles II 1660–1685
- James II 1685–1688
- William & Mary 1688–1702
- Anne 1702–1714
- George I 1714–1727
- George II 1727–1760
- George III 1760–1820

France
- Louis XIV 1643–1715
- Louis XV 1715–1774
- Louis XVI 1774–1793

Prussia
- Frederick I 1701–1713
- Frederick William I 1713–1740
- Frederick the Great 1740–1786

Russia
- Peter the Great 1682–1725
- Catherine the Great 1762–1791

Events

- Founding of English East India Co. 1600
- Netherlands revolt from Spain 1609
- Thirty Years War 1618–1648
- Galileo condemned by Inquisition 1632
- Revocation of Edict of Nantes 1685
- *Principia* by Newton 1687
- England's Glorious Revolution 1688
- Diderot's *Encyclopedia* 1747–1772
- Watt's improved steam engine 1775
- American revolution 1775–1783
- *Wealth of Nations* 1776
- French revolution 1789–1815

22 *Art: Baroque, Rococo, and Neoclassic*

The Baroque Age, ca. 1580–1700

An age of expansion following the Renaissance era of discovery, the Baroque was a time of conflicts and contradictions that encompassed extremes: Louis XIV and Rembrandt; Bernini and Descartes; Milton and Bach. In architecture and the visual arts the Baroque began in the last quarter of the sixteenth century and extended into the eighteenth, culminating in the supreme expression of the Baroque: the music of Bach and Handel (see chap. 23).

The characteristics of Baroque art are movement, intensity, tension, and energy, traits that are perhaps more natural to music than to the more static arts of painting, sculpture, and architecture. Nevertheless, revolutionary innovations in all of the arts produced a Baroque style that can be extravagant, excessive, or even grotesque. Baroque art has a fascination all its own, particularly when it is not judged by such other standards as, for example, the classical canons of balance, restraint, and control of the High Renaissance style.

The sometimes contradictory variations of the Baroque style can be studied in terms of three broad categories of patrons: the Counter-Reformation Church of Rome; the aristocratic courts of Louis XIV of France and the Stuarts of England; and the bourgeois merchants of Holland. Though drive, intensity, and contrast are common characteristics of all Baroque art, the style will be considered here as reactions to the needs of these patrons and labeled Counter-Reformation, Aristocratic, and Bourgeois Baroque art.

Counter-Reformation Baroque

Founded in 1534 by Ignatius of Loyola, the Society of Jesus (Jesuits) formed the spearhead of the Counter-Reformation. The mother church of the order, Il Gesu (Church of Jesus) was the first building in the new style, becoming a model for church design throughout the Catholic world,

Figure 22.1 G. B. Vignola (plan) and G. C. della Porta (facade), Il Gesu, 1568–1584, Rome.

Figure 22.2 Interior, Il Gesu

especially in Latin America (fig. 22.1). The four pairs of pilasters on each level visually stabilize the facade and add a rhythmic punctuation that the evenly spaced columns of the classical style do not have (see fig. 18.5). Baroque architecture, from its very beginning, is characterized by the strong accents of paired columns or pilasters. The dramatic effect of paired pilaster and column framing a central portal under a double cornice exemplifies the theatricality of the Baroque style, making the entrance seem like an invitation to hurry into the church. The proportions of the two stories and the framing volutes are derived from Alberti's Santa Maria Novella (see fig. 18.14), while the classical pediment is reminiscent of Alberti and Palladio (see fig. 18.43). Il Gesu is not a wholly new design but rather a skillful synthesis of existing elements into a new and dramatic style.

In the interior (fig. 22.2), chapels recessed in the walls replace side aisles, making the richly decorated central space a theatre for the enactment of the Lord's Supper. Light pours through the dome windows and upon the high altar in this architectural embodiment of the militant and mystical Society of Jesus.

The twin towers of the Cathedral of Salzburg (fig. 22.3) characterize a style of Baroque architecture prevalent north of the Alps, in Latin America, and in the Western United States. When covered with stucco whitewashed a gleaming white, this style of Baroque became California Mission architecture. Anchored by paired pilasters on both sides, the facade is set back from the bold towers framing a two-level front that climaxes in an elaborately designed pediment embellished with sculptures. The large flat surface areas of this Early Baroque church will, in later buildings, be filled with niches and sculpture to create a more elaborate and restless facade (see fig. 22.9).

The Baroque style of painting appeared abruptly in the person of the northern Italian artist called Caravaggio (ca-ra-VOD-jo; 1573–1610), perhaps the first artist to deliberately shock not only the public but also his fellow artists. The most important Italian painter of the seventeenth century, Caravaggio was militantly opposed to classical concepts like clarity and restraint. Using chiaroscuro and nonrealistic dramatic lighting, his paintings had an intense psychological impact that profoundly influenced most Baroque artists, including Rembrandt and Velasquez. In his *Crucifixion of St. Peter* (fig. 22.4), Caravaggio placed his figures in the immediate foreground, starkly outlined against an indeterminate background. Sentenced by the Romans to die on the cross, Peter insisted that he, unlike his Master, must be crucified upside down and we, viewing the agonizing scene at eye level, are drawn inexorably into the violence of the tragedy. The details are realistic, from the dirty feet of one executioner to the nail-pierced feet of Peter. The composition is designed for maximum impact. In the complex interplay of the slashing diagonals the figure of Peter is completely depicted, while the three executioners are shown only partially. The lighting is theatrical, intensifying a dramatic effect made more vivid by Caravaggio's innovative use of chiaroscuro.

Caravaggio's life was as dramatic as his art. A man of violent passions, he killed another man in a fight and, badly wounded, fled Rome for Naples. Later thrown into prison, he violated his oath of obedience and escaped to Sicily, but later returned to Naples where he was nearly fatally wounded in another fight. Destitute and ill with malaria, he died during a violent rage over a misunderstanding on the very day that his papal pardon was announced. In sharp contrast to his turbulent life, his *Supper at Emmaus* (fig. 22.5) is a low-keyed, personal drama. As recounted in Luke 24: 28–31, Christ was invited to supper by two of his disciples who, at the moment that he raised his hand to bless the food, recognized their risen Lord. The disciple on the left raises his hands in astonishment, while the other clutches the corner of the table. Unaware of the import of the discovery, the two servants are puzzled but dutiful. Set against a dark background, the eye-level composition invites the viewer to participate, to sit at the table between the two disciples.

In his life and in his art Caravaggio was at odds with his time, but Gianlorenzo Bernini (bear-NEE-nee; 1598–1680) was the Counter-Reformation personified. A superbly gifted sculptor/architect with a virtuosity comparable to that of Michelangelo, Bernini was regarded in his own century as not only its best artist but also its greatest man. He himself saw that his renown would decline with the waning of Counter-Reformation energy, but his emotional art has now regained some of its luster. His *David* (fig. 22.6) is a young warrior tensely poised over his discarded armor and harp, every muscle strained to hurl the fatal stone at an unseen Goliath, who seems to be approaching from behind and above the level of the viewer. When compared with Michelangelo's *David* (see colorplate 5) we experience the intense energy of the Baroque, so much so that there is an impulse to leap out of the way of the stone missile. The bit lip is Bernini's own expression as copied from a mirror, and realism is further heightened by the grip of David's foot on the actual base of the statue.

Figure 22.3 Solari, Cathedral of Salzburg, 1614, Austria.

Figure 22.4 Caravaggio, *Crucifixion of St. Peter,* 1601. Oil on canvas, 90 × 69″. Santa Maria del Popolo, Rome.

Figure 22.5 Caravaggio, *Supper at Emmaus,* ca. 1600. Oil on canvas, 69 × 55½″. (Brera Museum, Milan.)

Figure 22.6 Gianlorenzo Bernini, *David,* 1623. Marble, life size. Borghese Gallery, Rome.

Rome was Bernini's city and he left his stamp on it literally everywhere, but nowhere so effectively as in his enhancement of St. Peter's (fig. 22.7). The oval piazza, together with the embracing arms of the colossal colonnade, form a spectacular entrance to the largest church in Christendom. The 284 massive Doric columns are 39′ high and are topped with 15′ statues of 96 saints, demarcating a piazza that can accommodate about 250,000 people. Bernini used the pavement design, the Egyptian obelisk, and the two fountains to unify the piazza and give it human scale.

Once in the awesome nave of the church, the visitor is surrounded by other manifestations of Bernini's genius: monumental sculptures, the Throne of St. Peter, elegant relief carvings, even the patterned marble floor. Under Michelangelo's soaring dome stands the Baldacchino (ball-da-KEY-no; fig. 22.8), an 85′-high canopy over the tomb of St. Peter. The title is derived from the Italian: *baldacco* is a silk cloth draped as a canopy over important people or places. In this case, the drapery is bronze as is the entire canopy, including the intricate designs covering the four columns. The Baldacchino was commissioned by the Barberini pope Urban VIII, who ordered the bronze plates removed from the dome of the Pantheon (see colorplate 8) and melted down, prompting the pope's physician to remark that, "What the barbarians didn't

Figure 22.7 St. Peter's Basilica, Rome. Apse and dome by Michelangelo (1547–1564); nave and facade by Carlo Maderno (1607–1626); Colonnade and piazza by Gianlorenzo Bernini (1617–1667).

do the Barberini did." Bernini patterned the serpentine column design after the twisted marble columns saved from Old St. Peter's, which were thought by Constantine to have survived from King Solomon's Temple. Some critics refer to the Baldacchino as architecture and others as sculpture; in either case, it is an artistic triumph under difficult circumstances. It had to be large enough to be significant under Michelangelo's enormous dome but not disproportionate to the size of the nave. Bernini himself called the solution one that "came out well by luck."

Bernini was Pope Urban VIII's favorite, but by no means the only artist supported by the lavish building program that drained the Vatican treasury. One of Bernini's severest critics was the rival architect Francesco Borromini (BOR-o-ME-nee; 1599–1644), a brooding and introspective genius who resented Bernini's favored status and grand reputation. Rejecting Bernini's predilection for rich marbles and lavishly painted stucco, Borromini concentrated on the interplay of elaborate curves and lines. In the small monastic Church of S. Carlo alle Quattro Fontane (fig. 22.9), Borromini used a series of intersecting ellipses in an undulating facade richly embellished with columns, sculpture, plaques, and scrolls, all in stone and relying for their effect on design rather than on opulent materials. The impression of restless, mystical passion must have had great appeal, for this small Baroque church was emulated throughout southern Europe.

Figure 22.8 Gianlorenzo Bernini, Baldacchino, 1624–1633. St. Peter's Basilica, Rome.

Figure 22.9 Francesco Borromini, S. Carlo alle Quattro Fontane, begun 1638. Rome.

Figure 22.10 Gianlorenzo Bernini, *Ecstasy of St. Theresa,* 1645–1652. Marble and gilt, life size. Cornaro Chapel, Sta. Maria della Vittoria, Rome.

The appeal of Bernini's *Ecstacy of St. Theresa* (fig. 22.10) is emotional, mystical, spiritual, and, withal, palpably sensual. Based on the writings of St. Theresa, the Spanish mystic, the saint is depicted in the throes of rapture as the angel is about to pierce her with the golden arrow of Divine Love. Epitomizing the Roman High Baroque, the altarpiece has become a stage for a theatrical work of intense religiosity, a visual counterpart of the *Spiritual Exercises* of Ignatius of Loyola that Bernini himself practiced every day.

The Roman Baroque style, with regional variations, became dominant throughout Catholic Europe. In Venice, Baldassare Longhena's (1598–1682) Church of Sta. Maria della Salute (fig. 22.11) was built at the entrance to the Grand Canal, becoming one of the landmarks of that opulent city. Truly Baroque mainly in its multiplicity of shapes and forms, the church also reflects local Byzantine and Renaissance principles, even including a Roman triumphal arch for the main facade at the right. The lofty dome is supported by eighteen huge spiral buttresses that appear to be derived from the modest volutes of Il Gesu (see fig. 22.1).

With all its splendor, complexity, and opulence, the Baroque became the reigning style throughout the Catholic world. That does not mean, however, that every Baroque church was well designed. Lesser architects adopted elements of the style, but failed to achieve the artistic effect of, say, a Borromini design. The Church of San Moise (fig. 22.12) is a case in point; Baroque has run amok. The facade is a compendium of every Baroque characteristic and device of the time, designed to be "Baroque." The intention was earnest but the effect is stultifying, a kind of negative testimony to the architectural genius of artists like Bernini and Borromini.

The fervent mysticism of Counter-Reformation Spain was expressed in the Mannerism of El Greco (see chap. 18) and, in the seventeenth century, in the art of Francisco de Zurbarán (zoor-ba-RAHN; 1598–1664). Influenced by Caravaggio though he never studied in Italy, Zurbarán translates spiritual ideas into poetic visual reality. His *Agnus Dei* (fig. 22.13) presents the Lamb of God as a symbol of Christ the perpetual sacrifice. With loving attention to detail he contrasts the delicate curls with the altar cloth, emphasizing the serenity of the sacrifice and the severity of the site. Reflecting the tenets of the Quietists, the most mystical of Spanish sects, the mood encompasses passivity, spiritual solitude, faith, and silence in the presence of God.

Figure 22.11 Baldassare Longhena, Sta. Maria della Salute, 1631–1687, Venice.

Figure 22.12 A. Tremignon and E. Meyring, Church of San Moise, on the Grand Canal, Venice.

Figure 22.13 Francisco de Zurburan, *Agnus Dei*, 1635–1640. Oil on canvas, 20½ × 13¼″. The San Diego Museum of Art. San Diego, California.

Unlike his Spanish contemporaries, Diego Velasquez (ve-LASS-kis; 1599–1660) was not interested in religious subjects. Allegorical figures, swirling clouds, and rhapsodic faces were never a part of a unique style that was concerned with nature and the optical effects of light. During his studies in Italy he became fascinated with the paintings of Titian and Tintoretto, but cared not at all for the style of Raphael, nor was he influenced by Rubens even though the latter was a personal friend. A court painter to King Philip IV for thirty years, Velasquez worked with the effects of light on objects and colors, producing candid portraits that never descended to the level of common courtly pictures. His *Maids of Honor* (fig. 22.14) is his acknowledged masterpiece and one of the most celebrated works of the century. The painting is a symphony of

Figure 22.14 Diego Velasquez, *Maids of Honor (Las Meninas)*, 1656. Oil on canvas, 10′5″ × 9′. Prado Museum, Madrid.

deep pictorial space, light, and images of reality, from what we actually see in the room to the implied presence of the king and queen, whose images are reflected in the mirror. The painter himself looks back at us as he works on a painting that is probably the one at which we are looking. At the front of the picture plane, light falls on the dog with the child's foot placed on its back, on the court dwarf, and, in the near foreground, on the Infanta Margarita and her two attendants. Standing behind a lady-in-waiting and wearing the cross of the Order of Santiago, the artist pauses with paintbrush poised; slightly deeper in the middle ground we see a couple engaged in conversation. The mirror on the back wall reveals the presence of the artist's patrons and, behind the courtier in the open doorway, space recedes to infinity. What looks at first like a genre scene in the artist's studio is actually a stunning spacial composition of five or six receding planes. As it is usually displayed in the Prado Museum, the painting faces a mirror on the opposite wall in which the spectator sees an electrifying image of receding space, an illusion that further confuses reality because the mirror includes the viewer as part of the painting. Space was a major preoccupation of the Baroque from the large interior space of Baroque churches to the great piazza fronting St. Peter's and the fascinating illusion of deep space in the *Maids of Honor.*

Aristocratic Baroque

Peter Paul Rubens (1577–1640) lived during an age marked by extremes. Galileo, Kepler, and Descartes were helping shape a new vision of the world, but there was also the dark and bloody side of witchcraft trials, the Inquisition, and the ferocious Thirty Years' War. Throughout his entire lifetime Rubens's own country, the Netherlands, was engaged in a struggle for independence from Spain, and yet Rubens painted works that jubilantly praised the human spirit and celebrated the beauty of the natural world. He was not indifferent to human suffering—far from it—but his temperament was wholly sunny and positive. He possessed a rare combination of good health, good looks, good sense, a talent for business, phenomenal artistic ability, and a remarkable intellect. He was fluent in six modern languages and classical Latin, and was reputed to be capable of listening to a learned lecture while painting, conversing, and dictating letters. One of the most gifted and accomplished painters who ever lived, Rubens amassed a fortune and enjoyed it all.

In only eight years of study in Italy, Rubens mastered the classical style of ancient Rome plus those of the High and Late Renaissance. Upon completing a series of paintings for Marie de' Medici, the Dowager Queen of France, he established his reputation as the preeminent painter for kings, nobles, and princes of the church. His *Assumption of the Virgin* (colorplate 33), though considerably smaller than his many giant works, is filled with the boundless energy that characterizes all his work. The diametric opposite of Caravaggio's stark realism, the figures are richly and colorfully garbed, with pink and chubby cherubs and solicitous angels effortlessly wafting the Virgin into heaven. The rich sensual quality of Rubens's work was prized by aristocratic patrons and by the church; glamour, splendor, and glory gave favorable answers to the doubts and questions of the faithful, assuring them that heaven and earth alike were equally beautiful.

In his large-scale *Rape of the Daughters of Leucippus* (colorplate 34), Rubens depicts Castor and Pollux, the sons of Jupiter, abducting two mortal maidens with whom they have fallen in love. In a design like an ascending spiral, Rubens has built his colors up in rich, contrasting textures: the luminous flesh of the opulent bodies; the deeply tanned, muscular gods; sparkling armor; and shimmering horseflesh. The low horizon increases the illusion of the ascension to the realm of the gods and adds to the buoyancy of a composition that is explosive with energy. Only the passive cupid is isolated from the intense action. The nudes are designed to complement each other, adding to the balance of the composition; what is concealed in one is revealed in the other.

No one knows how many assistants Rubens employed in his huge studio in Antwerp. As a court painter he paid no guild tax and therefore kept no records of the people who copied popular works or roughed out canvases that the master would complete and sell at a price based on the square footage and the personal contribution of Rubens. Of the few assistants who were successful in their own right, Anthony van Dyck (1599–1641) is by far the most notable. Unable to develop his talents in the overpowering presence of his teacher, van Dyck left to seek his fortune, which he found in abundance at the court of Charles I of England. With his aristocratic and refined style, van Dyck became the century's foremost portrait painter for court and church, producing elegant portrayals that always improved on the appearance of the model. While working in Genoa before settling down in the English court, van Dyck painted a portrait of the *Marchesa Elena Grimaldi* (fig. 22.15). A model of the art of portraiture in the grand manner, van Dyck designed the angled parasol to balance the dark mass at the bottom. Contributing to the illusion of the Marchesa's regal height, the classical columns add just the right touch of aristocratic confidence and dignity. Van Dyck had a unique ability to portray his subjects as they wished to appear without, however, stepping over the line to mere sycophancy.

Throughout his mature career Nicolas Poussin (poo-SAN; 1594–1665) painted in the grand manner but in a style entirely different from van Dyck and, especially, Rubens. Emphasizing line, lucidity, and control, Poussin chose only lofty subject matter drawn from ancient history, mythology, and biblical stories.

Figure 22.15 Anthony van Dyck, *Marchesa Elena Grimaldi,* ca. 1623. Oil on canvas, 97 × 68″. Widener Collection. National Gallery of Art, Washington, D.C.

He was an elitist, an aristocrat of paint and canvas, a French Classicist in an age of Romantic exuberance. Religious subject matter was treated, he thought, in a base and vulgar manner in most of the works by Caravaggio and his followers. Poussin's Baroque Classical style attracted followers just as did the quite different Baroque style of Rubens, touching off a controversy between "Rubenists" and "Poussinists" that may never be resolved. The basic disagreement was between color and line. Line and drawing were absolute values in representing things according to the Poussinists, and color was merely accidental because it depended on light. Color was, of course, what fascinated Rubens and his followers, who painted the colorful world as they perceived it, while the Poussinists constructed idealized forms of the world as it should be. Actually, the conflict was not just Rubenists versus Poussinists but the eternally opposing views of artists who were, in general, inclined towards romanticism as opposed to artists who were classically oriented. Romanticism in the nineteenth century is a stylistic period and is not to be confused with romantic or classical tendencies of artists in any period. When considered in very

broad terms, the Renaissance was classically oriented, while the Baroque was inclined towards romanticism except, of course, for Poussin. Classicists emphasize objectivity, rationality, balance, and control; Romanticists stress subjectivity, nonrationality, and the restless expression of emotion. Leonardo, Raphael, Poussin, Haydn, and Mozart are classicists; Tintoretto, the later Michelangelo, El Greco, Rubens, Verdi, Tchaikovsky, and Delacroix are romanticists.

In *Holy Family on the Steps* (colorplate 35) Poussin has designed an upward-angled perspective that is enforced by the steps across the bottom of the painting. Reminiscent of Raphael's style that Poussin studied so assiduously, the triangular composition is slightly off center, putting the head of Christ almost precisely in the mathematical center of the painting. From vases to temples the setting is Roman and the mode is derived, according to Poussin, from the *ethos* of the Greek musical scales (see chap. 8), which in this case may be the sweetly lyrical quality of the Ionic scale. Appearing at first to be starkly geometric, the drama and classical beauty of the work are apparent in the balance of solids and voids, cylinders and cubes, and in the balanced contrast of hard stone and soft foliage, drapery, and cooly supple flesh. To compare this work with *The Assumption of the Virgin* (see colorplate 33) is to perceive and to understand the difference between Classicism and Romanticism in the broad sense in which these terms are used here.

French tastes were attuned to a rationalized version of the Baroque as represented in the work of Poussin and, on a grand scale, in the royal palace at Versailles. Soon after Louis XIV assumed full control of the government (ca. 1661), French classicism was deliberately used to create a "royal style" that reinforced and enhanced the absolute rule of the king of France. Classical architecture has, since that time, been used by banks to indicate their financial stability and by rulers and dictators from Napoleon to Hitler, Mussolini, and Stalin to symbolize authority, control, and power.

Originally a hunting lodge for Louis XIII, the Palace at Versailles was rebuilt and vastly enlarged for Louis XIV, the self-styled Sun King whose power was so immense that he supposedly declared that *"L'état, c'est moi"* (I am the state). He certainly said, "It is legal because I wish it." Designed initially by Louis le Vau (luh-VO; 1612–1670) and completed by Jules Hardouin Mansart (man-SAR; 1646–1708), the Palace was oriented along an east-west axis with the western front facing the extensive gardens (fig. 22.16). Far too large to photograph in its entirety, the view shown is of the southwest wing of the three-wing Garden Front. The design is basically classical, with three floors and windows equally spaced and lined up above each other in diminishing size from ground-level French doors to the square top windows. The paired Ionic columns on the two projecting fronts are Baroque and intended to enliven an exterior that would otherwise be bland and boring.

Figure 22.16 Louis le Vau and Jules Hardouin Mansart, Palace of Versailles, 1669–1685.

Figure 22.17 East front, Palace of Versailles

Facing squarely into the morning sun, the east front has three courts (fig. 22.17). The vast outer court extends from the ornamental outer gates (not shown) up to the pair of elevated classical temple fronts and was intended for court functionaries. Restricted to the nobility, the second court begins at the corner of the temple fronts and ends at the outer limit of the inner Marble Court (fig. 22.18). Used only by the royal family, this court faced the Royal Apartments, located on the top floor where the morning sun could greet the Sun King—and vice versa. Indeed, the "rising" *(levée)* was a major daily ritual attended by members of the court selected for the honor. The facade of the king's wing rises from Baroque paired columns on the ground floor through French doors above, and on up to the Royal Apartment on the top floor, surmounted by an elaborate sunburst, the latter a characteristic Baroque device possibly invented by Bernini for his Throne of St. Peter.

The vastness of the palace can be overpowering except when viewed as intended, as the principle structure set within the spacious formal gardens designed by André le Nôtre (lu NO-truh; 1613–1700), which are classical in every way except for Baroque scale and extension of space. Every flower, shrub, hedge, and tree is set precisely in place and enlivened by reflecting pools and 1,200 fountains, a superb setting for a king who imposed his will even upon nature. Since the king's minister of finance concealed the costs, there are no reliable figures on what it cost to build and maintain Versailles, but today the French

Figure 22.18 Marble Court, Palace of Versailles

Figure 22.19 Frans Hals, *Portrait of an Officer,* ca. 1640. Oil on canvas, 33¾ × 27″. Andrew W. Mellon Collection. National Gallery of Art, Washington, D.C.

government can afford to operate the fountains just during the summer tourist months, and then only on Sunday evenings.

Bourgeois Baroque

Dutch art flourished in an environment utterly unlike the regal splendor of France or the flamboyant Baroque of the southern Catholic countries. Freed at last from the Spanish yoke, Holland became a prosperous trading nation: Protestant, hardworking, and predominantly middle class. Calvinism opposed images in churches, and there was no royal court or hereditary nobility, meaning that there were no traditional patrons of the arts. The new patrons were private collectors and there were many. Just about everyone in the nation of nearly two million inhabitants wanted paintings for their living rooms, and schools at Amsterdam, Haarlem, Delft, and Utrecht labored to supply a demand somewhat comparable to the Golden Age of Greece or fifteenth-century Florence.

The first of the great Dutch masters, Frans Hals (1580/85–1666) was one of history's most brilliant portraitists. There is no precedent for the liveliness of his canvases or the spontaneous brilliance of his brushwork. In *Portrait of an Officer* (fig. 22.19), a portly gentleman with hand on hip, his head jauntily tilted, stares at the viewer. Large surfaces are treated casually but the lacework is delicately precise. Not a deep character study, this is a portrait of a passing acquaintance captured in a brief moment but rendered as a momentary but uncompromising truth.

Judith Leyster (LIE-ster; 1609–1660) specialized in genre paintings, especially of musicians, and was one of the few artists prior to this century who could suggest musical performance through form, line, and color. In *Self-Portrait* (fig. 22.20) Leyster portrays herself in formal dress but in a relaxed and casual pose that echoes, in a lower key, the laughing violinist on her canvas who is playing the instrument rather than

Figure 22.20 Judith Leyster, *Self-Portrait,* ca. 1635. Oil on canvas, 29⅜ × 25⅝″. Gift of Mr. and Mrs. Robert Woods Bliss. National Gallery of Art, Washington, D.C.

just holding it. Influenced by the Utrecht school of Caravaggio disciples and her teacher, Frans Hals, her style is clearly her own. However, it was not until this century that "Leyster" replaced "Hals" on several paintings that she had completed during her late teens or early twenties. Dutch artists were proud of their craft, and this attitude is reflected in the jaunty ease and confident self-assertion of the artist. Italian artists of the High Renaissance promoted the idea of the artist as a noble creator, but in bourgeois Holland, superlative skills in the crafts were valued on their own merits.

Some Dutch artists like Hals specialized in portraits, while Leyster painted genre scenes, and others concentrated on history or landscapes. Rembrandt van Rijn (van rhine; 1606–1669), however, worked with consummate ease in all areas. He is, in fact, one of a handful of supreme masters of the entire European tradition. Calvinism frowned on religious images, which may explain why sculpture was not popular, but on the other hand, the Reformed Church rejected all authority except individual conscience. This meant, in effect, that artists could study the Bible and create sacred images as they personally envisioned them, which is precisely what Rembrandt did. He could not accept the stern God of the Calvinists and he never painted a Last Judgment. He was concerned instead with the human drama of the Old Testament, the loving and forgiving God of the New Testament, and the life and Passion of Christ. In *The Descent from the Cross* (colorplate 37) the two main focal points of the drama are the body of Christ and the face of his fainting mother. Eliminating all superfluous details with his characteristic dark background, the artist conveys the tenderness with which the broken body is being lowered from the cross. The composition is extremely tight, concentrating our attention on the key figures and, through the skillful use of chiaroscuro, flooding the canvas with the most profound grief. Not even Rembrandt himself surpassed the expressive combination of space and light.

Rembrandt's portrayal of *The Apostle Bartholomew* (fig. 22.21) is a powerful study of Christ's disciple, who was flayed alive while on a preaching mission in Armenia. During the Middle Ages he was sometimes portrayed holding some of his own flesh in his hands, but Rembrandt creates instead a resurrected disciple holding the knife that symbolizes his martyrdom. That Rembrandt chose to depict this lesser-known apostle is curious and may refer to the Massacre of St. Bartholomew. The largely middle-class Huguenots (French Protestants) were opposed to both the pope and the king. On 24 August 1572 (St. Bartholomew's Day) more than 30,000 Huguenots were massacred by fanatical followers of Catherine de' Medici, the regent, and her son, King Charles IX. Pope Gregory XIII (1572–1585) celebrated the occasion by singing a *Te Deum* and having a medal struck to memorialize the event, but throughout Protestant Europe, reaction to the slaughter was intensely bitter and

Figure 22.21 Rembrandt van Rijn, *The Apostle Bartholomew*, 1657. Oil on canvas, 64¾ × 55¾". Timkin Gallery, San Diego Museum of Art, San Diego, California.

long-lasting. A devout Protestant who followed only his own conscience, Rembrandt was opposed to the authority of Calvin, not to mention a pope or a king. His monumental study of the martyred apostle could therefore symbolize the martyrdom of the Huguenots who died on the saint's day.

Jan Vermeer (yahn ver-MEER; 1632–1675) did not paint monumental subject matter with the passion of Rembrandt, but he did have a special magic that transmuted everyday reality into eternal symbols. Fewer than forty paintings survive, and all but three are of sparsely furnished interiors of modest size. Vermeer has, in fact, done for ordinary rooms what High Renaissance artists did for ordinary human bodies: elevated them to the level of universals. With an eye for detail comparable to van Eyck's, Vermeer's speciality is light, natural light streaming into the interior, usually from the left, filling a space punctuated by objects and figures seemingly suspended in light. In *Woman Holding a Balance* (fig. 22.22) Vermeer has created an apparently simple scene of a woman, probably his wife Catharina in one of her eleven pregnancies, holding an empty balance. With jewelry on the table and a painting of the Last Judgment on the wall, there is a temptation to assume that this is a moral analogy, a weighing of worldly possessions against a background of divine judgment. Dutch Calvinists would

Figure 22.22 Jan Vermeer, *Woman Holding a Balance,* ca. 1657. Oil on canvas, 16¾ × 15″. Andrew W. Mellon Collection. National Gallery of Art, Washington, D.C.

not have had a Last Judgment anywhere in the house, but this may be Catharina's room and she, unlike her husband, was Catholic. Nevertheless, the mood is introspective and her expression serene. Married to a painter who in his lifetime never sold a painting, a man of extravagant tastes with a host of creditors, this painting may represent nothing more nor less than a woman contentedly contemplating jewelry received from a loving husband. The highest level of art may not be to encourage laughter, passion, or tears but to invoke dreams, and dreams are perhaps best left unexplained.

After his premature death, Vermeer's paintings were used to satisfy creditors who undoubtedly had no more appreciation of his worth than a society that had ignored him. Not rediscovered until the 1860s, his use of color and light was a revelation to the Impressionists, who thought themselves the first to discover that shadows were not black but also had color. In *The Girl with a Red Hat* (colorplate 38), there is a technical mastery that, in combination with Vermeer's scientific study of light, makes this one of the finest works of the artist's brief mature period. Here, as if they were visualized molecules, we see floating globules of colored light. Light glints from an eye, an earring, and the lips of a young woman unexpectedly caught in a soft-focus candid "photograph." Under the

spectacular hat, light and shadow are painted in subtle gradations of color emphasized by the gleaming white ruff. Vermeer applied paint to canvas with a dexterity and charm that has never been equaled.

Vermeer exploited color and light, while Jacob van Ruisdael (ROIS-dale; 1628–1682) specialized in space. The finest Dutch landscape painter and one of the greatest in Western art, Ruisdael painted the immensity of space from memory and imagination. In *Wheatfields* (colorplate 36) the vast and brooding sky, forecasting a coming storm, takes up two-thirds of the canvas. Ruisdael's landscapes are frequently devoid of people, and when they are present, as here, they are inconsequential figures compared with the magnificence of nature. The atmospheric perspective encourages the illusion that we are looking into space so deep that it verges on infinity.

Seventeenth century Dutch burghers are justly famed for their support of the art of painting, and Dutch museums are today filled to overflowing with "Dutch masters" and "little Dutch masters." Many painters of that golden age acquired wealth and fame, but for whatever reason, Rembrandt, Hals, and Vermeer, the greatest of the Dutch school, all died in poverty.

Rococo Art, ca. 1715–1789

With the death of Louis XIV in 1715, the academic classical art of the Baroque had lost its chief patron. It was with great relief that the French court abandoned the Palace and the Baroque, moving back to Paris and to a new way of life in their elegant townhouses, where manners and charm were far more interesting than grandeur and geometric order. This was the Age of Enlightenment and of the Rococo style of art, contradictory but not mutually exclusive. In fact, the Enlightenment and the American and French revolutions cannot be fully understood without knowing what the Rococo was all about. That Rococo is merely Baroque made small or Baroque made light are bromides that do have a certain element of truth, but Rococo is also a style in its own right. Royalty and nobility became obsolete during the Enlightenment, and Rococo art illustrates with astonishing accuracy the superficial values of an aristocracy whose days were numbered. The imposing Baroque forms were reduced to depictions of the pursuit of pleasure and escape from boredom. Rococo art was not decadent but the society that it portrayed most certainly was.

Jean Antoine Watteau (vah-TOE; 1684–1721), the first and greatest French Rococo artist, was born of Flemish parents in Valenciennes, a city that had been French for only six years. Yet, he transformed French art from the classicism of Poussin into a new style of gaiety and tenderness, casual but elegant, that even today is recognized as Parisian in the sophisticated

Figure 22.23 Antoine Watteau, *A Pilgrimage to Cythera*, 1717. Oil on canvas, 76½ × 51″. The Louvre, Paris.

tradition later reinforced by artists like Renoir and Degas. Watteau's *A Pilgrimage to Cythera* (fig. 22.23), an early Rococo work, is also the most important. Cythera was the legendary island of love of Venus, whose statue at the right presides over the amorous festivities. Grouped couple by couple, the elegantly garbed party is preparing to board a fanciful boat attended by cherubs, but not without a wistful backward glance at the pleasures enjoyed on the isle of love. Characteristic of Rococo design is the reverse **C** (Ɔ) that can be traced from the heads at the lower left, curves past the couple on the hillock, and turns back to the left along the delicate tips of the tree branches. Though it is a large painting, the scene is remarkably intimate. Each couple is totally preoccupied with each other and forms a distinct unit as they talk, smile, whisper, or touch. Beneath the frivolity and charm there is a warm feeling of good people and good times. Watteau has transformed the amorous dalliances of an idle and privileged class into lyric poetry.

Venus was queen of the Rococo at its height in the 1750s, and François Boucher (boo-SHAY; 1703–1770) was her most talented interpreter. The protégé of Madame de Pompadour, mistress of Louis XV and arbiter of Rococo style, Boucher was a master of the sensual and frequently erotic art of the period. With astounding energy and great virtuosity he produced paintings, designed tapestries, decorated porcelain, and created opera and ballet settings. With his

many students and widely circulated engravings, he became the most influential artist in Europe. His *Venus Consoling Love* (colorplate 39) depicts a slim and delicate beauty who would be more comfortable at the French court than on Mount Olympos. She was, in fact, at the French court, for this is one of Boucher's many portraits of Mme. de Pompadour, to whom the painting belonged. Here are the characteristic ivory, pink, blue, silver, and gold colors of the Rococo, all elegantly detailed by one of the great virtuosos of the painter's brush. The painting is frankly pretty, and meant to be, but its design, though very subtle, is a carefully controlled interplay of sinuous curves. Nowhere is there a straight line. A study of the apparent diagonals of the goddess's body discloses a series of curves, flattering curves of supple and creamy flesh. This is an idealized version of Pompadour, totally different from other Boucher paintings that reveal the intellectual brilliance of an enlightened woman who assisted in the publication of Diderot's *Encyclopedia*. Her physician, Dr. Quesway, quoted her foreboding remark, *"Après moi le déluge!"* (After me the flood!, i.e., disaster), and Voltaire wrote, on the occasion of her death in 1764, that he would miss her because "She was one of us; she protected Letters to the best of her power."

Colorplate 33 Peter Paul Rubens, *The Assumption of the Virgin,* ca. 1626. Oil on panel, 49⅜ × 37⅛″. Samuel H. Kress Collection. National Gallery of Art, Washington, D.C.

Colorplate 34 Peter Paul Rubens, *Rape of the Daughters of Leucippus,* ca. 1618. Oil on canvas, 7'3" × 6'10". Alte Pinakothek, Munich.

Colorplate 35 Nicolas Poussin, *Holy Family on the Steps,* 1648. Oil on canvas, 38¼ × 27″. Samuel H. Kress Collection. National Gallery of Art, Washington, D.C.

Colorplate 36 Jacob van Ruisdael, *Wheatfields.* Oil on canvas, 51¼ × 39⅜. Metropolitan Museum of Art, New York. Bequest of Bejamin Altman, 1913.

Colorplate 37 Rembrandt van Rijn, *The Descent from the Cross,* 1653. Oil on canvas, 56¼ × 43¾″. Widener Collection. National Gallery of Art, Washington, D.C.

Colorplate 38 Jan Vermeer, *The Girl with a Red Hat,* ca. 1660. Oil on wood, 9⅛ × 7⅛″. Andrew W. Mellon Collection. National Gallery of Art, Washington, D.C.

Colorplate 39 François Boucher, *Venus Consoling Love,* 1751. Oil on canvas, 42⅛ × 33⅜″. Gift of Chester Dale. National Gallery of Art, Washington, D.C.

Figure 22.25 Étienne Falconet, *Madame de Pompadour as the Venus of the Doves.* Samuel H. Kress Collection. National Gallery of Art, Washington, D.C.

Figure 22.24 Jean-Honoré Fragonard, *A Young Girl Reading,* ca. 1776. Oil on canvas, 32 × 25½″. Gift of Mrs. Mellon Bruce in memory of her father Andrew W. Mellon, 1961. National Gallery of Art, Washington, D.C.

The most eminent pupil of Boucher and Chardin and the last of the great Rococo artists, Jean-Honoré Fragonard (frah-go-NAR; 1732–1806) lived to see the revolution destroy the Rococo age and all it represented. A master of the elegantly erotic paintings that delighted his patrons, Fragonard also had a technical skill and an eye for composition that enabled him to distill the essence of a personal and warmly intimate scene, such as *A Young Girl Reading* (fig. 22.24).

The spirit of the age in three-dimensional form is represented by Étienne Falconet (fal-ca-NAY; 1716–1791) in his harmonious sculptural group entitled *Madame de Pompadour as the Venus of the Doves* (fig. 22.25). The coquettish eroticism that delighted this decadent society is clearly evident in this lighthearted work, so typical of the figures that decorated Sèvres porcelain, music boxes, snuff boxes, and other accoutrements of the good life of idleness and luxury.

But there was another current, one that celebrated the sober virtues of the middle class. Jean-Baptiste-Simeon Chardin (shar-DAN; 1699–1779) sought the underlying nobility that could be found in scenes of daily life. Nothing was so humble but that his brush could reveal its charm. His depiction of *The Kitchen Maid* (fig. 22.26) has a natural dignity in sharp contrast to the artificiality of the courtly Rococo style.

Figure 22.26 Jean-Baptiste-Simeon Chardin, *The Kitchen Maid.* 1738. Oil on canvas, 18½ × 14¾″. Samuel H. Kress Collection. National Gallery of Art, Washington, D.C.

Figure 22.27 Johann Michael Fischer, Church of Ottobeuren, begun ca. 1720. Bavaria.

Figure 22.29 Cherubs, Ottobeuren

Figure 22.28 Interior, Ottobeuren

Chardin painted what he saw, which was, essentially, light falling on pleasing shapes: face, apron, basin, turnips. The result is a quietly beautiful composition by the finest still-life painter of the eighteenth century.

Rococo architecture is charming and beguiling in small structures and, when tastefully done, even in large buildings. The Benedictine Church of Ottobeuren (fig. 22.27) has twin towers derived from Baroque designs but unified with superimposed pilasters punctuated with decorative windows. The outward-thrusting middle section is characteristic of the Rococo, both assertive and inviting.

The interior of the church (fig. 22.28) is a celestial symphony of white stucco, gold gilt, and profuse decoration set off to best advantage by the north-south

orientation of the building and the large clear-glass windows. All of the elegantly textured decorations are carved wood, and the "marble" columns are actually wood painted to look like marble. The spritely Rococo cherubs (fig. 22.29) and even the dangling tassel are painted wood. The virtuosity of the woodcarvers of Bavaria is magnificently celebrated in Ottobeuren.

Neither the artificial elegance of the French Rococo nor the exuberance of Bavarian Rococo had a place in an English society that was generally more sober than the French and, unlike Catholic Bavaria, solidly Protestant. In both subject matter and style, Thomas Gainsborough's (1727–1788) portrait of *Mrs. Richard Brinsley Sheridan* (fig. 22.30) symbolizes the dashing, worldly taste of English high society. This is the beautiful singer who married Sheridan, the wit, brilliant member of Parliament, and writer of plays like *School for Scandal* and *The Rivals*. Here nature is artificial, arranged as a proper background to highlight the natural beauty and unpretentious air of the sitter. In contrast to the sprightly sophistication of Boucher's women, Mrs. Sheridan is the very picture of the tasteful elegance so admired by British society.

Figure 22.30 Thomas Gainsborough, *Mrs. Richard Brinsley Sheridan*, ca. 1783. Oil on canvas, 66½ × 60½". Andrew W. Mellon Collection. National Gallery of Art, Washington, D.C.

Figure 22.31 Inigo Jones, Queen's House, north facade, 1610–1618. Greenwich.

Figure 22.32 Inigo Jones, Palladian Bridge, 1647–1653. Wilton House, Wiltshire.

Neoclassic Art

The visual arts of the Renaissance and the Baroque made little impact on English culture. Apparently preoccupied with their justly celebrated achievements in dramatic literature, poetry, and music, the English continued to build in the Gothic and Tudor styles and to import painters like Holbein, Rubens, and van Dyck. After the visit to Italy of Inigo Jones (1573–1652), the king's surveyor (architect), a revolution began in English architecture. Jones's middle-class British sensibilities were offended by the extravagance of Michelangelo's style, but he was profoundly impressed with Palladio's architectural designs. Jones did not copy Palladian buildings, but instead selected classical characteristics as a basis for his own architectural style. His Queen's House (fig. 22.31) is the first English building designed in the Neoclassic style that would become so prominent in England and North America. Chaste and clean with the poise of pure Roman classicism, the house has slight rustication on the ground floor derived from an early Renaissance style long since abandoned by the

Italians (see fig. 18.13). With simple window openings and matching lower and upper balustrades, the curving double stairway adds a discreet touch of dignity and grace.

Along with his design for the stately home called Wilton House, Jones included the so-called Palladian Bridge (fig. 22.32), an influential concept that combined Roman triumphal arches with an Ionic colonnade. The arches were transformed with simple classical pediments instead of Roman squared-off tops. The entire structure is lighter and more graceful because the columns are proportionately taller than their classical models.

English architecture was influenced by Palladian and Baroque characteristics more rapidly than anyone might have anticipated. In 1666 King Charles II commissioned Christopher Wren (1632–1723) to design a new dome for the Gothic Cathedral of St. Paul's, a design that Wren planned in the "Roman manner." A professor of astronomy at Oxford and an amateur architect, Wren soon had more than he bargained for; the Great Fire of 1666 destroyed most of London, necessitating a major rebuilding program with Wren as the chief architect. Of the more than fifty churches

Figure 22.33 Christopher Wren, St. Paul's Cathedral, 1675–1710, west facade, London.

Figure 22.34 James Gibbs, St. Martin-in-the-Fields, 1721–1726, Tralfager Square, London.

that Wren designed, the most important project was the new St. Paul's, an eclectic design influenced by Jones, Palladio, and the French and Italian Baroque, and masterfully synthesized by Wren (fig. 22.33). St. Paul's is one of a limited number of English buildings with Baroque characteristics, but overall the design is dominated by the classical dome that is reminiscent, on a massive scale, of Bramante's Tempietto (see fig. 18.31). Punctuated by paired Corinthian columns in the Baroque manner, the facade is basically classical, but the ornate twin towers are similar to Borromini's curvilinear style (see fig. 22.9). None of Wren's London churches is quite like any other, though most are classical; some have towers, others steeples, and a few domes.

The Church of St. Martin-in-the-Fields (fig. 22.34) was designed by James Gibbs (1682–1754) as influenced by Wren, with whom he studied. Essentially a Roman temple with a classical steeple, this is a prototype of similar churches constructed throughout the United States, especially in New England. Usually of wood frame and clapboard construction and painted white, these classical buildings became one of the most familiar church designs in nineteenth century America.

Variations on the Palladian style spread throughout England in the designs of stately homes and their interiors, including furniture. The drawing room of

Townhouse No. 1 of Crescent Circle (fig. 22.35) contains an Axminster carpet, a fireplace of Italian Carrara marble, Sheraton cabinettes, Chippendale card table, and a Heppelwhite sofa and wooden chairs, all in the Neoclassic style. The 1798 piano is Neoclassic as are the spacious windows. The two mirrors add a Rococo touch to an interior design that, with many variations, became fashionable in comparable American homes of the late eighteenth and early nineteenth centuries.

In France the Rococo style was deemed too frivolous for public buildings and the Baroque style too elaborate, leaving the way open for a French version of Neoclassicism. Ange-Jacques Gabriel (1698–1782), court architect for Louis XV, made his reputation with his design for the Petit Trianon on the grounds of Versailles (fig. 22.36). Restrained, symmetrical, and exquisitely proportioned, the diminutive palace was contructed by and for Mme. de Pompadour who was, in effect, the ruler of France in place of the weak and inept Louis XV. Clearly reflecting her classical architectural tastes, the Petit Trianon is in the austere Augustan style of Republican Rome, a style that became dominant in Paris and other French cities during the second half of the eighteenth century.

The philosophes of the Enlightenment were, as might be expected, hostile to the Rococo style. Their attitude accounts for the sudden fame of Jean-Baptiste Greuze (grooz; 1725–1805), who was praised by

Figure 22.35 Drawing room, No. 1 Crescent Circle, Bath, England.

Figure 22.36 Ange-Jacques Gabriel, Petit Trianon, 1762–1768, south facade, Versailles.

Figure 22.37 Jean-Baptiste Greuze, *The Village Bride,* 1761. Oil on canvas, 46½ × 36″. The Louvre, Paris.

Diderot and other philosophes for paintings depicting bourgeois life. Diderot thought that paintings such as *The Village Bride* (fig. 22.37) celebrated the virtues of the simple life and the sterling moral values of the sober and sedate middle class. Greuze's work did please, but not the middle class; rather, it appealed to the philosophes who, along with the upper middle class and aristocracy, lived a life depicted more accurately by Boucher. The charming rusticity of Greuze's painting with a gentle patriarch, blushing bride, gawky bridegroom, and chickens pecking on the floor was sentimental, as phony and romanticized as Rococo paintings with their idyllic landscapes and the elite playing at being gods, goddesses, shepherds, and shepherdesses. Worse yet, they were hypocritical. Greuze's rural maidens, wide-eyed in their simpering innocence, are painted with sly sensual touches and erotic undertones that make the frankly amoral paintings of Boucher look positively poetic and moral.

The gap between the aristocracy and the middle class was possibly no greater than it had been for generations, but by the last quarter of the century it became far more noticeable. The philosophes expounded on the gap along with revolutionary political and economic ideas that were no longer theories but active principles in England's American colonies. When it became apparent that the art of Greuze and his imitators did not truly reflect their revolutionary fervor, the philosophes turned to Neoclassic art. Excavations at Pompeii and Herculaneum, begun in 1748 under the aegis of King Charles of Bourbon, were bringing to light a new chapter from the history of ancient Rome, sparking a renewed interest in antiquity that was not confined to the arts. Political theorists who were advocating democratic equality, fervent patriotism, and the rule of reason thought they had found all this in Republican Rome.

A far more gifted artist than Greuze, Jacques Louis David (da-VEED; 1748–1825) developed his Neoclassic style during his studies in Rome (1775–1781).

Figure 22.38 Jacques Louis David, *The Death of Sokrates,* 1787. Oil on canvas, 78 × 59″. The Metropolitan Museum of Art, New York. Wolfe Fund, 1931.

Refusing to merely copy Roman statues and paintings, to become an antiquarian, he chose instead to be a propagandist, to place his talent at the service of revolutionary ideals. David used the forms of ancient art to extol the virtues of patriotism and democracy. Painted shortly before the French Revolution, *The Death of Sokrates* (fig. 22.38) became one of the most popular paintings of the century and set the tone for didactic art of the highest quality. Sokrates the Greek philosopher is depicted here as the apostle of reason, the patron saint of Roman Stoics like Epictetus and Marcus Aurelius. With the body of a young athlete and the face of a benign sage, Sokrates dominates a sharply focused composition similar to the dramatic chiaroscuro of Caravaggio. The figures of the twelve disciples, no coincidence, are rendered as precisely as marble statues, precision of detail being a David trademark. David's message is unmistakable: men of principle should be willing to die in defense of their ideals. Nobles and tradesmen, philosophers and priests, seemingly everyone bought engravings of the painting, including Louis XVI, who admired its noble sentiments.

David's works, with their detailed, meticulous realism and appeal to reason, were conceived and executed as cries for revolution. During the revolution itself David was a member of the Convention that sentenced Louis XVI and Marie Antoinette to death. For twenty-five years he was a virtual dictator of the arts in France. Following his dicta, Rococo salons were stripped of their sensuous paintings and curvaceous furnishings, remodeled in Neoclassic style, and equipped with furniture patterned after Greek vase paintings and Pompeiian murals. Fashionable men and women adopted Roman names such as Portia and Brutus, styled their hair in the antique manner, and even costumed themselves in classical togas. Madame Tallien (fig. 22.39), a leading figure in revolutionary salons, is shown in the approved new look of the revolution as painted by an unknown artist in the style of David.

Figure 22.39 School of David, *Portrait of Madame Tallien.* San Diego Museum of Art, San Diego, California.

Figure 22.41 Jean Antoine Houdon, *Voltaire,* ca. 1775. Chester Dale Collection. National Gallery of Art, Washington, D.C.

Figure 22.40 Unknown French Artist, *Mlle. du Val d'Ognes,* ca. 1800. Oil on canvas, height 63½". Metropolitan Museum; of Art, New York. Bequest of Isaac D. Fletcher.

David was a highly successful artist with many students and, of course, numerous imitators. As with any well-known artist, paintings were sometimes attributed to him so that they would fetch a higher price, which is what happened with the portrait of *Mlle. du Val d'Ognes* (fig. 22.40). Purchased in 1917 as a David for $200,000, the painting has since been attributed by some critics to Constance Marie Charpentier (1767–1849), a Parisian artist who studied with David and several other noted painters. Winner of a gold medal and an exhibitor in ten salons, her work appears to be hidden away either in private collections or behind the names of more famous artists. That the painting could ever have been attributed to David is very odd. While the style is Neoclassic, the brushwork firm and lucid, and the garb elegantly classical, the mood is totally alien to David's style. Strangely haunting, there is a brooding and unreal quality about the work that prompted critics to use terms like "merciless portrait," "unforgettable," and "mysterious masterpiece." These remarks were made while the painting still bore the name of David, but they are no less appropriate even if the artist's name might be Charpentier.

Portrait sculpture, as might be expected, was a natural for the Neoclassic style, but there were no sculptors comparable to David. Jean Antoine Houdon (ooh-DON; 1741–1828), the finest French sculptor of the age, was admired by the philosophes, many of whom he portrayed with great accuracy. His portrait of Voltaire (fig. 22.41) is a realistic depiction of the aging philosopher, clearly communicating his personality with twinkling eyes and wry and cynical smile.

Figure 22.42 Antonio Canova, *Pauline Borghese as Venus,* 1805. Marble, life size. Borghese Gallery, Rome.

Figure 22.43 Gilbert Stuart, *Mrs. Richard Yates,* 1793. Oil on canvas, 30¼ × 25″. Andrew W. Mellon Collection. National Gallery of Art, Washington, D.C.

Houdon was friendly with other revolutionaries, like George Washington and Benjamin Franklin, and created a portrait of Franklin and two statues of Washington. Despite his revolutionary background and realistic portraits, Houdon could win only reluctant acceptance from Napoleon, who much preferred the Neoclassic style of Italian sculptor Antonio Canova (ka-NO-va; 1757–1822), whose art along with that of David became propaganda tools for the Empire. Canova's lovely study of *Pauline Borghese as Venus* (fig. 22.42) is an idealized version of feminine charm, a very sensual portrait of Napoleon's sister and, though classical, an evocation of imperial luxury rather than the noble dignity of Republican Rome.

The Neoclassic style found a home in the new republic of the New World. The leading American painter, Gilbert Stuart (1755–1828), painted many founding fathers, particularly George Washington, whose portrait on the dollar bill is from Gilbert Stuart. In his portraits Stuart displayed a mastery of flesh tones, having discovered, like the Impressionists, that flesh coloration was a combination of colors. His portrait of *Mrs. Richard Yates* (fig. 22.43) is typical of the Neoclassic style in a new democracy in which neither dress nor background gives a clue to the social status of the sitter. European portraiture customarily added a proper setting and adornment indicating a regal or noble subject. In this portrait of the wife of a New York importer we see a cooly poised and confident woman. Her strongly featured face with the raised eyebrows and slightly drooping eyelids is faintly skeptical, the face of a shrewd and capable Yankee.

As U.S. minister to France, Thomas Jefferson (1743–1826) had an opportunity to study French Neoclassic architecture and, especially, Roman architecture in France and Italy. He was fascinated by the Maison Carrée (see fig. 10.7) in southern France and was determined to introduce Roman architecture into the United States. Jefferson's design of the Capitol of Virginia (fig. 22.44) was patterned after the

Figure 22.44 Thomas Jefferson, State Capitol, 1785–1789, Richmond, Virginia.

Maison Carrée, but with Ionic capitals and constructed of wood painted gleaming white. Larger than the Roman temple, the Virginia Capitol building has an aura of noble dignity precisely as intended by its designer.

Neoclassicism is popular because it is easily comprehended. Political themes and purposes aside, the classical impulse is towards physical and intellectual perfection as embodied in buildings that express the essence of poised, serene beauty. The Greeks not only invented the style but perfected it, and for twenty-five centuries the Western world has copied it.

Almost entirely immune to Renaissance and Baroque styles, England responded enthusiastically to the Palladian-inspired architecture of Inigo Jones and the essentially Neoclassic designs of Christopher Wren and James Gibbs. Sponsored in France by Mme. de Pompadour, the Neoclassic style dominated the vast building program of the second half of the eighteenth century. Prerevolutionary classicism found its strongest expression in the art of David and Houdon, and found a home in America as represented in the work of Gilbert Stuart and Thomas Jefferson.

Neoclassicism spanned the eighteenth and nineteenth centuries as a prerevolutionary and then a postrevolutionary style. It served the needs of a society struggling to free itself from oppression and, paradoxically, a Napoleonic age that utilized Neoclassicism as a symbol of law, order, and authority.

Summary

The word *Baroque* was coined by eighteenth century classicists as a disdainful term denoting the art of an extravagant, disorderly, contradictory, and sometimes bizarre age. Powerful forces that were to shape the modern world were reflected in the Counter-Reformation style promoted by the Church of Rome, the Aristocratic style of absolute monarchs, and the Bourgeois style of the Protestant middle class of Holland.

The mother church of the Jesuits, Il Gesu, was the first church of a style that reached its apogee in the art of Bernini. The dramatic chiaroscuro and gritty realism of Caravaggio influenced every painting school in Europe including the Spanish mystic Zurbarán and Velasquez, the master of pictorial space.

The expressive and exuberant style of Rubens made him the top court painter of the century, while van Dyck painted courtly portraits of aristocratic patrons. The first and foremost of the Baroque Classicists, Poussin emphasized drawing and design over Rubenesque color and emotion, setting off a conflict between Poussinists and Rubenists that defined and illustrated the contradictory forces of the seventeenth century. Aristocratic art dominated the age as it dominated no other, as symbolized by the magnificent palace of Louis XIV at Versailles. Representing the divine right monarchy of Louis XIV, Versailles also connoted the emergence of France as the most influential and powerful nation in Europe.

With no princely or priestly patrons, the artists of Calvinist Holland produced works commissioned by a prosperous middle class that had an apparently insatiable taste for paintings. Although they were artistically the most successful, Hals, Rembrandt, and Vermeer fared less well financially than many lesser artists.

The decorative and delightfully erotic Rococo style was as much a part of the Enlightenment as the learned speculation of the philosophes. The art of Watteau, Boucher, Fragonard, and Falconet mirrored the elegance, idleness, and artificiality of the French nobility, while Chardin concentrated on painting objects and scenes of everyday life. In Austria and in Bavaria, churches like Ottobeuren represented a festive Catholic Rococo style, while in England the style was manifested in a more restrained British manner, as seen in the art of Gainsborough.

Bibliography

Banister, Fletcher. *A History of Architecture on the Comparative Method.* New York: Charles Scribner's Sons, 1963. A superb reference book with fine diagrams, floor plans, and descriptions of styles, and all the great buildings in history, but especially valuable for the Baroque. (Available in paperback edition.)

Bazin, Germain. *Baroque and Rococo Art.* New York: Frederick A. Praeger, Inc., 1964. Fine, general study. (Available in paperback edition.)

Brown, Dale, et al. *The World of Velasquez 1599–1660.* New York: Time-Life Books, 1969. The title is apt, but gives no indication of how thoroughly Velasquez is studied and how well. A slim volume, but magnificent.

Fosca, Francois. *The Eighteenth Century: Watteau to Tiepolo.* Translated by Stuart Gilbert. Geneva: Albert Skira, 1952. A book with illustrations "as pretty as a picture." Text of exceptional literary quality.

Friedlaender, Walter. *Nicolas Poussin: A New Approach.* New York: Harry R. Abrams, Inc., 1964. Makes Poussin come to life and makes his works understandable in terms of history and philosophy.

Hinks, Roger P. *Michelangelo Merisi da Caravaggio: His Life . . . His Legend . . . His Works.* London: Faber & Faber, 1953. A lively, well-documented, and well-illustrated work.

Kalnein, Wend G., and Michael Levey. *Art and Architecture of the Eighteenth Century in France.* Baltimore, Md.: Penguin, 1973. Excellent coverage.

Kitson, Michael. *The Age of Baroque.* New York: McGraw-Hill Book Company, 1965. Lively and well-rounded study of the art and the age. (Available in paperback edition.)

Levey, Michael. *Rococo to Revolution: Major Trends in European Painting.* New York: Frederick A. Praeger, Inc., 1966. A very handy and informative general study. Well illustrated. (Available in paperback edition.)

Pope-Hennessy, John. *Italian High Renaissance and Baroque Sculpture.* London: Phaidon Publishers, Inc., 1963. An outstanding work. Despite its title, this book is not a summary but a penetrating study. Well documented and well illustrated.

Rosenberg, Jakob. *Rembrandt.* 2 vols. Cambridge: Harvard University Press, 1948. Among the thousands of works on Rembrandt, this is one of the best. (Available in paperback edition.)

Schneider, Pierre, et al. *The World of Watteau 1684–1721.* New York: Time-Life Books, 1967. A delightful book, as charming as the artists, works, and society it presents.

Soehner, Halldor, and Arno Schonberger. *The Rococo Age.* New York: McGraw-Hill Book Company, 1960. This is one of the *Search . . .* author's favorite art books and he recommends it highly. He warns that you need muscles or a stout table to hold it. This is a case of a good thing coming in a very big package.

Trapier, Elizabeth. *Velasquez.* New York: Hispanic Society of America, 1948. One of the very few scholarly books on this artist in English. Highly recommended.

Wallace, Robert. *The World of Bernini 1598–1680.* New York: Time-Life Books, 1970. Superb critical study, beautifully illustrated, helpful graphs. The books in the Time-Life Library of Art are valuable to students and laymen alike. The texts are easy and pleasant to read; the layouts are superior to most standard art books, and the illustrations equal to those of the best art-book publishers. Although the books in the Time-Life Series are so pleasant, lively, and inexpensive, many critics have not given them the time and appraisal they deserve.

Wildenstein, Georges, ed. *The Paintings of Fragonard.* London: Phaidon Publishers, Inc., 1960. Wildenstein has written or edited many monographs on French painters of the eighteenth and nineteenth centuries. In many cases these are the only books of any importance on these artists presented in English.

Wittkower, Rudolf. *Art and Architecture in Italy, 1600–1750.* Baltimore: The Pelican History of Art, Penguin Books, 1958. This is a well-illustrated architectural history that explains the why and how of Baroque art.

————. *Gian Lorenzo Bernini, the Sculptor of the Roman Baroque.* London: Phaidon Publishers, Inc., 1955. This is one of the finest works on any sculptor in any period. Beautifully illustrated.

23 *Music: Baroque, Rococo, and Classical*

Baroque Music (1600–1750)

Modern music, music as we know it, began sometime around the year 1600 as the Renaissance waned and the new Age of Reason began to take shape. The unbroken line of development leading from early organum to the smoothly flowing symmetry of the a cappella vocal music of the Golden Age of Polyphony came to an end. The old world of *private* music for the church, the courts, and a cultural elite steadily declined in influence and importance. The modern world in which music became a *public* art was taking shape amidst the intellectual, political, and social ferment of the seventeenth century.

Stimulated by exploration, scientific discovery, the emergence of capitalism, the middle class, and the modern state, and the continuing conflict between Reformation and Counter-Reformation, *audiences* of the common man were created. Churches could no longer take the piety of their communicants for granted; they were obliged to build structures with a maximum of floor space, structures that resembled theatres more than they did Gothic or Renaissance churches. In a setting bursting with agitated forms and twisting, curving shapes with elaborate decorative details, these audiences were preached to, firmly and fervently.

This new *Baroque* style was applied to all public buildings whether they were churches, concert halls, or opera houses. Even the Baroque palaces (such as Versailles) of ruling heads of state assumed a quasi-public character in their dual roles as royal residences and showcases of national prestige and power.

There was a consistent dualism in the Baroque era, a sometimes precarious balance of opposing forces: church and state, aristocracy and affluent middle class. Baroque architecture achieved a sculptured effect by balancing the massiveness of its basic structure with elaborate decoration and exploitation of three-dimensional effects. Even the cylindrical columns of the facades were grouped in pairs.

Baroque music displayed the same dualism with balanced vocal-instrumental groups, consistent use of two-part (binary) forms and the reduction of the church modes to only two modes: major and minor.

The emergence of instrumental music to a position of equal importance with vocal music practically eliminated the a cappella style. All Baroque vocal music had an instrumental accompaniment whether it was a mass, motet, oratorio, passion, cantata, or opera. Purely instrumental music established new forms such as the balanced participation of small and large groups in the concerto grosso and the pieces for two solo instruments with keyboard accompaniment (called trio sonatas). Even the dynamics were dualistic, with consistent use of alternating loud and soft passages.

Keyboard Music

Harpsichord

Dance Suite Dancing has been a fundamental activity since the dim dawn of the human race—dances to appease the gods, exorcise evil spirits, invoke fertility—and for the sheer exhilaration of physical and emotional release. Dancing attained a new prestige during the seventeenth-century Age of Kings, with magnificent balls in the great courts. The lords and ladies refined lusty and sometimes crude peasant dances into a social art of grace and charm without, however, discarding the omnipresent eroticism of social dancing.

During the early Baroque period short instrumental pieces were composed in the manner and style of various popular dances. The exotic and erotic Sarabande, for example, was transformed into a stylized and sophisticated art form that sometimes subtly implied what the original boldly proclaimed. Later on, a similar process changed the waltz from an "indecent" dance into a popular social dance, leading finally to an art form; for example, "The Blue Danube" by Johann Strauss, Jr. Late twentieth-century composers are more than likely to accord similar treatment to dances of the 1980s.

During the seventeenth century these stylized dances were combined in collections of chamber music called *dance suites* and played by harpsichords, other solo instruments, and various instrumental ensembles. There are usually five or six dances (or movements) in a suite, each a different type of dance with a standard sequence, which can be described as A–C–S–O–G: Allemande, Courante, Sarabande, Optional dance(s), Gigue. The dance suite was truly international in character; the original folk dances were, respectively, German, French, Spanish, and English (jig). Each dance suite had, however, a basic unity; that is, *each dance was in the same key.*

"Each dance was in the same *key*"—a significant statement about this period and one that goes beyond the mere technicalities of music. The new "key" to reality was the rational world of Descartes and, later, the mechanistic world of Newton. After Descartes, philosophers and scientists of the Enlightenment unlocked the door leading to a new world in which, they thought, they could begin to examine and to comprehend a rational universe of order and logic. The single key of Baroque compositions can be compared, in function, with Newton's law of universal gravitation; music and physics attempt to explain motion in the simplest possible terms.

For the first time in history music acquired what was considered to be a firm and rational foundation: a key. Many centuries before, the multitudinous modes of the Greeks were reduced to the eight church modes that formed the musical material of everything from plainsong through Renaissance polyphonic music. The Baroque saw the emergence of two new concepts: (1) all music written in a consistent pitch relationship called a key, with a choice of either major or minor mode, and (2) a temporary disenchantment with the complexities of polyphonic music in favor of blocks of sound called chords or harmony.

By exploiting homophonic music (one sound, i.e., one block of harmony following another) and a fixed pitch relationship, composers were merely reflecting the new view of reality. The "old music" was gradually replaced by less complicated music which was considered to be lucid and rational, though of course always expressive. This is not to say that this was a conscious decision by anyone or that there was instant recognition of the drastic changes that had taken place. Rather, musicians, like all artists, reacted to the new view of reality with a combination of old and new techniques that gave a new sound to a new age.

This new sound, as in the music of Johann Sebastian Bach (1685–1750), can be considered the beginning of modern music. Compositions by twentieth-century composers such as Stravinsky, Prokofiev, and Bartók are more closely related to the music of Bach than Bach's work relates, in turn, to the Renaissance. Palestrina, Lassus, and other Renaissance musicians were writing for the Church and for an educated aristocracy. Bach, though sometimes serving as a court composer, also performed routine services which ranged from conducting choir rehearsals to composing music for next Sunday's worship service.

The music of Bach is admired for its artistry and for its superb craftsmanship. In his own day, however, Bach composed much of his music in response to specific demands. Many of his organ works were written and performed for church services and for special programs. His sacred cantatas, written for particular Sundays of the liturgical year, were normally performed only once. Having served their purpose, they were consigned to storage where, many years later, a young Mozart could discover them and exclaim, "Now here is a man from whom I can learn," or words to that effect.

Much of Bach's output was intended for performance by amateur musicians and, more importantly, to be listened to by audiences composed essentially of the middle-class burghers of Germany. This middle class, of increasing influence and affluence, was becoming the primary audience of not only that period but of all subsequent periods. Today's mass audience is a logical development of the processes that began during the eighteenth century.

The following dance suite for harpsichord is typical of solo keyboard music of the Baroque. The setting for a performance could be as simple as an amateur performing in the parlor of a middle-class home or as elaborate as a professional performance on a gold-encrusted harpsichord at a royal court.

The dance suite was based on actual dances from the past, dances that were codified, stylized, and refined into a succession of dance movements for a listening rather than a dancing audience. Following are only the titles and major themes of the suite.[1]

French Suite no. 1 in d Minor

J. S. Bach (1685–1750)
Total Time: 12:30

Allemande (Fr., *German*, i.e., a German dance)

Courante (Fr., *courir*, to run, a running dance)

Sarabande (from Spain)

Minuet I (French dance of rustic origin)

Minuet II

Gigue (from sixteenth-century English or Irish jig)

Organ

Fugue Intellectuals of the Age of Enlightenment believed that there was a basic explanation for the rational order of the universe—and the discoveries of Isaac Newton seemed (at that time) to support this point of view. Composers of the era mirrored this view with their consistent use of a single musical concept called, variously, *motive, theme, subject, melody,* or *tune.* They wrote *monothematic* (one theme) compositions and depended upon their craftsmanship, intellectual agility, and musical sensitivity to keep their one-theme compositions from becoming exercises in monotony. Not all Baroque composers succeeded and not even the best composers consistently won this game of intellectual musicianship.

The musical rules for writing monothematic dance suites, fugues, inventions, preludes, passacaglias, and so forth were well established by the eighteenth century; even children could follow the rules for writing a fugue with all of the clever devices for making something interesting out of a single musical idea—but the result was frequently dull, duller, or dullest. Those who emerged victorious in the contest were great craftsmen such as J. S. Bach, who added the vital spark of creative genius: men who could take a single theme and spin a web of glorious sound. Bach brought fugue writing to its highest point of artist perfection; his *Art of Fugue,* written for a keyboard instrument, is considered the epitome of the art and the craft.

The prime instrument for the performance of fugues and other monothematic styles was the pipe organ. Baroque organs were the only solo instruments capable of filling Baroque churches and concert halls with a variety and volume of sound unequaled by any other instrument. The clarity and grandeur of these magnificent instruments has never been surpassed. The proof of this statement can still be heard throughout Europe; many of the original instruments have never ceased pouring forth the unique color and brilliance of the Baroque (fig. 23.1).

Two of the most challenging of all Baroque musical forms were the fugue and the passacaglia. The Baroque period became a veritable wasteland of bad fugues but, as usual, the good ones survived. The passacaglia (even an unsuccessful one) was a comparative rarity because only a minority of brave souls tackled its formidable musical-intellectual challenge (an example of a supremely successful passacaglia follows the fugue outlined below).

A fugue has been called the strictest free form in music *and* the freest strict form in music. Both statements happen to be true, because the composer is limited to a theme which must occur throughout the composition in essentially its original form. However, there is no prescribed length for the composition nor

---

1. Please consult the Appendix, "Music Listening and Notation," for the rules on reading music.

any standard methods of achieving variety amidst the almost constant restatement of the theme in one voice or another. Writing a fugue is a thoroughly rational procedure that tests the composer's craft: making musical sense out of what is essentially a mathematical exercise. And now to the rules of the game.

A *fugue* is an exercise in ingenuity. The composer uses a single theme (called *subject*) which is played (or sung) several times by each voice throughout a composition, for example, four voices in a four-part fugue. Fugues have staggered entries (begin with one voice, add a second voice, third voice, etc.) exactly like the imitative entries of Renaissance choral music. In fugue, however, there is only the single subject, with variety provided in part by *episodes,* or sections in which none of the voices have the subject.

After the first voice has sounded the subject, a second voice answers (starts the subject) while the first voice moves into a *counter subject,* which is a secondary theme used against (counter to) the subject. There may be two or even three counter subjects, and they may be used every time the subject appears. A typical opening fugal pattern would look like this:

1. Subject _____ Counter Subject 1

        2. Subject _____

(sometimes called Answer)

Following is an organ fugue by J. S. Bach. The long subject is given in its entirety, for it is typical of Bach's strong, rhythmical themes. The fugue is referred to as "Little" because Bach wrote another, more elaborate fugue in the same key of g minor, referred to as "Great."

Figure 23.1 Baroque pipe organ, dating from the fifteenth century with eighteenth-century casework, Grote Kerk, Haarlem, Holland. Organ designers were as concerned with the exterior design of the case as with the tone quality of the pipes.

Organ Fugue in g Minor ("Little")

J. S. Bach
Time: 4:00

Subject

Passacaglia A *passacaglia,* like the fugue, is a polyphonic form using a single basic theme. The resemblance ends there, however, because the passacaglia theme is played over and over in the same key, usually in the lowest voice, while the composer devises *variations* of rhythm, melody, and (sometimes) harmony in the upper voices. This was a challenging form for gifted composers because of the problems posed by what could be the monotonous repetition of a single theme.

Based as it is on an old dance form, the Baroque passacaglia is moderately slow in tempo and is in triple meter. The theme usually begins on the third beat of the measure, with a *pickup.* The form is sometimes described as *variations on a ground* (ground = bass).

The following passacaglia uses an eight-measure theme, plus twenty variations of eight measures each. In other words, there is a new variation every twenty-four beats. Although never stopping its forward motion the piece is divided into four distinct sections:

   I. Variations 1–8: gradual buildup in texture and volume

II. Variations 9–13: reduction to somewhat lighter texture followed by a gradual increase in volume and texture
III. Variations 14–15: sharp reduction to very light texture
IV. Variations 16–20: strong buildup to thick texture and forceful climax in final variation

The passacaglia moves directly into a fugue based on the first portion of the theme.

Passacaglia in c Minor

J. S. Bach
Time: 7:20

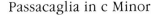

Instrumental

Trio Sonata

Baroque music was particularly notable for the widespread development of private music-making by zealous performers who played or sang for the sheer joy of making their own music. Not all of them were as skilled as professionals, but self-expression was more important than technical proficiency. These multitudes of musicians whose personal pleasure was more than sufficient payment for performance were *amateurs:* true lovers of music in the best meaning of the term.

Musical instruments became necessary functional furniture for a burgeoning middle class that was becoming ever more affluent. Baroque music was, in many respects, ready-made for amateur performances (or vice versa?), because composers never indicated the exact speed or tempo of their compositions nor did they do more than provide occasional directions regarding dynamics (relative loudness or softness). These procedures gave amateurs considerable margin for error. Moreover, specific directions as to which instruments were to be used were frequently left to the discretion (and resources) of the performers.

The ubiquitous trio sonata (see detailed description below) provided ideal material for amateurs because it was written in the conventional form of two melodic lines plus generalized directions for keyboard accompaniment. The two melodies could be performed by any two available instruments and the accompaniment by any keyboard instrument (clavichord, harpsichord, or pipe organ). The pivotal figure in trio sonatas (and large compositions) was the keyboard performer; it was assumed that he or she was the most competent musician, which was usually the case. He provided the foundation for the *continuation* of the piece, which led to the adoption of the Italian word *continuo* to describe the function of the keyboard musician. It was up to him to fill in the harmony and to cover up the blank spots whenever the possibly less-expert musicians played wrong notes, lost their place, or otherwise strayed from grace.

Baroque chamber music (but also including operatic arias) was highly improvisational inasmuch as performers were expected to add their personal touches to a given melodic line. Compositions were "personalized" in terms of available instruments, the expertise and imagination of performers, and, most importantly, the musical challenge presented by the composer. Not until jazz appeared on the scene during the latter part of the nineteenth century did performers again have the individual freedom that was accorded amateur and professional musicians of the Baroque period.

The typical trio sonata was performed by four instruments: two violins, harpsichord, and cello. There were, however, three lines of music: one for each violin and a bass line for cello and harpsichord which included a musical shorthand (called *figured bass*) for the chords to be played on the harpsichord. The harpsichordist was free to fill in the harmonies as necessary since the function was to improvise a suitable accompaniment.

Trio sonatas usually had a four-movement sequence of slow–fast–slow–fast. By the early part of the seventeenth century the familiar Italian words used to indicate approximate tempos were in common use, namely, *allegro, adagio, andante, presto,* and the like. The two violins would be used in imitation throughout each movement. In slow movements the second violin would follow closely after the first violin. In fast movements, however, the second entrance would be delayed until the first violin had played a complete theme.

The following trio sonata is entitled *Sonata da chiesa,* which is a generic term for a church sonata of a more profound nature than a *sonata da camera* (chamber sonata), such as a dance suite.

Sonata da chiesa in e Minor, opus 3, no. 7[2]

Arcangelo Corelli (1653–1713)
Total Time: 6:20

I (First Movement)

Theme a
Grave (very slow)

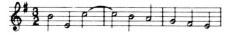

II

Theme a
Allegro (fast)

III

Theme a
Adagio (slow)

IV

Theme a
Allegro

                   repeated
many
times

Concerto

The classic Baroque concerto was the *concerto grosso* in which a small group of soloists *(concertino)* performed in conjunction with a full orchestra *(tutti* or *concerto grosso).* Bach, Handel, and Vivaldi did write *solo concertos* for single instruments but Baroque composers preferred the sonority of the concertino as it blended and contrasted with the full orchestra.[3] Baroque concerto grossos usually have the following characteristics:

Three movements: fast–slow–fast
Tuttis (Italian, *all*): soloist(s) and orchestra play
    together
Solo passages with orchestral accompaniment
Orchestral interludes
Echo effects: *forte* (loud) passages followed
    immediately by *piano* (soft) passages

One of the inimitable sounds of the period was that of the Baroque trumpet. Formerly limited to use in warfare and at royal courts, the trumpet became a favorite instrument because of its bright tone quality and its rich, full sound.

The following concerto for two trumpets and orchestra exploits many of the capabilities of high-pitched Baroque trumpets. The contrasts between light and dark are highlighted by the contrasts between the glittering tones of the trumpets and the sonorous sounds of the strings.

Concerto in C Major for Two Trumpets and Orchestra

Antonio Vivaldi (1685–1743)
Total Time: 8:10

I

The first movement has a main section that is played three times and is connected by variations of three melodic ideas.

Allegro

Theme a

II

The slow movement (*largo*) is only six measures in length and amounts to a soft orchestral interlude between fast movements.

III

There are three main themes, usually started by Trumpet I and imitated by Trumpet II.

Allegre moderato (moderately fast)

Theme a

f (forte)

Theme b

Theme c

Vocal-Instrumental

Chorale

When Martin Luther failed to convince Rome that the Church was long overdue for internal reform he was, in effect, forced into an external reformation. Among his basic ideas was his concern for congregational

---

2. "Opus 3" means this is the third large collection of trio sonatas by the composer (*opus* = work). That this is the seventh trio sonata in the collection is indicated by "no. 7."

3. A composition for solo instrument and keyboard accompaniment is a *sonata.*

participation in the service of worship. Congregational singing was of special importance to Luther because it tended to bind the congregation and the clergy together in a common endeavor. Also, music had, in Luther's opinion, a spiritual, transcendental quality that enriched and elevated the worship service. Unlike John Calvin, Luther, once a priest of the Church of Rome, culled the rich musical heritage of the Church, selecting and adapting plainsong to the needs and capabilities of Protestant congregations. For the first time in many centuries common people once again took an active part in worship as they raised their voices in song.

By definition, a *chorale* is a hymn tune of the German Protestant church. The tempo is usually slow and the musical form is A–A–B (bar form). Bar form has a repeated phrase of A followed by a new phrase identified as B. The following chorale is derived from the Easter sequence *Victimae paschali laudes.*

Chorale: *Christ lag in Todesbanden*
(Christ Lay in Death's Dark Prison)

Text by Martin Luther
(total of seven verses)

Harmonized by J. S. Bach
Time: 1:35

The typical Lutheran service of the eighteenth century began at 7:00 A.M. and concluded at noon. In the larger churches professional musicians (such as Bach) were expected to teach school during the week, maintain the organ, train a volunteer choir, compose special instrumental and vocal music for each Sunday of the year, and play the organ and direct the choir during the Sunday service. Each Sunday occupied a special place in the liturgical year, with special emphasis upon Christmas, the Epiphany, Easter, and Pentecost. The music for each Sunday of the liturgical calendar had to correspond with the special meaning of that Sunday from opening chorale prelude through the hymns, the cantata, and concluding postlude.

Chorale Prelude

An organ composition consisting of variations on a chorale melody is called a *chorale prelude.* The variations are to be played *before* the congregation sings the chorale, hence the term *prelude.* The intention of the organist is to set the general mood of the chorale so the congregation can sing it with more understanding.

The following chorale prelude is based on the melody *Christ lag in Todesbanden.* The tempo is now slower because Bach has added a descending, undulating accompaniment pattern. This constant downward movement is a bit of characteristic tone painting and represents the body of Christ buried in the tomb.

Chorale Prelude: *Christ lag in Todesbanden*

J. S. Bach
Time: 1:35

Cantata

A *cantata* (Italian, *cantare*,[4] to sing) is a set of movements for soloist(s), chorus (usually), and instrumental accompaniment based on a continuous narrative text. The text may be either secular or sacred, but the latter form is more familiar, primarily due to the large output of sacred cantatas by Johann Sebastian Bach.[5]

The following cantata is based entirely on the chorale illustrated in the two versions outlined above. The seven verses by Martin Luther are separated into seven different movements preceded by a brief instrumental introduction. Because the melody is present in some form in each verse the piece is called a *chorale cantata*.

Cantata no. 4: *Christ lag in Todesbanden*

J. S. Bach
Time: 22:10 (complete)

Sinfonia (orchestra prelude)[6]

Verse I—four-part chorus (SATB) and orchestra
Chorale melody (A–A–B): sung by sopranos in *augmentation* (each note twice as long as in original melody)

Text:
Christ lay by death enshrouded, *from* mortal sin to save us.
He is again arisen, *eternal* life He gave us.
So now let us be joyful, and *magnify* Him thankfully
And *singing Hallelujah, Hallelujah!*

The singing of a new line of text is indicated with the italicized words above.

Verse II—soprano, alto, and orchestra
Chorale melody divided between two voices
Striding bass figure used throughout:

Text:
O Death, none could lay thee low, no child of man subdue thee.
Our sin brought all this to pass, for there is no health in us.
Therefore soon came Death, Ah soon, and threw over us his net,
To hold us captive fast imprisoned, Hallelujah!

Verse III—Tenors and orchestra
Chorale melody with embellishments for the Hallelujah's
Orchestral figure used throughout:

Text:
Jesus Christ, our God's own son, for us to earth descended.

And all our sin has He atoned, and so Death's rule has ended.
All Death's power here below is now a vain, an empty show;
His sting is lost forever, Hallelujah!

Verse IV—four-part chorus and orchestra
Chorale melody sung by altos; other parts based on the melody and used in imitation

Text:
It was a wonderful array, with Life and Death embattled,
For Life is victor over Death, Death is swallowed up in victory.
So the saying comes to pass, Death swallowed up in victory.
O Grave, where is thy victory? Hallelujah.

Verse V—basses and orchestra
Chorale melody in triple meter with embellishments, especially with the concluding Hallelujah's; chorale melody also in orchestra

Text:
For us the Easter lamb was slain, God's promised boon bestowing.
High hung He there upon the Cross, with Love supernal glowing.
His Blood sprinkled on our door, with Faith bade Death to pass o'er.
The Slayer can no more harm us. Hallelujah!

Verse VI—sopranos, tenors, and orchestra
Chorale melody: both voices in imitation
Jumping bass figure throughout:

Text:
So let us keep this Holy Feast, with glad and gay rejoicing
For us the Sun is shining bright, our Lord Himself is risen.
Lighted by His glowing Grace, our radiant Hearts are glorified.
The Night of Sin is now over. Hallelujah!

Verse VII—four-part chorus and orchestra
Exactly the same form as the original chorale given on page 193

---

4. As compared with *sonata* (Italian, *sonare,* to sound). A "sounding piece" is one played by instruments.

5. Bach, however, also wrote a cantata extolling the virtues of a new beverage introduced in Europe: "The Coffee Cantata."

6. Orchestra composed of two flutes, three oboes, four trumpets, two timpani, violins I and II, violas, continuo (harpsichord or organ and cello).

Opera

Opera (Italian, from Latin *opera,* work) is generally considered to be the most "Baroque" of all of the artistic media of the age. Opera began as a "reform" movement in the late sixteenth century as an attempt to return to what was mistakenly thought to be the proper combination of words and music used by the ancient Greeks. Text was all-important, vocal lines were sparse, and accompaniment minimal. However, within a remarkably short period of time opera developed into a full-blown music drama with elaborate sets, costumes, and choruses. Despite various regional differences in style between Florence, Rome, Venice, Vienna, Paris, and London, opera became the most spectacular and popular art form of the period.

"Art form" may not be the proper term for some purists, because opera was a collage of the arts and crafts of music, poetry, acting, dance, set design, costuming, lighting, and so forth. Elaborate opera houses were built all over Europe for an art form which, in a manner of speaking, put the vitality of an era on stage for all to see and hear.[7]

Italian operas became the favorite artistic import for most of the nations of western Europe. French nationalism, however, strongly resisted the dominance of Italian music. Critics lambasted Italian operas as being too long, monotonous, too arty, archaic in language, and with flamboyant singing that obscured the sound and the sense of the words, thus leaving no appeal to the logical French mind. Additionally, the male sopranos and altos—the *castrati*—were said to horrify the women and to cause the men to snicker.

But the most important reasons why the French resisted Italian opera were probably because of drama and the dance. As drama, Italian opera was not in the same league with the theatre of Corneille, Racine, and Molière. Dance—French ballet—was central to the French musical stage but only minimal in Italian opera.

The struggle between French and Italian music finally became an actual confrontation when the noted Italian opera composer, Cavalli, was commissioned to write a festive opera for the wedding of Louis XIV. It was at this point that the director of the king's music, Jean Baptiste Lully (1632–1687)—born Gianbattista Lulli in Florence—turned the occasion to his advantage. The opera was indeed performed in 1662 for the king's wedding and it was monumental, lasting some six hours. However, each act concluded with one of Lully's large-scale ballets. The French reaction to this spectacle was interesting: the entire production was seen, not as a music drama with interpolated dances, but as a gigantic ballet with operatic interludes. Cavalli returned to Italy, vowing never to write another opera while Lully continued his intrigues becoming, in time, as absolute a sovereign in music as Louis XIV was in affairs of state. Capping a highly successful career, Lully died with one of the greatest fortunes ever amassed by a musician.

Italian opera did prevail in England where all attempts at establishing English opera were ultimately futile. The German-born George Frederick Handel (1685–1759) dominated the London theatrical scene with forty operas in thirty years, all Italian. Despite the consistently high quality of his music, Handel's operas were, in the long run, financial failures. London nobility was too weak to support opera and the court was not interested. The middle class was definitely not interested in musical entertainment designed for the nobility and sung in a foreign language.

The enormous success of *The Beggar's Opera* (1728) by John Gay and Johann Pepusch served to highlight the precarious state of opera in London. Called a "Newgate Pastoral" by Jonathan Swift, this ballad opera combined political satire with parodies of Italian opera. A twentieth-century version of this perennial musical play by Bertolt Brecht and Kurt Weill is entitled *Threepenny Opera,* "because beggars can pay only three-pence admission."

In the latter part of his career Handel turned from composing operas for the nobility to writing oratorios for the middle class. He had written Anglican church music and oratorios since he first settled in London, but he did not concentrate on oratorios until after his operatic period. His most celebrated work, the *Messiah* (1741), receives many performances today, while his other oratorios and his operas are less in demand.

Rococo (1725–1775)

The last stage of the Baroque period is characterized by an even more ornate style called *Rococo* (from the French, *rocaille,* rock, and *coquilles,* shells). The Baroque principles of design were applied to surfaces rather than to outlines. The grandeur of the Baroque was scaled down to an emphasis on interior design and decorative scroll and shell work, resulting in a sort of domesticated, sometimes decadent, Baroque.

In music, *rococo* is the "gallant style," a highly refined art of elegant pleasantness suitable for intimate social gatherings in fashionable salons. Among the chief exponents were François Couperin and Domenico Scarlatti with Rococo styles comparable to the painting of Watteau, Boucher, and Fragonard, the sculpture of Falconet, and the designs of Cuvilliés.

The Amalienburg lodge (fig. 23.2), located on the grounds of Nymphenburg Palace near Munich, represents the epitome of Rococo refinement, grace, and elegance: opulence on a small scale. The central mirror in figure 23.2 reflects an outside window, indicating a room large enough for masked balls but small enough to be intimate. Approximately thirty couples could dance to a small chamber orchestra or listen to a harpsichord recital.

---

7. The books listed in the Bibliography contain extensive information on Baroque operas, composers, and opera houses.

Figure 23.2 François Cuvilliés, Hall of Mirrors, The Amalienburg, Nymphenburg Palace, Munich, 1734–1739.

The room is a compendium of Rococo characteristics: white plaster ceiling with lacy silver tendrils, lavish use of mirrors, all with curvilinear frames, light blue walls with silver insets and shell-like decoration, parquet floor, elaborately carved furniture in silver with cabriole legs and, highlighting the room, an array of exquisite chandeliers.

The following harpsichord composition is as representative of Rococo music as the Hall of Mirrors is of Rococo decoration. The texture of the piece is light and airy, and the melodic line is replete with curving embellishments.

Piece for Clavecin: *La Galante*

François Couperin (1668–1733)
Time: 2:10

The principal theme is used throughout in imitation. The form or structure of the piece is still two-part, called binary and described as A–B. Even with the Rococo title the piece is in fact a *gigue*.

Theme

Key: E Major

Classicism in Music (1760–1827)

The Classical period in music dates from about 1760, the beginning of Haydn's mature style, to about 1827, the year of Beethoven's death. Haydn, Mozart, and Beethoven were musical giants in what has been called the Golden Age of Music, an era of extraordinary musical achievements. Other eras have perhaps been as musically productive but none have become so mutually identifiable as the Classical period, the Golden Age, and the musical output of Haydn, Mozart, and Beethoven.

The basic homophonic style of Classicism has many antecedents in several earlier periods of music. It is therefore appropriate to briefly review these earlier periods.

Music in the Renaissance was primarily polyphonic and written in the old liturgical modes. Some Renaissance music, English madrigals in particular, was quite homophonic and was, moreover, tonal; that is, it was written in either a major or a minor key rather than in a liturgical mode. The music of Gabrielli in Venice was also strongly homophonic with a preference for sonorous harmonies rather than the multiple melody lines used by Renaissance composers like Josquin, Lassus, and Palestrina.

At the beginning of the seventeenth century there was a relatively brief period of strongly homophonic music as composers attempted to recreate what they thought was the text-oriented musical style of the ancient Greeks. These experiments in words and music led to the development of the new style of music called opera. Opera, the epitome of the new Baroque style, quickly became elaborate and ornate and combined homophonic and polyphonic music. The vocal-instrumental music of the age developed a new and complex style of polyphony, culminating in the music of Handel and Bach.

The Rococo style used Baroque ornamentation, but the style was much more homophonic, less profound, and more stylishly elegant. Some of the characteristics of the Rococo, notably less complex homophonic techniques, were incorporated into a new style called *Classicism, Neoclassicism,* or *Viennese Classicism* (Haydn, Mozart, Beethoven). Classicism is the preferred term for music of the period while Neoclassicism is generally applied to the sister arts.

At no time are the stylistic periods of the arts precisely synchronized. Careful study of the comparative outline given (table 23.1) will indicate that the prevailing world views of the periods since the Renaissance are reflected in the arts at different points in time. Any number of inferences can be drawn regarding the influence of an era on the arts and the arts on each other. It is important to remember, however, that the artistic production of specific individuals is of paramount concern. The uniqueness of the works of art reflects the uniqueness of the individual, the artist who creates these works.

The Classical period of music might also be called the Advanced Age of the Amateur Musician. Baroque music, with its figured bass accompaniments and demands for improvisation, was partially the province of the professional but with real possibilities for gifted amateurs. On the other hand, the latter part of the eighteenth century featured modern notation, with every note written down plus indications for interpretation (tempo, dynamics, etc.), thus providing a better opportunity for music-making by middle- and upper-class amateurs.

Table 23.1 Comparison of Stylistic Periods of the Arts

	Approximate Dates	Important Individuals
Period: Baroque	1600–1700	Descartes, Galileo, Kepler, Bacon, Spinoza
Artistic Style: Baroque		
Architecture	1575–1740	Bernini, Wren, Mansart, Perrault, LeVau
Music	1600–1750	Corelli, Lully, Vivaldi, Handel, Bach, Purcell
Painting	1600–1720	Rubens, Rembrandt, Steen, Hals, Vermeer, Van Dyck, Velasquez
Sculpture	1600–1720	Bernini
Period: The Enlightenment	1687–1789	Newton, Voltaire, Diderot, Locke, Hume, Kant, Rousseau, Frederick II, Jefferson, Franklin
Artistic Style: Rococo		
Architecture	1715–1760	Erlach, Hildebrandt, Asam, Cuvilliés, Fischer
Music	1725–1775	Couperin, some of Haydn and Mozart
Painting	1720–1789	Watteau, Chardin, Boucher, Fragonard
Sculpture	1770–1825	Clodion, Falconet
Artistic Style: Neoclassic		
Architecture	1750–1830	Chalgrin, Vignon, Fontaine
Music (Classicism)	1760–1827	Haydn, Mozart, Beethoven, Gluck
Painting	1780–1850	David, Ingres
Sculpture	1800–1840	Canova, Thorwalden, Houdon

The vastly increased demand for music for all occasions resulted in a flood of new compositions (mostly instrumental). There were serenades for outdoor parties, chamber music for indoor gatherings, symphonies for the newly established symphony orchestras, and operas for the increasing number of private and public opera houses. The newly invented piano (ca. 1710 by Cristofori), with its ability to play soft and loud (full name, *pianoforte*) on the single keyboard, rapidly replaced harpsichord and clavichord as the standard home instrument for amateur performance. Amateur chamber music societies were organized for the presentation of programs ranging from sonatas to duets, trios, and so forth, for the various instruments, including the quartets for a homogeneous group of string instruments called, naturally enough, string quartets.

All of this musical activity was of little benefit to those who tried to earn a living with their music. Eighteenth-century musicians were, on the whole, accorded a rather lowly position on the social scale. Typically, composers like Franz Joseph Haydn worked for a noble family like the Esterhazy, wore servant's livery, and sat "below the salt" at the dinner table. Not until the latter part of his life did Haydn achieve any financial independence, and he had to go to the London concert scene to do it. Ironically, the descendants of the once powerful Esterhazy family are notable today only to the extent that some of Haydn's unpublished music may still be in their possession.

Haydn

The professional life of Franz Joseph Haydn (1732–1809) was quite typical of the vicissitudes of a musical career, and yet, Haydn fared a bit better than many of his contemporaries. In a short sketch that he contributed to a 1776 yearbook, Haydn wrote that he sang at court in Vienna and in St. Stephen's Cathedral until his services were terminated at the latter. His services were eminently satisfactory but his voice changed and he was summarily dismissed.

> When my voice finally changed I barely managed to stay alive by giving music lessons to children for about eight years. In this way many talented people are ruined: they have to earn a miserable living and have no time to study.

There were numerous musical opportunities for a musician in Vienna, and most of them paid very little. Musicians were forced to hold down a number of positions in order to survive. Haydn had as many as three jobs on a Sunday morning: playing violin at one church, the organ at another, and singing in the choir at a third. When he finally achieved full employment with the Esterhazy family, he was quite willing, at that time, to relinquish a certain amount of personal freedom.

Haydn, as the first of the composers in the Classical style, led the way in establishing some basic instrumental ensembles like the symphony orchestra and the string quartet. Large enough to produce a rich, full tone but small enough to be intimate and to leave room for personal expression, the string quartet was the preferred classical musical group. Consisting of first and second violin, viola, and cello, corresponding to the SATB division of voices in choral music, the three members of the violin family can achieve a fine balance of unified tone.

The following string quartet by Haydn was composed early in his career and has both Rococo and Classical characteristics. The forms are classical and the melodies quite Rococo in their lightness, clarity, and elegance. The first, second, and last movements use *sonata form,* an important invention of the period. Classical composers had tired of the late Baroque proclivity for ever more elaborate and sometimes ponderous polyphony. A simpler homophonic style began to emerge and to gradually replace the polyphonic manipulation of a single musical theme. By abandoning the polyphonic, vocal-instrumental style, composers were faced with a dilemma: how to develop a coherent style of purely instrumental music. A certain unity was inherent in vocal music because of the text. Without a text, composers were faced with the possibility of a chaotic mass of instrumental sounds.

Sonata form[8] was an eighteenth-century solution to the problem of the design of instrumental music. In a very real sense, the invention of sonata form reflected the Enlightenment ideals of a structure that was lucid, logical, and symmetrical.

The technical term *sonata form* is a label for a procedure that uses a *dual subject* rather than the single subject of the Baroque style. The first of these two subjects is usually vigorous and dynamic while the second is generally quieter and more lyrical. The two subjects should be, musically speaking, logical parts of the whole; the second subject should somehow complement and balance the first.

In the first movement of the Haydn quartet given below *theme a* is straightforward and vigorous; *theme b* is smoother and more lyrical and with the stipulation that it be played "sweetly." The two subjects (themes) of sonata form are connected by a *bridge,* a transitional passage, which leads smoothly from *theme a* to *theme b.* Following *theme b* there is a closing section called a *codetta.* The complete unit of two themes with connecting transition and closing section contains all the thematic material which has been presented or to which the ear has been *exposed.* This unit is called an *exposition* and can be outlined as indicated below. During the Classical period expositions were normally repeated, as indicated by the sets of double dots.

Exposition

‖: *Theme a*   Bridge   *Theme b*   Codetta :‖

After the basic material has been presented in the exposition, the composer then proceeds to manipulate and exploit selected thematic material in the *development* section. Any and all material may be subjected to a variety of treatment.

Near the end of the development section, the composer usually introduces the *return,* a transitional section which prepares the way for a *recapitulation* of the material from the exposition. The recapitulation does repeat, more or less, the material from the exposition, but there are subtle variances that help avoid monotony.

After the codetta of the recapitulation, the composer may add a final *coda* if it is felt that something is needed to bring the movement to a satisfactory conclusion.

A complete sonata form can be outlined as follows:

String Quartet in F Major, opus 3, no. 5

Franz Joseph Haydn (1732–1809)
Total Time: 13:20

This is the famous Serenade movement. The first violin plays *con sordino* (with mute) accompanied by the other instruments playing *pizzicato* (plucking the strings). The effect is like an outdoor serenade for violin and guitar.

---

8. Sonata form was not limited to sonatas which are compositions for solo instruments plus accompaniment. The form was also used for trios, quartets, concertos, and symphonies.

III

Theme a

F:

Theme a (Trio)

B♭:

IV

Theme a

p I

Theme b

p V

Mozart

The nature of musical genius has been a subject of considerable interest to twentieth-century psychologists. The exact nature of the qualities that can be labeled "genius" remains tantalizingly elusive. Thus, the accomplishments of Wolfgang Amadeus Mozart (1756–1791), possibly the greatest musical genius who ever lived, are both awesome and inexplicable.

Mozart devoted virtually his entire life to the composition and performance of music. Like Haydn, he had to endure the slights of a society as yet unready and unwilling to recognize, let alone support, his incredible gifts. Unlike Haydn, he never found a noble patron. His brief, poverty-stricken life and eventual burial in an unmarked grave testify eloquently to the status of a musician in Vienna during the Golden Age of Music.

There are many accounts of Mozart's precocity but none more typical of his manner of composition—and life-style—than the occasion of the premiere of his opera, *Don Giovanni.* The opera was complete except for the overture which was, according to the composer, "finished." On the day of the premiere, Mozart was busily engaged in shooting billiards, one of his favorite occupations. In reply to urgent questioning, he reiterated that he had completed the overture. Upon being pressed to produce a musical score he finally admitted that the piece was indeed completed—in his head—and that he had not gotten around to writing it down. Many cups of coffee later, the complete parts, still dripping with wet ink, were rushed to the opera house where the orchestra, with no time left for rehearsing, sight-read the music. Characteristically, the thousands of musical notes which Mozart had mentally arranged added up to a masterpiece in the field of operatic overtures.

The following symphony by Mozart was probably not written down as hastily as the operatic overture but, stylistically, the similarities are many for only several years separated the two works. The symphony is supremely concise and lucid, stylish and elegant, and powerful but always lyrical. In Mozart's hands, the symphony orchestra sings like one instrument.

Symphony no. 40 in g Minor (1788)

Wolfgang Amadeus Mozart (1756–1791)
Total time: 27:20
(complete symphony)

I

Theme a

g: *p*

Theme b

B♭:   *p*

II

Theme a

E♭:   *p*

Theme b

p

Ternary Form (A-B-A or Minuet-Trio-Minuet)

Minuet
Theme a (in minor)

Trio
Theme a (in major)

Theme a

Theme b

The modern symphony orchestra was developed during the Classical period. Standard components were a nucleus of a full body of strings plus woodwinds and sometimes trumpets and timpani. Mozart's Symphony no. 40 used the following instrumentation: flute, two oboes, two clarinets, two bassoons, two French horns, violin I, violin II, viola, cello, bass.

A *symphony* may be defined as a sonata for orchestra, just as the quartet by Haydn was a sonata for string quartet. The first, second, and last movements are in sonata form. The form of the third movement can be described as Minuet–Trio–Minuet. As with the Haydn quartet, only the basic themes are given.

A summary of Mozart's musical compositions is given below. The list indicates at least three things: (1) the breadth of Mozart's musical interests; (2) the kinds of music required of Mozart (most of his work was commissioned); and (3) the incredible productivity of a sometimes destitute young musician who died in his thirty-sixth year.

Vocal

Secular

    57 Arias
    24 Operas and other stage works
    19 Duets and trios
    37 Songs
    Many cadenzas

Sacred

     8 Cantatas
    37 Kyries and other works
     7 Litanies and vespers
    19 Masses
    17 Church sonatas (organ)
     4 Oratorio arrangements

Instrumental

Piano

    10 Piano duets
    35 Minuets and variations
    12 Trios, quartets, quintets
    33 Sonatas and fantasias
    30 Piano concertos
     9 Miscellaneous compositions
    Many cadenzas

Violin, Strings, Orchestra

    40 Violin sonatas
    11 Violin concertos
     5 String duets and trios
    25 String quartets
     6 String quintets
    13 Miscellaneous chamber works
    13 Miscellaneous concertos
    52 Symphonies
   101 Serenades, divertimenti, cassations, etc.

Beethoven

Ludwig van Beethoven (1770–1827), unlike Haydn and Mozart, forged a place for himself as an economically independent musician. He was not above selling the same composition to different publishers and, in fact, did so quite often. He reasoned that the publishers had cheated composers long enough; he was merely collecting retribution for a long chain of abuses.

Beethoven's finances were generally sound though somewhat chaotic. His health, on the other hand, was another matter. He began to notice a hearing loss at an early age, a loss that gradually evolved into total deafness. This deafness became, at times, almost more than a musician could bear.

The fact that some of Beethoven's greatest music was composed while he was completely deaf is a testament to his genius and to his unconquerable spirit. He himself conducted the premiere of his Ninth Symphony, that powerful and imposing work dedicated to the exalted ideal of the Brotherhood of Man. At the conclusion of the symphony he remained facing the orchestra, solitary in his silence, and thinking that the work had failed. Finally, someone turned him about to face the thunderous applause of an audience that was both inspired and deeply moved.

Beethoven's Third Symphony, the *Eroica,* was originally dedicated to Napoleon, whom Beethoven regarded as a true Faustian man (see chap. 24). There were many victims of Napoleon's march to power—"while man's desires and aspirations stir, he cannot choose but err"—but it appeared that he was using his energy to make the world a better place in which people could work out their freedom. However, Napoleon declared himself emperor, and Beethoven furiously erased his name from the dedicatory page of the *Eroica,* leaving the work implicitly dedicated to the heroic impulses of a Faustian man or, simply, to an unknown hero.

Beethoven poured the very essence of classical symphonic music into his Fifth Symphony, a work which has often been cited as the perfect symphony. Though sometimes threatening to break the bounds of classical form, Beethoven, in the Fifth, channeled his titanic energy into the driving rhythms of this mighty work. The Fifth Symphony is a summary of many aspects of Beethoven's genius: the terse, surging energy of the first movement, the moving and mellow lyricism of the second movement, the exuberant vitality of the scherzo, and the sheer drive of the finale.

The orchestra as Beethoven knew it was simply not large and expressive enough for this symphony. He enlarged his tonal palette by adding instruments at both ends of the spectrum and then adding trombones in the middle to obtain the full and rich sound that he had to have. Following is the instrumentation for the enlarged orchestra needed to perform Beethoven's Fifth Symphony: piccolo, two flutes, two oboes, two clarinets, two bassoons, contra-bassoon, two French horns, two trumpets, three trombones, two timpani, sixteen violin I, fourteen violin II, ten viola, eight cello, six bass. (The number of strings can vary; these are approximations.)

The first movement is in sonata form. The second movement is a theme and variations. The theme is stated and then followed by a series of increasingly elaborate variations. Rather than a minuet, Beethoven uses a scherzo for the third movement, which is faster and more dynamic. For the fourth movement Beethoven uses sonata form with a very long coda.

The Fifth Symphony achieves a maximum effect with the utmost economy of musical materials. Essentially, the entire symphony is built out of one musical interval and one rhythmic pattern:

Interval of 3rd plus pattern of

This *motive* is so brief that it is referred to as a *germ motive* from which the entire symphony is germinated.

Symphony no. 5 in c Minor, opus 67 (1808)

Ludwig van Beethoven (1770–1827)
Total Time: 30:45

I

II

Theme and variations: Theme, four variations, restatement of theme and coda

Scherzo: form is Scherzo-Trio-Scherzo (A-B-A)
Note: Scherzo is similar in form to the minuet but faster and more vigorous.

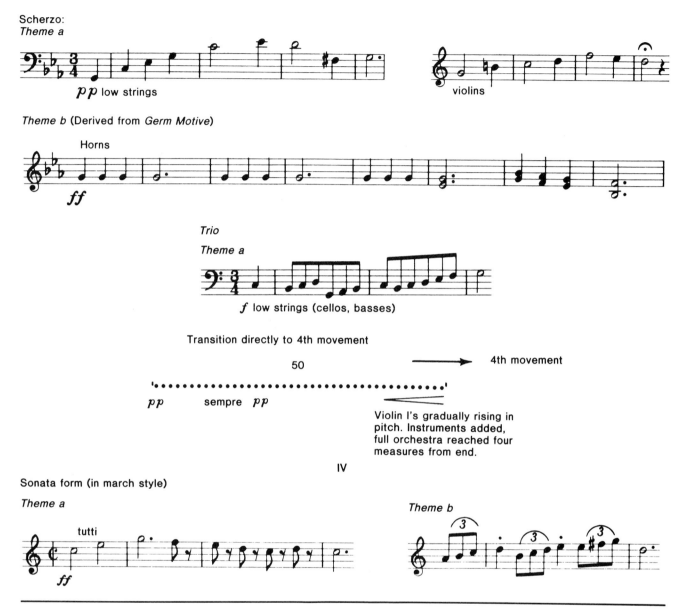

Scherzo:
Theme a

pp low strings

violins

Theme b (Derived from *Germ Motive*)

Horns

ff

Trio

Theme a

f low strings (cellos, basses)

Transition directly to 4th movement

50

4th movement

pp   sempre *pp*

Violin I's gradually rising in pitch. Instruments added, full orchestra reached four measures from end.

IV

Sonata form (in march style)

Theme a

tutti

ff

Theme b

The Fifth Symphony is a prime example of the Classical style: logical, direct, and to the point, objective, controlled, achieving maximum effect with a minimum of means (use of the germ motive). Beethoven is considered by some to be a pivotal figure in musical styles standing midway between classicism and the dawning Age of Romanticism; however, his heroic style and even his introspective later works all testify to his fundamental classical outlook, namely, his rational control of his own destiny. Beethoven's music served *him;* he was the master who, with disciplined creativity, molded (and sometimes hammered) his musical materials into the structured sounds of the Classical style.

Summary

From about 1600 to 1750, the Baroque style built a new kind of music on the classical foundations of the Renaissance. The flexible modal system of the past was narrowed down to a single tonal center, or *key,* with the modal possibilities reduced to two: major or minor. Compensating for the limiting of tonal materials to a single major or minor key were the new possibilities for building compositions in terms of contrasting keys and modulating from one key to another.

Baroque *dance suites,* based in a single key, combined stylized dance types of three or four national origins into a coherent sequence of contrasting movements (A–C–S–O–G) in binary form.

With the establishment of a tonal center, the *fugue* became one of the basic monothematic styles of the Baroque. Composers could manipulate both the fugal subject and various major and minor key relations. The *passacaglia,* on the other hand, remained in the same key throughout, with variations built out of varying textures and rhythmic patterns.

The ubiquitous *trio sonata* was perhaps most representative of Baroque music-making because of the emphasis on instrumental music with improvised accompaniment in the *continuo* part. *Concertos* were more formal because of the larger number of instrumentalists involved, but the continuo still played an important accompanying part for orchestra and soloist(s).

Following the Reformation, the German sacred songs called *chorales* assumed an important place in congregational singing and in organ literature in the form of *chorale preludes. Cantatas, oratorios,* and *operas* were the most important vocal forms of the Baroque although there was still a tradition of composing masses and motets.

The surface elements of the ornate Baroque style assumed a primary emphasis in the style called Rococo. The Rococo, or "gallant style" of music (1725–1775), with its light, airy texture and elegant ornamentation served as a bridge between the sumptuous Baroque and the gracefully refined style of the Classical period.

During the Classical period (1760–1827), instrumental musicians, whether professional or amateur, came into their own. The improvement in musical instruments and the great interest in amateur performance encouraged the composition of chamber music *(sonatas, string quartets,* etc.) and orchestral music ranging from *serenades* for soirees to *symphonies* for the growing number of concert halls. Monothematic polyphony was replaced by a dual-subject (bi-thematic) structure called *sonata form* in which composers could combine two contrasting subjects into an expressive and balanced whole.

The Classical period, coinciding with the height of the Age of Enlightenment, created chamber music and the symphony orchestra virtually as they are known today. Even more important, music progressed from a more or less private concern of the aristocracy or the church to a public art available to all.

Listening Outline (Fourth Stage)

Note: This outline lists a maximum of elements to listen for each time that the work is played. Hearing everything even with repeated auditions is not crucial but having an objective listening procedure is important, and that is the purpose of this guide.

I. Listening outline
   A. Medium
      1. Vocal (text: English, French, Italian, German, Latin, other)
      2. Instrumental
      3. Vocal and instrumental (text)
   B. Tempo—very slow, slow, moderate, fast, very fast
   C. Loudness—soft, medium loud, loud, combination
   D. Number of performers
      1. Solo
      2. Ensemble
         a) Small (2 to 5)
         b) Medium (6 to 20)
         c) Medium large (21 to 59)
         d) Large (60 to 100 or more)
   E. Rhythm
      1. Regular beat (or pulsation)
      2. Pulsation irregular or indistinct
   F. Meter
      1. Duple (2 beats per measure)
      2. Triple (3 beats per measure)
      3. Quadruple (4 beats per measure)
   G. Texture
      1. One melody, unaccompanied (monophonic)
      2. Melody with accompaniment (homophonic)
      3. Simultaneous melodies (polyphonic)
   H. Form
      1. AB (two-part) or variant
      2. ABA (three-part) or variant
      3. Sonata form
      4. Theme and variations
      5. Rondo
      6. Other
II. Conclusions
   A. Period
      1. Medieval (600–1420)
      2. Renaissance (1420–1600)
      3. Baroque (1600–1750)
      4. Rococo (1725–1775)
      5. Classical (1760–1827)
   B. General musical form

Vocal

Gregorian chant	Sequence-trope
Madrigal	Troubadour/
Mass	Trouvère tradition
Motet	Song
	Other

Vocal and Instrumental

Accompanied song	Motet
	Opera
Cantata	Oratorio
Chorale	Other
Mass	

Instrumental

Chorale prelude	String quartet (trio,
Concerto grosso	quintet)
Dance suite	Symphony
Sonata	Trio sonata
Concerto	Other

C. National origin—Austria, England, Flanders, France, Germany, Italy, Western Europe, other

N.B. See the Glossary for terms that may be unfamiliar.

Record List

Except for special records and standard anthologies, specific records are not listed.

1. Bach, J.S. French Suite no. 1. In *Six French Suites*. Valenti, harpsichord. 2-Westminster 9300/1.
2. Bach, J.S. Fugue in G Minor. Schweitzer. Angel COLC—89. *Or:* Recordings of Bach's organ works by Biggs, Weinrich, Richter, Walcha, Dupré.
3. Bach, J.S. Passacaglia in C Minor. In *Passacaglia and Fugue in C minor*. Biggs, organ. Columbia ML—5661; MS—6261.
4. Corelli, A. Sonata da Chiesa in E Minor. In *Masterpieces of Music before 1750* (referred to as *Masterpieces*), 3 volumes. Haydn Society 9038/9040.
5. Vivaldi, A. "Concerto in C Major for Two Trumpets and Orchestra."
6. Bach, J.S. Chorale: *Christ Lag in Todesbanden*. In *Masterpieces*.
7. Bach, J.S. Chorale Prelude: *Christ Lag in Todesbanden*. In *Masterpieces*.
8. Bach, J.S. Cantata: *Christ Lag in Todesbanden*. Shaw Chorale. Victor LM—2273; LSC—2273 (German).
9. Pepusch, Johann. *The Beggar's Opera*.
10. Weill, Kurt. *Threepenny Opera*.
11. Handel, George Frederick. *Messiah*.
12. Couperin, F. Piece for Clavecin: *La Galante*. In *Masterpieces*.
13. Scarlatti, D. Sonata for Harpsichord. Longo 104 in C Major.
14. Haydn, Franz Joseph. *String Quartet in F Major*. Allegri Quartet. Westminster 19111; 17111.
15. Mozart, Wolfgang Amadeus. *Symphony no. 40 in G Minor*. Karajan, Vienna Phil. Victor LM—2535; LSC—2535.
16. Beethoven, Ludwig van. *Symphony no. 5 in C Minor*. Ormandy, Philadelphia Orch. Columbia ML—5098.

Bibliography

Bukofzer, Manfred. *Music in the Baroque Era*. New York: W. W. Norton, 1947. Comprehensive and detailed.
Kirby, F.E. *Music in the Classical Period, An Anthology with Commentary*. New York: Macmillan, 1979. Excellent selection of music scores.
Palisca, Claude. *Baroque Music*. Englewood Cliffs, N.J.: Prentice-Hall, 1968. Fairly technical survey.
Pauly, Reinhard. *Music in the Classic Period*. Englewood Cliffs, N.J.: Prentice-Hall, 1965. Survey of the style with a minimum of technical obstacles.
Rosen, Charles. *The Classical Style: Haydn, Mozart, Beethoven*. New York: W. W. Norton, 1972. Winner of the 1972 National Book Award for Arts and Letters.

Unit 8

The Middle Modern World, 1789–1914

24 Revolution, Romanticism, Realism

Power and Politics

With the advantage of 20–20 hindsight we can see the rise of nationalism, colonialism, and imperialism to an inexorable climax in the Great War that was supposed to end all wars. Catchwords along the way were national honor, fame, and glory but the brutal realities were envy, greed, destruction, and death. Amidst the thunder of the Guns of August the Romantic Century was laid to rest on the static battlefields of Europe, along with half a generation of young men.

Revolution to Waterloo

By 1792 the French Revolution was faltering. There had been a noble "Declaration of the Rights of Man and the Citizen," feudalism had been abolished, the monastic orders suppressed and church properties confiscated, but the enemies of France were assaulting the borders and internal disorder was increasing. The execution of Robespierre in 1793 ended the Terror but it took the establishment of the Directory in 1795 to temporarily stabilize the state. Composed of men of conspicuous wealth, the Directory ruled from 1795 to 1799 with the assistance of the military, most notably the Corsican general Napoleon Buonaparte (1769–1821). Under the guise of saving the revolution Napoleon seized power in a coup d'état in 1799 and declared himself First Consul. Proclaiming himself emperor in 1804, Napoleon launched a course of conquest that engulfed much of Europe and part of Africa. Waterloo (June 18, 1815) was an anticlimax to the fall of a conqueror who lost his entire Grand Army of 500,000 men on the scorched steppes of Russia.

Napoleon saw himself as the enlightened, benevolent despot who had saved the revolution (fig. 24.1), but he had to maintain order with the army and, especially, his secret police. He did establish the Code of Napoleon, a model of modern civil laws that buried the inequities of the *ancien régime* and set the stage for the rise of the middle class. The Napoleonic legend of the military and political genius who fostered liber-

Figure 24.1 Jacques Louis David, *Napoleon in His Study*, 1812. Oil on canvas, 80½ × 49¼". Wearing the Legion of Honor, Napoleon is pictured by his court painter as a conscientious ruler who has stayed up until 4:12 A.M. working for his subjects. Samuel H. Kress Collection. National Gallery of Art, Washington, D.C.

alism and nationalism contains, therefore, elements of truth. The ideals of the French Revolution did, in time, inspire the spread of democracy throughout the Western world. The other side of the coin was dark and bloody; the Napoleonic wars caused enormous destruction of lives and property.

The French were fascinated by Napoleon as leader and legend but the rest of Europe viewed him much as did Lord Byron, who wrote his "Ode to Napoleon Buonaparte" upon learning of the Emperor's abdication and banishment to Elba in 1814. Following are the first and last stanzas of a vitriolic nineteen-stanza poem exulting in the downfall of a tyrant who could have been the equal, according to Byron, of an American general.

Literary Selection

ODE TO NAPOLEON BUONAPARTE
Lord Byron

'T is done—but yesterday a King!
    And arm'd with Kings to strive—
And now thou art a nameless thing:
    So abject—yet alive!
Is this the man of thousand thrones,
Who strew'd our earth with hostile bones,
    And can he thus survive?
Since he, miscall'd the Morning Star,
Nor man nor fiend hath fallen so far.

Where may the wearied eye repose,
    When gazing on the Great;
Where neither guilty glory glows,
    Nor despicable state?
Yes—one—the first—the last—the best—
The Cincinnatus of the West,
    Whom envy dared not hate,
Bequeath'd the name of Washington,
To make man blush there was but one!

                April 10, 1814

Napoleon's conquerors were deep in deliberations at the Congress of Vienna when he escaped from Elba and rallied his still loyal armies for a Hundred Days campaign that ended, once and for all, on the field of Waterloo. Final banishment to the remote island of St. Helena and a heavy guard assured the allies of a peace on their terms.

Called the "peace concert of Europe," the Congress of Vienna involved Austria, Prussia, Russia, and England, but its guiding spirit was Prince Clemens von Metternich (MEH–ter–NIKH; 1773–1859), the chief minister of Austria. A reactionary and arch defender of the old order, Metternich sought and achieved a balance of power that favored Austria and reinforced established monarchies at the expense of all liberal movements, marking the period of 1815–1848 as the Age of Metternich. Napoleon's foreign minister, Prince Charles Maurice de Talleyrand (1754–1838), betrayed Napoleon, won easier peace terms for his country, and effected the restoration of the Bourbon kings with Louis XVIII (1814–1824), the brother of Louis XVI.

The Revolutions of 1830 and 1848

The heavy-handed, reactionary rule of Charles X (1824–1830), who succeeded Louis XVIII, led to the July Revolution of 1830 in which the workers of Paris challenged the government. When the troops and police refused to fire on the rioters, the king quickly abdicated, delighting the liberals who, with visions of major social improvements, saw a possibility of relieving the misery of the workers who were oppressed by the monarchy and the Industrial Revolution. Upon invitation of the Chamber of Deputies, Louis Philippe (1830–1848) assumed rule of a "bourgeois monarchy," which catered to the wealthy middle class and ignored the industrial workers. The brief July Revolution sparked violence in Germany, Italy, Spain, Portugal, Poland, and Belgium, all of which was put down by force except in Belgium which, in 1831, won its independence from Holland.

A wave of revolutions swept Europe in 1848, the year in which Marx and Engels published *The Communist Manifesto*. The suppressed forces of liberalism erupted in France, Prussia, Austria, Hungary, Bohemia, Croatia, and the Italian possessions of the Hapsburgs. Repression was even more severe than in 1830 but, as Marx had written, "The specter of Communism" was haunting Europe.

The Industrial Revolution

Between 1750 and 1850 there were, in England, striking changes in the economic structure as the nation moved from an agrarian society to modern industrialism. The change had been astonishingly rapid because so many important factors already existed: capitalism, international trade, mercantilism, colonialism, the Protestant work ethic. England already had hand-operated domestic (cottage) industries; what was needed was power to drive the machinery and this became available when, in 1769, James Watt patented an improved version of the steam engine that Thomas Newcomen had invented in ca. 1700 to pump water out of mine shafts.[1]

Why was England the original home of the Industrial Revolution rather than prosperous Holland or rich and powerful France? American economic historian W. W. Rostow suggests that national pride and confidence were buoyed by a series of English military victories but, more importantly, that the mix of needed resources was best in England:

> Britain, with more basic industrial resources than the Netherlands; more nonconformists, and more ships than France; with its political, social, and religious revolution fought out by 1688—Britain alone was in a position to weave together cotton manufacture, coal and iron technology, the steam-engine and ample foreign trade to pull it off.[2]

With its head start England became the textile center of the world but, after 1850, Belgium, France, Germany, and the United States were also involved not only in industrialization but in dramatic changes in communications, agricultural chemistry, machinery, and transportation. Railroads and steamships helped turn northern Europe and North America into an energetic and highly competitive complex that, in effect, functioned like an economic community.

Development of the Western Nations

Only in France did the 1848 revolution succeed and then just briefly. The Second Republic lasted from 1848 to 1852, followed by the Second Empire of Napoleon III (1852–1870). Deliberately provoked by Bismarck, the Franco-Prussian War (1870–1871) toppled the inept emperor and humiliated the nation. The Third Republic of 1871 finally exorcised absolutism in France but the Dreyfus Affair (1894–1906) nearly ripped the nation asunder. Falsely accused of treason, Captain Alfred Dreyfus (dry–fus; 1859–1935) was cashiered from the army and given a life sentence on Devil's Island. Generally speaking, anti-Semites, royalists, militarists, and Catholics backed the army while republicans, socialists, intellectuals, and anticlericals supported Dreyfus. Émile Zola, for example, was jailed for his inflammatory newspaper article: "J'Accuse" (1898). It took a civil court to exonerate Dreyfus and reinstate him in the army as a major. Monarchists and Catholics were discredited, paving the way for the separation of Church and State.

Otto Fürst von Bismarck (1815–1898), the premier of Prussia (1862–1890), personally created the German Empire in 1871 when he had William I of Prussia proclaimed emperor (1871–1888). Consolidating his gains after the Danish War (1864), Austro-Prussian War (1866), and Franco-Prussian War (1870–1871), the "iron chancellor" made a unified Germany the new power in Europe. William II (1888–1918), the grandson of Queen Victoria, had his own ideas about royal power and dismissed his chancellor in 1890. Bismarck criticized the Kaiser unceasingly as the emperor armed his nation for the conflict that erupted in 1914. William II abdicated in 1918.

Under the reign of Francis II (1792–1835) Austria was defeated on four different occasions by the French. Ferdinand (1835–1848) had frequent fits of insanity, which left Metternich free to govern in his name. The 1848 revolution drove Ferdinand from the throne and Metternich from power but the monarchy continued under the ill-fated Francis Joseph (1848–1916), Emperor of Austria and King of Hungary (1867–1916). The emperor's brother, Maximilian I, was installed by Napoleon III as Emperor of Mexico (1864–1867) but executed by the revolutionary forces of Juarez after the French emperor withdrew his troops. Elizabeth, the wife of Francis Joseph, was assassinated in 1898 by an Italian anarchist and his only son, Archduke Rudolf, was found dead along with his mistress Baroness Maria Vetsera at Mayerling. Thought to possibly be a double suicide, the tragedy remains a mystery. Heir-apparent to Francis Joseph, his grandnephew Archduke Francis Ferdinand (1863–1914) and his wife were assassinated on June 28, 1914, by a Serbian nationalist at Sarajevo, leading to the ultimate tragedy of World War I.

Ruled by the Turks since 1456, Greece finally began, in 1821, a rebellion that engaged the romantic imagination of the Western world. Ancient Greece was the birthplace of democracy and of Western culture, and Philhellenic (pro-Greek) committees in Europe and America sent supplies and money while demanding that civilized nations intervene directly, which, eventually, England, France, and Russia did. The war was ferocious with Greek peasants slaughtering every Turk in sight and the Turks retaliating, for example, by killing or selling into slavery all 30,000 residents of the island of Chios, which inspired Delacroix's painting of *Massacre at Chios*. Lord Byron could not resist the siren call of Greek independence and died

---

1. Reinvented would be a more appropriate word. The ancient Greeks were apparently the first to invent the steam engine. Judging by the drawings of Heron (or Hero) of Alexandria (ca. second century A.D.), steam power was used in toy gadgets that caused birds to sing and Tritons to blow their horns. See Brumbaugh, Robert S. *Ancient Greek Gadgets and Machines.* Westport, Conn.: Greenwood Press, 1975.

2. W. W. Rostow, *The Stages of Economic Growth* (New York: Cambridge University Press, 1960), p. 33.

there in 1824. By 1832 independence had been achieved but Greek nationalism was not fully victorious until after World War II.

Early in the nineteenth century Italy was temporarily unified under Napoleon, but the Congress of Vienna again reduced it to petty states. After abortive revolts in 1821, 1830, and 1848, Giuseppe Garibaldi (1807–1882) spearheaded the Risorgimento (rie–sor–jie–MEN–toe; resurgence) which, by 1861, established Italy as the first political entity since the demise of the Roman Empire. Victor Emmanuel II (1861–1878) was supported by Garibaldi and Camillo Benzo Cavour (1810–1861) as the first monarch of the Kingdom of Italy. By 1870 the Papal States had been incorporated into the kingdom but not until 1929 was Vatican City established as a separate sovereign state of 108 acres.

Plagued by Czarist repression and widespread corruption, poverty, and ignorance, Russia was the most backward country in Europe. Czar Alexander I (1801–1825) attempted some reforms but, under the influence of Metternich, he became a reactionary and his successor, Nicholas I (1825–1855), was even more rigid. The campaign of Nicholas to dominate southeast Europe led to the Crimean War (1853–1856) in which the allied powers of Turkey, England, France, and Sardinia stopped, for a time, Russian expansionism. The main campaign was the siege of the Russian Naval Base at Sevastopol but the war itself was notorious for the appalling neglect of wounded soldiers and general incompetence of command. Florence Nightingale organized field hospitals but nothing could save the troops from tragic blunders epitomized by the futile gallantry of the Light Brigade. Tennyson's poem typifies the romantic fantasies about honor and glory that were later to end in the Great War.

Literary Selection

THE CHARGE OF THE LIGHT BRIGADE
Alfred, Lord Tennyson

I

Half a league, half a league,
   Half a league onward,
All in the valley of Death
   Rode the six hundred.
'Forward, the Light Brigade!
Charge for the guns!' he said:
Into the valley of Death
   Rode the six hundred.

II

'Forward, the Light Brigade!'
Was there a man dismay'd?
Not tho' the soldier knew
   Some one had blunder'd:
Their's not to make reply,
Their's not to reason why,
Their's but to do and die:
Into the valley of Death
   Rode the six hundred.

III

Cannon to right of them,
Cannon to left of them,
Cannon in front of them
   Volley'd and thunder'd;
Storm'd at with shot and shell,
Boldly they rode and well,
Into the jaws of Death,
Into the mouth of Hell
   Rode the six hundred.

IV

Flash'd all their sabres bare,
Flash'd as they turn'd in air
Sabring the gunners there,
Charging an army, while
   All the world wonder'd:
Plunged in the battery-smoke
Right thro' the line they broke;
Cossack and Russian
Reel'd from the sabre-stroke
   Shatter'd and sunder'd.
Then they rode back, but not
   Not the six hundred.

V

Cannon to right of them,
Cannon to left of them,
Cannon behind them
   Volley'd and thunder'd;
Storm'd at with shot and shell,
While horse and hero fell,
They that had fought so well
Came thro' the jaws of Death,
Back from the mouth of Hell,
All that was left of them,
   Left of six hundred.

VI

When can their glory fade?
O the wild charge they made!
   All the world wonder'd.
Honour the charge they made!
Honour the Light Brigade,
   Noble six hundred!

The reign of Alexander II (1855–1881) was about as authoritarian as that of Nicholas I but he did belatedly liberate about forty million serfs with his 1861 Emancipation Act. The assassination of Alexander II led to the brutally oppressive regime of Alexander III (1881–1894) and the inept but equally oppressive reign of Nicholas II (1894–1917), the last of the czars.

The long reign of England's George III (1760–1820) actually ended in 1811 when the king became totally insane. Functioning as Prince Regent (1811–1820) and then king, George IV (1820–1830) led a wildly profligate life that earned the hatred of his subjects. William IV (1830–1837) agreed to the Reform Bill of 1832 that extended suffrage to property-owning subjects, thus still excluding the great mass of workers. His niece, Victoria (1837–1901), reestablished the prestige of the crown while presiding over the enormous expansion of the British Empire, symbolized by her crowning as Empress of India in 1876. Though the English monarchy was largely decorative, Victoria determinedly took her role seriously, presiding over the conversion of the country into a political democracy with humanitarian reforms and a measure of social and economic democracy. The British developed a liberal democracy at home while pursuing aggressive imperialism abroad.

Several decades before Victoria's death Victorian earnestness and sobriety had become, for many writers and artists, increasingly boring. Many were ready for a new era and certainly Edward VII (1901–1910) was ready to rule, having been Prince of Wales for sixty years. The Edwardian Age was as flashy and flamboyant as the king himself. Frivolity and high living were eminently fashionable for those who could afford to live in the grand manner. The accession of George V (1910–1936) restored some measure of decorum but all that ended in the late summer of 1914.

Inspired in part by the doctrine of Manifest Destiny, the United States tripled its size during the nineteenth century and increased its population nearly twentyfold. Even more remarkable was the fact that the nation could expand so enormously and still maintain its union. The Civil War (1861–1865) was a cruel test sufficient to destroy perhaps any other nation. Though slavery was an inflammatory issue the conflict was between widely divergent ways of life and different economic structures. Mainly industrial, the North was vigorous and aggressive in the spirit of Calvinism while the South was primarily agricultural with a relaxed and cavalier life-style. Despite the ferocious fighting, the constant threats of wholesale reprisals and other vengeful measures were never realized. Jefferson Davis did spend two years in prison but this was followed by thirty years of peaceful existence. Just as remarkable, Lee surrendered to Grant at Appomattox, the war was over, and that fact was accepted by the South as the final end of a rebellion that would never again be seriously considered. Reconstruction might have proceeded less radically had Lincoln not been assassinated but, nevertheless, his views seemed to temper northern radicals and encourage the moderates. In his memorable Second Inaugural Address, given just five weeks before the end of the war, Lincoln set the tone of what would ultimately prove to be the sanest and wisest attitude in the aftermath of the nation's internal agony.

Literary Selection

SECOND INAUGURAL ADDRESS

March 4, 1865
Abraham Lincoln

Fellow-countrymen: At this second appearing to take the oath of the presidential office, there is less occasion for an extended address than there was at the first. Then a statement, somewhat in detail, of a course to be pursued, seemed fitting and proper. Now, at the expiration of four years, during which public declarations have been constantly called forth on every point and phase of the great contest which still absorbs the attention and engrosses the energies of the nation, little that is new could be presented. The progress of our arms, upon which all else chiefly depends, is as well known to the public as to myself; and it is, I trust, reasonably satisfactory and encouraging to all. With high hope for the future, no prediction in regard to it is ventured.

On the occasion corresponding to this four years ago, all thoughts were anxiously directed to an impending civil war. All dreaded it—all sought to avert it. While the inaugural address was being delivered from this place, devoted altogether to saving the Union without war, insurgent agents were in the city seeking to destroy it without war—seeking to dissolve the Union, and divide effects, by negotiation. Both parties deprecated war; but one of them would make war rather than let the nation survive; and the other would accept war rather than let it perish. And the war came.

One-eighth of the whole population were colored slaves, not distributed generally over the Union, but localized in the Southern part of it. These slaves constituted a peculiar and powerful interest. All knew that this interest was, somehow, the cause of the war. To strengthen, perpetuate, and extend this interest was the object for which the insurgents would rend the Union, even by war; while the government claimed no right to do more than to restrict the territorial enlargement of it.

Neither party expected for the war the magnitude or the duration which it has already attained. Neither anticipated that the cause of the conflict might cease with, or even before, the conflict itself should cease. Each looked for an easier triumph, and a result less fundamental and astounding. Both read the same Bible, and pray to the same God; and each invokes his aid against the other. It may seem strange that any men should dare to ask a just God's assistance in wringing their bread from the sweat of other men's faces; but let us judge not, that we be not judged. The prayers of both could not be answered—that of neither has been answered fully.

The Almighty has his own purposes. "Woe unto the world because of offenses! for it must needs be that offenses come; but woe to that man by whom the offense cometh." If we shall suppose that American slavery is one of those offenses which, in the providence of God, must needs come, but which, having continued through his appointed time, he now wills to remove, and that he gives to both North and South this terrible war, as the woe due to those by whom the offense came, shall we discern therein any departure from those divine attributes which the believers in a living God always ascribe to him? Fondly do we hope—fervently do we pray—that this mighty scourge of war may speedily pass away. Yet, if God wills that it continue until all the wealth piled by the bondman's two hundred and fifty years of unrequited toil shall be sunk, and until every drop of blood drawn with the lash shall be paid by another drawn with the sword, as was said three thousand years ago, so still it must be said, "The judgments of the Lord are true and righteous altogether."

With malice toward none; with charity for all; with firmness in the right, as God gives us to see the right, let us strive on to finish the work we are in; to bind up the nation's wounds; to care for him who shall have borne the battle, and for his widow, and his orphan—to do all which may achieve and cherish a just and lasting peace among ourselves, and with all nations.

The End of an Era

The Industrial Revolution was a major factor in the complex chain of events leading to the "Great War." Germany, England, France, and Russia were competing in the quality and price of industrial products while also searching for new colonial markets that would absorb some of their booming production. In Europe, after the unification of Germany and Italy, there was very little territory "available" for annexation. There were, in other words, more predatory nations than there were suitable victims. In order to protect what they had and hoped to acquire, nations enlarged their armies and navies and equipped them with the latest technology in munitions and weaponry.

Another crucial factor leading to war was the issue of national identity. As late as the 1860s citizens of Florence generally saw themselves as Florentines or Tuscans; residents of Normandy were Norman rather than French; the population of Munich was Bavarian first and German second, and so on. The physical unification of Germany and Italy stimulated a sense of national identity symbolized by the powerful image of Great Britain as a sovereign nation, with national pride fueled by feelings of national superiority. When James Thomson wrote,

> The nations not so blest as thee,
>   Must in their turn, to tyrants fall;
> Whilst thou shalt flourish great and free,
>   The dread and envy of them all.
>   Rule Britannia! Britannia rules the waves!
>   Britons will never be slaves.

he had no idea of sharing the waves or anything else with other nations.

The Romantic idea of the sovereign individual was enlarged to include each citizen as a critical component in the noble and heroic image of the sovereign state. There was for the Romantic no true identity separate from the homeland, as Sir Walter Scott emphasized.

Literary Selection
BREATHES THERE THE MAN
Sir Walter Scott

Breathes there the man with soul so dead
Who never to himself hath said,
    This is my own, my native land!
Whose heart hath ne'er within him burned,
As home his footsteps he hath turned
    From wandering on a foreign strand!
If such there breathe, go, mark him well;
For him no minstrel raptures swell;
High though his titles, proud his name,
Boundless his wealth as wish can claim,
Despite those titles, power, and pelf,
The wretch, concentred all in self,
Living, shall forfeit fair renown,
And, doubly dying, shall go down
To the vile dust from whence he sprung,
Unwept, unhonored, and unsung.

In their efforts to avoid open warfare, the major nations made alliances that attempted to maintain a balance of power. To guard against French power Bismarck effected a Triple Alliance (1882) of Germany, Austria-Hungary, and Italy. France and Russia countered in 1894 with a Dual Alliance that made Germany uneasy about a two-front war and, in 1907, England joined the two nations in what was called a "close understanding" (Triple Entente). The tinderbox was the Balkans where nationalist ambitions were continually clashing. Russia wanted to make the Black Sea a Slavic lake but Britain saw a Russian thrust as a threat to the empire. By this time Turkey, the "sick man of Europe," was virtually powerless, newly independent Serbia was a threat to the Austro-Hungarian Empire, and Germany had her eye on Balkan conquests. The high level of international tension was extremely dangerous because all nations were armed to the teeth.

Nationalist activities touched a spark to the Balkan tinder and nationalist stubbornness, duty, and honor provoked a war that many diplomats and statesmen believed was a better alternative than seeing their nation humiliated by loss of face. On June 28, 1914, a Serbian nationalist assassinated the Austrian Archduke Francis Ferdinand and his wife. After obtaining Germany's backing for whatever Austria proposed to do about Serbia, a true "blank check," Austria issued an ultimatum that the Serbs could not wholly accept.

Because it was inconsistent with "national honor," Austria turned down a British proposal for a compromise conference and declared war on Serbia on July 28, 1914, despite German attempts to withdraw the blank check. Russia began to mobilize but slowed things down as Germany insisted that the Austrians could be made to compromise. Fearing that her enemies would quickly overwhelm her, the Russian government again ordered full mobilization and Germany responded with an ultimatum to cease mobilizing or face a fight. With no Russian response Germany began mobilizing on August 1 and declared war on Russia the same day, which says something about German preparedness. French mobilization also began on August 1 and Germany declared war on Russia's ally on August 3. Britain dithered and delayed until Germany announced her intention to violate Belgium's neutrality as established in 1839; when Britain declared war on August 4 the German chancellor sneeringly remarked that the English had gone to war over a "scrap of paper." Actually, as pointed out by Barbara Tuchman,[3] the German Staff had laid plans years before the war to violate Belgium's neutrality. The "scrap of paper" remark inflamed world and British public opinion, which solidly backed a government that had honored its treaty and thus the nation. The response was typified by Thomas Hardy's poem, "Cry of the Homeless."

Literary Selection

CRY OF THE HOMELESS

After the Prussian Invasion of Belgium
Thomas Hardy

"Instigator of the ruin—
    Whichsoever thou mayst be
Of the masterful of Europe
    That contrived our misery—
Hear the wormwood-worded greeting
    From each city, shore, and lea
      Of thy victims:
      "Conqueror, all hail to thee!"

"Yea: 'All hail!' we grimly shout thee
    That wast author, fount, and head
Of these wounds, whoever proven
    When our times are throughly read.
'May thy loved be slighted, blighted,
    And forsaken,' be it said
      By thy victims,
      'And thy children beg their bread!'

"Nay: a richer malediction!—
    Rather let this thing befall
In time's hurling and unfurling
    On the night when comes thy call;
That compassion dew thy pillow
    And bedrench thy senses all
      For thy victims,
      Till death dark thee with his pall."

August 1915

Generally speaking, the war was fought with twentieth-century weapons (machine guns, tanks, poison gas, artillery) and nineteenth-century tactics (mass frontal assaults, artillery duels, use of cavalry). There were many theatres of action but the 300–mile Western Front was the main meat grinder with mass charges launched between trenches into point-blank machine gun fire. In four years sixteen nations had casualties (killed, died, wounded, missing) of nearly 40 million. One example will suffice to illustrate the extent of the slaughter. In the center of the French village of Sully-sur-Loire there stands a war memorial designed as a tall obelisk. On one side are listed, in categories, those from the village who died in World War II. The categories themselves communicate much about the conflict with Nazi Germany: "Killed in Action," "Murdered by the Gestapo," "Died in Concentration Camp," and "Missing." Eight names are engraved on the World War II side. On the opposite side the single category is "Killed in Action": There are ninety-six names.

As some historians have noted, World War I began as the most popular war in history. Just about everyone was spoiling for a fight, a chance to demonstrate the great fighting spirit of their country, to prove their valor and nobility, to honor their country. All these Romantic notions died in the trenches and are buried from Flanders Fields to Verdun. Throughout Western history no event has ended an era with such finality as did the Great War.

Literature, Philosophy, and Science

A maze of conflicting ideas and contentious national identities, the nineteenth century produced an exceptional number of gifted writers, thinkers, and scientists, with some of the more important figures considered here. Included are representative persons and representative works in sufficient detail to adequately survey the period.

Romanticism

More an attitude to be explored than a term to be defined, Romanticism began around 1780 as a reaction against the Enlightenment. The Romantic Movement itself lasted from about 1780 to about 1830 but Romantic ideas and issues were present in a variety of forms right up to 1914.

In its initial stages Romanticism was mainly a German movement but the inspiration came from Jean Jacques Rousseau (1712–1778). Rousseau began his *Social Contract* (1762) with a ringing declamation: "Man is born free and everywhere he is in chains." According to Rousseau, the source of the trouble was too much education and of the wrong kind at that. Self-forged chains could not be thrown off with more

---

3. Barbara Tuchman, *The Guns of August* (New York: Macmillan, 1962).

"progress"; instead, people must emulate the Noble Savage by returning to a state of innocence in nature. Civilization had corrupted us, claimed Rousseau, but a return to nature was the proper antidote. More a call to action than a coherent program, just what Rousseau meant by "back to nature" has been debated for centuries. Some idea of his attitude can be obtained from Rousseau's analysis of the "wrong kind of education":

> Astronomy was born of superstition, eloquence of ambition, hatred, falsehood, and flattery; geometry of avarice; physics of an idle curiosity; and even moral philosophy of human pride. Thus the arts and sciences owe their birth to our vices; and we should be less doubtful of their advantages, if they had sprung from our virtues.
>
> Their evil origin is, indeed, but too plainly reproduced in their objects. What would become of the arts were they not cherished by luxury? If men were not unjust, of what use were jurisprudence? What would become of history if there were no tyrants, wars, or conspiracies? In a word, who would pass his life in barren speculations if everybody, attentive only to the obligations of humanity and the necessities of nature, spent his whole life in serving his country, obliging his friends, and relieving the unhappy?
>
> from *Discourse on the Arts and Sciences,* 1749,
> by Jean Jacques Rousseau

Literary Selection
ÉMILE
Jean Jacques Rousseau (1712–1778)

Rousseau presented his ideas about the proper education of children in the form of a novel. In the two brief selections given here we see first an opening essay on the nature of education, and, second, an example of the proper education of the pupil Emile.

Book I

Everything is good as it comes from the hand of the Author of things; everything degenerates in the hand of man. He forces a piece of ground to nourish harvests alien to it, a tree to bear fruit not its own; he mingles and confounds climates, elements, seasons; he mutilates his dog, his horse, his slave; he turns everything upside down, he disfigures everything; he loves deformity and monsters. He does not want anything to be as nature made it, not even man; it must be groomed for him, like a riding-school horse; it must conform to his whim like a tree in his garden. . . .

It is you I address, gentle and far-seeing mother, who know that you must withdraw yourself from the established highway and protect the tender sapling from the shock of human opinion! Cultivate, water the young plant before it dies; its fruits will one day be your greatest joy. Build early a protecting wall about the soul of your child; another may mark out the boundary, but you alone must erect the barrier.

Plants are formed by cultivation and men by education. If a man were born tall and strong, his height and strength would be worthless to him until he had learned to make use of them; both could be harmful to him, in keeping others from thinking he needed help; left to himself, he could die of misery before he understood his own needs. We pity the childish state; we do not see that the human race would have perished if man had not started out as a child.

We are born feeble, we need strength; we are born deprived of everything, we need help; we are born stupid, we need judgment. Everything we lack at our birth, but need when we are grown, is given by our education.

This education comes to us from nature, from men, or from things. The internal development of our faculties and organs is the education of nature; the use we learn to make of this development is the education of men; and the acquisition of our own experience from the objects which affect us is the education of things.

Each one of us, then, is fashioned by three sorts of teachers. The pupil in whom their various teachings clash is badly educated, and will never be at peace with himself; the one in whom they all emphasize the same purpose and tend towards the same ends, goes straight to his goal and lives harmoniously. Such an one is well educated.

Now, of these three different educations, that of nature is the only one that does not depend on us at all; that of things depends on man only in certain respects. That of man is the only one of which we are truly the masters: even here we are in control only theoretically; for who can hope to direct completely the discourse and actions of all those surrounding a child?

Since, then, education is an art, it is almost impossible that it should be successful, for the circumstances necessary to its success are determined by no one person. All that one can do with the greatest care is, more or less, to approach the goal, but one needs good luck to reach it.

What is this goal? It is the very same as nature's; that has just been proved. Since the combination of these educations is necessary for their perfecting, it is toward the one over which we have no control that we must direct the other two. But perhaps this word nature is too vague a term; we must try here to define it.

Nature, we are told, is only habit. What does that mean? Are there not habits which are developed only with effort, and which never stifle nature? Such is, for example, the habit of plants, the vertical direction of which is interfered with. Once the restraints are removed, the plant retains the inclination which it has been forced to take; but even so the sap has not changed its primitive direction, and, if the plant continues to thrive, its growth will return to the vertical. It is the same with the tendencies of man. As long as we stay in one situation, we keep those which are the result of custom and which are the least natural to us; but as soon as the situation changes the learned habit stops and the natural returns. Education is certainly a habit. Now are there not people who forget and lose their education and others who retain it? From whence comes this difference? If we limit the meaning of nature to the habits which conform to the natural, we may spare ourselves this nonsense.

We are born sensitive, and from our birth we are affected in diverse ways by the objects which surround us. As soon as we have, so to speak, the consciousness of our sensations, we are disposed to seek out or to flee from the objects which produce them, first according as to whether they are agreeable or displeasing to us, then according to the harmony or discord which we find between ourselves and these objects, and finally according to the judgments which we form concerning the idea of happinesss and perfection which our reason gives us. These judgments are extended and strengthened in accordance with our becoming more sensitive and more enlightened; but limited by our habits, they are changed more or less by our opinions. Before this change, they are what I call nature in us.

It is to these primitive urges, then, that we must relate everything; and this could be done if our three educations were merely different; but what is to be done when they are opposed?—when, instead of educating a man for himself, we wish to educate him for others, then harmony is impossible. Forced to combat nature or social institutions, we must choose between making a man or a citizen; for one cannot do both at the same time.

All small societies, when confined and close-knit, draw away from the world at large. Every patriot is intolerant of foreigners; they are mere men, they have no worth to him. This difficulty is inevitable but it is a slight one. It is essential to be kind to the people with whom one lives. Outside, the Spartan was ambitious, miserly, unrighteous; but disinterestedness, justice, and concord reigned within his walls. Beware of those citizens of the world who study their books for dutiful acts which they disdain to carry out at home. This kind of philosopher loves the barbarian in order to be free from loving his neighbor.

The natural man is all for himself; he is a numerical unity, the absolute entity, in harmony only with himself or his equals. The civil man (the man in society) is but a fractional unit belonging to the denominator whose sole value is in relation to the whole, which is the social body. Good social institutions are those that know best how to strip man of his nature, to take from him his real existence and give him one which is only relative, and to add his personality to the common unity; to the end that each individual will no longer think of himself as one, but as a part of the whole, no longer a thinking being except in the group. A Roman citizen was neither a Caius nor a Lucius: he was a Roman. . . .

A woman of Sparta had five sons in the army and awaited news of the battle. A helot arrived and she asked for news, trembling. "Your five sons have been killed." "Ignoble slave, did I ask you that?" "We are victorious!" The mother ran to the temple and gave thank-offerings to the gods. There is your citizen.

One who, in civilized society, hopes to maintain the pre-eminence of the natural does not know what he asks. Always at odds with himself, forever vacillating between his inclinations and his duty, he will never be either man or citizen; he will be no good to himself or others. He will be one of those contemporary men, a Frenchman, an Englishman, a citizen. He will be a nonentity.

To be something, to be himself and always whole, a man must act as he speaks, he must be sure always of the road he must take, take it resolutely and follow it always. I am waiting for someone to show me such a prodigy to know if he is man or citizen, or how he undertakes to be both at the same time.

From these necessarily opposed aims come two forms of contrary institutions: the one held in common and public, the other individual and private.

If you want to get an idea of public education, read Plato's *Republic.* It is not at all a political work, as those who judge a book only by its title believe it to be: it is the finest treatise on education that anyone ever wrote.

When people want to return to a never-never land, they think of Plato's institution: if Lycurgus[4] had done no more than put his in writing, I should find it much more fanciful. Plato simply purified the heart of man: Lycurgus denaturalized it.

That public system exists no longer, and can exist no longer, because where there is no nation there can be no citizen. These two words *Nation* and *Citizen* should be removed from modern languages. I know quite well the reason for this, but I do not want to discuss it: it has nothing to do with my subject.

Those laughable institutions they call "colleges" I do not think of in connection with public education. Neither do I count the education of the world, because this education leads toward two contrary goals, and misses both of them; it is useful only to produce two-faced men, who seem always to defer to others but who are really interested only in pleasing themselves. Now this behavior, being common to all, deceives no one in particular. It is so much wasted effort.

From these contradictions arises the one which we feel constantly within ourselves. Pulled by nature and by man in opposite directions; forced to divide ourselves among these different compulsions, we make compromises which lead neither to one goal nor the other. Thus besieged and vacillating during the whole course of our life, we end it without having found peace within ourselves and without having been any good to ourselves or others.

There remains finally private education, or that of nature, but what can a man mean to others if he is educated only for himself. If perhaps the proposed double object could be resolved into one, by removing the contradictions of man we could remove a great obstacle to his happiness. To make a judgment, we must see the finished man; we must have observed his tendencies, seen his progress, followed his advance; in a word, we must know the natural man. I believe you will have taken some steps (made some progress) in our research after having read this discussion.

What must we do to fashion this rare being?—much, without doubt: that is, prevent anything from being done. When it is only a question of sailing against the wind, we tack; but if the sea is high and we want to stay in one place, we must drop anchor. Take care, young pilot, that your cable does not slip or your anchor drag, and that your vessel does not drift without your noticing it.

In the social order where every place is allocated, each one must be educated for his niche. If a man leaves the place for which he was prepared, he no longer fits anywhere. Education is useful to the extent that destiny harmonizes it with the vocation of the parents; in all other instances, it is harmful to the student, if only for the prejudices it gives him. In Egypt, where the son was

---

4. Lycurgus, the Spartan king, did not write about education; he established the actual system of training in Sparta to which Rousseau refers.

obliged to step into his father's place, education at least had an assured purpose: but among us where only classes remain, and where men change from one to the other constantly, no one knows whether, in educating his son to take his place, a father may be working against the son's best interests.

In the natural order, since men are equal, their common calling is man's estate, and whoever is well educated for this, cannot fill unworthily any position which relates to it. Whether I destine my pupil for the army, the church, the bar, is of little importance. No matter what the calling of his parents, nature calls him to human life. Living is the trade I should like to teach him. Leaving my hands, he will not be, I admit, magistrate, soldier, or priest; he will be first of all a man: everything that a man should be, he will know how to be, when called on, as well as any man; and in vain will fortune change his place, for he will always be at home. . . .

* * *

. . . For a time we had noticed, my pupil and I, that amber, glass, wax, different substances when they were rubbed would attract straws, and that others did not attract them. By chance we discovered one which had a still stranger attribute, which was to attract from quite a distance and without being rubbed, filings and other bits of iron. How long this quality amused us without our being able to perceive anything beyond it! Finally we found that this characteristic was communicated to the iron even magnetized in a certain sense. One day we went to the fair; a juggler attracted with a piece of bread a wax duck floating on a basin of water. Very much astonished, we did not call him a sorcerer, however, for we did not know what a sorcerer was. Continually struck with effects of which we did not know the causes, we were in no hurry to make judgments, and remained quietly ignorant until we found the answer.

On returning to our lodging, as a result of talking about the duck at the fair we began to try to imitate it. We took a well-magnetized needle, covered it with white wax which we shaped like a duck as best we could, in such a way that the needle traversed the body and the eye formed the beak. We placed the duck on the water and brought near the beak a key, and we saw, with what joy you may imagine, that our duck followed the piece of bread. To observe in what direction the duck faced when left quiet on the water was something for us to do another time. As for the present, full of our plans, we asked for nothing more.

The same evening we returned to the fair with some prepared bread in our pockets and as soon as the magician performed his trick, our little savant, who could hardly contain himself, said that this trick was not difficult and that he could do as well himself. He was taken at his word and at once took from his pocket the bread containing the bit of iron. As he approached the table his heart was pounding, and, almost trembling, he held out the bread. The duck came and followed it; the child cried out and quivered with joy. As people clapped and the assembly acclaimed him, his head was completely turned and he was beside himself. The juggler, overwhelmed, came, nevertheless to embrace and congratulate him and to request the honor of his presence the next day, adding that we would take pains to assemble a still larger crowd to applaud his cleverness. My proud little naturalist wanted to make a speech, but I shut him up at once and took him away, overwhelmed with praise.

The child with evident excitement counted the minutes the next day. He invited everyone he met; he wanted the whole human race to witness his glory. He could hardly wait for the time to come, he was ready ahead of time, we flew to the meeting place; the room was already full. As he entered, his young heart swelled. Other tricks had to come first; the juggler surpassed himself and did astonishing things. The child saw nothing of all this; he was agitated, he perspired, his breathing was labored. He spent the time fingering the bread in his pocket with a hand trembling with impatience. At last it was his turn; the master announced him ceremoniously. He approached a little ashamedly, he brought out the bread. New vicissitude of human things!—the duck, so tame the day before, had become wild today. Instead of presenting its beak, it turned tail and fled; it avoided the bread and the hand which held it with the same care with which it had formerly followed them. After a thousand useless attempts, each one jeered at, the child whined, said that he was being duped, that this was another duck substituted for the first one, and defied the juggler to attract it.

The juggler, without replying, took a piece of bread and held it out to the duck; which at once followed the bread and came to the hand which held it. The child took the same piece of bread, but far from succeeding better than before, he saw the duck make fun of him and do pirouettes all around the basin; he went off at last, quite upset, and did not dare expose himself to catcalls.

Then the juggler took the bread that the child had brought and made use of it as successfully as with his own: he drew out the iron (magnet) before the people, more laughter at our expense: then with the bread thus emptied he attracted the duck as before. He did the same thing with another piece, cut by a third person, he did the same with his glove, with the end of his finger; finally he went off to the center of the room and in an emphatic tone such as show people use, declaring that the duck would obey his voice no less than his gesture, he spoke and the duck obeyed: he told it to go to the right and it turned right; to come back, and it came; to turn and it turned; the movement followed close upon the order. The redoubled applause was a still greater insult to us. We slipped out without being noticed, and shut ourselves up in our room, without going about to tell everyone of our prowess, as we had planned to do.

The next morning there was a knock at the door, I opened it; there stood the juggler. He mildly objected to our behaviour. What had he done to us that we would undertake to discredit his tricks and deprive him of a livelihood? What is so marvelous after all about drawing along a wax duck to cause us to purchase that ability at the expense of the living of an honest man? "By my faith, gentlemen, if I had some other talent by which to earn my living, I should hardly take pride in this one. You ought to know that a man who has spent his life continually practicing this miserable trade would know more about it than you who have spent only a few minutes on it. If I did not show you my finest tricks at once, it was because a man must not be in a hurry to display foolishly all he knows. I always take care to keep my best tricks for a great occasion, and beyond that I have still greater ones to halt young upstarts. Also, gentlemen, I come in goodwill to disclose the secret which embarrassed you so much, requesting that you will not make use of it to harm me, and that you will be more restrained another time."

Then he showed us his apparatus, and we saw with the utmost surprise that it was nothing but a strong, well mounted magnet which a child hidden under the table moved about without our realizing it.

The man put away his apparatus and after we had expressed our thanks and our apologies, we wanted to give him a present; he refused it. "No, gentlemen, I am not pleased enough with you to accept your gift; I leave you in my debt in spite of yourselves; this is my only revenge. Learn that there is generosity in all classes; I get paid for my tricks but not for my lessons."

Exercises

1. What are the three aspects of education according to Rousseau? What should be the aim of the two aspects that people can do anything about?
2. What distinction does Rousseau make between the *person* and the *citizen?* What is his opinion of the citizen?
3. Some of today's educators claim that vocational training is of little value because job requirements are changing so rapidly. What would Rousseau say about this problem?
4. In terms of the person and the citizen what sort of education would Rousseau advocate, then, to accomplish his purpose?

Johann Gottfried von Herder (1744–1803) was the leader of the precursor of Romanticism, the *sturm und drang* (SHTOORM oont DRAHNG) movement in German literature, a term derived from Klinger's novel *Die Wirrwarr; oder Sturm und Drang* ("Chaos; or storm and stress"). A passionate opponent of French rationalism of the Enlightenment, Herder emphasized the *Volksgeist* (spirit of the people) in Germany, claiming that each *volk* found its *geist* in its language, literature, and religion. This was, in effect, a cultural nationalism that became the basis of later German nationalism.

In his early writings Johann Wolfgang von Goethe (GUHR-tuh; 1749–1832) was one of the leading exponents of the movement. Written after an unhappy love affair, his *The Sorrows of Young Werther* (1774) was a morbidly sensitive tale full of sentiment and gloomy feelings that culminated in the suicide of the tragic Werther. Though Goethe was later to regret the storm and stress of his little book, it made him an instant celebrity.

The philosopher Friedrich William Joseph von Schilling (1775–1854) contributed to the Romantic Movement with his theory that nature and mind were inseparable and differed only in degree rather than in kind. For Schilling the creative artist was the "ideal Romantic man," a genius who presented his work as instinctively created apart from any conscious effort.

From this Nietzsche was to evolve his idea of the creative genius as a "superman" who was "beyond good and evil."

Second only to Goethe in German literature, Friedrich von Schiller (1759–1805) was influenced by Kant and, in turn, was a major influence on modern German literature. An idealist who hated tyranny, Schilling had a vision of the universal fellowship of all humankind. It was his poem "An die Freude" (to joy) that Beethoven used as the "Ode to Joy" in the final movement of his mighty Ninth Symphony.

Arthur Schopenhauer (1788–1860) also contributed to the Romantic Movement with his generally pessimistic theories. According to Schopenhauer, reality is a blind driving force manifested in individuals as Will. Individual wills inevitably clash, causing strife and pain, from which there is no escape except by a negation of the will. Temporary escape is possible, however, through creative acts in art and science.

According to Schopenhauer and other romantics, creativity emerges from the unconscious but there are also instinctual drives that conflict with the creative impulses. In other words, the unconscious cuts both ways and the Romantics were vividly aware of the "night-side" that could release demonic destruction, as Schopenhauer pointed out in *The World of Will and Idea* (1818). Blind human will achieves only unhappiness or, as Goya said, "The sleep of reason produces monsters" (see chap. 26). Schopenhauer concluded that reason had to permit the release of creativity while simultaneously controlling the passions, but he was not optimistic about the results.

To summarize the Romantic Movement is difficult if we consider only what these individual writers and philosophers advocated. What most Romantics were opposed to gives a clearer picture, and the Enlightenment was their main target. Geometric thinking, empiricism, Neoclassicism, all were areas subject to reason and, said the Romantics, all had become mechanized and dehumanized. The great Newton had become only a materialist and a narrow materialist at that.

All Romantics emphasized individuality, the irrational component of the human personality and a sense of the infinite, a search for religious reality beyond sensible experience to find God in nature and within the human heart. Far from a return to orthodoxy, the impulse to recreate wonder in the world by finding God in nature was common to many Romantics except for poets like Byron and Shelley, who sought no God at all. The closest thing to a Romantic consensus lay in the emphasis on the primacy of humane concerns, the celebration of the emotional nature of human beings, and the necessity for creative activity through the exercise of an unfettered imagination.

Romanticism in England

Romanticism was effectively expressed in nineteenth-century art and music, in historical novels, Gothic tales, and romantic stories of love and adventure. In no one medium is the Romantic mood better expressed, for an English-speaking audience, than in the work of the English poets.

William Blake (1757–1827)

A self-proclaimed mystic with minimal formal schooling, Blake was a fundamentalist Protestant who believed that the Bible was the sole source of religious knowledge. Very much an individualist, he detested institutionalized religion, claiming that the human imagination was the sole means of expressing the Eternal. Blake referred to people as the Divine Image, the possessors of the humane virtues of mercy, pity, peace, and love. Equally gifted as an artist, Blake illustrated all but one of his volumes of poetry plus the Book of Job, Dante, and the poems of Thomas Gray.

From the collection called the *Songs of Innocence,* the following two poems celebrate the joy of the simple pastoral life and that of the Christian life. Written in 1789, they coincide with the beginning of the French Revolution that, for Blake, held so much promise of a better life for all people.

Literary Selections

INTRODUCTION
William Blake

Piping down the valleys wild,
Piping songs of pleasant glee,
On a cloud I saw a child,
And he laughing said to me:

'Pipe a song about a Lamb!'   5
So I piped with merry cheer.
'Piper, pipe that song again;'
So I piped: he wept to hear.

'Drop thy pipe, thy happy pipe;
Sing thy songs of happy cheer:'   10
So I sang the same again,
While he wept with joy to hear.

'Piper, sit thee down and write
In a book, that all may read.'
So he vanish'd from my sight,   15
And I pluck'd a hollow reed,

And I made a rural pen,
And I stain'd the water clear,
And I wrote my happy songs
Every child may joy to hear.   20

THE LAMB
William Blake

Little Lamb, who made thee?
    Dost thou know who made thee?
Gave thee life, and bid thee feed,
By the stream and o'er the mead;
Gave thee clothing of delight,   5
Softest clothing, woolly, bright;
Gave thee such a tender voice,
Making all the vales rejoice?
    Little Lamb, who made thee?
    Dost thou know who made thee?   10
Little Lamb, I'll tell thee,
    Little Lamb, I'll tell thee:
He is called by thy name,
For He calls Himself a Lamb.
He is meek, and He is mild;   15
He became a little child.
I a child, and thou a lamb,
We are called by His name.
    Little Lamb, God bless thee!
    Little Lamb, God bless thee!   20

Blake's *Songs of Experience* are concerned with the sick and corrupt world in which good and evil co-exist. In "The Tiger" Blake asks the age-old question: did the good God create evil?

THE TIGER
William Blake

Tiger! Tiger! burning bright
In the forests of the night,
What immortal hand or eye
Could frame thy fearful symmetry?

In what distant deeps or skies   5
Burnt the fire of thine eyes?
On what wings dare he aspire?
What the hand dare seize the fire?

And what shoulder, and what art,
Could twist the sinews of thy heart?   10
And when thy heart began to beat,
What dread hand? and what dread feet?

What the hammer? what the chain?
In what furnace was thy brain?
What the anvil? what dread grasp   15
Dare its deadly terrors clasp?

When the stars threw down their spears,
And water'd heaven with their tears,
Did he smile his work to see?
Did he who made the Lamb make thee?   20

Tiger! Tiger! burning bright
In the forests of the night,
What immortal hand or eye,
Dare frame thy fearful symmetry?

Exercise

1. In his *The Marriage of Heaven and Hell* Blake wrote that "Attraction and Repulsion, Reason and Energy, Love and Hate are necessary to Human Existence." Is this attitude reflected in the poems about the lamb and the tiger? Is the tiger, in other words, wholly evil or a symbol of necessary vigor and energy?

William Wordsworth (1770–1850)

The greatest of the English nature poets, Wordsworth was influenced by Rousseau and the spirit of the French Revolution. Strongly opposed to the flowery artificiality of Neoclassic poetry, Wordsworth and Samuel Taylor Coleridge published *Lyrical Ballads* (1798), which contained a new poetic manifesto. Wordsworth referred to his poetry as "emotion recollected in tranquility" but, as he stated in his manifesto, he deliberately chose to write in "the language of conversation in the middle and lower classes of society." Indicating that "Tintern Abbey" was in a new style, Wordsworth chose the simple title of "Lines" to evoke a world soul that, for him, was present in all nature. The poem is divided into four sections. In the first section (11. 1–23) the poet sets a meditative scene; in the second scene (11. 23–58) are the poet's thoughts about the significance of the landscape. In the heart of the poem, the third section (11. 59–112), Wordsworth reviews the meanings the landscape had for him at different stages of his life. The Friend in the final section (11. 112–160) is the poet's sister, Dorothy, whom he tries to convince that the landscape will restore her tranquility.

Literary Selections

LINES

Composed a Few Miles above Tintern Abbey, on Revisiting the Banks of the Wye During a Tour
July 13, 1798
William Wordsworth

Five years have past; five summers, with the length
Of five long winters! and again I hear
These waters, rolling from their mountain-springs
With a sweet inland murmur.—Once again
Do I behold these steep and lofty cliffs,
That on a wild secluded scene impress
Thoughts of more deep seclusion; and connect
The landscape with the quiet of the sky.
The day is come when I again repose
Here, under this dark sycamore, and view   10

These plots of cottage-ground, these orchard-tufts,
Which at this season, with their unripe fruits,
Are clad in one green hue, and lose themselves
Among the woods and copses, nor disturb
The wild green landscape. Once again I see
These hedgerows, hardly hedgerows, little lines
Of sportive wood run wild: these pastoral farms,
Green to the very door; and wreaths of smoke
Sent up, in silence, from among the trees!
With some uncertain notice, as might seem   20
Of vagrant dwellers in the houseless woods,
Or of some Hermit's cave, where by his fire
The Hermit sits alone.

          These beauteous Forms,
Through a long absence, have not been to me
As is a landscape to a blind man's eye:
But oft, in lonely rooms, and 'mid the din
Of towns and cities, I have owed to them,
In hours of weariness, sensations sweet,
Felt in the blood, and felt along the heart;
And passing even into my purer mind,   30
With tranquil restoration:—feelings too
Of unremembered pleasure: such, perhaps,
As have no slight or trivial influence
On that best portion of a good man's life,
His little, nameless, unremembered acts
Of kindness and of love. Nor less, I trust,
To them I may have owed another gift,
Of aspect more sublime; that blessed mood,
In which the burthen of the mystery,
In which the heavy and the weary weight   40
Of all this unintelligible world,
Is lightened:—that serene and blessed mood,
In which the affections gently lead us on,—
Until, the breath of this corporeal frame
And even the motion of our human blood
Almost suspended, we are laid asleep
In body, and become a living soul:
While with an eye made quiet by the power
Of harmony, and the deep power of joy,
We see into the life of things.

          If this   50
Be but a vain belief, yet, oh! how oft,
In darkness, and amid the many shapes
Of joyless daylight; when the fretful stir
Unprofitable, and the fever of the world,
Have hung upon the beatings of my heart,
How oft, in spirit, have I turned to thee,
O sylvan Wye! Thou wanderer thro' the woods,
How often has my spirit turned to thee!

    And now, with gleams of half-extinguished thought,
With many recognitions dim and faint,   60
And somewhat of a sad perplexity,
The picture of the mind revives again:
While here I stand, not only with the sense
Of present pleasure, but with pleasing thoughts
That in this moment there is life and food
For future years. And so I dare to hope,
Though changed, no doubt, from what I was when first

I came among these hills; when like a roe
I bounded o'er the mountains, by the sides
Of the deep rivers, and the lonely streams,   70
Wherever nature led: more like a man
Flying from something that he dreads, than one
Who sought the thing he loved. For nature then
(The coarser pleasures of my boyish days,
And their glad animal movements all gone by)
To me was all in all.—I cannot paint
What then I was. The sounding cataract
Haunted me like a passion: the tall rock,
The mountain, and the deep and gloomy wood,
Their colours and their forms, were then to me   80
An appetite; a feeling and a love,
That had no need of a remoter charm,
By thought supplied, or any interest
Unborrowed from the eye.—That time is past,
And all its aching joys are now no more,
And all its dizzy raptures. Not for this
Faint I, nor mourn nor murmur; other gifts
Have followed, for such loss, I would believe,
Abundant recompence. For I have learned
To look on nature, not as in the hour   90
Of thoughtless youth; but hearing oftentimes
The still, sad music of humanity,
Nor harsh nor grating, though of ample power
To chasten and subdue. And I have felt
A presence that disturbs me with the joy
Of elevated thoughts: a sense sublime
Of something far more deeply interfused,
Whose dwelling is the light of setting suns,
And the round ocean and the living air,
And the blue sky, and in the mind of man: 100
A motion and a spirit, that impels
All thinking things, all objects of all thought,
And rolls through all things. Therefore am I still
A lover of the meadows and the woods,
And mountains; and of all that we behold
From this green earth; of all the mighty world
Of eye and ear, both what they half create,
And what perceive; well pleased to recognise
In nature and the language of the sense,
The anchor of my purest thoughts, the nurse,   110
The guide, the guardian of my heart, and soul
Of all my moral being.
                            Nor perchance,
If I were not thus taught, should I the more
Suffer my genial spirits to decay:
For thou art with me, here, upon the banks
Of this fair river; thou, my dearest Friend,
My dear, dear Friend, and in thy voice I catch
The language of my former heart, and read
My former pleasures in the shooting lights
Of thy wild eyes. Oh! yet a little while   120
May I behold in thee what I was once,
My dear, dear Sister! and this prayer I make,
Knowing that Nature never did betray
The heart that loved her; 'tis her privilege,
Through all the years of this our life, to lead
From joy to joy: for she can so inform
The mind that is within us, so impress
With quietness and beauty, and so feed
With lofty thoughts, that neither evil tongues,
Rash judgments, nor the sneers of selfish men,   130
Nor greetings where no kindness is, nor all
The dreary intercourse of daily life,
Shall e'er prevail against us, or disturb

Our cheerful faith, that all which we behold
Is full of blessings. Therefore let the moon
Shine on thee in thy solitary walk;
And let the misty mountain winds be free
To blow against thee: and in after years,
When these wild ecstasies shall be matured
Into a sober pleasure, when thy mind   140
Shall be a mansion for all lovely forms,
Thy memory be as a dwelling-place
For all sweet sounds and harmonies; oh! then,
If solitude, or fear, or pain, or grief,
Should be thy portion, with what healing thoughts
Of tender joy wilt thou remember me,
And these my exhortations! Nor, perchance
If I should be where I no more can hear
Thy voice, nor catch from thy wild eyes these gleams
Of past existence, wilt thou then forget   150
That on the banks of this delightful stream
We stood together; and that I, so long
A worshipper of Nature, hither came
Unwearied in that service: rather say
With warmer love, oh! with far deeper zeal
Of holier love. Nor wilt thou then forget,
That after many wanderings, many years
Of absence, these steep woods and lofty cliffs,
And this green pastoral landscape, were to me
More dear, both for themselves and for thy sake!   160

The following sonnet mourns a world so overwhelmed with materialism that it may lose its spiritual qualities. Proteus and Triton are from Greek
mythology and symbolize the poet's conviction that
the wonders of nature that delighted the ancients
cannot, in the long run, be destroyed by the Industrial Age. Wordsworth was a Romantic optimist.

THE WORLD IS TOO MUCH WITH US
William Wordsworth

The world is too much with us; late and soon,
Getting and spending, we lay waste our powers;
Little we see in Nature that is ours;
We have given our hearts away, a sordid boon!
This Sea that bares her bosom to the moon,
The winds that will be howling at all hours,
And are up-gathered now like sleeping flowers,
For this, for everything, we are out of tune;
It moves us not.—Great God! I'd rather be
A Pagan suckled in a creed outworn;
So might I, standing on this pleasant lea,
Have glimpses that would make me less forlorn;
Have sight of Proteus rising from the sea;
Or hear old Triton blow his wreathéd horn.

Exercises

1. In his "Lines" Wordsworth describes two
   memorable periods in his life (11. 65–83 and
   83–111). How are these periods characterized?
   Changes have taken place since the poet's first
   visit to this almost magical place. Has the scene
   changed, the poet himself, or both?

2. If Wordsworth were to write "The World Is Too Much With Us" today would he be as optimistic about the survival of nature's wonders? Why or why not?

Samuel Taylor Coleridge (1772–1834)

Though he did not consider himself a Romantic poet, Coleridge did make a classic Romantic statement: "Each man is meant to represent humanity in his own way, combining its elements uniquely." Coleridge set great store on imagination over fancy, claiming that fancy was only the ability to copy or elaborate on previous examples; imagination was the ability to create new worlds. "Kubla Khan" is a notable example of an inspired vision whether or not, as Coleridge claimed, the poem was composed during an opium reverie and later written down. Coleridge and many other Romantics were fascinated with the exotic Orient. The grandson of Mongol conqueror Genghis Khan, Kubla Khan (1215?–1294) founded the Yuan dynasty of China and sponsored Marco Polo as his agent to the West.

Literary Selection

KUBLA KHAN
Samuel Taylor Coleridge

In Xanadu did Kubla Khan
    A stately pleasure-dome decree:
Where Alph, the sacred river, ran
Through caverns measureless to man
    Down to a sunless sea.
So twice five miles of fertile ground
With walls and towers were girdled round:
And here were gardens bright with sinuous rills,
Where blossomed many an incense-bearing tree
And here were forests ancient as the hills,   10
Enfolding sunny spots of greenery.

But oh! that deep romantic chasm which slanted
Down the green hill athwart a cedarn cover!
A savage place! as holy and enchanted
As e'er beneath a waning moon was haunted
By woman wailing for her demon-lover!
And from this chasm, with ceaseless turmoil seething,
As if this earth in fast thick pants were breathing,
A mighty fountain momently was forced,
Amid whose swift half-intermitted burst   20
Huge fragments vaulted like rebounding hail,
Or chaffy grain beneath the thresher's flail:
And 'mid these dancing rocks at once and ever
It flung up momently the sacred river.
Five miles meandering with a mazy motion
Through wood and dale the sacred river ran,
Then reached the caverns measureless to man,
And sank in tumult to a lifeless ocean:
And 'mid this tumult Kubla heard from far
Ancestral voices prophesying war!   30
    The shadow of the dome of pleasure
    Floated midway on the waves;
    Where was heard the mingled measure
    From the fountain and the caves.

It was a miracle of rare device,
A sunny pleasure-dome with caves of ice!
    A damsel with a dulcimer
    In a vision once I saw:
    It was an Abyssinian maid,
    And on her dulcimer she played,   40
    Singing of Mount Abora.
    Could I revive within me
    Her symphony and song,
    To such a deep delight 'twould win me,
That with music loud and long,
I would build that dome in air,
That sunny dome! those caves of ice!
And all who heard should see them there,
And all should cry, Beware! Beware!
His flashing eyes, his floating hair!   50
Weave a circle round him thrice,
And close your eyes with holy dread,
For he on honey-dew hath fed,
And drunk the milk of Paradise.

        1797

Exercise

1. Coleridge claimed that "Kubla Khan" appeared to him in a dream and that what he later wrote down was "a fragment." But, is the poem incomplete? Could it be that the first thirty-six lines are an exercise in creative imagination and the remainder a lament over the loss of poetic power? In these terms is the poem complete or incomplete?

George Noel Gordon, Lord Byron (1788–1824)

The most flamboyant and controversial personality of the age, Lord Byron epitomizes the Romantic hero. With his egotism and superhuman vigor he gloried in physical and mental license, learning relatively late and only in part the virtue of moderation. He wrote his words, he said, "as a tiger leaps" and aimed many of them at conventional social behaviour, cant, and hypocrisy. Much of his poetry was prosaic when compared with the iridescent style of Shelley and Keats but, as he said, his genius was eloquent rather than poetical. His reputation was early and firmly established with *Childe Harold's Pilgrimage*, a poetic travelogue, but his masterpiece is *Don Juan*, a work full of irony and pathos of which Byron wrote in the Dedication:

I want a hero: an uncommon want,

. . .

But can't find any in the present age
Fit for my poem (that is, for my new one):
So, as I said, I'll take my friend Don Juan.

Literary Selections

The lovely lyric that follows was inspired by Lady Wilmot Horton, whom Byron had seen in a ballroom wearing a mourning dress decorated, strangely enough, with numerous spangles.

SHE WALKS IN BEAUTY
Lord Byron

She walks in beauty, like the night
    Of cloudless climes and starry skies;
And all that 's best of dark and bright
    Meet in her aspect and her eyes:
Thus mellow'd to that tender light
    Which heaven to gaudy day denies.

One shade the more, one ray the less,
    Had half impair'd the nameless grace
Which waves in every raven tress,
    Or softly lightens o'er her face;
Where thoughts serenely sweet express
    How pure, how dear their dwelling-place.

And on that cheek, and o'er that brow,
    So soft, so calm, yet eloquent,
The smiles that win, the tints that glow,
    But tell of days in goodness spent,
A mind at peace with all below,
    A heart whose love is innocent!

June 12, 1814

Byron was a revolutionary in spirit but his inspiration was based upon classical art and its emphasis upon emotion controlled by the intellect. The Greek revolt against the Turks provided Byron with the opportunity to become a revolutionary Graecophile. Several years before sailing for Greece on July 14, 1823 (Bastille Day), he wrote the following ironic lines:

WHEN A MAN HATH NO FREEDOM TO FIGHT FOR AT HOME
Lord Byron

When a man hath no freedom to fight for at home,
    Let him combat for that of his neighbours;
Let him think of the glories of Greece and of Rome,
    And get knock'd on the head for his labours.

To do good to mankind is the chivalrous plan,
    And is always as nobly requited;
Then battle for freedom wherever you can,
    And, if not shot or hang'd, you'll get knighted.

Almost to the day of his premature death Byron was torn between the heroic defiance of Prometheus and the worldly, cynical defiance of Don Juan. In the end, he chose the Promethean way and died during the Greek struggle for independence.

PROMETHEUS
Lord Byron

Titan! to whose immortal eyes
    The sufferings of mortality,
    Seen in their sad reality,
Were not as things that gods despise;
What was thy pity's recompense?
A silent suffering, and intense;
The rock, the vulture, and the chain,
All that the proud can feel of pain,
The agony they do not show,
The suffocating sense of woe,   10
    Which speaks but in its loneliness,
And then is jealous lest the sky
Should have a listener, nor will sigh
    Until its voice is echoless.

Titan! to thee the strife was given
    Between the suffering and the will,
    Which torture where they cannot kill;
And the inexorable Heaven,
And the deaf tyranny of Fate,
The ruling principle of Hate,   20
Which for its pleasure doth create
The things it may annihilate,
Refused thee even the boon to die:
The wretched gift eternity
Was thine—and thou hast borne it well.
All that the Thunderer wrung from thee
Was but the menace which flung back
On him the torments of thy rack;
The fate thou didst so well foresee,
But would not to appease him tell;   30
And in thy Silence was his Sentence,
And in his Soul a vain repentance,
And evil dread so ill dissembled,
That in his hand the lightnings trembled.
Thy Godlike crime was to be kind,
    To render with thy precepts less
    The sum of human wretchedness,
And strengthen Man with his own mind;
But baffled as thou wert from high,
Still in thy patient energy,   40
In the endurance, and repulse
    Of thine impenetrable Spirit,
Which Earth and Heaven could not convulse,
    A mighty lesson we inherit:
Thou art a symbol and a sign
    To Mortals of their fate and force;
Like thee, Man is in part divine,
    A troubled stream from a pure source;
And Man in portions can foresee
His own funereal destiny;   50
His wretchedness, and his resistance,
And his sad unallied existence:
To which his Spirit may oppose
Itself—and equal to all woes,
    And a firm will, and a deep sense,
Which even in torture can descry
    Its own concenter'd recompense,
Triumphant where it dares defy,
And making Death a Victory.

Diodati, July, 1816

Though unable to moderate his course, Byron was fully aware of the causes of his self-destruction, as revealed in several lines from his poignant "Epistle to Augusta:"

I have been cunning in mine overthrow,
The careful pilot of my proper woe.
Mine were my faults, and mine be their reward.
My whole life was a contest, since the day
That gave me being, gave me that which marr'd
The gift,—a fate, or will, that walk'd astray.

Exercises

1. Two contrary aspects of Byron's personality are evidenced in "She Walks in Beauty" and "When a Man Hath No Freedom." How would you describe these very different aspects?
2. Prometheus was the Titan who stole fire from Mount Olympos and gave it to humankind. Zeus, the Thunderer in the poem, had him chained to a rock where a vulture perpetually tears out his liver. What does Prometheus symbolize for Byron? Greece under Turkish tyranny? Himself? Both?

Percy Bysshe Shelley (1792–1822)

Shelley and his friend John Keats established romantic verse as the prime poetic tradition of the period; to this day "Shelley and Keats" and "Romantic poetry" are virtually synonymous. A lifelong heretic who was expelled from Oxford because of his pamphlet *The Necessity of Atheism,* Shelley saw all humankind as the Divine Image to whom poets spoke as the "unacknowledged legislators of the world" *(A Defense of Poetry).* His masterpiece is *Prometheus Unbound,* a lyrical drama in four acts in which he gave full expression to his "passion for reforming the world." Also composed at Leghorn, Italy, and published with *Prometheus Unbound* was "To a Skylark," the composition of which was described by Mrs. Shelley:

> It was on a beautiful summer evening while wandering among the lanes, whose myrtle hedges were the bowers of the fireflies, that we heard the caroling of the skylark, which inspired one of the most beautiful of his poems.

Literary Selections

TO A SKYLARK
Percy Bysshe Shelley

Hail to thee, blithe spirit!
  Bird thou never wert,
That from heaven, or near it,
  Pourest thy full heart
In profuse strains of unpremeditated art.   5

Higher still and higher
  From the earth thou springest
Like a cloud of fire;
  The blue deep thou wingest,
And singing still dost soar, and soaring ever singest.   10
  In the golden lightning
    Of the sunken sun,
  O'er which clouds are brightning,
    Thou dost float and run;
Like an unbodied joy whose race is just begun.   15
  The pale purple even
    Melts around thy flight;
  Like a star of heaven,
    In the broad day-light
Thou art unseen, but yet I hear thy shrill delight,   20
  Keen as are the arrows
    Of that silver sphere,
  Whose intense lamp narrows
    In the white dawn clear,
Until we hardly see, we feel that it is there.   25
  All the earth and air
    With thy voice is loud,
  As, when night is bare,
    From one lonely cloud
The moon rains out her beams, and heaven is overflowed.   30
  What thou art we know not;
    What is most like thee?
  From rainbow clouds there flow not
    Drops so bright to see,
As from thy presence showers a rain of melody.   35
  Like a poet hidden
    In the light of thought,
  Singing hymns unbidden,
    Till the world is wrought
To sympathy with hopes and fears it heeded not: 40
  Like a high-born maiden
    In a palace tower,
  Soothing her love-laden
    Soul in secret hour
With music sweet as love, which overflows her bower: 45
  Like a glow-worm golden
    In a dell of dew,
  Scattering unbeholden
    Its aërial hue
Among the flowers and grass, which screen it from the view: 50
  Like a rose embowered
    In its own green leaves,
  By warm winds deflowered,
    Till the scent it gives
Makes faint with too much sweet these heavy-winged thieves: 55
  Sound of vernal showers
    On the twinkling grass,
  Rain-awakened flowers,
    All that ever was
Joyous, and clear, and fresh, thy music doth surpass: 60
  Teach us, sprite or bird,
    What sweet thoughts are thine:
  I have never heard
    Praise of love or wine
That panted forth a flood of rapture so divine.   65

Chorus Hymenaeal,
   Or triumphal chaunt,
Matched with thine would be all
   But an empty vaunt,
A thing wherein we feel there is some hidden want.   70

   What objects are the fountains
      Of thy happy strain?
   What fields, or waves, or mountains?
      What shapes of sky or plain?
What love of thine own kind? what ignorance of pain?   75

   With thy clear keen joyance
      Languor cannot be:
   Shadow of annoyance
      Never came near thee:
Thou lovest; but ne'er knew love's sad satiety.   80

   Waking or asleep,
      Thou of death must deem
   Things more true and deep
      Than we mortals dream,
Or how could thy notes flow in such a crystal stream?   85

   We look before and after,
      And pine for what is not:
   Our sincerest laughter
      With some pain is fraught;
Our sweetest songs are those that tell of saddest
   thought.   90

   Yet if we could scorn
      Hate, and pride, and fear;
   If we were things born
      Not to shed a tear,
I know not how thy joy we ever should come near.   95

   Better than all measures
      Of delightful sound,
   Better than all treasures
      That in books are found,
Thy skill to poet were, thou scorner of the ground!   100

   Teach me half the gladness
      That thy brain must know,
   Such harmonious madness
      From my lips would flow,
The world should listen then, as I am listening now.   105

"Ode to a West Wind" was, according to Shelley:

. . . conceived and chiefly written in a wood that
skirts the Arno near Florence, and on a day when
that tempestuous wind, whose temperature is at once
mild and animating, was collecting the vapours
which pour down the autumnal rains. They began, as
I foresaw, at sunset with a violent tempest of hail and
rain, attended by that magnificent thunder and
lightning peculiar to the Cisalpine regions.

ODE TO THE WEST WIND
Percy Bysshe Shelley

I

O, wild West Wind, thou breath of Autumn's being,
Thou, from whose unseen presence the leaves dead
Are driven, like ghosts from an enchanter fleeing,

Yellow, and black, and pale, and hectic red,
Pestilence-stricken multitudes: O, thou,   5
Who chariotest to their dark wintry bed

The wingèd seeds, where they lie cold and low,
Each like a corpse within its grave, until
Thine azure sister of the spring shall blow

Her clarion o'er the dreaming earth, and fill   10
(Driving sweet buds like flocks to feed in air)
With living hues and odours plain and hill:

Wild Spirit, which art moving every where;
Destroyer and preserver; hear, O, hear!

II

Thou on whose stream, 'mid the steep sky's
   commotion,   15
Loose clouds like earth's decaying leaves are shed,
Shook from the tangled boughs of Heaven and Ocean,

Angels of rain and lightning: there are spread
On the blue surface of thine airy surge,
Like the bright hair uplifted from the head   20
Of some fierce Mænad, even from the dim verge
Of the horizon to the zenith's height
The locks of the approaching storm. Thou dirge

Of the dying year, to which this closing night
Will be the dome of a vast sepulchre,   25
Vaulted with all thy congregated might

Of vapours, from whose solid atmosphere
Black rain, and fire, and hail will burst: O, hear!

III

Thou who didst waken from his summer dreams
The blue Mediterranean, where he lay,   30
Lulled by the coil of his crystàlline streams,

Beside a pumice isle in Baiæ's bay,
And saw in sleep old palaces and towers
Quivering within the wave's intenser day,

All overgrown with azure moss and flowers   35
So sweet, the sense faints picturing them! Thou
For whose path the Atlantic's level powers

Cleave themselves into chasms, while far below
The sea-blooms and the oozy woods which wear
The sapless foliage of the ocean, know   40

Thy voice, and suddenly grow grey with fear,
And tremble and despoil themselves: O, hear!

IV

If I were a dead leaf thou mightest bear;
If I were a swift cloud to fly with thee;
A wave to pant beneath thy power, and share   45

The impulse of thy strength, only less free
Than thou, O, uncontroulable! If even
I were as in my boyhood, and could be

The comrade of thy wanderings over heaven,
As then, when to outstrip thy skiey speed   50
Scarce seemed a vision; I would ne'er have striven

As thus with thee in prayer in my sore need.
Oh! lift me as a wave, a leaf, a cloud!
I fall upon the thorns of life! I bleed!

A heavy weight of hours has chained and bowed   55
One too like thee: tameless, and swift, and proud.

V

Make me thy lyre, even as the forest is:
What if my leaves are falling like its own!
The tumult of thy mighty harmonies

Will take from both a deep, autumnal tone,   60
Sweet though in sadness. Be thou, spirit fierce,
My spirit! Be thou me, impetuous one!

Drive my dead thoughts over the universe
Like withered leaves to quicken a new birth!
And, by the incantation of this verse,   65

Scatter, as from an unextinguished hearth
Ashes and sparks, my words among mankind!
Be through my lips to unawakened earth
The trumpet of a prophecy! O, wind,
If Winter comes, can Spring be far behind?   70

Exercises

1. How does Shelley achieve the seemingly
   effortless buoyancy of "To a Skylark"? Consider
   the rhythm and the use of words like *blithe,
   springest, soar, float,* and many others.
2. The central image in the "Ode to the West
   Wind" is, of course, the wind itself. What does
   the wind represent? Consider the fact that in
   Latin and Greek, the words for wind, breath,
   soul, and inspiration are identical or
   interrelated. Could the wind symbolize a
   quickening of the inner spirit in response to the
   exterior movement? What is the significance of
   an *Autumn* wind? How many images are there
   of the cycle of life and death?

Mary Wollstonecraft Godwin Shelley (1797–1851)

Though not a poet, Mary Shelley deserves special
mention here. She was the daughter of noted feminist
Mary Wollstonecraft (1759–1797), author of *Vindi-
cation of the Rights of Women* (1792), and the equally
notable social reformer William Godwin (1756–1836),
a disciple of Jeremy Bentham and a man who strongly
influenced Shelley's reforming zeal. Shelley had left
Harriet, his wife, for Mary and moved to the continent
where he later married her. While reading ghost
stories one evening, Lord Byron suggested that each
should write a tale of the supernatural. Mary Shelley's
contribution was *Frankenstein; or, The Modern Prometheus* (1818). Using the central themes of Faustian
ambition and Promethean creativity, Mary told the
story of the scientist Frankenstein who dared to create life itself and, in so doing, dehumanized himself
and brought destruction on all those he loved. Frankenstein's creation needed love and sympathy but was
greeted instead with disgust and revulsion. Symbolizing Romantic ideas of isolation and alienation,
Frankenstein's creation turned from a search for love
to hatred of all humankind and murderous destruction. Mary Shelley's story is even more influential today
as a modern myth about the horrifying potential of
human creativity like, for example, nuclear weapons,
when divorced from ethical considerations.

John Keats (1795–1821)

Generally speaking, the verse of both Keats and Shelley have a musicality that sets their work apart from
all other Romantic poetry. Though trained as an
apothecary and not even thinking of becoming a poet
until he was eighteen, Keats began writing poetry with
a sense of urgency and forebodings of an early death
(his mother and, later, his brother died of the disease
that was to carry him off: tuberculosis). Keats was the
first to admit that his first volume of poetry had many
flaws but not that it was "alternately florid and arid,"
as one critic bitingly observed. Keats's own reaction
to a barrage of criticism was quite relaxed: "About a
twelvemonth since, I published a little book of verses;
it was read by some dozen of my friends, who lik'd it;
and some dozen whom I was unacquainted with, who
did not."

Keats is the only Romantic poet whose sonnets
have been compared with those by Shakespeare,
which he studied in depth and concluded that "He
has left nothing to say about nothing or anything."
Nevertheless, when the British Museum acquired the
Elgin marbles that Lord Elgin had taken from the Parthenon in Athens (see chap. 7), Keats's reaction was
a sonnet memorable for its subtle imagery and mixed
feelings of personal mortality and artistic immortality.

Literary Selections

ON THE ELGIN MARBLES

John Keats

My spirit is too weak; mortality
    Weighs heavily on me like unwilling sleep,
    And each imagined pinnacle and steep
Of godlike hardship tells me I must die
Like a sick eagle looking at the sky.
    Yet 'tis a gentle luxury to weep,
    That I have not the cloudy winds to keep
Fresh for the opening of the morning's eye.
Such dim-conceived glories of the brain,
    Bring round the heart an indescribable feud;
So do these wonders a most dizzy pain,
    That mingles Grecian grandeur with the rude
Wasting of old Time—with a billowy main
    A sun, a shadow of a magnitude.

Keats generally obeyed his own rule of stopping
his writing when the poetry ceased to come "as easily
as leaves upon a tree," which accounts, at least in part,
for the seemingly effortless style of his poetry. In his
contemplation of a Grecian urn (see, for example, fig.
7.56) Keats succeeds in fusing his personality with the
urn, partaking, as he said, of "fellowship with essence."

ODE ON A GRECIAN URN

John Keats

I

Thou still unravished bride of quietness,
    Thou foster-child of silence and slow time,
Sylvan historian, who canst thus express
    A flowery tale more sweetly than our rhyme:
What leaf-fringed legend haunts about thy shape   5
    Of deities or mortals, or of both,
        In Tempe or the dales of Arcady?
    What men or gods are these? What maidens loath?
What mad pursuit? What struggle to escape?
        What pipes and timbrels? What wild ecstacy?   10

II

Heard melodies are sweet, but those unheard
    Are sweeter; therefore, ye soft pipes, play on;
Not to the sensual ear, but, more endeared,
    Pipe to the spirit ditties of no tone.
Fair youth, beneath the trees, thou canst not leave   15
    Thy song, nor ever can those trees be bare;
        Bold lover, never, never canst thou kiss,
Though winning near the goal—yet, do not grieve;
    She cannot fade, though thou hast not thy bliss,
        For ever wilt thou love, and she be fair!   20

III

Ah, happy, happy boughs! that cannot shed
    Your leaves, nor ever bid the spring adieu;
And, happy melodist, unwearied,
    For ever piping songs for ever new;
More happy love! more happy, happy love!   25
    For ever warm and still to be enjoyed,
        For ever panting, and for ever young;
All breathing human passion far above,
    That leaves a heart high-sorrowful and cloyed,
        A burning forehead, and a parching tongue.   30

IV

Who are these coming to the sacrifice?
    To what green altar, O mysterious priest,
Leadest thou that heifer lowing at the skies,
    And all her silken flanks with garlands drest?
What little town by river or sea-shore,   35
    Or mountain-built with peaceful citadel,
        Is emptied of this folk, this pious morn?
And, little town, thy streets for evermore
    Will silent be; and not a soul to tell
        Why thou art desolate, can e'er return.   40

V

O Attic shape! Fair attitude! with brede
    Of marble men and maidens overwrought,
With forest branches and the trodden weed;
    Thou, silent form, dost tease us out of thought
As doth eternity: Cold Pastoral!   45
    When old age shall this generation waste,
        Thou shalt remain, in midst of other woe
    Than ours, a friend to man, to whom thou sayest,
"Beauty is truth, truth beauty,"—that is all
    Ye know on earth, and all ye need to know.   50

Most Romantics adored what they imagined the Middle Ages to have been; none would have tolerated for a moment the reality of the medieval world. "La Belle Dame sans Merci" ("The Lovely Lady without Pity") is perhaps the finest example of Romantic medievalism. Though the title is taken from a medieval poem by Alain Chartier, the ballad is the poet's own magical version of the ageless myth of the hapless mortal who succumbed to the irresistible charms of a supernatural and pitiless seductress. The first three stanzas are addressed to the distraught knight by an unknown questioner; the balance of the poem forms his anguished reply.

LA BELLE DAME SANS MERCI

John Keats

O what can ail thee, knight-at-arms,
    Alone and palely loitering?
The sedge has withered from the lake,
    And no birds sing.

O what can ail thee, knight-at-arms,
    So haggard and so woe-begone?
The squirrel's granary is full,
    And the harvest's done.

I see a lily on thy brow,
    With anguish moist and fever dew;
And on thy cheek a fading rose
    Fast withereth too.

I met a lady in the meads,
    Full beautiful—a faery's child;
Her hair was long, her foot was light,
    And her eyes were wild.

I set her on my pacing steed,
    And nothing else saw all day long;
For sidelong would she bend, and sing
    A faery's song.

I made a garland for her head,
    And bracelets too, and fragrant zone;
She looked at me as she did love,
    And made sweet moan.

She found me roots of relish sweet,
    And honey wild, and manna-dew;
And sure in language strange she said,
    "I love thee true."

She took me to her elfin grot,
    And there she wept and sighed full sore:
And there I shut her wild, wild eyes
    With kisses four.

And there she lulled me asleep,
    And there I dreamed—Ah! woe betide!
The latest dream I ever dreamed,
    On the cold hill-side.

I saw pale kings and princes too,
    Pale warriors—death-pale were they all;
Who cried, "La Belle Dame Sans Merci
    Hath thee in thrall!"

I saw their starved lips in the gloam,
    With horrid warning gaped wide;
And I awoke, and found me here
    On the cold hill's side.

And this is why I sojourn here,
    Alone and palely loitering;
Though the sedge is withered from the lake,
    And no birds sing.

Exercises

1. In "To the Elgin Marbles" what does the poet mean by *shadow* and by *magnitude?* Consider the fact that the Elgin Marbles were fragments of some of the finest sculptures on the Parthenon. The Parthenon itself was, and is, the most beautiful temple in Greece but it was, 2,500 years ago, only one of many lovely Greek temples.
2. Who or what speaks the final two lines of "Ode on a Grecian Urn"? Also, what does *Beauty is truth, truth beauty* really mean? If this statement refers to everyday life it doesn't make much sense. Suppose, instead, that the reference is to great art. Do sublime works of art like a Grecian urn crystalize truth and that's why beauty is truth?
3. How does Keats maintain the medieval mood in "La Belle Dame sans Merci"? Look, for example, at obvious words like *thee, knight-at-arms,* and *dancing steed* and subtle words like *meads, garland,* and *elfin.*

Johann Wolfgang von Goethe (GUHR–tu; 1749–1832)

Germany's greatest writer achieved instant fame with the publication of *The Sorrows of Young Werther* (1774), a morbid tale that captured the imagination of all Europe. Werther's hopeless longing for his best friend's wife was autobiographical, but Werther's subsequent suicide was merely in the tradition of romantic despair, emulated, tragically, by a number of young men who died of a bullet in the brain while holding a copy of the novel. Calling Romanticism "a sickness," Goethe proceeded to write novels and plays in the Neoclassic style. A "Renaissance man" rather than a "Romantic hero," Goethe made important contributions to botany, the theory of evolution, physics, and devoted much of the rest of his life to the retelling of the legend of Dr. Johannes Faustus (ca. 1480–1540), who supposedly sold his soul to the Devil (Mephistopheles) in exchange for youth, knowledge, and power. Goethe's *Faust* (1808–1832) became the mythic symbol for the restless search for the meaning of life, and the will to wrest the fullest possibilities from a lifetime of titanic deeds. In his relentless drive to enlarge the meaning of life the "Faustian man" is Romantic, but his will to power and knowledge was always and inevitably doomed to failure. In the final analysis, Faust's salvation lay in his heroic self-regeneration and his acceptance of his own mortality.

Late in his long career Goethe again became a romantic poet but, as usual, in his own original fashion. Long attracted to poetry of the Middle East, Goethe published his *West-Eastern Divan* (1819), his last important body of lyric poetry, in which he sought wisdom, piety, and peace through a central motif of love. Inspired by a translation of the *Divan* of Hafiz, a fourteenth-century Persian poet, Goethe wrote twelve books of mostly love poetry. One book was devoted to the conquests of Timur (Tamerlane), the Mongol conqueror of Hafiz's homeland. In Goethe's mind Timur's ravages were paralleled by Napoleon's Russian campaign of 1812, including the scorched-earth policy of the Russian defenders that sealed the fate of the Grand Army. Goethe's thesis was that love and peace were not possible until after Napoleon had been eliminated.

Literary Selection

VII. BOOK OF TIMUR
Johann Wolfgang von Goethe

I

The Winter and Timur

So around them closed the winter
With resistless fury. Scattering
Midst them all his icy breathings.
Winds he lashed from every quarter
As a hostile troop against them;
Over them gave power tyrannic
To his frost-fanged storm and tempest.
Down he came to Timur's council,
Shrilled his threat and spake on this wise:
"Slack and slow, O man forbidden,
Be thy march, unrighteous tyrant!
Longer yet shall hearts be wasted,
Scorching in thy flames and burning?
Art thou of the damnèd spirits
One? Behold, I am the other.
Hoar of head art thou; I likewise;
Stark we make the land and mortals.

Mars thou art; I am Saturnus,
Stars that strike with baneful influence,
Dreadfullest in their conjunction.
Souls thou slayest; airs of heaven
Dost thou freeze; my airs are colder
Than thou e'er canst be. Thy savage
Host, they martyrize the faithful
With a thousand several tortures.
Well, in these my days, God grant it,
Direr ill shall be discovered.
I, by God, in nought will spare thee!
Let God hear what gift I proffer!
Ay, by God, from death's cold shudder
Nought, O greybeard, shall defend thee,
Not the broad hearth's glow of fuel,
Not the flame-leaps of December."

Goethe's idealized lovers were Hatem (Goethe) and Zuleika (Marianne von Willemer).

III

Hatem

Now that Zuleika is thy name
I should also named be.
When thy beloved thou dost acclaim
Hatem—that the name shall be.
'Tis but to have me known aright,
And no presumption shall there be;
Who names himself St George's Knight
Pretends not like St George to be.
Not Hatem Thai, who every gift could give,
I, in my poverty, can be;
Not Hatem Zograi, wealthiest that did live
Of all the poets, might I be;
Yet up to both mine eyes to lift—
That shall not wholly blameful be;
To take bliss and to give the gift,
Will ever noble joyance be.
Self-love in joy's exchange—sweet thrift—
Rapture of Paradise shall be!

IV

Hatem

It is not Opportunity
    Makes thieves, herself she heads the roll;
For from my heart, its treasury,
    All that was left of love she stole.
To thee the spoil she has consigned,
    The sum of all my life had won;
So now, made poor, I look to find
    My very life from thee alone.
But even already pity charms
    Those lustrous eyes to which I sued,
And I may welcome in thine arms
    The fortune of my life renewed.

V

Zuleika

Since of my joys your love is chief,
    I chide not Opportunity;
For if with you she played the thief,
    How has her booty gladdened me.
But wherefore "theft"? Of free choice give
    Yourself to me! though for my part
Too willingly would I believe—
    Yes, I am she who stole your heart.
What you have given thus freely brings
    Noble return, to match your stake—
My rest, my opulent life; these things
    I joy to give; 'tis yours to take!
Mock not! No word of being "made poor!"
    Are we not rich, of love possessed?
I hold you in my arms, and sure
    Such fortune reckons with the best.

IX

Hatem

Interpret this! In truth I can:
    Have I not often by your side
Told how the Doge Venetian
    Maketh the sea his bride?

The ring in the Euphrates fell
    From off your finger even so.
Ah! thousand songs celestial,
    Sweet dreams, from thee shall flow!
But I, from farthest Hindustan,
    Made for Damascus, hoping there
With the next starting caravan,
    Toward the Red Sea to fare.
Your stream, the grove, the terrace, this,
    Has bound me to, as wedded mate;
Here shall my spirit, till love's last kiss,
    To you be dedicate.

X

Zuleika

Skilled am I to read men's glances;
One says—"Ah, I love, I suffer!
Live in longing, live despairing!"
And what more a maiden knoweth.
All such speech can nought avail me,
All such speech unmoved must leave me;
But, my Hatem, these your glances
Give the day its gleam and glory.
For they say, "She yonder glads me,
As nought else on earth can gladden;
Lo, I look on roses, lilies,
Pomp and wealth of every garden,
Look on cypress, myrtle, violets,
Sprung to adorn the world with beauty,
And adorned she stands a marvel,
Compassing us with sweet surprises,
Quickening us, restoring, blessing,
So that health returns upon us,
And we sigh again for sickness."
Then you looked upon Zuleika,
And in sickness found a healing,
In your healing found a sickness,
Smiled and turned your eyes upon her,
As you never smiled on others.
And Zuleika felt the glance's
Ever-living speech—"She glads me
As nought else on earth has gladdened."

Exercise

1. Compare the language of the five love poems
   with that of "The Winter and Timur." In the
   latter, phrases like *resistless fury, icy breathings,*
   and *frost-fanged storm* are fierce in meaning
   and in sound. Look for other phrases that have
   the same quality. Try reading the Timur poem
   aloud and then one of the love poems. How do
   the rhythms and sounds differ?

Hegel and Marx

The most important German philosopher after Kant, Georg Wilhelm Hegel (HAY-gul; 1770–1831) influenced European and American philosophers, historians, theologians, and political theorists. Described by Bertrand Russell as "the hardest to understand of all the great philosophers," the discussion of Hegel will be limited here to those doctrines that influenced Karl Marx. Hegel believed in an all-encompassing Absolute, a world Spirit that expressed itself in the historical process. Basing his logic on the "triadic dialectic," Hegel stated that for every concept (thesis) there was its opposite idea (antithesis). Out of the dynamic interaction between the two extremes would emerge a synthesis which, in turn, would become a new and presumably higher thesis. Absolute Being, for example, is a thesis while Absolute Unbeing is its antithesis. The synthesis is Absolute Becoming, meaning that the universe is eternally recreating itself.

The notable cultures of the past were, according to Hegel, stages in the evolutionary development of the world Spirit toward perfection and freedom. Human beings and their institutions must inevitably clash because all are subject to error but, nevertheless, they must act and, through striving, find the "path of righteousness." Essentially Faustian in the conviction that perfectability was attainable only through continuous activity and unavoidable conflict, Hegel's philosophy of history was evolutionary. Not only all humankind but the world itself was progressing ever upward, away from imperfection and toward the Absolute.

By mid-century the horrible working conditions and dismal lives of factory workers concerned social reformers thoughout Europe. Many spoke out against the exploitation of the working class but none so dramatically as the Communists.

Literary Selection

MANIFESTO OF THE COMMUNIST PARTY

Karl Marx and *Friedrich Engels*

A specter is haunting Europe—the specter of communism. All the powers of old Europe have entered into a holy alliance to exorcise this specter: Pope and Czar, Metternich and Guizot, French Radicals and German police spies.

Where is the party in opposition that has not been decried as communistic by its opponents in power? Where the Opposition that has not hurled back the branding reproach of communism, against the more advanced opposition parties, as well as against its reactionary adversaries?

Two things result from this fact:

I. Communism is already acknowledged by all European powers to be itself a power.

II. It is high time that Communists should openly, in the face of the whole world, publish their views, their aims, their tendencies, and meet this nursery tale of the specter of communism with a manifesto of the party itself.

To this end, Communists of various nationalities have assembled in London, and sketched the following manifesto, to be published in the English, French, German, Italian, Flemish, and Danish languages.

I

Bourgeois and Proletarians

The history of all hitherto existing society is the history of class struggles.

Freeman and slave, patrician and plebeian, lord and serf, guildmaster and journeyman, in a word, oppressor and oppressed, stood in constant opposition to one another, carried on an uninterrupted, now hidden, now open fight, a fight that each time ended, either in a revolutionary reconstitution of society at large, or in the common ruin of the contending classes.

In the earlier epochs of history, we find almost everywhere a complicated arrangement of society into various orders, a manifold gradation of social rank. In ancient Rome we have patricians, knights, plebeians, slaves; in the Middle Ages, feudal lords, vassals, guildmasters, journeymen, apprentices, serfs; in almost all of these classes, again, subordinate gradations.

The modern bourgeois society that has sprouted from the ruins of feudal society, has not done away with class antagonisms. It has but established new classes, new conditions of oppression, new forms of struggle in place of the old ones.

Our epoch, the epoch of the bourgeoisie, possesses, however, this distinctive feature: It has simplified the class antagonisms. Society as a whole is more and more splitting up into two great classes directly facing each other—bourgeoisie and proletariat. . . .

The Communists disdain to conceal their views and aims. They openly declare that their ends can be attained only by the forcible overthrow of all existing social conditions. Let the ruling classes tremble at a Communist revolution. The proletarians have nothing to lose but their chains. They have a world to win.

Workingmen of all countries, unite!

Because he believed in the basic goodness of human beings, Karl Marx (1818–1883), along with his collaborator Friedrich Engels (1820–1895), formulated a doctrine of inevitable progress that would lead to the perfect classless society in which private property and the profit motive would be relics of the imperfect past. From Hegel he took the dialectic, not as world Spirit but as material forces, a concept espoused by the German philosopher Ludwig Feuerbach (1804–1872). In effect, Marx turned Hegel's dialectic upside down, contending that it was not consciousness that determined human existence but the social existence of people that defined their consciousness.

For Marx, the way people made a living, their "means of production," determined their beliefs and institutions. To demonstrate the working out of dialectical materialism Marx concentrated on the feudal society of the Middle Ages. The ruling class consisted of the nobility and clergy as the thesis. With the development of trade an increasingly affluent middle class, the bourgeoisie, rose as the antithesis in the class struggle. Following the American and French revolutions the bourgeois class merged with the vanquished nobility as the synthesis. Traders, bankers, and factory owners made up the ruling class of capitalists, the new thesis, while the oppressed workers, the proletariat, were the antithesis. The final class struggle between capitalists and workers would, according to Marx, inevitably result in victory for the proletariat, who would take over the means of production. Under the "dictatorship of the proletariat" the entire capitalist apparatus would be collectivized. With only one class remaining the class struggle would cease. The state, according to Marx, with its laws, courts, and police served only to oppress the proletariat and thus would no longer be necessary and would therefore "wither away."

The inevitable march of history to a classless society did not happen, of course, as Marx had predicted. In order to better protect the working class democratic governments have had to regulate industry and adopt various degrees of "state socialism." The theoretical dictatorship of the proletariat still functions in the U.S.S.R. with no signs of withering away of the state in Russia or in any country controlled by Marxist-Leninist ideology. Hard-core Marxists still contend that the revolution will have to be worldwide before the withering away can take place.[5]

Charles Darwin (1809–1882)

Anaximander of Miletus (610–ca. 547 B.C.) postulated an elementary theory of evolution, but it was not until the nineteenth century that the theories of Erasmus Darwin, Jean-Baptiste de Lamarch, Thomas Malthus, and the detailed naturalistic observations of Charles Darwin finally led to Darwin's publication of *On the Origin of Species by Means of Natural Selection* (1859). After serving as naturalist on the surveying ship *Beagle* (1831–1836) Darwin read in Thomas Malthus's *On Population* (1798), the thesis that population increased by geometric ratio (1, 2, 4, 16, etc.), while the food supply increased arithmetically (1, 3, 5, 7, 9, etc.). The limited food supply, Malthus observed, naturally checked unlimited population increases. Darwin wrote:

> It at once struck me that under the circumstances favorable variations would tend to be preserved and unfavorable ones destroyed. The result of this would be the formation of a new species. Here then I had a theory by which to work.

This is the doctrine of natural selection, the result of chance permitting the survival of the fittest.

Darwin proceeded from three facts to his deductions:

Fact 1. All organisms tend to increase geometrically.

Fact 2. The population of a given species remains more or less constant.

Fact 3. Within any species there is considerable variation.

Deduction 1. With more young produced than can survive there must be competition for survival.

Deduction 2. The variations within a species means that a higher percentage of those with favorable variations will survive and, conversely, a higher percentage of those with unfavorable variations will die or fail to reproduce. This is natural selection. Furthermore, the favorable variations are generally transmitted by heredity, meaning that natural selection will tend to maintain and act to improve the ability of the species to survive.

Modern evolution theory confirms Darwin's facts and deductions as outlined above, but adds some significant variations in terms of modifications, mutations, and recombinations. Modification is a variation due to external or internal factors and is not the result of inheritance. Take, for example, two brothers, one leading an active and healthy life and the other immersed in alcoholism. The odds on survival are not difficult to predict.

The copying of genes in the process of reproduction is not always precise. A copy that differs slightly from the original is a mutation and the mutated gene will continue to reproduce itself unless the mutation results in an unfavorable variation that increases the chances against survival. Mutations tend, on the whole, to result in unfavorable variations.

Darwin was not aware of the full implications of Gregor Mendel's (1822–1884) experiments in genetics, specifically the fact that sexual reproduction results in a recombination of existing genetic units that may produce or modify inheritable combinations. Take, for example, twelve children born of the same parents. Though there is generally a familial resemblance, each child will be distinctly different because of the different recombination of genes.

Darwin was reluctant to publish his theories until he learned that Alfred Russel Wallace (1823–1913) had independently developed a theory of evolution. Both men submitted a paper to the Linnean Society on the theory of natural selection; both papers were read on July 1, 1858, and later published. Even when Darwin published his *Origin of Species* the following year he considered his work a brief abstract of twenty-five years of detailed studies.

---

5. For a detailed analysis of current Soviet problems see Marshall I. Goldman, *USSR in Crisis: The Failure of an Economic System* (New York: W. W. Norton and Company, 1983).

Darwin's work provoked a great controversy, of course, because it denied supernatural intervention in the functioning of the universe. He could and did ride out the theological storm but not the attacks of naturalists who claimed a special place for *homo sapiens* separate from other species. In the introduction to his *The Descent of Man* (1871) Darwin noted that he had many notes on the origin or descent of man but that he was determined "not to publish, as I thought that I should thus only add to the prejudices against my views." Indeed, his *Origin of Species* implied "that man must be included with other organic beings in any general conclusion respecting his manner of appearance on this earth." *The Descent of Man* is therefore a response to hostile naturalists and a sequel to the *Origin of Species* in which Darwin discussed the evolution of *homo sapiens* from lower forms of life. The conclusion of this work reveals Darwin as a realist and as an optimist.

Literary Selection

THE DESCENT OF MAN
Charles Darwin

The main conclusion arrived at in this work, namely, that man is descended from some lowly organised form, will, I regret to think, be highly distasteful to many. But there can hardly be a doubt that we are descended from barbarians. The astonishment which I felt on first seeing a party of Fuegians on a wild and broken shore will never be forgotten by me, for the reflection at once rushed into my mind—such were our ancestors. These men were absolutely naked and bedaubed with paint, their long hair was tangled, their mouths, frothed with excitement, and their expression was wild, startled, and distrustful. They possessed hardly any arts, and like wild animals lived on what they could catch; they had no government, and were merciless to every one not of their own small tribe. He who has seen a savage in his native land will not feel much shame, if forced to acknowledge that the blood of some more humble creature flows in his veins. For my own part I would as soon be descended from that heroic little monkey, who braved his dreaded enemy in order to save the life of his keeper, or from that old baboon, who descending from the mountains, carried away in triumph his young comrade from a crowd of astonished dogs—as from a savage who delights to torture his enemies, offers up bloody sacrifices, practices infanticide without remorse, treats his wives like slaves, knows no decency, and is haunted by the grossest superstitions.

Man may be excused for feeling some pride at having risen, though not through his own exertions, to the very summit of the organic scale; and the fact of his having thus risen, instead of having been aboriginally placed there, may give him hope for a still higher destiny in the distant future. But we are not here concerned with hopes or fears, only with the truth as far as our reason permits us to discover it; and I have given the evidence to the best of my ability. We must, however, acknowledge, as it seems to me, that man with all his noble qualities, with sympathy which feels for the most debased, with benevolence which extends not only to other men but to the humblest living creature, with his god-like intellect which has penetrated into the movements and constitution of the solar system—with all these exalted powers—Man still bears in his bodily frame the indelible stamp of his lowly origin.

What is the status of Darwinism today? Is the theory of evolution simply a theory, a kind of glorified hypothesis that may be knocked down by contradictory scientific evidence or because someone comes up with a better theory? In *Nature*, a leading British scientific journal, a lead editorial states:

The first requirement of any theory, good or bad, is that it should be consistent with such phenomena as there are, and logically consistent. Darwinism is consistent with the data to which Darwin had access more than a century ago. One of the remarkable features of the theory is that it remains consistent with the vastly greater body of data now available.

On the grounds of internal consistency, Darwinism has also triumphed quite remarkably. Today's molecular biology has provided an independent (and potentially extremely powerful) method of telling the relationships between species and groups of species, many of them only distantly related to each other. The result is a striking confirmation of the general character of the relationships suggested by Darwin and his contemporaries. To be sure, it is not possible to tell from a comparison of the structures of proteins found in primates whether people are more closely related to gorillas or chimpanzees, but that only goes to fill out Darwin's notion of divergent evolution from some common stock. At the same time, however, the quite remarkable constancy of some materials, the histone proteins for example, is vividly suggestive of the common origin of all living things, and of their persistence over time. The way in which the theory of evolution has been able to survive such a long succession of discoveries bearing on the mechanism of inheritance—the rediscovery of Mendelism, the discovery of chromosomes, the recognition of what genes are and the recognition that genes are usually pieces of double-stranded DNA—is striking evidence of its overwhelming consistency. No theory of such a grand scale in the physical sciences has done as well in the past century.[6]

Social Darwinism

Herbert Spencer (1820–1903) was an English philosopher and an advocate not only of evolution in nature but in human institutions as well. "Survival of the fittest," the phrase coined by Spencer, meant, claimed the Social Darwinists, that the rich were better adapted

---

6. "How true is the theory of evolution?" *Nature* 290 (12 March 1981): 75–76.

to the rigors of competitive life; they were, in short, more fit to survive than the poor. Opposed to governmental intervention in economic affairs, trade unions, and socialist ideas like welfare, powerful capitalists like John D. Rockefeller and Andrew Carnegie claimed that unrestrained competition had a scientific basis comparable to evolution in nature. This position was, of course, an attempt to justify laissez-faire capitalism.

On a larger scale, Social Darwinism helped reinforce the idea that some nations were more fit than rival nations and defeating a rival in warfare would demonstrate that superiority. Indeed, it became almost a moral duty, in evolutionary terms, to conquer an inferior people and populate their lands with fitter human beings. Late nineteenth-century imperialism thus had an ideal social philosophy to justify the growth of empire. Cecil Rhodes, the British imperialist, even held the view that a world of Anglo-Saxons was the best of all possible worlds, thus adding racism to the social evolution theory. In 1845 a journalist and diplomat named John Louis O'Sullivan coined the term *manifest destiny* which, when reinforced by social evolution, provided the justification of American imperialism.

In the fullness of time Darwinian ideas spread into every corner of the intellectual domain: anthropology, sociology, history, literature, art, music, legal and political institutions. Just about everything was investigated in terms of origin, development, and survival or disappearance.

There is no denying the enormous influence of evolutionary theory in all of these areas, but great care has to be taken when applying a scientific theory to nonscientific areas. "Natural selection," for scientists, means the way things work in nature and no more than that. Social Darwinists used evolutionary theory to justify individuality and unfettered competition as if the marketplace were a scientific laboratory. Scientific terminology was selected to undergird the way things were supposed to be. "Survival of the fittest" was intended to prove that the wealthy and powerful were fit and no one else. As a matter of fact, the most fit in Darwin's natural world were those who left, over a period of time, the most dependents who could survive natural selection. Not necessarily the smartest, biggest, or strongest, just survivors.

Furthermore, the same conservative Social Darwinists who claimed that a capitalistic economy was a struggle for existence with only the fittest surviving refused, for the most part, to compete in a free market. They wanted high tariffs to protect them from foreign competition and would tolerate no competition for improved wages and working conditions on the part of organized labor. Those who argued so persuasively for competition, like Rockefeller and Carnegie, effectively eliminated almost all competition so that they could enjoy their virtual monopolies in steel and oil. In the final analysis, Social Darwinism is a misnomer in terms of using Darwin's name. The true social philosophy of America's Robber Barons at the height of laissez-faire capitalism can best be summed up in the memorable statement of Cornelius Vanderbilt: "The public be damned!"

It was only in nature that ruthless competition was natural. Competition in business, however ruthless, appears to be practical and efficient providing no one is cheating. In terms of human nature, however, neither natural nor business competition seems to present an acceptable pattern for human behavior. Ethical and humane considerations must be applied to human beings.

Liberalism

Jeremy Bentham (1748–1832) was the founder of the rationalist philosophy of utilitarianism, a doctrine whose central idea is that actions are not right or wrong in themselves; they can be judged only by their consequences. Utilitarianism is based on the assumption that all human beings pursue happiness and that they do this by seeking pleasure and avoiding pain. The criterion of the value of deeds is their utility, that is, whether or not they lead to the greatest happiness of the greatest number. Bentham's ethics are, in effect, an inversion of those of Kant. Kant calls for action as a duty and on principle; Bentham's values are based on the consequences of actions.

Bentham believed, along with classical (laissez-faire) economists, that government governs best when it governs least, and that it should be relatively passive in social affairs. He was, however, an ardent reformer and his detailed studies of English institutions convinced him that the pleasure derived by some in the pursuit of self-interest caused pain for others, sometimes many, many others. He and his followers, the Philosophic Radicals, came to believe that the state should intervene to help provide the greatest happiness for the greatest number. Their influence helped bring about considerable administrative, legal, and economic reforms that broadened, in the twentieth century, into the concept of the welfare state.

James Mill was a disciple of Bentham and the director of a rigorous "educational experiment" for his son, John Stuart Mill (1806–1873). At the age of three, young Mill had learned Greek and, at seven, was reading Plato's dialogues. During the following year he taught Latin to his sister. By the time John Stuart Mill started college, he had what he called a twenty-five-year headstart on his classmates. There were drawbacks, however. "I grew up," Mill wrote in his celebrated *Autobiography* (1873) "in the absence of love and in the presence of fear." Referring to himself as a "reasoning machine," Mill had a breakdown at twenty from which he recovered by turning to music and the Romantic poets, especially Coleridge and Wordsworth. It was also during this period of crisis that Mill met Harriet Taylor, the wife of a London merchant. A woman of remarkable intellect comparable to that of Mill, Harriet was his intense Platonic love and intellectual companion until 1851, when her husband died and they were finally married. The belated education in music and art plus the association with Harriet, whom Mill credited with much assistance in his writing, helped make Mill the foremost humanitarian liberal of the century.

Mill adopted utilitarianism at an early age but distinguished pleasures by qualities rather than mere quantities as Bentham had done. For Mill the greatest pleasures were intellectal, ranking far above sensual pleasures. As he said, he would "rather be Sokrates dissatisfied than a fool satisfied." Mill's position was comparable to that of the Epicureans when he said that "human beings have faculties more elevated than the animal appetites, and when once conscious of them, do not regard anything as happiness which does not include their gratification." Among the greatest pleasures for Mill were freedom of thought, speech, and action, but only up to the point where this freedom might impinge upon that of another individual. His famous political essay *On Liberty* (1859) explores the "nature and limits of power which can be legitimately exercised over the individual." His arguments in defense of free speech in a democratic society are just as convincing today, and his warning against "the tyranny of the majority" is equally apropos for our own age.

In order to help secure the greatest good for the greatest number, Mill was an extremely active reformer, pressing for extended suffrage, measures to protect children and actions to improve the lot of the poor. Virtually alone among intellectuals of his time, Mill was convinced that women were the intellectual equals of men. Vigorously opposed to the inferior status of women, he wrote the *Subjection of Women* (1869), a strongly worded book that was responsible for some changed laws and a number of changes in opinions. Though he did not reject classical economics, Mill did see that modifications were necessary and, moreover, long overdue. In the midst of self-righteous, materialistic Victorians, Mill's sane and sophisticated voice was like a liberal breath of fresh air.

Victorian Poets

By the late Victorian period England was a bustling and prosperous country. Mechanized, industrialized, and urbanized, it was also a tiny island on whose flag the sun never set, the most powerful and far-flung empire the world had ever known. Early Romantics had envisioned a new society flourishing in a golden age, but late Victorians witnessed endless colonial wars, smoke blanketing the countryside from hundreds of belching smokestacks, and miles of dreary row houses inhabited by overworked and underpaid factory workers. The Industrial Revolution had defiled nature but, after Darwin, there was no solace in a nature "red with tooth and claw." What, then, was the role of the poet?

Alfred, Lord Tennyson (1809–1892)

The most representative poet of the late Victorian era, Tennyson reflected the mood of the period in poetry that was contemplative, sad, quiet, melancholy, sometimes wistful, and often pessimistic. The old optimism of the Early Romantics was gone.

Literary Selections

In the following poem Mariana, from Shakespeare's *Measure for Measure,* waits in the "moated grange" (farmhouse complex) for the lover who has deserted her. The scene painting is remarkably consistent with the dark and hopeless feelings of the abandoned Mariana and is, in fact, the embodiment of her feelings.

MARIANA
Alfred, Lord Tennyson

> "Mariana in the moated grange."
> *Measure for Measure*

With blackest moss the flower plots
    Were thickly crusted, one and all;
The rusted nails fell from the knots
    That held the pear to the gable wall.
The broken sheds looked sad and strange: 5
    Unlifted was the clinking latch;
    Weeded and worn the ancient thatch
Upon the lonely moated grange.
        She only said, "My life is dreary,
           He cometh not," she said;   10
        She said, "I am aweary, aweary,
           I would that I were dead!"

Her tears fell with the dews at even;
    Her tears fell ere the dews were dried;
She could not look on the sweet heaven,   15
    Either at morn or eventide.
After the flitting of the bats,
    When thickest dark did trance the sky,
    She drew her casement curtain by,
And glanced athwart the glooming flats.   20
        She only said, "The night is dreary,
           He cometh not," she said;
        She said, "I am aweary, aweary,
           I would that I were dead!"

Upon the middle of the night,   25
    Waking she heard the nightfowl crow;
The cock sung out an hour ere light;
    From the dark fen the oxen's low
Came to her; without hope of change,
    In sleep she seemed to walk forlorn,   30
    Till cold winds woke the gray-eyed morn
About the lonely moated grange.
        She only said, "The day is dreary,
           He cometh not," she said;
         She said, "I am aweary, aweary,   35
           I would that I were dead!"

About a stonecast from the wall
    A sluice with blackened waters slept,
And o'er it many, round and small,
    The clustered marish-mosses crept.   40

Hard by a poplar shook alway,
    All silver-green with gnarlèd bark:
    For leagues no other tree did mark
The level waste, the rounding gray.
        She only said, "My life is dreary,   45
            He cometh not," she said;
        She said, "I am aweary, aweary,
            I would that I were dead!"

And ever when the moon was low,
    And the shrill winds were up and away,   50
In the white curtain, to and fro,
    She saw the gusty shadows sway.
But when the moon was very low,
    And wild winds bound within their cell,
    The shadow of the poplar fell   55
Upon her bed, across her brow.
        She only said, "The night is dreary,
            He cometh not," she said;
        She said, "I am aweary, aweary,
            I would that I were dead!"   60

All day within the dreamy house,
    The doors upon their hinges creaked;
The blue fly sung in the pane; the mouse
    Behind the moldering wainscot shrieked,
Or from the crevice peered about.   65
    Old faces glimmered through the doors,
    Old footsteps trod the upper floors,
Old voices called her from without.
        She only said, "My life is dreary,
            He cometh not," she said;   70
        She said, "I am aweary, aweary,
            I would that I were dead!"

The sparrow's chirrup on the roof,
    The slow clock ticking, and the sound
Which to the wooing wind aloof   75
    The poplar made, did all confound
Her sense; but most she loathed the hour
    When the thick-moted sunbeam lay
    Athwart the chambers, and the day
Was sloping toward his western bower.   80
        Then, said she, "I am very dreary,
            He will not come," she said;
        She wept, "I am aweary, aweary,
            Oh God, that I were dead!"

Tennyson wrote often about contemporary events such as "The Charge of the Light Brigade," but his best poetry is about the past, particularly the classical past. In "Ulysses" the Greek hero has returned, after twenty years, to Penelope, his "aged wife," and Telemachus, a dutiful son who is content to stay at home and "make mild a rugged people." Ulysses is always the man of action, the embodiment of the Faustian man, whose mission in life is succinctly stated in the last line of the poem.

ULYSSES
Alfred, Lord Tennyson

It little profits that an idle king,
By this still hearth, among these barren crags,
Matched with an aged wife, I mete and dole
Unequal laws unto a savage race,
That hoard, and sleep, and feed, and know not me.

I cannot rest from travel: I will drink
Life to the lees: all times I have enjoyed
Greatly, have suffered greatly, both with those
That loved me, and alone; on shore, and when
Through scudding drifts the rainy Hyades   10
Vext the dim sea. I am become a name;
For always roaming with a hungry heart
Much have I seen and known: cities of men
And manners, climates, councils, governments,
Myself not least, but honored of them all,—
And drunk delight of battle with my peers,
Far on the ringing plains of windy Troy.
I am a part of all that I have met;
Yet all experience is an arch wherethrough
Gleams that untraveled world, whose margin fades   20
For ever and for ever when I move.
How dull it is to pause, to make an end,
To rust unburnished, not to shine in use!
As though to breathe were life! Life piled on life
Were all too little, and of one to me
Little remains: but every hour is saved
From that eternal silence, something more,
A bringer of new things; and vile it were
For some three suns to store and hoard myself,
And this gray spirit yearning in desire   30
To follow knowledge, like a sinking star,
Beyond the utmost bound of human thought.

    This is my son, mine own Telemachus,
To whom I leave the scepter and the isle—
Well-loved of me, discerning to fulfill
This labor, by slow prudence to make mild
A rugged people, and through soft degrees
Subdue them to the useful and the good.
Most blameless is he, centered in the sphere
Of common duties, decent not to fail   40
In offices of tenderness, and pay
Meet adoration to my household gods,
When I am gone. He works his work, I mine.

    There lies the port: the vessel puffs her sail:
There gloom the dark broad seas. My mariners,
Souls that have toiled, and wrought, and thought with
    me—
That ever with a frolic welcome took
The thunder and the sunshine, and opposed
Free hearts, free foreheads—you and I are old;
Old age hath yet his honor and his toil;   50
Death closes all: but something ere the end,
Some work of noble note, may yet be done,
Not unbecoming men that strove with Gods.
The lights begin to twinkle from the rocks:
The long day wanes: the slow moon climbs: the deep
Moans round with many voices. Come, my friends,
'Tis not too late to seek a newer world.
Push off, and sitting well in order smite
The sounding furrows; for my purpose holds
To sail beyond the sunset, and the baths   60
Of all the western stars, until I die.
It may be that the gulfs will wash us down:
It may be we shall touch the Happy Isles,
And see the great Achilles, whom we knew.
Though much is taken, much abides; and though
We are not now that strength which in old days
Moved earth and heaven, that which we are, we
    are,—
One equal temper of heroic hearts,
Made weak by time and fate, but strong in will
To strive, to seek, to find, and not to yield.   70

Exercise

1. In Tennyson's version is Ulysses a noble hero who refuses to submit meekly to old age and death or is he an arrogant, self-centered old man with little concern for his family? Why shouldn't he be "Matched with an aged wife"? Penelope is younger than Ulysses and she did wait twenty faithful years for her husband to return from his Odyssey. Whatever your opinion, is he believeable as a human being?

Matthew Arnold (1822–1888)

As a poet and literary critic Arnold was as pessimistic about human beings and their institutions as were his colleagues, but through sheer force of will he created a cheerful demeanor and purposive character for himself. Possibly the most anti-Victorian figure in Victorian England, Arnold was an apostle of high culture and a lifelong enemy of Puritanism, the "Barbarians" (the aristocracy), and the "Philistines" (the middle class). His melancholic and despairing view of human alienation in a hostile universe is memorably expressed in "Dover Beach." When the poet says to his female companion, "Ah love, let us be true to one another!" the objective is not love but survival. Arnold was a realist, not a romantic.

Literary Selection

DOVER BEACH
Matthew Arnold

[First published 1867.]

The sea is calm to-night,
The tide is full, the moon lies fair
Upon the Straits;—on the French coast, the light
Gleams, and is gone; the cliffs of England stand,
Glimmering and vast, out in the tranquil bay.
Come to the window, sweet is the night air!
Only, from the long line of spray
Where the ebb meets the moon-blanch'd sand,
Listen! you hear the grating roar
Of pebbles which the waves suck back, and fling,   10
At their return, up the high strand,
Begin, and cease, and then again begin,
With tremulous cadence slow, and bring
The eternal note of sadness in.

    Sophocles long ago
Heard it on the Aegaean, and it brought
Into his mind the turbid ebb and flow
Of human misery; we
Find also in the sound a thought,
Hearing it by this distant northern sea.   20

The sea of faith
Was once, too, at the full, and round earth's shore
Lay like the folds of a bright girdle furl'd;
But now I only hear
Its melancholy, long, withdrawing roar,

Retreating to the breath
Of the night-wind down the vast edges drear
And naked shingles of the world.
Ah, love, let us be true
To one another! for the world, which seems   30
To lie before us like a land of dreams,
So various, so beautiful, so new,
Hath really neither joy, nor love, nor light,
Nor certitude, nor peace, nor help for pain;
And we are here as on a darkling plain
Swept with confused alarms of struggles and flight,
Where ignorant armies clash by night.

Exercises

1. Compare the liquid and nasal sounds of lines 1–8 with the much harsher sounds of lines 9–14. Notice, also, that the opening lines describe a lovely seascape, with a discordant tone entering at line 9 in both sounds and sense.
2. What was it that Sophokles heard long ago and far away?
3. What happened to the "sea of faith"? Why?
4. The verbs in lines 1–8 are positive but, in lines 30–31, the world *seems* like a land of dreams. What is the world really like?
5. What are the many implications inherent in the last line? Consider the levels of meaning in each of the key words—*ignorant, armies, clash, night*—and then reflect on the entire line. How far have we come from the opening lines?

Thomas Hardy (1840–1928)

Though he denied being a pessimist, the novels, short stories, and poems of Thomas Hardy reveal a pessimism every bit as profound as that of Matthew Arnold. Like Arnold, Hardy was a realist. He claimed that human effort could make the world a better place, but his prose and poetry are brimming over with sadness over the waste and frustration of life. Though he outlived the Victorian Age, Hardy's output typifies the late Victorian mood of ironic sadness as, for example, in "Neutral Tones" in which the imagery is consistent and convincing.

Literary Selections

NEUTRAL TONES
Thomas Hardy

We stood by a pond that winter day,
And the sun was white, as though chidden of God,
And a few leaves lay on the starving sod;
    —They had fallen from an ash, and were gray.

Your eyes on me were as eyes that rove   5
Over tedious riddles of years ago;
And some words played between us to and fro
    On which lost the more by our love.

The smile on your mouth was the deadest thing
    Alive enough to have strength to die;   10
And a grin of bitterness swept thereby
    Like an ominous bird a-wing. . . .

Since then, keen lessons that love deceives,
    And wrings with wrong, have shaped to me
Your face, and the God-cursed sun, and a tree,   15
    And a pond edged with grayish leaves.
1898

One of the last and probably the most unpopular of England's colonial wars, the Boer War (1899–1902) was a brutal struggle that forced the South Africans (Afrikaaners) to submit to British domination. "Drummer Hodge" is a lament for an English soldier buried where a "kopje-crest" (Afrikaans, small hill) breaks the veldt (Afrikaans, prairie), a stranger to this part of the world who did not know the meaning of a dry tableland region called "the broad Karoo."

DRUMMER HODGE
Thomas Hardy

They throw in Drummer Hodge, to rest
    Uncoffined—just as found:
His landmark is a kopje-crest
    That breaks the veldt around;
And foreign constellations west   5
    Each night above his mound.

Young Hodge the Drummer never knew—
    Fresh from his Wessex home—
The meaning of the broad Karoo,
    The Bush, the dusty loam,   10
And why uprose to nightly view
    Strange stars amid the gloam.

Yet portion of that unknown plain
    Will Hodge forever be;
His homely Northern breast and brain   15
    Grow to some Southern tree,
And strange-eyed constellations reign
    His stars eternally.
1902

Written on the last day of the nineteenth century, "The Darkling Thrush" morosely defines a century that ends, for Hardy, with a whimper, and anticipates a new hundred years that seems to offer little hope of anything better.

THE DARKLING THRUSH
Thomas Hardy

I leant upon a coppice gate
    When Frost was specter-gray,
And Winter's dregs made desolate
    The weakening eye of day.
The tangled bine-stems scored the sky   5
    Like strings of broken lyres,
And all mankind that haunted nigh
    Had sought their household fires.

The land's sharp features seemed to be
    The Century's corpse outleant,   10
His crypt the cloudy canopy,
    The wind his death-lament.

The ancient pulse of germ and birth
    Was shrunken hard and dry,
And every spirit upon earth   15
    Seemed fervorless as I.

At once a voice arose among
    The bleak twigs overhead
In a fullhearted evensong
    Of joy illimited;   20
An aged thrush, frail, gaunt, and small,
    In blast-beruffled plume,
Had chosen thus to fling his soul
    Upon the growing gloom.

So little cause for carolings   25
    Of such ecstatic sound
Was written on terrestrial things
    Afar or nigh around,
That I could think there trembled through
    His happy good-night air   30
Some blessed Hope, whereof he knew
    And I was unaware.
1902

Hardy wrote the following poem in April 1914 to describe, with foreboding, gunnery practice in the English Channel. The war began four months later.

CHANNEL FIRING
Thomas Hardy

That night your great guns, unawares,
Shook all our coffins as we lay,
And broke the chancel window-squares,
We thought it was the Judgment Day
And sat upright. While drearisome   5
Arose the howl of wakened hounds:
The mouse let fall the altar-crumb,
The worms drew back into the mounds,

The glebe cow drooled. Till God called, "No;
It's gunnery practice out at sea   10
Just as before you went below;
The world is as it used to be:

"All nations striving strong to make
Red war yet redder. Mad as hatters
They do no more for Christés sake   15
Than you who are helpless in such matters.

"That this is not the judgment hour
For some of them's a blessed thing,
For if it were they'd have to scour
Hell's floor for so much threatening. . . .   20

"Ha, ha. It will be warmer when
I blow the trumpet (if indeed
I ever do; for you are men,
And rest eternal sorely need)."

So down we lay again. "I wonder,   25
Will the world ever saner be,"
Said one, "than when He sent us under
In our indifferent century!"

And many a skeleton shook his head.
"Instead of preaching forty year,"   30
My neighbor Parson Thirdly said,
"I wish I had stuck to pipes and beer."

Again the guns disturbed the hour,
Roaring their readiness to avenge,
As far inland as Stourton Tower,   35
And Camelot, and starlit Stonehenge.
1914

Exercises

1. Why are the stars *strange* in "Drummer Hodge"? How was he buried? What does this imply about the treatment of living soldiers?
2. In "The Darkling Thrush" Hardy uses words gloomy in sense and sound such as *spectre-gray, dregs, desolate,* and *broken.* What are some of the other depressing words? Why does Hardy choose the image of a joyfully singing thrush? What effect does this have on the generally morbid tone of the poem?
3. In "Channel Firing" why does the poet select the names Stourton Tower, Camelot, and Stonehenge? Consider the following facts: Stourton Tower was built in the eighteenth century to commemorate King Alfred's ninth-century victory over the Danes, Camelot was the fabled sixth-century home of King Arthur, and Stonehenge is a mysterious circle of enormous stones dating from about 1800 B.C.

Romanticism and Realism in America

For the United States the nineteenth century was the great age of expansion, from thirteen colonies to forty-five states, three territories, Alaska, Hawaii, the Philippines, Puerto Rico, Guam, and American Samoa. The vast physical growth and economic development was not paralleled, however, by significant developments in the fine and literary arts—not for some time. Early in the century writers were still intimidated by British letters but seeking ways to declare their literary independence. The emergence of Romanticism in England struck a responsive spark in America, and writers like Washington Irving (1783–1859), William Cullen Bryant (1794–1878), and James Fenimore Cooper (1789–1851) produced romantic works in a new American style. Because of limited space we will begin with the next generation of writers and trace the development of American literature from Romanticism to Realism with selected poetry, short stories, and an essay by representative American authors.

Edgar Allen Poe (1809–1849)

One of the few literary figures with an international reputation that this nation has produced, Poe was a brilliant literary critic, poet, and writer of highly imaginative short stories. Among the first to condemn crass American materialism, Poe devoted himself wholly to his art, becoming the first American to live his life entirely as an artist. Poe defined poetry as "the creation of beauty" and contended that all poetry should appeal equally to reason and emotion. Poe felt that all poetry should be composed in terms of beauty, restraint, and unity of effect and, indeed, his poetry is the embodiment of his theory of art. Inspired by the loss of a beautiful woman, "Annabel Lee" is a lyric masterpiece in a lucid and musical style.

Literary Selections

ANNABEL LEE
Edgar Allen Poe

It was many and many a year ago,
    In a kingdom by the sea,
That a maiden there lived whom you may know
    By the name of Annabel Lee;
And this maiden she lived with no other thought
    Than to love and be loved by me.

I was a child and she was a child,
    In this kingdom by the sea,
But we loved with a love that was more than love,
    I and my Annabel Lee;
With a love that the wingèd seraphs of heaven
    Coveted her and me.

And this was the reason that, long ago,
    In this kingdom by the sea,
A wind blew out of a cloud, chilling
    My beautiful Annabel Lee;
So that her highborn kinsmen came
    And bore her away from me,
To shut her up in a sepulchre
    In this kingdom by the sea.

The angels, not half so happy in heaven,
    Went envying her and me;
Yes! that was the reason (as all men know,
    In this kingdom by the sea)
That the wind came out of the cloud by night,
    Chilling and killing my Annabel Lee.

But our love it was stronger by far than the love
    Of those who were older than we,
    Of many far wiser than we;
And neither the angels in heaven above,
    Nor the demons down under the sea,
Can ever dissever my soul from the soul
    Of the beautiful Annabel Lee:

For the moon never beams, without bringing me dreams
    Of the beautiful Annabel Lee;
And the stars never rise, but I feel the bright eyes
    Of the beautiful Annabel Lee;
And so, all the night-tide, I lie down by the side
Of my darling—my darling—my life and my bride,
    In her sepulchre there by the sea,
    In her tomb by the sounding sea.

Exercise

1. This is one of the most musical of all Poe's poems. How does he achieve this effect? Consider the rhythm and the word selection, particularly the use of repeated words and phrases.

THE FALL OF THE HOUSE OF USHER
Edgar Allen Poe

Poe felt that the primary purpose of his prose tales was to make an emotional impact upon the reader. He considered fear the most basic emotion and drew upon the supernatural for material, exploring what is today called the subconscious. In the twilight zone between sleeping and waking Poe found the senses to be most alert and the emotions less inhibited. Called a "grotesque" by its author, "The Fall of the House of Usher" is a tale of death, decadence, and evil, with undertones intimating that the supernatural was somehow involved.

During the whole of a dull, dark, and soundless day in the autumn of the year, when the clouds hung oppressively low in the heavens, I had been passing alone, on horseback, through a singularly dreary tract of country; and at length found myself, as the shades of the evening drew on, within view of the melancholy House of Usher. I know not how it was—but, with the first glimpse of the building, a sense of insufferable gloom pervaded my spirit. I say insufferable; for the feeling was unrelieved by any of that half-pleasurable, because poetic, sentiment with which the mind usually receives even the sternest natural images of the desolate or terrible. I looked upon the scene before me—upon the mere house, and the simple landscape features of the domain, upon the bleak walls, upon the vacant eye-like windows, upon a few rank sedges, and upon a few white trunks of decayed trees— with an utter depression of soul which I can compare to no earthly sensation more properly than to the after-dream of the reveller upon opium: the bitter lapse into every-day life, the hideous dropping off of the veil. There was an iciness, a sinking, a sickening of the heart, an unredeemed dreariness of thought which no goading of the imagination could torture into aught of the sublime. What was it—I paused to think—what was it that so unnerved me in the contemplation of the House of Usher? It was a mystery all insoluble; nor could I grapple with the shadowy fancies that crowded upon me as I pondered. I was forced to fall back upon the unsatisfactory conclusion, that while, beyond doubt, there *are* combinations of very simple natural objects which have the power of thus affecting us, still the analysis of this power lies among considerations beyond our depth. It was possible, I reflected, that a mere different arrangement of the particulars of the scene, of the details of the picture, would be sufficient to modify, or perhaps to annihilate, its capacity for sorrowful impression; and acting upon this idea, I reined my horse to the precipitous brink of a black and lurid tarn that lay in unruffled lustre by the dwelling, and gazed down—but with a shudder even more thrilling than before—upon the remodelled and inverted images of the gray sedge, and the ghastly tree-stems, and the vacant and eye-like windows.

Nevertheless, in this mansion of gloom I now proposed to myself a sojourn of some weeks. Its proprietor, Roderick Usher, had been one of my boon companions in boyhood; but many years had elapsed since our last meeting. A letter, however, had lately reached me in a distant part of the country—a letter from him—which in its wildly importunate nature had admitted of no other than a personal reply. The MS. gave evidence of nervous agitation. The writer spoke of acute bodily illness, of a mental disorder which oppressed him, and of an earnest desire to see me, as his best and indeed his only personal friend, with a view of attempting, by the cheerfulness of my society, some alleviation of his malady.

It was the manner in which all this, and much more, was said—it was the apparent *heart* that went with his request—which allowed me no room for hesitation; and I accordingly obeyed forthwith what I still considered a very singular summons.

Although as boys we had been very intimate associates, yet I really knew little of my friend. His reserve had been always excessive and habitual. I was aware, however, that his very ancient family had been noted, time out of mind, for a peculiar sensibility of temperament, displaying itself, through long ages, in many works of exalted art, and manifested of late in repeated deeds of munificent yet unobtrusive charity, as well as in a passionate devotion to the intricacies perhaps even more than to the orthodox and easily recognizable beauties, of musical science. I had learned, too, the very remarkable fact that the stem of the Usher race, all time-honored as it was, had put forth at no period any enduring branch; in other words, that the entire family lay in the direct line of descent, and had always, with very trifling and very temporary variation, so lain. It was this deficiency, I considered, while running over in thought the perfect keeping of the character of the premises with the accredited character of the people, and while speculating upon the possible influence which the one, in the long lapse of centuries, might have exercised upon the other—it was this deficiency, perhaps, of collateral issue, and the consequent undeviating transmission from sire to son of the patrimony with the name, which had, at length, so identified the two as to merge the original title of the estate in the quaint and equivocal appellation of the "House of Usher"—an appellation which seemed to include, in the minds of the peasantry who used it, both the family and the family mansion.

I have said that the sole effect of my somewhat childish experiment, that of looking down within the tarn, had been to deepen the first singular impression. There can be no doubt that the consciousness of the rapid increase of my superstition—for why should I not so term it?—served mainly to accelerate the increase itself. Such, I have long known, is the paradoxical law of all sentiments having terror as a basis. And it might have been for this reason only, that, when I again uplifted my eyes to the house itself, from its image in the pool, there grew in my mind a strange fancy—a fancy so ridiculous, indeed, that I but mention it to show the vivid force of the sensations which oppressed me. I had so worked upon my imagination as really to believe that about the whole mansion and domain there hung an atmosphere peculiar to themselves and their immediate vicinity: an atmosphere which had no affinity with the air of heaven, but which had reeked up from the decayed trees, and the gray wall, and the silent tarn: a pestilent and mystic vapor, dull, sluggish, faintly discernible, and leaden-hued.

Shaking off from my spirit what *must* have been a dream, I scanned more narrowly the real aspect of the building. Its principal feature seemed to be that of an excessive antiquity. The discoloration of ages had been great. Minute fungi overspread the whole exterior, hanging in a fine tangled web-work from the eaves. Yet all this was apart from any extraordinary dilapidation. No portion of the masonry had fallen; and there appeared to be a wild inconsistency between its still perfect adaptation of parts and the crumbling condition of the individual stones. In this there was much that reminded me of the specious totality of old wood-work which has rotted for long years in some neglected vault, with no disturbance from the breath of the external air. Beyond this indication of extensive decay, however, the fabric gave little token of instability. Perhaps the eye of a scrutinizing observer might have discovered a barely perceptible fissure, which, extending from the roof of the building in front, made its way down the wall in a zigzag direction, until it became lost in the sullen waters of the tarn.

Noticing these things, I rode over a short causeway to the house. A servant in waiting took my horse, and I entered the Gothic archway of the hall. A valet, of stealthy step, thence conducted me, in silence, through many dark and intricate passages in my progress to the studio of his master. Much that I encountered on the way contributed, I know not how, to heighten the vague sentiments of which I have already spoken. While the objects around me—while the carvings of the ceilings, the sombre tapestries of the walls, the ebon blackness of the floors, and the phantasmagoric armorial trophies which rattled as I strode, were but matters to which, or to such as which, I had been accustomed from my infancy—while I hestitated not to acknowledge how familiar was all this—I still wondered to find how unfamiliar were the fancies which ordinary images were stirring up. On one of the staircases, I met the physician of the family. His countenance, I thought, wore a mingled expression of low cunning and perplexity. He accosted me with trepidation and passed on. The valet now threw open a door and ushered me into the presence of his master.

The room in which I found myself was very large and lofty. The windows were long, narrow, and pointed, and at so vast a distance from the black oaken floor as to be altogether inaccessible from within. Feeble gleams of encrimsoned light made their way through the trellised panes, and served to render sufficiently distinct the more prominent objects around; the eye, however, struggled in vain to reach the remoter angles of the chamber, or the recesses of the vaulted and fretted ceiling. Dark draperies hung upon the walls. The general furniture was profuse, comfortless, antique, and tattered. Many books and musical instruments lay scattered about, but failed to give any vitality to the scene. I felt that I breathed an atmosphere of sorrow. An air of stern, deep, and irredeemable gloom hung over and pervaded all.

Upon my entrance, Usher arose from a sofa on which he had been lying at full length, and greeted me with a vivacious warmth which had much in it, I at first thought, of an overdone cordiality—of the constrained effort of the *ennuyé* man of the world. A glance, however, at his countenance, convinced me of his perfect sincerity. We sat down; and for some moments, while he spoke not, I gazed upon him with a feeling half of pity, half of awe. Surely man had never before so terribly altered, in so brief a period, as had Roderick Usher! It was with difficulty that I could bring myself to admit the identity of the wan being before me with the companion of my early boyhood. Yet the character of his face had been at all times remarkable. A cadaverousness of complexion; an eye large, liquid, and luminous beyond comparison; lips somewhat thin and very pallid, but of a surpassingly beautiful curve; a nose of a delicate Hebrew model, but with a breadth of nostril unusual in similar formations; a finely moulded chin, speaking, in its want of prominence, of a want of moral energy; hair of a more than weblike softness and tenuity; these features, with an inordinate expansion above the regions of the temple, made up

altogether a countenance not easily to be forgotten. And now in the mere exaggeration of the prevailing character of these features, and of the expression they were wont to convey, lay so much of change that I doubted to whom I spoke. The now ghastly pallor of the skin, and the now miraculous lustre of the eye, above all things startled and even awed me. The silken hair, too, had been suffered to grow all unheeded, and as, in its wild gossamer texture, it floated rather than fell about the face, I could not, even with effort, connect its arabesque expression with any idea of simple humanity.

In the manner of my friend I was at once struck with an incoherence, an inconsistency; and I soon found this to arise from a series of feeble and futile struggles to overcome an habitual trepidancy, an excessive nervous agitation. For something of this nature I had indeed been prepared, no less by his letter than by reminiscences of certain boyish traits, and by conclusions deduced from his peculiar physical conformation and temperament. His action was alternately vivacious and sullen. His voice varied rapidly from a tremulous indecision (when the animal spirits seemed utterly in abeyance) to that species of energetic concision—that abrupt, weighty, unhurried, and hollow-sounding enunciation—that leaden, self-balanced and perfectly modulated guttural utterance—which may be observed in the lost drunkard, or the irreclaimable eater of opium, during the periods of his most intense excitement.

It was thus that he spoke of the object of my visit, of his earnest desire to see me, and of the solace he expected me to afford him. He entered, at some length, into what he conceived to be the nature of his malady. It was, he said, a constitutional and a family evil, and one for which he despaired to find a remedy—a mere nervous affection, he immediately added, which would undoubtedly soon pass off. It displayed itself in a host of unnatural sensations. Some of these, as he detailed them, interested and bewildered me; although, perhaps, the terms and the general manner of the narration had their weight. He suffered much from a morbid acuteness of the senses; the most insipid food was alone endurable; he could wear only garments of certain texture; the odors of all flowers were oppressive; his eyes were tortured by even a faint light; and there were but peculiar sounds, and these from stringed instruments, which did not inspire him with horror.

To an anomalous species of terror I found him a bounden slave. "I shall perish," said he, "I *must* perish in this deplorable folly. Thus, thus, and not otherwise, shall I be lost. I dread the events of the future, not in themselves, but in their results. I shudder at the thought of any, even the most trivial, incident, which may operate upon this intolerable agitation of soul. I have, indeed, no abhorrence of danger, except in its absolute effect—in terror. In this unnerved—in this pitiable condition, I feel that the period will sooner or later arrive when I must abandon life and reason together, in some struggle with the grim phantasm, FEAR."

I learned moreover at intervals, and through broken and equivocal hints, another singular feature of his mental condition. He was enchained by certain superstitious impressions in regard to the dwelling which he tenanted, and whence, for many years, he had never ventured forth—in regard to an influence whose supposititious force was conveyed in terms too shadowy here to be re-stated—an influence which some peculiarities in the mere form and substance of his family mansion, had, by dint of long sufferance, he said, obtained over his spirit—an effect which the physique of the gray walls and turrets, and of the dim tarn into which they all looked down, had, at length, brought about upon the morale of his existence.

He admitted, however, although with hestitation, that much of the peculiar gloom which thus afflicted him could be traced to a more natural and far more palpable origin—to the severe and long-continued illness, indeed to the evidently approaching dissolution, of a tenderly beloved sister—his sole companion for long years, his last and only relative on earth. "Her decease" he said, with a bitterness which I can never forget, "would leave him (him the hopeless and the frail) the last of the ancient race of the Ushers." While he spoke, the lady Madeline (for so was she called) passed slowly through a remote portion of the apartment, and, without having noticed my presence, disappeared. I regarded her with an utter astonishment not unmingled with dread, and yet I found it impossible to account for such feelings. A sensation of stupor oppressed me, as my eyes followed her retreating steps. When a door, at length, closed upon her, my glance sought instinctively and eagerly the countenance of the brother; but he had buried his face in his hands, and I could only perceive that a far more than ordinary wanness had overspread the emaciated fingers through which trickled many passionate tears.

The disease of the lady Madeline had long baffled the skill of her physicians. A settled apathy, a gradual wasting away of the person, and frequent although transient affections of a partially cataleptical character, were the unusual diagnosis. Hitherto she had steadily borne up against the pressure of her malady, and had not betaken herself finally to bed; but, on the closing in of the evening of my arrival at the house, she succumbed (as her brother told me at night with inexpressible agitation) to the prostrating power of the destroyer; and I learned that the glimpse I had obtained of her person would thus probably be the last I should obtain—that the lady, at least while living, would be seen by me no more.

For several days ensuing, her name was unmentioned by either Usher or myself; and during this period I was busied in earnest endeavors to alleviate the melancholy of my friend. We painted and read together; or I listened, as if in a dream, to the wild improvisations of his speaking guitar. And thus, as a closer and still closer intimacy admitted me more unreservedly into the recesses of his spirit, the more bitterly did I perceive the futility of all attempt at cheering a mind from which darkness, as if an inherent positive quality, poured forth upon all objects of the moral and physical universe, in one unceasing radiation of gloom.

I shall ever bear about me a memory of the many solemn hours I thus spent alone with the master of the House of Usher. Yet I should fail in any attempt to convey an idea of the exact character of the studies, or of the occupations, in which he involved me, or led me the way. An excited and highly distempered ideality threw a sulphureous lustre over all. His long improvised dirges will ring forever in my ears. Among other things, I hold painfully in mind a certain singular perversion and amplification of the wild air of the last waltz of Von Weber. From the paintings over which his elaborate fancy brooded, and which grew, touch by touch, into vagueness at which I shuddered the more thrillingly because I

shuddered knowing not why;—from these paintings (vivid as their images now are before me) I would in vain endeavor to educe more than a small portion which should lie within the compass of merely written words. By the utter simplicity, by the nakedness of his designs, he arrested and overawed attention. If ever mortal painted an idea, that mortal was Roderick Usher. For me at least, in the circumstances then surrounding me, there arose, out of the pure abstractions which the hypochondriac contrived to throw upon his canvas, an intensity of intolerable awe, no shadow of which felt I ever yet in the contemplation of the certainly glowing yet too concrete reveries of Fuseli.

One of the phantasmagoric conceptions of my friend, partaking not so rigidly of the spirit of abstraction, may be shadowed forth, although feebly, in words. A small picture presented the interior of an immensely long and rectangular vault or tunnel, with low walls, smooth, white, and without interruption or device. Certain accessory points of the design served well to convey the idea that this excavation lay at an exceeding depth below the surface of the earth. No outlet was observed in any portion of its vast extent, and no torch or other artificial source of light was discernible; yet a flood of intense rays rolled throughout, and bathed the whole in a ghastly and inappropriate splendor.

I have just spoken of that morbid condition of the auditory nerve which rendered all music intolerable to the sufferer, with the exception of certain effects of stringed instruments. It was, perhaps, the narrow limits to which he thus confined himself upon the guitar, which gave birth, in great measure, to the fantastic character of his performances. But the fervid *facility* of his impromptus could not be so accounted for. They must have been, and were, in the notes, as well as in the words of his wild fantasias (for he not unfrequently accompanied himself with rhymed verbal improvisations), the result of that intense mental collectedness and concentration to which I have previously alluded as observable only in particular moments of the highest artificial excitement. The words of one of these rhapsodies I have easily remembered. I was, perhaps, the more forcibly impressed with it, as he gave it, because, in the under or mystic current of its meaning, I fancied that I perceived, and for the first time, a full consciousness, on the part of Usher, of the tottering of his lofty reason upon her throne. The verses, which were entitled "The Haunted Palace," ran very nearly, if not accurately, thus:—

I

In the greenest of our valleys
  By good angels tenanted,
Once a fair and stately palace—
  Radiant palace—reared its head.
In the monarch Thought's dominion,
  It stood there;
Never seraph spread a pinion
  Over fabric half so fair.

II

Banners yellow, glorious, golden,
  On its roof did float and flow,
(This—all this—was in the olden
  Time long ago)
And every gentle air that dallied,
  In that sweet day,
Along the ramparts plumed and pallid,
  A wingèd odor went away.

III

Wanderers in that happy valley
    Through two luminous windows saw
Spirits moving musically
    To a lute's well-tunèd law,
Round about a throne where, sitting,
    Porphyrogene,
In state his glory well befitting,
    The ruler of the realm was seen.

IV

And all with pearl and ruby glowing
    Was the fair palace door,
Through which came flowing, flowing, flowing,
    And sparkling evermore,
A troop of Echoes whose sweet duty
    Was but to sing,
In voices of surpassing beauty,
    The wit and wisdom of their king.

V

But evil things, in robes of sorrow,
    Assailed the monarch's high estate;
(Ah, let us mourn, for never morrow
    Shall dawn upon him, desolate!)
And round about his home the glory
    That blushed and bloomed
Is but a dim-remembered story
    Of the old time entombed.

VI

And travellers now within that valley
    Through the red-litten windows see
Vast forms that move fantastically
    To a discordant melody;
While, like a ghastly rapid river,
    Through the pale door
A hideous throng rush out forever,
    And laugh—but smile no more.

I well remember that suggestions arising from this ballad led us into a train of thought, wherein there became manifest an opinion of Usher's which I mention not so much on account of its novelty, (for other men have thought thus,) as on account of the pertinacity with which he maintained it. This opinion, in its general form, was that of the sentience of all vegetable things. But in his disordered fancy the idea had assumed a more daring character, and trespassed, under certain conditions, upon the kingdom of inorganization. I lack words to express the full extent, or the earnest *abandon* of his persuasion. The belief, however, was connected (as I have previously hinted) with the gray stones of the home of his forefathers. The conditions of the sentience had been here, he imagined, fulfilled in the method of collocation of these stones—in the order of their arrangement, as well as in that of the many fungi which overspread them, and of the decayed trees which stood around—above all, in the long undisturbed endurance of this arrangement, and in its reduplication in the still waters of the tarn. Its evidence—the evidence of the sentience—was to be seen, he said (and I here started as he spoke), in the gradual yet certain condensation of an atmosphere of their own about the waters and the walls. The result was discoverable, he added, in that silent, yet importunate and terrible influence which for centuries had moulded the destinies of his family, and which made *him* what I now saw him—what he was. Such opinions need no comment, and I will make none.

Our books—the books which, for years, had formed no small portion of the mental existence of the invalid—were, as might be supposed, in strict keeping with this character of phantasm. We pored together over such works as the Ververt and Chartreuse of Gresset; the Belphegor of Machiavelli; the Heaven and Hell of Swedenborg; the Subterranean Voyage of Nicholas Klimm by Holberg; the Chiromancy of Robert Flud, of Jean D'Indaginé, and of De la Chambre; the Journey into the Blue Distance of Tieck; and the City of the Sun of Campanella. One favorite volume was a small octavo edition of the *Directorium Inquisitorum,* by the Dominican Eymeric de Gironne; and there were passages in Pomponius Mela, about the old African Satyrs and Ægipans, over which Usher would sit dreaming for hours. His chief delight, however, was found in the perusal of an exceedingly rare and curious book in quarto Gothic—the manual of a forgotten church—*the Vigilæ Mortuorum secundum Chorum Ecclesiæ Maguntinæ.*

I could not help thinking of the wild ritual of this work, and of its probable influence upon the hypochondriac, when one evening, having informed me abruptly that the lady Madeline was no more, he stated his intention of preserving her corpse for a fortnight, (previously to its final interment,) in one of the numerous vaults within the main walls of the building. The worldly reason, however, assigned for this singular proceeding, was one which I did not feel at liberty to dispute. The brother had been led to his resolution (so he told me) by consideration of the unusual character of the malady of the deceased, of certain obtrusive and eager inquiries on the part of her medical men, and of the remote and exposed situation of the burial-ground of the family. I will not deny that when I called to mind the sinister countenance of the person whom I met upon the staircase, on the day of my arrival at the house, I had no desire to oppose what I regarded as at best but a harmless, and by no means an unnatural, precaution.

At the request of Usher, I personally aided him in the arrangements for the temporary entombment. The body having been encoffined, we two alone bore it to its rest. The vault in which we placed it (and which had been so long unopened that our torches, half smothered in its oppressive atmosphere, gave us little opportunity for investigation) was small, damp, and entirely without means of admission for light; lying, at great depth, immediately beneath that portion of the building in which was my own sleeping apartment. It had been used, apparently, in remote feudal times, for the worst purposes of a donjon-keep, and in later days as a place of deposit for powder, or some other highly combustible substance, as a portion of its floor, and the whole interior of a long archway through which we reached it, were carefully sheathed with copper. The door, of massive iron, had been, also, similarly protected. Its immense weight caused an unusually sharp grating sound, as it moved upon its hinges.

Having deposited our mournful burden upon tressels within this region of horror, we partially turned aside the yet unscrewed lid of the coffin, and looked upon the face of the tenant. A striking similitude between the brother and sister now first arrested my attention; and Usher, divining, perhaps, my thoughts, murmured out some few words from which I learned that the deceased and himself had been twins, and that sympathies of a scarcely intelligible nature had always existed between them. Our glances, however, rested not long upon the dead—for we could not regard her unawed. The disease which had thus entombed the lady in the maturity of youth, had left, as usual in all maladies of a strictly cataleptical character, the mockery of a faint blush upon the bosom and the face, and that suspiciously lingering smile upon the lip which is so terrible in death. We replaced and screwed down the lid, and, having secured the door of iron, made our way, with toil, into the scarcely less gloomy apartments of the upper portion of the house.

And now, some days of bitter grief having elapsed, an observable change came over the features of the mental disorder of my friend. His ordinary manner had vanished. His ordinary occupations were neglected or forgotten. He roamed from chamber to chamber with hurried, unequal, and objectless step. The pallor of his countenance had assumed, if possible, a more ghastly hue—but the luminousness of his eye had utterly gone out. The once occasional huskiness of his tone was heard no more; and a tremulous quaver, as if of extreme terror, habitually characterized his utterance. There were times, indeed, when I thought his unceasingly agitated mind was laboring with some oppressive secret, to divulge which he struggled for the necessary courage. At times, again, I was obliged to resolve all into the mere inexplicable vagaries of madness, for I beheld him gazing upon vacancy for long hours, in an attitude of the profoundest attention, as if listening to some imaginary sound. It was no wonder that his condition terrified—that it infected me. I felt creeping upon me, by slow yet certain degrees, the wild influences of his own fantastic yet impressive superstitions.

It was, especially, upon retiring to bed late in the night of the seventh or eighth day after the placing of the lady Madeline within the donjon, that I experienced the full power of such feelings. Sleep came not near my couch, while the hours waned and waned away. I struggled to reason off the nervousness which had dominion over me. I endeavored to believe that much, if not all, of what I felt was due to the bewildering influence of the gloomy furniture of the room—of the dark and tattered draperies which, tortured into motion by the breath of a rising tempest, swayed fitfully to and fro upon the walls, and rustled uneasily about the decorations of the bed. But my efforts were fruitless. An irrepressible tremor gradually pervaded my frame; and at length there sat upon my very heart an incubus of utterly causeless alarm. Shaking this off with a gasp and a struggle, I uplifted myself upon the pillows, and, peering earnestly within the intense darkness of the chamber, hearkened—I know not why, except that an instinctive spirit prompted me—to certain low and indefinite sounds which came, through the pauses of the storm, at long intervals, I knew not whence. Overpowered by an intense sentiment of horror, unaccountable yet unendurable, I threw on my clothes with haste, (for I felt that I should sleep no more during the night,) and endeavored to arouse myself from the pitiable condition into which I had fallen, by pacing rapidly to and fro through the apartment.

I had taken but few turns in this manner, when a light step on an adjoining staircase arrested my attention. I presently recognized it as that of Usher. In an instant afterward he rapped with a gentle touch at my door, and entered, bearing a lamp. His countenance was, as usual, cadaverously wan—but, moreover, there was a species of mad hilarity in his eyes—an evidently restrained hysteria

in his whole demeanor. His air appalled me—but anything was preferable to the solitude which I had so long endured, and I even welcomed his presence as a relief.

"And you have not seen it?" he said abruptly, after having stared about him for some moments in silence—"you have not then seen it?—but, stay! You shall." Thus speaking, and having carefully shaded his lamp, he hurried to one of the casements, and threw it freely open to the storm.

The impetuous fury of the entering gust nearly lifted us from our feet. It was, indeed, a tempestuous yet sternly beautiful night, and one wildly singular in its terror and its beauty. A whirlwind had apparently collected its force in our vicinity; for there were frequent and violent alterations in the direction of the wind; and the exceeding density of the clouds (which hung so low as to press upon the turrets of the house) did not prevent our perceiving the life-like velocity with which they flew careering from all points against each other, without passing away into the distance. I say that even their exceeding density did not prevent our perceiving this; yet we had no glimpse of the moon or stars, nor was there any flashing forth of the lightning. But the under surfaces of the huge masses of agitated vapor, as well as all terrestrial objects immediately around us, were glowing in the unnatural light of a faintly luminous and distinctly visible gaseous exhalation which hung about and enshrouded the mansion.

"You must not—you shall not behold this!" said I, shudderingly, to Usher, as I led him with a gentle violence from the window to a seat. "These appearances, which bewilder you, are merely electrical phenomena not uncommon—or it may be that they have their ghastly origin in the rank miasma of the tarn. Let us close this casement; the air is chilling and dangerous to your frame. Here is one of your favorite romances. I will read, and you shall listen;—and so we will pass away this terrible night together."

The antique volume which I had taken up was the "Mad Trist" of Sir Launcelot Canning; but I had called it a favorite of Usher's more in sad jest than in earnest; for, in truth, there is little in its uncouth and unimaginative prolixity which could have had interest for the lofty and spiritual ideality of my friend. It was, however, the only book immediately at hand; and I indulged a vague hope that the excitement which now agitated the hypochondriac might find relief (for the history of mental disorder is full of similar anomalies) even in the extremeness of the folly which I should read. Could I have judged, indeed, by the wild overstrained air of vivacity with which he hearkened, or apparently hearkened, to the words of the tale, I might well have congratulated myself upon the success of my design.

I had arrived at that well-known portion of the story where Ethelred, the hero of the Trist, having sought in vain for peaceable admission into the dwelling of the hermit, proceeds to make good an entrance by force. Here, it will be remembered, the words of the narrative run thus:—

"And Ethelred, who was by nature of a doughty heart, and who was now mighty withal, on account of the powerfulness of the wine which he had drunken, waited no longer to hold parley with the hermit, who, in sooth, was of an obstinate and maliceful turn, but, feeling the rain upon his shoulders, and fearing the rising of the tempest, uplifted his mace outright, and with blows made quickly room in the plankings of the door for his gauntleted hand; and now pulling therewith sturdily, he so cracked, and ripped, and tore all asunder, that the noise of the dry and hollow-sounding wood alarumed and reverberated throughout the forest."

At the termination of this sentence I started, and for a moment paused; for it appeared to me (although I at once concluded that my excited fancy had deceived me)—it appeared to me that from some very remote portion of the mansion there came, indistinctly, to my ears, what might have been, in its exact similarity of character, the echo (but a stifled and dull one certainly) of the very cracking and ripping sound which Sir Launcelot had so particularly described. It was, beyond doubt, the coincidence alone which had arrested my attention; for, amid the rattling of the sashes of the casements, and the ordinary commingled noises of the still increasing storm, the sound, in itself, had nothing, surely, which should have interested or disturbed me. I continued the story:—

"But the good champion Ethelred, now entering within the door, was sore enraged and amazed to perceive no signal of the maliceful hermit; but, in the stead thereof, a dragon of a scaly and prodigious demeanor, and of a fiery tongue, which sate in guard before a palace of gold, with a floor of silver; and upon the wall there hung a shield of shining brass with this legend enwritten—

Who entereth herein, a conqueror hath bin;
Who slayeth the dragon, the shield he shall win.

And Ethelred uplifted his mace, and struck upon the head of the dragon, which fell before him, and gave up his pesty breath, with a shriek so horrid and harsh, and withal so piercing, that Ethelred had fain to close his ears with his hands against the dreadful noise of it, the like whereof was never before heard."

Here again I paused abruptly, and now with a feeling of wild amazement; for there could be no doubt whatever that, in this instance, I did actually hear (although from what direction it proceeded I found it impossible to say) a low and apparently distant, but harsh, protracted, and most unusual screaming or grating sound—the exact counterpart of what my fancy had conjured up for the dragon's unnatural shriek as described by the romancer.

Oppressed, as I certainly was, upon the occurrence of this second and most extraordinary coincidence, by a thousand conflicting sensations, in which wonder and extreme terror were predominant, I still retained sufficient presence of mind to avoid exciting, by any observation, the sensitive nervousness of my companion. I was by no means certain that he had noticed the sounds in question; although, assuredly, a strange alteration had during the last few minutes taken place in his demeanor. From a position fronting my own, he had gradually brought round his chair, so as to sit with his face to the door of the chamber; and thus I could but partially perceive his features, although I saw that his lips trembled as if he were murmuring inaudibly. His head had dropped upon his breast—yet I knew that he was not asleep, from the wide and rigid opening of the eye as I caught a glance of it in profile. The motion of his body, too, was at variance with this idea—for he rocked from side to side with a gentle yet constant and uniform sway. Having rapidly taken notice of all this, I resumed the narrative of Sir Launcelot, which thus proceeded:—

"And now, the champion, having escaped from the terrible fury of the dragon, bethinking himself of the brazen shield, and of the breaking up of the enchantment which was upon it, removed the carcass from out of the way before him, and approached valorously over the silver pavement of the castle to where the shield was upon the wall; which in sooth tarried not for his full coming, but fell down at his feet upon the silver floor, with a mighty great and terrible ringing sound."

No sooner had these syllables passed my lips, than—as if a shield of brass had indeed, at the moment, fallen heavily upon a floor of silver—I became aware of a distinct, hollow, metallic and clangorous, yet apparently muffled reverberation. Completely unnerved, I leaped to my feet; but the measured rocking movement of Usher was undisturbed. I rushed to the chair in which he sat. His eyes were bent fixedly before him, and throughout his whole countenance there reigned a stony rigidity. But, as I placed my hand upon his shoulder, there came a strong shudder over his whole person; a sickly smile quivered about his lips; and I saw that he spoke in a low, hurried, and gibbering murmur, as if unconscious of my presence. Bending closely over him, I at length drank in the hideous import of his words.

"Not hear it?—yes, I hear it, and *have* heard it. Long—long—long—many minutes, many hours, many days, have I heard it—yet I dared not—oh, pity me, miserable wretch that I am!—I dared not—I *dared* not speak! *We have put her living in the tomb!* Said I not that my senses were acute? I *now* tell you that I heard her first feeble movements in the hollow coffin. I heard them—many, many days ago—yet I dared not—*I dared not speak!* And now—to-night—Ethelred—ha! ha!—the breaking of the hermit's door, and the death-cry of the dragon, and the clangor of the shield!—say, rather, the rending of her coffin, and the grating of iron hinges of her prison, and her struggles within the coppered archway of the vault! Oh, whither shall I fly? Will she not be here anon? Is she not hurrying to upbraid me for my haste? Have I not heard her footstep on the stair? Do I not distinguish that heavy and horrible beating of her heart? Madman!"—here he sprang furiously to his feet, and shrieked out his syllables, as if in the effort he were giving up his soul—*"Madman! I tell you that she now stands without the door!"*

As if in the superhuman energy of his utterance there had been found the potency of a spell, the huge antique panels to which the speaker pointed threw slowly back, upon the instant, their ponderous and ebony jaws. It was the work of the rushing gust—but then without those doors there *did* stand the lofty and enshrouded figure of the lady Madeline of Usher. There was blood upon her white robes, and the evidence of some bitter struggle upon every portion of her emaciated frame. For a moment she remained trembling and reeling to and fro upon the threshold—then, with a low moaning cry, fell heavily inward upon the person of her brother, and, in her violent and now final death-agonies, bore him to the floor a corpse, and a victim to the terrors he had anticipated.

From that chamber, and from that mansion, I fled aghast. The storm was still abroad in all its wrath as I found myself crossing the old causeway. Suddenly there shot along the path a wild light, and I turned to see whence a gleam so unusual could have issued; for the vast house and its shadows were alone behind me. The radiance was that of the full, setting, and blood-red moon, which now shone vividly through that once barely-discernible fissure, of which I have before spoken as extending from the roof of the building, in a zigzag direction, to the base. While I gazed, this fissure rapidly widened—there came a fierce breath of the whirlwind—the entire orb of the satellite burst at once upon my sight—my brain reeled as I saw the mighty walls rushing asunder—there was a long tumultuous shouting sound like the voice of a thousand waters—and the deep and dank tarn at my feet closed sullenly and silently over the fragments of the *"House of Usher."*

Exercises

1. Poe called his fanciful tales "arabesques" because his intention was to disclose and arouse unusual mental states. As in most of his tales, it is difficult to tell the difference between appearance and reality. For example, are the twins Roderick and Madeline real persons or are they complementary parts of a single personality?
2. Does the poem embedded in the story describe a palace, a person, or both? The *banners yellow* could be blond hair, with eyes described as *luminous windows*. The *fair palace door* of *pearl and ruby* could be a mouth emitting a *troop of echoes,* and so on.
3. Did the House of Usher bring on its own destruction or was the supernatural somehow involved? How?
4. Does the literal destruction of the house at the end constitute a climax or an anticlimax? Explain your answer.

Ralph Waldo Emerson (1803–1882)

Poe was a conscious representative of a Southern tradition in literature, that of a romantic Virginia Cavalier. Just as consciously, Emerson and his colleagues were New England Romantics who reconciled romantic abstractions with the hardheaded realities of Yankee individualism. The creed of Emerson, Thoreau, Margaret Fuller, and others was transcendentalism, a belief that human beings and the universe were in perfect harmony and moving in a Hegelian manner toward perfection. High-minded and highly individualistic, transcendentalism stressed the individual's conscience as the sole judge in spiritual matters, total self-reliance in all matters, and the necessity for social reforms.

For Poe poetry was beauty but Emerson viewed it as a necessary function for the individual who was seeking truth. Emerson wrote his essays but, in a sense, he thought that his poems wrote him. Many of Emerson's poems are the result of the poet's attempts to perceive the deeper meaning of nature, such as "The Rhodora," which was emblematic of the beauty bestowed by spirit on the world and implanted in human beings.

Literary Selections

The Rhodora

On Being Asked, Whence is the Flower?
Ralph Waldo Emerson

In May, when sea-winds pierce our solitudes,
I found the fresh Rhodora in the woods,
Spreading its leafless blooms in a damp nook,
To please the desert and the sluggish brook.
The purple petals, fallen in the pool,
Made the black water with their beauty gay;
Here might the red-bird come his plumes to cool,
And court the flower that cheapens his array.
Rhodora! if the sages ask thee why
This charm is wasted on the earth and sky,
Tell them, dear, that if eyes were made for seeing,
Then Beauty is its own excuse for being:
Why thou wert there, O rival of the rose!
I never thought to ask, I never knew:
But, in my simple ignorance, suppose
The self-same Power that brought me there brought you.

Like many other romantics, particularly Hegel, Emerson was influenced by Oriental philosophy and religion. His "Brahma" is a tightly constructed parable about the unity that underlies the world and all that is in it.

BRAHMA
Ralph Waldo Emerson

If the red slayer think he slays,
    Or if the slain think he is slain,
They know not well the subtle ways
    I keep, and pass, and turn again.

Far or forgot to me is near;
    Shadow and sunlight are the same;
The vanished gods to me appear;
    And one to me are shame and fame.

They reckon ill who leave me out;
    When me they fly, I am the wings;
I am the doubter and the doubt,
    And I the hymn the Brahmin sings.

The strong gods pine for my abode,
    And pine in vain the sacred Seven;
But thou, meek lover of the good!
    Find me, and turn thy back on heaven.

Emerson's most famous poem is the "Concord Hymn" that memorialized the first battle of the Revolutionary War.

CONCORD HYMN

Sung at the Completion of the Battle
Monument, July 4, 1837

Ralph Waldo Emerson

By the rude bridge that arched the flood,
   Their flag to April's breeze unfurled,
Here once the embattled farmers stood
   And fired the shot heard round the world.

The foe long since in silence slept;
   Alike the conqueror silent sleeps;
And Time the ruined bridge has swept
   Down the dark stream which seaward creeps.

On this green bank, by this soft stream,
   We set to-day a votive stone;
That memory may their deed redeem,
   When, like our sires, our sons are gone.

Spirit, that made those heroes dare
   To die, and leave their children free,
Bid Time and Nature gently spare
   The shaft we raise to them and thee.

Exercises

1. In "The Rhodora" Emerson says *that if eyes were made for seeing,/Then beauty is its own excuse for being.* What does this mean? That beauty is as necessary as sight? In "Grecian Urn" Keats wrote that *beauty is truth, truth beauty.* Was Emerson thinking along the same lines or was he referring to nature rather than art?

2. "Brahma" contains a number of paradoxes like *shadow and sunlight are the same.* What are the other paradoxes and what do these imply?

Henry David Thoreau (1817–1862)

Emerson and Thoreau were close friends all their lives but no two people were less alike personally or more alike in their transcendentalist conviction that individuals should lead active and responsible lives. Thoreau felt that most people lived lives of "quiet desperation" and made his point at Walden Pond by coexisting for two years in harmony with nature. His account of his experiences in *Walden* (1854) was his masterwork, but his thoughtful essay on "Civil Disobedience" was largely unread in his own day. Inspired probably by a night in jail because of his refusal, on principle, to pay a poll tax, "Civil Disobedience" was a major influence on Mahatma Gandhi and, later, on Martin Luther King, Jr.

Literary Selection

CIVIL DISOBEDIENCE

Henry David Thoreau

I heartily accept the motto, "That government is best which governs least;" and I should like to see it acted up to more rapidly and systematically. Carried out, it finally amounts to this, which also I believe,—"That government is best which governs not at all; and when men are prepared for it, that will be the kind of government which they will have. Government is at best but an expedient; but most governments are usually, and all governments are sometimes, inexpedient. The objections which have been brought against a standing army, and they are many and weighty, and deserve to prevail, may also at last be brought against a standing government. The standing army is only an arm of the standing government. The government itself, which is only the mode which the people have chosen to execute their will, is equally liable to be abused and perverted before the people can act through it. Witness the present Mexican war, the work of comparatively a few individuals using the standing government as their tool; for, in the outset, the people would not have consented to this measure.

This American government,—what is it but a tradition, though a recent one, endeavoring to transmit itself unimpaired to posterity, but each instant losing some of its integrity? It has not the vitality and force of a single living man; for a single man can bend it to his will. It is a sort of wooden gun to the people themselves. But it is not the less necessary for this, for the people must have some complicated machinery or other, and hear its din, to satisfy that idea of government which they have. Governments show thus how successfully men can be imposed on, even impose on themselves, for their own advantage. It is excellent, we must all allow. Yet this government never of itself furthered any enterprise, but by the alacrity with which it got out of its way. *It* does not keep the country free. *It* does not settle the West. *It* does not educate. The character inherent in the American people has done all that has been accomplished; and it would have done somewhat more, if the government had not sometimes got in its way. For government is an expedient by which men would fain succeed in letting one another alone; and, as has been said, when it is most expedient, the governed are most let alone by it. Trade and commerce, if they were not made of india-rubber, would never manage to bounce over the obstacles which legislators are continually putting in their way; and, if one were to judge these men wholly by the effects of their actions and not partly by their intentions, they would deserve to be classed and punished with those mischievous persons who put obstructions on the railroads.

But, to speak practically and as a citizen, unlike those who call themselves no-government men, I ask for, not at once no government, but *at once* a better government. Let every man make known what kind of government would command his respect, and that will be one step toward obtaining it.

After all, the practical reason why, when the power is once in the hands of the people, a majority are permitted, and for a long period continue, to rule is not because they are most likely to be in the right, nor because this seems fairest to the minority, but because they are physically the strongest. But a government in which the majority rule in all cases cannot be based on justice, even as far as men understand it. Can there not be a government in which majorities do not virtually decide right and wrong, but conscience?—in which majorities decide only those questions to which the rule of expediency is applicable? Must the citizen ever for a moment, or in the least degree, resign his conscience to the legislator? Why has every man a conscience, then? I think that we should be men first, and subjects afterward. It is not desirable to cultivate a respect for the law, so much as for the right. The only obligation which I have a right to assume is to do at any time what I think right. It is truly enough said that a corporation has no conscience; but a corporation of conscientious men is a corporation *with* a conscience. Law never made men a whit more just; and, by means of their respect for it, even the well-disposed are daily made the agents of injustice. A common and natural result of an undue respect for law is, that you may see a file of soldiers, colonel, captain, corporal, privates, powder-monkeys, and all, marching in admirable order over hill and dale to the wars, against their wills, ay, against their common sense and consciences, which makes it very steep marching indeed, and produces a palpitation of the heart. They have no doubt that it is a damnable business in which they are concerned; they are all peaceably inclined. Now, what are they? Men at all? or small movable forts and magazines, at the service of some unscrupulous man in power? Visit the Navy-Yard, and behold a marine, such a man as an American government can make, or such as it can make a man with its black arts,—a mere shadow and reminiscence of humanity, a man laid out alive and standing, and already, as one may say, buried under arms with funeral accompaniments, though it may be,—

"Not a drum was heard, not a funeral note,
  As his corse to the rampart we hurried;
Not a soldier discharged his farewell shot
  O'er the grave where our hero we buried."

The mass of men serve the state thus, not as men mainly, but as machines, with their bodies. They are the standing army, and the militia, jailers, constables, *posse comitatus,* etc. In most cases there is no free exercise whatever of the judgment or of the moral sense; but they put themselves on a level with wood and earth and stones; and wooden men can perhaps be manufactured that will serve the purpose as well. Such command no more respect than men of straw or a lump of dirt. They have the same sort of worth only as horses and dogs. Yet such as these even are commonly esteemed good citizens. Others—as most legislators, politicians, lawyers, ministers, and office-holders—serve the state chiefly with their heads; and, as they rarely make any moral distinctions, they are as likely to serve the devil, without *intending* it, as God. A very few—as heroes, patriots, martyrs, reformers in the great sense, and *men*—serve the state with their consciences also, and so necessarily resist it for the most part; and they are commonly treated as

enemies by it. A wise man will only be useful as a man, and will not submit to be "clay," and "stop a hole to keep the wind away," but leave that office to his dust at least:—

"I am too high-born to be propertied,
To be a secondary at control,
Or useful serving-man and instrument
To any sovereign state throughout the world."

He who gives himself entirely to his fellow-men appears to them useless and selfish; but he who gives himself partially to them is pronounced a benefactor and philanthropist.

How does it become a man to behave toward this American government to-day? I answer, that he cannot without disgrace be associated with it. I cannot for an instant recognize that political organization as *my* government which is the *slave's* government also.

All men recognize the right of revolution; that is, the right to refuse allegiance to, and to resist, the government, when its tyranny or its inefficiency are great and unendurable. But almost all say that such is not the case now. But such was the case, they think, in the Revolution of '75. If one were to tell me that this was a bad government because it taxed certain foreign commodities brought to its ports, it is most probable that I should not make an ado about it, for I can do without them. All machines have their friction; and possibly this does enough good to counterbalance the evil. At any rate, it is a great evil to make a stir about it. But when the friction comes to have its machine, and oppression and robbery are organized, I say, let us not have such a machine any longer. In other words, when a sixth of the population of a nation which has undertaken to be the refuge of liberty are slaves, and a whole country is unjustly overrun and conquered by a foreign army, and subjected to military law, I think that it is not too soon for honest men to rebel and revolutionize. What makes this duty the more urgent is the fact that the country so overrun is not our own, but ours is the invading army.

Paley, a common authority with many on moral questions, in his chapter on the "Duty of Submission to Civil Government," resolves all civil obligation into expediency; and he proceeds to say that "so long as the interest of the whole society requires it, that is, so long as the established government cannot be resisted or changed without public inconveniency, it is the will of God . . . that the established government be obeyed,—and no longer. This principle being admitted, the justice of every particular case of resistance is reduced to a computation of the quantity of the danger and grievance on the one side, and of the probability and expense of redressing it on the other." Of this, he says, every man shall judge for himself. But Paley appears never to have contemplated those cases to which the rule of expediency does not apply, in which a people, as well as an individual, must do justice, cost what it may. If I have unjustly wrested a plank from a drowning man, I must restore it to him though I drown myself. This, according to Paley, would be inconvenient. But he that would save his life, in such a case, shall lose it. This people must cease to hold slaves, and to make war on Mexico, though it cost them their existence as a people.

In their practice, nations agree with Paley; but does any one think that Massachusetts does exactly what is right at the present crisis?

"A drab of state, a cloth-o'-silver slut,
To have her train borne up, and her soul trail in the dirt."

Practically speaking, the opponents to reform in Massachusetts are not a hundred thousand politicians at the South, but a hundred thousand merchants and farmers here, who are more interested in commerce and agriculture than they are in humanity, and are not prepared to do justice to the slave and to Mexico, *cost what it may.* I quarrel not with far-off foes, but with those who, near at home, coöperate with, and do the bidding of, those far away, and without whom the latter would be harmless. We are accustomed to say, that the mass of men are unprepared; but improvement is slow, because the few are not materially wiser or better than the many. It is not so important that many should be as good as you, as that there be some absolute goodness somewhere; for that will leaven the whole lump. There are thousands who are *in opinion* opposed to slavery and to the war, who yet in effect do nothing to put an end to them; who, esteeming themselves children of Washington and Franklin, sit down with their hands in their pockets, and say that they know not what to do, and do nothing; who even postpone the question of freedom to the question of free trade, and quietly read the prices-current along with the latest advices from Mexico, after dinner, and, it may be, fall asleep over them both. What is the price-current of an honest man and patriot to-day? They hesitate, and they regret, and sometimes they petition; but they do nothing in earnest and with effect. They will wait, well disposed, for others to remedy the evil, that they may no longer have it to regret. At most, they give only a cheap vote, and a feeble countenance and God-speed, to the right, as it goes by them. There are nine hundred and ninety-nine patrons of virtue to one virtuous man. But it is easier to deal with the real possessor of a thing than with the temporary guardian of it.

All voting is a sort of gaming, like checkers or backgammon, with a slight moral tinge to it, a playing with right and wrong, with moral questions; and betting naturally accompanies it. The character of the voters is not staked. I cast my vote, perchance, as I think right; but I am not vitally concerned that that right should prevail. I am willing to leave it to the majority. Its obligation, therefore, never exceeds that of expediency. Even voting *for the right* is *doing* nothing for it. It is only expressing to men feebly your desire that it should prevail. A wise man will not leave the right to the mercy of chance, nor wish it to prevail through the power of the majority. There is but little virtue in the action of masses of men. When the majority shall at length vote for the abolition of slavery, it will be because they are indifferent to slavery, or because there is but little slavery left to be abolished by their vote. *They* will then be the only slaves. Only *his* vote can hasten the abolition of slavery who asserts his own freedom by his vote.

I hear of a convention to be held at Baltimore, or elsewhere, for the selection of a candidate for the Presidency, made up chiefly of editors, and men who are politicians by profession; but I think, what is it to any independent, intelligent, and respectable man what decision they may come to? Shall we not have the advantage of his wisdom and honesty, nevertheless? Can we not count upon some independent votes? Are there not many individuals in the country who do not attend conventions? But no: I find that the respectable man, so called, has immediately drifted from his position, and despairs of his country, when his country has more reason to despair of him. He forthwith adopts one of the candidates thus selected as the only *available* one, thus proving that he is himself *available* for any purposes of the demagogue. His vote is of no more worth than that of any unprincipled foreigner or hireling native, who may have been bought. O for a man who is a *man,* and, as my neighbor says, has a bone in his back which you cannot pass your hand through! Our statistics are at fault: the population has been returned too large. How many *men* are there to a square thousand miles in this country? Hardly one. Does not America offer any inducement for men to settle here? The American has dwindled into an Odd Fellow,—one who may be known by the development of his organ of gregariousness, and a manifest lack of intellect and cheerful self-reliance; whose first and chief concern, on coming into the world, is to see that the almshouses are in good repair; and, before yet he has lawfully donned the virile garb, to collect a fund for the support of the widows and orphans that may be; who, in short, ventures to live only by the aid of the Mutual Insurance company, which has promised to bury him decently.

It is not a man's duty, as a matter of course, to devote himself to the eradication of any, even the most enormous, wrong; he may still properly have other concerns to engage him; but it is his duty, at least, to wash his hands of it, and, if he gives it no thought longer, not to give it practically his support. If I devote myself to other pursuits and contemplations, I must first see, at least, that I do not pursue them sitting upon another man's shoulders. I must get off him first, that he may pursue his contemplations too. See what gross inconsistency is tolerated. I have heard some of my townsmen say, "I should like to have them order me out to help put down an insurrection of the slaves, or to march to Mexico;—see if I would go;" and yet these very men have each, directly by their allegiance, and so indirectly, at least, by their money, furnished a substitute. The soldier is applauded who refuses to serve in an unjust war by those who do not refuse to sustain the unjust government which makes the war; is applauded by those whose own act and authority he disregards and sets at naught; as if the state were penitent to that degree that it hired one to scourge it while it sinned, but not to that degree that it left off sinning for a moment. Thus, under the name of Order and Civil Government, we are all made at last to pay homage to and support our own meanness. After the first blush of sin comes its indifference; and from immoral it becomes, as it were, *un*moral, and not quite unnecessary to that life which we have made.

The broadest and most prevalent error requires the most disinterested virtue to sustain it. The slight reproach to which the virtue of patriotism is commonly liable, the noble are most likely to incur. Those who, while they disapprove of the character and measures of a government, yield to it their allegiance and support are undoubtedly its most conscientious supporters, and so frequently the most serious obstacles to reform. Some are petitioning the State to dissolve the Union, to disregard the requisitions of the President. Why do they not dissolve it themselves,—the union between themselves and the State,—and refuse to pay their quota into its treasury? Do not they stand in the same relation to the State that the State does to the Union? And have not the same reasons prevented the State from resisting the Union which have prevented them from resisting the State?

How can a man be satisfied to entertain an opinion merely, and enjoy *it?* Is there any enjoyment in it, if his opinion is that he is aggrieved? If you are cheated out of a single dollar by your neighbor, you do not rest satisfied with knowing that you are cheated, or with saying that you are cheated, or even with petitioning him to pay you your due; but you take effectual steps at once to obtain the full amount, and see that you are never cheated again. Action from principle, the perception and the performance of right, changes things and relations; it is essentially revolutionary, and does not consist wholly with anything which was. It not only divides States and churches, it divides families; ay, it divides the *individual,* separating the diabolical in him from the divine.

Unjust laws exist: shall we be content to obey them, or shall we endeavor to amend them, and obey them until we have succeeded, or shall we transgress them at once? Men generally, under such a government as this, think that they ought to wait until they have persuaded the majority to alter them. They think that, if they should resist, the remedy would be worse than the evil. But it is the fault of the government itself that the remedy *is* worse than the evil. *It* makes it worse. Why is it not more apt to anticipate and provide for reform? Why does it not cherish its wise minority? Why does it cry and resist before it is hurt? Why does it not encourage its citizens to be on the alert to point out its faults, and *do* better than it would have them? Why does it always crucify Christ, and excommunicate Copernicus and Luther, and pronounce Washington and Franklin rebels?

One would think, that a deliberate and practical denial of its authority was the only offence never contemplated by government; else, why has it not assigned its definite, its suitable and proportionate, penalty? If a man who has no property refuses but once to earn nine shillings for the State, he is put in prison for a period unlimited by any law that I know, and determined only by the discretion of those who placed him there; but if he should steal ninety times nine shillings from the State, he is soon permitted to go at large again.

If the injustice is part of the necessary friction of the machine of government, let it go, let it go: perchance it will wear smooth,—certainly the machine will wear out. If the injustice has a spring, or a pulley, or a rope, or a crank, exclusively for itself, then perhaps you may consider whether the remedy will not be worse than the evil; but if it is of such a nature that it requires you to be the agent of injustice to another, then, I say, break the law. Let your life be a counter-friction to stop the machine. What I have to do is to see, at any rate, that I do not lend myself to the wrong which I condemn.

As for adopting the ways which the State has provided for remedying the evil, I know not of such ways. They take too much time, and a man's life will be gone. I have other affairs to attend to. I came into this world, not chiefly to make this a good place to live in, but to live in it, be it good or bad. A man has not everything to do, but something; and because he cannot do *everything,* it is not

necessary that he should do *something* wrong. It is not my business to be petitioning the Governor or the Legislature any more than it is theirs to petition me; and if they should not hear my petition, what should I do then? But in this case the State has provided no way: its very Constitution is the evil. This may seem to be harsh and stubborn and unconciliatory; but it is to treat with the utmost kindness and consideration the only spirit that can appreciate or deserves it. So is all change for the better, like birth and death, which convulse the body.

I do not hesitate to say, that those who call themselves Abolitionists should at once effectually withdraw their support, both in person and property, from the government of Massachusetts, and not wait till they constitute a majority of one, before they suffer the right to prevail through them. I think that it is enough if they have God on their side, without waiting for that other one. Moreover, any man more right than his neighbors constitutes a majority of one already.

I meet this American government, or its representative, the State government, directly, and face to face, once a year—no more—in the person of its tax-gatherer; this is the only mode in which a man situated as I am necessarily meets it; and it then says distinctly, Recognize me; and the simplest, most effectual, and, in the present posture of affairs, the indispensablest mode of treating with it on this head, of expressing your little satisfaction with and love for it, is to deny it then. My civil neighbor, the tax-gatherer, is the very man I have to deal with,—for it is, after all, with men and not with parchment that I quarrel,—and he has voluntarily chosen to be an agent of the government. How shall he ever know well what he is and does as an officer of the government, or as a man, until he is obliged to consider whether he shall treat me, his neighbor, for whom he has respect, as a neighbor and well-disposed man, or as a maniac and disturber of the peace, and see if he can get over this obstruction to his neighborliness without a ruder and more impetuous thought or speech corresponding with his action. I know this well, that if one thousand, if one hundred, if ten men whom I could name,—if ten *honest* men only,—ay, if *one* HONEST man, in this State of Massachusetts, *ceasing to hold slaves,* were actually to withdraw from this copartnership, and be locked up in the county jail therefor, it would be the abolition of slavery in America. For it matters not how small the beginning may seem to be: what is once well done is done forever. But we love better to talk about it: that we say is our mission. Reform keeps many scores of newspapers in its service, but not one man. If my esteemed neighbor, the State's ambassador, who will devote his days to the settlement of the question of human rights in the Council Chamber, instead of being threatened with the prisons of Carolina, were to sit down the prisoner of Massachusetts, that State which is so anxious to foist the sin of slavery upon her sister,— though at present she can discover only an act of inhospitality to be the ground of a quarrel with her,—the Legislature would not wholly waive the subject the following winter.

Under a government which imprisons any unjustly, the true place for a just man is also a prison. The proper place to-day, the only place which Massachusetts has provided for her freer and less desponding spirits, is in her prisons, to be put out and locked out of the State by her own act, as they have already put themselves out by their principles. It is there that the fugitive slave, and the Mexican prisoner on parole, and the Indian come to plead the wrongs of his race should find them; on that separate, but more free and honorable, ground, where the State places those who are not *with* her, but *against* her,—the only house in a slave State in which a free man can abide with honor. If any think that their influence would be lost there, and their voices no longer afflict the ear of the State, that they would not be as an enemy within its walls, they do not know by how much truth is stronger than error, nor how much more eloquently and effectively he can combat injustice who has experienced a little in his own person. Cast your whole vote, not a strip of paper merely, but your whole influence. A minority is powerless while it conforms to the majority; it is not even a minority then; but it is irresistible when it clogs by its whole weight. If the alternative is to keep all just men in prison, or give up war and slavery, the State will not hesitate which to choose. If a thousand men were not to pay their tax-bills this year, that would not be a violent and bloody measure, as it would be to pay them, and enable the State to commit violence and shed innocent blood. This is, in fact, the definition of a peaceable revolution, if any such is possible. If the tax-gatherer, or any other public officer, asks me, as one has done, "But what shall I do?" my answer is, "If you really wish to do anything, resign your office." When the subject has refused allegiance, and the officer has resigned his office, then the revolution is accomplished. But even suppose blood should flow. Is there not a sort of blood shed when the conscience is wounded? Through this wound a man's real manhood and immortality flow out, and he bleeds to an everlasting death. I see this blood flowing now.

I have contemplated the imprisonment of the offender, rather than the seizure of his goods,—though both will serve the same purpose,—because they who assert the purest right, and consequently are most dangerous to a corrupt State, commonly have not spent much time in accumulating property. To such the State renders comparatively small service, and a slight tax is wont to appear exorbitant, particularly if they are obliged to earn it by special labor with their hands. If there were one who lived wholly without the use of money, the State itself would hesitate to demand it of him. But the rich man—not to make any invidious comparison—is always sold to the institution which makes him rich. Absolutely speaking, the more money, the less virtue; for money comes between a man and his objects, and obtains them for him; and it was certainly no great virtue to obtain it. It puts to rest many questions which he would otherwise be taxed to answer; while the only new question which it puts is the hard but superfluous one, how to spend it. Thus his moral ground is taken from under his feet. The opportunities of living are diminished in proportion as what are called the "means" are increased. The best thing a man can do for his culture when he is rich is to endeavor to carry out those schemes which he entertained when he was poor. Christ answered the Herodians according to their condition. "Show me the tribute-money," said he;—and one took a penny out of his pocket;—if you use money which has the image of Cæsar on it, and which he has made current and valuable, that is, *if you are men of the State,* and gladly enjoy the advantages of Cæsar's government, then pay him back some of his own when he demands it. "Render therefore to Cæsar that which is Cæsar's, and to God those things which are God's,"—leaving them no wiser than before as to which was which; for they did not wish to know.

When I converse with the freest of my neighbors, I perceive that, whatever they may say about the magnitude and seriousness of the question, and their regard for the public tranquility, the long and the short of the matter is, that they cannot spare the protection of the existing government, and they dread the consequences to their property and families of disobedience to it. For my own part, I should not like to think that I ever rely on the protection of the State. But, if I deny the authority of the State when it presents its tax-bill, it will soon take and waste all my property, and so harass me and my children without end. This is hard. This makes it impossible for a man to live honestly, and at the same time comfortably, in outward respects. It will not be worth the while to accumulate property; that would be sure to go again. You must hire or squat somewhere, and raise but a small crop, and eat that soon. You must live within yourself, and depend upon yourself always tucked up and ready for a start, and not have many affairs. A man may grow rich in Turkey even, if he will be in all respects a good subject of the Turkish government. Confucius said: "If a state is governed by the principles of reason, poverty and misery are subjects of shame; if a state is not governed by the principles of reason, riches and honors are the subjects of shame." No: until I want the protection of Massachusetts to be extended to me in some distant Southern port, where my liberty is endangered, or until I am bent solely on building up an estate at home by peaceful enterprise, I can afford to refuse allegiance to Massachusetts, and her right to my property and life. It costs me less in every sense to incur the penalty of disobedience to the State than it would to obey. I should feel as if I were worth less in that case.

Some years ago, the State met me in behalf of the Church, and commanded me to pay a certain sum toward the support of a clergyman whose preaching my father attended, but never I myself. "Pay," it said, "or be locked up in the jail." I declined to pay. But, unfortunately, another man saw fit to pay it. I did not see why the schoolmaster should be taxed to support the priest, and not the priest the schoolmaster; for I was not the State's schoolmaster, but I supported myself by voluntary subscription. I did not see why the lyceum should not present its tax-bill, and have the State to back its demand, as well as the Church. However, at the request of the selectmen, I condescended to make some such statement as this in writing:—"Know all men by these presents, that I, Henry Thoreau, do not wish to be regarded as a member of any incorporated society which I have not joined." This I gave to the town clerk; and he has it. The State, having thus learned that I did not wish to be regarded as a member of that church, has never made a like demand on me since; though it said that it must adhere to its original presumption that time. If I had known how to name them, I should then have signed off in detail from all the societies which I never signed on to; but I did not know where to find a complete list.

I have paid no poll-tax for six years. I was put into a jail once on this account, for one night; and, as I stood considering the walls of solid stone, two or three feet thick, the door of wood and iron, a foot thick, and the iron grating which strained the light, I could not help being struck with the foolishness of that institution which treated me as if I were mere flesh and blood and bones, to be locked up. I wondered that it should have concluded at length that this was the best use it could put me to, and had never thought to avail itself of my services in some way. I saw that, if there was a wall of stone between me and my townsmen, there was a still more difficult one to climb or break through before they could get to be as free as I was. I did not for a moment feel confined, and the walls seemed a great waste of stone and mortar. I felt as if I alone of all my townsmen had paid my tax. They plainly did not know how to treat me, but behaved like persons who are underbred. In every threat and in every compliment there was a blunder; for they thought that my chief desire was to stand the other side of that stone wall. I could not but smile to see how industriously they locked the door on my meditations, which followed them out again without let or hindrance, and *they* were really all that was dangerous. As they could not reach me, they had resolved to punish my body; just as boys, if they cannot come at some person against whom they have a spite, will abuse his dog. I saw that the State was half-witted, that it was timid as a lone woman with her silver spoons, and that it did not know its friends from its foes, and I lost all my remaining respect for it, and pitied it.

Thus the State never intentionally confronts a man's sense, intellectual or moral, but only his body, his senses. It is not armed with superior wit or honesty, but with superior physical strength. I was not born to be forced. I will breathe after my own fashion. Let us see who is the strongest. What force has a multitude? They only can force me to obey a higher law than I. They force me to become like themselves. I do not hear of *men* being *forced* to live this way or that by masses of men. What sort of life were that to live? When I meet a government which says to me, "Your money or your life," why should I be in haste to give it my money? It may be in a great strait, and not know what to do: I cannot help that. It must help itself; do as I do. It is not worth the while to snivel about it. I am not responsible for the successful working of the machinery of society. I am not the son of the engineer. I perceive that, when an acorn and a chestnut fall side by side, the one does not remain inert to make way for the other, but both obey their own laws, and spring and grow and flourish as best they can, till one, perchance, overshadows and destroys the other. If a plant cannot live according to its nature, it dies; and so a man.

The night in prison was novel and interesting enough. The prisoners in their shirt-sleeves were enjoying a chat and the evening air in the doorway, when I entered. But the jailer said, "Come, boys, it is time to lock up;" and so they dispersed, and I heard the sound of their steps returning into the hollow apartments. My roommate was introduced to me by the jailer as "a first-rate fellow and a clever man." When the door was locked, he showed me where to hang my hat, and how he managed matters there. The rooms were whitewashed once a month; and this one, at least, was the whitest, most simply furnished, and probably the neatest apartment in the town. He naturally wanted to know where I came from, and what brought me there; and, when I had told him, I asked him in my turn how he came there, presuming him to be an honest man, of course; and, as the world goes, I believe he was. "Why," said he, "they accuse me of burning a barn; but I never did it." As near as I could discover, he had probably gone to bed in a barn when drunk, and

smoked his pipe there; and so a barn was burnt. He had the reputation of being a clever man, had been there some three months waiting for his trial to come on, and would have to wait as much longer; but he was quite domesticated and contented, since he got his board for nothing, and thought that he was well treated.

He occupied one window, and I the other; and I saw that if one stayed there long, his principal business would be to look out the window. I had soon read all the tracts that were left there, and examined where former prisoners had broken out, and where a grate had been sawed off, and heard the history of the various occupants of that room; for I found that even here there was a history and a gossip which never circulated beyond the walls of the jail. Probably this is the only house in the town where verses are composed, which are afterward printed in a circular form, but not published. I was shown quite a long list of verses which were composed by some young men who had been detected in an attempt to escape, who avenged themselves by singing them.

I pumped my fellow-prisoner as dry as I could, for fear I should never see him again; but at length he showed me which was my bed, and left me to blow out the lamp.

It was like traveling into a far country, such as I had never expected to behold, to lie there for one night. It seemed to me that I never had heard the town clock strike before, nor the evening sounds of the village; for we slept with the windows open, which were inside the grating. It was to see my native village in the light of the Middle Ages, and our Concord was turned into a Rhine stream, and visions of knights and castles passed before me. They were the voices of old burghers that I heard in the streets. I was an involuntary spectator and auditor of whatever was done and said in the kitchen of the adjacent village inn,—a wholly new and rare experience to me. It was a closer view of my native town. I was fairly inside of it. I never had seen its institutions before. This is one of its peculiar institutions; for it is a shire town. I began to comprehend what its inhabitants were about.

In the morning, our breakfasts were put through the hole in the door, in small oblong-square tin pans, made to fit, and holding a pint of chocolate, with brown bread, and an iron spoon. When they called for the vessels again, I was green enough to return what bread I had left; but my comrade seized it, and said that I should lay that up for lunch or dinner. Soon after he was let out to work at haying in a neighboring field, whither he went every day, and would not be back till noon; so he bade me good-day, saying that he doubted if he should see me again.

When I came out of prison,—for some one interfered, and paid that tax,—I did not perceive that great changes had taken place on the common, such as he observed who went in a youth and emerged a tottering and gray-headed man; and yet a change had to my eyes come over the scene,—the town, and State, and country,—greater than any that mere time could effect. I saw yet more distinctly the State in which I lived. I saw to what extent the people among whom I lived could be trusted as good neighbors and friends; that their friendship was for summer weather only; that they did not greatly propose to do right; that they were a distinct race from me by their prejudices and superstitions, as the Chinamen and Malays are; that in their sacrifices to humanity they ran no risks, not even to their property; that after all they were not so noble but they treated the thief as he had treated them, and hoped, by a certain outward observance and a few prayers, and by walking in a particular straight though useless path from time to time, to save their souls. This may be to judge my neighbors harshly; for I believe that many of them are not aware that they have such an institution as the jail in their village.

It was formerly the custom in our village, when a poor debtor came out of jail, for his acquaintances to salute him, looking through their fingers, which were crossed to represent the grating of a jail window, "How do ye do?" My neighbors did not thus salute me, but first looked at me, and then at one another, as if I had returned from a long journey. I was put into jail as I was going to the shoemaker's to get a shoe which was mended. When I was let out the next morning, I proceeded to finish my errand, and, having put on my mended shoe, joined a huckleberry party, who were impatient to put themselves under my conduct; and in half an hour,—for the horse was soon tackled,—was in the midst of a huckleberry field, on one of our highest hills, two miles off, and then the State was nowhere to be seen.

This is the whole history of "My Prisons."

I have never declined paying the highway tax, because I am as desirous of being a good neighbor as I am of being a bad subject; and as for supporting schools, I am doing my part to educate my fellow-countrymen now. It is for no particular item in the tax-bill that I refuse to pay it. I simply wish to refuse allegiance to the State, to withdraw and stand aloof from it effectually. I do not care to trace the course of my dollar, if I could, till it buys a man or a musket to shoot one with,—the dollar is innocent,—but I am concerned to trace the effects of my allegiance. In fact, I quietly declare war with the State, after my fashion, though I will still make what use and get what advantage of her I can, as is usual in such cases.

If others pay the tax which is demanded of me, from a sympathy with the State, they do but what they have already done in their own case, or rather they abet injustice to a greater extent than the State requires. If they pay the tax from a mistaken interest in the individual taxed, to save his property, or prevent his going to jail, it is because they have not considered wisely how far they let their private feelings interfere with the public good.

This, then, is my position at present. But one cannot be too much on his guard in such a case, lest his action be biased by obstinacy or an undue regard for the opinions of men. Let him see that he does only what belongs to himself and to the hour.

I think sometimes, Why, this people mean well, they are only ignorant; they would do better if they knew how: why give your neighbors this pain to treat you as they are not inclined to? But I think again, This is no reason why I should do as they do, or permit others to suffer much greater pain of a different kind. Again, I sometimes say to myself, When many millions of men, without heat, without ill will, without personal feeling of any kind, demand of you a few shillings only, without the possibility, such is their constitution, of retracting or altering their present demand, and without the possibility, on your side, of appeal to any other millions, why expose yourself to this overwhelming brute force? You do not resist cold and hunger, the winds and the waves, thus obstinately; you quietly submit to a thousand similar

necessities. You do not put your head into the fire. But just in proportion as I regard this as not wholly a brute force, but partly a human force, and consider that I have relations to those millions as to so many millions of men, and not of mere brute or inanimate things, I see that appeal is possible, first and instantaneously, from them to the Maker of them, and, secondly, from them to themselves. But if I put my head deliberately into the fire, there is no appeal to fire or to the Maker of fire, and I have only myself to blame. If I could convince myself that I have any right to be satisfied with men as they are, and to treat them accordingly, and not according, in some respects, to my requisitions and expectations of what they and I ought to be, then, like a good Mussulman and fatalist, I should endeavor to be satisfied with things as they are, and say it is the will of God. And, above all, there is this difference between resisting this and a purely brute or natural force, that I can resist this with some effect; but I cannot expect, like Orpheus, to change the nature of the rocks and trees and beasts.

I do not wish to quarrel with any man or nation. I do not wish to split hairs, to make fine distinctions, or set myself up as better than my neighbors. I seek rather, I may say, even an excuse for conforming to the laws of the land. I am but too ready to conform to them. Indeed, I have reason to suspect myself on this head; and each year, as the tax-gatherer comes round, I find myself disposed to review the acts and position of the general and State governments, and the spirit of the people, to discover a pretext for conformity.

"We must affect our country as our parents,
And if at any time we alienate
Our love or industry from doing it honor,
We must respect effects and teach the soul
Matter of conscience and religion,
And not desire of rule or benefit."

I believe that the State will soon be able to take all my work of this sort out of my hands, and then I shall be no better a patriot than my fellow-countrymen. Seen from a lower point of view, the Constitution, with all its faults, is very good; the law and the courts are very respectable; even this State and this American government are, in many respects, very admirable, and rare things, to be thankful for, such as a great many have described them; but seen from a point of view a little higher, they are what I have described them; seen from a higher still, and the highest, who shall say what they are, or that they are worth looking at or thinking of at all?

However, the government does not concern me much, and I shall bestow the fewest possible thoughts on it. It is not many moments that I live under a government, even in this world. If a man is thought-free, fancy-free, imagination-free, that which *is not* never for a long time appearing *to be* to him, unwise rulers or reformers cannot fatally interrupt him.

I know that most men think differently from myself; but those whose lives are by profession devoted to the study of these or kindred subjects content me as little as any. Statesmen and legislators, standing so completely within the institution, never distinctly and nakedly behold it. They speak of moving society, but have no resting-place without it. They may be men of a certain experience and discrimination, and have no doubt invented ingenious and even useful systems, for which we sincerely thank them; but all their wit and usefulness lie within certain not very wide limits. They are wont to forget that the world is not governed by policy and expediency. Webster never goes behind government, and so cannot speak with authority about it. His words are wisdom to those legislators who contemplate no essential reform in the existing government; but for thinkers, and those who legislate for all time, he never once glances at the subject. I know of those whose serene and wise speculations on this theme would soon reveal the limits of his mind's range and hospitality. Yet, compared with the cheap professions of most reformers, and the still cheaper wisdom and eloquence of politicians in general, his are almost the only sensible and valuable words, and we thank Heaven for him. Comparatively, he is always strong, original, and, above all, practical. Still, his quality is not wisdom, but prudence. The lawyer's truth is not Truth, but consistency or a consistent expediency. Truth is always in harmony with herself, and is not concerned chiefly to reveal the justice that may consist with wrong-doing. He well deserves to be called, as he has been called, the Defender of the Constitution. There are really no blows to be given by him but defensive ones. He is not a leader, but a follower. His leaders are the men of '87. "I have never made an effort," he says, "and never propose to make an effort; I have never countenanced an effort, and never mean to countenance an effort, to disturb the arrangement as originally made, by which the various States came into the Union." Still thinking of the sanction which the Constitution gives to slavery, he says, "Because it was a part of the original compact,—let it stand." Notwithstanding his special acuteness and ability, he is unable to take a fact out of its merely political relations, and behold it as it lies absolutely to be disposed of by the intellect,—what, for instance, it behooves a man to do here in America to-day with regard to slavery,—but ventures, or is driven, to make some such desperate answer as the following, while professing to speak absolutely, and as a private man,—from which what new and singular code of social duties might be inferred? "The manner," says he, "in which the governments of those States where slavery exists are to regulate it for their own consideration, under their responsibility to their constituents, to the general laws of propriety, humanity, and justice, and to God. Associations formed elsewhere, springing from a feeling of humanity, or any other cause, have nothing whatever to do with it. They have never received any encouragement from me, and they never will."

They who know of no purer sources of truth, who have traced up its stream no higher, stand, and wisely stand, by the Bible and the Constitution, and drink at it there with reverence and humility; but they who behold where it comes trickling into this lake or that pool, gird up their loins once more, and continue their pilgrimage toward its fountain-head.

No man with a genius for legislation has appeared in America. They are rare in the history of the world. There are orators, politicians, and eloquent men, by the thousand; but the speaker has not yet opened his mouth to speak who is capable of settling the much-vexed questions of the day. We love eloquence for its own sake, and not for any truth which it may utter, or any heroism it may inspire. Our legislators have not yet learned the comparative value of free trade and of freedom, of union, and of rectitude, to a nation. They have no genius or talent for comparatively humble questions of taxation and finance, commerce and manufactures and agriculture. If we were left solely to the wordy wit of legislators in Congress for our guidance, uncorrected by the seasonable experience and the effectual complaints of the people, America would not long retain her rank among the nations. For eighteen hundred years, though perchance I have no right to say it, the New Testament has been written; yet where is the legislator who has wisdom and practical talent enough to avail himself of the light which it sheds on the science of legislation?

The authority of government, even such as I am willing to submit to,—for I will cheerfully obey those who know and can do better than I, and in many things even those who neither know nor can do so well,—is still an impure one: to be strictly just, it must have the sanction and consent of the governed. It can have no pure right over my person and property but what I concede to it. The progress from an absolute to a limited monarchy, from a limited monarchy to a democracy, is a progress toward a true respect for the individual. Even the Chinese philosopher was wise enough to regard the individual as the basis of the empire. Is a democracy, such as we know it, the last improvement possible in government? Is it not possible to take a step further towards recognizing and organizing the rights of man? There will never be a really free and enlightened State until the State comes to recognize the individual as a higher and independent power, from which all its own power and authority are derived, and treats him accordingly. I please myself with imagining a State at last which can afford to be just to all men, and to treat the individual with respect as a neighbor; which even would not think it inconsistent with its own repose if a few were to live aloof from it, not meddling with it, nor embraced by it, who fulfilled all the duties of neighbors and fellow-men. A State which bore this kind of fruit, and suffered it to drop off as fast as it ripened, would prepare the way for a still more perfect and glorious State, which also I have imagined, but not yet anywhere seen.

Exercises

1. Thoreau wrote that the war with Mexico (1846–1848) was "the work of comparatively a few individuals using the standing government as their tool." Was his view essentially correct? Was this an unprovoked war of conquest?
2. Do you agree with the statement that "a government in which the majority rules in all cases cannot be based on justice"? What would John Stuart Mill say?
3. Thoreau predicted that the majority would eventually vote for the abolition of slavery "because they are indifferent to slavery, or because there is but little slavery left to be abolished by their vote." Did his prediction come to pass?
4. Thoreau criticizes presidential conventions because delegates have made themselves "*available* for any purposes of the demagogue." Is there any truth in this? How *do* Democrats and Republicans select their presidential candidates?

5. According to Thoreau, "The soldier is applauded who refuses to serve in an unjust war by those who do not refuse to sustain the unjust government which makes the war." His essay, particularly this statement, was a major force during the Vietnam War. Can you see why? What, on the other hand, is a "just" war?

6. Thoreau asks if we should be content to obey unjust laws. What did he elect to do and what, briefly stated, were his reasons? Do you agree with him? Did Mahatma Gandhi and Martin Luther King agree with his point of view?

Walt Whitman (1819–1892)

In his essay on "The Poet" Emerson wrote that the poet has a special mission because "the experience of each new age requires a new confession, and the world seems always waiting for its poet." It was the age of affirmation of American aspirations and the exuberant voice of American democracy was that of Walt Whitman, which Emerson himself immediately recognized. Upon receiving the first edition of *Leaves of Grass* (1855), Emerson wrote Whitman that this was "the most extraordinary piece of wit and wisdom that America has yet contributed" and greeted the poet "at the beginning of a great career." Few writers, not to mention an indifferent general public, were as perceptive as Emerson and even he later advised Whitman to go easy on the erotic poetry, advice which Whitman consistently ignored. *Leaves of Grass* was to be the poet's only book. Through nine editions (1855–1892) it grew with his life and, in effect, became his life. "This is no book," wrote Whitman, "who touches this touches a man."

A poet of many voices, Whitman rejected the genteel tradition and what he called "book-words," selecting instead the language of the common people, a unique blend of journalistic jargon, everyday speech, and a great variety of foreign words and phrases. A pantheist, mystic, and ardent patriot, Whitman advocated humanity, brotherhood, and freedom, not only in the United States but throughout the world.

The following chantlike poem is in Whitman's "catalog style" and illustrates his lusty mode as the "bard of democracy."

Literary Selections
I HEAR AMERICA SINGING
Walt Whitman

I hear America singing, the varied carols I hear,
Those of mechanics, each one singing his as it should be blithe and strong,
The carpenter singing his as he measures his plank or beam,
The mason singing his as he makes ready for work, or leaves off work,
The boatman singing what belongs to him in his boat, the deck-hand singing on the steamboat deck,
The shoemaker singing as he sits on his bench, the hatter singing as he stands,
The wood-cutter's song, the ploughboy's on his way in the morning, or at noon intermission or at sundown,
The delicious singing of the mother, or of the young wife at work, or of the girl sewing or washing,
Each singing what belongs to him or her and to none else,
The day what belongs to the day—at night the party of young fellows, robust, friendly,
Singing with open mouths their strong melodious songs.

Always an ardent supporter of the Union, Whitman was so distressed about the "peculiar institution" of slavery that he became an active Abolitionist. His involvement in the Civil War became personal when he began caring for his wounded brother George in an Army hospital, and stayed on to nurse others stricken by the war. The following poem is from *Drum-Taps,* which was added to *Leaves of Grass* in 1865.

BY THE BIVOUAC'S FITFUL FLAME
Walt Whitman

By the bivouac's fitful flame,
A procession winding around me, solemn and sweet and slow—but first I note,
The tents of the sleeping army, the fields' and woods' dim outline,
The darkness lit by spots of kindled fire, the silence,
Like a phantom far or near an occasional figure moving,
The shrubs and trees, (as I lift my eyes they seem to be stealthily watching me,)
While wind in procession thoughts, O tender and wondrous thoughts,
Of life and death, of home and the past and loved, and of those that are far away;
A solemn and slow procession there as I sit on the ground,
By the bivouac's fitful flame.

Whitman found in the tragic death of Abraham Lincoln the symbol for all the men and women who had suffered and died in America's most terrible war. The following poem is both a magnificent elegy for a fallen leader and a profound statement of Whitman's love and compassion for all humankind.

WHEN LILACS LAST IN THE DOORYARD BLOOM'D
Walt Whitman

1

When lilacs last in the dooryard bloom'd,
And the great star early droop'd in the western sky in the night,
I mourn'd, and yet shall mourn with ever-returning spring.
Ever-returning spring, trinity sure to me you bring,
Lilac blooming perennial and drooping star in the west,
And thought of him I love.

2

O powerful western fallen star!
O shades of night—O moody, tearful night!
O great star disappear'd—O the black murk that hides the
   star!
O cruel hands that hold me powerless—O helpless soul
   of me!
O harsh surrounding cloud that will not free my soul.

3

In the dooryard fronting an old farm-house near the
   white-wash'd palings,
Stands the lilac-bush tall-growing with heart-shaped
   leaves of rich green,
With many a pointed blossom rising delicate, with the
   perfume strong I love,
With every leaf a miracle—and from this bush in the
   dooryard,
With delicate-color'd blossoms and heart-shaped leaves of
   rich green,
A sprig with its flower I break.

4

In the swamp in secluded recesses,
A shy and hidden bird is warbling a song.

Solitary the thrush,
The hermit withdrawn to himself, avoiding the
   settlements,
Sings by himself a song.

Song of the bleeding throat,
Death's outlet song of life, (for well dear brother I know,
If thou wast not granted to sing thou would'st surely die.)

5

Over the breast of the spring, the land, amid cities,
Amid lanes and through old woods, where lately the
   violets peep'd from the ground, spotting the gray
   débris,
Amid the grass in the fields each side of the lanes, passing
   the endless grass,
Passing the yellow-spear'd wheat, every grain from its
   shroud in the dark-brown fields uprisen,
Passing the apple-tree blows of white and pink in the
   orchards,
Carrying a corpse to where it shall rest in the grave,
Night and day journeys a coffin.

6

Coffin that passes through lanes and streets,
Through day and night with the great cloud darkening
   the land,
With the pomp of the inloop'd flags with the cities draped
   in black,
With the show of the States themselves as of crape-veil'd
   women standing,
With processions long and winding and the flambeaus of
   the night,
With the countless torches lit, with the silent sea of faces
   and the unbared heads,
With the waiting depot, the arriving coffin, and the
   sombre faces,
With dirges through the night, with the thousand voices
   rising strong and solemn,
With all the mournful voices of the dirges pour'd around
   the coffin,
The dim-lit churches and the shuddering organs—where
   amid these you journey,
With the tolling tolling bells' perpetual clang,
Here, coffin that slowly passes,
I give you my sprig of lilac.

7

(Nor for you, for one alone,
Blossoms and branches green to coffins all I bring,
For fresh as the morning, thus would I chant a song for
   you O sane and sacred death.

All over bouquets of roses,
O death, I cover you over with roses and early lilies,
But mostly and now the lilac that blooms the first,
Copious I break, I break the sprigs from the bushes,
With loaded arms I come, pouring for you,
For you and the coffins all of you O death.)

8

O western orb sailing the heaven,
Now I know what you must have meant as a month since I
   walk'd,
As I walk'd in silence the transparent shadowy night,
As I saw you had something to tell as you bent to me
   night after night,
As you droop'd from the sky low down as if to my side,
   (while the other stars all look'd on,)
As we wander'd together the solemn night, (for
   something I know not what kept me from sleep,)
As the night advanced, and I saw on the rim of the west
   how full you were of woe,
As I stood on the rising ground in the breeze in the cool
   transparent night,
As I watch'd where you pass'd and was lost in the
   netherward black of the night,
As my soul in its trouble dissatisfied sank, as where you
   sad orb,
Concluded, dropt in the night, and was gone.

9

Sing on there in the swamp,
O singer bashful and tender, I hear your notes, I hear
   your call,
I hear, I come presently, I understand you,
But a moment I linger, for the lustrous star has detain'd
   me,
The star my departing comrade holds and detains me.

10

O how shall I warble myself for the dead one there I
   loved?
And how shall I deck my song for the large sweet soul
   that has gone?
And what shall my perfume be for the grave of him I love?

Sea-winds blown from east and west,
Blown from the Eastern sea and blown from the Western
   sea, till there on the prairies meeting,
These and with these and the breath of my chant,
I'll perfume the grave of him I love.

11

O what shall I hang on the chamber walls?
And what shall the pictures be that I hang on the walls,
To adorn the burial-house of him I love?

Pictures of growing spring and farms and homes,
With the Fourth-month eve at sundown, and the gray
    smoke lucid and bright,
With floods of the yellow gold of the gorgeous, indolent,
    sinking sun, burning, expanding the air,
With the fresh sweet herbage under foot, and the pale
    green leaves of the trees prolific,
In the distance the flowing glaze, the breast of the river,
    with a wind-dapple here and there,
With ranging hills on the banks, with many a line against
    the sky, and shadows,
And the city at hand with dwellings so dense, and stacks
    of chimneys,
And all the scenes of life and the workshops, and the
    workmen homeward returning.

12

Lo, body and soul—this land,
My own Manhattan with spires, and the sparkling and
    hurrying tides, and the ships,
The varied and ample land, the South and the North in
    the light, Ohio's shores and flashing Missouri,
And ever the far-spreading prairies cover'd with grass and
    corn.

Lo, the most excellent sun so calm and haughty,
The violet and purple morn with just-felt breezes,
The gentle soft-born measureless light,
The miracle spreading bathing all, the fulfill'd noon,
The coming eve delicious, the welcome night and the
    stars,
Over my cities shining all, enveloping man and land.

13

Sing on, sing on you gray-brown bird,
Sing from the swamps, the recesses, pour your chant from
    the bushes,
Limitless out of the dusk, out of the cedars and pines.

Sing on dearest brother, warble your reedy song,
Loud human song, with voice of uttermost woe.

O liquid and free and tender!
O wild and loose to my soul—O wondrous singer!
You only I hear—yet the star holds me, (but will soon
    depart,)
Yet the lilac with mastering odor holds me.

14

Now while I sat in the day and look'd forth,
In the close of the day with its light and the fields of
    spring, and the farmers preparing their crops,
In the large unconscious scenery of my land with its lakes
    and forests,
In the heavenly aerial beauty, (after the perturb'd winds
    and the storms,)
Under the arching heavens of the afternoon swift passing,
    and the voices of children and women,
The many-moving sea-tides, and I saw the ships how they
    sail'd,
And the summer approaching with richness, and the
    fields all busy with labor,

And the infinite separate houses, how they all went on,
    each with its meals and minutia of daily usages,
And the streets how their throbbings throbb'd, and the
    cities pent—lo, then and there,
Falling upon them all and among them all, enveloping
    me with the rest,
Appear'd the cloud, appear'd the long black trail,
And I knew death, its thought, and the sacred knowledge
    of death.

Then with the knowledge of death as walking one side of
    me,
And the thought of death close-walking the other side of
    me,
And I in the middle as with companions, and as holding
    the hands of companions,
I fled forth to the hiding receiving night that talks not,
Down to the shores of the water, the path by the swamp
    in the dimness,
To the solemn shadowy cedars and ghostly pines so still.

And the singer so shy to the rest receiv'd me,
The gray-brown bird I know receiv'd us comrades three,
And he sang the carol of death, and a verse for him I love.

From deep secluded recesses,
From the fragrant cedars and the ghostly pines so still,
Came the carol of the bird.

And the charm of the carol rapt me,
As I held as if by their hands my comrades in the night,
And the voice of my spirit tallied the song of the bird.

Come lovely and soothing death,
Undulate round the world, serenely arriving, arriving,
In the day, in the night, to all, to each,
Sooner or later delicate death.

Prais'd be the fathomless universe,
For life and joy, and for objects and knowledge curious,
And for love, sweet love—but praise! praise! praise!
For the sure-enwinding arms of cool-enfolding death.

Dark mother always gliding near with soft feet,
Have none chanted for thee a chant of fullest welcome?
Then I chant for thee, I glorify thee above all,
I bring thee a song that when thou must indeed come,
*   come unfalteringly.*

Approach strong deliveress,
When it is so, when thou hast taken them I joyously sing
*   the dead,*
Lost in the loving floating ocean of thee,
Laved in the flood of thy bliss O death.

From me to thee glad serenades,
Dances for thee I propose saluting thee, adornments and
*   feastings for thee,*
And the sights of the open landscape and the high-spread
*   sky are fitting,*
And life and the fields, and the huge and thoughtful night.

The night in silence under many a star,
The ocean shore and the husky whispering wave whose
*   voice I know,*
And the soul turning to thee O vast and well-veil'd death,
And the body gratefully nestling close to thee.
Over the tree-tops I float thee a song,
Over the rising and sinking waves, over the myriad fields
*   and the prairies wide,*
Over the dense-pack'd cities all and the teeming wharves
*   and ways,*
I float this carol with joy, with joy to thee O death.

15

To the tally of my soul,
Loud and strong kept up the gray-brown bird,
With pure deliberate notes spreading filling the night.

Loud in the pines and cedars dim,
Clear in the freshness moist and the swamp-perfume,
And I with my comrades there in the night.

While my sight that was bound in my eyes unclosed,
As to long panoramas of visions.

And I saw askant the armies,
I saw as in noiseless dreams hundreds of battle-flags,
Borne through the smoke of the battles and pierc'd with
    missiles I saw them,
And carried hither and yon through the smoke, and torn
    and bloody,
And at last but a few shreds left on the staffs, (and all in
    silence,)
And the staffs all splinter'd and broken.

I saw battle-corpses, myriads of them,
And the white skeletons of young men, I saw them,
I saw the debris and debris of all the slain soldiers of the
    war,
But I saw they were not as was thought,
They themselves were fully at rest, they suffer'd not,
The living remain'd and suffer'd, the mother suffer'd,
And the wife and the child and the musing comrade
    suffer'd,
And the armies that remain'd suffer'd.

16

Passing the visions, passing the night,
Passing, unloosing the hold of my comrades' hands,
Passing the song of the hermit bird and the tallying song
    of my soul,
Victorious song, death's outlet song, yet varying ever-
    altering song,
As low and wailing, yet clear the notes, rising and falling,
    flooding the night,
Sadly sinking and fainting, as warning and warning, and
    yet again bursting with joy,
Covering the earth and filling the spread of the heaven,
As that powerful psalm in the night I heard from recesses,
Passing, I leave thee lilac with heart-shaped leaves,
I leave there in the door-yard, blooming, returning
    with spring.

I cease from my song for thee,
From my gaze on thee in the west, fronting the west,
    communing with thee,
O comrade lustrous with silver face in the night.

Yet each to keep and all, retrievements out of the night,
The song, the wondrous chant of the gray-brown bird,
And the tallying chant, the echo arous'd in my soul,
With the lustrous and drooping star with the countenance
    full of woe,
With the holders holding my hand nearing the call of the
    bird,
Comrades mine and I in the midst, and their memory ever
    to keep, for the dead I loved so well,
For the sweetest, wisest soul of all my days and lands—
    and this for his dear sake,
Lilac and star and bird twined with the chant of my soul,
There in the fragrant pines and the cedars dusk and dim.

Exercises

1. "I Hear America Singing" clearly represents Whitman as the poet of democracy. What are the uniquely American aspects of this poem? Is there, for example, any hint of a hierarchy?
2. What is the mood of "By the Bivouac's Fitful Flame" and how is this accomplished? Consider rhythm, word choice, and, especially, the use of *and*.
3. Whitman's elegy for Lincoln is built on three symbols: the blooming lilac, the hermit thrush singing, and the evening star drooping in the West. Which symbol refers to Lincoln? What meanings are implied in the other two symbols?

Herman Melville (1819–1891)

Born in the same year as Whitman and also influenced by Emerson, Melville had not one but two literary careers. Like Whitman, Melville was fascinated by the sea and images of the sea, but Whitman's vision was essentially positive while Melville's was ironic and tragic, the viewpoint of a realist as opposed to Whitman the romantic. Several years after publishing his greatest novel, *Moby-Dick* (1851), Melville turned, for reasons still unknown, to an exclusive preoccupation with poetry. (He did leave at his death the manuscript of *Billy Budd* but with no clues as to when it was written.) Melville's ten-year career as a prose writer and thirty-year sequel as a poet were as unnoticed by the general public of the time as was the poetry of Whitman.

Deeply disturbed over the coming war, Melville followed the self-appointed mission of the Abolitionist John Brown who, in his zeal to free the slaves, had secured support from Emerson, Thoreau, and many others. Brown's capture of the U.S. Arsenal at Harper's Ferry was a major step in his campaign, but the government recaptured the Arsenal and hanged John Brown. Melville's brooding poem uses the image of the dead Abolitionist as a prologue to war.

Literary Selections

THE PORTENT
Herman Melville

Hanging from the beam,
    Slowly swaying (such the law),
Gaunt the shadow on your green,
    Shenandoah!
The cut is on the crown
(Lo, John Brown),
And the stabs shall heal no more.

Hidden in the cap
    Is the anguish none can draw;
So your future veils its face,
    Shenandoah!
But the streaming beard is shown
(Weird John Brown),
    The meteor of the war.

1859

One of the bloodiest conflicts of the Civil War, the Battle of Shiloh (April 6–7, 1862) cost the lives of thousands of soldiers, including Stonewall Jackson, and forecast both the terrible battles to come and the inevitable defeat of the Confederacy. No one, not even Whitman, wrote more eloquently and sadly about the war than did Herman Melville.

SHILOH

A Requiem
(April, 1862)
Herman Melville

Skimming lightly, wheeling still,
    The swallows fly low
Over the field in clouded days,
    The forest-field of Shiloh—
Over the field where April rain
Solaced the parched ones stretched in pain
Through the pause of night
That followed the Sunday fight
    Around the church of Shiloh—
The church so lone, the log-built one,
That echoed to many a parting groan And natural prayer
    Of dying foemen mingled there—
Foemen at morn, but friends at eve—
    Fame or country least their care:
(What like a bullet can undeceive!)
    But now they lie low,
While over them the swallows skim,
    And all is hushed at Shiloh.

Though Melville's sympathies lay with the North, he saw the war as equally tragic for North and South with neither side wholly right or wholly wrong.

ON THE SLAIN COLLEGIANS
Herman Melville

Youth is the time when hearts are large,
    And stirring wars
Appeal to the spirit which appeals in turn
    To the blade it draws.
If woman incite, and duty show
    (Though made the mask of Cain),
Or whether it be Truth's sacred cause,
    Who can aloof remain
That shares youth's ardor, uncooled by the snow
    Of wisdom or sordid gain?

The liberal arts and nurture sweet
Which give his gentleness to man—
    Train him to honor, lend him grace
Through bright examples meet—
That culture which makes never wan

With underminings deep, but holds
    The surface still, its fitting place,
    And so gives sunniness to the face
And bravery to the heart; what troops
    Of generous boys in happiness thus bred—
    Saturnians through life's Tempe led,
Went from the North and came from the South,
With golden mottoes in the mouth,
    To lie down midway on a bloody bed.
Woe for the homes of the North,
And woe for the seats of the South:
All who felt life's spring in prime,
And were swept by the wind of their place and time—
    All lavish hearts, on whichever side,
Of birth urbane or courage high,
Armed them for the stirring wars—
Armed them—some to die.
        Apollo-like in pride,
Each would slay his Python—caught
The maxims in his temple taught—
    Aflame with sympathies whose blaze
Perforce enwrapped him—social laws,
    Friendship and kin, and by-gone days—
Vows, kisses—every heart unmoors,
And launches into the seas of wars.
What could they else—North or South?
Each went forth with blessings given
By priests and mothers in the name of Heaven;
        And honor in all was chief.
Warred one for Right, and one for Wrong?
So put it; but they both were young—
Each grape to his cluster clung,
All their elegies are sung.

The anguish of maternal hearts
    Must search for balm divine;
But well the striplings bore their fated parts
    (The heavens all parts assign)—
Never felt life's care or cloy.
Each bloomed and died an unabated Boy;
Nor dreamed what death was—thought it mere
Sliding into some vernal sphere.
They knew the joy, but leaped the grief,
Like plants that flower ere comes the leaf—
Which storms lay low in kindly doom,
And kill them in their flush of bloom.

The naval battle between the ironclads *Merrimac* and *Monitor* (March 9, 1862) symbolized for Melville the inhuman mechanization of war. He was a realist, the first poet to describe *modern* warfare for what it really was: killing people by means of advanced technology.

A UTILITARIAN VIEW OF THE MONITOR'S FIGHT
Herman Melville

Plain be the phrase, yet apt the verse,
    More ponderous than nimble;
For since grimed War here laid aside
His painted pomp, 'twould ill befit
    Overmuch to ply
    The rhyme's barbaric cymbal.

Hail to victory without the gaud
     Of glory; zeal that needs no fans
Of banners; plain mechanic power
     Plied cogently in War now placed—
        Where War belongs—
     Among the trades and artisans.

Yet this was battle, and intense—
     Beyond the strife of fleets heroic;
Deadlier, closer, calm 'mid storm;
No passion; all went on by crank,
        Pivot, and screw,
     And calculations of caloric.

Needless to dwell; the story's known.
     The ringing of those plates on plates
Still ringeth round the world—
The clangor of that blacksmith's fray.
        The anvil-din
     Resounds this message from the Fates:

War shall yet be, and to the end;
     But war-paint shows the streaks of weather;
War yet shall be, but warriors
Are now but operatives; War's made
        Less grand than Peace,
     And a singe runs through lace and feather.

Melville's ambivalent feelings about the sea are summed up in "Pebbles." The sea was a cruel and lonely world, inhuman and dangerous but, at the same time, Melville felt that it had restorative powers that could purify the spirit. Nevertheless, man "sails on sufferance there."

PEBBLES
Herman Melville

I

Though the Clerk of the Weather insist,
     And lay down the weather-law,
Pintado and gannet they wist
That the winds blow whither they list
     In tempest or flaw.

II

Old are the creeds, but stale the schools,
     Revamped as the mode may veer,
But Orm from the schools to the beaches strays,
And, finding a Conch hoar with time, he delays
     And reverent lifts it to ear.
That Voice, pitched in far monotone,
     Shall it swerve? Shall it deviate ever?
The Seas have inspired it, and Truth—
     Truth, varying from sameness never.

III

In hollows of the liquid hills
     Where the long Blue Ridges run,
The flattery of no echo thrills,
     For echo the seas have none;
Nor aught that gives man back man's strain—
The hope of his heart, the dream in his brain.

IV

On ocean where the embattled fleets repair,
Man, suffering inflictor, sails on sufferance there.

V

Implacable I, the old implacable Sea:
     Implacable most when most I smile serene—
Pleased, not appeased, by myriad wrecks in me.

VI

Curled in the comb of yon billow Andean,
     Is it the Dragon's heaven-challenging crest?
Elemental mad ramping of ravening waters—
     Yet Christ on the Mount, and the dove in her nest!

VII

Healed of my hurt, I laud the inhuman Sea—
Yea, bless the Angels Four that there convene;
For healed I am even by their pitiless breath
Distilled in wholesome dew named rosmarine.

Exercises

1. In "The Portent" what is the effect of the words *Shenandoah* and *Weird?* What vistas are opened up? What feelings?
2. During the Battle of Shiloh the Union lost over 13,000 men and the Confederacy nearly 11,000, but the latter was hailed as the "victor." Consider the paradoxes in the situation and in the poem like, for example, the church at the center of the conflict and the strange mixture of friend and foe.
3. In "On the Slain Collegians" does Melville view the Civil War as necessary?
4. Compare the word choice in the "Collegians" with those describing the *Monitor's* fight. Notice in both poems how sound and sense tend to be synonymous, which is, of course, a characteristic of good poetry. Try reading both poems aloud.
5. Melville's ambivalence about the sea is reflected in almost every line of "Pebbles." Consider words and phrases like *reverent, implacable, I smile serenely, ravening waters,* and many more.

Mark Twain (1835–1910)

The second half of the century saw the emergence of realism in American literature and throughout the Western world. There was a new interest in common people and everyday facts of life. Among the new realists were Dickens, Thackeray, and George Eliot in England, Zola and Balzac in France, and William Dean Howells (1837–1921) in the United States. As editor-in-chief of the influential *Atlantic Monthly,* Howells advocated realism and supported regional writers. Mark Twain (pseudonym of Samuel Langhorne Clemens) was, however, the only major writer to emerge from what can be called the grass-roots movement.

The first important author to be born west of the Mississippi, Mark Twain, more than any other writer of his time, symbolized the power and exuberance of the expansive American spirit that blossomed after the Civil War. Twain spoke and wrote in the voice of the people in celebration of the winning of the west. (The later, darker Twain will not be considered here.) His major works include *Innocents Abroad* (1869) and *Roughing It* (1872) but his masterwork can be considered as a kind of trilogy: *The Adventures of Tom Sawyer* (1876); *Life on the Mississippi* (1883); and *The Adventures of Huckleberry Finn* (1885). Perhaps his best short story, "The Notorious Jumping Frog of Calaveras County" was an oft-told tale but it took a Mark Twain to give it form and style. The story is reprinted below but in actuality, this is only the first of a three-part exercise by the inimitable Twain. Upon learning that a French critic had called it a good story that, however, was not funny, Twain translated the tale into French and then translated *that* version into English. Twain concluded that the original was funny but that the French-into-English version was awkward and unfunny. The point is, of course, that Twain's American English was so idiomatic that it was untranslatable.

Literary Selection

THE NOTORIOUS JUMPING FROG OF CALAVERAS COUNTY
Mark Twain

In compliance with the request of a friend of mine, who wrote me from the East, I called on good-natured, garrulous old Simon Wheeler, and inquired after my friend's friend, Leonidas W. Smiley, as requested to do, and I hereunto append the result. I have a lurking suspicion that *Leonidas W.* Smiley is a myth; that my friend never knew such a personage; and that he only conjectured that if I asked old Wheeler about him, it would remind him of his infamous *Jim* Smiley, and he would go to work and bore me to death with some exasperating reminiscence of him as long and as tedious as it should be useless to me. If that was the design, it succeeded.

I found Simon Wheeler dozing comfortably by the bar-room stove of the dilapidated tavern in the decayed mining camp of Angel's, and I noticed that he was fat and bald-headed, and had an expression of winning gentleness and simplicity upon his tranquil countenance. He roused up, and gave me good day. I told him that a friend of mine had commissioned me to make some inquiries about a cherished companion of his boyhood named *Leonidas W.* Smiley—*Rev. Leonidas W.* Smiley, a young minister of the Gospel, who he had heard was at one time a resident of Angel's Camp. I added that if Mr. Wheeler could tell me anything about this Rev. Leonidas W. Smiley, I would feel under many obligations to him.

Simon Wheeler backed me into a corner and blockaded me there with his chair, and then sat down and reeled off the monotonous narrative which follows this paragraph. He never smiled, he never frowned, he never changed his voice from the gentle-flowing key to which he tuned his initial sentence, he never betrayed the slightest suspicion of enthusiasm; but all through the interminable narrative there ran a vein of impressive earnestness and sincerity, which showed me plainly that, so far from his imagining that there was anything ridiculous or funny about his story, he regarded it as a really important matter, and admired its two heroes as men of transcendent genius in *finesse.* I let him go on in his own way, and never interrupted him once.

"Rev. Leonidas W. H'm, Reverend Le—well, there was a feller here once by the name of *Jim* Smiley, in the winter of '49—or maybe it was the spring of '50—I don't recollect exactly, somehow, though what makes me think it was one or the other is because I remember the big flume warn't finished when he first come to the camp; but anyway, he was the curiousest man about always betting on anything that turned up you ever see, if he could get anybody to bet on the other side; and if he couldn't he'd change sides. Any way that suited the other man would suit *him*—any way just so's he got a bet, *he* was satisfied. But still he was lucky, uncommon lucky; he most always come out winner. He was always ready and laying for a chance; there couldn't be no solit'ry thing mentioned but that feller'd offer to bet on it, and take ary side you please, as I was just telling you. If there was a horse-race, you'd find him flush or you'd find him busted at the end of it; if there was a dog-fight, he'd bet on it; if there was a cat-fight, he'd bet on it; if there was a chicken-fight, he'd bet on it; why, if there was two birds setting on a fence, he would bet you which one would fly first; or if there was a camp-meeting, he would be there reg'lar to bet on Parson Walker, which he judged to be the best exhorter about here, and so he was too, and a good man. If he even see a straddle-bug start to go anywheres, he would bet you how long it would take him to get to—to wherever he was going to, and if you took him up, he would foller that straddle-bug to Mexico but what he would find out where he was bound for and how long he was on the road. Lots of the boys here has seen that Smiley, and can tell you about him. Why, it never made no difference to *him*—he'd bet on *any* thing—the dangdest feller. Parson Walker's wife laid very sick once, for a good while, and it seemed as they warn't going to save her; but one morning he come in, and Smiley up and asked him how she was, and he said she was considerable better—thank the Lord for his inf'nite mercy—and coming on so smart that with the blessing of Prov'dence she'd get well yet; and Smiley, before he thought, says, 'Well, I'll resk two-and-a-half she don't anyway.'

"Thish-yer Smiley had a mare—the boys called her the fifteen-minute nag, but that was only in fun, you know, because of course she was faster than that—and he used to win money on that horse, for all she was so slow and always had the asthma, or the distemper, or the consumption, or something of that kind. They used to give her two or three hundred yards' start, and then pass her under way; but always at the fag end of the race she'd get excited and desperate like, and come cavorting and straddling up, and scattering her legs around limber, sometimes in the air, and sometimes out to one side among the fences, and kicking up m-o-r-e dust and raising m-o-r-e racket with her coughing and sneezing and blowing her nose—and *always* fetch up at the stand just about a neck ahead, as near as you could cipher it down.

"And he had a little small bull-pup, that to look at him you'd think he warn't worth a cent but to set around and look ornery and lay for a chance to steal something. But as soon as money was up on him he was a different dog; his under-jaw'd begin to stick out like the fo'castle of a steamboat, and his teeth would uncover and shine like the furnaces. And a dog might tackle him and bully-rag him, and bite him, and throw him over his shoulder two or three times, and Andrew Jackson—which was the name of the pup—Andrew Jackson would never let on but what *he* was satisfied, and hadn't expected nothing else—and the bets being doubled and doubled on the other side all the time, till the money was all up; and then all of a sudden he would grab that other dog jest by the j'int of his hind leg and freeze to it—not chaw, you understand, but only just grip and hang on till they throwed up the sponge, if it was a year. Smiley always come out winner on that pup, till he harnessed a dog once that didn't have no hind legs, because they'd been sawed off in a circular saw, and when the thing had gone along far enough, and the money was all up, and he come to make a snatch for his pet holt, he see in a minute how he'd been imposed on, and how the other dog had him in the door, so to speak, and he 'peared surprised, and then he looked sorter discouraged-like, and didn't try no more to win the fight, and so he got shucked out bad. He give Smiley a look, as much as to say his heart was broke, and it was *his* fault, for putting up a dog that hadn't no hind legs for him to take holt of, which was his main dependence in a fight, and then he limped off a piece and laid down and died. It was a good pup, was that Andrew Jackson, and would have made a name for hisself if he'd lived, for the stuff was in him and he had genius—I know it, because he hadn't no opportunities to speak of, and it don't stand to reason that a dog could make such a fight as he could under them circumstances if he hadn't no talent. It always makes me feel sorry when I think of that last fight of his'n, and the way it turned out.

"Well, thish-yer Smiley had rat-tarriers, and chicken cocks, and tomcats and all them kind of things, till you couldn't rest, and you couldn't fetch nothing for him to bet on but he'd match you. He ketched a frog one day, and took him home, and said he cal'lated to educate him; and so he never done nothing for three months but set in his back yard and learn that frog to jump. And you bet you he *did* learn him, too. He'd give him a little punch behind, and the next minute you'd see that frog whirling in the air like a doughnut—see him turn one summerset, or maybe a couple, if he got a good start, and come down flat-footed and all right, like a cat. He got him up so in the matter of ketching flies, and kep' him in practice so constant, that he'd nail a fly every time as fur as he could see him. Smiley said all a frog wanted was education, and he could do 'most anything—and I believe him. Why, I've seen him set Dan'l Webster down here on this floor—Dan'l Webster was the name of the frog—and sing out, 'Flies, Dan'l, flies!' and quicker'n you could wink he'd spring straight up and snake a fly off'n the counter there, and flop down on the floor ag'in as solid as a gob of mud, and fall to scratching the side of his head with his hind foot as indifferent as if he hadn't no idea he'd been doin' any more'n any frog might do. You never see a frog so modest and straight-for'ard as he was, for all he was so gifted. And when it come to fair and square jumping on a dead level, he could get over more ground at one straddle than any animal of his breed you ever see. Jumping on a dead level was his strong suit, you understand; and when it come to that, Smiley would ante up money on him as long as he had a red. Smiley was monstrous proud of his frog, and well he might be, for fellers that had traveled and been everywheres all said he laid over any frog that ever *they* see.

"Well, Smiley kep' the beast in a little lattice box, and he used to fetch him down-town sometimes and lay for a bet. One day a feller—a stranger in the camp, he was—come acrost him with his box, and says:

"'What might it be that you've got in the box?'

"And Smiley says, sorter indifferent-like, 'It might be a parrot, or it might be a canary, maybe, but it ain't—it's only just a frog.'

"And the feller took it, and looked at it careful, and turned it round this way and that, and says, 'H'm—so 'tis. Well, what's *he* good for?'

"'Well,' Smiley says, easy and careless, 'he's good enough for *one* thing, I should judge—he can outjump any frog in Calaveras County.'

"The feller took the box again, and took another long, particular look, and give it back to Smiley, and says, very deliberate, 'Well,' he says, 'I don't see no p'ints about that frog that's any better'n any other frog.'

"'Maybe you don't,' Smiley says. 'Maybe you understand frogs and maybe you don't understand 'em; maybe you've had experience, and maybe you ain't only a amature, as it were. Anyways, I've got *my* opinion, and I'll resk forty dollars that he can outjump any frog in Calaveras County.'

"And the feller studied a minute, and then says, kinder sadlike, 'Well, I'm only a stranger here, and I ain't got no frog; but if I had a frog, I'd bet you.'

"And then Smiley says, 'That's all right—that's all right—if you'll hold my box a minute, I'll go and get you a frog.' And so the feller took the box, and put up his forty dollars along with Smiley's, and set down to wait.

"So he set there a good while thinking and thinking to himself, and then he got the frog out and prized his mouth open and took a teaspoon and filled him full of quail-shot—filled him pretty near up to his chin—and set him on the floor. Smiley he went to the swamp and slopped around in the mud for a long time, and finally he ketched a frog, and fetched him in, and give him to this feller, and says:

"'Now, if you're ready, set him alongside of Dan'l, with his fore paws just even with Dan'l's, and I'll give the word.' Then he says, 'One—two—three—*git!*' and him and the feller touched up the frogs from behind, and the new frog hopped off lively, but Dan'l give a heave, and hysted up his shoulders—so—like a Frenchman, but it warn't no use—he couldn't budge; he was planted as solid as a church, and he couldn't no more stir than if he was anchored out. Smiley was a good deal surprised, and he was disgusted too, but he didn't have no idea what the matter was, of course.

"The feller took the money and started away; and when he was going out at the door, he sorter jerked his thumb over his shoulder—so—at Dan'l, and says again, very deliberate, 'Well,' he says, '*I* don't see no p'ints about that frog that's any better'n any other frog.'

"Smiley he stood scratching his head and looking down at Dan'l a long time, and at last he says, 'I do wonder what in the nation that frog throw'd off for—I wonder if there ain't something the matter with him—he 'pears to look mighty baggy, somehow.' And he ketched

Dan'l by the nap of the neck, and hefted him, and says, 'Why blame my cats if he don't weigh five pound!' and turned him upside down and he belched out a double handful of shot. And then he see how it was, and he was the maddest man—he set the frog down and took out after that feller, but he never ketched him. And—"

[Here Simon Wheeler heard his name called from the front yard, and got up to see what was wanted.] And turning to me as he moved away, he said: "Just set where you are, stranger, and rest easy—I ain't going to be gone a second."

But, by your leave, I did not think that a continuation of the history of the enterprising vagabond *Jim* Smiley would be likely to afford me much information concerning the Rev. *Leonidas W.* Smiley, and so I started away.

At the door I met the sociable Wheeler returning, and he buttonholed me and recommenced:

"Well, thish-yer Smiley had a yaller one-eyed cow that didn't have no tail, only just a short stump like a bannanner, and—"

However, lacking both time and inclination, I did not wait to hear about the afflicted cow, but took my leave.

Exercise

1. This tale became a humorous classic because it is a virtual compendium of comic elements and devices. Almost immediately we are told that Simon Wheeler was an old windbag who launches right into a "monotonous narration." This is a story within a story highlighted by the comic character and folksy dialect of bald-headed Simon. The other major character, Jim Smiley, will bet on anything, even whether or not Parson Walker's wife will live or die. The imagery is graphic, there's lots of local color, and the "tables turned" theme provides the proper comic twist. Identify some of the images, elements of local color, and exaggerations like the mare called the "fifteen-minute nag." Do not overlook the bull pup named Andrew Jackson. In short, just how complex is this story?

Emily Dickinson (1830–1886)

The poetry of the "recluse of Amherst" is also realistic. Twain's universe was the exterior world; Dickinson's was that of the inner world of her own psyche. Published years after her death, her 1,775 poems were written as if they were entries in a diary, the private thoughts of a private person who took just a little from society and shut out all the rest. Her gemlike, frequently cryptic verses are unique, unlike poetry of any writer of any age.

Literary Selections

X
IN A LIBRARY
Emily Dickinson

A precious, mouldering pleasure 't is
To meet an antique book,
In just the dress his century wore;
A privilege, I think,

His venerable hand to take,
And warming in our own,
A passage back, or two, to make
To times when he was young.

His quaint opinions to inspect,
His knowledge to unfold
On what concerns our mutual mind,
The literature of old;

What interested scholars most,
What competitions ran
When Plato was a certainty,
And Sophocles a man;

When Sappho was a living girl,
And Beatrice wore
The gown that Dante deified.
Facts, centuries before,

He traverses familiar,
As one should come to town
And tell you all your dreams were true:
He lived where dreams were sown.

His presence is enchantment,
You beg him not to go;
Old volumes shake their vellum heads
And tantalize, just so.

XXII
Emily Dickinson

I had no time to hate, because
The grave would hinder me,
And life was not so ample I
Could finish enmity.

Nor had I time to love; but since
Some industry must be,
The little toil of love, I thought,
Was large enough for me.

VI
A SERVICE OF SONG
Emily Dickinson

Some keep the Sabbath going to church;
I keep it staying at home,
With a bobolink for a chorister,
And an orchard for a dome.

Some keep the Sabbath in surplice;
I just wear my wings,
And instead of tolling the bell for church,
Our little sexton sings.
God preaches,—a noted clergyman,—
And the sermon is never long;
So instead of getting to heaven at last,
I'm going all along!

XLVI
DYING
Emily Dickinson

I heard a fly buzz when I died;
    The stillness round my form
Was like the stillness in the air
    Between the heaves of storm.

The eyes beside had wrung them dry,
    And breaths were gathering sure
For that last onset, when the king
    Be witnessed in his power.

I willed my keepsakes, signed away
    What portion of me I
Could make assignable,—and then
    There interposed a fly,

With blue, uncertain, stumbling buzz,
    Between the light and me;
And then the windows failed, and then
    I could not see to see.

XVII

Emily Dickinson

I never saw a moor,
I never saw the sea;
Yet know I how the heather looks.
And what a wave must be.

I never spoke with God,
Nor visited in heaven;
Yet certain am I of the spot
As if the chart were given.

X

Emily Dickinson

I died for beauty, but was scarce
Adjusted in the tomb,
When one who died for truth was lain
In an adjoining room.

He questioned softly why I failed?
"For beauty," I replied.
"And I for truth,—the two are one;
We brethren are," he said.

And so, as kinsmen met a night,
We talked between the rooms,
Until the moss had reached our lips,
And covered up our names.

XI

Emily Dickinson

Much madness is divinest sense
To a discerning eye;
Much sense the starkest madness.
'T is the majority
In this, as all, prevails.
Assent, and you are sane;
Demur,—you're straightway dangerous,
And handled with a chain.

XXVII
THE CHARIOT
Emily Dickinson

Because I could not stop for Death,
He kindly stopped for me;
The carriage held but just ourselves
And Immortality.

We slowly drove, he knew no haste,
And I had put away
My labor, and my leisure too,
For his civility.

We passed the school where children played,
Their lessons scarcely done;
We passed the fields of gazing grain,
We passed the setting sun.

We paused before a house that seemed
A swelling of the ground;
The roof was scarcely visible,
The cornice but a mound.

Since then 't is centuries; but each
Feels shorter than the day
I first surmised the horses' heads
Were toward eternity.

Exercises

1. How, in Poem X, does the poet feel about books and how does she convey that feeling?
2. Why is hate, in Poem XXII, greater than love?
3. Would you call Poem VI pantheistic? Is it opposed to conventional religion or merely indifferent?
4. Is the fly in Poem XLVI metaphorical or real? Why did you answer as you did? Why did she use legal terms in stanza 3?
5. Compare *beauty* and *truth* in Poem X with Keats's statement about beauty and truth in "Grecian Urn." Are the two versions similar? Identical?
6. Is the divine madness in Poem XI like that of the Fool in *King Lear?* Explain your answer.
7. Poem XXVII contains many of the unusual metaphors for which Dickinson is famous. What are some of them? How effective are they?

Paul Laurence Dunbar (1872–1906)

Emancipation had released the slaves from bondage only to suspend Black Americans somewhere between African cultures to which they could not return and an American culture that refused to admit them. The first black poet to reach a national audience, Dunbar wrote a poignant poem about the situation, a poem that is still quoted today.

Literary Selection

Sympathy

Paul Laurence Dunbar

I know what the caged bird feels, alas!
    When the sun is bright on the upland slopes;
When the wind stirs soft through the springing grass,
And the river flows like a stream of glass;
    When the first bird sings and the first bud opes,
And the faint perfume from its chalice steals—
I know what the caged bird feels!

I know why the caged bird beats his wing
    Till its blood is red on the cruel bars;
For he must fly back to his perch and cling
When he fain would be on the bough a-swing;
    And a pain still throbs in the old, old scars
And they pulse again with a keener sting—
I know why he beats his wing!

I know why the caged bird sings, ah me,
    When his wing is bruised and his bosom sore,—
When he beats his bars and he would be free;
It is not a carol of joy or glee,
    But a prayer that he sends from his heart's deep core,
But a plea, that upward to Heaven he flings—
I know why the caged bird sings!

Exercises

1. The *caged bird* is a metaphor for what? Is it a multiple metaphor? Please explain.
2. What is implied by the peaceful images in stanza 1? The violent images in stanza 2?
3. Who or what will free the caged bird?

Stephen Crane (1871–1900)

Though sometimes identified as a writer in the realistic style called naturalism, Crane was actually influenced by Monet, Renoir, and other Impressionists. A journalist by profession and a war correspondent, Crane used word-painting in a manner comparable to the Impressionists' use of color. His *The Red Badge of Courage* (1895) is perhaps the finest short novel in the English language and "The Open Boat" and "The Blue Hotel" rank at the top of American short stories. Of Crane's poems, the following two seem most appropriate to conclude this survey of nineteenth-century life and literature.

Literary Selections
Stephen Crane

Do not weep, maiden, for war is kind.
Because your lover threw wild hands toward the sky
And the affrighted steed ran on alone,
Do not weep.
War is kind.
    Hoarse, booming drums of the regiment,
    Little souls who thirst for fight
    These men were born to drill and die.
    The unexplained glory flies above them,
    Great is the battle-god, great, and his kingdom—
    A field where a thousand corpses lie.

Do not weep, babe, for war is kind.
Because your father tumbled in the yellow trenches,
Raged at his breast, gulped and died,
Do not weep.
War is kind.
    Swift blazing flag of the regiment,
    Eagle with crest of red and gold,
    These men were born to drill and die.
    Point for them the virtue of slaughter,
    Make plain to them the excellence of killing
    And a field where a thousand corpses lie.

Mother whose heart hung humble as a button
on the bright splendid shroud of your son,
Do not weep.
War is kind.

Stephen Crane

A man said to the universe:
"Sir, I exist!"
"However," replied the universe,
"The fact has not created in me
A sense of obligation."

Bibliography

Recommended are two books that provide excellent overviews of the period.

1. Burchell, S. C. *Age of Progress*. Great Ages of Man. New York: Time Incorporated, 1966. Good bibliography.
2. *Age of Optimism (1803–1896)*. Vol. 5, Milestones of History. New York: Newsweek, 1970.

Following are a few of the good, more-specialized books.

3. Bloom, Harold, and Lionel Trilling, eds. *Romantic Prose and Poetry*. New York: Oxford University Press, 1973.
4. Hofstadter, Richard. *Social Darwinism in American Thought*. New York: George Braziller, 1959.
5. Kroeber, Karl. *Romantic Landscape Vision: Constable and Wordsworth*. Madison, Wis.: University of Wisconsin Press, 1975.
6. Packham, Morse, ed. *Romanticism: The Culture of the Nineteenth Century*. New York: George Braziller, 1965.

Time Chart for the Middle Modern World, 1789–1914

	1800	1825	1850	1875	1900	1925

Artists

Goya 1746–1828
Constable 1776–1837
Ingres 1780–1867
Gericault 1791–1824
Corot 1796–1875
Delacroix 1799–1863
Daumier 1808–1879
Millet 1814–1875
Courbet 1819–1877
Manet 1832–1883
Degas 1834–1917
Whistler 1834–1903
Homer 1836–1910
Cézanne 1839–1906
Rodin 1840–1917
Monet 1840–1926
Renoir 1841–1919
Morisot 1841–1895
Cassatt 1844–1926
Rousseau 1844–1910
van Gogh 1853–1890
Seurat 1859–1891
Toulouse-Lautrec 1864–1901
Munch 1864–1944

Musicians

Schubert 1797–1828
Berlioz 1803–1869
Mendelssohn 1809–1847
Chopin 1810–1849
Liszt 1811–1886
Brahms 1833–1897
Tchaikovsky 1840–1893
Puccini 1858–1924
Debussy 1862–1918
Strauss 1864–1949

Literary Figures

Rousseau 1718–1778
Goethe 1749–1832
Schiller 1759–1805
Blake 1757–1827
Wordsworth 1770–1850
Coleridge 1772–1834
Byron 1788–1824
Shelley 1792–1822
Mary Shelley 1797–1851
Keats 1795–1821
Emerson 1803–1882
Tennyson 1809–1892
Poe 1809–1849
Thoreau 1817–1860
Whitman 1819–1892
Melville 1819–1891
Arnold 1822–1888
Dickinson 1830–1886
Twain 1835–1910
Hardy 1840–1928
Crane 1871–1900
Dunbar 1872–1906

Government

England
George III 1760–1820
George IV 1820–1830
William IV 1830–1837
Victoria 1837–1901
Edward VII 1901–1910
George V 1910–1936

France
Napoleon 1804–1812
Louis XVIII 1814–1824
Charles X 1824–1830
Louis Philippe 1830–1848
Second Republic 1848–1852
Napoleon III 1852–1870
Third Republic 1871–

Germany
William I 1871–1888
William II 1888–1918

Russia
Alexander I 1801–1825
Nicholas I 1825–1855
Alexander II 1855–1881
Alexander III 1881–1894
Nicholas II 1894–1918

Italy
Victor Emmanuel II 1861–1878
Humbert I 1878–1900
Victor Emmanuel III 1900–1946

Time Chart for the Middle Modern World, 1789–1914 (cont.)

	1800	1825	1850	1875	1900	1925
Events		• Congress of Vienna 1815 • Age of Metternich 1815–1848 • French July revolution 1830	• Wave of revolutions 1848 • *Communist Manifesto* • Crimean War 1853–1856 • *Origin of Species* 1859 • American Civil War 1861–1865 • Liberation of Russian serfs 1861 • Lincoln's Emancipation Proclamation 1863 • Franco-Prussian War 1870–1871 • Dreyfuss Affair 1894–1906 • World War I 1914–1918			

25

Romanticism in Music

The ever-changing sequence of artistic styles can be seen in broad perspective as a constant back and forth movement between two extremes. In painting, these outer boundaries are represented by the Rubenists, who emphasized color, and Poussinists, who advocated line and drawing. In nineteenth-century painting Delacroix was a Rubenist; Ingres and David were the Poussinists. These extremes are referred to, in music, as *romanticism* and *classicism*. As in painting, the emphasis of romantic music is on color and that of classical music is on the primacy of line and design. Music is a different medium, of course, and perhaps more abstract than painting; the distinctions and parallels are therefore less finely drawn. As an exercise in extremes, the opposing concepts can be stated in many different ways:

Classicism	Romanticism
intellectual	emotional
objective	subjective
rational	nonrational
tranquil	restless
simple	ornate
Apollonian	Dionysian

At no time can an artistic style be classified as wholly classic or wholly romantic. An inclination in favor of either extreme results in a classification of the style *as* that extreme, a process that can be compared to a seesaw touching ground at one end because of a slight shift of balance. Although it is manifestly foolish to consider all of Mozart's music, for example, as intellectual but not emotional, tranquil, and simple rather than ornate and restless, the fact remains that Mozart's music is essentially classic in its meticulous detail, restraint, and clarity of design.

Nineteenth-century music generally follows the romantic mode and is concerned primarily with either miniature or large-scale works, with comparatively little in between. There are intimate art songs for solo voice and piano and single-movement piano pieces at one extreme, and large symphonic works and even larger vocal-instrumental works at the other. The emphasis is on tone color (or sound), that fourth element of music (melody, harmony, rhythm, tone color). Piano pieces are "characteristic" compositions written specifically for that instrument; songs are written for specific voice types; symphonies are scored for a greater range of instrumental tone color and a greater volume of sound. The international aspects of seventeenth- and eighteenth-century music are replaced by highly individualistic styles of writing and strong nationalistic expression. The "Austrian" quality of the classical music of Haydn and Mozart is not germane to any study of their compositions. During the romantic period the "German" characteristics of Wagner, Schubert, and Schumann and the "Italian" qualities of Verdi, Rossini, and Donizetti are part of the stylistic picture. In other words, nineteenth-century music reflects the rise of nationalism.

German Lieder

An important aspect of the Romantic movement was the inauguration of a new style, the setting of preexisting poetry—almost always Romantic poetry—to music in an artful matching of mood and meaning. Nationalism was again a prominent characteristic, for the new style was keyed to the meticulous setting of poetry in the original language, and the language was German.

In 1814, the Viennese composer Franz Schubert (1797–1828) set to music the poem "Gretchen am Spinnrade" from Goethe's *Faust*. The resultant combination was a new artistic medium called a *lied* (Ger., song); the German art song movement or style was referred to as *lieder* (songs). The generic term *lieder* is applied to the German Romantic songs of Schubert, Schumann, Brahms, and others, though *lied* is the word Germans also use when they refer to just any song.

Composers had written songs, in all languages, before Schubert wrote the first lied. Lieder are not just songs, however, for composers displayed a remarkable unity of purpose—the recreation of a poem in musical terms—along with a typically Romantic range of personal styles. Schubert wrote lieder and Brahms wrote lieder; both were adept at the art of merging poetry and music, but Brahms does not sound like Schubert. The Romantic movement was notable for the personal touch, for individuality at all costs. Romantic artists sought personalized expression in a variety of contrasting and even paradoxical procedures: large-scale works coexisting with miniatures, Neo-Gothic (new-old styles were in) with Neo-Classic, Neo-Baroque with Neo-Romanesque, and quite logically, somehow, Mary Shelley's *Frankenstein* with Goethe's *Faust*.

Art songs, or lieder, were important miniatures in an era that indulged itself with the grandiose or doted on the diminutive. There was remarkably little middle ground, for the Romantic sought the heights and the depths and had little patience with the ordinary. Complexity was preferred; simplicity was abhorred. If one art form was good then two art forms were even better. Art songs represented the essence of Romanticism for they combined the arts of poetry and music into a new and rarefied style.

First came the poem and then the song, which attempts to capture the feelings, the mood, indeed the essence of what the poet is trying to communicate. The rhythm, inflection, sound, and meaning of the language are corroborated and heightened by the composer's own personal language of melody, harmony, rhythm, and tone color.

Following is a lied by Schubert based on a poem from *Faust* by Goethe. German art songs are not translated because translations spoil the interrelation of words and music. The German text with English translation is provided so that the listener can follow one and understand the other. The song is made up of ten verses, as indicated by the numbers in the text.

Gretchen am Spinnrade (1814)
(Margaret at the Spinning Wheel)

Franz Schubert (1797–1828)
Poem by Goethe (from *Faust*)

Synopsis: Margaret sits in her room at the spinning wheel and sings of her love for Faust, knowing that this love will prove fatal. The scene occurs near the end of Part I of *Faust*.

Accompaniment pattern in the piano

sempre legato—"always smooth," imitating the whirring of the spinning wheel.

sempre staccato—"always staccato," imitating the working of the treadle.

1. Mei-ne Ruh' ist hin, mein Herz ist schwer;
   ich fin-de, ich fin-de sie nim-mer und nim-mer-mehr.
   (My peace is gone, My heart is sore:
   I shall find it never And never more.)
2. Wo ich ihn nicht hab', ist mir das Grab,
   die gan-ze Welt ist mir ver-gällt.
   (He has left my room An empty tomb
   He has gone and all My world is gall.)
3. Mein ar-mer Kopf ist mir ver-rückt,
   mein ar-mer Sinn ist mir zer-stückt.
   (My poor head Is all astray,
   My poor mind Fallen away.)
4. Mei-ne Ruh' ist hin, mein Herz ist schwer;
   ich fin-de, ich fin-de sie nim-mer und nim-mer-mehr.
   (My peace is gone, My heart is sore;
   I shall find it never And never more.)
5. Nach ihm nur schau' ich zum Fen-ster hin-aus,
   (Tis he that I look through The window to see
   He that I open The door for—he!)
6. nach ihm nur geh' ich aus dem Haus.
   Sein ho-her Gang, sein' ed-le Ge-stalt,
   sei-nes Mun-des Lä-cheln, sei-ner Au-gen Ge-walt,
   (His gait, his figure, So grand, so high,
   The smile of his mouth, The power of his eye.)
7. und sei-ner Re-de Zau-ber-fluss,
   sein Hän-de-druck und ach, sein Kuss! (Piano)
   (And the magic stream Of his words—what bliss
   The clasp of his hand And, ah, his kiss!)
8. Mei-ne Ruh' ist hin, mein Herz ist schwer;
   ich fin-de, ich fin-de sie nim-mer und nim-mer-mehr.
   (My peace is gone, My heart is sore:
   I shall find it never And never more.)
9. Mein Bu-sen drängt sich nach ihm hin.
   Ach, dürft' ich fas-sen und hal-ten ihn!
   (My heart's desire Is so strong, so vast;
   Ah, could I seize him And hold him fast.)
10. und küs-sen ihn, so wie ich wollt'
    an sei-nen Küs-sen ver-ge-hen sollt',
    O köont' ich ihn küs-sen, so wie ich wollt',
    an sei-nen Küs-sen ver-ge-hen sollt',
    an sei-nen Küssen ver-ge-hen sollt'!
    Mei-ne Ruh' ist hin, mein Herz ist schwer'.
    (Piano)
    (And kiss him forever Night and day,
    And on his kisses Pass away!)

Piano Music

The Romantic emphasis upon the uniqueness of the individual was symbolized by the dominance of the piano as the single most popular musical instrument, as typical of the Romantic era as the guitar is of contemporary life. The piano was ubiquitous because it could accompany lieder, blend into a chamber music ensemble or, in a piano concerto, dominate a symphony orchestra. Its prime attraction, however, was its independence, for it was a superb solo instrument.

Figure 25.1 Eugene Delacroix, *Frédéric Chopin,* 1838. Oil on canvas, 18 × 15″. Delacroix (see chap. 26) seldom painted portraits on commission; instead, he depicted some of his personal friends, the victims, like himself, of what he and other artists called the "Romantic agony." The Louvre, Paris.

Eighteenth-century pianos were relatively small with a clear and delicate tone. Nineteenth-century pianos were larger, more sonorous than clear, and loud enough to fill the largest concert hall. The range of tone was representative of the Romantic propensity for extremes. Whether playing the tender "Lullaby" by Brahms or the thunderous "Revolutionary Etude" by Chopin, the pianist was a commanding figure throughout the entire Romantic period. The pianist continues to dominate today's concert world, possibly because of the uninterrupted popularity of the Romantic repertoire.

The nineteenth century was an age of virtuosos. Franz Liszt and Frédéric Chopin were spectacular performers on the piano and, equally remarkable, was Niccolo Paganini, the virtuoso of the violin. Virtuosity and showmanship were so widely admired that, for example, Paganini would conclude a concert with a razor blade hidden in his right hand. Near the end of an already sensational performance he would deftly cut the violin strings, one by one, until he could triumphantly conclude on the last remaining string.

Franz Liszt was fond of planting a female admirer in the front row of the concert hall. At the most dramatic moment the young lady, obviously overcome by the beauty and power of Liszt's playing, would rise slowly to her feet and ecstatically faint away. The master would rush to her side, carry her on stage and, holding her artistically draped body over one arm, triumphantly conclude the composition with one hand.

Frédéric Chopin (sho–pan; 1810–1849) was a fine concert pianist but he did not confuse virtuoso performance with the circus showmanship of Liszt and Paganini (fig. 25.1). Although he was successful in the concert hall he gave fewer than seventy-five public concerts in his entire career. In terms of temperament and style, he was much more at home in the fashionable salons of Paris. The so-called poet of the keyboard developed a highly personal style that represents the epitome of the Romantic spirit. Chopin's music can be heard as a kind of musical poetry not unlike the blending of words and music in German art songs. The formal designs of his music—sonata form, binary and ternary forms—are quite traditional but the content is unique. Some of the range of

Chopin's piano style can be appreciated by considering three representative pieces: a ballade, an étude, and a prelude (see p. 271).

Ballade in g Minor is loosely related to the medieval French verse in which the refrain comes at the end of the stanza. In this dramatic and rhapsodic composition Chopin uses sonata form and reverses themes *a* and *b* in the recapitulation, after which he brings the work to a vigorous close with a brilliant coda.

Ballade in g Minor, op. 23

Form: Modified Sonata

Frédéric Chopin (1810–1849)
Time: 7:00

Theme a

Theme b

Chopin wrote a number of *études,* compositions for concentrated study of technical problems in piano playing. That these studies are more than mere exercises is typical of Chopin's unique musicality. The E-Major Etude is a study in piano touch. The right hand must bring out the songlike melody but subor-

dinate the undulating accompanying figure even though the two elements are played by the same hand. The contrasting middle section, for all its brilliance, is probably less difficult technically than the delicate handling of the main theme.

Étude in E Major, op. 10, no. 3

Form: Ternary (A–B–A)

Chopin
Time: 3:45

Theme a

legato

Theme b
(poco piu animato)

Chopin wrote twenty-four *preludes* in opus 28, each in a different key. The last prelude in the series is one of his most unusual and powerful compositions. As befits a prelude, which for Chopin is a short piano piece in one movement, there is only one subject. In the d-minor Prelude, the subject is limited almost entirely to a d-minor chord (d–f–a); in fact, the left hand plays the same d-minor chord for the first ten measures, and over one-third of the piece is devoted to this single chord. From the unchanging har-

mony of the opening section through the five statements of the theme to the final three low d's on the keyboard the accumulative effect is almost hypnotic.[1]

---

1. Should a brief refresher course in reading music be needed you may again consult the Appendix: Music Listening and Notation.

Prelude in d Minor, op. 28, no. 24

Form: Single Subject

Chopin
Time: 2:20

d-minor chord

Table 25.1 Comparative Sizes of Orchestras

	Mozart (1788)	Beethoven (1808)	Strauss (1895)
Woodwinds	flute 2 oboes 2 clarinets 2 bassoons	piccolo 2 flutes 2 oboes 2 clarinets 2 bassoons	piccolo 3 flutes 3 oboes English horn 3 clarinets bass clarinet 3 bassoons contrabassoon
Brass	2 French horns	2 French horns 2 trumpets 3 trombones	8 French horns 6 trumpets 3 trombones tuba
Percussion		timpani	timpani, snare drum, bass drum, cymbals, triangle
Strings	violin I violin II viola cello bass	violin I violin II viola cello bass	violin I violin II viola cello bass

The Symphony

The symphony was one of the primary forms of the nineteenth century but not all composers chose to follow the symphonic tradition. Those who did write symphonies sometimes adopted classical practices, altered them to suit their purposes, or simply rejected them completely. In order to achieve an overview of the remarkable variety of orchestral music, we will consider a symphonic work by each of six different composers: Felix Mendelssohn, Hector Berlioz, Franz Liszt, Richard Strauss, Peter I. Tchaikovsky, and Johannes Brahms. However, before taking up the Romantic tradition in symphonic literature it is necessary to consider the development of the orchestra itself.

The greatly augmented symphony orchestra with its strong brass and percussion sections and enlarged body of woodwinds provided a particularly effective medium for Romantic music. The classic orchestra had a nucleus of strings plus a small woodwind section and just a few brass and percussion instruments. The nineteenth-century orchestra added full sections of woodwinds and brass which could play as independent sections as well as filling in the ensemble. The comparative size of the orchestra over a period of a single century is illustrated in table 25.1.

Orchestra size grew even beyond the enormous ensemble specified by Strauss before being reduced to an average-sized modern orchestra that could play most symphonic music and still meet a sizable payroll. The additional instrumentalists needed for works by Strauss and others are now hired especially for the occasion. Figure 25.2 is a seating plan observed in principle by most modern orchestras. Because of their limited volume the strings are seated in front and the woodwinds in the center; brass, bass instruments, and percussion bring up the rear (also see fig. 25.3).

Felix Mendelssohn (1809–1847) was the grandson of the great Jewish philosopher Moses Mendelssohn. His father was a wealthy banker and his mother a woman with an exceptional cultural background. In addition to his superior intellect and rarefied socioeconomic background, Mendelssohn was endowed with a wealth of musical talent.

Mendelssohn admired classical forms and followed them closely. However, the classical spirit was acquired rather than assimilated and the classical forms that he used became more like noble gestures rather than natural expressions. Because of the clarity of his writing and his control of the emotional content Mendelssohn is best described as a classical Romanticist.

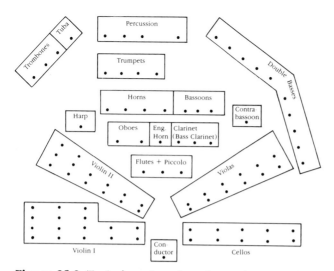

Figure 25.2 Typical seating plan of a modern symphony orchestra.

Figure 25.3 A modern symphony orchestra

The Fourth Symphony was written during an extended sojourn in Italy. The symphony is called "Italian," probably because of the sunny first theme of the opening movement and the brilliant *Saltarello* which forms the last movement and which was probably inspired by a carnival in Rome that the composer had observed. Mendelssohn characteristically avoided anything that was overdone or in bad taste. The orchestra, therefore, was virtually the same size as that used by Mozart.

Symphony no. 4 in A Major, op. 90 (1833)

"Italian"

Felix Mendelssohn (1809–1847)
Total Time: 30:00

I

Form: Sonata

Theme a

Allegro vivace

Theme b

II

Form: Ternary (A-B-A)

Principal theme

Andante con moto

III

Form: Minuet-Trio-Minuet

Minuet   Trio

Con moto moderato

IV

Form: Modified theme and variations

Theme

Presto

Hector Berlioz (bear–lee–OS; 1803–1869) was a red-headed Romantic from the south of France, a revolutionary artist whose only personal instrument was the guitar but whose preferred instrument was the entire symphony orchestra. Despite his flamboyance—his lifetime dream was hearing ten thousand trumpets from a mountaintop—he was a solid musician and an orchestral innovator who strongly influenced Liszt, Wagner, Tchaikovsky, and Strauss.

One of Berlioz's most successful and most controversial works was his *Symphonie Fantastique* which he completed in 1830, only three years after the death of Beethoven. Berlioz had been influenced by the popular *Confessions of an English Opium Eater* (1821) by Thomas de Quincey and contemplated using the idea of an opium dream in conjunction with his music. He also fell madly in love with a Shakespearean actress named Harriet Smithson. It is now impossible to tell what the components were of this frenzied, desperate love affair which, strangely enough, led to marriage, a union which was both short-lived and disastrous.

Berlioz was completely entranced with what he saw as the Romantic elements in Shakespeare's plays. He was therefore as stagestruck by the Shakespearean women played by Miss Smithson as he was infatuated with the actress herself. In the midst of their stormy marriage, Berlioz combined his conception of Shakespeare's women, his passion for Miss Smithson, and his interest in opium into the fanciful story line (program) that led to the creation of the *Symphonie Fantastique.*

Berlioz considered classical forms as merely empty shells. Instead he concentrated on an *idée fixe,* a single theme that would be the common thread for each of the five movements of his daring new symphony. The idée fixe was a kind of *leit motif*—a procedure that Wagner was to exploit—that represented both the ideal of perfect love and the artist's idealized version of Harriet Smithson.

Following are the titles of the five movements plus a brief explanation of what the composer apparently had in mind when he wrote the music.

I. *Rêveries—Passions* (Daydreams—Passions). The artist, despairing of ever possessing his beloved, attempts to poison himself with opium. What follows in this and in the other movements are a series of opium-induced dreams, fantasies, and nightmares. This first movement is a frequently euphoric reverie about the artist's passion for his beloved.

II. *Un bal* (A ball). There is a fancy ball at which the beloved appears, slipping in and out of the dancers. The idée fixe, representing the beloved, is heard as she appears among the dancers.

III. *Scène aux champs* (Scene in the country). An idyllic scene of calm serenity in the bucolic countryside.

IV. *Marche au supplice* (March to the scaffold). In his delirium, the artist imagines he has killed his beloved and that he is being taken on a tumbrel to the guillotine.

V. *Songe d'une nuit de Sabbat* (Dream of a Witches' Sabbath). Following his execution the artist dreams that he is present at a gruesome Witches' Sabbath complete with a parody of the *Dies irae* (Day of Judgment) as a part of a Black Mass. The idée fixe is also parodied as his beloved appears as a debased prostitute.

Symphonie Fantastique, op. 14 (1830)
(Épisode de la vie d'un artiste)

Hector Berlioz
Total Time: 48:00

I (Daydreams—Passions)

Idée fixe

II (A ball)

Principal theme (following Intro.)

III (Scene in the country)

Principal theme (following Intro.)

IV (March to the scaffold)

Theme a (following Intro.)

Theme b

V (Dream of a Witches' Sabbath)

Dies irae

Franz Liszt (1811–1886) felt that it was possible to create organized musical compositions without forcing the ideas into the traditional forms of the Classical period. He used programs for much of his music—hence the term *program music*—but operated from a different point of view than did Berlioz.

Liszt was dedicated to the Romantic ideal of uniting the various arts. He respected the uniqueness of the musical language but he advocated the addition of extramusical concepts that would "humanize" the music and make it more meaningful to the listener.

> The musician who is inspired by nature exhales in tones nature's most tender secrets without copying them. . . . Since his language is more arbitrary and more uncertain than any other . . . and lends itself to the most varied interpretations, it is not without value . . . for the composer to give in a few lines the spiritual sketch of his work and . . . convey the idea which served as the basis for his composition. . . . This will prevent faulty elucidations, hazardous interpretations, idle quarrels with intentions the composer never had, and endless commentaries which rest on nothing.[2]

Franz Liszt was perhaps the only composer of program music to understand the real meaning of Beethoven's preface to his Sixth Symphony: "More the expression of sentiment than painting." Richard Strauss contended that a tone poem could, for example, "describe a teaspoon" so that all listeners could envision a similar image. Liszt denied the capability of music to be this literal and to be this limited. Instead, he created the symphonic poem, a new art form that followed the dictates of Beethoven. He stated broad concepts for his programs and then dissolved these concepts into the wonderfully abstract language of music.

Les Preludes, the most famous of Liszt's twelve symphonic poems, was inspired by a *meditation poétique* by the mystical French poet Alphonse de Lamartine. The musical score is prefaced by a quotation from Lamartine that expresses a favorite Romantic theme—man pitted against Fate:

> What is our life but a series of preludes to that unknown song whose first solemn note is tolled by Death? Love is the enchanted dawn of every existence, but where is the life in which the first enjoyment of bliss is not dispelled by some tempest? Yet no man is content to resign himself for long to the benificent charms of Nature; when the trumpet sounds, he hastens to danger's post, so that in the struggle he may regain full consciousness of himself, and the possession of all his powers.

Liszt uses a germ motive that, unlike Berlioz's idée fixe, ties the work together in a process of continuous transformation. Constructed in six sections, the piece begins with the germ motive, followed by section 1 in which the motive becomes majestic. In section 2 the motive turns into a love song in a pastoral mood, followed by a new, tender love theme in section 3. The pace quickens dramatically in section 4 and then relaxes into a bucolic mood in section 5. In section 6 the two love themes are transformed into rousing battle calls and the piece concludes triumphantly in a typically romantic burst of exaltation.

---

2. Franz Liszt, *Gesammelte Schriften,* Leipzig, 1881–1910, p. 104.

Les Preludes (1854)
Symphonic Poem

Franz Liszt (1811–1886)

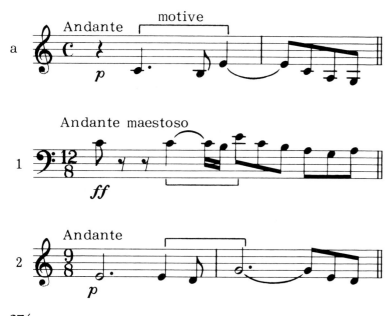

Richard Strauss (1864–1949) exploited the large symphony orchestra in a manner very similar to Liszt's treatment of the piano and Paganini's performances on the violin. The orchestra became, in his hands, an enormous virtuoso instrument. One of the great orchestrators, Strauss expanded to an unprecedented degree the techniques of individual musicians and the capabilities of the orchestra as a whole.

Notoriously reluctant to try new ideas, symphonic musicians bristled and balked whenever a new Strauss composition was placed on their music stands. Strauss was asking them to play sequences of notes that they had never played before and sometimes to play in a manner that had never occurred to them. Certain patterns of notes were so new that musicians deemed them impossible to play. More, perhaps, than any composer of his time, Strauss was responsible for the increased playing skills of symphonic musicians. Even today the music of Strauss is considered difficult to play. The designation of "impossible" is reserved for later composers who continue to confront and to challenge the orchestral musicians.

The *tone poem* (or *symphonic poem*) was the favorite form of program music for the large orchestra. Originated by Franz Liszt and developed by Richard Strauss, the tone poem generally utilized a dramatic narrative as the basis for an extended one-movement composition. The music would attempt to describe such grandiose conceptions as *A Hero's Life, Death and Transfiguration,* the affairs of a lover (*Don Juan*), and the adventures of a practical joker (*Till Eulenspiegel's Merry Pranks*). The tone poem about the practical joker is one of the most successful ventures in this genre, principally because of the vivid, dramatic music and tightly-knit construction. The story is by no means the only one that can be associated with the music but, nevertheless, it is the story that the composer had in mind when he wrote the music.

Till Eulenspiegel was an actual fourteenth-century character who achieved considerable notoriety as a sometimes likable rogue, swindler, prankster, and scoundrel. The Strauss tone poem is built around a selection of Till's adventures, including the final adventure of being brought to justice for his many offenses.

Till Eulenspiegel's Merry Pranks (1895)

Richard Strauss (1864–1949)
Total Time: 14:00

Form: Through-composed. Because of the sequence of events in the dramatic narrative, there is no repetition of thematic material as there would be in absolute music.

There are two themes (*a* and *b*) which are used throughout the piece and which represent Till himself:

There are six scenes and an epilogue. There is a primary theme in each section and repeated material in the epilogue.

1. *Till in the Marketplace*
2. *Till the Priest*
3. *Till in Love*
4. *Till and the Philistines*
5. *To Be or Not to Be Himself*
6. *Till's Sad End*

Following is a brief synopsis of the events in each section:

Introduction
The two Till themes (*a* and *b*) are presented.

1. Till in the Marketplace
After a pause, the 'a' theme is heard and we have a typical market scene with much bustling activity, women gossiping in their stalls and so forth. Till slips into the square, mounts a horse and careens through the square, making a shambles of it. Leaving consternation in his wake, he rides out of sight.

2. Till the Priest
Till appears as a caricature of a priest, dripping unction and morality. He is not really comfortable in the role and abandons it quickly when a pretty girl walks by.

3. Till in Love
A short violin solo signals this latest adventure as Till follows the girl, catches up with her and does his best to make a good impression. His advances are repulsed and he storms off swearing vengeance on all humankind.

4. Till and the Philistines
The hopping theme announces the arrival of some musty professors and doctors. Till falls in with them and amazes all and sundry with his brilliance as he propounds one ridiculous notion after another. Quickly becoming bored with such stodgy scholars, Till leaves them behind in a state of shocked amazement.

5. To Be or Not to Be Himself
In the longest section of the piece Till wrestles with his conscience, such as it is. The question is whether he should continue in his erratic, exciting, and sometimes scandalous life or reform and settle down with the good burghers who have been the butt of so many of his pranks. After considerable indecision he finally decides to remain true to his real nature and continue as the scoundrel he has always been. This decision is announced by a jubilant orchestra.

6. Till's Sad End
At almost the very moment he decides to be himself the snare drum roll announces that Till has been dragged off to face the stern justice of the court. The low, threatening chords hurl the charges at Till, who answers impudently the first two times (solo clarinet). The answer to the third volley of charges is an anguished squeal from the clarinet and Till is marched to the scaffold. An ominous drop in pitch (interval of a M7) portrays the dropping of the trap door. His soul takes flight to the accompaniment of fluttering clarinet and flute and the mortal Till is no more. A short pizzicato string passage leads to the Epilogue.

7. Epilogue
The 'a' theme is heard for the last time. In retrospect Till becomes an amusing devil and immortal rogue, as indicated by the triumphant close for full orchestra.

Peter Ilich Tchaikovsky (chy–KOF–skee; 1840–1893) seldom succeeded in mastering musical forms, but he was remarkably skillful in his handling of the symphonic orchestra. The lush sounds of Tchaikovsky's orchestra have become a kind of hallmark for the dramatic intensity and emotional extremes of the Romantic movement.

Tchaikovsky's orchestral music ranges from ponderous melodrama to vapid sentimentality and yet, at his best, he has created enormously popular works for ballet—*Swan Lake, The Nutcracker, Sleeping Beauty*—and three successful symphonies, the

Fourth, the Fifth, and the Sixth. His symphonies are cast in Classical forms but there is little concern with the development of thematic ideas in the Classical sense. Rather there are broadly sweeping melodies or powerful dramatic themes that are developed, in a manner of speaking, through the exploitation of the orchestral colors of the symphonic ensemble itself. The Russian preference for variations on a theme and for bold color changes is never heard to better advantage than in the symphonic music of Tchaikovsky.

Symphony no. 5 in e Minor, op. 64 (1888)

Peter I. Tchaikovsky (1840–1893)
Total Time: 53:00

The Romantic affinity for lush lyricism, storm and stress, grandiose display, and programmatic music was reflected in varying degrees in the music of all the nineteenth-century composers. *Johannes Brahms* (1833–1897), however, was supremely conscious of the heritage of Classical music and particularly the monumental contributions of Beethoven. He waited until rather late in his career to write his first symphony; critics were quick to label this powerful work "the Beethoven Tenth."

Brahms made deliberate attempts to exert some sort of control over his inherent Romantic tendencies. In his four symphonies, as in most of his music, Brahms utilized Baroque and Classical models but exploited them in a personal style that is a unique combination of Classical and Romantic traits.

Considered in his own time as something of a reactionary, the composer "born too late," Brahms actually helped pave the way for the swing of the pendulum back to Classic concepts that have been prominent in much of the music of the twentieth century. Among the many unusual circumstances in the development of artistic styles, nothing is more ironic than the appearance of Brahms in the avant-garde of modern music while his contemporaries, the self-styled modernists Liszt, Strauss, and Wagner, are now seen as archetypes of nineteenth-century Romanticism.

In his Third Symphony, Brahms turns a typically frugal amount of musical material into a major symphonic work. He builds the entire composition out of a three-note *motto*:

The notes F–A–F are derived from the words *frei aber froh* (free but happy) which was supposedly the motto that Brahms used to indicate his life-style. Unlike the motto in Tchaikovsky's Fifth Symphony, which is a complete, self-contained melody, this pattern is a motive from which Brahms generates a variety of musical ideas.

Symphony no. 3 in F Major, op. 90 (1883)

Johannes Brahms (1833–1897)
Total Time: 31:40

I

Form: Sonata

II

Form: Sonata

Theme a: clarinets, bassoons

Theme b

III

Form: Ternary

Theme a

Cellos

mp expressivo

Theme b

IV

Form: Sonata, with delayed Development coming between *a* and *b* in the Recapitulation. Also uses the motto of the first movement and the *b* theme of the second movement.

Theme a

Theme b

Opera

Opera underwent drastic changes in style and intent during the nineteenth century. Early in the century, Beethoven's *Fidelio* (1805) represented what might be called international opera. With the emergence of Romanticism there was a corresponding rise in national schools of opera with Italy dominating the European (and American) scene.

Italian opera, as typified by Verdi's *Rigoletto* (1851), was a mélange of melodramatic plots, popular-type melodies, and "effective" solos and ensembles. There was more emphasis upon *bel canto* (beautiful singing) than upon logical development of plot and character. Later operas, Verdi's *Aida* (1871) for example, evidenced an ever-increasing concern with dramatic values culminating, perhaps inevitably, in the complex music dramas of Richard Wagner.

Wagner conceived of opera, his *Tristan und Isolde* (1859) for example, as a super art form, a viewpoint roughly comparable to Byron's conception of himself as a super hero and Nietzsche's theory of a superman.

Wagner's insistence upon the musical-literary totality of his myth-based music dramas provoked strong reactions in favor of so-called realism in subject matter and a new simplicity in musical treatment. A similar reaction against academic painting led to the emergence of such Romantic Realists as Millet and Corot of the Barbizon School and, especially, the Realists Daumier and Courbet. A comparable movement in literature, called Naturalism, was led by Émile Zola.

Giacomo Puccini (poo–CHEE–nee; 1858–1924) was perhaps the leading Realist in operatic literature. His tragic operas, *La Bohème, Madame Butterfly,* and *Tosca,* are among the most popular works in the standard repertoire of leading opera companies. *La Bohème* is the opera selected for inclusion here because with it one can perhaps best persuade a neophyte that a theatrical work in which everything is sung is actually a viable means of expressive communication. The field of opera has suffered for far too long from the misguided notion that it is esoteric and "highbrow" and thus not fit for middle-class consumption.

The text of *La Bohème* was drawn from Henri Murger's *Scenes de la Vie en Bohème,* the time is 1830, and the setting is an artist's garret in the Bohemian section of the Latin Quarter of Paris. The characters in order of appearance are: Marcello, a painter, *baritone;* Rodolfo, a poet, *tenor;* Colline, a philosopher, *bass;* Schaunard, a musician, *baritone;* Benoit, a landlord, *bass;* Mimi, an embroiderer, *soprano;* Parpignol, a toy vendor, *tenor;* Musetta, a shop girl, *soprano;* Alcindoro, a councilor of state, *bass;* Customhouse sergeant, *bass;* Students, working girls, citizens, shopkeepers, street vendors, soldiers, waiters, boys and girls, etc. Following is a brief summary of the plot.

La Bohème (1896)

Giacomo Puccini (1858–1924)

Act I

Scene: In the Attic   Time: 35:00

Four struggling young artists, Rodolfo, Marcello, Colline, and Schaunard are living together in the garret. Mimi timidly knocks at the door and asks Rodolfo to light her candle. It is love at first sight, to coin a phrase, and they eventually exit upstage center, singing a love duet.

Act II

Scene: In the Latin Quarter   Time: 17:00

The four artists and Mimi convene at a cafe. Musetta, Marcello's former girlfriend, appears on the arm of Alcindoro, her current admirer. Musetta uses her considerable charms to rekindle Marcello's interest in her and all march offstage behind a passing military band.

Act III

Scene: A toll gate at an entrance to Paris   Time: 24:00

Musetta and Marcello can be heard in the tavern in the background. Mimi appears and asks Marcello to help her separate from Rodolfo. As Rodolfo comes out of the tavern he exclaims that he has decided to leave Mimi. She then tells him that she must return to another lover but they cling together knowing that they must part when spring comes.

Act IV

Scene: In the Attic   Time: 28:00

The four bachelors and Musetta are in the apartment when Mimi appears, desperately ill. The friends rush out seeking food, medicine, and a doctor, leaving Mimi and Rodolfo alone. They return in time to witness Mimi's death.

The plot of *La Bohème* is commonplace. The characterization is fixed from the outset rather than developed. The mutual attraction of the young lovers is instant and total without any attempt at verisimilitude. The stormy romance of Musetta and Marcello remains at that entry level. *La Bohème* reads, on paper, like a third-rate soap opera.

Then why has this opera been so enormously popular for almost a century? Surely it is not because of the plot, the characterization, the pathos of the tragic love affair. Perhaps it is because Rodolfo and Mimi represent some profound truths about life, suffering, love, and death. Hardly.

In the parlance of the theatre, *La Bohème* is effective when placed "on the boards" because "it plays." It is believable because it sings and sings gloriously. From the vivacious opening measures audiences willingly, even eagerly, suspend their disbelief.

Mimi then sings "I am Mimi" and Rodolfo is enchanted.

Rodolfo sings to Mimi of his hopes and aspirations as a poet.

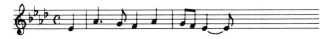

For the conclusion of Act I Puccini uses Rodolfo's melody in a soaring love duet. The musical language of love has rarely sounded better.

In order to learn how to listen to an opera, one should listen to an opera: *La Bohème* in this case. The preceding remark is not facetious or condescending.

The obvious is sometimes obscured by an academic fog of talking rather than doing. Listen to the opera all the way through with nothing more in mind than enjoying Puccini's singable melodies. Listen again with the idea of identifying the different characters by voice register (soprano, baritone, etc.) and by characterization; for example, Musetta's melodies tend to be flamboyant while Mimi's melodies are gentle and very lyrical.

Check the plot using liner notes, one of the many opera guides, or even the musical score, which has interesting stage directions and an English translation. All current recordings are in Italian but, after all, music is the closest thing we have to an international language.

Listen again to each act as you identify the interplay of personalities and ideas. Listen again to each act while visualizing, in your mind's eye, sets, costumes, Mimi, Rodolfo, Musetta, Marcello, and the others. Finally, put aside all details, settle back and listen to Puccini's melodies work their magic. Ultimately you will want to see the opera on the stage, where it belongs. If at all possible do not settle for a second-rate production. Puccini deserves better.

Impressionism in Music

By the end of the nineteenth century the main stream of Romanticism had about run its course. The decline was marked by the appearance of what was thought to be the *new* style of *Impressionism.* Just as the Renaissance had faded into Mannerism and the Baroque into Rococo, the refined essence of Romanticism was distilled into a final stage named after the painting style of Monet, Degas, Renoir, and others.

The so-called Impressionistic music of Debussy and Ravel—Debussy detested the term *Impressionism*—spearheaded a French revolt against the domination of German Romanticism and particularly the overwhelming exuberance of Wagner. The competition of German and French nationalism was a major factor in the Impressionist movement. Debussy cultivated an art that was subtle, delicate, and discreet, an art that was a sensuous rather than an emotional experience. For Debussy, German Romanticism was ponderous and tedious while French music possessed the Gallic spirit of elegance and refinement.

Many similarities exist between the painting of the Impressionists and the sophisticated music of Debussy and Ravel. The Impressionists tried to capture the play of color and light; favorite images included dappled sunlight through leaves and the play of light on water, fields, flowers, and buildings. The musicians dealt with an art of movement that attempted to translate this interplay of color and light into shimmering and sensual sounds.

Closely related to Impressionism in painting and music was the Symbolism of Mallarmé, Verlaine, and Baudelaire. They achieved an indefiniteness with words that had been the privilege of music alone. They likened their poetry to music and sought tone color in word sounds and symbolic meanings of words rather than any definite meaning. Word plays, as with the tonal play of Impressionistic music, was, according to Verlaine, "the gray song where the indefinite meets the precise."

The effects that musical Impressionism achieved were the result of a number of innovations and extensions of musical resources.

Modes The old church modes came into favor again during late Romanticism and were exploited further by the Impressionists. The effects they sought were counter to the clear tonality of the major-minor system. The modes, among other scales, provided a wider range of colors and the desirable vagueness of tonality.

Other Scales The strong Oriental influence was reflected in the use of the *pentatonic scale* (five-tone scale), that is the basis for the folk music of Bali, China, and other Oriental cultures.

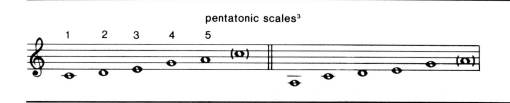

pentatonic scales[3]

Particularly appropriate for the vague tonalities and drifting harmonies of Impressionism was the *whole-tone scale.* This was a six-tone scale with a whole step between each pitch. With all tones equidistant, there was no clear tonal center. In fact, there were only two whole-tone scales possible: one starting on a white note and ending on a black note, and the other starting on a black note and ending on a white note.

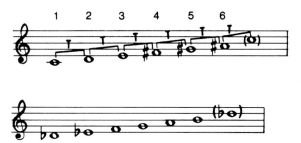

Form Classical forms were generally abandoned in favor of the vague outlines, drifting quality, and dreamlike effects so basic to the style. This is not to say that the music is formless—there is a beginning, middle, and end—but rather that the forms are subtle and dictated by the effects of impressions sought by the composer.

Orchestration The massed woodwind and/or brass sounds of the orchestras of Brahms, Strauss, Wagner, and so forth, were anathema to the Impressionists. They replaced the dark and ponderous sound of the Germanic orchestras with a much lighter, shimmering effect and much more individualistic use of instruments. They delighted in the exotic sounds of the English horn and the flutes and clarinets in the low register. Violins frequently played in extremely high registers and were often muted. Trumpets and horns

were frequently muted. The characteristic sounds of the orchestra were supplemented by the harp, triangle, lightly brushed cymbals, and the bell tones of the small keyboard instrument called the *céleste.* The treatment of the pure sounds of the individual instruments was very much like the use of tiny brushstrokes of pure colors by the painters.

The piano remained a favorite instrument for the Impressionists, but the sounds had little in common with the style, for example, of Chopin. The emphasis was on coloration, sensation, subtle harmonic effects, a great delicacy of tone. Everything was programmatic, whether a tonal description of a specific event or the evocation of a general idea, image, or sensation.

In the following piano composition, Debussy describes the Breton legend of the sunken cathedral of Ys which, on certain mornings, rises out of the misty sea with its bells tolling and with monks intoning their prayers and singing Gregorian chant. After a brief moment the cathedral sinks again below the surface, and rippling waters gradually close over its lofty towers. Because of its detailed program, this composition is Romantic in style. The other two compositions by Debussy (*Sails* and *Prelude to the Afternoon of a Faun*) are less explicit and are therefore more in the style of Impressionism.

---

3. These scales can be played using only the black keys of the piano. Pentatonic scales are commonly used in many cultures outside the Orient; for example, Scotland, American Indian, American folk songs.

La Cathédrale Engloutie, Preludes, vol. I, no. X
(1910) *(The Engulfed Cathedral)*

Form: a–b–á–c–b–ć–a²   Claude Debussy (1862–1918)
Three-note motive throughout plus the three themes

Theme a   Theme b   Theme c

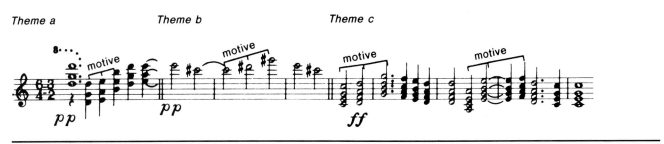

Below is another composition from the same set of preludes which bears only the symbolic title of *Voiles (Sails).* The listener is free to make any association in keeping with the music and the one-word clue that the composer has placed at the *end* of the composition. The musical techniques that make the piece *sound* the way it does can of course be studied and analyzed. It would not be proper, however, to inform the listener which sensations or images should be called to mind. The title and the music are quite sufficient; the listener can take it from there.

The piece uses the whole-tone scale throughout, except for a brief section on the pentatonic scale.

Voiles, Preludes, vol. I, no. II (1910) *(Sails)*

Form: **Ternary**
         (more or less)   Claude Debussy

Theme a

Whole-tone scale

Pentatonic scale

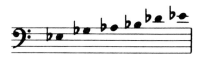

The delicate subtleties and discreet coloration of Impressionism appear to best effect in the carefully chosen palette of the orchestra. For his *Prelude to the Afternoon of a Faun,* Debussy used the following instrumentation:

3 flutes	Antique cymbals
2 oboes	(small, tuned cymbals)
English horn	violin I
2 clarinets	violin II
2 bassoons	viola
4 French horns	cello
2 harps	bass

Debussy's music was inspired by a study of the poem "Ecologue" by Stéphane Mallarmé. All poetry is difficult to translate and that of the Symbolists is impossible. The general feeling of the mood that Debussy attempted to portray can be better understood by reading the following paraphrase of Mallarmé's poem:

A faun—a simple, sensuous, passionate being—wakens in the forest at daybreak and tries to recall his experience of the previous afternoon. Was he the fortunate recipient of an actual visit from nymphs, white or golden goddesses, divinely tender and indulgent? Or is the memory he seems to retain nothing but the shadows of a vision, no more substantial than the arid rain of notes from his own flute? He cannot tell. Yet surely there was, surely there is, an animal whiteness among the brown reeds of the lake that shines out yonder? Were they, are they, swans? No! But Naiads plunging? Perhaps!

Vaguer and vaguer grows the impression of this delicious experience. He would resign his woodland godship to retain it. A garden of lilies, golden-headed, white-stalked, behind the trellis of red roses? Ah! the effort is too great for his poor brain. Perhaps if he selects one lily from the garth of lilies, one benign and beneficent yielder of her cup to thirsty lips, the memory, the ever-receding memory, may be forced back. So, when he has glutted upon a branch of grapes, he is wont to toss the empty skins into the air and blow them out in a visionary greediness. But no, the delicious hour grows vaguer; experience or dreams, he will now never know which it was. The sun is warm, the grasses yielding; and he curls himself up again, after worshipping the efficacious star of wine, that he may pursue the dubious ecstasy into the more helpful boskages of sleep.[4]

Prélude à l'Après-midi d'un Faune (1895)

Claude Debussy

Form: Ternary. The piece is built on one main theme (*a*) which goes through a series of transformations before returning in its original form. There are four other themes that appear at least twice and that should be identified (themes *b, c, d,* and *e*).

Theme a
flute

Theme b
clarinet

Theme c
oboe

Theme d
woodwinds

Theme e
oboe

Summary

Some of the elements of nineteenth-century Romanticism were present in the later works of Beethoven, but the lyric strains of full-blown Romanticism were paramount in the vocal and instrumental works of Franz Schubert. The characteristic style of German art songs (*lieder*) was created by the composer from Vienna and further developed by the German composers Schumann, Brahms, and Wolf. Frédéric Chopin made the piano his personal instrument with his unique style, and the very nature of Romanticism reinforced this individuality of personal expression. The music of Liszt, Strauss, Tchaikovsky, Verdi, and most emphatically, Richard Wagner reflected this intensely subjective approach to artistic experience. They, like Rousseau, if not better than other men, were "at least different."

The decline of absolute music in favor of a full range of miniature to grandiose program music was probably the most significant musical characteristic of the century. The abstract titles of the eighteenth century (sonata, serenade, symphony) were, to a considerable extent, abandoned for descriptive or poetic titles. In addition, there were dreamy *nocturnes,* cute *capriccios,* and dashing *rhapsodies* distinguished more by sound and fury than by strong intrinsic design. Filled with emotion for its own sake and thus unabashedly sentimental, and lacking also the disciplined energy of the pre-Napoleonic era, Romantic music provided the sounding board of the age.

The creation of the tone poem seemed to be the inevitable result of a Romantic propensity for reinforcing music with the literary arts. Two arts seemed to be better than one. By the same token, six trumpets were better than two and a hundred-piece orchestra superior to a sixty-piece orchestra. If the trend to monumental Napoleonic ideas had continued, the French Romantic, Hector Berlioz might have eventually recruited the ten thousand trumpets playing from a mountaintop that he so ardently longed to hear.

The latter part of the century saw a gradual leveling off in the growth of the symphony orchestra. The tone poems of Strauss and the huge vocal-instrumental works of Mahler and Bruckner represented a point of no return, a stage reached after a reaction against the grandiloquence had already set in. Brahms reacted against the extravagant use of musical materials and orchestral sounds by deliberately returning to the more disciplined practices of an earlier age. Debussy, Ravel, and other Impressionists also reacted negatively by sharply reducing the orchestra in order to concentrate on the pure tone colors of individual instruments. However, they did continue in the Romantic tradition of program music, carrying it to its ultimate conclusion with techniques similar to the symbolism of Mallarmé and Verlaine. The transition from nineteenth-century Romanticism to the so-called New Music of the twentieth century was accomplished in large part by the Impressionists, who inaugurated many of the materials of modern music while writing the final chapter of Romantic music.

Listening Outline (Fifth Stage)

I. Listening Outline
  A. Medium
    1. Vocal (text: English, French, German, Russian, Latin, other)
    2. Instrumental
    3. Vocal and instrumental (text)
  B. Tempo—very slow, slow, moderate, fast, very fast
  C. Loudness—very soft, soft, medium loud, very loud, combination
  D. Number of performers
    1. Solo
    2. Ensemble
      a) Small (2 to 5)
      b) Medium (6 to 20)
      c) Medium large (21 to 59)
      d) Large (60 to 100)
      e) Very large (over 100)
  E. Rhythm
    1. Metric (regular beat or pulsation)
    2. Nonmetric (pulsation irregular or indistinct)
  F. Meter
    1. Duple (2 beats per measure)
    2. Triple (3 beats per measure)
    3. Quadruple (4 beats per measure)
    4. Other (5 or 7 beats per measure)
  G. Texture
    1. Monophonic (unaccompanied melody)
    2. Homophonic (melody with accompaniment)
    3. Polyphonic (2 or more simultaneous melodies)

4. Edmund Gosse, "French Profiles," *The Collected Essays of Edmund Gosse,* William Heinemann, Ltd., London, 1905. Needless to say the "faun" of this fantasy is in no way related to a "fawn."

H. Form
1. AB (two-part)
2. ABA (three-part)
3. Sonata form
4. Theme and variations
5. Rondo
6. Tone (Symphonic) poem (may have sections or movements; may be through-composed with no repeated themes; may have a single theme used throughout)
7. Other

II. Conclusions
A. Period
1. Medieval (600–1420)
2. Renaissance (1420–1600)
3. Baroque (1600–1750)
4. Rococo (1725–1775)
5. Classical (1760–1827)
6. Romantic (ca. 1814–1900)
7. Impressionism (ca. 1880–1920)

B. General musical form

Vocal

Gregorian chant	Sequence-trope
Madrigal	Troubadour/
Mass	Trouvère tradition
Motet	Song
	Other

Vocal and Instrumental

Accompanied song	Motet
Lied	Opera
Cantata	Oratorio
Chorale	Other
Mass	

Instrumental

Chorale prelude	Symphony
Concerto	Trio sonata
Dance suite	Tone poem
Sonata	Characteristic
String quartet (trio, quintet)	piece (Ballade, Rhapsody, Nocturne, etc.)

C. National origin—Austria, England, Flanders, France, Germany, Italy, Russia, Scandinavia, United States

N.B. See the Glossary for unfamiliar terms.

Record List

Specific records are not listed except for a few exceptional recordings.

1. Schubert, Franz. Lied: "Gretchen am Spinnrade."
2. Chopin, Frédéric. "Ballade in G Minor." Rubinstein. *Ballades 1,2,3,4.* Victor LM—2370; LSC—2370.
3. ———. "Etude in E Major." Slencyznska. *Études, Op. 10 and 25.* 2—Decca 9890/1.
4. ———. "Prelude in D Minor." *Preludes, Op. 28.* Brailowski, Columbia ML—5444; MS—6119.
5. Mendelssohn, Felix. "Symphony No. 4 in A Major."
6. Berlioz, Hector. "Symphonie Fantastique."
7. Liszt, Franz. "Les Préludes."
8. Strauss, R. *Till Eulenspiegel.* Bernstein, N.Y. Phil. (and "Humor in Music"). Columbia ML—5625; MS—6225.
9. Tchaikovsky, Peter. "Symphony No. 5 in E Minor."
10. Brahms, Johannes. *Symphony No. 3 in F Major.*
11. Puccini, Giacomo. *La Bohème.* 2—Seraphim S—6099. Or: 2—RCA LSC—6095. Or: 2—London 1208.
12. Debussy, Claude. "La Cathedrale Engloutie" and "Voiles," *Preludes for Piano.* Book 1, Haas, DGG—18831; 138831.
13. ———. *Prelude à l'Après–midi d'un Faune.* Ansermet, London 9228; 6024.

Bibliography

Conrad, Peter. *Romantic Opera and Literary Form.* Berkeley, Calif.: University of California Press, 1977. Intriguing cross relationships.

Dannreuther, E. *The Romantic Period.* New York: Cooper Square Publishers, 1973. Quite a thorough exposition of the varieties of Romantic expression.

Einstein, Alfred. *Music in the Romantic Era.* New York: W.W. Norton, 1947. The definitive text for the period but not overly technical.

Plantinga, Leon. *Romantic Music.* New York: W. W. Norton, 1982. Introductory text.

26

Nineteenth-Century Art: Conflict and Diversity

The Romantic Movement and the Neoclassic Style

The Romantic movement first manifested itself in literature and music: the poetry of Wordsworth and Coleridge, the songs of Schubert, and the operas of Carl Maria von Weber. The visual arts were, however, in thrall to David, Napoleon's court painter, and to Napoleon's determination to confirm the legitimacy of his empire with the classical architecture of Imperial Rome. In 1806 Napoleon commissioned Jean Francis Chalgrin (shal–GREN; 1739–1811) to construct a mighty arch to honor the victories of the French fighting forces (fig. 26.1). Placed in the center of twelve radiating avenues, the arch is 164′ high and 148′ wide, larger than the triumphal arch of any Caesar. It stands today at the climax of the Avenue des Champs Elysées over the tomb of the Unknown Soldier, commemorating French imperial glory and the military triumphs of an emperor who did not live to see its completion.

The Church of St. Mary Magdalen, known as The Madeleine (fig. 26.2), was originally begun in 1764 and later razed to be replaced with a building modeled after the Pantheon in Rome. Napoleon ordered that structure replaced by a new temple, a massive building dedicated to the glory of the Grand Army. The Madeleine has fifty-two majestic Corinthian columns running completely around the building, each 66′ tall. The eight-column front and complete peristyle are reminiscent of the Parthenon (see fig. 7.44) but the 23′ high podium is of Roman origin and similar to the Maison Carrée (see fig. 10.7). Napoleon's Temple of Glory is a skillful synthesis of Graeco-Roman elements into a unified and imposing design.

Jean-Auguste-Dominique Ingres (ang'r; 1780–1867) was only nine years old when the revolution began and was never an enthusiastic supporter of Napoleon's self-proclaimed revolutionary ideals. Ingres was, however, David's most talented pupil and an advocate of a Neoclassic style that had evolved from revolutionary art into state-endorsed dogma. Contending that David's style was too heavily incised, Ingres developed a fluid drawing technique influenced by Pompeiian frescoes and patterned after elegant linear figures of Greek vase paintings (see fig. 7.56). His *Grand*

Figure 26.1 Jean François Chalgrin (and others), Arch of Triumph, 1806–1836. Place Charles de Gaulle, Paris.

Figure 26.2 Pierre Vignon, The Madeleine, 1806–1842, Paris.

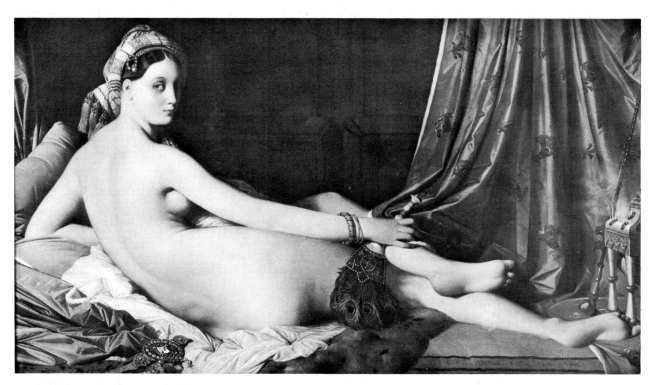

Figure 26.3 Jean-Auguste-Dominique Ingres, *Grand Odalisque,* 1814. Oil on canvas, 35¼ × 63¾". The Louvre, Paris.

Odalisque (fig. 26.3) is not a classical version of feminine beauty, however; but a superb example of the artist's unique mix of Neoclassic and Romantic ideas. The reclining-nude pose can be traced to Titian and the smoothly-flowing contours of the sculpturesque body are cooly Classical; but, the subject is an odalisque, a harem slave girl who represents an exotic concept dear to the Romantics. The small head, elongated limbs, and languid pose are very mannered in the decorative style of Parmigianino (see fig. 18.41).

The first of the illustrious painters of the Romantic era, Francisco de Goya (GO–ya; 1746–1828) was unique even in a time of remarkably individualistic artists. A contemporary of David, with whom he had nothing in common, Goya was influenced by Velasquez and Rembrandt but not at all by antiquity or the Renaissance. Appointed painter to the court of Spain in 1799, Goya created many acutely candid studies of a royal family that presided over a corrupt and decadent administration. His portrait of *Carlos IV of Spain as Huntsman* (fig. 26.4) is a devastating study of an arrogant and pompous monarch. Possibly symbolizing the plight of the Spanish people, the dog sits humbly and meekly at the feet of a vacant-faced king whom Goya has posed as if he were a mighty hunter.

Colorplate 40 Eugene Delacroix, *Arabs Skirmishing in the Mountains,* 1863. Oil on canvas, 36⅜ × 29⅜″. Chester Dale Fund, 1966. National Gallery of Art, Washington, D.C.

Colorplate 41 John Constable, *Wivenhoe Park, Essex,* 1816. Oil on canvas, 22⅛ × 39⅞″. (Widener Collection. National Gallery of Art, Washington, D.C.)

Colorplate 42 Winslow Homer, *Breezing Up*, 1876. Oil on canvas, 24⅛ × 38⅛″. Gift of the W. L. and May T. Mellon Foundation, 1943. National Gallery of Art, Washington, D.C.

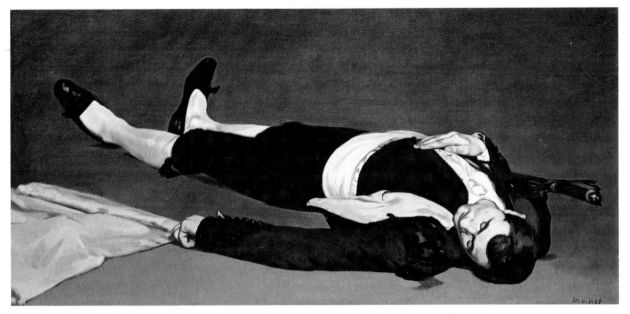

Colorplate 43 Edouard Manet, *The Dead Toreador,* 1864. Oil on canvas, 29⅞ × 60⅜″. Widener Collection. National Gallery of Art, Washington, D.C.

Colorplate 44 Edgar Degas, *Four Dancers,* ca. 1899. Oil on canvas, 59¼ × 71¼″. Chester Dale Collection, 1962. National Gallery of Art, Washington, D.C.

Colorplate 45 Claude Monet, *Rouen Cathedral, West Façade Sunlight,* 1894. Oil on canvas, 39½ × 26″. Chester Dale Collection, 1962. National Gallery of Art, Washington, D.C.

Colorplate 46 Auguste Renoir, *Girl with a Watering Can,* 1876. Oil on canvas, 39½ × 28¾″. Chester Dale Collection, 1962. National Gallery of Art, Washington, D.C.

Colorplate 47 Paul Cézanne, *Le Château Noir,* ca. 1904. Oil on canvas, 29 × 38″. Gift of Eugene and Agnes Meyer, 1958. National Gallery of Art, Washington, D.C.

Colorplate 48 Paul Gauguin, *Self-Portrait,* 1889. Oil on wood, 31¼ × 20¼″. Chester Dale Collection, 1962. National Gallery of Art, Washington, D.C.

Colorplate 49 Georges Seurat, *Sunday Afternoon on the Island of La Grande Jatte,* 1884–1886. Oil on canvas, 10'6" × 6'9". Courtesy the Art Institute of Chicago.

Colorplate 50 Henri Matisse, *The Blue Window,* 1911, Autumn. Oil on canvas 51½ × 35⅜″. Collection, The Museum of Modern Art, New York. Abby Aldrich Rockefeller Fund.

Colorplate 51 Pablo Picasso, *Still Life,* 1918. Oil on canvas, 54¼ × 38¼″. Chester Dale Collection, 1962. National Gallery of Art, Washington, D.C.

Figure 26.4 Francisco de Goya, *Carlos IV of Spain as Huntsman,* ca. 1799. Oil on canvas, 18¼ × 11¾″. Andrew W. Mellon Collection. National Gallery of Art, Washington, D.C.

Figure 26.5 Francisco de Goya, *Maria Luisa, Queen of Spain,* ca. 1799. Oil on canvas, 18¼ × 11¾″. Andrew W. Mellon Collection. National Gallery of Art, Washington, D.C.

The portrait of *Maria Luisa, Queen of Spain* (fig. 26.5) reveals an equally arrogant personality. Elegantly gowned and wearing pointed slippers on her tiny feet, the queen towers over a muted landscape. Goya has vividly captured the malicious glint in her eyes and the cruelty implicit in her tight mouth. The monarchs are not only portrayed as insolent but there is also an aura of evil. If these characteristics are so evident, why did the royal family retain Goya as their court painter? They may have been dazzled by the artist's skillful painting of their splendid costumes but they were, in fact, too stupid to view themselves as Goya, and posterity, see them.

Goya extended his critical appraisal of the royal family to a general view of human folly, vice, and stupidity as depicted in a series of paintings and engravings called *The Caprices.* Then, Napoleon's 1808 occupation of Spain provided the artist with a powerful new subject: the bestiality and utter futility of war. Goya and many of his countrymen had hoped for

French reforms of the debased Spanish court; instead, the merciless brutality of French soldiers provoked an equally savage resistance. In a series of unforgettable etchings called *The Disasters of War,* Goya brilliantly depicted the sordid consequences of warfare. His *Grande hazaña! Con muertos!* (Great exploit! In casualties!; fig. 26.6) conveys the horror of mutilation and violent death with a startling economy of means. Euripides (see his *Trojan Woman* in vol. 1) and Goya stand virtually alone in their convincing portrayals of the senselessness of warfare.

Goya's art was intensely personal and impossible to classify. He was a true Romantic, however, in his concern about placing too much faith in the primacy of reason, that goddess of an Enlightenment that led to a violent revolution, the Reign of Terror, and, ultimately, to Napoleon. In an etching entitled "The Sleep of Reason Produces Monsters," Goya illustrated the primitive, bestial instincts that were unleashed whenever reason was not eternally vigilant. Goya left

Spain in 1824 during another period of repression and died in exile in France. His art was not known outside Spain until late in the Romantic movement.

The most talented French painter of early Romanticism, Théodore Gericault (ZHAY-ree-ko; 1791–1824), won artistic immortality with his painting of *The Raft of the Medusa* (fig. 26.7). Like other Romantic artists, Gericault seized upon a contemporary event (in 1816), in this case a tragedy that caused a national scandal. Jammed with colonists bound for French West Africa, the *Medusa* ran aground off the African coast because of the incompetence of the ship's captain, who then filled the *Medusa's* six boats with his own party and sailed to shore. About 150 men and one woman were left to shift for themselves.[1] In the painting, the few remaining survivors on their makeshift raft have just sighted a rescue ship on the horizon and are frantically signaling for help. Gericault researched the tragedy like an investigative reporter, interviewing survivors, studying corpses in the morgue, even building a raft in his studio. The result is not just a realistic reporting of the event but a drama of heroic proportions of men against the sea. The slashing diagonals and vivid chiaroscuro lead our eye to the triangle formed by the extended arms, with the waving figure at the apex; all movement is projected forward toward the distant sail. Gericault's graphic realism was characteristic of the Romantic intent to shock the sensibilities of the viewer and evoke an emotional response. Government attempts to cover up the errors of a French naval officer stirred the public to a frenzy and focused attention on the painting as a political statement, much to the artist's dismay, rather than as a compelling work of art.

Figure 26.6 Francisco de Goya, *Grande hazaña! Con muertos!*, from *The Disasters of War,* ca. 1814. Etching, edition of 1863. Private collector.

1. For details of the century's worst French scandal prior to the Dreyfus Case see Alexander McKee's *Death Raft: The Human Drama of the Medusa Shipwreck* (New York: Warner Books, Inc., 1977).

Figure 26.7 Théodore Gericault, *The Raft of the Medusa,* 1818–1819. Oil on canvas, ca. 16′ × 23′. The Louvre, Paris.

Figure 26.8 François Rude, *La Marseillaise (The Departure of the Volunteers in 1792)*, 1833–1836. Stone, ca. 42 × 26'. Arch of Triumph, Paris.

Following Gericault's early death as a result of a riding accident, Eugène Delacroix (de–la–KWRAH; 1799–1863), a peerless colorist, became the leading Romantic artist. The first major French artist to visit Islamic countries, Delacroix was fascinated with the colorful vitality of North African cultures. In *Arabs Skirmishing in the Mountains* (colorplate 40) he demonstrates a vibrant range of intense hues and strong contrasts of light and dark. As the artist wrote in one of his journals, "the more the contrast the greater the force." His ability to capture the illusion of movement makes the dramatic impact of the pitched battle all the more convincing. Continuing the squabble between color and line (Romanticism vs. Classicism), Delacroix was the Rubenist and his rival, Ingres (see fig. 26.3), the Poussinist of the nineteenth century. For a colorist like Delacroix the perfect style, as he said, was a combination of Michelangelo and Goya, whose works were then being rediscovered.

Romantic painters were enamored with the sister arts: the plays of Shakespeare, medieval romances, English romantic poetry, and, especially, music. Delacroix preferred, surprisingly, the classical style of Mozart to the flamboyant romanticism of his French contemporary Hector Berlioz (see chap. 25) but was a personal friend of Frédéric Chopin, whose poetic piano music had a special appeal, not only for Delacroix, but also for many writers and artists of the time. His portrait of Chopin (see fig. 25.1) epitomizes the melancholy suffering of the Romantic genius.

Though there were no Romantic sculptors the caliber of Goya and Delacroix, François Rude (1784–1855) did design a notable work for the Arch of Triumph. His *La Marseillaise* (fig. 26.8), the only distinguished sculpture on the Arch, is a dramatic patriotic work depicting citizen-soldiers leaving to defend the borders of the new republic against foreign invaders. Done in very high relief and dressed in Roman armor, when they are dressed, the volunteers are urged on by Bellona, the Roman war goddess, portrayed here as a Goddess of Victory singing the stirring call to arms of the French National Anthem: *La Marseillaise.*

In England, Romantic art responded more to Rousseau's back-to-nature movement than it did to the ideological drive of the revolution and subsequent Napoleonic wars; England had already had a revolution. English Romantic poets—Wordsworth, Coleridge, Shelley, Keats—described the beauties of nature in highly personal terms. Landscape was prominent in their poetry but not as description for its own sake; rather, poets responded to aspects of the natural scene that stimulated their thinking, leading to meditations on nature that, as Wordsworth observed, involved the "Mind of Man." On the other hand, nature was frequently the subject matter for Romantic painters. John Constable (1776–1837), one of the finest of all English painters, studied landscapes with a scientific objectivity. Rather than simply recording tangible objects he sought the intangible qualities of atmosphere, light, and, especially, the sky. The justly-famed "Constable sky" is the dominating element in his poetic response to the peaceful scene at *Wivenhoe Park, Essex* (colorplate 41). Sunlight shining on the wind-driven clouds and the effect of sunshine on fields and water have a luminosity rivaling even the Dutch masters, and the entire canvas has a freshness never before achieved in painting. The lustrous sky is the crowning glory of the picture, triumphantly confirming the artist's claim that this area was the "principle instrument for expressing sentiment." After his first exposure to Constable's work, Delacroix repainted the sky of an already completed work, and the Impressionists were no less dazzled by the skies of Constable.

Many Romantic writers and architects were antiquarians, researching history for authentic details of the glorious past. Sir Walter Scott wrote what he called romances, historical novels like *Ivanhoe* that were set in medieval England. Scott's obsession with the past led him to the construction of an elaborate country estate resembling a medieval castle that he named Abbotsford, after a river crossing used by medieval

Figure 26.9 Abbotsford, home of Sir Walter Scott, on the Tweed River, Scotland. Begun ca. 1820.

Figure 26.10 Alfred Waterhouse, Museum of Natural History, 1873–1879, London.

abbots (fig. 26.9). The medieval tower is a decorative appendage to a baronial mansion of gables, clustered chimney pots, Neoclassic windows, and elaborate gardens in the casual English manner. Scott's vision of himself as the lord of a manor led to a prodigious production of novels just to make the payments on his romantic dream house.

Typical of the concern with the medieval past, the Museum of Natural History (fig. 26.10) was patterned after Italian Romanesque church designs. The elaborate arches, columns, and other details are now placed on the exterior of a secular public building. Romanesque churches were built by skilled stonemasons but Neoromanesque buildings of the Victorian Age used cast-iron skeletons covered with mass-produced elements of Romanesque details.

The largest and most successful architectural recollection of the past were the Houses of Parliament, designed by Sir Charles Barry (1795–1860) with the assistance of Gothic scholar Augustus Welby Pugin (1812–1852; fig. 26.11). The English felt, as did the French and Germans, that the Gothic style was the perfect expression of the national past, a heritage both noble and Christian. The Parliamentary Commission specified that the design for the new seat of government be either Gothic or Elizabethan and nothing else. Barry favored the Neoclassic style but Pugin convinced him that the English Late Gothic style was the proper glorification of the British spirit and a celebration of medieval craftsmanship in the face of mass-produced items of the Industrial Age. Actually, the body of the building is symmetrical in the Palladian manner surmounted by a Gothic fantasy of turrets, towers, and battlements.

Figure 26.11 Barry and Pugin, The Houses of Parliament, London.

Figure 26.12 Victorian Gothic mansion, ca. 1885, Eureka, California.

Inspired by the design of Parliament, the Gothic Revival style of about 1855–1885 was enthusiastically adopted by English and American architects. Constructed during the height of the Revival by a timber contractor, the Victorian Gothic mansion in California (fig. 26.12) is a wooden frame structure with an incredible variety of surface decoration and detail. "More is better" was a Victorian preference that is exuberantly realized in this prize example of American Gothic.

Realism

Countering the Romantic fantasies of their literary and artistic contemporaries, the Realists concentrated on the real world as they perceived it, with an objective matter-of-factness that alienated the followers of Gericault and Delacroix. Settling near the village of Barbizon in the Forest of Fontainebleau south of Paris, painters of the Barbizon School imitated Rousseau's

back-to-nature movement while simultaneously escaping the disorder and confusion of the 1848 Revolution. Rousseau's "noble savage" was interpreted by Barbizon associate François Millet (me–YAY; 1814–1875) as a heroic peasant who exemplified the dignity of working the land. In *The Sower* (fig. 26.13) Millet's peasant has the monumentality of Michelangelo and an earthy quality comparable to the bourgeois Dutch tradition. Himself the son of peasants, Millet chose to live the life of a peasant, sympathetically depicting his protagonists as actors in a kind of divine drama in a style antithetic to the French academic tradition.[2]

---

2. Disdained since about 1860 as artistically inferior, French academic art has, since about 1965, experienced a rebirth. See, for example, *The Encyclopedia of World Art,* vol. XVI (New York: McGraw-Hill Book Company, 1983), pp. 230–231.

Figure 26.13 François Millet, *The Sower*, ca. 1850. Oil on canvas, 39¾ × 32½″. Shaw Collection. Museum of Fine Arts, Boston.

Figure 26.14 Joan-Baptiste-Camille Corot, *Forest of Fontainebleau*, ca. 1830. Oil on canvas, 69⅛ × 95¼″. Chester Dale Collection, 1962. National Gallery of Art, Washington, D.C.

Figure 26.15 Honoré Daumier, *Le Ventre Legislatif*, 1834. Lithograph. The Arizona State University Art Collections, Arizona State University. Gift of Oliver B. James.

Though he did not consider himself a member of the Barbizon School, Jean-Baptiste-Camille Corot (ko–ROW; 1796–1875) lived in the area and shared their strong commitment to direct visual experience. In the *Forest of Fontainebleau* (fig. 26.14) Corot painted the full range of light and dark values, depicting visual reality at a single moment in time. Working very quickly, Corot sought the underlying rhythm of nature, composing his landscapes so that the magic moment of truth would be revealed to all. One of the finest Western landscape painters, Corot became as the poet Baudelaire said he would, "the master of an entire younger generation."

Corot, Millet, and the Barbizon School can be described as Romantic Realists for there is an element of escapism in their work. In Paris, however, the realities of political and social unrest before and after the 1848 Revolution were of far greater concern to a hard-bitten Realist like Honoré Daumier (doe–me–AY; 1808–1879). Known to his contemporaries as a caricaturist, Daumier created over 4,000 lithographs[3] satirizing the major and minor foibles of the day. In his caricature of *Le Ventre Legislatif* ("The Legislative Belly"; fig. 26.15) Daumier depicted the venality, pomposity, and stupidity of the collective "Legislative Belly," i.e., "Body." With devastating candor Daumier gives us a cast of politicians all too well known in the body politic of democratic societies.

Daumier's political caricatures once landed him in jail but that did not curtail his acid pen; in a series of lithographs called *Ancient History* the artist lambasted the Neoclassicists. *Pygmalion* (fig. 26.16) is a comical rendering of the classical myth about the sculptor who fell in love with his beautiful creation and invited her to come to life. Daumier pictured the sculptor as a journeyman stone hacker astonished by the flirtatious response of a dumpy, unattractive Galatea.

---

3. One of the graphic arts, lithography is a printmaking process that was widely popular in the nineteenth century for newspaper and magazine illustrations. In lithography (Gk., "writing on stone") the design is drawn on stone or a metal plate with a greasy printing ink and then reproduced by the standard printing process.

Figure 26.16 Honoré Daumier, *Pygmalion,* from the series *Histoire Ancienne.* Private collection.

Figure 26.17 Honoré Daumier, *The Washerwoman,* ca. 1863. Oil on panel, 19¼ × 13″. The Louvre, Paris.

Daumier was just as forceful a contemporary social critic in oils as he was in his lithographs, claiming that scenes of contemporary everyday life had to be painted because "one must be of one's own time." In *The Washerwoman* (fig. 26.17) he used a strong chiaroscuro in the manner of Rembrandt, whom he greatly admired, to depict the weariness of a mother who is tenderly assisting her child up the steps. Looming large against the vague urban background, the figure has a monumental nobility that is comparable, though on a much smaller scale, with Michelangelo's grandiose figures on the Sistine Chapel ceiling.

Realism in art was given a name and a leader in the person of Gustave Courbet (koor–BAY; 1819–1877), who even took the time to issue a "Manifesto of Realism." At the Andler Keller, one of the first Parisian beer halls, the swaggering, flamboyant Courbet held forth as the apostle of the physical world of visible objects. "Show me an angel," he once remarked, "and I will paint you an angel." Courbet found his natural subjects in the common people of his home village of Ornans in eastern France. As he said, "to paint a bit of country, one must know it. I know my country." *Burial at Ornans* (fig. 26.18) depicts a rural scene on a monumental scale normally reserved for epic historical events. Much to the consternation of the critics, Courbet turned the somber reality of this simple country funeral into a noble occasion that he

called "true history." Combining religious symbolism with realism, Courbet included the dog as it was depicted in the Office of the Dead in medieval manuscripts; the people were all painted from life in innumerable sittings demanded by the artist. Composed on a horizontal S-curve, the figures of clergy, pallbearers, friends, and relatives stand in poses ranging from indifference to composed grief. The staff with the crucifix is positioned to give the illusion of Christ's actual death on Golgotha. This and other paintings were rejected by the Universal Exposition, leading to the construction of a shed, called by Courbet "The Pavilion of Realism," for the exhibition of his uncompromising works.

Realism spread throughout Europe as artists were attracted to the style but it was especially popular in the United States, where pragmatism and realism were characteristics of the American way of life. Beginning his career as an illustrator for *Harper's Weekly,* Winslow Homer (1836–1910) was influenced by Corot and Courbet, but not at the expense of his American point

Figure 26.18 Gustave Courbet, *Burial at Ornans,* 1849–1850. Oil on canvas, ca. 10'3" × 21'9". The Louvre, Paris.

of view. Homer lived during what Mark Twain had called the Gilded Age, a grossly materialistic era of pretentious opulence, but his style was firmly fixed in genre paintings in the mode of American realism. In *Breezing Up* (colorplate 42) Homer celebrated his lifelong love affair with the sea in a joyous composition of wind, salt air, and sparkling sea. Fatigued but happy with the day's catch, the fisherman and boys are returning home. With the catboat placed at eye level and slanting away from the viewer, we are drawn into an illusion of movement and the feeling of a job well done. Exemplifying Homer's statement, "When I have selected a thing carefully, I paint it exactly as it appears," the details are finely drawn: wrinkled clothes, light sparkling from metal fittings, a lighthouse at the lower left, a wheeling gull at the upper right. Homer's ability to give the illusion of light emanating from his canvases paralleled the development of French Impressionism across the ocean from his native New England.

Homer's career was remarkably divergent from that of his older contemporary, author Herman Melville. Both were New Englanders and fascinated by the sea but Homer's vision was generally positive while Melville's was darkly ambiguous. Homer covered the Civil War as an illustrator for *Harper's Weekly;* Melville wrote two volumes of war poems that were totally unknown at the time. Homer was a highly successful and popular painter; Melville was not recognized as one of America's greatest writers until many years after his obscure death. Ironically, both were Realists (see chap. 24 for some of Melville's poetry).

Realism in painting can be compared, to some extent, with the development of late nineteenth-century architecture. Abandoning copies of older styles, architects turned to modern building materials to design functional structures serving specific purposes. Epitomizing the new attitude toward utilitarian design, the Crystal Palace (fig. 26.19) was constructed of 5,000 prefabricated iron columns and girders and nearly 300,000 panes of glass. A greenhouse designer by profession, Sir Joseph Paxton (1801–1865) oversaw the construction of an immense structure that covered nineteen acres in Hyde Park and contained almost a million square feet of floor space. Assembled in only four months, the Crystal Palace housed London's "Great Exhibition of the Works of All Nations," a triumphant display of the miracles wrought by the Industrial Revolution. The theme of the exhibition was "Progress" as represented by the mechanized marvels within the glittering structure, itself a symbol of the "Age of Progress." The first of many similar buildings, the Crystal Palace was dismantled after the exhibition and reassembled south of London where, in 1936, it was destroyed by fire. Though cast-iron structures were vulnerable to fire, the Crystal Palace did establish the practicality of metal as a building material. With the 1856 invention of the Bessemer process of making steel the technology was already available for the construction of twentieth-century high-rise buildings.

Figure 26.19 Joseph Paxton, Crystal Palace, 1850–1851, London.

The first high-rise structure in the world was designed by an engineer, Gustave Eiffel (I–fel; 1832–1923), for the Paris Exhibition of 1889, another celebration of technological advances. Rising to an imposing height of 984', the Eiffel Tower (fig. 26.20) symbolized the Age of Progress in modern France. Like a giant erector set, it was assembled on the site; prefabricated and prepunched girders were bolted together in a masterful demonstration of precision design and production. Though denounced from the outset by purists who objected to the violation of the Parisian skyline, the tower stands today as the enduring symbol of the City of Light.

Impressionism

In one respect Impressionism was an outgrowth of Realism but in another it was a revolutionary artistic movement almost as profound in its effect as the Early Renaissance in Italy. Impressionists saw themselves as the ultimate Realists whose main concern was the perception of optical sensations of light and color. Whether or not the Impressionists were consciously aware of photographic techniques, scientific research in optics, or the physiology of the eye is not important; they painted as if the world were not matter in space but a source of sensations of light and color. Objects were perceived as agents for the absorption and reflection of light; there were no sharp edges, indeed, no lines in nature. In nature, form and space were implied by infinitely varied intensities of color and light, and shadows were not black but colored in relation to the objects casting the shadows. This is Impressionist theory in essence but the individual artists developed styles, of course, that sometimes contradicted the theories.

Figure 26.20 Gustave Eiffel, Eiffel Tower, 1889, Paris

Figure 26.21 Edouard Manet, *Déjeuner sur l'herbe,* 1863. Oil on canvas, 7′ ×
8′10″. The Jeu de Paume, Paris.

A major innovator in Western painting, Édouard
Manet (ma–NAY; 1832–1883) was not an Impressionist but his influence on the movement was critical. Realizing that modeled transitions did not exist in nature,
he worked instead in planes. Also one of the first artists to paint with pure colors, eliminating dark shadows that had been used for centuries, Manet was a
pioneer in the use of light as his subject; light was the
actual subject matter of the painting that he submitted in 1863 to the jury of the Paris Salon. An unconventional painting with a conventional title, *Déjeuner
sur l'herbe (Luncheon on the Grass;* fig. 26.21) was
refused by the jury but exhibited in a special Salon
des Refusés, where it caused a storm of controversy.
Though the ostensible subject matter was possibly
derived from Giorgione's *Fête Champêtre* (see fig.
18.33), the contemporary dress of the men in combination with the unconcerned nakedness of the
woman deeply shocked the public; even Courbet, who
did not object to the nude, criticized the work as flat
and formless. Manet had almost totally abandoned
Renaissance perspective, accepting the canvas for
what it really was: a two-dimensional surface. The hue
and cry over the work bewildered the artist; the subject, after all was *light* as clustered around the nude,
the background figure, the still life in the left foreground. The grouping of the dark areas further emphasized the harsh light of day, giving the painting a
powerful visual impact. For Manet and the Impressionists the objects and figures in their paintings were
sometimes treated impersonally, as opportunities to

depict light sensations. Frequently detached and
nonjudgmental, Manet and the Impressionists, except for Renoir, were often more entranced with optical sensations than with humanity.

The public, however, was not detached and it was
very judgmental. The reaction to Manet's *Olympia* (fig.
26.22) that he exhibited at the 1865 Salon caused one
of the greatest scandals in art history. Critics called
Manet "a buffoon" and the nude a "female gorilla"
and "yellow-bellied odalisque," while boisterous
crowds flocked to see a work that another critic advised pregnant women and proper young ladies to
avoid at all costs. Manet had painted his model, Vic-
torine Meurend (who also posed for the Déjeuner),
as an elegant and worldly-weary lady of the evening.
With an orchid in her hair and wearing only a black
ribbon around her neck, she stares disdainfully at the
viewer while ignoring the bouquet proferred by her
maid. Critics were no more incensed about the fla-
grant nakedness than with the black-on-black coloration of the maid's face against the background, not
to mention the black cat at the foot of the suggestively
rumpled bed, also painted against a black background. The picture became a *cause célèbre,* pitting
modernists against traditionalists. In his novel *Of
Human Bondage* Somerset Maugham gleefully described the Latin Quarter in which reproductions of
Olympia were prominent in virtually every student
room, bar, and sidewalk cafe. Even today the picture
is distinctly modern. Manet forces his viewers to look

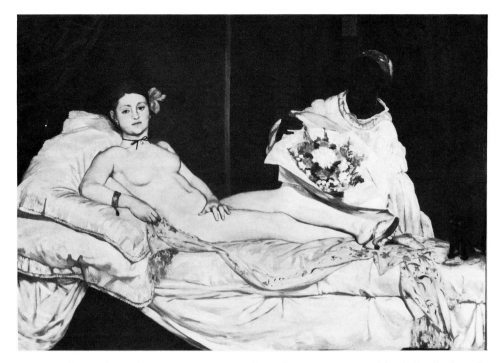

Figure 26.22 Edouard Manet, *Olympia*. 1863. Oil on canvas, 51¼ × 74¾″. The Jeu de Paume, Paris.

at his flat picture rather than *into* it. The traditional boxlike space behind the frontal picture plane has been eliminated, presenting a situation that leaves much to the imagination. A comparison of *Olympia* and the *Odalisque* of Ingres (see fig. 26.3) reveals the difference, at that time, between acceptable nudity and the disagreeable reality of a naked prostitute.

Manet was the first Western artist to reject Renaissance perspective as fraudulent, as basically contrary to the reality of an arrangement of colors and shapes on a flat surface. In *The Dead Toreador* (colorplate 43) he continued to antagonize a public that expected to see a dramatic depiction of a bullfighter fatally gored in the ring. Again, this is not a narrative but a striking arrangement of white, olive, pink, and black against a neutral background. Manet, like many of his contemporaries, was influenced by the newly popular Japanese prints in which two-dimensionality, line, and flat color planes were basic components of the style.

Following the innovations of Manet, who went on to experiment in other directions, the Impressionists developed a definite system with its own aesthetic principles. For centuries artists had been painting what they knew but the Impressionists were more interested in painting what they saw. The recent development of paint tubes and canisters liberated artists from the messy and time-consuming process of mixing pigments; more importantly, portable paints freed

artists from their studios, enabling them to roam the countryside and paint *en plein air* (in open air). To see and capture the wondrous glories of nature and revel in the evanescent effects of sunlight became the new aesthetic.

The spokesman and chief painter of the Impressionist style was Claude Monet (mo–NAY; 1840–1926), who throughout his long and productive career relied wholly upon his visual perceptions. For him, especially, there were no objects like trees, houses, or figures but some green here, a patch of blue there, a bit of yellow over here, and so on. Monet was "only an eye" said his contemporary, Paul Cézanne, "but what an eye!" The mechanics of vision were a major concern of Monet and the other Impressionists. To achieve intensity of color, pigments were not combined on the palette but laid on the canvas in primary hues so that the eye could do the mixing. A dab of yellow, for example, placed next to one of blue is perceived, from a distance, as green, a brilliant green because the eye accomplishes the optical recomposition. Further, each color leaves behind a visual sensation which is its afterimage or complementary color. The afterimage of red is blue-green and that of green is the color red. The adjacent placement of red and green reinforces each color through its afterimage, making both red and green more brilliant. Impressionists generally painted with pure pigments in the colors of the spectrum; conspicuously absent from the spectrum and thus from Impressionist canvases was black, a favorite of academic painters. Monet contended that black was not a color and he was scientifically correct; black is the absence of color. This, of course, did not keep artists like Degas and Manet *(The Dead Toreador)* from using black with dramatic effect.

Portable paints in the open sunlight and color perception were two components of Impressionist technique. The third component was speed. Making natural light explode on canvas necessitated quick brushstrokes that captured a momentary impression of reflected light, a reflection that changed from minute to minute. Monet's procedure was to paint furiously for seven or eight minutes and then move quickly to another canvas to capture a different light. Should a painting require additional effort he would return to the same spot the following day at precisely the same time, a procedure he followed in his many paintings of Rouen Cathedral done at different times of day. Early in the morning the elaborate Gothic facade would appear to be quite solid but later in the day, as in *Rouen Cathedral, West Façade Sunlight* (colorplate 45), the stonework has dissolved into a luminous haze of warm colors. *Impressionism* is a term used derisively by a critic who, upon seeing Monet's 1872 painting entitled *Impression, Sunrise,* remarked that it was "only an impression." That the term is generally apropos is apparent in Monet's impression of sunlight on medieval stonework.

Monet was a magnificent "eye" whose achievements are far more appreciated today than in his own time. On the other hand, the work of his celebrated contemporary, Auguste Renoir (ren–o'AR; 1841–1919), has always had great appeal, possibly because Renoir portrayed people rather than buildings, landscapes, or lily ponds. The finest painter of luscious nudes since Rubens, Renoir had a unique ability to create the illusion of soft and glowing human flesh. He painted females of all ages, once exclaiming that if "God had not created woman I don't know whether I would have become a painter!" *Girl with a Watering Can* (colorplate 46) is a marvel of iridescent color. Renoir's associates were astonished by his carefree approach to painting but, "if painting weren't fun," protested the artist, "you may be sure that I wouldn't do it." That joyous attitude is readily apparent in this luminous evocation of happy innocence.

Edgar Degas (DAY–gah; 1834–1917) also specialized in women, but mainly women in their casual but graceful roles as ballet dancers. Delighting in studying forms in motion, he drew dancers and race horses and, in so doing, gained a remarkable vitality in his work. *Four Dancers* (colorplate 44) was one of his last large oil paintings but it also shows the influence of the pastel medium that he used in most of his later works. Of all the Impressionists, Degas was most interested in photography, both in taking pictures and in basing some of his works on photographs. This off-stage ballet scene has the appearance of a candid

Figure 26.23 Berthe Morisot, *In the Dining Room,* 1881–1883. Oil on canvas, 24½ × 19¾". Chester Dale Collection, 1962. National Gallery of Art, Washington, D.C.

snapshot of dancers limbering up and checking their costumes before going on stage. Actually, Degas posed dancers in his studio to orchestrate the illusion of spontaneity that he wanted. It should be noted that Degas's concern with composition and his use of black make his style less impressionistic than the style of Monet.

The Impressionists were a cohesive group of avant-garde artists that revolved around the central personality of Manet. The regular meeting place of Manet's "school" was the Café Guerbois, where Manet, Monet, Renoir, Degas, Whistler, the photographer Nadar, Émile Zola, Baudelaire, and others congregated to argue passionately about the role of the modern artist. Berthe Morisot (more–uh–so; 1841–1895) was a member of the group but, as a proper young woman, she was denied the opportunity to socialize at the cafe with her colleagues. A student of both Corot and Manet, she had the unusual distinction of having her work accepted by both the Impressionists and the Salon. In her *In the Dining Room* (fig. 26.23) she depicted her maid and little white dog in a setting in which the forms are silhouetted as elements in a design literally flooded with light. An enthusiastic admirer of her art, the Symbolist poet Stéphane Mallarmé, wrote in his catalog for an exhibition of her work: "To make poetry in the plastic arts demands that the artist portray on the surface the luminous secret of things, simply, directly, without extraneous detail." And so she did.

Figure 26.24 Mary Cassatt, *The Bath,* ca. 1891–1892. Oil on canvas, 39¼ × 26″. Courtesy, The Art Institute of Chicago.

Both of the American painters who exhibited with the Impressionists, Cassatt and Whistler, drew their inspiration from their techniques but each developed a different and very personal style. Mary Cassatt (1844–1926) was American by birth and training and, though she lived in France for much of her life, is considered by the French to be the best artist America has yet produced. The influence of two-dimensional Japanese woodcuts is apparent in *The Bath* (fig. 26.24) but the extraordinary quality of the lines is uniquely her own. Both decorative and functional, the fluid lines enclose what seems at first to be a simple domestic scene. But, this is a highly stylized composition that we look down upon, an intimate and tender moment presented in a closed form that shuts out the viewer, and the world. We experience the rich warmth of the scene but we are not a part of it.

James McNeill Whistler (1834–1903), like Henry James, considered American civilization, such as it was, an embarrassment. Like James, Whistler became an expatriate, even denying that he was born in Lowell, Massachusetts: "I shall be born when and where I want, and I do not choose to be born in Lowell."

Whistler was highly critical, naturally, of American realists like Winslow Homer (see colorplate 42), advocating instead "art for art's sake." The Impressionists were sufficiently artistic for his tastes and he adapted some of their modern techniques to his uniquely personal style. Subject matter, he felt, was of no importance; in his *Arrangement in Gray and Black, No. 1* (fig. 26.25) Whistler contended that no one could possibly be interested in the artist's mother. The lasting popularity of "Whistler's Mother" contradicts his thesis, for there is a very personal feeling here. Color, line, pattern, and composition communicate a serenity that is both a portrait and an abstract composition.

During the eighteenth and nineteenth centuries sculpture failed to keep pace with painting and architecture. The work of Houdon (see fig. 22.41) was significant but the sculptures of Daumier and Degas were scarcely known at the time. And then there was Auguste Rodin (ro–DAN; 1840–1917), the greatest sculptor since Bernini, a dynamo of a man who captured the spontaneity and immediacy of Impressionism in three-dimensional form. Like Renoir and Degas, Rodin was concerned with the human figure but, totally unlike any Impressionist, his figures are depicted in moments of stress or tension. Intended originally as a study for *St. John the Baptist Preaching, The Walking Man* (fig. 26.26) is a study in motion and motion is all that we sense. Headless and armless, there is no expression or gesture to distract our attention from the strongly striding torso moving its muscular legs in long steps. The surface shimmers with light, shaped by the artist to further heighten the illusion of motion.

Rodin's commission for *The Gates of Hell* produced a number of figures extracted from a monumental work that was never completely finished. Sitting atop the Gates and brooding over Rodin's conception of Dante's *Inferno, The Thinker* (fig. 26.27) is a prodigious work of tension in repose. Similar to Michelangelo's superhuman forms that Rodin studied in detail, the figure is sunk in deep thought. What is he thinking of? Rodin said at one time that it was Dante contemplating his poem and another time that this was a dreamer and then a creator. Whether writer, dreamer, or creator, *The Thinker* remains a fascinating enigma.

Post-Impressionism

Post-Impressionism is a catchall term for some highly individual artists who reacted against the purely visual emphasis of Impressionism. The first and foremost of the Post-Impressionists, Paul Cézanne (say–ZAN; 1839–1906) was, in fact, one of the giants of European painting. His art lay somewhere between representation and abstraction, an intellectualized approach to applying paint to canvas. For Cézanne the whole purpose of painting was to express the emotion that the forms and colors of the natural world

Figure 26.25 James McNeill Whistler, *Arrangement in Gray and Black, No. 1,* ca. 1877. Oil on canvas, 57 × 64½″. The Louvre, Paris.

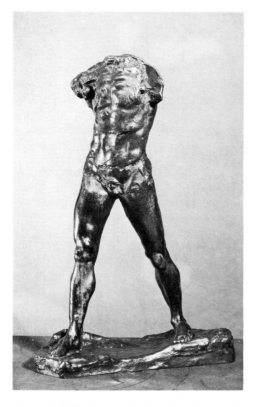

Figure 26.26 Auguste Rodin, *The Walking Man,* 1877–1878. Gift of Mrs. John W. Simpson. National Gallery of Art, Washington, D.C.

Figure 26.27 Auguste Rodin, *The Thinker,* 1879–1889. Gift of Mrs. John W. Simpson. National Gallery of Art, Washington, D.C.

Figure 26.29 Vincent van Gogh, *The Olive Orchard*, 1889. Oil on canvas, 28¾ × 36¼″. Chester Dale Collection, 1962. National Gallery of Art, Washington, D.C.

Figure 26.28 Vincent van Gogh, *La Mousmé*, 1888. Oil on canvas, 28⅞ × 22¾″. Chester Dale Collection, 1942. National Gallery of Art, Washington, D.C.

evoked in the artist. His landscapes look like his native Provence but not literally; everything has been clarified and concentrated. Cézanne took liberties with ordinary visual experience that challenge our perceptions and force us to view the world in a new way, in Cézanne's way. In *Le Château Noir* (colorplate 47) Cézanne gave the building a brooding air of mystery in keeping with the local legend that it was haunted by the ghost of an alchemist. In common with his other landscapes, there are no living creatures and the forms of the dense forest and the arcane building on its rocky spur are synthesized with the artist's characteristically muted blue-green and orange hues. The Impressionists used color to dissolve form and space; Cézanne did precisely the opposite by using color to define form in a very tangible space. Cézanne constructed his paintings slowly, methodically, with an intellectual control comparable to the art of Poussin. *Le Château Noir* has what he called a "durable museum quality" because Cézanne painted not just what he saw but what he knew.

Cézanne sold some of his paintings for as little as nine dollars but the Dutch artist, Vincent van Gogh (van–GO; 1853–1890), sold only one painting during his ten-year career, depending entirely on his brother for support. Van Gogh began as an Impressionist but changed his style drastically after studying Japanese prints, which he found "extremely clear, never tedious, as simple as breathing." Though van Gogh never attained this degree of facility he did learn to treat the picture surface as an area to be decorated in masses of flat or slightly broken color. In *La Mousmé* (fig. 26.28) he painted a young girl from Provence, to which he had moved in 1888 to capture in the brilliant sunlight some of the beauty that he imagined existed in Japan. The word *mousmé* was taken from a contemporary romantic novel in which it was used to characterize the innocent charm of youthful Japanese teahouse attendants. Poised motionless against a neutral background and holding some oleander flowers, the thirteen-year-old peasant girl seems totally removed from everyday experience. She represents the artist's aim "to paint men and women with that quality of the eternal which used to be suggested by the halo."

Twice confined to a hospital in Arles after a mental breakdown in 1889, van Gogh resumed painting and continued to produce during his subsequent year-long confinement in a mental asylum at St. Remy. Though sometimes permitted to paint outdoors when accompanied by a guard, *The Olive Orchard* (fig. 26.29) was painted "from memory," as he wrote his brother Theo. In late works such as this, van Gogh was intent on getting large quantities of paint onto the canvas, squeezing colors directly from the tube and then working them with brush and palette knife. The result was a very thick impasto that makes the paintings three-dimensional in the manner of topographical models. The flamelike cypress and writhing olive trees of Provence fascinated the artist. In this decorative and swirling composition the olive pickers are seemingly suspended in space as part of the design.

Painted in a field near the asylum, *The Starry Night* (see colorplate 4, vol. 1) is an ecstatic vision of the power and glory of the universe. A tall cypress flames toward the whirling and exploding stars of a cosmic drama unknown to the inhabitants of the

Figure 26.30 Paul Gauguin, *Vision after the Sermon (Jacob Wrestling with the Angel),* 1888. Oil on canvas, 36¼ × 28¾″. National Galleries, Edinburgh. Courtesy National Galleries of Scotland.

peaceful village below. This expressive work represents the artist's reverent celebration of the wonders of nature and is not, as some have contended, symptomatic of his illness.

Moving northwest of Paris to the village of Auvers-sur-Oise after his release from the asylum, van Gogh completed about sixty paintings during the last two months of his tragic life. There has never been an acceptable explanation for his fits of madness nor why he chose to commit suicide at age thirty-seven. In none of his work, however, is there even a hint of madness. At his funeral his friend and physician, Dr. Paul Gachet, said, "He was an honest man and a great artist. He had only two aims: humanity and art. It was the art that . . . will insure his survival."

Van Gogh's onetime friend, Paul Gauguin (go–GAN; 1848–1903) has been a kind of folk hero for desk-bound romantics who dream of dropping out of the rat race to pursue their artistic muse. The reality of Gauguin's life and career is, however, not the stuff of dreams. An amateur painter for many years, Gauguin had naively assumed that he would be as successful as a full-time painter as he had been as a stockbroker. Within three years after giving up his career in 1883, everything was gone: wife, family, money; he found himself living on borrowed funds at a run-down country inn in Brittany. Fascinated by the peasant costumes and deep piety of Breton women, Gauguin painted *Vision after the Sermon (Jacob Wrestling with the Angel)* (fig. 26.30) as a symbolic religious drama. The peasant women have just left the church after perhaps hearing a sermon by the priest (at the far right) about Jacob's bout with the angel, at which they are staring. Painted in flat, boldly outlined colors, the picture reveals Gauguin's keen perception of the power of belief and imagination in the almost medieval world of the Breton peasant.

A rebel at odds with conventional behavior and society in general, Gauguin was seldom bothered with self-doubt. Writing to his absent wife, he proclaimed that "I am a great artist and I know it." Probably inspired by Japanese prints, as was much of his work, his *Self-Portrait* (colorplate 48) includes a slight oriental cast to the eyes in this strikingly off-centered composition. Presenting himself with an ironic halo, his temptations are symbolized by the sharply outlined apples and the snake that he holds like a cigarette. Painted in the manner of a cloisonné enamel, the vivid colors are divided by incised lines, with everything flattened except the arrogant but sadly reflective face of a man who once wrote that he felt "like a brigand, which, for that matter, I am to many people."

Forever restless, Gauguin was drawn to the warm climate of Provence where he roomed briefly, and quarreled, with van Gogh, and then drifted to tropical climates: Panama, Martinique, Tahiti, and the Marquesas, where he died. In Tahiti Gauguin found, he thought, an antidote to the sickness of European civilization, a "primitive life" that would nurture his style. Actually, the Society Islands were governed by

Figure 26.31 Paul Gauguin, *Fatata te Miti (By the Sea)*, 1892. Oil on canvas, 26¾ × 36″. Chester Dale Collection, 1942. National Gallery of Art, Washington, D.C.

the French and Gauguin had evolved his tropical style before settling down in Polynesia. Gauguin's dream of "solitude under the tropical sun" was compromised by illness, poverty, and harassment by French authorities but, nevertheless, his work acquired a new vigor. *Fatata te Miti* (fig. 26.31) is a masterful evocation of sun, sea, and Polynesian beauties in a decorative composition that illustrates the artist's theories about resemblances between abstract patterns and music. It may have been this painting (or the one discussed below) that the Symbolist poet Mallarmé called a "musical poem that needs no libretto."

Critics of the time found Gauguin's colors bizarre and his drawing crude but the public accepted the content of his paintings as actual illustrations of Tahitian life and customs. Though Gauguin admitted that his Tahiti was a subjective interpretation of what was "vaguest and most universal in nature," we still have a romantic image of Tahiti in Gauguin's mode. In *Where Do We Come From? What Are We? Where Are We Going?* (see colorplate 1, vol. 1) Gauguin executed what he called his "spiritual testament," completed shortly before his abortive suicide attempt. Stating that "I will never do anything better or even like it," Gauguin painted this as a voyage of discovery, not as a statement of his rather confused ideas about birth, life, and death. The painting is a fusion of antitheses: sunlight and moonlight; night and day; the warmness of life and the coldness of death. The cycle of life can be read from childhood on the right to the old woman waiting for death at the left. Ultimately, this work attests, as Gauguin said, to "the futility of words," not to mention the futility of life.

Causing nearly as much controversy as works by Manet, Georges Seurat (sue–RAH; 1859–1891) exhibited *Sunday Afternoon on the Island of La Grande Jatte* (colorplate 49) at the eighth and final Impressionist show of 1886. Critics had a field day lambasting the dots of color, the "procession of pharaohs," and a "clearance sale of Nuremberg toys." Favorable critics, and there were some, labeled the new style Neoimpressionism or Divisionism, while Paris wits chose the word "confettism." Seurat himself used the term "chromo-luminarium" to describe a method of painting with tiny dots using the colors of the spectrum. Aspiring to paint in a scientific manner based on the optical theories of Helmholtz and others, Seurat used his *petit points,* his dots, to construct a monumental composition of "museum quality," as advocated by Cézanne. The scene is a popular summer resort near Paris where middle-class city dwellers could bathe, picnic, and promenade. Though the dots of pure color were supposed to fuse in the eye this does not happen, save in the luminosity of the river. Instead, the spectator is conscious of the myriads of dots that, in a nonchromatic way, contribute as units of scale to the grandeur that Seurat achieved; his optical theories were, in practice, more artistic than scientific. In addition, he developed a control of line, proportions, and masses of light and shade that make this a classical composition in the manner of Poussin and David. In its psychological impact the work is curiously modern. People, animals, hats, and parasols are structural and decorative elements, as isolated from each other as they are from the viewer. A typical

Figure 26.32 Henri de Toulouse-Lautrec, *Quadrille at the Moulin Rouge,* 1892. Gouache on cardboard, 31½ × 23¾". Chester Dale Collection, 1942, National Gallery of Art, Washington, D.C.

Figure 26.33 Henri Rousseau, *The Equatorial Jungle,* 1909. Oil on canvas, 55¼ × 51". Chester Dale Collection, 1942. National Gallery of Art, Washington, D.C.

Impressionist genre scene has become a melancholic comment on alienation and isolation in late Victorian society, symbolizing the underlying pessimism of the age.

The bawdy night life of Parisian society was vividly depicted by Henri de Toulouse-Lautrec (tu–LOSE–la–TREK; 1864–1901), who delighted in portraying people at cabarets, theatres, the races, and brothels. He especially enjoyed the tawdry gaiety of Montmartre's most colorful music hall, the Moulin Rouge. In *Quadrille at the Moulin Rouge* (fig. 26.32) he portrayed the earthy vitality of the dancer Gabrielle as she hikes her skirts to begin the quadrille, a dance that grew out of the high-kicking cancan. Confronted by the professional dancer is an elegant and refined patron of the establishment, who reaches obediently for her skirt to begin the dance. Far more concerned with the human comedy than most Impressionists were, Toulouse-Lautrec, like Daumier, has given us, in his paintings and inimitable posters, vivid pictures of the Gilded Age.

The most influential of the Post-Impressionists were Cézanne and an obscure toll collector named Henri Rousseau (1844–1910). An isolated and enigmatic genius who began painting late in life, Rousseau taught himself to paint "alone," as he said, "and without any master but nature." His naive ideal was what he called the "truth" of the camera; he was actually convinced that his paintings were as "realistic" as a photograph. His jungle landscapes were painted

with a startling directness of vision that influenced Picasso and others, but, these were tropics of the mind produced by the magical vision of a simple man who, apparently, never left France. Nothing in *The Equatorial Jungle* (fig. 26.33) is identifiable in botanical terms. What we see is a brooding and sinister jungle inhabited by a mysterious bird (a vulture?) and two strange-looking animals. There is an eerie and timeless stillness about this exotic, compelling scene that communicates the wonder that the artist must have felt as he painted his visions, images so real that, as he told his colleagues, they actually terrified the painter.

Van Gogh, Gauguin, Seurat, and Rousseau were critical of the disease of civilization but their pervasive pessimism was not limited to French urban culture. The Norwegian painter Edvard Munch (MOONK; 1864–1944), manipulated themes of evil, terror, and death to depict the plight, as he saw it, of *fin de siècle* European civilization, themes similar to those of the English poets Matthew Arnold and Thomas Hardy (see chap. 24). In *The Scream* (fig. 26.34) Munch portrayed a terror-stricken person whose sexual and facial identity has been obliterated by a piercing scream that is echoed in undulating lines of the landscape. Like his friend and associate, Henrik Ibsen, Munch dealt with the unbearable tensions of the modern world that led to anxiety, alienation, and, as here, terror. Though his iconography was intensely personal, Munch's pessimistic vision strongly influenced the later German Expressionist movement (see chap. 29).

A rather impromptu special event, the *banquet Rousseau,* symbolically marks the end of the old era and the advent of the twentieth-century avant-garde.

Figure 26.34 Edvard Munch, *The Scream,* 1893. Oil on canvas, 36 × 29″. Nationalgallereit, Oslo.

Held in the studio of Picasso in 1908, three years after the revolutionary show of the Fauves (see chap. 29), the guest of honor was Henri Rousseau, nearing the end of his career and still unrecognized by the public. Guests included artists Georges Braque and Marie Laurecin, writers Apollinaire, Max Jacob, Gertrude Stein, and other luminaries of the new epoch. Picasso had ordered the food for the wrong day but there was ample wine and abundant good spirits, with violin entertainment provided by the guest of honor. The only real tribute the unassuming little toll collector cum painter ever received prompted him to whisper confidentially to Picasso that, "after all, you and I are both great painters: I in the Modern style and you in the Egyptian." Though Picasso's "Egyptian" style was actually his African mask period, Henri Rousseau's remark turned out be correct on both counts.

Summary

Romanticism was a reaction in all the arts against the Enlightenment. For a time, however, the visual arts in France were in the service of Napoleon and David, his court painter. The Arch of Triumph and Church of the Madeleine made significant contributions to the Neoclassic face of Paris and the paintings of Ingres established an academic style against which later artists were to rebel.

Painting in a style uniquely his own, Goya was one of the most important painters of the century. The French Romantic style was established by the dramatic work of Gericault and continued by the peerless colorist Delacroix. John Constable was the leading Romantic landscape painter in England while Romantic architecture was revivalist, as manifested in the Gothic Revival Houses of Parliament.

By the second half of the century Realists like Millet, Corot, Daumier, and Courbet dominated the Parisian art scene while, in America, Winslow Homer was a leading artist in the ongoing tradition of American realism. Imaginative uses of industrial technology saw the construction of prefabricated structures like the Crystal Palace and the Eiffel Tower.

Led by the innovations of Manet, the Impressionist movement became the avant-garde of European art. Considering themselves the ultimate Realists, Monet, Renoir, Degas, Morisot, Cassatt, and others helped establish Impressionism as one of the most influential of all artistic styles. Whistler did his own personal version of modern art and, in Paris, Rodin produced the most dramatic and expressive sculpture since the High Renaissance.

Reacting against the visual emphasis of Impressionism in very personal terms, the Post-Impressionists included Cézanne, who distilled on canvas the forms and colors of the natural world, and Seurat, who used a similar approach but with dots of color. Van Gogh and Gauguin used vivid colors to create very expressive works while Toulouse-Lautrec portrayed the high life and low life of his age. Rousseau created works from his private dream world that were a revelation to Picasso and others of the new avant-garde. Like many artists and writers of the late Victorian era, Munch reacted against modern urban society with themes of alienation and terror. It can be said that a century which began with the Arch of Triumph ended with *The Scream.*

Bibliography

Elsen, Albert E. *In Rodin's Studio: A Photographic Record of Sculpture in the Making.* Ithaca: Cornell University Press, 1980. A unique opportunity to see the process of Rodin's work.

Prideaux, Tom, et al. *The World of Delacroix.* New York: Time-Life Books, 1966. The focus is on Delacroix but his important contemporaries are also included.

———. *The World of Whistler 1834–1903.* New York: Time-Life Books, 1970. The Time-Life series is uniformly well written and the reproductions are framable.

Rewald, John. *The History of Impressionism.* New York: Museum of Modern Art, 1973. Any book by Rewald on Impressionism and Post-Impressionism is highly recommended.

———. *Post-Impressionism from van Gogh to Gauguin.* New York: Museum of Modern Art, 1956.

———. *Georges Seurat.* New York: George Wittenborn, Inc., 1979.

Schneider, Pierre, et al. *The World of Manet 1832–1883.* Time-Life Books, 1968. The approach is scholarly and the writing is clear and concise.

Shapiro, Meyer. *Vincent van Gogh.* New York: Doubleday, 1980. This is one of the few books on van Gogh that is not more romantic and expressionistic than the subject. Highly recommended.

Wallace, Robert, et al. *The World of van Gogh 1853–1890.* New York: Time-Life Books, 1969. Concise biographies of van Gogh and other artists who have been romanticized in literature and in the movies.

Unit 9

The Twentieth Century

27

Things Fall Apart: The Center Cannot Hold

Historical Overview, 1918–1939

World War I can be viewed as Act 2 in a drama that began in 1871 with Bismarck's formation of the German Empire and concluded with World War II as Act 3 in a tragedy that engulfed most of the world. The period of 1918–1939 can be seen, in retrospect, as an entr'acte that set the stage for the last act.

When the Armistice between the Allies and Germany and her allies was agreed upon for November 11, 1918, the stated intent was to stop the fighting and arrange for a just peace. The Treaty of Versailles that was signed on June 28, 1919, was, however, harshly punitive. Germany and her allies were forced to accept the "war guilt" clause and, further, to accept *all* responsibility for causing the war. War reparations were to be paid to all 32 allies; Germany lost virtually her entire armed services, overseas colonies, and portions of her land area, including the critical Polish Corridor that divided Germany and gave Poland a passage to the sea. Woodrow Wilson's attempts to curb the nationalistic zeal of Britain's Lloyd George and France's Clemenceau were essentially futile. Even Wilson's prize project, the League of Nations that was part of the Peace of Versailles, ended, finally, in failure caused, in part, by the refusal of the United States to join this valiant, doomed attempt to civilize the conduct of nations. The League of Nations did settle a few disputes but was powerless to prevent Japan's invasion of Manchuria in 1931, Mussolini's invasion of Ethiopia in 1935, and Germany's withdrawal from the League to rearm.

The Allies had led the Germans to believe that Kaiser Wilhelm II and his imperial government were primarily responsible for the war. But it was the new Weimar Republic that signed the dictated peace and it was, therefore, the Republic that bore the onus of German humiliation at the conference table. Moreover, the Treaty of Versailles made no provision for the economic rehabilitation of Europe nor were there any assurances for the futures of new nations like Czechoslovakia and Yugoslavia, which had been carved out of the dismembered Austro-Hungarian empire. The Treaty of Versailles caused more discontent and unrest than even the 1815 Congress that had ended the Napoleonic wars.

The March 1917 revolution in Russia had disposed of the czar but the new Provisional government, despite rising unrest, continued to pursue the war. V. I. Lenin (1870–1924) capitalized on new defeats at the front to seize the government and establish the All-Russian Congress of the Soviets. Concluding a separate disastrous peace with Germany, Lenin established a dictatorship of the Communist party that barely survived the ferocious Civil War of 1917–1920. Under Leon Trotsky (1877–1940) a new Red Army destroyed the rebel White armies and then helped Lenin solidify his hold on the government. Following Lenin's death in 1924, a power struggle between Trotsky and Joseph Stalin (1879–1953) saw Stalin emerge, in 1927, as the absolute dictator of the Soviet Union. Stalin's agents assassinated Trotsky in Mexico in 1940.

The new democracies were beset by economic difficulties in the 1920s and assaulted by Communists on the left and hardcore nationalists on the right. Benito Mussolini (1883–1945) marched on Rome in 1922 and assumed full dictatorial powers by 1926. Designed to produce a corporate totalitarian state, the doctrines of Italian fascism stressed the dominance of the state and the subordination of the individual, the desirability of war, and the Social Darwinian "right" of Italy to expand at the expense of "inferior" nations.

The initial successes of Italian fascism impressed not only the older Western democracies but also many malcontents in Germany, who bitterly resented the war guilt clause of the Treaty of Versailles. Compounding the discontent, the German military clique fostered the belief that Germany had never been defeated on the field of battle; she had been betrayed at home, said the military, by pacifist liberals. Following the disastrous inflation of 1923 the National Socialist German Workers Party (Nazis) launched a propaganda campaign that capitalized on German belief in the sellout at Versailles; coupled with the barrage was a virulent anti-Semitism that blamed the Jews for many of Germany's postwar problems while proclaiming the absolute supremacy of the Aryan master race. Led by Adolf Hitler (1889–1945), a spellbinding political orator, the Nazis achieved their first significant power when, in 1933, President von Hindenburg appointed Hitler as Chancellor of the Republic. Utilizing the emergency powers of Article 48 of the constitution, Hitler eradicated all opposition with his bloody purge of 1934. He was now absolute ruler of a Third Reich that was to last for "a thousand years."

The direct road to World War II began, probably, with the Japanese seizure of Manchuria in 1931, followed by her withdrawal from the League of Nations in 1933, and her invasion of China in 1937.

Germany withdrew from the League in 1933 to begin arming for war, which was also the year in which Dachau, the first concentration camp, was opened. In 1936 Hitler occupied the Rhineland in defiance of the Treaty of Versailles, a step that is now seen as the last opportunity for England and France to avert war in Europe.

Italy challenged the League of Nations by invading Ethiopia in 1935. The League's feeble response was to vote economic sanctions that failed miserably. No longer a member of the League, Germany supplied arms and supplies for her future ally.

The Spanish Civil War of 1936–1939 had the effect of polarizing world opinion between the fascists and monarchists of "loyalist" Francisco Franco (1892–1975) and rebel factions led by socialists, communists, and an assortment of liberals. Hitler backed Franco, using the opportunity to field-test his new war machines. It was German bombers that attacked the undefended Basque town of Guernica, an atrocity immortalized by Picasso in his *Guernica* (see fig. 29.11).

After signing a Rome-Berlin treaty with Mussolini in 1936, Hitler launched his campaign for a union (*anschluss*) with German-speaking Austria, which he occupied in early 1938. The next target was the German-speaking Sudeten area of Czechoslovakia. After working up a full-scale crisis with his oratory, Hitler agreed to a four-power conference at Munich on September 29, 1938. Hitler, Mussolini, British Prime Minister Neville Chamberlain and Premier Édouard Daladier of France conferred in an atmosphere of conciliation artfully orchestrated by Hitler. Chamberlain returned to England proclaiming "peace in our time" but, actually, England and France had helped dismember hapless Czechoslovakia. Hitler acquired the Sudetenland at Munich and all of Czechoslovakia by the following spring.

The final step was Poland, which was fated to be divided between Germany and Russia. On August 23, 1939, Germany and Russia signed a nonagression pact that relieved Hitler of his concerns about waging a two-front war. On September 1, 1939, the German armies rolled into Poland and, on September 3, 1939, England and France honored their commitment to Poland by declaring war on Germany. The Peace of Versailles that was supposed to confirm the Great War as the "war to end all wars" had lasted a scant twenty years.

The Culture-Epoch Theory and the Twentieth Century

Our distance from past ages enables us to perceive the periods when a culture was balanced, when the balance tipped into chaos, when the adjustment began that led to a new period of balance, and so on. Analyzing our own age is far more difficult, perhaps impossible, yet as thinking beings, we try to understand where we are and where we might be going. First, let us review the culture-epoch theory.

Philosophers of history have found many patterns that seem to account for the growth, flowering, and decay of civilizations. In this book we are using a modified and simplified form of the *culture-epoch theory* as a framework upon which to arrange our materials. This theory is neither more nor less "true" than any of a half-dozen other theories that attempt to account for changes throughout the recorded story of mankind.

According to the culture-epoch theory, a culture is founded upon whatever conception of reality is held by the great majority of people over a considerable period of time. This is true even though the majority may not be aware of any concept of reality or, more probably take it so much for granted that they are not aware it is simply a human idea, held on faith. Thus, for most people at the time this is written, a typewriter is real, a physical tree is real, and all things which can be seen, heard, smelled, felt, or tasted are real.

As a matter of fact, a number of scientists, philosophers, and religious thinkers have given us different concepts of reality, which have also been widely held. These thinkers have contemplated the millions of forms of life, many of them bearing resemblances to others, yet each one different; they have examined the forms of earth, air, fire, and water; they have wondered about the processes of change by which a tree today may, at some time in the future, disintegrate into earth and reappear in some totally alien form. They have watched such nontangible things as sunlight and air becoming leaf and branch. Pondering these things, they come inevitably to the ultimate question: "What is the nature of reality?"

To reach an answer, they usually focus on a few profound inquiries, some of which may be given here. For example, they might say, "We see change all around us. We see grass eaten and turn into cow. We see cow eaten and turn into man. We see man disintegrate and turn into earth. If all these changes can take place, what are the universal elements of which all things are composed?" Or they might say, "We see an individual human, John Doe, as baby, as youth, as adult, as senile old man, as corpse. From one moment to the next, he is never the same. Yet he is always the same, John Doe, a distinct being. Can it be that nothing is permanent, that reality is a process rather than a thing or group of things? If we have change, then, how does the process take place? And more important, we know that we live in a world of constant change, but what force directs the process?"

"Nonsense," retorts another group of thinkers. "That which is in a constant state of flow cannot be real. Only that which is permanent and unchanging can be real. What, then, in the universe is permanent, unchanging in itself, yet is able to transform itself, manifest itself, or produce from itself the countless forms which we see around us?"

These are some of the basic questions the pure thinker contemplates. The answers are various concepts of reality.

Based upon the idea of reality accepted as "true," specialized thinkers build different thought-structures that underlie visible institutions. These include a philosophy of justice from which particular forms of law and government spring; a philosophy of education which dictates the nature of our schools and the material taught in them; a religious philosophy that becomes apparent in churches and creeds; and an economic philosophy that yields its particular ways of producing and distributing goods and services, including the token-systems used as money. Other philosophies and institutions could be named, but these are some that greatly affect our daily living.

When these are formed, we have a complete culture, but always by the time such a pattern is established, we have forces at work which tend to destroy it. The destroyers are new pure thinkers who note inconsistencies within the idea of reality itself, and who question postulates or find contradictions.

From these new thinkers (philosophers, scientists, theologians) comes a new idea of reality so convincing it cannot be brushed aside. It must be accepted. Suddenly the whole structure of the culture finds itself without foundation. The justice and the law appropriate in the old culture no longer fit on the new foundation; the old education is no longer appropriate; old religious beliefs no longer describe our position in relation to God; old ways of making things and distributing them no longer suffice.

At this time people are plunged into a *period of chaos,* the first step in the formation of a new epoch.

The symptoms of the period of chaos lie around us now in such profusion that they scarcely need description. In the latter part of the twentieth century this is where we live. New and shocking ideas, moralities, and beliefs are introduced and discarded; terrorists attack established governments; civil strife and wars of conquest rage; everyone damages the environment; over everything looms the menace of nuclear obliteration. At the mercy of events beyond their control, some people try to turn back the clock to better, more peaceful days; others seek refuge and security in fundamentalist beliefs; still others retreat to paramilitary armed camps; many just mindlessly camp in front of their television sets, hoping, perhaps, that all the problems will somehow vanish. In other words, we see in the late twentieth century a period of chaos that may or may not be giving evidence of resolution, but more on that later.

Out of the turmoil and confusion of chaotic periods of past cultures there emerges the *period of adjustment.* At this point notable artists, whether painters, writers, sculptors, composers, or creators in some other medium, make their important contributions to society. Pheidias and Sokrates of ancient Athens, the master builders of Gothic cathedrals, Michelangelo, Beethoven, Goethe, Picasso, Sartre, Stravinsky, these innovators suggest the new line, shape, and pattern for a new culture, a new period of balance.

What is the role of the artist in the development of a cultural pattern? The artist does not necessarily know all about new ideas of reality. The artist in our time, for example, need not know all about Einstein's Special and General theories of Relativity (which are discussed below). The artist is simply a person of greater sensitivity than others, and with fine skills in one medium. As a sensitive person, the artist feels perhaps more keenly than the rest of us the tensions of the time—the pulls of this belief and the pulls of a contradictory one. An artist will not rest until he or she has explored this confusing experience and discovered some meaning, some significance therein. The great artist is always the composer (whether musician, writer, painter, architect, sculptor, choreographer, movie director), the person who puts things together in new relationships and finds new meanings for experience.

It comes down to this: styles in beauty change as the basic characteristics of people change. Or perhaps it works the other way; perhaps as new glimpses of beauty are caught by the artists, people themselves change to conform to the new beauty.

However it may happen, the artist, especially in the period of chaos and early in the period of adjustment within a culture-epoch, personally feels the stresses, tensions, and turmoil of the period. The artist explores conflicts within, which are the conflicts of the general population as well, and creates new structures, new designs, to synthesize the elements of conflict and give new meaning to experience. Some works of art, probably depending upon the individual artist's breadth of vision and ability to compose insight into significance, are seized upon as symbols of new pattern and new truth in society. They express the new idea of beauty and truth.

At this point another element of the population—we may call them the *intellectuals*—enters the picture. They are people like ourselves, college students and faculty members, government officials, ministers, business executives, and many others who think seriously about things and who, like the artists, have been troubled by the conflict of their times. They still are working within the period of adjustment in an epoch. They become aware of new meanings and patterns produced by the artists, and they start reshaping these designs into new philosophies of justice, of economics, of religion, and the like, and begin to build concrete institutions out of the philosophies that they have created. Through their work, order slowly emerges out of chaos.

When their work is finished, we come to the third period within a culture-epoch, the *period of balance*. At this point, the idea of reality, the philosophies which underlie our basic institutions, and the institutions themselves are all in harmony. Early in a period of balance, life must be very satisfying; everyone must know the reason for getting up in the morning to face the day. But if balance lasts too long, life begins to get dull. The big jobs seem to be done, and decadence, boredom, and deterioration may set in. The long and painful decline of the Roman Empire was just such a period.

But change comes inevitably. At the beginning of the twentieth century physicists were assuring young scientists that the great discoveries in physics had all been made and that only little tidying-up jobs remained. At the same time, Einstein was beginning his work, which was to supersede all our knowledge in physics. Just when people have been certain of everything in their periods of balance, new pure thinkers come along to upset the whole apple cart into a new epoch.

The last period of cultural balance extended from about 1600 to about 1918, though forces were already in motion in the late nineteenth and early twentieth centuries that were to destroy the old order. From before 1918 to the dawn of the nuclear age in the 1950s there was certainly a period of chaos. Are we now in a period of adjustment? Are we moving to a new age and, if so, what will be the new realities?

During the past several decades new attitudes have become increasingly important. We know through evolutionary studies, for example, that all living things are evolving (everything in the cosmos, in fact) and that all are interrelated. On our own tiny world homo sapiens does not have dominion over the world or over so-called lower forms of life. The balance of life in our world is precarious; we know, or should know, that we cannot alter our environment without worldwide repercussions and we cannot damage our environment without ultimately harming ourselves.

This holistic view of living things expands to include our concept of the cosmos as expressed by Einstein and others, and applies to the inner world of the human personality as expressed by Freud and other psychologists. Contemporary holistic views of evolving personality, society, the environment, and the cosmos suggest a coming new age that may be called a world in process, a world in which everything is in a continual stage of becoming. Goal-oriented cultures of the past may be replaced by change-oriented cultures of the future. Once people begin viewing their cultural identities as journeys rather than as destinations, the new age may have begun.

In this and the following chapters we will consider the contributions of Einstein and Freud, the Electronic Age, the Global Village, and the reactions of many artists to the chaos, adjustment, and new directions of the twentieth century.

Einstein and Relativity

The old social order had ended in 1918 but the predictable world-machine described by Newtonian science had ended even earlier. In 1900 Max Planck (1858–1947) took a major step away from visible perceptions of the physical world to a theory that described the microcosmos by using mathematical abstractions. While studying the radiant energy given off by heated bodies, Planck discovered that energy radiated not in unbroken streams but in discontinuous bits or portions that he called *quanta*. In terms of both emission and absorption of atomic and subatomic particles, Planck hypothesized that the energy transfer was discontinuous and involved a unit of energy (quantum) that could be calculated using what is called Planck's Constant. He concluded that the energy in each quantum could be computed by using the equation $E = hv$, in which v is the frequency of the radiation and h is Planck's Constant. Roughly a decimal point followed by 26 zeroes and ending in 6624, this miniscule number remains one of nature's most fundamental constants.

In conjunction with Quantum Theory, Werner Heisenberg (1901–1976) developed, in 1927, his "Principle of Uncertainty," which states, in effect, that theory can accurately predict the behavior of statistically large numbers of particles but not the behavior of individual particles. Using principles now known to science, it is impossible to simultaneously determine the position and velocity of, for example, an electron. If the position is observed, that act of observing will alter its velocity and, conversely, the more accurate the determination of its velocity the more indefinite is the position of the electron. The old science relied on a study of cause and effect (or causality and determinism) but the Principle of Uncertainty undermined these formerly sturdy pillars. In philosophy, the uncertainty of cause and effect in the physical world led to renewed arguments for the existence of free will. If physical events cannot be determined precisely and cannot be predicted, then perhaps the still relatively unknown capabilities of the human intellect might be a decisive factor in the destiny of mankind.

Albert Einstein (1879–1955) postulated that light photons were also quanta and went on to develop his Special Theory of Relativity (1905). In essence, his Special Theory rests on the hypothesis that neither space nor time has an objective reality. Space is an arrangement of perceived objects and time has no independent existence apart from our measurements of a sequence of events. Our clocks are geared to our solar system. What we call an hour is actually a measurement of an arc of 15 degrees in space based on the apparent movement of the sun. A year is, therefore, the time it takes the earth to orbit the sun, which is 365¼ days. Mercury has an 88-day year and other planets have their own time frame. As Einstein said, time is subjective and based on how people remember events as a sequence of "earlier" and "later," associating a greater number with the later event, an association that is defined by means of a clock.

In particular, Einstein's Special Theory stipulates that the velocity of light is constant for all uniformly moving systems anywhere in the universe. There is neither absolute space nor absolute time but the velocity of light is the absolute speed limit of the universe. There can be no fixed interval of time independent of the system to which it is referred nor can there be simultaneity independent of an established reference. Einstein assumes, for example, that there is an observer seated beside a railroad track who sees a bolt of lightning at the far left (bolt A) and another at the far right (bolt B). Assuming that the observer is positioned precisely between A and B, the bolts will be perceived as simultaneous because all events have the same frame of reference. Now, assume that a train is moving along the track from right

to left at the brisk speed of light (186,284 miles/second) and that another observer (2) is riding on the top of the train. Assume, further, that observer 2 is exactly opposite observer 1 at the precise moment that bolts A and B strike. Observer 2 will perceive bolt A but not bolt B. The train is moving away from bolt B at the speed of light, meaning that the light waves of bolt B will never catch up with the train. Observer 2 is in a different frame of reference than is observer 1.

Based on his Special Theory, Einstein determined that with an increase in velocity, the mass of an object will also increase relative to an observer. Because motion is a form of kinetic energy, the increase in motion that leads to an increase in mass means that the mass has increased in energy. Einstein computed the value of the equivalent mass (m) in any unit of energy (e), leading to the equation that mass is equal to its energy over the square of the speed of light (c^2), or $m = e/c^2$. The remaining algebraic step results in the equation $e = mc^2$, the most famous equation of our age. As Einstein demonstrated mathematically, mass and energy were equivalent. What we normally call mass is concentrated energy that, with the proper trigger, can be released. The detonation of the first atomic device at Alamogordo, New Mexico, on July 16, 1945, demonstrated the transmutation of matter into energy in the forms of light, heat, sound, and motion.

Newton's laws still satisfactorily explain phenomena based on human experiences but they are too limited for modern physics. Einstein's laws of motion are based on the relativity of distance, time, and mass, what he called the "four-dimensional space-time continuum," that is, three dimensions of space and one of time. Relativity thus gives scientists the means to accurately and completely describe the workings of nature.

Einstein later expanded his system into the General Theory of Relativity in which he examined what it is that guides all moving systems. His Special Theory had stated that the velocity of light was constant for all uniformly moving systems. His General Theory is broader and states that the laws of nature are the same for all systems regardless of their states of motion. The basic premise of his Special Theory held true, that all motion, uniform or nonuniform, had to be judged within some system of reference because absolute motion did not exist. He could not, however, distinguish between the motion caused by inertial forces (acceleration, centrifugal forces, etc.) and motion caused by gravitation. This led to his Principle of the Equivalence of Gravitation and Inertia, a new theory of gravitation more accurate and complete than Newton's Law of Universal Gravitation. Newton had postulated gravitation as a force or attraction but Einstein's Law of Gravitation simply describes the behavior of objects in a gravitational field by describing the paths they follow.

Gravitation, for Einstein, was a form of inertia, leading him to conclude that light, like any material body, was subject to gravitation when passing through a very strong gravitational field. He then proved that light travels in a predictable curve given sufficient gravitational pull. Einstein's universe has no straight lines. Euclidian geometry defines a straight line as the shortest distance between two points but, in space, there are only vast circles delineating all of space that, though it is finite, is unbounded.

As Einstein observed, Relativity defined the outer limits of our knowledge and Quantum Theory defined the inner limits. What bothered him was that the two systems are unrelated to each other: "The idea that there are two structures of space independent of each other, the metric-gravitational and the electromagnetic is intolerable to the theoretical spirit." A persistent believer in the fundamental uniformity and harmony of nature, Einstein devoted the latter part of his career to a search for a Unified Field Theory that would construct a bridge between Relativity and Quantum Mechanics. The search continues.

Freud and the Inner World

Though he had written his celebrated *The Interpretation of Dreams* in 1900 and *The Psychopathology of Everyday Life* in 1904, the psychological theories of Sigmund Freud (1856–1939) did not become influential until after World War I. A rational social and humanitarian scientist, Freud developed cogent theories of the role of the unconscious in human actions and the irrational aspects of human behavior. Though there have been subsequent modifications of some of his theories, Freudian psychology remains one of the dominant systems of the century.

Freud evolved a theory of the tripartite personality consisting of the id, ego, and superego. There are no clear boundaries between these concepts but each can be described in isolation. Representing our biological endowment, the id (Latin, "it") resides in our unconscious as an amalgam of our drives and instincts. Hunger, thirst, elimination, and sex are some of the drives that compel us to avoid pain and to seek pleasure through gratification. Either through action or wish fulfillment pentup energy is discharged and tension relieved. Freud considered life and love as positive life forces (libido or Eros) and aggressiveness, destruction, and the death wish as negative forces.

The ego is the reality principle, the thinking, conscious self that interacts with objective reality. The well-developed ego controls the id, determining when and how instinctive drives are satisfied.

The superego is a combination of the moral code of the parents and the person, a kind of conscience that is a product of socialization and cultural traditions. Motivated by fear of punishment and desire for approval, the superego can be perhaps best described as a synthesis of the ego-ideal and conscience. The

psychological rewards for the superego are feelings of pride and accomplishment; psychological punishment causes feelings of guilt and inferiority.

The well-balanced personality has a strong ego generally in control of the id and superego, restraining the id while recognizing the censorship of the superego. A neurotic person has lost some control, for whatever reason, over conscious actions, giving in to aggressive instincts from the id, or succumbing to feelings of guilt and inferiority exacted by the superego. Psychosis is a serious mental illness in which the patient has lost all touch with reality.

Freud invented what he called psychoanalysis, a systematic therapy for the treatment of neurosis. The task of the analyst was to help the patient uncover repressed matter, mainly through free association and the interpretation of dreams. Essentially, the analyst assisted the patient in understanding the reasons for abnormal behavior; once the patient uncovered the repressions that caused undesirable actions, the ego could consciously deal with the problem. Recognition of the basic problem(s) would help restore emotional balance.

Partly because he treated mostly neurotic patients, and partly because any new idea is likely to carry its originator to extremes, Freud rode his interpretations very hard in one particular direction. For him, practically all of the mental disorders that he treated were ultimately traceable to one basic frustration: the denial of the life force, the libido—that is, the sexual drive. All symbols were apparently, for him, reducible to sexual symbols. Freud's discovery that sexuality goes far back into childhood, even infancy, was a radical departure from the views of his day. It is, therefore, quite understandable that the sexual factor should loom so large in his investigations, for there is no one of the human drives that is so hedged about with all sorts of taboos. Even in our own time, which is supposedly sexually liberated, there are a variety of sexual mores, both in the ways one should act and the ways in which one should not.

Later psychologists have pointed out that human beings are motivated by, in addition to sex, social and cultural factors and their interpersonal relationship with their analyst. Freud, however, has not been entirely superseded; we have derived many benefits from his work. He challenged the mechanistic view of human personality by insisting that human beings were complex individuals and not simply power switchboards; by so doing he opened the way for later humanistic psychology. Freud also brought the whole problem of mental and emotional well-being or illness to the attention of society. Even in his time mental illness was frequently regarded as possession of the mind by evil spirits or, at best, a disgraceful condition that should be hidden away or locked up in a madhouse. Mental patients were treated like lepers, shut away and forgotten. Freud changed all that by demonstrating that emotionally disturbed individuals were truly ill and that their illness could be treated.

Though his intimate knowledge of human nature made him critical and pessimistic he was convinced, nevertheless, that knowledge gained through scientific investigation was the best way to understand and deal with the human condition.

Literary Selection

CIVILIZATION AND ITS DISCONTENTS
Sigmund Freud (1856–1939)

Freud had long been disturbed about negative aspects of the sex drive such, for example, as sadism. For him love did indeed "make the world go around" while sadism, though it was related to Eros, was aggressively destructive. How can the goodness of Eros be reconciled with the cruelty of sadism? The answer, as Freud points out in the following selection, is that life-enhancing Eros has an antithesis that seeks to destroy life. He calls the latter an instinct for death, a death wish that is forever locked in combat with the positive life-force of Eros. Sadism is therefore a manifestation of the aggressiveness of the death wish, a perversion of Eros, erotic but destructive. Furthermore, Freud points out, there are nonerotic aggressive instincts that threaten the stability of the individual and even that of society itself. His view of the aggressive, destructive instinct as a threat to civilization underscores the pervasive pessimism of the period between world wars, not to mention our own age.

VI

Never before in any of my previous writings have I had the feeling so strongly as I have now that what I am describing is common knowledge . . . that I am using up paper and ink to expound things which are self-evident. If it should appear that the recognition of a special independent instinct of aggression would entail a modification of the psycho-analytical theory of instincts, I should be glad to seize upon the idea.

We shall see that this is not so, that it is merely a matter of coming to grips with a conclusion to which we long ago committed ourselves, following it to its logical consequences. Analytic theory has evolved gradually enough, but the theory of instincts has groped its way forward. And yet that theory was so indispensable that something had to be put in its place. In my perplexity I made my starting point Schiller's aphorism that hunger and love make the world go around. Hunger represents the instinct for self-preservation while love strives after objects; its chief function is preservation of the species. Thus first arose the contrast between ego instincts and object instincts. To denote the energy of the latter I introduced the term "libido." An antithesis was thus formed between the ego instincts and the libidinal instincts directed towards objects, i.e., love in its widest sense. One of these object instincts, the sadistic, stood out in that its aim was so very unloving; moreover, it clearly allied itself with the ego instincts, and its kinship with instincts of mastery without libidinal purpose could not be concealed. Nevertheless, sadism plainly belonged

to sexual life—the game of cruelty could take the place of the game of love. Neurosis appeared as the outcome of a struggle between self-preservation and libido, a conflict in which the ego was victorious but at the price of great suffering.

Modifications in this theory became essential as our inquiries advanced from the repressed to the repressing forces, from the object instincts to the ego. The decisive step was the introduction of the concept of narcissism, i.e., the discovery that the ego is cathected with libido, that the ego is the libido's original home and, to some extent, its headquarters. This narcissistic libido turns towards objects, becoming object libido, and can change back into narcissistic libido. The concept of narcissism made possible an analytic understanding of the traumatic neuroses as well as many diseases bordering on the psychoses. It was not necessary to abandon the view that the transference-neuroses are attempts of the ego to guard itself against sexuality but the concept of the libido was jeopardized. Since the ego instincts, too, were libidinal, it seemed inevitable that we should make libido coincide with instinctual energy in general, as Jung had already advocated. Yet I retained a groundless conviction that the instincts could not all be of the same kind. It was in *Beyond the Pleasure Principle* (1920) that the repetition-compulsion and the conservative character of instinctual life first struck me. While speculating on the origin of life and of biological parallels, I concluded that, beside the instinct preserving the organic substance and binding it into ever larger units, there must exist an antithesis, which would seek to dissolve these units and reinstate their antecedent inorganic state; that is, a death instinct as well as Eros. The phenomena of life would be explicable from the interplay and counteracting effects of the two. Demonstrating the working of this hypothetical death instinct was not easy. Manifestations of Eros were conspicuous enough; one might assume that the death instinct worked within the organism towards its disintegration but that was no proof. A more fruitful idea was that part of the instinct is diverted towards the external world and surfaces as an instinct of aggressiveness and destructiveness. In this way the instinct could serve Eros in that the organism was destroying something other than itself. One can suspect that the two kinds of instinct seldom—perhaps never—appear in isolation from each other, but are alloyed with each other in varying and very different proportions. In sadism, long known to us as a component instinct of sexuality, we observe a particularly strong alloy between trends of love and the destructive instinct; while its counterpart, masochism, would be a union between destructiveness directed inwards and sexuality.

The assumption of the existence of an instinct of death or destruction has met with resistance even in analytic circles; I am aware that there is a frequent inclination rather to ascribe whatever is dangerous and hostile in love to an original bipolarity in its own nature. To begin with it was only tentatively that I put forth the views I have developed here, but in the course of time they have gained such a hold upon me that I can no longer think in any other way. To my mind, they are far more serviceable from a theoretical viewpoint than any other possible ones; they provide that simplification, without either ignoring or doing violence to the facts, for which we strive in scientific work. I know that in sadism and masochism we have always seen before us manifestations of the destructive instinct (directed outwards and inwards), strongly alloyed with erotism; but I can no longer understand how we can have overlooked the ubiquity of non-erotic aggressivity and destructiveness and can have failed to give it its due place in our interpretation of life. I remember my own defensive attitude when the idea of an instinct of destruction first emerged in psycho-analytic literature, and how long it took before I became receptive to it. That others should have shown, and still show, the same attitude of rejection surprises me less. For "little children do not like it" when there is talk of the inborn human inclination to "badness," to aggressiveness and destructiveness, and so to cruelty as well. God has made them in the image of His own perfection; nobody wants to be reminded how hard it is to reconcile the undeniable existence of evil— despite the protestations of Christian Science—with His all-powerfulness or His all-goodness.

The name "libido" can once more be used to denote the manifestations of the power of Eros in order to distinguish them from the energy of the death instinct. It must be confessed that we have much greater difficulty in grasping that instinct; we can only suspect it, as it were, as something in the background behind Eros, and it escapes detection unless its presence is betrayed by its being alloyed with Eros. It is in sadism, where the death instinct twists the erotic in its own sense and yet at the same time fully satisfies the erotic urge, that we succeed in obtaining the clearest insight into its nature and its relation to Eros. But even where it emerges without any sexual purpose, in the blindest fury of destructiveness, we cannot fail to recognize that the satisfaction of the instinct is accompanied by an extraordinarily high degree of narcissistic enjoyment, owing to its presenting the ego with a fulfillment of the latter's old wishes for omnipotence. The instinct of destruction, moderated and tamed, and, as it were, inhibited in its aim, must, when it is directed towards objects, provide the ego with the satisfaction of its vital needs and with control over nature. This is how things appear to us now; future research and reflection will no doubt bring further light which will decide the matter.

In all that follows I adopt the viewpoint, therefore, that the inclination to aggression is an original, self-subsisting instinctual disposition in man, and that it constitutes the greatest impediment to civilization. At one point I was led to the idea that civilization was a special process in the service of Eros, whose purpose is to combine single human individuals, and after that families, then races, peoples and nations, into one great unity, the unity of mankind. Why this has to happen, we do not know; the work of Eros is precisely this. These collections of men are to be libidinally bound to one another. Necessity alone, the advantages of work in common, will not hold them together. But man's aggressive instinct, the hostility of each against all and of all against each, opposes this programme of civilization. This aggressive instinct is the derivative and the main representative of the death instinct which we have found alongside of Eros and which shares world-dominion with it. And now, I think, the meaning of the evolution of civilization is no longer obscure to us. It must present the struggle between Eros and Death, between the instinct of life and the instinct of destruction as it works itself out in the human species.

Exercises

1. Discuss the difference between ego instincts and object instincts.
2. How does Freud explain sadism and masochism?
3. Try explaining the strains of contemporary society in terms of the struggle between Eros and Death.

Whatever illusions the nineteenth century may have preserved about the perfectability of human behavior and human institutions perished during the four dreadful years of World War I. Much of the art and literature of the postwar period reflected a profound pessimism, a feeling that Western civilization carried the seeds of its own destruction. (See the Dada art movement in chap. 29.) The following poems and essays express some of the prevailing sentiments, some of the loneliness, alienation, and despair experienced by the postwar generation. And little did anyone know that within less than a generation, the Great War was to receive a number.

Literary Selections

THE LOVE SONG OF J. ALFRED PRUFROCK

Thomas Stearns Eliot (1888–1965)

Written in England around the beginning of World War I, *Prufrock* is a dramatic monologue of a middle-aged and frustrated social misfit who is vainly trying to adjust to a petty and superficial society. The larger perspective is that of bankrupt idealism, a decaying of nations, societies, and religious institutions. With juxtaposed images enlarged by dramatic echoes of Hesiod, Dante, and Shakespeare, Eliot builds a mood of futility and despair.

S'io credesse che mia risposta fosse
A persona che mai tornasse al mondo,
Questa fiamma staria senza piu scosse.
Ma perciocche giammai di questo fondo
Non torno vivo alcun s'i'odo il vero,
Senza tema d'infamia ti rispondo.[1]

---

1. "If I thought I were making answer to one that might return to view the world, this flame should evermore cease shaking. But since from the abyss, if I hear true, none ever came alive, I have no fear of infamy, but give thee answer due." The speaker is Guido da Montefeltro, who was condemned to Hell as a Counsellor of Fraud (Dante, *Inferno*, XXVII, 61–66). Dante had asked him why he was being punished and Guido, still fearful of what might be said about him, answers truthfully because he thinks Dante is also dead. Prufrock, like Guido, is fearful of society's judgment.

Let us go then, you and I,
When the evening is spread out against the sky
Like a patient etherized upon a table;
Let us go, through certain half-deserted streets,
The muttering retreats
Of restless nights in one-night cheap hotels
And sawdust restaurants with oyster-shells:
Streets that follow like a tedious argument
Of insidious intent
To lead you to an overwhelming question . . .   10
Oh, do not ask, 'What is it?'
Let us go and make our visit.

In the room the women come and go
Talking of Michelangelo.

The yellow fog that rubs its back upon the window-panes,
The yellow smoke that rubs its muzzle on the window-
        panes
Licked its tongue into the corners of the evening,
Lingered upon the pools that stand in drains,
Let fall upon its back the soot that falls from chimneys,
Slipped by the terrace, made a sudden leap,   20
And seeing that it was a soft October night,
Curled once about the house, and fell asleep.

And indeed there will be time
For the yellow smoke that slides along the street,
Rubbing its back upon the window-panes;
There will be time, there will be time
To prepare a face to meet the faces that you meet;
There will be time to murder and create,
And time for all the works and days of hands[2]
That lift and drop a question on your plate;   30
Time for you and time for me,
And time yet for a hundred indecisions,
And for a hundred visions and revisions,
Before the taking of a toast and tea.

In the room the women come and go
Talking of Michelangelo.

And indeed there will be time
To wonder, 'Do I dare?' and, 'Do I dare?'
Time to turn back and descend the stair,
With a bald spot in the middle of my hair—   40
(They will say: 'How his hair is growing thin!')
My morning coat, my collar mounting firmly to the chin,
My necktie rich and modest, but asserted by a simple
        pin—
(They will say: 'But how his arms and legs are thin!')
Do I dare
Disturb the universe?
In a minute there is time
For decisions and revisions which a minute will reverse.

For I have known them all already, known them all:—
Have known the evenings, mornings, afternoons,   50
I have measured out my life with coffee spoons;
I know the voices dying with a dying fall
Beneath the music from a farther room.
        So how should I presume?

And I have known the eyes already, known them all—
The eyes that fix you in a formulated phrase,
And when I am formulated, sprawling on a pin,
When I am pinned and wriggling on the wall,
Then how should I begin
To spit out all the butt-ends of my days and ways?   60
        And how should I presume?

And I have known the arms already, known them all—
Arms that are braceleted and white and bare
(But in the lamplight, downed with light brown hair!)
Is it perfume from a dress
That makes me so digress?
Arms that lie along a table, or wrap about a shawl.
        And should I then presume?
        And how should I begin?

        . . . . . .

Shall I say, I have gone at dusk through narrow
        streets   70
And watched the smoke that rises from the pipes
Of lonely men in shirt-sleeves, leaning out of
        windows? . . .

I should have been a pair of ragged claws
Scuttling across the floors of silent seas.

        . . . . . .

And the afternoon, the evening, sleeps so peacefully!
Smoothed by long fingers,
Asleep . . . tired . . . or it malingers,
Stretched on the floor, here beside you and me.
Should I, after tea and cakes and ices,
Have the strength to force the moment to its crisis?   80
But though I have wept and fasted, wept and prayed,
Though I have seen my head (grown slightly bald)
        brought in upon a platter,
I am no prophet—and here's no great matter;[3]
I have seen the moment of my greatness flicker,
And I have seen the eternal Footman hold my coat, and
        snicker,
And in short, I was afraid.

And would it have been worth it, after all,
After the cups, the marmalade, the tea,
Among the porcelain, among some talk of you and me,
Would it have been worth while,   90
To have bitten off the matter with a smile,
To have squeezed the universe into a ball[4]
To roll it toward some overwhelming question,
To say: 'I am Lazarus, come from the dead,[5]
Come back to tell you all, I shall tell you all'—
If one, settling a pillow by her head,
        Should say: That is not what I meant at all,
        That is not it, at all.

        . . . . . .

And would it have been worth it, after all,
Would it have been worth while,   100

_____

2. *Works and days* recalls Hesiod's poem entitled *Works and Days* (ca. 750 B.C.). Ironically contrasting with Prufrock's frivolous world, Hesiod's poem extols the virtues of hard labor on the land.

3. *I am no prophet,* i.e., no John the Baptist, who was beheaded by Herod and his head brought in on a tray to please Salome, Herod's stepdaughter (Matthew 14: 3–11). Prufrock views himself as a sacrificial victim but he is neither saint nor martyr.

4. *Universe into a ball* recalls "Let us roll all our strength and all our sweetness up into a ball" from the poem "To a Coy Mistress" by Andrew Marvell (see chap. 21). Prufrock's attempt to raise the conversation to a cosmic level with an allusion to a love poem is doubly ironic; the imaginary lady casually brings the discussion back to trivialities (11. 96–98).

5. *Lazarus* was raised from the grave by Christ (John 11:1–44). Can this society be brought back from the dead?

After the sunsets and the dooryards and the sprinkled
        streets,
After the novels, after the teacups, after the skirts that trail
        along the floor—
And this, and so much more?—
It is impossible to say just what I mean!
But as if a magic lantern threw the nerves in patterns on a
        screen:
Would it have been worth while
If one, settling a pillow or throwing off a shawl,
And turning toward the window, should say:
        'That is not it at all,
        That is not what I meant, at all.'   110

. . . . . .

No! I am not Prince Hamlet, nor was meant to be;
Am an attendant lord, one that will do
To swell a progress, start a scene or two,
Advise the prince; no doubt, an easy tool,[6]
Deferential, glad to be of use,
Politic, cautious, and meticulous;
Full of high sentence, but a bit obtuse;
At times, indeed, almost ridiculous—
Almost, at times, the Fool.
I grow old . . . I grow old . . .   120
I shall wear the bottoms of my trousers rolled.[7]
Shall I part my hair behind? Do I dare to eat a peach?
I shall wear white flannel trousers, and walk upon the
        beach.
I have heard the mermaids singing, each to each.
I do not think that they will sing to me.
I have seen them riding seaward on the waves
Combing the white hair of the waves blown back
When the wind blows the water white and black.
We have lingered in the chambers of the sea
By sea-girls wreathed with seaweed red and brown   130
Till human voices wake us, and we drown.

Exercises

1. What kind of a society is implied in which "the
   women come and go Talking of Michelangelo"
   (11. 13–14)?
2. Compare Eliot's references to time in lines
   23–26 with the first line of Marvell's "To his
   Coy Mistress" in chapter 21. How do the
   meanings differ?
3. What is implied in line 32 by "time yet for a
   hundred indecisions"?
4. What kind of life has Prufrock led that can be
   measured "with coffee spoons" (line 51)?
5. Describe, in your own words, Prufrock's
   physical appearance, personality, and social
   conduct.

THE SECOND COMING
William Butler Yeats (1865–1939)

This poem, written by Yeats in 1920, conveys a sense
of the dissolution of civilization. His image of the
cycle of history is a "gyre" (a spiral turning, pronounced with a hard *g*). Imagine a falconer losing
control of his falcon as the bird soars in widening circles and eventually breaks away. Lines 4–8 refer to the
Russian Revolution of 1917 but they can also be taken
as a portent of the rise of fascism in the twenties and
thirties. *Spiritus Mundi* is the soul of the universe
which connects all human souls in what Yeats calls
the "Great Memory," or universal subconscious.

Turning and turning in the widening gyre
The falcon cannot hear the falconer;
Things fall apart: the center cannot hold;
Mere anarchy is loosed upon the world,
The blood-dimmed tide is loosed, and everywhere
The ceremony of innocence is drowned;
The best lack all conviction, while the worst
Are full of passionate intensity.

Surely some revelation is at hand:
Surely the Second Coming is at hand.
The Second Coming! Hardly are those words out
When a vast image out of the *Spiritus Mundi*
Troubles my sight: somewhere in the sands of the desert
A shape with lion body and the head of a man,
A gaze blank and pitiless as the sun,
Is moving its slow thighs, while all about it
Reel shadows of the indignant desert birds.
The darkness drops again; but now I know
That twenty centuries of stony sleep
Were vexed to nightmare by a rocking cradle,
And what rough beast, its hour come round at last,
Slouches towards Bethlehem to be born?

Exercises

1. What does the poet mean, in lines 7 and 8, by
   the "best" and the "worst"?
2. There is a name for a shape with the head of a
   man and the body of a lion. What is it and why
   does Yeats evoke this image?
3. What is the implication of the "rocking cradle"?
4. Describe the feeling aroused by the last two
   lines of the poem.

DULCE ET DECORUM EST
Wilfred Owen (1893–1918)

Perhaps the most promising English poet to die in the
war, Wilfred Owen, unlike most of his contemporaries, saw no honor or glory in a conflict that he referred
to as "this deflowering of Europe." The closing quotation of this somber poem is from the poet Horace:
"It is sweet and fitting to die for one's country." Owen

---

6. *Advise the prince* apparently refers to Polonius, the king's
adviser in *Hamlet*. The cross-reference is to Guido da
Montefeltro, also a false counsellor.

7. Cuffed (rolled) trousers were stylish at the time. Middle-aged
and socially inept, Prufrock tries to appear young and
fashionable.

apparently hoped that this "old lie" would never again lead nations to war. He was killed in action on November 4, 1918, one week before the Armistice that ended the fighting.

Bent double, like old beggars under sacks,
Knock-kneed, coughing like hags, we cursed through
    sludge,
Till on the haunting flares we turned our backs
And towards our distant rest began to trudge.
Men marched asleep. Many had lost their boots   5
But limped on, blood-shod. All went lame; all blind;
Drunk with fatigue; deaf even to the hoots
Of tired, outstripped Five-Nines that dropped behind.

Gas! Gas! Quick, boys!—An ecstasy of fumbling,
Fitting the clumsy helmets just in time;   10
But someone still was yelling out and stumbling
And flound'ring like a man in fire or lime . . .
Dim, through the misty panes and thick green light,
As under a green sea, I saw him drowning.
In all my dreams, before my helpless sight,   15
He plunges at me, guttering, choking, drowning.

If in some smothering dreams you too could pace
Behind the wagon that we flung him in,
And watch the white eyes writhing in his face,
His hanging face, like a devil's sick of sin;   20
If you could hear, at every jolt, the blood
Come gargling from the froth-corrupted lungs,
Obscene as cancer, bitter as the cud
Of vile, incurable sores on innocent tongues,—
My friend, you would not tell with such high zest   25
To children ardent for some desperate glory,
The old Lie: Dulce et decorum est
Pro patria mori.

Exercises

1. Notice the many participles in lines 2 and 3. Is their effect active or passive?
2. Read line 6 aloud while listening to the sounds. How many weak syllables are there? Strong syllables? What is the effect?

SHINE, PERISHING REPUBLIC
Robinson Jeffers (1887–1962)

Postwar America was a world power but Jeffers saw the darker side, a crass and materialistic nation mired "in the mould of its vulgarity." The reader can determine whether the poem, written in 1924, is still apropos.

While this America settles in the mould of its vulgarity,
    heavily thickening to empire.
And protest, only a bubble in the molten mass, pops and
    sighs out, and the mass hardens.
I sadly smiling remember that the flower fades to make
    fruit, the fruit rots to make earth.

Out of the mother; and through the spring exultances,
    ripeness and decadence; and home to the mother.
You making haste haste on decay: not blameworthy; life is
    good, be it stubbornly long or suddenly
A mortal splendor: meteors are not needed less than
    mountains: shine perishing republic.
But for my children, I would have them keep their
    distance from the thickening center: corruption
Never has been compulsory, when the cities lie at the
    monster's feet there are left the mountains.
And boys, be in nothing so moderate as in love of man, a
    clever servant, insufferable master.
There is the trap that catches noblest spirits, that
    caught—they say—God, when he walked on earth.

Exercises

1. Identify the images that refer to the cycle of life and death.
2. What is implied by "meteors are not needed less than mountains"?
3. Jeffers wrote in 1924 that "corruption Never has been compulsory." Does this still apply in the 1980s? Consider, for example, air, water, and noise pollution, especially acid rain. Can we avoid this pollution? Stop it? How?

YET DO I MARVEL
Countee Cullen (1887–1946)

One of the leaders of a 1920s literary movement called the Harlem Renaissance, Cullen can be seen, at first glance, as a voice of moderation compared with black protests since World War II. Cullen's references are from the Western literary tradition (Greek mythology, Dante) and the form is that of a sonnet, but line 12 is derived from the last two lines of "The Tiger" by William Blake:"What immortal hand or eye/Dare frame thy fearful symmetry?" (see chap. 24). Blake asks how a good God can put evil in the world; Cullen ponders a similar question about the evil of racism. The tone is moderate, the sentiment is not.

I doubt not God is good, well-meaning, kind,
And did He stoop to quibble could tell why
The little buried mole continues blind,
Why flesh that mirrors Him must some day die,
Make plain the reason tortured Tantalus   5
Is baited by the fickle fruit, declare
If merely brute caprice dooms Sisyphus
To struggle up a never-ending stair.
Inscrutable His ways are, and immune
To catechism by a mind too strewn   10
With petty cares to slightly understand
What awful brain compels His awful hand.
Yet do I marvel at this curious thing:
To make a poet black, and bid him sing!

                   1924, 1925

Exercises

1. How many images are there of the way things are? Consider, for example, blind moles, Tantalus, and Sisyphus. (Tantalus was condemned by Zeus to stand up to his chin in water that receded everytime he tried to drink. Above his head hung fruit that the wind kept perpetually out of his reach. His name has given us the verb *tantalize*. The Myth of Sisyphus may be found in chap. 28.)

2. The last line implies that people who can write poetry *must* write poetry. Why is this so? Does the same compulsion hold true for painters, composers, and sculptors? Give some examples.

THE CRACK-UP (FEBRUARY, 1936)
F. Scott Fitzgerald (1896–1940)

Though many writers of the twenties saw themselves as a Lost Generation, working and reworking the wasteland motif, the pace of the Roaring Twenties was geared to explosive economic growth—the postwar boom. Jazz, bootleg booze, and flappers dancing the Charleston symbolized a frenetic era which was hurtling towards the Wall Street panic of 1929 and the subsequent worldwide depression of the thirties—while in the wings Adolf Hitler was tuning up the Nazi war machine.

A paradigm of the boom and bust cycle was F. Scott Fitzgerald, the literary darling of the twenties and a bankrupt movie script writer of the depression years. The following selection describes, in painful detail, Fitzgerald's personal burn-out but it can also be read as a case history of the extended entr'acte between act 2 and act 3 of worldwide warfare.

Of course all life is a process of breaking down, but the blows that do the dramatic side of the work—the big sudden blows that come, or seem to come, from outside—the ones you remember and blame things on and, in moments of weakness, tell your friends about, don't show their effect all at once. There is another sort of blow that comes from within—that you don't feel until it's too late to do anything about it, until you realize with finality that in some regard you will never be as good a man again. The first sort of breakage seems to happen quick—the second kind happens almost without your knowing it but is realized suddenly indeed.

Before I go on with this short history, let me make a general observation—the test of a first-rate intelligence is the ability to hold two opposed ideas in the mind at the same time, and still retain the ability to function. One should, for example, be able to see that things are hopeless and yet be determined to make them otherwise. This philosophy fitted on to my early adult life, when I saw the improbable, the implausible, often the "impossible," come true. Life was something you dominated if you were any good. Life yielded easily to intelligence and effort, or to what proportion could be mustered of both. It seemed a romantic business to be a successful literary man—you were not ever going to be as famous as a movie star but what note you had was probably longer-lived—you were never going to have the power of a man of strong political or religious convictions but you were certainly more independent. Of course within the practice of your trade you were forever unsatisfied—but I, for one, would not have chosen any other.

As the twenties passed, with my own twenties marching a little ahead of them, my two juvenile regrets—at not being big enough (or good enough) to play football in college, and at not getting overseas during the war—resolved themselves into childish waking dreams of imaginary heroism that were good enough to go to sleep on in restless nights. The big problems of life seemed to solve themselves, and if the business of fixing them was difficult, it made one too tired to think of more general problems.

Life, ten years ago, was largely a personal matter. I must hold in balance the sense of the futility of effort and the sense of the necessity to struggle; the conviction of the inevitability of failure and still the determination to "succeed"—and, more than these, the contradiction between the dead hand of the past and the high intentions of the future. If I could do this through the common ills—domestic, professional and personal—then the ego would continue as an arrow shot from nothingness to nothingness with such force that only gravity would bring it to earth at last.

For seventeen years, with a year of deliberate loafing and resting out in the center—things went on like that, with a new chore only a nice prospect for the next day. I was living hard, too, but: "Up to forty-nine it'll be all right," I said. "I can count on that. For a man who's lived as I have, that's all you could ask."

—And then, ten years this side of forty-nine, I suddenly realized that I had prematurely cracked.

II

Now a man can crack in many ways—can crack in the head—in which case the power of decision is taken from you by others! or in the body, when one can but submit to the white hospital world; or in the nerves. William Seabrook in an unsympathetic book tells, with some pride and a movie ending, of how he became a public charge. What led to his alcoholism or was bound up with it, was a collapse of his nervous system. Though the present writer was not so entangled—having at the time not tasted so much as a glass of beer for six months—it was his nervous reflexes that were giving way—too much anger and too many tears.

Moreover, to go back to my thesis that life has a varying offensive, the realization of having cracked was not simultaneous with a blow, but with a reprieve.

Not long before, I had sat in the office of a great doctor and listened to a grave sentence. With what, in retrospect, seems some equanimity, I had gone on about my affairs in the city where I was then living, not caring much, not thinking how much had been left undone, or what would become of this and that responsibility, like people do in books; I was well insured and anyhow I had been only a mediocre caretaker of most of the things left in my hands, even of my talent.

But I had a strong sudden instinct that I must be alone. I didn't want to see any people at all. I had seen so many people all my life—I was an average mixer, but more than average in a tendency to identify myself, my ideas, my destiny, with those of all classes that I came in contact with. I was always saving or being saved—in a single morning I would go through the emotions ascribable to Wellington at Waterloo. I lived in a world of inscrutable hostiles and inalienable friends and supporters.

But now I wanted to be absolutely alone and so arranged a certain insulation from ordinary cares.

It was not an unhappy time. I went away and there were fewer people. I found I was good-and-tired. I could lie around and was glad to, sleeping or dozing sometimes twenty hours a day and in the intervals trying resolutely not to think—instead I made lists—made lists and tore them up, hundreds of lists: of cavalry leaders and football players and cities, and popular tunes and pitchers, and happy times, and hobbies and houses lived in and how many suits since I left the army and how many pairs of shoes (I didn't count the suit I bought in Sorrento that shrunk, nor the pumps and dress shirt and collar that I carried around for years and never wore, because the pumps got damp and grainy and the shirt and collar got yellow and starch-rotted). And lists of women I'd liked, and of the times I had let myself be snubbed by people who had not been my betters in character or ability.

—And then suddenly, surprisingly, I got better.

—And cracked like an old plate as soon as I heard the news.

That is the real end of this story. What was to be done about it will have to rest in what used to be called the "womb of time." Suffice it to say that after about an hour of solitary pillow-hugging, I began to realize that for two years my life had been a drawing on resources that I did not possess, that I had been mortgaging myself physically and spiritually up to the hilt. What was the small gift of life given back in comparison to that?—when there had once been a pride of direction and a confidence in enduring independence.

I realized that in those two years, in order to preserve something—an inner hush maybe, maybe not—I had weaned myself from all the things I used to love—that every act of life from the morning tooth-brush to the friend at dinner had become an effort. I saw that for a long time I had not liked people and things, but only followed the rickety old pretense of liking. I saw that even my love for those closest to me was become only an attempt to love, that my casual relations—with an editor, a tobacco seller, the child of a friend, were only what I remembered I *should* do, from other days. All in the same month I became bitter about such things as the sound of the radio, the advertisements in the magazines, the screech of tracks, the dead silence of the country—contemptuous at human softness, immediately (if secretively) quarrelsome toward hardness—hating the night when I couldn't sleep and hating the day because it went toward night. I slept on the heart side now because I knew that the sooner I could tire that out, even a little, the sooner would come that blessed hour of nightmare which, like a catharsis, would enable me to better meet the new day.

There were certain spots, certain faces I could look at. Like most Middle Westerners, I have never had any but the vaguest race prejudices—I always had a secret yen for the lovely Scandinavian blondes who sat on porches in St. Paul but hadn't emerged enough economically to be part of what was then society. They were too nice to be "chickens" and too quickly off the farmlands to seize a

place in the sun, but I remember going round blocks to catch a single glimpse of shining hair—the bright shock of a girl I'd never know. This is urban, unpopular talk. It strays afield from the fact that in these latter days I couldn't stand the sight of Celts, English, Politicians, Strangers, Virginians, Negroes (light or dark), Hunting People, or retail clerks, and middlemen in general, all writers (I avoided writers very carefully because they can perpetuate trouble as no one else can)—and all the classes as classes and most of them as members of their class. . . .

Trying to cling to something, I liked doctors and girl children up to the age of about thirteen and well-brought-up boy children from about eight years old on. I could have peace and happiness with these few categories of people. I forgot to add that I liked old men—men over seventy, sometimes over sixty if their faces looked seasoned. I liked Katharine Hepburn's face on the screen, no matter what was said about her pretentiousness, and Miriam Hopkins' face, and old friends if I only saw them once a year and could remember their ghosts.

All rather inhuman and undernourished, isn't it? Well, that, children, is the true sign of cracking up.

It is not a pretty picture. Inevitably it was carted here and there within its frame and exposed to various critics. One of them can only be described as a person whose life makes other people's lives seem like death—even this time when she was cast in the usually unappealing role of Job's comforter. In spite of the fact that this story is over, let me append our conversation as a sort of postscript:

"Instead of being so sorry for yourself, listen—" she said. (She always says "Listen," because she thinks while she talks—*really* thinks.) So she said: "Listen. Suppose this wasn't a crack in you—suppose it was a crack in the Grand Canyon."

"The crack's in me," I said heroically.

"Listen! The world only exists in your eyes—your conception of it. You can make it as big or as small as you want to. And you're trying to be a little puny individual. By God, if I ever cracked, I'd try to make the world crack with me. Listen! The world only exists through your apprehension of it, and so it's much better to say that it's not you that's cracked—it's the Grand Canyon."

"Baby et up all her Spinoza?"

"I don't know anything about Spinoza. I know—" She spoke, then, of old woes of her own, that seemed, in the telling, to have been more dolorous than mine, and how she had met them, over-ridden them, beaten them.

I felt a certain reaction to what she said, but I am a slow-thinking man, and it occurred to me simultaneously that of all natural forces, vitality is the incommunicable one. In days when juice came into one as an article without duty, one tried to distribute it—but always without success; to further mix metaphors, vitality never "takes." You have it or you haven't it, like health or brown eyes or honor or a baritone voice. I might have asked some of it from her, neatly wrapped and ready for home cooking and digestion, but I could never have got it—not if I'd waited around for a thousand hours with the tin cup of self-pity. I could walk from her door, holding myself very carefully like cracked crockery, and go away into the world of bitterness, where I was making a home with such materials as are found there—and quote to myself after I left her door:

"Ye are the salt of the earth. But if the salt hath lost its savour, wherewith shall it be salted?"
Matthew 5–13.

Handle with Care (*March,* 1936)

In a previous article this writer told about his realization that what he had before him was not the dish that he had ordered for his forties. In fact—since he and the dish were one, he described himself as a cracked plate, the kind that one wonders whether it is worth preserving. Your editor thought that the article suggested too many aspects without regarding them closely, and probably many readers felt the same way—and there are always those to whom all self-revelation is contemptible, unless it ends with a noble thanks to the gods for the Unconquerable Soul.

But I had been thanking the gods too long, and thanking them for nothing. I wanted to put a lament into my record, without even the background of the Euganean Hills to give it color. There weren't any Euganean hills that I could see.

Sometimes, though, the cracked plate has to be retained in the pantry, has to be kept in service as a household necessity. It can never again be warmed on the stove nor shuffled with the other plates in the dishpan; it will not be brought out for company, but it will do to hold crackers late at night or to go into the ice box under left-overs. . .

Hence this sequel—a cracked plate's further history.

Now the standard cure for one who is sunk is to consider those in actual destitution or physical suffering—this is an all-weather beatitude for gloom in general and fairly salutory day-time advice for everyone. But at three o'clock in the morning, a forgotten package has the same tragic importance as a death sentence, and the cure doesn't work—and in a real dark night of the soul it is always three o'clock in the morning, day after day. At that hour the tendency is to refuse to face things as long as possible by retiring into an infantile dream—but one is continually startled out of this by various contacts with the world. One meets these occasions as quickly and carelessly as possible and retires once more back into the dream, hoping that things will adjust themselves by some great material or spiritual bonanza. But as the withdrawal persists there is less and less chance of the bonanza—one is not waiting for the fade-out of a single sorrow, but rather being an unwilling witness of an execution, the disintegration of one's own personality. . .

Unless madness or drugs or drink come into it, this phase comes to a dead-end, eventually, and is succeeded by a vacuous quiet. In this you can try to estimate what has been sheared away and what is left. Only when this quiet came to me, did I realize that I had gone through two parallel experiences.

The first time was twenty years ago, when I left Princeton in junior year with a complaint diagnosed as malaria. It transpired, through an X-ray taken a dozen years later, that it had been tuberculosis—a mild case, and after a few months of rest I went back to college. But I had lost certain offices, the chief one was the presidency of the Triangle Club, a musical comedy idea, and also I dropped back a class. To me college would never be the same. There were to be no badges of pride, no medals, after all. It seemed on one March afternoon that I had lost every single thing I wanted—and that night was the first time that I hunted down the spectre of womanhood that, for a little while, makes everything else seem unimportant.

Years later I realized that my failure as a big shot in college was all right—instead of serving on committees, I took a beating on English poetry; when I got the idea of

what it was all about, I set about learning how to write. On Shaw's principle that "If you don't get what you like, you better like what you get," it was a lucky break—at the moment it was a harsh and bitter business to know that my career as a leader of men was over.

Since that day I have not been able to fire a bad servant, and I am astonished and impressed by people who can. Some old desire for personal dominance was broken and gone. Life around me was a solemn dream, and I lived on the letters I wrote to a girl in another city. A man does not recover from such jolts—he becomes a different person and, eventually, the new person finds new things to care about.

The other episode parallel to my current situation took place after the war, when I had again over-extended my flank. It was one of those tragic loves doomed for lack of money, and one day the girl closed it out on the basis of common sense. During a long summer of despair I wrote a novel instead of letters, so it came out all right, but it came out all right for a different person. The man with the jingle of money in his pocket who married the girl a year later would always cherish an abiding distrust, an animosity, toward the leisure class—not the conviction of a revolutionist but the smoldering hatred of a peasant. In the years since then I have never been able to stop wondering where my friends' money came from, nor to stop thinking that at one time a sort of *droit de seigneur* might have been exercised to give one of them my girl.

For sixteen years I lived pretty much as this latter person, distrusting the rich, yet working for money with which to share their mobility and the grace that some of them brought into their lives. During this time I had plenty of the usual horses shot from under me—I remember some of their names—*Punctured Pride, Thwarted Expectation, Faithless, Show-off, Hard Hit, Never Again.* And after awhile I wasn't twenty-five, then not even thirty-five, and nothing was quite as good. But in all these years I don't remember a moment of discouragement. I saw honest men through moods of suicidal gloom—some of them gave up and died; others adjusted themselves and went on to a larger success than mine; but my morale never sank below the level of self-disgust when I had put on some unsightly personal show. Trouble has no necessary connection with discourage-ment—discouragement has a germ of its own, as different from trouble as arthritis is different from a stiff joint.

When a new sky cut off the sun last spring, I didn't at first relate it to what had happened fifteen or twenty years ago. Only gradually did a certain family resemblance come through—an over-extension of the flank, a burning of the candle at both ends; a call upon physical resources that I did not command, like a man over-drawing at his bank. In its impact this blow was more violent than the other two but it was the same in kind—a feeling that I was standing at twilight on a deserted range, with an empty rifle in my hands and the targets down. No problem set—simply a silence with only the sound of my own breathing.

In this silence there was a vast irresponsibility toward every obligation, a deflation of all my values. A passionate belief in order, a disregard of motives or consequences in favor of guess work and prophecy, a feeling that craft and industry would have a place in any world—one by one, these and other convictions were swept away. I saw that the novel, which at my maturity was the strongest and supplest medium for conveying thought and emotion from one human being to another, was becoming subordinated to a mechanical and communal art that, whether in the hands of Hollywood merchants or Russian idealists, was capable of reflecting only the tritest thought, the most obvious emotion. It was an art in which words were subordinate to images, where personality was worn down to the inevitable low gear of collaboration. As long past as 1930, I had a hunch that the talkies would make even the best selling novelist as archaic as silent pictures. People still read, if only Professor Canby's book of the month—curious children nosed at the slime of Mr. Tiffany Thayer in the drugstore libraries—but there was a rankling indignity, that to me had become almost an obsession, in seeing the power of the written word subordinated to another power, a more glittering, a grosser power. . .

I set that down as an example of what haunted me during the long night—this was something I could neither accept nor struggle against, something which tended to make my efforts obsolescent, as the chain stores have crippled the small merchant, an exterior force, unbeatable—

(I have the sense of lecturing now, looking at a watch on the desk before me and seeing how many more minutes—).

Well, when I had reached this period of silence, I was forced into a measure that no one ever adopts voluntarily: I was impelled to think. God, was it difficult! The moving about of great secret trunks. In the first exhausted halt, I wondered whether I had ever thought. After a long time I came to these conclusions, just as I write them here:

(1) That I had done very little thinking, save within the problems of my craft. For twenty years a certain man had been my intellectual conscience. That was Edmund Wilson.

(2) That another man represented my sense of the "good life," though I saw him once in a decade, and since then he might have been hung. He is in the fur business in the Northwest and wouldn't like his name set down here. But in difficult situations I had tried to think what *he* would have thought, how *he* would have acted.

(3) That a third contemporary had been an artistic conscience to me—I had not imitated his infectious style, because my own style, such as it is, was formed before he published anything, but there was an awful pull toward him when I was on a spot.

(4) That a fourth man had come to dictate my relations with other people when these relations were successful: how to do, what to say. How to make people at least momentarily happy (in opposition to Mrs. Post's theories of how to make everyone thoroughly uncomfortable with a sort of systematized vulgarity). This always confused me and made me want to go out and get drunk, but this man had seen the game, analyzed it and beaten it, and his word was good enough for me.

(5) That my political conscience had scarcely existed for ten years save as an element of irony in my stuff. When I became again concerned with the system I should function under, it was a man much younger than myself who brought it to me, with a mixture of passion and fresh air.

So there was not an "I" any more—not a basis on which I could organize my self-respect—save my limitless capacity for toil that it seemed I possessed no more. It was strange to have no self—to be like a little boy left alone in a big house, who knew that now he could do anything he wanted to do, but found that there was nothing that he wanted to do—

(The watch is past the hour and I have barely reached my thesis. I have some doubts as to whether this is of general interest, but if anyone wants more, there is plenty left, and your editor will tell me. If you've had enough, say so—but not too loud, because I have the feeling that someone, I'm not sure who, is sound asleep—someone who could have helped me to keep my shop open. It wasn't Lenin, and it wasn't God.)

Pasting It Together (*April,* 1936)

I have spoken in these pages of how an exceptionally optimistic young man experienced a crack-up of all values, a crack-up that he scarcely knew of until long after it occurred. I told of the succeeding period of desolation and of the necessity of going on, but without benefit of Henley's familiar heroics, "my head is bloody but unbowed." For a check-up of my spiritual liabilities indicated that I had no particular head to be bowed or unbowed. Once I had had a heart but that was about all I was sure of.

This was at least a starting place out of the morass in which I floundered: "I felt—therefore I was." At one time or another there had been many people who had leaned on me, come to me in difficulties or written me from afar, believed implicitly in my advice and my attitude toward life. The dullest platitude monger or the most unscrupulous Rasputin who can influence the destinies of many people must have some individuality, so the question became one of finding why and where I had changed, where was the leak through which, unknown to myself, my enthusiasm and my vitality had been steadily and prematurely trickling away.

One harassed and despairing night I packed a brief case and went off a thousand miles to think it over. I took a dollar room in a drab little town where I knew no one and sunk all the money I had with me in a stock of potted meat, crackers and apples. But don't let me suggest that the change from a rather overstuffed world to a comparative asceticism was any Research Magnificent—I only wanted absolute quiet to think out why I had developed a sad attitude toward sadness, a melancholy attitude toward melancholy and a tragic attitude toward tragedy—*why I had become identified with the objects of my horror or compassion.*

Does this seem a fine distinction? It isn't: identification such as this spells the death of accomplishment. It is something like this that keeps insane people from working. Lenin did not willingly endure the sufferings of his proletariat, nor Washington of his troops, nor Dickens of his London poor. And when Tolstoy tried some such merging of himself with the objects of his attention, it was a fake and a failure. I mention these because they are the men best known to us all.

It was dangerous mist. When Wordsworth decided that "there had passed away a glory from the earth," he felt no compulsion to pass away with it, and the Fiery Particle. Keats never ceased his struggle against t. b. nor in his last moments relinquished his hope of being among the English poets.

My self-immolation was something sodden-dark. It was very distinctly not modern—yet I saw it in others, saw it in a dozen men of honor and industry since the war. (I heard you, but that's too easy—there were Marxians among these men.) I had stood by while one famous contemporary of mine played with the idea of the Big Out for half a year; I had watched when another, equally eminent, spent months in an asylum unable to endure any contact with his fellow men. And of those who had given up and passed on I could list a score.

This led me to the idea that the ones who had survived had made some sort of clean break. This is a big word and is no parallel to a jail-break when one is probably headed for a new jail or will be forced back to the old one. The famous "Escape" or "run away from it all" is an excursion in a trap even if the trap includes the south seas, which are only for those who want to paint or sail them. A clean break is something you cannot come back from; that is irretrievable because it makes the past cease to exist. So, since I could no longer fulfill the obligations that life had set for me or that I had set for myself, why not slay the empty shell who had been posturing at it for four years? I must continue to be a writer because that was my only way of life, but I would cease any attempts to be a person—to be kind, just or generous. There were plenty of counterfeit coins around that would pass instead of these and I knew where I could get them at a nickel on the dollar. In thirty-nine years an observant eye has learned to detect where the milk is watered and the sugar is sanded, the rhinestone passed for diamond and the stucco for stone. There was to be no more giving of myself—all giving was to be outlawed henceforth under a new name, and that name was Waste.

The decision made me rather exuberant, like anything that is both real and new. As a sort of beginning there was a whole shaft of letters to be tipped into the waste basket when I went home, letters that wanted something for nothing—to read this man's manuscript, market this man's poem, speak free on the radio, indite notes of introduction, give this interview, help with the plot of this play, with this domestic situation, perform this act of thoughtfulness or charity.

The conjuror's hat was empty. To draw things out of it had long been a sort of sleight of hand, and now, to change the metaphor, I was off the dispensing end of the relief roll forever.

The heady villainous feeling continued.

I felt like the beady-eyed men I used to see on the commuting train from Great Neck fifteen years back—men who didn't care whether the world tumbled into chaos tomorrow if it spared their houses. I was one with them now, one with the smooth articles who said:

"I'm sorry but business is business." Or:

"You ought to have thought of that before you got into this trouble." Or:

"I'm not the person to see about that."

And a smile—ah, I would get me a smile. I'm still working on that smile. It is to combine the best qualities of a hotel manager, an experienced old social weasel, a headmaster on visitors' day, a colored elevator man, a pansy pulling a profile, a producer getting stuff at half its market value, a trained nurse coming on a new job, a body-vendor in her first rotogravure, a hopeful extra swept near the camera, a ballet dancer with an infected toe, and of course the great beam of loving kindness common to all those from Washington to Beverly Hills who must exist by virtue of the contorted pan.

The voice too—I am working with a teacher on the voice. When I have perfected it the larynx will show no ring of conviction except the conviction of the person I am talking to. Since it will be largely called upon for the elicitation of the word "Yes," my teacher (a lawyer) and I are concentrating on that, but in extra hours. I am learning to bring into it that polite acerbity that makes people feel that far from being welcome they are not even tolerated and are under continual and scathing analysis at every moment. These times will of course not coincide with the smile. This will be reserved exclusively for those from whom I have nothing to gain, old worn-out people or young struggling people. They won't mind—what the hell, they get it most of the time anyhow.

But enough. It is not a matter of levity. If you are young and you should write asking to see me and learn how to be a sombre literary man writing pieces upon the state of emotional exhaustion that often overtakes writers in their prime—if you should be so young and so fatuous as to do this, I would not do so much as acknowledge your letter, unless you were related to someone very rich and important indeed. And if you were dying of starvation outside my window, I would go out quickly and give you the smile and the voice (if no longer the hand) and stick around till somebody raised a nickel to phone for the ambulance, that is if I thought there would be any copy in it for me.

I have now at last become a writer only. The man I had persistently tried to be became such a burden that I have "cut him loose" with as little compunction as a Negro lady cuts loose a rival on Saturday night. Let the good people function as such—let the overworked doctors die in harness, with one week's "vacation" a year that they can devote to straightening out their family affairs, and let the underworked doctors scramble for cases at one dollar a throw; let the soldiers be killed and enter immediately into the Valhalla of their profession. That is their contract with the gods. A writer need have no such ideals unless he makes them for himself, and this one has quit. The old dream of being an entire man in the Goethe-Byron-Shaw tradition, with an opulent American touch, a sort of combination of J. P. Morgan, Topham Beauclerk and St. Francis of Assisi, has been relegated to the junk heap of the shoulder pads worn for one day on the Princeton freshman football field and the overseas cap never worn overseas.

So what? This is what I think now: that the natural state of the sentient adult is a qualified unhappiness. I think also that in an adult the desire to be finer in grain than you are, "a constant striving" (as those people say who gain their bread by saying it) only adds to this unhappiness in the end—that end that comes to our youth and hope. My own happiness in the past often approached such an ecstasy that I could not share it even with the person dearest to me but had to walk it away in quiet streets and lanes with only fragments of it to distil into little lines in books—and I think that my happiness, or talent for self delusion or what you will, was an exception. It was not the natural thing but the unnatural—unnatural as the Boom; and my recent experience parallels the wave of despair that swept the nation when the Boom was over.

I shall manage to live with the new dispensation, though it has taken some months to be certain of the fact. And just as the laughing stoicism which has enabled the American Negro to endure the intolerable conditions of his existence has cost him his sense of the truth—so in my case there is a price to pay. I do not any longer like the postman, nor the grocer, nor the editor, nor the cousin's husband, and he in turn will come to dislike me, so that life will never be very pleasant again, and the sign *Cave Canem* is hung permanently just above my door. I will try to be a correct animal though, and if you throw me a bone with enough meat on it I may even lick your hand.

Exercises

1. Why does the writer refer to himself as a "cracked plate"? Why not a cup, or saucer, or piece of crystal? Why does he go on to say that "the cracked plate has to be retained in the pantry, has to be kept in service as a household necessity"? Could this analogy have something to do with the idea of suicide?
2. What does Fitzgerald mean when he says he is one now with the "men who didn't care whether the world tumbled into chaos tomorrow if it spared their houses"? What kind of a person was he before his "crackup"?

THE ETHICS OF LIVING JIM CROW, 1937

An Autobiographical Sketch

Richard Wright (1908–1960)

Raised in poverty in Mississippi, Richard Wright became a powerful spokesman for human rights and human dignity at a time when black artists and writers were finally being taken seriously. *Native Son* (1940) is his finest novel, followed by *Black Boy* (1945) and numerous books dealing with America's race problems. Before World War II few white Americans were aware of the effects of Jim Crow laws and customs in the North and, especially, in the South. Though such practices are no longer legal or condoned by responsible citizens, Jim Crow attitudes, both Black and White, persist as a disturbing reality in the long struggle for equal opportunity for all Americans. Neither polemical nor didactic, Wright's reflective essay is an artist's statement about how Jim Crow affected his life.

I

My first lesson in how to live as a Negro came when I was quite small. We were living in Arkansas. Our house stood behind the railroad tracks. Its skimpy yard was paved with black cinders. Nothing green ever grew in that yard. The only touch of green we could see was far away, beyond the tracks, over where the white folks lived. But cinders were good enough for me and I never missed the green growing things. And anyhow cinders were fine weapons. You could always have a nice hot war with huge black cinders. All you had to do was crouch behind the brick pillars of a house with your hands full of gritty ammunition. And the first woolly black head you saw pop out from behind another row of pillars was your target. You tried your very best to knock it off. It was great fun.

I never fully realized the appalling disadvantages of a cinder environment till one day the gang to which I belonged found itself engaged in a war with the white boys who lived beyond the tracks. As usual we laid down our cinder barrage, thinking that this would wipe the white boys out. But they replied with a steady bombardment of broken bottles. We doubled our cinder barrage, but they hid behind trees, hedges, and the sloping embankment of their lawns. Having no such fortifications, we retreated to the brick pillars of our homes. During the retreat a broken milk bottle caught me behind the ear, opening a deep gash which bled profusely. The sight of blood pouring over my face completely demoralized our ranks. My fellow-combatants left me standing paralyzed in the center of the yard, and scurried for their homes. A kind neighbor saw me, and rushed me to a doctor, who took three stitches in my neck.

I sat brooding on my front steps, nursing my wound and waiting for my mother to come from work. I felt that a grave injustice had been done me. It was all right to throw cinders. The greatest harm a cinder could do was leave a bruise. But broken bottles were dangerous; they left you cut, bleeding, and helpless.

When night fell, my mother came from the white folks' kitchen. I raced down the street to meet her. I could just feel in my bones that she would understand. I knew she would tell me exactly what to do next time. I grabbed her hand and babbled out the whole story. She examined my wound, then slapped me.

"How come yuh didn't hide?" she asked me. "How come yuh awways fightin'?"

I was outraged, and bawled. Between sobs I told her that I didn't have any trees or hedges to hide behind. There wasn't a thing I could have used as a trench. And you couldn't throw very far when you were hiding behind the brick pillars of a house. She grabbed a barrel stave, dragged me home, stripped me naked, and beat me till I had a fever of one hundred and two. She would smack my rump with the stave, and, while the skin was still smarting impart to me gems of Jim Crow wisdom. I was never to throw cinders any more. I was never to fight any more wars. I was never, never, under any conditions, to fight *white* folks again. And they were absolutely right in clouting me with the broken milk bottle. Didn't I know she was working hard every day in the hot kitchens of the white folks to make money to take care of me? When was I ever going to learn to be a good boy? She couldn't be bothered with my fights. She finished by telling me that I ought to be thankful to God as long as I lived that they didn't kill me.

All that night I was delirious and could not sleep. Each time I closed my eyes I saw monstrous white faces suspended from the ceiling, leering at me.

From that time on, the charm of my cinder yard was gone. The green trees, the trimmed hedges, the cropped lawns grew very meaningful, became a symbol. Even today when I think of white folks, the hard, sharp outlines of white houses surrounded by trees, lawns, and hedges are present somewhere in the background of my mind. Through the years they grew into an overreaching symbol of fear.

It was a long time before I came in close contact with white folks again. We moved from Arkansas to Mississippi. Here we had the good fortune not to live behind the railroad tracks, or close to white neighborhoods. We lived in the very heart of the local

Black Belt. There were black churches and black preachers; there were black schools and black teachers; black groceries and black clerks. In fact, everything was so solidly black that for a long time I did not even think of white folks, save in remote and vague terms. But this could not last forever. As one grows older one eats more. One's clothing costs more. When I finished grammar school I had to go to work. My mother could no longer feed and clothe me on her cooking job.

There is but one place where a black boy who knows no trade can get a job, and that's where the houses and faces are white, where the trees, lawns, and hedges are green. My first job was with an optical company in Jackson, Mississippi. The morning I applied I stood straight and neat before the boss, answering all his questions with sharp yessirs and nosirs. I was very careful to pronounce my *sirs* distinctly, in order that he might know that I was polite, that I knew where I was, and that I knew he was a *white* man. I wanted that job badly.

He looked me over as though he were examining a prize poodle. He questioned me closely about my schooling, being particularly insistent about how much mathematics I had had. He seemed very pleased when I told him I had had two years of algebra.

"Boy, how would you like to try to learn something around here?" he asked me.

"I'd like it fine, sir," I said, happy. I had visions of "working my way up." Even Negroes have those visions.

"All right," he said. "Come on."

I followed him to the small factory.

"Pease," he said to a white man of about thirty-five, "this is Richard. He's going to work for us."

Pease looked at me and nodded.

I was then taken to a white boy of about seventeen.

"Morrie, this is Richard, who's going to work for us."

"Whut yuh sayin' there, boy!" Morrie boomed at me.

"Fine!" I answered.

The boss instructed these two to help me, teach me, give me jobs to do, and let me learn what I could in my spare time.

My wages were five dollars a week.

I worked hard, trying to please. For the first month I got along O.K. Both Pease and Morrie seemed to like me. But one thing was missing. And I kept thinking about it. I was not learning anything and nobody was volunteering to help me. Thinking they had forgotten that I was to learn something about the mechanics of grinding lenses, I asked Morrie one day to tell me about the work. He grew red.

"Whut yuh tryin' 't' do, nigger, get smart?" he asked.

"Naw; I ain' tryin' t' git smart," I said.

"Well, don't, if yuh know whut's good for yuh!"

I was puzzled. Maybe he just doesn't want to help me, I thought. I went to Pease.

"Say, are yuh crazy, you black bastard?" Pease asked me, his gray eyes growing hard.

I spoke out, reminding him that the boss had said I was to be given a chance to learn something.

"Nigger, you think you're *white*, don't you?"

"Naw, sir!"

"Well, you're acting mighty like it!"

"But, Mr. Pease, the boss said . . ."

Pease shook his fist in my face.

"This is a *white* man's work around here, and you better watch yourself!"

From then on they changed toward me. They said good-morning no more. When I was just a bit slow in performing some duty, I was called a lazy black son-of-a-bitch.

Once I thought of reporting all this to the boss. But the mere idea of what would happen to me if Pease and Morrie should learn that I had "snitched" stopped me. And after all the boss was a white man, too. What was the use?

The climax came at noon one summer day. Pease called me to his workbench. To get to him I had to go between two narrow benches and stand with my back against a wall.

"Yes sir," I said.

"Richard, I want to ask you something," Pease began pleasantly, not looking up from his work.

"Yes, sir," I said again.

Morrie came over, blocking the narrow passage between the benches. He folded his arms, staring at me solemnly.

I looked from one to the other, sensing that something was coming.

"Yes, sir," I said for the third time.

Pease looked up and spoke very slowly.

"Richard, *Mr.* Morrie here tells me you called me *Pease*."

I stiffened. A void seemed to open up in me. I knew this was the showdown.

He meant that I had failed to call him Mr. Pease. I looked at Morrie. He was gripping a steel bar in his hands. I opened my mouth to speak, to protest, to assure Pease that I had never called him simply *Pease,* and that I had never had any intentions of doing so, when Morrie grabbed me by the collar, ramming my head against the wall.

"Now be careful, nigger!" snarled Morrie, baring his teeth. "*I* heard yuh call 'im *Pease!* 'N' if yuh say yuh didn't, yuh're callin' me a *lie,* see?" He waved the steel bar threateningly.

If I had said: No, sir, Mr. Pease, I never called you *Pease* I would have been automatically calling Morrie a liar. And if I had said: Yes, sir, Mr. Pease, I called you *Pease,* I would have been pleading guilty to having uttered the worst insult that a Negro can utter to a southern white man. I stood hesitating, trying to frame a neutral reply.

"Richard, I asked you a question!" said Pease. Anger was creeping into his voice.

"I don't remember calling you *Pease,* Mr. Pease," I said cautiously. "And if I did, I sure didn't mean . . ."

"You black son-of-a-bitch! You called me *Pease,* then!" he spat, slapping me till I bent sideways over a bench. Morrie was on top of me, demanding:

"Didn't you call 'im *Pease?* If yuh say yuh didn't, I'll rip yo' gut string loose with this bar, yuh black granny dodger! Yuh can't call a white man a lie 'n' git erway with it, you black son-of-a-bitch!"

I wilted. I begged them not to bother me. I knew what they wanted. They wanted me to leave.

"I'll leave," I promised. "I'll leave right *now.*"

They gave me a minute to get out of the factory. I was warned not to show up again, or tell the boss.

I went.

When I told the folks at home what had happened, they called me a fool. They told me that I must never again attempt to exceed my boundaries. When you are working for white folks, they said, you got to "stay in your place" if you want to keep working.

II

My Jim Crow education continued on my next job, which was portering in a clothing store. One morning, while polishing brass out front, the boss and his twenty-year-old son got out of their car and half dragged and half kicked a Negro woman into the store. A policeman standing at the corner looked on, twirling his nightstick. I watched out of the corner of my eye, never slackening the strokes of my chamois upon the brass. After a few minutes, I heard shrill screams coming from the rear of the store. Later the woman stumbled out, bleeding, crying, and holding her stomach. When she reached the end of the block, the policeman grabbed her and accused her of being drunk. Silently, I watched him throw her into a patrol wagon.

When I went to the rear of the store, the boss and his son were washing their hands at the sink. They were chuckling. The floor was bloody and strewn with wisps of hair and clothing. No doubt I must have appeared pretty shocked, for the boss slapped me reassuringly on the back.

"Boy, that's what we do to niggers when they don't want to pay their bills," he said, laughing.

His son looked at me and grinned.

"Here, hava cigarette," he said.

Not knowing what to do, I took it. He lit his and held the match for me. This was a gesture of kindness, indicating that even if they had beaten the poor old woman, they would not beat me if I knew enough to keep my mouth shut.

"Yes, sir," I said, and asked no questions.

After they had gone, I sat on the edge of a packing box and stared at the bloody floor till the cigarette went out.

That day at noon, while eating in a hamburger joint, I told my fellow Negro porters what had happened. No one seemed surprised. One fellow, after swallowing a huge bite, turned to me and asked:

"Huh! Is tha' all they did t' her?"

"Yeah. Wasn't tha' enough?" I asked.

"Shucks! Man, she's a lucky bitch!" he said, burying his lips deep into a juicy hamburger. "Hell, it's a wonder they didn't lay her when they got through."

III

I was learning fast, but not quite fast enough. One day, while I was delivering packages in the suburbs, my bicycle tire was punctured. I walked along the hot, dusty road, sweating and leading my bicycle by the handlebars.

A car slowed at my side.

"What's the matter, boy?" a white man called.

I told him my bicycle was broken and I was walking back to town.

"That's too bad," he said. "Hop on the running board."

He stopped the car. I clutched hard at my bicycle with one hand and clung to the side of the car with the other.

"All set?"

"Yes, sir," I answered. The car started.

It was full of young white men. They were drinking. I watched the flask pass from mouth to mouth.

"Wanna drink, boy?" one asked.

I laughed as the wind whipped my face. Instinctively obeying the freshly planted precepts of my mother, I said:

"Oh, no!"

The words were hardly out of my mouth before I felt something hard and cold smash me between the eyes. It was an empty whisky bottle. I saw stars, and fell backwards from the speeding car into the dust of the road, my feet becoming entangled in the steel spokes of my bicycle. The white men piled out and stood over me.

"Nigger, ain' yuh learned no better sense'n tha' yet?" asked the man who hit me. "Ain' yuh learned t' say *sir* t' a white man yet?"

Dazed, I pulled to my feet. My elbows and legs were bleeding. Fists doubled, the white man advanced, kicking my bicycle out of the way.

"Aw, leave the bastard alone. He's got enough," said one.

They stood looking at me. I rubbed my shins, trying to stop the flow of blood. No doubt they felt a sort of contemptuous pity, for one asked:

"Yuh wanna ride t' town now, nigger? Yuh reckon yuh know enough t' ride now?"

"I wanna walk," I said, simply.

Maybe it sounded funny. They laughed.

"Well, walk, yuh black son-of-a-bitch!"

When they left they comforted me with:

"Nigger, yuh sho better be dawn glad it wuz us yuh talked t' tha' way. Yuh're a lucky bastard, 'cause if yuh'd said tha' t' somebody else, yuh might've been a dead nigger now."

IV

Negroes who have lived South know the dread of being caught alone upon the streets in white neighborhoods after the sun has set. In such a simple situation as this the plight of the Negro in America is graphically symbolized. While white strangers may be in these neighborhoods trying to get home, they can pass unmolested. But the color of a Negro's skin makes him easily recognizable, makes him suspect, converts him into a defenseless target.

Late one Saturday night I made some deliveries in a white neighborhood. I was pedaling my bicycle back to the store as fast as I could, when a police car, swerving toward me, jammed me into the curbing.

"Get down and put up your hands!" the policemen ordered.

I did. They climbed out of the car, guns drawn, faces set, and advanced slowly.

"Keep still!" they ordered.

I reached my hands higher. They searched my pockets and packages. They seemed dissatisfied when they could find nothing incriminating. Finally, one of them said:

"Boy, tell your boss not to send you out in white neighborhoods after sundown."

As usual, I said:

"Yes, sir."

V

My next job was as hall-boy in a hotel. Here my Jim Crow education broadened and deepened. When the bell-boys were busy, I was often called to assist them. As many of the rooms in the hotel were occupied by prostitutes, I was constantly called to carry them liquor and cigarettes. These women were nude most of the time. They did not bother about clothing, even for bell-boys. When you went into their rooms, you were supposed to take their nakedness for granted, as though it startled you no more than a blue vase or a red rug. Your presence awoke in them no sense of shame, for you were not regarded as human. If they were alone, you could steal side-long glimpses at them. But if they were receiving men, not a flicker of your eyelids could show. I remember one incident vividly. A new woman, a huge, snowy-skinned blonde, took a room on my floor. I was sent to wait upon her. She was in bed with a thick-set man; both were nude and uncovered. She said she wanted some liquor and slid out of bed and waddled across the floor to get her money from a dresser drawer. I watched her.

"Nigger, what in hell you looking at?" the white man asked me, raising himself upon his elbows.

"Nothing," I answered, looking miles deep into the blank wall of the room.

"Keep your eyes where they belong, if you want to be healthy!" he said.

"Yes, sir."

VI

One of the bell-boys I knew in this hotel was keeping steady company with one of the Negro maids. Out of a clear sky the police descended upon his home and arrested him, accusing him of bastardy. The poor boy swore he had had no intimate relations with the girl. Nevertheless, they forced him to marry her. When the child arrived, it was found to be much lighter in complexion than either of the two supposedly legal parents. The white men around the hotel made a great joke of it. They spread the rumor that some white cow must have scared the poor girl while she was carrying the baby. If you were in their presence when this explanation was offered, you were supposed to laugh.

VII

One of the bell-boys was caught in bed with a white prostitute. He was castrated and run out of town. Immediately after this all the bell-boys and hall-boys were called together and warned. We were given to understand that the boy who had been castrated was a "mighty, mighty lucky bastard." We were impressed with the fact that next time the management of the hotel would not be responsible for the lives of "trouble-makin' niggers." We were silent.

VIII

One night, just as I was about to go home, I met one of the Negro maids. She lived in my direction, and we fell in to walk part of the way home together. As we passed the white night-watchman, he slapped the maid on her buttock. I turned around, amazed. The watchman looked at me with a long, hard, fixed-under stare. Suddenly, he pulled his gun and asked:

"Nigger, don't yuh like it?"

I hesitated.

"I asked yuh don't yuh like it?" he asked again, stepping forward.

"Yes, sir," I mumbled.

"Talk like it, then!"

"Oh, yes, sir!" I said with as much heartiness as I could muster.

Outside, I walked ahead of the girl, ashamed to face her. She caught up with me and said:

"Don't be a fool! Yuh couldn't help it!"

This watchman boasted of having killed two Negroes in self-defense.

Yet, in spite of all this, the life of the hotel ran with an amazing smoothness. It would have been impossible for a stranger to detect anything. The maids, the hall-boys, and the bell-boys were all smiles. They had to be.

IX

I had learned my Jim Crow lessons so thoroughly that I kept the hotel job till I left Jackson for Memphis. It so happened that while in Memphis I applied for a job at a branch of the optical company. I was hired. And for some reason, as long as I worked there, they never brought my past against me.

Here my Jim Crow education assumed quite a different form. It was no longer brutally cruel, but subtly cruel. Here I learned to lie, to steal, to dissemble. I learned to play that dual role which every Negro must play if he wants to eat and live.

For example, it was almost impossible to get a book to read. It was assumed that after a Negro had imbibed what scanty schooling the state furnished he had no further need for books. I was always borrowing books from men on the job. One day I mustered enough courage to ask one of the men to let me get books from the library in his name. Surprisingly, he consented. I cannot help but think that he consented because he was a Roman Catholic and felt a vague sympathy for Negroes, being himself an object of hatred. Armed with a library card, I obtained books in the following manner: I would write a note to the librarian, saying: "Please let this nigger boy have the following books." I would then sign it with the white man's name.

When I went to the library, I would stand at the desk, hat in hand, looking as unbookish as possible. When I received the books desired I would take them home. If the books listed in the note happened to be out, I would sneak into the lobby and forge a new one. I never took any chances guessing with the white librarian about what the fictitious white man would want to read. No doubt if any of the white patrons had suspected that some of the volumes they enjoyed had been in the home of a Negro, they would not have tolerated it for an instant.

The factory force of the optical company in Memphis was much larger than that in Jackson, and more urbanized. At least they liked to talk, and would engage the Negro help in conversation whenever possible. By this means I found that many subjects were taboo from the white man's point of view. Among the topics they did not like to discuss with Negroes were the following: American white women; the Ku Klux Klan; France, and how Negro soldiers fared while there; French women; Jack Johnson; the entire northern part of the United States; the Civil War; Abraham Lincoln; U.S. Grant; General Sherman; Catholics; the Pope; Jews; the Republican Party; slavery; social equality; Communism; Socialism; the 13th and 14th Amendments to the Constitution; or any topic calling for positive knowledge or manly self-assertion on the part of the Negro. The most accepted topics were sex and religion.

There were many times when I had to exercise a great deal of ingenuity to keep out of trouble. It is a southern custom that all men must take off their hats when they enter an elevator. And especially did this apply to us blacks with rigid force. One day I stepped into an elevator with my arms full of packages. I was forced to ride with my hat on. Two white men stared at me coldly.

Then one of them very kindly lifted my hat and placed it upon my armful of packages. Now the most accepted response for a Negro to make under such circumstances is to look at the white man out of the corner of his eye and grin. To have said: "Thank you!" would have made the white man *think* that you *thought* you were receiving from him a personal service. For such an act I have seen Negroes take a blow in the mouth. Finding the first alternative distasteful, and the second dangerous, I hit upon an acceptable course of action which fell safely between these two poles. I immediately—no sooner than my hat was lifted—pretended that my packages were about to spill, and appeared deeply distressed with keeping them in my arms. In this fashion I evaded having to acknowledge his service, and, in spite of adverse circumstance, salvaged a single shred of personal pride.

How do Negroes feel about the way they have to live? How do they discuss it when alone among themselves? I think this question can be answered in a single sentence. A friend of mine who ran an elevator once told me:

"Lawd, man! Ef it wuzn't fer them polices 'n' them ol' lynchmobs, there wouldn't be nothin' but uproar down here!"

Exercises

Near the end of this essay the author lists, as of 1937, the following topics that "were taboo from the white man's point of view": "American white women; the Ku Klux Klan; France, and how Negro soldiers fared while there; French women; Jack Johnson; the entire northern part of the United States; the Civil War; Abraham Lincoln; U. S. Grant; General Sherman; Catholics; the Pope; Jews; the Republican Party; slavery; social equality; Communism; Socialism; the 13th and 14th Amendments to the Constitution."

1. Is this true today and, if so, to what extent?
2. Are some topics no longer applicable and, if so, which ones? Why?
3. Are there any new topics?
4. In your conversations with another person who differs from you—race, religion, sex, nationality—do you find yourself avoiding certain topics? Which topics? Why?

Bibliography

Miller, Richard. *Bohemia: The Proto-Culture Then and Now.* Chicago: Nelson-Hall Publishers, 1970. From the Bohemians of 1830 through the beats, hippies, yippies, and so forth.

Our Twentieth-Century World, 1903–1969. Milestones of History, vol. VI. New York: Newsweek Books, 1970.

This Fabulous Century: Sixty Years of American Life. Alexandria, Va.: Time-Life Books, 1969, 1970. From 1870 to 1970 in eight volumes. Vivid overview.

28

Ideas and Conflicts That Motivate the Twentieth Century

Historical Overview, 1939–1980s

The Great Depression following the breakdown of economic systems was "cured" by the escalating production of weapons for war. England and France frantically, and belatedly, prepared for the resumption of hostilities with Germany in a war notably different from any other in mankind's interminable history of violence.

Soldiers fought in fields and pastures in the nineteenth century, in the trenches in 1914–1918, but in 1939–1945 the furious new battlefield described in the poem given below was the air itself. The bomber was the cost-efficient delivery system of World War II; targets included not only opposing armies but myriads of cities and their millions of inhabitants. Whether blasting Berlin and London, fire-bombing Dresden and Tokyo, or nuking Hiroshima and Nagasaki, civilian casualties vastly outnumbered those of the military, and warfare was total. The conflict between Eros and man's aggressive instincts, as described by Freud, seems canted towards the death wish. Mankind appears capable of limitless destruction until there is nothing left to destroy.

THE FURY OF AERIAL BOMBARDMENT
Richard Eberhart (1904—)

You would think the fury of aerial bombardment
Would rouse God to relent; the infinite spaces
Are still silent. He then looks on shock-pried faces
History, even, does not know what is meant.

You would feel that after so many centuries
God would give man to repent; yet he can kill
As Cain could, but with multitudinous will,
No farther advanced than in his ancient furies.

Was man made stupid to see his own stupidity?
Is God by definition indifferent, beyond us all?
Is the eternal truth man's fighting soul
Wherein the Beast ravens in its own avidity?

Of Van Wettering I speak, and Averill,
Names on a list, whose faces I do not recall
But they are gone to early death, who late in school
Distinguished the belt feed lever from the belt holding
pawl.

World War II ended on August 14, 1945, with the Japanese surrender, and the whole world expected a new era of peace and stability. The United States, with its nuclear monopoly and enormous industrial capacity, emerged as an unrivaled superpower; having learned some bitter lessons from the League of Nations, the United Nations began to function as the first real consortium of nations; with the assistance of the Marshall Plan, war-ravaged nations launched recovery programs that, in some cases, verged on the miraculous. The new era of peace and stability lasted four years, from 1945 to Russia's detonation of its own atomic bomb in 1949. The sharply reduced power of the Western European nations and the shambles of the old colonial order left a vacuum that was filled by the United States and Russia, now two superpowers who were engaged in a continued struggle for world dominance. Mutual nuclear deterrence, a "balance of terror," has kept nuclear weapons in their silos but so-called conventional wars abounded. If a major war is defined as one in which there are more than a thousand combatants, there have been about 100 major wars since 1945. African and Asian nationalism, endless Middle East crises, the wars in Korea and Vietnam, OPEC, the looming shadow of the People's Republic of China, the litany of the trials and tribulations of our era is endless and yet, somehow, the world blunders on short of Armageddon.

Since World War II the United States has become more democratic, but it hasn't been easy. The so-called Second Reconstruction in American history began in the late 1940s with presidential decrees that banned discrimination in federal jobs and ordered desegregation of the armed forces. The target of the first stage of the civil rights movement, segregation in public education was struck down by the landmark Supreme Court decision of 1954. Despite sometimes violent opposition the nation's schools were gradually integrated while, at the same time, other forms of discrimination were challenged with boycotts, sit-ins, and "freedom rides." Congress enacted, in 1957, the first civil rights legislation since 1865, followed by voting legislation in 1960, and, in 1964, by a comprehensive Civil Rights Act that banned discrimination on the basis of race, sex, nationality, or religion in public places, employment, and unions.

By 1965 the attack on segregation was essentially completed and stage two of the civil rights movement had begun. The rising demand was for equal opportunity, not only for jobs but in every area in American life. Mounting dissatisfaction with ghetto life, *de facto* segregation, and deteriorating urban environments fueled frustrations that writers like Langston Hughes early saw as unbearable. Hughes, the leading writer of the Harlem Renaissance, summed up the smoldering situation in 1951 with a prophetic eleven-line poem:

HARLEM
Langston Hughes (1902–1967)

What happens to a dream deferred?

    Does it dry up
    like a raisin in the sun?
    Or fester like a sore—
    And then run?   5
    Does it stink like rotten meat?
    Or crust and sugar over—
    like a syrupy sweet?

    Maybe it just sags
    like a heavy load.   10

    Or *does it explode?*

Harlem, Detroit, Watts, and other urban centers erupted in the 1960s and extreme violence did not subside until after 1969. Equal opportunity for many Blacks, Hispanics, Native Americans, and other minorities remains a "dream deferred."

During the two decades of civil rights activism other fundamental changes were beginning to quietly transform American life. Once a nation of farmers, the Industrial Revolution made laborers the dominant work force. By the mid 1950s, however, white-collar workers outnumbered blue-collar laborers and, by the early 1980s, the manufacturing work force had dwindled to about 13 percent and farmers to 3 percent of the working population. The United States had shifted from an industrial society to an information society based on high technology; computers, communication satellites, robots, and other electronic hardware and software herald what has been called the Age of Information, the Computer Age, the Communications Age. According to John Naisbitt[1] 75 percent of all jobs will involve computers in some way by about 1985. Smokestack industries like steel, textiles, and shipbuilding will continue to decline in the Western world as heavy industry expands in Third World countries. Alvin Toffler[2] predicts individualized entertainment and information services that will become available to everyone, and a whole new range of social, political, psychological, and religious adaptions throughout the Western world and around the Pacific Basin (Japan, Hong Kong, Singapore, Korea, Taiwan, Australia).

---

1. John Naisbitt, *Megatrends: Ten New Directions Transforming Our Lives* (New York: Warner Books, Inc., 1982).

2. Alvin Toffler, *The Third Wave* (New York: William Morrow and Co., 1980).

Literary Selection

The Accelerative Thrust, from FUTURE SHOCK

Alvin Toffler (b. 1928)

Not too many years ago children lived in a world not very different from that of their parents or grandparents. Information about the rest of the globe was confined to the printed word and technology was not even a word. The velocity of change was, metaphorically speaking, about ten miles an hour—the speed of a horse and buggy. In a society that was evolving almost imperceptibly, children tended to adopt the values, religion, and political party of their parents.

Today's world is so vastly different that comparisons boggle the mind. It has been estimated, for example, that our society has experienced more change during the past half-century than in all the preceding two or three million years. The acceleration of change appears to be the single most important influence on our lives. We can choose a philosophical, religious, or humanistic point of view (probably very different from that of our parents) but we can neither avoid nor deny the reality of a future that so insistently crowds upon the present.

During the late sixties Alvin Toffler wrote a book whose title, *Future Shock,* has become a metaphor for the frustrations and anxieties thrust on us by the onslaught of relentless change. Rather than trying to describe futuristic hardware, Toffler, in his book, is concerned with the "human side of tomorrow" and with the understandable reluctance of people to recognize and to accept the existence of what he calls the "accelerative thrust." Only after understanding current changes can we begin to cope—try to cope—with future shock. Future shock is even more of a problem now than in the late sixties, which is why a section from Toffler's still-timely book is reprinted here. On the other hand, as mentioned in the introduction, the shock of change may be replaced by the recognition of change as necessary and proper in a coming age in which process is the new reality.

Early in March, 1967, in eastern Canada, an eleven-year-old child died of old age.

Ricky Gallant was only eleven years old chronologically, but he suffered from an odd disease called progeria—advanced aging—and he exhibited many of the characteristics of a ninety-year-old person. The symptoms of progeria are senility, hardened arteries, baldness, slack, and wrinkled skin. In effect, Ricky was an old man when he died, a long lifetime of biological change having been packed into his eleven short years.

Cases of progeria are extremely rare. Yet in a metaphorical sense the high technology societies all suffer from this peculiar ailment. They are not growing old or senile. But they *are* experiencing super-normal rates of change.

Many of us have a vague "feeling" that things are moving faster. Doctors and executives alike complain that they cannot keep up with the latest developments in their fields. Hardly a meeting or conference takes place today without some ritualistic oratory about "the challenge of change." Among many there is an uneasy mood—a suspicion that change is out of control.

Not everyone, however, shares this anxiety. Millions sleepwalk their way through their lives as if nothing had changed since the 1930's, and as if nothing ever will. Living in what is certainly one of the most exciting periods in human history, they attempt to withdraw from it, to block it out, as if it were possible to make it go away by ignoring it. They seek a "separate peace," a diplomatic immunity from change.

One sees them everywhere: Old people, resigned to living out their years, attempting to avoid, at any cost, the intrusions of the new. Already-old people of thirty-five and forty-five, nervous about student riots, sex, LSD, or miniskirts, feverishly attempting to persuade themselves that, after all, youth was always rebellious, and that what is happening today is no different from the past. Even among the young we find an incomprehension of change: students so ignorant of the past that they see nothing unusual about the present.

The disturbing fact is that the vast majority of people, including educated and otherwise sophisticated people, find the idea of change so threatening that they attempt to deny its existence. Even many people who understand intellectually that change is accelerating, have not internalized that knowledge, do not take this critical social fact into account in planning their own personal lives.

Time and Change

How do we *know* that change is accelerating? There is, after all, no absolute way to measure change. In the awesome complexity of the universe, even within any given society, a virtually infinite number of streams of change occur simultaneously. All "things"—from the tiniest virus to the greatest galaxy—are, in reality, not things at all, but processes. There is no static point, no nirvana-like un-change, against which to measure change. Change is, therefore, necessarily relative.

It is also uneven. If all processes occurred at the same speed, or even if they accelerated or decelerated in unison, it would be impossible to observe change. The future, however, invades the present at differing speeds. Thus it becomes possible to compare the speed of different processes as they unfold. We know, for example, that compared with the biological evolution of the species, cultural and social evolution is extremely rapid. We know that some societies transform themselves technologically or economically more rapidly than others. We also know that different sectors within the same society exhibit different rates of change—the disparity that William Ogburn labeled "cultural lag." It is precisely the unevenness of change that makes it measurable.

We need, however, a yardstick that makes it possible to compare highly diverse processes, and this yardstick is time. Without time, change has no meaning. And without change, time would stop. Time can be conceived as the intervals during which events occur. Just as money permits us to place a value on both apples and oranges, time permits us to compare unlike processes. When we say that it takes three years to build a dam, we are really saying it takes three times as long as it takes the earth to circle the sun or 31,000,000 times as long as it takes to sharpen a pencil. Time is the currency of exchange that makes it possible to compare the rates at which very different processes play themselves out.

Given the unevenness of change and armed with this yardstick, we still face exhausting difficulties in measuring change. When we speak of the rate of change, we refer to the number of events crowded into an arbitrarily fixed interval of time. Thus we need to define the "events." We need to select our intervals with precision. We need to be careful about the conclusions we draw from the differences we observe. Moreover, in the measurement of change, we are today far more advanced with respect to physical processes than social processes. We know far better, for example, how to measure the rate at which blood flows through the body than the rate at which a rumor flows through society.

Even with all these qualifications, however, there is widespread agreement, reaching from historians and archaeologists all across the spectrum to scientists, sociologists, economists and psychologists, that, many social processes are speeding up—strikingly, even spectacularly.

Subterranean Cities

Painting with the broadest of brush strokes, biologist Julian Huxley informs us that "The tempo of human evolution during recorded history is at least 100,000 times as rapid as that of pre-human evolution." Inventions or improvements of a magnitude that took perhaps 50,000 years to accomplish during the early Paleolithic era were, he says, "run through in a mere millennium toward its close; and with the advent of settled civilization, the unit of change soon became reduced to the century." The rate of change, accelerating throughout the past 5000 years, has become, in his words, "particularly noticeable during the past 300 years."

C. P. Snow, the novelist and scientist, also comments on the new visibility of change. "Until this century . . ." he writes, social change was "so slow, that it would pass unnoticed in one person's lifetime. That is no longer so. The rate of change has increased so much that our imagination can't keep up." Indeed, says social psychologist Warren Bennis, the throttle has been pushed so far forward in recent years that "No exaggeration, no hyperbole, no outrage can realistically describe the extent and pace of change. . . . In fact, only the exaggerations appear to be true."

What changes justify such super-charged language? Let us look at a few—change in the process by which man forms cities, for example. We are now undergoing the most extensive and rapid urbanization the world has ever seen. In 1850 only four cities on the face of the earth had a population of 1,000,000 or more. By 1900 the number had increased to nineteen. But by 1960, there were 141, and today world urban population is rocketing upward at a rate of 6.5 percent per year, according to Edgar de Vries and J. P. Thysse of the Institute of Social Science in The Hague. This single stark statistic means a doubling of the earth's urban population within eleven years.

One way to grasp the meaning of change on so phenomenal a scale is to imagine what would happen if all existing cities, instead of expanding, retained their present size. If this were so, in order to accommodate the new urban millions we would have to build a duplicate

city for each of the hundreds that already dot the globe. A new Tokyo, a new Hamburg, a new Rome and Rangoon—and all within eleven years. (This explains why French urban planners are sketching subterranean cities—stores, museums, warehouses and factories to be built under the earth, and why a Japanese architect has blueprinted a city to be built on stilts out over the ocean.)

The same accelerative tendency is instantly apparent in man's consumption of energy. Dr. Homi Bhabha, the late Indian atomic scientist who chaired the first International Conference on the Peaceful Uses of Atomic Energy, once analyzed this trend. "To illustrate," he said, "let us use the letter 'Q' to stand for the energy derived from burning some 33,000 million tons of coal. In the eighteen and one half centuries after Christ, the total energy consumed averaged less than one half Q per century. But by 1850, the rate had risen to one Q per century. Today, the rate is about ten Q per century." This means, roughly speaking, that half of all the energy consumed by man in the past 2,000 years has been consumed in the last one hundred.

Also dramatically evident is the acceleration of economic growth in the nations now racing toward super-industrialism. Despite the fact that they start from a large industrial base, the annual percentage increases in production in these countries are formidable. And the rate of increase is itself increasing.

In France, for example, in the twenty-nine years between 1910 and the outbreak of the second world war, industrial production rose only 5 percent. Yet between 1948 and 1965, in only seventeen years, it increased by roughly 220 percent. Today growth rates of from 5 to 10 percent per year are not uncommon among the most industrialized nations. There are ups and downs, of course. But the direction of change has been unmistakable.

Thus for the twenty-one countries belonging to the Organization for Economic Cooperation and Development—by and large, the "have" nations—the average annual rate of increase in gross national product in the years 1960–1968 ran between 4.5 and 5.0 percent. The United States grew at a rate of 4.5 percent, and Japan led the rest with annual increases averaging 9.8 percent.

What such numbers imply is nothing less revolutionary than a doubling of the total output of goods and services in the advanced societies about every fifteen years—and the doubling times are shrinking. This means, generally speaking, that the child reaching teen age in any of these societies is literally surrounded by twice as much of everything newly man-made as his parents were at the time he was an infant. It means that by the time today's teen-ager reaches age thirty, perhaps earlier, a second doubling will have occurred. Within a seventy-year lifetime, perhaps five such doublings will take place—meaning, since the increases are compounded, that by the time the individual reaches old age the society around him will be producing thirty-two times as much as when he was born.

Such changes in the ratio between old and new have, as we shall show, an electric impact on the habits, beliefs, and self-image of millions. Never in previous history has this ratio been transformed so radically in so brief a flick of time.

The Technological Engine

Behind such prodigious economic facts lies that great, growling engine of change—technology. This is not to say that technology is the only source of change in society. Social upheavals can be touched off by a change in the chemical composition of the atmosphere, by alterations in climate, by changes in fertility, and many other factors. Yet technology is indisputably a major force behind the accelerative thrust.

To most people, the term technology conjures up images of smoky steel mills or clanking machines. Perhaps the classic symbol of technology is still the assembly line created by Henry Ford half a century ago and made into a potent social icon by Charlie Chaplin in *Modern Times*. This symbol, however, has always been inadequate, indeed, misleading, for technology has always been more than factories and machines. The invention of the horse collar in the middle ages led to major changes in agricultural methods and was as much a technological advance as the invention of the Bessemer furnace centuries later. Moreover, technology includes techniques, as well as the machines that may or may not be necessary to apply them. It includes ways to make chemical reactions occur, ways to breed fish, plant forests, light theaters, count votes or teach history.

The old symbols of technology are even more misleading today, when the most advanced technological processes are carried out far from assembly lines or open hearths. Indeed, in electronics, in space technology, in most of the new industries, relative silence and clean surroundings are characteristic—even sometimes essential. And the assembly line—the organization of armies of men to carry out simple repetitive functions—is an anachronism. It is time for our symbols of technology to change—to catch up with the quickening changes in technology, itself.

This acceleration is frequently dramatized by a thumbnail account of the progress in transportation. It has been pointed out, for example, that in 6000 B.C. the fastest transportation available to man over long distances was the camel caravan, averaging eight miles per hour. It was not until about 1600 B.C. when the chariot was invented that the maximum speed was raised to roughly twenty miles per hour.

So impressive was this invention, so difficult was it to exceed this speed limit, that nearly 3,500 years later, when the first mail coach began operating in England in 1784, it averaged a mere ten mph. The first steam locomotive, introduced in 1825, could muster a top speed of only thirteen mph, and the great sailing ships of the time labored along at less than half that speed. It was probably not until the 1880's that man, with the help of a more advanced steam locomotive, managed to reach a speed of one hundred mph. It took the human race millions of years to attain that record.

It took only fifty-eight years, however, to quadruple the limit, so that by 1938 airborne man was cracking the 400-mph line. It took a mere twenty-year flick of time to double the limit again. And by the 1960's rocket planes approached speeds of 4000 mph, and men in space capsules were circling the earth at 18,000 mph. Plotted on a graph, the line representing progress in the past generation would leap vertically off the page.

Whether we examine distances traveled, altitudes reached, minerals mined, or explosive power harnessed, the same accelerative trend is obvious. The pattern, here and in a thousand other statistical series, is absolutely clear and unmistakable. Millennia or centuries go by, and then, in our own times, a sudden bursting of the limits, a fantastic spurt forward.

The reason for this is that technology feeds on itself. Technology makes more technology possible, as we can see if we look for a moment at the process of innovation. Technological innovation consists of three stages, linked together into a self-reinforcing cycle. First, there is the creative, feasible idea. Second, its practical application. Third, its diffusion through society.

The process is completed, the loop closed, when the diffusion of technology embodying the new idea, in turn, helps generate new creative ideas. Today there is evidence that the time between each of the steps in this cycle has been shortened.

Thus it is not merely true, as frequently noted, that 90 percent of all the scientists who ever lived are now alive, and that new scientific discoveries are being made every day. These new ideas are put to work much more quickly than ever before. The time between original concept and practical use has been radically reduced. This is a striking difference between ourselves and our ancestors. Appollonius of Perga discovered conic sections, but it was 2000 years before they were applied to engineering problems. It was literally centuries between the time Paracelsus discovered that ether could be used as an anaesthetic and the time it began to be used for that purpose.

Even in more recent times the same pattern of delay was present. In 1836 a machine was invented that mowed, threshed, tied straw into sheaves and poured grain into sacks. This machine was itself based on technology at least twenty years old at the time. Yet it was not until a century later, in the 1930's, that such a combine was actually marketed. The first English patent for a typewriter was issued in 1714. But a century and a half elapsed before typewriters became commercially available. A full century passed between the time Nicholas Appert discovered how to can food and the time canning became important in the food industry.

Today such delays between idea and application are almost unthinkable. It is not that we are more eager or less lazy than our ancestors, but we have, with the passage of time, invented all sorts of social devices to hasten the process. Thus we find that the time between the first and second stages of the innovative cycle—between idea and application—has been cut radically. Frank Lynn, for example, in studying twenty major innovations, such as frozen food, antibiotics, integrated circuits and synthetic leather, found that since the beginning of this century more than sixty percent has been slashed from the average time needed for a major scientific discovery to be translated into a useful technological form. Today a vast and growing research and development industry is consciously working to reduce the lag still further.

But if it takes less time to bring a new idea to the marketplace, it also takes less time for it to sweep through the society. Thus the interval between the second and third stages of the cycle—between application and diffusion—has likewise been sliced, and the pace of diffusion is rising with astonishing speed. This is borne out by the history of several familiar household appliances. Robert B. Young at the Stanford Research

Institute has studied the span of time between the first commercial appearance of a new electrical appliance and the time the industry manufacturing it reaches peak production of the item.

Young found that for a group of appliances introduced in the United States before 1920—including the vacuum cleaner, the electric range, and the refrigerator—the average span between introduction and peak production was thirty-four years. But for a group that appeared in the 1939–1959 period—including the electric frying pan, television, and washer-dryer combination—the span was only eight years. The lag had shrunk by more than 76 percent. "The post-war group," Young declared, "demonstrated vividly the rapidly accelerating nature of the modern cycle."

The stepped-up pace of invention, exploitation, and diffusion, in turn, accelerates the whole cycle still further. For new machines or techniques are not merely a product, but a source, of fresh creative ideas.

Each new machine or technique, in a sense, changes all existing machines and techniques, by permitting us to put them together into new combinations. The number of possible combinations rises exponentially as the number of new machines or techniques rises arithmetically. Indeed, each new combination may, itself, be regarded as a new super-machine.

The computer, for example, made possible a sophisticated space effort. Linked with sensing devices, communications equipment, and power sources, the computer became part of a configuration that in aggregate forms a single new super-machine—a machine for reaching into and probing outer space. But for machines or techniques to be combined in new ways, they have to be altered, adapted, refined or otherwise changed. So that the very effort to integrate machines into super-machines compels us to make still further technological innovations.

It is vital to understand, moreover, that technological innovation does not merely combine and recombine machines and techniques. Important new machines do more than suggest or compel changes in other machines—they suggest novel solutions to social, philosophical, even personal problems. They alter man's total intellectual environment—the way he thinks and looks at the world.

We all learn from our environment, scanning it constantly—though perhaps unconsciously—for models to emulate. These models are not only other people. They are, increasingly, machines. By their presence, we are subtly conditioned to think along certain lines. It has been observed, for example, that the clock came along before the Newtonian image of the world as a great clock-like mechanism, a philosophical notion that has had the utmost impact on man's intellectual development. Implied in this image of the cosmos as a great clock were ideas about cause and effect and about the importance of external, as against internal, stimuli, that shape the everyday behavior of all of us today. The clock also affected our conception of time so that the idea that a day is divided into twenty-four equal segments of sixty minutes each has become almost literally a part of us.

Recently, the computer has touched off a storm of fresh ideas about man as an interacting part of larger systems, about his physiology, the way he learns, the way he remembers, the way he makes decisions. Virtually every intellectual discipline from political science to family psychology has been hit by a wave of imaginative

hypotheses triggered by the invention and diffusion of the computer—and its full impact has not yet struck. And so the innovative cycle, feeding on itself, speeds up.

If technology, however, is to be regarded as a great engine, a mighty accelerator, then knowledge must be regarded as its fuel. And we thus come to the crux of the accelerative process in society, for the engine is being fed a richer and richer fuel every day.

Knowledge as Fuel

The rate at which man has been storing up useful knowledge about himself and the universe has been spiraling upward for 10,000 years. The rate took a sharp upward leap with the invention of writing, but even so it remained painfully slow over centuries of time. The next great leap forward in knowledge-acquisition did not occur until the invention of movable type in the fifteenth century by Gutenberg and others. Prior to 1500, by the most optimistic estimates, Europe was producing books at a rate of 1000 titles per year. This means, give or take a bit, that it would take a full century to produce a library of 100,000 titles. By 1950, four and a half centuries later, the rate had accelerated so sharply that Europe was producing 120,000 titles a year. What once took a century now took only ten months. By 1960, a single decade later, the rate had made another significant jump, so that a century's work could be completed in seven and a half months. And, by the mid-sixties, the output of books on a world scale, Europe included, approached the prodigious figure of 1000 titles per *day*.

One can hardly argue that every book is a net gain for the advancement of knowledge. Nevertheless, we find that the accelerative curve in book publication does, in fact, crudely parallel the rate at which man discovered new knowledge. For example, prior to Gutenberg only 11 chemical elements were known. Antimony, the 12th, was discovered at about the time he was working on his invention. It was fully 200 years since the 11th, arsenic, had been discovered. Had the same rate of discovery continued, we would by now have added only two or three additional elements to the periodic table since Gutenberg. Instead, in the 450 years after his time, some seventy additional elements were discovered. And since 1900 we have been isolating the remaining elements not at a rate of one every two centuries, but of one every three years.

Furthermore, there is reason to believe that the rate is still rising sharply. Today, for example, the number of scientific journals and articles is doubling, like industrial production in the advanced countries, about every fifteen years, and according to biochemist Philip Siekevitz, "what has been learned in the last three decades about the nature of living beings dwarfs in extent of knowledge any comparable period of scientific discovery in the history of mankind." Today the United States government alone generates 100,000 reports each year, plus 450,000 articles, books and papers. On a worldwide basis, scientific and technical literature mounts at a rate of some 60,000,000 pages a year.

The computer burst upon the scene around 1950. With its unprecedented power for analysis and dissemination of extremely varied kinds of data in unbelievable quantities and at mindstaggering speeds, it has become a major force behind the latest acceleration in knowledge acquisition. Combined with other increasingly powerful analytical tools for observing the invisible universe around us, it has raised the rate of knowledge acquisition to dumbfounding speeds.

Francis Bacon told us that "Knowledge . . . is power." This can now be translated into contemporary terms. In our social setting, "Knowledge is change"—and accelerating knowledge-acquisition, fueling the great engine of technology, means accelerating change.

The Flow of Situations

Discovery. Application. Impact. Discovery. We see here a chain reaction of change, a long, sharply rising curve of acceleration in human social development. This accelerative thrust has now reached a level at which it can no longer, by any stretch of the imagination, be regarded as "normal." The normal institutions of industrial society can no longer contain it, and its impact is shaking up all our social institutions. Acceleration is one of the most important and least understood of all social forces.

This, however, is only half the story. For the speed-up of change is a psychological force as well. Although it has been almost totally ignored by psychology, the rising rate of change in the world around us disturbs our inner equilibrium, altering the very way in which we experience life. Acceleration without translates into acceleration within.

This can be illustrated, though in a highly oversimplified fashion, if we think of an individual life as a great channel through which experience flows. This flow of experience consists—or is conceived of consisting—of innumerable "situations." Acceleration of change in the surrounding society drastically alters the flow of situations through this channel.

There is no neat definition of a situation, yet we would find it impossible to cope with experience if we did not mentally cut it up into these manageable units. Moreover, while the boundary lines between situations may be indistinct, every situation has a certain "wholeness" about it, a certain integration.

Every situation also has certain identifiable components. These include "things"—a physical setting of natural or man-made objects. Every situation occurs in a "place"—a location or arena within which the action occurs. (It is not accidental that the Latin root "situ" means place.) Every social situation also has, by definition, a cast of characters—people. Situations also involve a location in the organizational network of society and a context of ideas or information. Any situation can be analyzed in terms of these five components.

But situations also involve a separate dimension which, because it cuts across all the others, is frequently overlooked. This is duration—the span of time over which the situation occurs. Two situations alike in all other respects are not the same at all if one lasts longer than another. For time enters into the mix in a crucial way, changing the meaning or content of situations. Just as the funeral march played at too high a speed becomes a merry tinkle of sounds, so a situation that is dragged out has a distinctly different flavor or meaning than one that strikes us in staccato fashion, erupting suddenly and subsiding as quickly.

Here, then, is the first delicate point at which the accelerative thrust in the larger society crashes up against the ordinary daily experience of the contemporary individual. For the acceleration of change, as we shall show, shortens the duration of many situations. This not only drastically alters their "flavor," but hastens their passage through the experiential channel. Compared with life in a less rapidly changing society, more situations now flow through the channel in any given interval of time—and this implies profound changes in human psychology.

For while we tend to focus on only one situation at a time, the increased rate at which situations flow past us vastly complicates the entire structure of life, multiplying the number of roles we must play and the number of choices we are forced to make. This, in turn, accounts for the choking sense of complexity about contemporary life.

Moreover, the speeded-up flow-through of situations demands much more work from the complex focusing mechanisms by which we shift our attention from one situation to another. There is more switching back and forth, less time for extended, peaceful attention to one problem or situation at a time. This is what lies behind the vague feeling noted earlier that "Things are moving faster." They are. Around us. And through us.

There is, however, still another, even more powerfully significant way in which the acceleration of change in society increases the difficulty of coping with life. This stems from the fantastic intrusion of novelty, newness into our existence. Each situation is unique. But situations often resemble one another. This, in fact, is what makes it possible to learn from experience. If each situation were wholly novel, without some resemblance to previously experienced situations, our ability to cope would be hopelessly crippled.

The acceleration of change, however, radically alters the balance between novel and familiar situations. Rising rates of change thus compel us not merely to cope with a faster flow, but with more and more situations to which previous personal experience does not apply. And the psychological implications of this simple fact, which we shall explore later in this book, are nothing short of explosive.

"When things start changing outside, you are going to have a parallel change taking place inside," says Christopher Wright of the Institute for the Study of Science and Human Affairs. The nature of these inner changes is so profound, however, that, as the accelerative thrust picks up speed, it will test our ability to live within the parameters that have until now defined man and society. In the words of psychoanalyst Erik Erikson, "In our society at present, the 'natural course of events' is precisely that the rate of change should continue to accelerate up to the as-yet-unreached limits of human and institutional adaptability."

To survive, to avert what we have termed future shock, the individual must become infinitely more adaptable and capable than ever before. He must search out totally new ways to anchor himself, for all the old roots—religion, nation, community, family, or profession—are now shaking under the hurricane impact of the accelerative thrust. Before he can do so, however, he must understand in greater detail how the effects of acceleration penetrate his personal life, creep into his behavior and alter the quality of existence. He must, in other words, understand transience.

Exercises

1. Toffler implies that millions of people are neither aware nor concerned about future shock. Why is it so important to be able to understand the nature and rate of change? How can concerns about the future make your life more rewarding and perhaps more interesting?

2. Select a contemporary product or process and trace the rapidity of change from initiation to current status. Subjects might include, for example, the space shuttle, robotics, communication satellites, the increases in memory capacity and speed of computers, and so forth.

3. Try being your own futurist. Select, say, the year 2001 and predict the characteristics of a city: appearance, design, transportation, communications, economics, government, taxes, education, work opportunities, leisure activities, etc. You should study each area in terms of past development, trying to determine whether any area will be improved or refined or whether certain aspects will call for new inventions. You should check with the readings given below.

Suggested Reading

The world is moving so fast that books are partially outdated by the time they appear in print. (In fact, print publishing may be becoming obsolete.) Instead, we are recommending several magazines which are devoted to future studies.

Next Magazine. Next Press. 703 Third Avenue. New York, NY 10017.

Futures, The Journal of Forecasting and Planning. IPC Business Press Ltd. Oakfield House. Perrymount Road. Haywards Heath, Sussex, RH16 3DH, England.

Futuribles. Analyse, Prévision, Prospective. Revue mensuelle de l'Association Internationale Futuribles. 55 rue de Varenne, 75007 Paris, France.

The Futurist. World Future Society. Post Office Box 30369. Bethesda Branch, Washington, D.C., 20014.

Developing technology tends to follow a line of least resistance. The first book printed with movable type, the Gutenberg Bible, looked like a handwritten manuscript. The first automobiles were called "horseless carriages" because they were indeed carriages with motors. Computer technology first followed two general lines of development: nonthreatening games that tend to make computers "user friendly" and improvements in existing technology like, for example, the word processor. Still to come is a third line of development. No one can really predict the different directions that computers will take except to say that, inevitably, there will be startling new applications of computer technology.

Einstein gave us new conceptions of space, and the age of computers and telecommunications has forced us to recognize space as a concept connected by electronics and not just as a physical reality connected by interstate highways. Telecommunication conferences with participants sitting at video consoles in London, Paris, Rome, and New York are old hat and this is only the beginning. The world has shrunk to a global village. No one can say what the globalization of culture will lead to but the prognosis can be optimistic. The possibility of instantaneous close contact with people and their institutions can lead to closer human ties than at any time in human history.

Philosophy

Probably every philosophical system ever invented has surfaced at one time or another during this troubled century. One of the most influential of these philosophies, existentialism, is more of a mood or attitude than a complete philosophical system. Formulated during World War II by French writer Jean Paul Sartre during his years with the French Resistance, existentialism had an immediate appeal for a desperate world. Actually, the roots of the movement go back to several disparate personalities of the nineteenth century, particularly Kierkegaard, a Danish anticlerical theologian, and Nietzsche, a German atheist.

Friedrich Nietzsche (NEE-chuh; 1844–1900) stressed the absurdity of human existence and the inability of our reason to understand the world. Himself a passionate individualist, Nietzsche proclaimed the will to power as the only value in the face of a meaningless world. He rejected any ideas or system that would limit the freedom of the individual, particularly Christianity, which taught, he contended, a "slave morality" of sympathy, kindness, humility, and pity, qualities beneficial only to the weak and the helpless. His "noble" man was a superman, an incarnate will to power, who would rise above the herd, the "bungled and the botched," to establish a "master morality" of aristocratic qualities like strength, nobility, pride, and power. "God is dead," Nietzsche proclaimed, meaning that all absolute systems from Plato onwards had died with the God of the Judeo-Christian tradition.

A fervent admirer of the culture of ancient Greece, Nietzsche evolved an influential aesthetic theory of the Apollonian and Dionysian modes. The Apollonian mode is intellectual. It draws an aesthetic veil over reality, creating an ideal world of form and beauty. The Apollonian found expression in Greek mythology, in Homer's epic poems, in sculpture, painting, architecture, and Greek vases.

The Dionysian, somewhat like Freud's id, is the dark, turgid, and formless torrent of instinct, impulse, and passion that tends to sweep aside everything in its path. Tragedy and music are typical Dionysian art forms that transmute existence into aesthetic phenomena without, however, drawing a veil over authentic existence. The Dionysian represents existence in aesthetic form and affirms this, says Nietzsche, in the human condition. True culture, for Nietzsche, was a unity of life forces, the dark Dionysian element combined with the love of form and beauty that characterizes the Apollonian. The highest product of this balanced culture is the creative genius, the superman.

Adolf Hitler drew on Nietzsche's purported work, *The Will to Power,* for key ideas about German superiority, the Master Race (Nietzsche's superman), and anti-Semitism. Scholars finally proved, by 1958, that Nietzsche did not write *The Will to Power.* After his death, Nietzsche's proto-Nazi sister combined his notebook jottings with thirty forged letters and other fabrications to publish the volume in her brother's name. Actually, Nietzsche was more anti- than pro-German, referring to Germans as "blond beasts of prey" and casting scorn on "their repulsive habit of stimulating themselves with alcohol." Far from a racist, Nietzsche saw all the races on the globe blending into a uniform color of beige and he called anti-Semites "another name for failures."

The basic theme of Nietzsche's life and thought was the antipolitical individual who sought self-perfection far from the modern world. His desire was "to live for one's education free from politics, nationality, and newspapers." For him, knowledge was power and the will to power was the use of education for the betterment of humankind. "Above all," he said, "become who you are!"

A melancholy and lonely Dane, Soren Kierkegaard (KEER–kuh–gard; 1813–1855) was almost totally unnoticed in his own time, even more so than Nietzsche. Kierkegaard's concern, like that of Nietzsche, was with the individual, whom he saw as an actor on the stage of life. For each individual there was, according to Kierkegaard, the possibility of three ascending levels of existence along life's way: aesthetic, ethical, and religious. The aesthetic level was that of the pleasure seeker, and the only goals were newer pleasant sensations. Eventually, the futile pursuit of pleasure ends in despair and life is absurd. The only way to rise above the aesthetic level is to recognize the reality of choice.

The second level is that of the ethical, which does not eliminate the aesthetic mode but rises above it. The ethical life is not, however, the same as advocating abstract ethical theories; one can know about ethical theories and still be an unethical slob. The ethical person, for Kierkegaard, is actively committed to long-range purposes, dedicated to the continuity of life, free to choose and be bound to a commitment. Choice is a necessity in the ethical life and, Kierkegaard says, the only absolutely ethical choice is between good and evil. But, this is not enough. We are virtually helpless in facing the evils and injustices of everyday life; these evils can be overcome only by an outpouring of love and generosity beyond human justice and human powers. Such love and generosity is possible only if something transcending us breaks into history and works in our lives. Kierkegaard believed that the breakthrough of the eternal into history had happened with the birth of Christ.

To recapitulate: after the vain pursuit of pleasure we feel despair; through choice we can raise ourselves to the ethical level and become committed to our responsibilities but this eventually proves insufficient, we become a "knight of infinite resignation." At this point we can choose to leap beyond reason to the religious mode of existence using the passion called faith ("where reason ends there begins faith").

Faith, for Kierkegaard, means total commitment to the inner personality of God. We cannot cleverly argue our way to God; we either accept God completely or reject Him completely. The second and final leap of faith is into the arms of Jesus. However, Kierkegaard says, this leap to the God-man of Christian history is conceptually absurd. The intensity of the leap of faith to God is vastly increased by the second venture to the level of Christianity, which is unintelligible. As Kierkegaard wrote, "In an unpermissible and unlawful way people have become *knowing* about Christ, for the only permissible way is to be *believing.*"

These absolute ventures are total personal decisions taken in absolute loneliness with the utmost responsibility. The isolation of the individual in such a decision is absolute and this, says Kierkegaard, is what it means to be a human being. These leaps of faith make an existing individual. Speculative philosophy, according to Kierkegaard, plus the Christian establishment and the press had confused basic facts: "Christendom has done away with Christianity without being quite aware of it."

Values, for Kierkegaard, were not esoteric essences: "Good and evil are ways of existing and the human good is to exist authentically." Conversely, evil is an unauthentic, ungenuine existence. Authentic existence is a matter of choice and the existing person knows the risk and feels the dread of individual responsibility. But, as Kierkegaard observed, "dread is the possibility of freedom" and "man is condemned to freedom."

Kierkegaard was a theistic existentialist; Jean Paul Sartre (SAR–truh; 1905–1980) was an atheistic existentialist. Kierkegaard made two leaps of faith: to God and then to the God-man of Christian history. Sartre, on the other hand, contended that the idea of God was self-contradictory, that the man called Christ could not be both divine and human because the terms are mutually exclusive. In other words, said Sartre, divine means nonhuman and human means that which is not divine. You cannot draw a circular square or a square circle. And, if there is no God, there are no fixed values, no absolute right or wrong or good or bad. In *The Brothers Karamazov* Dostoevsky has one of his characters say, "But you see, if there were no God, everything would be possible." And that is precisely Sartre's point, that human beings are the sole source of values and anything is possible.

Sartre's basic premise was that existence precedes essence. First, a person *is;* what he or she becomes is settled in the course of existence. For the existentialist things in the world just *are;* only human beings can create themselves. Liberty is unrestricted, our capacity for choice is unrestricted, and making choices is what makes us human. The only meaning that life has is in the meaning of the values that we choose. Values are not waiting to be discovered; we invent values. To the question "What meaning is there in life?" the existentialist replies, "only what you put into life." But, as Sartre warns, the exercise of freedom is inseparably linked with responsibility:

> Man is condemned to be free; because once thrown into the world, man is responsible for everything he does.

You can never choose anything, wrote Sartre, without realizing that this is the choice you wish all humankind to make. If you choose truth then you want everyone to be truthful; if you choose to steal then you are willing that everyone should be a thief. In every choice you have chosen for all humankind, a crushing responsibility, a condition that Sartre calls *anguish.*

What are the values for which the existentialist is willing to assume responsibility? The answer has a curiously old-fashioned ring: the values are those of individualism; value is *in* the individual; value *is* the individual. The supreme virtue is responsible choice, what we call integrity, and the ultimate vice is self-deception. The Greeks said that we should "know thyself" and the existentialist fervently agrees. What you choose determines what you will become but, Sartre emphasizes, you can change, you can redirect your steps. What gives meaning to life is not what *happens* to us but what we ourselves *do*. We are actors on the stage of life. As Sartre said: "Man is encompassed by his own existence and there is no exit." In 1947 Sartre wrote in *Existentialism:*

> Existentialism is nothing less than an attempt to draw all the consequences of a coherent atheistic position. It isn't trying to plunge man into despair at all. But if one calls every attitude of unbelief despair, like the Christian, then the word is not being used in its original sense. Existentialism isn't so atheistic that it wears itself out showing that God doesn't exist. Rather, it declares that even if God did exist, that would change nothing. There you've got our point of view. Not that we believe that God exists, but we think the problem of his existence is not the issue. In this sense existentialism is optimistic, a doctrine of action, and it is plain dishonesty for Christians to make no distinction between their own despair and ours and then to call us despairing.

Existentialism owes its popularity in no small part to repeated failures in politics, economics, and social organizations that have scarred our century. Whatever shortcomings the movement may have, it is not just a body of philosophical speculations but an attitude that helps a great many people in this muddled world to pursue a personal freedom, a way of life that seeks quality rather than quantity.

Literary Selections

The following works highlight just a few of the problems of our troubled century.

THE WALL
Jean Paul Sartre (1905–1980)

In this classic existential short story Sartre stresses the following themes: mindless brutality (representing the indifferent universe), the absence of values or meaning (life has only as much meaning as we ourselves choose to provide), and loneliness (we lead a solitary existence and we die alone). Life is depicted as meaningless and absurd throughout the story, climaxing in the ultimate absurdity on the last page. That the protagonist is a Communist and that the setting is the Spanish Civil War is incidental; the narrator could be on either side of any war.

They pushed us into a big white room and I began to blink because the light hurt my eyes. Then I saw a table and four men behind the table, civilians, looking over the papers. They had bunched another group of prisoners in the back and we had to cross the whole room to join them. There were several I knew and some others who must have been foreigners. The two in front of me were blond with round skulls; they looked alike. I supposed they were French. The smaller one kept hitching up his pants; nerves.

It lasted about three hours; I was dizzy and my head was empty; but the room was well heated and I found that pleasant enough: for the past 24 hours we hadn't stopped shivering. The guards brought the prisoners up to the table, one after the other. The four men asked each one his name and occupation. Most of the time they didn't go any further—or they would simply ask a question here and there: "Did you have anything to do with the sabotage of munitions?" Or "Where were you the morning of the 9th and what were you doing?" They didn't listen to the answers or at least didn't seem to. They were quiet for a moment and then looking straight in front of them began to write. They asked Tom if it were true he was in the International Brigade; Tom couldn't tell them otherwise because of the papers they found in his coat. They didn't ask Juan anything but they wrote for a long time after he told them his name.

"My brother José is the anarchist," Juan said, "you know he isn't here any more. I don't belong to any party, I never had anything to do with politics."

They didn't answer. Juan went on, "I haven't done anything. I don't want to pay for somebody else."

His lips trembled. A guard shut him up and took him away. It was my turn.

"Your name is Pablo Ibbieta?"

"Yes."

The man looked at the papers and asked me, "Where's Ramon Gris?"

"I don't know."

"You hid him in your house from the 6th to the 19th."

"No."

They wrote for a minute and then the guards took me out. In the corridor Tom and Juan were waiting between two guards. We started walking. Tom asked one of the guards, "So?"

"So what?" the guard said.

"Was that the cross-examination or the sentence?"

"Sentence," the guard said.

"What are they going to do with us?"

The guard answered dryly, "Sentence will be read in your cell."

As a matter of fact, our cell was one of the hospital cellars. It was terrifically cold there because of the drafts. We shivered all night and it wasn't much better during the day. I had spent the previous five days in a cell in a monastery, a sort of hole in the wall that must have dated from the middle ages: since there were a lot of prisoners and not much room, they locked us up anywhere. I didn't miss my cell; I hadn't suffered too much from the cold but I was alone; after a long time it gets irritating. In the cellar I had company. Juan hardly ever spoke: he was afraid and he was too young to have anything to say. But Tom was a good talker and he knew Spanish well.

There was a bench in the cellar and four mats. When they took us back we sat and waited in silence. After a long moment, Tom said, "We're screwed."

"I think so too," I said, "but I don't think they'll do anything to the kid."

"They don't have a thing against him," said Tom. "He's the brother of a militiaman and that's all."

I looked at Juan: he didn't seem to hear. Tom went on, "You know what they do in Saragossa? They lay the men down on the road and run over them with trucks. A Moroccan deserter told us that. They said it was to save ammunition."

"It doesn't save gas," I said.

I was annoyed at Tom: he shouldn't have said that.

"Then there's officers walking along the road," he went on, "supervising it all. They stick their hands in their pockets and smoke cigarettes. You think they finish off the guys? Hell no. They let them scream. Sometimes for an hour. The Moroccan said he damned near puked the first time."

"I don't believe they'll do that here," I said. "Unless they're really short on ammunition."

Day was coming in through four airholes and a round opening they had made in the ceiling on the left, and you could see the sky through it. Through this hole, usually closed by a trap, they unloaded coal into the cellar. Just below the hole there was a big pile of coal dust; it had been used to heat the hospital, but since the beginning of the war the patients were evacuated and the coal stayed there, unused; sometimes it even got rained on because they had forgotten to close the trap.

Tom began to shiver. "Good Jesus Christ, I'm cold," he said. "Here it goes again."

He got up and began to do exercises. At each movement his shirt opened on his chest, white and hairy. He lay on his back, raised his legs in the air and bicycled.

I saw his great rump trembling. Tom was husky but he had too much fat. I thought how rifle bullets or the sharp points of bayonets would soon be sunk into this mass of tender flesh as in a lump of butter. It wouldn't have made me feel like that if he'd been thin.

I wasn't exactly cold, but I couldn't feel my arms and shoulders any more. Sometimes I had the impression I was missing something and began to look around for my coat and then suddenly remembered they hadn't given me a coat. It was rather uncomfortable. They took our clothes and gave them to their soldiers leaving us only our shirts—and those canvas pants that hospital patients wear in the middle of summer. After a while Tom got up and sat next to me, breathing heavily.

"Warmer?"

"Good Christ, no. But I'm out of wind."

Around eight o'clock in the evening a major came in with two *falangistas*. He had a sheet of paper in his hand. He asked the guard, "What are the names of those three?"

"Steinbock, Ibbieta and Mirbal," the guard said.

The major put on his eyeglasses and scanned the list: "Steinbock . . . Steinbock . . . Oh yes . . . You are sentenced to death. You will be shot tomorrow morning." He went on looking. "The other two as well."

"That's not possible," Juan said. "Not me."

The major looked at him amazed. "What's your name?"

"Juan Mirbal," he said.

"Well, your name is there," said the major. "You're sentenced."

"I didn't do anything," Juan said.

The major shrugged his shoulders and turned to Tom and me.

"You're Basque?"

"Nobody is Basque."

He looked annoyed. "They told me there were three Basques. I'm not going to waste my time running after them. Then naturally you don't want a priest?"

We didn't even answer.

He said, "A Belgian doctor is coming shortly. He is authorized to spend the night with you." He made a military salute and left.

"What did I tell you," Tom said. "We get it."

"Yes," I said, "it's a rotten deal for the kid."

I said that to be decent but I didn't like the kid. His face was too thin and fear and suffering had disfigured it, twisting all his features. Three days before he was a smart sort of kid, not too bad; but now he looked like an old fairy and I thought how he'd never be young again, even if they were to let him go. It wouldn't have been too hard to have a little pity for him but pity disgusts me, or rather it horrifies me. He hadn't said anything more but he had turned grey; his face and hands were both grey. He sat down again and looked at the ground with round eyes. Tom was good hearted, he wanted to take his arm, but the kid tore himself away violently and made a face.

"Let him alone," I said in a low voice, "you can see he's going to blubber."

Tom obeyed regretfully; he would have liked to comfort the kid, it would have passed his time and he wouldn't have been tempted to think about himself. But it annoyed me: I'd never thought about death because I never had any reason to, but now the reason was here and there was nothing to do but think about it.

Tom began to talk. "So you think you've knocked guys off, do you?" he asked me. I didn't answer. He began explaining to me that he had knocked off six since the beginning of August; he didn't realize the situation and I could tell he didn't *want* to realize it. I hadn't quite realized it myself, I wondered if it hurt much, I thought of bullets, I imagined their burning hail through my body. All that was beside the real question; but I was calm: we had all night to understand. After a while Tom stopped talking and I watched him out of the corner of my eye; I saw he too had turned grey and he looked rotten; I told myself "Now it starts." It was almost dark, a dim glow filtered through the airholes and the pile of coal and made a big stain beneath the spot of sky; I could already see a star through the hole in the ceiling: the night would be pure and icy.

The door opened and two guards came in, followed by a blonde man in a tan uniform. He saluted us. "I am the doctor," he said. "I have authorization to help you in these trying hours."

He had an agreeable and distinguished voice. I said, "What do you want here?"

"I am at your disposal. I shall do all I can to make your last moments less difficult."

"What did you come here for? There are others, the hospital's full of them."

"I was sent here," he answered with a vague look. "Ah! Would you like to smoke?" he added hurriedly, "I have cigarettes and even cigars."

He offered us English cigarettes and *puros,* but we refused. I looked him in the eyes and he seemed irritated. I said to him, "You aren't here on an errand of mercy. Besides, I know you. I saw you with the fascists in the barracks yard the day I was arrested."

I was going to continue, but something surprising suddenly happened to me; the presence of this doctor no longer interested me. Generally when I'm on somebody I don't let go. But the desire to talk left me completely; I shrugged and turned my eyes away. A little later I raised my head; he was watching me curiously. The guards were sitting on a mat. Pedro, the tall thin one, was twiddling his thumbs, the other shook his head from time to time to keep from falling asleep.

"Do you want a light?" Pedro suddenly asked the doctor. The other nodded "Yes": I think he was about as smart as a log, but he surely wasn't bad. Looking in his cold blue eyes it seemed to me that his only sin was lack of imagination. Pedro went out and came back with an oil lamp which he set on the corner of the bench. It gave a bad light but it was better than nothing: they had left us in the dark the night before. For a long time I watched the circle of light the lamp made on the ceiling. I was fascinated. Then suddenly I woke up, the circle of light disappeared and I felt myself crushed under an enormous weight. It was not the thought of death, or fear; it was nameless. My cheeks burned and my head ached.

I shook myself and looked at my two friends. Tom had hidden his face in his hands. I could only see the fat white nape of his neck. Little Juan was the worst, his mouth was open and his nostrils trembled. The doctor went to him and put his hand on his shoulder to comfort him: but his eyes stayed cold. Then I saw the Belgian's hand drop stealthily along Juan's arm, down to the wrist. Juan paid no attention. The Belgian took his wrist between three fingers, distractedly, the same time drawing back a little and turning his back to me. But I leaned backward and saw him take a watch from his pocket and look at it for a moment, never letting go of the wrist. After a minute he let the hand fall inert and went and leaned his back against the wall, then, as if he suddenly

remembered something very important which had to be jotted down on the spot, he took a notebook from his pocket and wrote a few lines. "Bastard," I thought angrily, "let him come and take my pulse. I'll shove my fist in his rotten face."

He didn't come but I felt him watching me. I raised my head and returned his look. Impersonally, he said to me, "Doesn't it seem cold to you here?" He looked cold, he was blue.

"I'm not cold," I told him.

He never took his hard eyes off me. Suddenly I understood and my hands went to my face: I was drenched in sweat. In this cellar, in the midst of winter, in the midst of drafts, I was sweating. I ran my hands through my hair, gummed together with perspiration; at the same time I saw my shirt was damp and sticking to my skin: I had been dripping for an hour and hadn't felt it. But that swine of a Belgian hadn't missed a thing; he had seen the drops rolling down my cheeks and thought: this is the manifestation of an almost pathological state of terror; and he had felt normal and proud of being alive because he was cold. I wanted to stand up and smash his face but no sooner had I made the slightest gesture than my rage and shame were wiped out; I fell back on the bench with indifference.

I satisfied myself by rubbing my neck with my handkerchief because now I felt the sweat dropping from my hair onto my neck and it was unpleasant. I soon gave up rubbing, it was useless; my handkerchief was already soaked and I was still sweating. My buttocks were sweating too and my damp trousers were glued to the bench.

Suddenly Juan spoke. "You're a doctor?"

"Yes," the Belgian said.

"Does it hurt . . . very long?"

"Huh? When . . . ? Oh, no," the Belgian said paternally. "Not at all. It's over quickly." He acted as though he were calming a cash customer.

"But I . . . they told me . . . sometimes they have to fire twice."

"Sometimes," the Belgian said, nodding. "It may happen that the first volley reaches no vital organs."

"Then they have to reload their rifles and aim all over again?" He thought for a moment and then added hoarsely, "That takes time!"

He had a terrible fear of suffering, it was all he thought about: it was his age. I never thought much about it and it wasn't fear of suffering that made me sweat.

I got up and walked to the pile of coal dust. Tom jumped up and threw me a hateful look: I had annoyed him because my shoes squeaked. I wondered if my face looked as frightened as his: I saw he was sweating too. The sky was superb, no light filtered into the dark corner and I had only to raise my head to see the Big Dipper. But it wasn't like it had been: the night before I could see a great piece of sky from my monastery cell and each hour of the day brought me a different memory. Morning, when the sky was a hard, light blue, I thought of beaches on the Atlantic; at noon I saw the sun and I remembered a bar in Seville where I drank *manzanilla* and ate olives and anchovies; afternoons I was in the shade and I thought of the deep shadow which spreads over half a bull-ring leaving the other half shimmering in sunlight; it was really hard to see the whole world reflected in the sky like that. But now I could watch the sky as much as I pleased, it no longer evoked anything in me. I liked that better. I came back and sat near Tom. A long moment passed.

Tom began speaking in a low voice. He had to talk, without that he wouldn't have been able to recognize himself in his own mind. I thought he was talking to me but he wasn't looking at me. He was undoubtedly afraid to see me as I was, grey and sweating: we were alike and worse than mirrors of each other. He watched the Belgian, the living.

"Do you understand?" he said. "I don't understand."

I began to speak in a low voice too. I watched the Belgian. "Why? What's the matter?"

"Something is going to happen to us that I can't understand."

There was a strange smell about Tom. It seemed to me I was more sensitive than usual to odors. I grinned. "You'll understand in a while."

"It isn't clear," he said obstinately. "I want to be brave but first I have to know. . . . Listen, they're going to take us into the courtyard. Good. They're going to stand up in front of us. How many?"

"I don't know. Five or eight. Not more."

"All right. There'll be eight. Someone'll holler 'aim!' and I'll see eight rifles looking at me. I'll think how I'd like to get inside the wall, I'll push against it with my back . . . with every ounce of strength I have, but the wall will stay, like in a nightmare. I can imagine all that. If you only knew how well I can imagine it."

"All right, all right!" I said, "I can imagine it too."

"It must hurt like hell. You know, they aim at the eyes and the mouth to disfigure you," he added mechanically. "I can feel the wounds already; I've had pains in my head and in my neck for the past hour. Not real pains. Worse. This is what I'm going to feel tomorrow morning. And then what?"

I well understood what he meant but I didn't want to act as if I did. I had pains too, pains in my body like a crowd of tiny scars. I couldn't get used to it. But I was like him, I attached no importance to it. "After," I said, "you'll be pushing up daisies."

He began to talk to himself: he never stopped watching the Belgian. The Belgian didn't seem to be listening. I knew what he had come to do; he wasn't interested in what we thought; he came to watch our bodies, bodies dying in agony while yet alive.

"It's like a nightmare," Tom was saying. "You want to think something, you always have the impression that it's all right, that you're going to understand and then it slips, it escapes you and fades away. I tell myself there will be nothing afterwards. But I don't understand what it means. Sometimes I almost can . . . and then it fades away and I start thinking about the pains again, bullets, explosions. I'm a materialist, I swear it to you; I'm not going crazy. But something's the matter. I see my corpse; that's not hard but I'm the one who sees it, with my eyes. I've got to think . . . think that I won't see anything anymore and the world will go on for the others. We aren't made to think that, Pablo. Believe me: I've already stayed up a whole night waiting for something. But this isn't the same: this will creep up behind us, Pablo, and we won't be able to prepare for it."

"Shut up," I said, "Do you want me to call a priest?"

He didn't answer. I had already noticed he had the tendency to act like a prophet and call me Pablo, speaking in a toneless voice. I didn't like that: but it seems all the Irish are that way. I had the vague impression he smelled of urine. Fundamentally, I hadn't much sympathy for Tom and I didn't see why, under the pretext of dying together, I should have any more. It would have been different with some others. With Ramon Gris, for example. But I felt alone between Tom and Juan. I liked that better, anyhow: with Ramon I might have been more deeply moved. But I was terribly hard just then and I wanted to stay hard.

He kept on chewing his words, with something like distraction. He certainly talked to keep himself from thinking. He smelled of urine like an old prostate case. Naturally, I agreed with him, I could have said everything he said: it isn't *natural* to die. And since I was going to die, nothing seemed natural to me, not this pile of coal dust, or the bench, or Pedro's ugly face. Only it didn't please me to think the same things as Tom. And I knew that, all through the night, every five minutes, we would keep on thinking things at the same time. I looked at him sideways and for the first time he seemed strange to me: he wore death on his face. My pride was wounded: for the past 24 hours I had lived next to Tom, I had listened to him, I had spoken to him and I knew we had nothing in common. And now we looked as much alike as twin brothers, simply because we were going to die together. Tom took my hand without looking at me.

"Pablo, I wonder . . . I wonder if it's really true that everything ends."

I took my hand away and said, "Look between your feet, you pig."

There was a big puddle between his feet and drops fell from his pants-leg.

"What is it," he asked, frightened.

"You're pissing in your pants," I told him.

"It isn't true," he said furiously. "I'm not pissing. I don't feel anything."

The Belgian approached us. He asked with false solicitude. "Do you feel ill?"

Tom did not answer. The Belgian looked at the puddle and said nothing.

"I don't know what it is," Tom said ferociously. "But I'm not afraid. I swear I'm not afraid."

The Belgian did not answer. Tom got up and went to piss in a corner. He came back buttoning his fly, and sat down without a word. The Belgian was taking notes.

All three of us watched him because he was alive. He had the motions of a living human being, the cares of a living human being; he shivered in the cellar the way the living are supposed to shiver; he had an obedient, well-fed body. The rest of us hardly felt ours—not in the same way anyhow. I wanted to feel my pants between my legs but I didn't dare; I watched the Belgian, balancing on his legs, master of his muscles, someone who could think about tomorrow. There we were, three bloodless shadows; we watched him and we sucked his life like vampires.

Finally he went over to little Juan. Did he want to feel his neck for some professional motive or was he obeying an impulse of charity? If he was acting by charity it was the only time during the whole night.

He caressed Juan's head and neck. The kid let himself be handled, his eyes never leaving him, then suddenly, he seized the hand and looked at it strangely. He held the Belgian's hand between his own two hands and there was nothing pleasant about them, two grey pincers gripping this fat and reddish hand. I suspected what was going to happen and Tom must have suspected it too: but the Belgian didn't see a thing, he smiled paternally. After a moment the kid brought the fat red hand to his mouth and tried to bite it. The Belgian pulled away quickly and stumbled back against the wall. For a second he looked at us with horror, he must have suddenly understood that we were not men like him. I began to laugh and one of the guards jumped up. The other was asleep, his wide open eyes were blank.

I felt relaxed and over-excited at the same time. I didn't want to think any more about what would happen at dawn, at death. It made no sense. I only found words or emptiness. But as soon as I tried to think of anything else I saw rifle barrels pointing at me. Perhaps I lived through my execution twenty times; once I even thought it was for good: I must have slept a minute. They were dragging me to the wall and I was struggling; I was asking for mercy. I woke up with a start and looked at the Belgian: I was afraid I might have cried out in my sleep. But he was stroking his moustache, he hadn't noticed anything. If I had wanted to, I think I could have slept a while; I had been awake for 48 hours. I was at the end of my rope. But I didn't want to lose two hours of life: they would come to wake me up at dawn, I would follow them, stupefied with sleep and I would have croaked without so much as an "Oof!"; I didn't want that, I didn't want to die like an animal, I wanted to understand. Then I was afraid of having nightmares. I got up, walked back and forth, and, to change my ideas, I began to think about my past life. A crowd of memories came back to me pell-mell. There were good and bad ones—or at least I called them that *before.* There were faces and incidents. I saw the face of a little *novillero* who was gored in Valencia during the *Feria,* the face of one of my uncles, the face of Ramon Gris. I remembered my whole life: how I was out of work for three months in 1926, how I almost starved to death. I remembered a night I spent on a bench in Granada: I hadn't eaten for three days. I was angry, I didn't want to die. That made me smile. How madly I ran after happiness, after women, after liberty. Why? I wanted to free Spain, I admired Pi y Margall, I joined the anarchist movement, I spoke in public meetings: I took everything as seriously as if I were immortal.

At that moment I felt that I had my whole life in front of me and I thought, "It's a damned lie." It was worth nothing because it was finished. I wondered how I'd been able to walk, to laugh with the girls: I wouldn't have moved so much as my little finger if I had only imagined I would die like this. My life was in front of me, shut, closed, like a bag and yet everything inside of it was unfinished. For an instant I tried to judge it. I wanted to tell myself, this is a beautiful life. But I couldn't pass judgment on it; it was only a sketch; I had spent my time counterfeiting eternity, I had understood nothing. I missed nothing: there were so many things I could have missed, the taste of *manzanilla* or the baths I took in summer in a little creek near Cadiz; but death had disenchanted everything.

The Belgian suddenly had a bright idea. "My friends," he told us, "I will undertake—if the military administration will allow it—to send a message for you, a souvenir to those who love you. . . ."

Tom mumbled, "I don't have anybody."

I said nothing. Tom waited an instant then looked at me with curiosity. "You don't have anything to say to Concha?"

"No."

I hated this tender complicity: it was my own fault, I had talked about Concha the night before. I should have controlled myself. I was with her for a year. Last night I would have given an arm to see her again for five minutes. That was why I talked about her, it was stronger than I was. Now I had no more desire to see her, I had nothing more to say to her. I would not even have wanted to hold her in my arms: my body filled me with horror because it was grey and sweating—and I wasn't sure that her body didn't fill me with horror. Concha would cry when she found out I was dead, she would have no taste for life for months afterward. But I was still the one who was going to die. I thought of her soft, beautiful eyes. When she looked at me something passed from her to me. But I knew it was over: if she looked at me *now* the look would stay in her eyes, it wouldn't reach me. I was alone.

Tom was alone too but not in the same way. Sitting cross-legged, he had begun to stare at the bench with a sort of smile, he looked amazed. He put out his hand and touched the wood cautiously as if he were afraid of breaking something, then drew back his hand quickly and shuddered. If I had been Tom I wouldn't have amused myself by touching the bench; this was some more Irish nonsense, but I too found that objects had a funny look: they were more obliterated, less dense than usual. It was enough for me to look at the bench, the lamp, the pile of coal dust, to feel that I was going to die. Naturally I couldn't think clearly about my death but I saw it everywhere, on things, in the way things fell back and kept their distance, discreetly, as people who speak quietly at the bedside of a dying man. It was *his* death which Tom had just touched on the bench.

In the state I was in, if someone had come and told me I could go home quietly, that they would leave me my life whole, it would have left me cold: several hours or several years of waiting is all the same when you have lost the illusion of being eternal. I clung to nothing, in a way I was calm. But it was a horrible calm—because of my body; my body, I saw with its eyes, I heard with its ears, but it was no longer me; it sweated and trembled by itself and I didn't recognize it any more. I had to touch it and look at it to find out what was happening, as if it were the body of someone else. At times I could still feel it, I felt sinkings, and fallings, as when you're in a plane taking a nosedive, or I felt my heart beating. But that didn't reassure me. Everything that came from my body was all cockeyed. Most of the time it was quiet and I felt no more than a sort of weight, a filthy presence against me; I had the impression of being tied to an enormous vermin. Once I felt my pants and I felt they were damp; I didn't know whether it was sweat or urine, but I went to piss on the coal pile as a precaution.

The Belgian took out his watch, looked at it. He said, "It is three-thirty."

Bastard! He must have done it on purpose. Tom jumped; we hadn't noticed time was running out; night surrounded us like a shapeless, somber mass, I couldn't even remember that it had begun.

Little Juan began to cry. He wrung his hands, pleaded, "I don't want to die. I don't want to die."

He ran across the whole cellar waving his arms in the air then fell sobbing on one of the mats. Tom watched him with mournful eyes, without the slightest desire to console him. Because it wasn't worth the trouble: the kid made more noise than we did, but he was less touched: he was like a sick man who defends himself against his illness by fever. It's much more serious when there isn't any fever.

He wept: I could clearly see he was pitying himself; he wasn't thinking about death. For one second, one single second, I wanted to weep myself, to weep with pity for myself. But the opposite happened: I glanced at the kid, I saw his thin sobbing shoulders and I felt inhuman: I could pity neither the others nor myself. I said to myself, "I want to die cleanly."

Tom had gotten up, he placed himself just under the round opening and began to watch for daylight. I was determined to die cleanly and I only thought of that. But ever since the doctor told us the time, I felt time flying, flowing away drop by drop.

It was still dark when I heard Tom's voice: "Do you hear them?"

Men were marching in the courtyard.

"Yes."

"What the hell are they doing? They can't shoot in the dark."

After a while we heard no more. I said to Tom, "It's day."

Pedro got up, yawning, and came to blow out the lamp. He said to his buddy, "Cold as hell."

The cellar was all grey. We heard shots in the distance.

"It's starting," I told Tom. "They must do it in the court in the rear."

Tom asked the doctor for a cigarette. I didn't want one; I didn't want cigarettes or alcohol. From that moment on they didn't stop firing.

"Do you realize what's happening," Tom said.

He wanted to add something but kept quiet, watching the door. The door opened and a lieutenant came in with four soldiers. Tom dropped his cigarette.

"Steinbock?"

Tom didn't answer. Pedro pointed him out.

"Juan Mirbal?"

"On the mat."

"Get up," the lieutenant said.

Juan did not move. Two soldiers took him under the arms and set him on his feet. But he fell as soon as they released him.

The soldiers hesitated.

"He's not the first sick one," said the lieutenant. "You two carry him; they'll fix it up down there."

He turned to Tom. "Let's go."

Tom went out between two soldiers. Two others followed, carrying the kid by the armpits. He hadn't fainted; his eyes were wide open and tears ran down his cheeks. When I wanted to go out the lieutenant stopped me.

"You Ibbieta?"

"Yes."

"You wait here; they'll come for you later."

They left. The Belgian and the two jailers left too, I was alone. I did not understand what was happening to me but I would have liked it better if they had gotten it over with right away. I heard shots at almost regular intervals; I shook with each one of them. I wanted to scream and tear out my hair. But I gritted my teeth and pushed my hands in my pockets because I wanted to stay clean.

After an hour they came to get me and led me to the first floor, to a small room that smelt of cigars and where the heat was stifling. There were two officers sitting smoking in the armchairs, papers on their knees.

"You're Ibbieta?"

"Yes."

"Where is Ramon Gris?"

"I don't know."

The one questioning me was short and fat. His eyes were hard behind his glasses. He said to me, "Come here."

I went to him. He got up and took my arms, staring at me with a look that should have pushed me into the earth. At the same time he pinched my biceps with all his might. It wasn't to hurt me, it was only a game: he wanted to dominate me. He also thought he had to blow his stinking breath square in my face. We stayed for a moment like that, and I almost felt like laughing. It takes a lot to intimidate a man who is going to die; it didn't work. He pushed me back violently and sat down again. He said, "It's his life against yours. You can have your if you tell us where he is."

These men dolled up with their riding crops and boots were still going to die. A little later than I, but not too much. They busied themselves looking for names in their crumpled papers, they ran after other men to imprison or suppress them; they had opinions on the future of Spain and on other subjects. Their little activities seemed shocking and burlesqued to me; I couldn't put myself in their place, I thought they were insane. The little man was still looking at me, whipping his boots with the riding crop. All his gestures were calculated to give him the look of a live and ferocious beast.

"So? You understand?"

"I don't know where Gris is," I answered. "I thought he was in Madrid."

The other officer raised his pale hand indolently. This indolence was also calculated. I saw through all their little schemes and I was stupefied to find there were men who amused themselves that way.

"You have a quarter of an hour to think it over," he said slowly. "Take him to the laundry, bring him back in fifteen minutes. If he still refuses he will be executed on the spot."

They knew what they were doing: I had passed the night in waiting; then they had made me wait an hour in the cellar while they shot Tom and Juan and now they were locking me up in the laundry; they must have prepared their game the night before. They told themselves that nerves eventually wear out and they hoped to get me that way.

They were badly mistaken. In the laundry I sat on a stool because I felt very weak and I began to think. But not about their proposition. Of course I knew where Gris was; he was hiding with his cousins, four kilometers from the city. I also knew that I would not reveal his hiding place unless they tortured me (but they didn't seem to be thinking about that). All that was perfectly regulated, definite and in no way interested me. Only I would have liked to understand the reasons for my conduct. I would rather die than give up Gris. Why? I didn't like Ramon Gris any more. My friendship for him had died a little while before dawn at the same time as my love for Concha, at the same time as my desire to live. Undoubtedly I thought highly of him: he was tough. But it was not for this reason that I consented to die in his place; his life had no more value than mine; no life had value. They were going to slap a man up against a wall and shoot at him till he died, whether it was I or Gris or somebody else made no difference. I knew he was more useful than I to the cause of Spain but I thought to hell with Spain and anarchy; nothing was important. Yet I was there, I could save my skin and give up Gris and I refused to do it. I found that somehow comic; it was obstinacy. I thought, "I must be stubborn!" And a droll sort of gaiety spread over me.

They came for me and brought me back to the two officers. A rat ran out from under my feet and that amused me. I turned to one of the *falangistas* and said, "Did you see the rat?"

He didn't answer. He was very sober, he took himself seriously. I wanted to laugh but I held myself back because I was afraid that once I got started I wouldn't be able to stop. The *falangista* had a moustache. I said to him again, "You ought to shave off your moustache, idiot." I thought it funny that he would let the hairs of his living being invade his face. He kicked me without great conviction and I kept quiet.

"Well," said the fat officer, "have you thought about it?"

I looked at them with curiosity, as insects of a very rare species. I told them, "I know where he is. He is hidden in the cemetery. In a vault or in the gravediggers' shack."

It was a farce. I wanted to see them stand up, buckle their belts and give orders busily.

They jumped to their feet. "Let's go. Molés, go get fifteen men from Lieutenant Lopez. You," the fat man said, "I'll let you off if you're telling the truth, but it'll cost you plenty if you're making monkeys out of us."

They left in a great clatter and I waited peacefully under the guard of *falangistas*. From time to time I smiled, thinking about the spectacle they would make. I felt stunned and malicious. I imagined them lifting up tombstones, opening the doors of the vaults one by one. I represented this situation to myself as if I had been someone else: this prisoner obstinately playing the hero, these grim *falangistas* with their moustaches and their men in uniform running among the graves; it was irresistibly funny. After half an hour the little fat man came back alone. I thought he had come to give the orders to execute me. The others must have stayed in the cemetery.

The officer looked at me. He didn't look at all sheepish. "Take him into the big courtyard with the others," he said. "After the military operations a regular court will decide what happens to him."

"Then they're not . . . not going to shoot me? . . ."

"Not now, anyway. What happens afterwards is none of my business."

I still didn't understand. I asked, "But why . . . ?"

He shrugged his shoulders without answering and the soldiers took me away. In the big courtyard there were about a hundred prisoners, women, children and a few old men. I began walking around the central grass-plot, I was stupefied. At noon they let us eat in the mess hall. Two or three people questioned me. I must have known them, but I didn't answer: I didn't even know where I was.

Around evening they pushed about ten new prisoners into the court. I recognized Garcia, the baker. He said, "What damned luck you have! I didn't think I'd see you alive."

"They sentenced me to death," I said, "and then they changed their minds. I don't know why."

"They arrested me at two o'clock," Garcia said.

"Why?" Garcia had nothing to do with politics.

"I don't know," he said. "They arrest everybody who doesn't think the way they do. He lowered his voice. "They got Gris."

I began to tremble. "When?"

"This morning. He messed it up. He left his cousin's on Tuesday because they had an argument. There were plenty of people to hide him but he didn't want to owe anything to anybody. He said, 'I'd go and hide in Ibbieta's place, but they got him, so I'll go hide in the cemetery.' "

"In the cemetery?"

"Yes. What a fool. Of course they went by there this morning, that was sure to happen. They found him in the gravediggers' shack. He shot at them and they got him."

"In the cemetery!"

Everything began to spin and I found myself sitting on the ground: I laughed so hard I cried.

Exercises

1. Why was there no real connection between the information the prisoners supplied at the interrogation and their death sentences? Why was the sentence read to them in their cell rather than in the interrogation room?
2. What significance is there in the narrator being held in a hospital cellar after spending several days in the cell of a medieval monastery?
3. What is the significance of running trucks over prisoners rather than shooting them? Does it save ammunition (while using gas) or does it make any difference?
4. Juan Mirbal contends that he did not do anything, that there is no reason for him to die. If, as appears likely, he was accidentally caught up in events, what is implied here in terms of Existential themes?
5. What is the significance of the major's assumption that the prisoners do not want a priest?
6. What characteristics of Existential belief are symbolized by the Belgian doctor? You should consider the various words used to describe the doctor and his actions.
7. Why does Tom feel impelled to "understand" what is going to happen to him? Why does the narrator feel that this is irrelevant?
8. The narrator contemplates "the pretext of dying together." What does this imply? Look also at other references to dying.
9. What attitudes do the prisoners have about a possible life after death?
10. What does the narrator mean by the statement "I had spent my time counterfeiting eternity"?
11. Why does the narrator have no desire to see Concha? What does this signify?
12. Consider the words "alone" and "lonely." How are they used?
13. Why is the narrator locked in the laundry after his interrogation about Ramon Gris?
14. Why did it, as the narrator said, make no difference whether he or Ramon Gris was shot?
15. Why, at the end, did the narrator laugh so hard that he cried?

THE MYTH OF SISYPHUS

Albert Camus (1913–1966)

Both Sartre and Albert Camus were active in the French Resistance and both won the Nobel Prize for literature. Camus's brilliant novel, *The Stranger,* superbly delineates the existential themes of absurdity, anguish, despair, and alienation but Camus always denied that he was an existentialist. He claimed instead that the world was so absurd that the philosopher should logically contemplate suicide. The alternative, for Camus, was to dismiss the world and lead an active, heroic life. The hero of ordinary life is the person who resolutely shoulders the responsibilities that life imposes, knowing full well that all is futile and meaningless, an attitude that is exemplified in the essay "The Myth of Sisyphus." In Greek mythology Sisyphus was a rogue-hero who delighted in tricking the gods. When death (Thanatos) came for him Sisyphus tied him up and no one died until Zeus intervened. Sisyphus was then taken to Hades but won a temporary leave so that he could return to the world to punish his wife for not giving him a proper burial. Actually, Sisyphus had instructed her to throw his body in the street so that he had an excuse for returning. Once free of Hades he refused to return and finally died of old age. The gods were so furious that, through all eternity, they required Sisyphus to roll a huge stone up a hill only to have it plunge back down once it reached the crest. The divine plan was to keep Sisyphus too busy to plan another escape but, as Camus concludes, "One must imagine Sisyphus happy" in the act of doing.

The gods had condemned Sisyphus to ceaselessly rolling a rock to the top of a mountain, whence the stone would fall back of its own weight. They had thought with some reason that there is no more dreadful punishment than futile and hopeless labor.

If one believes Homer, Sisyphus was the wisest and most prudent of mortals. According to another tradition, however, he was disposed to practice the profession of highwayman. I see no contradiction in this. Opinions differ as to the reasons why he became the futile laborer of the underworld. To begin with, he is accused of a certain levity in regard to the gods. He stole their secrets. Ægina, the daughter of Æsopus, was carried off by Jupiter. The father was shocked by that disappearance and complained to Sisyphus. He, who knew of the abduction, offered to tell about it on condition that Æsopus would give water to the citadel of Corinth. To the celestial thunderbolts he preferred the benediction of water. He was punished for this in the underworld. Homer tells us also that Sisyphus had put Death in chains. Pluto could not endure the sight of his deserted, silent empire. He dispatched the god of war, who liberated Death from the hands of her conqueror.

It is said also that Sisyphus, being near to death, rashly wanted to test his wife's love. He ordered her to cast his unburied body into the middle of the public square. Sisyphus woke up in the underworld. And there, annoyed by an obedience so contrary to human love, he obtained from Pluto permission to return to earth in order to chastise his wife. But when he had seen again the face of this world, enjoyed water and sun, warm stones and the sea, he no longer wanted to go back to the infernal darkness. Recalls, signs of anger, warnings were of no avail. Many years more he lived facing the curve of the gulf, the sparkling sea, and the smiles of earth. A decree of the gods was necessary. Mercury came and seized the impudent man by the collar and, snatching him from his joys, led him forcibly back to the underworld, where his rock was ready for him.

You have already grasped that Sisyphus is the absurd hero. He *is,* as much through his passions as through his torture. His scorn of the gods, his hatred of death, and his passion for life won him that unspeakable penalty in which the whole being is exerted toward accomplishing nothing. This is the price that must be paid for the passions of this earth. Nothing is told us about Sisyphus in the underworld. Myths are made for the imagination to breathe life into them. As for this myth, one sees merely the whole effort of a body straining to raise the huge stone, to roll it and push it up a slope a hundred times over; one sees the face screwed up, the cheek tight against the stone, the shoulder bracing the clay-covered mass, the foot wedging it, the fresh start with arms outstretched, the wholly human security of two earth-clotted hands. At the very end of his long effort measured by skyless space and time without depth, the purpose is achieved. Then Sisyphus watches the stone rush down in a few moments toward that lower world whence he will have to push it up again toward the summit. He goes back down to the plain.

It is during that return, that pause, that Sisyphus interests me. A face that toils so close to stones is already stone itself! I see that man going back down with a heavy yet measured step toward the torment of which he will never know the end. That hour like a breathing-space which returns as surely as his suffering, that is the hour of consciousness. At each of those moments when he leaves the heights and gradually sinks toward the lairs of the gods, he is superior to his fate. He is stronger than his rock.

If this myth is tragic, that is because its hero is conscious. Where would his torture be, indeed, if at every step the hope of succeeding upheld him? The workman of today works every day in his life at the same tasks, and this fate is no less absurd. But it is tragic only at the rare moments when it becomes conscious. Sisyphus, proletarian of the gods, powerless and rebellious, knows the whole extent of his wretched condition: it is what he thinks of during his descent. The lucidity that was to constitute his torture at the same time crowns his victory. There is no fate that cannot be surmounted by scorn.

If the descent is thus sometimes performed in sorrow, it can also take place in joy. This word is not too much. Again I fancy Sisyphus returning toward his rock, and the sorrow was in the beginning. When the images of earth cling too tightly to memory, when the call of happiness becomes too insistent, it happens that melancholy rises in man's heart: this is the rock's victory, this is the rock itself. The boundless grief is too heavy to bear. These are our nights of Gethsemane. But crushing truths perish from being acknowledged. Thus, Œdipus at the outset obeys fate without knowing it. But from the moment he knows, his tragedy begins. Yet at the same moment, blind and desperate, he realizes that the only bond linking him to the world is the cool hand of a girl.

Then a tremendous remark rings out: "Despite so many ordeals, my advanced age and the nobility of my soul make me conclude that all is well." Sophocles' Œdipus, like Dostoevsky's Kirilov, thus gives the recipe for the absurd victory. Ancient wisdom confirms modern heroism.

One does not discover the absurd without being tempted to write a manual of happiness. "What! by such narrow ways—?" There is but one world, however. Happiness and the absurd are two sons of the same earth. They are inseparable. It would be a mistake to say that happiness necessarily springs from the absurd discovery. It happens as well that the feeling of the absurd springs from happiness. "I conclude that all is well," says Œdipus, and that remark is sacred. It echoes in the wild and limited universe of man. It teaches that all is not, has not been, exhausted. It drives out of this world a god who had come into it with dissatisfaction and a preference for futile sufferings. It makes of fate a human matter, which must be settled among men.

All Sisyphus' silent joy is contained therein. His fate belongs to him. His rock is his thing. Likewise, the absurd man, when he contemplates his torment, silences all the idols. In the universe suddenly restored to its silence, the myriad wondering little voices of the earth rise up. Unconscious, secret calls, invitations from all the faces, they are the necessary reverse and price of victory. There is no sun without shadow, and it is essential to know the night. The absurd man says yes and his effort will henceforth be unceasing. If there is a personal fate, there is no higher destiny, or at least there is but one which he concludes is inevitable and despicable. For the rest, he knows himself to be the master of his days. At that subtle moment when man glances backward over his life, Sisyphus returning toward his rock, in that slight pivoting he contemplates that series of unrelated actions which becomes his fate, created by him, combined under his memory's eye and soon sealed by his death. Thus, convinced of the wholly human origin of all that is human, a blind man eager to see who knows that the night has no end, he is still on the go. The rock is still rolling.

I leave Sisyphus at the foot of the mountain! One always finds one's burden again. But Sisyphus teaches the higher fidelity that negates the gods and raises rocks. He too concludes that all is well. This universe henceforth without a master seems to him neither sterile nor futile. Each atom of that stone, each mineral flake of that night-filled mountain, in itself forms a world. The struggle itself toward the heights is enough to fill a man's heart. One must imagine Sisyphus happy.

Exercises

1. Imagine several children on a sandy beach busily constructing a large sand castle. A passerby maliciously stomping on a tower leads to a brief but violent confrontation. Finally the builders complete their elaborate fairy-tale structure just as the encroaching tide tentatively laps at the outer walls. The construction crew observes attentively as the noble turrets subside into the swirling water and then, losing interest, pick up their things and set off for the beach house. Why was there a fight over the mutilated tower but only calm acceptance of the watery demise of the castle? How is all of this analogous to Sisyphus and his rock?

2. Consider now the millionaire who feels that he must aim for a hundred million, then a billion, or more. How much money will be enough, or is money even the main focus? How does this relate to Sisyphus?

3. Let us say that the gods have relented and that, as Sisyphus muscles the rock into place, it teeters for a moment and then remains firmly in place. Describe Sisyphus's feelings. Have the gods indeed relented or have they devised a more fiendish form of punishment?

Existentialism: Postscript

The same type of character as Sisyphus is found in Camus's novel *The Plague* (written, one recognizes, after Camus had split from Existentialism but maintaining the same attitude toward the hero) in Monsieur Grand, who does his daily duties as a clerk in the city government; in his spare time he carefully tabulates the number of dead in the plague; and he vainly tries to communicate with the world through his novel—which never gets written beyond the first sentence.

Beyond this everyday sort of hero, some Existentialists, particularly the Christian Existentialists, imagine that a person can become a sort of superhero when he or she infuses pointless life with meaning, and thereby creates meaning in the universe. Some of the Christian Existentialists believe that Christ was such a figure; and that, if the actuality for such Being exists within one individual, then it is also a potentiality for all humanity.

A large number of philosophers and Christian theologians have advanced and developed this Christian Existentialist point of view. Among them are Ernst Block and the Dutch Roman Catholic theologian, E. Schillebeeckx. Oversimplifying greatly, they view God as the Creative Purpose of the World; the End toward which the world is moving. Block has referred to Him as "the God who is not yet"; Schillebeeckx as the God who is "wholly new." This concept is a far cry from the standard view of a God who was complete and whole from the beginning of time, and who rules the world either as loving Father or as Great Engineer. Instead, He is constantly inventing Himself or being invented here on earth, exactly as the Existentialist person, moment by moment, invents himself or herself.

Literary Selections

On the Road, from THE WHITE ALBUM

Joan Didion (b. 1934)

A sense of loss of national purpose brooded over the land. Where is America heading? Joan Didion, in the selection given below, replies, "nowhere." She does, however, describe, in devastating detail, where we are now. Her impressionistic picture of a puzzled nation depicts transcience, superficiality, and boredom. Values are skewed and mobility is an illusion: "Time was money. Money was progress. Decisions were snap." A self-indulgent, business-oriented nation rethinks the sixties, the fifties. Where did we go wrong?

Where are we heading, they asked in all the television and radio studios. They asked it in New York and Los Angeles and they asked it in Boston and Washington and they asked it in Dallas and Houston and Chicago and San Francisco. Sometimes they made eye contact as they asked it. Sometimes they closed their eyes as they asked it. Quite often they wondered not just where we were heading but where we were heading "as Americans," or "as concerned Americans," or "as American women," or, on one occasion, "as the American guy and the American woman." I never learned the answer, nor did the answer matter, for one of the eerie and liberating aspects of broadcast discourse is that nothing one says will alter in the slightest either the form or the length of the conversation. Our voices in the studios were those of manic actors assigned to do three-minute, four-minute, seven-minute improvs. Our faces on the monitors were those of concerned Americans. On my way to one of those studios in Boston I had seen the magnolias bursting white down Marlborough Street. On my way to another in Dallas I had watched the highway lights blazing and dimming pink against the big dawn sky. Outside one studio in Houston the afternoon heat was sinking into the deep primeval green of the place and outside the next, that night in Chicago, snow fell and glittered in the lights along the lake. Outside all these studios America lay in all its exhilaratingly volatile weather and eccentricity and specificity, but inside the studios we shed the specific and rocketed on to the general, for they were The Interviewers and I was The Author and the single question we seemed able to address together was *where are we heading.*

> "8:30 A.M. to 9:30 A.M.: LIVE on WFSB TV/THIS MORNING.
> "10 A.M. to 10:30 A.M.: LIVE on WINF AM/THE WORLD TODAY.
> "10:45 A.M. to 11:45 A.M.: PRESS INTERVIEW with HARTFORD COURANT.
> "12 noon to 1:30 P.M.: AUTOGRAPHING at BARNES AND NOBLE.
> "2 P.M. to 2:30 P.M.: TAPE at WDRC AM/FM.
> "3 P.M. to 3:30 P.M.: PRESS INTERVIEW with THE HILL INK.
> "7:30 P.M. to 9 P.M.: TAPE at WHNB TV/WHAT ABOUT WOMEN."

From 12 noon to 1:30 P.M., that first day in Hartford, I talked to a man who had cut a picture of me from a magazine in 1970 and had come round to Barnes and Noble to see what I looked like in 1977. From 2 P.M. to 2:30 P.M., that first day in Hartford, I listened to the receptionists at WDRC AM/FM talk about the new records and I watched snow drop from the pine boughs in the cemetery across the street. The name of the cemetery was Mt. St. Benedict and my husband's father had been buried there. "Any Steely Dan come in?" the receptionists kept asking. From 8:30 A.M. until 9 P.M., that first day in Hartford, I neglected to mention the name of the book I was supposed to be promoting. It was my fourth book but I had never before done what is called in the trade a book tour. I was not sure what I was doing or why I was doing it. I had left California equipped with two "good" suits, a box of unanswered mail, Elizabeth Hardwick's *Seduction and Betrayal,* Edmund Wilson's *To the Finland Station,* six Judy Blume books and my eleven-year-old daughter. The Judy Blume books were along to divert my daughter. My daughter was along to divert me. Three days into the tour I sent home the box of unanswered mail to make room for a packet of Simon and Schuster press releases describing me in favorable terms. Four days into the tour I sent home *Seduction and Betrayal* and *To the Finland Station* to make room for a thousand-watt hair blower. By the time I reached Boston, ten days into the tour, I knew that I had never before heard and would possibly never again hear America singing at precisely this pitch: ethereal, speedy, an angel choir on Dexamyl.

Where were we heading. The set for this discussion was always the same: a cozy oasis of wicker and ferns in the wilderness of cables and cameras and Styrofoam coffee cups that was the actual studio. On wicker settees across the nation I expressed my conviction that we were heading "into an era" of whatever the clock seemed to demand. In green rooms across the nation I listened to other people talk about where we were heading, and also about their vocations, avocations, and secret interests. I discussed L-dopa and biorhythm with a woman whose father invented prayer breakfasts. I exchanged makeup tips with a former Mouseketeer. I stopped reading newspapers and started relying on bulletins from limo drivers, from Mouseketeers, from the callers-in on call-in shows and from the closed-circuit screens in airports that flashed random stories off the wire ("CARTER URGES BARBITURATE BAN" is one that got my attention at La Guardia) between advertisements for *Shenandoah.* I gravitated to the random. I swung with the nonsequential.

I began to see America as my own, a child's map over which my child and I could skim and light at will. We spoke not of cities but of airports. If rain fell at Logan we could find sun at Dulles. Bags lost at O'Hare could be found at Dallas/Fort Worth. In the first-class cabins of the planes on which we traveled we were often, my child and I, the only female passengers, and I apprehended for the first time those particular illusions of mobility which power American business. Time was money. Motion was progress. Decisions were snap and the ministrations of other people were constant. Room service, for example, assumed paramount importance. We needed, my eleven-year-old and I, instant but erratically timed infusions of consommé, oatmeal, crab salad and asparagus vinaigrette.

We needed Perrier water and tea to drink when we were working. We needed bourbon on the rocks and Shirley Temples to drink when we were not. A kind of irritable panic came over us when room service went off, and also when no one answered in the housekeeping department. In short we had fallen into the peculiar hormonal momentum of business travel, and I had begun to understand the habituation many men and a few women have to planes and telephones and schedules. I had begun to regard my own schedule—a sheaf of thick cream-colored pages printed with the words "SIMON & SCHUSTER/A DIVISION OF GULF & WESTERN CORPORATION"—with a reverence approaching the mystical. We wanted 24-hour room service. We wanted direct-dial telephones. We wanted to stay on the road forever.

WE SAW AIR AS OUR ELEMENT. In Houston the air was warm and rich and suggestive of fossil fuel and we pretended we owned a house in River Oaks. In Chicago the air was brilliant and thin and we pretended we owned the 27th floor of the Ritz. In New York the air was charged and crackling and shorting out with opinions, and we pretended we had some. Everyone in New York had opinions. Opinions were demanded in return. The absence of opinion was construed as opinion. Even my daughter was developing opinions. "Had an interesting talk with Carl Bernstein," she noted in the log she had been assigned to keep for her fifth-grade teacher in Malibu, California. Many of these New York opinions seemed intended as tonic revisions, bold corrections to opinions in vogue during the previous week, but since I had just dropped from the sky it was difficult for me to distinguish those opinions which were "bold" and "revisionist" from those which were merely "weary" and "rote." At the time I left New York many people were expressing a bold belief in "joy"—joy in children, joy in wedlock, joy in the dailiness of life—but joy was trickling down fast to show-business personalities. Mike Nichols, for example, was expressing his joy in the pages of *Newsweek,* and also his weariness with "lapidary bleakness." Lapidary bleakness was definitely rote.

We were rethinking the Sixties that week, or Morris Dickstein was.

We were taking another look at the Fifties that week, or Hilton Kramer was.

I agreed passionately. I disagreed passionately. I called room service on one phone and listened attentively on the other to people who seemed convinced that the "texture" of their lives had been agreeably or adversely affected by conversion to the politics of joy, by regression to lapidary bleakness, by the Sixties, by the Fifties, by the recent change in administrations and by the sale of *The Thorn Birds* to paper for one-million-nine.

I lost track of information.

I was blitzed by opinion.

I began to see opinions arcing in the air, intersecting flight patterns. The Eastern shuttle was cleared for landing and so was lapidary bleakness. John Leonard and joy were on converging vectors. I began to see the country itself as a projection on air, a kind of hologram, an invisible grid of image and opinion and electronic impulse. There were opinions in the air and there were planes in the air and there were even people in the air: one afternoon in New York my husband saw a man jump from a window and fall to the sidewalk outside the Yale Club. I mentioned this to a *Daily News* photographer who was taking my picture. "You have to catch a jumper in the act to make the paper," he advised me. He had caught two in the act but only the first had made the paper. The second was a better picture but coincided with the crash of a DC–10 at Orly. "They're all over town," the photographer said. "Jumpers. A lot of them aren't even jumpers. They're window washers. Who fall."

What does that say about us as a nation. I was asked the next day when I mentioned the jumpers and window washers on the air. *Where are we headed.* On the 27th floor of the Ritz in Chicago my daughter and I sat frozen at the breakfast table until the window washers glided safely out of sight. At a call-in station in Los Angeles I was told by the guard that there would be a delay because they had a jumper on the line. "I say let him jump," the guard said to me. I imagined a sky dense with jumpers and fallers and DC–10s. I held my daughter's hand at takeoff and landing and watched for antennae on the drive into town. The big antennae with the pulsing red lights had been for a month our landmarks. The big antennae with the pulsing red lights had in fact been for a month our destinations. "Out I–10 to the antenna" was the kind of direction we had come to understand, for we were on the road, on the grid, on the air and also in it. *Where were we heading.* I don't know where you're heading, I said in the studio attached to the last of these antennae, my eyes fixed on still another of the neon FLEETWOOD MAC signs that flickered that spring in radio stations from coast to coast, but I'm heading home.

Exercises

Replete with vivid images, this selection is a mine of metaphors and pungent phrases. The following questions should be only the beginning of your explorations into deeper meanings.

1. Consider "manic actors assigned to do three-minute improvs." What does this tell you about our life-style? About TV?
2. What is the face of a "concerned American"? How often have you seen politicians wearing this face?
3. What is implied by "I never learned the answer nor did the answer matter"? Consider the basic question, "where are we going as Americans?"
4. The author first praised America's eccentricity and specificity but added, "inside the studios we shed the specific and rocketed on to the general." What is implied? Mediocrity?
5. What does the absence of similes do for the style?
6. At one point the question, "where are we heading" is followed by a typed schedule of appointments. What is implied about our day-to-day lives?
7. Ostensibly the writer is describing a book promotional tour. What are the deeper implications? Why is there no mention of the book in question, not even the title? Is this country promoting things of intrinsic or extrinsic value?

8. Consider the setting for the panel discussions which "was always the same: a cozy oasis of wicker and ferns in the wilderness of cables and cameras and Styrofoam cups." An oasis in what? Who really uses wicker furniture? Are the ferns real? And what about the ubiquitous Styrofoam cups? Add up the scene and what do you have?

9. Describe the implications of "the peculiar hormonal momentum of business travel." Words like "momentum," "planes," "telephones," and "schedules" are used but there is no mention of destinations or accomplishments. Is this another elaborate metaphor for self-delusion or false values? The lack of a national purpose? How many metaphors can you find which communicate these general ideas?

THE RIVER

Flannery O'Connor (1925–1964)

In her novels and short stories Flannery O'Connor is a detached and ironic observer of the human condition, no matter how cruel, vulgar, or grotesque life in the South might be. The forlorn little boy in this melancholy story is a psychologically battered child, a pathetic victim of neglect and ignorance. His childish search for acceptance is literal and includes the acquisition of a meaningful name like Bevel, a book about a mysterious person named Jesus, and baptism, not as symbolic, but as a way to a better existence in the embrace of the River of Life.

The child stood glum and limp in the middle of the dark living room while his father pulled him into a plaid coat. His right arm was hung in the sleeve but the father buttoned the coat anyway and pushed him forward toward a pale spotted hand that stuck through the half-open door.

"He ain't fixed right," a loud voice said from the hall.

"Well then for Christ's sake fix him," the father muttered. "It's six o'clock in the morning." He was in his bathrobe and barefooted. When he got the child to the door and tried to shut it, he found her looming in it, a speckled skeleton in a long pea-green coat and felt helmet.

"And his and my carfare," she said. "It'll be twict we have to ride the car."

He went in the bedroom again to get the money and when he came back, she and the boy were both standing in the middle of the room. She was taking stock. "I couldn't smell those dead cigarette butts long if I was ever to come sit with you," she said, shaking him down in his coat.

"Here's the change," the father said. He went to the door and opened it wide and waited.

After she had counted the money she slipped it somewhere inside her coat and walked over to a watercolor hanging near the phonograph. "I know what time it is," she said, peering closely at the black lines crossing into broken planes of violent color. "I ought to.

My shift goes on at 10 P.M. and don't get off till 5 and it takes me one hour to ride the Vine Street car."

"Oh, I see," he said; "well, we'll expect him back tonight, about eight or nine?"

"Maybe later," she said. "We're going to the river to a healing. This particular preacher don't get around this way often. I wouldn't have paid for that," she said, nodding at the painting, "I would have drew it myself."

"All right, Mrs. Connin, we'll see you then," he said, drumming on the door.

A toneless voice called from the bedroom, "Bring me an icepack."

"Too bad his mamma's sick," Mrs. Connin said. "What's her trouble?"

"We don't know," he muttered.

"We'll ask the preacher to pray for her. He's healed a lot of folks. The Reverend Bevel Summers. Maybe she ought to see him sometime."

"Maybe so," he said. "We'll see you tonight," and he disappeared into the bedroom and left them to go.

The little boy stared at her silently, his nose and eyes running. He was four or five. He had a long face and bulging chin and half-shut eyes set far apart. He seemed mute and patient, like an old sheep waiting to be let out.

"You'll like this preacher," she said. "The Reverend Bevel Summers. You ought to hear him sing."

The bedroom door opened suddenly and the father stuck his head out and said, "Good-by, old man. Have a good time."

"Good-by," the little boy said and jumped as if he had been shot.

Mrs. Connin gave the watercolor another look. Then they went out into the hall and rang for the elevator. "I wouldn't have drew it," she said.

Outside the gray morning was blocked off on either side by the unlit empty buildings. "It's going to fair up later," she said, "but this is the last time we'll be able to have any preaching at the river this year. Wipe your nose, Sugar Boy."

He began rubbing his sleeve across it but she stopped him. "That ain't nice," she said. "Where's your handkerchief?"

He put his hands in his pockets and pretended to look for it while she waited. "Some people don't care how they send one off," she murmured to her reflection in the coffee shop window. "You pervide." She took a red and blue flowered handkerchief out of her pocket and stooped down and began to work on his nose. "Now blow," she said and he blew. "You can borry it. Put it in your pocket."

He folded it up and put it in his pocket carefully and they walked on to the corner and leaned against the side of a closed drugstore to wait for the car. Mrs. Connin turned up her coat collar so that it met her hat in the back. Her eyelids began to droop and she looked as if she might go to sleep against the wall. The little boy put a slight pressure on her hand.

"What's your name?" she asked in a drowsy voice. "I don't know but only your last name. I should have found out your first name."

His name was Harry Ashfield and he had never thought at any time before of changing it. "Bevel," he said.

Mrs. Connin raised herself from the wall. "Why ain't that a coincident!" she said. "I told you that's the name of this preacher!"

"Bevel," he repeated.

She stood looking down at him as if he had become a marvel to her. "I'll have to see you meet him today," she said. "He's no ordinary preacher. He's a healer. He couldn't do nothing for Mr. Connin though. Mr. Connin didn't have the faith but he said he would try anything once. He had this griping in his gut."

The trolley appeared as a yellow spot at the end of the deserted street.

"He's gone to the government hospital now," she said, "and they taken one-third of his stomach. I tell him he better thank Jesus for what he's got left but he says he ain't thanking nobody. Well I declare," she murmured, "Bevel!"

They walked out to the tracks to wait. "Will he heal me?" Bevel asked.

"What you got?"

"I'm hungry," he decided finally.

"Didn't you have your breakfast?"

"I didn't have time to be hungry yet then," he said.

"Well when we get home we'll both have us something," she said. "I'm ready myself."

They got on the car and sat down a few seats behind the driver and Mrs. Connin took Bevel on her knees. "Now you be a good boy," she said, "and let me get some sleep. Just don't get off my lap." She lay her head back and as he watched, gradually her eyes closed and her mouth fell open to show a few long scattered teeth, some gold and some darker than her face; she began to whistle and blow like a musical skeleton. There was no one in the car but themselves and the driver and when he saw she was asleep, he took out the flowered handkerchief and unfolded it and examined it carefully. Then he folded it up again and unzipped a place in the innerlining of his coat and hid it in there and shortly he went to sleep himself.

Her house was a half-mile from the end of the car line, set back a little from the road. It was tan paper brick with a porch across the front of it and a tin top. On the porch there were three little boys of different sizes with identical speckled faces and one tall girl who had her hair up in so many aluminum curlers that it glared like the roof. The three boys followed them inside and closed in on Bevel. They looked at him silently, not smiling.

"That's Bevel," Mrs. Connin said, taking off her coat. "It's a coincident he's named the same as the preacher. These boys are J. C., Spivey, and Sinclair, and that's Sarah Mildred on the porch. Take off that coat and hang it on the bed post, Bevel."

The three boys watched him while he unbuttoned the coat and took it off. Then they watched him hang it on the bed post and then they stood, watching the coat. They turned abruptly and went out the door and had a conference on the porch.

Bevel stood looking around him at the room. It was part kitchen and part bedroom. The entire house was two rooms and two porches. Close to his foot the tail of a light-colored dog moved up and down between two floor boards as he scratched his back on the underside of the house. Bevel jumped on it but the hound was experienced and had already withdrawn when his feet hit the spot.

The walls were filled with pictures and calendars. There were two round photographs of an old man and woman with collapsed mouths and another picture of a man whose eyebrows dashed out of two bushes of hair and clashed in a heap on the bridge of his nose; the rest of his face stuck out like a bare cliff to fall from. "That's Mr. Connin," Mrs. Connin said, standing back from the stove for a second to admire the face with him, "but it don't favor him any more." Bevel turned from Mr. Connin to a colored picture over the bed of a man wearing a white sheet. He had long hair and a gold circle around his head and he was sawing on a board while some children stood watching him. He was going to ask who that was when the three boys came in again and motioned for him to follow them. He thought of crawling under the bed and hanging onto one of the legs but the three boys only stood there, speckled and silent, waiting, and after a second he followed them at a little distance out on the porch and around the corner of the house. They started off through a field of rough yellow weeds to the hog pen, a five-foot boarded square full of shoats, which they intended to ease him over into. When they reached it, they turned and waited silently, leaning against the side.

He was coming very slowly, deliberately bumping his feet together as if he had trouble walking. Once he had been beaten up in the park by some strange boys when his sitter forgot him, but he hadn't known anything was going to happen that time until it was over. He began to smell a strong odor of garbage and to hear the noises of a wild animal. He stopped a few feet from the pen and waited, pale but dogged.

The three boys didn't move. Something seemed to have happened to them. They stared over his head as if they saw something coming behind him but he was afraid to turn his own head and look. Their speckles were pale and their eyes were still and gray as glass. Only their ears twitched slightly. Nothing happened. Finally, the one in the middle said, "She'd kill us," and turned, dejected and hacked, and climbed up on the pen and hung over, staring in.

Bevel sat down on the ground, dazed with relief, and grinned up at them.

The one sitting on the pen glanced at him severely. "Hey you," he said after a second, "if you can't climb up and see these pigs you can lift that bottom board off and look in thataway." He appeared to offer this as a kindness.

Bevel had never seen a real pig but he had seen a pig in a book and knew they were small fat pink animals with curly tails and round grinning faces and bow ties. He leaned forward and pulled eagerly at the board.

"Pull harder," the littlest boy said. "It's nice and rotten. Just lift out thet nail."

He eased a long reddish nail out of the soft wood.

"Now you can lift up the board and put your face to the . . ." a quiet voice began.

He had already done it and another face, gray, wet and sour, was pushing into his, knocking him down and back as it scraped out under the plank. Something snorted over him and charged back again, rolling him over and pushing him up from behind and then sending him forward, screaming through the yellow field, while it bounded behind.

The three Connins watched from where they were. The one sitting on the pen held the loose board back with his dangling foot. Their stern faces didn't brighten any but they seemed to become less taut, as if some great need had been partly satisfied. "Maw ain't going to like him lettin out thet hawg," the smallest one said.

Mrs. Connin was on the back porch and caught Bevel up as he reached the steps. The hog ran under the house and subsided, panting, but the child screamed for five minutes. When she had finally calmed him down, she gave him his breakfast and let him sit on her lap while he ate it. The shoat climbed the two steps onto the back porch and stood outside the screen door, looking in with his head lowered sullenly. He was long-legged and hump-backed and part of one of his ears had been bitten off.

"Git away!" Mrs. Connin shouted. "That one yonder favors Mr. Paradise that has the gas station," she said. "You'll see him today at the healing. He's got the cancer over his ear. He always comes to show he ain't been healed."

The shoat stood squinting a few seconds longer and then moved off slowly. "I don't want to see him," Bevel said.

They walked to the river, Mrs. Connin in front with him and the three boys strung out behind and Sarah Mildred, the tall girl, at the end to holler if one of them ran out on the road. They looked like the skeleton of an old boat with two pointed ends, sailing slowly on the edge of the highway. The white Sunday sun followed at a little distance, climbing fast through a scum of gray cloud as if it meant to overtake them. Bevel walked on the outside edge, holding Mrs. Connin's hand and looking down into the orange and purple gulley that dropped off from the concrete.

It occurred to him that he was lucky this time that they had found Mrs. Connin who would take you away for the day instead of an ordinary sitter who only sat where you lived or went to the park. You found out more when you left where you lived. He had found out already this morning that he had been made by a carpenter named Jesus Christ. Before he had thought it had been a doctor named Sladewall, a fat man with a yellow mustache who gave him shots and thought his name was Herbert, but this must have been a joke. They joked a lot where he lived. If he had thought about it before, he would have thought Jesus Christ was a word like "oh" or "damm" or "God," or maybe somebody who had cheated them out of something sometime. When he had asked Mrs. Connin who the man in the sheet in the picture over her bed was, she looked at him a while with her mouth open. Then she had said, "That's Jesus," and she had kept on looking at him.

In a few minutes she had got up and got a book out of the other room. "See here," she said, turning over the cover, "this belonged to my great grandmamma." She wouldn't part with it for nothing on earth." She ran her finger under some brown writing on a spotted page. "Emma Stevens Oakley, 1832," she said. "Ain't that something to have? And every word of it the gospel truth." She turned the next page and read him the name: "The Life of Jesus Christ for Readers Under Twelve." Then she read him the book.

It was a small book, pale brown on the outside with gold edges and a smell like old putty. It was full of pictures, one of the carpenter driving a crowd of pigs out of a man. They were real pigs, gray and sour-looking, and Mrs. Connin said Jesus had driven them all out of this one man. When she finished reading, she let him sit on the floor and look at the pictures again.

Just before they left for the healing, he had managed to get the book inside his innerlining without her seeing him. Now it made his coat hang down a little farther on one side than the other. His mind was dreamy and serene as they walked along and when they turned off the highway onto a long red clay road winding between banks of honeysuckle, he began to make wild leaps and pull forward on her hand as if he wanted to dash off and snatch the sun which was rolling away ahead of them now.

They walked on the dirt road for a while and then they crossed a field stippled with purple weeds and entered the shadows of a wood where the ground was covered with thick pine needles. He had never been in woods before and he walked carefully, looking from side to side as if he were entering a strange country. They moved along a bridle path that twisted downhill through crackling red leaves, and once, catching at a branch to keep himself from slipping, he looked into two frozen green-gold eyes enclosed in the darkness of a tree hole. At the bottom of the hill, the woods opened suddenly onto a pasture dotted here and there with black and white cows and sloping down, tier after tier, to a broad orange stream where the reflection of the sun was set like a diamond.

There were people standing on the near bank in a group, singing. Long tables were set up behind them and a few cars and trucks were parked in a road that came up by the river. They crossed the pasture, hurrying, because Mrs. Connin, using her hand for a shed over her eyes, saw the preacher already standing out in the water. She dropped her basket on one of the tables and pushed the three boys in front of her into the knot of people so that they wouldn't linger by the food. She kept Bevel by the hand and eased her way up to the front.

The preacher was standing about ten feet out in the stream where the water came up to his knees. He was a tall youth in khaki trousers that he had rolled up higher than the water. He had on a blue shirt and a red scarf around his neck but no hat and his light-colored hair was cut in sideburns that curved into the hollows of his cheeks. His face was all bone and red light reflected from the river. He looked as if he might have been nineteen years old. He was singing in a high twangy voice, above the singing on the bank, and he kept his hands behind him and his head tilted back.

He ended the hymn on a high note and stood silent, looking down at the water and shifting his feet in it. Then he looked up at the people on the bank. They stood close together, waiting; their faces were solemn but expectant and every eye was on him. He shifted his feet again.

"Maybe I know why you come," he said in the twangy voice, "maybe I don't.

"If you ain't come for Jesus, you ain't come for me. If you just come to see can you leave your pain in the river, you ain't come for Jesus. You can't leave your pain in the river," he said. "I never told nobody that." He stopped and looked down at his knees.

"I seen you cure a woman oncet!" a sudden high voice shouted from the hump of people. "Seen that woman git up and walk out straight where she had limped in!"

The preacher lifted one foot and then the other. He seemed almost but not quite to smile. "You might as well go home if that's what you come for," he said.

Then he lifted his head and arms and shouted, "Listen to what I got to say, you people! There ain't but one river and that's the River of Life, made out of Jesus' Blood. That's the river you have to lay your pain in, in the River of Faith, in the River of Life, in the River of Love, in the rich red river of Jesus' Blood, you people!"

His voice grew soft and musical. "All the rivers come from that one River and go back to it like it was the ocean sea and if you believe, you can lay your pain in that River and get rid of it because that's the River that was made to carry sin. It's a River full of pain itself, pain itself, moving toward the Kingdom of Christ, to be washed away, slow, you people, slow as this here old red water river round my feet.

"Listen," he sang, "I read in Mark about an unclean man, I read in Luke about a blind man, I read in John about a dead man! Oh you people hear! The same blood that makes this River red, made that leper clean, made that blind man stare, made that dead man leap! You people with trouble," he cried, "lay it in that River of Blood, lay it in that River of Pain, and watch it move away toward the Kingdom of Christ."

While he preached, Bevel's eyes followed drowsily the slow circles of two silent birds revolving high in the air. Across the river there was a low red and gold grove of sassafras with hills of dark blue trees behind it and an occasional pine jutting over the skyline. Behind, in the distance, the city rose like a cluster of warts on the side of the mountain. The birds revolved downward and dropped lightly in the top of the highest pine and sat hunch-shouldered as if they were supporting the sky.

"If it's this River of Life you want to lay your pain in, then come up," the preacher said, "and lay your sorrow here. But don't be thinking this is the last of it because this old red river don't end here. This old red suffering stream goes on, you people, slow to the Kingdom of Christ. This old red river is good to Baptize in, good to lay your faith in, good to lay your pain in, but it ain't this muddy water here that saves you. I been all up and down this river this week," he said. "Tuesday I was in Fortune Lake, next day in Ideal, Friday me and my wife drove to Lulawillow to see a sick man there. Them people didn't see no healing," he said and his face burned redder for a second. "I never said they would."

While he was talking a fluttering figure had begun to move forward with a kind of butterfly movement—an old woman with flapping arms whose head wobbled as if it might fall off any second. She managed to lower herself at the edge of the bank and let her arms churn in the water. Then she bent farther and pushed her face down in it and raised herself up finally, streaming wet; and still flapping, she turned a time or two in a blind circle until someone reached out and pulled her back into the group.

"She's been that way for thirteen years," a rough voice shouted. "Pass the hat and give this kid his money. That's what he's here for." The shout, directed out to the boy in the river, came from a huge old man who sat like a humped stone on the bumper of a long ancient gray automobile. He had on a gray hat that was turned down over one ear and up over the other to expose a purple bulge on his left temple. He sat bent forward with his hands hanging between his knees and his small eyes half closed.

Bevel stared at him once and then moved into the folds of Mrs. Connin's coat and hid himself.

The boy in the river glanced at the old man quickly and raised his fist. "Believe Jesus or the devil!" he cried. "Testify to one or the other!"

"I know from my own self-experience," a woman's mysterious voice called from the knot of people, "I know from it that this preacher can heal. My eyes have been opened! I testify to Jesus!"

The preacher lifted his arms quickly and began to repeat all that he had said before about the River and the Kingdom of Christ and the old man sat on the bumper, fixing him with a narrow squint. From time to time Bevel stared at him again from around Mrs. Connin.

A man in overalls and a brown coat leaned forward and dipped his hand in the water quickly and shook it and leaned back, and a woman held a baby over the edge of the bank and splashed its feet with water. One man moved a little distance away and sat down on the bank and took off his shoes and waded out into the stream; he stood there for a few minutes with his face tilted as far back as it would go, then he waded back and put on his shoes. All this time, the preacher sang and did not appear to watch what went on.

As soon as he stopped singing, Mrs. Connin lifted Bevel up and said, "Listen here, preacher, I got a boy from town today that I'm keeping. His mamma's sick and he wants you to pray for her. And this is a coincident—his name is Bevel! Bevel," she said, turning to look at the people behind her, "same as his. Ain't that a coincident, though?"

There were some murmurs and Bevel turned and grinned over her shoulder at the faces looking at him. "Bevel," he said in a loud jaunty voice.

"Listen," Mrs. Connin said, "have you ever been Baptized, Bevel?"

He only grinned.

"I suspect he ain't ever been Baptized," Mrs. Connin said, raising her eyebrows at the preacher.

"Swang him over here," the preacher said and took a stride forward and caught him.

He held him in the crook of his arm and looked at the grinning face. Bevel rolled his eyes in a comical way and thrust his face forward, close to the preacher's. "My name is Bevvvuuuuul," he said in a loud deep voice and let the tip of his tongue slide across his mouth.

The preacher didn't smile. His bony face was rigid and his narrow gray eyes reflected the almost colorless sky. There was a loud laugh from the old man sitting on the car bumper and Bevel grasped the back of the preacher's collar and held it tightly. The grin had already disappeared from his face. He had the sudden feeling that this was not a joke. Where he lived everything was a joke. From the preacher's face, he knew immediately that nothing the preacher said or did was a joke. "My mother named me that," he said quickly.

"Have you ever been Baptized?" the preacher asked.

"What's that?" he murmured.

"If I Baptize you," the preacher said, "you'll be able to go to the Kingdom of Christ. You'll be washed in the river of suffering, son, and you'll go by the deep river of life. Do you want that?"

"Yes," the child said, and thought, I won't go back to the apartment then, I'll go under the river.

"You won't be the same again," the preacher said. "You'll count." Then he turned his face to the people and began to preach and Bevel looked over his shoulder at the pieces of the white sun scattered in the river.

Suddenly the preacher said, "All right, I'm going to Baptize you now," and without more warning, he tightened his hold and swung him upside down and plunged his head into the water. He held him under while he said the words of Baptism and then he jerked him up again and looked sternly at the gasping child. Bevel's eyes were dark and dilated. "You count now," the preacher said. "You didn't even count before."

The little boy was too shocked to cry. He spit out the muddy water and rubbed his wet sleeve into his eyes and over his face.

"Don't forget his mamma," Mrs. Connin called. "He wants you to pray for his mamma. She's sick."

"Lord," the preacher said, "we pray for somebody in affliction who isn't here to testify. Is your mother sick in the hospital?" he asked. "Is she in pain?"

The child stared at him. "She hasn't got up yet," he said in a high dazed voice. "She has a hangover." The air was so quiet he could hear the broken pieces of the sun knocking in the water.

The preacher looked angry and startled. The red drained out of his face and the sky appeared to darken in his eyes. There was a loud guffaw from the bank and Mr. Paradise shouted, "Haw! Cure the afflicted woman with the hangover!" and began to beat his knee with his fist.

"He's had a long day," Mrs. Connin said, standing with him in the door of the apartment and looking sharply into the room where the party was going on. "I reckon it's past his regular bedtime." One of Bevel's eyes was closed and the other half closed; his nose was running and he kept his mouth open and breathed through it. The damp plaid coat dragged down on one side.

That would be her, Mrs. Connin decided, in the black britches—long black satin britches and barefoot sandals and red toenails. She was lying on half the sofa, with her knees crossed in the air and her head propped on the arm. She didn't get up.

"Hello Harry," she said. "Did you have a big day?" She had a long pale face, smooth and blank, and straight sweet-potato-colored hair, pulled back.

The father went off to get the money. There were two other couples. One of the men, blond with little violet-blue eyes, leaned out of his chair and said, "Well Harry, old man, have a big day?"

"His name ain't Harry. It's Bevel," Mrs. Connin said.

"His name is Harry," *she* said from the sofa. "Whoever heard of anybody named Bevel?"

The little boy had seemed to be going to sleep on his feet, his head drooping farther and farther forward; he pulled it back suddenly and opened one eye; the other was stuck.

"He told me this morning his name was Bevel," Mrs. Connin said in a shocked voice. "The same as our preacher. We been all day at a preaching and healing at the river. He said his name was Bevel, the same as the preacher's. That's what he told me."

"Bevel!" his mother said. "My God! what a name."

"This preacher is name Bevel and there's no better preacher around," Mrs. Connin said. "And furthermore," she added in a defiant tone, "he Baptized this child this morning!"

His mother sat straight up. "Well the nerve!" she muttered.

"Furthermore," Mrs. Connin said, "he's a healer and he prayed for you to be healed."

"Healed!" she almost shouted. "Healed of what for Christ's sake?"

"Of your affliction," Mrs. Connin said icily.

The father had returned with the money and was standing near Mrs. Connin waiting to give it to her. His eyes were lined with red threads. "Go on, go on," he said, "I want to hear more about her affliction. The exact nature of it has escaped. . ." He waved the bill and his voice trailed off. "Healing by prayer is mighty inexpensive," he murmured.

Mrs. Connin stood a second, staring into the room, with a skeleton's appearance of seeing everything. Then, without taking the money, she turned and shut the door behind her. The father swung around, smiling vaguely, and shrugged. The rest of them were looking at Harry. The little boy began to shamble toward the bedroom.

"Come here, Harry," his mother said. He automatically shifted his direction toward her without opening his eye any farther. "Tell me what happened today," she said when he reached her. She began to pull off his coat.

"I don't know," he muttered.

"Yes you do know," she said, feeling the coat heavier on one side. She unzipped the innerlining and caught the book and a dirty handkerchief as they fell out. "Where did you get these?"

"I don't know," he said and grabbed for them. "They're mine. She gave them to me."

She threw the handkerchief down and held the book too high for him to reach and began to read it, her face after a second assuming an exaggerated comical expression. The others moved around and looked at it over her shoulder. "My God," somebody said.

One of the men peered at it sharply from behind a thick pair of glasses. "That's valuable," he said. "That's a collector's item," and he took it away from the rest of them and retired to another chair.

"Don't let George go off with that," his girl said.

"I tell you it's valuable," George said. "1832."

Bevel shifted his direction again toward the room where he slept. He shut the door behind him and moved slowly in the darkness to the bed and sat down and took off his shoes and got under the cover. After a minute a shaft of light let in the tall silhouette of his mother. She tiptoed lightly across the room and sat down on the edge of his bed. "What did that dolt of a preacher say about me?" she whispered. "What lies have you been telling today, honey?"

He shut his eye and heard her voice from a long way away, as if he were under the river and she on top of it. She shook his shoulder. "Harry," she said, leaning down and putting her mouth to his ear, "tell me what he said." She pulled him into a sitting position and he felt as if he had been drawn up from under the river. "Tell me," she whispered and her bitter breath covered his face.

He saw the pale oval close to him in the dark. "He said I'm not the same now," he muttered. "I count."

After a second, she lowered him by his shirt front onto the pillow. She hung over him an instant and brushed her lips against his forehead. Then she got up and moved away, swaying her hips lightly through the shaft of light.

He didn't wake up early but the apartment was still dark and close when he did. For a while he lay there, picking his nose and eyes. Then he sat up in bed and looked out the window. The sun came in palely, stained gray by the glass. Across the street at the Empire Hotel, a colored cleaning woman was looking down from an upper window, resting her face on her folded arms. He got up and put on his shoes and went to the bathroom and then into the front room. He ate two crackers spread with anchovy paste, that he found on the coffee table, and drank some ginger ale left in a bottle and looked around for his book but it was not there.

The apartment was silent except for the faint humming of the refrigerator. He went into the kitchen and found some raisin bread heels and spread a half jar of peanut butter between them and climbed up on the tall kitchen stool and sat chewing the sandwich slowly, wiping his nose every now and then on his shoulder. When he finished he found some chocolate milk and drank that. He would rather have had the ginger ale he saw but they left the bottle openers where he couldn't reach them. He studied what was left in the refrigerator for a while—some shriveled vegetables that she had forgot were there and a lot of brown oranges that she bought and didn't squeeze; there were three or four kinds of cheese and something fishy in a paper bag; the rest was a pork bone. He left the refrigerator door open and wandered back into the dark living room and sat down on the sofa.

He decided they would be out cold until one o'clock and that they would all have to go to a restaurant for lunch. He wasn't high enough for the table yet and the waiter would bring a highchair and he was too big for a highchair. He sat in the middle of the sofa, kicking it with his heels. Then he got up and wandered around the room, looking into the ashtrays at the butts as if this might be a habit. In his own room he had picture books and blocks but they were for the most part torn up; he found the way to get new ones was to tear up the ones he had. There was very little to do at any time but eat; however, he was not a fat boy.

He decided he would empty a few of the ashtrays on the floor. If he only emptied a few, she would think they had fallen. He emptied two, rubbing the ashes carefully into the rug with his finger. Then he lay on the floor for a while, studying his feet which he held up in the air. His shoes were still damp and he began to think about the river.

Very slowly, his expression changed as if he were gradually seeing appear what he didn't know he'd been looking for. Then all of a sudden he knew what he wanted to do.

He got up and tiptoed into their bedroom and stood in the dim light there, looking for her pocketbook. His glance passed her long pale arm hanging off the edge of the bed down to the floor, and across the white mound his father made, and past the crowded bureau, until it rested on the pocketbook hung on the back of a chair. He took a car-token out of it and half a package of Life Savers. Then he left the apartment and caught the car at the corner. He hadn't taken a suitcase because there was nothing from there he wanted to keep.

He got off the car at the end of the line and started down the road he and Mrs. Connin had taken the day before. He knew there wouldn't be anybody at her house because the three boys and the girl went to school and Mrs. Connin had told him she went out to clean. He passed her yard and walked on the way they had gone to the river. The paper brick houses were far apart and after

a while the dirt place to walk on ended and he had to walk on the edge of the highway. The sun was pale yellow and high and hot.

He passed a shack with an orange gas pump in front of it but he didn't see the old man looking out at nothing in particular from the doorway. Mr. Paradise was having an orange drink. He finished it slowly, squinting over the bottle at the small plaid-coated figure disappearing down the road. Then he set the empty bottle on a bench and, still squinting, wiped his sleeve over his mouth. He went in the shack and picked out a peppermint stick, a foot long and two inches thick, from the candy shelf, and stuck it in his hip pocket. Then he got in his car and drove slowly down the highway after the boy.

By the time Bevel came to the field speckled with purple weeds, he was dusty and sweating and he crossed it at a trot to get into the woods as fast as he could. Once inside, he wandered from tree to tree, trying to find the path they had taken yesterday. Finally he found a line worn in the pine needles and followed it until he saw the steep trail twisting down through the trees.

Mr. Paradise had left his automobile back some way on the road and had walked to the place where he was accustomed to sit almost every day, holding an unbaited fishline in the water while he stared at the river passing in front of him. Anyone looking at him from a distance would have seen an old boulder half hidden in the bushes.

Bevel didn't see him at all. He only saw the river, shimmering reddish yellow, and bounded into it with his shoes and his coat on and took a gulp. He swallowed some and spit the rest out and then he stood there in water up to his chest and looked around him. The sky was a clear pale blue, all in one piece—except for the hole the sun made—and fringed around the bottom with treetops. His coat floated to the surface and surrounded him like a strange gay lily pad and he stood grinning in the sun. He intended not to fool with preachers any more but to Baptize himself and to keep on going this time until he found the Kingdom of Christ in the river. He didn't mean to waste any more time. He put his head under the water at once and pushed forward.

In a second he began to gasp and sputter and his head reappeared on the surface; he started under again and the same thing happened. The river wouldn't have him. He tried again and came up, choking. This was the way it had been when the preacher held him under—he had had to fight with something that pushed him back in the face. He stopped and thought suddenly: it's another joke, it's just another joke! He thought how far he had come for nothing and he began to hit and splash and kick the filthy river. His feet were already treading on nothing. He gave one low cry of pain and indignation. Then he heard a shout and turned his head and saw something like a giant pig bounding after him, shaking a red and white club and shouting. He plunged under once and this time, the waiting current caught him like a long gentle hand and pulled him swiftly forward and down. For an instant he was overcome with surprise; then since he was moving quickly and knew that he was getting somewhere, all his fury and his fear left him.

Mr. Paradise's head appeared from time to time on the surface of the water. Finally, far downstream, the old man rose like some ancient water monster and stood empty-handed, staring with his dull eyes as far down the river line as he could see.

Exercises

1. There are many clues in the opening section about the child, his parents, about how he is treated. He stands, for example, nameless, "glum and limp." Though his right arm was caught in the sleeve his father buttoned his coat anyway and "pushed him forward toward a pale spotted hand." Not a person, just a hand. Why didn't his mother see him off? Why does the child jump when his father says good-by? Why was the child without a handkerchief and without breakfast? Why did he claim that his name was Bevel?
2. Why did the child take the sitter's handkerchief?
3. What were the circumstances when the child was beaten up in the park?
4. The rampant hog is a metaphor for what?
5. How does Mrs. Connin differ from "an ordinary sitter" and what does this imply?
6. How is it possible that the child had never heard of Jesus Christ? Why did he steal the book about Jesus?
7. The preacher claimed that he was not a healer. Was he sincere?
8. Who should make the decision to baptize a child? A baby-sitter? A preacher?
9. Was it, somehow, inevitable that the fisherman's name was Mr. Paradise?

TENEBRAE

Denise Levertov (b. 1923)

No other war in American history has had the impact of Vietnam. Conflicting postmortems are still appearing and the spectre of Agent Orange shadows the lives of many Vietnam veterans. Written in 1967 during the protest march on the Pentagon, Levertov's poem, "Tenebrae,"[3] remains as an indictment and an elegy.

Heavy, heavy, heavy, hand and heart.
We are at war,
bitterly, bitterly at war.

And the buying and selling
buzzes at our heads, a swarm   5
of busy flies, a kind of innocence.

Gowns of gold sequins are fitted,
sharp-glinting. What harsh rustlings
of silver moiré there are,
to remind me of shrapnel splinters.   10

And weddings are held in full solemnity
not of desire but of etiquette,
the nuptial pomp of starched lace;
a grim innocence.

And picnic parties return from the beaches   15
burning with stored sun in the dusk;
children promised a TV show when they get home
fall asleep in the backs of a million station wagons,
sand in their hair, the sound of waves
quietly persistent at their ears.   20

They are not listening.
Their parents at night
dream and forget their dreams.
They wake in the dark
and make plans. Their sequin plans   25
glitter into tomorrow.
They buy, they sell.
They fill freezers with food.
Neon signs flash their intentions
into the years ahead.   30
And at their ears the sound
of the war. They are
not listening, not listening.

Exercises

1. Compare the contrasting words and images between rampant materialism and the reality of warfare.
2. What turned *a kind of innocence* into *a grim innocence?*
3. What intentions do neon signs flash?
4. Are they *not listening* because they cannot hear, or will not hear?

A SOLDIER'S EMBRACE

Nadine Gordimer (b. 1923)

In her novels and short stories South Africa's Nadine Gordimer is primarily concerned with the apartheid policies of the Afrikaaner government. In her novel *July's People* (1981), for example, the black revolution, which Gordimer and other white liberals feel is inevitable, has already happened and South Africans, black and white, are trying to adjust to the new order. In "A Soldier's Embrace" the revolution has also succeeded but Gordimer's poignant story of the strange ambivalence of race relations has no geographical boundaries. Her setting is Africa but winning freedom from oppression could take place anywhere in the world.

The day the cease-fire was signed she was caught in a crowd. Peasant boys from Europe who had made up the colonial army and freedom fighters whose column had marched into town were staggering about together outside the barracks, not three blocks from her house in whose rooms, for ten years, she had heard the blurred parade-ground bellow of colonial troops being trained to kill and be killed.

The men weren't drunk. They linked and swayed across the street; because all that had come to a stop, everything *had* to come to a stop: they surrounded cars, bicycles, vans, nannies with children, women with loaves

3. Tenebrae (Latin, darkness), are church services for the last three days of Holy Week that commemorate the suffering and death of Christ. The candles that are lighted at the beginning of the service are extinguished one by one after each Psalm is sung or read, symbolizing the darkness that fell on the land at the time of the crucifixion.

of bread or basins of mangoes on their heads, a road gang with picks and shovels, a Coca-Cola truck, an old man with a barrow who bought bottles and bones. They were grinning and laughing amazement. That it could be: there they were, bumping into each other's bodies in joy, looking into each other's rough faces, all eyes crescent-shaped, brimming greeting. The words were in languages not mutually comprehensible, but the cries were new, a whooping and crowing all understood. She was bumped and jostled and she let go, stopped trying to move in any self-determined direction. There were two soldiers in front of her, blocking her off by their clumsy embrace (how do you do it, how do you do what you've never done before) and the embrace opened like a door and took her in—a pink hand with bitten nails grasping her right arm, a black hand with a big-dialled watch and thong bracelet pulling at her left elbow. Their three heads collided gaily, musk of sweat and tang of strong sweet soap clapped a mask to her nose and mouth. They all gasped with delicious shock. They were saying things to each other. She put up an arm round each neck, the rough pile of an army haircut on one side, the soft negro hair on the other, and kissed them both on the cheek. The embrace broke. The crowd wove her away behind backs, arms, jogging heads; she was returned to and took up the will of her direction again—she was walking home from the post office, where she had just sent a telegram to relatives abroad: ALL CALM DON'T WORRY.

The lawyer came back early from his offices because the courts were not sitting although the official celebration holiday was not until next day. He described to his wife the rally before the Town Hall, which he had watched from the office-building balcony. One of the guerilla leaders (not the most important; he on whose head the biggest price had been laid would not venture so soon and deep into the territory so newly won) had spoken for two hours from the balcony of the Town Hall. 'Brilliant. Their jaws dropped. Brilliant. They've never heard anything on that level: precise, reasoned—none of them would ever have believed it possible, out of the bush. You should have seen de Poorteer's face. He'd like to be able to get up and open his mouth like that. And be listened to like that. . .' The Governor's handicap did not even bring the sympathy accorded to a stammer; he paused and gulped between words. The blacks had always used a portmanteau name for him that meant the-crane-who-is-trying-to-swallow-the-bullfrog. One of the members of the black underground organization that could now come out in brass-band support of the freedom fighters had recognized the lawyer across from the official balcony and given him the freedom fighters' salute. The lawyer joked about it, miming, full of pride. 'You should have been there—should have seen him, up there in the official party. I told you—really—you ought to have come to town with me this morning.'

'And what did you do?' She wanted to assemble all details.

'Oh I gave the salute in return, chaps in the street saluted *me* . . . everybody was doing it. *It was marvellous*. And the police standing by; just to think, last month—only last week—you'd have been arrested.'

'Like thumbing your nose at them,' she said, smiling. 'Did anything go on around here?'

'Muchanga was afraid to go out all day. He wouldn't even run up to the post office for me!' Their servant had come to them many years ago, from service in the house of her father, a colonial official in the Treasury.

'But there was no excitement?'

She told him: 'The soldiers and some freedom fighters mingled outside the barracks. I got caught for a minute or two. They were dancing about; you couldn't get through. All very good-natured.—Oh, I sent the cable.'

An accolade, one side a white cheek, the other a black. The white one she kissed on the left cheek, the black one on the right cheek, as if these were two sides of one face.

That vision, version, was like a poster; the sort of thing that was soon peeling off dirty shopfronts and bus shelters while the months of wrangling talks preliminary to the take-over by the black government went by.

To begin with, the cheek was not white but pale or rather sallow, the poor boy's pallor of winter in Europe (that draft must have only just arrived and not yet seen service) with homesick pimples sliced off by the discipline of an army razor. And the cheek was not black but opaque peat-dark, waxed with sweat round the plump contours of the nostril. As if she could return to the moment again, she saw what she had not consciously noted: there had been a narrow pink strip in the darkness near the ear, the sort of tender stripe of healed flesh revealed when a scab is nicked off a little before it is ripe. The scab must have come away that morning: the young man picked at it in the troop carrier or truck (whatever it was the freedom fighters had; the colony had been told for years that they were supplied by the Chinese and Russians indiscriminately) on the way to enter the capital in triumph.

According to newspaper reports, the day would have ended for the two young soldiers in drunkenness and whoring. She was, apparently, not yet too old to belong to the soldier's embrace of all that a land-mine in the bush might have exploded for ever. That was one version of the incident. Another: the opportunity taken by a woman not young enough to be clasped in the arms of the one who (same newspaper, while the war was on, expressing the fears of the colonists for their women) would be expected to rape her.

She considered this version.

She had not kissed on the mouth, she had not sought anonymous lips and tongues in the licence of festival. Yet she had kissed. Watching herself again, she knew that. She had—god knows why—kissed them on either cheek, his left, his right. It was deliberate, if a swift impulse: she had distinctly made the move.

She did not tell what happened not because her husband would suspect licence in her, but because he would see her—born and brought up in the country as the daughter of an enlightened white colonial official, married to a white liberal lawyer well known for his defence of blacks in political trials—as giving free expression to liberal principles.

She had not told, she did not know what had happened.

She thought of a time long ago when a school camp had gone to the sea and immediately on arrival everyone had run down to the beach from the train, tripping and tearing over sand dunes of wild fig, aghast with ecstatic shock at the meeting with the water.

De Poorteer was recalled and the lawyer remarked to one of their black friends, 'The crane has choked on the bullfrog. I hear that's what they're saying in the Quarter.'

The priest who came from the black slum that had always been known simply by that anonymous term did not respond with any sort of glee. His reserve implied it was easy to celebrate; there were people who 'shouted freedom too loud all of a sudden.'

The lawyer and his wife understood: Father Mulumbua was one who had shouted freedom when it was dangerous to do so, and gone to prison several times for it, while certain people, now on the Interim Council set up to run the country until the new government took over, had kept silent. He named a few, but reluctantly. Enough to confirm their own suspicions—men who perhaps had made some deal with the colonial power to place its interests first, no matter what sort of government might emerge from the new constitution? Yet when the couple plunged into discussion their friend left them talking to each other while he drank his beer and gazed, frowning as if at a headache or because the sunset light hurt his eyes behind his spectacles, round her huge-leaved tropical plants that bowered the terrace in cool humidity.

They had always been rather proud of their friendship with him, this man in a cassock who wore a clenched fist carved of local ebony as well as a silver cross round his neck. His black face was habitually stern—a high seriousness balanced by sudden splurting laughter when they used to tease him over the fist—but never inattentively ill-at-ease.

'What was the matter?' She answered herself; 'I had the feeling he didn't want to come here.' She was using a paper handkerchief dipped in gin to wipe greenfly off the back of a pale new leaf that had shaken itself from its folds like a cut-out paper lantern.

'Good lord, he's been here hundreds of times.'

'—Before, yes.'

What things were they saying?

With the shouting in the street and the swaying of the crowd, the sweet powerful presence that confused the senses so that sound, sight, stink (sweat, cheap soap) ran into one tremendous sensation, she could not make out words that came so easily.

Not even what she herself must have said.

A few wealthy white men who had been boastful in their support of the colonial war and knew they would be marked down by the blacks as arch exploiters, left at once. Good riddance, as the lawyer and his wife remarked. Many ordinary white people who had lived contentedly, without questioning its actions, under the colonial government, now expressed an enthusiastic intention to help build a nation, as the newspapers put it. The lawyer's wife's neighbourhood butcher was one. 'I don't mind blacks.' He was expansive with her, in his shop that he had occupied for twelve years on a licence available only to white people. 'Makes no difference to me who you are so long as you're honest.' Next to a chart showing a beast mapped according to the cuts of meat it provided, he had hung a picture of the most important leader of the freedom fighters, expected to be first President. People like the butcher turned out with their babies clutching pennants when the leader drove through the town from the airport.

There were incidents (newspaper euphemism again) in the Quarter. It was to be expected. Political factions, tribally based, who had not fought the war, wanted to share power with the freedom fighters' Party. Muchanga no longer went down to the Quarter on his day off. His friends came to see him and sat privately on their hunkers near the garden compost heap. The ugly mansions of the rich who had fled stood empty on the bluff above the sea, but it was said they would make money out of them yet— they would be bought as ambassadorial residences when independence came, and with it many black and yellow diplomats. Zealots who claimed they belonged to the Party burned shops and houses of the poorer whites who lived, as the lawyer said, 'in the inevitable echelon of colonial society', closest to the Quarter. A house in the lawyer's street was noticed by his wife to be accommodating what was certainly one of those families, in the outhouses; green nylon curtains had appeared at the garage window, she reported. The suburb was pleasantly overgrown and well-to-do; no one rich, just white professional people and professors from the university. The barracks was empty now, except for an old man with a stump and a police uniform stripped of insignia, a friend of Muchanga, it turned out, who sat on a beer-crate at the gates. He had lost his job as night-watchman when one of the rich people went away, and was glad to have work.

The street had been perfectly quiet; except for that first day.

The fingernails she sometimes still saw clearly were bitten down until embedded in a thin line of dirt all round, in the pink blunt fingers. The thumb and thick fingertips were turned back coarsely even while grasping her. Such hands had never been allowed to take possession. They were permanently raw, so young, from unloading coal, digging potatoes from the frozen Northern Hemisphere, washing hotel dishes. He had not been killed, and now that day of the cease-fire was over he would be delivered back across the sea to the docks, the stony farm, the scullery of the grand hotel. He would have to do anything he could get. There was unemployment in Europe where he had returned, the army didn't need all the young men any more.

A great friend of the lawyer and his wife, Chipande, was coming home from exile. They heard over the radio he was expected, accompanying the future President as confidential secretary, and they waited to hear from him.

The lawyer put up his feet on the empty chair where the priest had sat, shifting it to a comfortable position by hooking his toes, free in sandals, through the slats. 'Imagine, Chipande!' Chipande had been almost a protégé—but they didn't like the term, it smacked of patronage. Tall, cocky, casual Chipande, a boy from the slummiest part of the Quarter, was recommended by the White Fathers' Mission (was it by Father Mulumbua himself?—the lawyer thought so, his wife was not sure they remembered correctly) as a bright kid who wanted to be articled to a lawyer. That was asking a lot, in those days—nine years ago. He never finished his apprenticeship because while he and his employer were soon close friends, and the kid picked up political theories from the books in the house he made free of, he became so involved in politics that he had to skip the country one jump ahead of a detention order signed by the crane-who-was-trying-to-swallow-the-bullfrog.

After two weeks, the lawyer phoned the offices the guerilla-movement-become-Party had set up openly in the town but apparently Chipande had an office in the former colonial secretariat. There he had a secretary of his own; he wasn't easy to reach. The lawyer left a message. The lawyer and his wife saw from the newspaper pictures he hadn't changed much: he had a beard and had adopted the Muslim cap favoured by political circles in exile on the East Coast.

He did come to the house eventually. He had the distracted, insistent friendliness of one who has no time to re-establish intimacy; it must be taken as read. And it must not be displayed. When he remarked on a shortage of accommodation for exiles now become officials, and the lawyer said the house was far too big for two people, he was welcome to move in and regard a self-contained part of it as his private living quarters, he did not answer but went on talking generalities. The lawyer's wife mentioned Father Mulumbua, whom they had not seen since just after the cease-fire. The lawyer added, 'There's obviously some sort of big struggle going on, he's fighting for his political life there in the Quarter.' 'Again,' she said, drawing them into a reminder of what had only just become their past.

But Chipande was restlessly following with his gaze the movements of old Muchanga, dragging the hose from plant to plant, careless of the spray; 'You remember who this is, Muchanga?' she had said when the visitor arrived, yet although the old man had given, in their own language, the sort of respectful greeting even an elder gives a young man whose clothes and bearing denote rank and authority, he was not in any way overwhelmed nor enthusiastic—perhaps he secretly supported one of the rival factions?

The lawyer spoke of the latest whites to leave the country—people who had got themselves quickly involved in the sort of currency swindle that draws more outrage than any other kind of crime, in a new state fearing the flight of capital: 'Let them go, let them go. Good riddance.' And he turned to talk of other things—there were so many more important questions to occupy the attention of the three old friends.

But Chipande couldn't stay. Chipande could not stay for supper; his beautiful long velvety black hands with their pale lining (as she thought of the palms) hung impatiently between his knees while he sat forward in the chair, explaining, adamant against persuasion. He should not have been there, even now; he had official business waiting, sometimes he drafted correspondence until one or two in the morning. The lawyer remarked how there hadn't been a proper chance to talk; he wanted to discuss those fellows in the Interim Council Mulumbua was so warily distrustful of—what did Chipande know?

Chipande, already on his feet, said something dismissing and very slightly disparaging, not about the Council members but of Mulumbua—a reference to his connection with the Jesuit missionaries as an influence that 'comes through'. 'But I must make a note to see him sometime.'

It seemed that even black men who presented a threat to the Party could be discussed only among black men themselves, now. Chipande put an arm round each of his friends as for the brief official moment of a photograph, left them; he who used to sprawl on the couch arguing half the night before dossing down in the lawyer's pyjamas. 'As soon as I'm settled I'll contact you. You'll be around, ay?'

'Oh, we'll be around.' The lawyer laughed, referring, for his part, to those who were no longer. 'Glad to see you're not driving a Mercedes!' he called with reassured affection at the sight of Chipande getting into a modest car. How many times, in the old days, had they agreed on the necessity for African leaders to live simply when they came to power!

On the terrace to which he turned back, Muchanga was doing something extraordinary—wetting a dirty rag with Gilbey's. It was supposed to be his day off, anyway; why was he messing about with the plants when one wanted peace to talk undisturbed?

'Is those thing again, those thing is killing the leaves.'

'For heaven's sake, he could use methylated for that! Any kind of alcohol will do! Why don't you get him some?'

There were shortages of one kind and another in the country, and gin happened to be something in short supply.

Whatever the hand had done in the bush had not coarsened it. It, too, was suede-black, and elegant. The pale lining was hidden against her own skin where the hand grasped her left elbow. Strangely, black does not show toil—she remarked this as one remarks the quality of a fabric. The hand was not as long but as distinguished by beauty as Chipande's. The watch a fine piece of equipment for a fighter. There was something next to it, in fact looped over the strap by the angle of the wrist as the hand grasped. A bit of thong with a few beads knotted where it was joined as a bracelet. Or amulet. Their babies wore such things; often their first and only garment. Grandmothers or mothers attached it as protection. It had worked; he was alive at cease-fire. Some had been too deep in the bush to know, and had been killed after the fighting was over. He had pumped his head wildly and laughingly at whatever it was she—they—had been babbling.

The lawyer had more free time than he'd ever remembered. So many of his clients had left; he was deputed to collect their rents and pay their taxes for them, in the hope that their property wasn't going to be confiscated—there had been alarmist rumours among such people since the day of the cease-fire. But without the rich whites there was little litigation over possessions, whether in the form of the children of dissolved marriages or the houses and cars claimed by divorced wives. The Africans had their own ways of resolving such redistribution of goods. And a gathering of elders under a tree was sufficient to settle a dispute over boundaries or argue for and against the guilt of a woman accused of adultery. He had had a message, in a round-about way, that he might be asked to be consultant on constitutional law to the Party, but nothing seemed to come of it. He took home with him the proposals for the draft constitution he had managed to get hold of. He spent whole afternoons in his study making notes for counter or improved proposals he thought he would send to Chipande or one of the other people he knew in high positions: every time he glanced up, there through his open windows was Muchanga's little company at the bottom of the garden. Once, when he saw they had straggled off, he wandered down himself to clear his head (he got drowsy, as he never did when he used to work twelve hours a day at the office). They ate dried shrimps, from the market: that's what they were doing! The ground was full of bitten-off heads and black eyes on stalks. His wife smiled. 'They bring them. Muchanga won't go near the market since the riot.' 'It's ridiculous. Who's going to harm him?'

There was even a suggestion that the lawyer might apply for a professorship at the university. The chair of the Faculty of Law was vacant, since the students had demanded the expulsion of certain professors engaged during the colonial regime—in particular of the fuddy-duddy (good riddance) who had gathered dust in the Law chair, and the quite decent young man (pity about him) who had had Political Science. But what professor of Political Science could expect to survive both a colonial regime and the revolutionary regime that defeated it? The lawyer and his wife decided that since he might still be appointed in some consultative capacity to the new government it would be better to keep out of the university context, where the students were shouting for Africanization, and even an appointee with his credentials as a fighter of legal battles for blacks against the colonial regime in the past might not escape their ire.

Newspapers sent by friends from over the border gave statistics for the number of what they termed 'refugees' who were entering the neighbouring country. The papers from outside also featured sensationally the inevitable mistakes and misunderstandings, in a new administration, that led to several foreign businessmen being held for investigation by the new regime. For the last fifteen years of colonial rule, Gulf had been drilling for oil in the territory, and just as inevitably it was certain that all sorts of questionable people, from the point of view of the regime's determination not to be exploited preferentially, below the open market for the highest bidder in ideological as well as economic terms, would try to gain concessions.

His wife said, 'The butcher's gone.'

He was home, reading at his desk; he could spend the day more usefully there than at the office, most of the time. She had left after breakfast with her fisherman's basket that she liked to use for shopping, she wasn't away twenty minutes. 'You mean the shop's closed?' There was nothing in the basket. She must have turned and come straight home.

'Gone. It's empty. He's cleared out over the weekend.'

She sat down suddenly on the edge of the desk; and after a moment of silence, both laughed shortly, a strange, secret, complicit laugh. 'Why, do you think?' 'Can't say. He certainly charged, if you wanted a decent cut. But meat's so hard to get, now; I thought it was worth it—justified.'

The lawyer raised his eyebrows and pulled down his mouth: 'Exactly.' They understood; the man probably knew he was marked to run into trouble for profiteering—he must have been paying through the nose for his supplies on the black market, anyway, didn't have much choice.

Shops were being looted by the unemployed and loafers (there had always been a lot of unemployed hanging around for the pickings of the town) who felt the new regime should entitle them to take what they dared not before. Radio and television shops were the most favoured objective for gangs who adopted the freedom fighters' slogans. Transistor radios were the portable

luxuries of street life; the new regime issued solemn warnings, over those same radios, that looting and violence would be firmly dealt with but it was difficult for the police to be everywhere at once. Sometimes their actions became street battles, since the struggle with the looters changed character as supporters of the Party's rival political factions joined in with the thieves against the police. It was necessary to be ready to reverse direction, quickly turning down a side street in detour if one encountered such disturbances while driving around town. There were bodies sometimes; both husband and wife had been fortunate enough not to see any close up, so far. A company of the freedom fighters' army was brought down from the north and installed in the barracks to supplement the police force; they patrolled the Quarter, mainly. Muchanga's friend kept his job as gatekeeper although there were armed sentries on guard: the lawyer's wife found that a light touch to mention in letters to relatives in Europe.

'Where'll you go now?'

She slid off the desk and picked up her basket. 'Supermarket, I suppose. Or turn vegetarian.' He knew that she left the room quickly, smiling, because she didn't want him to suggest Muchanga ought to be sent to look for fish in the markets along the wharf in the Quarter. Muchanga was being allowed to indulge in all manner of eccentric refusals; for no reason, unless out of some curious sentiment about her father?

She avoided walking past the barracks because of the machine guns the young sentries had in place of rifles. Rifles pointed into the air but machine guns pointed to the street at the level of different parts of people's bodies, short and tall, the backsides of babies slung on mothers' backs, the round heads of children, her fisherman's basket—she knew she was getting like the others: what she felt was afraid. She wondered what the butcher and his wife had said to each other. Because he was at least one whom she had known. He had sold the meat she had bought that these women and their babies passing her in the street didn't have the money to buy.

It was something quite unexpected and outside their own efforts that decided it. A friend over the border telephoned and offered a place in a lawyers' firm of highest repute there, and some prestige in the world at large, since the team had defended individuals fighting for freedom of the press and militant churchmen upholding freedom of conscience on political issues. A telephone call; as simple as that. The friend said (and the lawyer did not repeat this even to his wife) they would be proud to have a man of his courage and convictions in the firm. He could be satisfied he would be able to uphold the liberal principles everyone knew he had always stood for; there were many whites, in that country still ruled by a white minority, who deplored the injustices under which their black population suffered etc. and believed you couldn't ignore the need for peaceful change etc.

His offices presented no problem; something called Africa Seabeds (Formosan Chinese who had gained a concession to ship seaweed and dried shrimps in exchange for rice) took over the lease and the typists. The senior clerks and the current articled clerk (the lawyer had always given a chance to young blacks, long before other people had come round to it—it wasn't only the secretary to the President who owed his start to him) he managed to get employed by the new Trades Union Council; he still knew a few blacks who remembered the times he had acted for black workers in disputes with the colonial government. The house would just have to stand empty, for the time being. It wasn't imposing enough to attract an embassy but maybe it would do for a Charge d'Affaires—it was left in the hands of a half-caste letting agent who was likely to stay put: only whites were allowed in, at the country over the border. Getting money out was going to be much more difficult than disposing of the house. The lawyer would have to keep coming back, so long as this remained practicable, hoping to find a loophole in exchange control regulations.

She was deputed to engage the movers. In their innocence, they had thought it as easy as that! Every large vehicle, let alone a pantechnicon, was commandeered for months ahead. She had no choice but to grease a palm, although it went against her principles, it was condoning a practice they believed a young black state must stamp out before corruption took hold. He would take his entire legal library, for a start; that was the most important possession, to him. Neither was particularly attached to furniture. She did not know what there was she felt she really could not do without. Except the plants. And that was out of the question. She could not even mention it. She did not want to leave her towering plants, mostly natives of South America and not Africa, she supposed, whose aerial tubes pushed along the terrace brick erect tips extending hourly in the growth of the rainy season, whose great leaves turned shields to the spatter of Muchanga's hose glancing off in a shower of harmless arrows, whose two-hand-span trunks were smooth and grooved in one sculptural sweep down their length, or carved by the drop of each dead leaf-stem with concave medallions marking the place and building a pattern at once bold and exquisite. Such things would not travel; they were too big to give away.

The evening she was beginning to pack the books, the telephone rang in the study. Chipande—and he called her by her name, urgently, commandingly—'What is this all about? Is it true, what I hear? Let me just talk to him—'

'Our friend,' she said, making a long arm, receiver at the end of it, towards her husband.

'But you can't leave!' Chipande shouted down the phone. '*You* can't go! I'm coming round. *Now.*'

She went on packing the legal books while Chipande and her husband were shut up together in the living-room.

'He cried. You know, he actually cried.' Her husband stood in the doorway, alone.

'I know—that's what I've always liked so much about them, whatever they do. They feel.'

The lawyer made a face: there it is, it happened; hard to believe.

'Rushing in here, after nearly a year! I said, but we haven't seen you, all this time . . . he took no notice. Suddenly he starts pressing me to take the university job, raising all sorts of objections, why not this . . . that. And then he really wept, for a moment.'

They got on with packing books like builder and mate deftly handling and catching bricks.

And the morning they were to leave it was all done; twenty-one years of life in that house gone quite easily into one pantechnicon. They were quiet with each other, perhaps out of apprehension of the tedious search of their possessions that would take place at the border; it was said that if you struck over-conscientious or officious freedom fighter patrols they would even make you unload a piano, a refrigerator or washing machine. She had bought Muchanga a hawker's licence, a hand-cart, and stocks of small commodities. Now that many small shops owned by white shopkeepers had disappeared, there was an opportunity for humble itinerant black traders. Muchanga had lost his fear of the town. He was proud of what she had done for him and she knew he saw himself as a rich merchant; this was the only sort of freedom he understood, after so many years as a servant. But she also knew, and the lawyer sitting beside her in the car knew she knew, that the shortages of the goods Muchanga could sell from his cart, the sugar and soap and matches and pomade and sunglasses, would soon put him out of business. He promised to come back to the house and look after the plants every week; and he stood waving, as he had done every year when they set off on holiday. She did not know what to call out to him as they drove away. The right words would not come again; whatever they were, she left them behind.

Exercises

1. What was symbolized by the embrace of a white European soldier, a black African freedom fighter, and a white woman? What went wrong after that? Why did it go wrong?

2. Consider the role of the black priest who did not want to come to the lawyer's home *after* freedom.

3. Muchanga, the old black servant, is a key figure in the story. At first he wasn't enthusiastic about greeting the returned black leader. Later, he stays with the lawyer and his wife but refuses to take orders from them. What happened to change his attitude? Does he represent the great mass of people who used to work for white families?

4. What was the significance of the African amulet worn next to a fine (European) watch?

5. Perhaps the most important statement was made by the lawyer's wife when she said, about Chipande, "I know—that's what I've always liked so much about them, whatever they do. They feel." What is implied?

6. What were the "right words" that were left behind?

29

Art in the Twentieth Century: Shock Waves and Reactions

Art is either a plagiarist or a revolutionist.
Paul Gauguin

Would you realize what Revolution is, call it Progress; and would you realize what Progress is, call it Tomorrow.
Victor Hugo

Prelude

The beginnings of contemporary art can be traced back to the revolutionary innovations of Édouard Manet, especially as exemplified in his *Olympia* (see fig. 26.22). Manet had insisted that the actual subject matter was "light" but the new conception was even more fundamental than that; the artist's response to the rapidly changing world about him was, in effect, visible on the canvas. *Olympia* was a naked prostitute from Manet's contemporary world. She gazed unconcernedly at a shocked public that still expected art to be an academic enterprise, art that drew its subject matter from myths and legends and instructed the viewer in the beauty of color and line. This was, however, the Age of Progress, the industrial era of cities, factories, slums, trains, Marx, Darwin, and Bismarck. The Renaissance tradition was no longer adequate or even appropriate. The Impressionists did paint from nature but Monet also painted, many times, a Parisian train station crowded with powerful locomotives emitting clouds of steam. Gauguin fled to Polynesia to escape a civilization that he saw as corrupt and diseased. Cézanne's sources were nature, people, and objects of the world in which he lived, not stories and myths of the past. The contemporary world was the basis for the new reality of painting. The stage was set for the advent of modernism.

Artistic Styles to 1945

Painting and Sculpture

Fauvism and Expressionism   Modern art was in the air in 1905, especially in Collioure, a fishing port on the French Mediterranean coast a few miles from the Spanish border. Summering there with his family and a fellow artist, Henri Matisse (ma–TEESS; 1869–1954) saw some Tahitian paintings by Gauguin and was forcibly reminded of Gauguin's contention that color was whatever the artist perceived it to be. Still searching for a style, Matisse had become dissatisfied with copying nature as an Impressionist and he refused to even consider the dots-of-color technique of Seurat. At age thirty-six he found his style in Collioure. In the sparkling southern light he began painting in bold colors with broad and exuberant brushstrokes; he would delight in color for the rest of a long and marvelously productive career. When he displayed some of his Collioure pictures in Paris at the 1905 Salon d'Automne critics were outraged, claiming that the "blotches of barbaric color" bore no relationship to real painting. There was, in fact, a whole roomful of wildly colorful paintings by Matisse, his Collioure colleague André Derain, and other French artists. Perhaps seeking to localize the repercussions, the judges assigned all of their paintings to Room VII, leading the horrified public to believe that this was an organized school with Matisse, the eldest, as its leader. A critic's remark about a roomful of Fauves (foves, "wild beasts")[1] gave the group a name, and critical and public hostility helped create a movement. For a public still unfamiliar with the works of van Gogh and Gauguin, Fauve paintings were shocking. Color was, after all, *true;* apples were red and trees were green. In *The Blue Window* (colorplate 50) Matisse has painted a landscape that is also a still life. The lampshade is green but the beautifully rounded trees in the background are blue. They are, nevertheless, still perceived as trees in an elegantly cool and decorative composition of curving shapes within a series of carefully proportioned rectangles. Color has been freed to become whatever the artist wants it to be.

In an earlier work, *La Coiffure* (fig. 29.1), Matisse reveals the influence of Japanese prints, works similar to those that so affected the styles of van Gogh and Gauguin. Matisse was not, however, a tortured creator like the two lonely Post-Impressionists. Throughout his sixty-year career he was a hard-working but consistently cheerful painter and sculptor who seemingly paid not the slightest attention to the woes of the world, not even the two terrible wars that his country had endured. He was neither insensitive nor indifferent; his concern was with the creation of beauty in a world that had become most unbeautiful.

Georges Rouault (roo–OH; 1871–1958) was, on the other hand, obsessed with the plight of humankind in the twentieth century. Deeply religious, unlike most modern artists, he was unable to accept the

Figure 29.1 Henri Matisse, *La Coiffure,* 1901. Oil on canvas, 37¼ × 31¼". Chester Dale Collection, 1962. National Gallery of Art, Washington, D.C.

joyful hedonism of Matisse or even the relaxed styles of other Fauves. His sympathies lay with clowns and other circus performers, whom he saw as symbols for the tragic victims of society; he was extremely hostile toward corrupt judges and the demimonde of criminals and prostitutes. *Nude with Upraised Arms* (fig. 29.2) is a tortuous study of agitated lines and crude, fleshy form. Clearly judgmental about the woman's ancient profession, the painting has, nevertheless, a ripe sensuality that contrasts sharply with the gracefully decorative nude by Matisse.

Beginning about the same time as Fauvism, German Expressionism was influenced by the French movement and by the anguished work of Edvard Munch (see fig. 26.34). The leading Expressionist sculptor, Ernst Barlach (1870–1938), displays a medieval, craftsmanlike quality in his work. Even though the medium is bronze his *Shivering Woman* (fig. 29.3) has the appearance of a wood carving. Monumental in mass despite its small scale, the huddled figure is a powerful study of concentrated misery. The art of the German avant-garde has an intense emotional content reminiscent of the work of Grünewald (see colorplate 32).

---

1. Though commonly translated as "wild beasts," *fauves* actually means deer; the French call wild beasts *les grands fauves.*

Figure 29.2 Georges Rouault, *Nude with Upraised Arms,* 1906. Oil on canvas, 24¾ × 18¾″. Chester Dale Collection, 1962. National Gallery of Art, Washington, D.C.

Figure 29.3 Ernst Barlach, *Shivering Woman.* Bronze, height 10″, width 6″. The University Art Collections, Arizona State University, Tempe. Gift of Oliver B. James.

German artists were more concerned with political and social conditions before and after World War I than were the French, and none more so than Käthe Kollwitz (1867–1945). Both a sculptor and a graphic artist, Kollwitz became, in 1919, the first female member of the Prussian Academy. A Socialist and a feminist, she concentrated on themes of poverty and injustice, and the problem of being a woman and mother in militaristic Prussia. In *The Only Good Thing About It* (fig. 29.4) the exhausted mother stares numbly at the viewer, her newborn baby on her chest, her other child nestled down in the bed. The baby is presumably a girl. When first published the print had a caption that read: "If they are not used as soldiers they at least deserve to be treated as children." Kollwitz's lifelong campaign against German militarism began even before her personal tragedies. Her only son was killed in combat in World War I and her only grandson met the same fate in World War II.

With his satirical drawings George Grosz (1893–1959) became a prominent spokesman for the antiwar movement in Germany during the 1920s. At first identified with the Berlin Dadists (see Dada below), Grosz developed a pessimistic Expressionist style influenced by the powerful imagery of Grünewald and Bosch (see fig. 18.17). His opposition to the Nazi movement forced him to flee Germany in 1932

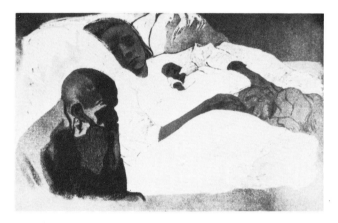

Figure 29.4 Käthe Kollwitz, *The Only Good Thing About It,* 1909. Print. Kunstbibliothek, West Berlin.

Figure 29.5 George Grosz, *I Am Glad I Came Back,* 1943. Oil on masonite, 28 × 20″. The University Art Collections, Arizona State University, Tempe. Gift of Oliver B. James.

Figure 29.6 Pablo Picasso, *The Tragedy,* 1903. Oil on wood, 41½ × 27⅛″. Chester Dale Collection, 1962. National Gallery of Art, Washington, D.C.

for the United States, where he realized his dream of becoming an American citizen. Painted during the horror of a war that he, among many, had forseen, *I Am Glad I Came Back* (fig. 29.5) depicts a grinning skeleton peering through parted draperies at the holocaust of World War II. Symbolically, the work is a vision of the rebirth of the Four Horsemen of the Apocalypse: War, Famine, Pestilence, and Death.

The expressive qualities of strong color impressed some Russian artists also, especially Wassily Kandinsky (1866–1944). Paradoxically, Russia had a long history of strong colors derived from its Byzantine tradition, which Kandinsky came to realize as he studied the intense colors of richly ornamented peasant houses, furniture, and clothing. Moving to Munich to study the movement, he began painting in the German Expressionist style. It was not until about 1908 that he discovered, apparently accidentally, that color could operate independently of subjects. Red, for example, need not be on an apple nor green on a tree; colors could function in expressive compositions without representing specific objects. Called the first Abstract Expressionist as early as 1919, Kandinsky developed theories about the spiritual qualities of colors and the interrelationship of music and art. In

Panel 3 (also known as *Summer;* vol. 1, colorplate 5) he created what can be described as "visual poetry" or "visual music," a celebration of the warmth and brightness of summer.

Cubism and Other Abstractions The most famous and successful artist of this century, Pablo Picasso (1881–1973), was a one-man art movement whose innovations throughout a long and enormously productive career make him impossible to classify or categorize. He is discussed under this heading because he, along with Georges Braque (bra'ak; 1882–1963), invented Cubism. Working in his native Spain after a discouraging first attempt at a career in Paris, Picasso painted *The Tragedy* (fig. 29.6) as a somber monochromatic study, in blue, of sorrowing figures in a timeless setting by an unknown sea. There have been numerous explanations for the artist's brief Blue Period (ca. 1903–1904) but the likeliest appears to be his prolonged melancholy at this stage of his career.

After deciding, in 1904, to live in Paris permanently, Picasso was still poverty-stricken, but his first mistress helped brighten his life and his style. The last of the circus-theme paintings of his Rose Period

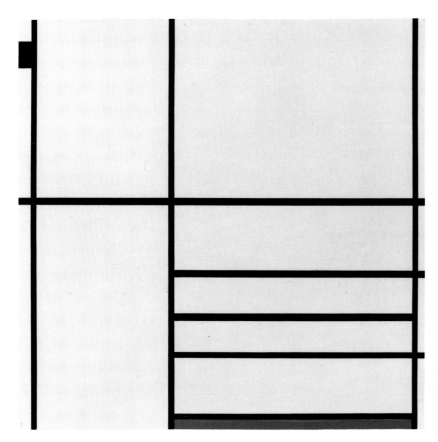

Colorplate 52 Piet Mondrian, *Composition in White, Black, and Red,* 1936. Oil on canvas, 41 × 40¼″. Collection, The Museum of Modern Art, New York. Gift of the Advisory Committee.

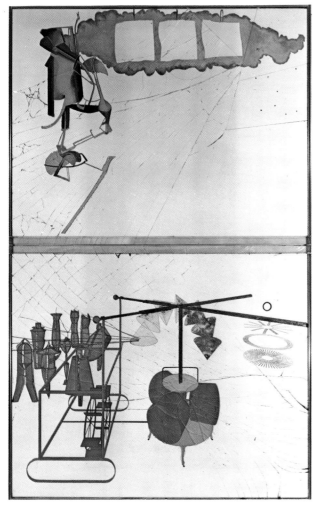

Colorplate 53 Marcel Duchamp, *The Bride Stripped Bare by Her Bachelors, Even,* 1915–1923. Oil, lead wire and foil, and dust and varnish on plate glass (in two parts), 9′ 1¼″ × 5′ 9⅛″. Philadelphia Museum of Art. Bequest of Katherine S. Dreier.

Colorplate 54 Joan Miro, *Person Throwing a Stone at a Bird,* 1926. Oil on canvas, 36¼ × 29″. Collection, The Museum of Modern Art, New York. Acquired through the Lillie P. Bliss Bequest.

Colorplate 55 Jackson Pollack, *Number 1,* 1948. Oil on canvas, 9′8″ × 5′8″. Collection, The Museum of Modern Art, New York. Purchase.

Colorplate 56 Willem de Kooning, *Woman I,* 1950–1952. Oil on canvas, 75⅞ × 58″. Collection, The Museum of Modern Art, New York. Purchase.

Colorplate 57 Mark Rothko, *Number 10,* 1950. Oil on canvas, 90⅜ × 57⅛″. Collection, The Museum of Modern Art, New York. Gift of Philip Johnson.

Colorplate 58 Paul Klee, *Fish Magic,* 1925. Oil and watercolor, varnished, 38⅝ × 30¼". Philadelphia Museum of Art. Louise and Walter Arensberg Collection.

Colorplate 59 Otto Duecker, *Russell, Terry, J. T., and a Levi Jacket,* 1979. Oil on masonite cutouts. Courtesy, The Elaine Horwitch Galleries, Scottsdale.

Figure 29.7 Pablo Picasso, *Family of Saltimbanques,* 1905. Oil on canvas, 90⅜ × 83¾". Chester Dale Collection, 1962. National Gallery of Art, Washington, D.C.

(ca. 1904–1905), the *Family of Saltimbanques* (fig. 29.7) was his first large painting, a kind of summary that concluded the period. The Jester stands between Harlequin at the left along with two boy acrobats. Like objects in a still life, the figures are expressionless and motionless. As was his custom, Picasso has portrayed some members of his "gang," including himself as Harlequin, but there is no explanation for the isolated woman at the right.

Picasso could have painted in the lyrical Rose Period style indefinitely. By 1906 his works were selling so well that he had become, next to Matisse, perhaps the best-known painter in Paris. And so, having mastered the style, he moved on to a new style. His studies of ancient Iberian sculptures and African masks and figures like the *Dogon Ancestor Figure* (fig. 29.8) led him to produce a painting of five nude women that astonished and horrified art dealers, and even his friends. Unlike anything ever seen in art, *Les Demoiselles d'Avignon* (fig. 29.9) represented a breakthrough as epochal as Masaccio's *The Tribute Money* (see fig. 18.9) at the beginning of the Italian Renaissance. Masaccio established Renaissance perspective; with this painting Picasso destroyed it. Just about all the rules were broken: flat picture plane with no one-point perspective; angular and fragmented bodies; distorted faces with enormous eyes; two figures wearing grotesque Africanlike masks. With a remarkable economy of means Picasso created tense and massive figures whose heads and facial features are seen simultaneously in full face and profile, marking a great step forward in the evolution of Cubism. A friend of the artist added the title later, a reference to a brothel on Avignon Street in Barcelona.

Figure 29.8 African, *Dogon Ancestor Figure* (2 views). Wood, 8⅝ × 2¼ × 2". The University Art Collections, Arizona State University, Tempe. Gift of Dr. and Mrs. Richard Bessom.

Figure 29.9 Pablo Picasso, *Les Demoiselles d'Avignon,* 1907. Oil on canvas, 8′ × 7′8″. Collection, The Museum of Modern Art, New York.

Figure 29.10 Pablo Picasso, *The Lovers,* 1923. Oil on canvas, 51¼ × 38¼". Chester Dale Collection, 1962. National Gallery of Art, Washington, D.C.

Picasso and Braque took Cubism through several phases, from a faceting of three-dimensional figures to flattened images and rearranged forms. In *Still Life* (colorplate 51) Picasso uses forms from the "real" world to confuse reality and illusion. All is two-dimensional but shadows cast by objects on the tilted tabletop further add to the confusion. What is reality here? Actually, colors and forms on canvas. Inspired in part by Cézanne's compressed forms (see colorplate 47), Cubism was a refutation of our Mediterranean classical heritage as the sole criteria for creating and viewing art. Though Picasso did not forsake Cubism, his studies in Rome of ancient and Renaissance art led to Neoclassic works like *The Lovers* (fig. 29.10). Recalling both classical sculpture and the style of Raphael, the two figures are conceived with bulk and monumentality but outlined with sure, delicate lines.

Inspired by a new German mistress with blond hair and high-bridged nose, Picasso painted her in a number of colorful works, of which his personal favorite was *Girl Before a Mirror* (see colorplate 7, vol. 1). Standing nude before a mirror, she is young and innocent but the mirror image is older and darker, mysterious and sultry. The wide range of vivid colors set off by heavy dark lines is reminiscent of medieval stained glass, perhaps indicating that Picasso had in mind Eve the Temptress or even a modern-day version of the Madonna.

During the afternoon of April 26, 1937, the Spanish Civil War came home to the Spanish artist living in Paris. German bombers virtually destroyed the Basque town of Guernica and, 25 sketches and one month later, Picasso had completed his anguished protest against the brutal destruction of a defenseless town (fig. 29.11). The central figure is a wounded horse that, according to the artist, represents the people, while the bull symbolizes not Fascism but brutality and darkness. Possibly representing the threatened Light of Reason, a light bulb is superimposed on the blazing sun. Painted on an enormous scale in a stark black, white, and gray, the work is a monumental protest against the impersonal brutality of modern warfare. At the bottom center is one small symbol of life: a fragile flower above the broken sword. Picasso decreed that the work would remain on loan to the Museum of Modern Art in New York until democracy was restored in Spain, a condition that was deemed satisfied in 1982.

In the United States, Georgia O'Keeffe (b. 1887), whose training was entirely American, applied abstract concepts to American themes. Her *Horse's Skull on Blue* (fig. 29.12) evokes the mood of the Southwest, to which she moved permanently after the death of her husband, the celebrated photographer Alfred Stieglitz (1864–1946). Together they had operated the Little Gallery of the Photo-Secession that Stieglitz had earlier opened at 291 Fifth Avenue in New York. At "291," as the art world called it, they had shown, for the first time in America, works by Cézanne, Picasso, Toulouse-Lautrec, Rodin, Matisse, Brancusi, and Henri Rousseau.

American abstract artists, like their European counterparts, had to combat the hostility of a public accustomed to representational art and the resistance of both academicians and the Ash Can school (discussed below under Realism). The modernists of "291" ended the internecine warfare by inducing academicians and Ash Can artists to form, in 1911, the Association of American Artists and Painters. An exhibition of contemporary American art was to be the first project, but the end result was the epochal New York Armory Show of 1913, still the most controversial exhibition ever staged in this country. Convinced that the public was ready for new ideas, the organizers included European modernists in what was officially called the International Exhibition of Modern Art. Works by Cézanne, Rousseau, Gauguin, van Gogh, Matisse, Duchamp, and Picasso astounded and infuriated artists, critics, and, most of all, the public. The shocked organizers dismissed the public reaction as militant ignorance, which it was, but American modernists were dismayed to see how far behind they themselves were. The Armory Show was "the greatest single influence that I have experienced" said Stuart Davis (1894–1964) as he altered his style and, like many American artists, sailed to Paris. His cubistic *Radio Tubes* (fig. 29.13) is a characteristically whimsical celebration of American technology at a time

Figure 29.11 Pablo Picasso, *Guernica,* 1937. Oil on canvas, 25′ 5¾″ × 11′5½″. The Prado Museum, Madrid.

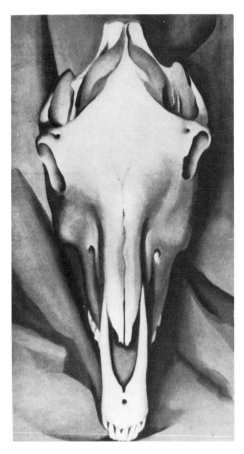

Figure 29.12 Georgia O'Keeffe, *Horse's Skull on Blue,* 1930. Oil on canvas, 30 × 16″. The University Art Collections, Arizona State University, Tempe. Gift of Oliver B. James.

Figure 29.13 Stuart Davis, *Radio Tubes,* 1940. Gouache, 22 × 14″. The University Art Collections, Arizona State University, Tempe. Gift of Oliver B. James.

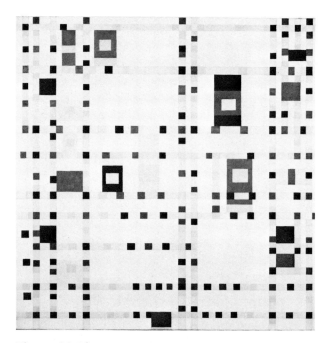

Figure 29.14 Piet Mondrian, *Broadway Boogie Woogie,* 1942–1943. Oil on canvas, 50 × 50″. Collection, The Museum of Modern Art, New York. Given anonymously.

Figure 29.15 Constantin Brancusi, *The Kiss,* 1908. Limestone, height 23″. The Philadelphia Museum of Art. Louise and Walter Arensberg Collection.

when advanced technology was naively thought to be uniquely American. Contending that the camera was the proper instrument for recording facts, Davis believed, as did most modernists, that his function was to make new statements. Though influenced by European Cubism, *Radio Tubes* is, in its own way, as American as the work of Georgia O'Keeffe.

Though he was attracted to the work of the French Cubists, the Dutch artist Piet Mondrian (1872–1944) felt that their art did not express what he called "pure reality." He sought "plastic expression" in a basic reality made up solely of colors and forms. *Composition in White, Black, and Red* (colorplate 52) is a precisely balanced work in a style generally called Geometric Abstraction. Of the sixteen rectangles no two are of the same size or shape nor are all the heavy black lines the same width. The poised serenity of Mondrian's "compositions" is as classical as a Greek temple. Mondrian's ideas influenced many artists but they have also been popularized, in simplified and sometimes distorted versions, in fashion, interior, and advertising design.

Both Mondrian and Kandinsky produced nonrepresentational art and both believed that their paintings were analogous to music. Though this analogy may not be apparent in colorplate 52, unless in conjunction with the music of Mozart, Mondrian's *Broadway Boogie Woogie* (fig. 29.14) is different; it pulses with the rhythm and vitality of New York's Great White Way. Along with European artists Marc Chagall, Max Ernst, Yves Tanguy, Thomas Mann, Bertolt Brecht, and others, Mondrian lived in New York as a refugee from Hitler and the German armies.

Though he did not live to see the defeat of Nazi Germany, this work and a companion piece called *Victory Boogie Woogie* embodied the artist's admiration for America.

The Roumanian sculptor Constantin Brancusi (bran–KOOSH; 1876–1957) was first influenced by Rodin when studying in Paris but developed an abstract style that was to influence many artists. An ancestor of cubist sculture, the amusing *The Kiss* (fig. 29.15) reduces this kind of personal interaction to its essentials, to a meaningful minimum. His *Bird in Space* (fig. 29.16) conveys, in an elegantly swelling shape, the soaring spirit of flight. It is a magnificent work of transcendental beauty that epitomizes the sculptor's statement: "I bring you pure joy."

Fantasy, Dada, and Surrealism Fantasy plays a large part in twentieth-century art, and the Russian artist Marc Chagall (shah–GALL; b. 1889) has been a leading exponent. Chagall combines Fauve color and Cubist forms with a personal vision of his early life in a Russian village. In *I and the Village* (fig. 29.17) cow and peasant speak to each other; a peasant marches up the street after his wife, who floats upside down; and a magic tree grows out of a hand. Chagall's paintings are meant to be enjoyed as pictorial arrangements of images that fascinated the artist and enchant the viewer.

Figure 29.16 Constantin Brancusi, *Bird in Space,* ca. 1928. Polished bronze, unique cast, ca. 54″ high. Collection, The Museum of Modern Art, New York.

Figure 29.17 Marc Chagall, *I and the Village,* 1911. Oil on canvas, 75⅝ × 59⅝″. Collection, The Museum of Modern Art, New York. Mrs. Simon Guggenheim Fund.

The German-Swiss artist Paul Klee (klay; 1879–1940) was a master of fantasy. Through his teaching at the Bauhaus (see fig. 29.29) and his painting, Klee was one of the most influential artists of the century. Rejecting illusionistic art as obsolete, he turned to the art of children and primitives as inspirations for his paintings. *Fish Magic* (colorplate 58) is a whimsical fantasy of disparate objects placed, with infinite care, in harmonious relationships. Nothing in this work is invented. As a shrewd observer of nature and people, Klee coded his findings and arranged them on canvas. Everything is from the real world but transformed into a magical composition.

The fantasies of Giorgio de Chirico (day KEE–re–ko; 1888–1979) were as subjective as those of Chagall but infused with pessimism and melancholy. Born in Greece of Italian parents, de Chirico first studied in Athens but, like many artists of the time, wound up in Paris where he studied the Old Masters in the Louvre. Strongly influenced by the German philosopher Nietzsche (see chap. 28), de Chirico looked upon himself as a metaphysical painter who explored the mysteries of life. In *The Nostalgia of the Infinite* (fig. 29.18) he used a distorted Renaissance perspective in a characteristic dreamlike cityscape in which everything is real, except that it isn't. Pennants are flying vigorously from a sinister and threatening tower in front of which two miniscule figures cast disproportionately long shadows. Like most of his images, this building actually exists in Turin but the strange juxtaposition creates another reality that is not of the waking world.

As early as 1914 it had become obvious to some artists that World War I marked the low point of a bankrupt Western culture. By 1916, exiles from the war that was consuming Europe had formed, in neutral Switzerland, the Cabinet Voltaire, a loose-knit and contentious group devoted to attacking everything that Western civilization held dear. For whatever reason, these writers, artists, musicians, and poets chose the word *Dada* to identify their iconoclastic movement. Dada was an idea whose time had come, for it happened even earlier in New York with the arrival, in 1915, of Marcel Duchamp (due–SHAWM; 1887–1968). Duchamp was always the greatest exponent of the "anti-art" movement known as Dada, having already turned "found" objects into art by, for example, hanging a snow shovel on a gallery wall and labelling it *In Advance of a Broken Arm.* He made

Figure 29.18 Giorgio de Chirico, *The Nostalgia of the Infinite,* ca. 1913–1914, dated 1911 on the painting. Oil on canvas, 53¼ × 25½". Collection, The Museum of Modern Art, New York. Purchase.

the first mobile in 1913 by fastening an inverted bicycle wheel to the top of a stool and presenting it as a sculpture with moving parts. Typical of his assault on the citadel of formal art was the reproduction of the *Mona Lisa* to which he added a moustache and a goatee and the title of *L.H.O.O.Q.* which, when pronounced letter by letter in French means "She's got a hot ass."

Duchamp found a congenial home in Stieglitz's "291" and began work on his Dada masterpiece enigmatically titled *The Bride Stripped Bare by Her Bachelors, Even,* more commonly referred to as *The Large Glass* (colorplate 53). The following analysis is based on Duchamp's notes which, given the artist's proclivity for paradox and irony, may be accepted, modified, or rejected. According to Duchamp, this is the story of a bride, located in the upper section and symbolized by an internal combustion engine with a reservoir of love gasoline and a magneto of desire. She is lusted after by the nine bachelors in the left lower section: the reddish-brown molds resembling chessmen. Each bachelor is a stereotype of what were, at the time, masculine occupations: priest, delivery boy, policeman, warrior, gendarme, undertaker's assistant, busboy, stationmaster, and flunky. Capillary tubes carry gas from each bachelor mold to the center of the glass and to one of seven funnels, where the gas solidifies into large needles. These needles, in turn, break into spangles of frosty gas and then into liquid drops of semen that splash into the bride's domain. At the moment depicted in the glass the bride is stripped but she remains undefiled; bride and bachelors are caught between desire and possession/surrender. Duchamp intended the work to be humorous and sexual, satirizing machines, people, and social conventions. He succeeded on all counts.

The leading German Dadaist, Kurt Schwitters (1887–1948), collected trash from wastebaskets and gutters to compose collages of the detritus of civilization. When once asked what art was, Schwitters responded with, "What isn't?" *Sichtbar* (fig. 29.19), meaning "visible," proves that an artist can arrange the unlikeliest materials into a meaningful statement. Like so many of his constructions, this work visualizes the modern city as a compressor and energizer of life, constantly changing, leaving behind the rubbish of yesterday.

Though Schwitters continued to collect and arrange his Dada collages, completely filling several three-story houses in the process, the movement was generally absorbed by the Surrealists, who coalesced around the Manifesto of Surrealism issued in 1924 by the writer André Breton, a disciple of Sigmund Freud (see chap. 27). Surrealism in art is, briefly stated, the theory that dreams, and those waking moments when subconscious images overwhelm our intellect, furnish us with material far more relevant to our lives than traditional subject matter. The world of psychic experience, as explored by Freud and others, was to be combined with consciousness to create a super-reality *(surréalité)* called Surrealism.

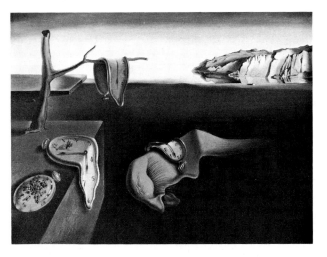

Figure 29.20 Salvador Dali, *The Persistence of Memory,* 1931. Oil on canvas, 13 × 9¼″. Collection, The Museum of Modern Art, New York. Given anonymously.

Figure 29.21 Meret Oppenheim, *Luncheon in Fur,* 1936. Fur-covered cup, saucer, and spoon. Collection, The Museum of Modern Art, New York.

Figure 29.19 Kurt Schwitters, *Sichtbar,* 1923. Collage, ca. 7 × 5″. Estate of Kurt Schwitters. Courtesy Marlborough Gallery, New York.

Surrealism was an organized movement in revolt against conventional art and society but there was no single style. Artists like Joan Miro (ME–row; 1893–1983) drew upon their personal dream world. In *Person Throwing a Stone at a Bird* (colorplate 54) Miro does not abstract the human image but seems, instead, to humanize abstractions. In a witty and humorous style, sometimes called Biomorphic Abstraction, he creates an amoebic person with one huge foot, bulbous body, and orange and yellow eye. This being seems to fall back in wonder as an oblong stone falls in a delineated trajectory toward an appealing bird with a crescent torso from which a longline neck projects to a lavendar head topped by a flaming cock's comb. This is super-reality. "Everything in my pictures exists," stated Miro; "there is nothing abstract in my pictures."

Still the professed spokesman of the movement, Salvador Dali (DAH–lee; b. 1904) stresses paradox, disease, decay, and eroticism. *The Persistence of Memory* (fig. 29.20) is a tiny painting of a vast landscape in which watches hang limply and dejectedly. A strange chinless creature with protruding tongue (alive? dead?) lies in the foreground of a Renaissance perspective construction lit by an eerie glow. A dead tree grows out of a table (?) on which the only flat watch lies, a metal timepiece infested with sinister-looking bugs. Anything is possible in dreams.

Startling distortions or juxtapositions are basic to Surrealism as Meret Oppenheim's (b. 1913) surrealistic object *Luncheon in Fur* (fig. 29.21) demonstrates. The absurdity of a fur-lined teacup has become a symbol of Surrealism. Her now familiar but bizarre ensemble is typical of the push-pull effect of many Surrealist works. Our intellect is titillated but our senses of touch and taste are outraged.

With the exception of one artist there has been little significant surrealist sculpture. Surrealists believed in automatism, in just letting a painting happen, and shaping solid objects is too painstaking an endeavor to be directed by the subconscious. Only Alberto Giacometti (zhak–ko–MET–ti; 1901–1966) succeeded in creating three-dimensional equivalents

Figure 29.22 Alberto Giacometti, *The Palace at 4 A.M.,* 1932–1933. Wood, glass, wire, and string, 25 × 28 × 15¾". Collection, The Museum of Modern Art, New York. Purchase.

Figure 29.23 Alton Pickens, *The Blue Doll,* 1942. Oil on canvas, 42⅞ × 35". Collection, The Museum of Modern Art, New York. James Thrall Soby Fund.

Figure 29.24 Yves Tanguy, *The Stone in the Tree,* 1942. Oil on canvas, 24 × 18". The University Art Collections, Arizona State University, Tempe. Gift of Oliver B. James.

of surrealist pictures. *The Palace at 4* A.M. (fig. 29.22) is an airy cage with a skeletal backbone in a smaller cage at the right and the figure of a woman on the left, the latter possibly representing the artist's mother. In the center is a spoon shape with which the artist said he identified and, at the upper right, the skeleton of a prehistoric bird that supposedly greets the dawn at 4 A.M. The air of dreamlike mystery is all pervasive.

Dreams can also be nightmares. In *The Blue Doll* (fig. 29.23) the American Surrealist Alton Pickens (b. 1917) depicts the murder of a doll, or perhaps two dolls. The distorted and brutal figures dominate an eerie and terrifying scene that is the stuff of nightmares.

Yves Tanguy (tawn–geay; 1900–1955) was a member of the original Surrealist group in Paris. After his escape from the Nazis in 1939 he was associated with the New York group of emigrées and later became an American citizen. He was, like Rousseau, an untrained artist. Throughout his career he painted vast and desolate landscapes inhabited by strange, haunting objects. *The Stone in the Tree* (fig. 29.24) depicts an endless space with no reference points. The eerie objects are not totally lifeless, seeming to possess a flicker of life left over from a destroyed universe. The artist appears to be portraying (in 1942!) our world after the ultimate nightmare of a nuclear holocaust.

Realism in America From the early days of the Republic there has always been a strain of Realism on the American scene, a tradition separate from European Realists like Courbet and Millet. While European artists were experimenting with Impressionism, Americans like Thomas Eakins (1844–1916) and Winslow Homer (see colorplate 42) continued to paint reality as they perceived it. At the beginning of this century Robert Henri (hen–RYE; 1865–1929) founded a new school of realism called The Eight. Working almost entirely in New York, the followers of Henri painted city scenes of tenement life and

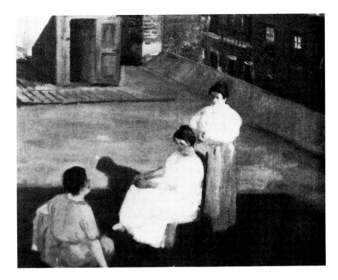

Figure 29.25 John Sloan, *Roof Gossips,* ca. 1912. Oil on canvas, 24 × 20″. The University Art Collections, Arizona State University, Tempe. Gift of Oliver B. James.

Figure 29.26 Edward Hopper, *Cottage, Cape Cod,* 1942. Oil on canvas, 27 × 19″. The University Art Collections, Arizona State University, Tempe. Gift of Oliver B. James.

everyday activities of, mainly, the working class. A derogatory remark by a critic gave still another new style a label. After the caustic comment that they "even painted ash cans," The Eight became known as the Ash Can school. John Sloan (1871–1951), a leading artist of the school, painted *Roof Gossips* (fig. 29.25) as if the three women on the tenement roof were the subject of a casual snapshot. Actually, the work is an artful composition of lines and forms. Reminiscent of the high viewpoint of Mary Cassatt's *The Bath* (see fig. 26.25), we witness an intimate and relaxed scene but are not a part of it. Academicians were critical of the gritty realism of Sloan and the Ash Can school but did join with them and the avant-garde of "291" to present the Armory Show the year after this work was painted.

A student of Henri's in the early 1900s, Edward Hopper (1882–1967) was more concerned with formal design than were his Ash Can colleagues. He did not paint people in everyday life but sought subjects like old houses and buildings along the coast of Maine and on Cape Cod. His *Cottage, Cape Cod* (fig. 29.26), like most of his paintings, rests on a solid horizontal base from which the rising verticals and slanting diagonals outline a house "with sunlight on the side" as Hopper preferred to paint. The broad, uncluttered planes, sunlight, and shadows give the house a brooding air of loneliness and melancholy.

Best described as Social Realists, Diego Rivera, José Orozco, and David Siqueiros were the most important Mexican mural painters of the century. Diego Rivera (1886–1957), though he lived and studied in Europe for many years, disavowed modernism in his zeal to create a distinctly Mexican style in the Socialist spirit of the protracted Mexican revolution (1910–1940). Like most of his subjects, *Niña Parada* (fig. 29.27) is one of the common people, a stocky child with a heavy body and broad, impassive face.

Figure 29.27 Diego Rivera, *Niña Parada,* 1937. Oil on canvas, 31½ × 23½″. The University Art Collections, Arizona State University, Tempe. Gift of Oliver B. James.

Figure 29.28 Antonio Gaudi, Church of the Holy Family, 1883–1926. Barcelona.

Figure 29.29 Walter Gropius, Workshop of the Bauhaus, 1925–1926. Dessau, Germany.

Despite her obvious youth she looks considerably older. Weary and endlessly patient, she represents a class that for centuries had been downtrodden and exploited.

Architecture

Art Nouveau was a turn-of-the-century style that grew out of an English Arts and Crafts movement to revive medieval craftsmanship. Determined to raise interior and decorative design to the eminence enjoyed by painting and sculpture, Art Nouveau artists and craftsmen developed an elaborate curvilinear style that assiduously avoided straight lines and right angles. Line drawings by Aubrey Beardsley (1872–1898) and multicolored lamps by Louis Comfort Tiffany (1848–1933) were Art Nouveau, as was the basic style of the Spanish architect Antonio Gaudi (gow–D; 1852–1926). In his Church of the Holy Family (fig. 29.28) Gaudi went beyond the Art Nouveau style to architectural innovations never seen before or since. Working with a church that had already been started as a Gothic revival structure, Gaudi added four bottle-shaped spires pierced by innumerable holes and topped by glittering crystal decorations. Although the enormous building is primarily of cut stone, it looks eroded and dessicated, organic rather than man-made. Much of the exterior is studded with bright ceramic decorations, with more scheduled to be added if and when the building is completed.

Art Nouveau tried, unsuccessfully, to deny the Industrial Age but the work of the design school called Bauhaus (BOUGH–house) exploited modern technology. As director of Bauhaus, Walter Gropius (1883–1969) promoted instruction in not only painting, sculpture, and architecture, but also in the crafts, with everything oriented toward the latest in technology and industrial design. The workshop (fig. 29.29) is a four-story box with an interior steel skeleton enclosed by window walls of glass, the latter a Gropius invention. The design established the principles of the International Style that was to dominate architectural design into the 1970s. Expensive to heat and to cool, not to mention washing the windows, International Style buildings appear as anomalies in the energy-conscious 1980s. For half a century, however, they were the essence of modernity.

The International Style was brilliantly developed by the Swiss painter-architect Charles-Edouard Jeanneret known as Le Corbusier (luh core–BOOS–iay; 1887–1965). For Le Corbusier, houses were "machines for living," as efficient as airplanes were for flying. Totally devoid of ornament, his Villa Savoye (fig. 29.30) is partially supported by the slender columns but rests mostly on a recessed unit containing service functions, servants quarters, entrance hall, and staircase to the living quarters on the second level.

Figure 29.30 Le Corbusier, Villa Savoye, 1929. Poissy-sur-Seine, France.

The living room is separated from an open interior terrace by floor-to-ceiling panes of glass, making the terrace a basic part of living arrangements.

International Style buildings are, in effect, disdainful of their environment, thrusting away from the earth to create their own internal space. America's greatest architect, Frank Lloyd Wright (1867–1959), disagreed totally with this concept. Wright's buildings are generally organic, seemingly a natural consequence of their environment. One of his most imaginative designs is the Kaufmann House (fig. 29.31). Built on a site that would challenge any architect and which obviously inspired Wright, the house is situated on a steep and rocky hillside over a waterfall. Combining native rock construction with daring cantilevers colored beige to blend with the environment, the structure cannot even be imagined on any other site. The Villa Savoye and Falling Water represent, between them, opposite theories of modern design; subsequent developments tended to fall somewhere between the two extremes.

Artistic Styles Since 1945

Painting and Sculpture

Action Painting: Abstract Expressionism After World War II, New York replaced Paris as the artistic capital of the Western world. The acknowledged leader of a new artistic movement was Jackson Pollock (1912–1956), who was once a Social Realist. Pollock's personal style of Abstract Expressionism began to

Figure 29.31 Frank Lloyd Wright, Kaufmann House ("Falling Water"), 1936. Bear Run, Pennsylvania.

bloom when he quit easel painting and, instead, tacked a large, unstretched canvas to the floor. Walking all around the canvas he became completely absorbed as he dropped, dripped, poured, and spattered paint on the canvas. Though he had no preconceived ideas when he began a canvas he could, as he said, "control the flow of the paint," and he did complete works with brushstrokes as needed. His *Number 1* (colorplate 55) is an intricate and complex interplay of curvilinear lines and controlled spatters illustrating, as he remarked, "energy made visible." Pollock's energetic involvement in the act of painting led to the term Action Painting as a general descriptor of the movement.

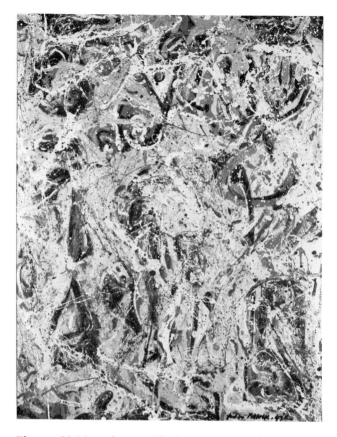

Figure 29.32 Jackson Pollock, *Galaxy,* 1946. Joslyn Art Museum, Omaha, Nebraska. Gift of Miss Peggy Guggenheim.

Pollock's style of Abstract Expressionism totally abandoned all recognizable forms and shapes, a remarkable achievement in itself. His *Galaxy* (fig. 29.32) has both lines and shapes; forms rest upon forms that cover still other forms. As our eyes move endlessly over the vitalized canvas we seem to perceive distant, indistinct solar systems through a blizzard of molecular dots that themselves appear to be faraway stars.

The Dutch-American artist Willem de Kooning (b. 1904) works in violent motions using a brush heavy with paint. His favorite theme is that of the eternal woman: earth mother and goddess of fertility. *Woman I* (colorplate 56) is a giant, earthy figure of a woman painted in slashing brushstrokes. An energetic portrayal of a goddess cum movie queen and sex symbol, this is one man's view of the other half of the human race.

In his mature style Mark Rothko (1903–1970) covered large canvases with luminous, softly bleeding rectangles of color. *Number 10* (colorplate 57) is an extremely subtle combination of softly glowing colors separated by ragged, foggy edges. Compared with the dynamics of Pollock and de Kooning, this is Abstract Expressionism in a gentle and meditative mood in a style frequently called Color Field.

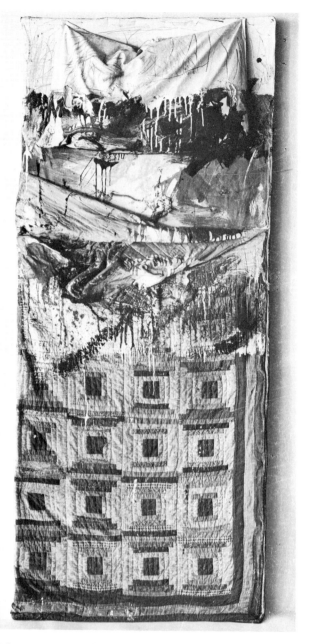

Figure 29.33 Robert Rauschenberg, *Bed,* 1955. Combine painting, 74 × 31″. Leo Castelli, New York.

Reaction against Action: Pop Art The emotional fervor of Abstract Expressionism burned itself out in about fifteen years, to be superseded by a Dada-type reaction. The self-confidence of America after World War II had been jolted by the Korean conflict, the Cold War, and the buildup in Vietnam. A new breed of artists was skeptical of American accomplishments and chose the banalities of American life to satirize the superficiality of American culture. First called Neo-Dadaists, these artists used recognizable subject matter from American popular culture: soup cans, comic strips, road signs, and cult figures from Rock music and commercial Hollywood movies.

Figure 29.34 Robert Rauschenberg, *Monogram,* 1959. Construction, 48 × 72 × 72". Moderna Museet, Stockholm, Sweden.

The movement was labeled Pop Art when it burst on the national scene in 1962, but Robert Rauschenberg (b. 1925) had been working his way from Abstract Expressionism to Pop Art since the mid 50s. His *Bed* (fig. 29.33) includes a pillow and quilt over which he has splashed paint. Real objects have been combined with paint, destroying their original, familiar meaning so that they become part of a composition with an independent existence. Neither sculpture nor painting, this is, as the artist says, a combine that unites two-dimensional and three-dimensional art.

There are recognizable objects in Rauschenberg's *Monogram* (fig. 29.34) like the old tire, stuffed Angora goat, and pieces of stenciled signs. The goat and tire were once waste that has been recycled, so to speak. Paradoxically, they are still distasteful objects, retaining their identity and creating a tension between themselves and the total work. They should not be there but they are, undeniably, there, forever and ever. Rauschenberg has stated that painting is related to art and to life and that his function is to "act in the gap between the two."

Another early leader of the Pop movement, Jasper Johns (b. 1930), painted familiar images like flags, targets, maps, and numbers. Commenting that they were so common that they had become almost invisible, Johns felt that everyday images could be known in their own right. Numerals, for example, can be given identities (fig. 29.35). *Figure 6* is as delicate as a subtle tracery; *Figure 7* is soft and lacking in clarity, as enigmatic as the *Mona Lisa* that peers at us; *Figure 8* is reminiscent of the chiaroscuro in Rembrandt's late

etchings; and *Figure 9* is bold and assertive. The tension between the two-dimensionality of the numerals and their psychological depth is striking.

Rauschenberg and Johns generally retain the painterly quality of Abstract Expressionism, but Roy Lichtenstein (b. 1923) adopted the mechanical techniques and imagery of comic strips, including the Benday dots used in newspaper reproductions of the comics. He also used the hard lines of comic strips but his paintings are monumental in scale. His cold and impersonal portrayal of a *Drowning Girl* (fig. 29.36) is an indictment of the casual and callous attitudes of many Americans toward violence in comic strips, in the streets, in Vietnam. The technique is that of the "low art" of the comics but the result is a potent artistic statement. Lichtenstein, for obvious reasons, selected nothing from comic strips like *Peanuts*.

Andy Warhol (b. 1925) began his career as a commercial artist, working with images and methods that provided a whole vocabulary of banality. His Campbell's Soup cans, Coca-Cola bottles, and multiple portraits of celebrities have made him the best known of Pop artists. *The American Man (Portrait of Watson Powell)* (fig. 29.37) is the first known portrait by a Pop artist to be commissioned by a businessman for a corporate collection. This multi-portrait suggests the continuity of filmstrips except that the thirty-two images vary only in the subtle changes of light and dark. With his serialized multi-images Warhol establishes a boredom that can become hypnotic.

EAT, SLEEP, LOVE are some of the words that Robert Indiana (b. Robert Clark of Indiana in 1928) extracts from signs to treat as subject matter. LOVE, as in the reiterated "make love not war" slogan of anti-war protestors of the 60s, is the subject of Indiana's jewelry designs, painting, sculpture, and printing. *The Black and White Love* (fig. 29.38) is a complex design that resonates with multiple meanings. Is this the word that makes the world go round? Indiana's handcut aluminum sculpture of *Love* (fig. 29.39) is boldly provocative, forcing the viewer to wonder why the "O" can't stand upright. Is LOVE askew or is it the society that uses the word so readily?

Early in the Pop movement Claes Oldenburg (b. 1929) specialized in creating sculptures like his classic six-foot hamburger. Later he turned to soft vinyl sculptures of everyday objects: shirts, ties, electrical outlets, and the like, all ten or twenty times actual size. Oldenburg's capacity for innovation is astounding, sometimes amusing, like his 4' clothespins, sometimes frightening, like his proposal for a park monument in the shape of an H-bomb mushroom cloud.

a.

b.

c.

d.

Figure 29.35 Jasper Johns, *Black Numerals,* 1966. a. *Figure 6,* b. *Figure 7,* c. *Figure 8,* d. *Figure 9,* 1968. Lithographs, 37 × 30″ each. Copyright Gemini G. E. L., 1968.

Figure 29.36 Roy Lichtenstein, *Drowning Girl,* 1963. Oil and synthetic polymer paint on canvas, 67⅝ × 66¾″. Collection, The Museum of Modern Art, New York. Gift of Philip Johnson and Mr. and Mrs. Bagley.

Figure 29.37 Andy Warhol, *The American Man (Portrait of Watson Powell),* 1964. Silkscreen ink and acrylic on canvas, 10′8⅞ × 5′4⅜″. Courtesy, The American Republic Insurance Company, Des Moines, Iowa.

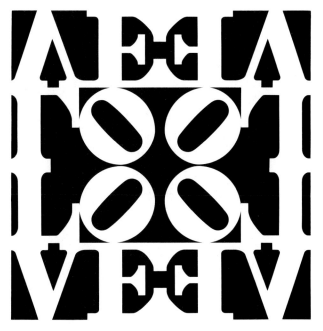

Figure 29.38 Robert Indiana, *The Black and White Love,* ca. 1966. Silkscreen. Printed by Multiples, New York.

Figure 29.39 Robert Indiana, *Love,* 1960. Aluminum, 12 × 12 × 6″. Published by Multiples, New York. Edition of six.

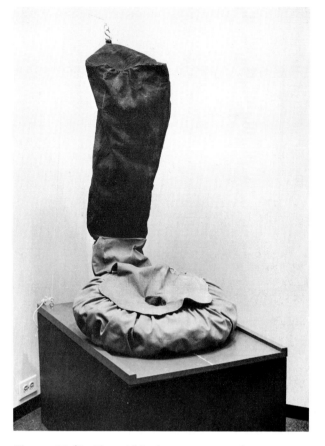

Figure 29.40 Claes Oldenburg, *Proposal for a Giant Balloon in the Form of a Typewriter Eraser—Structural Model,* 1970. Painted canvas, spray enamel, liquitex, and shredded foam rubber, 58″ high. Collection of the High Museum, Atlanta, Georgia. Courtesy of the Margo Leavin Gallery, Los Angeles.

His *Proposal for a Giant Balloon in the Form of a Typewriter Eraser* (fig. 29.40) is monumental even in the structural model and the mind boggles at the thought of the eraser soaring through the sky.

The sculptures of Edward Kienholz (b. 1927) have been called Pop but his work is also expressionistic and surreal. He combines painting, sculpture, collage, and the stage to depict the shabbiness, stupidity, and cruelty of modern urban life: an abandoned patient in a desolate mental ward; patrons in a seedy cafe; lovers on the back seat of a decrepit car. In a satirical vein, *The Friendly Grey Computer—Star Gauge Model #54* (fig. 29.41) appears, at first, to be "user friendly." A second look shows, however, a human being who has turned into a mechanized contraption that clanks and whirrs. Or has Model #54 swallowed the user?

Color, Geometry, and Optics   One of the first graduates of the Bauhaus, Josef Albers (1888–1976) emigrated to the United States in 1933, where his work influenced the development of abstract geometric

Figure 29.41 Edward Kienholz, *The Friendly Grey Computer—Star Gauge Model #54,* 1965. Motorized assemblage, 40 × 39⅛ × 24½″. Collection, The Museum of Modern Art, New York. Gift of Jean and Howard Lipman.

painting and Op art. His *Homage to the Square* paintings were a serialization similar to Monet's paintings of haystacks and lily ponds, a process, not a solution. Working with three or four squares of different colors, Albers explored, in hundreds of paintings, the interaction of colors and straight lines. *Homage to a Square: Ascending* (fig. 29.42) has a yellow square surrounded by white, surrounded in turn by grey, and framed by powder blue. The overall effect of this particular scheme is a remarkable serenity quite unlike Rothko's glowing colors and fuzzy lines (see color-plate 57).

Kenneth Noland (b. 1924) was influenced by Albers and Mondrian but chose abstract images painted boldly and with immaculate precision. Sometimes called a "hard-edge" painter, Noland is known for his immense paintings of chevron or wedge shapes. *Cirium of 1964* (fig. 29.43) is simple, bold, and enormous.

Working against the currents of Abstract Expressionism and Geometric Abstraction, Helen Frankenthaler (b. 1928) stained the raw canvas to achieve a limpid freshness quite unlike the work of other artists. In *Monoscape* (fig. 29.44) large amorphous forms seem to float like pools of mercury. The tension is heightened by the interplay of the unstable shapes and the flat, pristine background.

Figure 29.42 Josef Albers, *Homage to the Square: Ascending,* 1953. Oil on composition board, 43½" square. Whitney Museum of American Art, New York.

Figure 29.43 Kenneth Noland, *Cirium of 1964.* Arcylic on canvas, 18′ × 8′9″. Joslyn Art Museum, Omaha, Nebraska.

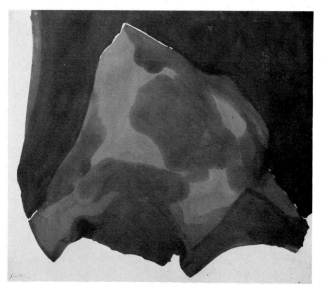

Figure 29.44 Helen Frankenthaler, *Monoscape,* 1969. Joslyn Art Museum, Omaha Nebraska.

Figure 29.45 Louise Nevelson, *Illumination—Dark,* 1961. Wood and bronze reliefs, 10'5" × 9'½" × 5" deep. Whitney Museum of American Art, New York.

Figure 29.46 Bridget Riley, *Current,* 1964. Synthetic-resin paint on composition board, ca. 58⅞ × 53⅜″. Collection, The Museum of Modern Art, New York. Philip Johnson Fund.

The assemblage of sculptures of Louise Nevelson (b. 1900) reflect the geometric forms of pre-Columbian sculpture, but her overriding interest in working with wood can be traced to her father's career as a cabinetmaker and her involvement with the wood in his shop. *Illumination—Dark* (fig. 29.45) is a large wooden wall on which the artist has arranged selected pieces of wood culled from old houses to form a three-dimensional geometric abstraction. With bronze-painted shapes against the flat black background of the wall, the piece resembles both a cupboard and a cityscape like the artist's native New York. As Nevelson has said, she "putters endlessly" with the design until she gets it right. The result here is a subtle blend of delicacy, mystery, and strength.

American painters like Albers and Noland were concerned with straight lines but the British artist Bridget Riley (b. 1931) worked with the possibilities inherent in curved lines. *Current* (fig. 29.46) is a terse composition that communicates directly with the eye and the optic nerve. Though she has been called an Op artist (from Optical art), Riley's style goes beyond merely confusing or tricking the eye. What we have here is a new way of perceiving and experiencing motion.

Figure 29.47 Jean Dubuffet, *Portrait of Henri Michaux,* 1947. Oil and other substances on canvas, 51½ × 38⅜″. The Sidney and Harriet Janis Collection. Gift of the Museum of Modern Art, New York.

Fantasy, Expressionism, and Surrealism Jean Dubuffet (due–boo–FAY; b. 1901), the most notable French artist since World War II, found his inspiration in strangely different areas: art of the insane, children's art, and graffiti. Dubuffet painted intuitively, somewhat like the Abstract Expressionists, but his subjects were fantastic figures and landscapes. He combined pigments with different mixtures of plaster, sand, or twigs to make a thick impasto that he scratched and scored to make grotesque figures like his *Portrait of Henri Michaux* (fig. 29.47). The artist referred to this style as *art brut,* which can be translated as brutal art or ugly art; both are apropos. Whatever the label, this attack on conventional artistic standards, even in the twentieth century, has a powerful primordial quality that both attracts and repels.

The Irish-born Francis Bacon (b. 1901) paints tormented visions distorted to the point of insanity. Preoccupied with deformity and disease, he selects works by Old Masters and restates them as anguished symbols of contemporary life. *Number VII from Eight*

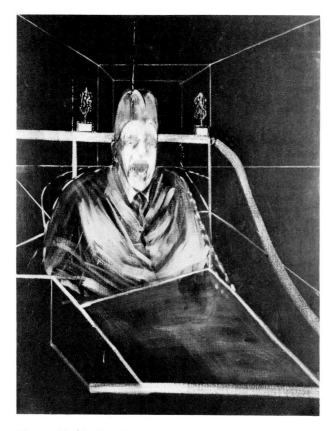

Figure 29.48 Francis Bacon, *Number VII from Eight Studies for a Portrait,* 1953. Oil on canvas, 60 × 46⅛". Collection, The Museum of Modern Art, New York. Gift of Mr. and Mrs. William A. M. Burden.

Figure 29.49 Leonel Gongora, *Velasquez Painting Gongora,* 1961. Oil on canvas, ca. 50 × 36". The University Art Collections, Arizona State University, Tempe.

Figure 29.50 Roy de Forest, *Inside the Bull,* 1973. Polymer on canvas, 72¾ × 66¾". American Art Heritage Fund. Arizona State University Art Collections, Tempe.

Studies for a Portrait (fig. 29.48) is based on the portrait of Pope Innocent X (1644–1655) by Velasquez, who depicted the pope as a powerful, intelligent, and cooly confident pontiff. Bacon uses Renaissance perspective but places the pope in an isolation booth where his anguished screams tear his head asunder.

Velasquez also costars in a fantasy work by Leonel Gongora (GONG–go–ra; b. 1932), a Colombian painter who was educated in the United States. Both a tribute to the Spanish tradition and a fanciful manipulation of reality, *Velasquez Painting Gongora* (fig. 29.49) depicts the youthful artist in seventeenth-century garb standing before a portrait of Velasquez. The reference is to the *Maids of Honor* by Velasquez (see fig. 22.14) in which Velasquez looks directly at the viewer as Gongora does in this painting. The mirror that reflects the images of the king and queen in *Maids of Honor* has become the portrait of an older Velasquez, creating the illusion that the portrait is a reflection of the Spanish artist as he paints Gongora. Reality is adroitly confused and extended in both space and time.

Fantasy becomes light-hearted in the work of the innovative California painter and sculptor Roy de Forest (b. 1930), who delights in exploring states beyond seriousness. *Inside the Bull* (fig. 29.50) depicts

a cruise ship sailing by a tropical isle with one palm tree and a candy-eyed native. The gentle bull stands calmly over a white Spitz dog with fiery red eyes. Fanciful, delightful, semipsychedelic, and replete with incongruities, this style can be described as "funk art" in the manner of the funky sounds of Soul Jazz (see chap. 30).

The best-known American Indian artist, Fritz Scholder (b. 1937), shows the influence of Expressionism and Pop Art but his subject matter sets him apart from both styles. Scholder uses serialism to

Figure 29.51 Fritz Scholder, *Waiting Indian No. 4,* 1970 Oil on canvas, 70 × 64″. The University Art Collections, Arizona State University, Tempe.

Figure 29.53 Alexander Calder, *Many Pierced Discs,* 65 × 49″. The University Art Collections, Arizona State University, Tempe.

Figure 29.52 Philip Curtis, *Farewell,* 1961. Collection of Edward Jacobson, Phoenix, Arizona.

portray the paradoxical position of Native Americans in American life. With a poignant irony he has depicted stereotypes: a Super Chief eating an ice cream cone; a drunken Indian clutching a can of beer like a tomahawk; a Hollywood Indian and his captive Anglo maiden. Scholder's work is satirical and searching, depicting the degradation and basic nobility of his people. *Waiting Indian No. 4* (fig. 29.51) stands majestically in a barren landscape. In his awesome dignity he refuses to accept any part of a stereotype in the Anglo world.

Philip Curtis (b. 1907) combines a remarkable gift for fantasy with classical techniques of the Renaissance tradition. *Farewell* (fig. 29.52) pictures a family waving good-bye to a little girl who frantically returns their gestures from the caboose of a train. Belatedly, we realize that the child and the parting train are part of a billboard and our senses reel with the enigma. Curtis steadfastly maintains that he is not a Surrealist but critics are unconvinced. There are no apparent Freudian undertones but this is a super-reality beyond everyday experience.

For centuries sculptors have labored to give their works the illusion of movement. Alexander Calder (1898–1976) invented abstract works that actually moved. Influenced by Surrealism and geometric abstractions, Calder created the true mobile. *Many Pierced Discs* (fig. 29.53) is a fantasy of abstract shapes wired together and delicately balanced so that it can respond to the slightest breeze. An indoor rather than an outdoor mobile that is activated by the wind, this work rests on its pedestal in an art gallery where it can gently gyrate and bow to museum visitors.

Figure 29.54 Mark di Suvero, *Side Frames*, 1979. Steel, 24' long × 12' wide × 16' high. Courtesy of ConStruct, Chicago.

Figure 29.55 Henry Moore, *Girl Seated Against a Square Wall*, 1958–1959. Bronze, 41¾ × 33⁷⁄₁₆″. Museum of Art, The University of Arizona. Gift of Edward J. Gallagher, Jr.

Mark di Suvero's (b. 1933) *Side Frames* (fig. 29.54) is a giant outdoor mobile, an abstract fantasy on a grand scale. A large pendant is held, seemingly tenuously, by a cable attached to a long balanced beam. Despite the work's monumental size the pendant is completely free to sway or twist in the wind. Di Suvero's works are energy structures, metallic lyrics of action and reaction.

Henry Moore (b. 1898) is the most important English artist in any medium. Like Calder, he was influenced by Surrealism but went on to develop his unique abstract figural style. In *Girl Seated Against a Square Wall* (fig. 29.55) the figure is abstracted into a depersonalized version of the female concept. The attenuated legs, arms, neck, and the tiny head recall the Mannerist emotionalism of El Greco. The arms encapsulate and press space to the torso, just as the girl's legs and the bench's supports emphasize and contrast space and bulk. Space, for Moore, is as important as solids; this figure is surrounded by a much larger space as suggested by the floor and square wall.

Minimal Art Minimal Art began in the 1960s as a movement to reduce art to basics: one shape or one color or one idea. Also called Primary Structures or Primary Art, the style is easier to observe than to discuss. *Sentaro* (fig. 29.56) by Tony DeLap (b. 1927) is a sculpture/painting reduced to a basic shape and a single color. This is a beautiful hunk of a bright red rectangular box that seemingly floats within its plastic

Figure 29.56 Tony DeLap, *Sentaro,* 1967. Aluminum, wood, plexiglass, and lacquer, 16 × 16 × 5″ deep. American Art Heritage Fund. Arizona State University Art Collections, Tempe.

Figure 29.57 David Smith, *Cubi XV.* Steel, 10′5⅛″ × 4′10½″. The San Diego Museum of Art, San Diego, California.

case. DeLap used commercial staining and spraying techniques so that the saturated painting/sculpture is a solid color field with no trace of brushwork or other manipulation by the artist. The vitality and spontaneity of Abstract Expressionism has given way to a laid-back restraint comparable to Cool Jazz (see chap. 30).

American sculptor David Smith (1906–1965) applied his experience of working in an automotive plant and locomotive factory to sculpting with steel which, as he said, "had little art history." His *Cubi XV* (fig. 29.57) is a gravity-defying combination of simple geometric components that set up a lively interplay of forms and space. The stainless steel is highly polished, with controlled light patterns that make the metal surface as sensual as works by Brancusi (see fig. 29.16) or Verrocchio (see fig. 18.15).

For an exhibition in Washington's Corcoran Gallery, Ronald Bladen (b. 1918) created a giant *X* of painted wood (fig. 29.58) that virtually filled a classical two-story hall. The spectator can not only walk around the sculpture but through it as well. Large-scale Minimalist works such as this offer valid alternatives to representational public monuments which, more often than not, are forgettable clichés. The understated elegance and enormous power of the Washington Memorial to the veterans of the Vietnam War is a case in point.

Varieties of Realism   Though never absent from the American scene, Realism has again become a major factor in a variety of styles called New Realism, Magic Realism, or Photorealism. The sculptor Duane Hanson (b. 1925) makes casts of living people and paints the resulting figures to look completely lifelike, including real clothing and accessories. Richard Estes (b. 1936) projects a slide directly on canvas and makes a precise copy with an airbrush. Hanson selects subjects like gaudily-dressed tourists, junkies, and overweight shoppers, while Estes paints banal cityscapes totally devoid of people. In their subject matter Hanson and Estes follow the orientation of Pop Art but other artists use photorealism in a more positive vein. In *The Glass Table* (fig. 29.59) John Moore (b. 1941) uses a superb technique to depict the light and airy corner of a room. The table waits invitingly for someone to walk in and sit down.

Figure 29.58 Ronald Bladen, *X,* 1967. Wood, 22′8″ × 24′6″. Courtesy Fishback Gallery, New York.

Figure 29.59 John Moore, *The Glass Table,* 1975. Acrylic on canvas, 90 × 75″. The University Art Collections, Arizona State University, Tempe. Gift of the Childe Hassam Fund, 1975.

Ben Schonzeit (b. 1942) reveals an apparent fidelity to photographic reality in his *Tools* (fig. 29.60) but close observation discloses crisp tactile details on the right and soft focus on the left. To see a 2′-tall nib of an ink pen and brushheads almost as large is disconcerting, perhaps more so than some Surrealist anomalies. With his enormous *Tools* Schonzeit transforms his viewers into, in effect, a Lilliputian-sized audience. On the other hand, gargantuan movie screens and the sight of 6″-high football players racing about a TV screen may have innoculated the public against size-shock.

Our society has apparently learned to accept many real/unreal mystifications of the everyday world. Indeed, when Otto Duecker (b. 1948) paints larger-than-life-sized figures, cuts them out, and arranges them in galleries, homes, and warehouses, we are inclined to accept them as "real." In *Russell, Terry, J.T., and a Levi Jacket* (colorplate 59) we see the artist posed in front of his four cutouts and appearing, in this photograph, somehow less real than his creations.

James Havard (b. 1937) is a leading artist in a new generation of American abstract painters. He challenges one's concept of reality by creating illusionistic nonobjective paintings in a style called Abstract Illusionism. His *Cane Garden* (fig. 29.61) deliberately violates the unity of canvas and what is painted on it. Havard gives every stroke of paint a texture, bulk, even shadows, all of which seem to rest upon, but not become a part of, a solid-colored canvas. In fact, Havard's work is a painting of a nonobjective painting. What is real? Earlier, it was stated that each generation develops its own concepts of reality. For the present century, frequently called the Age of Uncertainty, it might be more accurate to point out that several concepts of reality are acceptable or, possibly, tolerable.

Hispanic and Black Artists

Contemporary artists of Hispanic or African heritages are just as involved with mainstream art as their colleagues; artists are, after all, contributing members of the international community of artists, more involved with breaking down national or ethnic barriers than erecting them. An overview of past and present developments by Hispanic and black artists is given here because American society has, primarily in the past, had barriers that excluded minorities from the mainstream of American life, barriers that, in effect, created a history of Hispanic and black art and artists. Moreover, when minority artists worked in prevailing styles their art was frequently downgraded as "imitative." When their work expressed their ethnic heritage it was all too often criticized because it did not conform to establishment attitudes about what art should be, a no-win situation that is finally largely in the past.

There are no typical Hispanic (or Mexican American or Chicano) artists nor are there any styles that are clearly Hispanic. The most common attribute of Hispanic artists is that they, in general, live in the American Southwest in areas formerly belonging to Mexico. Some are influenced by the pre-Columbian past while others deny it. The European tradition that Spain brought to Mexico influences some artists and repels others. They are bilingual, their roots are in pre-Columbian times, followed by three centuries of Spanish rule and a century and a half of American culture. Their culture is complex, their tradition rich, and their search for identity as Americans is what much of their art, and culture, is all about.

The most important influences early in the century were those of Mexican muralists José Orozco (1883–1949) and Rufino Tamayo (b. 1899), both of whom executed major works while living in this country. Antonio García (b. 1901) and Porfirio Salinas (b. 1912) are leading artists of the first generation of Hispanic painters. Both are realists with García specializing in portraiture and Salinas in landscapes of his native Texas. In the second generation Edward Chávez (b. 1917) and Michael Ponce de León (b. 1922) have gained national prominence. Chávez is an abstractionist in the cubist mode while de León is a printmaker who specializes in bas-relief prints. Influenced by Pop Art, Melesio Casas (b. 1929) has done a series of paintings based on movies and TV advertising that he calls "Humanscapes." Sculptor Manuel Neri (b. 1930) is influenced by pre-Columbian art and Orozco and paints sculptures that he has hacked out of plaster. Ralph Ortiz (b. 1934) is a Destructive artist. For his Piano Destruction Concert Ortiz attacks with an ax an upright piano that has plastic bags of animal blood suspended inside. The resulting mess of blood-stained keys, splinters, and strings is, according to Ortiz, an artistic realization of violence that symbolizes the violence and destruction of the real world. Luis Jimenez (b. 1940) creates polychromed sculptures made of epoxy and fiberglass. Influenced by Pop Art and popular culture, Jimenez's works are lusty, humorous, and charged with explosive energy, particularly works like *Rodeo Queen* and *California Chick,* not to mention his show that he called *Texas Sweet Funk.*

American artists of African ancestry have contributed to the arts in America since Jamestown was founded in 1619. Joshua Johnson (1765–1830), the most celebrated of Black artisan-painters, painted family portraits, some of which are in the National

Figure 29.60 Ben Schonzeit, *Tools,* 1974. Acrylic on canvas, 60 × 44″. Courtesy, Ponderosa System, Inc., Dayton, Ohio.

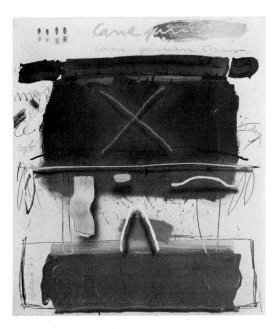

Figure 29.61 James Havard, *Cane Garden,* 1979. Courtesy, The Elaine Horwitch Galleries, Scottsdale.

Figure 29.62 Joshua Johnson, *The Westwood Children*, ca. 1807. Oil on canvas, 41⅛ × 46″. Gift of Edgar William and Bernice Chrysler Garbisch, 1959. National Gallery of Art, Washington, D.C.

Gallery, though most have been retained by descendents of the original families. His *The Westwood Children* (fig. 29.62) has a charming modern appeal with its artful asymmetrical arrangement of the children, the dog, and the tree outside. The children are dressed in identical outfits but each is distinguished by hair style, placement of the feet, and the held objects.

Influenced by the mysticism of the Hudson River School, Robert S. Duncanson (1817–1872) was recognized in his own time as an outstanding landscape painter. His *Blue Hole, Flood Waters, Little Miami River* is one of the finest works in the romantic style of the Hudson River tradition. Artist Edward M. Bannister (1828–1901) was described by a friend as impelled to pursue an artistic career after reading in a New York newspaper that "while the Negro may harbor an appreciation of art, he is unable to produce it." Refusing to accept patronage for the usual study in Europe, Bannister developed a landscape style in the Hudson River tradition that, in 1876, became nationally recognized when he won a gold medal at the Philadelphia Centennial Exposition.

Sculptor Edmonia Lewis (1843–ca. 1900) also won an award at the Philadelphia Exposition but her career was very different from that of Bannister. Bannister avoided racial themes; Lewis exploited racial issues. Created in the Neoclassic style, her sculpture *Forever Free* celebrated the thirteenth amendment to the constitution that prohibited slavery.

A student of Thomas Eakins at the Pennsylvania Academy of Art, Henry O. Tanner (1859–1937) was the first black American artist to achieve an international reputation with his election to the French Academy. Like many other artists whose ethnic background placed them in a minority population, Tanner

rejected the label, at the time, of Negro artist. Whether black, Hispanic, Indian, or even American, American artists like Tanner insisted upon recognition in their own right without stereotypical labels. Tanner did not disavow his heritage but he did insist that he was an artist who happened to be black and who happened to be an American. Not surprisingly, a dichotomy still exists among some black artists who seek acceptance as mainstream artists but who are proud of their heritage.

A notable artist in the manner of colonial artisan-painters, Horace Pippin (1888–1946) was a self-taught painter whose style can be described as modernized abstractions of folk art traditions. Unlike the French primitive Henri Rousseau, Pippin's work was acclaimed in his lifetime and acquired by major American museums.

Hale Woodruff's (b. 1900) most notable work is the three-panel series, *The Amistad Murals,* at Talladega College in Alabama. The subject is the 1839 revolt of Africans aboard the Spanish slave ship who, after seizing the ship, were captured by an American ship and tried in New Haven for mutiny. With the assistance of John Quincy Adams and other Abolitionists, the Africans were finally returned to their homeland.

Richmond Barthé (b. 1901) is one of the most prolific and successful American sculptors. Notable among his creations are the *African Dancer* and *The Blackberry Woman,* which were acquired by the Whitney Museum of American Art. Long a notable and influential art teacher at Howard University, Lois Maillol Jones (b. 1905) is an accomplished textile designer and painter of cityscapes and landscapes in the spirit of Cézanne. Particularly outstanding are her Haitian paintings and her *Africa* series of 1971.

Romare Beardon (b. 1914) began his career as a cartoonist. After studying with George Grosz he developed a painting style based on Cubist techniques. His mature works are powerful collages of the black experience, but genre art rather than propaganda. Juxtaposing African motifs and contemporary black figures,Beardon redefines the human image "in terms of the Negro experience I know best."

One of the most celebrated artists at mid-century was Jacob Lawrence (b. 1917), who uses vigorous silhouetted patterns and narrative subject matter. Deeply committed to black history in America, Lawrence is perhaps best known for the series *The Migration of the Negro* (1940–1941) and his *Harlem* series of 1943. *Daybreak—A Time to Rest* (fig. 29.63) is related, like much of his work, to the life of a black hero: Harriet Tubman, a famed conductor on the Underground Railway, in a children's book entitled *Harriet and the Promised Land,* which he illustrated. The work is balanced between a dream world and reality, an artful juxtaposition of identifiable images and abstractions. The huge feet are pointed north but even when traveling the route to freedom, there must be a time to rest and to dream of the promised land.

Figure 29.63 Jacob Lawrence, *Daybreak—A Time to Rest*, 1967. Tempera on masonite, 30 × 24″. Gift of an anonymous donor, 1973. National Gallery of Art, Washington, D.C.

Charles White (b. 1918), like Hale Woodruff and Jacob Lawrence, was employed during the Depression by the W.P.A. Art Project. In a style influenced by Mexican muralists Diego Rivera and David Siqueiros, White completed powerful murals like, for example, *The Contribution of the Negro to American Democracy* (1943) at Hampton Institute. White later specialized in lithographs and charcoal and ink drawings because he felt that he could communicate better with his intended audience of black Americans. Always a strong social critic, White's later works, such as his *Wanted Poster* series of the turbulent 1960s, reveal a lot of anger. Admittedly propaganda pieces, this series is, nevertheless, artistically eloquent.

Norma Morgan (b. 1928) divides her time between England and the United States, considering herself an artist born in America, and not necessarily a black artist. Noted for her "magic-realist" etchings and copper engravings, her *David in the Wilderness* is owned by the Museum of Modern Art. Norma Morgan is considered a mainstream artist but there is a movement called Blackstream of which Benny Andrews (b. 1930) is a leading member. His *Trash* (1972) is a large and powerful work that attacks American junk culture while, at the same time, depicting Andrews's consistent theme that black artists are creating art as uniquely American as jazz.

Benny Andrews and other Blackstream artists like Milton Johnson, Joe Everstreet, Raymond Saunders, and Malcolm Bailey all depict the strength of black people under adverse conditions. Each of them has contributed to American art the vitality and uniqueness of the black experience, qualities that are not derived from European cultures. The current generation of black artists is, in effect, breaking down ethnic and national barriers. First and foremost, they are artists successfully reinforcing the cultural pluralism that is the real strength of this complex nation.

Art in the 1980s

Contemporary artistic styles are wildly pluralistic with no one style predominating. A renewed interest in figural painting called, for want of a better term, "New Painting," is significant but some older styles persist and innovations abound. Art in the 80s is, in general, no longer a Bohemian activity and New York is no longer the primary center of artistic activity. Artists like Julian Schnabel, David Salle, and Laurie Anderson are making a living out of art by promoting a "fast track" art market rivaling the hyped success of Rock stars and soap-opera personalities. The marketing of art and "art stars" has become another American enterprise with the implication that "success" is more important than aesthetics. Where this will lead is anybody's guess but just a listing of contemporary styles, attitudes, and movements will indicate the range of artistic activity in the current decade.

New Painting	Primitivism
French Nouveau Realisme	Naïves
Italian Arte Povera	Abstractionists
Pop and Post-Pop	Nul/Zero
Fluxus	Environmental Art
Conceptual Art	Performance Art
Minimalism	Body Art
German-Italian	Noise or Sound Art
"transavantgarde"	Vague Art
Earth Art	

Whether any one style will predominate in the manner of Impressionism or Cubism is unlikely, given the rapid interactions of our Global Village in the Communications Age. Artistic influences are international but artists are always individuals. They will pursue their own goals, creating artworks faster than critics can conjure up labels and this is as it should be. Works of art are always best judged on their own merits regardless of style, school, or movement.

Architecture

Before World War II skyscraper designs were generally eclectic, clothing steel skeletons with older styles. The innovations of Louis Sullivan (1856–1924) and Frank Lloyd Wright were more influential in Europe than at home and the International Style had yet to make much of an impression outside of Europe. Until

Figure 29.64 Wallace K. Harrison, Le Corbusier, and others, Secretariat Building of the United Nations, 1947–1950. New York.

Figure 29.65 Gio Ponti, Pier Luigi Nervi, and Arturo Danosso, Pirelli Tower, 1956–1959. Milan, Italy.

Figure 29.66 Ludwig Mies van der Rohe, Gallery of the Twentieth Century, 1962–1968. West Berlin.

the 1950s New York skyscrapers were circumscribed by the demands of clients and rigid zoning restrictions. Buildings had to occupy every square foot of expensive real estate but zoning ordinances required that some sunlight had to fall into manmade canyons. The result was the so-called ziggurat, a setback design with upper floors terraced back from the street.

What was to become an international Renaissance in architecture, mainly International Style, was launched with the design of the United Nations complex in New York. Because modern buildings were so complicated most were designed by a group of architects and engineers. Wallace K. Harrison (b. 1895) headed an international team that designed the Secretariat Building (fig. 29.64) in the shape of a giant slab, as suggested by Le Corbusier. Clothed on the sides in glass and on the ends in marble, the structure was the first American building to embody the Bauhaus tradition. Because it occupied only a portion of the riverfront site, it avoided the setback restrictions that can be seen in the Empire State Building (on the left) and Chrysler Building (on the right).

The Pirelli Tower in Milan (fig. 29.65) represents an imaginative variation on the International Style. Gio Ponti designed the sleek and subtly proportioned facade while the innovative structural design was by Nervi, the self-styled "architectural engineer." Though it has thirty-three floors and is 416' high, the entire building is suspended from two giant transverse spines 79' apart. The floors are cantilevered from the pylons, making the columnless office space within totally open and thus completely flexible.

The German architect Ludwig Mies van der Rohe (1886–1969) was initially influenced by Gropius but developed his own Minimalist version of International Style. Illustrating his motto that "less is more," his art museum in West Berlin (fig. 29.66) is classically simple, refined, and elegant.

Figure 29.67 Le Corbusier, Notre-Dame-du-Haut, 1950–1955. Ronchamp, France.

Figure 29.68 Interior, Notre-Dame-du-Haut.

Though he was an influential pioneer of the International Style, Le Corbusier later abandoned his boxes on stilts (see fig. 29.30) for a more sculptural style. His design for the pilgrimage chapel of Notre-Dame-du-Haut (fig. 29.67) was revolutionary, unlike any other building. The plan is irregular in every respect. Thick, curving white walls are topped by a heavy overhanging roof and flanked by a tall white tower on the left and a shorter tower on the right. The towers are decorative but they also transmit natural light to the two altars within. Window openings are cut through the massive walls to make tunnels of light (fig. 29.68). Randomly placed, the windows are of differ-

ent sizes and cut through the walls in a variety of angles. Stained glass is used but each window has a different design and color scheme. The overall effect is intimate and magical.

Frank Lloyd Wright designed many buildings based on the circle but none as dramatic as the Solomon R. Guggenheim Museum in New York (fig. 29.69). The front circle is the administrative unit with the gallery behind. The structure is essentially a cylinder rising in expanding circles. This is the antithesis, in every respect, of the International Style. Inside the building (fig. 29.70) a circular ramp rises to the top in six complete turns around a 90' well that

Figure 29.69 Frank Lloyd Wright, The Solomon R. Guggenheim Museum, 1943–1959. New York.

Figure 29.70 Interior, Solomon R. Guggenheim Museum

Figure 29.71 Eero Saarinen, TWA Terminal. 1956–1962. JFK International Airport, New York.

climaxes in a skylight dome. Visitors are taken to the top in an elevator, permitting them to walk on a continuous downhill grade while inspecting artworks placed on the outside wall. The design necessarily limits how art is displayed but the interior of the Guggenheim is one of Wright's boldest and most successful concepts.

New York's JFK International Airport is an uninspired collection of architectural clichés with the sole exception of the TWA Terminal (fig. 29.71). Designed by Eero Saarinen (1910–1961), the structure is a triumph, a curvilinear enclosure of space that actually looks like an air terminal. Built of reinforced concrete, the continuously curving surfaces symbolize flight in a manner reminiscent of Brancusi's *Bird*

Figure 29.72 Interior, TWA Terminal

Figure 29.73 R. Buckminster Fuller, American Pavilion, EXPO 67. Montreal, Canada.

Figure 29.74 Moshe Safdie and associates, Habitat, EXPO 67. Montreal, Canada.

in Space (see fig. 29.16). The interior of the terminal (fig. 29.72) reveals a graceful interplay of flowing curves with a minimum of vertical supports. Functional as well as aesthetically appealing, the design effectively guides passengers to and from the aircraft.

R. Buckminster Fuller (1895–1983) was an unconventional architect-engineer who, among other things, invented the geodesic dome. Composed of mutually sustaining tetrahedrons and octahedrons, these spheroids can be constructed almost anywhere, out of virtually any material, and at very low cost. Used at first for greenhouses and temporary structures, the first large geodesic dome appeared at EXPO 67 as the American Pavilion (fig. 29.73). Because the design is eminently practical on any scale, Fuller even envi-

sioned cities under geodesic domes with full control of the climate. Air and noise pollution may, of course, present a problem or two.

At the same exposition, Moshe Safdie (b. 1945) presented a new concept in urban habitation called Habitat (fig. 29.74). Various sized housing units, each a complete apartment, are attached to a zigzag concrete framework. Each Habitat can be extended in any direction and assembled in a variety of heights, giving the occupants a diversified range of views and perspectives. When compared with sterile high-rise apartment buildings with every floor the same size, the Habitat concept offers a practical and aesthetic form of multiple dwellings for people who like living in clustered units.

Figure 29.75 Utzon, Hall, Todd, and Littleton, Sydney Opera House, 1959–1972. Bennelong Point, Sydney, Australia.

Figure 29.76 Renzo Piano and Richard Rogers, Georges Pompidou National Center for Art and Culture (Beaubourg), 1977. Paris. View of east side.

Figure 29.77 Philip Johnson, Model for Chippendale skyscraper. New York.

The design competition for the new opera house in Sydney, Australia, was won by Danish architect Joern Utzon (b. 1918) in 1956, but it took thirteen years and several more architects and engineers to figure out how to build the unique concept (fig. 29.75). A cultural center that includes opera house, exhibition hall, theatre, and other facilities, the soaring gull-wing design faced with brilliant white ceramic tiles is a visual triumph, thanks in part to its location on one of the world's great harbors.

Even before its dedication the Pompidou National Center for Arts and Culture (fig. 29.76) provoked a storm of controversy. The building is, in effect, turned inside out. Brilliantly painted structural supports, heating and cooling ducts, elevators, and staircases form the exterior, leaving the interior open to any arrangement by using movable partitions. Designed as a center for art, music, drama, film, and industrial arts, the structure also contains a Public Information Center (media library) and a variety of bars and restaurants. A prime tourist attraction and beehive of cultural activities, the building is perhaps more detested by many Parisians than even the Eiffel Tower. Sobriquets are legion: *art brut,* boiler room, factory, kinetic architecture, honest architecture, indecent architecture, science fiction architecture, and so on and on. Set in the midst of historical Paris, the Pompidou is, to say the least, quite noticeable.

Outside of a few well-proportioned International Style buildings, rectangular glass boxes have become three-dimensional platitudes: sterile, inefficient, and boring. Some recent designs are more energy-efficient and, whether Romantic or Classical, deliberately antithetical to outdated modernism in the mode of the International Style. Philip Johnson's (b. 1906) classical design for his so-called Chippendale skyscraper (fig. 29.77) has an entrance reminiscent of Brunelleschi's Pazzi Chapel (see fig. 18.5). The pediment is similar to eighteenth-century furniture designed in England by Thomas Chippendale (1718–1779). Between entrance and pediment the building (currently under construction for AT&T) is still a straight-line high-rise minus windows.

Summary

The multiplicity of styles and innumerable artists of the present century cannot be adequately covered in a chapter or even in a set of books. The discussion of most major styles and some of the important artists should be considered as a preamble to continuing studies of what today's artists are creating. Twentieth-century art is as accessible in this country as Renaissance art is in Italy and can be viewed in any good-sized American city. Most of the illustrations for this chapter, for example, were drawn from the collections of fourteen American museums and galleries from New York to the West Coast. Following is a summary in outline form, providing both a review of the chapter and a framework for personal initiative.

I. Artistic Styles to 1945
  A. Painting and Sculpture
    1. Prelude
      a) Édouard Manet
      b) Impressionism: Monet et al
      c) Post-Impressionism: Cézanne et al
    2. Fauvism
      a) Henri Matisse
      b) Georges Rouault
    3. Expressionism
      a) Wassily Kandinsky (Abstract Expressionism)
      b) Ernst Barlach
      c) Käthe Kollwitz
      d) George Grosz
    4. Cubism
      a) Pablo Picasso (including Blue and Rose Periods and Neoclassicism)
      b) Stuart Davis
    5. Abstractionists
      a) Georgia O'Keeffe
      b) Piet Mondrian (geometric, plasticism)
      c) Constantin Brancusi
    6. Fantasy
      a) Marc Chagall
      b) Paul Klee
      c) Giorgio de Chirico (metaphysical)
    7. Dada
      a) Marcel Duchamp
      b) Kurt Schwitters
    8. Surrealism
      a) Joan Miro
      b) Salvador Dali
      c) Meret Oppenheim
      d) Alberto Giacometti
      e) Alton Pickens
      f) Yves Tanguy
    9. Realism in America
      a) John Sloan (Ash Can school)
      b) Edward Hopper
      c) Diego Rivera (Social Realism)
  B. Architecture
    1. Antonio Gaudi (Art Noveau and Expressionism)
    2. Walter Gropius (International Style)
    3. Le Corbusier (International Style)
    4. Frank Lloyd Wright (Organic architecture)
II. Artistic Styles since 1945
  A. Painting and Sculpture
    1. Abstract Expressionism
      a) Jackson Pollock
      b) Willem de Kooning
      c) Mark Rothko (Color Field)
    2. Pop Art
      a) Robert Rauschenberg
      b) Jasper Johns
      c) Roy Lichtenstein
      d) Andy Warhol
      e) Robert Indiana
      f) Claes Oldenburg
      g) Edward Kienholz
    3. Color, Geometry, and Optics
      a) Josef Albers (geometric)
      b) Kenneth Noland (hard-edge)
      c) Helen Frankenthaler (abstract color)
      d) Louise Nevelson (geometric abstraction)
      e) Bridget Riley (curved lines, optics)
    4. Fantasy, Expressionism, and Surrealism
      a) Jean Dubuffet *(art brut)*
      b) Francis Bacon (fantasy/ expressionism)
      c) Leonel Gongora (fantasy/ expressionism)
      d) Roy de Forest (fantasy/funk)
      e) Fritz Scholder (Pop/Expressionism)
      f) Philip Curtis (Surrealism)
      g) Alexander Calder (abstract fantasy/ kinetic)
      h) Mark di Suvero (abstract fantasy/ kinetic)
      i) Henry Moore (abstract figural)
    5. Minimal Art
      a) Tony DeLap
      b) David Smith
      c) Ronald Bladen

6. Varieties of Realism
    a) John Moore (New Realism)
    b) Ben Schonzeit (altered Photorealism)
    c) Otto Duecker (Photorealism Cutouts)
    d) James Havard (Abstract Illusionism)
7. Hispanic and Black Artists (overview)
    a) Joshua Johnson (artisan-painter)
    b) Jacob Lawrence (image/abstraction)
B. Architecture
    1. Wallace Harrison (International Style)
    2. Ponti and Nervi (International Style)
    3. Ludwig Mies van der Rohe (Minimalist International Style)
    4. Le Corbusier (sculptural architecture)
    5. Frank Lloyd Wright (functional/organic)
    6. Eero Saarinen (functional/expressionism)
    7. R. Buckminster Fuller (geodesic dome)
    8. Moshe Safdie (Habitat)
    9. Joern Utzon (Expressionism)
    10. Piano and Rogers (*art brut*/kinetic architecture)
    11. Philip Johnson (Neoclassicism)

WARNING!: The above outline with artists placed neatly in pigeonholes is a generalized approximation and guide and only that. Artists, as stated before, are individuals and their works are unique. Treat the text and outline as points of departure, keeping in mind that artists do change their styles and that, art critics notwithstanding, we are still too close in time to many styles to make valid judgments. Mozart, for example, had no idea that he was a Classical composer; he was criticized in his day as an avant-garde composer.

Finally, consider art as what anyone elects to present to us as art, as evidence of human creativity. If we do not like an artwork perhaps it communicates something we already know but refuse to acknowledge. Paradoxically, a work of art that tells us something we know and understand can leave us dissatisfied. We do want the artist to challenge our emotions, our intellect, our knowledge. The more we study art the more likely we are to respond to and to seek out challenges.

Bibliography

An exhaustive bibliography would be nearly endless and therefore pointless. Rather, the following list is highly selective but with a wide range of interesting and useful books.

Arnason, H. H. *History of Modern Art.* New York: Harry N. Abrams, Inc., 1968. A large general study and well illustrated. As is only proper for a book like this, the bibliography is truly exhaustive.

Bearden, Romare and Harry Henderson. *Six Black Masters of American Art.* New York: Doubleday & Company, 1972. The six masters are Joshua Johnson, Robert S. Duncanson, Henry D. Tanner, Horace Pippin, Augusta Savage, and Jacob Lawrence. Bearden could have included himself.

Broude, Norma and Mary D. Garrard, eds. *Feminism and Art History: Questioning the Litany.* New York: Harper and Row, 1982. An excellent collection of thoughtful essays that raise many issues like, for example, the fact that art historians have concentrated on the work of "white males over a five-hundred year period in a small section of the world." One recommendation: "Don't just write women into art history but rewrite art history."

Fax, Elton C. *Black Artists of the New Generation.* New York: Dodd, Mead & Company, 1977. Twenty important contemporary artists almost equally divided between men and women.

Fine, Elsa Honig. *The Afro-American Artist: A Search for Identity.* New York: Holt, Rinehart and Winston, 1971. An excellent general history. Highly recommended.

Giedion, Siegfried. *Space, Time and Architecture.* Cambridge, Mass.: Harvard University Press, 1973. A classic study.

Greenberg, Clement. *Art and Culture: Critical Essays.* Boston: Beacon Press, 1961. Valuable series of essays by one of the most influential American art critics of the century.

Hamilton, George Heard. *19th and 20th Century Art.* Englewood Cliffs, N.J.: Prentice-Hall, 1972. A well-illustrated, generalized overview of art in the modern world.

Hughes, Robert. *The Shock of the New.* New York: Alfred A. Knopf, 1981. This is the book that grew out of the TV series Hughes did for BBC, which has been shown on public television in this country. The writing is both dazzling and fascinating. Hughes is seldom timid about his opinions and critical remarks.

Johnson, Ellen, ed. *American Artists on Art: from 1940 to 1980.* New York: Harper and Row, 1982. Cogent comments from important artists of every major movement and a few minor movements.

Lippard, Lucy R. *Pop Art.* New York: Frederick A. Praeger, Inc., 1966. Probably the finest general study of the style, as enjoyable and amusing as the style itself.

Lowe, Sue Davidson. *Stieglitz: A Memoir/Biography.* New York: Farrar Straus Giroux, 1983. A personal account of the career of one of the most influential artists of the century.

Lucie-Smith, Edward. *Art in the Seventies.* Oxford: Phaidon Press, 1980. Perhaps the only authoritative guide to a confusing but exciting decade.

Peterson, Karen and J. J. Wilson. *Women Artists; Recognition and Appraisal from the Early Middle Ages to the Twentieth Century.* A quotation from page 6 sums up the thrust of the book: "The only places we have not found women artists are where we have not yet looked."

Quirarte, Jacinto. *Mexican American Artists.* Austin: University of Texas Press, 1973. A good overview that includes an extensive bibliography.

Rubinstein, Charlotte Streifer. *American Women Artists: from Early Indian Times to the Present.* Boston: G. K. Hall & Co., 1982. This is the first comprehensive chronological survey of American women artists. The scholarship is impressive and the bibliography is enormous.

Russell, John. *The Meanings of Modern Art.* New York: Harper and Row, 1981. In his preface Russell writes that his book is based on two beliefs: "In art, as in the sciences, ours is one of the big centuries. The other is that the history of art, if properly set out, is the history of everything." If only one book can be read on modern art let this be the book. Suggested Readings are wonderful.

Tomkins, Calvin. *Off the Wall: Robert Rauschenberg and the Art World of Our Time.* New York: Penguin Books, 1981. Paperback. There is no better book about the astonishingly creative 1950s and 1960s.

Tomkins, Alvin, et al. *The World of Marcel Duchamp.* New York: Time-Life, 1966. This is one of the most informative and enjoyable (at times hilarious) biographical-historical studies to appear in art literature.

Periodicals

There are many fine art magazines published in English. Highly recommended are:

American Art Review
American Craft
Artforum
Art in America
Art International
ARTnews

30 *Modern Music*

Twentieth-century music has developed in what are essentially two phases. Phase one is a continuation and development of instruments, forms, and styles inherited from the rich tradition of Bach, Beethoven, and Brahms. Phase two began in the 1950s with the electronic age. Though the past is still influential, this is essentially a new world of music using an incredible variety of electronic sounds, instruments, synthesizers, computer composition and computer performance, and the innovations continue to proliferate.

In terms of our musical heritage Igor Stravinsky (1882–1971) is perhaps the one contemporary composer whose career best summarizes the ceaseless experimentation and multiplicity of styles of the first three-quarters of this century. He exploited all the "neo" styles from Neo-Gothic to Neo-Romantic, pausing along the way to try his hand, unsuccessfully, at modern jazz. Thoroughly grounded in the music of the past—he admired the music of Bach above all—he was a superb musical craftsman as well as a bold and daring innovator. Always associated with the European avant-garde, he influenced Diaghilev, Cocteau, Picasso, and Matisse and was, in turn, influenced by all of them.

The first and perhaps strongest impetus came from Diaghilev, who commissioned several ballet scores for the Ballet Russe de Monte Carlo of which the first was *The Firebird.* Following the successful *Firebird,* Stravinsky produced the popular *Petrouchka* ballet score and then turned his attention to the ballet *The Rite of Spring.*

Success was not immediate for this daringly original work. The 1913 premiere in Paris set off a full-scale riot between Stravinsky's avant-garde partisans and his far more numerous detractors. The audience was restless before the music even began; the two camps of "liberal artist" and "conservative establishment" had, in effect, already chosen up sides. The liberals were as determined to like the work as the conservatives were bent on open hostility.

The high register bassoon solo at the very beginning of the piece provoked some sneers and even some audible laughs from the conservative camp and the situation went downhill from there. Things had gotten totally out of hand by the time the police arrived, with the consequence that the premiere performance was never completed. On a special television program aired many years later Stravinsky sat in that Parisian hall in the same seat which he had occupied in 1913. When asked what he did during the riot, Stravinsky replied, "I just stood up, told all of them to go to hell and walked out."

The Rite of Spring[1], subtitled *Pictures of Pagan Russia*, exploits a very large symphonic orchestra and uses many unique instrumental effects to portray the primitive ceremonies.

2 Piccolos	4 Tubas
2 Flutes	Small Timpani
Alto Flute	4 Timpani
4 Oboes	Bass Drum
English Horn	Other Percussion: Triangle,
E♭ Clarinet	Cymbals, Antique
3 B♭ Clarinets	Cymbals, Tam Tam
Bass Clarinet	(gong), Snare Drum,
3 Bassoons	Tambourine, Guiro
Contrabassoon	(serrated gourd with
8 French Horns	stick)
D Trumpet	Violin I
4 C Trumpets	Violin II
Bass Trumpet	Viola
3 Trombones	Cello
	Bass

The ballet is built around the spring fertility rites of ancient Russia. The scenes include the invocation of the coming of spring, various spring dances, games of the rival tribes, the selection of the sacrificial virgin, and finally, her sacrificial dance of death. The music is divided into two main parts with eight sections to Part I and six sections to Part II. In general, the music is *through-composed,* because each section is a specific scene in a dramatic sequence. Parts I and II are separate, but there are no breaks between sections.

Le Sacre du Printemps (1913)
(The Rite of Spring)

Igor Stravinsky (1882–1971)
Total Time: 32:25

Part I: The Adoration of the Earth

Section A. Introduction (Adoration of the Earth)
Meter: Many but principally *duple*
The invocation of the birth of spring. On stage a group of girls is seen sitting before the sacred mound, each girl holding a long garland. The tribal sage appears and leads them towards the mound.
Theme One: Bassoon (Phrygian mode)
Theme Two: English horn (Pentatonic)

Section B. Dance of the Youths and Maidens
Meter: Duple, with strong syncopations
Theme One: Strings (rhythmic patterns)
Theme Two: Bassoons
Theme Three: French horn
Section C. Dance of Abduction
Meter: Constantly changing
Theme One: Trumpet, piccolo, flutes in Fanfare style (Dorian mode)
Section D. Spring Rounds
There are four couples left on stage. Each man lifts a girl on his back and, with a solemn and measured tread, begins making the Rounds of Spring.
Theme One: Soprano and bass clarinets (Pentatonic)
Theme Two: Flutes, violins (Dorian)
Section E. Games of the Rival Cities
The young warriors of the rival tribes display their prowess. Near the end of the section the sage pushes his way through the crowd.
Theme One: Muted trumpet, horns (Aeolian)
Theme Two: Muted trumpets (Mixolydian)
The two themes, representing the rival tribes, alternate throughout.
Section F. Entrance of the Sage
After making his entrance near the end of the preceding scene the village wise man (portrayed by four tubas) assumes direction of the proceedings.
Section G. Adoration of the Earth
The dancers prostrate themselves in adoration of the mystic powers of the earth. This section is only *four measures* long and features bassoons, timpani, and string bass and closes with a very soft, dissonant chord in the strings.
Section H. Dance of the Earth
An exuberant dance in praise of the fertility of the earth.

Part II: The Sacrifice

Section A. Introduction (Pagan Night)
The sage and the girls sit motionless around the fire in front of the sacred mound. They must choose the girl who is to be sacrificed to ensure the earth's fertility.
Section B. Mystic Circles of the Adolescents
The girls dance the mystic circles until one stands suddenly transfixed as she realizes that she is the chosen one.
Section C. Dance to the Glorified One
In honor of the sacrificial victim there is a vigorous dance which builds up to a frenzied climax.
Section D. Evocation of the Ancestors
Strong rhythmic and dance patterns to invoke the blessings of the ancestors.
Section E. Ritual Performance of the Ancestors
Undulating, pulsating rhythmic patterns to which the village elders perform a shuffling, swaying dance.
Section F. Sacrificial Dance
The chosen one begins a frenzied dance and continues until she collapses and dies. The men carry her body to the foot of the sacred mound as an offering to the gods of fertility.

---

1. Recordings of musical examples are listed at the end of each chapter on music. The Record List always follows the exact sequence in which examples are presented.

Atonality

Atonality was a musical idea whose time had come. Strictly speaking, atonality is a twentieth-century technique which arbitrarily declares the twelve different notes in an octave to be created free and equal. No one tone would predominate; there would be no tonal center, no tonic, no tonality. Curiously symptomatic of the twentieth century, the new system was associated with mathematics and, by coincidence, the system demanded true equality of *black* notes with *white* notes.

Modern science depends on highly sophisticated mathematics and, quite naturally, modern musicians developed their system of what might be called mathematical music. Atonal composers used no more than simple arithmetic, but this was quite sufficient for their manipulations of notes, rhythm, texture, and so forth. Following is a brief description of the process of change from tonal to atonal music, a development which, in retrospect, appears to have been inevitable. Also included are some games that people can play with twelve-tone arithmetic.

Tonal music, which had superseded the modes during the seventeenth century, was based on the idea that the seven tones of a diatonic scale belonged to a key and that the other five tones were outside the key. Composers relied more and more on the five tones outside the key to give color and variety to their music. By the end of the nineteenth century musicians such as Wagner and Brahms were regularly using all of the tones as a twelve-tone system of tonality revolving around a central pitch called tonic, or tonal center.

key of C Major

diatonic scale

outside the key

chromatic tones

After World War I, Arnold Schoenberg (SHURN–burg; 1874–1951) developed a system in which all twelve tones were considered to be exactly equal and therefore with no tonal center. There would be no dissonance or consonance as such because all the pitches could be used in any combination and without reference to the predominance of any single pitch. This system of twelve equal musical pitches is called *atonality,* or the *dodecaphonic (twelve-tone) system.*

Without a tonic pitch to give the music some sort of unity, it was necessary to devise another kind of unifying system. This new device was called a *tone row,* or *basic set.* Composers invented melodic sequences of the twelve tones, using each tone only once and refraining from using any sequence of notes which would imply a key (tonality). Since it is neither necessary nor desirable to limit the twelve different tones to one octave, a basic set (tone row) could look like this:

Basically, the twelve-tone system lends itself to polyphonic rather than homophonic writing. Almost anyone can devise and use a mixture of polyphonic and homophonic techniques. Because of the infinite possibilities of manipulating the row, the problem becomes one of *selectivity,* selecting those possibilities which make sense musically.

Twelve-tone composition is not solely a musical process but partly a mathematical and/or mechanical procedure. The finished composition might be very different and original in sound (and it might not). Whether it is good or bad music (or something in between) still remains the province of the composer, who makes up one or more tone rows, manipulating, selecting, and modifying until he gets the *musical results* he wants. Twelve-tone technique is neither a virtue nor a vice; it is merely a means to an end. It may assist the composer in discovering new melodic, rhythmic, and harmonic ideas and different combinations of these ideas. It will not do a thing for the finished product; that rests within the sphere of the creative individual.

Alban Berg (1885–1935) was one of the most musically creative of the twelve-tone composers. His style is also notable for clear, clean orchestral writing. For his Violin Concerto he used a small, versatile orchestra with a delicate contrapuntal texture. Following is the instrumentation for the Violin Concerto (the instruments in parentheses are doubled by the same instrumentalists):

2 Flutes (2 Piccolos)
Alto Saxophone
  (clarinet)
Bass Clarinet
Contrabassoon
2 Trumpets
Tuba
Strings

2 Oboes (2 English
  Horns)
2 Clarinets
2 Bassoons
4 Horns
2 Trombones
  Timpani, Bass Drum,
  Cymbals, Snare
  Drum, Tam Tam,
  Triangle

His tone row for the Violin Concerto was not a mechanical contrivance but a point of departure for pure music making. He deliberately chose a row which had clear tonal implications, a mixture of *g minor* (the primary tonality), *a minor,* and a portion of the whole-tone scale. The following is the tone row for the Violin Concerto:

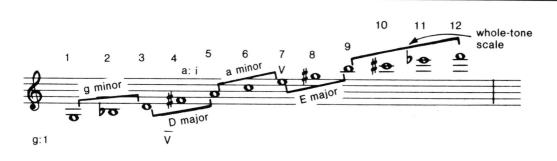

Violin Concerto (1935)

Alban Berg (1885–1935)
Total Time: 25:15

There are two separate movements, each divided into two distinct sections:
 I Andante; Allegretto
II Allegro; Adagio

I Andante

Form: Ternary (103 measures)
Tempo: Andante   Time: 4:00

Theme a (Row)
solo violin

Theme b
solo violin

Form: Ternary, i.e., Scherzo——————— Trio———
——— Scherzo
Tempo: Allegretto

Theme a
solo violin

Theme b
solo violin

Trio I (*Theme a*)
strings

Trio II (*Theme b*)
flute

Coda (Carinthian folk tune) (*Theme c*)
horn

II Allegro

Form: Ternary
Tempo: Allegro ("But always rubato, free as in a cadenza")

The movement is one long violin cadenza which is played in a rhapsodic manner as specified in the composer's tempo indication. This particular cadenza is no mere display of virtuosity but a unified movement featuring brilliant solo work and orchestral accompaniment. Theme b dominates the movement.
Theme a: Tutti
Theme b: Horn
Theme c: Solo Violin

II Adagio (Continued)

Form: Variations on the chorale *Oh, Eternity, Thou Word of Thunder* from Bach's Cantata no. 60, *It is Enough! So Take My Spirit Lord* (95 measures)
Tempo: Adagio

Theme (harmonization by J. S. Bach, melody in Lydian mode)

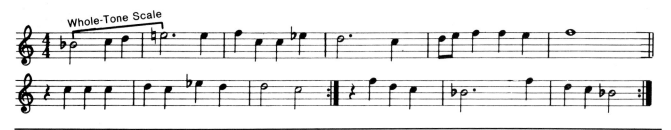

The styles of twentieth-century music are many and varied, as befits a dynamic art in a rapidly changing age. The vogue of neoprimitivism (*The Rite of Spring* and other similar compositions) had its day; Romanticism, whether called Neo-Romantic or Post-Romantic, continues to have some influence; nationalism is once again a characteristic of the works of some composers. One trend has been toward Classicism, as in the works of the twelve-tone school and, among many others, the music of the Russian composer Serge Prokofiev (1891–1953).

Prokofiev went through a primitive phase, and his music does have certain nationalistic characteristics. He has had exceptional success with descriptive music, as attested to by his motion-picture scores and the universally popular *Peter and the Wolf*. The bulk of his writing, however, has a classical orientation and deals mainly with the abstract forms of sonata, concerto, and symphony. His Fifth Symphony is written for the large orchestra in which Russian composers take particular delight. The musical content is rich, expressive, and often highly dramatic. The form is lucidly classical, logical, and controlled.

Symphony no. 5 in B♭ Major, op. 100 (1944)

Serge Prokofiev (1891–1953)
Total Time: 44:00

I

Form: Sonata
Tempo: Andante

Theme a

Theme b

Scherzo

Theme a

Theme b

Violin I muted

II

Form: Ternary (Scherzo-Trio-Scherzo)
Tempo: Allegro marcato

Trio

Theme a

Theme b

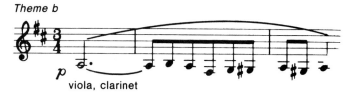

III
Form: Ternary
Tempo: Adagio

Theme a

IV
Form: Rondo (Primary theme *a* alternating with secondary themes *b, c,* and so forth to give A–B–A–C–A–B–A). The introduction uses material from the first movement.
Tempo: Allegro giocoso

Theme a

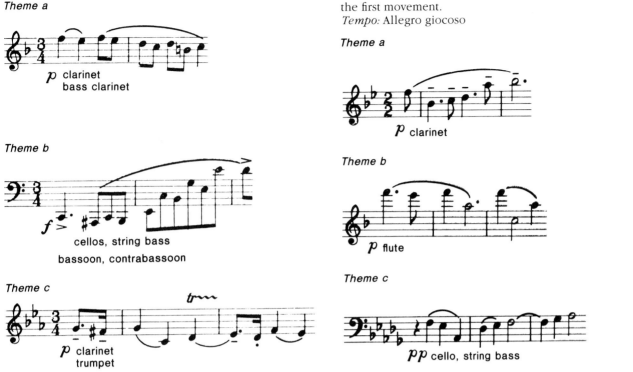

Theme b

Theme b

Theme c

Theme c

Béla Bartók (1881–1945) was one of the outstanding composers of the century. Born in Hungary, he escaped the Nazi terror and settled in New York City where he made a meager living as a piano teacher and as a concert pianist. Only after his death was there any significant recognition of the consistently high quality of his music. The shy, soft-spoken Hungarian refugee has written some powerful music characterized by great intensity and depth of feeling, music which sings and plays without becoming flippant, music which is sometimes somber and occasionally tragic in tone but which is not dejected or self-pitying. His work consistently manifests an affirmative life-force which epitomizes the man and his music.

Béla Bartók's style was an amalgam of Hungarian folk music, great rhythmic ingenuity, and a fundamental allegiance to Classical forms. He delighted in the folk music of southeastern Europe because it helped free him from the tyranny of the major-minor system; moreover, many of his rhythmic conceptions were derived from folk dances of the same area. His preoccupation with formal unity and coherence led him to a unique style of *continuous variations,* a dynamic and thoroughly modern style of relentless tension and growth.

His Concerto for Orchestra, which sounds like a contradiction in terms, is an orchestral piece in which nearly all of the instruments are treated in a soloistic manner. The virtuoso in this case is the entire orchestra. There are five movements, each very different in content, but all a part of the dynamic drive which culminates in the fifth and last movement. His sonata form is called "modified sonata form" because of his consistent application of the continuous variation principle. In other words, his recapitulations are never simple restatements of expositions but variations on those statements. The traditional ternary form is used for the second movement but even here the return to the A section is a varied rather than a literal one. The third and fourth movements exploit the *arch form* which is so much of a part of Bartók's style: A–B–C–B–A. Bartók's continuous variations, however, modify this form to A–B–C–B′–A′.

Concerto for Orchestra (1943)

Béla Bartók (1881–1945)
Total Time: 37:00

I

Form: Modified sonata form
Tempo: Andante non troppo
    Allegro vivace

Introduction
Theme One
low strings

p legato

Theme Two
tpt.

pp

Exposition Allegro vivace

Theme a
violins

f

Theme b
oboe

p dolce

II "Game of Pairs"

Form: Ternary (All material varied in the closing section)
Tempo: Allegretto scherzando

This movement is in the nature of an exercise for a succession of pairs of instruments. The movement begins with a snare drum solo followed by two bassoons a *sixth* apart. The bassoons remain a sixth apart throughout their solo section; no other harmonic interval is used. The bassoons are followed by two oboes a *third* apart, a pair of clarinets a *seventh* apart, two flutes a *fifth* apart, and two muted trumpets in *seconds.* Bartók deliberately imposed on his own creativity a problem of trying to write in a rigorously predetermined pattern and still maintain interest and musical value, a typical exercise in ingenuity which artists seem to delight in inflicting on themselves.

Section A
Introduction: Snare drum

Theme One: Bassoons in sixths (m6)

p

Theme Two: Oboes in thirds (m3)

p

Theme Three: Clarinets in sevenths (m7)

p   3

Theme Four: Flutes in fifths (p5)

8va - - - - - -

mf

Theme Five: Muted trumpets in seconds (m2)

p

Section B
Theme a (Chorale theme)
Brass Choir

III "Elegia"
Form: Arch (A–B–C–B'–A')
Tempo: Andante non troppo

Introduction

string basses

Section A
Theme a

Section B
Theme b
Violins, cl.

Section C
Theme c
violas

IV "Intermezzo Interrotto" (Interrupted Intermezzo)
   Theme *c* is a parody of material from Dmitri Shostakovitch's Seventh (Leningrad) Symphony. The listener can form his own judgment as to Bartók's opinion of the symphony.
Form: Arch (A–B–C–B'–A')
Tempo: Allegretto

Section A
Theme a

oboe

Section B
Theme b

violas

Section C
Theme c

clarinet *accellerando*

V "Finale"
Form: Modified sonata form
Tempo: Presto

Introduction
Pesante   horn

Theme a
Presto   violins

Theme b
bassoon

Theme c
trumpet

Some contemporary composers have reacted against the prevailing Classical concepts of the twentieth century as well as against the innovations of composers who are experimenting with computer compositions and the manipulation of electronic tapes. These modern-day Neo-Romantics are still primarily interested in program music, major-minor tonality, tertiary harmony, and large vocal and instrumental ensembles. They have adopted some modern techniques but have incorporated them into what is essentially a nineteenth-century framework.

Carl Orff, in his cantata *Carmina Burana* (see chapter 16 on medieval music in vol. 1), used the poetry of the medieval goliards to write what he calls a "dramatic cantata." The wandering scholars, defrocked monks, vagabonds, minstrels, rascals, artists, and dreamers who were known as goliards rebelled against the strictures of society and protested the rule of the establishment, in this case the Church and the aristocracy.

The text of Orff's cantata was selected from the thirteenth-century collection of goliard poems which was discovered in Bavaria in the Benedictine monastery of Benediktbeuren, hence the name *Carmina Burana (Songs of Beuren)*. These *cantiones profanae* (secular songs) were written in a mixture of Latin, French, and German. They sing of nature and the joys of love, the tavern, and the free life. There is a strong undercurrent of protest against the cruel fate of those who do not conform to the conventions of society.

Carmina Burana is a concert piece for soloists, boy's chorus, small chorus, large chorus, and a large orchestra augmented by two pianos, five timpani, and a large percussion section (glockenspiel, xylophone, castanets, drums, ancient cymbals, etc.). Orff selected twenty-four verses and divided them into four sections:

Introduction—1,2

In the Spring—3–10

In the Tavern—11–14

The Court of Love—15–25 (verse 25 is a repeat of the opening verse)

There is no thematic development. The music consists of a series of clear-cut stanzas, many of which are repeated with a change of dynamics, orchestration, and the like.

Carmina Burana; Cantiones Profanae (1936)

Carl Orff (1895–1982)
Total Time: 50:40

Introduction
1. "O fortune variable as the moon." Large chorus and orchestra.
2. "I lament fortune's blows." Men's chorus, piano, bassoons.

In the Spring
3. "The bright face of spring shows itself to the world." (Imitation of Gregorian chant.) Small chorus, woodwinds, pianos.

4. "The sun, pure and fine, tempers all." Baritone solo, strings.

5. "Behold the spring, welcome and long awaited." Chorus, orchestra.

6. *On the lawn.* Dance, orchestral.

7. "The noble wood is filled with buds and leaves. Where is my love?" Large chorus, small chorus, orchestra.

8. "Shopkeeper, give me color to paint my cheeks, so that the young men will not resist my charm." Sopranos, large chorus, small chorus, orchestra.

9. *Round dance* in three sections for orchestra. Large chorus; small chorus.

10. "Were the world all mine from the sea to the Rhine, I would gladly forsake it all if the Queen of England were in my arms." Large chorus, orchestra.

In the Tavern

11. "In rage and bitterness I talk to myself." Baritone solo.

12. "The roasted swan sings 'Once I dwelt in the lake and was a beautiful swan. O miserable me! Now I am roasted black!'" Tenor solo (falsetto) and orchestra.

13. "I am the Abbot of Cluny, and I spend my time with drinkers." Baritone solo and men's chorus.

14. "When we are in the tavern we don't care who has died." Male chorus, orchestra.

The Court of Love

15. "The God of Love flies everywhere." Boys' choir, orchestra.

16. "Day and night and all the world against me." Baritone solo, orchestra.

17. "There stood a maid in a red tunic." Soprano solo, orchestra.

18. "My heart is filled with sighing." Baritone solo, chorus, orchestra.

19. "When a boy and a girl are alone together, happy is their union." Male sextet.

20. "Come, come, do not let me die." Double chorus, orchestra.

21. "My mind is torn between opposites; between love's desire and chastity." Soprano solo, orchestra.

22. "Pleasant is the season, O maidens, so rejoice you lads!" Baritone, soprano, boys' choir, chorus, orchestra.

23. "Sweetest boy, I give myself completely to you!" Soprano solo.

24. "Hail to thee most beautiful." Chorus and orchestra.

25. "O fortune, variable as the moon." (Repeat of opening chorus.)

Music of Today

The musical selections presented so far represent a cross section of established classics of the first half of the century. There has been an explosive growth of movements and styles since World War II which includes pre-World War II composers (and their techniques) who still exert a powerful influence and, in addition, a growing number of post-war avant-garde composers.

The Futurists gave concerts of noises before World War I with imaginative use of explosions, snorts, hisses, murmurs, screams, howls, laughter, sobs, and sighs, for example, which influenced the Dadaists and the music of Varèse. With their insistence upon songs of factories, warships, cars, and planes and exploitation of machine and electrical power they also influenced such artists as Leger. Although they were outside the mainstream of traditional European music and few of their works survived, they opened the door to post-World War II exploitation of the world of acoustic phenomena.

Next to the development of new ideas in European music, some of the most important experimental work was taking place in the United States. What had been a more or less transplanted European tradition led to a distinctive American sound in the development of jazz (to be discussed later) and the startling innovations of Charles Ives (1874–1954). Ives was a one-man movement who anticipated just about every important musical development of the past half century: serial and aleatory music,[2] mixed meters and tempos, blocks of sound, free forms, the possibilities of accidental or chance acoustical experiences, assemblages, collages, and even early manifestations of Pop art. However, despite an impressive array of avant-garde techniques, Ives was still a traditional New Englander who wanted to maintain his philosophical relationship with the recent literary past. His important *Concord Sonata* for piano has the four movements named after the Transcendentalists: Emerson, Hawthorne, the Alcotts, and Thoreau.

To understand what Ives is getting at in his music it is necessary to recognize the music that he quotes, the church hymns, dance music, and military band music. These quotes are comments on life in the small towns and rural areas of America. His nostalgic *Three Places in New England,* for orchestra, is replete with quotes from Americana and illustrates a concern for his American heritage as profound as that of Walt Whitman.

Three Places in New England (1903–1911)

Charles Ives (1874–1954)

I *The "St. Gaudens" in Boston Common: Col. Shaw and His Colored Regiment.*
Following are the opening lines of a poem which Ives wrote into the score:
Moving,—Marching—Faces of Souls!
Marked with generations of pain,
Part-freers of a Destiny,
Slowly restlessly—swaying us on with you
Towards other Freedom!

II *Putnam's Camp, Redding, Connecticut.*
Ives wrote: "Near Redding Center is a small park preserved as a Revolutionary Memorial; for here General Israel Putnam's soldiers had their winter quarters in 1778–1779. Long rows of stone camp fireplaces still remain to stir a child's imagination. The scene is a "4th of July" picnic held under the auspices of the First Church and the Village Cornet Band. The child wanders into the

---

2. Aleatory (AY-lee-uh-TORE-e) or chance music.

woods and dreams of the old soldiers, of the hardships they endured, their desire to break camp and abandon their cause, and of how they returned when Putnam came over the hills to lead them. The little boy awakes, he hears the children's songs and runs down past the monument to "listen to the band" and join in the games and dances.

III *The Housatonic at Stockbridge.*
Ives quotes the poem of that name by Robert Underwood Johnson:

Contented river! in thy dreamy realm—
The cloudy willow and the plumy elm . . .
Thou hast grown human laboring with men
At wheel and spindle; sorrow thou dost ken . . .
Wouldst thou away!
I also of much resting have a fear;
Let me thy companion be
By fall and shallow to the adventurous sea!

The twelve-tone composition of the Viennese School of Schoenberg, Berg, and Webern (VAY–burn) went into temporary decline with the growing power of fascist dictatorships in the thirties and war in the forties. Many composers fled for their lives from totalitarian states which demanded simplistic music in a national style in conformance with the military monoliths which the arts were commanded to serve. Schoenberg emigrated to the United States, Berg died in 1935, but Webern stayed on in Vienna quietly creating rigorous twelve-tone music which was to captivate post-war composers. Ironically Webern survived tyranny and the war only to be accidentally killed by an American soldier shortly after the end of the war.

The music of Anton Webern (1883–1945) is difficult to characterize apart from the sound: a kind of cubistic pointillism with meaningful breathing space. He has written some of the most beautiful rests in music—the sounds of silence. He uses few notes in a short space of time, manipulating isolated, contrasted tone colors in a space-time continuum. All is rigorous, precise, twelve-tone mathematics, but the result combines the isolation of single tones with the disassociation of sequential events which somehow make up a total musical interrelationship. Although half of his limited production was devoted to vocal music, his mature style is fully illustrated in two instrumental pieces: Symphony, op. 21 (1928) and Variations for Orchestra, op. 30 (1940).

The opening measures of Webern's Symphony, opus 21, are given below as a visual illustration of the restraint and precision of his music.

Partly because of the presence of Schoenberg, twelve-tone composition in the United States flourished during the war, and later reoccupied most of Europe, with the exception of Iron Curtain countries, which continued to condemn its dissonant complexities as "bourgeois decadence." The American composer Milton Babbitt (b. 1916), among others, expanded twelve-tone writing from a method into an elaborate system called *serial technique* or *serial composition.* Although the old method was never a matter of simply arranging the twelve pitches into a row, the new procedure systematized other elements of music such as rhythm, harmony, tempo, dynamics, timbre, and so forth. For example, a serial composition could contain mathematical permutations of twelve pitches, a sixteen-unit rhythmic organization, a sequence of twenty-nine chords, and fourteen timbres (tone colors). When one considers the fact that there are approximately half a billion ways of arranging just the twelve pitches, the mathematical possibilities of serial technique systems approach infinity. Whether or not these combined mathematical procedures produce music worth listening to is strictly up to a composer who has to choose from an infinitely greater range of possibilities than ever confronted Stravinsky, not to mention Bach or Beethoven.

Symphony for Small Orchestra, op. 21 (1928)

Anton Webern (1883–1945)

Following are examples of serial techniques using six notes in a horizontal (melodic) pattern, vertical (harmonic) pattern, and in a rhythmic pattern:

Melodic

Rhythmic

Harmonic

In the fifties Babbitt began working in electronic music with the R.C.A. Electronic Sound Synthesizer. Electronic music uses artificial tones produced by electronic means as, for example, in the earlier and far simpler instrument called the Hammond organ. Babbitt's experience with synthesized music affected such nonelectronic works as *All Set* for jazz ensemble and *Sounds and Words* for soprano with piano accompaniment. He went on to juxtapose the two types of music in a work combining voice and synthesizer in a setting of Dylan Thomas's *Vision and Prayer*.

Olivier Messiaen (mes–YAYN; b. 1908) is a leading proponent of European serial composition and also the teacher of Stockhausen and Boulez, two of the most important avant-garde composers. As an expert ornithologist and student of Eastern music, Messiaen utilizes authentic bird calls and Hindu *talas* and *ragas* within a highly original serial system. Examples of his work include many organ compositions plus such representative orchestral works as *Oiseaux exotiques* (1956) and *Chronochromie* (1960).

After the war a new program of studies was inaugurated in Darmstadt, Germany to help German (and other European) composers catch up on artistic developments, particularly in the United States, which had been blacked out by the Nazi nightmare. Leading figures in the movement were Stockhausen and especially Pierre Boulez (boo–LESZ; b. 1925), a French composer whose professed musical influences were Debussy, Stravinsky, and Webern. However, in line with the classic French approach to artistic theory, Boulez has related his musical work to the literary production of Mallarmé, James Joyce, and the diaries of Paul Klee. Characteristic works include a setting of Surrealist poems entitled *Le Marteau sans maître* and his Third Piano Sonata.

While the serialists pursue the manifold possibilities of their systems, other composers have concentrated on the exploitation of noise and timbre first introduced by the pre-World War I Futurists. Traditionally, tone color has been more ornamental than essential to Western music and the incorporation of "noise" was unthinkable. But musical sounds as such are only a miniscule part of the modern world of acoustical phenomena. We are surrounded and often engulfed by noise which ranges from city traffic, electrical appliances, and factory din to the "noises" of nature: sounds of the animal world, thunder, rain, hail, seasounds, windsounds, and so forth.

Previous Western cultures have tended to rank "musical" sounds (simple acoustical events with regular pitch vibrations) above "noise" (a complex mixture of regular and irregular vibrations). Some modern composers have attempted to express the sounds of nature in traditional musical terms while at the same time incorporating "noise-making" instruments of the percussion section such as drums, rattles, gourds, and cymbals. Because of the ever-growing interest in different cultures, non-Western percussion instruments were introduced in the nineteenth century and extensively used in the twentieth century. Traditionalists scorned these intruders as nonpitched and therefore antimusical, but innovative composers enthusiastically employed the possibilities of combining timbre and noise into a new musical fabric which violated virtually every precept of conventional melody and harmony.

Webern was the first modern composer to emphasize tone color as a musical idea in its own right, but Edgard Varèse (1883–1965) was the first outstanding composer to write a major work—*Ionisation* (1931) for thirteen percussionists and forty instruments—based on a new musical conception utilizing noise and timbre. Although critics vigorously attacked Varèse throughout his long career for his "insane barbarous and atrocious" treatment of music, *Ionisation* has become a classic work—and it has yet to be determined where music leaves off and sheer, unadulterated noise begins. During the war years Varèse's influence waned but returned with full force when he turned his talents to the *musique concrète* which was developed in the late forties by technicians at the French National Radio. Musique concrète uses preexisting recorded sounds (tones and noises), thus establishing the important idea that all aural impressions are available as raw material for creative composers. Varèse provided what are probably the two most significant compositions in this genre with *Deserts* (1954) for tape and instrumental ensemble and *Poème Electronique,* commissioned to be played by over four hundred spinning loudspeakers at the 1958 Brussels World's Fair.

As indicated above in the work of Babbitt, the Darmstadt school, Varèse, and the Paris school, many roads of contemporary music lead to several varieties of electronic music. In fact, electronic music appears to be a natural consequence in the evolution of Western music. In the early predominantly vocal era, the singer was his own instrument. During the Baroque period there was a general parity between vocal and instrumental music, after which instrumental music clearly dominated vocal music. The musician now used what amounted to a mechanical extension for his music making, with varying degrees of disassociation between performer and instrument; for example, wind players are in close contact with their instruments, string players have some direct control, but keyboard instruments, especially the pipe organ, are quite mechanical. The evolution from a personal instrument (the voice) to an instrument once removed (e.g., the trumpet) has now reached a twice-removed instrument which is wholly the product of technology and which is entirely removed from direct human contact.

This instrumental evolution seems to reflect the condition of contemporary culture in which so many activities are carried on untouched by human hands. Computers are talking to computers while many people find it ever more difficult to communicate with each other. One might argue that the exclusion of human beings from the production of musical sounds spells the death of art and the triumph of technology. On the other hand, there is some evidence that the new possibilities in the manipulation of sound can open up a whole new era of musical forms while simultaneously stimulating new vitality in vocal and instrumental music. If this optimistic view proves to be the correct one, it will bear out the thesis emphasized throughout this book: the ferment and rapid change in contemporary life is apparently a necessary prelude to a more humane society which may already be taking form. In any event, the work in electronic music is basically a reflection of the current crisis-dilemma-opportunity situation now operative in contemporary life, and electronic music, along with all our highly developed technology, is here to stay. What happens with machines is still the prerogative of those who build the machines.

Over thirty years ago—in 1951—the electronic studio of Cologne Radio was put into operation, thus semi-officially launching the age of electronic music. Other studios were subsequently opened in Paris, Milan, Tokyo, and at Columbia University and the Bell Laboratories in the United States—and many more are now in operation. Karlheinz Stockhausen (b. 1928) of the Cologne Studio has been a leader in a medium which has particular importance in his work: he could create new forms out of his basic idea of serial control of transformation and thus break down conventional distinctions between clarity and complexity and, most especially, between noise and pitch. Representative compositions include Op. 1970 and Solo for Electronic Instrument with Reverberation.

After the mid-fifties, the nature of avant-garde music began to change, due largely to the leadership of Stockhausen. Total serialism grew into new materials based on the many ways of transforming textures, colors, and sound densities. From the earlier "controlled chance" compositions, with some options controlled by the composer and others by the performer, the movement has shifted to multiple forms

of control and chance and so-called "open forms" with chance the major factor. Aleatory music (Latin, *alea:* dice) is a general term describing various kinds of music in which chance, unpredictability, ambiguity, and even sheer chaos is realized in performance. If strict serial music represents a kind of Newtonian, mathematical determinism, then aleatory music represents its exact opposite: a symbolic rolling of musical dice just to see what will happen.

This conflict between determined calculation and chance is a musical equivalent to the current situation in science. The precision of the Newtonian world-machine has been supplanted by a modern science which is forced to settle for contingent proofs, complementary truths, and/or mathematical concepts of uncertainty. Quantum mechanics recognizes the element of chance and its language has even been carried over, however ineffectively, into aesthetic theories. Strict mathematical concepts (except for "pure" mathematics), whether in science or art, can lead only to dead ends: scientific "truths" which are jarred by further gains in knowledge and strict mathematics in music which lead to the sterility of nonart. Chance music is therefore a corollary of modern science, and especially of both the profundity and absurdity of contemporary life.

The American composer John Cage (b. 1912) was among the first to experiment with chance music. In the late thirties he worked with a "prepared piano" which was designed to produce percussive sounds and noises that were unrelated to its traditional sound. Since the early fifties he has produced works of indeterminate length, of chance operations, of chance media (a concert of a group of radios tuned to different stations), and similar techniques. One of his most widely discussed compositions is a piano solo titled *4' 33"* during which the pianist merely sits quietly at the piano for this period of time, after which he bows and leaves the stage. Obviously the composition "sounds" different at each performance because of the variance in noise from the audience. This composition would have to be considered the ultimate in Minimal art as well as an achievement somewhat comparable in everyday life to the "non-wheat" which a farmer produces in exchange for government money. Carrying this idea to its logical conclusion would have the government paying artists for nonpoetry, nonnovels, and nonpaintings. The ultimate absurdity would seem to have been reached and Dada would reign supreme.

And Dada is related to chance music, or vice versa, just as are Cage's ideas of the Chinese chance technique of coin throwing from the *I Ching* and his fascination with Zen Buddhism. Chance music concerts may include instructions on manuscripts such as: "Start when you like and repeat as often as necessary," "Hold this note as long as you like and then go on to the next one," "Wait till the spirit moves you and then make up your own piece," and so forth. Performers are also instructed to destroy their instruments, stare at the audience, propel vehicles about the stage, blow sirens, flash lights, and perform other stimulating activities. The end result might be called Aimless Theatre rather than theatre of the absurd, although there appear to be common elements. For an encore there may or may not be a full-blown Happening followed by the ultimate absurdity—leaving the concert hall to return to "real" life.

Pierre Boulez has done extensive work with aleatory music but his work is not at the mercy of blind chance as in the case with Cage, or myopic chance as with Stockhausen. Boulez himself states that chance is guided; the work leaves much to the discretion of the performer and can thus be seen from several angles, something like the mobiles of Calder.

Contemporary music contains perhaps more than its fair share of politically motivated music. Soviet composers like Dmitri Shostakovitch (1906–1975) were expected to follow the party line and supposedly his well-known Fifth Symphony did so. In his *Memoirs* (smuggled out of Russia and published in 1979) Shostakovitch revealed some startlingly different ideas. According to him the Fifth Symphony was meant to describe Stalin's Great Terror of 1936–1937. The Seventh Symphony, called the Leningrad, was actually planned before the war; the so-called invasion theme, with its fearsomely swelling fortissimo, had nothing to do with the Nazi attack. "I was thinking," wrote Shostakovitch, "of other enemies of humanity [namely Stalin and his killers] when I composed the theme." "The majority of my symphonies are tombstones," stated Shostakovitch. "Too many of our people died and were buried in places unknown to anyone. . . . I'm willing to write a composition for each of the victims, but that's impossible, and that's why I dedicate my music to them all."

During the thirties many artists, in a quest for Utopia, moved over to the party line but most moved back again after Utopia was more clearly seen as Shostakovitch had experienced it first-hand, a brutal totalitarian empire. In the fifties the themes changed to pacifism, antiwar and individual freedom. Britain's Benjamin Britten (1913–1979) wrote his notable *War Requiem* for the rededication of Coventry Cathedral after its destruction by German bombers during the war. In Italy, Dallapiccola (b. 1904) has become a persuasive artist dedicated to universal humanism. His techniques follow Schoenberg and Berg but his humanistic philosophy is expressed in works such as *Canti di Prigionia (Songs of Imprisonment)* and the opera *Il prigioniero (The Prisoner)*.

Not all contemporary music is of the avant-garde variety. Paul Hindemith (1895–1963) was a Neoclassicist in his retention of tonal writing and his devotion to the style of J. S. Bach. He also advocated *Gebrauchmusik* (useful music) and wrote music for all ages and degrees of musical skills and for numerous special events which called for appropriate music. One of his best works is the symphonic version of *Mathis der Maler,* a moving depiction in sound of the *Isenheim Altarpiece* by Matthias Grünewald (1480–1528). Kurt Weill (1900–1950), after he met the

playwright Bertolt Brecht, deliberately rejected the complexities of modern music. In conjunction with Brecht he wrote *The Threepenny Opera* and *The Fall of the House of Mahagony.* These two operas were partly responsible for the renaissance of musical theatre in America which began with Rodgers and Hammerstein's *Oklahoma!* and continued through their *South Pacific, Carousel,* and *The Sound of Music.* Bernstein's *West Side Story,* Lerner and Loewe's *My Fair Lady* and *Camelot,* and Newley's *The Roar of the Greasepaint; The Smell of the Crowd* are notable contributions to the musical theatre. The finest talent in contemporary music theatre is unquestionably Stephen Sondheim, who writes both words and music. His musicals include *West Side Story* (lyrics), *A Funny Thing Happened on the Way to the Forum, A Little Night Music, Pacific Overtures,* and *Sweeney Todd.*

George Gershwin (1898–1937) may be one of America's best composers. Criticized by musical snobs as being "popular" and thus, for some strange reason, beyond the pale, his music has endured and much of it has become a part of the standard repertory. The *Rhapsody in Blue, An American in Paris,* and the Concerto in F have all become known throughout the world as truly representative of American music. *Of Thee I Sing* is now recognized as musical theatre at its satirical best and *Porgy and Bess*—a smash hit at La Scala in Milan—is perhaps America's finest opera.

Following are brief descriptions of additional major American composers along with one or more representative compositions by each.

Earle Browne (b. 1926) wrote *Available Forms II for Large Orchestra, Four Hands* for two conductors who choose from among thirty-eight "sound events."

Elliott Carter's (b. 1908) Concerto for Orchestra was commissioned for the 125th anniversary of the New York Philharmonic Society. It is a major work by a superb craftsman in the Post-Renaissance tradition.

Aaron Copland's (b. 1900) Suite from the Ballet *Appalachian Spring* and the ballet score *Rodeo* have become modern classics.

George Crumb (b. 1929) wrote *Echoes of Time and the River: Four Processionals for Orchestra* (cf. Thomas Wolfe) using all titles as poetic metaphors rather than for specific meanings.

Time Cycle, Four Songs for Soprano and Orchestra by Lukas Foss (b. 1922) uses a literary "time-motive" with each poem referring to time, clocks, or bells.

Symphony no. 3 by Roy Harris (1898–1979) was the first symphony by an American composer to achieve worldwide acclaim.

Carl Ruggles (1876–1971) took the title of his orchestral work *Sun-Treader* from Robert Browning's tribute to Shelley.

Symphony no. 6 by William Schuman (b. 1910) was commissioned by the Dallas Symphony Orchestra.

As with so many important orchestral works, the Symphony no. 3 by Roger Sessions (b. 1896) was commissioned by a symphony orchestra, in this case the Boston Symphony.

Samuel Barber (b. 1910) bases his *Knoxville: Summer of 1915* on a fragment by the writer James Agee.

Windows by Jacob Druckman (b. 1928) won the Pulitzer Prize for 1972, a fitting recognition for a major work.

Synchrony was a collaborative effort between Henry Cowell (1897–1965) and Martha Graham.

Lou Harrison's (b. 1917) Symphony on G is serially based on twelve tones while literally basing itself on the note "G."

Mysterious Mountain by Alan Hovhaness (b. 1911) is written in the manner of a romantic symphony but with a variety of modern techniques.

Wallingford Riegger's (1885–1961) Symphony no. 3 is a blending of traditional and twelve-tone techniques.

George Rochberg (b. 1918) uses two six-note groups derived from a single twelve-tone row for his Symphony no. 2.

Gunther Schuller (b. 1925) composed his tonal impressions of visual art with his *Seven Studies on Themes of Paul Klee.* Schuller has been a leader in the movement known as "third-stream jazz" which attempts to combine jazz with chamber and/or symphonic music.

The Plow that Broke the Plains by Virgil Thompson (b. 1896) is an orchestral suite extracted from the score of a documentary film about the drought of the 1930s.

Charles Wuorinen (b. 1938) wrote his Concerto for Amplified Violin and Orchestra after winning a Pulitzer Prize in 1970 for an electronic composition.

Following are brief descriptions of additional major European composers—by country—with representative compositions.

Austria

Ernst Krenek (b. 1900) has written a jazz opera entitled *Jonny spielt auf.* Perhaps his most important work is the opera *Karl V,* a prophetic piece predating the rise of Hitler.

Egon Wellesz (1885–1974) has been almost equally famous as a composer and as a musicologist. His finest stage work is the *Bakchantinnen,* based on Euripides' *The Bacchae.*

One of the most curious figures in twentieth-century music is Joseph Mathias Hauer (1883–1959), an inventor of a twelve-tone system. Unlike Schoenberg, who refused to violate his twelve-tone row, Hauer contended, among other things, that there were 479,001,600 possible combinations of twelve notes. His theories may be more interesting than his music.

Hans Erich Apostel (b. 1901) has been strangely neglected, possibly because his music is starkly austere, conceived as an architectonic act with a minimum of romantic accoutrements.

Czechoslovakia

Vieteslav Nóvak (1870–1949) was strongly influenced by the more flamboyant qualities of Slovak folksong. *The Storm,* a symphony-like cantata, is his best dramatic work.

Leoš Janáček (1854–1928) was perhaps the most important Czech composer of this century. Major works include: *Diary of a Young Man Who Disappeared, Concertino* for seven instruments, Quartet no. 2, *Sinfonietta,* and the *Glagolitic Mass.*

One of the more strikingly original composers is Alois Hába (1893–1973) who developed a technique of microtones which includes quarter-tone, sixth-tone, and twelfth-tone scales.

The work of Bohuslav Martinu (1890–1959) is the most cosmopolitan in outlook. Perhaps his long residence in France, Switzerland, and the United States accounts for this, and yet his music remains Czech to the core. His compositions include four symphonies and two piano concertos.

Eugen Suchon (b. 1908) is a Slovak composer whose sociological-psychological drama *Krutnava* is the first Slovak national opera.

Petr Eben (b. 1929) is a traditionalist who draws as much from Gregorian chant as he does from contemporary techniques. His compositions include the large-scale orchestral work *Vox clamantis.*

England

William Walton (1929–1982) achieved early fame with his *Facade,* a setting for a series of "nonsense" poems by Edith Sitwell. His dramatic cantata *Belshazzar's Feast* is one of the great choral works of the century.

Michael Tippett (b. 1905) produced nothing of any lasting value before his mid-thirties. *The Midsummer Marriage, King Priam,* and *The Knot Garden* are his three operas, all of which have aroused considerable controversy. Critical opinion ranges from condemnation to acclaim with very little in a moderated middle ground. All three works are actually very significant contributions to the operatic stage and any or all of them may find a permanent place in the opera house. His oratorio, *A Child of Our Time,* transforms a Nazi pogrom against the Jews into a formidable image of terrible reality.

Maxwell Davies (b. 1930) is possibly the leading British composer of the younger generation. He is both a modernist and a traditionalist in works such as *L'Homme armé* (based on the fifteenth-century mass) and *Revelation and Fall.*

France

Darius Milhaud (1892–1974) was one of the most prolific composers of the century. His music for Cocteau's pantomime, *Le Boeuf sur le Toit,* set the standard for a chic, hard, chrome-plated music. His later works include the operas *Bolivar* and *David* and the suite *Opus Americanum.*

Arthur Honegger (1892–1955) made his reputation with *Le Roi David,* a biblical drama for chorus and orchestra. Perhaps his most significant works are his dramatic oratorios *Amphion* and *Jeanne d'Arc au bûcher.*

Francis Poulenc (1899–1963) channeled his enormous talent into two disparate directions, an ultra-Parisian side of music halls, circus bands, and street-corner ensembles along with a devotion to serious sacred music. He set Cocteau's *Cocardes* to the sounds of a street-corner ensemble. For Diaghilev, he wrote a brilliant score for the ballet *Les Biches.* During World War II, he played a prominent part in the "musical resistance" movement and wrote one of his finest works during the German occupation, the cantata *Figure humaine* which ends with a hymn to Liberté. His choral works are monumental: Mass in G, *Litanies à la Vierge noire de Rocamadour, Stabat Mater, Gloria,* and *Sept repons des tenebras.* The role of Francis Poulenc in twentieth-century music is unique because of the unabashed pleasure-giving quality of his music. Even his religious works are never morbid or sentimental for he wore his religion happily. Even when he was at his witty, Parisian best he was never banal, trivial, or superficial. Above all, he staunchly refused to take anything seriously, which may be the most eloquent testimony of all to this musical blithe spirit.

Germany

Hans Werne Henze (b. 1926) has precocious talents which, after early success in Germany, he moved to Italy where he indulged himself in Italian romanticism—a Rimbaud cantata *Being Beauteous* and *Nocturnes and Arias.* By 1970, his Italian dream had ended as he faced a mind-blowing Rolling Stones concert in Rome and the attempted assassination of a students' revolutionary leader. His angry protest piece *Versuch uber Schweine* was one result of his politicalization. Henze's conversion to Marxism was also marked by his controversial *Raft of the Medusa.*

Gyorgy Ligeti (b. 1923) worked with Stockhausen at the electronic studios in Cologne. His technique is exemplified in his *Aventures* and *Nouvelles Aventures* in which the "language" used is limited to phonetic sounds with no meaning. His most notable pieces to date are the *Requiem* and the *Lux Aeterna.*

Mauricio Kagel (b. 1931) of Buenos Aires worked in the electronic studios at Cologne and taught at the Darmstadt electronic complex. His music can be said to eternally rejuvenate itself and, at each moment of performance, to produce new sounds and other surprises. His *Transicion,* written for piano, percussion, and two tape recorders, uses a pianist playing in the traditional manner, a percussionist striking various parts of the piano, these sounds recorded—and distorted—on the first tape recorder, and the whole concert hall scene recorded by the second tape recorder and played back during the performance.

Greece

Iannis Xenakis (b. 1922) has emerged as an important avant-garde composer. He collaborated with Le Corbusier in designing the Philips Pavilion for the Brussels World's Fair and wrote music for it. His *Stratégie* for two orchestras and two conductors is a contest between the two instrumental ensembles in which the conductors are given certain specifications about the nineteen sections of the composition and, at the conclusion of the battle, the applause of the audience determines the winner.

Holland

Peter Schat (b. 1935) has studied with Pierre Boulez and figures prominently in many avant-garde programs as a serial composer with aleatory and improvisational passages in the manner of John Cage.

Italy

Luciano Berio (b. 1925) achieved prominence with his pioneering of the Milan Radio electronic music studio. He has the ability to write music ideally suited to the nature of individual instruments, such as his *Sequenzas.* Probably his best and most original work is *Circles,* written to poems by e e cummings.

Poland

Witold Lutoslawski (b. 1913) strives to extend the frontiers of music while remaining within the bounds of the Post-Renaissance tradition. In *Trois poèmes d'Henri Michaux,* he uses various methods of producing sound—exclusive of singing—varying between quiet whispers and violent calls, cries, and screams.

Russia

Nikolai Myaskovsky (1881–1950) is representative of the neutral, easily forgotten artisan-composers which the Soviet Union has vigorously promoted.

Aram Khachaturian (1903–1978) reflects vivid Armenian folksongs in works like the Piano Concerto, Violin Concerto, and his very popular ballets.

Scandinavia

Bengt Hambraeus (b. 1928) was the first Scandinavian composer to write an electronic piece, albeit in Cologne, with his *Doppelrohr II.*

Bo Nilsson (b. 1937) explores unusual and striking sonorities, as in the *Brief an Gôsta Oswald* for three sound groups.

Spain

Joaquin Turina (1882–1949) had a vast output including, for example, forty-nine different series of piano music. He is at his best in orchestral works such as *La Procesión del Rocio* and *Danzas Fantásticas.*

Manual de Falla (1876–1946) was one of the notable composers of the century. His contributions to the repertoire include *Love the Sorcerer, The Three-Cornered Hat, Nights in the Gardens of Spain,* the *Retalbo,* and the Harpsichord Concerto.

Oscar Esplá (1886–1971) is the third of the Spanish masters of the twentieth century. His best works include *El Sueno de Eros, La Nochebuena del Diablo,* and *Don Quijote valando las armas.*

Switzerland

Frank Martin (1890–1974) based his major work, *Le vin herbé,* on the Tristan legend. His *In terra pax* was written for the end of World War II.

Rolf Lieberman (b. 1910) has also made a name for himself as an operatic director in Germany. His best-known work is his Concerto for Jazzband and Symphony Orchestra.

Summary

Twentieth-century music, like the music of every age, effectively mirrors the prevailing patterns of the century. The impending catastrophe of World War I was forecast in the primitive barbarity of Stravinsky's *The Rite of Spring.* Reflecting the rational, intellectual aspects of the Age of Analysis were the serial techniques of Alban Berg as he exploited the self-imposed discipline of the tone row to achieve the musical results of the Violin Concerto.

Prokofiev's Neoclassical Fifth Symphony displayed another kind of discipline, that of casting modern tonal materials in classical forms and making the forms serve the music. Orff's *Carmina Burana* gives some indication of the persistence of the Romantic tradition in a century which seems to have little time for sentiment. Bartòk's Concerto for Orchestra, with its continuous variation technique, seems to epitomize the age, the restless, ever-changing forms of contemporary life.

The pre-World War I Futurists began the exploration of the musical possibilities of noise and timbre which Varèse later developed into a uniquely modern musical style.

Charles Ives anticipated many of the innovations of avant-garde twelve-tone composers such as Schoenberg, Berg, and Webern and, after World War II, the avant-garde developed the twelve-tone method into complete serial systems.

Electronic music in various forms (*musique concrète* and synthesizers) exerted an ever-growing influence as reflected in much or all of the work of Babbitt, Messiaen, Boulez, Stockhausen, Varèse, and Cage. Aleatory music, with or without electronic assistance, is not dominating the musical scene but it is certainly making strong waves.

Britten, Shostakovich, and Dallapiccola, among others, have used a variety of styles to convey sociopolitical viewpoints, while Hindemith concentrated on expanding the resources of tonal music and Weill deliberately rejected the complexities of contemporary music in favor of a synthesis of traditional styles (including jazz) which influenced the development of modern musical theatre.

American composers have made important contributions to the international scene. Gershwin, Copeland, Harris, Sessions, and Barber, among others, have contributed a variety of significant contemporary music. European composers continue to dominate Western music though not as exclusively as they have in the past. Krenek, Janacek, Martinu, Walton, Tippett, Milhaud, and Honegger have continued the Post-Renaissance tradition; Ligeti, Kagel, Xenakis, Berio, and Nilsson have been leaders in experimental music utilizing electronic resources.

The essence of much of the music of this century can be summarized in the phrase "Things fall apart: the center cannot hold." The old musical centers of clear-cut keys, major-minor tonality, and traditional musical instruments are no longer apropos. Composers have been trying to find and/or establish new centers, new ways of relating to a rapidly changing world.

The search for new musical values has utilized mathematics (twelve-tone and serial techniques), technology (electronic media), the sounds of people, and the sounds of nature. Traditional music has been bent, borrowed, violated, and ignored. The search goes on and, probably, only the next century can look back and describe where the search has led us and what twentieth-century music was all about.

Jazz in America

Jazz is a uniquely different style of music, the result of a fusion—collision might be a better word—of certain elements of African and American musical cultures. Aside from the music of the American Indian, music in the United States was of European origin and under the influence of European musical styles. This influence extended to both North and South America.

Given the broad influence of European civilization and the presence of African slaves and freedmen throughout the United States, the islands of the Caribbean, Central and South America, the singular and significant fact remains that jazz is a style of music that originated solely in the United States. By the turn of the century, Negro spirituals, ragtime, blues, and jazz were established types or styles of music. None of these styles, however, existed at this time anywhere else in the Western Hemisphere.

The French, Spanish, Portuguese, and even English cultures of the West Indies, Central and South America seemed to have provided a climate in which African arts, crafts, customs, and religious beliefs could coexist with their European counterparts: a climate in which transplanted Africans could maintain a considerable portion of their customs mixed, of course, with many elements of Western culture, Christianity in particular. For whatever reasons, and there appear to be many, the dominant white culture of the American South was not as tolerant of African customs as were the transplanted European cultures south of the United States. There existed a strong conflict between white and black Americans in almost every area of life: religion, folklore, music, art, dance, and social and political customs. This continuing cultural conflict, it should be pointed out, is only one complex area amidst the persistent problems of race relations and need not be equated with strife in areas such as civil liberties, equality of educational, housing, and job opportunities. Fundamental differences in the ways of living built up by a group of human beings, namely *culture*, may very well lie at the heart of some of the problems, but those considerations lie outside the scope of this book.

In summary, jazz is a musical style that evolved out of a three-century history of cultural and racial conflict, a clash between an inflexible dominant culture and a powerful and persistent subculture with its own age-old beliefs and customs.

The elements of jazz are those of any music: melody, harmony, rhythm, and tone color. It is the Afro-American mixture, however, that makes the difference. The development of any style of music normally follows an evolutionary process *within* a single culture. Outside influences, when they appear, tend to be transformed and absorbed into the stylistic development. For example, the Viennese waltz is a modified, speeded-up version of an old Austrian folk dance called the *ländler*. The landler was Austrian; the changes were compatible with Austrian concepts of melody, harmony, rhythm, and tone color. The finished product was in all respects a result of Austrian culture and the musical genius of one Johann Strauss, Jr. It would be ludicrous to remove the Strauss melody and insert a Russian boat song, an Irish jig, or an American Indian rain dance. Scale, harmony, rhythm, and tone color would be all wrong because an incompatible melody was introduced into a foreign context.

In a manner of speaking, jazz sounds the way it does because it *is* a compound of several different and even opposing concepts of melody, rhythm, and tone color. In very general terms, jazz can be defined as a style of music that consists of Afro-European melody, European harmony, African rhythm, and Afro-European tone color. A built-in conflict of musical styles lies at the root of jazz and probably accounts, at least in part, for the feelings of dislocation and sometimes anguish and even pain on the part of performers and listeners.

The fundamental conflict in the materials of jazz occurs in *scale* and *tuning*. Equal temperament, with its twelve equal semitones in each octave, is the tuning standard for Western music. On the other hand, African melody was and is based on the tones present in the overtone series. The distances between pitches range from whole steps and half steps, similar to those in the tempered scale, to other intervals *between* half steps, including *quarter tones* (tones approximately midway between, say, C♯ and D♭). African harmony is quite rudimentary; melody, rhythm, and tone color are far more important.

African melodies, with their different-sized intervals, were sung in a culture that did not use such a variety of intervals, that built musical instruments in equal temperament, a culture in which African songs were often characterized as out of tune, primitive, and/or a poor imitation of "proper" singing.

The Elements of Jazz

Scale   The combining of African scales with the European diatonic scale produced a hybrid called the *blues scale*.[3] In terms of the equal-tempered piano the blues scale can be described as a diatonic scale plus three *blue notes*: flatted 3rd, 5th, and 7th scale degrees.

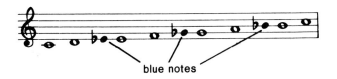

blue notes

---

3. The blues scale is not African in itself although its origins necessarily lie in African music. Rather it is an Afro-American scale, and it is the elemental component out of which jazz is made.

In a single melody line there can be a mixture of diatonic notes and blue notes:

In actual performance the blues scale might be described as a pentatonic scale plus flatted 5th (g♭ or f♯):

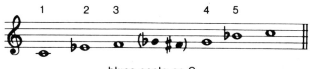

blues scale on C

The blues scale on C can be used *against* the three primary triads in several different ways:

Blues scales all based on C
x = blue notes

Blues scales based on chord roots, C, F, G:
x = blue notes

A simple melodic line using only the blues scale on C would sound like this when played against the primary diatonic chords (the name of the chord is given in parentheses):

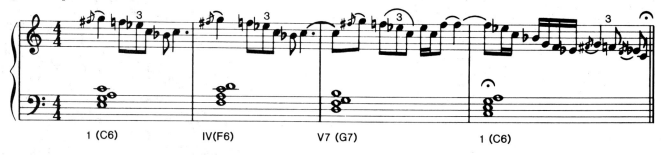

A melody such as the one above would be written the same way whether played on the piano, on another instrument, or sung; however, the melody would be performed in equal temperament only on the piano. In any other medium (vocal or instrumental) the flatted 3rd might be the same pitch as the piano E♭ or several other slightly higher pitches *between* E♭ and E♮ (there is no commonly used notational system which can accurately indicate these pitches):

The vocalist or instrumentalist can produce any of the preceding pitches, slide from one to another or play with or "worry" the notes. The best that the pianist can do is strike E♭ and E♮ together as a substitute for the note in between.

Rhythm Rhythm is the main ingredient in African music: highly developed, intricate, complex, as sophisticated in its own way as the harmonic system of Western culture. The African rhythms which have crossed over into jazz and into much of our modern concert music are but a relatively simple portion of a whole world of elaborate percussion music. Compare, for example, the single rhythmic pattern of an

Indian dance

or that of a waltz

with the simultaneous rhythms of a quartet of African percussionists:

Guiro (scratched gourd)

High Drum   Right Hand / Left Hand

Middle Drum

Low Drum

There are two interrelated fundamental characteristics of African rhythm: *beat* and *syncopation.* Emerging from the simultaneous rhythm patterns is a *subjective beat,* a rhythmic pulsation which is not necessarily played by any one drummer but which results from the combination of the whole. The beat is

implicit. This beat (whether explicit or implicit) is so much a part of jazz that it can be called its *heartbeat* or *pulse.* Jazz can thus be defined as the "beauty of the beat."

Syncopation is a displacement or shifting of accents so they disagree with natural metrical accents.

Natural accents

Syncopations

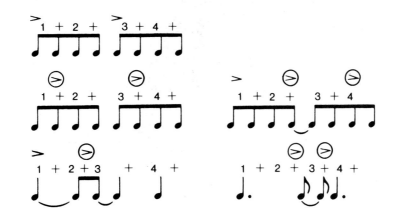

Syncopation has the effect of tugging at the beat, a process that emphasizes the existence of the basic pulse by setting up a conflict with that pulse. The pull of syncopation on the ongoing beat gives a kind of *swing* to the music, a buoyant resiliency which is a fundamental characteristic of jazz.

Tone Color   The story is told of the World War II air base in Africa which stockpiled aviation gasoline in steel drums. The drums were unloaded and stacked by native laborers, one of whom accidentally dropped a drum and noticed a booming, reverberant tone as the heavy drum hit the hard ground. His neighbor immediately dropped his drum in order to discover its tone color. Within a very few minutes, in their delight at discovering new tone colors, the entire crew was enthusiastically engaged in dropping, hitting, and scraping gasoline drums.

Beating on logs, sticks, bones, metal, or drums, scratching gourds, shaking rattles, all are activities designed to exploit tone colors within a rhythmic framework. An African drummer can obtain several dozen different timbres as he uses his thumbs, fingers, flat of the hand, or fist on various areas of a drumhead. All that is necessary for a percussion instrument is a distinctive tone color with virtually no limit to the number and variety of possible tone colors.

Distinctive tone color in jazz is not confined to the drums. It extends to the colors obtained by using mutes, hats, plungers, handkerchiefs, or anything else that will give variety to the timbre of instruments such as trumpet and trombone. Instrumentalists also use growls, slurs, slides, and so forth in what is basically an attempt to give an expressive range and personal quality to their music. The colors may be cool or hot or anything in between; in any event, jazz musicians are concerned with their sound, the distinctive coloration of their performance.

Harmony   Harmony is one of the most highly developed elements of Western culture but of only slight importance in African music. Consequently, the fusion of African and American music was essentially a combining of African melody, rhythm, and tone color with an established harmonic system. The result, as stated before, was a synthesis of conflicting stylistic elements and the beginning of a new style of music called jazz.

Primary Origins of Jazz

Jazz probably came into existence at one or more places in the American South some time between the end of the Civil War and the last decade of the nineteenth century (ca. 1890). The precise date may never be pinpointed because jazz was a compound of preexisting music.

There are many types of black music, some probably dating back to the arrival of the first slaves in the early part of the seventeenth century and others gradually developing in response to, or despite, the Amer-

ican environment. The African vocal tradition survived and adjusted to the new conditions and the new religion (Christianity). The instrumental tradition, however, was generally repressed by the planters who suspected, and rightly so, that African drums could communicate such matters as possible slave rebellion. The planters were also concerned about breaking up tribal units and traditions, little suspecting that tribal histories were perpetuated by the drummers and the language of the drum script.[4] The banjo (African, *banjar*) did survive but European instruments were gradually taken up by black musicians. The outline below specifies the various types of vocal music, ceremonies, instrumental styles and ensembles, dances, and stage presentations which lie, in varying degrees, at the roots of jazz.

Black Music in America

Vocal Music (with and without accompaniment)	**Instrumental Music** Creole music (dances, woodwind instruments)
Secular	**Sacred**
Work songs	Spirituals
Hollers	Ring shouts
Street cries	Gospel songs
Ballads	Jubilees
Blues	Song-sermon
Marches	(semivocal)
Brass bands	Voodoo ceremonies
Ragtime	(dances, singing,
Minstrel shows (vocal	percussion)
and instrumental)	

The sound of the music is the only practical way for gaining an understanding of any music, and particularly the many styles of black folk music. Following are pre-jazz styles (as outlined above), including specific examples, their background, and characteristics.

African Music

1. "Dundun Drums" (talking drums). In *Dances of the Yoruba of Nigeria*. Folkways FE 4441.
2. "Religious Drumming to the Deity Orishania," The Yoruba, Nigeria. In *African and Afro-American Drums*. Folkways FE 4502.

---

4. Some African languages, especially the varieties of Bantu, used different pitch levels of vowel sounds for different word meanings. Tribal historians were highly select drummers who were trained to play the *talking drum* by beating out the word rhythms while at the same time varying the pitch by means of a stretched membrane. Thus, the drum script was almost a vocal sound which could be transmitted over considerable distances with the use of relay drummers.

Pre-Jazz Styles (Black Folk Music)

Work Song

Background and Characteristics Directly and closely related to African work songs. Strong, regular beat, blues scale, syncopations,[5] usually unaccompanied solo song but may use guitar or banjo accompaniment. Associated with manual labor that tends to a rhythmic regularity, such as rowing a boat, driving railroad spikes, and chopping wood.

Examples
1. Leadbelly. "Juliana Johnson." In *Jazz*, Vol. I. Folkways FV 2801.
2. Leadbelly. "Looky Yonder Where de Sun Done Gone." In *Last Session,* Vol. I. Folkways 2941.

Holler (Field Holler)

Background and Characteristics Sung to non-rhythmic fieldwork such as picking cotton or hoeing corn. Unaccompanied, irregular beat, narrative or singsong text, varied repetition of words and phrases, some prolonged syllables with elaborated melodic line.

Examples
1. "Old Hannah."In *Jazz,* Vol. I. Folkways FV 2801.
2. Leadbelly. "Bring Me Li'l' Water, Silvey." *Take This Hammer.* Verve, Folkways 9001; S9001.

Street Cry

Background and Characteristics Song to accompany the selling of fruits, vegetables, fish, and so forth in the streets of a city or village. Unaccompanied, constant repetition of the name of the product with varying inflections on the words, including changes in pitch and tone quality. Conversion of words to consistent rhythmic patterns, a prevailing characteristic of most black music. The ends of phrases frequently use a *falsetto break* in which the voice slides up an octave or so in pitch and abruptly breaks off.

Examples
1. "Strawberry Woman" and "Crab Man." In *Porgy and Bess: Original Sound Track Recording.* Columbia OL—5410; OS—2016.
2. Van Wey, Adelaide. "Sweet Oranges" and "Blue Berries." *New Orleans Creole Songs and Cries,* 10″. Folkways 2202.

Ballad

Background and Characteristics Narrative song in numerous verses. African heroic songs of kings, hunters, and warriors are translated into ballads about folk heroes such as John Henry, the steel-driving man.

Example
1. Leadbelly. "John Henry." In *Jazz,* Vol. I. Folkways FV 2801.

Blues

Background and Characteristics The most important single influence in the development of jazz. There are two kinds of blues: folk (rural blues) and urban (true jazz blues). Only the folk blues will be considered here. (See page 428 for Urban Blues.)

The blues reflect African customs and musical traditions, but they are native to America. The blues are personal, subjective, introspective, a way of protesting misfortune and identifying trouble. Singing the blues is a survival technique for counteracting bad times, loneliness, and despair.

Blues lyrics usually consist of three lines of poetry. The first line is repeated (possibly with a slight variation) followed by a third line which completes the thought. Because blues are usually improvised, the repeating of the second line gives the singer a better chance to make up the last line. There may be only one verse or there may be many verses in a narrative blues. Favorite subjects are love, traveling, and trouble, but almost anything makes a fit subject, as shown by the following blues poems.

Love:

Love is like a faucet, you can turn it off or on (twice)
But when you think you've got it, it's done turned off and gone.

Traveling:

I went to the deepot, an' looked upon de boa'd. (twice)
It say: dere's good times here, dey's better down de road.

Proverbs:

My momma tole me, my daddy tole me too: (twice)
Everybody grin in yo' face, ain't no friend to you.

Images:

Ef blues was whiskey, I'd stay drunk all de time. (twice)
Blues ain't nothin' but a po'man's heart disease.

Comedy:

Want to lay my head on de railroad line, (twice)
Let the train come along and pacify my mind.

Tragedy:

(one line images)
Got the blues but too dam mean to cry.
Standin' here lookin' one thousand miles away.
I hate to see the evenin' sun go down.
Been down so long, Lawd, down don't worry me.

---

5. All these styles use blue notes and syncopations unless otherwise specified.

The music of the blues is quadruple meter and is eight, twelve, sixteen, and sometimes twenty bars in length. The *twelve-bar blues* is the most common of all patterns. It accompanies the three-phrase rhymed couplet in the most popular poetic meter of iambic pentameter. The harmony is limited to the primary triads.

Chilly Winds

Examples

1. "Careless Love." Brownie McGhee. *Blues.* Folkways 3557; or: *Wilbur de Paris Plays, Jimmy Witherspoon Sings, New Orleans Blues.* Atlantic 1266.
2. "Every Night When the Sun Goes Down." Elizabeth Knight. *Hootenanny Tonight.* Folkways 2511.
3. "Joe Turner Blues." Big Bill Broonzy. *Sings Country Blues.* Folkways 2326; or: *Louis Armstrong Plays W. C. Handy.* Columbia CL—591.

Spiritual

Background and Characteristics Many derived from Protestant hymns but with significant changes in melody and rhythm. Usually improvised, especially during church services or prayer meetings. Most common pattern is solo verse with group refrain. Call and response patterns (song leader alternating with group response) also quite common. The texts are variations of existing hymns, paraphrases of biblical passages, or sometimes wholly original. They are notable for vividness of imagery, the relating of biblical stories with direct and telling simplicity, and a strong concern for the sounds and rhythms of words.

Examples

1. "Didn't It Rain." Mahalia Jackson. *Newport 1958: Mahalia Jackson.* Columbia CL—1244.
2. "Michael Row the Boat Ashore." *We Shall Overcome: Songs of the Freedom Riders.* Folkways FH 5591.

3. "Down by the Riverside." *Pete Seeger at Carnegie Hall.* Folkways 2412; or: Mahalia Jackson. *Bless This House.* Columbia CL—899; CS—8761.
4. "Every Time I Feel the Spirit." Josh White. *Chain Gang Songs.* Elektra 158; 7158; or: Marian Anderson. *Spirituals.* RCA Victor, LM 2032.

Ring Shout

Background and Characteristics Similar to an African circle dance in form and character. Usually performed outdoors after a service. A ring would be formed and a spiritual sung to start it moving, accompanied by hand claps and foot stomping. The same spiritual would be sung over and over, usually with added verses until the cumulative effect would be hypnotic.

Example

1. "Come an' Go with Me." Odetta. *Odetta Sings Ballads and Blues.* Tradition 1010; or *Guy Carawan Sings,* Vol. II. Folkways 3548; or Hally Wood. *Hootenanny at Carnegie Hall.* Folkways 2512.

Gospel Song

Background and Characteristics Many derived from Protestant gospel songs. They differ from hymns and spirituals mostly in the texts, which are more personal and subjective. "I," "me," "my" (sometimes "we") are the key words in songs that tend to reduce the religious experience to a personal viewpoint. Melody and harmony are generally simpler than in spirituals.

Examples
1. "My God Is Real." Mahalia Jackson. *Newport 1958: Mahalia Jackson.* Columbia CL—1244.
2. "We Shall Overcome." *We Shall Overcome: Songs of the Freedom Riders.* Folkways FH 5591.

Jubilee

Background and Characteristics   A type of spiritual which sings jubilantly of the Year of Jubilee "When the Saints Go Marching In."

Example
1. "When the Saints Go Marching In." Many jazz recordings available

Song-Sermon

Background and Characteristics   Delivered from the pulpit and usually beginning with a scriptural quotation. The vocal delivery of the minister proceeds from the spoken word to a kind of intoned chant and culminating in ringing declamation and vocalized phrases on higher and higher pitches. The African custom of responding verbally to the utterance of important personages such as a tribal chieftan is reflected in the congregational response to the song-sermon. There are shouts of "amen," "yes sir," "hallelujah," and impromptu wordless crooning.

Examples
1. "Dry Bones." *Jazz,* Vol. I. Folkways VB 2801.
2. "It Ain't Necessarily So." *Porgy and Bess.* Columbia OL—5410.

Voodoo (Vodun)

Background and Characteristics   Voodoo is the name given to the combination of African and Catholic religious rites and beliefs which was developed in Haiti by the Dahomeans of West Africa and which still exists in the West Indies and portions of the United States. Voodoo rites took place in Congo Square in New Orleans before being driven underground. Voodoo helped perpetuate African customs and music and probably made a significant contribution to Afro-American music and to the development of jazz.

Examples
1. *Drums of Haiti.* Folkways 4403.
2. *Cuba: Cult Music.* Folkways 4410.
3. *Jamaica: Cult Rhythms.* Folkways 4461.

Minstrel Show

Background and Characteristics   Dating from about mid-nineteenth century, minstrel shows were generally sentimentalized "scenes of plantation life" performed by an all-male, all-white cast. Characteristic black elements were present in some of the group dances, the use of rhythmic "bones," tambourine, and banjo, the soft shoe dances and the cakewalk finale (see "Ragtime"). The romantic ballads, basso profundo, silver-voiced tenor, sliding trombones, and southland chorus were, at best, distantly related to black music. Stephen Collins Foster's songs (many of them based on black folk music) were a popular staple. Minstrelsy dealt with stereotypes which no longer exist, if they ever did, but it can be credited with disseminating a portion of black musical culture throughout the United States and Europe and preparing the way for the more authentic music of a later period.

Example
1. *A Complete Authentic Minstrel Show.* Somerset SF—1600.

Ragtime

Background and Characteristics   A written-down style of music originally composed for the piano and featuring syncopated rhythmic patterns over a regular left-hand accompaniment in duple meter. The essentials of ragtime probably were in existence prior to the Civil War although Scott Joplin is formally credited as the first to write ragtime in the mid-1890s. Blacks in their slave quarters liked to imitate the fancy balls in the plantation house by staging a cakewalking contest. The highest-stepping couple "took the cake." The basic cakewalk patterns consisted of duple meter plus two kinds of melodic syncopations:

There is a considerable body of ragtime piano literature, most of which is too difficult for the average pianist to play. Consequently, there is much watered-down semi-ragtime popular music from the period 1900–1920. Almost any piece of music can be "ragged" by changing the meter to duple, if necessary, and converting the rhythms into ragtime patterns. In developed ragtime these syncopations would include the two patterns illustrated above plus the more difficult pattern of four-note groups in which every third note is accented:

Examples

1. "Original Rags." Scott Joplin. *Ragtime: Piano Roll Classics.* Riverside RLP 12—126.
2. Joseph Lamb. *Classic Ragtime.* Folkways 3562.
3. *Reunion in Ragtime.* Stereoddities S 1900.
4. "Golliwog's Cake Walk" from the *Children's Corner Suite* by Claude Debussy. Angel 35067; or: Columbia ML—4539; or: Columbia ML—5967; MS—6567.
5. Scott Joplin. *Ragtime Songs (for piano).* Nonesuch 71248.

The Styles of Jazz

New Orleans Style

Background and Characteristics   New Orleans style jazz probably began in the 1890s as brass band performances of spirituals and gospel songs, and ragtime versions of standard band marches. This is the so-called *traditional jazz* which, in a more discreet version played by white musicians, became known as Dixieland jazz. The original New Orleans style, however, still exists and is normally referred to as such.

Brass bands secured many of their instruments from the pawn shops of the South where they had been deposited after the Civil War by returning military bandsmen. The instrumentation was fairly typical of marching bands: trumpets, trombones, tuba, snare drum, bass drum, and usually one clarinet. The bands played and paraded for all special functions but especially for the funeral processions. According to a long-standing tradition the bands played spirituals and dirges on the way to the cemetery and some of the same music in a jazz idiom on the way back from the cemetery.

New Orleans jazz is ensemble jazz; everyone plays all the time. In general, the first trumpet has the melody, the clarinet a moving obbligato above the trumpet, and the trombone a contrapuntal bass below the lead trumpet. The material is normally gospel songs, spirituals, and marches, and the meter invariably duple. ("In the churches they sang the spirituals. In the bright New Orleans sun, marching down the street, they played them.") Needless to say, all the music was played by ear and everyone was free to improvise a suitable part for himself. ("You play your part and I play mine. You don't tell me what you want and I don't tell you. We will all variate on the theme.") The texture was polyphonic, a crude but dynamic grouping of musical voices improvising simultaneously on the melodic and harmonic framework of preexisting music. One word can describe New Orleans jazz: *exuberant.*

Examples

1. "Medley of Hymns."*Jazz Begins.* Atlantic 1297.
2. "Just a Closer Walk with Thee." Young Tuxedo Jazz Band. *Jazz Begins.* Atlantic 1297.
3. "High Society." Sweet Emma Barrett and her Dixieland Boys. *New Orleans: The Living Legends,* 2 Volumes. Riverside 356—7.

Urban Blues

Background and Characteristics   Urban blues are the heart of the true jazz idiom. The accompaniment has changed from the folk (or country) blues guitar to piano or jazz band. The subject matter revolves around the problems of urban (ghetto) life. The feeling is still bittersweet, and the form has crystallized into the classic twelve-bar blues accompanying the rhymed couplet in iambic pentameter. The blues may be sung or played by any instrument. The urban blues appeared as a recognizable style in the 1920s (on records).

Examples

1. "Mean Old Bed Bug Blues." Bessie Smith. *Jazz,* Vol. 2. Folkways FJ 2802.
2. "How Long Blues." *Jazz,* Vol. 2. Folkways FJ 2802.
3. "Back Water Blues." Dinah Washington. *Newport '58: Dinah Washington.* Mercury MG 36141.
4. *What is Jazz.* Leonard Bernstein. Columbia CL—919. Illustrations of jazz styles using "Empty Bed Blues"; topics include blues scale, a Swahili song, blue notes, rhythm, beat, syncopation, tone color, harmony, form, and a "Macbeth Blues"

Chicago Style

Background and Characteristics   With the closing of Storyville, New Orleans's legal red-light district (1897–1917), jazz musicians began moving North in increasing numbers. Prohibition and the resultant practice of bootlegging helped make the Roaring Twenties city of Chicago the host for unemployed musicians playing the new and exciting sounds of jazz. Briefly stated, Chicago jazz is New Orleans jazz moved indoors. The ensemble used on the march in the New Orleans sun now played in crowded speakeasies for dances like the Fox Trot, Shimmy, Black Bottom, and Charleston.

Some of the simultaneous improvising remains, but the bands are playing many popular songs in a more homophonic but still lively and swinging style. The meter is mostly duple, but the instrumentation has changed. The piano, a newcomer to jazz, furnishes the rhythmic harmonic background; drums, guitar or banjo, tuba, or string bass, the rhythm. Varying combinations of trumpet, clarinet, trombone, and saxophone (another newcomer) play the melody and harmony. March tempos have been superseded by a range of tempos suitable for the various dances. The one word for Chicago style would be *frenetic.*

Examples

1. "Black Bottom Stomp." Jelly Roll Morton's Hot Peppers. *Jazz*, Vol. 5. Folkways FJ 2805.
2. "Somebody Stole My Gal." Bix Beiderbecke. *Jazz*, Vol. 6. Folkways FJ 2806.
3. "Margie." Bix Beiderbecke. *Jazz*, Vol. 6. Folkways FJ 2806.
4. "China Boy." Eddie Condon. *Chicago Jazz Album*. Decca 8029.

Swing (ca. 1935–1945)

Background and Characteristics   The swing period of jazz began in the Depression years, the so-called Dancing Thirties. After the repeal of Prohibition in 1933 the speakeasies closed down and jazz musicians were again out of work. The migration turned in the direction of New York with its radio stations and large ballrooms, and the crowds of young dancers seeking evenings of economical entertainment.

The six- or eight-piece bands of the Chicago era were large enough for the tiny speakeasies but too small for spacious ballrooms. More musicians had to be added and stylistic changes made to accommodate them. The individuality of New Orleans and Chicago styles was subordinated to ensemble playing mixed with solo performances. The solution for handling larger numbers of players was the harmonized lead: brass sections of two trumpets and two trombones played as a unit with the first trumpet playing lead (melody) while the remaining instruments supplied the harmony. A saxophone section of three or four instruments also operated as a unit.

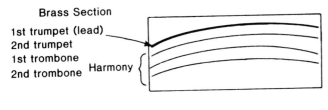

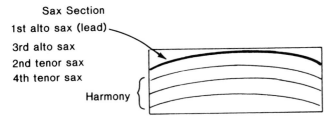

A rhythm section of piano, drums, guitar, and string bass supplied a solid four beats to a bar (quadruple meter) for the brass and sax sections, which played as independent units or as a full ensemble.

Stylistic Characteristics of Swing

1. Four heavy beats to a bar.
2. Three units: brass, saxes, rhythm.
3. Harmonized lead: brass and saxes.

4. Repertoire of popular songs in swing style plus a few jazz compositions from the preswing era. Little or no blues.
5. Extensive use of *riffs*, short rhythmic phrases or figures repeated a number of times. Riffs were used to give unity to the music, to help build up tension through constant repetition and to serve as contrasting and/or filling material against the harmonized lead in another section. Riffs were played by brass and saxes, separately or with two different figures simultaneously.

Examples

1. "A Tisket a Tasket." Ella Fitzgerald. *Original Hit Performances: The Late 30's.* Decca DL 4000.
2. "Don't Be That Way." Benny Goodman. *Carnegie Hall Jazz Concert*, Vol. I. Columbia CL—814.
3. "One O'Clock Jump." Benny Goodman. *Carnegie Hall Jazz Concert*, Vol. I. Columbia CL—814.
4. *Bei mir bist du schoen*. Benny Goodman. *Carnegie Hall Jazz Concert*, Vol. 3. Columbia CL—816.

Kansas City Jump (ca. 1935–1945)

Background and Characteristics   There are many similarities between the Kansas City, or jump style and swing, sometimes called stomp style. Swing was mainly the province of white bands while Kansas City was the preferred style for many black bands. There is little difference in the instrumentation; both used the four-beat style and both used riffs, especially Kansas City, which preferred saxes in unison for riffs.

However, Kansas City was blues-based rather than oriented toward popular songs. The harmonic progression of the twelve-bar blues furnished the framework for many compositions. Swing was generally written-down or arranged jazz; Kansas City used written arrangements and considerable group improvisation. Both styles used improvised solos. Kansas City avoided the heavy sound of swing meter by using four, even, rather light beats to a bar. The piano was much more prominent, both as a solo instrument and as the dominant instrument of the rhythm section.

Examples

1. "627 Stomp." Pete Johnson. *Kansas City Jazz.* Decca DL 3044.
2. "Piney Brown Blues." Joe Turner. Decca DL 8044.
3. "Doggin' Around." Count Basie. Decca DL 8044.
4. "One O'Clock Jump." *Original Hit Performances: The Late 30's.* Decca DL 4000.
5. "Woodchopper's Ball." Woody Herman. *Original Hit Performances: Into the 40's.* Decca DL 4001.

Boogie-Woogie

Background and Characteristics Boogie-woogie became popular during the thirties but apparently had been in existence long before then. Called Texas bass, or Texas walking bass, it probably originated in the southwestern United States as a piano style. Boogie-woogie uses a *basso ostinato* in the left hand and a variety of figures in the right hand, all within the framework of the twelve-bar blues. The left hand plays the same pattern in the "obstinate bass," changing to different notes only when the harmony changes. Eight notes to the bar is the most typical rhythmic pattern.

The combination of strong beat, boogie-woogie bass, twelve-bar blues, and vocal solo became popular in the thirties as Rhythm and Blues (in the black communities). In the fifties the style changed to the amplified "big beat" of rock 'n' roll.

Examples

1. "Slow Boogie." Jack Dupre. *Jazz,* Vol. 1. Folkways FV 2801.
2. "Honky Tonk Train Blues." Meade Lux Lewis. *Jazz,* Vol. 10. Folkways 2810.

Boogie-Woogie Bass Patterns

walking bass

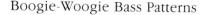

New Orleans Revival (1939–   )

Background and Characteristics Big band jazz of the swing era put the finishing touches on the fading fortunes of the old, free-swinging New Orleans style. A group of white San Francisco musicians took the first steps, in 1939, toward a revival of traditional jazz. Old jazzmen were brought out of retirement and old records studied. The end result was the development of a variety of approaches to traditional jazz under the general heading of New Orleans Revival. Some Revivalists used the ragtime piano (or no piano), banjo, tuba, clarinet, trumpet, trombone, and drums in the authentic two-beat New Orleans style. Many others mixed New Orleans with the four-beat characteristics of swing to achieve the style called Dixieland. Typical Dixieland jazz uses the "front line" of obbligato clarinet, lead trumpet, and fluid trombone (tailgate trombone) backed by drums, bass, and piano.

Examples

1. "Original Dixieland One-Step." Eddie Condon. *Jazz Omnibus.* Columbia CL—1020.
2. "Maryland My Maryland." Turk Murphy. Columbia CL—1020.
3. "Washington and Lee Swing." Mound City Six. *Dixieland from St. Louis.* Everest LPBR—5002.
4. *Come On and Hear.* Dukes of Dixieland. Decca 4708; 74708.
5. Pete Fountain. *Standing Room Only.* Coral 57474; 757474.

The Bop Revolution (ca. 1944–1950)

Background and Characteristics During the long musician's recording and broadcasting strike midway through World War II, an entirely new style of jazz was being developed. Upon the resumption of broadcasting and recording the unsuspecting public heard for the first time, in the style known as bop (or rebop or bebop), the startling sounds of the beginning of modern jazz.

The increasingly regimented big band swing and the by-now monotonous repetition of riffs had stifled most individual creativity. Bop took musical control away from the arranger and returned it to the performing musician.

Stylistic Characteristics of Bop

1. The heavy four-beat pattern employed by the full-rhythm section of the swing band was taken over by the *string bass,* giving a much lighter sound to the basic beat.
2. The drummer, freed from the necessity of maintaining the basic "four," kept the beat on the *cymbal,* reserving the *snare drum* for accompanying patterns and coordinated effects with the soloists. The *bass drum* was played intermittently for special effects, a practice called "bomb dropping."

3. The *piano* was also liberated from the tyranny of the basic four. The pianist accompanied, complimented, and augmented the soloists, a process known as "comping."
4. The *guitar* abandoned the regular strumming of chords and began to function as a melodic as well as a rhythmic instrument.
5. The bop style usually featured the unison playing of *trumpet* and *alto saxophone* in highly elaborated melodic and rhythmic patterns.
6. Quadruple meter was maintained, but riffs were abandoned completely. The band was reduced to a small ensemble of six or seven instruments (combo). Harmony was modernized with much use made of the "flatted fifth" of the blues scale.
7. The conventional pattern of paraphrasing an existing melody and "playing the changes," for instance, improvising upon the changes of harmony of a piece of music, became subordinated to the bop practice of adding new melodies to the existing harmonic patterns of standard songs. For example, the addition of a new melody to the chords of the old popular song "Whispering," produced a new composition entitled "Groovin' High."

Examples

1. "Groovin' High." Gillespie, Parker. *Groovin' High with Dizzy Gillespie.* Savoy MG—12020.
2. "Hot House." Gillespie, Parker. *Groovin' High with Dizzy Gillespie.* Savoy MG—12020.
3. "Salt Peanuts." Gillespie, Parker. *Groovin' High with Dizzy Gillespie.* Savoy MG—12020.
4. "52nd Street Theme." *The Amazing Bud Powell,* Vol. 1. Blue Note BLP—1503.
5. Charlie Parker. *Greatest Recording Session.* Savoy 12079.

Cool Jazz (ca. 1946–   )

Background and Characteristics   Derived from bop and originally known as "cool bop." Deliberate cooling off of the hot jazz of the bop style.

Stylistic Characteristics

1. Instrumentation oriented toward the cool sounds of flute, guitar (acoustic), Chinese cymbals, muted trumpet. Use of straight tone (without vibrato).
2. Emphasis on homophonic texture. Strong influence of the impressionists Debussy and Ravel.
3. Usually based on popular songs.
4. A soft, sometimes dreamy, lag-a-long, behind-the-beat style.

Examples

1. "Moon Dreams." Miles Davis. *Birth of the Cool.* Capitol TT—1974.
2. "September in the Rain." George Shearing. *The Very Best of George Shearing.* MGM 4169; S 4169.
3. "Lullaby of Birdland." George Shearing. MGM 4169.
4. "My Reverie." Barney Kessel. *Music to Listen to Barney Kessel By.* Contemporary 3521; 7521.
5. "Indian Summer." Barney Kessel. *Music to Listen to Barney Kessel By.* Contemporary 3521; 7521.
6. *Lee Konitz.* Pacific Jazz 38.
7. Miles Davis. *Original Quintet.* Prestige 7254; S—7254.

Progressive Jazz (ca. 1946–   )

Background and Characteristics   *Progressive* is the term sometimes used to encompass the whole field of modern jazz. The term was originally employed in the belief that *progress* could be made in the art of jazz. *Progress* is a term, however, more applicable to technology than to the arts; better television sets can undoubtedly be built, but more artistic television programs are by no means a concomitant development. The term *progressive jazz* will be used here to describe modern big band jazz.

Stylistic Characteristics

1. An amalgamation of the elements of swing, bop, and symphonic orchestra techniques and instrumentation.
2. Large ensembles characterized by the increased range and versatility of traditional jazz instruments plus the addition of symphonic instruments such as flute, oboe, English horn, bassoon, French horn, fluegelhorn, celeste, chimes, cello, violins, harp, harpsichord.
3. Influenced by twentieth-century composers such as Stravinsky, Bartók, Prokofiev, Schoenberg.
4. Heavy use of quartal harmony (chords built in fourths), polychords (superimposed tertiary chords), dissonance, and some twelve-tone techniques.
5. Exploitation of a variety of meters in addition to the traditional quadruple meter. Use of polymeters (simultaneous use of different meters).

Examples

1. "Misty." Stan Kenton. *Adventures in Jazz.* Capitol T—1796; ST—1796.
2. "Limehouse Blues." Stan Kenton. *Adventures in Jazz.* Capitol T—1796; ST—1796.
3. Stan Kenton. *Conducts L.A. Neophonic Orchestra.* Capitol MAS—2424; SMAS—2424.

4. Stan Kenton. *Greatest Hits.* Capitol T—2327; ST—2327.
5. "That's Where It Is." Woody Herman. *Encore: Woody Herman.* Philips 200092; 600092.
6. "Better Get It in Your Soul." Woody Herman. *Encore: Woody Herman.* Philips 200092.
7. Woody Herman. *Greatest Hits.* Columbia CL—2491; CS—9291.
8. Count Basie. *Big Band Scene '65.* Roulette 52117; S—52117.

Latin (Afro-Cuban, Afro-Brazilian; ca. 1946–   )

Background and Characteristics   The Latin style of jazz is based on the reservoir of Afro-American dance rhythms of the West Indies, Central and South America. Among the many dances of African origin are the Rhumba, Conga, Samba, Mambo, Afro, Bolero, Tango, Cha Cha, Meringue, Calinda, Bamboula, and Guaracha. Combining African rhythms and jazz produced the jazz samba (bossa nova); many more similar combinations will apparently be forthcoming. For example, the combination of Mexican mariachi music with elements of rock 'n' roll and jazz has produced the peripheral jazz sound of the Tijuana Brass.

Stylistic Characteristics   The use of Latin instruments is the hallmark of Latin Jazz:

Maracas—gourd rattles
Guiro—serrated gourd with scraper
Claves—percussion sticks
Conga drum—large single-skin drum
Bongo drums—pair of small, single-skin drums
Marimba—large xylophone with metal resonators
Cowbell, tambourine, snare drum and bass drum

The other basic characteristic of Latin-styled jazz is, of course, the use of continuous syncopated rhythms, with percussion instruments using the same patterns throughout a composition.

In many cases the Latin influence is used in combination with other jazz styles.

Examples

1. "The Girl from Ipanema." Stan Getz. *Getz-Gilberto.* Verve 8545; 68545.
2. "Bim Bom." Stan Getz. *Big Band Bossa Nova: Stan Getz.* Verve 8494; 68494.
3. "Morning of the Carnival." *New Wave: Dizzy Gillespie.* Philips 200070; 600070.
4. "Days of Wine and Roses." *Kessel/Jazz: Contemporary Latin Rhythms.* Reprise 6073; 9—6073.

Mainstream Jazz (ca. 1946–   )

Background and Characteristics   Mainstream is a continuation and updating of the swing tradition but without the stereotyped riffs and cumbersome written arrangements. Swing, the so-called classical period of jazz, has continued as a mainstream, middle-of-the-road style of jazz. As such it is not particularly concerned with exotic instrumentation or experimentation but rather with a communicable, emotional expression and the requirement that the music must always swing. There is no set instrumentation, but the quadruple meter of swing is standard.

Examples

1. *Mainstream,* 1958. Savoy 12127.
2. Benny Goodman. *Together Again!* Victor LPM—2698; LSP—2698.
3. Benny Goodman. *Greatest Hits.* Columbia CL—2483; CS—2983.
4. Lionel Hampton. *Taste of Hamp.* Glad–Hamp 1009; S—1009.

Hard Bop (1958–   )

Background and Characteristics   Hard bop is modern bop with the same uncompromising drive of the earlier style: dynamic melody line in unison and explosive attack and figuration in the various instruments, especially percussion. The instrumentation tends to remain with the five-piece ensemble: trumpet, alto sax, piano, drums, bass. The so-called East Coast school of jazz is oriented toward the hard bop sound mixed with soul jazz (see following).

Examples

1. "Room 608." *Horace Silver and the Jazz Messengers.* Blue Note 1518.
2. *The Jazz Messengers.* Savoy 12171.

Soul Jazz (ca. 1960–   )

Background and Characteristics   One of the strongest movements in recent years, soul jazz is a return to the church music ("soul music") roots of jazz. Soul emphasizes an emotional depth of communication and scorns the intellectual pretensions ("wigging") of white musicians in general and West Coast musicians in particular. "Soul" indicates more of an approach to jazz performance than any particular style, but there are certain characteristics that all "soul" tends to have in common.

Stylistic Characteristics

1. Heavy use of the "amen cadence," for example, subdominant chord moving to tonic chord to end a phrase (IV–I).
2. Preponderance of subdominant and dominant chords (IV and V).
3. Many open sounds of the perfect fifth and fourth and considerable use of the tritone (three whole steps or D5 or A4).
4. Considerable use of triple meter.
5. Exploitation of "funky" sounds such as tone colors, melodies, and rhythms derived from old work songs, folk blues, hollers, gospel songs. Also the use of "funky" rhythm (duple).

Examples

1. "Filet of Soul." Les McCann. *Shampoo.* Pacific Jazz 63; S-63.
2. "This Here." Cannonball Adderly. *Quintet in San Francisco.* Riverside 311; 1157.
3. Cannonball Adderly. *Them Dirty Blues.* Riverside 322; 1170.
4. Les McCann. *Soul Hits.* Pacific Jazz 78; S—78.
5. Grant Green. *His Majesty King Funk.* Verve 8627; 68627.
6. Ramsey Lewis. *Down to Earth.* Mercury 20536; 60536.
7. Bobby Timmons. *Workin' Out.* Prestige 7387; S—7387.

West Coast Jazz (ca. 1960–   )

Background and Characteristics   Jazzmen have been known to remark that East Coast jazz is jazz that is played on the East Coast and that, by the same token, West Coast musicians are playing West Coast jazz. The differences, however, encompass more than a New York or California locale. Many West Coast musicians have been preoccupied with polyphonic devices, 3/4, 5/4, 7/4, and mixed time signatures, classical forms (sonata, rondo, fugue), and various exotic sounds (oriental, Arabic, Hindu, etc.). Their East Coast critics contend that they have emphasized techniques at the expense of the swinging sound which is fundamental to all jazz styles.

Examples

1. "Blue Rondo a la Turk." Dave Brubeck. *Time Out.* Columbia CL—1397; CS—8192.
2. "Take Five." Dave Brubeck. *Time Out.* Columbia CL—1397; CS—8192.
3. Dave Brubeck. *Impressions of Japan.* Columbia CL—2212; CS—9012.
4. Dave Brubeck. *Time In.* Columbia CL—2512; CS—9312.
5. "The Fakir." Cal Tjader. *Several Shades of Jade.* Verve 8507; 68507.
6. "Cherry Blossoms." Cal Tjader. *Several Shades of Jade.* Verve 8507; 68507.
7. Cal Tjader. *Breeze from the East.* Verve 8575; 68575.
8. Shelly Mann. *West Coast.* Contemporary 3507.

Third-Stream Jazz (ca. 1960–   )

Background and Characteristics   Third-Stream jazz runs between the twin streams of classical music and jazz, borrowing techniques from both but attempting to stay in the jazz idiom. There had been earlier confrontations with classical music in the eras of ragtime ("ragging the classics") and swing ("swinging the classics"). Later jazz movements borrowed instrumental, melodic, harmonic techniques and musical forms from contemporary concert music. Third Stream went one step further with attempts to combine jazz quartets with string quartets and jazz combos with symphony orchestras, the latter in the manner of Baroque concerto grossos.

Some critics have contended that jazz and classical music are basically incompatible and others that Third-Stream music features fair to good jazz improvisation in a context of bad to mediocre string quartet or symphony orchestra writing. The experiments continue and the issue has yet to be resolved.

Examples

1. "Fugue in D Major." Swingle Singers. *Bach's Greatest Hits.* Philips 200097; 600097.
2. "Fugue in C Minor." Swingle Singers. *Bach's Greatest Hits.* Philips 200097; 600097.
3. "Largo." Swingle Singers. *Going Baroque.* Philips 200126; 600126.

Note: The preceding three examples are note-for-note performances of Bach's music. Originally written for harpsichord and/or orchestral instruments the music is here performed vocally with rhythmic syllables and accompanied by drums. No other changes have been made.

4. "Sketch." Modern Jazz and Beaux Arts Quartets. *Third Stream Music.* Atlantic 1345; S—1345.
5. "Allegro-Blues." From "Dialogues for Jazz Combo and Orchestra." Dave Brubeck. *The Dave Brubeck Quartet.* Columbia CL—1466; CS—8257.

Free Form Jazz (The "New Thing") (ca. 1960–   )

Background and Characteristics   The constant experimentation in all fields of twentieth-century music has, to a limited extent, carried over into jazz. A small but persistent vanguard of young musicians has been concentrating on the possibilities of free improvisation. In free improvisation there are no preexisting chord changes on which to improvise, no set patterns, no arbitrary limitations of any kind. Musicians are encouraged to a free self-expression which is responsible only to its own inner world of discipline and logic.

The results to date of free improvisation, simply called the New Thing, have caused considerable debate. Questions have been raised about the difference between freedom and license and about the problem of anarchy and sheer chaos when no one musician knows what his colleagues are doing. Communication between performers and the listening public is also a considerable problem which is far from resolution. Free Form jazz may indeed revitalize the whole field of modern jazz, or it may degenerate into the other extreme in which only the emancipated soloist knows what he is doing—if indeed he does know what he is doing.

Examples

1. "W.R.U." Ornette Coleman. *Ornette!* Atlantic 1378; S—1378.
2. Ornette Coleman. *Free Jazz/Collective Improvisation.* Atlantic 1364; S—1364.
3. "Pithecanthropus Erectus." Charlie Mingus. *Giant Steps.* Atlantic 1237.
4. Charlie Mingus. *Tonight at Noon.* Atlantic 1416; S—1416.
5. John Coltrane. *New Thing at Newport.* Impulse 94; S—94.
6. Ornette Coleman. *Town Hall Concert.* ESP Disc 1006; S—1006.

Liturgical Jazz (ca. 1960–   )

Background and Characteristics   A comparatively recent movement to incorporate jazz into church worship services has opened up an outlet for jazz which it had long been denied. Jazz has become a fixture in concert halls, in regional and international jazz festivals, in government-sponsored goodwill tours, and as the subject of scholarly conferences, learned treatises, and doctoral dissertations. Its return to its original association with religious practices appears to be a natural consequence of its acceptance as an independent art form. The early spirituals, ring shouts, jubilees, and gospel songs have come full circle as the jazz idiom to which they contributed so much has found a place in modern worship.

The use of jazz and jazz instruments has been a long-accepted practice in many black revivals, "storefront" churches, and tent meetings. The acceptance of jazz as another valid mode of musical expression has taken place in the prescribed formal patterns of some of the churches in the major Protestant denominations and a few Catholic churches. The prime moving force has been the attempt to update the liturgy by using some contemporary modes of thought and musical expression. Much of the liturgical music now

in use dates from the Romantic period and appears out of place in the late twentieth century. Some of the sentimental Romantic period music used to accompany hymns, chants, and responses is being replaced by older music (medieval, Renaissance, Baroque) as well as by twentieth-century music.

The practice of using contemporary modes of thought and artistic expression was a natural part of church practices in past centuries. In the Gothic era, for example, the Gothic church was a *modern* church, with sculptures and stained glass by modern artists and music by modern composers. The Gothic cathedral in all its parts was a new church for a new age. The same procedures held true for Renaissance and Baroque churches. Bach and his contemporaries were expected to write new music for almost every Sunday. On the other hand, the eclectic nineteenth century with its Neo-Gothic cathedrals, Neo-medieval country houses, Neo-Baroque opera houses, French Provincial and Renaissance mansions, Neo-Roman train stations, and Neo-Classic government buildings was preoccupied with the past; it failed to develop its own mode of expression. The artistic sterility of the Romantic century carried over into the present century, which had to make a special effort to break away from the borrowed past.

The modes of expression of a bygone era have tended to linger on in the formal religious practices of the twentieth century. The updating of these practices is a task to which many churches have dedicated themselves. The appearance (reappearance is probably a better word) of contemporary words, ideas, musical instruments, musical styles, dance, and drama within the churches is evidence of the impulse toward a more relevant church in contemporary life. The process of modernizing the musical language has even gone to the extreme of including "hootenanny masses" and rock 'n' roll services.

The resistance to liturgical jazz has come from a variety of sources for a variety of reasons. Some have mistakenly confused jazz with popular music. Others have reasoned that a music which was formerly associated with New Orleans bordellos, Chicago speakeasies, dance halls, and night clubs is obviously not good enough for church. This argument overlooks the fact that much of the music presently used in the church had similar humble origins. Moreover, there is no such category as "sacred music"; there is only music which is used in connection with sacred services.

Examples

1. "Introit." *20th Century Folk Mass.* Fiesta 2500.
2. "Kyrie." *20th Century Folk Mass.* Fiesta 2500.

Beaumont's so-called folk mass was a pioneer effort in the attempt to use contemporary music in the church. Referred to, unfortunately, as the Jazz Mass it is a prime example of what not to do. The piece is only distantly related to jazz, being an amalgam of warmed-over swing combined with a sentimental and pretentious Hollywood style. Its only virtue is a demonstration of the fact that the ancient texts of the church tend to shine forth with new vigor when set to newer musical ideas. The *20th Century Folk Mass* provides a pertinent reminder for all who attempt to use liturgical jazz, namely, that there is no substitute for quality. Bad to mediocre jazz badly performed has no place in church or concert hall.

The following examples of Paul Horn and Duke Ellington are of far better quality and demonstrate some of the possibilities of good liturgical jazz.

3. "Kyrie Eleison." *Jazz Suite on the Mass Texts.* Victor LPM—3414; LSP—3414.
4. "Credo in unum Deum." *Jazz Suite on the Mass Texts.* Victor LPM—3414; LSP—3414.

The Kyrie combines some elements of chant and medieval music with jazz scoring and improvisation. The Credo is an experiment in congregational participation and improvisation backed up by improvised commentary by Horn's alto sax.

5. "In the Beginning." Duke Ellington. *Concert of Sacred Music.* Victor LPM—3582; LSP—3582.
6. *Psalmkonzert* by Heinz Werner Zimmermann, Cantata 640 229; available from Barenreiter & Neuwerk, Sortiment, 35 Kassel-Wilhelmshohe, Heinrich-Schutz-Allee 35, Fernruf 30011—16.

The *Psalmkonzert* uses five-part mixed choir (SSATB), children's choir, three trumpets, string bass, and vibraphone. The style is a blend of jazz techniques with classical polyphonic practices. The resources used are within the reach of a good church music program without the necessity of having to go outside the church for a professional ensemble.

7. "Gloria in Excelsis Deo." *Vince Guaraldi at Grace Cathedral.* Fantasy 3367; 8367.
8. Joe Masters. *The Jazz Mass.* Columbia CL—2598; CS—9398.

The Evolution of Jazz

The evolution of jazz can best be summarized by providing a chart outlining the various periods, dates, styles, major centers, and major figures (see page 436). It is interesting to note that jazz has undergone approximately the same pattern of evolution in its single century of existence as has the music of Western civilization since the fall of Rome. For this reason the chart includes some major periods of Western culture as they are roughly approximated by the sequence of jazz styles. The outline should be considered as a very generalized overview of the evolution of the elusive art known as jazz.

Eclectic, Crossover, and Fusion

The heading of this section indicates a greater mixing of musical styles than ever before. The sounds of the seventies and eighties are compounded of many stylistic elements. Artificial barriers are coming down and "interdisciplinary" music appears to be increasingly important in our everyday musical life, not only in America but all around the globe.

Popular music (whatever *that* means) includes everything from a "top 40" rock performance with guitars at one hundred decibels to amalgams of folk-rock, jazz-rock, blues-rock and a combination or synthesis of any and all of these elements, including significant traces of classical, oriental, electronic, and country-and-western influences. The simplistic rock 'n' roll of the mid-fifties has been replaced by a far more sophisticated music utilizing whatever musical instruments, styles, and resources best serve the purposes of the performers.

Big band music of the World War II era is back on the jazz scene. Retrospective recordings of the half-century career of Duke Ellington top the jazz charts but Count Basie, Woody Herman, Bob Crosby, and others are in there swinging. The revival of the "classical" style of jazz (see the Outline of the Evolution of Jazz on page 436) has been explained as evidence of nostalgia for the days when issues were simpler, the good guys won, and energy was something a breakfast cereal provided. This may be so, at least in part, but the mindless and monotonous sounds of disco seem to have fostered a countermovement of real dance music. After all, the swing style was primarily a superb form of dance music, the very essence of the Dancing Thirties and Forties.

Current jazz styles range from traditional jazz in the New Orleans manner to Ragtime, Dixieland, Chicago, Bop, Mainstream, Free Jazz, and, as mentioned above, Big Band Swing. Added to this twentieth-century melange are the eclectic styles called *fusion* and *crossover*. Fusion dates from the early sixties as jazz-rock, now musically defined by *Downbeat* magazine as "an agreement between jazz, rock and funk." "Crossover," according to *Downbeat*, "downplays the rocking aspects, adding a recognizable dose of popular melody, sometimes transmitted vocally."

Practitioners of fusion include Miles Davis (later style), Tony Williams's Lifetime, John McLaughlin's Mahavishnu Orchestra, and the groups Return to Forever and Weather Report. Crossover musicians include Chuck Mangione, Bob James, and Grover Washington, Jr. Groups which are best described as fusion/crossover include Spyro Gyra, Seawind, Auracle, and Caldera.

Crossover groups are written off by regular jazz musicians as merely pop-type performers, and certainly there are some huge record sales which confirm this judgment. Fusion, however, is another matter. The central argument is purist versus fusion; pure jazz as opposed to jazz corrupted by undesirable elements; Mainstream against the Philistines. The intensity of the conflict between jazz purists and the fusion forces simply highlights the assurance that contemporary jazz is dynamic, vital, and flourishing; the swinging beat goes on—all over the globe.

Outline: The Evolution of Jazz

Western Culture	Jazz	Dates	Primary and Secondary Styles and Characteristics	Major Centers or Areas	Major Figures
Dark Ages	Folk Origins	Pre-Civil War	Work Songs, Hollers, Street Cries, Ballads, Blues, Spirituals, Ring Shouts, Gospel Songs, Jubilees, Song-sermons, Voodoo, Creole Music	Old South	unknown
		1840–1900	Minstrel Shows (Cakewalk)	U.S. and Europe	Stephen Collins Foster, E.P. Christy, Dan Emmett
Middle Ages	Traditional	1890–1918	Ragtime, Brass Bands: Spirituals, Gospel Songs, Jubilees, Blues and Ragtime Marches	New Orleans	Buddy Bolden, Bunk Johnson
Baroque	Pre-Classical	1918–1929	Advanced New Orleans Style	South, Midwest	King Oliver, Jelly Roll Morton, Louis Armstrong, Sidney Bechet, Kid Ory, Original Dixieland Jazz Band
			Chicago (Modified New Orleans Style)	Chicago	Bix Beiderbecke, Eddie Condon
			Beginning Big Band; Piano	New York	Fletcher Henderson, James P. Johnson, Fats Waller
	Transitional	1929–1934	Transition to Big Band Styles	New York	Fletcher Henderson, Duke Ellington
				Kansas City	Bennie Moten
Classical	Classical	1935–1945	Swing	New York (nationwide)	Fletcher Henderson, Benny Goodman, Coleman Hawkins, Teddy Wilson, Lionel Hampton, Art Tatum, Chick Webb, Roy Eldridge, Casa Loma
			Kansas City Jump	Kansas City	Count Basie, Lester Young, Woody Herman
			Boogie-Woogie	Midwest	Meade Lux Lewis, Pete Johnson, Albert Ammons
		1939–	New Orleans Revival, Dixieland	West Coast	Lu Watters, Turk Murphy, Bob Scobey, Bunk Johnson
Modern	Modern	1944–	Bop	New York	Charlie Parker, Dizzy Gillespie, Bud Powell
		1946–	Cool (Impressionism)	New York, West Coast	Miles Davis, Lee Konitz, George Shearing
			Progressive	West Coast	Stan Kenton, Woody Herman
			Latin	New York Los Angeles	Chano Pozo, Tito Puente, Machito, Gilberto, Schifrin
			Mainstream		Benny Goodman, Lionel Hampton, Count Basie
		1958–	Hard Bop	East Coast Detroit	Jazz Messengers
		1960–	Soul	East Coast	Cannonball Adderly, Les McCann, Ramsey Lewis, Bobby Timmons
			West Coast	West Coast	Dave Brubeck, Cal Tjader
			Third Stream	East and West Coast	Gunther Schuller, Modern Jazz Quartet, Brubeck
			Free Form (The New Thing)	New York	Ornette Coleman, John Coltrane, Charlie Mingus
			Liturgical		Paul Horn, Lalo Schifrin, Duke Ellington, Vince Guaraldi
		1970s and 1980s	Mainstream Fusion Crossover	International	Most jazz musicians. Miles Davis, Tony Williams, John McLaughlin, Chuck Mangione, Bob James, Grover Washington, Jr.

Summary

The many faces of contemporary jazz and the infinite variety of the whole pop-rock-jazz scene seem to span the spectrum of twentieth-century life and thought:

Dixieland—conservative, traditional, exuberant, the "happy" sound

Cool—romantic impressionism, always keeping its cool

Progressive—ever striving to incorporate and exploit new musical ideas

Mainstream—a bit of the old, a bit of the new, but mainly steering down the middle of the road

Hard Bop—uncompromising, blowing hard and hot

Soul—return to the roots, to unabashed emotion, to wholehearted involvement

West Coast—eclectic, intellectual, studying and incorporating the sounds of East and West, blending jazz and classical forms

Third Stream—a synthesis (as jazz was a synthesis) of jazz and the art music of Western culture

Free Jazz—freedom of expression of the creative individual

Liturgical Jazz—revitalization of music of the established churches

Eclectic—a variety of compounds with emphasis on pop, rock, folk, country-and-western, jazz, blues, classical, electronic

Fusion—elements of jazz, rock, funk

Crossover—some jazz with little rock and much pop

Listening Outline (Sixth Stage)

I. Listening Outline
  A. Medium
    1. Vocal (language of text)
    2. Instrumental
    3. Vocal and instrumental (text)
    4. Electronic
    5. Electronic and vocal (text)
  B. Tempo: very slow to very fast (*Largo* to *Presto*)
  C. Loudness: very soft to very loud (*pp* to *ff*)
  D. Number of performers
    1. Solo (instrument)
    2. Ensemble (duo, trio, quartet, quintet, jazz combo, jazz band, chamber orchestra, symphony orchestra, other)
  E. Rhythm: metric or nonmetric
  F. Meter: duple, triple, quadruple, quintuple, other
  G. Texture
    1. Monophonic, homophonic, polyphonic, combination
    2. Number of actual voices or parts (not necessarily identical with number of performers)
  H. Tonal organization
    1. Modal
    2. Major-minor
    3. Twelve-tone
    4. Micro-tone
    5. Mixed
  I. Form: AB, ABA, sonata, theme and variations, rondo, tone poem
  J. Construction
    1. Characteristic texts
    2. Characteristic rhythms
    3. Characteristic harmonies
    4. Melodic organization (motives, themes)
II. Conclusions
  A. Period (dates approximate)
    1. Medieval (600–1420)
    2. Renaissance (1420–1600)
    3. Baroque (1600–1750)
    4. Rococo (1725–1775)
    5. Classical (1760–1827)
    6. Romantic (1814–1900)
    7. Impressionism (1880–1920)
    8. Modern (1910–   )
  B. General musical form

Vocal

Electronic	Opera
Gregorian chant	Oratorio
Madrigal	Sequence/Trope
Mass	Song
Motet	Troubadour/
	Trouvère tradition

Instrumental

Characteristic piece (Ballade, Rhapsody, etc.)	Jazz combo (band)
	Rock/Pop
	Sonata
Chorale prelude	String quartet (trio, quintet)
Concerto	
Country-western	Symphony
Dance suite	Symphonic poem
Electronic	Trio sonata
	Other

Vocal and Instrumental

Accompanied song	Mass
Cantata	Motet
Chorale	Opera
Country-western	Oratorio
Electronic	Rock/Pop
Jazz	Symphony
Lieder	Other

  C. National origin: Europe, United States, Latin America, Africa, Asia, other

Music for Listening

The following list includes composers and works discussed in the chapter. Specific recordings are not listed except for a few special sets.

Record List

1. Stravinsky, Igor. *Le Sacre du Printemps.*
2. Berg, Alban. Concerto for Violin and Orchestra.
3. Prokofiev, Serge. Symphony no. 5 in B♭ Major.

4. Bartók, Béla. Concerto for Orchestra.
5. Orff, Carl. *Carmina Burana.*
6. Ives, Charles. *Concord Sonata.*
7. ———. *Three Places in New England.*
8. Webern, Anton. Symphony, op. 21 and Variations for Orchestra, op. 30 in Complete Works. 4—Columbia CK4L—232.
9. Messiaen, Olivier. *Oiseaux exotiques.*
10. ———. *Chronochromie.*
11. Boulez, Pierre. *Le Marteau sans maître.*
12. ———. Third Piano Sonata.
13. Varèse, Edgard. *Ionisation.*
14. ———. *Deserts.*
15. ———. *Poéme Electronique.*
16. Stockhausen, Karlheinz. Op. 1970.
17. ———. Solo for Electronic Instrument with Reverberation.
18. Shostakovich, Dmitri. Fifth Symphony.
19. Britten, Benjamin. *War Requiem.*
20. Dallapiccola, Luigi. *Canti di prigionio.*
21. Hindemith, Paul. *Mathis der Maler.*
22. Weill, Kurt. *The Threepenny Opera.*
23. ———. *The Fall of the House of Mahagony.*
24. Rodgers and Hammerstein. *Oklahoma!*
25. ———. *South Pacific.*
26. Lerner and Loewe. *My Fair Lady.*
27. Bernstein, Leonard. *West Side Story.*
28. Gershwin, George. *Porgy and Bess.*
29. ———. *An American in Paris.*
30. ———. *Rhapsody in Blue.*
31. ———. Concerto in F.

Note: All of the compositions discussed on pages 417–18 under additional major American composers are found in a two-volume set of records:

32. *The Outstanding Contemporary Orchestral Compositions of the United States,* produced by The International Contemporary Music Exchange, 58 West 58th St., Suite 29B, New York, N.Y. 10019.
33. Janáček, Leoś. *Diary of One Who Vanished.*
34. ———. Concertino for Piano and String Orchestra.
35. ———. Quartets.
36. ———. *Sinfonietta.*
37. ———. *Slavonic Mass* (M'sa Glagolskava).
38. Hába, Alois. Fantasy for Violin Solo in 1/4 Tones.
39. Martinu, Bohuslav. *Fastasia Concertante.*
40. ———. *Nonet.*
41. Walton, William. *Facade.*
42. ———. *Belshazzar's Feast.*
43. Tippett, Michael. *Child of Our Times.*
44. ———. *The Knot Garden.*
45. ———. *Midsummer Marriage.*
46. Milhaud, Darius. *Le Boeuf sur le Toit.*
47. Honegger, Arthur. *Le Roi David.*
48. Poulenc, Francis. *Les Biches.*
49. ———. Mass in G.
50. ———. *Litanies á la Vierge noire de Rocamadour.*
51. ———. *Stabat Mater.*
52. ———. *Gloria.*
53. Henze, Hans Werne. *Raft of the Medusa.*
54. ———. *Being Beauteous.*
55. Kagel, Mauricio. *Transicion II.*
56. Xenakis, Iannis. *Medea.*
57. Berio, Luciano. *Circles.*
58. ———. *Sequenza.*
59. ———. *Sequenza III.*
60. Lutoslawski, Witold. Concerto for Orchestra.
61. Khachaturian, Aram. *Gayne Ballet.*
62. ———. *Masquerade Suite.*
63. Nilsson, Bo. *Frequenzen.*
64. Turina, Joaquin. *Danzas Fantásticas.*
65. De Falla, Manuel. *El Amor Brujo.*
66. ———. *Nights in the Gardens of Spain.*
67. ———. *Three-Cornered Hat.*
68. ———. Harpsichord Concerto.
69. Martin, Frank. Concerto for Violin and Orchestra.
70. Lieberman, Rolf. *School for Wives.*

Electronic Music

71. *The Nonesuch Guide to Electronic Music,* HC—73018, Stereo, 2-record set. A comprehensive survey of electronic music and its creation. Included are recorded examples of electronic music on two stereophonic long-playing records, a meticulously prepared sixteen-page booklet containing notes on the recordings, an introduction to electronic-music theory, glossary, bibliography, symbolic notation, and the score to *Peace Three,* a new electronic composition presented here for the first time.
72. Berio, Luciano. *Sequenza VI* (1970). Victor LSC—3168.
73. *Switched-on-Bach.* Moog Synthesizer. Columbia MS—7194.
74. Henry & Wright. *Ceremony—An Electronic Mass.* A & M 4225.
75. Carlos. *Well-Tempered Synthesizer.* Columbia MS—7286.
76. White. *Flowers of Evil.* Limelight 86066.
77. Swickard. *Sermons of St. Francis,* for narrator and tape (moog). Orion 7021.
78. Dodge. *Earth's Magnetic Field.* Nonesuch 71250.

Listening Outline (Jazz)

Procedures exactly the same as for Listening Outline (Sixth Stage). Of course close attention should be paid to rhythm in all its aspects, the text, the blues scale and performance characteristics such as altered tone quality, "worrying" notes, deliberate alteration of pitch.

Conclusions

Styles are listed with the periods in which they apparently originated. Most of the styles exist as such just as, for example, the Baroque period still exists in the music of J. S. Bach. Moreover, some of today's music is patterned after the originals, for instance, folk blues, urban blues, New Orleans style, and the like. (See "Outline: Evolution of Jazz" on page 436.) This tends to be a characteristic of folk music and of jazz but does not apply to the world of sonatas and symphonies. Hardly anyone today is writing in the style of J. S. Bach.

Record List (Jazz)

Jazz records go out of print with alarming frequency. Following is a supplementary list, by style, of records which may be easier to obtain than those cited in the text.

Gospel Songs
1. Ward, Clara. *Hang Your Tears Out to Dry.* Verve 5002; 65002.
2. Ward Singers. *Meeting Tonight.* Savoy 14015.
3. Jackson, Mahalia. *Gospel Songs.* Grand Award 2—GA 33—326.
4. ———. *Gospel World.* Kenwood 501.

New Orleans Style
5. Ory, Kid. *Dixieland Marching Songs.* Verve 1026; 61026.
6. Jazz at Preservation Hall, vol. II. Atlantic 1409; S—1409, vol. III, Atlantic 1410; S—1410.
7. *Echoes of New Orleans.* Southland 239.

Urban Blues
8. Charles, Ray. *Genius Sings the Blues.* Atlantic 8052.
9. Holiday, Billie. *Lady Sings the Blues.* Verve 8099.
10. Jackson, Milt. *Ballads and Blues.* Atlantic 1242.
11. Lewis, Ramsey. *Bach to the Blues.* Argo 732; S—732.
12. Turner, Joe. *Boss of the Blues.* Atlantic 1234; S—1234.
13. Washington, Dinah. *Back to the Blues.* Roulette 25189; S—25189.
14. Witherspoon, Jimmy. *Evenin' Blues.* Prestige 7300; S—7300.
15. *Many Faces of Blues.* Savoy 12125.
16. Charles, Ray. *Portrait.* ABC S—625.
17. Franklin, Aretha. *Today I Sing the Blues.* Columbia CS—9956.

Chicago Style
18. *Chicago: The Living Legends.* 2 Riverside 389/390.
19. Condon, Eddie. *Legend.* Mainstream 56024; 6024.

20. *Bix Beiderbecke Story.* 3 Columbia CL—844/6.
21. *Chicago Jazz* (1923–29). Biograph 12005.
22. *Chicagoans* (1928–30). Decca 79231.

Swing
23. *Carnegie Hall Jazz Concert,* vol. 2. Columbia CL—815.
24. *Golden Age of Goodman.* Victor, LPM—1099.
25. *Encyclopedia of Jazz* (20s, 30s, 40s, 50s). 4 Decca DX—140.
26. Kenton, Stan. *Formative Years.* Decca 8259.
27. Time-Life Series: *The Swing Era.* Eight 3-record sets with booklet of recreated Swing classics from 1936–1937 through 1944–1945. Record numbers from STL 341 through 348.

Kansas City Jump
28. Herman, Woody. *Greatest Hits.* Columbia CL—2491; CS—9291.
29. Young, Lester. *Lester Leaps In.* Epic LN—3107.
30. Count Basie. *In Kansas City.* Victor LPV—514.
31. *Kansas City Piano (1936–1941).* Decca 79226.

New Orleans Revival
32. Fountain, Pete. *Taste of Honey.* Coral 57486; 757486.
33. Dukes of Dixieland. *Live at Bourbon Street.* Decca 4653; 74653.
34. *Best of Dixieland.* Victor LPM—2982; LSP—2982.
35. *Dixieland—New Orleans.* Mainstream 56003; 6003.

Progressive (Big Band) Jazz
36. Duke Ellington. *Far East Suite.* Victor LSP—3782.
37. ———. *Flaming Youth.* Victor LPV—568.
38. ———. *Hot in Harlem.* Decca 79241.
39. *Duke Ellington's 70th Birthday Concert.* Solid State.
40. Count Basie. *Basie on the Beatles.* Happy Tiger.
41. ———. *Just in Time.* Harmony 11371.
42. ———. *Manufacturers of Soul.* Brunswick 754134.
43. ———. *Standing Ovation.* Dot 25938.
44. ———. *Straight Ahead.* Dot 259002.
45. Herman, Woody. *Concerto for Herd.* Verve 68764.
46. ———. *Light My Fire.* Cadet S—819.
47. Kenton, Stan. *Deluxe Set.* 3—Capitol STCL—2989.
48. Rich, Buddy. *Keep the Customers Satisfied.* Liberty 11006.
49. ———. *Buddy and Soul.* Pacific Jazz 20158.
50. ———. *Mercy, Mercy.* Pacific Jazz 20133.
51. ———. *Super.* Verve 68778.
52. Davis, Miles. *Bitches Brew.* 2—Columbia GP 26.
53. Jones, Quincy. *Walking in Space.* A & M 3023.
54. ———. *Gula Matari.* A & M 3030.
55. Ellis, Don. *Don Ellis at Fillmore.* 2—Columbia G—30243.

56. ———. *Don Ellis Goes Underground.* Columbia CS—9889.
57. Severinsen, Doc. *Revival.* Command S—950.
58. Evans, Bill. *What's New.* Verve 68777.
59. Gillespie, Dizzy. *At Village Vanguard.* Solid 18034.
60. ———. *My Way.* Solid 18054.

Latin

61. *Getz/Gilberto No. 2.* Verve 8623; 68623.
62. Mann, Herbie. *Latin Fever.* Atlantic 1422; S—1422.
63. ———. *Latin Mann.* Columbia CL—2388; CS—9188.
64. Byrd, Charlie. *Bossa Nova Peloe Passaros.* Riverside 436; 9436.
65. Gibbs, Terry. *Latino!* Roost 2260; S—2260.
66. Stan Getz Quartet. *Didn't We!* Verve 68780.

Soul Jazz

67. Adderley, Cannonball. *Country Preacher.* Capitol SKAO—404.
68. ———. *In Person.* Capitol ST—162.
69. Mann, Herbie. *Memphis Underground.* Atlantic S—1522.
70. McCann, Les, and Eddie Harris. *Swiss Movement.* Atlantic S—1537.
71. Jazz Crusaders. *Lighthouse '69.* Pacific Jazz 20165.
72. Oscar Peterson Trio. *Great!* Prestige S—7620.
73. ———. *Soul-O.* Prestige S—7595.
74. Charlie Byrd Quintet. *Let It Be.* Columbia CS—1053.
75. ———. *Greatest Hits of 60's.* Columbia CS—9970.
76. *Great Soul Hits.* Brunswick 754129.

West Coast Jazz

77. Dave Brubeck Trio. *In Amsterdam.* Columbia CS—3353.
78. ———. *Gone With the Wind.* Harmony 11336.

Third-Stream Jazz

79. Schuller, Gunther. *Concertino for Jazz Quartet and Orchestra.* Atlantic 1359; S—1359.
80. "Transformation." Gunther Schuller. *Outstanding Jazz Compositions—20th Century.* 2—Columbia C2L—31; C2S—831.
81. Swingle Singers. *Rococo a Go Go.* Philips PHM—200—214; PHS—600—214.
82. Modern Jazz Quartet. *Space.* Apple STAO—3360.
83. ———. *Under the Jasmin Tree.* Apple ST—3353.

Free Form Jazz (The "New Thing")

84. Coltrane, John. *Last Trane.* Prestige 7378; S—7378.
85. Cherry, Don. *Don Cherry.* Blue Note 4226; 84226.
86. Coltrane, John. *Traneing In.* Prestige S—7651.

Anthologies

87. *Introduction to Jazz.* Decca 8244.
88. *Original Blue Note Jazz,* vol. 2. Blue 6506.
89. *Classic Jazz Piano Styles.* Victor LPV—543.
90. *Jazz Odyssey:*
    Vol. 1, *Sound of New Orleans.* 3—Columbia C3L—30.
    Vol. 2, *Sound of Chicago.* 3—Columbia C3L—32.
    Vol. 3, *Sound of Harlem.* 3—Columbia C3L—33.
91. *Encyclopedia of Jazz—20's, 30's, 40's, 50's.* 4—Decca DXS—7140.
92. *Encyclopedia of Jazz in the Sixties.* Verve 68677.
93. *Newport Jazz Festival All Stars* (1969). Odyssey 32160296.
94. *Three Decades of Music:*
    Vol. 1, *1939–49.* 2—Blue Note 89902.
    Vol. 2, *1949–59.* 2—Blue Note 89903.
    Vol. 3, *1959–69.* 2—Blue Note 89904.
95. *The Smithsonian Collection of Classic Jazz,* 5 albums, available through the Smithsonian Associates, distributed by W. W. Norton, New York.

Bluegrass

96. Monroe, Bill. *The Original Bluegrass Sound.* Columbia HL 7338.
97. ———. *A Voice from on High.* Decca DL 75135.
98. Scruggs, Earl. *Foggy Mountain Banjo.* LE 10043.
99. Stanley Brothers. *Mountain Song Favorites.* Nashville NLP 2014.

Modern Mainstream ("Straight-Ahead Jazz")

100. *Four Decades of Jazz.* A Musical History of Xanadu, Xanadu 5001.
101. Phillips, Flip, and Woody Herman. *Together.* Century CR—1090.
102. Herman, Woody, *Chick, Donald, Walter and Woodrow.* Century CR—1110.
103. Bill Evans Trio with Lee Konitz and Wayne Marsh. *Crosscurrents.* Fantasy F—9568.
104. Friesen, David, and John Stowell. *Through the Listening Glass.* Inner City IC 1061.
105. Byas, Don, and Bud Powell. *A Tribute to Cannonball.* Columbia JC 35755.
106. Ellington, Duke. *Giants of Jazz.* Time-Life Records JO2.
107. Jackie McLean with the Great Jazz Trio. *New Wine in Old Bottles.* Inner City IC6029.
108. Mitchell, Joni. *Mingus.* Asylum 5E—505.
109. Mingus, Charles. *Cumbia and Jazz Fusion.* Atlantic SO 8801.
110. Air. *Montreux Suisse.* Arista/Novus AN 3008.
111. Ray Linn and the Chicago Stompers. *Chicago Jazz.* Trend 515 (Chicago revival).
112. Ortiz, Luis "Perico." *Super Salsa.* New Generation NG 710 (Latin/Mainstream).

Bibliography (Classical Music)

Brindle, Reginald. *The New Music: The Avant-Garde Since 1945.* New York: Oxford University Press, 1975.

Ewen, David. *Composers of Tomorrow's Music: A Non-Technical Introduction to the Musical Avant-Garde Movement.* New York: Dodd, Mead & Company, 1971.

Hamm, Charles E., et al. *Contemporary Music and Music Cultures.* Englewood Cliffs, N.J.: Prentice-Hall, 1975.

Hansen, Peter. *An Introduction to Twentieth-Century Music.* Boston: Allyn & Bacon, 1978.

Horn, David. *The Literature of American Music in Books and Folk Music Collections: A Fully Annotated Bibliography.* Metuchen, N.J.: Scarecrow, 1977. First really comprehensive guide.

Mellers, Wilfred. *Music in a New Found Land.* New York: Stonehill Publishing, 1975. Good but opinionated study of American music; includes much jazz and some pop.

Nyman, Michael. *Experimental Music: Cage and Beyond.* New York: Schirmer Books, 1974.

Stuckenschmidt, H. H. *Twentieth Century Music.* New York: McGraw-Hill, 1969. A humanistic and socialistic approach.

Zaimont, Judith Lang, and Karen Famera, eds. and comps. *Contemporary Concert Music by Women: A Directory of the Composers and Their Works.* Westport, Conn.: Greenwood Press, 1981.

Bibliography (Jazz, Rock, Popular)

Artis, Bob. *Bluegrass.* New York: Hawthorn Books, 1975.

Bayliss, John F., ed. *Black Slave Narratives.* New York: Collier Books, Macmillan, 1970. Insightful and painful.

Belz, Carl. *The Story of Rock.* New York: Colophon Books, Harper & Row, Publishers, 1969. Thesis that rock has a long history as a folk art.

Berendt, Joachim. *Jazz Book: From New Orleans to Rock and Free Jazz.* New York: Lawrence Hill, 1975.

Berlin, Edward A. *Ragtime: A Musical and Cultural History.* Berkeley: University of California Press, 1980.

Blesh, Rudi, and Harriet Janis. *They All Played Ragtime.* New York: Evergreen, Grove Press, 1959. The classic study.

Castleman, Harry, and Walter Podrazik. *All Together Now.* New York: Ballantine, 1976. A landmark in rock-and-roll discography.

Charters, Samuel. *The Country Blues.* New York: Da Capo Press, 1975. Reissue of a standard work (1959).

Coryell, Julie, and Laura Friedman. *Jazz Rock Fusion.* New York: Dell, 1978.

Courlander, Harold. *Negro Folk Music U.S.A.* New York: Columbia University Press, 1963. Fascinating study.

Eisen, Jonathan. *The Age of Rock: Sounds of the American Cultural Revolution.* New York: Vintage Books, Random House, 1969.

Fink, Robert, and Robert Ricci. *The Language of Twentieth Century Music: A Dictionary of Terms.* New York: Schirmer Books, 1975. Basic vocabulary of jazz, rock, computer, chance, electronic, multimedia, musique concrete, and twelve-tone.

Gammond, Peter, and Charles Fox. *Jazz On Record: A Critical Guide.* Westport, Ct. 1978.

Gridley, Mark C. *Jazz Styles.* Englewood Cliffs, N.J.: Prentice-Hall, 1978.

Hentoff, Nat. *Jazz Is.* New York: Avon, 1978.

Hodier, Andre. *Jazz: Its Evolution and Essence.* New York: Grove, 1979. One of the very best books on the aesthetics of jazz.

Jones, LeRoi. *Blues People: Negro Music in White America.* New York: W. Morrow, 1963. Stylish sociological study.

———. *Black Music.* New York: Apollo Editions, 1968. Pungent, stimulating, controversial.

Malone, Bill. *Country Music.* Austin, Tx.: University of Texas Press, 1974. Probably the best single book on the subject.

Meeker, David. *Jazz in the Movies.* New Rochelle, N.Y.: Arlington House, 1978.

Morgenstern, Dan. *Jazz People.* New York: Abrams, 1978.

Oliver, Paul. *The Meaning of the Blues.* New York: Collier Books, Macmillan, 1963. Probably the best single book on the blues.

Ostransky, Leroy. *Jazz City: The Impact on our Cities of the Development of Jazz.* Englewood Cliffs, N.J.: Prentice-Hall, 1978.

Palmer, Robert. *Deep Blues.* New York: Viking Press, 1981. Concise and authoritative, the book revolves around the pungent, candid histories of the great blues performers.

Placksin, Sally. *American Women in Jazz: 1900 to the Present.* New York: Seaview Books, 1982. Overdue recognition of some very fine jazz musicians.

Sarlin, Bob. *Turn It Up! (I Can't Hear the Words).* New York: Simon & Schuster, 1973. Song-poets like Bob Dylan, Joni Mitchell, and others.

Stearns, Marshall. *The Story of Jazz.* New York: Oxford University Press, 1970. Still the best single book on jazz.

Periodicals

Downbeat, bi-weekly, 222 W. Adams St., Chicago, Illinois 60606. Most popular American periodical on jazz.

Jazz Journal, quarterly, 1/3 Upper James St., London WI, England. Largest and most popular English journal.

Journal of Jazz Studies, semi-annual, Rutgers Institute of Jazz Studies c/o Transaction, Inc., Rutgers University, New Brunswick, New Jersey 08903.

NAJE Educator, quarterly, NAJE, P.O. Box 724, Manhattan, Kansas 66502. Official periodical of the National Association of Jazz Educators.

A Basic Library of Good Music (Second Stage)

Following are fifty records which have been selected to help round out the basic collection as listed in chapter 3. From motets to marches to operas and covering four centuries of music, this includes a great variety of good music which you will always enjoy and to which you can continue to add as your taste develops through the years. (To safeguard your investment you could duplicate all of your records on cassettes.)

All listings are conventional stereo records except for a few recent releases which were recorded in quad, as indicated by a (Q) at the end of the serial number. We have suggested only one recording of each work but you can preview other versions before you make your final selections. You should also check compact discs with laser playback.

Romanticism (ca. 1820–1910)

Hector Berlioz (1803–1869) Inspired by Byron's poem, "Childe Harold," his *Harold in Italy* is both a viola concerto and a tone poem. Zukerman is the soloist with Berenboim and the Orchestre de Paris (Columbia M—34541).

Alexander Borodin (1833–1887) A full-time chemist and a part-time composer, Borodin's output was small but very good. If the Polovtsian Dances from his opera, *Prince Igor,* sound familiar, it is probably because a Broadway musical was based on the themes. Also included is *In the Steppes of Central Asia,* an exotic piece about a desert caravan. On the reverse side of the record is the dramatic *Night on Bald Mountain* (much used by the Disney studio) by Borodin's contemporary, Modest Mussorgsky. Eugene Ormandy directs the Philadelphia Orchestra (Columbia MS—6073).

Johannes Brahms (1833–1897) All four of Brahms's symphonies are popular throughout the world. When a critic was asked about his favorite Brahms symphony, the response was, "The one I am listening to at the time." Recommended at this time is Symphony no. 2 in D Major, op. 73 by the Royal Philharmonic Orchestra under Sir Thomas Beecham (Seraphim S—60083). Completing the record is the Academic Festival Overture which is based on four student songs and which Brahms wrote in response to an honorary doctor's degree.

His variations on a Theme by Haydn is a stimulating lesson in the art of writing a lot of variations on a simple melody. On the reverse side is the Enigma Variations by the English composer *Edward Elgar* (1857–1934). Each of the fourteen variations is a musical description of one of Elgar's friends. The entire theme and variations are based on another theme, which is never heard and which was known only to the composer. Thus the enigma. The London Symphony is conducted by Jochum (DG 2530586).

Frédéric Chopin (1810–1849) Of the two piano concertos we have selected Concerto no. 1 in E minor, op. 11 as recorded by Van Cliburn and the Philadelphia Orchestra under Eugene Ormandy (RCA LSC—3147).

Antonín Dvořák (1841–1904) During the late nineteenth century when Dvořák first visited the United States, he was told that America had no folk music to speak of. Returning to Czechoslovakia and using American folk music themes, he composed his Symphony no. 9 in E minor, "from the New World." Conducting this tribute to America's rich folk music tradition is Leonard Bernstein with the New York Philharmonic (Columbia M—31809).

César Franck (1822–1890) A mild-mannered music teacher and church organist, this Parisian composer wrote only one symphony but it became one of his most popular works: Symphony in D minor. Bernstein conducts the New York Philharmonic (Columbia M—31803).

William S. Gilbert (1836–1911) and *Arthur Sullivan* (1842–1900) Written to make money—and they made plenty—the Gilbert and Sullivan operettas are now classics. Recommended is *The Mikado* (excerpts) by the inimitable D'Oyly Carte Opera Company (London 25903).

Charles Gounod (1818–1893) His one opera has been enough to forever secure the reputation of this French composer. Singing *Faust* (excerpts) is Joan Sutherland, accompanied by the London Symphony (London 26139).

Edvard Grieg (1843–1907) His most popular work, the Piano Concerto in A minor, op. 16, is one of the two favorite concertos from the Romantic period. On the reverse side is the other favorite: Piano Concerto in A minor, op. 54 by *Robert Schumann* (1810–1856). Anda solos with the Berlin Philharmonic under Kubelik (DG 138888).

Gustav Mahler (1860–1911) The opulent lyricism of this German Romantic is never better than in the *Songs of a Wayfarer* for voice and orchestra. The soloist is Dietrich Fischer-Dieskau, the world's foremost baritone, accompanied by the Bavarian Radio Symphony under Kubelik (DG 2530630).

Felix Mendelssohn (1809–1847) This cheerful work is discussed in chapter 25: Symphony no. 4 in A Major, op. 90, "Italian," played by Eugene Ormandy and the Philadelphia Orchestra (Columbia MS—6628). On the back is his enchanting music for Shakespeare's *Midsummer Night's Dream.*

Modest Mussorgsky (1839–1881) One of the most original of all Russian composers, Mussorgsky based his piano suite on a friend's pictures at an exhibition. As orchestrated by Maurice Ravel the suite is crowded with vivid depictions of Russian life. *Maurice Ravel* (1875–1937) is himself represented on the second side. Commissioned by the dancer, Ida Rubinstein, to write an orchestral piece for a tabletop dancing scene in a Spanish tavern in which the rising tension climaxes in a barroom brawl, Ravel wrote the famous *Bolero* with its hypnotic orchestral crescendo. Herbert von Karajan conducts the Berlin Philharmonic (DG 139010).

Nikolai Rimski-Korsakov (1844–1908) Inspired by the thousand and one tales told by the princess in the Arabian Nights, *Scheherazade* is perhaps the composer's most popular work. Zubin Mehta conducts the Los Angeles Philharmonic (London 6950).

Gioacchino Rossini (1792–1868) Rossini made so much money writing hugely successful Italian operas that, on occasion, he could—and did—rent an entire train. Light and bright, the Overtures to *William Tell* and *The Barber of Seville* are perennial favorites. The back side features the tone poem, *The Pines of Rome*, by the Neo-Romantic Italian composer, *Ottorino Respighi* (1879–1936). The Hamburg Radio Symphony is conducted by Ghiglia (CMS/Summit 1058).

Franz Schubert (1797–1828) The Quintet in A Major, op. 114 for piano and string quartet is titled "The Trout," after Schubert's song of the same name, which forms one of the movements of the quintet. Featured with a string quartet is the brilliant young pianist Peter Serkin (Vanguard 71145).

Bedřich Smetana (1824–1884) An ardent nationalist, Smetana wrote a tone poem about Czechoslovakia's chief river, *The Moldau*. Also included is the lively overture to his opera, *The Bartered Bride*. On the second side are the Slavonic dances of *Antonin Dvořák* (1841–1904). The orchestra is the Israel Philharmonic with Kertesz conducting (London STS—15409).

Johann Strauss, Jr. (1825–1899) Excerpts from the waltz king's sparkling opera, *Die Fledermaus,* are sung in English by the Vienna State Opera (RCA LSC—2728).

Richard Strauss (1864–1949) Three tone poems, *Till Eulenspiegel's Merry Pranks* (see chapter 25), *Don Juan,* and *Also sprach Zarathustra,* are played by the Chicago Symphony under conductor George Solti (London 6978). The opening section of Zarathustra was used for the movie *2001: A Space Odyssey.*

Giuseppe Verdi (1813–1901) Perhaps the greatest Italian opera composer, Verdi is noted for his lovely, singable melodies, as in the arias sung on this recording by Leontyne Price (RCA ARL1—6840(Q). The back side features operatic duets by *Giocomo Puccini* (1858–1924).

Richard Wagner (1813–1883) Wagner's operatic overtures are justly famous: *The Flying Dutchman, Die Meistersinger,* and *Rienzi.* Concluding the record is the passionate prelude to *Tristan and Isolde* with Leonard Bernstein conducting the New York Philharmonic (Columbia M—31011).

The Classical Period (ca. 1760–1827)

Ludwig van Beethoven (1770–1827) Included here are five of his most important works, all of which have, coincidentally, titles.

Trio no. 6 in B flat Major, op. 97, *Archduke*. Stern, Rose, Istomin (Columbia MS—6819).

Piano Sonata no. 23 in F minor, op. 53, *Appassionata*. Vladimir Horowitz (Columbia M—34509).

Piano Concerto no. 5 in E flat Major, op. 73, *Emperor*. Arthur Rubinstein and the London Philharmonic under Daniel Berenboim (RCA ARL1—1420).

Symphony no. 3 in E flat Major, op. 55, *Eroica*. Solti and the Vienna Philharmonic (London 6778).

Symphony no. 9 in D minor, op. 125, *Choral*. Eugene Ormandy and the Philadelphia Orchestra (Columbia M—31818).

Franz Joseph Haydn (1732–1809) The featured work is the Quartet in E♭ Major, op. 33 no. 2, *Joke*. The joke has to do with the last movement. Haydn bet a friend that some silly people would start to applaud before the movement had finally ended. With his tricky ending he did indeed win his bet. Completing the record are the quartets, op. 3 no. 5 and op. 76 no. 2. Played by the Janáček Quartet (London 6385).

Wolfgang Amadeus Mozart (1756–1791) This recording by Bernstein and the New York Philharmonic (Columbia M—31825) has Mozart's last two—and greatest—symphonies: no. 40 in G minor, K.550 (see chapter 23) and no. 41 in C Major, K.551, *Jupiter*.

Impressionism (ca. 1880–1920)

Claude Debussy (1862–1918) The composer calls these three pieces nocturnes: *Nuages* (Clouds), *Fêtes* (Festivals), and *Sirènes*. Evoking the exotic atmosphere of Spain, *Iberia* closes the recording by Dorati and the National Symphony (London 6968).

Maurice Ravel (1875–1937) His *Daphnis and Chlöe:* Suite no. 2 is known especially for its musical impressions of the dawn. The *Mother Goose Suite* and the lovely *La Valse* conclude the record, which is played by the Los Angeles Philharmonic under Zubin Mehta (London 6698).

Baroque Music (1600–1750)

Carl Philipp Emanuel Bach (1714–1789) Of his twenty children J. S. Bach had four sons who were gifted composers, all by Maria Barbara Bach, his first wife and also his first cousin. These Sonatas for Flute and Harpsichord feature Jean Pierre Rampal, the world's leading flutist (Nonesuch 71034).

Johann Sebastian Bach (1685–1750)   Here are three very different kinds of music:

Cantata no. 4, Munich Bach Orchestra (DG ARC—198465). (See chap. 23.)

Concerto in D minor for Two Violins, Perlman and Zukerman and the English Orchestra under Berenboim (Angel S—36841).

Italian Concerto for Harpsichord, Richter (DG 2530035).

Giovanni Gabrielli (ca. 1554/57–1612)   Written for St. Mark's Cathedral in opulent Venice, these brilliant motets feature antiphonal choirs, brass, and organ as described in chapter 23. Negri, Smith Singers, Texas Boys Choir (Columbia M—30937).

George Frederick Handel (1685–1759)   The greatest of all oratorios, *The Messiah* (excerpts), is performed here by the Philharmonic Orchestra and Chorus under Otto Klemperer (Angel S—36324).

Twentieth Century

Béla Bartók (1881–1945)   Modern in technique and lyrical in sound, the Concerto for Violin and Orchestra (1938) is played by Isaac Stern and the New York Philharmonic conducted by Leonard Bernstein (Columbia MS—6002).

Manuel De Falla (1876–1946)   The true flavor is captured of *Nights in the Gardens of Spain,* played by Rubinstein with Ormandy conducting the Philadelphia Orchestra. (RCA LSC—3165). Backing the record is the concerto no. 2 in G minor by the French composer *Camille Saint-Saens* (1835–1921).

Carl Orff (1895–1982)   *Carmina Burana* (discussed in chapter 30) is a real challenge for performers and recording engineers. Try Ormandy and the Philadelphia Orchestra but you might prefer another version (Columbia M—31839).

Francis Poulenc (1899–1963)   Written by a modern French composer in a lively and light-hearted manner, the Gloria in G Major is performed by the National Radio Orchestra under Prêtre (Angel S—35953). His fine Organ Concerto in G minor concludes the record.

Serge Prokofiev (1891–1953)   The *Lieutenant Kije Suite* was extracted from a movie about a fictitious functionary in the Czar's army. On the reverse side is the *Hary Janos Suite* by the Hungarian composer *Zoltán Kodály* (1882–1967), which features a mad emperor and his court. Eugene Ormandy conducts the Philadelphia Orchestra (RCA ARL1—1325).

Arnold Schöenberg (1874–1951)   Variations for Orchestra is a twelve-tone work by the transplanted Austrian who ended up teaching at the University of Southern California. His *Transfigured Night,* a late romantic work, is found on the back side and played by von Karajan and the Berlin Philharmonic (DG 253–0627).

Dmitri Shostakovitch (1906–1975)   According to the composer's *Memoirs*—smuggled out of Russia and published in 1979—this (Symphony no. 5) and other symphonies are memorials for the millions of his countrymen who died under the murderous regime of Joseph Stalin. Russian musicians feel that the best performance of this dramatic work is by the New York Philharmonic under the direction of Leonard Bernstein (Columbia MS—6115). (See chap. 30.)

Jean Sibelius (1865–1957)   Here are three of the best-known works of Finland's greatest composer: *The Swan of Tuonela, Tapiola,* and *Valse Triste.* Herbert von Karajan conducts the Berlin Philharmonic (DG 139016).

Igor Stravinsky (1882–1971)   *Petrouchka,* one of the most successful ballets by the century's leading composer, is played by the New York Philharmonic under the direction of Pierre Boulez (Columbia M—31076).

Heitor Villa-Lobos (1887–1959)   Brazil's most famous composer wrote a series of six pieces as a tribute to J. S. Bach. This is Bachianas no. 5 as performed by folk singer Joan Baez and accompanied by eight cellos (Vanguard 79160).

Medieval and Renaissance Music

Please check the recordings as recommended in chapter 3 in volume 1.

Americana

Aaron Copland (b. 1900)   Two of his best ballet scores, *Appalachian Spring* and *Rodeo,* are conducted by Edouard Mata with the Dallas Symphony (RCA ARL1—2862). His *El Salon Mexico* completes the recording.

John Philip Sousa (1854–1932)   America's march king has never been recorded better than on the album entitled *Footlifters: A Century of American Marches.* Gunther Schuller leads The Incredible Columbia All-Star Band on this award-winning recording (Columbia 33513).

Kurt Weill (1900–1950)   Leaving Hitler's Germany in 1933, Weill settled in New York where he wrote outstanding musicals like *Lady in the Dark* and *Knickerbocker Holiday.* Recommended here is his brilliant social protest opera, *The Threepenny Opera,* which he wrote in conjunction with playwright Bertolt Brecht. Excerpts from the complete opera are performed by the New York Shakespeare Festival Company (Columbia PS—34326 (Q)).

31
Twentieth-Century Literature

Nowhere does our analogy of the broken center fit more exactly than in the field of contemporary literature. Amid the wreckage of old values, modern authors search for new meanings, new forms, and a new sense of personal identity and community.

One can propose almost any thesis about contemporary literature and support it with a large body of writing, for the wide experimentation of today has produced many types, moods, and themes. Perhaps the only defensible approach to "contemporary" literature is to make a few very wide and controversial generalizations about modern writing, and then to comment on a few specific literary works which seem to embody various trends and which are anthologized at the end of the chapter so that the student may read them and agree or disagree with the critical comments expressed here.

Perhaps the first of the generalizations that can be made is that the far-out writers of the latter part of our century have abandoned most of the restrictions on form and idea which were characteristic of a great deal of nineteenth-century writing. It is possible to find in our century at least two "literatures of the twentieth century," almost chronological and sequential, with the obvious break following World War II. The two types are related in that both are in revolt against the literary tradition of the nineteenth century and against the rigid structure of Victorian mores. The difference lies in the recognition of the early twentieth-century writers that a common core existed against which they might voice their protest; the writers since World War II are cast adrift, with little unifying force and few webs of connection, and with the urge, almost the necessity, to create anew the meanings and values of life and the consciousness of the race.

During the first part of the century, we witnessed the almost "conventional" revolt of which John Livingston Lowes wrote, "The ceaseless swing of the artistic pendulum is from the convention of a former age to the revolt of a new day, which in its turn becomes a convention from which still newer artists will in their turn revolt."[1]

---

1. John Livingston Lowes, *Convention and Revolt in Poetry,* New York, Gordon Press, n.d.

The poetic convention of the nineteenth century generally favored the tight-knit structure of recognizable stanzaic form: blank verse or couplet, tercet or quatrain, or other nameable unit. Exceptions are of course to be found, but in general a poem *looked* like a poem, because that was the way poems looked! The order and pattern and design appealed to an audience that liked design, approved of pattern, and believed in order.

But, about 1914, with such a group as the Imagist poets, the convention was challenged with "vers libre" ("free verse")—lines unrhymed and unmetrical. Not only is the form of Eliot's poem, *The Waste Land,* different from that of the past, but the meaning of his poem represents a revolt against the predominate optimism (or even the pessimism) of the nineteenth century. Yet with all the innovation of form and meaning, Eliot recognizes and works within the recognizable tradition. In the first place, the poem is not only to be felt and experienced, it must be thought out; it is an extremely intellectual poem within the rational tradition. Second, Eliot expects his reader to share a common background of meanings and knowledge.

At about the same time that Eliot was composing *The Waste Land,* Aldous Huxley was writing *Brave New World,* a novel that pictures a society pursuing our present value-system until it has killed nearly all human values. The novel attacked entrenched and accepted values, but it followed the patterned, chronologically structured form of the plotted novel, and made certain assumptions about the common center of meanings which were held by both the author and the reader. For instance, Huxley assumes a knowledge of Shakespeare, and, even more, he assumes that the reader shares with him a value system which says that Shakespeare is *good;* better than the Huxleyan depicted "feelies" (an extension of the movies) or a trip with mind-altering drugs.

The great body of "high-brow" literature since World War II and Existentialism cannot make these assumptions.

What has happened? Because World War II involved the obvious choice between freedom or submitting to an inhuman system, operated by a small group of power-mad men, all the rituals and emotions of patriotism seemed appropriate. Yet, when the conflict ended, the world went back to its old ways; the victors seemed to take more of a beating than the vanquished. Particularly in the United States, a period of introspection set in which allowed us to see our own guilts and the hollowness of much of our way of life. The old materialistic standards, as opposed to standards dealing with the quality of life itself, seemed no longer appropriate. The wars in Korea and especially Vietnam challenged much of the exuberance for the "rightness" of our value system.

At the same time, all over the Western world, we were introduced to philosophies of Existentialism which denied inherent intelligence and purpose in the universe, or inherent meaning to individual life.

Since that general philosophy has been introduced earlier, we need not repeat that discussion. The effect on an ever-growing number of intelligent, creative persons, however, has been to destroy the old center of certainty; to force them to peer over the brink of life and discover nothing but senseless void beyond. For many in this group of people, old value systems have been seriously questioned or destroyed completely. One may take courage in the increasingly large number of people, young and old, and certainly among most artists and writers, who have faced the problem of constantly "inventing" themselves and who have begun to suggest new meanings for life which are flexible and relative.

In all of this discussion, it must be borne in mind that these developments in literature are not entirely "new." Pessimism was not invented in the twentieth century; Existentialism had its immediate source in Kierkegaard in the nineteenth century and can be traced as far back as the Greek philosopher, Demokritos; new forms for literature (even Black Humor) have many antecedents; particularly the darkly humorous novel has a great-grandfather in Sterne's *Tristram Shandy.* Science fiction has a long history before our time. It would seem, instead, that the small, isolated, and relatively unknown trickles of thought and form in past centuries have flowed together to become the mainstream of literary creation.

Even the most superficial look at contemporary literature reveals at least three sets of taboos which have been swept away, and whose vanishing has had a profound effect on present-day writing.

The first of these is the loosening of social taboos on morality in general and sexual morality in particular. Not long ago it was almost impossible to buy a copy of Henry Miller's novels or D.H. Lawrence's *Lady Chatterly's Lover* in the United States, since they shocked our mass-sense of morality and were officially banned. Now social restrictions have become so relaxed that these particular books are not even very exciting in terms of raw sex. Almost all of the bare and athletic manifestations of love, as ends in themselves, have become rather dreary commonplaces. This trend toward complete sexual freedom has gone so far that it threatens to become self-defeating. One can scarcely say that when you've seen one nude, you've seen them all, but at least the element of shock has largely vanished.

A second aspect of this loss of what was once called "morality" is the change in our generally accepted ideas of *good* and *bad;* in a great deal of early contemporary writing, goodness seems to be a combination of luck and the functioning of the endocrine glands, or perhaps more simply, Not Being Caught. Examples of this—the antihero—are not hard to find. Saul Bellow's fine novel, *Seize the Day,* has Tommy Wilhelm as its protagonist, certainly one of the dirtiest slobs in literature, whose one redeeming feature is a response to humanity in the midst of a cold and negative environment. Even in such popular fiction as

John Le Carré's *The Spy Who Came in from the Cold,* the hero is one who has no sense of honor or patriotism (in an establishment which is equally amoral, although it is on "our side") until his personality finally warms to the plight of a single human being in an act of personal loyalty, not in terms of any generalization like patriotism or democracy. In much of our early recent fiction the terms *goodness* and *badness* have little meaning in their old contexts.

Herein lies one of the hopeful examples of new growth and new value systems. The completely negative antihero seems to have run his course, and a new picture of the hero has begun to emerge. The *old* hero was one who went forth in the world to do battle against enemies who were quite obviously bad guys. This hero clothed himself in noble generalities such as patriotism, honor, or love for the damsel-in-distress. Time after time he met the enemy, often suffering temporary defeat, but finally good triumphed, and the hero rode off into the sunset with the girl as prize. Except in highly commercial writing, this hero is dead. Then came the complete antihero who had few if any redeeming features. But in the two novels mentioned above, *Seize the Day* and *The Spy Who Came in from the Cold,* or McMurphy in Ken Kesey's *One Flew Over the Cuckoo's Nest,* we have the hero who accepts none of the glorious generalizations, whose shining armor may be a set of rags and a three-day growth of beard; but a hero who has faced the truth of the existential human condition and whose final heroism lies in an act of faith for human life, human dignity, and human love. This position is magnificently explained in the long conversation between Tarrou and Dr. Rieux in Camus's novel, *The Plague,* and it is exemplified very briefly in Hemingway's story, *A Clean, Well-lighted Place.* In these instances and many others, we see the discarding of old systems of value, but in the very rubble that they have created artists suggest new views of life and new values that promise fertility and growth both for now and the future.

There are, moreover, new heroes, some of them tragic, in recent fiction, but these protagonists are heroines. In Judith Rossner's *Looking for Mr. Goodbar* schoolteacher Theresa Dunn is a tragic victim of male-oriented society. Anne Tyler's *Dinner at the Homesick Restaurant* is concerned with the pain and destruction inflicted on a family by, initially, the desertion of the father. On the other hand, Isadore Wing in Erica Jong's *Fear of Flying* has been compared with no less than the irrepressible Wife of Bath. Based on John Cleland's eighteenth-century novel *Fanny Hill,* Jong's *Fanny* is an exuberant and triumphant feminist. Gail Godwin's *A Mother and Two Daughters* is a celebration of American life in feminine terms and a solid statement of faith in human capacity for good. Included in this chapter is Godwin's "A Sorrowful Woman," a somber story of a woman victimized by enforced domesticity.

A second taboo which has been removed from literary creation is the restriction to "polite" language; no English word is outside the pale for use in literature. Written language formerly reserved for the walls of restrooms now appears regularly in our "better" magazines—in fiction, poetry, and nonfiction. No moral judgment needs to be made of this new freedom. Certainly by the time any boy or girl has come to junior high school age, he or she is familiar with all the four-letter words; and, intrinsically, the word "excrement" is neither better nor worse than its four-letter synonym. One may wonder if this new freedom, like the freedom to disrobe, may soon become worn thin and lose its shock value. Writers who are now forced by the new convention to use the short Anglo-Saxon word may find a true freedom by choosing whatever language is best suited to the purpose of their artwork from the entire range of language.

A third restriction which has been removed from all writing is the necessity for rational or chronological structure in prose, for traditional "sense" in poetry. The old requirement that a literary work have a beginning, a middle, and an end is removed except for the requirements imposed by the printed page. For present-day writers the necessity for "plot" is no longer present. Plot may be defined as the working out of a theme, usually clearly stated, which is developed in chronological order by the confrontation of two "sides" in opposition, with the ultimate victory of one side over the other. Until the last quarter of a century (with notable exceptions, of course) this has been the standard structure for most fiction and drama. It is still used in most mass-appeal literature and in much artistic (as different from purely commercial) writing. But it is not necessary, and much of the important contemporary writing has discarded the usual flow-of-time convention as well as that of two forces in opposition. Except for the big Broadway shows, most theatre has discarded logical development in an attempt to achieve immediate and direct feeling which does not fit Aristotelian concepts of either thought or dramatic art. With the old structures no longer required, writers are now free to seek truth in many different ways. Experimentalism in form, sometimes successful, sometimes merely confusing, has become a commonplace in the writers' art.

Within its internal structure, one of the most noticeable characteristics of artistic literature in our time is its symbolic nature, for in much of the newer writing the authors use visible and tangible objects to represent some meaning which lies beyond words. The device is nothing new: Melville's *Moby Dick* is certainly something more than a mere white whale, and Sophokles' portrayal of the blindness of Tiresias or the self-blinding of Oedipus is a way of representing the gaining of spiritual sight as well as the purely physical fact of blindness. But modern literature abounds in symbolism to the point where the reading of a contemporary story or novel or poem frequently becomes the solving of a jigsaw puzzle in which one attempts to fit together all of the symbols into a pattern or patterns of significance.

Freudian symbols were once the most frequently encountered, but now one finds patterns of color symbolism; Christian symbolism abounds almost *ad nauseam;* symbols dealing with primitive initiation rites and fertility are very common. Another sort of symbol makes a parable of the entire work. William Carlos Williams's story, "The Use of Force," is an instance; the surface story of the doctor who tries to force a little girl to open her mouth, for purposes of diagnosis, becomes a cosmic situation that reveals all the violence and force in the world of men. The difference from the past lies perhaps in the degree of sophistication with which the modern writer employs such a device: the taste of the time delights in ingenuity, the intellectual delight of recognizing and following the hints and clues of the skillfully contrived tale, rather than the simple acceptance of face values. Here may be found one reason that plot is of less importance with many fiction writers than it has been in the past; they delight in taking a small surface incident and exploring it, probing down and down through various levels of meaning—sociological, psychological, philosophical, even mythical. It must be stated again that the device is not new in itself; great literature has always had different levels of significance; but it has become a very conscious method of writing in much of the fiction of the present century.

With these general remarks, we might turn to a few observations about the specific forms of writing of our time.

Poetry

The poetry of the present day is such an enormous and varied field that one could find illustration for any thesis he chose to propound. In this chapter are a number of poems illustrating ideas here dealt with; the selection is, necessarily, arbitrary. All one can say is, "Here is the evidence; does it ring true?"

The experimentalism characteristic of twentieth-century literature may, in the poetry of the time, be considered under three aspects: experiments in form, in subject, and in language. In a good poem, these aspects are so closely united as to be inseparable in their total effect, but it is sometimes rewarding to arbitrarily look at them separately.

We have already commented on the innovations in form which came into vogue with the "New Poets" about the time of World War I, and of which Eliot's *The Waste Land* and *The Love Song of J. Alfred Prufrock* (see chap. 27) are excellent examples. Robinson Jeffers's "Shine Perishing Republic" (see chap. 27) is another instance of free verse, with his characteristic long, flowing line. It is interesting to note the rhythmic effect of the poem, the phrasing often indicated by punctuation, but rhythm is not meter.

Perhaps the most strikingly different experiment is e. e. cumming's "anyone lived in a pretty how town" (included in this chapter). The poet delights in typographical eccentricity: lack of capitals or punctuation, frequent parentheses; the example quoted is mild in comparison with others among his poems. It is interesting to note his use, avoidance, and distortion of rhyme: *town-down, winter-did, same-rain.*

Innovation in subject-matter and form almost necessarily demands a difference in language. This does not simply mean that the modern poet talks about the artifacts of our culture—airplanes, or space travel, for example—but that he or she uses a deliberately distorted grammar, syntax, and logic. What will one say of cummings's "anyone lived in a pretty how town"? One must untangle the phrase, to find in it perhaps a sardonic amusement at a gushing cliché—"How pretty this little town is!" When this poet wishes to point out the passage of time, he does not say "time after time, as trees come out leaf by leaf"; he telescopes it to "when by now and tree by leaf," and the apparent nonsense suddenly becomes new sense.

Perhaps a longer look at a specific poem might clarify this insistence upon the difference in language. Dylan Thomas's "When All My Five and Country Senses" (included in this chapter) may seem pretty baffling at first reading. How can *fingers* forget *green thumbs* and what is the half-moon's *vegetable eye?* Certainly the poet is not talking with simple directness; his words do not "mean" with a single, unchanging meaning, but seem to move in several directions at once. Suppose we try to paraphrase in this fashion: "If all my five natural senses could perceive clearly, see—like my eyes—then even the sense of touch, that helped love grow, would 'see' with the passage of time how love grows old and is laid by, like fruit after harvest; the sense of hearing would 'see' love finished, driven away, ending in discord; the tongue, which is both taste and talk, would 'see' love's pains reluctantly ended; the sense of smell would 'see' love consumed as in a fire. But my heart has other means of perception of love, and these will go on beyond the decaying senses, so that my heart will still know love."

Or suppose that a conventional poet had tried to deal with the same idea in a conventional fashion:

Were all my wits perceptive as my eye
Each would tell the same sad tale of waste;
That Love, to which they witness, will go by
And pass beyond them without hope or haste—
Will vanish like a leaf, a smoke, a cry,
As fleeting as a sound or smell or taste.
This I know; but more than this I know:
Still will my heart love on, tho sense be gone:
Let hand or nostril, eye, ear, tongue, all go:
In other senses will my heart love on.

But paraphrase in prose or verse cannot convey the excitement and vitality of the original poem, with all its startling and centrifugal pulls. Here is not orderly sequence of thought, clearly conveyed; the mind leaps from "fingers" to "green thumbs" to the fertility-and-time association with "half-moon" and its "vegetable" (crescent? growing?) eye. It is not logical (neither is love!), but it is provocative and stimulating; not the mind alone, but the imagination, is stirred. One need not *like* the poem to be aware that here is something intensely alive and interesting, however unpredictable. The ambiguity is part of the effect; why is the "lynx tongue" "lashed to syllables"? Does "lashed" mean *bound, tied, confined,* or *whipped, stirred, driven?* The meanings are different to the point of contradiction, yet both may be appropriate. So, too, someone looking at the paraphrases above may exclaim, "Oh no! that's not it at all!"

Obviously the few poems included in this chapter cannot do justice to the range and variety of contemporary poetry; but there is enough to find illustration of the ideas presented here. Modern poetry (like that of any other period!) is not all incomprehensible nor gloomy; some of it is very much alive, and speaks our language. Further acquaintance with these and others like them will serve not merely as a comment on the times, but as enjoyment in the poems themselves, for their own sake.

Drama

For a number of reasons, modern drama has come very close to death and has had to resurrect itself in forms which are even stranger than are the forms for other types of literature. The reasons for its moribund state are easy to see: rising costs of production made big box-office necessary—therefore only those productions with a wide and not very subtle appeal could be produced. One answer to this problem has been the big musical show: *Oklahoma!, Camelot, West Side Story, Hello Dolly,* and many others. Revivals of time-tested and mass-approved dramatists have been another answer to the pressing financial problems which beset the legitimate theatre. Another factor which posed a threat to the live stage has been the usurpation by movies and television of the standard-brand, situation drama. Because of the width of the camera-eye, the possibility for an infinite number of settings, and because TV audiences numbering in the millions do not mind being interrupted every few minutes with a commercial, TV and film can present mass entertainment much more lavishly than live theatre.

While the bread and butter of the legitimate stage was being taken away from it in the early part of the century, all sorts of experimental theatres were springing up all over the world. In these, production costs were kept at a minimum—bare stages lacking any scenery grew commonplace; the "star" system was replaced by the use of good, young, and unknown actors who worked for Equity minimum wages—so that mass audiences were no longer necessary. With small, avant-garde audiences, dramatists were freed to try all sorts of experiments which would never be acceptable in the more tradition-bound Broadway theatre.

One of the first innovations was the attempt to bring the members of the audience into the play with mechanical innovations like the theatre-in-the-round. More recently an actor or several actors have simply stopped the rehearsed drama for a time to sit on the edge of the stage and talk to any members of the audience who have the courage to enter into the conversation. Then, the conversation period ended, the actors step back into their formal roles.

In no realm of literature has the Dionysiac, anti-rational abandonment found expression so much as in the theatre. Such dramas have become fairly commonplace; moving away from the usual concept of a play, they revert to the unplanned and unpredictable "Happening" as they consciously attempt to break down the logical, intellectualized part of human understanding and the barriers which it creates between people.

One of the significant directions in drama was the emergence of the Theatre of the Absurd, based, as the name implies, on the Existentialist concept of a meaningless universe. Probably the best-known play of this genre is Samuel Beckett's (b. 1903) *Waiting for Godot* (1954), which exhibits most of the qualities of the type. The drama takes place, not in sequential time, but in a timeless present. The characters wait for their own identity, but since in such a universe the individual must create himself, identity is never achieved. Such drama substitutes "tension" for what has traditionally been thought of as "conflict," but with the tension in the mind and emotions of the spectator. Since the tension is often left unresolved, as different from the neatly tied endings of the conventional play, the theatre-goer is left with tremendous questions in his mind which he must resolve for himself. Theatre which, in itself, seems to be nonlogical turns out to pose the greatest intellectual questions at exactly the point where they should be raised—in the mind of the individual. A questioning of values is left instead of the catharsis of the old Aristotelian definition. Indeed, Euripides anticipated this type of drama in the choral speeches with which he completes both *The Bacchae* and *Alcestis:*

Gods manifest themselves in many forms,
Bring many matters to surprising ends;
The things we thought would happen do not happen;
The unexpected, God makes possible:
And that is what has happened here today.

More recently Sam Shepard (b. 1943) has emerged as America's leading playwright. Shepard writes in a hyperrealistic mode comparable to the Photorealism (New Realism, Magic Realism) of artists like Richard Estes and Duane Hanson (see chap. 29). But, like abstract illusionist James Havard (see p. 391), Shepard's realism is illusory; the facts are there, it seems, but where reality begins and ends borders on a fifth dimension. Like his *Buried Child* (1979 Pulitzer prize) and *Curse of the Starving Class,* Shepard's *Fool for Love* (1983) is a lower middle-class family drama, in this case an elegaic myth of doomed incestuous love. Shepard's symbols are derived from junk food data and movie, TV, and auto mystiques that represent all that is tawdry and tacky in American life. In *True West* (1980) Shepard extols the mythic West, the Old West that is fast succumbing to cement mixers and bulldozers. In this and many other of his forty plus plays Shepard poses a basic question: must this New World become like the Old World just because so much of the Old World is becoming like us?

Modern Prose Fiction

Everything that has been said previously about literature in the twentieth century applies to the short story and the novel. As in poetry, one of the important concerns of the prose writer is to develop new forms, new methods of penetrating into the truths of human experience. Hitherto *plot* has been one of the chief methods by which fiction writers made their explorations. Many contemporary writers have abandoned this method of telling their story, with the result that form has become almost completely free.

Two forms of fiction, either new or renovated, have come into prominence in our century: black humor and science fiction. Of the first of these, Heller's novel *Catch 22* is the best known, and one of the best examples. Black humor *is* funny, but with a bitterness that stings. Basically it is satire against all the established ways of thought and action, but a satire which uses surrealistic techniques to achieve its purposes. The typical novel of this sort uses scenes which are sharply etched, with almost photographic naturalism. Yet the scenes and events exist in a crazy juxtaposition—as in a Dali painting—so that all ordinary sense is lost, and the mind which is accustomed to see logical relationships is utterly confounded. The reader is left with the sense of living through a funny nightmare in which time is compressed or expanded, in which space is purely relative and may change without warning to the intellect. The total impact of such a novel is that it is a crazy world, and if one were insane one would find it amusing—and then the reversal: maybe the world of the novel is sane and our conventional, Aristotelian minds are really the crazy part.

A brief discussion of *Catch 22* may serve to clarify the points we are making. (Chapter 39 of the novel is printed later in this chapter.) The central object of ridicule throughout the novel is our rational thought which goes around in a circle until it ends in total absurdity. The novel takes place on an Air Force base off the coast of Italy and seems to satirize military life, but a closer scrutiny reveals that it is a bitter attack against much of twentieth-century society and its values. The "Catch" is first revealed when Yossarian, a bombardier and the protagonist of the novel, objects

to flying more missions and goes to the medical officer, pleading insanity, in order to get sent home. The doctor explains to him that a man who expresses fear in a dangerous situation is necessarily sane, and therefore cannot be released. Yossarian asks about the men who are flying missions without protest. The doctor's explanation is simple: Those men are insane, but since they aren't asking to be relieved of duty he can't send them home. If they asked, they, like Yossarian, would show that they were sane and therefore be returned to duty. This is "Catch 22"; perfectly logical, totally absurd, and allowing no hope. Time after time, in many different situations throughout the early sections of the book, this same roundabout logic is revealed to establish an atmosphere of almost complete hopelessness.

Many other of the fallacies of our present way of life are satirized as well. One of these is our dependence upon paperwork rather than facts in making judgments; indeed ex-P.F.C. Wintergreen, a mail clerk, directs the actions of the military more completely than the generals through the handling and scrambling of messages. Another case in point concerns the suicidal mission to bomb the city of Bologna, when Yossarian sneaks down to the central map at headquarters and moves the ribbon which shows the Allied ground position above the city. This is discovered the next morning and word is transmitted from one level of command to the next that Bologna has been taken and the bombing mission is therefore unnecessary. For days this is believed until finally the true word gets through and the mission is rescheduled.

Perhaps the most bitter of attacks is made against the profit system as represented by the supply officer, Milo Minderbinder and his M and M Enterprises. Starting with the simple trading for supplies, he finally deals with both the enemy and his own side; at one point he directs the enemy bombing of his own airbase, at another he arranges a total battle, having charge of both sides. All this is with an enormous profit to himself, though he constantly reminds each person that the person "has a share" in M and M Enterprises. "Having a share" is certainly one of the great doublemeanings of the book.

The first two-thirds of the book are timeless, shifting from one incident to another with no regard to chronology. For Yossarian, however, the central incident is probably the death of his crewmate, Snowden. Snowden has been wounded by antiaircraft fire, and Yossarian is in the rear of the plane treating the obvious wound. Then he opens Snowden's flak suit and discovers the real and mortal wound as Snowden's guts spill out of the body. At this point Yossarian realizes that the world, friend or enemy, is really divided into two groups, the killers and the victims, and that he, as bombardier, has been one of the killers. He refuses this role and for a time goes naked (even when the general is pinning a medal on him) rather than wear the military uniform. The Snowden incident is referred to many times throughout the early part of the novel and is fully explained about two-thirds of the way through at a point when the story begins to exist in chronological time. This is the incident which leads to the first explanation of *Catch 22* and the hopelessness of the situation.

One pilot, Yossarian's tentmate, Orr, has seemed more insane than the rest throughout most of the book. His planes keep having engine trouble or are shot down over the sea. Orr always crash-lands his craft in the water, from which the crew is rescued as they work with the survival gear in the plane. Finally Orr lands in the sea, and all of the crew but he are rescued. It appears that he has drowned.

The novel ends with a scene in the hospital with Yossarian and other officers complaining that there is no hope, no hope at all. Then they receive word that Orr has successfully paddled his inflated life raft to neutral Sweden and is alive. The mood changes. Yossarian runs away to Rome with the promise that he, too, somehow, will reach Sweden. The other men, bound by various obligations, will not run for it, but the fact remains that hope remains. Man may not conquer, but he can refuse to be conquered. In spite of *Catch 22,* the individual can assert himself.

Science fiction as a type is not really new, for most utopian literature shares in its fantasy. Jules Verne and H.G. Wells wrote science fiction before our century. What is really new about it is its reacceptance as a serious genre. What had degenerated into comic strip stuff in the 1930s, somewhat below the level of serious thought, is now widely accepted. The difference lies in the reasons for writing science fiction. The utopians used it to show that things could be better. Jules Verne wrote high-quality, highly popular adventure literature. At the present time Sci-fi's purpose is to unchain the mind from its ordinary channels. As we move through "time-warps," we begin to live in a world in which A may not be A; in which not-A can very well be A. Serious science fiction is now one of the mind-expanding tools which opens new dimensions of thought and life for its devotees.

One of the most usual techniques for the fiction writer of this century is to take a relatively simple action or pattern of action and explore it in its depth, rather than running its length as the plot-story does. In such a case we usually have a surface action, with one or more levels of meaning revealed beneath that surface. It is often possible to distinguish sociological levels, philosophic or psychological levels, and mythical levels of significance. To reach these levels the author frequently uses the types of symbols which have been mentioned previously, and which very often yield meanings that are more felt than stated in words. At the moment it is interesting to compare some outstanding aspects of meaning which concern many writers of short stories and novels. These may be called the pessimism of modern fiction and its optimism.

Although one recognizes that some of the great writers of the nineteenth century were pessimistic, in that century and early in the present one, optimism was the dominant mood of most fiction, for goodness and virtue were, in the main, triumphant. About the time of the First World War, however, we find a very considerable change in the mood of the writers. Starting about that time we have the proletarian writers and the naturalistic writers who thought that society stifled the individual and turned life to tragedy or pathos or despair. Most of these novels are revolts against the materialistic goals which society has imposed upon people, which the individual persons accept, and which finally betray the individual. Theodore Dreiser's *An American Tragedy,* John Dos Passos's *Manhattan Transfer,* and even Aldous Huxley's *Brave New World* can be read as examples of this trend.

That these views of life are pessimistic there can be little doubt but they are not total, for they place the blame on forces external to man. If we could reform society, they seem to say, then the spirit of man could be liberated. Even in the bitter irony of *Brave New World* we have Helmholtz Watson who dreams beyond the bondages of his culture and who welcomes exile as a chance to create.

This mood of social criticism continued approximately from the end of the First World War, 1918, through the depression, and to the beginning of the Second World War. Steinbeck's *Grapes of Wrath* remains as one of the most notable products of the time, for below the surface story of the Joads during the depression (a social problem which has been almost completely forgotten) lie strong political and religious levels of significance which have enduring value.

One could cite many examples of pessimism expressed as social criticism, but, as we have said, such despair is not total. Hope remains that society itself may be reformed and with it may come the regeneration of the human spirit. To oversimplify, this is a pessimism which is still rooted in our present materialistic value system.

Very early, however, appeared another thought: that the universe itself was accidental and without purpose, that the conditions which support life on a mediocre planet arose as a part of the cosmic accident, and that the life or death of any man or group of men is completely insignificant. Such a point of view, expressed early in the century in Somerset Maugham's *Of Human Bondage,* makes any human plan or purpose or striving completely pointless. All forms of society become nothing more than traps to snare the individual into a senseless conformity. This type of pessimism might be called "proto-Existentialism."

Later such an American writer as William Faulkner explored the depths of pessimism in his series of novels dealing with Yoknapatawpha County, Mississippi. In these novels, using symbols of violence, rape, incest, fire, and insanity, Faulkner depicts the complete degeneracy of the aristocratic or commercial white man. In his Nobel Prize acceptance speech Faulkner stated his optimistic belief that man will not only endure, he will prevail. In the literary works themselves, however, one can still find only the expression of the lost and displaced nature of man in a universe that lacks pattern or purpose.

To conclude this discussion of the literature of our century, one sees first a welter of experimentation in forms and meanings, some successful, others not. The purpose of all the experimentation, however, is to free our minds; to take them out of old bondages which have hampered their search for truth. New meanings have required new forms, new language, new exploration in the realms of time, space, and consciousness. Throughout the century, doomsayers have predicted the demise of the novel as a literary form; literature in the 1980s proves them wrong. When Colombian novelist Gabriel García-Márquez received the 1982 Nobel Prize for Literature (see *One Hundred Years of Solitude* in this chapter), the international literary world was reminded that there are many active world-class novelists, some of which are: Saul Bellow, John Updike, and Doris Lessing (U.S.); Jorge Luis Borges (Argentina); Gunter Grass (West Germany); Nadine Gordimer (South Africa; see "A Soldier's Embrace" in chap. 28); Yokio Mishima (Japan); Aleksandr Solzhenitsyn (Russia/U.S.). In an age when print media are supposedly succumbing to the relentless onslaught of computer technology, more books (poetry, short stories, novels, biographies, drama, essays) are being published than at any time in history. No one can reasonably predict what the coming century holds but the literary arts are currently flourishing as perhaps never before.

Literary Selections

Chapters 27, 28, and 31 include a total of thirty-four works: seven short stories, eighteen poems, and selections from five essays and four novels. All told, these provide some indication of the variety of style and content of twentieth-century literature. For want of a better scheme, these concluding selections are arranged in chronological order based on the birthdates of the writers. We have, however, saved the chapter from *Catch 22* as perhaps the most appropriate conclusion for our bewildering, frustrating, and challenging age.

anyone lived in a pretty how town
e e cummings (1894–1962)

Playful syntax and novel versification, among other things, characterize the poetry of e e cummings. The line in the following poem about the growing up process is a case in point: "down they forgot as up they grew."

anyone lived in a pretty how town
(with up so floating many bells down)
spring summer autumn winter
he sang his didn't he danced his did.

Women and men(both little and small)
cared for anyone not at all
they sowed their isn't they reaped their same
sun moon stars rain

children guessed(but only a few
and down they forgot as up they grew
autumn winter spring summer)
that no one loved him more by more

when by now and tree by leaf
she laughed his joy she cried his grief
bird by snow and stir by still
anyone's any was all to her

someones married their everyones
laughed their cryings and did their dance
(sleep wake hope and then)they
said their nevers they slept their dream

stars rain sun moon
(and only the snow can begin to explain
how children are apt to forget to remember
with up so floating many bells down)

one day anyone died i guess
(and noone stooped to kiss his face)
busy folk buried them side by side
little by little and was by was

all by all and deep by deep
and more by more they dream their sleep
noone and anyone earth by april
wish by spirit and if by yes.

Women and men(both dong and ding)
summer autumn winter spring
reaped their sowing and went their came
sun moon stars rain

Exercises

1. Much of the poetry of cummings is very rhythmic with considerable use of what is called the "variable foot." In stanza 1, for example, the variation occurs in the third line. Try reading the poem aloud to hear how the variations set off the nimble words in the other lines.
2. Many of the phrases are disassociated from expected relationships. Try rephrasing some of these to see what happens to the rhythm. Do the conventional versions become rather commonplace?

WHEN ALL MY FIVE AND COUNTRY SENSES SEE
Dylan Thomas (1914–1953)

The carefully crafted work of Welsh poet Dylan Thomas consistently deals with the unity and process of life. Earlier in this chapter the following poem was analyzed but the essence of this poetry is primarily an aural experience. It should, therefore, be read aloud, and many times.

When all my five and country senses see,
The fingers will forget green thumbs and mark
How, through the halfmoon's vegetable eye,
Husk of young stars and handful zodiac,
Love in the frost is pared and wintered by.
The whispering ears will watch love drummed away
Down breeze and shell to a discordant beach,
And, lashed to syllables, the lynx tongue cry
That her fond wounds are mended bitterly,
My nostrils see her breath burn like a bush.
My one and noble heart has witnesses
In all love's countries, that will grope awake:
And when blind sleep drops on the spying senses,
The heart is sensual, though five eyes break.

Chapter 1 from INVISIBLE MAN
Ralph Ellison (b. 1914)

A searing novel about black America and white America, Ralph Ellison's *Invisible Man,* winner of the 1952 National Book Award, is both a folk novel and a polished work in the American literary tradition. Opening with a bizarre boxing match in a white man's "smoker" and culminating in an explosive race riot, this is the epic tale of one man's voyage to self-discovery, a man who is "invisible simply because people refuse to see me." Appearing originally as a short story and then as chapter 1, the following selection gives something of the flavor of a book which should be read in its entirety.

It goes a long way back, some twenty years. All my life I had been looking for something, and everywhere I turned someone tried to tell me what it was. I accepted their answers too, though they were often in contradiction and even self-contradictory. I was naïve. I was looking for myself and asking everyone except myself questions which I, and only I, could answer. It took me a long time and much painful boomeranging of my expectations to achieve a realization everyone else appears to have been born with: That I am nobody but myself. But first I had to discover that I am an invisible man!

And yet I am no freak of nature, nor of history. I was in the cards, other things having been equal (or unequal) eighty-five years ago. I am not ashamed of my grandparents for having been slaves. I am only ashamed of myself for having at one time been ashamed. About eighty-five years ago they were told that they were free, united with others of our country in everything pertaining to the common good, and, in everything social, separate like the fingers of the hand. And they believed it. They exulted in it. They stayed in their place, worked hard, and brought up my father to do the same. But my grandfather is the one. He was an odd old guy, my grandfather, and I am told I take after him. It was he who caused the trouble. On his deathbed he called my father to him and said, "Son, after I'm gone I want you to keep up the good fight. I never told you, but our life is a war and I have been a traitor all my born days, a spy in the enemy's country ever since I give up my gun back in the Reconstruction. Live with your head in the lion's mouth. I want you to overcome 'em with yeses, undermine 'em with grins, agree 'em to death and destruction, let 'em swoller you till they vomit or bust wide open." They thought the old man had gone out of his mind. He had been the meekest of men. The younger children were rushed from the room, the shades drawn and the flame of the lamp turned so low that it sputtered on the wick like the old man's breathing. "Learn it to the younguns," he whispered fiercely; then he died.

But my folks were more alarmed over his last words than over his dying. It was as though he had not died at all, his words caused so much anxiety. I was warned emphatically to forget what he had said and, indeed, this is the first time it has been mentioned outside the family circle. It had a tremendous effect upon me, however. I could never be sure of what he meant. Grandfather had been a quiet old man who never made any trouble, yet on his deathbed he had called himself a traitor and a spy, and he had spoken of his meekness as a dangerous activity. It became a constant puzzle which lay unanswered in the back of my mind. And whenever things went well for me I remembered my grandfather and felt guilty and uncomfortable. It was as though I was carrying out his advice in spite of myself. And to make it worse, everyone loved me for it. I was praised by the most lily-white men of the town. I was considered an example of desirable conduct—just as my grandfather had been. And what puzzled me was that the old man had defined it as *treachery*. When I was praised for my conduct I felt a guilt that in some way I was doing something that was really against the wishes of the white folks, that if they had understood they would have desired me to act just the opposite, that I should have been sulky and mean, and that that really would have been what they wanted, even though they were fooled and thought they wanted me to act as I did. It made me afraid that some day they would look upon me as a traitor and I would be lost. Still I was more afraid to act any other way because they didn't like that at all. The old man's words were like a curse. On my graduation day I delivered an oration in which I showed that humility was the secret, indeed, the very essence of progress. (Not that I believed this—how could I, remembering my grandfather?—I only believed that it worked.) It was a great success. Everyone praised me and I was invited to give the speech at a gathering of the town's leading white citizens. It was a triumph for our whole community.

It was in the main ballroom of the leading hotel. When I got there I discovered that it was on the occasion of a smoker, and I was told that since I was to be there anyway I might as well take part in the battle royal to be fought by some of my schoolmates as part of the entertainment. The battle royal came first.

All of the town's big shots were there in their tuxedoes, wolfing down the buffet foods, drinking beer and whiskey and smoking black cigars. It was a large room with a high ceiling. Chairs were arranged in neat rows around three sides of a portable boxing ring. The fourth side was clear, revealing a gleaming space of polished floor. I had some misgivings over the battle royal, by the way. Not from a distaste for fighting, but because I didn't care too much for the other fellows who were to take part. They were tough guys who seemed to have no grandfather's curse worrying their minds. No one could mistake their toughness. And besides, I suspected that fighting a battle royal might detract from the dignity of my speech. In those pre-invisible days I visualized myself as a potential Booker T. Washington. But the other fellows didn't care too much for me either, and there were nine of them. I felt superior to them in my way, and I didn't like the manner in which we were all crowded together into the servants' elevator. Nor did they like my being there. In fact, as the warmly lighted floors flashed past the elevator we had words over the fact that I, by taking part in the fight, had knocked one of their friends out of a night's work.

We were led out of the elevator through a rococo hall into an anteroom and told to get into our fighting togs. Each of us was issued a pair of boxing gloves and ushered out into the big mirrored hall, which we entered looking cautiously about us and whispering, lest we might accidentally be heard above the noise of the room. It was foggy with cigar smoke. And already the whiskey was taking effect. I was shocked to see some of the most important men of the town quite tipsy. They were all there—bankers, lawyers, judges, doctors, fire chiefs, teachers, merchants. Even one of the more fashionable pastors. Something we could not see was going on up front. A clarinet was vibrating sensuously and the men were standing up and moving eagerly forward. We were a small tight group, clustered together, our bare upper bodies touching and shining with anticipatory sweat; while up front the big shots were becoming increasingly excited over something we still could not see. Suddenly I heard the school superintendent, who had told me to come, yell, "Bring up the shines, gentlemen! Bring up the little shines!"

We were rushed up to the front of the ballroom, where it smelled even more strongly of tobacco and whiskey. Then we were pushed into place. I almost wet my pants. A sea of faces, some hostile, some amused, ringed around us, and in the center, facing us, stood a magnificent blonde—stark naked. There was dead silence. I felt a blast of cold air chill me. I tried to back away, but they were behind me and around me. Some of the boys stood with lowered heads, trembling. I felt a wave of irrational guilt and fear. My teeth chattered, my skin turned to goose flesh, my knees knocked. Yet I was strongly attracted and looked in spite of myself. Had the price of looking been blindness, I would have looked. The hair was yellow like that of a circus kewpie doll, the face heavily powdered and rouged, as though to form an abstract mask, the eyes hollow and smeared a cool blue, the color of a baboon's butt. I felt a desire to spit upon her as my eyes brushed slowly over her body. Her breasts were firm and round as the domes of East Indian temples, and I stood so close as to see the fine skin texture and beads of pearly perspiration glistening like dew around the pink and erected buds of her nipples. I wanted at one and the same time to run from the room, to sink through

the floor, or go to her and cover her from my eyes and the eyes of the others with my body; to feel the soft thighs, to caress her and destroy her, to love her and murder her, to hide from her, and yet to stroke where below the small American flag tattooed upon her belly her thighs formed a capital V. I had a notion that of all in the room she saw only me with her impersonal eyes.

And then she began to dance, a slow senuous movement; the smoke of a hundred cigars clinging to her like the thinnest of veils. She seemed like a fair bird-girl girdled in veils calling to me from the angry surface of some gray and threatening sea. I was transported. Then I became aware of the clarinet playing and the big shots yelling at us. Some threatened us if we looked and others if we did not. On my right I saw one boy faint. And now a man grabbed a silver pitcher from a table and stepped close as he dashed ice water upon him and stood him up and forced two of us to support him as his head hung and moans issued from his thick bluish lips. Another boy began to plead to go home. He was the largest of the group, wearing dark red fighting trunks much too small to conceal the erection which projected from him as though in answer to the insinuating low-registered moaning of the clarinet. He tried to hide himself with his boxing gloves.

And all the while the blonde continued dancing, smiling faintly at the big shots who watched her with fascination, and faintly smiling at our fear. I noticed a certain merchant who followed her hungrily, his lips loose and drooling. He was a large man who wore diamond studs in a shirtfront which swelled with the ample paunch underneath, and each time the blonde swayed her undulating hips he ran his hand through the thin hair of his bald head and, with his arms upheld, his posture clumsy like that of an intoxicated panda, wound his belly in a slow and obscene grind. This creature was completely hypnotized. The music had quickened. As the dancer flung herself about with a detached expression on her face, the men began reaching out to touch her. I could see their beefy fingers sink into the soft flesh. Some of the others tried to stop them and she began to move around the floor in graceful circles, as they gave chase, slipping and sliding over the polished floor. It was mad. Chairs went crashing, drinks were spilt, as they ran laughing and howling after her. They caught her just as she reached a door, raised her from the floor, and tossed her as college boys are tossed at a hazing, and above her red, fixed-smiling lips I saw the terror and disgust in her eyes, almost like my own terror and that which I saw in some of the other boys. As I watched, they tossed her twice and her soft breasts seemed to flatten against the air and her legs flung wildly as she spun. Some of the more sober ones helped her to escape. And I started off the floor, heading for the anteroom with the rest of the boys.

Some were still crying and in hysteria. But as we tried to leave we were stopped and ordered to get into the ring. There was nothing to do but what we were told. All ten of us climbed under the ropes and allowed ourselves to be blindfolded with broad bands of white cloth. One of the men seemed to feel a bit sympathetic and tried to cheer us up as we stood with our backs against the ropes. Some of us tried to grin. "See that boy over there?" one of the men said. "I want you to run across at the bell and give it to him right in the belly. If you don't get him, I'm going to get you. I don't like his looks." Each of us was told the same. The blindfolds were put on. Yet even then I had been going over my speech.

In my mind each word was as bright as flame. I felt the cloth pressed into place, and frowned so that it would be loosened when I relaxed.

But now I felt a sudden fit of blind terror. I was unused to darkness. It was as though I had suddenly found myself in a dark room filled with poisonous cottonmouths. I could hear the bleary voices yelling insistently for the battle royal to begin.

"Get going in there!"

"Let me at that big nigger!"

I strained to pick up the school superintendent's voice, as though to squeeze some security out of that slightly more familiar sound.

"Let me at those black sonsabitches!" someone yelled.

"No, Jackson, no!" another voice yelled. "Here, somebody, help me hold Jack."

"I want to get at that ginger-colored nigger. Tear him limb from limb," the first voice yelled.

I stood against the ropes trembling. For in those days I was what they called ginger-colored, and he sounded as though he might crunch me between his teeth like a crisp ginger cookie.

Quite a struggle was going on. Chairs were being kicked about and I could hear voices grunting as with a terrific effort. I wanted to see, to see more desperately than ever before. But the blindfold was tight as a thick skin-puckering scab and when I raised my gloved hands to push the layers of white aside a voice yelled, "Oh, no you don't, black bastard! Leave that alone!"

"Ring the bell before Jackson kills him a coon!" someone boomed in the sudden silence. And I heard the bell clang and the sound of the feet scuffling forward.

A glove smacked against my head. I pivoted, striking out stiffly as someone went past, and felt the jar ripple along the length of my arm to my shoulder. Then it seemed as though all nine of the boys had turned upon me at once. Blows pounded me from all sides while I struck out as best I could. So many blows landed upon me that I wondered if I were not the only blindfolded fighter in the ring, or if the man called Jackson hadn't succeeded in getting me after all.

Blindfolded, I could no longer control my motions. I had no dignity. I stumbled about like a baby or a drunken man. The smoke had become thicker and with each new blow it seemed to sear and further restrict my lungs. My saliva became like hot bitter glue. A glove connected with my head, filling my mouth with warm blood. It was everywhere. I could not tell if the moisture I felt upon my body was sweat or blood. A blow landed hard against the nape of my neck. I felt myself going over, my head hitting the floor. Streaks of blue light filled the black world behind the blindfold. I lay prone, pretending that I was knocked out, but felt myself seized by hands and yanked to my feet. "Get going, black boy! Mix it up!" My arms were like lead, my head smarting from blows. I managed to feel my way to the ropes and held on, trying to catch my breath. A glove landed in my mid-section and I went over again, feeling as though the smoke had become a knife jabbed into my guts. Pushed this way and that by the legs milling around me, I finally pulled erect and discovered that I could see the black, sweat-washed forms weaving in the smoky-blue atmosphere like drunken dancers weaving to the rapid drum-like thuds of blows.

Everyone fought hysterically. It was complete anarchy. Everybody fought everybody else. No group fought together for long. Two, three, four, fought one, then turned to fight each other, were themselves attacked.

Blows landed below the belt and in the kidney, with the gloves open as well as closed, and with my eye partly opened now there was not so much terror. I moved carefully, avoiding blows, although not too many to attract attention, fighting from group to group. The boys groped about like blind, cautious crabs crouching to protect their mid-sections, their heads pulled in short against their shoulders, their arms stretched nervously before them, with their fists testing the smoke-filled air like the knobbed feelers of hypersensitive snails. In one corner I glimpsed a boy violently punching the air and heard him scream in pain as he smashed his hand against a ring post. For a second I saw him bent over holding his hand, then going down as a blow caught his unprotected head. I played one group against the other, slipping in and throwing a punch then stepping out of range while pushing the others into the melee to take the blows blindly aimed at me. The smoke was agonizing and there were no rounds, no bells at three minute intervals to relieve our exhaustion. The room spun round me, a swirl of lights, smoke, sweating bodies surrounded by tense white faces. I bled from both nose and mouth, the blood spattering upon my chest.

The men kept yelling, "Slug him, black boy! Knock his guts out!"

"Uppercut him! Kill him! Kill that big boy!"

Taking a fake fall, I saw a boy going down heavily beside me as though we were felled by a single blow, saw a sneaker-clad foot shoot into his groin as the two who had knocked him down stumbled upon him. I rolled out of range, feeling a twinge of nausea.

The harder we fought the more threatening the men became. And yet, I had begun to worry about my speech again. How would it go? Would they recognize my ability? What would they give me?

I was fighting automatically when suddenly I noticed that one after another of the boys was leaving the ring. I was surprised, filled with panic, as though I had been left alone with an unknown danger. Then I understood. The boys had arranged it among themselves. It was the custom for the two men left in the ring to slug it out for the winner's place. I discovered this too late. When the bell sounded two men in tuxedoes leaped into the ring and removed the blindfold. I found myself facing Tatlock, the biggest of the gang. I felt sick at my stomach. Hardly had the bell stopped ringing in my ears than it clanged again and I saw him moving swiftly toward me. Thinking of nothing else to do I hit him smash on the nose. He kept coming, bringing the rank sharp violence of stale sweat. His face was a black blank of a face, only his eyes alive— with hate of me and aglow with a feverish terror from what had happened to us all. I became anxious. I wanted to deliver my speech and he came at me as though he meant to beat it out of me. I smashed him again and again, taking his blows as they came. Then on a sudden impulse I struck him lightly and as we clinched, I whispered, "Fake like I knocked you out, you can have the prize."

"I'll break your behind," he whispered hoarsely.

"For *them?*"

"For *me*, sonofabitch!"

They were yelling for us to break it up and Tatlock spun me half around with a blow, and as a joggled camera sweeps in a reeling scene, I saw the howling red faces crouching tense beneath the cloud of blue-gray smoke. For a moment the world wavered, unraveled, flowed, then my head cleared and Tatlock bounced before me. That fluttering shadow before my eyes was his jabbing left hand. Then falling forward, my head against his damp shoulder, I whispered,

"I'll make it five dollars more."

"Go to hell!"

But his muscles relaxed a trifle beneath my pressure and I breathed, "Seven?"

"Give it to your ma," he said, ripping me beneath the heart.

And while I still held him I butted him and moved away. I felt myself bombarded with punches. I fought back with hopeless desperation. I wanted to deliver my speech more than anything else in the world, because I felt that only these men could judge truly my ability, and now this stupid clown was ruining my chances. I began fighting carefully now, moving in to punch him and out again with my greater speed. A lucky blow to his chin and I had him going too—until I heard a loud voice yell, "I got my money on the big boy."

Hearing this, I almost dropped my guard. I was confused: Should I try to win against the voice out there? Would not this go against my speech, and was not this a moment for humility, for nonresistance? A blow to my head as I danced about sent my right eye popping like a jack-in-the-box and settled my dilemma. The room went red as I fell. It was a dream fall, my body languid and fastidious as to where to land, until the floor became impatient and smashed up to meet me. A moment later I came to. An hypnotic voice said FIVE emphatically. And I lay there, hazily watching a dark red spot of my own blood shaping itself into a butterfly, glistening and soaking into the soiled gray world of the canvas.

When the voice drawled TEN I was lifted up and dragged to a chair. I sat dazed. My eye pained and swelled with each throb of my pounding heart and I wondered if now I would be allowed to speak. I was wringing wet, my mouth still bleeding. We were grouped along the wall now. The other boys ignored me as they congratulated Tatlock and speculated as to how much they would be paid. One boy whimpered over his smashed hand. Looking up front, I saw attendants in white jackets rolling the portable ring away and placing a small square rug in the vacant space surrounded by chairs. Perhaps, I thought, I will stand on the rug to deliver my speech.

Then the M.C. called us, "Come on up here boys and get your money."

We ran forward to where the men laughed and talked in their chairs, waiting. Everyone seemed friendly now.

"There it is on the rug," the man said. I saw the rug covered with coins of all dimensions and a few crumpled bills. But what excited me, scattered here and there, were the gold pieces.

"Boys, it's all yours," the man said. "You get all you grab."

"That's right, Sambo," a blond man said, winking at me confidentially.

I trembled with excitement, forgetting my pain. I would get the gold and the bills, I thought. I would use both hands. I would throw my body against the boys nearest me to block them from the gold.

"Get down around the rug now," the man commanded, "and don't anyone touch it until I give the signal."

"This ought to be good," I heard.

As told, we got around the square rug on our knees. Slowly the man raised his freckled hand as we followed it upward with our eyes.

I heard, "These niggers look like they're about to pray!"

Then, "Ready," the man said. "Go!"

I lunged for a yellow coin lying on the blue design of the carpet, touching it and sending a surprised shriek to join those rising around me. I tried frantically to remove my hand but could not let go. A hot, violent force tore through my body, shaking me like a wet rat. The rug was electrified. The hair bristled up on my head as I shook myself free. My muscles jumped, my nerves jangled, writhed. But I saw that this was not stopping the other boys. Laughing in fear and embarrassment, some were holding back and scooping up the coins knocked off by the painful contortions of the others. The men roared above us as we struggled.

"Pick it up, goddamnit, pick it up!" someone called like a bass-voiced parrot. "Go on, get it!"

I crawled rapidly around the floor, picking up the coins, trying to avoid the coppers and to get greenbacks and the gold. Ignoring the shock by laughing, as I brushed the coins off quickly, I discovered that I could contain the electricity—a contradiction, but it works. Then the men began to push us onto the rug. Laughing embarrassedly, we struggled out of their hands and kept after the coins. We were all wet and slippery and hard to hold. Suddenly I saw a boy lifted into the air, glistening with sweat like a circus seal, and dropped, his wet back landing flush upon the charged rug, heard him yell and saw him literally dance upon his back, his elbows beating a frenzied tattoo upon the floor, his muscles twitching like the flesh of a horse stung by many flies. When he finally rolled off, his face was gray and no one stopped him when he ran from the floor amid booming laughter.

"Get the money," the M.C. called. "That's good hard American cash!"

And we snatched and grabbed, snatched and grabbed. I was careful not to come too close to the rug now, and when I felt the hot whiskey breath descend upon me like a cloud of foul air I reached out and grabbed the leg of a chair. It was occupied and I held on desperately.

"Leggo, nigger! Leggo!"

The huge face wavered down to mine as he tried to push me free. But my body was slippery and he was too drunk. It was Mr. Colcord, who owned a chain of movie houses and "entertainment palaces." Each time he grabbed me I slipped out of his hands. It became a real struggle. I feared the rug more than I did the drunk, so I held on, surprising myself for a moment by trying to topple *him* upon the rug. It was such an enormous idea that I found myself actually carrying it out. I tried not to be obvious, yet when I grabbed his leg, trying to tumble him out of the chair, he raised up roaring with laughter, and, looking at me with soberness dead in the eye, kicked me viciously in the chest. The chair leg flew out of my hand and I felt myself going and rolled. It was as though I had rolled through a bed of hot coals. It seemed a whole century would pass before I would roll free, a century in which I was seared through the deepest levels of my body to the fearful breath within me and the breath seared and heated to the point of explosion. It'll all be over in a flash, I thought as I rolled clear. It'll all be over in a flash.

But not yet, the men on the other side were waiting, red faces swollen as though from apoplexy as they bent forward in their chairs. Seeing their fingers coming toward me I rolled away as a fumbled football rolls off the receiver's fingertips, back into the coals. That time I luckily sent the rug sliding out of place and heard the coins ringing against the floor and the boys scuffling to pick them up and the M.C. calling, "All right, boys, that's all. Go get dressed and get your money."

I was limp as a dish rag. My back felt as though it had been beaten with wires.

When we had dressed the M.C. came in and gave us each five dollars, except Tatlock, who got ten for being last in the ring. Then he told us to leave. I was not to get a chance to deliver my speech, I thought. I was going out into the dim alley in despair when I was stopped and told to go back. I returned to the ballroom, where the men were pushing back their chairs and gathering in groups to talk.

The M.C. knocked on a table for quiet. "Gentlemen," he said "we almost forgot an important part of the program. A most serious part, gentlemen. This boy was brought here to deliver a speech which he made at his graduation yesterday. . . ."

"Bravo!"

"I'm told that he is the smartest boy we've got out there in Greenwood. I'm told that he knows more big words than a pocket-sized dictionary."

Much applause and laughter.

"So now, gentlemen, I want you to give him your attention."

There was still laughter as I faced them, my mouth dry, my eye throbbing. I began slowly, but evidently my throat was tense, because they began shouting, "Louder! Louder!"

"We of the younger generation extol the wisdom of that great leader and educator," I shouted, "who first spoke these flaming words of wisdom: 'A ship lost at sea for many days suddenly sighted a friendly vessel. From the mast of the unfortunate vessel was seen a signal: "Water, water; we die of thirst!" The answer from the friendly vessel came back: "Cast down your bucket where you are." The captain of the distressed vessel, at last heeding the injunction, cast down his bucket, and it came up full of fresh sparkling water from the mouth of the Amazon River.' And like him I say, and in his words, 'To those of my race who depend upon bettering their condition in a foreign land, or who underestimate the importance of cultivating friendly relations with the Southern white man, who is his next-door neighbor, I would say: "Cast down your bucket where you are"—cast it down in making friends in every manly way of the people of all races by whom we are surrounded. . . .' "

I spoke automatically and with such fervor that I did not realize that the men were still talking and laughing until my dry mouth, filling up with blood from the cut, almost strangled me. I coughed, wanted to stop and go to one of the tall brass, sand-filled spittoons to relieve myself, but a few of the men, especially the superintendent, were listening and I was afraid. So I gulped it down, blood, saliva and all, and continued. (What powers of endurance I had during those days! What enthusiasm! What a belief in the rightness of things!) I spoke even louder in spite of the pain. But still they talked and still they laughed, as though deaf with cotton in dirty ears. So I spoke with greater emotional emphasis.

I closed my ears and swallowed blood until I was nauseated. The speech seemed a hundred times as long as before, but I could not leave out a single word. All had to be said, each memorized nuance considered, rendered. Nor was that all. Whenever I uttered a word of three or more syllables a group of voices would yell for me to repeat it. I used the phrase "social responsibility" and they yelled:

"What's that word you say, boy?"

"Social responsibility," I said.

"What?"

"Social . . ."

"Louder."

". . . responsibility."

"More!"

"Respon—"

"Repeat!"

"—sibility."

The room filled with the uproar of laughter until, no doubt, distracted by having to gulp down my blood, I made a mistake and yelled a phrase I had often seen denounced in newspaper editorials, heard debated in private.

"Social. . ."

"What?" they yelled.

". . . equality—"

The laughter hung smokelike in the sudden stillness. I opened my eyes, puzzled. Sounds of displeasure filled the room. The M.C. rushed forward. They shouted hostile phrases at me. But I did not understand.

A small dry mustached man in the front row blared out, "Say that slowly, son!"

"What, sir?"

"What you just said!"

"Social responsibility, sir," I said.

"You weren't being smart, were you, boy?" he said, not unkindly.

"No, sir!"

"You sure that about 'equality' was a mistake?"

"Oh, yes, sir," I said. "I was swallowing blood."

"Well, you had better speak more slowly so we can understand. We mean to do right by you, but you've got to know your place at all times. All right, now, go on with your speech."

I was afraid. I wanted to leave but I wanted also to speak and I was afraid they'd snatch me down.

"Thank you, sir," I said, beginning where I had left off, and having them ignore me as before.

Yet when I finished there was a thunderous applause. I was surprised to see the superintendent come forth with a package wrapped in white tissue paper, and, gesturing for quiet, address the men.

"Gentlemen, you see that I did not overpraise this boy. He makes a good speech and some day he'll lead his people in the proper paths. And I don't have to tell you that this is important in these days and times. This is a good, smart boy, and so to encourage him in the right direction, in the name of the Board of Education I wish to present him a prize in the form of this. . . ."

He paused, removing the tissue paper and revealing a gleaming calfskin brief case.

". . . in the form of this first-class article from Shad Witmore's shop."

"Boy," he said, addressing me, "take this prize and keep it well. Consider it a badge of office. Prize it. Keep developing as you are and some day it will be filled with important papers that will help shape the destiny of your people."

I was so moved that I could hardly express my thanks. A rope of bloody saliva forming a shape like an undiscovered continent drooled upon the leather and I wiped it quickly away. I felt an importance that I had never dreamed.

"Open it and see what's inside," I was told.

My fingers a-tremble, I complied, smelling the fresh leather and finding an official-looking document inside. It was a scholarship to the state college for Negroes. My eyes filled with tears and I ran awkwardly off the floor.

I was overjoyed; I did not even mind when I discovered that the gold pieces I had scrambled for were brass pocket tokens advertising a certain make of automobile.

When I reached home everyone was excited. Next day the neighbors came to congratulate me. I even felt safe from grandfather, whose deathbed curse usually spoiled my triumphs. I stood beneath his photograph with my brief case in hand and smiled triumphantly into his stolid black peasant's face. It was a face that fascinated me. The eyes seemed to follow everywhere I went.

That night I dreamed I was at a circus with him and that he refused to laugh at the clowns no matter what they did. Then later he told me to open my brief case and read what was inside and I did, finding an official envelope stamped with the state seal; and inside the envelope I found another and another, endlessly, and I thought I would fall of weariness. "Them's years," he said. "Now open that one." And I did and in it I found an engraved document containing a short message in letters of gold. "Read it," my grandfather said. "Out loud!"

"To Whom It May Concern," I intoned. "Keep This Nigger-Boy Running."

I awoke with the old man's laughter ringing in my ears.

(It was a dream I was to remember and dream again for many years after. But at that time I had no insight into its meaning. First I had to attend college.)

Exercises

1. Why did the protagonist say that his grandfather's dying words "acted like a curse"?
2. Was the true function of the "battle royal" solely entertainment? Explain your answer.
3. What was implied in the way white males treated the naked blonde dancer? Was this at all comparable to the attitude toward blacks? In what ways?
4. The electrified rug was a metaphor for what?
5. Do you feel that the all-pervasive brutality in this story was exaggerated? If your answer was "yes" you might want to look much deeper into the history of race relations in this country and then examine your own attitude.

NAMING OF PARTS

Henry Reed (b. 1914)

It is springtime in the following poem, mating time, as soldiers name the mechanical components of a rifle. Ironically, the gun is both a destructive symbol and a phallic fertility symbol, with terminology appropriate to both war and love.

Today we have naming of parts. Yesterday,
We had daily cleaning. And tomorrow morning,
We shall have what to do after firing. But today,
Today we have naming of parts. Japonica
Glistens like coral in all of the neighboring gardens,
    And today we have naming of parts.

This is the lower sling swivel. And this
Is the upper sling swivel, whose use you will see,
When you are given your slings. And this is the pulling swivel,
Which in your case you have not got. The branches
Hold in the gardens their silent, eloquent gestures,
    Which in our case we have not got.

This is the safety catch, which is always released
With an easy flick of the thumb. And please do not let me
See anyone using his finger. You can do it quite easy
If you have any strength in your thumb. The blossoms
Are fragile and motionless, never letting anyone see
    Any of them using their finger.

And this you can see is the bolt. The purpose of this
Is to open the breech, as you see. We can slide it
Rapidly backwards and forwards: we call this
Easing the spring. And rapidly backwards and forwards
The early bees are assaulting and fumbling the flowers:
    They call it easing the Spring.

They call it easing the Spring: it is perfectly easy
If you have any strength in your thumb: like the bolt
And the breech, and the cocking piece, and the point of balance,
Which in our case we have not got; and the almond blossoms
Silent in all of the gardens and the bees going backwards and forwards,
    For today we have naming of parts.

Exercise

1. Some psychologists maintain that combat has a strong erotic component, that fighting and killing satisfy some kind of sexual drive. Would Freud agree? Before you answer, look again at the selection from *Civilization and Its Discontents* in chapter 27.

THE MAGIC BARREL
Bernard Malamud (b. 1914)

An ambiguous, ironic parable and quasi fantasy, Malamud's "The Magic Barrel" demonstrates the author's faith in the redemptive power of love. A rabbinical student approaching ordination, Leo Finkle foresees a "good" congregation if he can obtain a proper wife. Lacking the customary social contacts, he calls in a marriage broker named Pinye Salzman, who "smelled frankly of fish." Half con man and half impish messenger of God, Salzman valiantly extols the merits of his special (for a rabbi) female clientele while Finkle demurs and declines. After one dreary date with an aging school teacher who was expecting a true man of God, Finkle is reduced to despair combined with a significant increase in self-knowledge. Falling in love with a photograph accidentally left behind by Salzman, Finkle goes to meet his destiny in the form of Stella, Salzman's errant daughter. The question is: did Salzman plan all this? And, does Salzman's chanting prayer for the dead symbolize the demise of his integrity as a marriage broker? Finkle's loss of innocence? Stella's burial of a guilty past? All of the above?

Not long ago there lived in uptown New York, in a small, almost meager room, though crowded with books, Leo Finkle, a rabbinical student in the Yeshivah University. Finkle, after six years of study, was to be ordained in June and had been advised by an acquaintance that he might find it easier to win himself a congregation if he were married. Since he had no present prospects of marriage, after two tormented days of turning it over in his mind, he called in Pinye Salzman, a marriage broker whose two-line advertisement he had read in the *Forward*.

The matchmaker appeared one night out of the dark fourth-floor hallway of the graystone rooming house where Finkle lived, grasping a black, strapped portfolio that had been worn thin with use. Salzman, who had been long in the business, was of slight but dignified build, wearing an old hat, and an overcoat too short and tight for him. He smelled frankly of fish, which he loved to eat, and although he was missing a few teeth, his presence was not displeasing, because of an amiable manner curiously contrasted with mournful eyes. His voice, his lips, his wisp of beard, his bony fingers were animated, but give him a moment of repose and his mild blue eyes revealed a depth of sadness, a characteristic that put Leo a little at ease although the situation, for him, was inherently tense.

He at once informed Salzman why he had asked him to come, explaining that his home was in Cleveland, and that but for his parents, who had married comparatively late in life, he was alone in the world. He had for six years devoted himself almost entirely to his studies, as a result of which, understandably, he had found himself without time for a social life and the company of young women. Therefore he thought it the better part of trial and error—of embarrassing fumbling—to call in an experienced person to advise him on these matters. He remarked in passing that the function of the marriage broker was ancient and honorable, highly approved in the Jewish community, because it made practical the necessary without hindering joy. Moreover, his own parents had been brought together by a matchmaker. They had made, if not a financially profitable marriage—since neither had possessed any worldly goods to speak of—at least a successful one in the sense of their everlasting devotion to each other. Salzman listened in embarrassed surprise, sensing a sort of apology. Later, however, he experienced a glow of pride in his work, an emotion that had left him years ago, and he heartily approved of Finkle.

The two went to their business. Leo had led Salzman to the only clear place in the room, a table near a window that overlooked the lamp-lit city. He seated himself at the matchmaker's side but facing him, attempting by an act of will to suppress the unpleasant tickle in his throat. Salzman eagerly unstrapped his portfolio and removed a loose rubber band from a thin packet of much-handled cards. As he flipped through them, a gesture and sound that physically hurt Leo, the student pretended not to see and gazed steadfastly out the window. Although it was still February, winter was on its last legs, signs of which he had for the first time in years begun to notice. He now observed the round white moon, moving high in the sky through a cloud menagerie, and watched with half-open mouth as it penetrated a huge hen, and dropped out of her like an egg laying itself. Salzman, though pretending through eyeglasses he had just slipped on, to be engaged in scanning the writing on the cards, stole occasional glances at the young man's distinguished face, noting with pleasure the long, severe scholar's nose, brown eyes heavy with learning, sensitive yet ascetic lips, and a certain, almost hollow quality of the dark cheeks. He gazed around at shelves upon shelves of books and let out a soft, contented sigh.

When Leo's eyes fell upon the cards, he counted six spread out in Salzman's hand.

"So few?" he asked in disappointment.

"You wouldn't believe me how much cards I got in my office," Salzman replied. "The drawers are already filled to the top, so I keep them now in a barrel, but is every girl good for a new rabbi?"

Leo blushed at this, regretting all he had revealed of himself in a curriculum vitae he had sent to Salzman. He had thought it best to acquaint him with his strict standards and specifications, but in having done so, felt he had told the marriage broker more than was absolutely necessary.

He hesitantly inquired, "Do you keep photographs of your clients on file?"

"First comes family, amount of dowry, also what kind promises," Salzman replied, unbuttoning his tight coat and settling himself in the chair. "After comes pictures, rabbi."

"Call me Mr. Finkle. I'm not yet a rabbi."

Salzman said he would, but instead called him doctor, which he changed to rabbi when Leo was not listening too attentively.

Salzman adjusted his horn-rimmed spectacles, gently cleared his throat and read in an eager voice the contents of the top card:

"Sophie P. Twenty-four years. Widow one year. No children. Educated high school and two years college. Father promises eight thousand dollars. Has wonderful wholesale business. Also real estate. On the mother's side comes teachers, also one actor. Well known on Second Avenue."

Leo gazed up in surprise. "Did you say a widow?"

"A widow don't mean spoiled, rabbi. She lived with her husband maybe four months. He was a sick boy she made a mistake to marry him."

"Marrying a widow has never entered my mind."

"This is because you have no experience. A widow, especially if she is young and healthy like this girl, is a wonderful person to marry. She will be thankful to you the rest of her life. Believe me, if I was looking now for a bride, I would marry a widow."

Leo reflected, then shook his head.

Salzman hunched his shoulders in an almost imperceptible gesture of disappointment. He placed the card down on the wooden table and began to read another.

"Lily H. High school teacher. Regular. Not a substitute. Has savings and new Dodge car. Lived in Paris one year. Father is successful dentist thirty-five years. Interested in professional man. Well Americanized family. Wonderful opportunity."

"I knew her personally," said Salzman. "I wish you could see this girl. She is a doll. Also very intelligent. All day you could talk to her about books and theater and what not. She also knows current events."

"I don't believe you mentioned her age?"

"Her age?" Salzman said, raising his brows. "Her age is thirty-two years."

Leo said after a while, "I'm afraid that seems a little too old."

Salzman let out a laugh. "So how old are you, rabbi?"

"Twenty-seven."

"So what is the difference, tell me, between twenty-seven and thirty-two? My own wife is seven years older than me. So what did I suffer?—Nothing. If Rothschild's daughter wants to marry you, would you say on account her age, no?"

"Yes," Leo said dryly.

Salzman shook off the no in the yes. "Five years don't mean a thing. I give you my word that when you will live with her for one week you will forget her age. What does it mean five years—that she lived more and knows more than somebody who is younger? On this girl, God bless her, years are not wasted. Each one that it comes makes better the bargain."

"What subject does she teach in high school?"

"Languages. If you heard the way she speaks French, you will think it is music. I am in the business twenty-five years, and I recommend her with my whole heart. Believe me, I know what I'm talking, rabbi."

"What's on the next card?" Leo said abruptly.

Salzman reluctantly turned up the third card:

"Ruth K. Nineteen years. Honor student. Father offers thirteen thousand cash to the right bridegroom. He is a medical doctor. Stomach specialist with marvelous practice. Brother in law owns own garment business. Particular people."

Salzman looked as if he had read his trump card.

"Did you say nineteen?" Leo asked with interest.

"On the dot."

"Is she attractive?" He blushed. "Pretty?"

Salzman kissed his finger tips. "A little doll. On this I give you my word. Let me call the father tonight and you will see what means pretty."

But Leo was troubled. "You're sure she's that young?"

"This I am positive. The father will show you the birth certificate."

"Are you positive there isn't something wrong with her?" Leo insisted.

"Who says there is wrong?"

"I don't understand why an American girl her age should go to a marriage broker."

A smile spread over Salzman's face.

"So for the same reason you went, she comes."

Leo flushed. "I am pressed for time."

Salzman, realizing he had been tactless, quickly explained. "The father came, not her. He wants she should have the best, so he looks around himself. When we will locate the right boy he will introduce him and encourage. This makes a better marriage than if a young girl without experience takes for herself. I don't have to tell you this."

"But don't you think this young girl believes in love?" Leo spoke uneasily.

Salzman was about to guffaw but caught himself and said soberly, "Love comes with the right person, not before."

Leo parted dry lips but did not speak. Noticing that Salzman had snatched a glance at the next card, he cleverly asked, "How is her health?"

"Perfect," Salzman said, breathing with difficulty. "Of course, she is a little lame on her right foot from an auto accident that it happened to her when she was twelve years, but nobody notices on account she is so brilliant and also beautiful."

Leo got up heavily and went to the window. He felt curiously bitter and upbraided himself for having called in the marriage broker. Finally, he shook his head.

"Why not?" Salzman persisted, the pitch of his voice rising.

"Because I detest stomach specialists."

"So what do you care what is his business? After you marry her do you need him? Who says he must come every Friday night in your house?"

Ashamed of the way the talk was going, Leo dismissed Salzman, who went home with heavy, melancholy eyes.

Though he had felt only relief at the marriage broker's departure, Leo was in low spirits the next day. He explained it as arising from Salzman's failure to produce a suitable bride for him. He did not care for his type of clientele. But when Leo found himself hesitating whether to seek out another matchmaker, one more polished than Pinye, he wondered if it could be—his protestations to the contrary, and although he honored his father and mother—that he did not, in essence, care for the matchmaking institution? This thought he quickly put out of mind yet found himself still upset. All day he ran around in the woods—missed an important appointment, forgot to give out his laundry, walked out of a Broadway cafeteria without paying and had to run back with the ticket in his hand; had even not recognized his landlady in the street when she passed with a friend and courteously called out, "A good evening to you, Doctor Finkle." By nightfall, however, he had regained sufficient calm to sink his nose into a book and there found peace from his thoughts.

Almost at once there came a knock on the door. Before Leo could say enter, Salzman, commercial cupid, was standing in the room. His face was gray and meager, his expression hungry, and he looked as if he would expire on his feet. Yet the marriage broker managed, by some trick of the muscles, to display a broad smile.

"So good evening. I am invited?"

Leo nodded, disturbed to see him again, yet unwilling to ask the man to leave.

Beaming still, Salzman laid his portfolio on the table. "Rabbi, I got for you tonight good news."

"I've asked you not to call me rabbi. I'm still a student."

"Your worries are finished. I have for you a first-class bride."

"Leave me in peace concerning this subject." Leo pretended lack of interest.

"The world will dance at your wedding."

"Please, Mr. Salzman, no more."

"But first must come back my strength," Salzman said weakly. He fumbled with the portfolio straps and took out of the leather case an oily paper bag, from which he extracted a hard, seeded roll and a small, smoked white fish. With a quick motion of his hand he stripped the fish out of its skin and began ravenously to chew. "All day in a rush," he muttered.

Leo watched him eat.

"A sliced tomato you have maybe?" Salzman hesitantly inquired.

"No."

The marriage broker shut his eyes and ate. When he had finished he carefully cleaned up the crumbs and rolled up the remains of the fish, in the paper bag. His spectacled eyes roamed the room until he discovered, amid some piles of books, a one-burner gas stove. Lifting his hat he humbly asked, "A glass of tea you got, rabbi?"

Conscience-stricken, Leo rose and brewed the tea. He served it with a chunk of lemon and two cubes of lump sugar, delighting Salzman.

After he had drunk his tea, Salzman's strength and good spirits were restored.

"So tell me, rabbi," he said amiably, "you considered some more the three clients I mentioned yesterday?"

"There was no need to consider."

"Why not?"

"None of them suits me."

"What then suits you?"

Leo let it pass because he could give only a confused answer.

Without waiting for a reply, Salzman asked, "You remember this girl I talked to you—the high school teacher?"

"Age thirty-two?"

But, surprisingly, Salzman's face lit in a smile. "Age twenty-nine."

Leo shot him a look. "Reduced from thirty-two?"

"A mistake," Salzman avowed. "I talked today with the dentist. He took me to his safety deposit box and showed me the birth certificate. She was twenty-nine years last August. They made her a party in the mountains where she went for her vacation. When her father spoke to me the first time I forgot to write the age and I told you thirty-two, but now I remember this was a different client, a widow."

"The same one you told me about? I thought she was twenty-four?"

"A different. Am I responsible that the world is filled with widows?"

"No, but I'm not interested in them, nor for that matter, in school teachers."

Salzman pulled his clasped hand to his breast. Looking at the ceiling he devoutly exclaimed, "Yiddishe kinder, what can I say to somebody that he is not interested in high school teachers? So what then you are interested?"

Leo flushed but controlled himself.

"In what else will you be interested," Salzman went on, "if you not interested in this fine girl that she speaks four languages and has personally in the bank ten thousand dollars? Also her father guarantees further twelve thousand. Also she has a new car, wonderful clothes, talks on all subjects and she will give you a first-class home and children. How near do we come in our life to paradise?"

"If she's so wonderful, why wasn't she married ten years ago?"

"Why?" said Salzman with a heavy laugh. "—Why? Because she is *partikiler*. This is why. She wants the *best*."

Leo was silent, amused at how he had entangled himself. But Salzman had aroused his interest in Lily H., and he began seriously to consider calling on her. When the marriage broker observed how intently Leo's mind was at work on the facts he supplied, he felt certain they would soon come to an agreement.

Late Saturday afternoon, conscious of Salzman, Leo Finkle walked with Lily Hirschorn along Riverside Drive. He walked briskly and erectly, wearing with distinction the black fedora he had that morning taken with trepidation out of the dusty hat box on his closet shelf, and the heavy black Saturday coat he had thoroughly whisked clean. Leo also owned a walking stick, a present from a distant relative, but quickly put temptation aside and did not use it. Lily, petite and not unpretty, had on something signifying the approach of spring. She was au courant, animatedly, with all sorts of subjects, and he weighed her words and found her surprisingly sound— score another for Salzman, whom he uneasily sensed to be somewhere around, hiding perhaps high in a tree along the street, flashing the lady signals with a pocket mirror; or perhaps a clovenhoofed Pan, piping nuptial ditties as he danced his invisible way before them, strewing wild buds on the walk and purple grapes in their path, symbolizing fruit of a union, though there was of course still none.

Lily startled Leo by remarking, "I was thinking of Mr. Salzman, a curious figure, wouldn't you say?"

Not certain what to answer, he nodded.

She bravely went on, blushing, "I for one am grateful for his introducing us. Aren't you?"

He courteously replied, "I am."

"I mean," she said with a little laugh—and it was all in good taste, or at least gave the effect of being not in bad—"do you mind that we came together so?"

He was not displeased with her honesty, recognizing that she meant to set the relationship aright, and understanding that it took a certain amount of experience in life, and courage, to want to do it quite that way. One had to have some sort of past to make that kind of beginning.

He said that he did not mind. Salzman's function was traditional and honorable—valuable for what it might achieve, which, he pointed out, was frequently nothing.

Lily agreed with a sigh. They walked on for a while and she said after a long silence, again with a nervous laugh, "Would you mind if I asked you something a little bit personal? Frankly, I find the subject fascinating." Although Leo shrugged, she went on half embarrassedly, "How was it that you came to your calling? I mean was it a sudden passionate inspiration?"

Leo, after a time, slowly replied. "I was always interested in the Law."

"You saw revealed in it the presence of the Highest?"

He nodded and changed the subject. "I understand that you spent a little time in Paris, Miss Hirschorn?"

"Oh, did Mr. Salzman tell you, Rabbi Finkle?" Leo winced but she went on, "It was ages ago and almost forgotten. I remember I had to return for my sister's wedding."

And Lily would not be put off. "When," she asked in a trembly voice, "did you become enamored of God?"

He stared at her. Then it came to him that she was talking not about Leo Finkle, but of a total stranger, some mystical figure, perhaps even passionate prophet that Salzman had dreamed up for her—no relation to the living or dead. Leo trembled with rage and weakness. The trickster had obviously sold her a bill of goods, just as he had him, who'd expected to become acquainted with a young lady of twenty-nine, only to behold, the moment he laid eyes upon her strained and anxious face, a woman past thirty-five and aging rapidly. Only his self control had kept him this long in her presence.

"I am not," he said gravely, "a talented religious person," and in seeking words to go on, found himself possessed by shame and fear. "I think," he said in a strained manner, "that I came to God not because I loved Him, but because I did not."

This confession he spoke harshly because its unexpectedness shook him.

Lily wilted. Leo saw a profusion of loaves of bread go flying like ducks high over his head, not unlike the winged loaves by which he had counted himself to sleep last night. Mercifully, then, it snowed, which he would not put past Salzman's machinations.

He was infuriated with the marriage broker and swore he would throw him out of the room the minute he reappeared. But Salzman did not come that night, and when Leo's anger had subsided, an unaccountable despair grew in its place. At first he thought this was caused by his disappointment in Lily, but before long it became evident that he had involved himself with Salzman without a true knowledge of his own intent. He gradually realized—with an emptiness that seized him with six hands—that he had called in the broker to find him a bride because he was incapable of doing it himself. This terrifying insight he had derived as a result of his meeting and conversation with Lily Hirschorn. Her probing questions had somehow irritated him into revealing—to himself more than her—the true nature of his relationship to God, and from that it had come upon him, with shocking force, that apart from his parents, he had never loved anyone. Or perhaps it went the other way, that he did not love God so well as he might, because he had not loved man. It seemed to Leo that his whole life stood starkly revealed and he saw himself for the first time as he truly was—unloved and loveless. This bitter but somehow not fully unexpected revelation brought him to a point of panic, controlled only by extraordinary effort. He covered his face with his hands and cried.

The week that followed was the worst of his life. He did not eat and lost weight. His beard darkened and grew ragged. He stopped attending seminars and almost never opened a book. He seriously considered leaving the Yeshivah, although he was deeply troubled at the thought of the loss of all his years of study—saw them like pages torn from a book, strewn over the city—and at the devastating effect of his decision upon his parents. But he had lived without knowledge of himself, and never in the Five Books and all the Commentaries—mea culpa—had the truth been revealed to him. He did not know where to turn, and in all this desolating loneliness there was no *to whom,* although he often thought of Lily but not once could bring himself to go downstairs and make the call. He became touchy and irritable, especially with his landlady, who asked him all manner of personal questions; on the other hand, sensing his own disagreeableness, he waylaid her on the stairs and apologized abjectly, until mortified, she ran from him. Out of this, however, he drew the consolation that he was a Jew and that a Jew suffered. But gradually, as the long and terrible week drew to a close, he regained his composure and some idea of purpose in life: to go on as planned. Although he was imperfect, the ideal was not. As for his quest for a bride, the thought of continuing afflicted him with anxiety and heartburn, yet perhaps with this new knowledge of himself he would be more successful than in the past. Perhaps love would now come to him and a bride to that love. And for this sanctified seeking who needed a Salzman?

The marriage broker, a skeleton with haunted eyes, returned that very night. He looked, withal, the picture of frustrated expectancy—as if he had steadfastly waited the week at Miss Lily Hirschorn's side for a telephone call that never came.

Casually coughing, Salzman came immediately to the point: "So how did you like her?"

Leo's anger rose and he could not refrain from chiding the matchmaker: "Why did you lie to me, Salzman?"

Salzman's pale face went dead white, the world had snowed on him.

"Did you not state that she was twenty-nine?" Leo insisted.

"I give you my word—"

"She was thirty-five, if a day. *At least* thirty-five."

"Of this don't be too sure. Her father told me—"

"Never mind. The worst of it was that you lied to her."

"How did I lie to her, tell me?"

"You told her things about me that weren't true. You made me out to be more, consequently less than I am. She had in mind a totally different person, a sort of semi-mystical Wonder Rabbi."

"All I said, you was a religious man."

"I can imagine."

Salzman sighed. "This is my weakness that I have," he confessed. "My wife says to me I shouldn't be a salesman, but when I have two fine people that they would be wonderful to be married, I am so happy that I talk too much." He smiled wanly. "This is why Salzman is a poor man."

Leo's anger left him. "Well, Salzman, I'm afraid that's all."

The marriage broker fastened hungry eyes on him. "You don't want any more a bride?"

"I do," said Leo, "but I have decided to seek her in a different way. I am no longer interested in an arranged marriage. To be frank, I now admit the necessity of premarital love. That is, I want to be in love with the one I marry."

"Love?" said Salzman, astounded. After a moment he remarked, "For us, our love is our life, not for the ladies. In the ghetto they—"

"I know, I know," said Leo. "I've thought of it often. Love, I have said to myself, should be a by-product of living and worship rather than its own end. Yet for myself I find it necessary to establish the level of my need and fulfill it."

Salzman shrugged but answered, "Listen, rabbi, if you want love, this I can find for you also. I have such beautiful clients that you will love them the minute your eyes will see them."

Leo smiled unhappily. "I'm afraid you don't understand."

But Salzman hastily unstrapped his portfolio and withdrew a manila packet from it.

"Pictures," he said, quickly laying the envelope on the table.

Leo called after him to take the pictures away, but as if on the wings of the wind, Salzman had disappeared.

March came. Leo had returned to his regular routine. Although he felt not quite himself yet—lacked energy—he was making plans for a more active social life. Of course it would cost something, but he was an expert in cutting corners; and when there were no corners left he would make circles rounder. All the while Salzman's pictures had lain on the table, gathering dust. Occasionally as Leo sat studying, or enjoying a cup of tea, his eyes fell on the manila envelope, but he never opened it.

The days went by and no social life to speak of developed with a member of the opposite sex—it was difficult, given the circumstances of his situation. One morning Leo toiled up the stairs to his room and stared out the window at the city. Although the day was bright his view of it was dark. For some time he watched the people in the street below hurrying along and then turned with a heavy heart to his little room. On the table was the packet. With a sudden relentless gesture he tore it open. For a half-hour he stood by the table in a state of excitement, examining the photographs of the ladies Salzman had included. Finally, with a deep sigh he put them down. There were six, of varying degrees of attractiveness, but look at them long enough and they all became Lily Hirschorn: all past their prime, all starved behind bright smiles, not a true personality in the lot. Life, despite their frantic yoohooings, had passed them by; they were pictures in a brief case that stank of fish. After a while, however, as Leo attempted to return the photographs into the envelope, he found in it another, a snapshot of the type taken by a machine for a quarter. He gazed at it a moment and let out a cry.

Her face deeply moved him. Why, he could at first not say. It gave him the impression of youth—spring flowers, yet age—a sense of having been used to the bone, wasted; this came from the eyes, which were hauntingly familiar, yet absolutely strange. He had a vivid impression that he had met her before, but try as he might he could not place her although he could almost recall her name, as if he had read it in her own handwriting. No, this couldn't be; he would have remembered her. It was not, he affirmed, that she had extraordinary beauty—no, though her face was attractive enough; it was that *something* about her moved him. Feature for feature, even some of the ladies of the photographs could do better; but she leaped forth to his heart—had *lived,* or wanted to—more than just wanted, perhaps regretted how she had lived—had somehow deeply suffered: it could be seen in the depths of those reluctant eyes, and from the way the light enclosed and shone from her, and within her, opening realms of possibility: this was her own. Her he desired. His head ached and eyes narrowed with the intensity of his gazing, then as if an obscure fog had blown up in the mind, he experienced fear of her and was aware that he had received an impression, somehow, of evil. He shuddered, saying softly, it is thus with us all. Leo brewed some tea in a small pot and sat sipping it without sugar, to calm himself. But before he had finished drinking, again with excitement he examined the face and found it good: good for Leo Finkle. Only such a one could understand him and help him seek whatever he was seeking. She might, perhaps love him. How she had happened to be among the discards in Salzman's barrel he could never guess, but he knew he must urgently find her.

Leo rushed downstairs, grabbed up the Bronx telephone book, and searched for Salzman's home address. He was not listed, nor was his office. Neither was he in the Manhattan book. But Leo remembered having written down the address on a slip of paper after he had read Salzman's advertisement in the "personals" column of the *Forward.* He ran up to his room and tore through his papers, without luck. It was exasperating. Just when he needed the matchmaker he was nowhere to be found. Fortunately Leo remembered to look in his wallet. There on a card he found his name written and a Bronx address. No phone number was listed, the reason—Leo now recalled—he had originally communicated with Salzman by letter. He got on his coat, put a hat on over his skull cap and hurried to the subway station. All the way to the far end of the Bronx he sat on the edge of his seat. He was more than once tempted to take out the picture and see if the girl's face was as he remembered it, but he refrained, allowing the snapshot to remain in his inside coat pocket, content to have her so close. When the train pulled into the station he was waiting at the door and bolted out. He quickly located the street Salzman had advertised.

The building he sought was less than a block from the subway, but it was not an office building, nor even a loft, nor a store in which one could rent office space. It was a very old tenement house. Leo found Salzman's name in pencil on a soiled tag under the bell and climbed three dark flights to his apartment. When he knocked, the door was opened by a thin, asthmatic, gray-haired woman, in felt slippers.

"Yes?" she said, expecting nothing. She listened without listening. He could have sworn he had seen her, too, before but knew it was an illusion.

"Salzman—does he live here? Pinye Salzman," he said, "the matchmaker?"

She stared at him a long minute. "Of course."

He felt embarrassed. "Is he in?"

"No." Her mouth, though left open, offered nothing more.

"The matter is urgent. Can you tell me where his office is?"

"In the air." She pointed upward.

"You mean he has no office?" Leo asked.

"In his socks."

He peered into the apartment. It was sunless and dingy, one large room divided by a half-open curtain, beyond which he could see a sagging metal bed: The near side of a room was crowded with rickety chairs, old bureaus, a three-legged table, racks of cooking utensils, and all the apparatus of a kitchen. But there was no sign of Salzman or his magic barrel, probably also a figment of the imagination. An odor of frying fish made Leo weak to the knees.

"Where is he?" he insisted. "I've got to see your husband."

At length she answered, "So who knows where he is? Every time he thinks a new thought he runs to a different place. Go home, he will find you."

"Tell him Leo Finkle."

She gave no sign she had heard.

He walked downstairs, depressed.

But Salzman, breathless, stood waiting at his door.

Leo was astounded and overjoyed. "How did you get here before me?"

"I rushed."

"Come inside."

They entered. Leo fixed tea, and a sardine sandwich for Salzman. As they were drinking he reached behind him for the packet of pictures and handed them to the marriage broker.

Salzman put down his glass and said expectantly, "You found somebody you like?"

"Not among these."

The marriage broker turned away.

"Here is the one I want." Leo held forth the snapshot.

Salzman slipped on his glasses and took the picture into his trembling hand. He turned ghastly and let out a groan.

"What's the matter?" cried Leo.

"Excuse me. Was an accident this picture. She isn't for you."

Salzman frantically shoved the manila packet into his portfolio. He thrust the snapshot into his pocket and fled down the stairs.

Leo, after momentary paralysis, gave chase and cornered the marriage broker in the vestibule. The landlady made hysterical outcries but neither of them listened.

"Give me back the picture, Salzman."

"No." The pain in his eyes was terrible.

"Tell me who she is then."

"This I can't tell you. Excuse me."

He made to depart, but Leo forgetting himself, seized the matchmaker by his tight coat and shook him frenziedly.

"Please," sighed Salzman. *"Please."*

Leo ashamedly let him go. "Tell me who she is," he begged, "It's very important for me to know."

"She is not for you. She is a wild one—wild, without shame. This is not a bride for a rabbi."

"What do you mean wild?"

"Like an animal. Like a dog. For her to be poor was a sin. This is why to me she is dead now."

"In God's name, what do you mean?"

"Her I can't introduce to you," Salzman cried.

"Why are you so excited?"

"Why, he asks," Salzman said, bursting into tears. "This is my baby, my Stella, she should burn in hell."

Leo hurried up to bed and hid under the covers. Under the covers he thought his life through. Although he soon fell asleep he could not sleep her out of his mind. He woke, beating his breast. Though he prayed to be rid of her, his prayers went unanswered. Through days of torment he endlessly struggled not to love her; fearing success, he escaped it. He then concluded to convert her to goodness, himself to God. The idea alternately nauseated and exalted him.

He perhaps did not know that he had come to a final decision until he encountered Salzman in a Broadway cafeteria. He was sitting alone at a rear table, sucking the bony remains of a fish. The marriage broker appeared haggard, and transparent to the point of vanishing.

Salzman looked up at first without recognizing him. Leo had grown a pointed beard and his eyes were weighted with wisdom.

"Salzman," he said, "love has at last come to my heart."

"Who can love from a picture?" mocked the marriage broker.

"It is not impossible."

"If you can love her, then you can love anybody. Let me show you some new clients that they just sent me their photographs. One is a little doll."

"Just her I want," Leo murmured.

"Don't be a fool, doctor. Don't bother with her."

"Put me in touch with her, Salzman," Leo said humbly. "Perhaps I can be of service."

Salzman had stopped eating and Leo understood with emotion that it was now arranged.

Leaving the cafeteria, he was, however, afflicted by a tormenting suspicion that Salzman had planned it all to happen this way.

Leo was informed by letter that she would meet him on a certain corner, and she was there one spring night, waiting under a street lamp. He appeared carrying a small bouquet of violets and rosebuds. Stella stood by the lamp post, smoking. She wore white with red shoes, which fitted his expectations, although in a troubled moment he had imagined the dress red, and only the shoes white. She waited uneasily and shyly. From afar he saw that her eyes—clearly her father's—were filled with desperate innocence. He pictured, in her, his own redemption. Violins and lit candles revolved in the sky. Leo ran forward with flowers out-thrust.

Around the corner, Salzman, leaning against a wall, chanted prayers for the dead.

Exercises

1. We don't learn of Finkle's initial impression of Lily Hirschorn until he tells us at the *end* of the date. What does this imply?

2. Does love have to come before marriage or is it better to have an arranged marriage? Why do you answer as you do?

3. What is your prognosis for this marriage? Will it succeed or fail? Why?

LIFE, FRIENDS, IS BORING. WE MUST NOT SAY SO

John Berryman (1914–1972)

Berryman, like many other artists, saw the middle years of the century as a dreary procession of wars and other calamities. With his formally designed poetry he tried to relieve some of his personal anguish while making some kind of order in a disorderly world, a world that was worse than absurd; it was boring. Only three years after a critic had observed that Berryman "had come to poetic terms with the wreck of the modern world," the poet leaped to his death from a bridge in Minneapolis.

Life, friends, is boring. We must not say so.
After all, the sky flashes, the great sea yearns,
we ourselves flash and yearn,
and moreover my mother told me as a boy
(repeatedly) "Ever to confess you're bored
means you have no

Inner Resources." I conclude now I have no
inner resources, because I am heavy bored.
Peoples bore me,
literature bores me, especially great literature,
Henry bores me, with his plights & gripes
as bad as achilles,

who loves people and valiant art, which bores me.
And the tranquil hills, & gin, look like a drag
and somehow a dog
has taken itself & its tail considerably away
into mountains or sea or sky, leaving
behind: me, wag.

Exercises

1. Describe the missing "Inner Resources."
2. Why is great literature more boring than everyday literature?
3. Why the juxtaposition of "tranquil hills" and "gin"?

DEER IN THE WORKS

Kurt Vonnegut (b. 1922)

Mindless, destructive progress is the theme of the following satirical short story by Kurt Vonnegut. As part of a corporate entity with "federal" and "apparatus" in its title, the "Ilium Works" (Ilium is another name for ancient Troy), whose claim to fame is size ("second-largest industrial plant in America") makes unspecified things to meet "armament contracts." Pitted against a plant which "spewed acid fumes and soot" is a young journalist who has to settle for a job in promotion and publicity. Much like the naive journalist, a deer wanders into the "works," upsetting the routine and inviting the destruction accorded the environment. A deer is impeding progress? Shoot the deer!

The big black stacks of the Ilium Works of the Federal Apparatus Corporation spewed acid fumes and soot over the hundreds of men and women who were lined up before the red-brick employment office. It was summer. The Ilium Works, already the second-largest industrial plant in America, was increasing its staff by one third in order to meet armament contracts. Every ten minutes or so, a company policeman opened the employment-office door, letting out a chilly gust from the air-conditioned interior and admitting three more applicants.

"Next three," said the policeman.

A middle-sized man in his late twenties, his young face camouflaged with a mustache and spectacles, was admitted after a four-hour wait. His spirits and the new suit he'd bought for the occasion were wilted by the fumes and the August sun, and he'd given up lunch in order to keep his place in line. But his bearing remained jaunty. He was the last, in his group of three, to face the receptionist.

"Screw-machine operator, ma'am," said the first man.

"See Mr. Cormody in booth seven," said the receptionist.

"Plastic extrusion, miss," said the next man.

"See Mr. Hoyt in booth two," she said. "Skill?" she asked the urbane young man in the wilted suit. "Milling machine? Jig borer?"

"Writing," he said. "Any kind of writing."

"You mean advertising and sales promotion?"

"Yes—that's what I mean."

She looked doubtful. "Well, I don't know. We didn't put out a call for that sort of people. You can't run a machine, can you?"

"Typewriter," he said jokingly.

The receptionist was a sober young woman. "The company does not use male stenographers," she said. "See Mr. Dilling in booth twenty-six. He just might know of some advertising-and-sales-promotion-type job."

He straightened his tie and coat, forced a smile that implied he was looking into jobs at the Works as sort of a lark. He walked into booth twenty-six and extended his hand to Mr. Dilling, a man of his own age. "Mr. Dilling, my name is David Potter. I was curious to know what openings you might have in advertising and sales promotion, and thought I'd drop in for a talk."

Mr. Dilling, an old hand at facing young men who tried to hide their eagerness for a job, was polite but outwardly unimpressed. "Well, you came at a bad time, I'm afraid, Mr. Potter. The competition for that kind of job is pretty stiff, as you perhaps know, and there isn't much of anything open just now."

David nodded. "I see." He had had no experience in asking for a job with a big organization, and Mr. Dilling was making him aware of what a fine art it was—if you couldn't run a machine. A duel was under way.

"But have a seat anyway, Mr. Potter."

"Thank you." He looked at his watch. "I really ought to be getting back to my paper soon."

"You work on a paper around here?"

"Yes, I own a weekly paper in Dorset, about ten miles from Ilium."

"Oh—you don't say. Lovely little village. Thinking of giving up the paper, are you?"

"Well, no—not exactly. It's a possibility. I bought the paper soon after the war, so I've been with it for eight years, and I don't want to go stale. I might be wise to move on. It all depends on what opens up."

"You have a family?" said Mr. Dilling pleasantly.

"Yes. My wife, and two boys and two girls."

"A nice, big, well-balanced family," said Mr. Dilling. "And you're so young, too."

"Twenty-nine," said David. He smiled. "We didn't plan it to be quite that big. It's run to twins. The boys are twins, and then, several days ago, the girls came."

"You don't say!" said Mr. Dilling. He winked. "That would certainly start a young man thinking about getting a little security, eh, with a family like that?"

Both of them treated the remark casually, as though it were no more than a pleasantry between two family men. "It's what we wanted, actually, two boys, two girls," said David. "We didn't expect to get them this quickly, but we're glad now. As far as security goes—well, maybe I flatter myself, but I think the administrative and writing experience I've had running the paper would be worth a good bit to the right people, if something happened to the paper."

"One of the big shortages in this country," said Dilling philosophically, concentrating on lighting a cigarette, "is men who know how to do things, and know how to take responsibility and get things done. I only wish there were better openings in advertising and sales promotion than the ones we've got. They're important, interesting jobs, understand, but I don't know how you'd feel about the starting salary."

"Well, I'm just trying to get the lay of the land, now—to see how things are. I have no idea what salary industry might pay a man like me, with my experience."

"The question experienced men like yourself usually ask is: how high can I go and how fast? And the answer to that is that the sky is the limit for a man with drive and creative ambition. And he can go up fast or slow, depending on what he's willing to do and capable of putting into the job. We might start out a man like you at, oh, say, a hundred dollars a week, but that isn't to say you'd be stuck at that level for two years or even two months."

"I suppose a man could keep a family on that until he got rolling," said David.

"You'd find the work in the publicity end just about the same as what you're doing now. Our publicity people have high standards for writing and editing and reporting, and our publicity releases don't wind up in newspaper editors' wastebaskets. Our people do a professional job, and are well-respected as journalists." He stood. "I've got a little matter to attend to—take me about ten minutes. Could you possibly stick around? I'm enjoying our talk."

David looked at his watch. "Oh—guess I could spare another ten or fifteen minutes."

Dilling was back in his booth in three minutes, chuckling over some private joke. "Just talking on the phone with Lou Flammer, the publicity supervisor. Needs a new stenographer. Lou's a card. Everybody here is crazy about Lou. Old weekly man himself, and I guess that's where he learned to be so easy to get along with. Just to feel him out for the hell of it, I told him about you. I didn't commit you to anything—just said what you told me, that you were keeping your eyes open. And guess what Lou said?"

"Guess what, Nan," said David Potter to his wife on the telephone. He was wearing only his shorts, and was phoning from the company hospital. "When you come home from the hospital tomorrow, you'll be coming home to a solid citizen who pulls down a hundred and ten dollars a week, *every* week. I just got my badge and passed my physical!"

"Oh?" said Nan, startled. "It happened awfully fast, didn't it? I didn't think you were going to plunge right in."

"What's there to wait for?"

"Well—I don't know. I mean, how do you know what you're getting into? You've never worked for anybody but yourself, and don't know anything about getting along in a huge organization. I knew you were going to talk to the Ilium people about a job, but I thought you planned to stick with the paper another year, anyway."

"In another year I'll be thirty, Nan."

"Well?"

"That's pretty old to be starting a career in industry. There are guys my age here who've been working their way up for ten years. That's pretty stiff competition, and it'll be that much stiffer a year from now. And how do we know Jason will still want to buy the paper a year from now?" Ed Jason was David's assistant, a recent college graduate whose father wanted to buy the paper for him. "And this job that opened up today in publicity won't be open a year from now, Nan. Now was the time to switch—this afternoon!"

Nan sighed. "I suppose. But it doesn't seem like you. The Works are fine for some people; they seem to thrive on that life. But you've always been so free. And you love the paper—you know you do."

"I do," said David, "and it'll break my heart to let it go. It was a swell thing to do when we had no kids, but it's a shaky living now—with the kids to educate and all."

"But, hon," said Nan, "the paper is making money."

"It could fold like that," said David, snapping his fingers. "A daily could come in with a one-page insert of Dorset news,

or—"

"Dorset likes its little paper too much to let that happen. They like you and the job you're doing too much."

David nodded. "What about ten years from now?"

"What about ten years from now in the Works? What about ten years from now anywhere?"

"It's a better bet that the Works will still be here. I haven't got the right to take long chances any more, Nan, not with a big family counting on me."

"It won't be a very happy big family, darling, if you're not doing what you want to do. I want you to go on being happy the way you have been—driving around the countryside, getting news and talking and selling ads; coming home and writing what you want to write, what you believe in. You in the Works!"

"It's what I've got to do."

"All right, if you say so. I've had my say."

"It's still journalism, high-grade journalism," said David.

"Just don't sell the paper to Jason right away. Put him in charge, but let's wait a month or so, please?"

"No sense in waiting, but if you really want to, all right." David held up a brochure he'd been handed after his physical examination was completed. "Listen to this, Nan: under the company Security Package, I get ten dollars a day for hospital expenses in case of illness, full pay for twenty-six weeks, a hundred dollars for special hospital expenses. I get life insurance for about half what it would cost on the outside. For whatever I put into government bonds under the payroll-savings plan, the company will give me a five per cent bonus in company stock—twelve years from now. I get two weeks' vacation with pay each year, and after fifteen years, I get three weeks. Get free membership in the company country club. After twenty-five years, I'll be eligible for a pension of at least a hundred and twenty-five dollars a month, and much more if I rise in the organization and stick with it for more than twenty-five years!"

"Good heavens!" said Nan.

"I'd be a damn fool to pass that up, Nan."

"I still wish you'd waited until the little girls and I were home and settled, and you got used to them. I feel you were panicked into this."

"No, no—this is it, Nan. Give the little girls a kiss apiece for me. I've got to go now, and report to my new supervisor."

"Your what?"

"Supervisor."

"Oh. I thought that's what you said, but I couldn't be sure."

"Good-by, Nan."

"Good-by, David."

David clipped his badge to his lapel, and stepped out of the hospital and onto the hot asphalt floor of the world within the fences of the Works. Dull thunder came from the buildings around him, a truck honked at him, and a cinder blew in his eye. He dabbed at the cinder with a corner of his handkerchief and finally got it out. When his vision was restored, he looked about himself for Building 31, where his new office and supervisor were. Four busy streets fanned out from where he stood, and each stretched seemingly to infinity.

He stopped a passerby who was in less of a desperate hurry than the rest. "Could you tell me, please, how to find Building 31, Mr. Flammer's office?"

The man he asked was old and bright-eyed, apparently getting as much pleasure from the clangor and smells and nervous activity of the Works as David would have gotten from April in Paris. He squinted at David's badge and then at his face. "Just starting out, are you?"

"Yes sir. My first day."

"What do you know about that?" The old man shook his head wonderingly, and winked. "Just starting out. Building 31? Well, sir, when I first came to work here in 1899, you could see Building 31 from here, with nothing between us and it but mud. Now it's all built up. See that water tank up there, about a quarter of a mile? Well, Avenue 17 branches off there, and you follow that almost to the end, then cut across the tracks, and—Just starting out, eh? Well, I'd better walk you up there. Came here for just a minute to talk to the pension folks, but that can wait. I'd enjoy the walk."

"Thank you."

"Fifty-year man, I was," he said proudly, and he led David up avenues and alleys, across tracks, over ramps and through tunnels, through buildings filled with spitting, whining, grumbling machinery, and down corridors with green walls and numbered black doors.

"Can't be a fifty-year man no more," said the old man pityingly. "Can't come to work until you're eighteen nowadays, and you got to retire when you're sixty-five." He poked his thumb under his lapel to make a small gold button protrude. On it was the number "50" superimposed on the company trademark. "Something none of you youngsters can look forward to wearing some day, no matter how much you want one."

"Very nice button," said David.

The old man pointed out a door. "Here's Flammer's office. Keep your mouth shut till you find out who's who and what *they* think. Good luck."

Lou Flammer's secretary was not at her desk, so David walked to the door of the inner office and knocked.

"Yes?" said a man's voice sweetly. "Please come in."

David opened the door. "Mr. Flammer?"

Lou Flammer was a short, fat man in his early thirties. He beamed at David. "What can I do to help you?"

"I'm David Potter, Mr. Flammer."

Flammer's Santa-Claus-like demeanor decayed. He leaned back, propped his feet on his desk top, and stuffed a cigar, which he'd concealed in his cupped hand, into his large mouth. "Hell—thought you were a scoutmaster." He looked at his desk clock, which was mounted in a miniature of the company's newest automatic dishwasher. "Boy scouts touring the Works. Supposed to stop in here fifteen minutes ago for me to give 'em a talk on scouting and industry. Fifty-six per cent of Federal Apparatus' executives were eagle scouts."

David started to laugh, but found himself doing it all alone, and he stopped. "Amazing figure," he said.

"It *is*," said Flammer judiciously. "Says something for scouting and something for industry. Now, before I tell you where your desk is, I'm supposed to explain the rating-sheet system. That's what the Manuals say. Dilling tell you about that?"

"Not that I recall. There was an awful lot of information all at once."

"Well, there's nothing much to it," said Flammer. "Every six months a rating sheet is made out on you, to let you and to let us know just where you stand, and what sort of progress you've been making. Three people who've been close to your work make out independent ratings on you, and then all the information is brought together on a master copy—with carbons for you, me, and Personnel, and the original for the head of the Advertising and Sales Promotion Division. It's very helpful for everybody, you most of all, if you take it the right way." He waved a rating sheet before David. "See? Blanks for appearance, loyalty, promptness, initiative, cooperativeness—things like that. You'll make out rating sheets on other people, too, and whoever does the rating is anonymous."

"I see." David felt himself reddening with resentment. He fought the emotion, telling himself his reaction was a small-town man's—and that it would do him good to learn to think as a member of a great, efficient team.

"Now about pay, Potter," said Flammer, "there'll never be any point in coming in to ask me for a raise. That's all done on the basis of the rating sheets and the salary curve." He rummaged through his drawers and found a graph, which he spread out on his desk. "Here— now you see this curve? Well, it's the average salary curve for men with college educations in the company. See— you can follow it on up. At thirty, the average man makes this much; at forty, this much—and so on. Now, this curve above it shows what men with real growth potential can make. See? It's a little higher and curves upward a little faster. You're how old?"

"Twenty-nine," said David, trying to see what the salary figures were that ran along one side of the graph. Flammer saw him doing it, and pointedly kept them hidden with his forearm.

"Uh-huh." Flammer wet the tip of a pencil with his tongue, and drew a small "x" on the graph, squarely astride the average man's curve. "There *you* are!"

David looked at the mark, and then followed the curve with his eyes across the paper, over little bumps, up gentle slopes, along desolate plateaus, until it died abruptly at the margin which represented age sixty-five. The graph left no questions to be asked and was deaf to argument. David looked from it to the human being he would also be dealing with. "You had a weekly once, did you, Mr. Flammer?"

Flammer laughed. "In my naive, idealistic youth, Potter, I sold ads to feed stores, gathered gossip, set type, and wrote editorials that were going to save the world, by God."

David smiled admiringly, "What a circus, eh?"

"Circus?" said Flammer. "Freak show, maybe. It's a good way to grow up fast. Took me about six months to find out I was killing myself for peanuts, that a little guy couldn't even save a village three blocks long, and that the world wasn't worth saving anyway. So I started looking out for Number One. Sold out to a chain, came down here, and here I am."

The telephone rang. "Yes?" said Flammer sweetly. "Puh-*bliss*-itee." His benign smile faded. "No. You're kidding, aren't you? Where? Really—this is no gag? All right, Lord! What a time for this to happen. I haven't got anybody here, and I can't get away on account of the goddam boy scouts." He hung up. "Potter—you've got your first assignment. There's a deer loose in the Works!"

"Deer?"

"Don't know how he got in, but he's in. Plumber went to fix a drinking fountain out at the softball diamond across from Building 217, and flushed a deer out from under the bleachers. Now they got him cornered up around the metallurgy lab." He stood and hammered on his desk. "Murder! The story will go all over the country, Potter. Talk about human interest. Front page! Of all the times for Al Tappin to be out at the Ashtabula Works, taking pictures of a new viscometer they cooked up out there! All right—I'll call up a hack photographer downtown, Potter, and get him to meet you out by the metallurgy lab. You get the story and see that he gets the right shots. Okay?"

He led David into the hallway. "Just go back the way you came, turn left instead of right at fractional horsepower motors, cut through hydraulic engineering, catch bus eleven on Avenue 9, and it'll take you right there. After you get the story and pictures, we'll get them cleared by the law division, the plant security officer, our department head and buildings and grounds, and shoot them right out. Now get going. That deer isn't on the payroll—he isn't going to wait for you. Come to work today—tomorrow your work will be on every front page in the country, if we can get it approved. The name of the photographer you're going to meet is McGarvey. Got it? You're in the big time now, Potter. We'll all be watching." He shut the door behind David.

David found himself trotting down the hall, down a stairway, and into an alley, brushing roughly past persons in a race against time. Many turned to watch the purposeful young man with admiration.

On and on he strode, his mind seething with information: *Flammer, Building 31; deer, metallurgy lab; photographer. Al Tappin. No. Al Tappin in Ashtabula. Flenny the hack photographer. No. McCammer. No. McCammer is new supervisor. Fifty-six per cent eagle scouts. Deer by viscometer laboratory. No. Viscometer in Ashtabula. Call Danner, new supervisor, and get instructions right. Three weeks' vacation after fifteen*

years. Danner not new supervisor. Anyway, new supervisor in Building 319. No. Fanner in Building 39981983319.

David stopped, blocked by a grimy window at the end of a blind alley. All he knew was that he'd never been there before, that his memory had blown a gasket, and that the deer was not on the payroll. The air in the alley was thick with tango music and the stench of scorched insulation. David scrubbed away some of the crust on the window with his handkerchief, praying for a glimpse of something that made sense.

Inside were ranks of women at benches, rocking their heads in time to the music, and dipping soldering irons into great nests of colored wires that crept past them on endless belts. One of them looked up and saw David, and winked in tango rhythm. David fled.

At the mouth of the alley, he stopped a man and asked him if he'd heard anything about a deer in the Works. The man shook his head and looked at David oddly, making David aware of how frantic he must look. "I heard it was out by the lab," David said more calmly.

"Which lab?" said the man.

"That's what I'm not sure of," said David. "There's more than one?"

"Chemical lab?" said the man. "Materials testing lab? Print lab? Insulation lab?"

"No—I don't think it's any of those," said David.

"Well, I could stand here all afternoon naming labs, and probably not hit the right one. Sorry, I've got to go. You don't know what building they've got the differential analyzer in, do you?"

"Sorry," said David. He stopped several other people, none of whom knew anything about the deer, and he tried to retrace his steps to the office of his supervisor, whatever his name was. He was swept this way and that by the currents of the Works, stranded in backwaters, sucked back into the main stream, and his mind was more and more numbed, and the mere reflexes of self-preservation were more and more in charge.

He chose a building at random, and walked inside for a momentary respite from the summer heat, and was deafened by the clangor of steel sheets being cut and punched, being smashed into strange shapes by great hammers that dropped out of the smoke and dust overhead. A hairy, heavily muscled man was seated near the door on a wooden stool, watching a giant lathe turn a bar of steel the size of a silo.

David now had the idea of going through a company phone directory until he recognized his supervisor's name. He called to the machinist from a few feet away, but his voice was lost in the din. He tapped the man's shoulder. "Telephone around here?"

The man nodded. He cupped his hands around David's ear, and shouted. "Up that, and through the—" Down crashed a hammer. "Turn left and keep going until you—" An overhead crane dropped a stack of steel plates. "Four doors down from there is it. Can't miss it."

David, his ears ringing and his head aching, walked into the street again and chose another door. Here was peace and air conditioning. He was in the lobby of an auditorium, where a group of men were examining a box studded with dials and switches that was spotlighted and mounted on a revolving platform.

"Please, miss," he said to a receptionist by the door, "could you tell me where I could find a telephone?"

"It's right around the corner, sir," she said. "But I'm afraid no one is permitted here today but the crystallographers. Are you with them?"

"Yes," said David.

"Oh—well, come right in. Name?"

He told her, and a man sitting next to her lettered it on a badge. The badge was hung on his chest, and David headed for the telephone. A grinning, bald, big-toothed man, wearing a badge that said, "Stan Dunkel, Sales," caught him and steered him to the display.

"Dr. Potter," said Dunkel, "I ask you: is that the way to build a X-ray spectrogoniometer, or is that the way to build an X-ray spectrogoniometer?"

"Yes," said David. "That's the way, all right."

"Martini, Dr. Potter?" said a maid, offering a tray.

David emptied a Martini in one gloriously hot, stinging gulp.

"What features do you want in an X-ray spectrogoniometer, Doctor?" said Dunkel.

"It should be sturdy, Mr. Dunkel," said David, and he left Dunkel there, pledging his reputation that there wasn't a sturdier one on earth.

In the phone booth, David had barely got through the telephone directory's A's before the name of the supervisor miraculously returned to his consciousness: *Flammer!* He found the number and dialed.

"Mr. Flammer's office," said a woman.

"Could I speak to him, please? This is David Potter."

"Oh—Mr. Potter. Well, Mr. Flammer is somewhere out in the Works now, but he left a message for you. He said there's an added twist on the deer story. When they catch the deer, the venison is going to be used at the Quarter-Century Club picnic."

"Quarter-Century Club?" said David.

"Oh, that's really something, Mr. Potter. It's for people who've been with the company twenty-five years or more. Free drinks and cigars, and just the best of everything. They have a wonderful time."

"Anything else about the deer?"

"Nothing he hasn't already told you," she said, and she hung up.

David Potter, with a third Martini in his otherwise empty stomach, stood in front of the auditorium and looked both ways for a deer.

"But our X-ray spectogoniometer *is* sturdy, Dr. Potter," Stan Dunkel called to him from the auditorium steps.

Across the street was a patch of green, bordered by hedges. David pushed through the hedges into the outfield of a softball diamond. He crossed it and went behind the bleachers, where there was cool shade, and he sat down with his back to a wiremesh fence which separated one end of the Works from a deep pine woods. There were two gates in the fence, but both were wired shut.

David was going to sit there for just a moment, long enough to get his nerve back, to take bearings. Maybe he could leave a message for Flammer, saying he'd suddenly fallen ill, which was essentially true, or—

"There he goes!" cried somebody from the other side of the diamond. There were gleeful cries, shouted orders, the sounds of men running.

A deer with broken antlers dashed under the bleachers, saw David, and ran frantically into the open again along the fence. He ran with a limp, and his reddish-brown coat was streaked with soot and grease.

"Easy now! Don't rush him! Just keep him there. Shoot into the woods, not the Works."

David came out from under the bleachers to see a great semicircle of men, several ranks deep, closing in slowly on the corner of fence in which the deer was at bay. In the front rank were a dozen company policemen with drawn pistols. Other members of the posse carried sticks and rocks and lariats hastily fashioned from wire.

The deer pawed the grass, and bucked, and jerked its broken antlers in the direction of the crowd.

"Hold it!" shouted a familiar voice. A company limousine rumbled across the diamond to the back of the crowd. Leaning out of a window was Lou Flammer, David's supervisor. "Don't shoot until we get a picture of him alive," commanded Flammer. He pulled a photographer out of the limousine, and pushed him into the front rank.

Flammer saw David standing alone by the fence, his back to a gate. "Good boy, Potter," called Flammer. "Right on the ball! Photographer got lost, and I had to bring him here myself."

The photographer fired his flash bulbs. The deer bucked and sprinted along the fence toward David. David unwired the gate, opened it wide. A second later the deer's white tail was flashing through the woods and gone.

The profound silence was broken first by the whistling of a switch engine and then by the click of a latch as David stepped into the woods and closed the gate behind him. He didn't look back.

Exercises

1. Why is the protagonist named David?
2. Compare the company benefits with those David might have as the publisher of a small-town newspaper. What point is the author making about American life and private enterprise?
3. What was the significance of meeting a "fifty-year man"?
4. What is implied by Mr. Flammer's statement that 56 percent of the executives were Eagle scouts?
5. What are the implications of the categories on the rating sheets?
6. Review the different activities encountered by David as he looks for the deer. In which place would you like to work? Why or why not?
7. What will the firm do with the deer after it is killed? What does this imply?
8. Consider the significance of the scene with pursuers in full cry after the wounded deer. Is a deer a dangerous animal?
9. Would *you* let the deer go? Why or why not?

ADULTERY
James Dickey (b. 1923)

Sex in all its manifestations is a constant theme in all literature. The following poem by James Dickey extols the mystery and excitement of an adulterous affair for, as Dickey has written, "adultery seems to me to be the most potentially beautiful and fruitful relationship between men and women, and also the most calamitous and destructive." He goes on to point up the "paradox in the relationship of men and women: the more used to each other they are, the less exciting they are to each other." He feels that this is a terrible problem and things shouldn't be that way but, he concludes, "there *isn't* any justice in the world in that sense, and things *are* that way."

We have all been in rooms
We cannot die in, and they are odd places, and sad.
Often Indians are standing eagle-armed on hills

In the sunrise   open wide to the Great Spirit
Or gliding in canoes   or cattle are browsing on the
        walls
Far away   gazing down with the eyes of our children

Not far away   or there are men driving
The last railspike, which has turned
Gold in their hands. Gigantic forepleasure lives

Among such scenes, and we are alone with it
At last. There is always some weeping
Between us   and someone is always checking

A wrist watch by the bed to see how much
Longer we have left. Nothing can come
Of this   nothing can come

Of us: of me with my grim techniques
Or you who have sealed your womb
With a ring of convulsive rubber:

Although we come together,
Nothing will come of us. But we would not give
It up, for death is beaten

By praying Indians   by distant cows   historical
Hammers   by hazardous meetings that bridge
A continent. One could never die here

Never die   never die
While crying. My lover, my dear one
I will see you next week

When I'm in town. I will call you
If I can. Please get hold of   please don't
Oh God. Please don't any more I can't bear . . . Listen:

We have done it again   we are
Still living. Sit up and smile,
God bless you. Guilt is magical.

Exercises

1. Describe a room "we cannot die in."
2. Why does the poet use images of Indians "gliding in canoes" and cattle "browsing on the walls"?
3. Dickey refers to a railspike that has "turned gold" and later speaks of "historical hammers" and of bridging a continent. What actual event does he have in mind and what does this imply in the poem? Is there a double meaning here?
4. What is meant by the phrase "guilt is magical"?

Chapter 1
from ONE HUNDRED YEARS OF SOLITUDE
Gabriel Garcia Marquez (b. 1928)

Following is the first chapter of a novel which, according to the author, is completely lacking in seriousness. Gabriel Garcia Marquez intended, he says, to tell only the story of a family that lived in terror of incest and made every effort to avoid begetting a child with a pig's tail. Ultimately a monumental tour de force by a peerless spinner of yarns, *One Hundred Years of Solitude* relates the story of Macondo, founded in a world "so recent that many things lacked names," a village that, in seven generations, evolved from Eden to the Apocalypse. Historically, this tragi-comic novel is a synthesis of the various evils which have plagued much of South America from the revolts against Spanish rule to the ruthless exploitation by the United Fruit Company.

As a practitioner of absurd literature, Marquez fuses reality and fantasy using, among other things, hyperbole and preposterous distortions to negate reason and logic in order to reveal the discrepancies between human intentions and reality. In the selection given here José Arcadia Buendías, the credulous founder of Macondo, encounters the wonders of progress and modern science in the person of Melquíades, a "heavy gypsy" who, having died once and becoming bored with the solitude of death, is symbolically reborn with a new set of false teeth. In the climactic scene an ordinary object (ice), imbued with an aura of magic, represents both the advancement of science and the ultimate, inevitable destruction of Macondo by the banana boom. The book begins with one of the finest opening sentences in all literature.

Many years later, as he faced the firing squad, Colonel Aureliano Buendía was to remember that distant afternoon when his father took him to discover ice. At that time Macondo was a village of twenty adobe houses, built on the bank of a river of clear water that ran along a bed of polished stones, which were white and enormous, like prehistoric eggs. The world was so recent that many things lacked names, and in order to indicate them it was necessary to point. Every year during the month of March a family of ragged gypsies would set up their tents near the village, and with a great uproar of pipes and kettledrums they would display new inventions. First they brought the magnet. A heavy gypsy with an untamed beard and sparrow hands, who introduced himself as Melquíades, put on a bold public demonstration of what he himself called the eighth wonder of the learned alchemists of Macedonia. He went from house to house dragging two metal ingots and everybody was amazed to see pots, pans, tongs, and braziers tumble down from their places and beams creak from the desperation of nails and screws trying to emerge, and even objects that had been lost for a long time appeared from where they had been searched for most and went dragging along in turbulent confusion behind Melquíades' magical irons. "Things have a life of their own," the gypsy proclaimed with a harsh accent. "It's simply a matter of waking up their souls." José Arcadio Buendía, whose unbridled imagination always went beyond the genius of nature and even beyond miracles and magic, thought that it would be possible to make use of that useless invention to extract gold from the bowels of the earth. Melquíades, who was an honest man, warned him: "It won't work for that." But José Arcadio Buendía at that time did not believe in the honesty of gypsies, so he traded his mule and a pair of goats for the two magnetized ingots. Úrsula Iguarán, his wife, who relied on those animals to increase their poor domestic holdings, was unable to dissuade him. "Very soon we'll have gold enough and more to pave the floors of the house," her husband replied. For several months he worked hard to demonstrate the truth of his idea. He explored every inch of the region, even the riverbed, dragging the two iron ingots along and reciting Melquíades' incantation aloud. The only thing he succeeded in doing was to unearth a suit of fifteenth-century armor which had all of its pieces soldered together with rust and inside of which there was the hollow resonance of an enormous stone-filled gourd. When José Arcadio Buendía and the four men of his expedition managed to take the armor apart, they found inside a calcified skeleton with a copper locket containing a woman's hair around its neck.

In March the gypsies returned. This time they brought a telescope and a magnifying glass the size of a drum, which they exhibited as the latest discovery of the Jews of Amsterdam. They placed a gypsy woman at one end of the village and set up the telescope at the entrance to the tent. For the price of five reales, people could look into the telescope and see the gypsy woman an arm's length away. "Science has eliminated distance," Melquíades proclaimed. "In a short time, man will be able to see what is happening in any place in the world without leaving his own house." A burning noonday sun brought out a startling demonstration with the gigantic magnifying glass: they put a pile of dry hay in the middle of the street and set it on fire by concentrating the sun's rays. José Arcadio Buendía, who had still not been consoled for the failure of his magnets, conceived the idea of using that invention as a weapon of war. Again Melquíades tried to dissuade him, but he finally accepted the two magnetized ingots and three colonial coins in exchange for the magnifying glass. Úrsula wept in consternation. That money was from a chest of gold coins that her father had put together over an entire life of privation and that she had buried underneath her bed in hopes of a proper occasion to make use of it. José Arcadio Buendía made no attempt to console her, completely absorbed in his tactical experiments with the abnegation of a scientist and even at the risk of his own life. In an attempt to show the effects of the glass on enemy troops, he exposed himself to the concentration of the sun's rays and suffered burns which turned into sores that took a long time to heal. Over the protests of his wife, who was alarmed at such a dangerous invention, at one point he

was ready to set the house on fire. He would spend hours on end in his room, calculating the strategic possibilities of his novel weapon until he succeeded in putting together a manual of startling instructional clarity and an irresistible power of conviction. He sent it to the government, accompanied by numerous descriptions of his experiments and several pages of explanatory sketches, by a messenger who crossed the mountains, got lost in measureless swamps, forded stormy rivers, and was on the point of perishing under the lash of despair, plague, and wild beasts until he found a route that joined the one used by the mules that carried the mail. In spite of the fact that a trip to the capital was little less than impossible at that time, José Arcadio Buendía promised to undertake it as soon as the government ordered him to so that he could put on some practical demonstrations of his invention for the military authorities and could train them himself in the complicated art of solar war. For several years he waited for an answer. Finally, tired of waiting, he bemoaned to Melquíades the failure of his project and the gypsy then gave him a convincing proof of his honesty: he gave him back the doubloons in exchange for the magnifying glass, and he left him in addition some Portuguese maps and several instruments of navigation. In his own handwriting he set down a concise synthesis of the studies by Monk Hermann, which he left José Arcadio so that he would be able to make use of the astrolabe, the compass, and the sextant. José Arcadio Buendía spent the long months of the rainy season shut up in a small room that he had built in the rear of the house so that no one would disturb his experiments. Having completely abandoned his domestic obligations, he spent entire nights in the courtyard watching the course of the stars and he almost contracted sunstroke from trying to establish an exact method to ascertain noon. When he became an expert in the use and manipulation of his instruments, he conceived a notion of space that allowed him to navigate across unknown seas, to visit uninhabited territories, and to establish relations with splendid beings without having to leave his study. That was the period in which he acquired the habit of talking to himself, of walking through the house without paying attention to anyone, as Úrsula and the children broke their backs in the garden, growing banana and caladium, cassava and yams, ahuyama roots and eggplants. Suddenly, without warning, his feverish activity was interrupted and was replaced by a kind of fascination. He spent several days as if he were bewitched, softly repeating to himself a string of fearful conjectures without giving credit to his own understanding. Finally, one Tuesday in December, at lunchtime, all at once he released the whole weight of his torment. The children would remember for the rest of their lives the august solemnity with which their father, devastated by his prolonged vigil and by the wrath of his imagination, revealed his discovery to them:

"The earth is round, like an orange."

Úrsula lost her patience. "If you have to go crazy, please go crazy all by yourself!" she shouted. "But don't try to put your gypsy ideas into the heads of the children." José Arcadio Buendía, impassive, did not let himself be frightened by the desperation of his wife, who, in a seizure of rage, smashed the astrolabe against the floor. He built another one, he gathered the men of the village in his little room, and he demonstrated to them, with theories that none of them could understand, the possibility of returning to where one had set out by consistently sailing east. The whole village was convinced that José Arcadio Buendía had lost his reason, when Melquíades returned to set things straight. He gave public praise to the intelligence of a man who from pure astronomical speculation had evolved a theory that had already been proved in practice, although unknown in Macondo until then, and as a proof of his admiration he made him a gift that was to have a profound influence on the future of the village: the laboratory of an alchemist.

By then Melquíades had aged with surprising rapidity. On his first trips he seemed to be the same age as José Arcadio Buendía. But while the latter had preserved his extraordinary strength, which permitted him to pull down a horse by grabbing its ears, the gypsy seemed to have been worn down by some tenacious illness. It was, in reality, the result of multiple and rare diseases contracted on his innumerable trips around the world. According to what he himself said as he spoke to José Arcadio Buendía while helping him set up the laboratory, death followed him everywhere, sniffing at the cuffs of his pants, but never deciding to give him the final clutch of its claws. He was a fugitive from all the plagues and catastrophes that had ever lashed mankind. He had survived pellagra in Persia, scurvy in the Malayan archipelago, leprosy in Alexandria, beriberi in Japan, bubonic plague in Madagascar, an earthquake in Sicily, and a disastrous shipwreck in the Strait of Magellan. That prodigious creature, said to possess the keys of Nostradamus, was a gloomy man, enveloped in a sad aura, with an Asiatic look that seemed to know what there was on the other side of things. He wore a large black hat that looked like a raven with widespread wings, and a velvet vest across which the patina of the centuries had skated. But in spite of his immense wisdom and his mysterious breadth, he had a human burden, an earthly condition that kept him involved in the small problems of daily life. He would complain of the ailments of old age, he suffered from the most insignificant economic difficulties, and he had stopped laughing a long time back because scurvy had made his teeth drop out. On that suffocating noontime when the gypsy revealed his secrets, José Arcadio Buendía had the certainty that it was the beginning of a great friendship. The children were startled by his fantastic stories. Aureliano, who could not have been more than five at the time, would remember him for the rest of his life as he saw him that afternoon, sitting against the metallic and quivering light from the window, lighting up with his deep organ voice the darkest reaches of the imagination, while down over his temples there flowed the grease that was being melted by the heat. José Arcadio, his older brother, would pass on that wonderful image as a hereditary memory to all of his descendants. Ursula, on the other hand, held a bad memory of that visit, for she had entered the room just as Melquíades had carelessly broken a flask of bichloride of mercury.

"It's the smell of the devil," she said.

"Not at all," Melquíades corrected her. "It has been proven that the devil has sulphuric properties and this is just a little corrosive sublimate."

Always didactic, he went into a learned exposition of the diabolical properties of cinnabar, but Ursula paid no attention to him, although she took the children off to pray. That biting odor would stay forever in her mind linked to the memory of Melquíades.

The rudimentary laboratory—in addition to a profusion of pots, funnels, retorts, filters, and sieves—was made up of a primitive water pipe, a glass beaker with a long, thin neck, a reproduction of the philosopher's egg, and a still the gypsies themselves had built in accordance with modern descriptions of the three-armed alembic of Mary the Jew. Along with those items, Melquíades left samples of the seven metals that corresponded to the seven planets, the formulas of Moses and Zosimus for doubling the quantity of gold, and a set of notes and sketches concerning the processes of the Great Teaching that would permit those who could interpret them to undertake the manufacture of the philosopher's stone. Seduced by the simplicity of the formulas to double the quantity of gold, José Arcadio Buendía paid court to Ursula for several weeks so that she would let him dig up her colonial coins and increase them by as many times as it was possible to subdivide mercury. Ursula gave in, as always, to her husband's unyielding obstinacy. Then José Arcadio Buendía threw three doubloons into a pan and fused them with copper filings, orpiment, brimstone, and lead. He put it all to boil in a pot of castor oil until he got a thick and pestilential syrup which was more like common caramel than valuable gold. In risky and desperate processes of distillation, melted with the seven planetary metals, mixed with hermetic mercury and vitriol of Cyprus, and put back to cook in hog fat for lack of any radish oil, Ursula's precious inheritance was reduced to a large piece of burnt hog cracklings that was firmly stuck to the bottom of the pot.

When the gypsies came back, Ursula had turned the whole population of the village against them. But curiosity was greater than fear, for that time the gypsies went about the town making a deafening noise with all manner of musical instruments while a hawker announced the exhibition of the most fabulous discovery of the Naciancenes. So that everyone went to the tent and by paying one cent they saw a youthful Melquíades, recovered, unwrinkled, with a new and flashing set of teeth. Those who remembered his gums that had been destroyed by scurvy, his flaccid cheeks, and his withered lips trembled with fear at the final proof of the gypsy's supernatural power. The fear turned into panic when Melquíades took out his teeth, intact, encased in their gums, and showed them to the audience for an instant—a fleeting instant in which he went back to being the same decrepit man of years past—and put them back again and smiled once more with the full control of his restored youth. Even José Arcadio Buendía himself considered that Melquíades' knowledge had reached unbearable extremes, but he felt a healthy excitement when the gypsy explained to him alone the workings of his false teeth. It seemed so simple and so prodigious at the same time that overnight he lost all interest in his experiments in alchemy. He underwent a new crisis of bad humor. He did not go back to eating regularly, and he would spend the day walking through the house. "Incredible things are happening in the world," he said to Ursula. "Right there across the river there are all kinds of magical instruments while we keep on living like donkeys." Those who had known him since the foundation of Macondo were startled at how much he had changed under Melquíades' influence.

At first José Arcadio Buendía had been a kind of youthful patriarch who would give instructions for planting and advice for the raising of children and animals, and who collaborated with everyone, even in the physical work, for the welfare of the community. Since his house from the very first had been the best in the village, the others had been built in its image and likeness. It had a small, well-lighted living room, a dining room in the shape of a terrace with gaily colored flowers, two bedrooms, a courtyard with a gigantic chestnut tree, a well-kept garden, and a corral where goats, pigs, and hens lived in peaceful communion. The only animals that were prohibited, not just in his house but in the entire settlement, were fighting cocks.

Úrsula's capacity for work was the same as that of her husband. Active, small, severe, that woman of unbreakable nerves who at no moment in her life had been heard to sing seemed to be everywhere, from dawn until quite late at night, always pursued by the soft whispering of her stiff, starched petticoats. Thanks to her the floors of tamped earth, the unwhitewashed mud walls, the rustic, wooden furniture they had built themselves were always clean, and the old chests where they kept their clothes exhaled the warm smell of basil.

José Arcadio Buendía, who was the most enterprising man ever to be seen in the village, had set up the placement of the houses in such a way that from all of them one could reach the river and draw water with the same effort, and he had lined up the streets with such good sense that no house got more sun than another during the hot time of day. Within a few years Macondo was a village that was more orderly and hard-working than any known until then by its three hundred inhabitants. It was a truly happy village where no one was over thirty years of age and where no one had died.

Since the time of its founding, José Arcadio Buendía had built traps and cages. In a short time he filled not only his own house but all of those in the village with troupials, canaries, bee eaters, and redbreasts. The concert of so many different birds became so disturbing that Úrsula would plug her ears with beeswax so as not to lose her sense of reality. The first time that Melquíades' tribe arrived, selling glass balls for headaches, everyone was surprised that they had been able to find that village lost in the drowsiness of the swamp, and the gypsies confessed that they had found their way by the song of the birds.

That spirit of social initiative disappeared in a short time, pulled away by the fever of the magnets, the astronomical calculations, the dreams of transmutation, and the urge to discover the wonders of the world. From a clean and active man, José Arcadio Buendía changed into a man lazy in appearance, careless in his dress, with a wild beard that Úrsula managed to trim with great effort and a kitchen knife. There were many who considered him the victim of some strange spell. But even those most convinced of his madness left work and family to follow him when he brought out his tools to clear the land and asked the assembled group to open a way that would put Macondo in contact with the great inventions.

José Arcadio Buendía was completely ignorant of the geography of the region. He knew that to the east there lay an impenetrable mountain chain and that on the other side of the mountains there was the ancient city of Riohacha, where in times past—according to what he had been told by the first Aureliano Buendía, his grandfather—Sir Francis Drake had gone crocodile hunting with cannons and that he repaired them and stuffed them with straw to bring to Queen Elizabeth. In his youth, José Arcadio Buendía and his men, with wives and children, animals and all kinds of domestic implements, had crossed the mountains in search of an outlet to the sea, and after twenty-six months they gave up the expedition and founded Macondo, so they would not have to go back. It was, therefore, a route that did not interest him, for it could lead only to the past. To the south lay the swamps, covered with an eternal vegetable scum, and the whole vast universe of the great swamp, which, according to what the gypsies said, had no limits. The great swamp in the west mingled with a boundless extension of water where there were soft-skinned cetaceans that had the head and torso of a woman, causing the ruination of sailors with the charm of their extraordinary breasts. The gypsies sailed along that route for six months before they reached the strip of land over which the mules that carried the mail passed. According to José Arcadio Buendía's calculations, the only possibility of contact with civilization lay along the northern route. So he handed out clearing tools and hunting weapons to the same men who had been with him during the founding of Macondo. He threw his directional instruments and his maps into a knapsack, and he undertook the reckless adventure.

During the first days they did not come across any appreciable obstacle. They went down along the stony bank of the river to the place where years before they had found the soldier's armor, and from there they went into the woods along a path between wild orange trees. At the end of the first week they killed and roasted a deer, but they agreed to eat only half of it and salt the rest for the days that lay ahead. With that precaution they tried to postpone the necessity of having to eat macaws, whose blue flesh had a harsh and musky taste. Then, for more than ten days, they did not see the sun again. The ground became soft and damp, like volcanic ash, and the vegetation was thicker and thicker, and the cries of the birds and the uproar of the monkeys became more and more remote, and the world became eternally sad. The men on the expedition felt overwhelmed by their most ancient memories in that paradise of dampness and silence, going back to before original sin, as their boots sank into pools of steaming oil and their machetes destroyed bloody lilies and golden salamanders. For a week, almost without speaking, they went ahead like sleepwalkers through a universe of grief, lighted only by the tenuous reflection of luminous insects, and their lungs were overwhelmed by a suffocating smell of blood. They could not return because the strip that they were opening as they went along would soon close up with a new vegetation that almost seemed to grow before their eyes. "It's all right," José Arcadio Buendía would say. "The main thing is not to lose our bearings." Always following his compass, he kept on guiding his men toward the invisible north so that they would be able to get out of that enchanted region. It was a thick night, starless, but the darkness was becoming impregnated with a fresh and clear air. Exhausted by the long crossing, they hung up their hammocks and slept deeply for the first time in two weeks. When they woke up, with the sun already high in the sky, they were speechless with fascination. Before them, surrounded by ferns and palm trees, white and powdery in the silent morning light, was an enormous Spanish galleon. Tilted slightly to the starboard, it had hanging from its intact masts the dirty rags of its sails in the midst of its rigging, which was adorned with orchids. The hull, covered with an armor of petrified barnacles and soft moss, was firmly fastened into a surface of stones. The whole structure seemed to occupy its own space, one of solitude and oblivion, protected from the vices of time and the habits of the birds. Inside, where the expeditionaries explored with careful intent, there was nothing but a thick forest of flowers.

The discovery of the galleon, an indication of the proximity of the sea, broke José Arcadio Buendía's drive. He considered it a trick of his whimsical fate to have searched for the sea without finding it, at the cost of countless sacrifices and suffering, and to have found it all of a sudden without looking for it, as if it lay across his path like an insurmountable object. Many years later Colonel Aureliano Buendía crossed the region again, when it was already a regular mail route, and the only part of the ship he found was its burned-out frame in the midst of a field of poppies. Only then, convinced that the story had not been some product of his father's imagination, did he wonder how the galleon had been able to get inland to that spot. But José Arcadio Buendía did not concern himself with that when he found the sea after another four days' journey from the galleon. His dreams ended as he faced that ashen, foamy, dirty sea, which had not merited the risks and sacrifices of the adventure.

"God damn it!" he shouted. "Macondo is surrounded by water on all sides."

The idea of a peninsular Macondo prevailed for a long time, inspired by the arbitrary map that José Arcadio Buendía sketched on his return from the expedition. He drew it in rage, evilly, exaggerating the difficulties of communication, as if to punish himself for the absolute lack of sense with which he had chosen the place. "We'll never get anywhere," he lamented to Úrsula. "We're going to rot our lives away here without receiving the benefits of science." That certainty, mulled over for several months in the small room he used as his laboratory, brought him to the conception of the plan to move Macondo to a better place. But that time Úrsula had anticipated his feverish designs. With the secret and implacable labor of a small ant she predisposed the women of the village against the flightiness of their husbands, who were already preparing for the move. José Arcadio Buendía did not know at what moment or because of what adverse forces his plan had become enveloped in a web of pretexts, disappointments, and evasions until it turned into nothing but an illusion. Úrsula watched him with innocent attention and even felt some pity for him on the morning when she found him in the back room muttering about his plans for moving as he placed his laboratory pieces in their original boxes. She let him finish. She let him nail up the boxes and put his initials on them with an inked brush, without reproaching him, but knowing now that he knew (because she had heard him say so in his soft monologues) that the men of the village would not back him up in his undertaking. Only when he began to take down the door of the room did Úrsula dare ask him what he was doing, and he answered with a certain bitterness. "Since no one wants to leave, we'll leave all by ourselves." Úrsula did not become upset.

"We will not leave," she said. "We will stay here, because we have had a son here."

"We have still not had a death," he said. "A person does not belong to a place until there is someone dead under the ground."

Úrsula replied with a soft firmness:

"If I have to die for the rest of you to stay here, I will die."

José Arcadio Buendía had not thought that his wife's will was so firm. He tried to seduce her with the charm of his fantasy, with the promise of a prodigious world where all one had to do was sprinkle some magic liquid on the ground and the plants would bear fruit whenever a man wished, and where all manner of instruments against pain were sold at bargain prices. But Úrsula was insensible to his clairvoyance.

"Instead of going around thinking about your crazy inventions, you should be worrying about your sons," she replied. "Look at the state they're in, running wild just like donkeys."

José Arcadio Buendía took his wife's words literally. He looked out the window and saw the barefoot children in the sunny garden and he had the impression that only at that instant had they begun to exist, conceived by Úrsula's spell. Something occurred inside of him then, something mysterious and definitive that uprooted him from his own time and carried him adrift through an unexplored region of his memory. While Úrsula continued sweeping the house, which was safe now from being abandoned for the rest of her life, he stood there with an absorbed look, contemplating the children until his eyes became moist and he dried them with the back of his hand, exhaling a deep sigh of resignation.

"All right," he said. "Tell them to come help me take the things out of the boxes."

José Arcadio, the older of the children, was fourteen. He had a square head, thick hair, and his father's character. Although he had the same impulse for growth and physical strength, it was early evident that he lacked imagination. He had been conceived and born during the difficult crossing of the mountains, before the founding of Macondo, and his parents gave thanks to heaven when they saw he had no animal features. Aureliano, the first human being to be born in Macondo, would be six years old in March. He was silent and withdrawn. He had wept in his mother's womb and had been born with his eyes open. As they were cutting the umbilical cord, he moved his head from side to side, taking in the things in the room and examining the faces of the people with a fearless curiosity. Then, indifferent to those who came close to look at him, he kept his attention concentrated on the palm roof, which looked as if it were about to collapse under the tremendous pressure of the rain. Úrsula did not remember the intensity of that look again until one day when little Aureliano, at the age of three, went into the kitchen at the moment she was taking a pot of boiling soup from the stove and putting it on the table. The child, perplexed, said from the doorway, "It's going to spill." The pot was firmly placed in the center of the table, but just as soon as the child made his announcement, it began an unmistakable movement toward the edge, as if impelled by some inner dynamism, and it fell and broke on the floor. Úrsula, alarmed, told her husband about the episode, but he interpreted it as a natural phenomenon. That was the way he always was alien to the existence of his sons, partly because he considered childhood as a period of mental insufficiency, and partly because he was always too absorbed in his fantastic speculations.

But since the afternoon when he called the children in to help him unpack the things in the laboratory, he gave them his best hours. In the small separate room, where the walls were gradually being covered by strange maps and fabulous drawings, he taught them to read and write and do sums, and he spoke to them about the wonders of the world, not only where his learning had extended, but forcing the limits of his imagination to extremes. It was in that way that the boys ended up learning that in the southern extremes of Africa there were men so intelligent and peaceful that their only pastime was to sit and think, and that it was possible to cross the Aegean Sea on foot by jumping from island to island all the way to the port of Salonika. Those hallucinating sessions remained printed on the memories of the boys in such a way that many years later, a second before the regular army officer gave the firing squad the command to fire, Colonel Aureliano Buendía saw once more that warm March afternoon on which his father had interrupted the lesson in physics and stood fascinated, with his hand in the air and his eyes motionless, listening to the distant pipes, drums, and jingles of the gypsies, who were coming to the village once more, announcing the latest and most startling discovery of the sages of Memphis.

They were new gypsies, young men and women who knew only their own language, handsome specimens with oily skins and intelligent hands, whose dances and music sowed a panic of uproarious joy through the streets, with parrots painted all colors reciting Italian arias, and a hen who laid a hundred golden eggs to the sound of a tambourine, and a trained monkey who read minds, and the multiple-use machine that could be used at the same time to sew on buttons and reduce fevers, and the apparatus to make a person forget his bad memories, and a poultice to lose time, and a thousand more inventions so ingenious and unusual that José Arcadio Buendía must have wanted to invent a memory machine so that he could remember them all. In an instant they transformed the village. The inhabitants of Macondo found themselves lost in their own streets, confused by the crowded fair.

Holding a child by each hand so as not to lose them in the tumult, bumping into acrobats with gold-capped teeth and jugglers with six arms, suffocated by the mingled breath of manure and sandals that the crowd exhaled, José Arcadio Buendía went about everywhere like a madman, looking for Melquíades so that he could reveal to him the infinite secrets of that fabulous nightmare. He asked several gypsies, who did not understand his language. Finally he reached the place where Melquíades used to set up his tent and he found a taciturn Armenian who in Spanish was hawking a syrup to make oneself invisible. He had drunk down a glass of the amber substance in one gulp as José Arcadio Buendía elbowed his way through the absorbed group that was witnessing the spectacle, and was able to ask his question. The gypsy wrapped him in the frightful climate of his look before he turned into a puddle of pestilential and smoking pitch over which the echo of his reply still floated: "Melquíades is dead." Upset by the news, José Arcadio Buendía stood motionless, trying to rise above his affliction, until the group dispersed, called away by other artifices, and the puddle of the taciturn Armenian evaporated completely. Other gypsies confirmed later on that Melquíades had in fact succumbed to the fever on the beach at Singapore and that his body had been thrown into the deepest part of the Java Sea. The children

had no interest in the news. They insisted that their father take them to see the overwhelming novelty of the sages of Memphis that was being advertised at the entrance of a tent that, according to what was said, had belonged to King Solomon. They insisted so much that José Arcadio Buendía paid the thirty reales and led them into the center of the tent, where there was a giant with a hairy torso and a shaved head, with a copper ring in his nose and a heavy iron chain on his ankle, watching over a pirate chest. When it was opened by the giant, the chest gave off a glacial exhalation. Inside there was only an enormous, transparent block with infinite internal needles in which the light of the sunset was broken up into colored stars. Disconcerted, knowing that the children were waiting for an immediate explanation, José Arcadio Buendía ventured a murmur:

"It's the largest diamond in the world."

"No," the gypsy countered. "It's ice."

José Arcadio Buendía, without understanding, stretched out his hand toward the cake, but the giant moved it away. "Five reales more to touch it," he said. José Arcadio Buendía paid them and put his hand on the ice and held it there for several minutes as his heart filled with fear and jubilation at the contact with mystery. Without knowing what to say, he paid ten reales more so that his sons could have that prodigious experience. Little José Arcadio refused to touch it. Aureliano, on the other hand, took a step forward and put his hand on it, withdrawing it immediately. "It's boiling," he exclaimed, startled. But his father paid no attention to him. Intoxicated by the evidence of the miracle, he forgot at that moment about the frustration of his delirious undertakings and Melquíades' body, abandoned to the appetite of the squids. He paid another five reales and with his hand on the cake, as if giving testimony on the holy scriptures, he exclaimed:

"This is the great invention of our time."

Exercises

1. Consider the devices used in the opening sentence to catch the reader's attention. Do you know any other literary works that also have exceptionally effective opening sentences?
2. Based on just the first two paragraphs, describe the personalities of Melquíades and José Arcadio Buendía. What is it about the full name of Buendía that implies that he is a kind of Adam?
3. Describe Úrsula's personality as revealed in the third paragraph and comment on what she has to put up with from her husband.
4. Consider the procession of things that the gypsies bring to the village and relate this to the development of civilization.
5. Draw parallels between Adam, Eve, and the serpent and José, Úrsula, and Melquíades.
6. Describe Macondo and its setting. Could the Garden of Eden have been like this?
7. How do the new gypsies differ from the old gypsies and what does this imply?
8. What is signified by the block of ice in a tropical country?

TWO SONGS
Adrienne Rich (b. 1929)

In the following poem, reminiscent of the enthusiastic attitude of the ancient Greeks, Adrienne Rich speaks of lust that "too is a jewel."

1

Sex, as they harshly call it,
I fell into this morning
at ten o'clock, a drizzling hour
of traffic and wet newspapers.
I thought of him who yesterday
clearly didn't
turn me to a hot field
ready for plowing,
and longing for that young man
pierced me to the roots
bathing every vein, etc.
All day he appears to me
touchingly desirable,
a prize one could wreck one's peace for.
I'd call it love if love
didn't take so many years
but lust too is a jewel
a sweet flower and what
pure happiness to know
all our high-toned questions
breed in a lively animal.

2

That "old last act"!
And yet sometimes
all seems post coitum triste
and I a mere bystander.
Somebody else is going off,
getting shot to the moon.
Or, a moon-race!
Split seconds after
my opposite number lands
I make it—
we lie fainting together
at a crater-edge
heavy as mercury in our moonsuits
till he speaks—
in a different language
yet one I've picked up
through cultural exchanges . . .
we murmur the first moonwords:
Spasibo. Thanks. O.K.

Exercises

1. Why does the poet use the phrase "as they harshly call it"?
2. Discuss the images evoked by "a drizzling hour of traffic and wet newspapers."
3. Why does line 11 end with "etc."?
4. Describe the distinction made between love and lust.
5. What are "moonwords"? Are there several levels of meaning?

Flight on the Wind
from HOUSE MADE OF DAWN
N. Scott Momaday (b. 1934)

In *House Made of Dawn,* winner of the Pulitzer Prize in 1969, young Abel returns to tribal life, wondering if he can resume the ancient ways after living like an Anglo in the Army. The seemingly endless conflict of Anglo and Indian ways is symbolized by the excerpt given below in which the captured, shivering eagle represents an Indian view of life in America.

He had seen a strange thing, an eagle overhead with its talons closed upon a snake. It was an awful, holy sight, full of magic and meaning.

The Eagle Watchers Society was the sixth to go into the kiva at the summer and autumn rain retreats. It was an important society, and it stood apart from the others in a certain way. This difference—this superiority—had come about a long time ago. Before the middle of the last century there was received into the population of the town a small group of immigrants from the Tanoan city of Bahkyula, a distance of seventy or eighty miles to the east. These immigrants were a wretched people, for they had experienced great suffering. Their land bordered upon the Southern Plains, and for many years they had been an easy mark for marauding bands of buffalo hunters and thieves. They had endured every kind of persecution until one day they could stand no more and their spirit broke. They gave themselves up to despair and were then at the mercy of the first alien wind. But it was not a human enemy that overcame them at last; it was a plague. They were struck down by so deadly a disease that, when the epidemic abated, there were fewer than twenty survivors in all. And this remainder, too, should surely have perished among the ruins of Bahkyula had it not been for these *patrones,* these distant relatives who took them in at the certain risk of their own lives and the lives of their children and grandchildren. It is said that the cacique himself went out to welcome and escort the visitors in. The people of the town must have looked narrowly at those stricken souls who walked slowly towards them, wild in their eyes with grief and desperation. The Bahkyush immigrants brought with them little more than the clothes on their backs, but even in this moment of deep hurt and humiliation, they thought of themselves as a people. They carried three things that should serve thereafter to signal who they were: a sacred flute; the bull mask of Pecos; and the little wooden statue of their patroness *Maria de los Angeles,* whom they called Porcingula. Now, after the intervening years and generations, the ancient blood of this forgotten tribe still ran in the veins of men.

The Eagle Watchers Society was the principal ceremonial organization of the Bahkyush. Its chief, Patiestewa, and all its members were direct descendants of those old men and women who had made that journey along the edge of oblivion. There was a look about these men, even now. It was as if, conscious of having come so close to extinction, they had got a keener sense of humility than their benefactors, and paradoxically a greater sense of pride. Both attributes could be seen in such a man as old Patiestewa. He was hard, and he appeared to have seen more of life than had other men.

In their uttermost peril long ago, the Bahkyush had been fashioned into seers and soothsayers. They had acquired a tragic sense, which gave to them as a race so much dignity and bearing. They were medicine men; they were rainmakers and eagle hunters.

He was not thinking of the eagles. He had been walking since daybreak down from the mountain where that year he had broken a horse for the rancher John Raymond. By the middle of the morning he was on the rim of the Valle Grande, a great volcanic crater that lay high up on the western slope of the range. It was the right eye of the earth, held open to the sun. Of all the places that he knew, this valley alone could reflect the great spatial majesty of the sky. It was scooped out of the dark peaks like the well of a great, gathering storm, deep umber and blue and smoke-colored. The view across the diameter was magnificent; it was an unbelievably great expanse. As many times as he had been there in the past, each first new sight of it always brought him up short, and he had to catch his breath. Just there, it seemed, a strange and brilliant light lay upon the world, and all the objects in the landscape were washed clean and set away in the distance. In the morning sunlight the Valle Grande was dappled with the shadows of clouds and vibrant with rolling winter grass. The clouds were always there, huge, sharply described, and shining in the pure air. But the great feature of the valley was its size. It was too great for the eye to hold, strangely beautiful and full of distance. Such vastness makes for illusion, a kind of illusion that comprehends reality, and where it exists there is always wonder and exhilaration. He looked at the facets of a boulder that lay balanced on the edge of the land, and the first thing beyond, the vague, misty field out of which it stood, was the floor of the valley itself, pale and blue-green, miles away. He shifted the focus of his gaze, and he could just make out the clusters of dots that were cattle grazing along the river in the faraway plain.

Then he saw the eagles across the distance, two of them, riding low in the depths and rising diagonally towards him. He did not know what they were at first, and he stood watching them, their far, silent flight erratic and wild in the bright morning. They rose and swung across the skyline, veering close at last, and he knelt down behind the rock, dumb with pleasure and excitement, holding on to them with his eyes.

They were golden eagles, a male and a female, in their mating flight. They were cavorting, spinning and spiralling on the cold, clear columns of air, and they were beautiful. They swooped and hovered, leaning on the air, and swung close together, feinting and screaming with delight. The female was full-grown, and the span of her broad wings was greater than any man's height. There was a fine flourish to her motion: she was deceptively, incredibly fast, and her pivots and wheels were wide and full-blown. But her great weight was streamlined, perfectly controlled. She carried a rattlesnake; it hung shining from her feet, limp and curving out in the trail of her flight. Suddenly her wings and tail fanned, catching full on the wind, and for an instant she was still, widespread and spectral in the blue, while her mate flared past and away, turning round in the distance to look for her. Then she began to beat upward at an angle from the rim until she was small in the sky, and she let go of the snake. It fell, slowly, writhing and rolling, floating out like a bit of silver thread against the wide backdrop of the land. She held still above, buoyed up on the cold current, her crop and hackles gleaming like copper in the sun. The male swerved and sailed. He was younger than she and a little more than half as large. He was quicker, tighter in his moves. He let the carrion drift by; then suddenly he gathered himself and stooped, sliding down in a blur of motion to the strike. He hit the snake in the head, with not the slightest deflection of his course or speed, cracking its long body like a whip. Then he rolled and swung upward in a great pendulum arc, riding out his momentum. At the top of his glide he let go of the snake in turn, but the female did not go for it. Instead she soared out over the plain, nearly out of sight, like a mote receding into the haze of the far mountain. The male followed, and he watched them go, straining to see, saw them veer once, dip and disappear.

Now there was the business of the society. It was getting on towards the end of November, and the eagle hunters were getting ready to set forth to the mountains. He brooded for a time, full of a strange longing; then one day he went to old Patiestewa and told him of what he had seen. "I think you had better let me go," he said. The old chief closed his eyes and thought about it for a long time. Then he answered: "Yes, I had better let you go."

The next day the Bahkyush eagle watchers started out on foot he among them, northward through the canyon and into the high timber beyond. They were gone for days, holding up here and there at the holy places where they must pray and make their offerings. Early in the morning they came out of the trees on the edge of the Valle Grande. The land fell and reached away in the early light as far as the eye could see, the hills folding together and the gray grass rolling in the plain, and they began the descent. At midmorning they came to the lower meadows in the basin. It was clear and cold, and the air was thin and sharp like a shard of glass. They needed bait, and they circled out and apart, forming a ring. When the circle was formed, they converged slowly towards the center, clapping and calling out in a high, flat voice that carried only a little way. And as they closed, rabbits began to jump up from the grass and bound. They got away at first, many of them, while the men were still a distance apart, but gradually the ring grew small and the rabbits crept to the center and hid away in the brush. Now and then one of them tried to break away, and the nearest man threw his stick after it. These weapons were small curved clubs, and they were thrown with deadly accuracy by the eagle hunters, so that when the ring was of a certain size and the men only a few feet apart, very few of the animals got away.

He bent close to the ground, his arm cocked and shaking with tension. A great jackrabbit buck bounded from the grass, straight past him. It struck the ground beyond and sprang again, nearly thirty feet through the air. He spun round and hurled the stick. It struck the jackrabbit a glancing blow just as it bounded again, and it slumped in the air and fell heavily to the ground.

The clapping and calling had stopped. He could feel his heart beating and the sweat growing cold on his skin. There was something like remorse or disappointment now that the rabbits were still and strewn about on the ground. He picked one of the dead animals from the brush—it was warm and soft, its eyes shining like porcelain, full of the dull lustre of death—then the great buck, which was not dead but only stunned and frozen with fear. He felt the warm living weight of it in his hands; it was brittle with life, taut with hard, sinewy strength.

When he had bound the bait together and placed it in the sack, he gathered bunches of tall grass and cut a number of evergreen boughs from a thicket in the plain; these he tied in a bundle and carried in a sling on his back. He went to the river and washed his head in order to purify himself. When all was ready, he waved to the others and started off alone to the cliffs. When he came to the first plateau he rested and looked across the valley. The sun was high, and all around there was a pale, dry uniformity of light, a winter glare on the clouds and peaks. He could see a crow circling low in the distance. Higher on the land, where a great slab of white rock protruded from the mountain, he saw the eagle-hunt house; he headed for it. The house was a small tower of stone, built round a pit, hollow and open at the top. Near it was a shrine, a stone shelf in which there was a slight depression. There he placed a prayer offering. He got into the house, and with boughs he made a latticework of beams across the top and covered it with grass. When it was finished there was a small opening at the center. Through it he raised the rabbits and laid them down on the boughs. He could see here and there through the screen, but his line of vision was vertical, or nearly so, and his quarry would come from the sun. He began to sing, now and then calling out, low in his throat.

The eagles soared southward, high above the Valle Grande. They were almost too high to be seen. From their vantage point the land below reached away on either side to the long, crooked tributaries of the range; down the great open corridor to the south were the wooded slopes and the canyon, the desert and the far end of the earth bending on the sky. They caught sight of the rabbits and were deflected. They veered and banked, lowering themselves into the crater, gathering speed. By the time he knew of their presence, they were low and coming fast on either side of the pit, swooping with blinding speed. The male caught hold of the air and fell off, touching upon the face of the cliff in order to flush the rabbits, while the female hurtled in to take her prey on the run. Nothing happened; the rabbits did not move. She overshot the trap and screamed. She was enraged and she hurled herself around in the air. She swung back with a great clamor of her wings and fell with fury on the bait. He saw her the instant she struck. Her foot flashed out and one of her talons laid the jackrabbit open the length of its body. It stiffened and jerked, and her other foot took hold of its skull and crushed it. In that split second when the center of her weight touched down upon the trap he reached for her. His hands closed upon her legs and he drew her down with all of his strength. For one instant only did she recoil, splashing her great wings down upon the beams and boughs—and she very nearly broke from his grasp; but then she was down in the darkness of the well, hooded, and she was still.

At dusk he met with the other hunters in the plain. San Juanito, too, had got an eagle, but it was an aged male and poor by comparison. They gathered round the old eagle and spoke to it, bidding it return with their good will and sorrow to the eagles of the crags. They fixed a prayer plume to its leg and let it go. He watched it back away and crouch on the ground, glaring, full of fear and suspicion. Then it took leave of the ground and beat upward, clattering through the still shadows of the valley. It gathered speed, driving higher and higher until it reached the shafts of reddish-gold final light that lay like bars across the crater. The light caught it up and set a dark blaze upon it. It levelled off and sailed. Then it was

gone from sight, but he looked after it for a time. He could see it still in the mind's eye and hear in his memory the awful whisper of its flight on the wind. He felt the great weight of the bird which he held in the sack. The dusk was fading quickly into night, and the others could not see that his eyes were filled with tears.

That night, while the others ate by the fire, he stole away to look at the great bird. He drew the sack open; the bird shivered, he thought, and drew itself up. Bound and helpless, his eagle seemed drab and shapeless in the moonlight, too large and ungainly for flight. The sight of it filled him with shame and disgust. He took hold of its throat in the darkness and cut off its breath.

Exercises

1. What is symbolized by the image of an eagle holding a snake?
2. Consider the first full paragraph. Could this be a capsule history of what happened to Native Americans?
3. What kinds of feelings are invoked by the descriptions of the land? Can cities be described in this general manner?
4. Consider the mating flight of the two eagles and what this symbolizes.
5. Why was the old eagle freed? Why was the female killed?

A SORROWFUL WOMAN
Gail Godwin (b. 1937)

The following short story is a study of the gradual disintegration of a human personality. In keeping with the "once upon a time" lead, the style is similar to a fairy tale except that "happily ever after" does not happen. The reader should consider the monotonously repetitive tasks taken over by the husband and later shared with the live-in girl and compare these with the usual tasks of men in their jobs at the office or wherever. Then, consider how all of this relates to the final "legacy" of food, laundry, and sonnets.

Once upon a time there was a wife and mother one too many times

One winter evening she looked at them: the husband durable, receptive, gentle; the child a tender golden three. The sight of them made her so sad and sick she did not want to see them ever again.

She told the husband these thoughts. He was attuned to her; he understood such things. He said he understood. What would she like him to do? "If you could put the boy to bed and read him the story about the monkey who ate too many bananas, I would be grateful." "Of course," he said. "Why, that's a pleasure." And he sent her off to bed.

The next night it happened again. Putting the warm dishes away in the cupboard, she turned and saw the child's grey eyes approving her movements. In the next room was the man, his chin sunk in the open collar of his favorite wool shirt. He was dozing after her good supper.

The shirt was the grey of the child's trusting gaze. She began yelping without tears, retching in between. The man woke in alarm and carried her in his arms to bed. The boy followed them up the stairs, saying, "It's all right, Mommy," but this made her scream. "Mommy is sick," the father said, "go and wait for me in your room."

The husband undressed her, abandoning her only long enough to root beneath the eiderdown for her flannel gown. She stood naked except for her bra, which hung by one strap down the side of her body; she had not the impetus to shrug it off. She looked down at the right nipple, shriveled with chill, and thought, How absurd, a vertical bra. "If only there were instant sleep," she said, hiccuping, and the husband bundled her into the gown and went out and came back with a sleeping draught guaranteed swift. She was to drink a little glass of cognac followed by a big glass of dark liquid and afterwards there was just time to say Thank you and could you get him a clean pair of pajamas out of the laundry, it came back today.

The next day was Sunday and the husband brought her breakfast in bed and let her sleep until it grew dark again. He took the child for a walk, and when they returned, red-cheeked and boisterous, the father made supper. She heard them laughing in the kitchen. He brought her up a tray of buttered toast, celery sticks and black bean soup. "I am the luckiest woman," she said, crying real tears. "Nonsense," he said. "You need a rest from us," and went to prepare the sleeping draught, find the child's pajamas, select the story for the night.

She got up on Monday and moved about the house till noon. The boy, delighted to have her back, pretended he was a vicious tiger and followed her from room to room, growling and scratching. Whenever she came close, he would growl and scratch at her. One of his sharp little claws ripped her flesh, just above the wrist, and together they paused to watch a thin red line materialize on the inside of her pale arm and spill over in little beads. "Go away," she said. She got herself upstairs and locked the door. She called the husband's office and said, "I've locked myself away from him. I'm afraid." The husband told her in his richest voice to lie down, take it easy, and he was already on the phone to call one of the baby-sitters they often employed. Shortly after, she heard the girl let herself in, heard the girl coaxing the frightened child to come and play.

After supper several nights later, she hit the child. She had known she was going to do it when the father would see. "I'm sorry," she said, collapsing on the floor. The weeping child had run to hide. "What has happened to me, I'm not myself anymore." The man picked her tenderly from the floor and looked at her with much concern. "Would it help if we got, you know, a girl in? We could fix the room downstairs. I want you to feel freer," he said, understanding these things. "We have the money for a girl. I want you to think about it."

And now the sleeping draught was a nightly thing, she did not have to ask. He went down to the kitchen to mix it, he set it nightly beside her bed. The little glass and the big one, amber and deep rich brown, the flannel gown and the eiderdown.

The man put out the word and found the perfect girl. She was young, dynamic and not pretty. "Don't bother with the room, I'll fix it up myself." Laughing, she employed her thousand energies. She painted the room white, fed the child lunch, read edifying books, raced the boy to the mailbox, hung her own watercolors on the fresh-painted walls, made spinach soufflé, cleaned a spot from the mother's coat, made them all laugh, danced in stocking feet to music in the white room after reading the child to sleep. She knitted dresses for herself and played chess with the husband. She washed and set the mother's soft ash-blonde hair and gave her neck rubs, offered to.

The woman now spent her winter afternoons in the big bedroom. She made a fire in the hearth and put on slacks and an old sweater she had loved at school, and sat in the big chair and stared out the window at snow-ridden branches, or went away into long novels about other people moving through other winters.

The girl brought the child in twice a day, once in the later afternoon when he would tell of his day, all of it tumbling out quickly because there was not much time, and before he went to bed. Often now, the man took his wife to dinner. He made a courtship ceremony of it, inviting her beforehand so she could get used to the idea. They dressed and were beautiful together again and went out into the frosty night. Over candlelight he would say, "I think you are better, you know." "Perhaps I am," she would murmur. "You look . . . like a cloistered queen," he said once, his voice breaking curiously.

One afternoon the girl brought the child into the bedroom. "We've been out playing in the park. He found something he wants to give you, a surprise." The little boy approached her, smiling mysteriously. He placed his cupped hands in hers and left a live dry thing that spat brown juice in her palm and leapt away. She screamed and wrung her hands to be rid of the brown juice. "Oh, it was only a grasshopper," said the girl. Nimbly she crept to the edge of a curtain, did a quick knee bend and reclaimed the creature, led the boy competently from the room.

So the husband came alone. "I have explained to the boy," he said. "And we are doing fine. We are managing." He squeezed his wife's pale arm and put the two glasses on her table. After he had gone, she sat looking at the arm.

"I'm afraid it's come to that," she said. "Just push the notes under the door; I'll read them. And don't forget to leave the draught outside."

The man sat for a long time with his head in his hands. Then he rose and went away from her. She heard him in the kitchen where he mixed the draught in batches now to last a week at a time, storing it in a corner of the cupboard. She heard him come back, leave the big glass and the little one outside on the floor.

Outside her window the snow was melting from the branches, there were more people on the streets. She brushed her hair a lot and seldom read anymore. She sat in her window and brushed her hair for hours, and saw a boy fall off his new bicycle again and again, a dog chasing a squirrel, an old woman peek slyly over her shoulder and then extract a parcel from a garbage can.

In the evening she read the notes they slipped under her door. The child could not write, so he drew and sometimes painted his. The notes were painstaking at first; the man and boy offering the final strength of their day to her. But sometimes, when they seemed to have had a bad day, there were only hurried scrawls.

One night, when the husband's note had been extremely short, loving but short, and there had been nothing from the boy, she stole out of her room as she often did to get more supplies, but crept upstairs instead and stood outside their doors, listening to the regular breathing of the man and boy asleep. She hurried back to her room and drank the draught.

She woke earlier now. It was spring, there were birds. She listened for sounds of the man and the boy eating breakfast; she listened for the roar of the motor when they drove away. One beautiful noon, she went out to look at her kitchen in the daylight. Things were changed. He had bought some new dish towels. Had the old ones worn out? The canisters seemed closer to the sink. She inspected the cupboard and saw new things among the old. She got out flour, baking powder, salt, milk (he bought a different brand of butter), and baked a loaf of bread and left it cooling on the table.

The force of the two joyful notes slipped under her door that evening pressed her into the corner of the little room; she had hardly space to breathe. As soon as possible, she drank the draught.

Now the days were too short. She was always busy. She woke with the first bird. Worked till the sun set. No time for hair brushing. Her fingers raced the hours.

Finally, in the nick of time, it was finished one late afternoon. Her veins pumped and her forehead sparkled. She went to the cupboard, took what was hers, closed herself into the little white room and brushed her hair for a while.

"The girl upsets me," said the woman to her husband. He sat frowning on the side of the bed he had not entered for so long. "I'm sorry, but there it is." The husband stroked his creased brow and said he was sorry too. He really did not know what they would do without that treasure of a girl. "Why don't you stay here with me in bed," the woman said.

Next morning she fired the girl who cried and said, "I loved the little boy, what will become of him now?" But the mother turned away her face and the girl took down the watercolors from the walls, sheathed the records she had danced to and went away.

"I don't know what we'll do. It's all my fault, I know. I'm such a burden, I know that."

"Let me think. I'll think of something." (Still understanding these things.)

"I know you will. You always do," she said.

With great care he rearranged his life. He got up hours early, did the shopping, cooked the breakfast, took the boy to nursery school. "We will manage," he said, "until you're better, however long that is." He did his work, collected the boy from the school, came home and made the supper, washed the dishes, got the child to bed. He managed everything. One evening, just as she was on the verge of swallowing her draught, there was a timid knock on her door. The little boy came in wearing his pajamas. "Daddy has fallen asleep on my bed and I can't get in. There's not room."

Very sedately she left her bed and went to the child's room. Things were much changed. Books were rearranged, toys. He'd done some new drawings. She came as a visitor to her son's room, wakened the father and helped him to bed. "Ah, he shouldn't have bothered you," said the man, leaning on his wife. "I've told him not to." He dropped into his own bed and fell asleep with a moan. Meticulously she undressed him. She folded and hung his clothes. She covered his body with the bedclothes. She flicked off the light that shone in his face.

The next day she moved her things into the girl's white room. She put her hairbrush on the dresser; she put a note pad and pen beside the bed. She stocked the little room with cigarettes, books, bread and cheese. She didn't need much.

At first the husband was dismayed. But he was receptive to her needs. He understood these things.

"Perhaps the best thing is for you to follow it through," he said. "I want to be big enough to contain whatever you must do."

All day long she stayed in the white room. She was a young queen, a virgin in a tower; she was the previous inhabitant, the girl with all the energies. She tried these personalities on like costumes, then discarded them. The room had a new view of streets she'd never seen that way before. The sun hit the room in late afternoon and she took to brushing her hair in the sun. One day she decided to write a poem. "Perhaps a sonnet." She took up her pen and pad and began working from words that had lately lain in her mind. She had choices for the sonnet, ABAB or ABBA for a start. She pondered these possibilities until she tottered into a larger choice: she did not have to write a sonnet. Her poem could be six, eight, ten, thirteen lines, it could be any number of lines, and it did not even have to rhyme.

She put down the pen on top of the pad.

In the evenings, very briefly, she saw the two of them. They knocked on her door, a big knock and a little, and she would call Come in, and the husband would smile though he looked a bit tired, yet somehow this tiredness suited him. He would put her sleeping draught on the bedside table and say, "The boy and I have done all right today," and the child would kiss her. One night she tasted for the first time the power of his baby spit.

"I don't think I can see him anymore," she whispered sadly to the man. And the husband turned away, but recovered admirably and said, "Of course, I see."

The man and boy came home and found: five loaves of warm bread, a roast stuffed turkey, a glazed ham, three pies of different fillings, eight molds of the boy's favorite custard, two weeks' supply of fresh-laundered sheets and shirts and towels, two hand-knitted sweaters (both of the same grey color), a sheath of marvelous watercolor beasts accompanied by mad and fanciful stories nobody could ever make up again, and a tablet full of love sonnets addressed to the man. The house smelled redolently of renewal and spring. The man ran to the little room, could not contain himself to knock, flung back the door.

"Look, Mommy is sleeping," said the boy. "She's tired from doing all our things again." He dawdled in a stream of the last sun for that day and watched his father roll tenderly back her eyelids, lay his ear softly to her breast, test the delicate bones of her wrist. The father put down his face into her fresh-washed hair.

"Can we eat the turkey for supper?" the boy asked.

Exercises

1. Itemize the steps in the "abnormal" behavior of the wife from the opening paragraph on. Does this progression appear to be inevitable? What might the husband have done to stop this deterioration?
2. Consider the husband's solution of a live-in girl. What does this tell us about the husband and about his attitude toward his wife?
3. What is the significance of each of the gifts that the wife left for her son and her husband?
4. Why was it necessary for the child to be a boy? Why not a girl? Consider the implications of the final sentence.

MAN THINKING ABOUT WOMAN
Don L. Lee (b. 1942)

The first work is a love poem that should, like all poetry, be read aloud, taking care to pause at the caesuras (blank spots) but not between lines. The pauses add even more tenderness to what is already a gentle, lyric love song.

some thing is lost in me,
like
the way you lose old thoughts   that
somehow seemed unlost at the right time.
i've not known it or you many days;   5
we met as friends with an absence of strangeness.
it was the month
that my lines got longer & my metaphors softer.
it was the week   that
i felt the city's narrow breezes rush about   10
me
looking for a place to disappear
as   i walked the clearway,
sure footed in used sandals screaming to be replaced
your empty shoes (except for used stockings)   15
partially hidden beneath the dresser
looked at me,
as i sat thoughtlessly   waiting
for your touch.
that day,   20
as your body rested upon my chest
i saw the shadow of the
window blinds   beam
across the unpainted ceiling
going somewhere   25
like the somewhere i was going
when
the clearness of yr/teeth,
& the scars on yr/legs stopped me.
your beauty: un-noticed by regular eyes   is   30
like   a blackbird resting
on a telephone wire   that moves
quietly with the wind.
a southwind.

In the second poem Don Lee speaks as a black poet in a manner comparable to the Blackstream artists discussed in chapter 29. "Burned out hair" refers to hair straightened by a hot comb while "nappy-headed" is natural hair. The first reference implies denial of a heritage and the second a violent activism that seems equally unpalatable. The use of lowercase letters possibly reflects the influence of writer Imamu Amiri Baraka (formerly LeRoi Jones), not e e cummings. It is here an effective way to maintain a murmering, low-keyed mood that actually underscores the tension.

MIXED SKETCHES
Don L. Lee (b. 1942)

u feel that way sometimes
wondering:
as a nine year old sister
with burned out hair oddly
smiles at you and sweetly calls you   5
brother.
u feel that way sometimes
wondering:
as a blackwoman & her 6 children
are burned out of their apartment with no place   10
to go & a nappy-headed nigger comes running thru
our neighborhood with a match in his hand cryin
revolution.
u feel that way sometimes
wondering: 15
seeing sisters in two hundred dollar wigs & suits
fastmoving in black clubs in late surroundings   talking
about the late thoughts in late language waiting for late
        men
that come in with, "i don't want to hear bout nothing   20
black tonight."
u feel that way sometimes
wondering:
while eating on newspaper tablecloths
& sleeping on clean bed sheets that couldn't   25
stop bed bugs   as black children watch their
mothers leave the special buses returning from
special neighborhoods
to clean their "own" unspecial homes.
u feel that way sometimes   30
wondering:
wondering, how did we survive?

Exercises

1. In "Man Thinking about Woman" what is implied by the progression of the words *days, month, week,* and *that day?* What is a *narrow breeze?* What were the actual circumstances of this encounter?
2. Why is the second poem titled "Mixed Sketches"? The poem implies that there are three responses to racism. What are they?

NIKKI-ROSA
Nikki Giovanni (b. 1943)

The following poem is autobiographical and the poet did indeed become "famous or something." The poem was written in 1968 during the latter days of violent protests but it is a proud, clear statement of identity. Don Lee asks "how did we survive?" Nikki Giovanni provides one cogent answer. Woodlawn, in the poem, was a black suburb of Cincinnati, Ohio.

childhood remembrances are always a drag
if you're Black
you always remember things like living in Woodlawn
with no inside toilet
and if you become famous or something   5
they never talk about how happy you were to have your
      mother
all to your self and
how good the water felt when you got your bath from one
      of those
big tubs that folk in chicago barbecue in
and somehow when you talk about home   10
it never gets across how much you
understood their feelings
as the whole family attended meetings about Hollydale
and even though you remember
your biographers never understand   15
your father's pain as he sells his stock
and another dream goes
and though your're poor it isn't poverty that
concerns you
and though they fought a lot   20
it isn't your father's drinking that makes any difference
but only that everybody is together and you
and your sister have happy birthdays and very good
      christmasses
and I really hope no white person ever has cause to write
      about me
because they never understand Black love is Black
      wealth and they'll   25
probably talk about my hard childhood and never
      understand that
all the while I was quite happy.

Exercise

1. Are childhood remembrances "always a drag" if
   you are poor, white, and live in a slum, even if
   the slum is not a ghetto? How does black love
   differ from white love? In other words, is this a
   poem about racism or is it more about a loving
   family that produced a very fine American poet?

Chapter 39, The Eternal City, from CATCH 22

Joseph Heller (b. 1923)

Before starting this excerpt the reader should review
the discussion of *Catch 22* given earlier in this chapter.

By the end of chapter 38, Nately, one of Yossarian's companions, has been killed, and Nately's girlfriend, named only "Nately's whore," is pursuing
Yossarian relentlessly in an effort to kill him. (Can she
represent The Furies?) Yossarian has simply refused
to fly any more missions, but for various reasons he
cannot be court-martialed. His commanding officers
simply do not know what to do with him. If he can
get away with it, the other men will refuse to fly, too.

Chapter 39 is written in a surrealistic style with
the added ironies of black humor: the MPs do not arrest Aarfy, the super-conformist, although he has just
raped and killed a woman; when Yossarian is returned to the airbase he discovers that his commanding officers have decided to send him home.

This chapter, however, represents much more
than technique in writing. The title has a double
meaning. Rome has always been called "the eternal
city," but in this chapter it seems to represent Hell on
earth, its eternity a bitter comment on life in general.
The events within the chapter deal with a descent into
the underworld in the classic pattern of Virgil's and
Dante's descent. Another interesting parallel can be
drawn. Milo Minderbinder, who represents the profit
motive in society, can here be compared to Mephistopheles in Goethe's *Faust*. As Faust makes his journey into the classical underworld he is accompanied
by Mephistopheles until they encounter the "evil
Phorkyads." At that point Mephistopheles deserts
Faust exactly as Milo deserts Yossarian to pursue his
profits.

After the journey to Rome, the scene starts in the
comparative innocence of the brothel, now destroyed
by the military police, and continues through the
depths of human misery and cruelty, finally ending at
the apartment reserved for officers-on-leave, and ends
with the return to the airbase.

Yossarian was going absent without official leave with
Milo, who, as the plane cruised toward Rome, shook his
head reproachfully and, with pious lips pursed, informed
Yossarian in ecclesiastical tones that he was ashamed of
him. Yossarian nodded. Yossarian was making an uncouth
spectacle of himself by walking around backward with his
gun on his hip and refusing to fly more combat missions,
Milo said. Yossarian nodded. It was disloyal to his
squadron and embarrassing to his superiors. He was
placing Milo in a very uncomfortable position, too.
Yossarian nodded again. The men were starting to
grumble. It was not fair for Yossarian to think only of his
own safety while men like Milo, Colonel Cathcart,
Colonel Korn and ex-P.F.C. Wintergreen were willing to
do everything they could to win the war. The men with
seventy missions were starting to grumble because they
had to fly eighty, and there was a danger some of them
might put on guns and begin walking around backward,
too. Morale was deteriorating and it was all Yossarian's
fault. The country was in peril; he was jeopardizing his
traditional rights of freedom and independence by daring
to exercise them.

Yossarian kept nodding in the co-pilot's seat and
tried not to listen as Milo prattled on. Nately's whore was
on his mind, as were Kraft and Orr and Nately and
Dunbar, and Kid Sampson and McWatt, and all the poor
and stupid and diseased people he had seen in Italy,
Egypt and North Africa and knew about in other areas of
the world, and Snowden and Nately's whore's kid sister
were on his conscience, too. Yossarian thought he knew
why Nately's whore held him responsible for Nately's
death and wanted to kill him. Why the hell shouldn't she?
It was a man's world, and she and everyone younger had
every right to blame him and everyone older for every
unnatural tragedy that befell them; just as she, even in her
grief, was to blame for every man-made misery that
landed on her kid sister and on all other children behind
her. Someone had to do something sometime. Every
victim was a culprit, every culprit a victim, and somebody

had to stand up sometime to try to break the lousy chain of inherited habit that was imperiling them all. In parts of Africa little boys were still stolen away by adult slave traders and sold for money to men who disemboweled them and ate them. Yossarian marveled that children could suffer such barbaric sacrifice without evincing the slightest hint of fear or pain. He took it for granted that they did submit so stoically. If not, he reasoned, the custom would certainly have died, for no craving for wealth or immortality could be so great, he felt, as to subsist on the sorrow of children.

He was rocking the boat, Milo said, and Yossarian nodded once more. He was not a good member of the team, Milo said. Yossarian nodded and listened to Milo tell him that the decent thing to do if he did not like the way Colonel Cathcart and Colonel Korn were running the group was go to Russia, instead of stirring up trouble. Yossarian refrained from pointing out that Colonel Cathcart, Colonel Korn and Milo could all go to Russia if they did not like the way he was stirring up trouble. Colonel Cathcart and Colonel Korn had both been very good to Yossarian, Milo said; hadn't they given him a medal after the last mission to Ferrara and promoted him to captain? Yossarian nodded. Didn't they feed him and give him his pay every month? Yossarian nodded again. Milo was sure they would be charitable if he went to them to apologize and recant and promised to fly eighty missions. Yossarian said he would think it over, and held his breath and prayed for a safe landing as Milo dropped his wheels and glided in toward the runway. It was funny how he had really come to detest flying.

Rome was in ruins, he saw, when the plane was down. The airdrome had been bombed eight months before, and knobby slabs of white stone rubble had been bulldozed into flat-topped heaps on both sides of the entrance through the wire fence surrounding the field. The Colosseum was a dilapidated shell, and the Arch of Constantine had fallen. Nately's whore's apartment was a shambles. The girls were gone, and the only one there was the old woman. The windows in the apartment had been smashed. She was bundled up in sweaters and skirts and wore a dark shawl about her head. She sat on a wooden chair near an electric hot plate, her arms folded, boiling water in a battered aluminum pot. She was talking aloud to herself when Yossarian entered and began moaning as soon as she saw him.

"Gone," she moaned before he could even inquire. Holding her elbows, she rocked back and forth mournfully on her creaking chair. "Gone."

"Who?"

"All. All the poor young girls."

"Where?"

"Away. Chased away into the street. All of them gone. All the poor young girls."

"Chased away by who? Who did it?"

"The mean tall soldiers with the hard white hats and clubs. And by our *carabinieri*. They came with their clubs and chased them away. They would not even let them take their coats. The poor things. They just chased them away into the cold."

"Did they arrest them?"

"They chased them away. They just chased them away."

"Then why did they do it if they didn't arrest them?"

"I don't know," sobbed the old woman. "I don't know. Who will take care of me? Who will take care of me now that the poor young girls are gone. Who will take care of me?"

"There must have been a reason," Yossarian persisted, pounding his fist into his hand. "They couldn't just barge in here and chase everyone out."

"No reason," wailed the old woman. "No reason."

"What right did they have?"

"Catch-22."

"*What?*" Yossarian froze in his tracks with fear and alarm and felt his whole body begin to tingle. "*What* did you say?"

"Catch-22," the old woman repeated, rocking her head up and down. "Catch-22. Catch-22 says they have a right to do anything we can't stop them from doing."

"What the hell are you talking about?" Yossarian shouted at her in bewildered, furious protest. "How did you know it was Catch-22? Who the hell told you it was Catch-22?"

"The soldiers with the hard white hats and clubs. The girls were crying. 'Did we do anything wrong?' they said. The men said no and pushed them away out the door with the ends of their clubs. 'Then why are you chasing us out?' the girls said. 'Catch-22,' the men said. 'What right do you have?' the girls said. 'Catch-22,' the men said. All they kept saying was 'Catch-22, Catch-22,' What does it mean, Catch-22? What is Catch-22?"

"Didn't they show it to you?" Yossarian demanded, stamping about in anger and distress. "Didn't you even make them read it?"

"They don't have to show us Catch-22," the old woman answered. "The law says they don't have to."

"What law says they don't have to?"

"Catch-22."

"Oh, God damn!" Yossarian exclaimed bitterly. "I bet it wasn't even really there." He stopped walking and glanced about the room disconsolately. "Where's the old man?"

"Gone," mourned the old woman.

"Gone?"

"Dead," the old woman told him, nodding in emphatic lament, pointing to her head with the flat of her hand. "Something broke in here. One minute he was living, one minute he was dead."

"But he can't be dead!" Yossarian cried, ready to argue insistently. But of course he knew it was true, knew it was logical and true: once again the old man had marched along with the majority.

Yossarian turned away and trudged through the apartment with a gloomy scowl, peering with pessimistic curiosity into all the rooms. Everything made of glass had been smashed by the men with the clubs. Torn drapes and bedding lay dumped on the floor. Chairs, tables and dressers had been overturned. Everything breakable had been broken. The destruction was total. No wild vandals could have been more thorough. Every window was smashed, and darkness poured like inky clouds into each room through the shattered panes. Yossarian could imagine the heavy, crashing footfalls of the tall M.P.s in the hard white hats. He could picture the fiery and malicious exhilaration with which they had made their wreckage, and their sanctimonious, ruthless sense of right and dedication. All the poor young girls were gone. Everyone was gone but the weeping old woman in the bulky brown and gray sweaters and black head shawl, and soon she too would be gone.

"Gone," she grieved, when he walked back in, before he could even speak. "Who will take care of me now?"

Yossarian ignored the question. "Nately's girlfriend—did anyone hear from her?" he asked.

"Gone."

"I know she's gone. But did anyone hear from her? Does anyone know where she is?"

"Gone."

"The little sister. What happened to her?"

"Gone." The old woman's tone had not changed.

"Do you know what I'm talking about?" Yossarian asked sharply, staring into her eyes to see if she were not speaking to him from a coma. He raised his voice. "What happened to the kid sister, to the little girl?"

"Gone, gone," the old woman replied with a crabby shrug, irritated by his persistence, her low wail growing louder. "Chased away with the rest, chased away into the street. They would not even let her take her coat."

"Where did she go?"

"I don't know. I don't know."

"Who will take care of her?"

"Who will take care of me?"

"She doesn't know anybody else, does she?"

"Who will take care of me?"

Yossarian left money in the old woman's lap—it was odd how many wrongs leaving money seemed to right—and strode out of the apartment, cursing Catch-22 vehemently as he descended the stairs, even though he knew there was no such thing. Catch-22 did not exist, he was positive of that, but it made no difference. What did matter was that everyone thought it existed, and that was much worse, for there was no object or text to ridicule or refute, to accuse, criticize, attack, amend, hate, revile, spit at, rip to shreds, trample upon or burn up.

It was cold outside, and dark, and a leaky, insipid mist lay swollen in the air and trickled down the large, unpolished stone blocks of the houses and the pedestals of monuments. Yossarian hurried back to Milo and recanted. He said he was sorry and, knowing he was lying, promised to fly as many more missions as Colonel Cathcart wanted if Milo would only use all his influence in Rome to help him locate Nately's whore's kid sister.

"She's just a twelve-year-old virgin, Milo," he explained anxiously, "and I want to find her before it's too late."

Milo responded to his request with a benign smile. "I've got just the twelve-year-old virgin you're looking for," he announced jubilantly. "This twelve-year-old virgin is really only thirty-four, but she was brought up on a low-protein diet by very strict parents and didn't start sleeping with men until—"

"Milo, I'm talking about a little girl!" Yossarian interrupted him with desperate impatience. "Don't you understand? I don't want to sleep with her. I want to help her. You've got daughters. She's just a little kid, and she's all alone in this city with no one to take care of her. I want to protect her from harm. Don't you know what I'm talking about?"

Milo did understand and was deeply touched. "Yossarian, I'm proud of you," he exclaimed with profound emotion. "I really am. You don't know how glad I am to see that everything isn't always just sex with you. You've got principles. Certainly I've got daughters, and I know exactly what you're talking about. We'll find that girl. Don't you worry. You come with me and we'll find that girl if we have to turn this whole city upside down. Come along."

Yossarian went along in Milo Minderbinder's speeding M & M staff car to police headquarters to meet a swarthy, untidy police commissioner with a narrow black mustache and unbuttoned tunic who was fiddling with a stout woman with warts and two chins when they entered his office and who greeted Milo with warm surprise and bowed and scraped in obscene servility as though Milo were some elegant marquis.

"Ah, Marchese Milo," he declared with effusive pleasure, pushing the fat, disgruntled woman out the door without even looking toward her. "Why didn't you tell me you were coming? I would have a big party for you. Come in, come in, Marchese. You almost never visit us any more."

Milo knew that there was not one moment to waste. "Hello, Luigi," he said, nodding so briskly that he almost seemed rude. "Luigi, I need your help. My friend here wants to find a girl."

"A girl, Marchese?" said Luigi, scratching his face pensively. "There are lots of girls in Rome. For an American officer, a girl should not be too difficult."

"No, Luigi, you don't understand. This is a twelve-year-old virgin that he has to find right away."

"Ah, yes, now I understand," Luigi said sagaciously. "A virgin might take a little time. But if he waits at the bus terminal where the young farm girls looking for work arrive, I—"

"Luigi, you still don't understand," Milo snapped with such brusque impatience that the police commissioner's face flushed and he jumped to attention and began buttoning his uniform in confusion. "This girl is a friend, an old friend of the family, and we want to help her. She's only a child. She's all alone in this city somewhere, and we have to find her before somebody harms her. Now do you understand? Luigi, this is very important to me. I have a daughter the same age as that little girl, and nothing in the world means more to me right now than saving that poor child before it's too late. Will you help?"

"Si, Marchese, now I understand," said Luigi. "And I will do everything in my power to find her. But tonight I have almost no men. Tonight all my men are busy trying to break up the traffic in illegal tobacco."

"Illegal tobacco?" asked Milo.

"Milo," Yossarian bleated faintly with a sinking heart, sensing at once that all was lost.

"Si, Marchese," said Luigi. "The profit in illegal tobacco is so high that the smuggling is almost impossible to control."

"Is there really that much profit in illegal tobacco?" Milo inquired with keen interest, his rust-colored eyebrows arching avidly and his nostrils sniffing.

"Milo," Yossarian called to him. "Pay attention to me, will you?"

"Si, Marchese," Luigi answered. "The profit in illegal tobacco is very high. The smuggling is a national scandal, Marchese, truly a national disgrace."

"Is that a fact?" Milo observed with a preoccupied smile and started toward the door as though in a spell.

"Milo!" Yossarian yelled, and bounded forward impulsively to intercept him. "Milo, you've got to help me."

"Illegal tobacco," Milo explained to him with a look of epileptic lust, struggling doggedly to get by. "Let me go. I've got to smuggle illegal tobacco."

"Stay here and help me find her," pleaded Yossarian. "You can smuggle illegal tobacco tomorrow."

But Milo was deaf and kept pushing forward, nonviolently but irresistibly, sweating, his eyes, as though he were in the grip of a blind fixation, burning feverishly, and his twitching mouth slavering. He moaned calmly as though in remote, instinctive distress and kept repeating, "Illegal tobacco, illegal tobacco." Yossarian stepped out of the way with resignation finally when he saw it was hopeless to try to reason with him. Milo was gone like a shot. The commissioner of police unbuttoned his tunic again and looked at Yossarian with contempt.

"What do yo want here?" he asked coldly. "Do you want me to arrest you?"

Yossarian walked out of the office and down the stairs into the dark, tomblike street, passing in the hall the stout woman with warts and two chins, who was already on her way back in. There was no sign of Milo outside. There were no lights in any of the windows. The deserted sidewalk rose steeply and continuously for several blocks. He could see the glare of a broad avenue at the top of the long cobblestone incline. The police station was almost at the bottom: the yellow bulbs at the entrance sizzled in the dampness like wet torches. A frigid, fine rain was falling. He began walking slowly, pushing uphill. Soon he came to a quiet, cozy, inviting restaurant with red velvet drapes in the windows and a blue neon sign near the door that said: TONY'S RESTAURANT. FINE FOOD AND DRINK. KEEP OUT. The words on the blue neon sign surprised him mildly for only an instant. Nothing warped seemed bizarre any more in his strange, distorted surroundings. The tops of the sheer buildings slanted in weird, surrealistic perspective, and the street seemed tilted. He raised the collar of his warm woolen coat and hugged it around him. The night was raw. A boy in a thin shirt and thin tattered trousers walked out of the darkness on bare feet. The boy had black hair and needed a haircut and shoes and socks. His sickly face was pale and sad. His feet made grisly, soft, sucking sounds in the rain puddles on the wet pavement as he passed, and Yossarian was moved by such intense pity for his poverty that he wanted to smash his pale, sad, sickly face with his fist and knock him out of existence because he brought to mind *all* the pale, sad, sickly children in Italy that same night who needed haircuts and needed shoes and socks. He made Yossarian think of cripples and of cold and hungry men and women, and of all the dumb, passive, devout mothers with catatonic eyes nursing infants outdoors that same night with chilled animal udders bared insensibly to that same raw rain. Cows. Almost on cue, a nursing mother padded past holding an infant in black rags, and Yossarian wanted to smash her too, because she reminded him of the barefoot boy in the thin shirt and thin, tattered trousers and of all the shivering, stupefying misery in a world that never yet had provided enough heat and food and justice for all but an ingenious and unscrupulous handful. What a lousy earth! He wondered how many people were destitute that same night even in his own prosperous country, how many homes were shanties, how many husbands were drunk and wives socked, and how many children were bullied, abused or abandoned. How many families hungered for food they could not afford to buy? How many hearts were broken? How many suicides would take place that same night, how many people would go insane? How many cockroaches and landlords would triumph? How many winners were losers, successes failures, rich men poor men? How many wise guys were stupid? How many happy endings were unhappy endings? How many honest men were liars, brave men cowards, loyal men traitors, how many sainted men were corrupt, how many people in positions of trust had sold their souls to blackguards for petty cash, how many had never had souls? How many straight-and-narrow paths were crooked paths? How many best families were worst families and how many good people were bad people? When you added them all up and then subtracted, you might be left with only the children, and perhaps with Albert Einstein and an old violinist or sculptor somewhere. Yossarian walked in lonely torture, feeling estranged, and could not wipe from his mind the excruciating image of the barefoot boy with sickly cheeks until he turned the corner into the avenue finally and came upon an Allied soldier having convulsions on the ground, a young lieutenant with a small, pale, boyish face. Six other soldiers from different countries wrestled with different parts of him, striving to help him and hold him still. He yelped and groaned unintelligibly through clenched teeth, his eyes rolling up into his head. "Don't let him bite his tongue off," a short sergeant near Yossarian advised shrewdly, and a seventh man threw himself into the fray to wrestle with the ill lieutenant's face. All at once the wrestlers won and turned to each other undecidedly, for now that they held the young lieutenant rigid they did not know what to do with him. A quiver of moronic panic spread from one straining brute face to another. "Why don't you lift him and put him on the hood of that car?" a corporal standing in back of Yossarian drawled. That seemed to make sense, so the seven men lifted the young lieutenant up and stretched him out carefully on the hood of a parked car, still pinning each struggling part of him down. Once they had him stretched out on the hood of the parked car, they stared at each other uneasily again, for they had no idea what to do with him next. "Why don't you lift him up off the hood of that car and lay him down on the ground?" drawled the same corporal behind Yossarian. That seemed like a good idea, too, and they began to move him back to the sidewalk, but before they could finish, a jeep raced up with a flashing red spotlight at the side and two military policemen in the front seat.

"What's going on?" the driver yelled.

"He's having convulsions," one of the men grappling with one of the young lieutenant's limbs answered. "We're holding him still."

"That's good. He's under arrest."

"What should we do with him?"

"Keep him under arrest!" the M.P. shouted, doubling over with raucous laughter at his jest, and sped away in his jeep.

Yossarian recalled that he had no leave papers and moved prudently past the strange group toward the sound of muffled voices emanating from a distance inside the murky darkness ahead. The broad, rain-blotched boulevard was illuminated every half-block by short, curling lampposts with eerie, shimmering glares surrounded by smoky brown mist. From a window overhead he heard an unhappy female voice pleading, "Please don't. Please don't." A despondent young woman in a black raincoat with much black hair on her face passed with her eyes lowered. At the Ministry of Public Affairs on the next block, a drunken lady was backed up against one of the fluted Corinthian columns by a drunken young soldier, while three drunken comrades in arms sat watching nearby on the steps with wine bottles standing between their legs. "Pleeshe don't," begged the drunken lady. "I want to go home now. Pleeshe don't." One of the three sitting men cursed pugnaciously and hurled a wine bottle down at Yossarian when he turned to look up. The bottle shattered harmlessly far away with a brief and muted noise. Yossarian continued walking away at the same listless, unhurried pace, hands buried in his pockets. "Come on, baby," he heard the drunken soldier urge determinedly. "It's my turn now." "Pleeshe don't," begged the drunken lady. "Pleeshe don't." At the very next corner, deep inside the dense impenetrable shadows of a narrow, winding side street, he heard the mysterious, unmistakable sound of someone shoveling snow. The measured, labored, evocative scrape of iron shovel against concrete made his flesh crawl with terror as he stepped from the curb to cross the ominous alley and hurried onward until the haunting, incongruous noise had been left behind. Now he knew where he was; soon, if he continued without turning, he would come to the dry fountain in the middle of the boulevard, then to the officers' apartment seven blocks beyond. He heard snarling, inhuman voices cutting through the ghostly blackness in front suddenly. The bulb on the corner lamppost had died, spilling gloom over half the street, throwing everything visible off balance. On the other side of the intersection, a man was beating a dog with a stick like the man who was beating the horse with a whip in Raskolnikov's dream. Yossarian strained helplessly not to see or hear. The dog whimpered and squealed in brute, dumbfounded hysteria at the end of an old Manila rope and groveled and crawled on its belly without resisting, but the man beat it and beat it anyway with his heavy, flat stick. A small crowd watched. A squat woman stepped out and asked him please to stop. "Mind your own business," the man barked gruffly, lifting his stick as though he might beat her too, and the woman retreated sheepishly with an abject and humiliated air. Yossarian quickened his pace to get away, almost ran. The night was filled with horrors, and he thought he knew how Christ must have felt as he walked through the world, like a psychiatrist through a ward full of nuts, like a victim through a prison full of thieves. What a welcome sight a leper must have been! At the next corner a man was beating a small boy brutally in the midst of an immobile crowd of adult spectators who made no effort to intervene. Yossarian recoiled with sickening recognition. He was certain he had witnessed that same horrible scene sometime before. *Déjàvu?* The sinister coincidence shook him and filled him with doubt and dread. It was the same scene he had witnessed a block before, although everything in it seemed quite different. What in the world was happening? Would a squat woman step out and ask the man to please stop? Would he raise his hand to strike her and would she retreat? Nobody moved. The child cried steadily as though in drugged misery. The man kept knocking him down with hard, resounding open-palm blows to the head, then jerking him up to his feet in order to knock him down again. No one in the sullen, cowering crowd seemed to care enough about the stunned and beaten boy to interfere. The child was no more than nine. One drab woman was weeping silently into a dirty dish towel. The boy was emaciated and needed a haircut. Bright-red blood was streaming from both ears. Yossarian crossed quickly to the other side of the immense avenue to escape the nauseating sight and found himself walking on human teeth lying on the drenched, glistening pavement near splotches of blood kept sticky by the pelting raindrops poking each one like sharp fingernails. Molars and broken incisors lay scattered everywhere. He circled on tiptoe the grotesque debris and came near a doorway containing a crying soldier holding a saturated handkerchief to his mouth, supported as he sagged by two other soldiers waiting in grave impatience for the military ambulance that finally came clanging up with amber fog lights on and passed them by for an altercation on the next block between a single civilian Italian with books and a slew of civilian policemen with armlocks and clubs. The screaming, struggling civilian was a dark man with a face white as flour from fear. His eyes were pulsating in hectic desperation, flapping like bat's wings, as the many tall policemen seized him by arms and legs and lifted him up. His books were spilled on the ground. "Help!" he shrieked shrilly in a voice strangling in its own emotion as the policemen carried him to the open doors in the rear of the ambulance and threw him inside. "Police! Help! Police!" the doors were shut and bolted, and the ambulance raced away. There was a humorless irony in the ludicrous panic of the man screaming for help to the police while policemen were all around him. Yossarian smiled wryly at the futile and ridiculous cry for aid, then saw with a start that the words were ambiguous, realized with alarm that they were not, perhaps, intended as a call for police but as a heroic warning from the grave by a doomed friend to everyone who was *not* a policeman with a club and a gun and a mob of other policemen with clubs and guns to back him up. "Help! Police!" the man had cried, and he could have been shouting of danger. Yossarian responded to the thought by slipping away stealthily from the police and almost tripped over the feet of a burly woman of forty hastening across the intersection guiltily, darting furtive, vindictive glances behind her toward a woman of eighty with thick, bandaged ankles doddering after her in a losing pursuit. The old woman was gasping for breath as she minced along and muttering to herself in distracted agitation. There was no mistaking the nature of the scene; it was a chase. The triumphant first woman was halfway across the wide avenue before the second woman reached the curb. The nasty, small, gloating smile with which she glanced back at the laboring old woman was both wicked and apprehensive. Yossarian knew he could help the troubled old woman if she would only cry out, knew he could spring forward and capture the sturdy first woman and hold her for the mob of policemen nearby if the second woman would only give him license with a shriek of distress. But the the old woman passed by without even seeing him, mumbling in terrible, tragic vexation, and soon the first woman had vanished into the deepening layers of darkness and the old woman was left standing helplessly in the center of the thoroughfare, dazed, uncertain which way to proceed, alone. Yossarian tore his eyes from her and hurried away in shame because he had done nothing to assist her. He darted furtive, guilty glances back as he fled in defeat, afraid the old woman might now start following him, and he welcomed the concealing shelter of the drizzling, drifting, lightless, nearly opaque gloom. Mobs . . . mobs of policemen— everything but England was in the hands of mobs, mobs, mobs. Mobs with clubs were in control everywhere.

The surface of the collar and shoulders of Yossarian's coat was soaked. His socks were wet and cold. The light on the next lamppost was out, too, the glass globe broken. Buildings and featureless shapes flowed by him noiselessly as though borne past immutably on the surface of some rank and timeless tide. A tall monk passed, his face buried entirely inside a coarse gray cowl, even the eyes hidden. Footsteps sloshed toward him steadily through a puddle, and he feared it would be another barefoot child. He brushed by a gaunt, cadaverous, tristful man in a black raincoat with a star-shaped scar in his cheek and a glossy mutilated depression the size of an egg in one temple. On squishing straw sandals, a young woman materialized with her whole face disfigured by a God-awful pink and piebald burn that started on her neck and stretched in a raw, corrugated mass up both cheeks past her eyes! Yossarian could not bear to look, and shuddered. No one would ever love her. His spirit was sick; he longed to lie down with some girl he could love who would soothe and excite him and put him to sleep. A mob with a club was waiting for him in Pianosa. The girls were all gone. The countess and her daughter-in-law were no longer good enough; he had grown too old for fun, he no longer had the time. Luciana was gone, dead, probably; if not yet then soon enough. Aarfy's buxom trollop had vanished with her smutty cameo ring, and Nurse Duckett was ashamed of him because he had refused to fly more combat missions and would cause a scandal. The only girl he knew nearby was the plain maid in the officers' apartment, whom none of the men had ever slept with. Her name was Michaela, but the men called her filthy things in dulcet, ingratiating voices, and she giggled with childish joy because she understood no English and thought they were flattering her and making harmless jokes. Everything wild she watched them do filled her with enchanted delight. She was a happy, simple-minded, hard-working girl who could not read and was barely able to write her name. Her straight hair was the color of retting straw. She had sallow skin and myopic eyes, and none of the men had ever slept with her because none of the men had ever wanted to, none but Aarfy, who had raped her once that same evening and had then held her prisoner in a clothes closet for almost two hours with his hand over her mouth until the civilian curfew sirens sounded and it was unlawful for her to be outside.

Then he threw her out the window. Her dead body was still lying on the pavement when Yossarian arrived and pushed his way politely through the circle of solemn neighbors with dim lanterns, who glared with venom as they shrank away from him and pointed up bitterly toward the second-floor windows in their private, grim, accusing conversations. Yossarian's heart pounded with fright and horror at the pitiful, ominous, gory spectacle of the broken corpse. He ducked into the hallway and bolted up the stairs into the apartment, where he found Aarfy pacing about uneasily with a pompous, slightly uncomfortable smile. Aarfy seemed a bit unsettled as he fidgeted with his pipe and assured Yossarian that everything was going to be all right. There was nothing to worry about.

"I only raped her once," he explained.

Yossarian was aghast. "But you killed her, Aarfy! You killed her!"

"Oh, I had to do that after I raped her," Aarfy replied in his most condescending manner. "I couldn't very well let her go around saying bad things about us, could I?"

"But why did you have to touch her at all, you dumb bastard?" Yossarian shouted, "Why couldn't you get yourself a girl off the street if you wanted one? This city is full of prostitutes."

"Oh, no, not me," Aarfy bragged. "I never paid for it in my life."

"Aarfy, are you insane?" Yossarian was almost speechless. "You *killed* a girl. They're going to put you in jail!"

"Oh, no," Aarfy answered with a forced smile. "Not me. They aren't going to put good old Aarfy in jail. Not for killing *her*."

"But you threw her out the window. She's lying there dead in the street."

"She has no right to be there," Aarfy answered. "It's after curfew."

"Stupid! Don't you realize what you've done?" Yossarian wanted to grab Aarfy by his well-fed, caterpillar-soft shoulders and shake some sense into him. "You've murdered a human being. They *are* going to put you in jail. They might even *hang* you!"

"Oh, I hardly think they'll do that," Aarfy replied with a jovial chuckle, although his symptoms of nervousness increased. He spilled tobacco crumbs unconsciously as his short fingers fumbled with the bowl of his pipe. "No, sirree. Not to good old Aarfy." He chortled again. "She was only a servant girl. I hardly think they're going to make too much of a fuss over one poor Italian servant girl when so many thousands of lives are being lost every day. Do you?"

"Listen!" Yossarian cried, almost in joy. He pricked up his ears and watched the blood drain from Aarfy's face as sirens mourned far away, police sirens, and then ascended almost instantaneously to a howling, strident, onrushing cacophony of overwhelming sound that seemed to crash into the room around them from every side. "Aarfy, they're coming for you," he said in a flood of compassion, shouting to be heard above the noise. "They're coming to arrest you. Aarfy, don't you understand? You can't take the life of another human being and get away with it, even if she is just a poor servant girl. Don't you see? Can't you understand?"

"Oh, no," Aarfy insisted with a lame laugh and a weak smile. "They're not coming to arrest me. Not good old Aarfy."

All at once he looked sick. He sank down on a chair in a trembling stupor, his stumpy, lax hands quaking in his lap. Cars skidded to a stop outside. Spotlights hit the windows immediately. Car doors slammed and police whistles screeched. Voices rose harshly. Aarfy was green. He kept shaking his head mechanically with a queer, numb smile and repeating in a weak, hollow monotone that they were not coming for him, not for good old Aarfy, no sirree, striving to convince himself that this was so even as heavy footsteps raced up the stairs and pounded across the landing, even as fists beat on the door four times with a deafening, inexorable force. Then the door to the apartment flew open, and two large, tough, brawny M.P.s with icy eyes and firm, sinewy, unsmiling jaws entered quickly, strode across the room, and arrested Yossarian.

They arrested Yossarian for being in Rome without a pass.

They apologized to Aarfy for intruding and led Yossarian away between them, gripping him under each arm with fingers as hard as steel manacles. They said nothing at all to him on the way down. Two more tall M.P.s with clubs and hard white helmets were waiting outside at a closed car. They marched Yossarian into the back seat, and the car roared away and weaved through the rain and muddy fog to a police station. The M.P.s locked him up for the night in a cell with four stone walls. At dawn they gave him a pail for a latrine and drove him to the airport, where two more giant M.P.s with clubs and white helmets were waiting at a transport plane whose engines were already warming up when they arrived, the cylindrical green cowlings oozing quivering beads of condensation. None of the M.P.s said anything to each other either. They did not even nod. Yossarian had never seen such granite faces. The plane flew to Pianosa. Two more silent M.P.s were waiting at the landing strip. There were now eight, and they filed with precise, wordless discipline into two cars and sped on humming tires past the four squadron areas to the Group Headquarters building, where still two more M.P.s were waiting at the parking area. All ten tall, strong, purposeful, silent men towered around him as they turned toward the entrance. Their footsteps crunched in loud unison on the cindered ground. He had an impression of accelerating haste. He was terrified. Every one of the ten M.P.s seemed powerful enough to bash him to death with a single blow. They had only to press their massive, toughened, boulderous shoulders against him to crush all life from his body. There was nothing he could do to save himself. He could not even see which two were gripping him under the arms as they marched him rapidly between the two tight single-file columns they had formed. Their pace quickened, and he felt as though he were flying along with his feet off the ground as they trotted in resolute cadence up the wide marble staircase to the upper landing, where still two more inscrutable military policemen with hard faces were waiting to lead them all at an even faster pace down the long, cantilevered balcony overhanging the immense lobby. Their marching footsteps on the dull tile floor thundered like an awesome, quickening drum roll through the vacant center of the building as they moved with even greater speed and precision toward Colonel Cathcart's office, and violent winds of panic began blowing in Yossarian's ears when they turned him toward his doom inside the office, where Colonel Korn, his rump spreading comfortably on a corner of Colonel Cathcart's desk, sat waiting to greet him with a genial smile and said,

"We're sending you home."

Exercises

1. What, exactly, is Catch 22? Why is this so absurd?
2. Why did MP's smash *everything* in the whorehouse?
3. What is symbolized by "Nately's whore's kid sister" and the search for her?
4. Assuming that all of the events that Yossarian observes on his nighttime stroll are metaphors for the war, select several events and discuss what they represent.
5. How much of what happens in this chapter can be considered rational and reasonable? Irrational and unreasonable? Give some examples.

Summary

Time Chart for the Twentieth Century at the end of this chapter provides an overview of our bewildering century of violence and invention. The century has been one of interminable warfare, including the two most destructive wars in human history, but there have also been remarkable technological developments. Consider transportation, for example. The Wright brothers flew the first heavier-than-air flying machine in 1903. Thirty-one years later the jet engine was invented and, eighteen years after that, commercial jets were making the world much smaller. Goddard invented the liquid fuel rocket in 1926, the Russians put Sputnik into orbit twenty-one years later and, twelve years after that, an American astronaut walked on the moon.

Communications technology also developed in a rush. Twelve years after the beginning of commercial television transcontinental television became a reality; a decade later communication satellites were starting to beam television to the entire world. We do indeed live in a Global Community with the possibility, no mattter how faint, of evolving into a peaceful community in which human values will be more important than material possessions and national rivalries. High tech makes this possible but only human beings can make it a reality.

Suggested Reading

Rather than giving a definitive list of the "most important" literary works of this century we are providing a basic list of titles and authors, who have, in some way, contributed to the cultural tenor of our time. By using this bibliography as a basis for study and exploration students can select those authors or works which are of particular interest and thus create their personalized adventures in twentieth-century literature. Most of these titles are available in school and public libraries and most are published in paperback editions.

Fiction

Bellow, Saul. *Humboldt's Gift,* 1975.
Borges, Jorge Luis. *Labyrinths,* 1961.
Bowen, Elizabeth. *Death of the Heart,* 1939.
Camus, Albert. *The Stranger,* 1942; *The Fall,* 1957.
Celine, Louis-Ferdinand. *Death on the Installment Plan,* 1938.
Conrad, Joseph. *Heart of Darkness,* 1902.
Didion, Joan. *Play It as It Lays,* 1970.
Dos Passos, John. *U. S. A.,* 1937.
Dreiser, Theodore. *Sister Carrie,* 1900.
Farrell, James T. *Studs Lonigan,* 1935.
Faulkner, William. *The Sound and the Fury,* 1929.
Fitzgerald, F. Scott. *The Great Gatsby,* 1925.
Foley, Martha, editor. *Fifty Best American Short Stories, 1915–1965,* 1966.
Forster, E. M. *A Passage to India,* 1924.
Gide, André. *The Counterfeiters,* 1926.
Golding, William. *Lord of the Flies,* 1954.
Grass, Gunter. *The Tin Drum,* 1962.

Greene, Graham. *The Power and the Glory,* 1946.
Heller, Joseph. *Catch 22,* 1961.
Hemingway, Ernest. *For Whom the Bell Tolls,* 1940.
Huxley, Aldous. *Brave New World,* 1932.
James, Henry. *The Golden Bowl,* 1904.
Jones, James. *From Here to Eternity,* 1951.
Joyce, James. *Ulysses,* 1922.
Kafka, Franz. *The Trial,* 1937.
Kazantzakis, Nikos. *Zorba the Greek,* 1946.
Kerouac, John. *On the Road,* 1957.
Kesey, Ken. *One Flew Over the Cuckoo's Nest,* 1962.
Koestler, Arthur. *Darkness at Noon,* 1941.
Lawrence, D. H. *Sons and Lovers,* 1913.
Lessing, Doris. *The Golden Notebook,* 1962.
Lewis, Sinclair. *Babbitt,* 1922.
Mailer, Norman. *The Naked and the Dead,* 1948.
Malamud, Bernard. *The Fixer,* 1966.
Malraux, André. *Man's Fate,* 1934.
Mann, Thomas. *Buddenbrooks,* 1901.
Maugham, Somerset. *Of Human Bondage,* 1915.
McCullers, Carson. *The Heart Is a Lonely Hunter,* 1940.
Miller, Henry. *Tropic of Cancer,* 1934.
Mishima, Yukio. *The Decay of the Angel,* 1975.
Moravia, Alberto. *The Woman of Rome,* 1949.
Nabakov, Vladimir. *Lolita,* 1955.
Oates, Joyce Carol. *Then,* 1969.
O'Conner, Flannery. *Everything that Rises Must Converge,* 1965.
Orwell, George. *Nineteen Eighty-four,* 1949.
Pasternak, Boris. *Dr. Zhivago,* 1957.
Paton, Alan. *Cry the Beloved Country,* 1948.
Proust, Marcel. *Remembrance of Things Past,* 1934.
Pychon, Thomas. *V,* 1963.
Remarque, Erich Maria. *All Quiet on the Western Front,* 1929.
Renault, Mary. *The King Must Die,* 1958.
Richter, Conrad. *The Trees,* 1940.
Rolland, Romain. *Jean-Christophe,* 1912.
Roth, Philip. *Goodbye Columbus,* 1959.
Salinger, Jerome D. *Catcher in the Rye,* 1951.
Sartre, Jean-Paul. *Nausea,* 1949.
Sholokhov, Mikhail. *And Quiet Flows the Don,* 1934.
Solzhenitsyn, Aleksandr. *One Day in the Life of Ivan Denisovich,* 1963.
Steinbeck, John. *The Grapes of Wrath,* 1939.
Styron, William. *The Confessions of Nat Turner,* 1967.
Thurber, James. *The Thurber Carnival,* 1945.
Vidal, Gore. *Burr: A Novel,* 1973.
Vonnegut, Kurt. *Slaughterhouse Five,* 1969.
Warren, Robert Penn. *All the King's Men,* 1946.
Wolfe, Thomas. *You Can't Go Home Again,* 1940.
Woolf, Virginia. *To the Lighthouse,* 1927.
Wright, Richard. *Native Son,* 1940.

Drama

Albee, Edward. *Who's Afraid of Virginia Woolf,* 1962.
Anderson, Maxwell. *Winterset,* 1935.
Anouilh, Jean. *Becket,* 1960.
Baldwin, James. *Blues for Mr. Charlie,* 1965.
Beckett, Samuel. *Waiting for Godot,* 1952.
Brecht, Bertolt. *Mother Courage and Her Children,* 1949.
Cocteau, Jean. *Beauty and the Beast (film),* 1950.
Frisch, Max. *The Firebugs,* 1958.
Genet, Jean. *The Balcony,* 1956.
Ionesco, Eugene. *Exit the King,* 1961.
Maeterlinck, Maurice. *The Bluebird,* 1908.
Miller, Arthur. *Death of a Salesman,* 1949.
Odets, Clifford. *Awake and Sing,* 1935.
O'Neill, Eugene. *Long Day's Journey into Night,* 1956.
Osborne, John. *Look Back in Anger,* 1956.
Pinter, Harold. *The Homecoming,* 1967.
Pirandello, Luigi. *Six Characters in Search of an Author,* 1921.
Shaw, George Bernard. *Pygmalion,* 1912.
Synge, John. *Playboy of the Western World,* 1907.
Weiss, Peter. *Marat/Sade,* 1965.
Wilder, Thornton. *Our Town,* 1938.
Williams, Tennessee. *The Glass Menagerie,* 1945.

Poetry

Auden, W.H.	Rich, Adrienne
cummings, e e	Rilke, Rainer Maria
Eliot, T.S.	Robinson, Edwin Arlington
Ferlinghetti, Lawrence	Roethke, Theodore
Frost, Robert	Sandburg, Carl
Housman, A.E.	Sitwell, Edith
Hughes, Langston	Stevens, Wallace
Jeffers, Robinson	Thomas, Dylan
Plath, Sylvia	Yeats, William Butler
Pound, Ezra	Yevtushenko, Yevgeny

The Literature of Moving Images

Film can and should be studied as an art form but it is a medium that must be experienced, preferably in a theatre with an audience. With very few exceptions movies are made to make money in public showings before a mass audience. "Motion picture industry" is the term generally used to describe corporate enterprises that use a large number of highly skilled people: screenwriter, director, actors, cinematographer, film editor, film scorer, set and costume designers, and many others. Unlike a novel, say, by Albert Camus, a film cannot be credited to a single creator. Critics tend to lavish credit on the director as the person in charge but this is only a convention that tends to slight everyone else. One cannot, for example, think of director

Elia Kazan's *On the Waterfront* without recalling Marlon Brando's masterful performance. In the final analysis no film is better than its literary base, the screenplay itself, for this is where virtually all movies begin.

Movies are a prime mass entertainment medium the world over and, as commercial enterprises, about 99 percent of them are eminently forgettable. But from the beginning of motion pictures, there have been exceptions, movies that have made an artistic impact and that have withstood the test of time. Usually referred to as film classics, these are masterpieces that have effectively synthesized the efforts of many creators. Following is a list of movies that are generally regarded as true classics. Some, perhaps, are not to everyone's taste but all are notable works of art and all should be seen, preferably more than once. They are among the best of a new literature that began in this century. Following the standard procedure, credit for the movies is assigned to the directors but, in every case, the viewer should give due credit to all participants, both on and off camera.

Antonioni, Michelangelo. *L'Avventura.* Italy, 1959.
Bergman, Ingmar. *The Seventh Seal.* Sweden, 1956.
———. *Wild Strawberries.* Sweden, 1957.
Buñuel, Luis. *Belle de Jour.* France, 1968.
Chaplin, Charles. *The Gold Rush.* U.S., 1925.

Cocteau, Jean. *Beauty and the Beast.* France, 1947.
DeSica, Vittorio, *The Bicycle Thief.* Italy, 1948.
Eisenstein, Serge. *Potemkin.* Russia, 1925.
Fellini, Federico. *La Strada.* Italy, 1954.
———. *La Dolce Vita.* Italy, 1959.
Gance, Abel. *Napoleon.* France, 1925, 1982.
Griffith, David W. *Intolerance.* U.S., 1916.
Hitchcock, Alfred. *Vertigo.* U.S., 1958.
Kazan, Elia. *On the Waterfront.* U.S., 1954.
Kurosawa, Akira. *Roshomon.* Japan, 1950.
———. *Ikiru.* Japan, 1952.
———. *Seven Samurai.* Japan, 1954.
Lang, Fritz. *M.* Germany, 1931.
Penn, Arthur. *Bonnie and Clyde.* U.S., 1967.
Renoir, Jean. *La Grande Illusion.* France, 1938.
———. *Rules of the Game.* France, 1939, 1965.
Truffaut, Francois. *The 400 Blows.* France, 1959.
———. *Jules and Jim.* France, 1961.
Welles, Orson. *Citizen Kane.* U.S., 1941.
Wiene, Robert. *The Cabinet of Dr. Caligari.* Germany, 1919.
Wilder, Billy. *Some Like It Hot.* U.S., 1959.

1900–1980s

1900 Freud, *The Interpretation of Dreams;* quantum theory; beginnings of jazz in American South
 1901 First transatlantic radio telegraphic transmission
  1902 First phonograph recordings
   1903 Flight of Wright brothers; Picasso's Blue Period
    1905 Einstein's Special Theory of Relativity; first moving pictures by Edison; Fauves in Paris
     1906 San Francisco earthquake
      1907 Picasso, *Les Demoiselles d'Avignon*
       1909 F. L. Wright, Robie House; founding of NAACP; Diaghilev unveils Ballet Russe in Paris
        1911 Chagall, *I and the Village;* Matisse, *The Blue Window*
         1912 Kandinsky, *Concerning the Spiritual in Art*
          1913 Stravinsky, *Rite of Spring;* Armory Show in New York
           1914 World War I (to 1918)
            1915 Dada movement begins
             1916 Einstein's General Theory of Relativity
              1917 Lenin triumphs in Russia
               1918 Worldwide influenza epidemic kills ca. 20 million
                1919 Treaty of Versailles; Bauhaus founded
                 1920 Women win vote in U.S.; prohibition in U.S. (to 1933)
                  1920s Chicago style jazz; The Jazz Age
1921 Major powers meet in Limitation of Armaments Conference
 1922 Fascists seize power in Italy; Eliot, *The Wasteland;* radar invented
  1924 Breton, *First Surrealist Manifesto;* death of Lenin
   1925 Brancusi, *Bird in Space;* Gropius, Workshop of Bauhaus
    1926 First television transmission; first liquid fuel rocket
     1927 Stalin dictator in Russia; Lindbergh's flight to Paris
      1928 First sound movie; Weill, *Threepenny Opera*
       1929 Wall Street panic; beginning of Great Depression; Corbusier, Villa Savoye
        1930 Sinclair Lewis wins Nobel Prize for Literature; big band jazz flourishes (into 40s)
         1931 Sino-Japanese war (to 1945); Dali, *The Persistence of Memory*
          1932 Huxley, *Brave New World*
           1933 Hitler chancellor of Germany; Roosevelt begins New Deal
            1934 Discovery of antibiotics;
             1935 WPA Art Project (to 1940); Congress passes Social Security Act
              1936 F. L. Wright, Kaufmann House; Spanish Civil War (to 1939)
               1937 Picasso, *Guernica*
                1938 Germany annexes Austria; Czechoslovakia dismembered
                 1939 World War II (to 1945); first commercial television; invention of jet aircraft engine; automatic sequence
                       computer developed
                  1940 Richard Wright, *Native Son;* first successful plutonium fission
1941 Pearl Harbor bombed
 1942 Uranium fission, atomic reactor
  1943 Pollock's first exhibition; race riots in Detroit and New York
   1944 Beginnings of Bop (Modern) jazz
    1945 Atomic bomb on Hiroshima; New York becomes new international art center
     1946 Camus, *The Stranger;* Orwell, *1984;* Philippines win independence from U.S.
      1947 Beginning of Marshall Plan for Europe; transistor invented; United Nations Building
       1948 Israel becomes independent state; LP recordings marketed
        1949 Russia acquires atomic weapons; China goes Communist
         1950 Korean War (to 1953); U.S. military advisers sent to Vietnam
          1950s Beginnings of electronic music; art "happenings"; "beat" generation
           1951 Transcontinental television inaugurated
            1952 Hydrogen bomb exploded by U.S. in South Pacific
             1953 Death of Stalin; Beckett, *Waiting for Godot*
              1954 U.S. Supreme Court disallows segregation; DeGaulle returns to power
               1955 Rauschenberg, *Bed;* beginning of Civil Rights movement in South
                1956 Interstate highway system inaugurated; first transatlantic telephone cable
                 1957 Russia launches Sputnik; Congress passes first Civil Rights legislation since reconstruction
                  1958 Beginning of jet airline passenger service; LASAR beam invented
                   1959 Rauschenberg, *Monogram;* Wright's Guggenheim Museum completed
                    1960s Pop Art flourishes; Hippies, Yippies, protestors

1961 First manned orbital flight (Russia)
1962 Rachel Carson's *Silent Spring* launches environmentalist movement; Saarinen, TWA Terminal
1963 John F. Kennedy assassinated; quasars discovered
1964 Kubrick movie *Dr. Strangelove;* China explodes atom bomb
1965 Height of Beatlemania; foundation of the National Organization for Women
1966 Indiana, *The Black and White Love*
1967 First human heart transplant; Safdie, Habitat and Fuller, American Pavilion, EXPO 67
1968 Assassination of Martin Luther King and Robert Kennedy
1969 American moon walk; Rock Festival at Woodstock; race riots in Watts, Detroit, New York
1970 Toffler, *Future Shock*
1970s New Realism in art; art and technology; rapid advances in computors and robotics
1971 Shostakovitch, *Symphony No. 15*
1972 UN Conference on the Human Environment to study pollution
1973 First orbital laboratory (Skylab)
1974 First energy crisis; Nixon resigns presidency
1975 American withdrawal from Vietnam
1976 Moratorium lifted on Recombinant DNA technology (genetic engineering)
1977 Piano and Rogers, Pompidou Center, Paris
1978 Sadat of Egypt and Begin of Israel share Nobel Peace Prize; first "test-tube baby delivered in England
1979 Nobel Prize in Medicine awarded for invention of computed axial tomography (CAT scan); Iran takes Americans hostage at U.S. Embassy
1980s Age of Information and Communication; rapid developments in High Tech

Appendix *Music Listening and Notation*

Music listening is always enriched by a knowledge of basic facts such as those outlined herein. This appendix should, ideally, be studied for content and also used, along with the Glossary, as often as necessary in conjunction with the chapters on music.

Characteristics of Musical Sounds

Musical tones are sounds of definite pitch and duration, as distinct from noises and other less definite sounds. Musical tones have the four characteristics of *pitch, intensity, tone color,* and *duration,* which may be described as follows:

Pitch   The location of musical sound from low to high or high to low.

Intensity   Relative degree of softness or loudness.

Tone Color   The quality of a sound that distinguishes it from other musical sounds of the same pitch and intensity; for example, the different tone quality of a flute as contrasted with a clarinet. Also called *timbre.*

Duration   The length of time a tone is audible.

The Four Elements of Music

Rhythm, melody, harmony, and *tone color* are the essential elements of music. Composers and performers are concerned with each, while for the listener, they are experienced as a web of sound that makes it difficult to single out any one element. Each can, however, be considered in isolation as a guide to understanding.

Rhythm

Though little is known about prehistoric music, the earliest music was probably the beating out of rhythms long before the existence of either melody or speech. There is rhythm in the universe: our heartbeat, alternating day and night, the progression of the seasons, waves crashing on a beach. Manufactured rhythm can be heard in train wheels clicking on rails, a Ping-Pong game, or the clacking castanets of a Spanish dancer.

Essentially, rhythm is the organization of musical time, that is, everything that takes place in terms of sound and silence, accent and nonaccent, tension and relaxation. Rhythm can also be defined as the "melody of a monotone"; music can be recognized just by hearing its rhythm. For example, tapping out the rhythmic patterns of "Dixie" can bring that familiar melody to mind.

Rhythm is the name of the whole and is not to be confused with *beat,* which results from a certain regularity of the rhythmic patterns. Beat, or pulse, can be compared with the heartbeat or the pulse rate. The beat will usually be steady but it may temporarily speed up or slow down. It may be *explicit* (the uniform thump of a bass drum in a marching band) or *implicit* (resulting from combinations of rhythmic patterns). As soon as one duration follows another, there will be rhythm but not necessarily beat. Certain types of music (such as Gregorian chant) do not produce the regular pulsation called beat.

When beats are produced by the music in a repeating pattern of accents, the result is *meter. Metered* music is *measured* music, with groupings of two, three, or four beats (or combinations of these) in each *measure,* or *bar.*

Time Signatures

When there is a regular pattern of accented and unaccented beats, it is customary to use a *time signature* in which the upper figure indicates the number of beats in a measure and the lower figure (though not in every case), the unit of beat; that is, the note value the composer has selected to symbolize one beat. For example:

2 = two beats per measure (duple meter)
4 = ♩ unit of beat (quarter note receives one beat)

3 = three beats per measure (triple meter)
8 = ♪ unit of beat (eighth note receives one beat)

Melody

A melody is a horizontal organization of pitches or, simply, a succession of musical tones. Melodies may move with:

Conjunct (Stepwise) Motion

Disjunct (Skipping) Motion

Disjunct and Conjunct Motion

Harmony

Harmony exists when two or more pitches are sounded together. Western music has used harmony since about the ninth century. However, harmony is still not commonly used in the music of the Near, Middle, or Far East or Africa.

Individual Harmonies

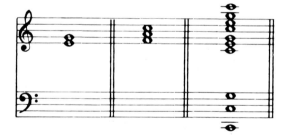

Melody with Harmony

Tone Color

Sometimes called timbre (TAM–ber), tone color is to music what color is to the painter. It is tone color that enables us to distinguish between a flute, a clarinet, and an oboe. A soprano voice is higher in pitch than a bass voice, but the tone color is also different. Through experience, everyone has learned to recognize the unique colors of many instruments. Further study leads to finer discriminations between similar instruments such as violin and viola, oboe and English horn, and so on. Composers select instruments for expressive purposes based largely on their coloration, whether singly or in combination. The full sound of a Beethoven symphony differs from a work by Richard Strauss, for example, because Strauss uses a wider range of instrumental colors.

Musical Literacy

The most abstract of the arts, music is sound moving in time. Factual information about music certainly helps the listener, but all the facts in the world can only assist the listening process; information about music can never replace the sound of music. One extremely useful method of instruction is to present major themes and ideas in musical notation, a practice common to virtually all books on music listening.

A practical approach to intelligent listening must include some instruction in musical literacy sufficient to read a single line of music. This is a simple process that can be quickly learned by young children and can be taught to an adult in a few minutes. The strangely prevalent folklore about musical notation being "too hard" or "too technical" has no foundation in fact, and probably refers to reading music as a performer, which is a very different matter that need not concern us here. As basic to music as the ABC's of written language but easier to understand, musical notation is an indispensable guide for music listeners. Learning to read music well enough to figure out a single line of music and to plunk it out on a piano is simply basic musical literacy.

Educated listeners quickly learn to enjoy picking out musical themes. This turns abstract sounds into tangible tunes, thus giving the listener an opportunity to preview the themes so that they can be anticipated in the music. Equally valuable is the repetition of themes after the listening experience. To summarize, picking out melodies is an aid to understanding, a helpful preview of music to be listened to, and a reminder of music already heard.

Approach the following material not with apprehension but with anticipation. Master the principles of musical notation with the positive attitude that this will materially assist not only in a better understanding of the music in this text but also lead, in time, to a lifetime of pleasurable listening.

Musical Notation

Pitch

The essential elements of our notational system were devised some ten centuries ago and subsequently altered and augmented to become a reasonably efficient means of communicating the composer's intentions to listener and performer. The system is based on the first seven letters of the alphabet and can best be illustrated by using a segment of the piano keyboard. The pitches range from low to high, from A through G in a repeating A–G pattern.

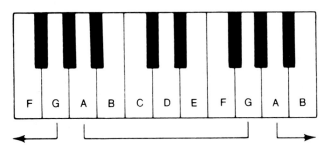

In order to know which of the eight A's available on the piano is the intended note, the following is necessary:

1. Use a musical *staff* of five lines and four spaces.

2. Use a symbol for a musical pitch, i.e., *note*.

3. Place the notes on the staff.

4. Indicate by means of a *clef sign* the *names* of the notes.

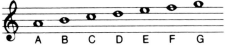

Clef (French, *key*) implies that the key to precise placement of the notes is the establishment of the letter name of *one* of the lines or spaces of the staff. There are two clefs in common use. Both are ornamental symbols derived from the letters G and F. The solid lines are the present clef signs and the dotted lines their original form:

The clefs are placed on the staff to indicate the location of the letters they represent. The lower portion of the G clef curls around the second line to fix the location of G; the two dots of the F clef are placed above and below the fourth line to show that this is the F line.

Once the five-line staff has received its pitch designations of G or F, the *staff* is subsequently identified as a *treble* or a *bass staff.*

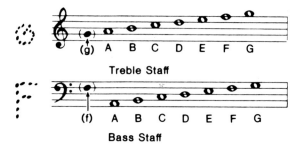

Treble Staff

Bass Staff

Both these staffs are segments of a complete system of lines and spaces called the *great staff*. The following illustration of the great staff includes notes arranged to form words, which is a quick way to learn to read music. Try putting your own words into notation.

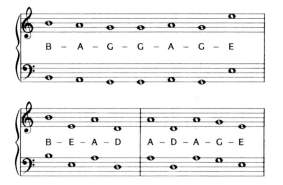

B – A – G – G – A – G – E

B – E – A – D   A – D – A – G – E

Not all melodies are composed so that they can be played on the white notes only of the piano. Sometimes another *key,* or different set of pitches, is used as demonstrated in the following examples:

Joy to the World

Key of C

Joy to the World

Key of D

In the second version the *key signature* indicates that all of the F's and C's have been raised a half step to the next closest note. A symbol called a sharp (♯) indicates raised notes. Key signatures can include up to seven sharps or flats.

The other common symbol that changes a note is the *flat* (♭), which lowers a note a half step to the next closest note. Following is the same melody written in the key of B♭. As indicated by the key signature, all the B's and E's have been lowered to B♭ and E♭.

Joy to the World

Key of B

You will note that the staff given above has an added short line, a *ledger line,* used to accommodate the last two notes.

A piano keyboard has *white* keys and *black* keys, with the black keys grouped in alternating sets of two and three. The white note, or key, immediately to the left of the two black keys is always C. There are eight C's; the C closest to the center is *middle C.* It is from this C that you can locate the notes of the themes.

Middle C   Middle C

On page 497 is a guide to the *chromatic scale,* which is all of the white and black keys in one octave.

Duration

The notation of the length of time of musical sounds (and silences) was developed in conjunction, more or less, with the notation of pitch. The modern *note-value* system consists of fractional parts of a whole unit, or *whole note* (𝅝), expressed in mathematical terms as 1/1. A *half note* (𝅗𝅥) is one-half the whole unit, or 1/2; a *quarter note* (♩) is one-quarter the unit, or 1/4; and so forth.

The *name* of the note value indicates the *number* of notes in the whole-note unit. There are four quarter notes ($4 \times 1/4 = 1/1$), eight eighth notes ($8 \times 1/8 = 1/1$), etc.

With note values smaller than the whole note, the relationships remain constant. There are two quarter notes in a half note ($2 \times 1/4 = 1/2$), two eighth notes in a quarter note ($2 \times 1/8 = 1/4$), etc.

Rhythmic notation is both relative and fixed. The duration of a whole note is dependent on the tempo (speed) and notation of music. It may have a duration of one second, eight seconds, or something in between. The interior relationships, however, never vary.

Chromatic Scale

A whole note has the same duration as two half notes, four quarter notes, and so forth. The mathematical relationship is fixed and precise. See the table below for an outline of the system.

Note and Rest Values

Note Value	Symbol
Whole note (basic unit)	𝅝
Half note	𝅗𝅥
Quarter note	♩
Eighth note	♪
Sixteenth note	𝅘𝅥𝅯

Rest Value	Symbol
Whole (note) rest	▬
Half rest	▬
Quarter rest	𝄽
Eighth rest	𝄾
Sixteenth rest	𝄿

Voices and Instruments

Choral ensembles are usually divided into four voice parts ranging from high to low: soprano and alto (women) and tenor and bass (men).

Instruments of the symphony orchestra and other ensembles are grouped by family, from highest pitch to lowest:

Strings	Woodwinds	Brass	Percussion
violin	piccolo	trumpet	snare drum
viola	flute	(and cornet)	timpani
cello	oboe	French horn	bass drum
bass	clarinet	trombone	cymbals
	bassoon	tuba	many others

Keyboard instruments include piano, harpsichord, and organ. The piano, originally called pianoforte, is based on the principle of hammers striking the strings; the harpsichord has a mechanism that plucks the strings. Built with two or more keyboards called manuals, organs either use forced air to activate the pipes or some version of an electronic reproduction of sound.

Musical Texture

The words for the three kinds of musical texture are derived from Greek and are virtually self-explanatory:

Monophonic (one sound)
Homophonic (same sound)
Polyphonic (many sounds)

Monophonic music has a single unaccompanied melody line. Much of the world's music is monophonic, including Chinese and Hindu music and, in Western civilizations, Gregorian chant and troubadour songs. Homophonic music has a principal melodic line accompanied by harmony, sometimes referred to as chordal accompaniment. While it is relatively unknown outside Western culture, homophonic comprises the bulk of our music including nearly all popular music. Polyphonic music has two or more melodies sounding simultaneously. Familiar rounds like "Three Blind Mice" and "Row, Row, Row Your Boat" are polyphonic, as is most Renaissance music. The music of baroque composers such as Bach, Handel, and many others is basically polyphonic.

Musical Form

Briefly stated, form in music is a balance of unity and variety. Too much unity becomes boring, while excessive variety leads to fragmentation and even chaos. Understanding form in music is a high priority for educated listeners. As Robert Schumann remarked, "Only when the form is quite clear to you will the spirit become clear to you."

The smallest unit of form is the *motive,* which to be intelligible must have at least two notes plus an identifiable rhythmic pattern. The principle motive in the first movement of Beethoven's Fifth Symphony has two different pitches in a four-note rhythmic pattern:

A musical phrase is a coherent group of notes roughly comparable to a literary phrase and having about the same function. Two related phrases form a *period,* in the manner of a literary sentence. In the period illustrated below, note that the first phrase has a transitional ending called a *half cadence,* while the second phrase ends solidly with a *full cadence.* Note also the extreme unity; the first three measures of both phrases are identical.

In large works the musical periods are used in various combinations to expand the material into sections comparable to paragraphs, and these are then combined to make still larger units.

Musical structure can be comprehended only *after* the music has arrived at wherever the composer intends it to go. Look again at "Ode to Joy." You can "see" its form only because the music is notated, which is why learning some notation is so important. When the music is played, your ear follows the line to the half cadence, which is then heard as a statement that demands completion. As the second phrase begins, there is aural recognition of its relationship to the first phrase. When the second phrase concludes with a gratifying full cadence, there is a kind of flashback to the memory of the first phrase. In other words, the conclusion of the second phrase is satisfying because it completes the thought of the still-remembered first phrase. The music conforms to its own inner logic; that is, the second phrase is a logical consequence of the first.

As a general rule, most music is constructed around two different but logically related (inner logic) musical ideas. We can call one idea *A* and the other *B.* One common musical form is two-part (binary), or simply A–B. An even more common form is three-part (ternary), or A–B–A. In two-part form the composer makes a musical statement (A), which is followed by a new section (B), which is sufficiently different to provide variety but not so different as to destroy the balance. The following hymn tune is a complete composition in two-part form, with two phrases in each section. Section B has the same rhythm as Section A, but the melody is a kind of inversion of the melody in A. The inner logic is maintained through the similarities.

The following complete hymn tune has a form related to two-part form: A–A¹–B, called A, A prime, B. Part A is followed by another A that is varied going into the cadence. Part B is properly different but related to A and A¹ by the similarity of measures 2, 6, and 10. In terms of measures, the structure of the piece can be diagrammed as:

A   A¹   B
2+2   2+2   2+2

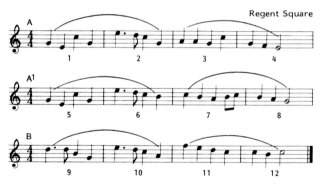

Three-part form operates on the principle of closing with the melody that began the piece, a rounding off of the material: A–B–A. The following example can be analyzed as A–A¹–B–A¹ and diagrammed as:

A   A¹   B   A¹
4 + 4   4 + 4   4 + 4   4 + 4.

This is the thirty-two-measure form most commonly used for popular songs.

There are, of course, other variants of AB and ABA forms as well as several other structures. However, the examples given illustrate the principle of a balance between unity and variety, of which unity is paramount. Perhaps because it is rather amorphous, music, more than any other art, emphasizes repetition, restating the material again and again, but mixing with enough variety to maintain interest. The forms illustrated can also be heard in the larger context of longer compositions. For example, "In the Gloaming" has 32 measures in a basic ABA form; a large symphonic work could have, say, 200 measures and be diagrammed as follows:

A	B	A	*or*	A	B	A¹	*or*	A	B	A¹
aba	aba	aba		aba¹	aba	aba¹		aa¹ba	aba	aa¹ba¹

The Listening Experience

Listening to music begins with the question, What do you hear? This is an objective question that has nothing whatever to do with a story you may imagine the music is telling, random associations the music happens to trigger, or any meaning that may be attributed to the music. For the educated listener the procedure is to objectively identify the sounds you hear, to determine how the sounds are produced, and to try to determine how the sounds are organized.

Composers do not pour out notes as if emptying a glass of water on a tabletop. They arrange their sounds in a sort of container in a manner that molds the container to the material it holds. Learning to comprehend the musical structure leads inevitably to the ability to *anticipate* the next melody, cadence, section, or whatever. Being able to anticipate what is to happen next means that you are tuned in to the web of sound, listening along with the pace of the music. Almost everyone has already acquired the ability to follow the progress of popular music and to anticipate what comes next in favorite recordings. As stated before, the larger world of classical music is only a step beyond the listening expertise of most individuals.

Glossary

Pronunciation: Approximations are given where necessary. The syllables are to be read as English words and with the capital letters accented.

Abbreviations: L., Latin; F., French; G., German; Gk., Greek; I., Italian; v., Vide (see).

Asterisks: An asterisk preceding a word or phrase indicates that a definition and/or illustration can be found under that heading.

Abbreviations: The musical abbreviations used are included here under one heading for easy reference.

Accel. *accelerando* (ah–chel–er–AHN–doe), becoming faster.

Br. bridge, connecting section between themes.

Bsn., Bssn. bassoon.

C.b. contra bass, that is, string bass.

Cl., clar. clarinet.

Cresc. *crescendo* (cray–SHEN–doe), becoming louder.

D.C. *da capo* (dah–KAH–po), repeat from the beginning.

D.S. *dal segno* (dahl–SEHN–yo), repeat from the sign.

Dim. *diminuendo,* becoming softer.

Eng. hn. English horn, alto oboe.

f *forte* (FORE–tay), loud.

ff *fortissimo,* very loud.

fff *fortississimo,* very, very loud.

Fl. flute.

fp *forte piano,* loud and immediately soft.

Hn., Fr. hn. French horn.

Low br., low brass, trombones and tubas (sometimes French horns).

Low stgs. low strings, that is, cello, string bass.

Low w.w.'s low woodwinds, that is, bass clarinet, bassoon, contra bassoon.

mf mezzo forte (MEH–dso), half loud (medium loud).

mp mezzo piano, half soft (medium soft).

Ob. oboe.

Picc. piccolo.

Pizz. *pizzicato,* strings plucked with the fingers.

p *piano* (pea–AHN–no), soft.

pp *pianissimo,* very soft.

ppp *pianississimo,* very, very soft.

Reeds clarinet, oboe, bassoon, bass clarinet, etc.

R.h., l.h. right hand, left hand (keyboard instruments).

Rit. *ritardando,* become slower.

SATB soprano, alto, tenor, bass (usually applied to vocal ensemble).

sf, sff, sfz *sforzando* (sfor–TSAHND–o), strongly accented.

Sn. drum snare drum, side drum.

Stgs. strings, that is, the string section of the orchestra (violin, viola, cello, bass).

Tpt. trumpet.

Tr. trill.

Trans. transition.

Trom. trombone.

Vla. viola.

Vlc. violoncello, cello.

Vln. violin.

W.w.'s woodwinds (flute, oboe, clarinet, bassoon).

A

Abacus The flat slab on top of a *capital.

Acanthus A plant whose thick leaves are reproduced in stylized form on *Corinthian capitals. (See fig. 10.8.)

A cappella (ah ka–PELL–ah; L.) Originally unaccompanied music sung "in the chapel." Term now applies to choral music without instrumental accompaniment.

Accent In music, stress or emphasis on a tone or chord. Regular accents are assumed in metrical music. Special accent marks are used as necessary:> ʌ sfz (sforzando), etc.

Accidental In music a sign used to add or cancel chromatic alterations, for example, ♯ (raise a semitone), ♭ (lower a semitone), x (raise a whole tone), ♭♭ (lower a whole tone), ♮ (cancel previous sharps or flats).

Acoustics The science of sound.

Aerial perspective See perspective.

Agnosticism (Gk., *agnostos,* unknowing) The impossibility of obtaining knowledge of certain subjects; assertion that people cannot obtain knowledge of God.

Agnus Dei (L., Lamb of God) Last item of the *Ordinary of the *Mass.

Agora In ancient Greece, a marketplace/public square.

Allegory A literary mode with a literal level of meanings plus a set of meanings above and beyond themselves. This second level may be religious, social, political, or philosophical, e.g., *The Faerie Queen* by Spenser is an allegory about Christian virtues.

Alleluia Latinization for the Hebrew *Halleluyah* ("praise ye the Lord"). Third item of the *proper of the *Mass.

Alto, Contralto The second highest part in choral music, that is, S A T B.

Ambulatory A passageway around the *apse of a church. (See fig. 15.33.)

Amphora Greek vase, usually quite large, with two handles and used to store food staples. (See fig. 7.23.)

Apocalypse Prophetic revelation; the Book of Revelation in the New Testament.

A posteriori (a–pos–TEER–e–or–e; L., following after) Reasoning from observed facts to conclusions; inductive; empirical.

A priori (a–pree–OAR–e) Reasoning from general propositions to particular conclusions; deductive; nonempirical.

Apse A recess, usually semicircular, in the east wall of a Christian church or, in a Roman *basilica, at the wall opposite to the general entrance way.

Arabesque Literally Arablike. Elaborate designs of intertwined flowers, foliage, and geometric patterns used in Islamic architecture. (See fig. 15.6.)

Arcade A series of connected *arches resting on columns. (See fig. 10.9.)

Arch A curved structure (semicircular or pointed) spanning a space, usually made of wedge-shaped blocks. Known to the Greeks, who preferred a *post and lintel system, but exploited by the Romans.

Archetype (Gk. *arche,* first; *typos,* form) The original pattern of forms of which things in this world are copies.

Architrave The lowest part of an *entablature, a horizontal beam or lintel directly above the *capital. (See figs. 7.20 and 18.13.)

Aria (I., AHR–yah; F., air) Solo song (sometimes duet) in *operas, *oratorios, *cantatas.

Arpeggio (ahr–PEJ–o; I., harplike) In music the playing of a *chord with the notes sounding in quick succession rather than simultaneously.

Ars antiqua (L., old art) Music of the late twelfth and thirteenth centuries.

Ars nova (L., new art) Music of the fourteenth century. Outstanding composers were Machaut (France) and Landini (Italy).

Art Nouveau A style of architecture, crafts, and design of the 1890s and a bit later characterized by curvilinear patterns. Examples include Tiffany lamps and the work of Beardsley and Klimt.

Art song Song intending an artistic combination of words and music, as distinct from popular song or folk song. (See chap. 25.)

Atheism (Gk., *a,* no; *theos,* god) The belief that there is no God; also means "not theistic" when applied to those who do not believe in a personal God.

Atonality A type of music in which there is no tonal center, no key note. v. Twelve-tone technique and serial composition. (See chap. 30.)

Atrium The court of a Roman house, roofless, and near the entrance. Also the open, colonnaded court attached to the front of early Christian churches. (See fig. 10.3.)

Aulos (OW–los) A shrill sounding oboelike instrument associated with the Dionysian rites of the ancient Greeks. Double-reed instrument normally played in pairs by one performer. (See fig. 8.2.)

Avant-garde (a–vahn–GARD) A French term meaning, literally, advanced guard, and used to designate innovators and experimentalists in the various arts.

B

Bagpipe A reed instrument with several pipes attached to a bag (skin reservoir). One or two pipes *(chanters)* have tone holes and are used for the melody. The longer pipes *(drones)* sustain the same notes throughout. Probably of Asiatic origin and imported by the Romans in first century, A.D.

Baldachino (ball–da–KEEN–o) A canopy over a tomb or altar of which the most famous is that over the tomb of St. Peter in St. Peter's in Rome; designed by Bernini. (See fig. 22.8.)

Ballad (L., *ballare,* to dance) Originally a dancing song. A narrative song, usually folk song but term also applied to popular songs.

Ballade Medieval *trouvère song. In the nineteenth and twentieth centuries dramatic piano pieces, frequently inspired by romantic poetry.

Balustrade A railing plus a supporting row of posts.

Banjo *Guitar family instrument, probably introduced into Africa by Arab traders and brought to America on the slave ships. The body consists of a shallow, hollow metal drum with a drumhead on top and open at the bottom. It has four or more strings and is played with fingers or plectrum.

Bar In music notation originally vertical lines through the staff (which are now called bar lines). Bar is synonymous with *measure.

Bar form Originated with German *minnesinger-*meistersinger tradition. A form of music with the first *phrase repeated followed by a different phrase, for example, A–A–B. Also see Form.

Bar Line v. Bar.

Barrel vault v. Vault.

Basilica In Roman architecture, a rectangular public building used for business or as a tribunal. (See fig. 12.9.) Christian churches that use a *cruciform plan are patterned after Roman basilicas. Though basilica is an architectural style, the Roman church calls a church a basilica if it contains the bones of a saint.

Bass "Low" musical voice as opposed to "high." Used in the following special ways: (1) lowest adult male voice; (2) bass clef has F on the fourth line; (3) short for bass viol., bass fiddle, double bass (string bass) in the orchestra; (4) prefixed to the name of an instrument to indicate the largest (and lowest) member of an instrumental family, for example, bass clarinet, bass trombone, etc.

Bass clef v. Bass (2).

Bay In Romanesque and Gothic churches the area between the columns.

Behaviorism School of psychology that restricts both animal and human psychology to the study of behavior; stress on the role of the environment and on conditioned responses to exterior stimuli.

Blank verse Unrhymed *iambic pentameter* (v. meter) in the English language, much used in Elizabethan drama.

Bourgeoisie The middle class; in Marxist theory the capitalist class, which is opposed to the proletariat, the lower or industrial working class.

Brass instruments Instruments of metal that produce a tone by vibrating the lips in a cup- or funnel-shaped mouthpiece. They include: (from high pitch to low) *trumpet, cornet, fluegelhorn, *French horn, baritone horn (euphonium), *trombone, *tuba.

Buttress Exterior support used to counter the lateral thrust of an *arch or *vault. A *pier buttress* is a solid mass of masonry added to the wall; a *flying buttress* is typically a pier standing away from the wall and from which an arch "flies" from the pier to connect with the wall at the point of outward thrust. (See fig. 15.37.)

C

Cadence Term in music applied to the concluding portion of a phrase (temporary cadence) or composition (permanent cadence).

Campanile Italian for bell tower, usually freestanding. The Leaning Tower of Pisa is a campanile. (See fig. 15.29.)

Canon (Gk., law, rule) A contrapuntal device in music in which one or more melodies strictly imitates an opening melody throughout its entire length. A canon is the strictest type of imitative *counterpoint. Canons that have no specified way to end but which keep going around are called "rounds," for example, "Three Blind Mice."

Canso A *troubadour song in *"bar form," for example, A–A–B.

Cantata (I., *cantare,* to sing) A "sung" piece as opposed to a "sound" (instrumental) piece, for example, sonata. The term is now generally used for secular or sacred choral works with orchestral accompaniment, which are on a smaller scale than *oratorios.

Cantilever A self-supporting projection which needs no exterior bracing; e.g., a balcony or porch can be cantilevered. (See fig. 29.31.)

Cantus firmus (L., fixed song) A preexisting melody used as the foundation for a *polyphonic composition. *Plainsong melodies were used for this purpose, but other sources included secular songs, Lutheran chorales, and scales. Any preexisting melody may serve as a cantus firmus.

Capital The top or crown of a column.

Cartoon A full-size preliminary drawing for a pictorial work, usually a large work such as a *mural, *fresco, or *tapestry. Also a humorous drawing.

Caryatid (care-ee-AT-id) A female figure that functions as a supporting column; male figures that function in a like manner are called *atlantes* (at-LAN-tees; plural of Atlas). (See fig. 7.51.)

Catharsis (Gk., *katharsis,* purge, purify) Purification, purging of emotions effected by tragedy (Aristotle).

Cella The enclosed chamber in a classical temple that contained the cult statue of the god or goddess after whom the temple was named.

Chamber music Term now restricted to instrumental music written for a limited number of players in which there is only one player to each part, as opposed to orchestral music, which has two or more players to some parts, for example, sixteen players on the first violin part. True chamber music emphasizes ensemble rather than solo playing.

Chanson (F., song) A major part of the *troubadour-*trouvère tradition, dating from the eleventh through the fourteenth centuries. Generic term for the general song production to a French text.

Chevet (sheh-VAY; F., pillow) The eastern end of a church, including *choir, *ambulatory, and *apse.

Chiaroscuro (kee-AR-oh-SKOOR-oh; I., light-dark) In the visual arts the use of gradations of light and dark to represent natural light and shadows.

Chinoiserie (she-nwaz-eh-REE; F.) Chinese motifs as decorative elements for craft objects, screens, wallpaper, and furniture; prominent in eighteenth-century Rococo style.

Choir That part of the church where the singers and clergy are normally accommodated; usually between the *transept and the *apse; also called chancel. (See fig. 15.40.)

Chorale A hymn tune of the German Protestant (Lutheran) church.

Chord In music the simultaneous sounding of three or more tones.

Chromatic (Gk., *chroma,* color) The use of notes that are foreign to the musical scale and have to be indicated by a sharp, flat, natural, etc. The *chromatic scale* is involved in these alterations. It consists of twelve tones to an octave, each a semitone apart.

Chromatic scale v. Chromatic.

Church modes   In music the medieval scale system of four basic modes (Dorian, Phrygian, Lydian, Mixolydian) and four related modes (Hypodorian, Hypophrygian, Hypolydian, Hypomixolydian). May also include Ionian and Aeolian, which are somewhat comparable to the *major-minor system.

Cire perdue   (seer pair–DUE; F., lost wax) A metal casting method in which the original figure is modeled in wax and encased in a mold; as the mold is baked the wax melts and runs out, after which the molten metal is poured into the mold.

Clavichord   The earliest type of stringed keyboard instrument (twelfth century). Probably developed from the *monochord. It is a 2′ × 4′ oblong box with a keyboard of about three octaves. The strings run parallel to the keyboard, as opposed to harpsichords and pianos, in which the strings run at right angles to the keyboard. The keys are struck from below by metal tangents fastened to the opposite ends of elongated keys. The tone is light and delicate but very expressive because the performer can control the loudness of each note. It was sometimes called a "table *clavier" because it was portable.

Clavier   Generic term for any instrument of the stringed keyboard family: clavichord, harpsichord, and piano.

Clef   (F., key) In music a symbol placed on the staff to indicate the pitches of the lines and spaces. There are three clefs in use today: G, F, and C. The G clef is used to indicate that the note on the second line is G (treble clef). The F clef is usually used to indicate that F is on the fourth line (bass clef).

Treble Clef   Bass Clef

The C clef places middle C on either the third line (alto clef) or fourth line (tenor clef).

Alto Clef   Tenor Clef

Clerestory   In a basilica or church, the second level, the wall that rises above the roof of the other parts and has numerous windows. (See fig. 12.11.)

Cloister   An inner court bounded by covered walks; a standard feature of monastery architecture.

Collage   (F., pasting) Paper and other materials pasted on a two-dimensional surface.

Colonnade   A series of spaced columns, usually connected by lintels. (See fig. 12.11.)

Column   A vertical support, usually circular, which has a base (except in *Doric style), shaft, and *capital. (See fig. 7.37.)

Comedy   A play or other literary work in which all ends well, properly, or happily. Opposite of *tragedy.

Con   (I., with) For example, *con moto* (with motion).

Concerto   (con–CHAIR–toe; I.) A musical work for one or more solo voices with orchestral accompaniment.

Conductus   In music a twelfth- or thirteenth-century metrical (as opposed to nonmetrical plainsong) song for one or more voices in a sacred or secular style. A conductus may be *monophonic or *polyphonic.

Contrapposto   (I., set against). Figural sculpture in which parts of the body (usually hips and legs, arms and shoulders) are set against each other along a central axis, setting up an alternation of tension and relaxation.

Contrapuntal   In the style of *counterpoint.

Corinthian   The most ornate style of Greek architecture, little used by the Greeks but preferred by the Romans; tall, slender, channeled columns topped by an elaborate capital decorated with stylized acanthus leaves. (See figs. 10.7 and 18.5.)

Cornice   The horizontal, projecting member crowning an *entablature.

Cosmology   Philosophic study of the origin and nature of the universe.

Counterpoint   The musical craft or technique of combining two or more melodies, of writing note against note *(punctus contra punctum)*. Music which consists of simultaneous melodies (two or more) is called *contrapuntal music or *polyphonic (many voiced) music.

Couplet   In poetry two successive rhymed lines in the same meter.

Credo   (L., I believe) Third item of the *Ordinary of the *Mass.

Crescendo, Decrescendo   (cray–SHEN-doe, day-cray–SHEN-doe; I.) Standard musical terminology for increasing or decreasing loudness. Also indicated by abbreviations *cresc.* and *decresc.,* or signs < and >.

Crocket   In Gothic architecture an ornamental device shaped like a curling leaf and placed on the outer angles of *gables and pinnacles. (See colorplate 20.)

Crossing   In a church, the space formed by the interception of the *nave and the *transepts.

Cruciform   The floor plan of a church in the shape of a Latin cross.

D

Daguerrotype   After L. J. M. Daguerre (1789–1851) the inventor. Photograph made on a silver-coated glass plate.

Determinism   (L., *de + terminus,* end) The doctrine that all events are conditioned by their causes and that people are mechanical expressions of heredity and environment; in short, we are at the mercy of blind, unknowing natural laws; the universe could care less.

Deus ex machina   (DAY–oos ex ma–KEE-na; L.) In Greek and Roman drama a deity who was brought in by stage machinery to resolve a difficult situation; any unexpected or bizarre device or event introduced to untangle a plot.

Dialectic   Associated with Plato as the art of debate by question and answer. Also dialectical reasoning using *syllogisms (Aristotle) or, according to Hegel, the distinctive characteristic of speculative thought.

Diatonic   (Gk., through the tones) Applied to musical scales in which each letter name is used once only, for example, c–d–e–f–g–a–b–(c), c–d–e♭–f–g–a♭–b♭–c, etc.

Dome A hemispherical vault; may be viewed as an arch rotated on its vertical axis.

Doric The oldest of Greek temple styles, characterized by sturdy *columns with no base and an unornamented cushionlike *capital. (See figs. 7.42 and 18.31.)

Drum The circular sections that make up the shaft of a *column; also the circular wall on which a *dome is placed. (See fig. 7.38.)

Drums Percussion musical instruments having a skin stretched over one or both ends of a frame.
1. *Timpani* (kettledrums) The skin is stretched over a metal half-sphere. They can be tuned to definite pitch.
2. *Side drum* (snare drum) Shallow drum with metal snares (taut wire coils) on the bottom drumhead. The tone is dry and crisp.
3. *Tenor drum* A larger and deeper version of the snare drum. The tone is similar to that of a tom-tom. It does not use snares.
4. *Bass drum* The largest drum used in the orchestra. The tone is rather booming.
5. *Conga drum* One head stretched over the top of a long cylinder.
6. *Bongo drums* Small pair of single-headed drums.
7. *Tambourine* A small single-headed drum with metal discs set around the frame.

Dualism In metaphysics, a theory that admits two independent substances, e.g., Plato's dualism of the sensible and intelligible worlds, Cartesian dualism of thinking and extended subjects, Kant's dualism of the noumenal and the phenomenal.

Dynamic marks Words or symbols indicating the relative degrees of loudness or softness in a musical performance. Some of the more important markings are summarized as follows:

Term	Symbol	Meaning
pianissimo (pea-uh-NEES-see-mo)	pp	very soft
piano (pea-AHN-no)	p	soft
mezzo piano (MEH-dso)	mp	half soft
mezzo forte (FORE-tay)	mf	half loud
forte	f	loud
fortissimo	ff	very loud
forte piano	fp	loud and immediately soft
sforzando (sforr-TSAHND-o)	sfz	strongly accented
also: *crescendo, *decrescendo		

E

Elegy A meditative poem dealing with the idea of death.

Elevation The vertical arrangements of the elements of an architectural design; a vertical projection.

Empiricism A proposition that the sole source of knowledge is experience, that no knowledge is possible independent of experience.

Engaged column A nonfunctional form projecting from the surface of a wall; used for visual articulation. (See fig. 10.7.)

Engraving The process of using a sharp instrument to cut a design into a metal plate, usually copper; also the print that is made from the plate after ink has been added.

Entablature That part of a building of post and lintel construction between the capitals and the roof. In classical architecture this includes the *architrave, *frieze, and *cornice. (See fig. 7.20.)

Entasis (EN-ta-sis) A slight convex swelling in the shaft of a *column.

Epic A lengthy narrative poem dealing with protagonists of heroic proportions and issues of universal significance, e.g., Homer's *Iliad.*

Epicurean One who believes that pleasure, especially that of the mind, is the highest good.

Epistemology A branch of philosophy that studies the origin, validity, and processes of knowledge.

Eschatology (Gk., *ta eschata,* death) That part of theology dealing with last things: death, judgment, heaven, hell.

Estampie (es-TAHM-pea) A dance form popular during the twelfth to fourteenth centuries. Consists of a series of repeated sections, for example, aa, bb, cc, etc.

Etching A kind of *engraving in which the design is incised into a wax-covered metal plate, after which the exposed metal is etched by a corrosive acid; the print made from the plate is also called an etching.

Ethos In ancient Greek music the "ethical" character attributed to the various modes. The Dorian was considered strong and manly; the Phrygian, ecstatic and passionate; the Lydian, feminine, decadent, and lascivious; the Mixolydian, mournful and gloomy.

Euphemism An innocuous term substituted for one considered to be offensive or socially unacceptable, e.g., "passing away" for "dying."

F

Facade One of the exterior walls of a building, usually the one containing the main entrance.

Fenestration The arrangement of windows or other openings in the walls of a building.

Fiddle Colloquialism for the violin. Also used to designate the bowed ancestors of the violin, particularly the medieval instrument used to accompany dances.

Finial In Gothic architecture an ornament fitted to the peak of an *arch; any ornamental terminating point, such as the screw-top of a lamp. (See colorplate 20.)

Flageolet (flaj-o-LET; F.) A small wind instrument, a forerunner of the *recorder.

Flamboyant Late Gothic architecture of the fifteenth or sixteenth centuries, which featured wavy lines and flamelike forms.

Flat v. Accidental.

Fleche (flesh; F., arrow) In architecture a slender spire above the intersection of the *nave and *transepts. (See fig. 15.37.)

Flute A *woodwind instrument made of wood (originally), silver, gold, or preferably platinum. It is essentially a straight pipe with keys, is held horizontally and played by blowing across a mouth (blow) hole located near one end. The tone is mellow in the bottom octave, becoming thinner and brighter up to the top of the range. Though many thousands of years old, the flute was not used in instrumental ensembles until the early eighteenth century, when it began to replace the *recorder.

Fluting The vertical grooves, usually semicircular, in the shaft of a *column or *pilaster.

Folk song A song of unknown (usually) authorship preserved by means of an oral tradition. A folk song is never composed by ''folk'' (or a committee); it is the creation of one or two individuals (words and/or music) and tends to be remembered and transmitted because the words and music are somehow pertinent to the environment in which it was created. Folk songs about special situations (labor unions, strikes, political causes, and movements, etc.) tend to fade away in time. Folk songs having something to do with the human condition may last indefinitely.

Foot A metrical unit in poetry such as the iamb ◡ /. Also see meter.

Foreshortening Creating the illusion in painting or drawing that the subject is projecting out of or into the frontal plane of a two-dimensional surface.

Form, Musical form Musical form is an intelligible structure that distinguishes music from haphazard sounds or noises. Since music is an intelligible ordering of tones all music has ''form,'' that is, it has a beginning, middle, and end; it exists in time. ''Form'' is therefore any organization or structuring of any combination, or all of the four elements of music (melody, harmony, rhythm, tone color). In general, music is ordered (formed) in such a manner as to possess enough unity to achieve coherence or continuity and sufficient variety to avoid monotony (short of chaos). All musical forms consist of varying relationships of unity and variety. There are many ways of organizing musical structure; following are a few of the more important forms.

  I. Single forms (pieces or single movements).
    A. Sectional (with clearly defined [more or less] interior divisions).
    B. Continuous.
      1. Through composed (no repetition). *Organum, some medieval *motets.
      2. Imitative (contrapuntal forms): *passacaglia, *fugue, Renaissance *masses, and *motets.
  II. Composite forms are simply compositions with two or more movements, for example, *symphony, *cantata, etc.

Free verse A verse that uses devices other than meter and rhyme.

Fresco (I., fresh) Painting on plaster, usually wet plaster on which the colors are painted, sinking in as the plaster dries and the fresco becomes part of the wall. (See fig. 18.38.)

Frets Thin strips of wood or metal fastened to the fingerboard of string instruments like the *viol and *guitar (but *not* members of the violin family). The frets are placed to mark specific notes.

Frieze In architecture decorated horizontal band, often embellished with carved figures and molding; the portion of an *entablature between the *architrave and the *cornice above.

Fugue *Polyphonic musical composition in which a single theme is developed by the different musical voices in succession. A favorite style of Baroque composers like Bach and Handel.

Fundamental In musical acoustics the lowest note of the overtone series. The generating tone for the series.

G

Gable In architecture the triangular section at the end of a pitched roof, frequently with a window below. (See fig. 21.12.)

Genre (ZHAN–re) In the pictorial arts a depiction of scenes of everyday life. (See fig. 22.26.)

Gittern English name for the medieval *guitar.

Glockenspiel A percussion instrument with rectangular metal bars laid out in a keyboard pattern. It is played with two mallets and has a sharp, bright tone.

Goliards Wandering Bohemians of the tenth through the thirteenth centuries: students, young ecclesiastics, dreamers, and the disenchanted.

Gospels In the Bible, New Testament accounts (Matthew, Mark, Luke, John) of the life and teachings of Christ.

Gouache (goo–AHSH; F.) Watercolor made opaque by adding zinc white.

Graphic arts Visual arts that are linear in character: drawing, engraving, printing, printmaking, typographic, and advertising design.

Greek cross A cross in which the four arms are of equal length.

Gregorian chant v. Plainsong.

Groin In architecture the edge (groin) formed by the intersection of two *vaults. (See figs. 15.26 and 15.27.)

Guitar A plucked string instrument with a flat body and six strings (modern guitar). Brought into Europe during the Middle Ages by the Moorish conquest of Spain.

H

Harmony In music the vertical (simultaneous) sound of two or more pitches. Harmonic development is a major achievement of Western music while remaining secondary in the rest of the world's music.

Harp A stringed instrument with a large triangular frame and about forty-five strings. In the modern harp the seven pedals change the pitches of the strings so that the harp can play chromatically, i.e., all twelve tones of the octave. The harp has been mentioned in recorded history since the days of the Babylonian Empire.

Harpsichord Actually a harp turned on its side and played by means of quills or leather tongues operated by a keyboard. It was the most common keyboard instrument of the sixteenth to eighteenth centuries and is again being built today in increasing numbers.

Hatching A series of closely spaced parallel lines in a drawing or print giving the effect of shading.

Hedonism The doctrine that pleasure or pleasant consciousness are intrinsically good; that pleasure is the proper—and the actual—motive for every choice.

Heroic couplet Two successive lines of rhymed iambic pentameter, e.g., Pope's *Essay on Man*.

Hieratic (HYE–uh–RAT–ik) Of or used by priests; priestly.

Hieroglyphic Symbols or pictures standing for a word, syllable, or sound; writing system of ancient Egyptians.

Homophonic (Gk., same sound) Music in which a single melodic line is supported by chords or other subordinate material (percussion instruments).

Horn The modern orchestral instrument, the French horn, is frequently referred to as a horn. Also, a generic designation for any instrument that has a mouthpiece through which the performer blows.

Hubris (HU–bris) *Tragic flaw,* i.e., excessive pride or arrogance that injures other people (not physically) and brings about the downfall of the person with the flaw.

Hue The name of a color. The chief colors of the spectrum are: red, yellow, blue (primary); green, orange, violet (secondary).

Hydraulis Ancient Greek pipe organ, probably invented in the Middle East 300–200 B.C. Air for the pipes was provided by hydraulic pressure and the pipes activated by a keyboard. Originally the tone was delicate and clear, but the Romans converted it into a noisy outdoor instrument by a large increase in air pressure.

Hymn A poem of praise. Usually, but not necessarily, sacred. The music accompanying a hymn is called the hymn tune.

I

Icon (EYE–kon; Gk., image) Two-dimensional representation of a holy person; in the Greek church a panel painting of a sacred personage. (See fig. 12.24.)

Iconography Visual imagery used to convey concepts in the visual arts; the study of symbolic meanings in the pictorial arts.

Illumination Decorative illustrations or designs, associated primarily with medieval illuminated manuscripts.

Impasto (I., paste) A painting style in which the pigment is laid on thickly, as in many of van Gogh's paintings. (See figs. 26.28 and 26.29.)

Intaglio (in–TAL–yo) A graphic technique in which the design is incised; used on seals, gems, and dies for coins and also for the kinds of printing and printmaking that have a depressed ink-bearing surface.

Ionic A style of Greek classical architecture using slender, *fluted *columns and *capitals decorated with scrolls and volutes. (See fig. 7.52.)

Isocepholy (I–so–SEPH–uh–ly) In the visual arts a convention that arranges figures so that the heads are at the same height. (See figs. 7.49 and 7.59.)

J

Jamb figure Sculpted figure flanking the portal of a Gothic church. (See fig. 15.39.)

Jongleur (zhon–GLEUR) French professional musicians (minstrels) of the twelfth and thirteenth centuries who served the *troubadours and *trouvères.

K

Keystone The central wedge-shaped stone in an arch; the last stone put in place and which makes the arch stable. (See fig. 15.35.)

Kithara (KITH–a-ra) The principal stringed instrument of the ancient Greeks. Essentially a larger version of the *lyre, it has a U-shaped form and usually seven to eleven strings running vertically from the cross arm down to the sound box at the base of the instrument. The legendary instrument of Apollo. (See fig. 8.3.)

Kyrie eleison (Gk., Lord have mercy) The first item of the *Ordinary of the *Mass.

L

Lantern In architecture a small decorative structure that crowns a *dome or roof. (See fig. 18.22.)

Latin cross A cross in which the vertical member is longer than the horizontal arm it bisects.

Legato (leh-GAH-toe; I.) Musical term meaning smooth, moving smoothly from note to note. Opposite of *staccato.

Libretto (I., little book) The text or words of an *opera, *oratorio, or other extended choral work.

Lied, Lieder (leet, LEE–der; G., song, songs). Term usually applied to the German romantic *art songs of Schubert, Schumann, Brahms, Wolf, and others. Also used for medieval songs, that is, *minnesinger and *meistersinger.

Lintel In architecture a horizontal crosspiece over an open space, which carries the weight of some of the superstructure. (See fig. 7.34.)

Lithography A printmaking process that uses a polished stone (or metal plate) on which the design is drawn with a crayon or greasy ink. Ink is chemically attracted only to the lines of the drawing, with a print made by applying paper to the inked stone. (See fig. 26.15.)

Liturgical Pertaining to public worship, specifically to the organized worship patterns of the Christian churches.

Liturgical drama Twelfth- and thirteenth-century enactments of biblical stories, frequently with music. Developed into the "mystery plays" of the fourteenth through sixteenth centuries.

Lituus (L.) Bronze trumpet used by the Roman armies. Shaped like the letter J.

Lost wax process v. *cire perdue.*

Lute   Plucked stringed instrument with a pear-shaped body and a fingerboard with *frets. It had eleven strings tuned to six notes (five sets of double strings plus a single string for the highest note). It was the most popular instrument of the sixteenth century and was used into the eighteenth century. Lutes are again being made, mainly for present-day performances of Renaissance music.

Lyre   (or Lyra) Ancient Greek instrument, a simpler form of the *kithara. The sound box was often made of a tortoise shell. Used mainly by amateurs. The larger kithara was used by professional musicians. (See fig. 8.1.)

Lyric   Poetry sung to the accompaniment of a lyre (Greek); troubadour and trouvère poetry intended to be sung; short poems with musical elements. (See fig. 8.1.)

M

Madrigal   Name of uncertain origin that refers to fourteenth-century vocal music or, usually, to the popular sixteenth-century type. Renaissance madrigals were free-form vocal pieces (usually set to love lyrics) in a *polyphonic style with intermixed *homophonic sections. Flemish, Italian, and English composers brought the madrigal to a high level of expressiveness in word painting and imagery. Madrigals were sometimes accompanied but mostly *a cappella. (See chap. 19.)

March   Music for a parade or procession. The *meter is usually duple (simple or compound) but is sometimes quadruple.

Mass   The central service of public worship of some Christian churches, principally the Roman Catholic church. The musical portions are indicated below.

Ordinary (same text)	Proper (text varies by the liturgical calendar)
Kyrie Eleison	Introit
Gloria in Excelsis Deo	Gradual
Credo in Unum Deum	Alleluia
Sanctus	Offertory
Agnus Dei	Communion

Materialism   The doctrine that the only reality is matter; that the universe is not governed by intelligence or purpose but only by mechanical cause and effect.

Measure   In music a group of beats set off by bar lines.

Meistersinger   (G., mastersinger) The highest level in the music-poetry guilds of Germany in the fifteenth and sixteenth centuries. Succeeding the earlier *minnesinger tradition the guilds held song schools and awarded prizes, with top prizes for creating new songs going to the "mastersingers."

Melisma   A melodic unit sung to one syllable; plainsong has frequent *melismatic* passages.

Melody   A succession of musical sounds, that is, the horizontal organization of music as compared with harmony, which is a vertical organization of tones. Melody is inseparable from rhythm because it has an up and down motion of pitches and, simply stated, long and short durations of rhythm.

Metaphor   A common form of figurative language that compares two dissimilar objects by stating that the two are identical, e.g., "the moon is blue."

Metaphysics   Philosophic inquiry into the ultimate and fundamental reality; "the science of being as such."

Meter   In music a grouping of beats into patterns of two, three, or four beats or combinations thereof; in English poetry the basic rhythmic pattern of stressed (—) and unstressed (∪) syllables. Metrical patterns include: *iambic* (∪ —), *trochaic* (— ∪), *anapestic* (∪ ∪ —), and *dactylic* (— ∪ ∪).

Metope   (MET–o–pay) In classical architecture the panel between two *triglyphs in a *Doric *frieze; may be plain or carved. The Parthenon metopes are all carved. (See fig. 7.50.)

Minnesinger   (G., from *minne,* love) German poet-musicians of noble birth of the thirteenth to fifteenth centuries (leading to the *meistersingers) who were influenced by the *troubadour-trouvère tradition of the age of chivalry. They composed *monophonic songs, usually in *bar form.

Minstrel   v. Jongleur.

Modes, rhythmic   A thirteenth-century system of music rhythmic notation based on the patterns of poetic meter. Rhythmic modes give the characteristic flavor to thirteenth-century *organum and *motets because of the constant repetition of the same rhythmic patterns. All modes were performed in so-called "perfect" meter, that is, triple.

Rhythmic Mode	Poetic Meter	Accent Pattern	Performed
I	Trochaic	— ∪	♩ ♪ ♩ ♪
II	Iambic	∪ —	♪♩ ♪♩
III	Dactylic	— ∪ ∪	♩. ♪♩
IV	Anapaestic	∪ ∪ —	♪♩ ♩.
V	Spondiac	— —	♩. ♩.
VI	Tribrachic	∪ ∪ ∪	♫♪ ♫♪

Monism   (Gk., *mones,* single) The philosophical position that there is but one fundamental reality. The classical advocate of extreme monism was Parmenides of Elea; Spinoza is a modern exponent.

Monochord   A device consisting of a single string stretched over a soundboard with a movable bridge. Used to demonstrate the laws of acoustics, especially the relationships between intervals and string lengths and the tuning of scales. (See fig. 16.2.)

Monophonic   (Gk., one sound) A single line of music without accompaniment or additional parts, as in *plainsong, *troubadour-trouvère-minnesinger songs, and some *folk songs, hollers, street cries, and blues.

Montage   (moan–TAHZH) A composition made of existing photographs, paintings, or drawings; in cinematography the effects achieved by superimposing images or using rapid sequences.

Mosaic   The technique of embedding bits of stone, colored glass, or marble in wet concrete to make designs or pictures for walls or floors. To achieve a complex interplay of light and shadows, the bits are set in the holding material with minute differences in the angles, as in the mosaics of San Vitale in Ravenna. (See colorplates 11 and 12.)

Motet   (from F., *mot,* word) The most important form of early *polyphonic music (ca. thirteenth to seventeenth centuries).

1. *Medieval motet* (thirteenth–fourteenth centuries). Usually 3 parts (triplum, motetus, tenor). The tenor "holds" to a *cantus firmus and the upper two voices sing different texts (sacred and/or secular).
2. *Renaissance* motet (fifteenth–sixteenth centuries). A four- or five-part composition, a cappella, generally polyphonic, with a single Latin text. A serious vocal piece intended for use in sacred services.

There are also Baroque motets (by J. S. Bach) for mixed chorus and orchestra (German text) and some Romantic motets (Brahms), again in the *a cappella style.

Motive   The smallest musical idea, usually part of a theme, which is used in various ways to give unity to musical expressions. Motives may be melodic (and rhythmic), purely rhythmic, harmonic or different combinations of these elements. Motives can be considered as building blocks of music or as a glue that holds music together.

Mullion   A vertical member that divides a window into sections; also used to support the glass in stained-glass windows.

Mural   A painting on a wall; a *fresco is a type of mural.

Myth   Stories explaining natural phenomena, customs, institutions, religious beliefs, and so forth of a people. Usually concerned with the supernatural, gods, goddesses, heroic exploits, and the like.

N

Narthex   A porch or vestibule of a church through which one passes to enter the *nave.

Natural   In music the sign ♮ used to cancel a previous sharp or flat. Also see accidentals.

Naturalism   The view that the universe requires no supernatural cause or government, that it is self-existent, self-explanatory, self-operating, and self-directing, that the universe is purposeless, deterministic, and only incidentally productive of man. In relation to literature sometimes defined as "realism on all fours." The dominant traits of literary naturalism are biological determinism (people are what they must be because of their genes) and environmental determinism (people are what they are because of where they were nurtured). It all comes out to nature versus nurture.

Nave   The main central space of a church running from the entrance to the *crossing of the *transepts; typically flanked by one or two side aisles. Name derived from *naval* because the barrel *vault ceiling has the appearance of the inside hull of a ship.

Nomos, Nome   (Gk., law, rule) In the Homeric tradition in ancient Greece the term is used to refer to the traditional phrases and melodies singers used to recite the epics and odes.

Notation   A set, any set, of symbols used to put music into written form. It should be pointed out that musical notation (even modern notation) can only approximate the sounds the composer wants. Actual performance practices must be based not only on a reading knowledge of music but also on an awareness of performance practices and the conventions of particular periods of music. Size of audience, acoustics of a room, and capabilities of the performer also affect the conversion of musical notation into actual music.

Notes and rest values   Modern musical system based on the whole and fractional divisions of a whole note, for example:

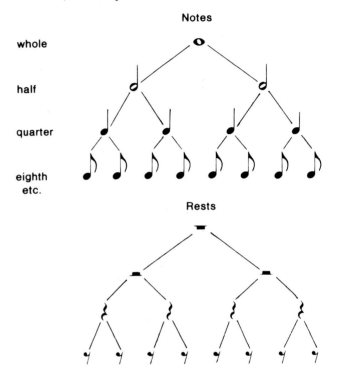

Notre Dame school   The composers of the twelfth- and thirteenth-century cathedral school at Notre Dame of Paris, most notably Leonin and Perotin. The Notre Dame school probably invented rhythmic notation for *polyphonic music.

O

Oboe   (from F., "high wind," that is, high-pitched instrument) A double-reed, soprano-range instrument with a conical bore (slightly expanding diameter from reed to bell). It has a nasal but mellow and poignant tone.

Odalisque   (oh–de–LISK) French word for a harem slave or concubine but used more broadly to refer to a reclining female figure, a favorite subject of painters like Ingres and Matisse. (See fig. 26.3.)

Ode   A formal lyric on a usually dignified theme, in exalted language, e.g., works by Horace.

Office hours   In the Roman Catholic church the services (usually observed only in monastic churches) that take place eight times a day (every three hours): Matins, Lauds, Prime, Terce, Sext, None, Vespers, and Compline. Musically the important services are Matins, Vespers, and Compline.

Ontology   (Gk., *on,* being + *logos,* logic) Philosophic inquiry into the ultimate nature of things, what it means to be.

Opera   (from I., *opera in musica,* work in music) A play in which the text is generally sung throughout to the accompaniment of an orchestra. Modern opera had its beginnings in Florence in the late sixteenth century when some musicians, poets, and scholars attempted a revival of Greek drama, which they assumed to have been sung throughout. Opera depends for its effect on communicating through song rather than other theatrical conventions such as blank verse. It is a complex synthesis of various arts: music, poetry, scenery, stagecraft, costume design, and acting. Because it is so complex it is expensive to produce (and attend) and therefore has a certain association with "society" as a prestige symbol. However, when a well-written opera is effectively staged, acted, and sung (in the language of the audience) the effect is not that of an esoteric status symbol but rather an overwhelming musical-theatrical-artistic experience.

Opus   (L., work) Abbreviated as op., it generally indicates the chronological order of "works" of music. When the designation is, for example, op. 2 no. 4, the work is the fourth part or portion of a composer's second major work. This designation is usually used for a related series of short compositions, for example, twenty-four *Preludes* by Chopin in his Opus 28.

Oratorio   A musical setting of a religious or epic theme for performance by soloists, chorus, and orchestra in a church or concert hall. Originally (early seventeenth century) they were similar to operas (sacred operas) with staging, costumes, and scenery. They are now usually presented in concert form, for example, *The Messiah,* by G. F. Handel.

Orchestra   (from Gk., *orcheisthai,* to dance) In ancient Greek theatres the circular or semicircular space in front of the stage used by the chorus; group of instrumentalists performing ensemble music, e.g. symphony orchestra.

Ordinary of the Mass   v. Mass.

Organ, Pipe organ   An instrument (see Hydraulis) of ancient origin consisting of from two to seven keyboards (manuals) and a set of pedals (usually thirty-two notes) for the feet. Organs have anywhere from a few hundred up to ten thousand individual pipes, a mechanical wind supply (electric blower), and a keyboard action that is either mechanical (directly connected to pipes with wooden "trackers"), pneumatic, or electric (opening the pipes with air or with electrical action). Some modern organs are so complex that they have built-in computers to assist with "registration," that is, the selection of which ranks (or sets) of pipes to use. Many pipe organ manufacturers are operating around the clock in an effort to keep up with the demand for what has been called the king of instruments. The pipe organ is not to be confused with the numerous electronic imitations, which attempt to reproduce the sound of real pipes.

Organum   (OR–ga–num; L.) The name given to the earliest types of *polyphonic music. Beginning with about the ninth century, organum was first strict, then parallel, free (contrary motion), and *melismatic. See (in the text) the section on medieval music for description and illustrations of the stages of organum.

Overture   Musical introduction to an *opera, *oratorio, or other large work; an independent orchestral work in one movement.

P

Pantheism   (Gk., *pan,* all, + *theos,* god) As a religious concept, the doctrine that God is immanent in all things.

Pediment   In classic architecture a triangular space at the end of a building framed by the *cornice and the ends of the sloping roof (*raking cornices). (See fig. 7.36.)

Pendentive   In architecture a concave triangular piece of masonry, four of which form a transition from a square base to support the circular rim of a *dome. (See fig. 12.20.)

Percussion   Instruments that are played by striking, shaking, scraping, etc. See separate articles for more detailed descriptions of individual instruments. Percussion instruments can be divided into two groups:

Instruments of definite pitch
Timpani
Glockenspiel or Bells
Celesta
Xylophone
Marimba
Chimes
Vibraphone

Instruments of indefinite pitch
Snare drum (side drum)
Tenor drum
Bass drum
Tambourine
Triangle
Cymbals
Tam-Tam (gong)
Castanets
Guiro
Maracas

Period   An inner division of music usually consisting of two or three *phrases.

Peristyle   A series of columns that surround the exterior of a building or the interior of a court, e.g., the Parthenon has a peristyle. (See figs. 7.46 and 26.2.)

Perspective   The illusion of a three-dimensional world on a two-dimensional surface. *Linear perspective* uses lines of projection converging on a vanishing point and with objects appearing smaller the further from the viewer. *Aerial (atmospheric) perspective* uses diminished color intensity and blurred contours for objects apparently deeper in space.

Phrase   A division of music larger than a *motive but smaller than a *period. It is a unit of melody (harmony and rhythm) of no specific length that expresses at least a comprehensible portion of a musical idea. It might be compared with a phrase of speech.

Pier   A mass of masonry, usually large, used to support arches or lintels; more massive than a *column and with a shape other than circular. (See fig. 15.1.)

Pieta   (pyay–TA; I., pity, compassion) Representations of the Virgin mourning the body of her Son. (See fig. 18.29.)

Pilaster   A flat vertical column projecting from the wall of a building; usually furnished with a base and capital in the manner of an *engaged column, which is rounded rather than rectangular like the pilaster.

Plainsong   The term generally used for the large body of nonmetrical, *monophonic, *liturgical music of the Roman Catholic church. Also called Gregorian chant.

Polyphony   (po–LIF–o–nee) *Polyphonic* (pol–ly–PHON–ik) "Many-voiced" music, that is, melodic interest in two or more simultaneous melodic lines. Examples of polyphonic music would be *canons and *rounds.

Positivism   Philosophic inquiry limited to problems open to scientific investigation. Traditional subjects such as aesthetics and metaphysics are dismissed as "meaningless" because their content cannot be subjected to verification.

Post and lintel   A structural system in which vertical supports or columns support horizontal beams. The lintel can span only a relatively short space because the weight of the superstructure centers on the mid-point of the horizontal beam. In a structural system using *arches the thrust is distributed to the columns supporting the bases of the arches, thus allowing for a greater span. The lintel is also called an *architrave. (See fig. 7.34.)

Pragmatism   (Gk., *pragma,* things done) Philosophic doctrine that the meaning of a proposition or course of action lies in its observable consequences and that its meaning is the sum of its consequences. In everyday life the favoring of practical means over theory; if something works it's good; if not, it's bad.

Primary colors   The *hues of red, yellow, and blue with which the colors of the spectrum can be produced. Primary colors cannot be produced by mixing.

Program music   Music intended to depict ideas, scenes, or other extramusical concepts. (See chap. 25.)

Proper of the Mass   v. Mass.

Proscenium   (Gk., *pro,* before; *skene,* stage) In traditional theatres the framework of the stage opening.

Psalm   A sacred song, poem, or hymn; the songs in the Old Testament book of The Psalms.

Psalter   Vernacular name for the book of The Psalms. v. Psalm.

Psaltery   Ancient or medieval instrument consisting of a flat soundboard over which a number of strings are stretched. A psaltery is plucked with the fingers. A similar instrument, the dulcimer, is played by striking the strings with hammers. The *harpsichord is a keyed psaltery. (See fig. 14.1.)

Putto   (I., plural *putti,* boy) The cherubs in Italian Renaissance painting and in rococo painting of the eighteenth century. (See colorplate 18.)

Q

Quatrain   A stanza of four lines, either rhymed or unrhymed.

R

Raking cornice   The end (cornice) on the sloping sides of a triangular *pediment.

Rebec   A small bowed medieval string instrument adapted from the Arabian *rebab.* It was one of the instruments from which the violin developed during the sixteenth century. (See fig. 16.3.)

Recorder   A straight, end-blown *flute, as distinct from the modern side-blown (transverse) flute. It was used from the Middle Ages until the eighteenth century and has been revived in the twentieth century.

Refrain   Recurring section of text (and usually music), e.g., verse-refrain.

Relief   In sculpture, carvings projecting from a background that is a part of the whole. Reliefs may be high (almost disengaged from the background) or low (*bas relief,* slightly raised above the background).

Reliquary   (F., remains) A receptacle for storing or displaying holy relics. (See colorplate 15.)

Rhythm   The temporal organization of music, for example, anything and everything that has to do with the motion of music, with the movement of sound in time. Rhythm is involved with pulsations (beats) that are either played or implied but it should not be confused with *meter, which is a regular pattern of beats or pulsations.

Rondo   A musical form with a primary theme alternating with several contrasting themes, e.g., ABACA.

Rotta   A medieval harp, probably originating with the Celts of western Europe. Also called a Celtic harp.

Round   In music a commonly used name for a circle *canon. At the conclusion of a melody the singer returns to the beginning, repeating the melody as often as desired. Examples: "Brother James," "Dona Nobis Pacem," and "Row, Row Your Boat."

S

Sanctuary   A sacred or holy place set aside for the worship of a god or gods; a place of refuge or protection.

Sanctus   (L., Holy) The fourth item in the *Ordinary of the *Mass.

Sarcophagus   A stone coffin. (See fig. 12.8.)

Satire   An indictment of human foibles using humor as a weapon, e.g., the relatively mild satires of Horace and the bitter ones of Juvenal.

Scale (L., ladder) The tonal material of music arranged in a series of rising or falling pitches. Because of the variety in the world's music there are many different scales. The basic scale of European music is the diatonic scale (C–D–E–F–G–A–B–C), i.e., the white keys of the piano. This arrangement of tones is also called a major scale or, more properly, a C major scale. Other commonly used scales are:

Minor	C–D–E♭–F–G–A♭–B♭–C
Whole tone	C–D–E–F♯–G♯–A♯–C
Pentatonic	C–D–F–G–A–C
Dorian mode	C–D–E♭–F–G–A–B♭–C
Phrygian mode	C–D♭–E♭–F–G–A♭–B♭–C

Scholasticism The philosophy and method of medieval theologians in which speculation was separated from observation and practice, revelation was regarded as both the norm and an aid to reason, reason respected authority, and scientific inquiry was controlled by theology.

Secondary colors Those *hues located between the *primary hues on a traditional color wheel: orange, green, and violet.

Semitone The smallest standard interval in Western music; half of a whole tone, for example, from C to C♯ on the piano keyboard.

Sempre (SEM–pra; I., Always).

Sequence A type of chant developed in the early Middle Ages in which a freely poetic text was added to the long *melisma at the end of the Alleluias. Subsequently separated from the Alleluias, the sequences became independent syllabic chants. The composition of many original sequences finally led to the banning of all but five sequences by the Council of Trent (1545–1563).

Serial composition A general term applied to twentieth-century music that uses a tone row (v. twelve-tone technique), but which also serializes other elements of music, such as *rhythm, *dynamics, and *timbre.

Sfumato (sfoo–MAH–toe) A hazy, smoky blending of color tones in a painting to create ambiguities of line and shape, as in Leonardo's *Ginevra diBenci.* (See colorplate 25.)

Sharp v. Accidental.

Shawm A double-reed instrument that preceded the *oboe.

Simile A comparison between two quite different things, usually using "like" or "as."

Snare drum v. Drum.

Sonata (I., *sonare,* to sound) An instrumental (sounding) piece which, in the seventeenth century, denoted a composition for a single instrument. Since about 1750 the term has come to mean a composition in several movements for a keyboard instrument or for solo instrument with keyboard accompaniment. "Duet sonatas" (solo instrument plus keyboard) usually have three movements (fast-slow-fast), while solo sonatas usually have four movements (fast-slow-moderate-fast).

Sonata form A term used for a structural design in which two contrasting themes appear in an initial exposure (exposition), after which one or both are altered, fragmented, and otherwise exploited (development). The form concludes with a return to the initial material (recapitulation) followed by a concluding section (coda) when necessary. Sonata form differs from other musical forms in that it is a dual thematic form with the two themes of approximately equal importance.

Sonnet A fourteen-line poem in iambic pentameter. Petrarch, the fourteenth-century Italian poet, used a rhyming scheme of *abbaabba* followed by *cde cde* or variants thereof. Shakespeare used a rhyming scheme of *abab cdcd efef gg,* or four *quatrains followed by a *rhymed couplet. (See chap. 20.)

Soprano The highest female singing voice, that is, S A T B. The term is also applied to the highest pitched instruments in a family of instruments, for example, soprano saxophones.

Spinet Originally a name for small *harpsichords with only one manual (keyboard). The term is used today for small upright pianos.

Squinch In architecture a device to effect a transition from a polygonal base to a circular dome. (See fig. 12.17 and accompanying explanation.)

Staff (musical) A set of five horizontal lines on which music is written. *Plainsong still uses a four-line staff.

Stele (STEE–lee) A carved slab of stone or pillar used especially by the Greeks as a grave marker. (See fig. 7.62.)

Still life In pictorial arts inanimate objects used as subject matter.

Stringed instruments Instruments in which the sound is produced by a stretched string. They may be divided into four main groups (see individual definitions for descriptions):

Stretched strings on a frame.
Plucked: zither.
Plucked, with keyboard: harpsichord, virginal, spinet.
Struck by hammer: dulcimer.
Struck by hammer, with keyboard: piano.
Strings touched by tangents: clavichord.

Instruments having a body and a neck.
Plucked: lute family (round back), guitar family (flat back).
Bowed: violin family, viols, vielle, rebec.

Instruments with projecting arms and crossbar: lyre, kithara.

Instrument with vertical strings: harp.

String quartet The standard chamber music ensemble of violin I and II, viola, cello. String quartets date from about 1750. In effect they are *sonatas for four instrumentalists.

Strophic A song in which the same music is used for all stanzas. When new music is used for each stanza the song is through-composed.

Stylobate The third of three steps of a Greek temple on which the *columns rest; essentially the platform on which the *cella and *peristyle are erected. (See fig. 7.49.)

Syllogism A form of deductive reasoning consisting of a major premise, minor premise, and a conclusion. Example: all men are mortal; Socrates is a man; therefore Socrates is mortal.

Symphony Since the classic era (1760–1827) the term stands for a *sonata for orchestra. Symphonies are played, naturally enough, by symphony orchestras and are usually (but not always) in a four-movement form.

Syncopation Stressing a beat or portion of a beat that is usually weak or unaccented. Most commonly used in jazz.

T

Tabor A medieval drum shaped like a long cylinder. Played with one stick to accompany a small *recorder, hence the standard combination of pipe and tabor.

Teleology (Gk., *telos,* end, completion) The theory of purpose, ends, goals, final cause; opposite of materialism.

Tempera A painting technique using pigment suspended in egg yolk.

Tempo The pace or speed of a musical composition. Since the seventeenth century, Italian terms have been used to give an approximation of the desired tempo. The invention of the metronome provides a more precise indication of a specific tempo. However, the size of an audience, the acoustics of a hall, and many other factors make the matter of tempo subject to a variety of interpretations. Some of the more common Italian tempo markings are given below, reading from slow tempo to progressively faster tempos:

Largo Slow, broad.

Grave (GRAH–vay) Slow, solemn.

Lento Slow.

Adagio (uh–DAH–jo) "At ease," slow.

Andante (ahn–DAHN–tay) "Walking tempo," that is, moderate.

Andante cantabile (kahn–TAH–bi–lay) In a singing manner.

Andante con moto Andante "with motion."

Andantino Slightly faster than andante.

Allegretto (ahl–luh–GRET–toe) Moderately lively.

Allegro (ahl–LEH–gro) "Cheerful," that is, fast.

Allegro appassionato With passion.

Allegro giocoso (joe–KO–so) Merrily.

Allegro marcato Emphatic.

Allegro moderato Moderately fast.

Allegro non troppo Fast but "not too fast."

Molto allegro "Much" fast, that is, very fast.

Vivace (vee–VAH–chay) Very fast.

Presto Very fast.

Presto con fuoco Very fast, "with fire."

Prestissimo Very, very fast.

Tenor (L., *tenere,* to hold) (1) Originally the part that "held" the melody on which early sacred polyphonic music was based. (2) The highest male voice (S A T B). (3) Prefix to the name of an instrument, for example, tenor saxophone.

Terra-cotta (I., baked earth) A baked clay used in ceramics and sculptures; a reddish color.

Tesserae (TESS–er–ee) Bits of stone and colored glass used in *mosaics.

Tetrachord In ancient Greek music a succession of four descending notes (a–g–f–e), which formed the nucleus of Greek music theory. Now loosely applied to any four-note segment of a scale.

Texture The melodic (horizontal) and harmonic (vertical) fabric of music, comparable to the horizontal and vertical aspects (warp and woof) of woven fabrics. There are three basic textures: *monophonic, *homophonic, *polyphonic. All music (except monophonic music) consists of a varying combination of vertical and horizontal relationships. A polyphonic texture with two distinct melodies still has a vertical aspect brought about by the harmonic intervals formed by the two melodies. A texture with two clearly defined melodies is necessarily described as polyphonic, providing there is also a realization of the harmonic implications of simultaneous melodies.

Thrust The outward force caused by the weight and design of an *arch or *vault, a thrust that must be countered by a *buttress. (See fig. 15.34.)

Timbre (tambr; F., tone color) Also used in English as a term referring to the coloration of musical tones, that is, the quality that enables a listener to distinguish, for example, between a flute, an oboe, and a clarinet. Tone color is the result of the relative strengths and weakness of the tones (partials) in the overtone series. In practical terms tone color is dependent on how a tone is produced (blowing, striking, bowing, etc.), the material used (wood, silver, platinum, etc.), and the abilities of individual performers. Two different trumpet players, for example, would produce a slightly different tone color when alternating on the same instrument.

Tone (1) In music a sound of well-defined pitch, as distinct from noise. (2) The distance of a whole step (two semitones).

Tone color v. Timbre.

Tragedy A serious play or other literary work with an unhappy or disastrous ending caused, in Greek drama, by *hubris on the part of the protagonist.

Transcendental Beyond the realm of the senses; rising above common thought or ideas; exalted.

Transept That part of a *cruciform-plan church whose axis intersects at right angles the long axis of the cross running from the entrance through the *nave to the *apse; the cross-arm of the cross.

Treble clef v. Clef.

Triforium In a Gothic cathedral, the gallery between the *nave arcades and the *clerestory; the triforium gallery opens on the nave with an *arcade. (See fig. 15.42.)

Triglyph Projecting block with vertical channels that alternates with *metopes in a *Dorian *frieze of a Greek temple. The ends of the marble beams are stylized versions of the wooden beams used in early temples.

Trombone   A tenor-baritone-range brass instrument with a cylindrical bore, played with a cup-shaped mouthpiece and a movable slide. The slide is the oldest method (fifteenth century) of changing the length of air column in a brass instrument, making the trombone the oldest member of the modern brass family.

Trompe-l'oeil   (trohmp LUH–yuh; F.) Illusionistic painting designed to convince the observer that what is seen is an actual three-dimensional object rather than a two-dimensional surface; literally, "eye fooling."

Trope   Additional text and/or music added to a preexisting *plainsong. The earliest tropes were *sequences. Troping became so widespread that it was banned by the Council of Trent. *Liturgical drama was a direct outgrowth of the trope.

Troubadour   Poet-musicians, mostly of aristocratic birth, of southern France (Provence) who, during the period ca. 1100–1300, cultivated the arts of poetry and music in chivalrous service to romantic love. Their music was *monophonic in style and popular in flavor but exerted considerable influence on the development of *polyphonic music.

Trouvère   Poet-musicians of central and northern France from ca. 1150–1300. Their music developed from the *troubadours and showed the same general characteristics except for the change in language from that of the south (Provençal) to the medieval forerunner of modern French.

Trumeau   A pillar or column placed in the center of a portal to help support the *lintel. (See fig. 15.28.)

Trumpet   A soprano-range brass instrument with basically a cylindrical bore and a cup mouthpiece. The modern trumpet lengthens the air column by using valves. The trumpet is the standard orchestral instrument and should not be confused with the instrument of shorter length and similar shape used frequently in military bands, namely, the *cornet*. The cornet has basically a conical bore and a milder and more mellow tone.

Tuba   The bass instrument of the brass family with conical bore, three to five valves, and played with a cup mouthpiece.

Twelve-tone technique   A twentieth-century procedure developed by Schoenberg and based on the equal tonal value of the twelve different notes within one octave. Basic to this system of *atonality is the tone row in which the twelve different notes are arranged in a nontonal pattern and used repeatedly with only mathematical variations: reverse order, change of octave, and so forth.

Tympanum   The space, usually elaborately carved, enclosed by the lintel and arch of a doorway; also, the space within the horizontal and *raking cornices of a *pediment. (See fig. 15.25.)

V

Vanishing point   In linear *perspective the point at which parallel lines converge on the horizon.

Vault   A masonry ceiling constructed on the principle of the arch. A *barrel vault* is an uninterrupted series of arches amounting to a very deep arch. (See fig. 15.14.)

Vibrato   (I., shaken) In music rapid but minute fluctuations of pitch that add a certain expressive quality to the pitch. Vocalists and string players traditionally use a vibrato on every note but other performers may or may not, depending on the circumstances.

Vielle   Medieval stringed instrument (twelfth to fifteenth centuries), succeeded by the *viol (sixteenth century), which in turn was replaced by the *violin family.

Viol   (VIE–ul) A family of bowed stringed instruments that were popular during the Renaissance and early Baroque periods and are being made again today. Three sizes were normally used, all with flat backs and sloping shoulders, and played sitting down with the instrument held between the knees. The string bass (bass viol) is the sole survivor of the viol family in the modern orchestra.

Viola   The alto-tenor member of the violin family. Slightly larger than the violin but with a rather muffled tone, the viola has been a regular member of the orchestra since the seventeenth century.

Violin   The violin emerged from the various bowed string instruments around 1600 and, with its brighter and more brilliant tone, replaced the *viols during the seventeenth century. As distinguished from the viol, it has a slightly rounded back and round shoulders. The best violins ever made were built in and around Cremona, Italy, from ca. 1600–1750 by the families Amati, Guarnierius, and Stradivarius.

Virelai   A form of medieval French poetry with a refrain before and after each stanza. Virelais were used by *trouvères and exploited during the Gothic period by Machaut and others.

Virginal   A *harpsichord used mainly in England and supposedly played by young ladies. The shape was frequently rectangular. When built in the standard two-keyboard form it was called a "pair of virginals."

Volute   The spiral scrolls of an *Ionian *capital.

Voussoir   (voo–SWAHR; F.) The wedge-shaped blocks of stone used to construct *arches and *vaults. (See fig. 15.34.)

W

Whole tone scale   v. Scales.

Woodcut   A wood block that has been carved so that the design stands out slightly from the block, comparable to printing type.

Woodwinds   A group of instruments most of which were, at one time, built of wood. There are three general types (see separate definitions for more detailed information):

Tube open at both ends
Piccolo
Flute
Alto flute

Double-reed instruments
Oboe
English horn
Bassoon
Contra bassoon

Single-reed instruments
Clarinet
Bass clarinet
Contra bass clarinet
Saxophone family

X

Xylophone   (Gk., wood sound) A percussion instrument consisting of a "keyboard" of hardwood bars and played with mallets. The tone is dry, brittle, and penetrating.

Credits

Photographs

Photographs by Robert C. Lamm except as indicated.

Figure 18.7   Alinari/Art Resource.
Figure 18.8   Museo Nazionale del Bargello, Florence.
Figure 18.9   Alinari/Art Resource.
Figure 18.11   Alinari/Art Resource.
Figure 18.12   Alinari/Art Resource.
Figure 18.13   Alinari/Art Resource.
Figure 18.15   Alinari/Art Resource.
Figure 18.16   Alinari/Art Resource.
Figure 18.17   Samuel H. Kress Collection. National Gallery of Art, Washington, D.C.
Figure 18.18   Andrew W. Mellon Collection. National Gallery of Art, Washington, D.C.
Figure 18.19   Art Reference Bureau.
Figure 18.20   Widener Collection. National Gallery of Art, Washington, D.C.
Figure 18.21   Art Reference Bureau.
Figure 18.22   Copyright A. C. L. Bruxelles.
Figure 18.23   Copyright A. C. L. Bruxelles.
Figure 18.24   National Gallery, London.
Figure 18.25   Andrew W. Mellon Collection. National Gallery of Art, Washington, D.C.
Figure 18.28   Alinari/Art Resource.
Figure 18.29   Alinari/Art Resource.
Figure 18.30   Alinari/Art Resource.
Figure 18.31   Alinari/Art Resource.
Figure 18.33   Art Reference Bureau.
Figure 18.38   Alinari/Art Resource.
Figure 18.39   Alinari/Art Resource.
Figure 18.41   Alinari/Art Resource.
Figure 18.42   Alinari/Art Resource.
Figure 18.43   Alinari/Art Resource.
Figure 18.45   The San Diego Museum of Art, San Diego, California.
Figure 18.46   University Art Collections, Arizona State University, Tempe. Gift of Mr. and Mrs. Read Mullen.
Figure 18.49   Musee Royaux des Beaux Arts, Brussels.
Figure 18.50   Alinari/Art Resource.
Figure 20.2   Copyright the Frick Collection, New York.
Figure 22.2   Art Reference Bureau.
Figure 22.4   Alinari/Art Resource.
Figure 22.5   Alinari/Art Resource.

Figure 22.10   Alinari/Art Resource.
Figure 22.13   The San Diego Museum of Art, San Diego, California.
Figure 22.14   Alinari/Art Resource.
Figure 22.21   Timkin Gallery, San Diego Museum of Art, San Diego, California.
Figure 22.22   Andrew W. Mellon Collection. National Gallery of Art, Washington, D.C.
Figure 22.23   Alinari/Art Resource.
Figure 22.24   Gift of Mrs. Mellon Bruce in memory of her father Andrew W. Mellon, 1961. National Gallery of Art, Washington, D.C
Figure 22.25   Samuel H. Kress Collection. National Gallery of Art, Washington, D.C.
Figure 22.26   Samuel H. Kress Collection. National Gallery of Art, Washington, D.C.
Figure 22.37   Alinari/Art Resource.
Figure 22.38   The Metropolitan Museum of Art. Wolfe Fund, 1931.
Figure 22.39   San Diego Museum of Art, San Diego, California.
Figure 22.40   Metropolitan Museum of Art, New York. Bequest of Isaac D. Fletcher.
Figure 22.41   Chester Dale Collection. National Gallery of Art, Washington, D.C.
Figure 26.3   Alinari/Art Resource.
Figure 26.4   Andrew W. Mellon Collection. National Gallery of Art, Washington, D.C.
Figure 26.5   Andrew W. Mellon Collection. National Gallery of Art, Washington, D.C.
Figure 26.7   Alinari/Art Resource.
Figure 26.8   Art Reference Bureau.
Figure 26.13   Shaw Collection. Museum of Fine Arts, Boston.
Figure 26.15   The Arizona State University Art Collections, Arizona State University. Gift of Oliver B. James.
Figure 26.17   Art Reference Bureau.
Figure 26.18   Art Reference Bureau.
Figure 26.21   Art Reference Bureau.
Figure 26.22   Art Reference Bureau.
Figure 26.25   Art Reference Bureau.
Figure 26.26   Gift of Mrs. John W. Simpson. National Gallery of Art, Washington, D.C.
Figure 26.30   National Galleries, Edinburgh. National Galleries of Scotland.
Figure 26.34   Art Reference Bureau.
Figure 29.1   National Gallery of Art, Washington, D.C.
Figure 29.2   Chester Dale Collection, 1962. National Gallery of Art, Washington, D.C.
Figure 29.6   National Gallery of Art, Washington, D.C.
Figure 29.8   The University Art Collections, Arizona State University, Tempe. Gift of Dr. and Mrs. Richard Besson.
Figure 29.9   Collection, The Museum of Modern Art, New York.
Figure 29.10   Chester Dale Collection, 1962. National Gallery of Art, Washington, D.C.
Figure 29.11   The Prado Museum, Madrid.
Figure 29.14   Collection, The Museum of Modern Art, New York. Given anonymously.
Figure 29.15   The Philadelphia Museum of Art. Louise and Walter Arensberg Collection.
Figure 29.16   Collection, The Museum of Modern Art, New York.
Figure 29.17   Collection, The Museum of Modern Art, New York. Mrs. Simon Guggenheim Fund.
Figure 29.18   Collection, The Museum of Modern Art, New York.
Figure 29.19   Courtesy Marlborough Gallery, New York.
Figure 29.20   Collection, The Museum of Modern Art, New York. Given anonymously.
Figure 29.22   Collection, The Museum of Modern Art, New York.
Figure 29.23   The Museum of Modern Art, New York. James Thrall Soby Fund.
Figure 29.27   The University Art Collections, Arizona State University, Tempe.
Figure 29.31   Art Reference Bureau.
Figure 29.32   Joslyn Art Museum, Omaha, Nebraska.
Figure 29.33   Leo Castelli, New York.
Figure 29.34   Moderna Museet, Stockholm, Sweden.
Figure 29.35   Copyright Gemini G. E. L., 1968.
Figure 29.36   Collection, The Museum of Modern Art, New York.
Figure 29.37   Courtesy, The American Republic Insurance Company, Des Moines, Iowa.
Figure 29.38   Multiples, New York.
Figure 29.39   Multiples, New York.
Figure 29.40   Collection of the High Museum, Atlanta, Georgia. Courtesy of the Margo Leavin Gallery, Los Angeles.
Figure 29.41   Collection, The Museum of Modern Art, New York.
Figure 29.42   Whitney Museum of American Art, New York.
Figure 29.43   Joslyn Art Museum, Omaha, Nebraska.
Figure 29.44   Joslyn Art Museum, Omaha, Nebraska.
Figure 29.45   Whitney Museum of American Art, New York.
Figure 29.46   Collection, The Museum of Modern Art, New York.
Figure 29.47   Collection, The Museum of Modern Art, New York.
Figure 29.48   Collection, The Museum of Modern Art, New York.
Figure 29.49   The University Art Collections, Arizona State University, Tempe.
Figure 29.50   American Art Heritage Fund. Arizona State University Art Collections, Tempe.

Literary Selections

Index

All B.C. dates are specified. Titles of works are set in italics with the artist's name in parentheses. Page numbers of black-and-white illustrations are in bold-face type; colorplates are specifically so designated. See the Glossary for definitions of technical terms.

George V, King of England (1865–1936), 211

Gericault, Théodore, French painter (1791–1824), 288–89, 291

Gershwin, George, American composer (1898–1937), 417

Gesú, Il (da Vignola and della Porta), 161, **162**, 166

Ghent Altarpiece (van Eyck), 32, **32**, 33, **33**

Ghiberti, Lorenzo, Florentine sculptor (ca. 1378–1455), 22

Ghirlandaio, Domenico, Florentine painter (1378–1455), 28, 30, 36

Giacometti, Alberto, Italian sculptor (1901–1966), 373–74

Gibbs, James, English architect (1682–1754), 178

Gilbert, William S. (1836–1911) and Sullivan, Arthur (1842–1900), English operetta team, 442

Ginevra de'Benci (Leonardo), 36, colorplate 25

Giorgione (Giorgio Barbarelli), Venetian painter (1478–1510), 31, 41–42, 47, 296

Giotto di Bondone, Florentine painter (1266–1337), 22, 24

Giovanni, Nikki, American poet (b. 1943), 481–82

Giovanni Arnolfini and His Bride (van Eyck), 34, **34**

Girl Before a Mirror (Picasso), 368, colorplate 7 (vol. 1)

Girl Seated Against a Square Wall (Moore), 388, **388**

Girl with a Watering Can (Renoir), 298, colorplate 46

Girl with the Red Hat, The (Vermeer), 173, colorplate 38

Glagolithic Mass (Janáček), 418

Glass Table, The (Moore), 389, **390**

Global village, 311, 338

Gloria (Poulenc), 419

Glorious Revolution, 131–33

God, 3–4, 6–7, 9–11, 130, 133, 217, 338–40, 348

Godwin, Gail, American writer (b. 1937), 447, 478–80

Godwin, William, English political philosopher (1756–1836), 225

Goethe, Johann, Wolfgang von, German poet and dramatist (1749–1832), 217, 227–28, 268, 311

Gongora, Leonel, Latin-American artist (b. 1932), 386

"Good-Morrow, The" (Donne), 138 (text)

Gordimer, Nadine, South African writer (b. 1923), 357–62, 452

Gospel song, 426–27

Gounod, Charles, French composer (1818–1893), 442

Goya y Lucientes, Francisco José de, Spanish painter (1746–1828), 217, 286–88, 289

Graham, Martha, American dancer and choreographer (b. ca. 1894), 418

Grande hazaña! Con muertos! (Goya), 287, **288**

Grand Odalisque (Ingres), 285–86, **286**, 297

Grant, Ulysses S(impson), General and United States president (1822–1885), 211

Grapes of Wrath (Steinbeck), 451

Grass, Günter, German writer and artist (b. 1927), 452

Gray, Thomas, English poet (1716–1771), 147–48, 218

Great War, The. *See* World War I

Greco, El (Kyriakos Theotokopoulos), Greek painter (1541–1614), 48, 388

Gretchen am Spinnrade (Schubert), 268 (text)

Greuze, Jean-Baptiste, French painter (1725–1805), 178, 180

Grieg, Edvard, Norwegian composer (1843–1907), 442

Gropius, Walter, German-American architect (1883–1969), 376, 394

Grosz, George, German-American artist (1893–1959), 365–66, 392

Grotius, Hugo, Dutch jurist (1583–1645), 15

Grünewald, Matthias (Mathis Gothart Nithart), German painter (1455–1528), 50, 364–65, 417

Guernica (Picasso), 310, 368, **369**

Guggenheim Museum (Wright), 395–96, **396**

Guilds, 3, 12

Guise, house of, French ducal family, 14

Gulliver's Travels (Swift), 144

Gunpowder, 130

Gutenberg, Johannes, German printer (1400–1468), 8

Gutenberg Bible, 338

Hába, Alois, Czechoslovakian composer (1893–1973), 418

Habitat (Safdie), 397, **397**

Hagia Sophia, Istanbul, 23

Halley, Edmund, English astronomer (1656–1742), 133

Hall of Mirrors, The Amalienburg, Nymphenburg Palace, Munich (Cuvilliés), **196**

Hals, Frans, Dutch painter (1580–1666), 171–73

Hambraeus, Bengt, Scandinavian composer (b. 1928), 420

Hamlet (Shakespeare), 14 (quote), 16 (quote)

Hammerstein, Oscar II, American lyricist (1895–1960), 417

Handel, George Frederick, German composer (1685–1759), 195–96, 444

Hanson, Duane, American artist (b. 1925), 389, 449

Hapsburgs, 12, 14

Hard bop jazz, 432

Hardy, Thomas, English novelist and poet (1840–1928), 213, 235–37, 304

Harlem (Hughes), 332 (text)

Harmonice Musices Odhecaton A (de Petrucci), 61

Harpsichord, 62, 188–89, 191, 195, 196

Harris, Roy, American composer (b. 1917), 417

Harrison, Lou, American composer (b. 1917), 418

Harrison, Wallace K., American architect (1895–1981), 394

Hauer, Joseph Mathias, Austrian composer (1883–1959), 418

Havard, James, American painter (b. 1945), 390–91, 449

Hawthorne, Nathaniel, American novelist (1804–1864), 413

Haydn, Franz Joseph, Austrian composer (1732–1809), 169, 196–200, 268, 443

Hegel, Georg Wilhelm Friedrich (1770–1831), 229

Heisenberg, Werner, German physicist (1901–1976), 313

Heller, Joseph, American novelist (b. 1923), 450–51, 482–88

Hello, Dolly! (Herman), 448

Hemingway, Ernest, American novelist and short-story writer (1899–1961), 447

Henri, Robert, American artist (1865–1929), 374, 375

Henry IV (Henry of Navarre), King of France (1553–1610), 14, 131

Henry V, King of England (1387–1422), 31–32

Henry VII, King of England (1457–1509), 49

Henry VIII, King of England (1491–1547), 9, 11, 14, 42, 50, 62

Henry the Navigator, Prince of Portugal (1394–1460), 8

Henze, Hans Werne, German composer (b. 1926), 419

Herculaneum, 180

Herder, Johann Gottfried von, German philosopher and poet (1744–1803), 217

Herman, Woodrow Charles (Woody), American jazz musician (b. 1913), 435

Hermes (Praxiteles), 24

Hero's Life, A (Strauss), 275

Hesiod, Greek poet (ca. 8th cent. B.C.), 316

Hindemith, Paul, German-American composer (1895–1963), 417

Historical and Critical Dictionary (Bayle), 136

Hitler, Adolf, German dictator (1889–1945), 310, 339

Hobbes, Thomas, English philosopher (1588–1679), 131

Holbein, Hans, the Younger, German painter (1497–1543), 49–50, 177

Holler (field holler), in music, 425

Holy Family, Church of the, Barcelona (Gaudi), 376, **376**